STUDIES IN
FINANCIAL
INSTITUTIONS
Commercial Banks

STUDIES IN FINANCIAL INSTITUTIONS
Commercial Banks

EDITED BY

Christopher M. James

Graduate School of Business
University of Florida
Gainesville

Clifford W. Smith, Jr.

William E. Simon Graduate School
of Business Administration
University of Rochester

McGRAW-HILL, INC.
New York   St. Louis   San Francisco   Auckland   Bogotá   Caracas
Lisbon   London   Madrid   Mexico City   Milan   Montreal   New Delhi
San Juan   Singapore   Sydney   Tokyo   Toronto

STUDIES IN FINANCIAL INSTITUTIONS
Commercial Banks

 This book is printed on recycled, acid-free paper containing a minimum of 50% total
recycled fiber with 10% postconsumer de-inked fiber.

2 3 4 5 6 7 8 9 0 DOH DOH 9 0 9 8 7 6 5 4

ISBN 0-07-032397-6

The editors were Kenneth A. MacLeod and Peitr Bohen;
the production supervisor was Elizabeth J. Strange.
R. R. Donnelley & Sons Company was printer and binder.

Library of Congress Cataloging-in-Publication Data

Studies in financial institutions: commercial banks / edited by
    Christopher M. James, Clifford W. Smith.
        p.   cm.—(McGraw-Hill series in advanced topics in finance
    and accounting)
    Includes bibliographical references.
    ISBN 0-07-032397-6
    1. Bank management—United States.   I. James, Christopher.
II. Smith, Clifford W.   III. Title: Commerical banks.   IV. Series.
HG1615.S776   1994
332.1'2'068—dc20   93-40434

CONTENTS

INTRODUCTION

This book contains reprints of articles that have been previously published in the *Journal of Financial Economics*, the *Journal of Finance*, the *Journal of Monetary Economics*, the *American Economics Review*, the *Journal of Political Economy*, the *Review of Economic Studies*, the *Journal of Money, Credit and Banking*, the *Journal of Financial and Quantitative Analysis*, the *Journal of Real Estate Finance and Economics*, the *American Real Estate and Urban Economics Association Journal*, and *Financial Management*. These papers address many of the topics that are frequently discussed in courses examining the commercial banking industry. The array of journals from which this collection of articles is drawn reflects the broad range of material relevant for such courses. By bringing together these papers, we focus attention on the progress that has been achieved in deriving a more basic understanding of the function of banks and the role of the banking industry in capital markets. We have used these papers in our courses and believe that they provide a productive core body of knowledge in this area.

We have tried to structure the book so it can fill various roles. In an advanced course on commercial banking or financial institutions, it can provide the basis for organizing the entire course. It can be employed as a valuable supplement in a lower-division commercial banking course or a course in financial institutions and markets, it can also be useful in a money and banking course in which the instructor wants to emphasize micro banking issues. Finally, it can be used with its companion book, *Studies in Financial Institutions: Nonbank Intermediaries*, in a broader financial institutions course at either the advanced undergraduate or MBA levels.

We have organized the readings into five parts. At the beginning of each is an introduction that provides a brief summary of the papers in the section as well as references to related papers that are not in this book. We show the readings in this book in **bold**, while related readings are not highlighted. All references in these section introductions appear at the end of the book.

We would like to acknowledge the assistance that all the authors and publishers gave us in producing this book of readings. We hope it will help to extend the knowledge contained in these papers to a broader cross-section of students in financial economics.

Christopher M. James
Clifford W. Smith, Jr.

ACKNOWLEDGMENTS

The editors wish to thank the following authors for permission to reprint their articles:

George J. Benston, School of Business Administration, Emory University

Mitchell Berlin, Stern School of Business, New York University

Ben S. Bernanke, Woodrow Wilson School, Princeton University

Fischer Black, Goldman Sachs

James A. Brickley, Simon Graduate School of Business Administration, University of Rochester

Stephen A. Buser, College of Business, The Ohio State University

Tim S. Campbell, School of Business Administration, University of Southern California

Yuk-Shee Chan, School of Business Administration, University of Southern California

Andrew H. Chen, Cox School of Business, Southern Methodist University

Douglas Diamond, Graduate School of Business, University of Chicago

Philip H. Dybvig, Olin School of Business, Washington University

Eugene F. Fama, Graduate School of Business, University of Chicago

Mark J. Flannery, Graduate School of Business Administration, University of Florida

Robert Gertner, Graduate School of Business, University of Chicago

Stuart G. Gilson, Graduate School of Business Administration, Harvard University

Stuart I. Greenbaum, Kellogg Graduate School of Management, Northwestern University

Alan C. Hess, Graduate School of Business Administration, University of Washington

Takao Hoshi, University of California – San Diego

Christopher M. James, College of Business Administration, University of Florida

Kose John, Stern School of Business, New York University

Edward J. Kane, Carroll School of Management, Boston College

Anil Kayshap, Federal Reserve

Michael Keeley, Cornerstone Research

William A. Kracaw, School of Business, Pennsylvania State University

Larry H. P. Lang, Stern School of Business, New York University

Jan G. Loeys, J. P. Morgan

George Pennacchi, School of Business, University of Illinois

Raghuran Rajan, Graduate School of Business, University of Chicago

Anthony Santomero, Wharton School, University of Pennsylvania

David Scharfstein, Sloan School of Management, MIT

Clifford W. Smith, Jr., Simon Graduate School of Business Administration, University of Rochester

Charles W. Smithson, Chase Manhattan Bank

Joseph Stiglitz, Stanford University

René M. Stulz, College of Business, The Ohio State University

Anjan Thakor, Graduate School of Business, Indiana University

Lee Macdonald Wakeman, TMG Financial Products

Jerold B. Warner, Simon Graduate School of Business Administration, University of Rochester

Andrew Weiss, Boston University

Karen H. Wruck, Graduate School of Business Administration, Harvard University

The editors wish to acknowledge the sources of the articles included in this volume:

American Economics Review

Joseph Stiglitz and Andrew Weiss, "Credit Rationing in Markets with Imperfect Information," Vol. 71 (1981), 393-410.

Ben S. Bernanke, "Nonmonetary Effects of the Financial Crisis in the Propagation of the Great Depression," Vol. 73 (1983), 257-276.

Michael Keeley, "Deposit Insurance, Risk, and Market Power in Banking," Vol. 80 (1990), 1183-1200.

American Real Estate and Urban Economics Association Journal

Clifford W. Smith, "Pricing Mortgage Originations," Vol. 10 (Fall 1982), 313-330.

Financial Management

Clifford W. Smith, Jr., Charles W. Smithson, and Lee Macdonald Wakeman, "The Market for Interest Rate Swaps," Vol. 17 (Winter 1988), 34-44.

Journal of Finance

George J. Benston and Clifford W. Smith, Jr., "A Transaction Cost Approach to the Theory of Financial Intermediation," Vol. 31 (1976), 215-231.

Tim S. Campbell and William A. Kracaw, "Information Production, Market Signalling, and the Theory of Financial Intermediation," Vol. 35 (1980), 863-882.

Stephen A. Buser, Andrew H. Chen and Edward J. Kane, "Federal Deposit Insurance, Regulatory Policy, and Optimal Bank Capital," Vol. 36 (1981), 51-60.

Mark J. Flannery and Christopher M. James, "The Effect of Interest Rate Changes on the Common Stock Returns of Financial Institutions," Vol. 39 (1984), 1141-1153.

George Pennacchi, "Loan Sales and the Cost of Bank Capital," Vol. 43 (1988), 375-396.

Mitchell Berlin and Jan G. Loeys, "Bond Covenants and Delegated Monitoring," Vol. 43 (June 1988), 397-412.

Robert Gertner and David Scharfstein, "A Theory of Workouts and the Effects of Reorganization Law," Vol. 46 (1991), 1189-1222.

Yuk-Shee Chan, Stuart I. Greenbaum, and Anjan Thakor, "Is Fairly Priced Deposit Insurance Possible?," Vol. 47 (1992), 227-246.

Raghuran Rajan, "Insiders and Outsiders: The Choice Between Informed and Arm's-Length Debt," Vol. 47 (1992), 1367-1400.

Journal of Financial and Quantitative Analysis

Clifford W. Smith, Jr., and René M. Stulz, "The Determinants of Firms," Vol. 20 (December 1985), 391-405.

Journal of Financial Economics

Fischer Black, "Bank Funds Management in an Efficient Market," Vol. 2 (1975), 323-339.

Christopher M. James, "Some Evidence on the Uniqueness of Bank Loans," Vol. 7 (1987), 217-235.

Clifford W. Smith, Jr. and Jerold B. Warner, "On Financial Contracting: An Analysis of Bond Covenants," Vol. 7 (1979), 111-161.

Karen Hopper Wruck, "Financial Distress, Reorganization, and Organizational Efficiency," Vol. 27 (1990), 419-444.

Stuart G. Gilson, Kose John and Larry H.P. Lang, "Troubled Debt Restructuring: An Empirical Study of Private Reorganization of Firms in Default," Vol. 27 (1990), 315-353.

Takao Hoshi, Anil Kayshap and David Scharfstein, "The Role of Banks in Reducing the Costs of Financial Distress in Japan," Vol. 27 (1990), 67-88.

James A. Brickley and Christopher M. James, "Access to Deposit Insurance, Insolvency Rules and the Stock Returns of Financial Institutions," Vol. 16 (1986), 345-372.

Journal of Money Credit and Banking

Anthony Santomero, "Modeling the Banking Firm: A Survey," Vol. 16 (1984), 576-602.

Journal of Monetary Economics

Eugene F. Fama, "What's Different about Banks," Vol. 15 (1985), 29-36.

Christopher M. James, "The Use of Loan Sales and Standby Letter of Credit by Commercial Banks," Vol. 22 (1988), 395-422.

Mark J. Flannery, "Capital Regulation and Insured Banks' Choice of Individual Loan Default Risks," Vol. 24 (September 1989), 235-258.

Journal of Political Economy

Philip H. Dybvig, "Bank Runs, Deposit Insurance, and Liquidity," Vol. 91, No. 3 (June 1983), 401-419.

Journal of Real Estate Finance and Economics

Alan C. Hess and Clifford W. Smith, Jr., "Elements of Mortgage Securitization," Vol. 1, No. 4, (December 1988), 331-346.

Review of Economic Studies

Douglas Diamond, "Financial Intermediation and Delegated Monitoring," Vol. 51, 393-414.

STUDIES IN FINANCIAL INSTITUTIONS
Commercial Banks

I

THE THEORIES OF THE BANKING FIRM

Advances in information economics, agency theory, and corporate finance have fundamentally changed the way financial economists view the role of commercial banks and other financial intermediaries in the economy. Prior to the late 1970s, the prevailing focus was on commercial banks as conduits of monetary policy. Growing out of macroeconomics, this perspective resulted from the fact that commercial banks were the only institutions that were authorized to offer checking accounts and thus played a key role in the money-supply process. As a result of this focus on banks as suppliers of liquidity, little attention was paid to the role of commercial banks in the capital acquisition process. Indeed, little attention was paid to the more fundamental question of why financial intermediaries exist.

In a competitive, frictionless capital market—that is, a market in which there are no information or contracting costs and all market participants are price takers—financial intermediaries that consume any real resources would not exist. In a frictionless capital market, individual borrowers and lenders can costlessly contract among themselves for the services that financial intermediaries provide. This argument makes clear that the *raison d'être* for financial intermediaries is the existence of frictions that make it costly to create, transfer, and enforce financial contracts.

While it may be easy to understand why the existence of financial institutions is predicated on costs, the precise nature of the costs that gives rise to financial intermediaries is less clearly understood. In the first article **Benston and Smith** (1976)[1] argue that the essential service provided by financial intermediaries is the reduction of contracting costs. Relevant contracting costs include the costs of becoming informed; costs of structuring, administering, and enforcing financial contracts (including the cost of search); and the cost of physically transferring financial claims. The demand for the products or services pro-

---

[1]References are listed at the end of the book.

duced by financial intermediaries, they argue, is derived from the consumer's demand to effect consumption decisions across time and goods in the least costly manner. Benston and Smith apply the contracting-cost theory of organizational development to explain the existence of financial institutions. In essence, the contracting-cost theory holds that organizations evolve to minimize the total costs of transacting. In this view, the theory of financial intermediation involves explaining why financial intermediaries have a comparative cost advantage in transacting.

Benston and Smith suggest that financial intermediaries potentially have a comparative cost advantage for several reasons. First, financial intermediaries are able to achieve scale economies as a consequence of specialization. Second, financial intermediaries' continued presence in a market allows the development of reputational capital that allows them to demand proprietary information useful in assessing the borrower's credit risk while credibly promising to keep the information confidential. Finally, financial intermediaries can reduce search costs through economies associated with centralized information production. For example, a market maker matching buy and sell orders reduces search costs for both potential purchasers and sellers of a security.

Black (1975) discusses how information and transaction costs affect the nature of commercial bank loan and deposit services. Black explores the implications a competitive and informationally efficient market for financial services has for bank funds-management decisions (that is, bank asset allocation, pricing, and financing decisions) and bank regulation. In his view, banks serve to reduce transaction costs for both depositors and loan customers essentially by serving as a clearinghouse for transactions. Specifically, the information that the bank acquires as part of an ongoing deposit relationship with a customer provides the bank with a comparative cost advantage in originating and monitoring commercial loans.

Black's analysis is useful because it highlights the importance of market contracting costs in shaping the banking industry. Just as our understanding of the factors affecting corporate capital-structure choices is enhanced by first examining financing decisions in the context of complete and frictionless markets, our understanding of the role of banks in the economy is enhanced by examining the role these institutions play in informationally efficient and relatively frictionless markets.

The Black and Benston and Smith analyses show that contracting costs are central to the theory of financial institutions. More recent work on the theory of financial intermediation focuses on a specific set of contracting costs: those involved in information production and monitoring. This research discusses why financial intermediaries have lower costs of producing precontract information and lower costs of monitoring borrowers after a loan is made.

The focus on the role of financial intermediaries in producing information and in monitoring the activities of borrowers results from the recognition that information asymmetries between borrowers and lenders can create significant adverse-selection and moral-hazard problems in financial transactions. [See, for example, Jensen and Meckling (1976) and Leland and Pyle (1977).] Information-based theories of financial intermediation focus on how intermediaries mitigate or resolve these information problems that are inherent in financial transactions. Adverse-selection problems arise from precontractual information asymmetries. The term "adverse selection" was coined in the insurance industry to refer to the situation where individuals with private information that they are above-average risks purchase the most insurance. Moral-hazard problems are problems that arise from post-contract information asymmetries. Specifically, "moral hazard" refers to the alteration of behavior after insurance is purchased or a loan is made.

The readings by **Campbell and Kracaw** (1980) and by **Diamond** (1984) focus on the role of financial intermediaries in reducing contracting costs arising from information asymmetries. Campbell and Kracaw examine the role of financial intermediaries in resolving free-rider or appropriability problems in information production. The appropriability problem in information production arises from the fact that once private information is disseminated, the producer is no longer able to profit from its use. For example, producing information that identifies mispriced securities is of little value if the information is immediately reflected in security prices. The direct sale of information is therefore limited by this appropriability problem. One way to avoid this problem is for the intermediary to sell information indirectly through selling claims on an income stream arising from the use of the information. (This assumes of course that investors cannot observe the portfolio the intermediary acquires with the private information that it produces.)

The indirect sale of information creates a potential moral-hazard problem. Without actually observing the information produced by the intermediary, one has difficulty evaluating the quality of that information. Indeed, the customer cannot be certain that the intermediary actually engages in costly information production. One mechanism for controlling this moral-hazard problem is for the intermediary to post a bond in the form of an equity investment, the value of which depends upon the quality of information produced. However, as Campbell and Kracaw indicate, in their model there is nothing intrinsic in the intermediation process itself that resolves appropriability and moral-hazard problems. For example, individual entrepreneurs bond the quality of information about the projects for which they seek funding by retaining a large equity stake in the corporation.

Diamond focuses on the question of whether there is something intrinsic in the intermediation process itself that serves to resolve the moral-hazard problem associated with the indirect sale of information. In his model, financial intermediaries serve to monitor the performance of borrowers after a loan is made. Suppose, however, that depositors cannot directly observe whether the intermediary actually monitors; specifically, suppose that even with efficient monitoring there is some uncertainty about the outcome of an individual investment project. As a result, observing a default on an individual transaction is difficult to interpret. The default on a particular loan may be the result of negligent monitoring or bad luck. Diamond shows that diversification across a large number of loans can resolve the moral-hazard problem.[2] In the limit, if the returns on the loans being monitored are independent, the uncertainty of the portfolio's cash flows is eliminated, allowing investors to infer the quality of monitoring that has occurred. Diamond thus demonstrates that there are economies of scale in information production intrinsic to the process of intermediation. Boyd and Prescott (1986) argue that coalitions of monitors also can control moral-hazard problems through a similar process of diversification.

The remaining readings in this part examine the implication of contracting costs for the pricing and portfolio decisions of commercial banks. The paper by **Santomero** (1984) provides a review of microeconomic models of the portfolio-allocation and capital-structure decisions commercial banks make. Santomero points out that the determinants of banks' portfolio and financing choices are inextricably linked to the nature of the markets in which banks operate and the nature of the contracting costs that give rise to financial institutions.

[2]Diamond assumes that there is a nonpecuniary penalty associated with default. This insures that the intermediary will make payment to investors when it has sufficient funds to do so.

The models of asset choice reviewed by Santomero generally assume that banks have some degree of market power in at least some of their loan markets. Given this assumption, the bank's asset portfolio choice is modeled as a discriminating monopolist choosing the optimal quantity of loans to supply in various markets. As Santomero points out, these asset-choice models provide little motivation for why bank loan markets should be viewed as imperfectly competitive. One fruitful area of recent research has been to distinguish between the degree of ex ante competition (that is, prior to the establishment of a lending relationship) and ex post competition (that is, after a relationship is established). If there are significant fixed costs associated with establishing a lending relationship, then it is costly for borrowers to switch banks. These sunk costs provide a potential cost advantage for the lending bank. [Additional implications for the borrower's choice between public debt and bank loans is discussed in the article by **Rajan** (1992) in Part II.]

Models of bank liability choice focus primarily on what determines the mix between deposit and equity financing. Again, the optimal scale and financing mix is inextricably linked to the assumed cost advantage that motivates the existence of financial institutions. For example, consider the choice between deposit and equity financing. In a frictionless capital market, the Modigliani and Miller (1958) capital-structure irrelevance proposition implies that bank value is unaffected by this choice. However, if banks provide transaction services that are bundled with the provision of deposits, then the bank's capital-structure decision is determined in part by the production technology used to produce intermediation services such as check processing and record keeping.

Another factor affecting the capital-structure decision in banking is deposit insurance. If the government insures bank deposits at less than actuarially fair rates, the market value of the bank depends on the subsidies obtained through underpriced insurance. As articles in Part IV of this book discuss, the value of the subsidies received from mispriced deposit insurance is a function of the bank's capital-structure decision.

Fama (1985) examines the incidence of the reserve-requirement tax on large negotiable certificates of deposit issued by commercial banks. Reserve requirements raise the cost of deposit financing to commercial banks by requiring banks to hold a portion of the deposit in non-interest-bearing cash or deposits at a Federal Reserve Bank.[3] Whether depositors pay this tax in the form of a lower interest rate on their deposits or borrowers pay the tax in the form of higher bank loan rates depends on the nature of nonbank substitutes for bank deposits and bank loans. Fama argues that since there exist close substitutes for bank certificates of deposit, depositors will not pay the tax. As a result, bank loan customers must pay the tax in the form of higher loan rates. However, the reserve tax can only be extracted from bank loan customers if there is something special or unique about bank loans relative to other forms of financing.

What is special about bank loans? Fama argues that bank loans are a form of debt in which the lender obtains information about the firm not available publicly. More important, bank access to this information serves to reduce information costs other creditors incur, as other creditors can free-ride on the information banks produce. Banks have a comparative advantage in making and monitoring loans, Fama argues, because of the information generated from a deposit relationship with a borrower. Fama's conjecture concerning the uniqueness of bank loans has spawned a large number of empirical studies directed at testing whether the identity of the lender is important. These studies are summarized in Part II.

---

[3]Reserve requirements on all time deposits were removed in 1990; however, they continue on transaction accounts.

A TRANSACTIONS COST APPROACH TO THE THEORY OF FINANCIAL INTERMEDIATION

GEORGE J. BENSTON AND CLIFFORD W. SMITH, JR.**

I. INTRODUCTION

IN OUR OPINION, a proper framework has yet to be developed for the analysis of financial intermediation. The traditional macroeconomic analysis views financial intermediaries as passive conduits through which monetary policy is effected.[1] Even when a more micro view is taken, though, the analyses often are restricted to studying the effect on the rate of change and allocation of money and credit of required and desired reserve ratios, ceiling rates imposed on loans and deposits, etc.[2]

Recent (and some past) writers criticize this approach.[3] These authors point out that since financial intermediaries are firms, they should be analyzed with the microeconomic tools that have been employed to analyze other industries. Yet, in this implementation, considerable divergence in approach can be found. For example, while Pesek [1970] and Towey [1974] describe one financial intermediary, banks, as producing money by employing loans as inputs, Hyman [1972] and Melitz and Pardue [1973] describe them as producing credit with deposits as inputs. Furthermore, although most authors suggest that the intermediaries maximize something, it is sometimes profits, sometimes growth, and sometimes (rather anthropomorphicly) utility (e.g., Klein [1971]). We believe that these approaches are not the most productive way to analyze financial intermediaries.

Essentially, we view the role of the financial intermediary as creating specialized financial commodities. These commodities are created whenever an intermediary finds that it can sell them for prices which are expected to cover all costs of their production, both direct costs and opportunity costs.

We see the demand for these financial commodities as a derived demand. Individuals derive utility from consumption, consumption today and consumption in the future. By acquiring financial commodities, inter-temporal and intra-temporal transfers of consumption may be achieved. Of course, there are many financial commodities other than those produced by financial intermediaries. The *raison d' être* for this industry is the existence of transactions costs.

** The University of Rochester Graduate School of Management.

1. For example, neither Friedman and Schwartz [1963] nor Cagan [1965] mention bank resource costs.

2. Admittedly, if the costs of production for this industry showed little variability over the period studied, these omissions may cause little difficulty. However, with the technological advancement in such areas as electronic funds transfer, this omission may pose serious problems for subsequent research.

3. See Pyle [1972] for a comprehensive review of this literature.

THE JOURNAL OF FINANCE, Vol. 31, No. 2, May 1976, pp. 215-231.

Several forms of financial intermediation have arisen to reduce these costs. The most basic form of financial intermediary is the market maker. He simply provides a market-place where potential buyers and sellers come together, thus lowering relevant information costs. An example of this form of intermediary is the New York Stock Exchange. It does not create assets, it only furnishes a physical location for buyers and sellers to transact. Without this intermediary, the task of locating a potential seller (much less the potential seller with the lowest reservation price) would be much more expensive. A somewhat more sophisticated form of financial intermediation is provided by a dealer who also takes a position at his own risk in the asset transacted. A market specialist on a securities exchange exemplifies this form of intermediation. A more complex form of financial intermediation is one in which new financial commodities are produced. This form of financial intermediary is exemplified by mutual funds, banks, and consumer finance companies. Thus, mutual funds allow individuals to purchase shares in diversified portfolios of securities, in odd amounts, for indefinite lengths of time, generally at a much lower transaction cost than could be achieved through the direct purchase of the underlying securites. This intermediary has a comparative advantage over a stock exchange in serving a particular group. Therefore, it exploits the returns to scale implicit in the structure of the transactions costs of a stock exchange by purchasing large blocks of securities, packaging those securities in a form that is demanded by some individuals, and selling the package at a price which covers all its costs. These examples illustrate the essential feature of financial intermediation—reduction of the transactions costs of effecting inter- and intra-temporal consumption decisions.[4]

II. Demand

A basic problem in the analysis of financial intermediaries may be the lack of an appropriate analytical framework within which to analyze the demand for the financial commodities produced by intermediaries. In the general analysis of consumer demand, individuals are assumed to possess an endowment and act according to the dictates of a utility function. The endowment is expended to purchase consumption goods in such a way as to maximize utility. We assume that individuals derive utility only from consumption, where by consumption we mean consuming different goods at many points in time, allowing for different states of the world. (Note that if this restriction were not imposed, any observed activity could be trivially deduced by an appropriate insertion of that phenomenon into the utility function, thus rendering the analytical apparatus empty.)

---

4. One point about the aggregate supply of the financial commodities created by financial intermediaries should be noted: it is always identically zero. The total long position in mutual fund shares held by the public is exactly offset by the short position in those shares taken by the fund itself. Similarly, the total long position in the installment loan market held by the customers of a consumer finance company is exactly offset by the short position in that market assumed by the finance company itself. This general proposition, that the supply of financial commodities created by financial intermediaries is identically zero, should highlight the fact that the increase in social welfare engendered by this industry comes about only through a reduction in the relevant transactions cost.

The individual's endowment may consist of securities plus his human wealth, the present value of his earnings. If the individual's preferred inter-temporal consumption pattern differs from his time-profile of earnings, he may rearrange his consumption pattern to achieve a more desired pattern. He does so by directly or indirectly acquiring a long or short position in assets (e.g., by purchasing equities or the financial commodities issued by financial intermediaries). Therefore, an individual's asset holdings do not yield utility in themselves. Assets are held for the inter- and intra-temporal rearrangement of consumption possibilities afforded by their holding.[5]

The foregoing explains, in part, why assets are held. We now turn to the question of which assets are held, or what the motivation is for holding the financial commodities created by financial intermediaries. It should be obvious that in a *perfect* market, a market with no frictions such as transactions costs, information costs, or indivisibilities, financial intermediaries would not exist. This argument focuses explicitly on the rationale for the existence of financial intermediaries—market imperfections.

Transactions Cost and Inter-Temporal Consumption

First we consider the consumer's demand for inter-temporal consumption. The well-known Sharpe-Lintner-Treynor-Mossin capital asset pricing model (CAPM) describes how the consumer can hold a portfolio of riskless and risky assets to achieve consumption patterns that maximize his utility. This model includes the essential elements appropriate to an analytical framework: consumption is the argument in the individual's preference function, at least two time periods are considered, the range of substitution involved in the portfolio decision is recognized, and risk is explicitly recognized. However, transactions costs are not incorporated.

In an earlier version of this paper, we demonstrate formally how general transactions costs can be included in Hamada's [1971] explication of the CAPM.[6] We draw the following conclusions. First, transactions costs reduce the amount of the consumer's present and future consumption should he want to consume other than his current period income. As a consequence, consumption only of current income and next period income may dominate borrowing and lending and investing in risk-free and risky assets. This conclusion is reinforced where transactions result in differing borrowing and lending rates. Both fixed and differential transactions costs result in a tendency of the individual's consumption patterns to follow his income pattern. Second, although in a perfect market it is never optimal to hold a portfolio with no risky assets, the existence of transactions costs may result in the optimal portfolio containing only riskless assets. Third, where a consumer can achieve a higher level of utility by purchasing risky assets even though he must incur transactions costs, the nature of these costs affect his choice of portfolio. If transactions costs are proportional for all risky assets, the market

---

5. We include here contingent consumption possibilities as, for example, are afforded by insurance.

6. This section of the paper was omitted because of space constraints. It is available from the authors upon request.

portfolio is still the optimal portfolio of risky assets,[7] though the amount that can be invested is reduced by the future value of the costs. However, the two fund property of the CAPM is lost virtually all other forms of transactions costs. If transactions costs are associated differentially with individual securities, the market portfolio will not be chosen. Essentially, the individual will add risky securities to his portfolio until the marginal net benefit of increased diversification is zero. The addition of more general increasing returns to scale in transactions costs will generate non-linearities in the model. Both the homogeneity properties associated with the map of the efficient frontier and the linearity of the capital market line will be lost. In particular, the consumer with a relatively small endowment and/or income may find the reduction in expected utility from paying transactions costs greater than the increase in expected utility from purchasing, borrowing or lending risky or risk-free assets.

The demand for the commodities produced by financial intermediaries, in general, is derived from the consumer's ability to achieve a higher level of utility by incurring lower levels of these transactions costs. In addition, individual specific transactions costs, such as the cost of transportation and inconvenience, also serve to reduce the consumer's consumption possibilities. These costs, we believe, are important for explaining the distribution of the consumer's demands among individual financial intermediaries. When several financial commodities can be obtained in a single location, the marginal transportation and inconvenience cost for services in addition to the first are virtually zero.[8] However, the continuing existence of thrift institutions, unit banks, and other limited service financial institutions suggest either that these costs are not overwhelmingly large or that government regulations prevent transactions cost saving changes. (These alternatives are considered further below.)

The addition of these costs would suggest that individuals' efficient opportunity sets would differ not only with the size of their portfolios, but also with physical location and the opportunity cost of their time. Thus the demands faced by financial intermediaries are also a function of the distribution of wealth among consumers.[9]

Transactions Costs and Intra-Temporal Consumption

The demand for financial commodities, such as demand deposits, is derived from the consumer's demand to effect intra-temporal consumption decisions across commodities. Demand deposits are acquired because of transactions costs, namely costs associated with barter and with the use of government supplied money.[10] Since it is costly to exchange assets for consumption goods, given some stochastic

---

7. Note, however, that if the individual begins with an endowment of risky securities, this property does not hold. See Zabel [1973].

8. Consequently, time deposit balances are positive in full-service commercial banks, even though thrift institutions are allowed to pay one-quarter percent more interest on their time deposits. (See Kardouche [1969]). This argument may also partially explain the observation that banks with extensive branching tend to dominate in states which permit branch banking.

9. In general, we expect that as the opportunity cost of the consumer's time increases, the value of full-service financial intermediaries to the consumer is likely to increase.

10. See Saving [1971], Feige and Parkin [1971], Brunner and Meltzer [1971] and Karni [1974] for recent analyses of the demand for money that consider explicitly the role of transactions costs.

expenditure patterns, individuals will choose to hold assets which have low transactions costs associated with conversion to consumption goods. This property of assets, the ability to be transformed into consumption goods at minimal transactions costs, is referred to as liquidity.[11] Given the continuum of liquidity and noting the generally negative correlation between liquidity and expected return, individuals will hold a portfolio of assets in which the marginal benefit of increased liquidity and the accompanying expected reduction in transactions costs is just equal to the marginal cost of the reduction in expected return.

Among these assets, demand deposits and loans provide liquidity at a relatively low transactions cost because they provide consumers with complete divisibility and permit him to monitor his activities at a relatively low cost. A demand deposit permits the consumer to purchase an asset or repay a debt with the exact amount required by writing a check. The cleared check provides him with a legally acceptable, validated record of the transaction. A treasury bill, on the other hand, usually must be converted to currency or a demand deposit before it can be used to effect transactions.

Loans made for the amounts and periods demanded similarly provide consumers with liquidity that obviates the need to incur the additional transactions costs of investing amounts not wanted. A debenture, on the other hand, involves a relatively large amount of funds for a relatively long period. Neither the amount nor the period may coincide with the consumption preferred by the consumer.

Transactions Costs and the Demand for Financial Commodities

To summarize, financial intermediaries meet consumers' demands for time-dated consumption by supplying units of generalized purchasing power that can be converted into goods or services at minimal transactions costs in the amounts and at the times demanded.[12] Included in the price of these financial commodities are amounts that compensate the financial institution for the costs of processing the paperwork required to record the transaction, to determine the likelihood that the borrower will repay his debt, to monitor his repayment of the debt and to acquire the funds borrowed. Also included are amounts (interest) that compensate other consumers for deferring present consumption.

Similarly, consumers who wish to consume in the future may invest their funds (currently owned claims over resources) with a financial intermediary. The intermediary provides them with an expected real return for the period over which they choose to invest. Furthermore, consumers generally can invest whatever amounts they wish for whatever period they wish.

---

11. Pierce [1966] following Tobin demonstrates that liquidity may be measured as the amount that can be acquired (either through the sale of an asset or through borrowing) over a given time period and state of the economy relative to the maximum amount that could be realized from the sale of the asset were time not a factor. Therefore, currency, being legal tender, is perfectly liquid. However mortgage loans, which require large information costs for a prospective buyer to ascertain valuation, are generally illiquid.

12. Thus, a consumer who wishes to acquire the services of an automobile now (and over time) in exchange for reduced consumption of other goods and services at specified amounts in the future may borrow $3800.00 and pay a bank $183.67 a month for 24 months. A manufacturer may acquire the productive services of a machine that costs $10,800.00, for which he contracts to return $11,880.00 one year hence.

Financial intermediaries are organized to meet these consumers' demands at relatively low transactions costs by producing financial commodities and services. The conditions that govern this production are considered in the next section.

III. PRODUCTION

General Considerations for the Production of Financial Commodities

The market price of a financial commodity is a function of the total cost of producing the financial commodity. We begin to examine the price charged by the firm by considering the behavior of an unregulated firm. (The impact of government regulation is considered in Section V.) The price of any financial commodity in an efficient, competitive market can be conceptually separated into three parts: one part depends only on the pure riskless rate (what in a two period world would correspond to the marginal rate of substitution between current and future consumption), one represents a premium for risk, and one is a compensation for the administration, monitoring, and processing costs imposed on the producer. To examine the first two parts, it is convenient to employ the analogy suggested by Black and Scholes [1973] between the valuation of a call option and the valuation of equity.[13] Black and Scholes demonstrate that in a frictionless world without taxes and bankruptcy costs that the value of equity (E) and debt (D) (defined as pure discount bonds) are functions of the value of the underlying assets (V), the face value of the debt (D^*), the time to maturity of the debt (T), the riskless rate of interest (r), and the variance rate on the assets (σ^2):[14]

$$V = E(V, D^*, T, r, \sigma^2) + D(V, D^*, T, r, \sigma^2) \tag{1}$$

where

$$\frac{\partial E}{\partial V} \frac{\partial E}{\partial T} \frac{\partial E}{\partial r} \frac{\partial E}{\partial \sigma^2} > 0 \qquad \frac{\partial E}{\partial D^*} < 0$$

$$\frac{\partial D}{\partial V} \frac{\partial D}{\partial D^*} > 0 \qquad \frac{\partial D}{\partial T} \frac{\partial D}{\partial r} \frac{\partial D}{\partial \sigma^2} < 0$$

13. See Smith [1976] for a review of the option pricing literature and the applications of the option pricing model to value other contingent claim assets.

14. These partial effects have intuitive interpretations: An increase in the value of the underlying assets directly increases the value of the equity and increases the coverage on the debt, thereby, lowering the probability of default. An increase in the face value of the debt increases the claim on the assets by the creditors thereby increasing the current value of the debt and, since equity is a residual claim, reduces its current value. An increase in the time to maturity of the debt or an increase in the riskless rate decreases the present value of the debt obligation. Finally, an increase in the variance rate on the assets increases the likelihood of the value of the assets being less than the face value of the debt at maturity, thereby lowering the current value of the debt and increasing the current value of the equity. Furthermore, in the presence of taxes, bankruptcy costs, and other agency costs, the debt-equity ratio would be an argument in the equity and debt functions. As pointed out by Long [1974] the Black-Scholes model cannot be directly applied in the presence of tax effects or agency costs which would make the value of the firm dependent upon the debt-equity ratio. However, it seems unlikely that qualitative results in (1) will be affected.

Even in the absence of transactions costs, any economic agent who purchases or sells a financial commodity must ascertain the values of these variables. The cost of assessing the riskless rate is very low, for it is exogeneous to the process and readily observable. However, assessment of the other relevant variables may entail high information costs. This task may be trivial in the case of an investment where repayment is guaranteed by a secure insuror (such as the FDIC, FSLIC, VA, FHA or NCUA). But for other investments, the assessment of the magnitudes of the variables is costly and the agents incurring these costs must be compensated.

In providing funds to a borrower, lenders are faced with the possibility that honesty on the part of the borrower may not be his best policy. For example, if a borrower obtains a loan based on his stated intention to purchase low risk assets with the proceeds, he can increase his equity by actually using the proceeds to purchase high risk assets. If the lender does not perceive that this action is possible (and therefore charges an interest rate which assumes that this action will in fact be taken), he will suffer a capital loss: the market value of the loan will fall because the agreed rate of interest is insufficient compensation for the risk of bankruptcy. Consequently, the lender must charge a price (interest rate) sufficient to compensate him for the riskiest choice of assets that the borrower might acquire. Furthermore, if the lender sets the interest rate at that level, the borrower must acquire assets at least as risky as those the lender implicitly expects him to purchase or he will over-compensate the lender.

As pointed out by Jensen and Meckling [1975], the cost of this conflict of interests between the borrower and the lender can be reduced by placing a restrictive covenant into the credit agreement. This covenant contractually limits the activities of the borrower and therefore allows the lender to offer a lower rate of interest on the loan. However, there are other methods which can be used to minimize this problem, specifically the pledging of collateral. If collateral is included in a credit agreement, then the information costs imposed on the lender may be significantly lowered. Instead of calculating the appropriate rate of interest based on the least favorable available action to the borrower, given the covenants in the instruments, the lender can base the rate on his estimate of the risks associated with the collateral. This procedure may be much less expensive to administer and monitor than the procedure of employing general, restrictive covenants.

Of course, in the case of financial commodities such as loans, trade-offs exist between these various ways of protecting one's self as a lender. Increasing the down payment required, pledging collateral, and inserting restrictive covenants into the credit agreements imply different combinations of information and monitoring costs over the life of the loan. It is expected that the combination of these instruments chosen would be such that the marginal reduction in expected costs would be equal for all instruments employed.

It also appears that, for certain types of loans, the information costs associated with ascertaining the magnitudes of the arguments in (1) are so high that it is preferable to employ instrumental variables instead. Consequently, financial intermediaries generally gather, check, and update information about borrowers, for frequently the historical record of past obligations is a good source of information about the likelihood of repayment. This information also may be quantified and summarized with the aid of credit scoring techniques and financial statement analysis.

The considerations discussed above are not specific to financial intermediaries—they are relevant to all financial commodities produced by economic agents. Now we turn to the question of why financial intermediaries usually perform these services rather than other services.

The Costs of Producing Financial Commodities

The production of financial commodities, like the production of any other good, requires the use of various forms of labor and capital goods. In the production of financial commodities, these inputs are more extensively employed in tasks of documentation, information and monitoring. Extensive documentation is necessary because financial commodities are claims that can be easily converted into generalized purchasing power or consumption goods by the holder with small transactions costs. Therefore, there must be little question that these claims are legally enforceable—so little question that the high legal costs associated with government enforcement of these contracts will be rarely employed.[15]

As suggested above, information costs are often relatively large for the production of financial commodities, especially for those that entail a promise to repay funds at a later date (e.g., loans). Where collateral is required to secure a loan, its value must be ascertained and kept current. This task is not difficult for assets that are continuously traded, such as listed securities; however, determination of the value of other assets may require specialized expertise. Though information and monitoring may be most useful for such financial commodities as loans; deposits and other commodities require these aspects of production to reduce frauds, litigation, and misunderstandings which are expected to be more costly. Financial intermediaries create financial commodities which require the performance of these tasks because they have a comparative advantage in processing documents, in acquiring information about borrowers' ability to repay debts, and in monitoring instruments that can be easily converted into generalized purchasing power.

Three sources of this comparative advantage may be delineated. First, the intermediary is able to achieve economies of scale as a consequence of specialization. Thus, routines designed for and information received about a consumer or types of consumers can be used to process other consumers;[16] further, specialized machinery and forms may be developed and designed.[17] Economies of specialization may make it cost-effective for some institutions to specialize in providing a single type of financial commodity to a specific group of customers (e.g., consumer

---

15. To reduce these enforcement costs and to minimize monitoring costs for the intermediary financial commodities are sometimes negotiable: a holder of a financial claim need prove only that he is a holder in due course, having not obtained the claim through fraud or theft. Consequently, negotiable commodities require extensive control and monitoring by the holder, since it is very difficult to prove that the bearer of such an instrument is not a holder in due course. Therefore, these transactions costs can be shifted directly from the issuer to the bearer.

16. Credit scoring for screening consumer loans and lending by bank officers who specialize in specific industries or types of real estate are examples.

17. Check sorting machines and loan forms and routines are examples.

finance companies), while others carry a limited line of related financial commodities (e.g., wholesale commercial banks, thrift institutions, and investment companies), and others are virtually financial department stores (e.g., full-service commercial banks).[18] Second, some important information, such as details about a borrower's financial condition, can be obtained by a financial institution at much lower cost than by others because the financial institution is expected to exhibit, and therefore can more easily acquire a reputation for exhibiting, discretion with that type of information.[19] Third, financial institutions can reduce the transactions costs associated with search. An individual who wishes to lend can search for another person who wishes to borrow, but this process is generally more expensive than having a market through which these transactions can be accomplished. (Note, however, that the process does not require a matching of borrower and lender, even within the same institution.)

Specialization and Diversification in the Production of Financial Commodities

It is generally the case (for reasons that are discussed below) that financial intermediaries tend to produce more than one kind of financial commodity. They tend to have many sources and uses of funds. They can obtain funds through equity, borrowing, accepting deposits of various kinds, etc. They can employ these funds by making loans, purchasing securities, building offices, buying equipment, etc. In equilibrium, the total cost of obtaining another dollar from any of these sources should be equal. In equilibrium, the total return from employing another dollar in any of these uses also should be equal. Consequently, financial intermediaries should not necessarily associate sources and uses of funds.

That financial intermediaries should not associate sources and uses of funds does not imply that the two sides of the balance sheet involve independent and separable decisions. As long as bankruptcy costs are positive, the structure of the two are related. For instance, real estate investment trust companies generally borrowed in the short term credit market and loaned in the intermediate or long term credit market. This practice exposed these trusts to interest rate risk which could have been hedged by matching the maturity structure of the assets and liabilities. When interest rates rose, the value of their assets fell by a much greater amount than did the value of their liabilities. This resulted in great financial difficulty for many of the trusts. Similarly, government regulations that essentially restrict thrift institutions to mortgage loans and savings deposits expose them to a higher probability of bankruptcy. Thus, a hedging of risks appears desirable. But it need not be achieved (and may not be achievable) by matching deposits from and loans to individuals (or any other group or type of consumers). What, then, determines whether and how financial institutions offer a specialized or diversified array of financial commodities and services?

---

18. Available evidence indicates that many financial institutions (such as thrift institutions) have achieved virtually all economies of scale available through specialization and consequently might benefit from economies of diversification were they not prohibited by law from producing additional financial commodities. (See Benston [1972].) These issues are considered further, below.

19. Private individuals may be denied access to this information for fear that it may be made available to competitors or others.

Financial intermediaries, as they presently are organized, offer a wide variety and combination of financial commodities and services. Aside from laws and government regulations (which, as we discuss in section V, are a principle determinant), several factors may account for this diversity. Among these are economies of scale from specialization, economies from diversification, economies to customers from purchasing financial commodities and services at a single location or from a single institution, and reduction of the probability of incurring bankruptcy costs. The available empirical evidence suggest that there exist economies of scale in the production of financial commodities. However, the financial intermediaries studied are sufficiently large to have achieved most of these economies with respect to the production of relatively homogeneous financial commodities.[20] Additionally, there appear to be some economies of scale from diversification.[21] Diversification also may be valued because it lowers the probability (and hence the expected cost) of bankruptcy. This occurs because the returns from investments in different types of loans, customer services, locations, etc., over different states of the world (such as general and local economic depressions, inflation, changes in consumers' tastes and preferences, changes in laws, and changes in the enforcement of regulations) are likely to be imperfectly correlated. Of course, it is expected that institutions will equate the marginal advantage from diversification with the marginal cost of less specialization.

A combination of economies from joint production and lower consumer-borne transactions costs, may explain why specific commodities and services generally are produced by financial intermediaries.[22] Reduced customer transactions costs also explains the offering of these services by many financial institutions. However, specialized financial intermediaries may have some comparative advantages over department store types of institutions.[23] But, as we discuss in section V, outdated laws and regulations may prevent change from occurring. First we consider the pricing of financial commodities and services.

IV. PRICING OF FINANCIAL COMMODITIES AND SERVICES

Several studies have suggested that, in the absence of government regulation and in the presence of efficient markets, financial institutions would unbundle charges for their products.[24] In equilibrium, given competitive markets, financial institutions would charge consumers the marginal cost of producing the commodities and

---

20. See Benston [1970], [1965], [1974], Bell and Murphy [1968], Longbrake and Haslem [1975], and Halpern and Mathewson [1975].

21. See Benston [1972], [1974], [1975], Halpern and Mathewson [1975], and Bell and Murphy [1968].

22. Safe deposit boxes, for example, require investments in vaults, alarm systems and guards. These also are required for safeguarding the currency and negotiable instruments used for fund transfers, deposits and loans.

23. For example, given the laws and consumers' tastes, specialized small loan companies may be able to supply high risk consumer cash loans at a lower transactions cost than can commercial banks. Changed conditions (such as changes in consumers' tastes and effective reductions in graduated legal ceiling rates on small loans as a consequence of inflation) may reduce the advantage of specialization to the point where the advantages from diversification dominate.

24. See, for example, Black [1975] and Knight [1975].

services demanded. Similarly, consumers would be rewarded according to the marginal value of the resources they made available to the intermediary. Thus charges would be levied for each check processed, each deposit made, each statement prepared and mailed, each note collected, each installment payment rendered, etc.

However, this analysis neglects the transactions cost of accounting for transactions. It is clear that, were it not for the prohibition of interest on demand deposits, we would observe direct interest payments rather than "free" checking or lower rates charged on loans to depositors, etc. But the cost of accounting for each service demanded by consumers might prevent complete unbundling from being cost-effective. Rather it seems likely that for some financial commodities financial institutions would estimate the average cost of processing a given type of account and pay (or charge) an interest rate and/or overall service charge that covers expected costs. This procedure would permit dispensing with the monitoring and accounting system required for the explicit charge system.[25] The issue, of course, is essentially an empirical one—which charging system (or combination of systems) requires the smallest costs net of benefits. However, government regulations impinge on the choice of method and on the ability of financial institutions to repackage and alter their commodities as technology and consumers' tastes change. We turn, next, to this question.

V. GOVERNMENT REGULATION

It is clear that any government regulation presents a constraint on those regulated that reduces aggregate welfare, with four possible exceptions: the constraints are not binding, there are externalities, the cost of government administration is reduced, and resources are redistributed among persons so that someone's welfare is increased. The following discussion is limited to considering the effect of specific regulations on the ability of financial institutions to meet consumers' demands efficiently. In general, we do not consider the welfare effects of these regulations on individuals (in part because we believe these to be unimportant).

Government regulations on financial intermediaries may be grouped as follows: (1) licensing, (2) price control, (3) credit allocation and (4) supervision. Each is discussed in turn.

First, unlike most other enterprises, financial intermediaries generally cannot be established without permission from some regulatory agency. In addition, bank-type financial institutions require regulatory permission to expand via branching, a method that is prohibited or restricted by many states, with expansion across state lines being generally prohibited. Financial intermediaries also are prohibited or restricted from offering specific financial commodities and services.[26] Licensing

25. It should be noted that before the prohibition of interest payments on demand depostis (in 1933), banks generally paid interest only on large account balances and generally did not charge for individual services rendered.

26. For example, only commercial banks can offer demand deposits. Thrift institutions cannot offer non-real estate related commercial loans. Consumer cash loans (except for real estate related and student loans) cannot be offered by thrift institutions in most states. Commercial banks cannot make equity investments or offer equity investment services to consumers.

regulations also may prevent financial intermediaries from organizing production of financial commodities and services in efficient ways. Restrictions on the intermediaries' ability to jointly produce and offer their output at locations of their choosing necessarily increases the transactions costs (including inconvenience costs) that some consumers must bear.

Second, control over the prices received and paid by financial intermediaries are imposed by the states and the federal government. State imposed usury laws place ceilings on the amounts that intermediaries can receive on loans.[27] As is the case for price controls generally, interest rate restrictions tend to misallocate resources. When they are effective, usury laws result in restricted availability of riskier and operationally more costly loans as financial intermediaries shift their funds to loans whose net yields are within legal limits. Since the ceilings are stated as rates per dollar and rarely are changed, inflation increases the effectiveness of the ceilings as the premium for inflation increases to the point where loans are not as profitable as other investments. Larger business loans are made in preference to smaller loans since, generally, larger loans require lower operating expenses per dollar loaned. Tie-in arrangements, such as compensating balances, are used which effectively increase the rate of interest charged. Smaller consumer loans are not offered, except as "loss leaders." (Bowsher [1975] and Benston [1975].) If the ceilings become sufficiently restrictive, consumers cease using the services of regulated financial intermediaries and, where the law permits, direct loans and other forms of disintermediation take their place. The net result seems to be a decline in welfare.

Ceilings on deposit payments similarly have dysfunctional effects. The argument that prohibiting interest payments on demand deposits is necessary to keep banks from making risky loans in an effort to offset the interest expense has been shown to be false (Benston [1964]). Rather the prohibition has the effect of a government administered oligopolistic cartel price enforcement. Ceilings on the rates paid on time and savings deposits also have the effect of raising transactions costs, as financial intermediaries and consumers attempt to evade the restrictions. Premiums and promotions are less valuable to consumers than their cash equivalents and disintermediation is generally more costly than intermediation. However, the cost to consumers of disintermediation may exceed the benefits (which appears to be the case for holders of smaller savings accounts).[28] The effect, then, of ceilings on the prices financial intermediaries may charge and pay for funds is to increase transactions costs (borne by the intermediaries and consumers) and misallocate resources.[29]

The third form of government regulation, control or credit allocation, takes at least four forms: (1) mortgage lending is encouraged by a variety of subsidies; (2) loans made to finance purchases of securities are discouraged by margin require-

27. See Bowsher [1975], pp. 20–21, for a table that summarizes the usury rates state by state.

28. See Pyle [1974] for an estimate of the opportunity losses incurred by savers from interest rate regulation.

29. The ceilings have been defended as necessary for the continued viability of specialized thrift institutions and beneficial to deserving groups (such as the housing industry, in the belief that the intermediaries' reduced cost of funds necessarily will be passed on to mortgages and that an interest rate

ments that call for relatively large amounts of collateral; (3) small consumer cash loans are limited by state imposed limitations on maturities and interest rate ceilings; and (4) mandatory credit allocation to groups and areas which presumably have been discriminated against have been proposed. Other controls have been attempted in the past, such as "moral suasion" by the Federal Reserve to discourage banks from making foreign and other undesirable loans and wartime controls on consumer loans and mortgages.[30]

Although there is doubt that subsidies on mortgage loans actually increase the stock of housing (Jaffee [1975] and Meltzer [1974]), there seems little doubt that controls reduce some forms of lending by financial intermediaries. In the short-run, such controls as margin requirements for loans to purchase securities can reduce the amount of funds allocated for this purpose. But, as Mayer [1975] concludes after an extensive review of the literature and analysis of credit allocation schemes: "…credit allocation is not an efficient system. The shifts in the distribution of credit which it tries to bring about are of doubtful value, and, in any case, credit allocation would be ineffective in the long run. But this would not prevent it from imposing substantial costs on the economy." (p. 91)[31]

Efforts of authorities to force or encourage financial intermediaries to lend specific groups or in specific areas also have been proposed.[32] It is possible that these efforts will succeed, particularly if the institutions have not been making loans as a consequence of misinformation or prejudice. However, if past experience is a guide, the net effect is likely to be the imposition of additional transactions costs with little effect on the allocation of credit.

Finally, financial intermediaries have almost always been subjected to rather close supervision by governmental authorities. This supervision takes the form of detailed reporting requirements (i.e., quarterly call reports by banks, monthly reports by savings and loan associations, annual statutory reports by life insurance companies, etc.) and (for bank-type intermediaries) direct examination. Several reasons explain this type of supervision: (1) the public-facility nature of most intermediaries, wherein the general public believes or is encouraged to believe that funds deposited in a financial intermediary are "safe," (2) the fact that the assets held by financial intermediaries can be misappropriated relatively easily if controls are not maintained, (3) the externalities that are believed to exist, wherein

---

differential in favor of thrift institutions will favor allocation of credit to mortgage loans). Even assuming that savers who find it too costly to disintermediate should (and do) support home builders and buyers, the effectiveness of this form of subsidy has been questioned by a large number of studies (see Meltzer [1974] and Jaffee [1971]). Since this argument explicitly assumes intermediaries associate sources and uses of funds, it is highly doubtful that this rationale is valid. The continued viability of financial intermediaries who are required by regulations to concentrate on mortgage loans and savings and time deposits, though, is in question as continued inflation increases the effectiveness of interest rate ceilings.

30. We also should mention that non-interest bearing required reserves in effect allocate resources from users of deposits to the federal government.

31. Also see Benston [1975] for an example of the effect of state imposed restrictions on driving almost all of the consumer finance companies in Maine out of business.

32. These proposals include mandatory mortgage loans in sections of a city presumably discriminated against (anti-red-lining), loans to black-owned businesses, loans to women, etc.

the failure of one intermediary affects others (bank-runs) and the economy in general, and (4) deposits are insured by government agencies (FDIC, FSLIC, NCUA).[33]

One important effect of close supervision is increased transactions costs. The supervised financial intermediaries must bear the direct cost of assessments and examination fees. They also absorb the costs of meeting the examiners' and supervisors' requests for data and the opportunity cost of complying with their orders. In equilibrium, these costs are borne by the purchasers of their output. However, the benefits from examination should be deducted from the costs. The principal benefit is the savings by consumers of the information and insurance costs that they otherwise would have to bear were the FDIC, FSLIC and NCUA not examining the institutions and insuring deposits and shares. These cost savings would appear to be relatively greater for holders of small deposits, since much of the cost of information about the operations of an institution is fixed with respect to the amount deposited. Borrowers, on the other hand, have much less interest in the safety of their creditors.

Conclusions on Government Regulation and Financial Intermediation

Goverment regulation increases the transactions costs of financial intermediation principally by restricting financial intermediaries from operating as efficiently as they otherwise would. Licensing restrictions increase the costs. Obviously, these restrictions increase the transactions costs of financial intermediation. Furthermore there appear to be few offsetting benefits for consumers, other than some reduction in information costs derived from the knowledge that the regulatory authorities can punish a poorly or fraudulently run intermediary by removing its license or refusing it permission to expand. Controls on interest payments and charges, mandatory credit policies and close supervision also result in higher transactions costs and asset misallocations. Only examination and deposit insurance appear to reduce some information and insurance costs that consumers otherwise would incur.

On the other hand, government regulations may benefit existing financial institutions at the expense of consumers and of would be competitors. This conclusion would be consistent with the capture hypothesis of regulation.

However, a mitigating factor should be mentioned. There is considerable contemporary evidence that financial institutions, acting in their own self-interest, have and are breaking down the regulatory barriers. The prohibition of interest payments on demand deposits is violated by "free" checking and, most recently, by negotiable orders of withdrawal (NOW) accounts and other demand deposit-like systems offered by thrift institutions. Automatic shifts between checking and savings deposits in commercial banks and the establishment and growth of money management funds also are examples of institutional methods of effectively paying interest on demand deposits. Place-of-business funds transfer terminals, located in food and other stores by savings and loan associations, are permitting them to offer demand deposit-like services at remote locations in unit banking areas. Approval of

---

33. These reasons are analyzed in Benston [1973] and, with the exception of the last reason, are found generally not to be valid.

these systems by the Federal Home Loan Bank Board in January 1974 led to the Comptroller of the Currency's approval in December 1974 of similar customer-bank-communication-terminals (CBCTs). These, in turn, are forcing a number of state authorities in unit banking states to approve their use by state banks.[34] Thus, the higher opportunity value of deposits appears to have made the same existing electronics technology economically feasible. The regulatory barriers are being breached. But, of course, the price paid by consumers is greater than had the barriers not initially existed.

V.   CONCLUSIONS

In this paper we have tried to show that the analysis of transactions costs is central to the theory of financial intermediation. Financial intermediaries produce financial commodities which can be used to effect consumers' inter-temporal, intra-temporal and state determined consumption decisions. Changes in technology and in consumer borne transactions costs alter the types of financial commodities produced, the way in which they are packaged, and the institutions that produce and sell them to consumers. Furthermore, government regulation essentially restricts financial intermediaries from changing the specific commodities they produce to meet changes in technology and consumer tastes. We believe a more complete analysis would show the relationship between specific types of transactions costs and the type of financial intermediary and financial commodity that should arise to reduce these costs. We feel that this approach represents an appropriate direction for future analysis.

REFERENCES

Bell, Frederick W. and Murphy, Neil B., *Costs in Commercial Banking: A Quantitative Analysis of Bank Behavior and Its Relations to Bank Regulation*, Research Report No. 41, Boston: Federal Reserve Bank of Boston, 1968.

Benston, George J., "Interest Payments on Demand Deposits and Bank Investment Behavior," *Journal of Political Economy*, LXXII, October 1964, pp. 431–449.

———. "Economies of Scale and Marginal Costs in Banking Operations," *The National Banking Review*, 2 June 1965, pp. 507–549.

———. "Cost of Operations and Economies of Scale in Savings and Loan Associations," in *Study of the Savings and Loan Industry*, Federal Home Loan Bank Board, Washington: U.S. Government Printing Office, 1970, pp. 971–1209.

———. "Savings Banking and the Public Interest," *Journal of Money, Credit and Banking*, IV, February 1972 (Part II), pp. 131–226.

———. "Bank Examination," *The Bulletin*, New York University, Institute of Finance, Nos. 89–90, May 1973, p. 73.

———. "The Costs to Consumer Finance Companies of Extending Consumer Credit," in *Technical Studies Volume II*, National Commission on Consumer Finance, U.S. Government Printing Office, Washington, D. C.: 1974, pp. 1–158.

———. "State Controls on Consumer Finance Company Loans: The Case of Maturity Regulation in Maine," in *Government Credit Allocation: Where Do We Go From Here?*, Institute for Contemporary Studies, San Francisco, Califormia and the Center for Research in Government Policy of the Graduate School of Management, The University of Rochester, New York, 1975, pp. 181–208.

---

34. See Lovati [1975] for a review of these developments.

Black, Fischer, "Bank Funds Management in an Efficient Market," *Journal of Financial Economics*, 2, December 1975, pp. 323–339.

———— and Scholes, Myron, "The Pricing of Options and Corporate Liabilities," *Journal of Political Economy*, 81, May-June 1973, pp. 637–659.

Bowsher, Norman N., "Usury Laws: Harmful When Effective," *Review*, Federal Reserve Bank of St. Louis, 56, August 1974, pp. 16–23.

Brunner, Karl and Meltzer, Allan H., "The Uses of Money: Money in the Theory of an Exchange Economy," *American Economic Review*, LXI, December 1971, pp. 784–805.

Cagen, Phillip, *Determinants and Effects of Changes in the Stock of Money*, New York, 1965.

Feige, Edgar L. and Parkin, Michael, "The Optimal Quantity of Money, Bonds, Commodity Inventories, and Capital," *American Economic Review*, LXI, June 1971, pp. 335–349.

Friedman, Milton and Schwartz, Anna J., *A Monetary History of the United States*, 1867–1960, Princeton, 1963.

Halpern, Paul J. and Mathewson, G. Frank, "Economies of Scale in Financial Institutions: A General Model Applied to Insurance," *Journal of Monetary Economics*, 1, 1975, pp. 203–220.

Hamada, Robert, "Investment Decision with a General Equilibrium Mean-Variance Approach," *Quarterly Journal of Economics*, LXXXV, November 1971, pp. 667–683.

Hyman, David, "A Behavioral Model for Financial Intermediation," *Economic and Business Bulletin*, Vol. 24, Spring-Summer 1972.

Jaffee, Dwight M., *Credit Rationing and The Commercial Loan Market*, New York: John Wiley and Sons, 1971.

————. "Housing Finance and Mortgage Market Policy," in *Government Credit Allocation: Where Do We Go From Here?*, Institute for Contemporary Studies, San Francisco, California and the Center for Research in Government Policy and Business of the Graduate School of Management, The University of Rochester, New York, 1975, pp. 93–122.

Jensen, Michael and Meckling, William, "Theory of the Firm: Managerial Behavior, Agency Costs, and Ownership Structure," Working Paper, The Graduate School of Management, The University of Rochester, New York.

Kardouche, George K., *The Competition for Savings*, New York: The Conference Board, 1969.

Karni, Edi, "The Value of Time and the Demand for Money," *Journal of Money, Credit and Banking*, VI:1, February 1974, pp. 45–64.

Klein, Michael, "A Theory of the Banking Firm," *Journal of Money, Credit and Banking*, III:2 (Part 1), May 1971.

Knight, Robert E., "Customer Profitability Analysis, Part II: Analysis Methods at Major Banks," *Monthly Review*, Federal Reserve Bank of Kansas City, October 1975, pp. 11–23.

Long, John, "Comment on the Pricing of Corporate Debt: The Risk Structure of Interest Rates," *Journal of Finance*, 29, May 1974.

Longbrake, William A. and Haslem, John A., "Productive Efficiency in Commercial Banking: The Effects of Size and Legal Form of Organization on the Cost of Producing Demand Deposit Services," *Journal of Money, Credit and Banking*, VII, August 1975, pp. 317–330.

Lovati, Jean M., "The Changing Competition Between Commercial Banks and Thrift Institutions for Deposits," *Review*, Federal Reserve Bank of St. Louis, July 1975, pp. 2–8.

Mayer, Thomas, "Credit Allocation: A Critical View," in *Government Credit Allocation: Where Do We Go From Here?*, Institute for Contemporary Studies, San Franscisco, California and the Center for Research in Government Policy of the Graduate School of Management, The University of Rochester, New York, 1975, pp. 39–92.

Melitz, Jacques and Pardue, Morris, "The Demand and Supply of Commercial Bank Loans," *Journal of Money, Credit and Banking*, V:2, May 1973, pp. 669–692.

Meltzer, Allan H., "Credit Availability and Economic Decisions: Some Evidence from the Mortgage and Housing Markets," *Journal of Finance*, XXIX:3, June 1974, pp. 763–777.

Pesek, Borris P., "Bank's Supply Function and the Equilibrium Quantity of Money," *Canadian Journal of Economics*, III:3, August 1970, pp. 357–383.

Pierce, James L., "Commercial Bank Liquidity," *Federal Reserve Bulletin*, 52, August 1966, pp. 1093–1101.

Pyle, David H., "Descriptive Theories of Financial Institutions," *Journal of Financial and Quantitiative Analysis*, December 1972, pp. 2009–2029.

———. "The Losses on Savings Deposits from Interest Rate Regulation," *The Bell Journal of Economics and Management Science*, 5:2, Autumn 1974, pp. 614–622.

Savings, Thomas R., "Transactions Costs and the Demand for Money," *American Economic Review*, LXI, June 1971, pp. 407–420.

Smith, Clifford, "Option Pricing: A Review," *Journal of Financial Economics*, 3, January/March 1976.

Towey, Richard E., "Money Creation and the Theory of the Banking Firm," *Journal of Finance*, XXXIX, March 1974, pp. 57–72.

Zabel, Edward, "Consumer Choice, Portfolio Decisions, and Transactions Costs," *Econometrica*, XXXXI, March 1973, pp. 321–335.

BANK FUNDS MANAGEMENT
IN AN EFFICIENT MARKET

Fischer BLACK*

Massachusetts Institute of Technology, Cambridge, Mass. 02139, U.S.A.

Received May 1975

This paper discusses general principles for choosing bank assets and liabilities, for deciding on when to make a loan and what interest rate to charge, for pricing funds transfer services such as the handling of checks, for establishing compensating balance requirements, and for dealing with government regulation. The discussion assumes markets are efficient and deals first with an unregulated environment and then with policies in the face of regulatory constraints. Most of the policies which would be optimal in an unregulated environment will be optimal in the regulated environment such as in the U.S. today, because it is relatively easy to get around most of the regulations that are applied to banks by the use of non-deposit liabilities, compensating balances and negative checking accounts.

1. Introduction

The phrase 'bank funds management' is meant to imply general principles for choosing bank assets and liabilities, for deciding on when to make a loan and what interest rate to charge, for pricing funds transfer services such as the handling of checks, and for dealing with government regulation. An 'efficient market' is one in which there are no opportunities to make special profits, given the transaction costs that exist in the market, and given the government regulations that may act as constraints.

If the market for financial services is efficient, then any bank that uses optimal methods of funds management (and has good management practices of other kinds) will make normal profits. A bank that uses other methods of funds management will make below normal profits.

If the market for financial services is not efficient in ways that can be identified, then a bank can make above-normal profits by taking advantage of any inefficiencies it finds. One kind of inefficiency that may exist is that transaction

*Sloan School of Management, Massachusetts Institute of Technology. This paper was written while I was at the Graduate School of Business, University of Chicago and was prepared for delivery at the Wells Fargo Conference on Capital Market Theory held in San Francisco on July 25–27, 1973. I am indebted to Myron Scholes for many discussions on these issues, and to Michael Jensen, Edward Kane, John McQuown, and Merton Miller for comments on an earlier draft.

costs of some kind may be too high. By finding ways to reduce these costs, a bank may make above normal profits.

Normal profits on an investment by a bank are defined in the same way as normal profits on an investment by any other kind of firm. In each period, the expected increase in value of the project plus any net cash inflows, divided by the start-of-period value of the project, should equal the short-term interest rate plus a risk premium proportional to the project's beta.[1]

Some of the questions we will ask in this paper are the following:

(1) Does the fact that a bank keeps cash available to pay depositors tend to reduce the interest rates that it can pay on its deposits?
(2) What is the function of compensating balances, used in connection with loans?
(3) For the banking system as a whole, what is the relation between loans and deposits?
(4) How can a bank prepare for a coming period of tight money?
(5) How much can a bank plan on being able to borrow in the federal funds market in an emergency?
(6) Can a bank's loan losses be reduced on loans to large companies if the loan officer makes regular visits to talk to management?
(7) Are many banks successful because they are consistently better at forecasting interest rates than their competitors?

One characteristic of an efficient market is that the price of any security reflects everything that more than a few people know about the issuer of the security. This means that if an investor can find out something about the issuer, other investors probably have the same information, so it is likely that the information is already discounted in the price of the security. In an efficient market, buying and selling securities on the basis of special information or interpretations of known facts is not likely to be profitable.[2]

Similarly, in an efficient market, it will not pay for a bank to take actions that increase reported earnings but have no effects on the bank's cash flows. And it will pay to take actions that increase the bank's cash flows, either now or in the future, even though there is a decrease in current reported earnings. An efficient market is not fooled by attempts to manipulate earnings.

Banking is probably the most regulated business in the United States. It may even be more regulated than public utilities. Many banking practices are a response to regulation, and would not exist if banking were unregulated. To highlight the effects of regulation, and the ways in which banks can get around

---

[1]For a discussion of the assumptions about efficient markets that make this definition of normal profits correct, see Fama and Miller (1972) or Sharpe (1970).

[2]For a more extensive discussion of portfolio management in an efficient market, see Black (1971).

many kinds of regulation, we will discuss bank funds management in an unregulated world, and will then go on to discuss ways of dealing with regulation.[3]

2. Unregulated banking

In this section, we will assume away ceilings on the interest that can be paid
on demand deposits or time deposits, ceilings on the interest that can be charged
on loans, restrictions on the location or number of bank branches or new banks,
restrictions on the types of loans that banks can make and the types of assets
they can hold, restrictions on the nature and amount of deposits they can accept
and securities they can issue, and requirements that they hold minimum amounts
of reserves and other assets.

It seems likely that without all of these restrictions, a great deal of the banking
business would be done by a few large banks that are national in scope. This
does not mean that competition would be reduced; a few large banks might well
compete more vigorously than many small banks do now. There would probably not be any sharp distinctions between banks and other kinds of financial
institutions. It is even possible that savings and loan associations and finance
companies would not exist as distinct institutions.

Deposits subject to withdrawal on demand would pay close to the 'wholesale
money rate', which we can take to be the federal funds rate. If deposits paid
more than the average federal funds rate, a bank would do better by borrowing
in the federal funds market. If deposits paid less than the average federal funds
rate, a bank would do better by offering a little more on deposits than other
banks, and lending in the federal funds market the money that is attracted from
other banks.

Note that the costs associated with handling deposits have little to do with
the dollar amount of a deposit. There are costs associated with opening and
closing an account, with sending out statements, with auditing, with deposits
and withdrawals, and with handling transfers by check or credit card. None of
these depend in any significant way on the size of an account. So in a competitive
world, they will not affect the interest rate paid on an account.

When competition is not restricted, we expect to find each product or service
offered by a firm priced at marginal cost, including the required profit on the
investment needed to provide that product or service. Thus we would expect to
find banks charging the 'full price' in this sense for all of the services connected
with deposits.

There would be a charge for opening or closing an account; a monthly charge
for maintaining the account; a charge for making deposits and withdrawals,

---

[3]For a discussion of the relation between monetary policy and banking in both an unregulated world and the existing environment, see Black (1970).

even if they are made in cash at the teller's window; and a charge for handling transfers by check or credit card that reflects all the costs involved.

' Thus a bank would make money on its demand deposit and funds transfer services, not by paying lower than market rates on its deposits, but by charging the full price for all the separate services related to deposits.

Since the costs to a bank of maintaining two accounts are higher than the costs of maintaining one account, competition will lead the bank to have only one account per customer. For borrowers, a bank would set up an account that can have either a positive or a negative balance. When the account has a positive balance, it will earn interest at the wholesale money rate. When it has a negative balance, it will be charged interest at a rate that depends on the amount of the loan, on the financial condition of the borrower, and on the nature of any collateral that may be assigned to the loan. When the balance in the account is negative, all deposits will serve to reduce the amount of the loan, and payments will increase the amount of the loan.

Normally, then, a loan will not involve a fixed schedule of payments. Whenever an individual borrower receives a salary payment, he will use it to reduce his loan. The amount of the loan will go up again as he pays for purchases. In any month in which he receives more than he pays out, the loan will be reduced. In any month in which he pays out more than he receives, the loan will be increased. As the amount of the loan changes, the interest rate on the loan will change, reflecting changes in the default risk and changes in the cost of administering the loan per dollar of loan.

It seems clear that a bank has more protection against loan defaults when it is getting all of an individual's salary deposits than when it is getting only a payment out of his salary. In principle, it can even find out quickly when the individual loses his job or gets a reduction in salary.

If the bank has more and better credit information about an individual, it will be able to offer him lower rates on his loan. The prospect of lower rates may even induce the individual to supply complete credit information to the bank at regular intervals. If the individual routes most of his receipts and payments through his loan account, they can serve as a continuing source of credit information.

Having a good quality credit file on an individual, including a substantial amount of historical information if the individual has been a customer for some time, should give the bank an edge over other lenders. It can offer lower rates to good credit risks and will be able to count on smaller default losses and lower collection costs than lenders who do not have the same information. Thus it seems natural that most credit would be provided by an individual's bank. He would make relatively little use of department store, oil company, and automobile finance company credit. Even if he incurred such debt at the time of a purchase, he would probably use his bank credit to pay it off.

It would be helpful to the bank to have certain kinds of formal collateral to secure an individual's loan. If the bank has financial assets as collateral with a value substantually greater than the amount of the loan, then it can charge an interest rate only slightly higher than the wholesale money rate plus the cost of keeping track of the collateral. Real estate is also an excellent form of collateral, though the cost of verifying title and appraising the property periodically is likely to be higher than the cost of keeping track of collateral in the form of securities. A natural kind of mortgage loan would be one where the interest rate fluctuates with wholesale money rates, but where the spread between the rate charged and the federal funds rate depends on the relation between the amount of the loan and the value of the property. If the property value increases fast enough, it may be possible that neither payments of interest nor payments of principal have to be made. If the property is collateral for the individual's single loan account, then the amount of the loan will fluctuate as he receives income and pays expenses. But he may be able to spend all of his income, leaving the value of the loan to increase at a rate equal to the rate of interest currently being charged. It seems possible that this sort of arrangement would reduce an individual's resistance to having a fluctuating interest rate on his mortgage loan. The ability to use real estate as collateral in buying other things, such as cars, means also that he would get a lower rate than he could get if he were only able to offer the car itself as collateral.

It would also be helpful to an individual's bank to receive information directly from his employer. Again, the bank can offer a lower interest rate on his loan if he has his employer send his salary checks directly to the bank. It is possible that a bank might offer a 'group loan' to the employees of a given company, where the interest rate would depend in part on the loss experience of the entire group of employees. (And in part on each individual's credit record.) The employer might even choose to subsidize some of the interest cost as a fringe benefit for employees. This would make group loans similar to group insurance policies. It seems likely that the savings in administrative costs would be as high for group loans as they are for group insurance policies.

The bank would offer credit to anyone with a reasonable credit record at a rate that depends on interest rates generally, on the cost of administering the loan, and on the likelihood of default. On riskier loans, rates would depend on general economic conditions. In a recession, the risk of default on a personal loan and the cost of administration and collection are likely to be higher, so the interest rate charged should be higher in a recession than in an expansion.

Now let us turn to the services a bank can provide to businesses. A corporate deposit would pay interest at the wholesale money rate, just like an individual's deposit. The deposit would be transferrable by check, so it would probably dominate investments in securities such as commercial paper. However, since the interest rate on a short-term debt security may differ somewhat from the interest rate on a demand deposit, a bank might also offer time deposits that have terms that are directly comparable to the terms on debt securities that are available in the marketplace. It seems likely that the bank could offer interest rates at least as high as those available on debt securities with comparable risk. And such a time deposit might automatically become a demand deposit at maturity, paying the going call money rate, unless the corporation wants to invest the money in a new time deposit.

Competitive pressures would force a bank toward pricing all of its services for corporations, like its services for individuals, separately. It would likely charge the full price for processing transactions and for its other services. It might even charge for the deposit and withdrawal of currency, to cover the costs of the transactions themselves and the cost of keeping supplies of currency in convenient locations.

A corporate bank account might have a very, very large negative balance. If the corporation has a loan from the bank, there is no reason for it to keep any other acount with the bank. It can use its receipts to reduce the amount of the loan, and the payments it makes can automatically increase the amount of the loan. The corporation might be charged interest each day on the average size of its loan for that day. In this situation, it is clear that the relation between 'current assets' and 'current liabilities' for the corporation is meaningless. Current liabilities might be far greater than current assets, because the demand loan might be enormous, but the corporation might be able to make substantial payments without any delay because it is able to increase the amount of its loan.

The bank might set up a schedule of interest rates for a corporate customer that depends on the amount borrowed. The interest rate will be affected by the increased cost of supervising the loan and by the increased risk of default as the amount borrowed goes up. When the loan is large compared to the customer's assets, the bank will want to exercise close control over his activities. Within this framework, the customer will choose the strategy for managing the size of his loan that he likes best. The interest rate can also depend on other factors, such as the value of the company's common stock, as we will see below.

When the bank is making a loan to a corporation, the basic protection that the bank has is the value of the corporation and its assets, not the corporation's cash flow or its ability to make payments on the debt at a specific point in time. The ultimate protection is the ability of the owners to sell equity shares in the corporation to get the money to reduce the size of the loan. The corporation's current and expected future cash flows are important only in that they affect the amount of money that can be raised in this way.

The easiest kind of loan to make is a loan to a corporation with outstanding common stock that trades regularly. It's not important that the stock be listed, only that it be traded at least every week or so, so the bank can observe the value that the market places on the company's common stock. The value of the company as a whole is the total value of its common stock, plus the value of its other liabilities, including the bank loan. When this value is substantially higher than the amount of the loan, the bank is in a relatively safe position.[4]

When the corporation has traded stock, the price of the stock will be the primary piece of credit information. The bank also needs information on the corporation's liabilities other than the bank loan, and information on whether the corporation is in default on any of the terms of the loan. In an efficient market, there is no reason for the bank to try to get information about the company and its prospects on its own. It is very unlikely that the bank will get any information that isn't already discounted by the stock price. And it will have no way of knowing when it has such a piece of information. If the bank's loan officers have the ability to obtain and identify information on companies that is not already identified, they would be better off as security analysts.

The interest rate on the loan can be made to depend on the price of the company's common stock, as well as on the size of the loan and other factors. When the stock price goes down, the interest rate can go up; and when the stock price goes up, the interest rate can go down. This will compensate the bank for the increased risk of default when the value of the company is low, and it will give the company an incentive to keep a substantial equity cushion to prevent the interest rate from going very high.

There might even be a formal arrangement that if the price of the company's stock falls far enough, it will have to issue additional common stock to raise money to reduce the amount of the loan. If the stock market is efficient, the fact that the stock price is lower than it may have been in the past does not imply that it is a bad time to sell stock. So the company should not object to an arrangement like this, especially if it reduces the interest rate on the loan.

The interest rate on a loan should also depend on the risk of the corporation, as measured by the variability through time of the value of the corporation. If the company has traded stock, then we can use the variance of the return on the stock (together with the nature of its other liabilities) as a measure of the risk of the corporation. The higher the variance of the return on the stock, the higher the risk of default, and the higher the cost of supervising the loan, and thus the higher the interest rate that should be charged.

If there are options traded on the corporation's stock, the bank can even use the option prices to get the market's estimate of the variance of the return on the stock. The value of an option depends on the future variance of the return on the stock, and on other variables that are almost all observable. So we can use the option formula to convert the price of an option into an estimate of the variance of the return on the stock.[5]

Note that the interest rate charged on a loan is a promised rate, not an expected rate. If the quoted interest rate depends in the right way on the variance of the value of the corporation, then the expected return on the loan will be the

---

[4]The basis for many of the statements in this section can be found in Black and Scholes (1973).

[5]The option formula is given in Black and Scholes (1973).

right function of the beta of the loan. For example, suppose the bank is asked to make a loan on a project whose success or failure is independent of the state of the economy. The project is the only collateral for the loan. If it succeeds, the loan will be paid back with interest. If the project fails, the entire amount loaned will be lost. There is a $\frac{2}{3}$ chance that the project will succeed, and a $\frac{1}{3}$ chance that the project will fail. The loan is for one year, and the one year riskless interest rate is 6 percent. The interest rate on this loan should be 59 percent plus the charge for administering the loan. If the interest rate is 59 percent, then the expected return on the loan will be 6 percent. [$\frac{2}{3} \cdot 1.59 = 1.06$.] Since the β of the collateral is zero, the β of the loan will be zero, and it is appropriate that its expected return be equal to the riskless interest rate.

Note that the fact that the bank may hold a portfolio of loans like this does not mean that the rate can be lower because some of the risk can be diversified away. If the bank had hundreds of loans like the one described above, all on projects whose outcomes are totally independent of one another, it would still charge the same rate on each loan. Because of its diversified portfolio, it would be quite sure of earning approximately 6 percent on its overall portfolio.

The interest rate on a corporate loan will also depend on the amount of protection that the loan agreement gives the lender. For example, if the lender is given control over specific kinds of collateral in the event of default, the interest rate can be reduced. Real estate, equipment, and accounts receivable are some of the obvious kinds of collateral that may be used. To protect the lender in the case of bankruptcy, it may make sense to structure parts of the loan as leases. If the bank owns the equipment and leases it to the company, giving the company an option to buy the equipment back for a very low price when the lease terminates, then the bank may find it relatively easy to claim the equipment in case of bankruptcy. For tax purposes, the corporation would own the equipment. But for purposes of bankruptcy court, the corporation would own only an option to buy the equipment at some point in the future, conditional on having made all the required lease payments.

It is important that the loan agreement specify the conditions under which a corporation can take on other liabilities, and the conditions under which it can significantly change the nature of its assets. In general, adding liabilities without a substantial increase in assets hurts the lender. Subtracting assets, or increasing the risk of the assets, also hurts the lender.

There are certain ways of writing the loan agreement that may reduce the administrative costs of bankruptcy substantially. For example, it may be possible to write the loan agreement so that if an event occurs that might normally force the company into bankruptcy court, the stockholders will lose all of their rights, and a new class of common stock will be issued and given to the bank to replace its loan. The bank would then have the right to the value of the entire company, if it is willing and able to satisfy the claims of any prior creditors.

Such a provision would require the consent of the stockholders, but might be worthwhile if it makes a significant difference in the interest rate charged on the loan, and in the value of the company.

In general, the tighter the loan agreement, the lower the interest rate can be on the loan. If the loan agreement allows the corporation to do things that will hurt the lender's position, then the interest rate charged will have to be high enough to cover the expected losses from these actions. If the corporation does not expect to do these things, then the loan agreement should specify that they can't be done, and this will allow the interest rate to be lower.

However, a lower interest rate need not be better for the company than a higher interest rate. The tighter the loan agreement, the higher the cost of administering the loan is likely to be. This cost reduces the value of the company. If the cost of enforcing the loan agreement were zero, the existence of a risky loan would not, in itself, have any effect on the value of the company. If there is a way to limit the risk to the lender without significant cost, a correctly priced high risk loan with few restrictions may be better for the company than a correctly priced low risk loan with many restrictions and a high administrative cost.

In discussing the factors involved in setting the interest rate on a loan, we have not mentioned the sources of the money that is being lent, or the alternative uses of that money, except that the federal funds market is both a potential source of funds and a potential alternative use for funds that are being lent out. It is clear too that those who have positive accounts at a bank are providing some of the funds that are being lent to those who have negative accounts. But it is important to keep in mind that a bank can use non-deposit funds to make loans. It can issue capital notes, or long-term bonds, or common stock. And it can borrow from other banks that have issued non-deposit liabilities.

If a bank has investments in notes or bonds or common stock, and it is faced with an increase in loan demand, it can sell these investments to get the funds to make additional loans. If markets are efficient, any time is a good time to sell (or buy) an investment. The fact that loan demand is increasing does not mean that bonds or other investments are likely to be underpriced.

The bank can also use its investments as collateral for borrowing funds, if it doesn't want to sell them. For example, this is what happens with repurchase agreements, where government securities are used as collateral for short-term loans.

Because of the variety of sources and uses of bank funds, there will be no special relation between bank deposits and bank loans, either for an individual bank or for banks as a group. There may be some banks that have common stock liabilities only, and thus make loans without having any deposits at all. And there may be some banks that have only positive accounts, and lend all of their money to other banks, making no loans at all to non-bank corporations. For the banking system as a whole, loans may be far greater than deposits.

Since a bank can count on getting funds from one or more of these sources at any time, there is no reason for it ever to ration loan money or loan customers. There can be no 'availability' problem. And, as with any corporate investment decision, there is no reason to take the source of funds into account when setting the price on a loan. If the expected return on the loan is commensurate with its beta, it's a good loan to make, whether the money to be loaned comes from deposits, or bonds, or stock.

Liquidity need not be a factor in a bank's decision-making. In the environment we are describing, liquidity is so freely available that it is literally costless. A bank account will provide as much liquidity as anyone could want, and positive accounts pay interest at the full federal funds rate. Negative accounts provide as much liquidity as positive accounts, and the interest rate charged on a negative account with good collateral will be only slightly higher than the federal funds rate.

As we have already noted, the fact that currency held by a bank does not pay interest need not affect the rates it pays and charges on its accounts. The costs of holding currency will be paid by those who use currency: by those who deposit currency in the bank or withdraw currency from the bank. If it were not for such customers, the bank would not have to hold currency. So the costs of holding currency should be covered, in a competitive world, by transaction charges for the deposit and withdrawal of currency.

If there is a central bank, and if deposits with the central bank do not pay interest, then banks will tend not to hold central bank deposits at all. If some banks demand payment in central bank funds for checks on other banks, the other banks will charge them the cost of holding the required central bank deposits. Banks who are willing to clear through the inter-bank loan market (the federal funds market) will not have to pay this cost. The charge for such transactions will pay the full cost of holding idle funds in central bank deposits.

Similarly, if government securities bear lower interest rates on a risk-adjusted basis than bank deposits or private securities, banks will generally not hold government securities. We might expect the rates on government securities to be slightly lower than rates on deposits with comparable maturity, because the risk of default on government securities will be slightly lower. But government securities should not have any liquidity advantages over deposits. It's hard to beat the liquidity of an asset that can be transferred for 25¢ or less.

Neither interest rate forecasts nor forecasts of cash flows would be necessary in this world. Since we are assuming that the securities markets are efficient, it would not help a bond investment officer to forecast interest rates so he will know what bonds to buy and sell. He cannot hope to get information that the market has not already discounted and to be able to recognize it as such. Similarly, forecasting interest rates will not help a bank decide what rates to pay on its liabilities of various maturities. It might as well take the rates given by the market, and pay the going rate on all of its liabilities.

Forecasting of cash flows is unnecessary because it is easy to deal with whatever cash flows the bank gets without advance notice. An unexpected cash inflow can be lent in the federal funds market, or, equivalently, deposited in another bank. The funds to meet an unexpected cash outflow can be borrowed in the federal funds market. If by any chance there were sometimes difficulty in locating a source of funds, this would create a profit opportunity that a bank could exploit by stepping in and becoming a dealer in federal funds. It seems likely that a simple, partially automated system could be created that would bring together borrowers and lenders of federal funds quite efficiently. And there should be no problem with the rate. By offering a rate slightly higher than the going rate, a bank should be able to get all the money it would ever want.

Because the federal funds market can be used to handle cash flows of any size, there is no reason to try to choose a maturity structure for the bank's bond portfolio that is related to the bank's cash flows. Diversification across maturities will have no value in helping the bank handle cash flows.

3. Dealing with regulation

It is quite clear that banking is not a 'natural monopoly' in the way that certain types of public utilities are. Economies of scale in banking do not seem great enough to put a bank that is moderate in size at a significant disadvantage relative to a large bank. So it is not clear why banking needs to be regulated at all. It certainly does not need the vast amount of detailed regulation that it gets. Currently, federal and state regulators must approve mergers, starting a new bank, and opening a new branch. Branching across state lines is prohibited entirely, and branching within states is often restricted or prohibited by law. Payment of interest on demand deposits is prohibited. Interest rates on deposits and loans are often subject to ceilings. The types of loans that banks can make are restricted. Bank examiners frown on risky loans and investments. They are concerned about the ratio of loans to deposits. Banks are required to keep fixed amounts of reserves on deposit with the central bank or with other designated banks.

One of the stated purposes of all this regulation is to keep depositors from bearing any losses when a bank fails. This does not seem to be too harmful as a regulatory goal, because the cost of this kind of regulation, if done in a reasonable way, should be very low. It may even be a beneficial form of regulation.

The simplest way to ensure that depositors do not bear losses when a bank suffers losses on its loans or investments is to require that a substantial portion of a bank's liabilities (at market value) be in forms other than deposits. The regulators might insist, for example, that the market value of a bank's non-deposit liabilities be at least equal to the value of its deposits. In case of a fall in the market value of its liabilities (caused, for example, by a fall in the value of its assets) a bank would have to sell more stock or bonds, or make its deposits less attractive to reduce the amount of its deposits.

If the bank's stock is publicly traded, this form of regulation is very easy to apply. The market value of the stock can be obtained by multiplying its price per share by the number of shares. The market value of the debt can be observed if it is publicly traded, or it can be estimated without much trouble given the risk and value of the common stock.[6]

If the bank's stock is not publicly traded, it may be harder to estimate its market value. To compensate for this, the regulators might require that the estimated market value of its non-deposit liabilities be greater than two or three times the value of its deposits, rather than just greater than the value of its deposits. In an efficient market, it is no more costly to get funds from non-deposit sources than to get deposits, so this would not be a hardship for smaller banks.

In addition, the government might guarantee to pay off itself any deposits where the bank's losses are so massive that the value of the bank declines to less than the value of its deposits. If the bank had to keep large amounts of capital at all times, as described above, this would be so unlikely that it seems unnecessary to call it insurance and have banks pay insurance premiums. In the absence of a major economic upheaval far worse than anything in U.S. history, this sort of loss is likely to occur only when fraud has occurred. In other words, this guarantee by the government would not require the administrative staff and detailed supervision of a bank's affairs that we have with the current deposit insurance system.

The economic function of reserve requirements in the current system, I believe, is simply to tax demand deposits.[7] Since banks do not earn interest on the reserves they have to hold against deposits, the amount they can pay on their deposits, directly or indirectly, is reduced. There may even be a certain logic to this tax. The interest paid on debt securities is generally subject to income taxes. When banks provide services to holders of demand deposits, the value of these services is generally not taxed. So reserve requirements may tend to equalize the taxation of deposits and debt securities.

Since a bank can get funds from so many sources other than deposits, such as bonds and common stock, government control of the total quantity of reserves does not imply government control of the total amount of bank lending. Government control of bank liabilities does not give it control over bank assets at all. Even when the government must approve any new issues of bonds or stock by banks, it does not have control over bank lending. Banks can issue large quantities of bonds and stock in periods when the government thinks it

---

[6]A discussion of the relation between the value and risk of a corporation's common stock and the value of its debt is given in Black and Scholes (1973).

[7]I have argued elsewhere [Black (1970)] that reserve requirements do not help the government control the overall level of economic activity.

wants to encourage bank lending, and can invest some of the money in corporate or government bonds. Then when the government is restricting new bank issues of securities, the banks can simply sell the bonds to get money to lend out.

Thus even in a regulated banking environment such as the one we have in the U.S. today, there are some relatively simple ways in which banks can keep the government from controling their lending activities by controlling their liabilities. If most banks do not use these methods, then a bank that does may find that it is able to earn significant profits by being able to make loans in periods of 'tight money' that other banks are not able to make.

The government can, on the other hand, choose to control bank lending directly. If it puts a quota on the amount that each bank can lend, then a bank will have to use other methods to minimize the impact of the regulation. In this case, a relatively simple alternative to making a loan is buying debt securities from the customer. Or letting someone else put up the money for a loan, and then doing the loan administration for the ultimate lender.

No matter what methods the government uses, short of direct control of the amount of loan administration done by a bank and all of its affiliates, it seems that a bank can virtually eliminate the impact of the regulation on its loan administration, and can make decisions on loans almost as if it were in an unregulated banking environment.

Similarly, there are some very effective ways for a bank to get around the regulation of interest rates that can be paid on deposits. It is well known that banks provide services to the holders of demand deposits to make up for the fact that they cannot pay interest directly. They charge less than the full price for processing checks, and they sometimes don't charge at all for depositing currency in an account or for withdrawing currency from an account. They provide fancy bank buildings, and a larger number of bank buildings than they would have if they were allowed to pay interest on demand deposits. These services may cost a bank as much as the full amount of interest it earns on its demand deposits, but they may not be worth that much to the bank's depositors. Thus the prohibition of interest payments on demand deposits may not give the banks any monopoly profits, because the potential monopoly profits are frittered away in inefficient forms of competition.

There is, however, one very effective way for a bank to get around maximum interest rates on both its deposits and its loans: the use of compensating balances in connection with loans. I believe that currently, the primary economic function of compensating balances is to give banks a way of paying interest on demand deposits.[8]

To illustrate the use of compensating balances to pay interest on demand deposits, let us imagine that demand deposits are not allowed to bear interest,

---

[8]For a discussion that comes close to this point, and references to the literature on compensating balances, see Wrightsman (1973).

and that a bank must keep reserves on deposit with the central bank equal to 10 percent of its demand deposits. A corporation that keeps a demand deposit that averages $2,000,000 wants to borrow $10,000,000 to buy some equipment. The bank is currently giving the corporation services such as reduced charges for processing its checks as a way of giving it some return on its balances. The current short-term interest rate is 6 percent, and the bank feels that an 8 percent rate would be appropriate for the $10,000,000 loan, in the light of the risk of default.

If the bank simply charged 8 percent on the loan, its interest income would be $800,000 per year. But its earnings on the $2,000,000 demand deposit, minus $200,000 in reserves, are $108,000 per year. So if it counts those earnings as part of its interest income, it needs to charge only 6.92 percent on the loan to bring its total income to $800,000 per year.

The bank can thus offer to lend the corporation $10,000,000 at 6.92 percent, if the corporation agrees to keep a balance averaging $2,000,000 at the bank. Thereafter the bank will not give the corporation any other services in return for its deposit. The bank will charge the full price for processing transfers of funds and for all other services.

In effect, the corporation is getting 5.4 percent interest on its demand deposit and the bank is getting 8 percent on its loan. So the use of compensating balances allows the effective interest rate on deposits to be higher than the stated rate of zero, and allows the effective interest rate on loans to be higher than the stated rate at the same time.

Note that it is important that the corporation be allowed to use its compensating balances as working balances. Sometimes, a bank making a loan will require that a corporation keep a minimum level of compensating balances rather than an average level. The minimum level is then not available for use as working balances. The corporation must keep working balances in addition to the minimum level of compensating balances. This type of compensating balance requirement makes sense only as a way of making the effective interest rate on the loan higher than the stated rate. For example, it might be useful when there is a problem with state usury laws, or when the federal government is pressuring the banks to keep their loan rates down. In the absence of pressures like these, it is better to make the loan without minimum compensating balances.

It is the reserve requirement that makes minimum compensating balances uneconomical. If the bank wants to make a $10,000,000 loan at 8 percent, it will get $800,000 in interest income. If it makes a $12,000,000 loan and requires a minimum compensating balance of $2,000,000, the corporation will still get $10,000,000 to use in buying equipment. But since the bank will now have to keep an additional $200,000 in reserves, it will have to get $812,000 in interest income. The bank will charge 6.77 percent on the $12,000,000 loan to generate this much interest income. The corporation will effectively be paying 8.12

percent on the $10,000,000 that it gets to use. Thus the corporation would be better off if the loan were made without minimum compensating balances.

It seems easier to use compensating balances to pay interest on corporate demand deposits than to use them to pay interest on individual demand deposits. However, it is used to some extent for individuals, as when a borrower is required to maintain a checking account while his loan is outstanding.

There is another device that can be used about as effectively as compensating balances to eliminate the cost of holding demand deposits at zero interest. This device also eliminates the problem of the bank's having to hold reserves against demand deposits. It involves letting a customer write checks on an account with a negative balance. It is sometimes called 'overdraft banking'.

To use this device, a bank sets up a line of credit for a customer, and allows him to increase the amount of his loan by writing checks on his account, and to decrease the amount of his loan by making deposits to his account. The customer can put all his cash flows through his loan account. Any cash inflows can reduce the amount of the loan, and any cash outflows can increase the amount of the loan. If his inflows are high enough that he is in danger of paying off the loan, he can use some of them to buy securities or other earning assets.

The interest rate on the loan can depend on the size of the loan, on the current federal funds rate, and on the customer's credit standing. More important, though, it can depend on the formal collateral that the customer can supply. A corporate customer might use Treasury Bills or prime commercial paper as collateral for its loan. This collateral is so good that the interest rate on the loan would be only slightly higher than the interest rate on the collateral.

Suppose that a corporate customer is keeping a demand deposit that fluctuates between zero and $4,000,000, with an average of $2,000,000. Unless the bank has effective ways of paying interest indirectly, the corporation is losing interest on an average of $2,000,000. Now suppose that the corporation withdraws its entire balance, and gets a loan for the amount by which the balance falls short of $4,000,000, and uses the $4,000,000 to buy Treasury Bills. It then gives the Treasury Bills to the bank as collateral for the loan, so the bank will charge an interest rate on the outstanding balance of the loan only slightly higher than the Treasury Bill rate. The charge for keeping the line of credit open will be negligible, because the risk to the bank is negligible so long as it has the collateral. The principal cost to the bank will simply be the cost of keeping track of the collateral.

Now the customer will be getting interest on $4,000,000 in Treasury Bills, and will be paying interest at a slightly higher rate on an average loan of $2,000,000. The amount of his loan will fluctuate between zero and $4,000,000. The corporation will be receiving net interest at slightly less than the Treasury Bill rate on its net assets, which will be averaging $2,000,000. In effect, the corporation will be getting interest on its demand deposit.

The same sort of thing can be done for an individual. He can use a savings account as collateral for his loan, or securities, or real estate that he may own. A natural way to set up a system like this for an individual who owns his home would be to give him a mortgage loan that can fluctuate in amount. When he writes checks, he will increase the amount of his mortgage, and when he deposits his salary and other cash inflows, he will reduce the amount of his mortgage. He will not need to hold a demand deposit that pays zero interest. He will, however, pay the full price for the processing of checks and other services that he gets from the bank.

Unfortunately, current laws limit severely the extent to which banks can make mortgage loans of this type. But it is possible that these laws will be changed in the near future.

4. Summary

In an efficient, unregulated, competitive market for banking services, a bank will pay the wholesale money rate on its deposits, and will charge the full price for its funds transfer services. It will allow transfers into and out of negative balances as well as positive balances. It may have large amounts of common stock and bonds outstanding in addition to its deposit liabilities. It may have a large continuously long or short position in the federal funds market.

A bank will quote rates on loans that depend on the rates on riskless loans with the same maturities; the size of the loan; the value and risk of the customer's assets, particularly those assets that are used as formal collateral for the loan; the customer's prospective cash inflows and outflows, and the uncertainty about them; and the amount of continuing information that the customer is willing to supply or have others supply on his credit condition. The rates that the bank quotes will not depend on whether the money is coming from deposits, bonds, or common stock; nor on the capital structure of the bank. The rate the bank quotes will depend on the total risk of the customer's assets and net cash flows, not just on that part of the risk that can't be diversified away.

Loans to corporations with common stock that trades frequently will be particularly easy to make. The variability of the price of the common stock can be used to measure the risk of the corporation, and the price of the common stock can be used to measure the current condition of the corporation. The interest rate charged on the loan can even be made an explicit function of the common stock price.

In an unregulated market for banking services, liquidity would be free. Positive and negative bank accounts would bear full market rates of interest, and would be transferrable for the price of processing a check. The fact that banks hold currency reserves will not cause them to change the interest rates they pay on deposits or loans.

Most of the above statements should be true even in a regulated banking environment, such as the one we have in the U.S. today, because it is relatively easy to get around most of the regulations that are applied to banks. Non-deposit liabilities make it possible for banks to avoid regulation of the total amount of their loans. Compensating balances and the use of negative checking accounts make it possible to avoid the prohibition on payment of interest on demand deposits and other interest rate ceilings.

References

Black, F., 1970, Banking and interest rates in a world without money, Journal of Bank Research 1, Autumn, 8–20.

Black, F., 1971, Implications of the random walk hypothesis for portfolio management, Financial Analysis Journal 27, March/April, 16–22.

Black, F. and M. Scholes, 1973, The pricing of options and corporate liabilities, Journal of Political Economy 81, May/June, 637–654.

Fama, E.F. and M.H. Miller, 1972, The theory of finance (Holt, Rinehart and Winston, New York).

Sharpe, W.F., 1970, Portfolio theory and capital markets (McGraw-Hill, New York).

Wrightsman, D., 1973, On the rationality of compensating balance requirements, Southern Economic Journal 39, Jan., 427–430.

Information Production, Market Signalling, and the Theory of Financial Intermediation

TIM S. CAMPBELL and WILLIAM A. KRACAW*

I. Introduction

CURRENT THEORIES OF FINANCIAL markets have been unable to successfully deal with the existence of financial intermediaries. In fact, there is very little theory which attempts to explain the purpose which intermediaries serve in capital markets. There is a relatively large literature dealing with portfolio choice of intermediaries, particularly commercial banks.[1] But all of this literature lacks a convincing analysis of the underlying rationale for the operation of the intermediary. The basic problem is that, in a perfect market environment, intermediaries could perform no unique financial service that investors would be unable to reproduce as easily. And, while it has long been understood that intermediation must develop as a response to costly market imperfections, few theories have been offered which provide a concrete explanation of the intermediary function.

A recent effort using an imperfect markets approach which relied on transactions costs to motivate financial intermediation was made by Benston and Smith [2]. Another reason for the intermediary function, proposed by Campbell [4], is to maintain the confidentiality of information about the firm's investment projects possessed by manager-insiders but valued by competing firms. As suggested by Leland and Pyle [15], however, there may be an even more powerful explanation which follows from the existence of informational asymmetries in capital markets. The specific hypotheses proposed by Leland and Pyle is that there is something intrinsic in intermediation which solves the problems of moral hazard and appropriability which inhibit the production of information. It is useful to think of their hypothesis as maintaining that information production is a sufficient condition for the emergence of intermediaries in an otherwise perfect capital

* Respectively Associate Professor of Finance, University of Utah and Assistant Professor of Management, Purdue University.

This paper was written while William Kracaw was a graduate student at the University of Utah. Thanks go to Sudipto Bhattacharya, John Finkelstein, and a referee for helpful comment.

[1] See Pyle [15] for survey of this literature.

market. The purpose of this paper is to develop a rigorous inquiry into the merits of the hypothesis posed by Leland and Pyle.

It is important to keep in mind, as the hypothesis of this paper is laid out, that there is a potentially powerful null hypothesis regarding the existence of financial intermediaries.[2] That hypothesis is that financial intermediaries are merely portfolio managers which would, in an unregulated competitive market, earn a competitive management fee. It follows that the unique kind of financial inter-mediation industry observed in the United States is a product of the regulatory environment. This view tends to minimize the significance for capital markets of information asymmetries. In general, this view hypothesizes that problems sur-rounding information are not critical in explaining intermediaries as we know them.

The ultimate explanation of the emergence of intermediaries to which this paper leads is eclectic. That is, the view taken in this paper is that none of the explanations which have appeared in the literature; i.e., to achieve economies in transactions costs, to protect confidentiality, or to produce information; stand alone as satisfactory explanations of intermediaries as we know them. Rather they are complementary explanations of intermediation. This paper concentrates on the information production role of intermediation and demonstrates that, contrary to the supposition of Leland and Pyle, intermediation, per se, is not sufficient to resolve the moral hazard and appropriability problems intrinsic in the market for information. But this does not imply that an important function of intermediaries is not the production of information. Our hypothesis is that intermediaries emerge as information producers because the production of infor-mation, the protection of confidentiality, the provision of transactions services, as well as other intermediary services, are naturally complimentary activities.

In addition to offering some insight into the role of financial intermediaries, this paper presents an important conclusion about the resolution of the moral hazard problem in financial markets which arises when there is imperfect infor-mation. It is demonstrated that initial wealth endowments resolve the moral hazard problem in that they function as a guarantee of the reliability of infor-mation. That is, the market will believe the signals of those who have a sufficient stake in the market that they have no incentive to misrepresent their information. This result leads to the important and general conclusion that initial wealth endowments act as a barrier to entry in the market for information and as a general constraint on reliability.

The general procedure adopted in this paper is to search for a Rational Expectations equilibrium in a capital market with imperfect information about the value of firms.[3] The concept of equilibrium employed here is somewhat broader than that which has been used in recent treatments of incentive signalling problems. The equilibrium sought is one where both the values of firms are accurately identified and this is accomplished in the most efficient manner. The

---

[2] See Fama [7] for a treatment of "banks" (defined in a broad sense) which is consistent with this null hypothesis.

[3] An anonymous referee deserves credit for the suggestion that the results be organized around a formally stated Rational Expectations equilibrium. This suggestion proved exceptionally helpful.

efficient Rational Expectations equilibrium defined here, in effect, requires equilibrium in both the capital market and the market for information.

The search for an equilibrium proceeds through a sequence of market regimes which are increasingly complicated but which provide increased avenues for resolution of the problems created by imperfect information. The treatment of this sequence of market regimes is organized into two sections. In each section investors know only the average value of firms in the market but may invest in costly information about the true value of firms. The distinguishing characteristic of Section II is that investors decisions on the profitability of information production depend solely on the returns they receive from the securities they purchase. The next section extends the results of Section II to include the possibility that owners of projects may offer investors side payments to either invest or not invest in information opportunities. This section demonstrates that investors acquire no advantage in the resolution of the moral hazard problem by organizing themselves as intermediaries.

In Section IV the final result of Section III is directly contrasted to the hypothesis posited by Leland and Pyle. This section is concluded with the argument that intermediaries evolve as important information producers if they jointly produce information about the value of firms as well as other services valued in the marketplace. This suggests that an important function of intermediation is the production of information about the value of investments, but that information production alone is not a satisfactory explanation of the intermediary's function. A brief final section points out the generality of the results.

II. IMPERFECT INFORMATION AND THE VALUES OF FIRMS: THE CASE OF NO SIDE-PAYMENTS

Introduction and Definition of Equilibrium

In this section we introduce the basic set of assumptions which will be used, with some crucial modifications, throughout the paper. We then consider a simple model of the market value of firms where investors have imperfect but symmetric information about the values of individual firms. This model is nearly identical to the basic model which has served as the starting point of other authors who have written on this and related topics, e.g., Akerlof and Ross. We then consider an extension of the basic model which allows asymmetric access to information by investors.

Each of the market regimes considered in this section and the next is analyzed to determine whether there exists a Rational Expectations equilibrium and whether the equilibrium is what will be labeled "efficient." A market regime will be said to have a Rational Expectations equilibrium if these conditions are met: (1) individual agents maximize their own wealth, taking prices of assets as given; (2) asset prices adjust in a tattonement process so that the asset market clears; (3) ex ante expectations of market participants are fulfilled. This Rational Expectations equilibrium will be said to be efficient if there are no opportunities for profitable production of information which are forgone in equilibrium.

The conditions for equilibrium are essentially the same as the equilibrium conditions employed in incentive signalling models, as for example in Spence [20], Ross [18] and Bhattacharya [3]. The equilibrium essentially says that the market provides some mechanism whereby the assets in the market become properly valued. But an efficient Rational Expectations equilibrium involves an additional and stronger condition.[4] This condition requires that the market must provide some mechanism for investments in information to take place which are profitable for investor-information producers acting as price-takers. Specifically, the market must provide a mechanism which allows investors to undertake any opportunity to identify the value of firms which is profitable when viewed as a price-taker. Therefore, an efficient Rational Expectations equilibrium requires not only that the information asymmetry is resolved but that it is resolved efficiently.

Assumptions Of The Analysis

There are two assumptions, one mentioned explicitly below and one only implicitly, which drive the analysis in this and the subsequent sections. The first is that there are no opportunities for costly signals of value by firms to the market which provide the basis for a successful incentive signalling scheme. Ross [18] has suggested that penalties incurred by managers in the event of bankruptcy may be just such a cost which allows capital structure to be a signal. In another context Leland and Pyle [15] have employed such a signal for owner-managers. Whatever the merits of these arguments (and these positions are not immune to criticism, see Chen and Kim [6] and Bhattacharya [3]) we assume that such perfect signals do not exist. Indeed, if they did there would be no room for the present analysis and no room for intermediaries as information producers.

The second assumption is that investors with informational advantages cannot privately use their information for profit. In fact, the assumption employed below of a tatonnement process for price determination assumes that private information immediately becomes a public good. While this may, at first glance, seem to be an unfortunate assumption, it is, in fact, chosen by design. When portfolios held by investors with information advantages are small relative to the market, they can invest their own funds based on their information with little impact on the market. If they seek to increase their profits beyond that obtainable from their own funds, they must persuade the market of the quality of their information. Their only other alternative is to wait for trading on their superior information to gradually increase their wealth.[5] But it is precisely the attempt to attract new funds based on superior information which is the subject of this

---

[4] In most incentive signalling models the distinction between these conditions is not particularly meaningful in that a signalling equilibrium satisfies both conditions. The additional element introduced here which makes the two conditions meaningful is the opportunity for investors to invest in information about the value of assets. This introduces profit·opportunities which create a meaningful distinction between the existence and efficiency of equilibrium. In effect, most existing analyses of signalling problems do not consider equilibrium with respect to both the valuation of firms and the production of information, whereas both are considered here.

[5] See Figlewski [8] for an analysis of market efficiency with this type of wealth redistribution.

analysis. The assumption that information, once acquired, becomes public through its use, focuses our analysis on the market where investors with information advantages are not an inconsequential part of the market.

This assumption creates the same difficulties encountered by Grossman [11]. If the return to information is to come from trading profits some noise must remain in market prices. On the other hand, it is not only possible, but enlightening to permit the firms whose value is being determined in the market to directly compensate investors for producing information.[6] This is the path down which the analysis of this section leads, though this section stops short of the formal introduction of side payments. Side payments form the basis for the analysis of Section III.

The specific assumptions underlying the model in this section are as follows.

(i) All firms in the market consist of profitable investment projects with one of two unique return distributions, either type A or type B.

(ii) The number of A assets or firms is N_A, and the number of B assets is N_B, $N = N_A + N_B$.

(iii) Investors are identical in all respects including the values they attach to particular return distributions, except that they have distinct wealth endowments, W_i.

(iv) Investors place values V_A and V_B on firms of type A and B where $V_A > V_B$.

(v) All investors have the same information about the identities of individual assets and their values. Specifically, investors know $\bar{V}$, the average or cross-sectional values of assets but not the identity of each individual firm.

(vi) The number of assets required to achieve the full benefits of diversification in an investors portfolio of accurately valued firms is equal to either N_A or N_B assets, whichever is lower. This means investors will lose nothing by limiting the size of their portfolio to N_A or N_B assets, if they believe all firms are properly valued.

(vii) Equilibrium prices are formed as in a tatonnement process where prices bid by investors are instantaneously known by all others.

(viii) Owners of firms are distinct from investors with capital. They undertake their investment projects and therefore receive value from their assets only by selling title to their projects to investors.

A Model of Market Value With Symmetric Information Among Investors, But No Opportunities For Information Production

Under these assumptions investors will value all N firms at $\bar{V}$. Even though investors know there are assets in the market worth more or less than $\bar{V}$ they have no way of reliably identifying undervalued or overvalued assets. Moreover, no investment strategy could consistently outperform that of purchasing equal

---

[6] It should be noted that Bhattacharya [3] points out that there is a problem in Ross' analysis in that the implications of side payments from the owners of overvalued firms are not fully developed.

fractions of all assets valued at $\bar{V}$.[7] While it is possible to derive excess returns, ex post, from randomly identifying a disproportionate number of undervalued assets, it is equally probable that equivalent losses may be the result. The expected value of a random selection of $n < N$ assets is still $n\bar{V}$; but a risk averse investor would require a premium to invest in those assets since a random portfolio also introduces additional portfolio risk resulting in the value of the portfolio being less than $n\bar{V}$.

If there are no better alternatives (as assumption (vii) implies) owners of A firms will be willing to accept this result. But since at $\bar{V}$, type A assets are undervalued by $V_A - \bar{V}$, individually, and $N_A(V_A - \bar{V})$ in total, it would be to the advantage of the owners of type A assets to communicate their identities, even at a cost, to the market. If information provided by firms regarding their true values were considered reliable by investors, competition among investors for undervalued assets would establish V_A and V_B as prevailing prices of A and B assets in equilibrium.[8] However, owners of overvalued firms have an equal incentive to maintain the status quo.

In order to see whether all firms will remain valued at $\bar{V}$ suppose that owners of undervalued projects advertised themselves to the market as owners of type A assets hoping that competition would restore the prices of their assets to V_A. They could even incur costs of distributing this information of $V_A - \bar{V}$ per asset and still be as well off as when the market price reflected average values. Owners of overvalued assets, however, should be willing to pay up to $\bar{V} - V_B$ to somehow maintain the market price at $\bar{V}$. To accomplish this they might pay up to $\bar{V} - V_B$ per asset to misrepresent themselves as owners of undervalued assets. Since owners of undervalued assets have no more incentive to establish the true qualities of assets than the owners of overvalued assets have to frustrate this result, the market would be unable to discern the true values of individual assets. Investors could not rely on any information imparted to the market by owners of projects. The moral hazard involved in the transfer of reliable information implies that the price of all firms will be $\bar{V}$.[9] The information asymmetry means that there will not be a Rational Expectations equilibrium.

---

[7] Actually, in the absence of information about the true identities of assets, the optimal investment strategy would be to purchase an equal portion of each asset, where the value invested in each asset is a function of the investor's relative market wealth, or,

$$V_{ik} = \frac{W_i}{N} \quad \text{and} \quad \sum_i W_i = \bar{V}N \forall\, i, k$$

V_{ik} = value of kth asset purchased by ith investor, and W_i = wealth invested in the market by the ith investor. In this fashion the most risk-return efficient investment is made which guarantees the investor returns worth, W_i, with no unnecessary portfolio risk.

[8] Wealth would be redistributed from owners of overvalued assets to the owners of undervalued assets in the amount $N_B(\bar{V} - V_B) = N_A(V_A - \bar{V})$.

[9] Leland and Pyle [14] suggest that another result is possible; that is, the market may fail due to the withdrawal of undervalued firms. This is an example of the problem discussed by Akerlof [1]. This requires either that there are a large number of unprofitable firms in the market so that, on average, firms are unprofitable, or that profitable firms withdraw to get a higher value elsewhere. The first possibility requires that there is no method by which firms with unprofitable projects can be

Market Value and the Incentive for Information Production

The conclusion that all firms in the market will trade at a value $\bar{V}$ is due to the fact that investors are precluded from gathering information about the true value of assets. Suppose, instead, that investors can obtain information, at a cost, that allows them to perfectly identify type A and B assets. Assumption (v) can be amended to include this possibility. The modified assumption is: (v) Each investor has costless access to the cross-sectional average value of firms, $\bar{V}$. In addition each investor has the ability to acquire information about the true value of all firms at a cost. For the ith investor the cost is C_i.[10]

One motivation for investors to undertake the investment in information might be to attempt to extract excess profits from the purchase of undervalued assets at $\bar{V}$. With this motive in mind, the investor would decide whether to invest in information by comparing the excess profits from investing his wealth in type A firms with the cost of acquiring information, i.e., he will invest if

$$\frac{W_i(V_A - \bar{V})}{\bar{V}} > C_i \tag{1}$$

where

W_i = wealth of the ith investor

$\dfrac{(V_A - \bar{V})}{\bar{V}}$ = the excess rate of return from investing in type A firms at $\bar{V}$.

C_i = cost of information for the ith investor.

Note that assumption (vi) insures that he loses nothing by restricting his portfolio to $N_A < N$ securities, once he has discovered the true identities of firms.

It would be profitable for investors to behave this way only if the information acquired were to remain private. This will generally not be the case when investors in the market are few and large enough that others are aware of their opportunities and actions. In markets where prices are efficient market signals of available information, the incentives for collecting information are significantly affected. Grossman [11] and Grossman and Stiglitz [12] have shown that in markets where asymmetries in information about the quality of assets exist, the market price may instantaneously and efficiently aggregate and summarize all available information about the quality of the asset. Under these conditions, information may be characterized as a public good (the value or usefulness of

---

discouraged from entering the market. For if firms are perceived to be profitable, on average, the market will still operate. This is considered explicitly in Campbell [5] and it seems unlikely that this problem will be significant. The possible existence of firms with unprofitable projects is not considered here. The other possibility is that undervalued firms withdraw because they believe they can receive a higher value in another place or at another time and the market will still function but only with low quality firms. Such possibilities are also excluded here by assumption (viii).

[10] There are a number of alternative possible specifications for information costs. This specification implicitly assumes economies in information production which makes it inefficient for any single investor to produce information about only part of the firms in the market and another investor produce information about another group of firms. Campbell [5] employs a specification which does not employ this assumption and a more general analysis of the implications of alternative specifications is presented in Kracaw [13].

information is undiminished as it becomes available to other investors) which cannot be protected so as to extract excess profits from the market.

To see the implication of this problem more clearly, imagine an investor with information production opportunities who undertakes the opportunity at cost, C_i, and successfully identifies each asset in the market. Due to the opportunity to extract excess profits from the market, the investor no longer purchases an equal fraction of each asset but chooses only type A assets (causing prices to rise by increasing competition for those assets). The effect of these actions is to signal other investors the true identities of the undervalued assets. In a tatonnement market the remaining investors react to new knowledge of the assets in the market by bidding up the prices of type A assets to V_A and bidding down type B assets to V_B. Because trades do not take place out of equilibrium, the information producer is unable to extract any excess returns by purchasing undervalued assets.[11] If such a strategy is attempted, the investor must incur the cost of information, C_i. The information producer, therefore, receives only market value for his investment, but incurs a cost, C_i.[12] Again, there is no Rational Expectations equilibrium.

III. THE MARKET VALUE OF FIRMS WITH SIDE PAYMENTS

Introduction

The preceding section showed that investors have no apparent incentives to acquire information that might identify the true values of firms, particularly if that information is costly. In the absence of investor supplied information, market prices reflect the average value of firms, $\bar{V}$, and a redistribution of wealth takes place from owners of undervalued firms to owners of overvalued firms. Our analysis thus far has neglected to deal with the incentive of undervalued firms to induce the production and use of that information. This section will describe a sequence of market regimes where owners of firms are free to offer side payments to the producers of information to either invest or not invest in information.

Monopolistic Access to Information

The analysis begins, as before, with a market for N assets where a number of investors have the ability to produce information at a cost. To simplify the analysis, we first assume that only one investor, investor i, has such an opportunity, at cost $C_i < N_A(V_A - \bar{V})$. Investor i is, therefore, a monopolist. This is

---

[11] The prospect of giving false signals as to identities of undervalued assets may seem to offer opportunities for excess profits by initially purchasing overvalued assets. However, the nature of the tatonnement process precludes success of these "false signals" in that all prices must be known to all in equilibrium. A false signal may initially bid up prices of overvalued assets, but eventual investment in undervalued assets serves as an opposite signal.

[12] Even if $C_i = 0$, no motivation exists for production of information since investment in only type A firms still leaves the producer of information exactly as well off as holding a fraction of all assets valued at $\bar{V}$. It is also impossible for information producers to extract gains by trading interests in assets since that action may be a signal as efficient as the market price.

formalized by adding the following sentence to assumption (v): "All investors except i have costs of information which exceed the total amount of under or overvaluation." At a market price, $\bar{V}$, the owners of undervalued firms stand to lose $N_A(V_A - \bar{V})$, the amount by which their firms are undervalued, to the owners of overvalued firms. Recovery of some or all of these potential losses is an incentive to firm A owners to induce the production and use of information.

If the owners of undervalued firms are aware of each other and are able to collude in their activities, then they may offer a side payment, S_A, to induce investor i to produce information and determine the true values of firms. The amount of the side payment is bounded above and below such that

$$C_i < S_A < N_A(V_A - \bar{V}). \tag{2}$$

As in Section II, since investors cannot improve their own positions by producing information, the minimum side payment which might induce that production would be C_i, enough to just cover the costs of production. On the other hand, the maximum side payment owners of A firms would be willing to make is $N_A(V_A - \bar{V})$. Anything more would leave them worse off than if they accepted $\bar{V}$. Thus, if $C_i < N_A(V_A - \bar{V})$ there will be incentives to produce information offered by owners of A firms in the form of side payments. The maximum net gain to investor i for producing information is $N_A(V_A - \bar{V}) - C_i$.

It should be obvious, however, that there will be incentives offered by owners of overvalued firms to forego information production, as well. Again, assuming the owners of overvalued firms have an equal opportunity to collude,[13] their maximum side payment should be no more than $N_B(\bar{V} - V_B)$. And, since the act of not producing information involves no cost on the part of the investor, the minimum feasible offer would be zero. The range of possible side payments from B firm owners to not produce information is,

$$0 < S_B < N_B(\bar{V} - V_B) \tag{3}$$

where S_B is the side payment offered by owners of B firms.

When there are positive costs of information acquisition, $C_i > 0$, a comparative advantage lies with owners of overvalued firms. Since by definition, the total amount of undervaluation equals the total amount of overvaluation (i.e., $N_A(V_A - \bar{V}) = N_B(\bar{V} - V_B)$), the maximum gross side payments affordable by both groups or owners is the same. But the maximum net gain to investor i is greater if he accepts side payments not to produce information because he avoids incurring the cost of information. When $C_i = 0$, there is no comparative advantage

---

[13] It is interesting to note that in the case where collusive opportunities are assumed to be restricted, some different results follow. For instance, suppose the cost of colluding between any 2 firms is Z, then the cost of colluding on the part of overvalued firms is ZN_B and that of undervalued firms is ZN_A. The maximum side payments (assuming that $Z < (\bar{V} - V_B)$ and $Z < (V_A - \bar{V})$) made by firms is

$$S_A = [(V_A - \bar{V}) - Z]N_A$$

$$S_B = [(\bar{V} - V_B) - Z]N_B$$

and relative power of persuasion rests with the group of fewer numbers.

to producing or not producing information and the impact of side payments on market equilibrium is, at best, indeterminate.[14, 15] Again, no well defined motives exist which induce investors to undertake production of information and this market regime fails to satisfy the conditions for existence of a Rational Expectations equilibrium.

Competition and Production of Reliable Information

In the remainder of this section, a market regime is described where competition exists for the side payments offered to produce information. It is demonstrated that a competitive information market performs quite differently from one that is monopolistic. We proceed by first examining a market where all information is reliable and define the incentives for its production. This is formalized by adding an additional assumption for this subsection: (IX) Investors are pathologically honest. In the following subsection this assumption is dropped and a market regime is described where unreliable information is produced if it is deemed profitable to do so. Mechanisms for resolving the moral hazard problem in the information market are then considered.

Suppose we complicate the analysis slightly by assuming that more than one investor in the market has the capability to produce profitably the same information. It is advantageous to simplify the analysis by assuming that only two investors (i and j) are able to produce the information at distinct costs, C_i and C_j. Also, we assume that $C_i < C_j$. Hence, the market here is different only by the inclusion of an additional, slightly less efficient, producer of information. This means assumption (v) now stipulates: Two investors i and j, have costs of information which are less than the total under or over-valuation and $C_i < C_j$.

When two investors are able to reveal the true values of firms, the owners of overvalued firms must induce both to forego information opportunities or lose the excess value they wish to retain. On the other hand, the owners of undervalued firms need only induce one or the other to invest in information in order to regain the value they otherwise might lose. More specifically, the owners of undervalued firms are able to offer a gross side payment of $N_A(V_A - \bar{V})$ to either information producer. If owners of overvalued firms offer side payments to both producers of information they must divide their resources, $N_B(\bar{V} - V_B)$, somehow. If, for

---

[14] Actually this result can be reached in either of two ways. Either the actual cost of obtaining information may be negligible, or the investor may interpret the side payment to collect information as a reliable signal of the identities of undervalued firms. This signal serves as an equally efficient means of determining the identities of firms as does undertaking the production of information, but at no cost. The important point, however, is that even if the side payment offers reveal the identities of firms to investor i, he is indifferent about passing that information on to the market due to the equality of gross side payments. Yet another possibility arises if the bidding itself is assumed to be public. In this instance overvalued firms could publicly mimic undervalued firms but with no intention of paying off if actually identified as overvalued. But they could then contract with an agent to bid against the undervalued firms. Ignoring any costs of the agency relationship this would lead to the same disequilibrium result.

[15] Stalemates of this sort will, in fact, work to the advantage of B firms since they benefit most from the status quo. Also, because the cost of inaction is unambiguously zero, the advantage would swing the incentive to not producing information, whenever C_i was anything but certain.

instance, they divide their resources evenly, the maximum side payments offered would be $\frac{1}{2} N_B(\bar{V} - V_B)$. And if, as in the case of offers to investor i,

$$N_A(V_A - \bar{V}) - C_i > \frac{1}{2} N_B(\bar{V} - V_B) \tag{4}$$

information production would be profitable. A similar condition exists for offers made to investor j. Only if investor j's cost of information were greater than $\frac{1}{2} N_B(\bar{V} - V_B)$ would the inequality above not be met and information not produced. Thus, if overvalued firms engage in a bidding contest with undervalued firms to influence producers of information they are no longer able to maintain the status quo.

In addition, the most efficient producer of information should emerge as the recipient of the side payment from A firms. This results from the fact that $C_i < C_j$. Investors i and j effectively bid for the side payment of A firms until,

$$C_j = S_A \tag{5}$$

where investor j can no longer profit by investing in information. At that point, investor i emerges as the most efficient producer of information receiving $S_A = C_j$ as payment for information. The profit generated by investor i in the process is

$$S_A - C_i = C_j - C_i \tag{6}$$

and firms are accurately and efficiently revalued in the market.

A general solution of equilibrium in a competitive information market where the owners of overvalued firms are assumed to attempt to simultaneously influence both producers of information, no longer favors the owners of overvalued firms. Even if those owners were allowed to concentrate their resources in one side payment to whichever investor A firms dealt with and cause the resolution of market equilibrium to be game-theoretic in nature, it still appears that owners of A firms will prevail. This is because it will always be to the advantage of one information producer, or the other, to contract with A firm owners because B firm owners can never successfully bribe both simultaneously. This conclusion will be insured if the owners of A firms can instigate side payment contracts conditional on investors not contracting with others.[16] Therefore, if there are competitive, information producers who are pathologically honest there will be an efficient Rational Expectations equilibrium because the low cost information producer will win a bidding contest to identify undervalued firms.

---

[16] Again, as in the monopolistic case, it appears possible that the mere action of offering side payments may serve as an adequate signal of the identities of the alternative groups. In that case information producers need not incur the cost of actually producing information but merely infer their identities from the side payment offers they receive. The result of this would be to reduce the gross side payments undervalued firms would have to make to reveal their identities. The overvalued firms could follow a strategy which would compel the undervalued firms to pay for information production. The strategy, would be to publicly mimic the true undervalued firms but with no intention of paying off, and employ an agent to bid against the undervalued firms but protect their identity. It is problematical whether undervalued firms might discover some incentive which would induce them to carry out such a strategy.

Moral Hazard and the Production of Unreliable Information

In the preceding section the Rational Expectations equilibrium depended on the existence of competitive and honest information producers. Under these conditions contracting for production of information was a simple process involving only the determination of the price at which information will be produced. One way to view the impact of the pathological honesty assumption is that it leads to a world of costless contracts. As long as information producers will behave honestly, regardless of the incentives to cheat, then potentially costly contract provisions which limit such incentives will be dispensible. However, when market participants act dishonestly if such behavior is profitable, as assumed in this subsection, more complex contracts may be necessary to ensure reliable performance. The costs of such contracts, and the incentives they create to induce reliable behavior are as important as the price of production.

There are basically two ways to structure contracts to deal with the problem of dishonesty. One way is to include provisions in the contract which permit the monitoring of the information producer to insure the honest production of information. But the costs of such monitoring activities are likely to be rather high and the problems of monitoring have been well developed, although in a somewhat different context (see Jensen and Meckling [13]). The other alternative, which is pursued here, is to devise contract provisions which offset the incentive to behave dishonestly. The particular incentive clause which is considered here as a contractive option is a requirement on investment by the information producer in the firms he claims are undervalued.

Suppose, that in the bidding situation described above, investor j realizes that he is able to extract profits from the market if he contracts dishonestly with the owners of firms. The way he can do this is to underbid investor i despite his own higher cost of producing information, but with no intention of actually producing that information. Investor j could randomly identify N_A firms and claim they were the true N_A firms. He could win the bidding with the more efficient investor i by bidding an amount, S_A, which is just under investor i's cost of producing information, C_i. This side payment of S_A could still be secured from firms since it is to the advantage of any firm to pay S_A/N_A to be revalued to V_A.

Of course, investor i will not be ignorant of the opportunities to misrepresent the identities of firms. He knows that investor j will underbid him with a dishonest bid once j's own cost of production has been reached. In effect, he knows that honesty is a losing strategy and will therefore have to withdraw from the market or follow j's lead. The question then becomes: What will be the outcome of the bidding process if both are dishonest when it is profitable to do so?

To evaluate the net gain from dishonest behavior it is necessary to consider the portfolio positions taken in the market by each investor-information producer. Each investor can certify his honesty, *up to a point*, by the position he takes in the market. To see this, consider the portfolio losses to which investors i and j will be subject if they commit their entire wealth endowment to the assets they claim are overvalued.[17] Pursuing the case of investor i, if he constructs a portfolio

---

[17] Given assumption (Vi), the market will assume that investors can hold such portfolios at no cost in terms of forgone diversification if they have actually identified the true undervalued firms.

of the N_A firms he had identified as undervalued, the expected value of this random selection of firms is $\bar{V}$. By paying V_A for these firms, or more appropriately a portion of each at a pro-rata value of V_A,[18] investor i's expected portfolio losses are

$$W_i \left[\frac{\bar{V} - V_A}{V_A} \right]. \tag{7}$$

At any prevailing side payment, S_A, offered in the market the incentive for any investor i, to produce unreliable information is given by

$$S_A - W_i \left[\frac{V_A - \bar{V}}{V_A} \right]. \tag{8}$$

Conversely, the corresponding incentive to produce reliable information is

$$S_A - C_i. \tag{9}$$

Therefore, there is a greater incentive for i to produce reliable information when

$$C_i < W_i \left[\frac{V_A - \bar{V}}{V_A} \right], \tag{10}$$

or when the costs of producing information are less than anticipated portfolio losses.

The problem facing the market is to determine the incentives of information producers to misrepresent the identities of firms. The ability of the market to accomplish this depends on its knowledge of characteristics of information producers. Suppose, temporarily, that the market already knew each potential information producers cost of production. In this case the bidding process would be needed to determine the most efficient information producer. The problem would be simply to insure that the low cost information producer did not have an incentive to cheat. One way to accomplish this is to require that the information producer have enough wealth committed to the undervalued firms that the inequality in (10) is satisfied. But suppose that the wealth endowment of the most efficient producer is insufficient to satisfy (10). In order to get reliable information, firms will have to contract with a less efficient producer who has sufficient wealth to be perceived as reliable, if one exists.

If knowledge of the relative costs of various producers is not known to the markets, as is assumed to be the case, then the bidding process will have to be used to establish the most efficient reliable information producer. By using the bidding process the market can still arrive at the same contract with the same producer as it would if knowledge of relative costs were initially available.[19] This

---

[18] More realistically, we mean investors will purchase an equal portion of each firm at a pro-rata value of V_A.

[19] Actually it is unlikely that the market will have an equilibrium which is totally free of cheating. For example the investor (i) that wins the bidding can secretly approach any one firm and threaten to identify it as a B firm unless it pays a bribe just short of $V_A - V_B$ which is sufficient to cover any losses incurred by the investor on his own investment in the firm. If the information producer does this to enough firms it will benefit them to pay another investor with a large portfolio to invest in information and reveal their true identity. But there is then the possibility that these investors may collude and share the original bribe. However, there is a greater incentive to blackmail true A firms than to seek bribes from B firms because the portfolio losses for the investor will be lower. This will tend to limit the number of incorrectly valued firms in the market.

is accomplished when the owners of undervalued firms accept the lowest bid (S_A) where it is clear that there is no incentive to misrepresent the identity of firms, i.e., the lowest value of S_A offered by any producer, say producer i, where

$$S_A < W_i \left[\frac{V_A - \bar{V}}{V_A} \right]. \tag{11}$$

When this condition holds for any producer i, he will expect to incur a net loss if he cheats. And, therefore, producer i can produce information profitably only if he does so reliably.

As long as there is at least one information producer who bids an amount S_A which satisfies (11) the moral hazard problem in the market for information will be solved. But, the Rational Expectations equilibrium which results will not be efficient. The emergence of a signal of reliability in the production of information enables the market to identify the true values of firms. However, it is because this signal is necessary to establish the reliability of information that the information itself may be produced inefficiently. This is because it is possible that the most efficient producers of information have insufficient endowments to signal reliability. Therefore, the efficiency of the Rational Expectations equilibrium depends on the distribution of wealth endowments and information costs across potential producers of information. What is necessary is that the most efficient information producer has sufficient wealth to signal reliability. Short of this, the efficiency condition will not be satisfied. It is interesting to note that while the emergence of a signal of reliability ensures that firms are identified. It also imposes a barrier to entry for information producers which may preclude entry to the most efficient producers.

Intermediation and the Moral Hazard Problem

If information producers are to successfully eliminate information asymmetries regarding the qualities of assets, it is clear that the information they produce must be perceived by the rest of the market as reliable. The establishment of reliability in the marketplace is concurrent with the resolution of any moral hazards which inhibit the production of information or diminish its integrity. Some authors have suggested that efficient information producers in the form of intermediaries may emerge to resolve these problems. Let us consider how information producers might organize themselves as intermediaries and how this form of organization affects the resolution of the moral hazard problem. In order to clearly specify the way the intermediary is organized, we begin with the simple case where information producers are pathologically honest. This will help us concentrate, momentarily, on explaining the ownership structure of the intermediary. Later, the moral hazard problem will be presented again as we relax the assumption of honest behavior.

Consider the ownership structure and mode of operation of an intermediary organized by information producer i. Suppose producer i forms an intermediary to collect sufficient funds from other investors to purchase all N_A undervalued firms at a price $N_A V_A - S_A$. If producer i is the most efficient producer of information bidding for the undervalued firms, then S_A is the competitive price of information which just underprices the next most efficient producer. Therefore the owners of undervalued firms receive full value for their assets, less the competitive price required to establish that value.

In return for their capital, investors in the intermediary receive a fraction of the assets of the intermediary worth $N_A V_A - S_A$. Given that the intermediaries assets are worth $N_A V_A$, their fraction of ownership, X, is,

$$X = \frac{N_A V_A - S_A}{N_A V_A} \qquad (12)$$

(therefore, the value of the claims held by those investors is $X(N_A V_A)$, or $N_A V_A - S_A$). As compensation for producing information which identifies the undervalued firms, producer i receives the competitive value of that information, S_A. He does so by receiving a fractional share of the assets of the intermediary of

$$1 - X = \frac{S_A}{N_A V_A} \qquad (13)$$

(the value of the claims of producer i against the intermediary is $(1 - X)(N_A V_A)$, or S_A).

When information producers are pathologically honest, the outcome of competitive bidding among intermediaries for undervalued assets is the same as it was among non-intermediary information producers. More efficient information producers are able to offer higher prices for undervalued assets since their costs of producing that information are lower. In the case of two producers i and j, if $C_i < C_j$, as was assumed before, then the intermediary formed by i is able to offer a higher price for the undervalued firms than can the intermediary formed by j. That is, i will offer $N_A V_A - S_A$ where $S_A = C_j$ and just price producer j out of the market. As a result, the investors in the intermediary formed by i receive market value for their investment, the owners of undervalued firms receive the fair market value of their assets (less information costs), and information producer i receives the competitive value of producing information about those assets and accrues profits of $S_A - C_i$.

Now suppose that information producers are no longer pathologically honest. As was the case above, information producers who organize intermediaries act essentially as investment brokers who invest the funds of their investors in supposed undervalued firms. In return they receive a fraction of the value of the assets they purchase. When information producers are not pathologically honest, this arrangement allows the information producer to profit by misrepresenting the value of his information. This results because the production of unreliable information is costless but by organizing an intermediary an information producer accrues a share of the assets he purchases, even though they may not be worth $N_A V_A$. For instance, producer j could organize an intermediary at no cost by selecting N_A firms randomly and financing that selection by issuing claims against supposed A firms. The value of a randomly chosen portfolio of N_A firms, and of the intermediary in this case, would $N_A \bar{V}$. The value of the share of the intermediary accruing to producer j is $(1 - X) N_A \bar{V}$, or substituting from (13), is $S_A(\bar{V}/$

V_A). So, as information producers engage in bidding for undervalued firms, when the price of producing information is bid down to $S_A = C_j$, investor j can continue to bid, in the expectation of making a profit by not incurring the cost of identifying the true undervalued firms. Investor i will recognize the incentive for j to behave dishonestly and will perceive that he will have to behave dishonestly in order to continue to bid against j. Without further constraints on reliability the bidding process will degenerate and no Rational Expectations equilibrium will be reached.

If investors in intermediaries were able to observe the competitive price of producing information as well as each intermediary's actual cost of production then the moral hazard problem is easily resolved. Investors could then compare the incentive to produce reliable information with that to produce unreliable information. Where, for producer i,

$$S_A - C_i > S_A(\bar{V}/V_A) \tag{14}$$

it is more profitable for producer i to produce accurate information than not. If, however, the cost of information production is not observable or if information production cannot be easily monitored then, as in the case of non intermediary information producers, it will not be feasible to directly make this comparison.

In markets where information costs are not observable, the resolution of the moral hazard problem lies, as in the previous section, in assuming that at least some information producers invest enough of their own wealth in the intermediary to establish their reliability. For instance, if producer i were to invest W_i in the assets of the intermediary he would receive returns from two sources. As before, producer i would receive a fraction of the assets of the intermediary of $S_A/N_A V_A$ in return for identifying undervalued firms. And producer i would receive the fair value of his own investment of W_i, or a fraction of the value of the intermediary of $W_i/N_A V_A$. The fraction of the intermediary accruing to other investors now is $(N_A V_A - W_i - S_A)/N_A V_A$ (since producer i furnishes some capital of his own, he need raise only $N_A V_A - W_i - S_a$ from outside sources).

In the event that producer i produces information reliably, at S_A, the change in the wealth of producer i is

$$S_A - C_i.$$

If, at the same price, he feigns the production of information, the change in wealth becomes,

$$S_A(\bar{V}/V_A) - W_i\left[\frac{(V_A - \bar{V})}{V_A}\right]$$

where the first term is the incentive to produce unreliable information and the second is the portfolio losses sustained in the process (i.e., the second term equals the fraction of the intermediary which the information producer has acquired with his own funds $W_i/N_A V_A$ times the total overvaluation of the intermediary, $(V_A - \bar{V})N_A$). When investors are able to observe the wealth invested by information producers then they can be assured that any information producer can be regarded as reliable when his losses on his own investment exceed the gain from cheating. Or, the reliability of any intermediary is established when W_i is large enough such that,

$$W_i \left[\frac{(V_A - \bar{V})}{V_A} \right] > S_A(\bar{V} V_A)$$

Investors will only invest in intermediaries which have large enough endowments to verify their reliability. Hence, some more efficient intermediaries may be precluded from the market by a market-imposed wealth constraint. In that case the Rational Expectations equilibrium is not efficient and owners of firms bear the costs of resolving moral hazards in the market as higher equilibrium prices for information are obtained.

IV. INFORMATION PRODUCTION AND THE ROLE OF INTERMEDIARIES

In the previous sections it has been demonstrated that a competitive market in information about the value of firms, where information producers have a sufficiently large stake in the value of their information, will function, but will not have an efficient Rational Expectations equilibrium. By this it is meant that the market for information will not fail and firms will not be valued according to the market average. But the avoidance of the moral hazard problem pertaining to the reliability of information is not accomplished costlessly. Specifically, the requirement that the portfolio of the investor-information producer be large enough to establish the reliability of his information creates a barrier to entry in the market for information. Highly efficient information producers with small portfolios will be unable to compete with less efficient producers who have sufficient wealth to establish their reliability. As a result, it is likely that information will be produced less efficiently than it otherwise might and the opportunities for collusion among information producers will be enhanced.

The analysis in the previous sections also demonstrates that intermediation does not in itself serve to resolve the problem of failure in the market for information. The moral hazard problem is resolved by the information producer having a large enough position in the market so as to be reliable. This can be accomplished either by investors observing the market portfolio of the large investor who, in the context of our model, wins the bidding; or by the winner accepting funds from other investors and acting as an intermediary. In the context of our model either solution works just as well because the crucial factors necessary for equilibrium are competition in the production of information and a sufficient stake in the market on the part of information producers that the quality of information is reliable.

It is fruitful to compare this conclusion with the suggestion made by Leland and Pyle [14] that intermediation resolves the problems encountered in the market for information. Leland and Pyle suggest that intermediaries resolve two problems which plague the market for information. The first is the public good nature of information which limits the saleability of information to investors. The second is the moral hazard problem of unreliable information.

Leland and Pyle argue that intermediation solves the first problem if it is presumed that investors cannot infer the intermediary's information by observing its portfolio. Throughout our analysis we have assumed the opposite. We have assumed that investors can observe the portfolios of other investors and that they presume that no investor values a firm at other than $\bar{V}$ without information which identifies the firm or an inducement from the firm to so indicate. Because Leland and Pyle ignore the possibility that firms rather than investors can profitably fund the production of reliable information by nonintermediaries, they are led to the conclusion that intermediation, per se, contributes to the avoidance of market failure. However, if there is some additional reason for undervalued firms to desire revaluation but without public knowledge of that revaluation, then intermediaries will be the preferred form of information producer. Leland and Pyle, however, offer no motivation for assuming that information cannot be inferred by observing portfolios.

The problem of the reliability of information is solved by intermediaries, according to Leland and Pyle, because, like entrepreneurs, they will communicate value to the market as a function of the size of the stake the information producer takes in the intermediary. It is important to note that Leland and Pyle's analysis assumes the existence of an incentive signalling equilibrium where there is a continuous valuation function which is positively dependent on the percentage of the firm or intermediary retained by the entrepreneur or information producer. Two comments on this approach are necessary. First, if there exists a signalling equilibrium, firms will be properly valued without the aid of intermediaries or other information producers (see the introduction to Section II). Second, where there does not exist an equilibrium incentive signalling scheme for firms, the moral hazard problem of the information market is resolved by the stake in the market held by the investor-information-producer. That is, it is not necessary to assume, a priori, the existence of an incentive signalling equilibrium for firms to resolve the moral hazard problem. But again there is nothing about intermediation, per se, which insures reliability.

Our analysis suggests that there must be some reason other than the difficulties created by asymmetric and costly information for intermediaries to emerge as an important type of information producer. The answer would seem to be that intermediaries can profitably emerge where they can jointly produce information as well as other products or services valued by investors. The obvious candidates for this joint production arrangement are the provision of liquidity or transactions services and the sale of insurance contracts. In addition, in the spirit of the assumptions made by Leland and Pyle, some firms may desire confidentiality and hence seek revaluation by the production of information through intermediaries rather than other types of market makers (see Campbell [4] for a more complete treatment of the confidentiality motive).

The hypothesis that intermediaries emerge through the joint production of information and other services desired by investors has the advantage that it encompasses other hypotheses which have been proposed. The explanations of intermediation available in the literature, e.g. Benston and Smith's [2] transactions cost argument and Leland and Pyle's asymmetric information argument, each have merit but do not seem, to us at least, to be independently persuasive. The alternative view that intermediaries prosper when they simultaneously produce information and provide other services seems to be a more promising explanation of intermediaries as we know them. A complete model of the joint-production approach to intermediation awaits a separate treatment.

V. Conclusions

The principal focus of this paper has been the theory of financial intermediation. But the results presented here have a broader applicability. The general conclusion of the paper deals with any market with asymmetric information where there is no signalling equilibrium with regard to the direct signals of the owners of assets but where there are opportunities for the purchasers of assets to produce information about their value. The conclusion is that there will generally not be a Rational Expectations equilibrium for the asset market and the market for information.

The problem is not that the market is unable to produce information which leads to the identification of the true value of assets. Rather, it is that this production of information will not be done efficiently or at least cost. The underlying reason for this is that efficient information producers may not have a sufficient stake in the market to persuade the market of their reliability. Each investor-information producer's initial wealth endowment acts as a constraint on reliability and as a barrier to entry in the information production industry. It remains to examine the implications for market structure of this conclusion.

REFERENCES

1. G. Akerlof. "The Market for 'Lemons': Qualitative Uncertainty and Market Mechanism." *Quarterly Journal of Economics*, 89 (August 1970).
2. G. Benston and C. W. Smith. "A Transactions Cost Approach to the Theory of Financial Intermediation." *Journal of Finance*, 31 (May 1976).
3. S. Bhattacharya. "Imperfect Information, Dividend Policy and 'The Bird in The Hand Fallacy.'" *Bell Journal of Economics*, 10 (Spring 1979).
4. T. Campbell. "Optimal Investment Financing Decisions and the Value of Confidentiality." *Journal of Financial and Quantitative Analysis* (December, 1979).
5. T. Campbell. "Asymmetric Information, Screening, and the Rationing of Corporate Debt." mimeo, University of Utah (May, 1979).
6. A. Chen and E. H. Kim. "Theories of Corporate Debt Policy, A Synthesis." *Journal of Finance*, 34 (May 1979).
7. E. F. Fama. "Banking and The Theory of Finance." unpublished manuscript, University of Chicago.
8. S. Figlewski. "Market Efficiency in a Market with Heterogeneous Information." *Journal of Political Economy*, 86 (August 1978).
9. N. Gonedes. "The Capital Market, The Market for Information, and External Accounting." *Journal of Finance*, 31 (May 1976).
10. N. Gonedes. "Capital Market Equilibrium for a Class of Heterogeneous Expectations in a Two-Parameter World." *Journal of Finance*, 31-1 (March 1976).
11. S. Grossman. "On the Efficiency of Competitive Stock Markets Where Traders Have Diverse Information." *Journal of Finance*, 31-2 (May 1976).

12. S. Grossman and J. E. Stiglitz. "Information and Competitive Price Systems", *American Economic Review* (May 1976).

13. Michael C. Jensen and William H. Meckling. "Theory of the Firm: Managerial Behavior, Agency Costs and Ownership Structure." *Journal of Financial Economics*, 3 (1976).

14. William A. Kracaw. "The Economics of Information and the Performance of Financial Markets." Doctoral Dissertation, University of Utah (1980).

15. H. E. Leland and D. H. Pyle. "Informational Asymmetries, Financial Structure, and Financial Intermediation." *Journal of Finance*, 32-2 (May 1977).

16. J. Lintner. "The Aggregation of Investors Diverse Judgements and Preferences in Purely Competitive Security Markets." *Journal of Financial and Quantitative Analysis*, 4-4 (Dec 1969).

17. D. H. Pyle. "Descriptive Theories of Financial Institutions Under Uncertainty." *Journal of Financial and Quantitative Analysis* (Dec 1972).

18. S. A. Ross. "The Determination of Financial Structure: The Incentive Signalling Approach". *Bell Journal of Economics* (Spring 1977).

19. M. Rothschild and J. Stiglitz. "Equilibrium in Competitive Insurance Markets: An Essay on the Economics of Imperfect Information." *Quarterly Journal of Economics* (Nov 1976).

20. A. M. Spence. "Job Market Signalling." *Quarterly Journal of Economics*, 87 (August 1973).

Financial Intermediation and Delegated Monitoring

This paper develops a theory of financial intermediation based on minimizing the cost of monitoring information which is useful for resolving incentive problems between borrowers and lenders. It presents a characterization of the costs of providing incentives for delegated monitoring by a financial intermediary. Diversification within an intermediary serves to reduce these costs, even in a risk neutral economy. The paper presents some more general analysis of the effect of diversification on resolving incentive problems. In the environment assumed in the model, debt contracts with costly bankruptcy are shown to be optimal. The analysis has implications for the portfolio structure and capital structure of intermediaries.

INTRODUCTION

This paper develops a theory of financial intermediation based on minimum cost production of information useful for resolving incentive problems. An intermediary (such as a bank) is delegated the task of costly monitoring of loan contracts written with firms who borrow from it. It has a gross cost advantage in collecting this information because the alternative is either duplication of effort if each lender monitors directly, or a free-rider problem, in which case no lender monitors. Financial intermediation theories are generally based on some cost advantage for the intermediary. Schumpeter assigned such a "delegated monitoring" role to banks,

> ... the banker must not only know what the transaction is which he is asked to finance and how it is likely to turn out but he must also know the customer, his business and even his private habits, and get, by frequently "talking things over with him", a clear picture of the situation (Schumpeter (1939), p. 116).

The information production task delegated to the intermediary gives rise to incentive problems for the intermediary; we can term these delegation costs. These are not generally analysed in existing intermediation theories, and in some cases one finds that the costs are so high that there is no net advantage in using an intermediary. Schumpeter made a similar point, although he did not consider incentives explicitly:

> ... traditions and standards may be absent to such a degree that practically anyone can drift into the banking business, find customers, and deal with them according to his own ideas. ... This in itself. . . is sufficient to turn the history of capitalist evolution into a history of catastrophes (Schumpeter (1939), p. 116).

This paper analyses the determinants of delegation costs, and develops a model in which a financial intermediary has a *net* cost advantage relative to direct lending and borrowing.

Diversification within the intermediary is key to the possible net advantage of intermediation. This is because there is a strong similarity between the incentive problem between an individual borrower and lender and that between an intermediary and its

Review of Economic Studies (1984) LI, 393–414

depositors. The possibility of diversification within the intermediary can make the incentive problems sufficiently different to make it feasible to hire an agent (the intermediary) to monitor an agent (the borrower). Diversification proves to be important even when everyone in the economy is risk neutral.

This model is related to two literatures. It relates to the single agent-single principal literature (e.g. Harris–Raviv (1979), Holmström (1979) and Shavell (1979)) which develops conditions when monitoring additional information about an agent will help resolve moral hazard problems. The analysis here extends this to costly monitoring in a many principal setting, where principals are security holders of a firm or depositors in an intermediary. The other related literature is that of financial intermediation based on imperfect information. Several interesting papers analyse the gross benefits of delegating some informational task to an intermediary without presenting explicit analysis of the costs and feasibility of this delegation (e.g. Leland–Pyle (1977) and Chan (1982)). In addition to developing a model in which overall feasibility of financial intermediation is analysed, we briefly apply our results to determine conditions when intermediation is feasible in the Leland–Pyle model.

The basic model developed is of an ex-post information asymmetry between potential lenders and a risk neutral entrepreneur who needs to raise capital for a risky project. In this environment, debt is shown to be the optimal contract between an entrepreneur and lenders. Because of the wealth constraint that an entrepreneur cannot have negative consumption (pay lenders more than he has), the debt contracts with which the entrepreneur can raise funds involve some costs. As an alternative to incurring these costs, it is possible for lenders (who contract directly with the entrepreneur) to spend resources monitoring the data which the entrepreneur observes. In the class of contracts written directly between entrepreneurs and lenders, the less costly of these two is optimal. However, the cost of monitoring may be very high if there are many lenders. If there are m outside security holders in a firm and it costs $K > 0$ to monitor, the total cost of direct monitoring is $m \cdot K$. This will imply either a very large expenditure on monitoring, or a free rider problem where no securityholder monitors because his share of the benefit is small. The obvious thing to do is for some securityholders to monitor on behalf of others, and we are then faced with analysing the provision of incentives for delegated monitoring.

There are many methods by which delegated monitoring might be implemented. We assume that the information monitored by a given person cannot be directly observed without cost by others. The analysis here focuses on a financial intermediary who raises funds from many lenders (depositors), promises them a given pattern of returns, lends to entrepreneurs, and spends resources monitoring and enforcing loan contracts with entrepreneurs which are less costly than those available without monitoring. The financial intermediary monitors entrepreneurs' information, and receives payments from the entrepreneurs which are not observed by depositors.

An example of useful costly information in a loan contract is a covenant which is costly to monitor. A common covenant is a promise that the firm's working capital will not fall below some minimum, unless "necessary for expansion of inventory". (See Smith–Warner (1979).) If it is costly to determine whether a shortfall is "necessary", and each of the bondholders has to incur this cost to enforce the contract, the contract using costly information is unlikely to be used if the number of bondholders is large. A contract specifying an uncontingent working capital requirement might be substituted, when the contingency would have been specified if there had been a single principal. In practice, loan covenants in bank loan contracts specify coarse contingencies which define a "default". Conditional on such a default, the intermediary monitors the situation and uses the information to re-negotiate the contract with new interest rates and contingent promises. A financial intermediary must choose an incentive contract such that it has incentives to monitor the information, make proper use of it, and make sufficient payments to depositors to attract deposits. Providing these incentives is costly, but we show that diversification serves to reduce these costs. As the number of loans to entrepreneurs with projects whose returns are independent (or independent conditional on observables) grows without bound, we show that costs of delegation approach zero, and that for some finite number of loans financial intermediation becomes viable, considering all costs.

Financial intermediaries in the world monitor much information about their borrowers in enforcing loan covenants, but typically do not directly announce the information or serve such an auditor's function. The intermediary in this model similarly does not announce the information monitored from each borrower, it simply makes payments to depositors. We show that debt is the optimal contract between the intermediary and depositors. The result that the delegation costs go to zero implies that asymptotically no other delegated monitoring structure will have lower costs. If there is an independent demand by entrepreneurs for monitoring without disclosure of the information monitored, for example to keep competitors from learning the information as suggested by Campbell (1979), then well diversified financial intermediaries can provide it (in addition to simple monitoring services) at almost no cost disadvantage.

Diversification is key to this theory, and it is interesting that because of the wealth constraint, diversification is important despite universal risk neutrality. To develop a more general intuition into the role of diversification, some analysis is presented of a related model with risk averse agents but no wealth constraint. Two types of diversification are considered in the context of two alternative financial intermediary models; one is the traditional diversification by sub-dividing independent risks, while the other is diversification by adding more independent risks of given scale. The latter is what Samuelson (1963) has termed a "fallacy of large numbers", because it does not always increase expected utility. This section may be of independent interest because it provides some conditions when the fallacy of large numbers is not a fallacy.

The basic model is outlined in Section 2. Delegated monitoring by a financial intermediary in the context of the basic model is analysed in Section 3. Section 4 explores the extension of the basic model to risk averse agents. Section 5 applies the analysis of section 4 to the model of Leland–Pyle. Section 6 concludes the paper.

2. A SIMPLE MODEL OF FIRM BORROWING

A model of risk neutral entrepreneurs who need to raise capital to operate a large investiment project is used to capture many of the aspects of the agency relationship between commerical borrowers and lenders. We specify a simple environment, and characterize optimal direct contracts between borrower and lender.

There are N entrepreneurs indexed by $i = 1, \ldots, N$ in the economy. For the balance of Section 2, we examine one of them, and do not use the index. The entrepreneur is endowed with the technology for an indivisible investment project with stochastic returns. The scale of inputs for the project greatly exceeds both his personal wealth and the personal wealth of any single lender. For simplicity, the entrepreneur's wealth is zero. Assume a one good economy with all consumption at the end of the period. The project requires inputs of the good today, and will produce output in one period. Normalize the required initial amount of inputs to one. The expectation of the output that will be produced at the end of the period exceeds R, the competitive interest rate in the economy. Therefore, the project would be undertaken if the risk neutral entrepreneur had available to him enough capital inputs.

The other investors in the economy are also risk neutral: call them lenders. To undertake the project, the entrepreneur must borrow sufficient resources from them to operate it at its scale of one. Because the interest rate is R, i.e. the lenders have access to a technology which will return R per unit of input, the entrepreneur must convince potential lenders that the rate of return which he will pay to them has an expected value of at least R. Each lender has available wealth of $1/m$, thus the entrepreneur must borrow from $m > 1$ lenders. The capital market is competitive—if convinced that their expected return equals or exceeds R (R/m per lender), lenders will make the loan.

Let the total output of the project be the random variable $\tilde{y}$. Assume that $\tilde{y}$ is bounded between zero and $\bar{y} < \infty$. The entrepreneur and all lenders agree on the probability distribution of $\tilde{y}$, in particular all agree that $E_{\tilde{y}}(\tilde{y}) > R + K$ (where $K > 0$ and is defined below) and that $y = 0$ is possible. The realization of $\tilde{y}$ does not depend on any actions of the entrepreneur.

A simple information asymmetry is introduced which will make the loan contracting problem non-trivial. The realization of $\tilde{y}$ is freely observed only by the entrepreneur. With output observed by the entrepreneur alone, he must be given incentives to make payments to lenders. At the end of the period, he will pay a liquidating dividend. It is always feasible for him to claim a very low value of y, and keep for himself the difference between the actual value and what he pays the others.

Let $z \geqq 0$ be the aggregate payment which the entrepreneur pays to the m lenders. If the realization of output is $\tilde{y} = y$, he then keeps $y - z$ for himself. Because consumption cannot be negative the payment which he pays cannot feasibly exceed y (plus any personal wealth he might have, assumed here to be zero). To induce the entrepreneur to select a value of $z > 0$, he must be provided with incentives. To raise captial to undertake the project, lenders must believe that the expectation of the value of z which he will select is at least R. The entrepreneur must choose an incentive contract which depends only on observable variables and makes lenders anticipate a competitive expected dividend. The only costlessly observable variable is the payment z itself.

Lenders know the distribution of $\tilde{y}$, and know that the entrepreneur chooses the payment z which is best for him given a realization $\tilde{y} = y$, and that $z \in [0, y]$. If y exceeded R with probability one, then a full information optimal contract would be feasible—the risk neutral entrepreneur would offer an uncontingent payment of R. (See Harris–Raviv (1979).)

It might appear that the assumption that $y = 0$ is a possible outcome of the project rules out any borrowing, because $z = 0$ must be feasible, and it does not appear incentive compatible for an entrepreneur to choose a payment $z > 0$ when he can choose $z = 0$ and retain the rest. However, we will allow contracts with non-pecuniary penalties: penalties where the entrepreneur's loss is not enjoyed by the lenders. This allows the agent's utility function to be defined over negative values of its domain without allowing negative consumption to "produce" goods. We will see that these penalties are best interpreted as bankruptcy penalties. Some examples include a manager's time spent in bankruptcy proceedings, costly "explaining" of poor results, search costs of a fired manager, and (loosely) the manager's loss of "reputation" in bankruptcy. Physical punishment is a less realistic example. Projects which could not be undertaken at all without the penalties can be operated using the penalties.

The optimal contract maximizes the risk neutral entrepreneur's expected return, given a minimum expected return to lenders of R. Let the function ϕ, from the non-negative reals to the non-negative reals, be the non-pecuniary penalty function, which depends on z, the payment to lenders selected by the entrepreneur. Assume that if the entrepreneur is indifferent between several values of z, he chooses the one preferred by the lender. The optimal contract with penalties $\phi^*(\cdot) \geqq 0$ solves[1]

$$\max_{\phi(\cdot)} E_{\tilde{y}}[\max_{z \in [0, \tilde{y}]} \tilde{y} - z - \phi(z)] \tag{1a}$$

$$\text{Subject to} \quad z \in \arg\max_{z \in [0, y]} y - z - \phi(z) \tag{1b}$$

and

$$E_{\tilde{y}}[\arg\max_{z \in [0, \tilde{y}]} \tilde{y} - z - \phi(z)] \geqq R, \tag{1c}$$

where the notation "arg max" denotes the set of arguments that maximize the objective function that follows.

Proposition 1. *The optimal contract which solves* (1) *is given by* $\phi^*(z) = \max(h - z, 0)$, *where h is the smallest solution to*

$$(P(\tilde{y} < h) \cdot E_{\tilde{y}}[\tilde{y}|y < h]) + (P(\tilde{y} \geqq h) \cdot h) = R. \tag{2}$$

That is, it is a debt contract with face value h and a non-pecuniary bankruptcy penalty equal to the shortfall from face, h, where h is the smallest face value which provides lenders with an expected return of R.

Proof. Given $\phi^*(z)$,

$$\arg\max_{z \in [0, y]} y - z - \phi^*(z) = \begin{cases} y & \text{if } y < h \\ h & \text{if } y \geqq h. \end{cases}$$

Using (2), this satisfies with equality the constraint (1c) of providing a competitive return to lenders. By construction, h is the smallest number such that if the constraints $z \leqq y$ and $z \leqq h$ are satisfied, the expectation of $\tilde{z}$ is at least R. Hence, to satisfy (1c), there must exist some payment $h^+ \geqq h$ which is incentive compatible. If $z = h^+$ is incentive compatible (fulfills (1b) given contract $\phi(z)$), it must be true that

$$y - h^+ - \phi(h^+) \geqq \max_{z' \in [0, h^+]} y - z' - \phi(z')$$

or for all $z' \in [0, h^+]$,

$$\phi(z') \geqq h^+ + \phi(h^+) - z'$$

$$\geqq h + \phi(h^+) - z'$$

$$\geqq h - z'$$

$$= \phi^*(z').$$

The final inequality follows from the requirement $\phi(z) \geqq 0$ for all z. Combined with the result that $\phi^*(z) = 0$ for all $z \geqq h$, this implies that $\phi^*(z)$ gives the smallest penalties such that it is incentive compatible to fulfill (1c), implying that $\phi^*(z)$ maximizes (1). ‖

The necessity of a positive probability of incurring the non-pecuniary penalty means that even the optimal contract is costly. Entrepreneurs could be made better off without making lenders worse off if $\tilde{y}$ were observable. In a one entrepreneur-one lender setting, where $\bar{y}$ could be observed at some cost, it would be observed so long as the cost were less than the expected non-pecuniary bankruptcy penalty, $E_{\bar{z}}[\phi^*(\tilde{z})] = E_{\bar{y}}[\phi^*(\tilde{y})]$.

In a setting where it is not possible to make $\bar{y}$ observable to lenders at some cost, the contracting problem is not influenced by the number of lenders—a contract with one lender who loans one unit is equivalent to a contract with m lenders who each loan $1/m$ units and the entrepreneur incurs a penalty of $\phi^*(z_j)/m$ on the basis of payments z_j to lender j. However, this is not true when costly monitoring is possible. By spending $K > 0$ in resources, a lender can observe $\bar{y}$, but other lenders do not automatically observe $\bar{y}$ as a result and other lenders cannot observe the payments by an entrepreneur to the lender who monitors. As a result, an entrepreneur and a given lender consider only the effect on a given lender's loan of $1/m$ units when deciding between a contract with costly penalties and one that avoids the bankruptcy penalties by costly monitoring.

We analyse the impact of an information technology which allows costly monitoring of the exact realization of output, y, for each entrepreneur. This information costs $K > 0$ for each principal to monitor, and the cost must be incurred before the output realization is known to anyone, including the entrepreneur. See Townsend (1979) for some interesting analysis of the optimal contingent monitoring policy when the decision to monitor can be made *after* the entrepreneur has made a payment to a lender. This additional complication is not introduced because given some specified probability of monitoring it would not influence our results.

If it is possible for lenders to observe the outcome at some cost, there are three types of contracting situations possible. The contract can be as described above, with no monitoring. A second possiblility is for each of the m lenders to spend resources to monitor the outcome. Thirdly, the lenders can delegate the monitoring to one or more monitoring agents. The least costly of these will be selected.

If there were a single lender so $m = 1$ (rather than $m > 1$ as we assume), monitoring would be valuable if its cost were less than the expected deadweight penalty without monitoring or $K \leqq E_{\bar{y}}[\phi^*(\tilde{y})]$. With many lenders and direct contracting between the entrepreneur and lenders, if each lender monitors, monitoring is valuable if and only if $m \cdot K \geqq E_{\bar{y}}[\phi^*(\tilde{y})]$. When m is large this is unlikely because each lender's loan is small. Even if this condition for valuable monitoring is satisfied, it implies a large expenditure on monitoring and some sort of delegated monitoring might be desirable in this case.

To obtain the benefits of monitoring, when m is large the task must be delegated rather than left to each individual lender. The entity doing the monitoring ("the monitor") must be provided with incentives to monitor and enforce the contract. We assume that the actions taken and the information observed by the monitor are not directly observed by the lenders. It will generally be costly to provide incentives to the monitor, and below we analyse these costs. The total cost of delegated monitoring is the physical cost of monitoring by the monitor, K, plus the expected cost of providing incentives to the monitor, which we call the cost of delegation and denote the cost per project by D. Delegated monitoring pays when

$$K + D \leqq \min \left[E_{\bar{y}}[\phi^*(\tilde{y})], (m \cdot K) \right].$$

The costs of delegation are analysed when the monitor is a financial intermediary who receives payments from entrepreneurs and makes payments to principals.

3. DELEGATED MONITORING BY A FINANCIAL INTERMEDIARY

A financial intermediary obtains funds from lenders and lends them to entrepreneurs. Economists have tried to explain this intermediary role by arguing that the financial intermediary has a cost advantage in certain tasks. When such tasks involve unobserved actons by the intermediary or the observation of private information, then an agency/incentive problem for the intermediary may exist. Any theory which tries to explain the role of intermediaries by an information cost advantage must net out the costs of providing incentives to the intermediary from any cost savings in producing information. Existing intermediary theories do not make this final step. We now introduce a financial intermediary between entrepreneurs and lenders (whom we call depositors from now on), and examine conditions when this intermediary function is viable considering all costs.

A financial intermediary is a risk neutral agent, with personal wealth equal to zero. The intermediary receives funds from depositors to lend to entrepreneurs and is delegated the task of monitoring the outcomes of entrepreneurs' projects on behalf of depositors. Monitoring the i-th entrepreneur costs the intermediary K units of goods.[2] Depositors can observe the payment they receive from the intermediary, but cannot observe the project outcomes, payments by entrepreneurs to the intermediary, or the resources expended by the intermediary in monitoring the outcomes.

Each entrepreneur's project requires one unit of initial capital. Each depositor has available capital of $1/m$, as in Section 2. An intermediary which contracts with N entrepreneurs has $m \cdot N$ depositors.

To analyse the conditions when intermediation is beneficial (when the monitoring cost savings exceed the delegation costs of providing incentives) we must first characterize the delegation costs. If the intermediary could monitor at no cost, it could enforce contracts with entrepreneurs which imposed no deadweight bankruptcy costs on them. However, there would remain an incentive problem for the intermediary, because the payments it receives from entrepreneurs are not observed by depositors. The intermediary could claim that payments from entrepreneurs were low, and pay a small amount to depositors. We now extend the results in Section 2 to analyse the optimal contract to provide incentives for an intermediary to make payments to depositors. We later show that it provides incentives to monitor as well.

Let us re-introduce the subscript i on the outcome y_i of the i-th entrepreneur. For $i = 1, \ldots, N$, the $\tilde{y}_i$ are distributed independently and all are bounded below by zero and above by the real number $\bar{y}$. The probability distribution functions of the $\tilde{y}_i$ are common knowledge to all. Let $g_i(\cdot)$ be the non-negative real valued function which is the payment to the intermediary by the i-th entrepreneur as a function of the outcome y_i, assuming the intermediary monitors y_i. Because y_i is then observed by the intermediary, this implies no deadweight penalties will be imposed on the i-th entrepreneur. If the intermediary does not monitor, it must use a contract with deadweight bankruptcy penalties, as in Section 2, but in that case there would be no reason to have an intermediary. Due to the constraint that an entrepreneur can pay only what he has, we require $g_i(y_i) \leqq y_i$. The intermediary monitoring N entrepreneurs receives total payments G_N when $\tilde{y}_1 = y_1$, $\tilde{y}_2 = y_2, \ldots, \tilde{y}_N = y_N$ equal to

$$G_N = \sum_{i=1}^{N} g_i(y_i).$$

Let $\tilde{G}_N$ be the random variable with realization G_N. It is bounded above by $\bar{G}_N$, and below by zero.

The intermediary must make total payments to depositors with expectation R per project, or $N \cdot R$ in total. Let Z_N be the total payment to depositors by entrepreneurs. The intermediary can pay only what it has, thus $Z_N \leqq G_N$. By an argument identical to that of Section 2, we see that deadweight bankruptcy penalties must be imposed on the intermediary unless the intermediary will always receive aggregate payments of at least $N \cdot R$, or $P(\tilde{G}_N \geqq N \cdot R) = 1$. Because of the constraint that entrepreneurs can pay the intermediary at most y_i, we know $P(\tilde{G}_N \geqq N \cdot R) \leqq P(\sum_{i=1}^{N} \tilde{y}_i \geqq N \cdot R)$. Any entrepreneur, i, with $P(\tilde{y}_i \geqq R) = 1$ could finance directly, with no bankruptcy penalties, thus entrepreneurs who choose to use intermediaries will lead the intermediary to incur expected deadweight bankruptcy penalties.

Let $\Phi(Z_N)$ be the deadweight non-pecuniary penalty imposed on the intermediary when payment Z_N is made to depositors. From Proposition 1, the optimal $\Phi(Z_N)$ which gives incentives to make payments with expectation $N \cdot R$, is given by

$$\Phi(Z_N) = \max [H_N - Z_N, 0],$$

where the constant H_N is the smallest solution to

$$\{(P(\tilde{G}_N < H_N) \cdot E_{\tilde{G}_N}[\tilde{G}_N \mid G_N < H_N]) + ([1 - P(\tilde{G}_N < H_N)] \cdot H_N)\} \geqq N \cdot R.$$

With this contract in place, the expected return of the intermediary is $E_{\tilde{G}_N}[\tilde{G}_N] - H_N$; therefore the intermediary chooses monitoring expenditure to maximize $E_{\tilde{G}_N}[\tilde{G}_N]$. The intermediary uses the same decision rule in the decision to monitor as it would if its expenditure on monitoring were freely observable. This implies that it contracts only with entrepreneurs for whom the value of monitoring exceeds its physical and delegation costs, and chooses to monitor them. The minimum cost contract which provides incentives for payment to depositors also provides incentives for monitoring. This implies that the optimal contract between the intermediary and depositors is also a debt contract.

Diversification and the viability of intermediation

For a financial intermediary to be viable, three conditions must be fulfilled. The depositors must receive an expected return of R per unit deposited. The intermediary must receive an expected return net of monitoring costs and any deadweight penalties incurred which is at least zero. Finally, each entrepreneur must retain an expected return at least as high as he would by contracting directly with depositors.

Everyone in the economy is risk netural, implying that a complete description of the optimality of any feasible set of contracts is the sum of monitoring costs and expectation of total deadweight bankruptcy penalties.

A financial intermediary which contracts with one entrepreneur (and m depositors) is not viable. This follows immediately from the constraint $g_1(y_1) \leqq y_1$, that the entrepreneur can pay no more than the outcome y_1, and the constraint $Z \leqq G_1 = g_1(y_1)$, that the intermediary can pay no more than it receives from the entrepreneur. An entrepreneur incurs a deadweight penalty whenever $y_1 < h$; an intermediary with one entrepreneur who pays g_i must also incur a penalty of at least the same magnitude when $g_i \leqq y_i \leqq H_1$ (and it is necessary that $H_1 \geqq h$ to provide depositors with a competitive return). The intermediary is not viable because it incurs at least as high a deadweight cost and in addition spends resources on monitoring.

The case of one entrepreneur demonstrates the potential hazard of neglecting the costs of delegation when considering financial intermediation. The per-entrepreneur cost of providing incentives to the intermediary is reduced as it contracts with more entrepreneurs with independently distributed projects. With independent and identically distributed projects, the per-entrepreneur cost, D_N, is a monotonically decreasing function of the number of entrepreneurs, N, because deadweight penalties are incurred when returns are in the extreme lower tail, and the probability of the average return across projects being in that tail is monotonically decreasing.[3]

The argument in footnote 3 shows that for all projects with less than perfect correlation, the delegation cost for N projects monitored by a single intermediary is less than the sum of the delegation costs for monitoring proper subsets of them by several intermediaries. Increasing returns to scale from delegation cost savings is a very general result. The assumption of independence allows a stronger result. The expected delegation cost per entrepreneur monitored by the intermediary gets arbitrarily small as N, the number of entrepreneurs with independently distributed projects, grows without bound. This implies that the total cost (per entrepreneur) of providing monitoring converges to K, the physical cost of monitoring. This is Proposition 2.

Proposition 2. *The cost of delegation, per entrepreneur monitored, D_N, approaches zero as $N \to \infty$ if entrepreneurs' projects have bounded returns, distributed independently.*

Proof. Choose payment schedules $g_i = g_i(y_i)$ to the intermediary for entrepreneurs $i = 1, \ldots, N$, such that

$$E_{\tilde{g}_i}[\tilde{g}_i] = R + K + D_N, \quad \text{where } D_N > 0 \text{ is a real number.}$$

This provides the i-th entrepreneur with an expected return given by

$$E_{\tilde{g}_i}[\tilde{g}_i] - R - D_N.$$

Choose the non-pecuniary bankruptcy penalties of the intermediary as

$$\Phi_N(Z_N) = \max\left[(Z_N - H_N), 0\right]$$

where $H_N = N \cdot (R + D_N/2)$.

Given this contract, the intermediary will choose payments Z_N to depositors equal to

$$Z_N = \begin{cases} G_N & \text{if } G_N \leqq H_N \\ H_N & \text{if } G_N > H_N \end{cases}.$$

The expected return of the intermediary net of expenditure NK on monitoring is

$$E_{\tilde{G}_N}(\tilde{G}_N) - H_N - NK = [N \cdot (R + K + D_N)] - \left[N \cdot \left(R + \frac{D_N}{2}\right)\right] - (N \cdot K)$$

$$= \frac{N}{2} D_N > 0.$$

(satisfying the constraint that this be non-negative.)

The aggregate expected return to depositors is given by

$$P_N \cdot E_{\tilde{G}_N}[\tilde{G}_N | G_N \leqq H_N] + (1 - P_N) \cdot H_N \quad \text{where } P_N \equiv P(\tilde{G}_N \leqq H_N).$$

Notice that $G_N \geqq 0$ implying $E_{\tilde{G}_N}[\tilde{G}_N | G_N \leqq H_N] \geqq 0$ and that the aggregate expected rerurn of depositors is greater than or equal to:

$$(1 - P_N) \cdot H_N = (1 - P_N) \cdot N \cdot \left(R + \frac{D_N}{2}\right)$$

$$> N \cdot R \quad \text{for small } P_N > 0$$

i.e. for $P_N \in (0, (D_N/2)/(R + D_N/2))$.

There exists $N^* < \infty$ such that $P_N < \delta$ for all $\delta > 0$, by the (weak) law of large numbers, because $E_{\tilde{G}_N}[\tilde{G}_N] > H_N$. This implies that the delegation cost D_N can be made arbitrarily small for large N. $\|$

Proposition 2 demonstrates the key role of diversification in the provision of delegated monitoring. The intermediary need not be monitored because it takes "full responsibility" and bears all penalties for any short-fall of payments to principals. The diversification of its portfolio makes the probability of incurring these penalties very small and allows the information collected by the intermediary to be observed only by the intermediary.

Proposition 1 characterized the optimal incentive compatible mechanism for financial intermediation, and this is the optimal incentive compatible mechanism with "privacy". It was the optimal mechanism when the agent monitoring entrepreneurs was constrained not to announce the values of the project outcomes he observed and could only use the information privately to enforce his contract with each entrepreneur. Proposition 2 shows that financial intermediation is, asymptotically, the optimal incentive compatible mechanism for financing entrepreneurs' projects, without imposing the constraint of "privacy".

If the number of entrepreneurs monitored is $N = 1$, then delegation costs are so large that intermediation is never viable. If $N \to \infty$, then expected delegation costs approach zero, and intermediation is viable whenever direct monitoring pays. There exists some $N > 1$ at which intermediation becomes just viable (when $D_N \leqq$ min $[E_{\bar{y}}[\phi^*(\bar{y})], m \cdot K]$). If the assumption is made that each entrepreneur's project has the same variance, then the expected delegation costs are a monotonically decreasing function of N. This leads to increasing returns to scale due to diversification, but asymptotic constant returns to scale because expected delegation costs per project are bounded below by zero, and they may be small for moderate values of N.

The incentive contract is debt with bankruptcy penalties and high leverage. Asymptotically, the debt is riskless (as $D_N \to 0$). The leverage is high, as the face value of the debt is $H(N) = N \cdot (R + D_N/2)$, while the expected future value of the intermediary (including value of the debt) is $N \cdot (R + D_N + K)$.

The importance of the diversification is not simply a way for principals to hold well-diversified portfolios. Principals are risk neutral, and are not made directly better off by the diversification. Diversification within the financial intermediary organization is important, and cannot be replaced by diversification across intermediaries by principals.

Correlated returns of entrepreneurs

The assumption of independently distributed project returns across entrepreneurs is quite strong. It can be weakened somewhat. Instead of independence, assume that entrepreneur's project returns depend on several common factors which are observable. Factors might include GNP, interest rates, input prices, etc. Since these are observable, they can be used as the basis for contingent contracts. There might exist futures markets for these variables, and the financial intermediary could hedge changes in these factors in those markets. An example is a bank's hedging of interest rate risk using interest rate futures. If there are not active futures markets, then the intermediary can write contracts with depositors which depend on the values of these factors, rather than taking responsibility for all risks. An example of this is matching the maturity of assets and liabilities by banks, which places all interest rate risk on depositors. In either case, the intermediary retains responsibility for (and potentially fails as a result of) all risks which are not observable.

The result of Proposition 2, that $D_N \to 0$ as $N \to \infty$ follows given this alternative assumption in place of independence. This is stated in the following corollary.

Corollary to Proposition 2.   *If it is common knowledge that the returns of the projects of entrepreneurs i = 1, ... N, are given by*

$$\tilde{y}_i = \sum_{j=1}^{M} [\beta_{ij} \cdot \tilde{F}_j] + \tilde{\varepsilon}_i$$

where the $\tilde{F}_j$ are observable ex post, the $\tilde{\varepsilon}_i$ are independent and bounded and $E[\tilde{y}_i] > R + K$, then the result of Proposition 2 follows.

Proof.   Choose $g_i(y_i) = \alpha_i \cdot y_i$ where

$$\alpha_i = \frac{R + K + D_N}{E_{\tilde{y}}[\tilde{y}_i]}.$$

Let the penalty contract be either

$$\phi(Z) = Z + [\sum_{i=1}^{N} \sum_{j=1}^{M} \alpha \cdot \beta_{ij} \cdot F_j] - H(N)$$

where

$$H(N) = \left[N \cdot \left(R + \frac{D_N}{2} \right) \right] - E[\sum_{i=1}^{N} \sum_{j=1}^{M} \alpha_i \cdot \beta_{ij} \cdot \tilde{F}_j],$$

or let $\phi(Z)$ be as in Proposition 2, and let the position in the futures market be $\sum_{i=1}^{N} \alpha_i \cdot \beta_{ij}$ in futures markets $j = 1, \ldots, M$. The transformed random variables are now independent, and the result Proposition 2 follows. ‖

The intermediary monitors firm specific information, which is independent across entrepreneurs, and hedges out all systematic risks. The description of the process generating project returns is consistent with the Arbitrage Pricing Theory of Ross (1976).

The intuition behind this result is that the intermediary must bear certain risks for incentive purposes, but that risks which have no incentive component because they are common information should be shared optimally.[4] There has been a debate among various bankers and bank regulators over the desirability of allowing hedging in futures markets by banks. Our analysis suggests a reason why it is desirable.

4. RISK AVERSION AND DIVERSIFICATION

Diversification proved to be important to reduce delegation costs despite universal risk neutrality because of the wealth constraint of non-negative consumption and the asymmetry of information about project outcomes. The wealth constraint gives rise to a special type of "risk aversion". In this section, we investigate the role of diversification within the intermediary when the agents within the intermediary are risk averse in the usual sense. To focus on risk sharing issues, we drop the wealth constraint to allow any promise to be made good. A complete re-analysis of the model of Section 2 is not presented. This section does not present a realistic intermediary model, but simply a further investigation of the role of diversification in reducing the costs of delegation.

The basic set-up is as in Section 2, each entrepreneur is endowed with a project with outcome $\tilde{y}_i$ which is freely observed only the entrepreneur, which has zero as a possible realization. Absent monitoring by lenders, no incentive compatible payment schedule can depend on the realization y_i, because the entrepreneur could always claim a low value occurred. For simplicity, assume that all agents in the economy, including the entrepreneurs, are identical and risk averse. Risk aversion implies that the payment to lenders will be a constant, rather than a random amount independent of $\tilde{y}_i$, (see Holmström (1979)). This implies that, absent monitoring, the risk averse entrepreneur bears all of the risk from fluctuations in $\tilde{y}_i$. This is inconsistent with the optimal risk sharing which would occur if $\tilde{y}_i$ were observed, and this provides a potential benefit from monitoring $\tilde{y}_i$. In this risk averse setting, we could introduce other actions, e.g. effort, which the entrepreneur could privately select to give rise to a more general motivation for monitoring. This would not change the essence of our results.

We focus again on delegated monitoring by a financial intermediary. A financial intermediary raises funds from depositors who do not monitor, lends these funds to entrepreneurs, and can offer improved risk sharing with an entrepreneur because the intermediary's monitoring reduces or eliminates the incentive problem. In Section 2, we showed that an intermediary monitoring a single entrepreneur would have an incentive problem just as severe as would an entrepreneur. Almost the same result is true here. Because depositors do not monitor the intermediary and cannot observe its information, incentive compatible payments from the intermediary to depositors cannot depend on outcomes, and will be constant. It is true, however, that a single intermediary and a single entrepreneur can now share $\tilde{y}_i$ risk, but this has little to do with intermediation. Any lender who spends resources to monitor $\tilde{y}_i$ can share risk with the entrepreneur without being called an "intermediary".

For a financial intermediary in an economy where everyone is risk averse to viably provide delegated monitoring services, it must have lower delegation costs than an entrepreneur. Equivalently, since risk sharing is the issue here, a viable financial intermediary which monitors many entrepreneurs with independently distributed projects must charge a lower Arrow-Pratt risk premium for bearing the risk of an entrepreneur's project than does the entrepreneur. This will carry over to more general settings, because if the intermediary can bear risks at a lower risk premium it will generally face a less severe trade-off between risk sharing and incentives, and can thus efficiently be delegated a monitoring task.

Two types of diversification

There are two ways in which an intermediary in an economy of risk averse agents might use diversification. They correspond to two different models of an intermediary. One model increases the number of agents working together within the intermediary organization as the intermediary monitors a larger number of entrepreneurs. The second model assumes that the intermediary consists of a *single* agent who monitors a large number of entrepreneurs with independent projects.

Beginning with the first model, assume that each identical agent ("banker") in the intermediary is risk averse, and that by spending resources to monitor, each banker within the intermediary can observe the information monitored by all other bankers within the intermediary. This implies that there are no incentive problems within the intermediary. The extreme assumption that incentive problems are absent is intended to capture the idea that there may be different mechanism for controlling incentive problems within an organization. This approach is followed in Ramakrishnan–Thakor (1983), to generalize the risk neutral analysis we present in Section 2. This model leads to the traditional "risk subdividing" type of diversification. This type of diversification works because each independent risk is shared by an increasing number of bankers. For example, each risk averse agent will obtain a higher expected utility if each of N agents invests in a fraction $1/N$ of N identical independent gambles than in any single one of the gambles.

The second type of diversification, "adding risks", occurs in the second model where a single banker bears 100% of N independent risks, with diversification occurring as N grows. This is quite different from risk subdivision, because it is not a form of risk sharing at all. The total risk imposed on the agent rises with N, while with subdivision of risks it falls with N. Samuelson (1963) termed diversification by adding risks a "fallacy of large numbers", because it is not true for all risk averse utility functions that the risk aversion toward the N-th independent gamble is a decreasing function of N. Samuelson provides no analysis of conditions when this type of diversification is beneficial, and I know of none in the literature.[5] We provide a partial characterization of conditions when the certainty equivalent of a given gamble is higher (and the risk premium lower) when another independent risky gamble is also held. That is, when is the per asset certainty equivalent higher with $N = 2$ than with $N = 1$?

We turn first to the relatively straightforward model of diversification by subdivision of risks. Assume that it takes one banker in the intermediary to monitor one entrepreneur, and this requires an expenditure in goods of K (or that the disutility of this monitoring task is additively separable). All bankers are identical, have increasing, concave utility of wealth functions $U(W)$. By spending K to monitor their entrepreneur, each banker can also observe information monitored by the other bankers within the intermediary, implying that there is no incentive problem within the intermediary. Depositors are not assumed to be able to observe any of the information generated within the intermediary, and are paid a fixed unconditional payment of NR. As $N \to \infty$, Ramakrishnan–Thakor (1983) shows that each banker bears an arbitrarily small risk, with perfect risk sharing within the intermediary.

The interpretation of this result is that the diversification which occurs when bankers within the intermediary can share independent risks does serve to reduce the severity of its incentive problem. This occurs because the incentive problem here imposes a constraint on optimal risk sharing, and if there is improved risk sharing within the intermediary (where incentive problems may be controlled directly, or absent as assumed here), then this is analogous to reducing the risk aversion of a single agent, which reduces the tradeoff between risk sharing and the provision of incentives.

In the second model, where the intermediary consists of a single agent, diversification by adding risks is at work. The intermediary agent monitoring N loans, receives payments from each entrepreneur and bears all of the risk because he pays an unconditional return, $N \cdot R$, to depositors. The financial intermediary can provide monitoring and risk sharing services superior to an individual lender if and only if his risk aversion toward the Nth independent risk is a decreasing function of N. Put another way, when there is no wealth constraint an intermediary monitoring a single entrepreneur ($N = 1$) is equivalent to direct monitoring by a lender. Intermediation becomes potentially viable when the delegation cost (equal to the risk premium here) is reduced by the centralization of monitoring to a single intermediary. This is therefore equivalent to the conditions when adding independent risks reduces per-entrepreneur risk aversion, which are the conditions when the fallacy of large numbers is not a fallacy.

To provide a partial characterization of conditions when the per-risk risk premium declines, we initially focus on the case of two risks. That is, given two bounded and independent random variables $\tilde{g}_1$ and $\tilde{g}_2$, when is the risk premium for bearing the risk of the bounded random variable $\tilde{g}_1 + \tilde{g}_2$ less than the sum of the two risk premia for bearing either risk separately. If both random variables represent payment schedules from entrepreneurs which a risk averse intermediary would voluntarily accept, both must have expectation greater than $R + K$, because the intermediary promises $N \cdot R$ to depositors and spends $N \cdot K$ on monitoring. It will ease exposition to provisionally assume

$E_{\tilde{g}_i}[\tilde{g}_1] = R + K$. In addition, define $x_i \equiv g_i - R - K$, for $i = 1, 2$. With this notation, the net effect of contracting to monitor an entrepreneur with payment schedule $\tilde{g}_1$ is equivalent to receiving the random variable $\tilde{x}_1$. (In this notation, our temporary assumption is $E_{\tilde{x}_i}[\tilde{x}_1] = 0$.)

An agent has a four times differentiable, increasing and strictly concave von Neuman-Morganstern utility function $U(W)$, and initial wealth W_0. The random variables $\tilde{x}_1$ and $\tilde{x}_2$ are bounded and independent. The risk premium, ρ_i, for bearing the risk, of the single random variable $x_i (i = 1, 2)$, satisfies

$$E_{\tilde{x}_i}[U(W_0 + \tilde{x}_i + \rho_i)] = U(W_0 + E_{\tilde{x}_i}[\tilde{x}_i]).$$

The risk premium, ρ_{1+2}, for bearing the risk of the random variable $\tilde{x}_1 + \tilde{x}_2$, satisfies

$$E_{\tilde{x}_1} E_{\tilde{x}_2}[U(W_0 + \tilde{x}_1 + \tilde{x}_2 + \rho_{1+2})] = U(W_0 + E_{\tilde{x}_1}[\tilde{x}_1] + E_{\tilde{x}_2}[\tilde{x}_2]).$$

Adding risks reduces the risk premium if

$$\rho_{1+2} < \rho_1 + \rho_2.$$

If $\tilde{x}_2$ is a small gamble, its risk premium is proportional to the Arrow-Pratt measure of absolute risk aversion or $-U''(W_0)/U'(W_0)$. Treating $\tilde{x}_1$ as part of the agent's endowment define the indirect utility function $V(x_2)$ of increments to wealth x_2, which is also von Neuman-Morganstern and defined as

$$V(x_2) = E_{\tilde{x}_1}[U(W_0 + \tilde{x}_1 + x_2)].$$

The expected utility of the agent bearing the risk of $\tilde{x}_1 + \tilde{x}_2$ is now expressed as $E_{\tilde{x}_2} V(\tilde{x}_2)$.

The incremental risk premium for bearing the risk of $\tilde{x}_2$, given that $\tilde{x}_1$ is in one's endowment is given by the Arrow-Pratt measure for the utility function $V(\cdot)$. The condition for $\rho_{1+2} < \rho_1 + \rho_2$ is for $V(\cdot)$ to be less risk averse than $U(\cdot)$, or

$$-\frac{E_{\tilde{x}_1}[U''(W_0 + \tilde{x}_1)]}{E_{\tilde{x}_1}[U'(W_0 + x_1)]} < -\frac{U''(W_0)}{U'(W_0)}.$$

Given our assumption that $E_{x_1}[\tilde{x}_1] = 0$, a sufficient condition can be directly obtained from Jensen's inequality. A sufficient condition is for the function $-U''(w)$ to be concave and $U'(w)$ to be convex, or $U''''(\cdot) \geq 0$ and $U'''(\cdot) \geq 0$ (with one inequality strict) over the range of $W_0 + \tilde{x}_1 + \tilde{x}_2$. (Clearly, $U'''' \leq 0$ and $U''' \leq 0$ (with one inequality strict) is sufficient for the reverse condition).

The assumption that $E_{\tilde{x}_1}[\tilde{x}_1] = 0$ is invalid if $\tilde{x}_1$ is a gamble which the agent accepts voluntarily. It is necessary to have $E_{\tilde{x}_1}[\tilde{x}_1] > 0$. Adding a voluntarily chosen gamble $\tilde{x}_1$ will not only place a mean preserving spread onto intitial wealth, it will increase mean wealth. To take account of the effect of this higher mean wealth on risk aversion, we augment the sufficient conditions described above with the condition for decreasing absolute risk aversion. This provides sufficient conditions for the "fallacy of large numbers" to be correct, rather than a fallacy, (for proof that this is equivalent to decreasing risk aversion, see Pratt (1964, Theorem 5) or Kihlstrom, Romer and Williams (1981, Corollary 2)).

The condition for decreasing absolute risk aversion at a point W is

$$U'''(W) > \frac{U''(W)^2}{U'(W)} > 0,$$

thus a sufficient condition is that over the entire domain of W

$$U'''(W) > \frac{U''(W)^2}{U'(W)}.$$

Combined with $U'''' \geqq 0$, we have a sufficient condition for diversification by adding risks to reduce the risk premium. Stronger characterizations can be obtained from stronger assumptions about the random variables $\tilde{x}_1$ and $\tilde{x}_2$.

These conditions extend beyond the case of $N = 2$, because if over the relevant domain $U'''(\cdot) \geqq 0$ then $V'''(\cdot) \geqq 0$ and if $U''''(\cdot) \geqq 0$ then $V''''(\cdot) \geqq 0$. Finally, straight forward extension of Pratt (1964, theorem 5) shows that if $-U''/U'$ is decreasing in the relevant domain, then $-V''/V'$ is decreasing as well. A third independent gamble will further reduce the risk premium: $\rho_{1+2+3} < \rho_{1+2} + \rho_3 < \rho_1 + \rho_2 + \rho_3$.

A few examples may help to illustrate what is at work. With constant absolute risk aversion $(-U''(W)/U'(W) = k$ for all $W)$, increasing the mean initial wealth is of no consequence and in addition,

$$\frac{-V''}{V'} = k \frac{E_{\tilde{w}}[U'(\tilde{W})]}{E_{\tilde{w}}[U'(W)]} = k,$$

implying that diversification by adding independent risks is of no consequence, because there are no wealth levels of lower risk aversion over which to average. The quadratic utility function $U(W) = W - (b/2)W^2$ has $U'''(\cdot) = U''''(\cdot) = 0$, therefore adding a zero mean gamble $\tilde{x}_1$ does not influence the risk aversion toward the independent gamble $\tilde{x}_2$. However, a voluntarily chosen gamble $\tilde{x}_1$ will have a positive expectation, and quadradic utility implies increasing absolute risk aversion. The per gamble risk premium will *increase* amd diversification will "hurt".

A simple example of a utility function which satisfies the conditions for diversification by adding risks to be beneficial is $U(W) = 0 \cdot 05 W^3 - 60 W^2 + 50,000 W - 4,450,000$ which is increasing and concave and has $U'''(\cdot) > 0$, $U''''(\cdot) = 0$, and decreasing absolute risk aversion over the domain $W \in [0, 400)$. Suppose initial wealth is 100, notice that $U(100) = 0$. The gamble

$$\tilde{x}_1 : \begin{array}{c} \overset{\frac{1}{2}}{\diagup} +32 \cdot 1983 \\ \underset{\frac{1}{2}}{\diagdown} -30 \end{array}$$

will be just acceptable; that is $E_{\tilde{x}_1}[U(100 + \tilde{x}_1)] = 0$. If $\tilde{x}_2$ is an independent identically distributed gamble, we find $E_{\tilde{x}_1} E_{\tilde{x}_2}[U(100 + \tilde{x}_1 + \tilde{x}_2)] = 209 \cdot 6$. The risk aversion toward the second gamble is reduced by accepting the first.

In contrast to diversification by subdividing risk, the value of diversification by adding risks depends critically on the form of agent's utility function. Given the lack of observability of preferences in practice, this limits the testability of this result on diversification when there is no binding wealth constraint. The results in Section 3, where the value of diversification arises only from binding wealth constraints, provide strong and testable results.

5. COMPARISON WITH LELAND–PYLE (1977) RESULTS

Leland–Pyle (1977) (L–P hereafter) develops an interesting model of costly signalling by entrepreneurs selling shares to the public. In contrast to the ex-post information asymmetry analysed in this paper, they focus on an *ex-ante* information asymmetry, where entrepreneurs know more than investors. This gives rise to an adverse selection problem, because if entrepreneurs of different types cannot be distinguished, all must sell securities at the same price, and there would be a large supply of securities by entrepreneurs with worthless projects. The model allows the entrepreneur an endogenous choice of investing in other assets or retaining equity in his project. L–P show that retained equity serves as a costly signal of the entrepreneur's information about value. It is costly, because in equilibrium a risk averse entrepreneur retains some "project specific risk" of his project which would be avoided under full information.

Some preliminary thoughts on a theory of financial intermediation are presented in L–P although no analysis is developed. They suggest that financial intermediaries might expend resources to observe entrepreneur's *ex-ante* information and use the information to offer to buy securities from entrepreneurs, offering improved risk sharing. Inter·mediaries might do this to capture cost savings compared with information collection by investors, or to solve underproduction of information problems analysed by Grossman–Stiglitz (1980) and Chan (1983). Although L–P do not mention diversification, they seem to suggest that the intermediary collects information about many entrepreneurs and then signals the *ex-ante* prospects of its portfolio using the same "retained equity" costly signal which entrepreneurs can use individually. Such intermediation will be viable only if the per-entrepreneur risk sharing cost of signalling by the intermediary is lower than the per-entrepreneur cost of direct signalling without an intermediary. This is analogous to the conditions for viable intermediation in the delegated monitoring model analysed above. It is interesting to investigate whether the types of diversification analysed in Section 4 facilitate intermediation here. In the process of doing this, we correct an error in L–P which was not criticial to their analysis of individual entrepreneur signalling, but which is central to our extending the analysis to diversification and intermediation.[6] We present results in the text, and sketch the analysis in the Appendix.

The formal L–P signalling model analyses an entrepreneur endowed with a project which has a mean return observed only by him. It is common knowledge that it has a normal distribution with known variance σ^2. The entrepreneur and all investors have exponential utility (constant absolute risk aversion). The entrepreneur's preferences are common knowledge. Traded securities are valued in the market using the Capital Asset Pricing Model and public information. This implies that known market wide risks are "priced", while "specific risks" (those uncorrelated with the market portfolio) are not priced. The market will bear specific risks at no risk premium. The entrepreneur signals by issuing unlimited liability (riskless) debt, and equity at market prices, and by trading in the "market portfolio", with signalling conditions enforced by retaining a non-trivial amount of equity and its associated specific risk. This signalling is costly because of imperfect risk sharing—the risk averse entrepreneur retains a large amount of specific risk which could be sold off to the market with no risk premium under full information.

We introduce financial intermediation and diversification into the L–P model by assuming that there are N entrepreneurs with projects whose returns are distributed independently and identically and are independent of the market portfolio. (The results extend to the case where projects are correlated with the market portfolio, but independent conditional on the observed market portfolio). In the appendix, we demonstrate that the results of Section 4 carry over to the L–P model.

Diversification by adding independent risks occurs if the intermediary is modeled as a single agent who like everyone else in the L–P model has exponential utility. As is suggested by the analysis in Section 4, such diversification has no effect, because with constant absolute risk aversion the risk aversion toward any gamble is not affected by the presence of any other independent gambles. This implies that an agent signalling a given project will choose to retain a given fraction of its equity in a signalling equilibrium, irrespective of other independent projects he must signal, and that the marginal impact on his expected utility is not influenced by other independent projects he must signal. This implies that financial intermediation based on diversification by adding risks is not viable given the L–P model because the intermediary signalling costs will be just as high as an entrepreneur's.

Diversification by subdividing risks occurs if there are N bankers working in the intermediary who all observe the *ex-ante* information of N entrepreneurs, and signal by each retaining equity in the intermediary's portfolio. Focusing for simplicity on the case of bankers with identical utility functions and identical independent projects with mean μ, and variance σ^2, this implies that each banker in the intermediary retains a fraction $1/N$ of total equity retained by insiders, and an equal fraction of each project. Because all bankers can observe each other's information and actions, they face no group moral hazard problem. Because of their risk sharing, we show that each banker's signalling decision is equivalent to that of a single entrepreneur signalling a project with mean $N\mu/N = \mu$ and variance $(1/N)^2 N\sigma^2 = \sigma^2/N$. As a result, diversification by subdividing risks has the same effect on each banker's expected utility as reducing the known variance of specific risk of a single project signalled directly by a single entrepreneur. We show in the Appendix that this diversification improves the expected utility of the agents in the intermediary (expected utility is a decreasing function of variance), implying that diversified intermediation is potentially viable. Put another way, the intermediary's signalling costs are lower than an entrepreneur's, because the intermediary's costs are equivalent to the signalling costs of an entrepreneur with a smaller variance of specific risk. This analysis corrects the erronous Proposition III in L–P, which states that an entrepreneur's expected utility is an *increasing* function of variance, and would have implied that even diversification by subdividing risk was counterproductive.

The results of our delegated monitoring intermediation model are consistent with the extension of the L–P analysis to intermediation. In particular, if the *ex-ante* information about the N entrepreneurs who contract with the intermediary is observed by the N bankers who as a team are the intermediary (diversification by subdividing risks), then the "delegated signalling" costs approach zero. The implication of this is an intermediary with primarily debt (deposits) in its capital structure and very little outside equity.

6. CONCLUSION

Diversification within the financial intermediary is the key to understanding why there is a benefit from delegating monitoring to an intermediary which is not monitored by its depositors. The intuitive reason for the value of diversification is slightly different in the model with risk neutral agents from the one with risk averse agents. In the risk neutral model, diversification is important because it increases the probability that the intermediary has sufficient loan proceeds to repay a fixed debt claim to depositors; in the limit, this probability is one, and the probability of incurring necessary bankruptcy costs goes to zero. In the model with risk aversion, but no binding constraints on non-negative consumption, diversification increases the intermediary's risk tolerance toward each loan, allowing the risk bearing necessary for incentive pruposes to be less costly. The general importance of diversification in financial intermediary theories is demonstrated by the similar results obtained from our analysis of a Leland–Pyle signalling model of intermediation.

Financial intermediaries allow better contracts to be used and allow Pareto superior allocations. This provides a positive role for financial intermediaries. The delegated monitoring model predicts well-diversified financial intermediaries with a capital structure which is mainly debt (deposits), with despite this high leverage, a low probability of default. These predictions are in line with reality for most intermediaries. In addition, the insight that intermediaries must bear certain risks for incentive purposes has an important implication for the regulatory controversy involving the desirability of allowing banks to hedge in interest rate futures markets. Because interest rate risk is freely observable, it ought to be shared optimally, and permitting banks to sell such risk in the futures market effectively allows them to do so. Because risk sharing within the intermediary is constrained by binding incentive compatibility constraints, there is a reason to allow the bank to hedge against these risks (although a possible alternative is for the bank to force borrowers to do this hedging).

Commerical banks and insurance companies are the most obvious applications of this model. Another interesting application of the diversification by subdividing model is conglomerate firms. To the extent that members of subsidiary divisions can monitor each others actions at low cost, the conglomerate can allow the managers of the divisions to share the risks which they as a group must bear for incentive purposes. In Diamond–Verrecchia (1982), it is argued that the risks which managers must bear for incentive purposes are the firm specific risks because these are not observable elsewhere. If the cost of within conglomerate monitoring is fixed, a possible implication of our results is that firms with high firm specific risk will be most likely to join together into conglomerates.

An interesting implication of the delegated monitoring model is that intermediary assets will be illiquid. This is because the intermediary is delegated the task of observing information about each loan which no one else but the entrepreneur/borrower observes. In one sense, such assets are totally illiquid, as the intermediary contracts to hold them and enforce the contract, rather than sell them. If the intermediary were to sell a loan and transfer the monitoring and enforcement to someone else, the acquirer would have to incur the monitoring costs again, duplicating the effort of the first intermediary. These costs would be in addition to any physical costs of transfering ownership. Adverse selection of which loan an intermediary chooses to sell could be another complication caused by the private information possessed by the intermediary. The centralization of monitoring each loan by a single intermediary will mean that there are not active markets for these assets. All of these phenomenon are related to the concept of illiquidity. The resulting illiquidity of assets leads to another reason why financial intermediaries might improve on the allocations provided by competitive exchange markets; see Diamond–Dybvig (1983), where asset illiquidity is simply a result of the specified production technology. An interesting extension of these two models would be a model of the liqudity implications of private information within an intermediary.

Many "markets" for information services induce the delegated private information production analysed in this paper. Further study of the implications of this arrangement should produce new insights into financial markets and institutions, and possibly other types of markets and organizations.

APPENDIX

To focus on the role of diversification in reducing the signalling costs of an intermediary below those of individual entrepreneurs, we compare signalling costs for $N = 1$ and $N = 2$. We view the intermediary as equivalent to an entrepreneur with 2 projects. We assume that the projects of entrepreneurs monitored by the intermediary are mutually independent and uncorrelated with the "market portfolio", the one other traded risky asset in the L–P model. We follow L–P and assume that projects are so small that we can neglect the effect of adding them to the market. This implies we can alternatively assume that the projects are independent conditional on the market portfolio, because trade in the market allows optimal linear sharing of market risk, and L–P analyze only linear risk sharing.

Agents in the intermediary have identical known exponential utility of wealth functions, $U(W) = -e^{-bW}$ where $b > 0$. Project i has returns $\tilde{x}_i + \mu_i$, where $\tilde{x}_i$ has a normal distribution with zero mean and known variance $\sigma_{x_i}^2$, and μ_i is known by the entrepreneur and intermediary, but not investors in the market. Given information which will be available to the market, the project is valued at its expectation, discounted by the rate of interest, r (because project is uncorrelated with the market, or alternatively, because investors are risk neutral). The intermediary chooses to retain a fraction α_i of the equity in the ith project, selling the remainder to outside investors and also issuing unlimited liability (riskless) debt. Absent some sort of self-selection or signalling mechanism, there will be a severe adverse selection problem. L–P solve for a fully separating signalling equilibrium, with sorting based on the value of α_i.

Using notation similar to L–P, define:

α_i = the fraction of the i-th project retained by the intermediary.

$\mu_i(\alpha_i)$ = the market's valuation schedule, expressing the μ_i inferred on the basis of α_i selected.

$V_i(\alpha_i)$ = the total market value of a project i implied by the schedule $\mu_i(\alpha_i)$. $V_i(\alpha_i) = \mu_i(\alpha_i)/(1+r)$.

W_0 = the initial wealth of the intermediary.

$\tilde{M}$ = the random return on the market portfolio.

β = the fraction of the market portfolio held by the intermediary.

V_M = price of the market portfolio.

K_i = initial outlay required for the ith project.

D_i = current value of riskless debt issued against i-th project (promise to pay $D_i(1+r)$).

Y = current value of riskless debt issued on "personal account". (The distinction between D_i and Y is not used here; we present it this way to be consistent with L–P.

r = riskless rate of interest.

W_1 = final wealth of intermediary.

$\sigma_{w_1}^2$ = variance of final wealth.

Given the assumption of exponential utility, and normal distributions of the projects and market portfolio, the intermediary maximizes $E[\tilde{W}_i] - (b/2)\sigma_{w_i}^2$. The budget constraint is:

$$W_0 + \alpha_1 D_1 + \alpha_2 D_2 + (1 - \alpha_1) V_1(\alpha_1) + (1 - \alpha_2) V_2(\alpha_2) - K_1 - K_2 - \beta V_M - Y = 0.$$
$$(A1)$$

Final wealth is

$$\tilde{W}_1 = \alpha_1[\tilde{x}_1 + \mu_1 - (1+r)D_1] + \alpha_2[\tilde{x}_2 + \mu_2 - (1+r)D_2] + \beta\tilde{M} + (1+r)Y. \quad (A2)$$

Substituting (A2) into (A1),

$$\tilde{W}_1 = \alpha_1[\tilde{x}_1 + \mu_1 - \mu_1(\alpha_1)] + \alpha_2[\tilde{x}_2 + \mu_2 - \mu_2(\alpha_2)] + \beta\tilde{M} - (1+r)V_M$$
$$+ (W_0 - K_1 - K_2)(1+r) + \mu_1(\alpha_1) + \mu_2(\alpha_2). \quad (A3)$$

The intermediary chooses α_1, α_2 and β to maximize $E[\tilde{W}_1] - (b/2)\sigma_{\tilde{W}_1}^2$. Noting that

$\tilde{x}_1$, $\tilde{x}_2$, and $\tilde{M}$ are independent, the optimal α_1^*, α_2^*, and β^* satisfy:

$$[\mu_1 - \mu_1(\alpha_1^*)] + (1 - \alpha_1^*)\mu_{\alpha_1}(\alpha_1) - \alpha_1 b\sigma_{x_1}^2 = 0, \tag{A4}$$

$$[\mu_2 - \mu_2(\alpha_2^*)] + (1 - \alpha_2^*)\mu_{\alpha_2}(\alpha_2) - \alpha_2 b\sigma_{x_2}^2 = 0, \tag{A5}$$

and

$$[E[\tilde{M}] - (1 + r)V_M] - \beta b\sigma_M^2 = 0. \tag{A6}$$

In a separating signalling equilibrium $\mu_i(\alpha_i) = \mu_i$. Solving (A4) and (A5) given this constraint yields

$$(1 - \alpha_i)\mu_{\alpha_i}(\alpha_i) = b\alpha_i\sigma_{x_i}^2 \quad \text{for } i = 1, 2. \tag{A7}$$

Solving the differential equation (A7) yields

$$\mu_i(\alpha_i) = -b\sigma_{x_i}^2[\log(1 - \alpha_i) + \alpha_i] + (1 + r)K_i, \tag{A8}$$

plus an arbitrary constant. The least cost solution not subject to unraveling, is shown in L–P to have the constant $= 0$, implying that the market value of the ith project is

$$V_i(\alpha_i) = \frac{1}{1 + r}[-b\sigma_{x_i}^2[\log(1 - \alpha_i) + \alpha_i]] + K_i. \tag{A9}$$

For simplicity we analyse the case of independent and identically distributed (i.i.d.) projects, where $\mu_1 = \mu_2 = \mu$ and $\sigma_{x_1}^2 = \sigma_{x_2}^2 = \sigma_x^2$.

Diversification by *subdividing* risks occurs with an intermediary which consists of two agents each with risk aversion b who each retain a fraction $\alpha/2$ of each of two projects. Because their decisions are separable, they each make a decision for each project which is equivalent to that of a single agent endowed with a single project with mean $\mu/2$ and variance $\sigma_x^2/4$. This, in turn, is equivalent to a project with mean $= \mu$ and variance $= \sigma_x^2/2$, because from (A8), if α_i solves $\mu_i = [\log(1 - \alpha_i) + \alpha_i]\sigma_{x_i}^2$, it also solves $a\mu_i = [\log(1 - \alpha_i) + \alpha_i] \cdot a\sigma_{x_i}^2$. We can therefore analyse the comparative static effect of diversification by sub-dividing risks on an intermediary's expected utility by analysing the effect of reducing the variance of specific risk of a single project $i = 1$, holding its mean constant (we suppress the subscript "i"). This is given by

$$\frac{dE[U(\tilde{W}_1)]}{d\sigma_x^2} = \frac{dE[\tilde{W}_1]}{d\sigma_x^2} - \frac{b}{2}\frac{d\sigma_{W_1}^2}{d\sigma_x^2}. \tag{A10}$$

Because $E[\tilde{x}_i] = 0$ and $\mu = \mu(\alpha)$, (A3) shows that $dE[\tilde{W}_1]/d\sigma_x^2 = 0$. Turning to the variance of final wealth, note that it is given by $\sigma_{W_1}^2 = \alpha^2\sigma_x^2 + \beta^2\sigma_M^2$, implying

$$\frac{d\sigma_{W_1}^2}{d\sigma_x^2} = 2\sigma_x^2\alpha\frac{d\alpha}{d\sigma_x^2} + \alpha^2\frac{d\sigma_x^2}{d\sigma_x^2} + \frac{d(\beta^2\sigma_M^2)}{d\sigma_x^2}. \tag{A11}$$

Inspecting (A4) and (A6), $d(\beta^2\sigma_M^2)/d\sigma_x^2 = 0$, and by definition $d\sigma_x^2/d\sigma_x^2 = 1$. In equilibrium $\mu(\alpha) = \mu$, so one can apply the implicit function theorem to (A8), and obtain

$$\frac{d\alpha}{d\sigma_x^2} = -\frac{d\mu(\alpha)/d\sigma_x^2}{d\mu(\alpha)/d\alpha} = \frac{(1 - \alpha)[\log(1 - \alpha) + \alpha]}{\alpha\sigma_x^2}.$$

Inserting this into (A10) and (A11), one obtains

$$\frac{dE[U(\tilde{W}_i)]}{d\sigma_x^2} = -b\left[(1 - \alpha)[\log(1 - \alpha) + \alpha] + \frac{\alpha^2}{2}\right] < 0.$$

This is negative because it is defined over $\alpha \in (0, 1)$, is zero at zero, and decreasing in α. This corrects Proposition III in L–P, where the final α^2 term was omitted, leading them to conclude that the sign of the entire expression was positive. The intuition behind the correct result is clear: signalling is costly because of inferior risk sharing, if there is very little risk, the cost is low (if $\sigma^2 = 0$, there is no risk for the entrepreneur to bear and no need to go public). Thus diversification by subdividing risks can serve as a basis for viable financial intermediation in a L–P setting. As N, the number of independent projects, and number of bankers within the intermediary, grows without bound, the per-project risk premium goes to zero, because the total variance of wealth, per banker in the intermediary (σ_x^2/N) goes to zero.

Diversification by *adding independent* risks is modelled by adding a second i.i.d. project to the intermediary's portfolio, while the intermediary consists of a single agent with constant risk aversion of b. Inspecting (A4) and (A5), one finds that no terms involving another independent project enter, thus $\alpha_1 = \alpha_2$ and both are equal to the level that would prevail if there were only one project. Therefore, adding additional i.i.d. projects is equivalent to adding i.i.d. lotteries, and given exponential utility the analysis in Section 4 shows that the risk premium per project is not influenced by the number of independent projects. Therefore, diversification by adding i.i.d. projects does not reduce signalling costs in the L–P model and cannot serve as a basis for viable financial intermediation. It would be interesing to extend the L–P model to a utility function which implies that this type of diversification has value.

First version received August 1982; *final version accepted December* 1983 *(Eds.).*

I am grateful to S. Bhattacharya, G. Connor, P. Dybvig, B. Grundy, O. Hart, B. Holmström, M. Machina, D. Pyle, D. Romer, S. Ross, J. Tobin and R. Verrecchia for helpful comments. An earlier version of this paper was part of my dissertation submitted to the Yale University Department of Economics.

NOTES

1. Note that this formulation is without loss of generality, and contract $\phi(z)$, which specifies a payment of goods to the entrepreneur by the lender and is not a non-pecuniary penalty, can be expressed as a net payment $\hat{z} = \phi(z) - z$.

2. There are two equivalent ways to model the monitoring cost. One, mentioned in the text, is for the financial intermediary to experience no disutility from monitoring and enforcement, but to spend K in resources. In this case, to avoid messy notation, re-normalize so that "one unit" is defined as the sum of the amount each project requires plus K, the amount spent on monitoring by the intermediary. Alternatively, one can assume that monitoring does not require resources, but that the intermediary experiences disutility from monitoring and has the linear utilty function of wealth $U(W, N) = W - NK$, where N is the number of entrepreneurs monitored. In this case, no renormalization is required.

3. For example, in the identically distributed case with 1 project, the delegation cost is

$$D_1 = E_{\tilde{g}_1}[H_1 - \tilde{g}_1 | g_1 \leqq H_1],$$

while with 2 projects the per project delegation cost is

$$D_2 = \tfrac{1}{2} E_{\tilde{g}_1} E_{\tilde{g}_2}[H_2 - \tilde{g}_1 - \tilde{g}_2 | g_1 + g_2 \leqq H_2].$$

We know that the minimum feasible value of $H_2 \leqq 2H_1$ because if $H_2 = 2H_1$, the expected return to depositors is at least $2R$. This implies $D \leqq D_1 - C$, where

$$C = P(\Omega) E[H_2 - \tilde{g}_1 - \tilde{g}_2 | \Omega]$$

and Ω is the event "$g_1 + g_2 \geqq H_1 \cdot 2$, and either $[g_1 \leqq H_1$ or $g_2 \leqq H_1]$". If $\tilde{g}_1$ and $\tilde{g}_2$ have continuous distributions, $P(\Omega) > 0$ unless they are perfectly correlated, implying $C > 0$.

4. See Diamond–Verrecchia (1982) and Holmström (1982) for implications of this observation for the theory of mangerial capital budgeting.

5. Some analysis is presented of risk aversion measured from a stochastic initial "wealth" position in Kihlstrom, Romer and Williams (1981), Machina (1982), and Ross (1981). These papers do not address the problem of adding risks.

6. The analysis of L–P presented here was stimulated by a referee's noting that this paper's results seemed opposed to those of Proposition III of L–P, and his conjecture that L–P Proposition III might be incorrect.

REFERENCES

CAMPBELL, T. (1979), "Optimal Investment Decisions and the Value of Confidentiality", *Journal of Financial and Quantitative Analysis*, **14**, 913–924.

CHAN, Y. (1983), "On the Positive Role of Financial Intermediation in Allocation of Venture Capital in a Market with Imperfect Information", *Journal of Finance*, **38**, 1543–1568.

DIAMOND, D. W. and DYBVIG, P. H. (1983), "Bank Runs, Deposit Insurance and Liquidity", *Journal of Political Economy*, **91**, 401–419.

DIAMOND, D. W. and VERRECCHIA, R. E. (1982), "Optimal Managerial Contracts and Equilibrium Security Prices", *Journal of Finance*, **37**, 275–287.

HARRIS, M. and RAVIV, A. (1979), "Optimal Incentive Contracts with Imperfect Information", *Journal of Economic Theory*, **20**, 231–259.

HOLMSTRÖM, B. (1979), "Moral Hazard and Observability", *Bell Journal of Economics*, **10**, 74–91.

HOLMSTRÖM, B. (1982), "Moral Hazard in Teams", *Bell Journal of Economics*, **13**, 324–340.

KIHLSTROM, R., ROMER, D. and WILLIAMS, S. (1981), "Risk Aversion with Random Initial Wealth", *Econometrica*, **49**, 911–920.

LELAND, H. and PYLE, D. (1977), "Informational Asymmetries, Financial Structure, and Financial Intermediation", *Journal of Finance*, **32**, 371–387.

MACHINA, M. (1983), "Temporal Risk and the Nature of Induced Preferences" (Working paper, University of California-San Diego, Department of Economics).

PRATT, J. (1964), "Risk Aversion in the Small and the Large", *Econometrica*, **69**, 122–136.

RAMAKRISHNAN, R. and THAKOR, A. (1983), "Information Reliability and a Theory of Financial Intermediation" (Working paper, Indiana University).

ROSS, S. A. (1976), "The Arbitrage Theory of Capital Asset Pricing", *Journal of Economic Theory*, **13**, 341–360.

ROSS, S. A. (1981), "Some Stronger Measures of Risk Aversion in the Small and the Large with Applications", *Econometrica*, **49**, 621–638.

SAMUELSON, P. (1963), "Risk and Uncertainty: A Fallacy of Large Numbers", *Scientia*.

SCHUMPETER, J. (1939) *Business Cycles* (New York: McGraw-Hill).

SHAVELL, S. (1979), "Risk Sharing and Incentives in the Principal and Agent Relationship", *Bell Journal of Economics*, **10**, 55–73.

SMITH, C. W. and WARNER, J. B. (1979), "On Financial Contracting: An Analysis of Bond Covenants", *Journal of Financial Economics*, **7**, 117–161.

TOWNSEND, R. M. (1979), "Optimal Contracts and Competitive Markets with Costly State Verification", *Journal of Economic Theory*, **21**, 1–29.

Modeling the Banking Firm

A Survey

ANTHONY M. SANTOMERO

THIS PAPER REPORTS on the status of the literature on micro bank modeling and assesses our understanding of the banking firm's optimal behavior. This is no mean task, for much has been written on banking, broadly defined, over the past couple of decades.

The review is developed in pieces. Each major subproblem is outlined and the analysis used to deal with the issue explicated. This is not the best way to summarize the development of a field, it should be immediately recognized. One would prefer to have a smooth continuum of development, moving the frontier of knowledge evenly through time and across subareas. Yet, this is rarely the way a field develops. More likely, individual questions attract attention and are the subjects of a substantial number of contributions. After a time, the field moves on to the new area of interest. The banking field is no exception.

Before embarking upon the review, however, a couple of lines should be devoted to previous attempts. There have been essentially three. First, Pyle (1972) analyzes the uncertainty portfolio models at a time when little existed in the literature, and hence one finds the review a bit vague and sketchy. Baltensperger's contributions (1978, 1980) are the next serious and rather extensive reviews. The quality of these

This paper was prepared for the Eighth Annual Economic Policy Conference of the Federal Reserve Bank of St. Louis, held on November 4–5, 1983. The author would like to thank Mark J. Flannery, Stephen M. Goldfeld, Michael L. Smirlock, and Richard Startz for their insights and discussions of earlier drafts.

ANTHONY M. SANTOMERO *is professor of finance, the Wharton School, University of Pennsylvania.*

Journal of Money, Credit, and Banking, Vol. 16, No. 4 (November 1984, Part 2)

comes through after reading the literature itself. This review, in fact, owes much to them.

1. WHY DO BANKS EXIST?

Before entering the analysis of the banking firm, it is, perhaps, relevant to ask why the institutional banking structure exists at all. This question has two functions. First, it allows us to discuss some of the more fundamental work in the banking area that centers upon the nature of the financial market structure that is being exploited by the banking firm. Second, it focuses our subsequent discussion of the behavioral models by specifying the nature of the role played by these institutions.

There are basically three approaches to the question of why internal financial institutions exist in the financial market. Each approach centers upon a specific portion of the bank's activity. The first relates to the role played by these institutions as asset transformers. Here, interest centers upon diversification potential and asset evaluation as a reason for these financial firms. The second refers to the nature of the liabilities issued and their central function in a monetary economy. Indeed, the existence of a medium of exchange creates an opportunity for its issuer to gain some form of seigniorage. Finally, some have emphasized the two-sided nature of these financial firms as critical in any explanation of their behavior. Although each of these explanations can find its roots in the seminal literature of financial inter-mediation, such as Goldsmith (1969) or Gurley and Shaw (1960), all have been specified more formally in the papers cited here.

A. Asset Transformation Function

Within this set of explanations for financial intermediation there are two distinct views, namely, asset diversification and asset evaluation functions of the financial firm. The first reason given is presented in the work of Klein (1973), Benston and Smith (1976), and Kane and Buser (1979). The authors argue that a fundamental role of intermediation is transformation of large-denomination financial assets into smaller units. Klein (1973) emphasizes the ability of the firm to exploit the sub-optimal portfolio choice of the depositor faced with unit constraints. The firm offers a risk-return combination in its financial assets that dominates the households' constrained set, even though economic profit is being earned by the bank providing such divisibility services. Benston and Smith (1976) make a similar argument concerning transaction cost minimization. Kane and Buser (1979) argue, at least implicitly, that these divisibility problems favor the use of a financial institution to diversify for both its depositors and equity holders. The latter authors also offer evidence to suggest that such diversification is supported by the portfolios held by the banking sector.

The second explanation on the asset side is currently receiving much attention. It argues that the bank is fundamentally an evaluator of credit risk for the uninitiated depositor. These banks function as a filter to evaluate signals in a financial environment with limited information. Financial agents are either pathologically honest or dishonest, but due to imperfect information, participants find it difficult to evaluate the quality of signals or the honesty of agents. This gives rise to financial intermediaries whose primary role is the evaluation and purchase of financial assets.

Leland and Pyle (1977) were the first to propose this view of financial intermediation. Much of the recent literature springs from their contribution. Starting with a firm's debt-equity decision, these authors argue that because of imperfect information concerning the value of the underlying project investors can glean some information about its quality by observing the willingness of the insider to invest equity capital in the endeavor. Accordingly, the financial structure of the firm adds information to the market. Leland and Pyle (1977) extend this approach to financial intermediation, arguing that this signaling problem could explain financial intermediation. The lack of adequate information on the quality of financial assets requires a set of firms whose primary output is signal evaluation. However, the output from such firms is quite fragile. Once resources are invested in obtaining such information, it becomes available to the market as a public good. The firm, therefore, has difficulty obtaining the return associated with its value. So, it is argued that capturing a return to information can be overcome if the firm that gathers the information becomes an intermediary, holding assets that are found to be of sufficient value.

Campbell and Kracaw (1980), however, counter that this solution to the information problem is conditional upon the assumptions made about the nature of information and its lack of general availability. First, they argue that portfolio choice by knowledgeable firms will be monitored and known in the market, so that honest intermediaries cannot hide portfolio choices. Second, they point out that, in the absence of prohibition, firms with low quality assets would find it in their best interest to produce false information. In this case, even honest firms would have information credibility problems. Therefore, given the uncertainty of the value of the intermediaries' information, the mere observation of the portfolio is not sufficient to resolve the signaling issue. Campbell and Kracaw's solution to the problem is similar in tone to the Leland and Pyle (1977) answer to the nonfinancial firm signaling problem. By dedicating wealth to the firm, the owner-managers of financial intermediaries demonstrate their commitment to the portfolio and signal the value of the underlying assets. They also argue that such firms can emerge which produce information and additional products, such as divisibility or liquidity as noted above. Diamond (1982) subsequently expands on this notion and demonstrates that diversification is an important characteristic in the information uncertainty equilibrium. His results, however, are dependent upon the assumed information and evaluation cost structure. Boyd and Prescott (1983), using a similar framework, note that financial institutions result in optimal consumption decisions with pathologically honest agents. They also argue that the dishonesty issue, which plays a relatively important part in the solutions of these information models, is overemphasized. Criminal charges make the cost of such dishonesty too high, they contend.

This information literature is still in its formative stages, at least as it relates to financial intermediation. Yet, it offers some interesting insights into the existence of the depository firm. The flow of information is obviously a key element in the market for financial assets, but, until now, the reasons for intermediation never clearly defined a role for it in the financial structure. Many questions remain to be answered, however. For instance, how important is honesty in firm information? Why is it so difficult for investors adequately to evaluate the project's specific risk? Are side payments to generate false information a realistic concern, particularly in a multiperiod setting?

B. The Role of the Bank's Liabilities

The second reason given to explain the existence of the banking firm is the central role played by its demand deposit liability as the medium of exchange. It has been many years since Clower's (1967) contribution pointed out the unique function of a monetary unit. The subsequent work of Niehans (1969, 1971, 1978) formalized the choice of monetary unit, and exchange patterns. Throughout, the central feature of a monetary unit is its ability to minimize the cost of transactions that convert income into the optimal consumption bundle. In fact, Barro and Santomero (1976), in their model of a monetary exchange economy, derive an effective price level for consumption goods as a direct result of the costs incurred in converting income into utility-yielding consumption goods.

Brunner and Meltzer (1971) take a different approach to the role of money, but one that is increasingly relevant in light of the recent literature on imperfect information rational macro models. To these authors, money holdings are part of the household's attempt to maximize a utility function in the first and second moments of consumption. Money allows the economic agent to search across the distribution of prices. As Starr (1972) points out, money balances are accepted even if the trade is not excess demand diminishing.

For whatever reason, money is held by the private sector. These balances, although subject to standard cost-minimization analytics, generate profit potential for the issuing institutions. The extent of these gains is dependent upon the characteristics of the money-type liability issued and the explicit pricing structure of the financial institution. The demand for money literature is replete with models that generate positive money balances. The obvious references here are Baumol (1952), Tobin (1956), Barro and Santomero (1972), Feige and Parkin (1971), Miller and Orr (1966), and Santomero (1974). Interested readers should refer to Laidler (1977) and Feige and Pearce (1977) for a thorough review.

The common feature of this literature is the determination of positive money holdings that are a function of transaction costs, uncertainty, and relative rates of return. The monetary mechanism, along with bank pricing decisions, offers the financial firm the opportunity to attract deposits, which may be reinvested at a positive spread. The extent of this profit will depend upon the nature of competition, as Black (1975) and Fama (1980b) point out, and the nature of the transactions network itself. Specific to the latter, the ease of transfer between accounts, the development of cash dispensing options nationwide, and the advent of home banking are all central to the evolution of the banking system's monopoly position.

C.   The Two-Sided Nature of the Financial Firm

The last line of argument explaining the existence of a banking firm centers upon the conditions necessary for banks to exist as internal financial firms. Here, the most quoted reference is Pyle (1971), which develops a model of the maximizing firm in a financial market with uncertain rates of return. Pyle concludes that covariance between the return on loans and deposits fosters intermediation by encouraging the risk-averse maximizer to transform deposits into loans. Sealey (1980) recently has extended this argument to consider the case where rates are set by the intermediary, rather than given by the open market. Here, a correlation between profits and the level of rates is shown to be equally important as an explanation for financial intermediation. In both cases, the covariance reduces the uncertainty around ex-pected profits and, due to concavity, encourages intermediation activity. Therefore, intermediation becomes possible because the firm can engage in risky arbitrage across markets that have different, though uncertain, interest rates. The firm's value is achieved by the expectation of a positive expected spread across markets, and a sufficiently small variance around this value.

An important question that is not asked in the Pyle (1971) framework is why such expected spreads exist in the financial markets. Presumably, it is because of the nature of its asset or liability services, but this is not modeled explicitly. The literature covered in the earlier two sections, however, offers several viable explana-tions for the existence of this positive spread for financial intermediaries. In each case, the reason involves some form of deviation from perfect market assumptions. Either there exists nontrivial transaction costs, or there are information problems, or bank liabilities have inherent monopoly potential. In the following sections we deal with optimal bank behavior to exploit such imperfections.

2.   THE OVERALL VIEW OF A BANKING FIRM'S PROBLEMS

A financial institution is viewed in the literature as a microeconomic firm that attempts to maximize an objective function in terminal wealth. It uses quantity and/or price variables, such as asset quantities or prices, as control variables. The extent of such choice is model specific and dependent upon the assumed environ-ment and the degree of regulation. Indeed, regulatory constraints may constrain the opportunity set of assets or liabilities, restrict the domain of the solution for one or more of the endogenous variables, or increase the monopoly position of the industry. In all of these cases the banking firm is viewed as seeking a mutatis mutandis solution to its optimization problem. The general form of the problem can be specified as

$$\max E[V(\tilde{W}_{t+\tau})] \tag{1}$$

subject to

$$W_{t+\tau} = W_t(1 + \tilde{\Pi}_{t+1})(1 + \tilde{\Pi}_{t+2})\ldots(1 + \tilde{\Pi}_{t+\tau}) \tag{2}$$

$$\tilde{\Pi}_{t+k} = \frac{\sum_i \tilde{r}_{A_i} A_i - \sum_j \tilde{r}_{D_j} D_j - C(A_i, D_j)}{W_{t+k-1}} = \frac{\tilde{\pi}_{t+k}}{W_{t+k-1}}, \tag{3}$$

where

> $V(\bullet)$ $\equiv$ the objective function, where $\partial V/\partial W_{t+\tau} > 0$ and $\partial^2 V/\partial W_{t+\tau}^2 \leqslant 0$
>
> $(\tilde{W}_{t+\tau})$ $\equiv$ the value of terminal wealth at the horizon time τ
>
> $\tilde{\Pi}_{t+k}$ $\equiv$ the stochastic profit per unit of capital during period $t + k$, where $0 \leqslant k \leqslant \tau$
>
> $\tilde{r}_{A_i}$ $\equiv$ the stochastic return from asset i
>
> A_i $\equiv$ the asset category i, where $1 \leqslant i \leqslant n$
>
> $\tilde{r}_{D_j}$ $\equiv$ the stochastic cost for deposit j
>
> D_j $\equiv$ the deposit category j, where $1 \leqslant j \leqslant m$
>
> $C(\bullet)$ $\equiv$ the operations cost function, where $\partial C/\partial A_i \geqslant 0$ $\forall i$ and $\partial C/\partial D_j \geqslant 0$ $\forall j$.

Equation (1) is the general form of the objective function to be maximized by the bank and as such allows for two distinct types of behavior. From the first derivative, more terminal wealth is preferred to less. However, the degree of marginal utility depends crucially upon the second derivative. The firm may be an expected value-maximizer or a risk-averse investor. Both choices have been made in the literature, depending upon the author's goals. Specifically, as will be outlined below, if the bank is viewed as selecting a mean-variance efficient portfolio, as in Parkin (1970), Pyle (1971), Hart and Jaffee (1974), or Koehn and Santomero (1980), some form of wealth concavity is assumed. On the other hand, if mean-variance efficiency is not a criterion, or, more generally, when the marginal rate of substitution between risk and return is not the focus of attention, expected profit maximization is assumed. This, of course, is consistent with a linear objective function in terminal wealth, that is, $\partial^2 V/\partial W_{t+\tau}^2 = 0$. Models by Klein (1971), Porter (1961), and Orr and Mellon (1961) are typical of this approach.

The choice is not irrelevant to our understanding of the motivation of the firm. Some would contend that it is at the heart of how one views the behavior of the financial institution. Specifically, when modeling the optimization problem, one implicitly defines the motivating force behind bank decisions by specifying the agent and his objectives for the firm. Two choices seem readily apparent, namely, equity investors, or bank management. For the former, a cogent argument can be offered in favor of a linear objective function. This is particularly true in a perfect capital market where financial intermediaries need not exist and the investor's opportunity set spans the institution's choice. Accordingly, any efficient bank portfolio can be perfectly duplicated or hedged by the investor.

In fact, if one views the investor's objective function as the relevant one for bank choice, a more appropriate approach would be one in which the bank's portfolio decisions are determined by global utility maximization of the owners. In this case, equation (1) would be replaced by the risk-averse utility function of the equity holder who views the bank's portfolio selection as a subset of his or her overall decisions. If the investor's opportunity set completely spanned that of the bank, nothing would be gained by the artificial separation of the portfolio choice problem. On the other hand, if any of the arguments of section 1 are correct, the bank's choice set differs from that of the investor due to its ability to exploit financial market opportunities that are not available to the nondepository institution. Yet, even in this case, a relevant factor in the choice of a bank portfolio is the covariance of the returns between the bank's equity with the other components of the investor's portfolio. This idea, however, has never been incorporated into bank modeling. Rather, the bank is viewed as determining a submaximization conditional upon an assumption about other personal wealth allocations being fixed. Consistent with this view, therefore, it is argued that a risk-neutral objective function should be selected for the banking firm to assure its investors efficient allocation, without regard to the risk level that may be hedged elsewhere in the investor's portfolio.

Yet, credible arguments have been offered in favor of the assumption of utility function concavity. The traditional corporate finance explanation rests upon the assumption that management is responsible for decision making and its inability to diversify its human capital. Fama (1980a) has developed this line of reasoning most completely. A similar argument has been made concerning the insufficient owner diversification by O'Hara (1981). In an industry in which only about 1 percent of the institutions have widely traded equity, the latter appears at least partially valid. The agency problems reported by Ross (1973) have also been used to motivate the concavity by Santomero (1983b). According to this view, investors with linear utility functions establish reward schedules for management that lead to risk-averse behavior. Draper and Hoag (1978) use a similar approach to intermediation based upon the information arguments above and Ross (1977). Recently, the presence of bankruptcy costs, first modeled rigorously by Stiglitz (1972), has added yet another explanation. Using this approach, the expected value maximizer behaves as if variance had negative value due to the probability of firm default with its attendant bankruptcy cost. Whether any or all of these reasons are sufficient to motivate the assumption of risk aversion is still open to question. Yet, most of the literature seems to have embraced this approach to the banking problem, at least when necessary.

Accepting concavity does not end the problem for the model builder, as the exact form of the objective or utility function must be specified. The common approach here is to rely upon the quadratic or the exponential forms. Alternatively, a simple two-term Taylor expansion is taken as indicative of the objective function, with appropriate caveats from Pratt (1964).

In equation (2), the general specification above is defined as a multiperiod valuation problem. Frequently, independence between periods is assumed so as to make the maximization a single-period analysis. This is clearly the case for portfolio models, which, to this author's knowledge, have never been cast in a multiperiod framework for the banking firm. On the other hand, important contributions have developed from a multiperiod view of the customer, loan, or deposit relationships. Goldfeld and Jaffee(1970), Flannery (1982), and Blackwell and Santomero (1982) are symptomatic of intertemporal approaches that show that balance sheet constraints make single-period problems dependent upon multiperiod decisions. This will be true, in general, even though those decisions are state variables at the time of quantity or pricing decision making. To motivate such models, some intertemporal stickiness must be asserted which is often difficult to model carefully. Accordingly, these intertemporal models frequently look like ad hoc specifications of reasonable a priori intuition.

Equation (3) defines profit per unit of capital invested by the owners of the firm or their management representatives. In the second specification, one sees that the optimization procedure involves the dual choice of leverage and portfolio components. Each has its own developed literature. The first involves the models to derive the optimal capital structure of a banking firm, for example, Taggart and Greenbaum (1978) and more recently Orgler and Taggart (1983). The second represents a large array of models of profit maximization, conditional upon leverage. In fact, most of the present review will devote itself to profit maximization or objective function maximization without reference to capitalization issues. Implicitly, the latter is assumed to be solved via a submaximization conditional upon the given portfolio or exogenously determined by regulatory standards.

Only recently have these two issues been brought together. Solving (1), (2), and (3) results in a joint decision of portfolio structure and leverage, along the lines of Pringle (1974), Kahane (1977), and Koehn and Santomero (1980). However, this is accomplished by using only the most general asset choice specification and ignoring operating cost considerations totally.

The issues surrounding operating or real resource costs have attracted increased attention lately as the industry itself views these operational issues of paramount importance. In fact, it plays a fairly central role in Baltensperger's (1978) review. This is because there is a large literature on the trade-off between rate spreads and production cost using, traditionally, a single-period profit-maximization framework. For example, the issue of reserve management, brought to our attention by Orr and Mellon (1961), involves such considerations. Sealey and Lindley (1977) and Towey (1974), have developed these models to consider appropriate product mix and scale. Mitchell (1979), Startz (1983), and others have recently been analyzing the interplay between explicit versus implicit charges for operating costs.

Finally, the pricing and quantity decisions in both the loan and deposit markets depend crucially upon the nature of market structure assumed, even in a single-period case. On the deposit side, there is a long literature on deposit rate setting based upon various assumed deposit market structures, for example, competitive, monopolistic, sticky, and tied-product relationships. Models by Goldfeld and Jaffee (1970), Klein (1972), Stigum (1976), Sealey (1980), and Flannery (1982) are representative of this genre. Likewise, but somewhat belatedly, the loan market decision has been analyzed. As above, we consider competitive, monopolistic, sticky, and tied-product relationships. The portfolio models of Hart and Jaffee (1974) and

Parkin (1970) are typical of the first; Porter (1961) and Klein (1971) are representative of the second. The sticky price paradigm, also known as the non-market-clearing or rationing literature, has its roots in Freimer and Gordon (1965), Jaffee and Modigliani (1969), and, more recently, Jaffee and Russell (1976) and Stiglitz and Weiss (1981). On the loan side, the pricing issue also includes a treatment of the interrelationship between the choice of interest rate and credit risk. This aspect of lending activity has received increased interest, with Ho and Saunders (1981), Deshmukh, Greenbaum, and Kanatas (1981), and Santomero (1983b) as examples of this approach.

To treat the individual areas listed above, it is necessary to concentrate much more heavily on the structure of the problem and its solution technique. For this reason, the subsequent sections are devoted to the individual issues raised in bank modeling. However, it is important to recognize that these individual problems feed directly into the global maximization problem outlined in equations (1), (2), and (3). For consistency's sake, one would like to have a decomposition procedure that results in an optimal global choice. Although this may be desirable, little academic work has attempted such a global reconciliation.

3. ASSET ALLOCATION MODELS

The first set of issues treated here will be those relating to asset choice. Models of asset allocation are primarily of two types, namely, reserve management models and portfolio composition models. The first of this set considers the problem of the optimal quantity of primary or secondary reserves to be held by a bank that is subject to stochastic reserve losses due to uncertain deposit levels. The second is devoted to the allocation across risky assets according to risk and return. As Patinkin (1965) points out, the separability of these two problems is not in general accurate as the opportunity cost associated with holding reserves is determined by the quantity of risk in the asset portfolio. However, this notion does not play a primary role in the modeling below.

A. Reserve Management Modeling

This literature has perhaps the oldest lineage in bank modeling, tracing its early roots to Edgeworth (1888). In addition, and perhaps more relevantly, the modeling of reserve management was started and largely completed in the two decades following the Orr and Mellon (1961) contribution. Subsequently, contributions and corrections have been made by Poole (1968), Modigliani, Rasche, and Cooper (1970), Cooper (1971), Frost (1971), Baltensperger (1972a, 1972b, 1974), Brown (1972), Knobel (1977), and Ratti (1979). Baltensperger (1980) has the most exact review of this area from which the present section draws.

The basic model of reserve management can be outlined as follows. Consider a bank that has two assets: noninterest bearing reserves, R, and earning assets, A, yielding r_A. Its deposits, credit lines, and loan repayments are all subject to random shifts without notice, with net bank withdrawals defined as X, with the density function $f(X)$. If net withdrawals exceed reserves, that is, $X > R$, the bank must undergo a proportional cost, c, to obtain the additional funds. The bank, therefore, wishing to maximize expected profit from its deposit balances, must maximize the following function:

$$\tilde{\pi} = r_A (D - R) - \int_R^\infty c (\tilde{X} - R) f(X) \, dX , \tag{4}$$

where loans are equal to deposits less reserves for expositional simplicity. The first-order conditions of this problem result in a reserve quantity that satisfies the condition

$$r_A = c \int_R^\infty f(X) \, dX , \tag{5}$$

that is, the opportunity cost of reserves, on the margin, must equal the expected reduction in operating or transactions costs devoted to reserve adjustments. This is the essential condition that must be met in reserve management models.

Poole (1968) notes that for a symmetric distribution with $E(X) = 0$, this condition implies that $c > 2r_A$. Both he and Baltensperger (1980) devote considerable time to explaining why this might be the case. For example, the cost of reserve deficiency, c, may not be linear; access to funds may be viewed as uncertain; and, administrative and regulatory hassles may ensue for firms with excessive dependence on the open market to adjust reserve positions.

Incorporating reserve requirements into the analysis further complicates the matter, but the economics are unaltered. Specifically, the existence of required reserves under a contemporaneous reserve requirement regime reduces the effect of an unexpected deposit drain by the amount of reserves held in its support. On the other hand, lagged reserve requirements, unless carryover provisions exist, appear to leave the analysis unaffected.

The Poole (1968) paper obtains another interesting result. Analyzing the effect of a mean preserving spread of $f(X)$, he concludes that increased uncertainty does *not* necessarily result in higher reserve positions. The economics of the result are that, with increased uncertainty, the bank is more likely to have both excess and deficient reserves. Inasmuch as the former encourages a reduction in reserves, the net effect of uncertainty on reserve assets is ambiguous.

Frost (1971) extends the reserve management issue to an environment where the bank inherits the previous reserve position. At any point in time, the ex post reserve position results from reserve planning and a single draw from the $f(X)$ distribution. The question addressed is whether reserves should be immediately adjusted to the ex ante optimal level for the next period. Here, the author applies a Miller and Orr (1966) approach to adjustment of reserves, where fixed adjustment costs and the previous period's endowment must be evaluated to determine if a movement to the optimal level is profitable. As is the case with all such models, a range of "nonoptimal" reserve positions exists where no adjustment will take place.

Baltensperger (1972b, 1974) and Baltensperger and Hellmuth (1976) extend this analysis of reserve management into its relationship with information and operating costs. They note that information on customer habits may reduce the variance of the underlying subjective distribution of stochastic withdrawals. The latter could reduce reserve costs sufficiently to warrant investment in such information. Accordingly, the profit function (4) should be written as

$$\pi = r_A(D - R) - \int_R^{\infty} c_1(X - R)f(X \mid \phi)\,dX - c_2\phi\,, \tag{6}$$

where ϕ is an information unit that costs c_2 to obtain. The ex ante expectation of the underlying deposit risk is dependent upon the quantity of information investment. The resultant first-order condition requires that the expected marginal return from information production be equal to its constant marginal cost.

In all, this literature is fairly self-contained and complete. It solves a problem that appears central to the banking environment and obtains fairly sensible results. However, it could be argued that, with the advent of a well-developed federal funds market, the overall importance of the problem as a micro banking issue is significantly reduced. In fact, casual empiricism suggests that total excess reserves amount to only about 0.1 percent of total bank assets, whereas the proportion of the academic literature associated with its determination is one hundred times that figure. This is, perhaps, unfair as the focus of the reserve management literature transcends just excess reserves and includes the quantity of short-term assets and the availability of credit facilities to meet reserve deficiencies. Yet, this feature of the reserve management problem is not part of the model framework. Indeed, the major shortcoming of this literature is its implicit assumption that all liquidity considerations can be reduced to the reserve management problem. It never squarely addresses the issues surrounding the definition of liquidity, its measurement in the balance sheet, or its optimal quantity. In an environment where liability management has gained increased importance as a liquidity and reserve adjustment tool, a dependence upon reserve items seems increasingly less relevant. In addition, given the interdependent nature of the individual withdrawals from any particular bank, the lack of consideration of contagion or bank-run phenomena seems to avoid a significant aspect of the bank's short-term funds management.

B. Portfolio Choice Models of Asset Allocation

Asset choice modeling in the literature generally takes two forms. Either the bank is viewed as possessing some degree of monopoly control over its loan price or the asset market is modeled as a perfectly competitive one where the bank must select appropriate quantities of loans of various characteristics. The first set is typified by Shull (1963), Klein (1971), and Porter (1961), and the second by the contributions of Pyle (1971), Parkin (1970), Hart and Jaffee (1974), and Sealey (1980).

The first group of papers seeks to obtain an optimal loan and/or asset size from the maximization of expected profit of the firm. In virtually all cases, the objective function is linear in profit. Frequently, uncertainty does not even exist, for example,

Shull (1963) or Stillson (1974). In all cases, the approach is a rather straightforward microeconomic setup from which the traditional marginal conditions result. A controversy central to this literature and perhaps one which separates it from work on the behavior of nonfinancial firms is the modeling of the most liquid, or highest elasticity, market.

In its simplest form, the typical model structure is a two-sided discriminating monopoly. Marginal revenue equals marginal cost. A variation in any one market feeds through the model to a comparative static shift in all marginal conditions. Shull (1963) exhibits such behavior.

Another approach, apparently initiated by Tobin (1958), has one market as a perfectly competitive one. Tobin used the discount window for this purpose, a position that was later rejected, at least implicitly, by Goldfeld and Kane (1966). Klein (1971) uses the government security market. Others have suggested it is the federal funds markets. In any case, the maximization associated with a model with one infinitely elastic source (use) of funds results in a general convergence of all marginal revenues and costs to this infinitely supplied (demanded) asset. Separation exists between asset allocation and deposit structure. Variations in demand for loans of one type have no effect on the other loan decisions. This result, first pointed out explicitly by Klein (1971), caused considerable debate, with comments by Pringle (1973) and Miller (1975) questioning the validity of the infinite elasticity assumption.

To formalize the discussion, one may view this type of model as the result of the following maximization process:

$$\max_{A_i, D_j} \pi = \sum_i r_{A_i} A_i - \sum_j r_{D_j} D_j , \qquad (7)$$

where

$$\frac{\partial r_{A_i}}{\partial A_i} < 0 \qquad \forall i$$

$$\frac{\partial r_{D_j}}{\partial D_j} > 0 \qquad \forall j \neq m$$

$$\frac{\partial r_{D_m}}{\partial D_m} = 0 .$$

The first-order conditions result in

$$\left(\frac{\partial r_{A_i}}{\partial A_i}\right) A_i + r_{A_i} = r_{D_m} = \left(\frac{\partial r_{D_j}}{\partial D_j}\right) + r_{D_j} . \qquad (8)$$

Baltensperger (1980) takes issue with this formulation of the bank's behavior on the grounds that no operating costs are included in the analysis and differential assets or deposits are indistinguishable within the formulation. Although both of these criticisms are entirely correct, they do not appear to be particularly relevant or fundamental. Stillson (1974) incorporates servicing costs, as do Towey (1974) and Sealey and Lindley (1977). In none of these cases does one find results that substantially affect the model's basic conclusions.

To obtain a nonobvious generalization through the use of operating costs or a production technology, one must go in the direction of Adar, Agmon, and Orgler (1975). There the authors argue that the banking firm has a joint production problem so that output mix is a critical determinant of operating expense. Within this framework, the equilibrium conditions from profit maximization are interdependent. Separation of loan decisions, as well as asset decisions from liability structure decisions, becomes impossible. This, of course, makes the operating cost function much more complex than it is generally considered to be in the theoretical literature. Perhaps it is also more realistic. In an era in which financial intermediaries are broadening their menu of financial series to include activities in both the deposit and securities areas, this joint production view of operating costs may warrant serious consideration.

Before turning from these simple micromodels of the firm it is worth noting what is not treated in most of these theoretical constructs. Almost without exception, these models represent the bank's problem as a single-period maximization. Intertemporal demand considerations are rarely explicitly modeled, in spite of the fact that the institutional literature spends much of its time discussing such problems. The customer relation that Hodgman (1963) and others have analyzed is rarely incorporated into bank models. Where it is, the treatment tends to be rather sterile, with the entire relationship captured by a geometric lag or by cross-product proportionality. Wood (1974) or Blackwell and Santomero (1982) are typical of such attempts, but represent only the most rudimentary approach to capture the dynamic effects of customer relationships.

Multiperiod firm maximization, too, is only peripherally treated. Where intertemporal concerns exist, the objective function is taken to be a multiperiod discounted valuation function. However, if the literature on agency costs is relevant, and there is a conflict between management and investor goals, it would be interesting to see a better development of this issue in the multiperiod environment. For example, my colleagues have argued that front-end fees in the syndication area have caused bank management to accept risk levels that would have been rejected if a present value decision rule had been used (see Guttentag and Herring 1980). Perhaps this could be due to a conflict between manager and investor discount rates or horizons. Unfortunately, without better multiperiod modeling, theory can say very little about this subject.

Where intertemporal models do exist (e.g., Wood 1974), the solutions have some curious characteristics. For example, consider a simple n period model, such as

$$\max_{r_t, r_{t+1}, \cdots} \quad \pi = \sum_{t=1}^{n} \beta^{t-1} \pi_t \,, \tag{9}$$

subject to

$$\pi_t = r_t l_t - r_{D_t} D_t,$$

where $l_t \equiv l(r_t, l_{t-1})$ and $\partial r_{D_t}/\partial D_t = 0$. The first-order conditions for $r_t, r_{t+1}, \ldots$ are

$$\frac{\partial \pi}{\partial r_t} = 0 = l_t + (r_t - r_{D_t})\frac{\partial l_t}{\partial r_t} + \beta(r_{t+1} - r_{D_{t+1}})\frac{\partial l_{t+1}}{\partial r_t} + \cdots. \qquad (10)$$

The implication of this optimal behavior may be characterized as follows. The bank will initially accumulate loans from period to period as a result of the build up of intertemporal demand based upon previous decisions. This increased loan demand implies that the interest rate will rise each period in spite of a constant cost of funds. This appears to be an awkward way of looking at the bank's dynamic behavior. Yet, only Blackwell and Santomero (1982) consider the properties of their model at the long-run stationary equilibrium.

The second approach to asset selection is the portfolio choice models using risk and return as criteria. The most elementary of these is the work of Pyle (1971), which set out to determine the necessary conditions for financial intermediation within a mean-variance framework. Using a three-asset case where there is a riskless asset, as well as loans and deposits in the intermediary, he derives the optimal behavior of the financial firm. Necessary and sufficient conditions for the existence of intermediation are also derived. The results imply that covariance of rates across the balance sheet is extremely important, and a positive loan premium and/or negative deposit premium must exist for the firm to make risky loans and to intermediate deposits.

These results appear fairly obvious, and Baltensperger (1980) argues that the major failing of the work is its inability to motivate this simple intuitive result. Yet, the paper has attracted quite a lot of attention, primarily because it clearly articulates the portfolio choice modeling of the financial firm.

The portfolio models, of which both Parkin (1970), and Pyle (1971, 1972) are the prototypes, have a rather standard set up. The investor or manager is viewed as maximizing a concave function in end of period profit, with a quadratic or exponential function often used to represent the firm's preference ordering.

$$E(\pi) - \left(\frac{b}{2}\right)\sigma_\pi^2, \qquad (11)$$

where profit and its variance are defined as

$$\pi = \sum_i r_{A_i} A_i - \sum_i r_{D_j} D_j$$

$$\sigma_\pi^2 = E[(\pi - E(\pi))^2].$$

The solution methodology of these papers is to define the characteristics of the feasible set of assets and/or liabilities of the firm. Then, asset choice is restricted to the efficient frontier, where additional return is only achievable at the expense of added variance. The bank, then, selects a point on the efficient frontier where the objective function's marginal rate of substitution between risk and return is equated with the market's opportunity set. Rather obviously, the determinants of the optimal solution are the specifications of the returns to each asset and liability, and the choice of the objective function of the bank. On the first of these, the return characteristics of the assets are assumed exogenously given and independent of bank decision making. This view significantly minimizes the effect of the bank on the asset return patterns through the manipulation of lending terms and conditions. However, if the entire set of assets from which the bank constructs its portfolio includes multiple pricing options for each loan category, this framework is theoretically correct. As far as the second factor determining the solution, section 2 notes the difficulty in determining the all-important objective function to be maximized.

The above reservations notwithstanding, these models lend new insight into the bank's portfolio selection. Hart and Jaffee (1974) is perhaps the best of the papers using this approach to examine the asset structure of the depository intermediary. Their results show that under some rather restrictive conditions, one can segment the scale of bank operations from its risk-return choice. Such a separation theorem can be developed for the bank in an environment in which no risk-free asset exists and a fully liability funded portfolio structure is assumed.

In total, the asset choice models get mixed reviews. One branch of the literature applies Economics 1 to the bank to obtain results that border on the trivial in retrospect, that is, marginal revenue equals marginal cost. It depends, to an excessive extent, on demand and supply curve slopes that are not well motivated or understood. Alternatively, the Tobin-Markowitz asset portfolio models are used for quantity choice in a perfect market. The results follow directly from the finance literature and add little more. Their insights, and they are many, come from the realization that the bank asset problem is a special case of the standard portfolio choice model. As such, that perception of asset management must become a part of the banking literature.

4. LIABILITY CHOICE MODELS

The modeling of the liability side of the balance sheet has taken two separate paths. For deposits, the modeling has been akin to the simple monopolistic modeling structure outlined for the asset side. For capital and leverage issues, the literature has used more sophisticated techniques, including bankruptcy considerations and models from corporate financial theory. We consider each in turn.

A. Deposit Modeling

A useful starting point for the analysis of liability modeling techniques is the simple deposit market form used by Klein (1971). Here, as indicated above, there is an infinitely elastic market from which an unlimited quantity of funds may be obtained. As noted in equation (7), the bank is a deposit rate setter with some monopolistic control over the deposit market. First-order conditions from such a setup indicate that the marginal cost of funds from each deposit source must equal the marginal cost (use) of funds from the competitive market, as in (7).

This model may be complicated by allowing production costs related either to balances held on deposits or to the number of accounts. Sealey and Lindley (1977), Klein and Murphy (1971), and Baltensperger (1972b) are typical of this genre. The solution of this type of model is a fairly obvious extension of the earlier work; that is, with production costs, the total marginal costs must be equilibrated. The analysis only becomes interesting when different types of production functions are integrated into the analysis. For example, Flannery (1982) considers the case of a quasi-fixed production process whereby the cost function relates to changes in deposit balances rather than (or in addition to) the level itself. Assuming that such customer-specific costs are shared by both the customer and bank, the model demonstrates that deposit-rate variation will be reduced relative to open-market rate movements. Flannery argues that such a production process can explain both the long-run customer relation and the tendency for deposit rates sometimes to lag behind open-market rates, both on the up and downside of the market. To Flannery, such quasi-fixed production technology explains the concept of "core" deposits.

Mitchell (1979) extends the analysis of the production or operating costs to a case where, due to regulatory constraints, explicit interest is incapable of rewarding the depositor sufficiently. Implicit payments then result from the willingness of the bank to absorb some of the real production costs associated with transactions in order to attract larger balances. Barro and Santomero (1972) and Santomero (1979), who treated the customer behavior within such a regime, demonstrate both the relevance and importance of such implicit payments. Mitchell (1979) and Startz (1983) go the next step to consider the effect of this implicit payment option on the behavior of the banking firm. Central to their analysis is the ability of the bank to subsidize banking activity, such as check cashing, funds transfers, and account maintenance costs, to encourage deposit balances. However, their treatment depends critically upon the relationship between such account activities and average balances. The basic model may be developed as follows. Denote the number of transactions using the deposit account as n and the cost and service charge per transaction as c and k, respectively. The profit function of (7) may be written more generally as

$$\pi = \sum_i r_{A_i} A_i - \sum_j r_{D_j} D_j - \sum_j [(c_j - k_j) n_j(D_j)]. \qquad (12)$$

The bank must now consider the return to deposit balances, the cost of deposit services, and the interrelationship between the two. Mitchell (1979) notes that increasing the explicit payments allowed on deposit balances within such a framework may result in either increases or decreases in implicit payments according to the relationship $n_j(D_j)$. Although this work is still in its formative stages, it does have some interesting implications for bank decision making and pricing. In fact, the whole area surrounding the relationship between various forms of payment, deposit reaction, and, ultimately, profitability needs further work in a real-world environment that is shifting to a greater extent to rate deregulation.

The movement of deposit rates relative to open-market interest rates is another area of continual attention in the literature. A simple neoclassical model of the firm argues that rates on deposits should move along with market rates. Yet, Weber (1966) and others have suggested that rates will move sluggishly for institutions with long-lived assets. The general argument is that due to the inability of the firm to achieve a satisfactory increase in the asset yields from its portfolio, the bank will be forced to adjust its deposit rates more slowly to overall market forces. The Weber hypothesis elicited a significant number of subsequent responses, of which the major contributors were Goldfeld and Jaffee (1970) and Stigum (1976).

The former authors demonstrate that on a theoretical plane the phenomenon can be explained by boundary conditions forced upon the firm by its balance sheet constraint. Specifically, consider a firm that maximizes the profit function contained in equation (7) and attracts assets and liabilities in period one. Optimum profit is obtained for that period and over the expected horizon, defined by expected rates and demand functions. Subsequently, however, assume that there is an unexpected decline in asset yields. The lower rates imply lower optimal deposit rates given a fixed liability schedule. However, if the asset portfolio is nonmarketable and relatively fixed in quantity, the bank may find itself in a position that requires it to pay whatever rate is necessary to finance its asset portfolio. Later upward movements in asset yields will, accordingly, not elicit an appropriate rate increase, as the initial deposit rate was a nonequilibrium choice by a constrained firm. As Goldfeld and Jaffee note, such sluggishness is introduced only because of the possibility that a corner solution will lead to perverse behavior. In the long run, such behavior is ruled out.

Stigum returns to this issue to present a more general treatment of the problem. Here, two innovations are offered. First, she considers the effect of sticky deposits on the analysis. Assuming that deposit balances can be written as a function of both current rates of return and the previous deposit balance, she demonstrates that deposit inertia will result in relatively sluggish movement in deposit rates even if no boundary condition is reached. This is an interesting insight into the pricing dynamics but the author offers little to motivate, in a rigorous economic sense, this deposit inertia. Flannery's (1982) joint cost-sharing framework is perhaps one such explanation from the industrial organization literature, as is Adar, et al. (1975). However, without adequate understanding of the cause of such sluggish deposit movement, it is difficult to be convinced that it is a satisfactory answer to the relative rate movement observed in the deposit markets.

The second generalization contained in Stigum (1976) is the addition of deposit uncertainty to the analysis of Goldfeld and Jaffee (1970). Considering both the case of risk neutrality and concavity, the author investigates the relative movement of rates. Not surprisingly, the degree of absolute risk aversion is a crucial determinant of bank behavior. This same factor comes into play in Sealey's (1980) slightly more general treatment of the deposit rate setting problem. In addition the latter author considers the correlation of loan and deposit rates as well. This critical feature of bank modeling will be discussed more fully below when issues related to the management of the total bank portfolio are discussed in section 5.

B. The Capital Decision

The capital decision of the financial firm is more complicated than it may first appear. This is true because the optimal choice of scale and leverage is determined by the assumed financial environment and the raison d'être of the firm. One must keep in mind the substantive contribution of Modigliani and Miller (1958), illustrating that in the absence of frictions and taxes there exists *no* optimal capital structure. Accordingly, to derive an optimal capital structure, one must determine, first, the role played by the financial institution and, second, the extent to which one wishes to deviate from the perfect market paradigm in explaining its operation. Pringle (1974) does so by asserting exogenous and fixed deviations from perfect market behavior, while at the same time assuming a CAPM valuation model. Not surprisingly, his results suggest that an optimal capital is obtained in this model whereby such imperfections are appropriately exploited. In his framework, there is a divergence between lending and borrowing rates, excess expected returns exist on loans, and capital cost diverges from the risk-adjusted open-market rate. The author shows that optimal capital is attained when the excess marginal revenue on loans equals the excess marginal cost of capital.

Taggart and Greenbaum (1978) develop their analysis of capital under the assumption that excess loan revenues and transaction service profits can be exploited by the value-maximizing firm. An extension of this approach by Orgler and Taggart (1983) argues that the optimal capital structure for the bank depends upon its efficiency of producing such intermediary services as check processing and record keeping, along with the interplay of private and corporate tax rates on profits. An interesting result obtained by the framework is its ability to explain variations in bank capital across firms by differential scale and efficiency of bank operations.

Kahane (1977) and Koehn and Santomero (1980) use the portfolio model approach, outlined above, on the bank capital issue. Starting from the general specification of (1), they optimize the bank's rate of return on capital by selecting a portfolio of assets and leverage position that optimizes shareholders' returns. The Koehn and Santomero paper is interesting because it analyzes the effect on bank portfolio behavior of a regulatory shift in capital adequacy regulations. The authors demonstrate that although capital increases as a fraction of assets, the resultant portfolio is unambiguously more risky than before the capital constraint. Essentially, the constrained firm attempts to offset some of the effect of the leverage limit by absorbing greater risk in its portfolio than before the regulation. Koehn (1979) finds a similar effect of asset restriction regulation. These results lend credence to the idea that regulation, if it is to be effective, must be combined with adequate understanding of the behavioral response of the banking firm.

Talmor (1980) uses a different approach, employing the gambler's ruin technology to the problem. According to this approach, appropriate capital involves the determination of an acceptable probability of bankruptcy and derives an optimal structure to achieve this ex ante acceptable level. Building on the work by Wilcox (1971) and Santomero and Vinso (1977), the paper derives the appropriate level of capital from a continuous time diffusion process whereby the management determines the appropriate ex ante probability of failure by portfolio choice. An interesting characteristic of the model is that the determinants of the process are derived endogenously from the underlying balance sheet of the bank.

For all its benefits, however, this approach has a fundamental problem. It is not clear how one defines the acceptable probability of failure. Presumably, the firm should be managed to optimize firm value for its stockholders. How one links this objective to an ex ante criterion for probability of failure is not developed in such models. This could be done by some form of general objective function in which bankruptcy costs affect shareholders' value, as was discussed in section 2. However, some would contend that the presence of regulation and deposit insurance precludes this market response mechanism from functioning adequately.

The mantle of regulation has in and of itself a built-in incentive to increase risk and leverage. The deposit insurance structure guarantees all depositors up to a statutory limit. For these depositors, the liability of the depository institution is de jure a riskless asset. Accordingly, there is no incentive for these depositors to respond to bank riskiness per se. The noninsured depositors would seem to require some assurance of the solvency of the institution before deposits are made. However, regulation has made their concerns less relevant in terms of the market disciplining the depository institution. Over the past several decades, failed institutions have been dealt with in a manner that has protected all depositors, rather than just the insured category. Assumption of the bank location and balance sheets has been the dominant form of regulatory action. Advances from the discount window to facilitate this manner of resolution lead Kareken and Wallace (1978) to conclude that such advances are essentially loans to the FDIC.

If one accepts this view that bank liabilities are essentially 100 percent insured, then the entire issue of bank capital and risk taking should be recast in terms of a discussion of insurance pricing. The role of the market to price the riskiness of the depository institution has been usurped by the regulator in its blanket insurance of the industry.

What remains, therefore, is to discuss the form and substance of the insurance and the impact it has and can have on the quantity of capital and risk held by the banking firm. Merton (1977) and Sharpe (1978) have made significant contributions in this direction. These papers apply the option pricing literature to the insurance of bank liabilities to obtain considerable insight into the deposit insurance problem. The basic approach used is to show that the payoff pattern of the insurance scheme is like a put option on the underlying assets of the institution. Then, using the work of Black and Scholes (1972), one can derive the optimal price for such insurance and its functional dependence.

Following Merton (1977), one may consider essentially three parties to the insurance of a liability of the bank: (a) the bank itself, (b) the depositor, and (c) the insurance company (Federal Deposit Insurance Corporation—FDIC). The bank offers the depositor a return, B, that compensates the latter for the time value of the funds left at the bank. These funds are commingled with the equity supplied by the bank's owners in the asset portfolio. After one period, the asset value is given by V, which is stochastic ex ante. If the ex post value of the asset portfolio is greater than B, that is, if $V \geq B$, the bank redeems the depositor's liability and the insurer plays no role. The equity holder receives the difference between V and B as a return on equity, presumably less the insurance fee charged by the FDIC. In the event that V is less than the maturity value of the liability, that is, if $V < B$, the depositor still receives the insured value, B, but, in this case, the return is paid partially by the residual value of the assets and partially from the insurance fund. The equity holder receives nothing, whereas the insurer receives $V - B$, which is unambiguously negative. One may rewrite the payoff pattern of the insurance fund equivalently as

$$\min[0, V - B] = \max[0, B - V].$$
(13)

This is identical to the payoff structure of a put option issued by the FDIC against the value of the assets at the bank. Using the Black-Scholes option pricing model to derive the optimal price per dollar, Merton (1977) derives the value of deposit insurance.

Sharpe (1978) develops this same perspective of the deposit insurance pricing problem using a state preference approach. His main insight is obtained by reversing the logic of the optimal deposit insurance pricing scheme. Specifically, the institutional realities in the United States are that FDIC insurance is granted under a fixed net insurance fee. Therefore, there is an inherent tendency for financial firms to accept higher risk levels than they would in the absence of the insurance subsidy. However, note that, given other factors, the value of a fair insurance fee declines as the capital-asset ratio increases. Sharpe points out that adequate capital is that quantity which would make the current fixed rate insurance fee the correct price for the underlying put option implicitly issued by the FDIC.

Buser, Chen, and Kane (1981) argue that appropriate pricing of insurance benefits may not be what the regulator wishes. They argue that the FDIC uses explicit and implicit costs to offset the inherent benefits accruing to the insured liability issuers. The latter includes capital regulation, safety regulations, community development accountability, and the like. Once accepting the benefits of insurance without paying the full cost explicitly, the institution can be manipulated by the regulator. However, the resultant profit of the firm must at least equal the uninsured case to maintain control.

In all, this literature on optimal bank capital is a bit vague and very model specific. This has led to a significant divergence between practice and theory as has been suggested in Santomero (1983a). Although more work needs to be done, the field seems to be awaiting a breakthrough in either of two areas. The corporate finance literature needs to develop further in order to aid in the search for a private determination of optimal capital. In addition, the interest expressed in variable pricing of deposit insurance must become much more of an institutional reality. Without both of these, the capital area remains murky.

5. TWO-SIDED MODELING

Thus far, the analysis has been focused upon the modeling of each side of the balance sheet. Frequently, the models discussed considered the entire portfolio choice problem, but for expositional convenience a review of the analysis was placed in either of the two sections above. For example, Klein (1971) considers the entire asset-liability management problem. However, the treatment is separable due to the structure of the infinitely elastic market. So, too, Parkin (1970) includes positive and negative assets within the portfolio choice under uncertainty, but the main insights gained from the model pertain to its asset choice structure.

Several models have recently appeared, however, which are intimately related to the two-sided nature of the banking problem. The first of these is the recent work by Deshmukh, et al. (1983), in which they look at the alteration in the financial intermediation process associated with increased interest rate variability. These authors argue that the typical bank serves as both an asset-transformer and broker. The former borrows funds at a fixed rate before interest rate uncertainty on the asset side is resolved, and the latter borrows only after interest rates are known. Increased rate volatility shifts the bank's activity more toward a brokerage function and away from the more traditional asset transformation function. The limited upside gain from higher rates is insufficient to compensate the bank for the reduced profit from asset transformation when rates decline. Accordingly, variability results in the shift to brokerage activity even for an expected profit-maximizing firm.

Ho and Saunders (1981) analyze the bank's brokerage function in more detail, using the finance literature on broker bid-and-ask spreads to explain bank margins. Using a diffusion process for rate movement and a concave objective function, they are able to define the optimum equilibrium spread for the banking firm. As one might anticipate, this margin is dependent upon the risk aversion of the firm and interest rate volatility.

One way of shedding interest rate risk is to construct a portfolio so as to immunize it from the effects of rate shifts. There is a whole literature on this problem and the method of application to the banking firm. Bierwag and Kaufman have been the mainstays in this duration and immunization literature, with their most recent work, Bierwag, Kaufman, and Toevs (1982). These contributions develop an appropriate measure of the interest rate exposure of both sides of the balance sheet and a portfolio structure that will not be adversely affected by interest rate movement. This is achieved by the use of Macauley's duration measure, among others, and the two-sided immunization of the balance sheet through duration matching.

This literature is interesting and critical to any treatment of actual bank interest rate exposure estimation. Its development, use, and limitations require more space than can be given here but interested readers can look elsewhere for a critique, for example, Haley (1982) and Bierwag and Toevs (1982).

Some caveats are in order. First, this technique involves the matching of present value changes associated with an arbitrarily small but specific variation in the yield curve. Rightly or wrongly, bankers worry much more about cash flow than the academic researcher. Inasmuch as regulation is frequently cast in current book value terms, this may be rational. By implication the banking firm may not wish to hedge its present value position. Second, one should keep in mind that there is a distinction between balance sheet hedging and equity-value immunization. These two concepts are in direct conflict inasmuch as a duration hedged balance sheet will cause the present value of the earnings stream, that is, the bank's equity value, to vary with rate movement. Third, duration matching requires active portfolio management, which may not be practical in the short run or for small institutions. In fact, Flannery (1981, 1983b) demonstrates that net current operating income is not affected by rate movements for large institutions, but is affected for smaller ones.

An allied area which must be discussed in the context of the banking firm is modeling interest rate risk taking. This area has only recently developed, though there was an early work by von Furstenberg (1973). Santomero (1983b) models the bank's choice between fixed and variable rate loans to analyze the payoff functions and to consider the optimal quantity of each in the overall portfolio. Dealing simultaneously with both credit and interest rate risk, it is demonstrated that both types of risk are likely to be present in the optimal portfolio choice. The driving force behind this analysis is the asymmetry of the variable rate payoff function, as noted by Deshmukh, et al. (1983) in a much different context. The paper demonstrates that credit or default risk is generally related to interest rate fluctuations. Using a concave utility function, marginal conditions require that the bank accept some nonzero interest rate exposure in order to minimize the sum of credit and interest rate risk.

In all, these models begin to investigate the financial firm as a true intermediary that deals simultaneously in both the asset and liability markets and bears both interest and credit risk. Yet much needs to be done before they can purport to explain bank behavior adequately. First, the credit risk decision must be more adequately integrated into the analysis than it has been heretofore. Rather than treating credit risk as a simple mean-variance-covariance decision process, serious consideration must be given to the interdependence both between interest rates and default probabilities and between credit risk at one firm precipitating failure at others. Second, the entire area of interest rate risk management and its optimal level needs further work. With the advent of a developed futures market, the average institution has the capability of shedding interest rate risk rather easily. Yet, little has been done to model this process or characterize the optimal solution. This, in particular, is an area that requires serious modeling and empirical investigation to bring the academic literature up to institutional realities.

6. CREDIT LINES AS AN EXAMPLE OF OFF-BALANCE SHEET RISK MANAGEMENT

While the profession has been building models of the banking firm from the perspective of optimal pricing and allocation of balance sheet items, the banking industry has been substantially expanding into off-balance sheet activity. Standby letters of credit, bankers acceptances, and credit lines have grown sufficiently to cause regulatory concern, as the board staff study illustrates (Board of Governors of the Federal Reserve System 1982). In addition, with the erosion of the traditional lines of commerce restrictions, banks have entered such standard securities market areas as futures trading, underwriting, private placement, and, most recently, discount brokerage. Yet, little has been done in the academic literature to integrate these activities into banking theory.

The only exception is the work on bank credit lines. Campbell (1978), Thakor (1982), and Thakor, Greenbaum and Hons (1981) represent significant advances. The basic approach taken by Campbell (1978) is the modeling of pricing with uncertainty in demand and cost. This has been the subject of a number of papers in the micro theory literature, most notably Leland (1972). The Thakor, et al. (1981) paper moves away from the construction of a general model of the market for credit lines in favor of an in-depth analysis of the optimal pricing of the instrument. The fundamental insight is that the bank is issuing a put option to the firm such that it stands ready to purchase a risky claim, the loan contract, over a given horizon. Then, using the intertemporal CAPM model of Merton (1973) to solve the value of the option, an optimal price is obtained.

There are weaknesses in the application of option pricing to this problem, however. Firstly, partial take-downs of the credit line make the pricing issue much more complex. Thakor, et al. argue that historical analysis and the decomposition of the total credit lines into a series of likely draw-downs can eliminate this difficult case. Yet, this is a somewhat heroic assertion. The option on the time of usage is at least as critical as the value associated with the resolution of price uncertainty. Yet, these models neglect the former in favor of the latter.

Secondly, even the price uncertainty resolution appears somewhat artificial. Credit lines have two pricing conventions, fixed and pegged. The former is a minor part of the market in which the bank specifies a fixed rate loan commitment to the firm for a reasonably short space of time. For these lines, the option pricing model is appropriate. For the large majority of commitments, however, the price of the loan commitment is tied to open-market rates. The option in this case relates to a hedge against the variability of the markup over prime or funding cost. The firm is betting either that credit tightness will increase bank margins or that the fortunes of the firm will deteriorate to such an extent that the upfront cost of the credit line is warranted. As the above authors point out, if the borrowers knew that the terms would be identical at draw-down and at commitment dates, there would be no incentive to purchase loan commitments. The uncertain availability, which cannot be modeled very neatly in these sorts of models, appears crucial to our understanding of the credit line market.

Others have taken another approach to the credit line literature, which is more along the lines of availability premiums. Wood (1975), for example, tries to deal with the firm reaction to a nonzero probability of lack of available funds. So, too, Blackwell and Santomero (1982) model the credit lines as a way for firms to jump positions on the queue of acceptable borrowers and therefore assure themselves access to credit. Thakor (1982) also recognizes this interrelationship between availability and credit lines. James (1981) goes further and argues that the decision of the firm as to how the cost of the commitment will be paid, that is, fee or balances, is a self-selection process. Firms that view themselves as more likely to require future funding will opt for fees over the freezing of needed balances.

7. CREDIT RATIONING MODELS

In traditional neoclassical theory of the firm, the lack of available credit is not a concern. According to the standard paradigm, demand equals supply at the equilibrium price. Yet, it has long been argued that nonprice rationing of credit is an integral part of the market. Although data on this issue is sketchy at best, many have attempted to develop models of the credit market and the banking firm that result in some nonprice rationing of credit demands. In fact, this has been somewhat of a growth area of the literature over the last decade. Accordingly, before ending a review of the banking field, an overview of the past and recent literature on credit rationing is appropriate.

Before entering a discussion of the models devoted to explaining the existence of credit rationing, a more exact specification of the phenomenon to be explained is in order. The traditional approach to the problem is to define a situation in which there is excess demand for credit at the "going interest rate" as a situation of credit rationing. Subsequent work by Freimer and Gordon (1965) and Stiglitz and Weiss (1981) suggests a more exact definition. Credit rationing occurs when a subset of firms seeking credit at the going rate are not granted such loans in spite of the fact that their objective characteristics are identical, or nearly so, to those firms receiving credit. This definition recognizes that some borrowers are not worthy of credit because of loan or project characteristics and are, therefore, formally rejected by the lending institution. Credit rationing situations have been further divided into cases of equilibrium rationing and dynamic rationing by Jaffee and Modigliani (1969). The definition of the former is a case where credit rationing occurs at the long-run equilibrium interest rate, whereas the latter exists in the transitory periods between such equilibriums.

A. *Rationing and the Customer Relation*

Models devoted to explanations of credit rationing have taken three approaches. The first, and oldest, is the literature that attributes credit rationing to the tied relationship between banks and their customers. Hodgman (1961) was the first to espouse this view, which argues that because of the intertemporal and cross-product relationship between a customer and the bank, preferential treatment is given to prime customers when credit tightening occurs. Accordingly, nonprime, small customers are rationed during periods of interest rate movement. Defining all credit rationing as dynamic and short-run, he argued that the bank was merely behaving as a multiperiod profit maximizer by favoring its best customers. In fact, standard textbooks in the field (e.g., Mason 1979) have made this central to the bank/customer relationship.

This line of analysis has some very serious problems. To make the analysis consistent, it is necessary to argue that the bank's best customers are ones that yield the bank super-normal returns in a present value sense. Therefore, when a period of credit rationing develops, they are given preferential treatment. However, it is unlikely that the bank's best and largest customers can be charged a rate that is sufficiently high to warrant such preferred treatment. In fact, Blackwell and Santomero (1982) have demonstrated that if large firms, with intertemporal demands for credit and multiperiod commitments to the banking institution, are priced correctly, they will, on the margin, be no more profitable than the smaller, less-sophisticated firm. Accordingly, if rationing becomes necessary, there is no reason to believe that they will be given additional consideration. In fact, the authors demonstrate that because of the higher elasticity of demand possessed by large customers with alternative funding options, these customers are less likely to receive credit preference during such periods of constraint in contrast to the traditional result. One is left with the feeling that this literature is of questionable worth.

B.   Rationing and Partial Price Discrimination

The second approach to credit rationing argues that there is something about the transactions cost structure that leads banks to refuse credit at the going interest rate. The most well known of these papers is the work of Jaffee and Modigliani (1969). According to this approach, the bank's offer curve for credit to any specific customer or customer group is defined by the standard profit-maximizing criteria. If the bank could operate as a discriminating monopolist, credit would never be rationed and each customer would be granted a profit-maximizing rate. However, if the bank is forced to charge a nonhomogeneous set of customers the same interest rate, then credit rationing will result. Such rationing results because, within the set of non-homogeneous borrowers, the bank can be shown to charge a rate that lies between the lowest and highest rates applicable to members of the group. For the subset of loans that should have been charged a higher rate than the optimal rate for the class, quantity rationing results. The least risky in the group and the riskless customers, on the other hand, are never rationed.

The major problem with the Jaffee-Modigliani approach to rationing is that the ultimate causes of the rationing are unsubstantiated assumptions about the loan market. Specifically, the model asserts that there is only a small set of loan prices that can be charged to the entire array of borrowers. It is, then, asserted that the bank knows the exact customer risk characteristics, even though it does not use such information to set loan prices. It can be argued that the first assumption is probably a reasonable view of the bank trying to deal with a large set of heterogeneous customers. Transaction costs presumably restrict the extent to which differential pricing is possible. It is not clear that this reasoning is consistent with the second assumption. If the bank, for economic reasons, only roughly categorizes its customers into broad groups, it is hard to accept the notion that it would find it profitable to maintain more explicit knowledge within each group. Yet such additional information is necessary to obtain the results of positive equilibrium and dynamic credit rationing.

Another problem with this approach to loan sorting is its stability. Any two banks within such a system will have, presumably, different groupings and group-specific interest rates. This would seem to imply that customers who are relatively less risky than the "average" within a group may find it desirable to shift to another bank. Their relative ranking would improve and borrowing costs decline as a result of such an action. In the limit, this type of behavior should result in adverse or unique selection and in the general absence of equilibrium credit rationing from the model. Although this may not in general be the case, there does not appear to be anything in the model setup to prohibit such a degenerate case.

C. Rationing and Information Problems

The third approach to credit rationing, and the one that appears most promising at the moment, is the information asymmetry or adverse selection approach. This was first suggested by Jaffee and Russell (1976), in which it was argued that expected value pricing of loan rates hides two different types of borrowers. When all loans are priced at a single rate, the bank attracts both honest and dishonest customers. The former fully anticipate repayment, whereas the latter will renege in all states where the implied cost is lower than repayment. An equilibrium competitive interest rate will be set so that the market rate incorporates the probability of default by dishonest or unlucky borrowers. They then demonstrate that variations in the loan rate from this equilibrium level could shift the relative proportion of honest borrowers so as to improve the expected profit for the financial institution. Essentially, by restricting the percentage of an investment project that is financed by the bank, the lender attracts more honest customers and a smaller loan loss experience. Barro (1976) considers a similar problem by treating the quantity of collateral as a determinant of the bank offer curve.

In a recent contribution, Stiglitz and Weiss (1981) extend this approach. Dealing again with customer groupings with low and high-risk characteristics, they demonstrate that as the interest rate charged to borrowers increases, the percentage of low quality loans may increase. They argue that without a priori knowledge of the quality of each loan applicant, the willingness to pay higher interest rates is a screening device in identifying high-risk borrowers. Therefore, the bank would prefer to charge a lower rate than to clear the loan market by discouraging the preferred borrowing group.

Taken as a whole, this credit rationing literature is diverse. On one side of the spectrum, a series of ad hoc assertions about extramarginal pricing is used to explain rationing. Next, we have an approach that dominated the literature for a long period of time, in which custom or costs mandate a small set of loan categories. These, in turn, bring about both equilibrium and dynamic rationing, but somehow do not cause the bank to subdivide its lending classes further. Finally, the recent literature on asymmetric information has been used to explain rationing. Here, equilibrium rationing exists by customers self-sorting in response to interest rate signals but not necessarily dynamic rationing. Although the last approach is clearly the most sophisticated, it also raises many questions. Yet, virtually no empirical work has been done over the past decade to answer them — or to assess the importance of this entire set of literature.

8. WHERE DO WE GO FROM HERE?

There has been much written over the past decade on the subject of bank behavior. This paper lists and discusses some two hundred contributions. To conclude my review of this literature, I offer some thoughts on the future directions of work on bank modeling.

The first point that springs from this review is that there is still much to be learned about financial institutions and their place in the economy. We seem to have converged upon a global view of the maximization process that the firm attempts. Nevertheless there is little solid work on the nature of the financial firm's product. The existence question remains vital to our understanding of these institutions and why they are capable of achieving their objectives in a relatively efficient capital market. On the asset side, more work clearly needs to be done along the imperfect information line of analysis in our explanation of the financial intermediation process. Whether it will be able to explain the evolution of banking, broadly defined, through new product innovation is an open question. On the liability side, understanding the evolution of the role and definition of money in a complex payments system appears central to the explanation of intermediation itself. Liability and transaction product innovation requires considerably more attention than it is currently receiving in the banking literature.

Within our existing view of bank behavior, the modeling of asset and liability management is fairly well formulated. But it is important to proceed further along the line of integrating the two sides of the balance sheet. Issues surrounding credit and interest rate risk management must be more adequately modeled. The recent work on the interaction of these risk factors moves us in the right direction, but much more needs to be done on risk taking, hedging, and diversification in the financial firm. Finally, economists must address the degree of competitiveness in the financial markets that surround the banking firm. In finance theory virtually no market imperfections are considered. Economists, on the other hand, have generally treated the bank as an imperfect competitor in markets that exhibit nonequilibrium pricing, price setting capability, and price discrimination. It would be worthwhile if we could reconcile these opposing views by incorporating modern finance theory in the theory of the banking firm.

WHAT'S DIFFERENT ABOUT BANKS?*

Eugene F. FAMA

University of Chicago, Chicago, IL 60637, USA

Negotiable certificates of deposit (CD's) trade in the capital market in competition with other securities like commercial paper and bankers' acceptances. If CD's must pay lenders competitive monetary interest, the reserve tax on CD's is borne by bank borrowers. Viability of the tax means there must be something special about bank loans that makes some borrowers willing to pay higher interest rates than those on other securities of equivalent risk. Moreover, there must be something special about banks that prevents other intermediaries from competing to assure that it never pays to finance loans with CD's.

1. Introduction

Banks are required to hold non-interest-bearing reserves against demand deposits. The banking literature treats the interests foregone on reserves as a tax on deposits. [See, for example, Black (1975).] The presumption is that banks earn the market interest rate on assets so the reserve tax falls on depositors. The viability of the demand deposit reserve tax is then explained in terms of special transactions services (redeemability for cash and the checking system for the transferring claims on wealth) that allow demand deposits to pay lower monetary interest than other securities of equivalent risk.

There is a problem in this conventional story about the incidence of the deposit reserve tax. Banks also finance assets with negotiable certificates of deposit (CD's). Although called 'deposits', negotiable CD's are transferable securities that trade in the capital market in competition with other similar instruments like commercial paper and bankers' acceptances. Unlike demand deposits, CD's provide no apparent transactions or liquidity services not also obtained from commercial paper or bankers acceptances. Thus, it seems reasonable to assume that CD's must yield lenders the same monetary interest as other securities of equivalent risk. The presumption is buttressed by table 1 which shows that during the 1967–83 period, average yields on high grade CD's and bankers' acceptances of the same maturity are almost identical. Likewise, the differences between average yields on CD's and commercial paper are trivial and not always of the same sign.

*The comments of Charles Plosser and the referee, David Romer, are gratefully acknowledged. This research is supported by the National Science Foundation.

Journal of Monetary Economics 15 (1985) 29–39. North-Holland

Table 1

Average, continuously compounded yields to maturity on high-grade certificates of deposit, bankers' acceptances, commercial paper, and Treasury bills; January 1967 to May 1983; $N = 197$.[a]

Instrument	Maturity		
	1 month	3 months	6 months
Certificates of deposit (CD's)	8.14	8.28	8.35
Bankers' acceptances (BA's)	8.13	8.25	8.36
Commercial paper	8.25	8.32	8.34
U.S. Treasury bills	6.86	7.31	7.61

[a] The data for CD's, BA's, and commercial paper are from Part IV, Table 1, of the *Analytical Record of Yields and Yield Spreads*, published by Salomon Brothers. The monthly data in the *Analytical Record* are secondary market quotes from Salomon traders for high-grade CD's and bankers' acceptances and for commercial paper rated A1–P1. The monthly Treasury bill quotes are from the Center for Research in Security Prices of the University of Chicago. The CD quotes and the discount quotes for BA's, commercial paper, and Treasury bills are transformed into annualized continuously compounded yields to maturity. The yields for each month are then averaged across months to get the average annualized yields in the table.

Unlike commercial paper and bankers acceptances, however, CD's are subject to a reserve requirement. If CD's must pay competitive monetary interest, the reserve tax on CD's is borne by bank borrowers. Viability of the tax then means there must be something special about bank loans that makes some borrowers willing to pay higher interest rates than those on the other securities of equivalent risk. Moreover, there must be something special about banks that prevents other intermediaries, like insurance companies and finance companies, whose liabilities are not subject to reserve requirements, from competing with banks to assure that it never pays to finance loans with CD's.

This paper presents a simple analysis that accommodates reserve requirements on demand deposits and CD's.

2. Reserve requirements and competitive banking

Fig. 1 summarizes demand and supply conditions for a banking sector in which individual banks are assumed to be perfectly competitive with one another in making loans and issuing demand deposits. The figure is a bit unusual in that the vertical axis shows the difference between i_B, an interest rate for a bank asset or liability, and i_m, the interest rate observed in the capital market on a non-bank security with risk equivalent to the bank asset or liability. Table 2 summarizes the various interest rates or costs in the analysis.

2.1. The supply of loanable funds

The cost to banks of a unit of demand deposits, i_D, includes monetary interest paid to depositors, the cost of unreimbursed services to depositors, and the interest foregone because of the reserve requirement. The special transactions services of demand deposits (access to a ready inventory of bank cash and to the checking system of exchange) allow the banking sector to issue deposits for which the per unit cost i_D is less than the market interest rate i_m. By raising either direct or service interest paid on deposits (raising $i_D - i_m$), the banking sector can induce a larger aggregate supply. If direct interest payments on demand deposits are unregulated, the demand deposit supply curve is horizontal when direct interest equals the market rate i_m, for example, at the point k in fig. 1. Because of the reserve requirement, the total cost i_D of a unit of deposits in the region where the supply curve is horizontal exceeds the market interest rate i_m. If the direct interest on demand deposits is restricted to a rate below i_m, the demand deposit supply curve is upward sloping throughout (the curve SD in fig. 1) as long as depositors consider some bank services less than perfect substitutes for direct interest.

The CD supply curve in fig. 1 is horizontal. This is consistent with the assumption (buttressed by the evidence of table 1) that CD's must pay holders the same monetary interest as other securities of equivalent risk. However, the total cost i_{CD} of a unit of CD's exceeds the market rate i_m because of the CD reserve requirement. Since the cost of CD's in fig. 1 is pictured net of i_m, the

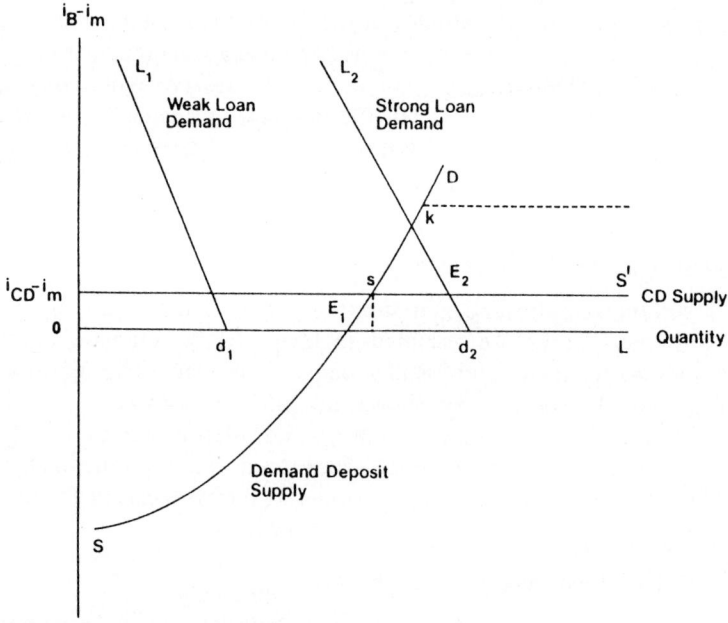

Fig. 1. Equilibrium in a competitive banking industry.

Table 2

Interest rate glossary.

Bank assets

i_m = interest rate observed in the capital market on non-bank securities like commercial paper.

i_L = interest rate charged on bank loans; does *not* include costs of making and monitoring loans.

Bank liabilities

i_D = cost of a unit of demand deposits; includes (a) direct interest paid to depositors, (b) interest foregone (paid to the central bank) because of the deposit reserve requirement, and (c) deposit servicing costs not reimbursed by depositors.

i_{CD} = cost of a unit of CD's; includes (a) direct interest paid to CD holders equal to what holders could get on non-bank securities of equivalent risk, (b) interest foregone (paid to the central bank) because of the CD reserve requirement, and (c) any issuing and maintenance costs.

CD supply curve can be horizontal even though the quantity of CD's issued by the banking sector can affect i_m.

Since the reserve requirement is higher for demand deposits than for CD's, there is an aggregate supply of demand deposits beyond which the cost of a unit of deposits exceeds that of a unit of CD's. This occurs at the point *s* in fig. 1. Below this point the industry supply curve for loanable funds is the demand deposit supply curve. At the point *s*, the banking sector switches from demand deposits to CD's. The aggregate supply curve for loanable funds is *SsS'*.

For simplicity the analysis of the supply of loanable funds is limited to demand deposits and CD's. However, the demand deposit supply curve can be interpreted as the aggregate of the supply curves for the class of liabilities (for example, small time deposits) that the banking sector does not issue in perfect competition with other suppliers. Moreover, the analysis is much the same when there are other classes of bank liabilities (for example, large time deposits) which, like CD's, are subject to reserve requirements but must yield holders the same return as non-bank securities of equivalent risk.

2.2. Industry equilibrium

2.2.1. Strong loan demand

Banks use CD's to finance loans when the loan demand schedule crosses the supply curve for loanable funds in the region where marginal supplies come from CD's, that is, to the right of the point *s* in fig. 1. The loan demand curve L_2 is an example.

The interest rate i_m is the market rate on securities with risks equivalent to those of bank loans. Assume that banks can buy all the open-market securities they want at the rate i_m. Thus, the demand curve for loanable funds becomes horizontal when it hits the quantity axis in fig. 1 (to the right of the point d_2 for the demand curve L_2).

With the loan demand curve L_2, industry equilibrium is at the point E_2. In this case (strong loan demand), equilibrium requires that banks issue loans to the point where the interest rate on loans, i_L, is equal to i_{CD}, the cost of a unit of CD's. Since banks always use the cheapest source of funds, they push demand deposits to the point where the cost of a unit of deposits, i_D, is also equal to i_{CD}.

The cost of a unit of CD's, i_{CD}, includes interest foregone because of the CD reserve requirement and the market interest rate i_m paid to CD holders. Since CD holders net the market rate i_m, the equilibrium condition $i_L = i_{CD}$ implies that the cost of the CD reserve requirement is borne by bank borrowers. Note that this is just an example of the standard result that an *ad valorem* tax is borne on the demand side when the supply curve is horizontal.

Perhaps more interesting, in equilibrium the banking sector issues deposits to the point where their cost is equal to the cost of CD's. The equilibrium condition $i_D = i_{CD} = i_L$ then implies that bank borrowers also bear the equivalent of the CD reserve requirement on the part of bank loans financed with demand deposits. This is in contrast to the conventional story in which demand depositors bear all the cost of the demand deposit reserve requirement. Moreover, since banks must cover all their lending costs, and since the loan rate i_L does not include the costs incurred by banks to issue and monitor loans, the condition $i_D = i_{CD} = i_L$ implies that such loan servicing costs must be borne by bank borrowers, in addition to the direct interest i_L charged on their loans.

Perhaps most important, the reserve requirement causes the cost of a unit of CD's to exceed the interest rate i_m on non-bank securities of equivalent risk. Thus, there must be something special about bank loans that makes some borrowers willing to pay interest rates greater than i_m on bank loans. Otherwise, CD's are not a viable means of financing loans. Moreover, there must be something special about banks that prevents other intermediaries, whose liabilities are not subject to reserve requirements, from competing with banks to assure that it never pays to finance bank loans with CD's. Some possible comparative advantages of banks as lenders are discussed in section 3.

2.2.2. Weak loan demand

The loan demand schedule L_1 in fig. 1 hits the quantity axis and becomes horizontal at the point d_1, to the left of the point E_1 where the demand deposit supply curve hits the axis. In this situation, the open-market interest rate i_m reigns supreme. The banking sector issues demand deposits to the point E_1 where the cost of a unit of deposits is $i_D = i_m$. Loans are issued to the point d_1 where the loan interest rate i_L is equal to i_m. The difference between the supply of deposits, E_1, and d_1 goes into some mix of loans and open-market securities. In this weak loan demand equilibrium, all bank assets are financed with deposits; banks issue no CD's.

Banks earn i_m on open-market securities. Thus, in addition to the interest rate $i_L = i_m$, borrowers again pay the service costs of making and monitoring their bank loans. I argue later, however, that monitoring services purchased from banks can actually help to explain the special attraction (comparative advantage) of bank loans for some borrowers.

The cost i_D of a unit of deposits in this weak loan demand equilibrium is also equal to the interest rate i_m on non-bank securities. However, i_D includes interest foregone on deposit reserves. Thus, an implication of $i_D = i_L = i_m$ is that the cost of the demand deposit reserve requirement is borne by depositors – the standard conclusion of the banking literature, for example, Black (1975). It is also an example of the standard conclusion that an *ad valorem* tax is borne by suppliers when an industry demand curve is infinitely elastic. We saw earlier, however, that the conclusion does not hold when bank loans are financed with both demand deposits and CD's. Then bank borrowers bear a part of the cost of the demand deposit reserve requirement equivalent to the cost of the CD reserve requirement.

Finally, there is an intermediate case where part of the demand deposit reserve tax is borne by bank borrowers even though banks do not finance loans with CD's. This occurs when the loan demand schedule crosses the demand deposit supply curve between the points E_1 and s is fig. 1.

2.3. Side issues

2.3.1. Bank portfolio composition

When banks finance in part with CD's, the cost of a unit of deposits or CD's is i_{CD}, and i_{CD} is greater than the return on open-market securities, i_m, because of the CD reserve requirement. Thus, CD financing implies that bank assets are concentrated in loans. Banks hold no open-market securities like Treasury bills. In fact, banks often issue CD's and hold open-market securities. This may in part result from the economics of deposit management. Since there are no active secondary markets for bank loans, an inventory of open-market securities that can be bought and sold at low cost can stand as a buffer between currency and loans to absorb unexpected variation in the redemption of demand deposits. In other words, holding some open-market securities lowers demand deposit servicing costs. Moreover, banks finance their holdings of Treasury securities in part with short-term repurchase agreements. Since repurchase agreements against Treasury securities are exempt from reserve requirements, financing Treasury securities in this way, while using CD's to finance loans, is consistent with the analysis.

At the end of 1983 commercial banks held $186.9 billion in Treasury securities and $250.6 billion in other securities. Repurchase agreements amounted to $85.5 billion, which is not sufficient to explain the Treasury security holdings. (See *Federal Reserve Bulletin*, May 1984, tables 1.24 and 1.25.) Whether the difference between total security holdings and repurchase agreements can be explained by incentives to lower deposit redemption costs is an interesting topic for future research.

2.3.2. Deposit insurance

Deposit insurance lowers the return required by some holders of CD's. If the price for the insurance charged to banks is not actuarially fair, the insurance subsidy helps offset the cost of the CD reserve requirement. If the offset is complete, we can observe that banks issue CD's to purchase open-market securities. In this case, however, the cost of CD's does not exceed the open-market rate i_m, and most of the interesting differences between weak and strong loan demand equilibria, for example, conclusions about who bears the cost of the demand deposit reserve requirement, disappear.

Deposit insurance does not necessarily undermine the analysis. First, it's not clear that deposit insurance is underpriced, at least for the banking sector as a whole. Fairly priced insurance fits easily in the analysis. Second, CD's are insured up to $100,000 to holders who qualify as physical persons, but negotiable CD's are commonly denominated in units of $1,000,000 or more. Finally, table 1 shows that average yields on negotiable CD's are systematically higher than those on Treasury bills of the same maturity and almost identical to those on high-quality bankers' acceptances and commercial paper. Thus, insurance is not a dominant factor in the pricing of CD's.

3. Bank loans and contracting costs in organizations

When the banking sector finances loans with CD's, interest rates on bank loans are higher than those on other securities of equivalent risk because of the CD reserve requirement. Thus, for some borrowers there must be something special about bank loans. Moreover, on the supply side, there must be something special about banks that prevents other intermediaries, like insurance companies and finance companies, whose liabilities are not subject to reserve requirements, from competing with banks to assure that it never pays to finance loans with CD's. The discussion that follows suggests an explanation of the comparative advantages of banks as lenders in the context of the more general problem of minimization of information costs in organizations. In short, information costs are used to explain why the demand curves for bank loans in fig. 1 are downward sloping rather than horizontal.

3.1. Inside and outside debt

To understand the role of bank loans in an organization's information process, it is useful to draw a distinction between outside debt and inside debt. Inside debt is defined as a contract where the debtholder gets access to information from an organization's decision process not otherwise publicly available. The debtholder may even participate in the decision process, for example, on the organization's board of directors. Bank loans are inside debt, as are the other types of debt commonly classified as private placements. In contrast, outside debt is defined as publicly traded debt where the debtholder relies on publicly available information generated by the organization or information purchased by the organization (for example, independent audits and bond ratings). Publicly traded bonds, commercial paper, bankers acceptances, and, of course, bank CD's are in this category. These distinctions between inside and outside debt are similar to the distinctions between inside and outside equity in Jensen and Meckling (1976).

3.2. The advantages of short-term inside debt

Fama and Jensen (1983a, b) observe that the contracts of most agents in organizations promise fixed payoffs or incentive payoffs tied to specific measures of performance. Such fixed payoff contracts are typical for labor, raw materials suppliers, managers and debtholders. Equity holders then contract for the right to net cash flows, that is, the time series of differences between revenues and promised payoffs to other agents.

Lower information costs incurred by agents to monitor their contracts translate into lower prices for their services. Competition pushes an organization to provide information jointly useful for evaluating the contracts of different agents to avoid duplication of information costs among agents [Fama and Jensen (1985)].

Bank loans are especially useful to avoid duplication of information costs. Bank loans usually stand last or close to last in the line of priority among contracts that promise fixed payoffs. Bank loans are short-term and the renewal process triggers periodic evaluation of the organization's ability to meet low-priority fixed payoff contracts. Positive renewal signals from bank loans mean that other agents with higher-priority fixed payoff claims need not undertake similar costly evaluations of their claims. Bank signals are credible since the bank backs its opinions with resources, or by declining resources.

The value of the signals from a bank about the credit worthiness of an organization's fixed payoff contracts is attested by the fact that many organizations pay periodic monitoring fees for lines of credit from banks even though they do not take the resources offered. Indeed, large corporations often purchase lines of credit from banks for the sole purpose of providing a signal about outside debt (commercial paper) to be issued publicly rather than held by the bank.

Like outside equity, outside (publicly traded) debt is issued predominantly by large corporations. Fama and Jensen (1983a, b) argue that outside equity involves high information and contracting costs that make it an uneconomical means of financing for small organizations. A similar argument applies to outside debt. In contrast, individuals and organizations of all types and sizes finance with bank loans. This suggests that contracting costs for bank loans debt are lower for individuals and small organizations than contracting costs for outside debt. For individuals and small organizations it's cheaper to give one agent (the banker) direct access to the organization's decision process than to produce the range of publicly available information that makes outside debt a viable means of financing.

In short, since a bank loan is a low-priority claim and the banker has access to inside information, in large and small organizations periodic signals from short-term bank loans about an organization's credit worthiness lower the information costs of other agents in the organization.[1] Moreover, for small organizations (and individuals) information and contracting costs for inside debt like bank loans are lower than for outside debt. Thus, we can explain why organizations (and individuals) are willing to pay higher interest rates on inside debt than we observe in the open capital market on outside debt of equivalent risk.

3.3. The comparative advantage of banks as inside lenders

These arguments do not explain why the supply side of the picture ever allows banks to charge higher than open-market interest rates because the cost of the reserve requirement on CD's must be passed on to bank borrowers. If the CD reserve tax is viable, bank costs of making and monitoring some kinds of inside loans must be lower than the costs of other intermediaries (for example, insurance and finance companies) by at least the cost of the CD reserve requirement.

Black (1975) suggests that banks have a cost advantage in making loans to depositors. The ongoing history of a borrower as a depositor provides informa-

---

[1] The absence of active secondary markets for bank loans suggests that they are based in part on inside information which is costly to transfer. See also Leland and Pyle (1977) and Diamond and Dybvig (1983).

tion that allows a bank to identify the risks of loans to depositors and to monitor the loans at lower cost than other lenders. The inside information provided by the ongoing history of a bank deposit is especially valuable for making and monitoring the repeating short-term loans (rollovers) typically offered by banks. Information from an ongoing deposit history also has special value when the borrower is a small organization (or individual) that does not find it economical to generate the range of publicly available information needed to finance with outside debt or equity.

Two facts tend to support these arguments. First, banks usually require that borrowers maintain deposits (often called compensating balances). Second, banks are the dominant suppliers of short-term inside debt. The inside debt or private placements offered by insurance and finance companies (which do not have the monitoring information provided by ongoing deposit histories) are usually much longer-term than bank loans.

4. Conclusions

Although called deposits, negotiable CD's are transferable securities that trade in the capital market in competition with other similar instruments like commercial paper and bankers' acceptances. Since CD's provide no apparent transactions or liquidity services not also obtained from commercial paper or bankers' acceptances, it is reasonable to assume that CD's must yield lenders the same monetary interest as other securities of equivalent risk. The assumption is supported by the yield comparisons in table 1.

Unlike commercial paper and bankers' acceptances, CD's are subject to a reserve requirement. If CD's must also pay competitive monetary interest, then the reserve tax on CD's is borne by bank borrowers. Viability of the reserve tax then means there must be something special about bank loans that makes borrowers willing to pay higher interest rates than those on open-market securities (outside debt) of equivalent risk. I suggest that for individuals and for some organizations, especially small organizations that do not have outside equity, the contracting costs for inside loans like bank loans are lower than for outside debt. Moreover, in all types of organizations, signals from short-term bank loans about an organization's credit worthiness can lower the information costs of other contracts.

On the supply side, if it pays to finance bank loans with CD's, then contracting costs for bank loans must be sufficiently lower than contracting costs for short-term inside loans from other intermediaries to make up the cost of the CD reserve requirement. I use Black's (1975) argument that because bank borrowers are usually also depositors, a bank has a low-cost ongoing history of financial information that gives it a comparative cost advantage in making and monitoring repeated short-term inside loans.

In short, the CD reserve tax is borne, by bank borrowers and its viability depends on special cost advantages of banks in servicing long-term depositor–borrowers. In contrast, the reserve tax on demand deposits is largely borne by depositors. Its viability depends on special transactions services (access to a ready inventory of bank cash and to the checking system for transferring claims on wealth) that allow deposits to pay lower interest than other securities of equivalent risk.

References

Black, Fischer, 1975, Bank funds management in an efficient market, Journal of Financial Economics 2, 323–339.

Diamond, Douglas W. and Philip H. Dybvig, 1983, Bank runs, deposit insurance, and liquidity, Journal of Political Economy 91, 401–419.

Fama, Eugene F. and Michael C. Jensen, 1983a, Separation of ownership and control, Journal of Law and Economics 26, 301–325.

Fama, Eugene F. and Michael C. Jensen, 1983b, Agency problems and residual claims, Journal of Law and Economics 26, 327–349.

Fama, Eugene F. and Michael C. Jensen, 1985, Organizational forms and investment decisions, Journal of Financial Economics 14, forthcoming.

Jensen, Michael C. and William H. Meckling, 1976, Theory of the firm: Managerial behavior, agency costs, and ownerships structure, Journal of Financial Economics 3, 306–360.

Klein, Benjamin, 1974, Competitive interest payments on bank deposits and the long-run demand for money, American Economic Review 65, 931–949.

Leland, Hayne E. and David H. Pyle, 1977, Information asymmetries, financial structure, and financial intermediation, Journal of Finance 32, 371–387.

II

BANK LENDING

The articles in this part examine the role of banks in the corporate capital acquisition process. Banks and other intermediaries can reduce the cost of obtaining outside capital by producing precontract information that mitigates the adverse-selection problems that arise between borrowers and lenders. In particular, when borrowers are better informed about the potential payoffs or the risk associated with their investment projects than lenders, an adverse-selection problem can arise whereby only the worst risks apply for a loan. Lenders, of course, recognize the potential for adverse selection and price loans to reflect this possibility. As a result, borrowers have a strong incentive to find ways to communicate precontract information in a reliable and cost-efficient way. As the articles in Part I suggest, an ongoing relationship with a commercial bank can reduce precontract information asymmetries and thereby lower the overall cost of capital. For example, Fama argues that banks are well informed, which implies that precontract information asymmetries are smaller in bank lending agreements than in public bond and equity issues.

The first article, by **James** (1987), provides an empirical test of Fama's (1985) hypothesis that private loans control information problems in the lending process. To test Fama's conjecture, James contrasts stock-price reactions to announcements of bank debt agreements with that of public securities offers. Smith (1986) notes that stock-price reactions to announcements of public debt and equity offerings are consistently either negative or not significantly different from zero; in no case is the stock-price reaction significantly positive. One explanation for this finding is that there exists an information asymmetry between the potential purchasers of new public securities and the managers of the firm who are presumed to act in the interests of existing shareholders [see Myers and Majluf (1985)]. Given this information asymmetry, management is expected to issue new securities when the market value of the firm is higher than management's assessment of firm value. As a result, investors revise downward their estimate of firm value in response to a public security offering. This adverse-selection problem could cause some companies to forgo profitable new investment opportunities.

One solution to the adverse-selection problem associated with public security offerings is to borrow from a well-informed private lender. A testable implication of this hypothesis is that share-price reactions associated with announcements of new bank loan agreements will be more favorable than the share-price reaction associated with new public security offerings. Consistent with this hypothesis, James finds a positive and statistically significant price reaction associated with announcements of bank loan agreements.

In addition to mitigating adverse-selection problems associated with public financing, commercial banks potentially lower the cost of borrowing by mitigating moral-hazard problems that can occur after a loan is made. For example, borrowers can have an incentive to shift funds to riskier projects after a loan is made because the borrowing firm's shareholders receive all the higher cash flows associated with these projects in the nondefault states and share the losses with debtholders in the default states. Moral hazard involves an opportunity loss because policies that maximize the value of shareholders' claims in a levered firm do not necessarily maximize the value of the firm.

One way to control moral hazard is through contractually restricting the actions that the borrower is permitted to take. Bank loan contracts and public bond contracts contain covenants that are designed to limit stockholders' opportunities to expropriate wealth from bondholders. In the second article, **Smith and Warner** (1979) examine ways in which debt contracts are written to control the conflict between borrowers and lenders. In particular, they examine how covenants restrict borrowers' actions in four areas: limitations on investment decisions, dividend policy, financing policy, and required bonding activities.

Some corporate decisions increase the borrower's wealth while reducing the wealth of lenders. In cases where wealth transfers are large enough, borrower's wealth can rise from decisions that reduce firm value. But rational lenders recognize these incentives faced by borrowers. When debt is issued, lenders forecast the value effects of future decisions. They understand that after issuance, actions which increase borrower wealth will tend to be taken. In an efficient market, the debt terms at issuance reflect an unbiased forecast of the effects of such future actions. Thus, on average, lenders will not suffer losses. However, the borrowers bear the costs of nonoptimal decisions motivated by wealth transfers from lenders. Therefore, effective control of this borrower-lender conflict can increase firm value.

Debt covenants that constrain activities such as asset sales or dividend payments are examples of voluntary contracts that can reduce the costs generated when stockholders of a levered firm follow a policy that deviates from firm-value maximization. The cost-reducing benefits of covenants accrue to the firm's owners through the higher price the bonds command at the time they are issued. Furthermore, if covenants lower the costs bondholders incur in monitoring stockholders, these cost reductions also are passed to stockholders through higher bond prices at issuance. Therefore, in structuring an optimal debt contract, the firm's managers face a tradeoff between the increased proceeds of the debt issue and reduced flexibility with respect to future policy choices.

In the third reading, **Smith** (1982) analyzes the structure of mortgage loan agreements. Mortgage loan contracts are complex agreements that include a variety of covenants restricting the actions of the borrower and requiring the borrower to periodically engage in certain activities such as the maintenance of the property and the acquisition of insurance. Smith argues that noninterest provisions of the loan contract, such as the amount of the down payment and covenants prohibiting the sale of the property, are efficient mechanisms to control the natural conflict of interest that arises between borrower and lender. More important, since the interest rate charged on a loan reflects the expected costs to the lender of moral hazard as well as the anticipated contracting costs in a competitive loan market, the borrower has a strong incentive to select contracts that minimize total contracting costs.

Writing complete state-contingent contracts is neither possible nor, with positive contracting costs, desirable. In the absence of complete state-contingent contracts, the borrower will have some discretion under the contract. In addition, incomplete contracts will involve an opportunity loss in the sense that the borrower will be restricted from undertaking certain activities that turn out to be in the best interest of the lender and the borrower.

The implications of imperfect precontract information and incomplete contracts for loan pricing and the allocation of credit are explored in **Stiglitz and Weiss** (1981). The adverse-selection problem that arises when information is costly implies that the rate the bank charges a pool of diverse customers will affect the composition of the pool. As a result, the profit-maximizing loan rate for the bank can result in excess demand for credit among the high-risk borrowers in the pool. Raising the loan rate to clear the market involves the loss of the lower-risk customers within the pool and thus a reduction in the bank's expected profits.

Moral-hazard problems arising from incomplete contracts can also restrict the bank's ability to adjust interest rates to clear the market. Specifically, the borrower's selection of projects will depend upon the promised rate the bank charges. As the promised rate changes, the optimal project choice for the borrower will change. As a result, the expected return to the bank does not necessarily increase as the promised rate on the loan is increased.

One solution to the problems raised by incomplete contracts is extensive monitoring on the part of the lender with the possibility of renegotiating the contract in the event of default or when the opportunity loss associated with the contract is large. As Smith and Warner explain, since renegotiation can mitigate opportunity losses associated with restrictive covenants, one would expect to observe tighter covenants associated with bond contracts that can be easily renegotiated.

Public debt is difficult and costly to renegotiate for several reasons. First, publicly held bonds are subject to the provisions of the Trust Indenture Act of 1939. This act specifies the role of the bond trustee and establishes rules concerning the modification of bond covenants. Important among the rules is the requirement of unanimous consent among the bondholders in order to change the maturity, principal, or coupon payments associated with a bond. The act also prescribes rules for the modification of other covenants (such as provisions for the maintenance of security). The Trust Indenture Act thus makes publicly held debt expensive to renegotiate. Bank and other privately placed debt claims are not subject to the Trust Indenture Act and as a result can be more easily renegotiated.

A second reason it is difficult to renegotiate public debt claims is that public bondholders may be poorly informed about the prospects of the firm. The lack of information arises in part from the fact that when public bonds are diffusely held, bondholders have little private incentive to monitor the firm, even when monitoring is in their collective interest. The lack of private incentives to monitor is a manifestation of a free-rider problem that arises because individual bondholders bear the costs of monitoring while the benefits of monitoring are shared among all bondholders. The free-rider problems associated with diffuse bondholder monitoring creates a demand for a centralized delegated monitor.

Berlin and Loeys (1988) examine the choice between loan contracts with limited monitoring (that is, public debt) and loan contracts with monitoring (that is, bank or privately placed debt). In their model, bond covenants are written on noisy publicly observable indicators of the financial condition of the firms. As a result, relying solely on contracts that do not specify monitoring involves opportunity losses. The covenants sometimes place the borrower in default even though, on the basis of private information, the firm is financially sound; at other times these noisy indicators fail to signal the firm's demise. Monitoring by a bank or other financial institution reduces this problem. However, monitoring also involves costs. In addition to the direct costs of monitoring, an incentive-compatible compensation contract for the monitor is needed to insure that the monitor indeed monitors the borrower. Unlike Diamond (1984), in Berlin and Loeys diversification is not assumed to resolve the agency problem between lenders and the delegated monitor. In the Berlin and Loeys model the incentive-compatible contract for the monitor is a contracting cost associated with delegated monitoring.

In Berlin and Loeys, the choice between public and private debt involves choosing the contractual arrangement that minimizes expected contracting costs of noisy covenant enforcement and delegated monitoring. When the informativeness of the financial indicators on which contracts are written is very high, contracts dominate delegated monitoring since the opportunity costs associated with relying on contracts are low. The less informative the financial indicators on which the terms of the contract depend, the greater the gains from monitoring and the more likely firms will rely on bank loans.

Rajan (1992) also examines the choice between public debt and bank loans. As in Berlin and Loeys, the contracting cost of public or "arm's length" debt arises from inefficient liquidation policies. In particular, with debt outstanding, there is an overinvestment problem in the sense that the owners of the firm will continue some projects that in the absence of debt would be abandoned. This inefficiency arises because it is assumed that public debt contracts cannot be made contingent on the firm's optimal liquidation decision (which in turn is based on private information). Private lenders are assumed to have access to better information about the value of the firm's assets. As a result, short-term private debt contracts can induce efficient liquidation policies.

The major contribution of Rajan's paper is to demonstrate the cost of bank financing that arises from the bank's monitoring and control function. Specifically, the information the bank obtains as part of its monitoring activities provides it with a competitive advantage vis à vis other lenders. As a result, it is costly for the firm to switch lenders and the bank is potentially in a position to extract rents from borrowers when short-term bank loans are renewed. While this prospect is priced into the loan contract at the initiation of the lending agreement, ex post, rents reduce the payoffs to shareholders associated with project continuation. As a result, short-term inside debt reduces the incentives of owners to exert effort. In Rajan's model the choice between bank loans and public debt involves a tradeoff of the incentive-distortion effects of monitoring against the overinvestment problems arising from public debt.

SOME EVIDENCE ON THE UNIQUENESS OF BANK LOANS*

Christopher JAMES

University of Oregon, Eugene, OR 97403, USA

Received April 1986, final version received June 1987

This paper presents evidence that banks provide some special service with their lending activity that is not available from other lenders. I find evidence that bank borrowers, not CD holders, bear the cost of reserve requirements on CDs. In addition, I find a positive stock price response to the announcement of new bank credit agreements that is larger than the stock price response associated with announcements of private placements or public straight debt offerings. Finally, I find significantly negative returns for announcements of private placements and straight debt issues used to repay bank loans.

1. Introduction

Although the economic rationale for commercial banks and other financial intermediaries is not well understood, recent theories of financial intermediation have focused on the role of banks in information production and transmittal [see, for example, Leland and Pyle (1977), Campbell and Kracaw (1980), and Diamond (1984)]. Banks and other intermediaries, the argument goes, have a cost advantage over other outsiders in producing and transferring information, either because of something intrinsic in the intermediation process, as Leland and Pyle and Diamond suggest, or because information production and the provision of transaction and other intermediary services are complementary activities. An implication of this view is that bank loans are different from publicly placed debt because banks know more about a company's prospects than other investors do.

The emphasis on information transmission contrasts sharply with an alternate hypothesis about the role of banks in the economy. The alternative holds that their special function is to provide transaction services through the issuance of demand deposits. On the asset side, banks are assumed to be simply passive portfolio managers [see Fama (1980)].

*A portion of this study was completed while I was visiting the University of Michigan. Thanks to James Brickley, Larry Dann, Mark Flannery, Ronald Lease, Wayne Mikkelson, Greg Niehaus, Megan Partch, Peggy Wier, seminar participants at the University of Oregon, University of Rochester, and New York University, an anonymous referee, and especially René Stulz (the editor) for helpful comments.

This paper provides evidence on whether commercial banks provide any special service with their lending activity that is not available from other lenders (i.e., on whether bank loans are unique). This evidence comes first from an examination of the incidence of the reserve requirement tax, and second from an analysis of the stock price response to announcements of bank loans, private placements of debt, and public straight debt issues.

My first examination extends research by Fama (1985), who studies the incidence of reserve requirements on bank certificates of deposit (CDs). He argues that because close substitutes for bank CDs, such as commercial paper or bankers' acceptances, exist and because CDs provide no special transaction services, reserve requirements on CDs must be borne by bank borrowers. In support of this conjecture, Fama finds no significant differences between the average yields on CDs and on high-grade commercial paper or bankers' acceptances. Fama concludes that because bank borrowers bear the cost of reserve requirements there must be something special about bank loans that distinguishes them from other types of privately placed and publicly placed debt.

A problem with Fama's conclusion is that the reserve requirement tax could be at least partially offset by a subsidy from the Federal Deposit Insurance Corporation (FDIC) in the form of deposit insurance supplied at less than actuarially fair prices. A more powerful test of the incidence of the reserve tax, provided here, examines the behavior of CD rates around changes in reserve requirements, when no offsetting changes in deposit insurance prices occur. My results support Fama's conclusion that the reserve tax is borne by bank borrowers.

A second source of evidence on the uniqueness of bank loans comes from a comparison of stock price responses to the announcements of bank loan agreements and other types of debt offerings. In analyzing the function of commercial banks, Kane and Malkiel (1965) and more recently Fama (1985) and Bernanke (1984), argue that bank loans are a form of inside debt, because banks have information about the borrower that is not available to other securities holders. As inside debt, bank loans are a way of avoiding the underinvestment problem associated with information asymmetries. Specifically, in the context of the Myers and Majluf model (1984), loans by banks (as inside debt) are similar to financial slack (internally generated funds). One testable implication of the bank-debt-as-inside-debt hypothesis is that because bank loans avoid the information asymmetries associated with public debt offerings, a non-negative stock price response will be associated with their announcement. For similar reasons, if private placements acquired by insurance companies are also inside debt, a non-negative stock price response is expected.

I examine the stock price response to publicly announced bank credit agreements, private placements, and publicly placed straight debt issues.

Abnormal performance is positive and statistically significant for bank loan announcements and nonpositive for publicly placed straight debt issues. These results are similar to those reported by Mikkelson and Partch (1986). Surprisingly, a negative and statistically significant stock price response is observed for debt placed privately with insurance companies. Most notably, I find a negative stock price response for private placements and straight debt issues used to repay bank loans. These results suggest that bank loans are unique, but they are not fully consistent with the inside-debt argument, as I discuss below.

The remainder of the paper is organized into five sections. In section 2, I analyze the incidence of the reserve requirement tax. In section 3, I describe my sample of bank credit agreements and debt offerings. The stock price effects associated with these borrowing arrangements are examined in section 4. In section 5, several explanations for the observed stock price behavior are explored. A brief conclusion is provided in section 6.

2. Incidence of the reserve requirement

The current reserve requirement on short-term CDs with original maturity of less than 180 days is 3%. In the absence of any special service provided to bank borrowers *or* any special service to CD holders, a reserve requirement tax would result in the elimination of CD financing. In a competitive deposit market other depositors (non-CD holders) will not bear the tax, because if a bank attempted to shift the tax to them, other banks not issuing CDs would bid them away. Bank stockholders cannot be expected to pay the tax because non-bank lenders (who are not subject to the reserve tax) would have a higher risk-adjusted return.

Fama (1985) argues that CD holders do not bear the reserve requirement tax and that therefore bank loans are special. This conclusion is based on his finding no significant difference between the yield on CDs and the yields on commercial paper and bankers' acceptances. Fama's evidence is not fully convincing, for two reasons. First, the reserve tax could be borne not by borrowers but by the FDIC through the provision of deposit insurance at less than actuarially fair prices. Second, CDs are insured only to $100,000, whereas the typical denomination is $1 million, so their rates may contain a default premium. If the default risk on CDs is greater than for commercial paper, observed yields on the two securities may be identical even though CD owners pay the reserve tax.

An alternative method of examining the incidence of the reserve tax is to examine the behavior of CD yields in relation to the yields on other money market instruments around changes in reserve requirements. Without any contemporaneous change in insurance costs, an increase in reserve require-

Table 1

Average annual yields to maturity on high-grade certificates of deposit, commercial paper, and Treasury bills and yield spreads (January 1977 to December 1984, sample size = 471).[a]

Panel A: Average annual yields (weekly data)

Instrument	3% reserve requirement period Jan. 1977–Nov. 1978 July 1980–Dec. 1984	5% reserve requirement period Nov. 1978–July 1980
90-day CDs	10.67	11.89
30-day CDs	10.52	11.59
90-day commercial paper	10.59	11.83
30-day commercial paper	10.40	11.51
90-day Treasury bills	9.74	10.66
30-day Treasury bills	9.11	10.01

Panel B: Average annual yield spread (in percent) between CDs and other money market instruments (standard errors in parentheses)

Spread[b]	3% reserve requirement period Jan. 1977–Nov. 1978 July 1980–Dec. 1984	5% reserve requirement period Nov. 1978–July 1980	Entire sample period
$SPCDTB_{90}$	0.931 (0.04)	1.211 (0.07)	0.992 (0.03)
$SPCDTB_{30}$	1.412 (0.05)	1.581 (0.09)	1.455 (0.04)
$SPCDCP_{90}$	0.073 (0.01)	0.038 (0.02)	0.065 (0.01)
$SPCDCP_{30}$	0.117 (0.01)	0.078 (0.02)	0.110 (0.01)

[a] Yields are based on weekly (Friday close) price quotes from the traders at Bank of America for high-grade CDs and for dealer-placed commercial paper rated A1–P1. All data were obtained from Data Resources Inc. DRI-FACS file.

[b] $SPCDTB_{90}$ = average annual yield spread between 90-day CDs and 90-day Treasury bills,
   $SPCDTB_{30}$ = average annual yield spread between 30-day CDs and 30-day Treasury bills,
   $SPCDCP_{90}$ = average annual yield spread between 90-day CDs and 90-day commercial paper,
   $SPCDCP_{30}$ = average annual yield spread between 30-day CDs and 30-day commercial paper.

ments should reduce the yield on CDs in relation to other yields if depositors pay the reserve tax.

Changes in the reserve requirements applied to CDs during the 1978–1980 period provide an opportunity to examine the incidence of the reserve tax. Effective November 2, 1978, and continuing through July 24, 1980, the Federal Reserve imposed a supplemental reserve requirement of 2% on all CDs in excess of $100,000. In addition, during this period, marginal reserve requirements of from 5% to 10% were imposed on CDs in excess of a base amount.[1]

---

[1] See table A7 of the *Federal Reserve Bulletin* for a list of reserve requirements.

The effect of these changes was to raise the reserve requirement on all large CDs from 3% to 5% and as high as 15% for CDs issued in excess of the base amount.

To examine the effect of these changes and the incidence of the reserve tax, I obtained weekly secondary market price quotes and computed yields for thirty- and ninety-day high-grade CDs, commercial paper, and Treasury bills. These data were obtained from Data Resources, Inc. (DRI), for the period January 1, 1977 to January 1, 1985.

Table 1 presents the average annual yield on CDs, commercial paper, and Treasury bills during the period in which a 3% reserve requirement was effective and the period in which a minimum 5% reserve requirement was imposed. Table 1 also contains the average spreads between CDs and other money market instruments for the 1977–1984 period. I find no statistically significant difference in the average spread between CDs and commercial paper or Treasury bills during the two periods. Assuming a competitive banking industry, the evidence presented in table 1 supports Fama's conclusion that bank borrowers and not CD holders bear the reserve tax.

3. Description of the sample and methodology

3.1. Random sample of firms

I am not aware of any source that provides information by company on new bank loan agreements. To obtain a sample of these financing events, I selected 300 companies at random from the population of firms contained in the 1983 Center for Research on Security Prices (CRSP) daily return file that were listed on the first trading day in 1974. I included companies in the sample if they were listed in the *Moody's Industrial, Transportation*, or *Utilities* manuals. (Excluded from the sample were financial companies.) I then searched the *Wall Street Journal Index* for information on each firm over the ten-year period 1974–1983 to identify all public straight debt offerings for cash, private placements of debt, and bank borrowing agreements that did not coincide with other financing, dividend, or earnings announcements.

The bank loan agreements in the sample consist of new credit agreements and the expansion of existing agreements. They include both extensions of lines of credit (commitments to lend) and term loans. The typical agreement, however, involves a line of credit where, at the firm's option, borrowing can be converted into a term loan.

Privately placed debt agreements consist of debt sold for cash to a restricted number of institutional investors. Most (approximately 70%) of the agreements involve an insurance company as the lender.

The total sample consists of 207 financing announcements. There are eighty announcements of bank loan agreements, thirty-seven announcements of

Table 2

Distribution by year of announcements of bank credit agreements, privately placed debt, and publicly placed straight debt for a random sample of 300 NYSE- and AMEX-traded non-financial firms (1974–1983).

Year of announcement	Bank loan agreements	Privately placed debt	Public straight debt
1974	9	4	5
1975	11	7	13
1976	7	7	8
1977	8	7	4
1978	1	8	6
1979	8	1	9
1980	11	1	10
1981	9	1	9
1982	10	1	16
1983	6	0	10
Total	80	37	90

private placements, and ninety announcements of public straight debt offerings. Table 2 presents the distribution of announcements by type of event by year for the period 1974–1983. Although there is no discernible time pattern for the number of bank loan or straight debt announcements, the number of private placement announcements decreases substantially after 1978.[2]

3.2. Descriptive statistics

Table 3 contains summary statistics for the debt offerings in my sample. Row 1 contains the amount of each type of offering. As table 3 indicates, public debt offerings are larger on average than private offerings. For bank loan agreements and private placements, the loan amounts reported may overstate the amount actually borrowed by the firm. In many cases these are commitments to lend, and the entries in row 1 of table 3 are based on the amount of the commitment.[3]

---

[2] The number and dollar volume of privately placed debt is reported in the *Investment Dealer's Digest*. The dollar value (in millions) and number of privately placed bond issues during the period are:

	1974	1975	1976	1977	1978
Dollar value	$8,214	11,856	17,811	21,797	18,511
Number of issues	696	685	717	1,017	900

	1979	1980	1981	1982	1983
Dollar value	15,270	10,750	10,860	10,397	10,360
Number of issues	786	640	556	531	525

[3] Private placements have many of the same features as bank loan agreements. The borrower is typically given an option to borrow up to some prespecified amount over a period of one to five years. See Zinbarg (1975).

Table 3

Descriptive statistics for commercial bank loans, privately placed debt, and publicly placed straight debt for a random sample of 300 NYSE- and AMEX-traded non-financial firms (1974–1983).[a]

Descriptive measure	Type of borrowing					
	Commercial bank loans (sample size = 80)		Privately placed debt (sample size = 37)		Public straight debt (sample size = 90)	
	Mean (Range)	Median	Mean (Range)	Median	Mean (Range)	Median
Debt amount (millions of dollars)	72.0 (4–800)	35.0	32.3 (5–120)	25.0	106.2 (10–1,000)	75.0
Firm size (millions of dollars)[b]	675 (28.6–10,311)	212	630 (20.2–6,365)	147	2,506 (47–59,540)	1,310
Debt amount/market value of common stock	0.72 (0.04–2.6)	0.46	0.52 (0.04–2.6)	0.25	0.26 (0.02–1.5)	0.15
Maturity of debt (years)[c]	5.6 (0.6–12)	6.0	15.34 (3–25)	15.0	17.96 (1–40)	20.0
Number of firms	52		34		43	
Number of firms with publicly traded debt outstanding[d]	25		16		30	

[a] Statistics given in the first row are the mean followed by the median. The range is provided in the second row.

[b] Firm size is for December 31 of the year immediately preceding the security offering or borrowing. Firm size equals the book value of all liabilities and preferred stock plus the market value of common stock outstanding. The market value of common stock is the product of the number of shares outstanding and the closing price per share at year-end preceding the announcement. Closing prices are from the *Security Owners Stock Guide*. The book value of liabilities and the number of shares outstanding are from *Moody's* manuals.

[c] Maturity of the loan or debt offering is from the *Wall Street Journal* article. No information on maturity was provided for twenty-four bank loans, two private placements, and nine straight debt offerings. For bank loans that are convertible to term loans, the maturity of the term loan is used.

[d] Firms are classified as having publicly traded debt if the *Moody's* manual report the firm had rated debt outstanding at year-end preceding the financing announcement.

Firms using private placements and bank loans are on average smaller than firms using public offerings of straight debt. The average firm size in both the bank loan sample and the private placement sample is about 25% of the average firm size in the straight debt sample. This finding is consistent with Brealey and Myers's (1985) view that private placements and bank loans typically involve small and medium-sized companies.

Row 4 of table 3 presents the average maturity of each type of borrowing. Bank loans are of considerably shorter maturity than either privately placed debt or straight debt. Indeed, the longest-term bank loan is twelve years, less than the median maturity of either privately placed or publicly placed debt.

3.3. Methodology

The market model is used to obtain estimates of abnormal stock returns around the announcement of the financing events. The announcement is defined as the date of the first report of the borrowing agreement or debt offering in the *Wall Street Journal*. The market model was estimated on daily returns for the period that begins 120 trading days before and ends 120 trading days following the announcement (event) date, excluding 41 trading days centered around the event date. The abnormal stock return or prediction error for firm j over day t is defined as

$$PE_{jt} = R_{jt} - \left(\hat{\alpha}_j + \hat{\beta}_j R_{mt} \right),$$

where R_{jt} is the rate of return of security j over period t, R_{mt} is the rate of return on the CRSP equal-weighted market index over period t, and $\hat{\alpha}_j$ and $\hat{\beta}_j$, are ordinary least squares estimates of firm j's market model parameters.

The daily prediction errors are averaged over all firms within a particular group to produce a daily portfolio average prediction error:

$$APE_t = 1/N \sum_{j=1}^{N} PE_{jt},$$

where N is the number of firms in the sample. I calculate a two-day announcement period abnormal return by summing the prediction errors for day -1 and day 0. This procedure incorporates the possibility that the announcement may have been made during trading hours the previous day and reported with a one-day lag.

Tests of statistical significance of the average prediction errors are based on standardized prediction errors. The two-day standardized prediction error for firm j is defined as

$$SPE_j = \sum_{t=-1}^{0} PE_{jt}/S_j,$$

where

$$S_j = \left[2V_j^2 \left[1 + \frac{1}{M} + \frac{(R_{mt} - R_m)^2}{\sum_{i=1}^{M} (R_{mi} - R_m)^2} \right] \right]^{1/2},$$

and V_j^2 is the residual variance of the market model regression for firm j, M is the number of days in the estimation period (199), and R_m is the mean market return over the estimation period.

Table 4

Average two-day percentage prediction errors (APE) on the announcement of commercial bank loans, privately placed debt, and publicly placed straight debt offerings for a random sample of 300 NYSE- and AMEX-traded non-financial firms (1974–1983).

Type of event	APE	Z-value[a]	Proportion negative[b] (sample size)
Bank loan agreement	1.93%	3.96	0.34[d] (80)
Private placement	−0.91%	−1.87	0.56 (37)
Public straight debt	−0.11%	−0.40	0.56 (90)
Bank loan agreement borrowing indicated[c]	1.71%	3.20	0.35[d] (71)
Bank loan agreement no borrowing indicated[d]	3.68%	1.71	0.23[e] (9)

[a] The null hypothesis is that the average standardized prediction error equals zero. $Z = \sqrt{N}\,(ASPE_t)$, where $ASPE_t$ is the average standardized prediction error and N is the number of firms in the sample.

[b] The null hypothesis is that the proportion of negative prediction errors equals 0.5. The test statistic is a Wilcoxon signed ranks statistic.

[c] Loan agreements in which the *Wall Street Journal* article describing the agreement indicates borrowing has occurred or is expected to occur under the loan agreement.

[d] Sign test statistic is significant at 0.05 level.

[e] Sign test statistic is significant at 0.01 level.

The average standardized prediction error is

$$ASPE_t = \frac{1}{N} \sum_{j=1}^{N} SPE_{jt}.$$

Assuming the individual prediction errors are cross-sectionally independent, the following Z-statistic can be computed:

$$Z = \sqrt{N}\,(ASPE_t),$$

which is asymptotically distributed unit normal under the hypothesis that the average standardized prediction error equals zero.

4. Stock price response to borrowing arrangements

Table 4 reports the average stock price response to the announcement of bank loan agreements, private placements, and public straight debt offerings. The average prediction error for bank loan agreements is positive and statistically significant at the 0.01 level. In addition, 66% of the prediction errors are positive.[4] There is no statistically significant difference between announcements of bank loan agreements in which immediate borrowing is indicated and announcements in which no immediate borrowing is indicated.

The positive stock price response to bank loan agreements contrasts with the non-positive response to public offerings of securities reported by other researchers.[5] As table 4 indicates, I also find a non-positive stock price response associated with the announcement of a public offering of straight debt. The average two-day prediction error associated with straight debt offerings is −0.11 percent, not statistically different from zero at the 0.10 level.

If the positive response to bank loan agreements is the result of some benefit from the intermediation process, but a benefit not unique to commercial banks, one would expect to observe a similar response to debt placed privately with insurance companies. As table 4 indicates, however, the average two-day prediction error associated with the announcement of privately placed debt is −0.91 percent, which is significantly different from zero at the 10% level (*p*-value of 0.063). Moreover, the difference between the average prediction error of bank loan agreements and of privately placed debt agreements is statistically significant at the 0.01 level.

5. Interpretation of the average stock price response

The difference in abnormal performance among announcements of bank loans, private placements, and straight debt offerings may arise because these debt offerings (or the borrowers using them) differ systematically in some important feature, such as the maturity of the issue or the purpose of the borrowing, that is unrelated to the identity of the lender. Alternatively, bank loans may differ from other types of borrowing because banks provide some special service with their lending activity. A testable implication of the second explanation is that the share price response to the announcement of bank loans will differ from the share price response to announcements of private placements or public debt offerings with characteristics similar to commercial bank loans.

In this section I examine the share price response associated with announcements of bank loans, private placements, and straight debt offerings grouped by stated purpose of the borrowing, the maturity of the offering, the default risk of the borrower, and the size of the borrower.

---

[4] Mikkelson and Partch (1986) also report a positive and statistically significant response to the announcement of bank credit agreements. They, however, focus on public securities offerings and do not explore differences in the stock price response associated with bank loan agreements and private placements.

[5] See Dann and Mikkelson (1984), Mikkelson and Partch (1986), Eckbo (1986), Asquith and Mullins (1986), and Masulis and Korwar (1986).

Table 5

Average two-day prediction errors (APE) on the announcement of commercial bank loans, privately placed debt, and publicly placed straight debt offerings grouped by stated purpose of the borrowing for a random sample of 300 NYSE- and AMEX-traded non-financial firms (1974–1983).

	Type of borrowing								
	Bank loan agreements[a] (sample size = 80)			Private placements (sample size = 37)			Public straight debt (sample size = 90)		
	APE (Z-value)[b]	Sample size	Average maturity[c]	APE (Z-value)	Sample size	Average maturity	APE (Z-value)	Sample size	Average maturity
Repay debt	1.14% (1.64)	17	6.5	0.51% (0.69)	5	14.2	-0.35% (-0.43)	32	17.4
Capital expenditure	1.20% (1.05)	24	5.9	-0.23% (0.02)	5	16.6	0.55% (1.63)	34	18.9
General corporate purposes	4.67% (2.54)	8	4.6	0.26% (0.31)	9	17.1	0.07% (0.24)	9	17.1
Repay bank loans	3.10% (2.35)	11	5.8	-2.07%[d] (-3.18)	18	14.4	-1.63%[c] (-1.74)	12	18.4
No purpose given	1.74% (1.79)	20	4.7	—	—	—	0.69% (0.73)	3	14.0

[a] Stated purpose is the primary purpose given in the *Wall Street Journal* article describing the borrowing. In cases in which multiple purposes are given, the first purpose listed is used to classify the event.

[b] The null hypothesis is that the average standardized prediction error equals zero. $Z = \sqrt{N}(\overline{ASPE_t})$, where $\overline{ASPE_t}$ is the average standardized prediction error and N is the number of firms in the sample.

[c] Maturity of the loan or debt offering is from the *Wall Street Journal* article describing the offering. Maturity is in years.

[d] The return is significantly different, at the 0.01 significance level, from the average prediction error for the sample of other private placements for which the stated purpose is other than repaying bank loans.

[c] This return is significantly different, at the 0.05 level, from the average prediction error for the sample of other straight debt issues for which the stated purpose is other than repaying bank loans.

5.1. Analysis of borrowing agreements by stated purpose

One explanation for the positive abnormal performance associated with bank loan agreements is based on the asymmetric information model of Myers and Majluf (1984). Bank loans may serve as a form of inside debt if banks have inside information about the value of the firm's growth prospects and bank loan rates reflect this information. Myers's and Majluf's model pertains to new financing, however, and offers no prediction about borrowing for other purposes. Examining the stock price response to bank loans grouped by stated purpose provides one test of the inside-debt hypothesis.

All borrowing announcements are placed into one of five purpose categories: (1) refinance debt, (2) capital expenditures, (3) general corporate purposes, (4) repayment of bank loans, and (5) no purpose given. The classification by purpose is based on information contained in the *Wall Street Journal* article describing the announcement. Where several purposes are stated, borrowing is classified by the first purpose listed or, where indicated, the primary purpose of the borrowing.

The average two-day prediction errors for bank loans, private placements, and straight debt offerings grouped by purpose are presented in table 5. Table 5 also includes the average maturity of each type of borrowing. The average prediction errors for bank loans are positive for all stated purposes, although general corporate purposes and the repayment or refinancing of bank debt are the only two categories in which the average prediction errors are statistically different from zero at the 0.01 level. There are, however, no significant differences (at the 0.10 level) between the mean returns for bank loans classified by purpose.

In only one category, the repayment of bank loans, is the average prediction error for private placements significantly different from zero. The average prediction error for this category is negative and appears to be the major component of the negative average prediction error associated with private placements reported in table 4. Moreover, the average prediction error for private placements used to repay bank loans is statistically different (at the 0.01 significance level) from that of private placements used for other purposes.

In the sample of straight debt offerings, only the repayment of bank loans category has an average prediction error significantly different from zero at the 0.10 level. The average two-day prediction error is -1.63 percent (p-value $= 0.08$).

Two findings in this section are of particular interest. First, there is no significant difference between the share price response to bank loans used to refinance debt (either existing bank loans or other debt offerings) and bank loans used for capital expenditures. The same conclusion is reached if the capital expenditures and general corporate purpose categories are combined. Therefore, the positive average abnormal returns associated with the announcement of new bank loans cannot be attributed solely to avoidance of information asymmetries associated with *new* investments. The second finding is the statistically significant decrease in share price for privately placed debt and straight debt used to refinance bank loans. This result is curious; why do managers use private placements to refinance bank loans, given the adverse share price reaction? One possible explanation is the difference in maturity between bank loans, private placements, and public debt offerings. This issue is explored in the next section.

5.2. Analysis of borrowing arrangements by maturity of the offers

The difference in average abnormal performance among borrowing arrangements may be attributed to differences in the average maturity of the issue. As table 3 indicates, bank loans have a shorter average maturity than do private placements and straight debt offerings in the sample.

Maturity of the debt issue may be important in explaining the differences in abnormal performance for several reasons. First, as suggested by Merton (1974) and Ho and Singer (1982), short-term debt may be less risky than long-term debt. In particular, Ho and Singer demonstrate that holding the market value of debt constant, an increase in the time to maturity of the debt will increase the elasticity of the value of the bond with respect to the value of the firm.[6] Myers and Majluf (1984) predict that the stock price response to the announcement of a new security issue depends on the sensitivity of the value of new securities to changes in firm value. This implies that the absolute value of the stock price response to the announcement of a debt offering should increase with the time to maturity of the offering.

Flannery (1986) provides a second reason for the importance of maturity. He argues that a firm's choice of maturity can provide a signal about management's assessment of earnings prospects. Flannery shows that, with transactions costs associated with new debt issues, managers who believe their firm is undervalued by outsiders can signal the true value of the firm by issuing short-term debt (i.e., debt repayable before cash flows are realized). When the undervalued firm's true prospects are revealed, refunding occurs at a lower default risk premium. Overvalued firms, on the other hand, find a short-term debt strategy more expensive because any initial cost savings from issuing short-term debt are more than offset by higher transaction costs of refinancing and higher subsequent refinancing costs (in terms of a higher default risk premium).

---

[6] With a discount bond, to maintain a constant market value of debt as its maturity increases the promised terminal payment to debt holders must also increase. In addition, note that the elasticity of risky debt equals the weighted average of the elasticity of equity for the unlevered firm and the elasticity of riskless debt (which is zero). An increase in the maturity of debt makes the expected payoff characteristics of debt more similar to those of equity (by raising the terminal payment) and therefore increases the elasticity of debt.

Easterbrook (1984) and Fama (1985) provide a third reason why maturity might matter. Both authors focus on the agency costs of monitoring managers. Easterbrook argues that the costs of monitoring are lower if the firm is frequently in the market for new capital.[7] The issuance of new securities triggers a review of the firm's earnings prospects by intermediaries (investment bankers and commercial banks). These intermediaries send reliable signals to existing as well as new claimants on the firm about the firm's ability to meet fixed-pay-off contracts. The intermediaries send reliable signals by bonding performance, directly through their own investment or indirectly through the value of their reputation. Fama (1985, p. 36) argues that bank loans avoid duplication of information costs:

> Bank loans usually stand last or close to last in the line of priority among contracts that promise fixed pay-offs. Bank loans are short-term and the renewal process triggers periodic evaluation of the organization's ability to meet low-priority fixed pay-off contracts. Positive renewal signals from bank loans mean that other agents with higher fixed pay-off claims need not undertake similar costly evaluations of their claims.

A firm's decision to commit to periodic evaluations can therefore provide a positive signal of management's assessment of the firm's earnings prospects.

The hypothesis that the positive share price response associated with bank loan announcements is due *solely* to the shorter maturity of bank loans I call the *maturity hypothesis*. If the difference in abnormal performance is due solely to the shorter maturity of bank loans, one would expect to observe a positive share price response for public straight debt offerings and private placements with maturities similar to those of bank loans.

The maturity hypothesis is not necessarily inconsistent with the hypothesis that banks provide some special service to borrowers. For example, Black (1975), Fama (1985), and Kane and Malkiel (1965) argue that banks have a cost advantage in making loans to depositors. The inside information provided by a continuing deposit history is particularly valuable, they argue, in making and monitoring repeating short-term loans. This argument explains why banks may have lower costs to originate short-term repeating loans but does not explain why firms use private placements or publicly placed long-term debt to refinance bank loans. If a continuing relationship between the bank and its loan customers results in lower costs of refinancing, banks also should have a comparative advantage in making long-term loans to these customers. There-

---

[7]Rozeff (1982) presents a similar argument in his analysis of the determinants of dividend payout ratios. He argues that dividend payments are a device that reduces the agency cost of equity by requiring the firm to acquire external funds more frequently. The suppliers of new funds require the firm to supply new information about the firm's earnings prospects. The agency cost savings from higher dividend payments are offset by higher transactions costs associated with new financing. These two opposing influences produce an optimum dividend payout ratio.

fore, although a change in a firm's earnings prospects may result in a shift in its maturity preference, it is not clear why this action also results in a change in the intermediary used (e.g., from banks to insurance companies). One explanation is that banks are constrained from making long-term loans.[8] This constraint could arise from regulatory pressure or a preference by banks for matching the maturity of their assets with the maturity of their liabilities.[9]

To test the maturity hypothesis, I divided the straight debt and private placement announcements into two groups, one consisting of offerings with a maturity of less than ten years and a second consisting of offerings with a maturity of ten years or more. I then analyzed the stock price response to borrowing announcements in the two groups.

My results are reported in table 6. Although the average prediction errors are larger for short-term offerings than for longer-term borrowing, the difference in average returns is not statistically significant. As an additional test of the maturity hypothesis I estimated the relation between the two-day prediction error and the maturity of the offering for each type of borrowing arrangement, using weighted least squares. The weights used in the regression analysis are the reciprocal of the standard error of each firm's abnormal returns. My results reveal no statistically significant relation between the share price response to the announcement of the offering and the maturity of the offering. These results, together with those reported in table 6, are inconsistent with the maturity hypothesis.

5.3. Other explanations

The other potential explanations for the differences in abnormal performance among borrowing arrangements are: differences in the risk of the debt issued, differences in the size of borrowing firms, and differences in the size of debt offering in relation to the size of borrowing firm. Smith and Warner (1977) argue that private placements contain more detailed restrictive covenants and are more likely to be used by riskier firms than is publicly placed debt. Differences in default risk may explain the differences in abnormal returns that I find. Alternatively, abnormal performance may be related to firm size. The announced ability to borrow may be good news for small firms (which borrow primarily from banks), but not much news at all for large firms (which

---

[8] The presence of a supply constraint is suggested by the lack of activity in the long-term commercial loan market. In my sample, only one bank loan has a maturity of more than ten years. The Federal Reserve Board's *Survey of the Terms of Bank Lending* indicates banks specialize in short-term loans. The survey for August 1985 indicates only 12% of commercial loans made have maturities of more than one year. These loans have an average maturity of four years.

[9] Although no federal regulations limit the maturity of commercial loans, a factor used in bank examinations to determine asset quality and capital requirements is the maturity mismatch of a bank's assets and liabilities. See Spong (1985).

Table 6

Average two-day percentage prediction errors (APE) on the announcement of private placements and straight debt offerings classified by maturity for a random sample of 300 NYSE- and AMEX-traded non-financial firms (1974–1983).

Type of event	APE	Z-value[a]	Sample size	Average maturity[b]
Straight debt, maturity less than 10 years	0.766%	1.625[c]	25	5.4 years
Straight debt, maturity greater than 10 years	−0.441%	−0.537	57	21 years
Private placements, maturity less than 10 years	−0.232%	−0.193	5	5.6 years
Private placements, maturity greater than 10 years	−1.011%	−2.002	32	17 years

[a] The null hypothesis is that the average standardized prediction error equals zero. $Z = \sqrt{N}(ASPE_t)$, where $ASPE_t$ is the average standardized prediction error and N is the number of firms in the sample.

[b] Maturity of the loan or debt offering is from the *Wall Street Journal* article describing the offering.

[c] Significantly different (at the 0.10 level) from the APE for straight debt issues with maturity greater than ten years at the 0.10 level.

use publicly placed debt) that have other ways of disseminating information. Bank borrowing may therefore be simply a proxy for firm size. Finally, the relative size of the offering may be an important determinant of the stock price response if it serves as a proxy for changes in leverage.

As a proxy for the default risk of the borrower, I obtained for each firm the rating of its most recently issued debt prior to each announcement in my sample. Debt ratings are from the *Moody's* manual. Panel A in table 7 provides the proportion of firms with debt outstanding in three rating categories: AA or better, A, and BAA and below. The proportion of firms in each rating category, as well as the proportion of firms with rated debt is similar for the private placement and bank loan samples. A higher proportion of the straight debt offerings is in the AA or better and A rated categories. If the rating of outstanding debt provides a proxy for default risk, firms announcing new bank loans and private placements have a higher default risk than those announcing straight debt offerings.

Myers and Majluf (1984) predict that abnormal performance is related to the sensitivity of the value of the securities issued to changes in the firm value. Default risk can affect the sensitivity. Panel B of table 7 provides two-day average prediction errors for each type of borrowing grouped by rating. For each type of borrowing arrangement, the abnormal returns are larger the higher the debt rating. This result is consistent with the prediction of Myers's and Majluf's model. The results in table 7 are *not* consistent, however, with the hypothesis that differences in default risk explain the difference in stock price

Table 7

Debt ratings for a random sample of 300 NYSE- and AMEX-traded non-financial firms announcing bank loan agreements, private placements, and straight debt offerings (1974–1983), and average two-day percentage prediction errors for firms grouped by rating of outstanding debt.

| | Panel A: Debt rating[a] | | | |
Type of event	Proportion of firms rated AA or better[b]	Proportion of firms rated A	Proportion of firms rated BAA or below	Proportion of firms with rated debt
Bank loan agreements	0.12 (5)	0.10 (4)	0.78 (25)	0.48 (34)
Private placements	0.12 (2)	0.20 (3)	0.68 (11)	0.47 (16)
Public straight debt offerings	0.31 (20)	0.41 (27)	0.28 (18)	0.69 (65)

| | Panel B: Average two-day prediction errors by debt rating[c] | | |
	Rated A or better	Rated BAA or below	Not rated
Bank loan agreements	3.89% (2.82)	1.77% (1.92)	1.76% (2.184)
Private placements	1.18% (1.68)	0.30% (0.211)	−2.03% (−2.90)
Public straight debt offerings	0.40% (1.72)	−0.32% (−1.42)	−1.08% (−1.45)

[a]Rating refers to the bond rating of the most recently issued debt prior to announcement. Ratings were obtained from *Moody's* manuals.
[b]Sample size is in parentheses.
[c]Z-value in parentheses; the null hypothesis is that the average standardized prediction error equals zero. $Z = \sqrt{N}(ASPE_t)$, where $ASPE_t$ is the average standardized prediction error and N is the number of firms in the sample.

response to different types of borrowing agreements. The proportion of firms in each rating category is similar for bank loans and private placements, but the abnormal return associated with bank loans is positive (on average and in each rating category), whereas the abnormal return for private placements is negative.

As table 3 indicates, firms in the bank loan sample are smaller than firms in the straight debt sample. To determine whether differences in firm size can explain differences in abnormal performance I estimate the following cross-sectional equation:

$$STRET_i = \alpha_1 + \alpha_2 STMVCS_i + \alpha_3 Issue\ I + \alpha_4 Issue\ II + \varepsilon_i, \qquad (1)$$

where $STRET_i$ is the two-day standardized prediction error for firm i;

$STMVCS_i$ is the market value of common stock divided by the standard error of the two-day prediction errors for firm i; *Issue I* equals 1 if issue is a private placement, zero otherwise; *Issue II* equals 1 if issue is a straight debt offering, zero otherwise; and ε_i is the error term.

The results are presented below (*t*-statistics in parentheses):

$$STRET_i = 0.305 + 1.17E^{-9}STMVCS_i - 0.554 \ Issue \ I - 0.306 \ Issue \ II,$$
$$(1.75) \quad (1.61) \qquad\qquad (-1.97) \qquad\quad (-1.83)$$

$$R^2 = 0.05.$$

The results indicate no statistically significant relation between the stock price response to the borrowing announcement and the size of the firm after controlling for issue type. These results indicate that differences in abnormal returns among borrowing agreements are not the result of differences in firm size.

I obtain similar results when firm size is measured as the sum of the market value of common stock and the book value of all other liabilities. In addition, I find no statistically significant relation between abnormal returns and firm size within each type of borrowing arrangement. Finally, I obtain similar results when the relative size of the offer, defined as the ratio of the amount of the offering to the market value of the firm's outstanding common stock, is substituted for the size variable in eq. (1).

6. Summary and conclusions

Significant positive abnormal returns accrue to stockholders of firms announcing new bank loan agreements, whereas negative abnormal returns accrue to stockholders of firms announcing private placements. In addition, negative and statistically significant abnormal returns are associated with the announcement of private placements and straight debt issues used to retire bank debt.

One possible explanation for the difference in abnormal performance is that bank loans differ in some important feature such as maturity. Alternatively, bank loans may differ from other types of borrowing because of some special service provided by banks with their lending activity. An analysis of differences in the maturity, borrower default risk, borrower size, and purpose of the borrowing indicates that differences in abnormal performance are not due *solely* to differences in characteristics of the loan or characteristics of the borrowers. This result, together with the evidence concerning the incidence of reserve requirements, suggests that banks provide some special service not available from other lenders. Further research is needed to identify that unique service or unique attribute of bank loans, and to explain its relation to the market value of the firm.

References

Asquith, Paul and David Mullins, 1986, Equity issues and offering dilution, Journal of Financial Economics 15, 61–90.

Bernanke, Ben, 1983, Non-monetary effects of the financial crisis in the propagation of the great depression, American Economic Review 73, 257–276.

Black, Fisher, 1975, Bank fund management in an efficient market, Journal of Financial Economics 2, 323–339.

Brealey, Richard and Stewart Myers, 1984, Principles of corporate finance (McGraw Hill, New York).

Campbell, Tim and William Kracaw, 1980, Information production, market signaling, and the theory of intermediation, Journal of Finance 35, 863–882.

Dann, Larry and Wayne Mikkelson, 1984, Convertible debt issuance, capital structure change and financing-related information: Some new evidence, Journal of Financial Economics 13, 157–186.

Diamond, Douglas, 1984, Financial intermediation and delegated monitoring, Review of Economic Studies 51, 393–414.

Easterbrook, Frank, 1984, Two agency-cost explanations of dividends, American Economic Review 74, 650–660.

Eckbo, Espen, 1986, Valuation effects of corporate debt offerings, Journal of Financial Economics 15, 119–152.

Fama, Eugene, 1980, Banking and the theory of finance, Journal of Monetary Economics 10, 10–19.

Fama, Eugene, 1985, What's different about banks?, Journal of Monetary Economics 15, 29–36.

Flannery, Mark J., 1986, Asymmetric information and risky debt maturity choice, Journal of Finance 41, 19–38.

Ho, Thomas, S.Y. and Ronald Singer, 1982, Bond indenture provisions and the risk of corporate debt, Journal of Financial Economics 10, 375–406.

Kane, Edward and Burton Malkiel, 1965, Bank portfolio allocation, deposit variability and the availability doctrine, Quarterly Journal of Economics 79, 113–134.

Leland, Haynes and David Pyle, 1977, Information asymmetries, financial structure and financial intermediaries, Journal of Finance 32, 371–387.

Masulis, Ronald and Ashok Korwar, 1986, Seasoned equity offerings: An empirical investigation, Journal of Financial Economics 15, 91–118.

Merton, Robert, 1974, On the pricing of corporate debt: The risk structure of interest rates, Journal of Finance 29, 449–465.

Mikkelson, Wayne and Megan Partch, 1986, Valuation effects of securities offerings and the issuance process, Journal of Financial Economics 15, 31–60.

Myers, Stewart and Nicholas Majluf, 1984, Corporate financing and investment decisions when firms have information that investors do not have, Journal of Financial Economics 13, 157–187.

Rozeff, Michael S., 1982, Growth, beta and agency costs as determinants of dividend payout ratios, Journal of Financial Research 5, 249–259.

Smith, Clifford and Jerold Warner, 1979, On financial contracting: An analysis of bond covenants, Journal of Financial Economics 7, 111–161.

Spong, Kenneth, 1985, Banking regulation: Its purposes, implementation and effects (Federal Reserve Bank of Kansas City, KS).

Zinbarg, Edward, 1975, The private placement loan agreement, Financial Analyst Journal 31, 33–52.

ON FINANCIAL CONTRACTING

An Analysis of Bond Covenants*

Clifford W. SMITH, Jr. and Jerold B. WARNER

University of Rochester, Rochester, NY 14627, USA

Received September 1978, revised version received May 1979

With risky debt outstanding, stockholder actions aimed at maximizing the value of their equity claim can result in a reduction in the value of both the firm and its outstanding bonds. We examine ways in which debt contracts are written to control the conflict between bondholders and stockholders. We find that extensive direct restrictions on production/investment policy would be expensive to employ and are not observed. However, dividend and financing policy restrictions are written to give stockholders incentives to follow a firm-value-maximizing production/investment policy. Taking into account how contracts control the bondholder-stockholder conflict leads to a number of testable propositions about the specific form of the debt contract that a firm will choose.

1. Introduction and summary

The conflict of interest between the firm's bondholders and its stockholders has been discussed by a number of authors. For example, Fama/Miller (1972, p. 179) indicate that under certain circumstances 'it is easy to construct examples in which a production plan that maximizes shareholder wealth does not maximize bondholder wealth, or vice versa'.[1] Citing an extreme case of the bondholder-stockholder conflict, Black (1976) points out that 'there is no easier way for a company to escape the burden of a debt than to pay out all of its assets in the form of a dividend, and leave the creditors holding an empty shell'.

In this paper, we examine how debt contracts are written to control the bondholder-stockholder conflict. We investigate the various kinds of bond covenants which are included in actual debt contracts. A bond covenant is a provision, such as a limitation on the payment of dividends, which restricts the firm from engaging in specified actions after the bonds are sold.

*This research is supported by the Managerial Economics Research Center, Graduate School of Management, University of Rochester. We are indebted to numerous colleagues, both those at the University of Rochester and elsewhere, for their help on this paper. We are especially grateful to Michael C. Jensen for his assistance.
[1]See also, Modigliani/Miller (1958, p. 293), Black/Cox (1976), Jensen/Meckling (1976), Miller (1977a), and Black/Miller/Posner (1978).

Our description of the specific provisions in debt contracts is based primarily on an American Bar Foundation compendium entitled *Commentaries on Indentures*. This volume contains both the standardized provisions which are included in the debt contract (the 'boilerplates') and a practitioner-oriented discussion of their use.

1.1. Sources of the bondholder–stockholder conflict

Corporations are 'legal fictions which serve as a nexus for a set of contracting relationships among individuals'.[2] To focus on the contract between the bondholders and the corporation, we assume that costs of enforcing other contracts are zero. For example, we assume that contracts between stockholders and managers costlessly induce managers to act as if they own all the firm's equity.

The corporation has an indefinite life and the set of contracts which comprise the corporation evolves over time: as the firm's investment opportunity set changes decisions are made about the real activities in which the firm engages and the financial contracts the firm sells. With risky bonds outstanding, management, acting in the stockholders' interest, has incentives to design the firm's operating characteristics and financial structure in ways which benefit stockholders to the detriment of bondholders. Because investment, financing, and dividend policies are endogenous, there are four major sources of conflict which arise between bondholders and stockholders:

Dividend payment. If a firm issues bonds and the bonds are priced assuming the firm will maintain its dividend policy, the value of the bonds is reduced by raising the dividend rate and financing the increase by reducing investment. At the limit, if the firm sells all its assets and pays a liquidating dividend to the stockholders, the bondholders are left with worthless claims.

Claim dilution. If the firm sells bonds, and the bonds are priced assuming that no additional debt will be issued, the value of the bondholders' claims is reduced by issuing additional debt of the same or higher priority.

Asset substitution. If a firm sells bonds for the stated purpose of engaging in low variance projects[3] and the bonds are valued at prices commensurate

---

[2]Jensen/Meckling (1976, p. 310).

[3]The importance of the variance rate is derived from the option pricing analysis of Black/Scholes (1973). In section A.1 of the appendix we discuss the determinants of the value of a bond issue where the bonds are single-payment contracts, and the market is efficient and competitive, without transactions costs, information costs, other agency costs, or taxes. The option pricing analysis assumes that the value of the firm will be independent of its financial structure. Our concern in this paper is with a world in which covenants can change the value of the firm. Hence a critical assumption of the option pricing analysis is violated; the value of the firm will, in general, be a function of the covenants which are offered. The option pricing

with that low risk, the value of the stockholders' equity rises and the value of the bondholders' claim is reduced by substituting projects which increase the firm's variance rate.[4]

Underinvestment.   Myers (1977) suggests that a substantial portion of the value of the firm is composed of intangible assets in the form of future investment opportunities. A firm with outstanding bonds can have incentives to reject projects which have a positive net present value if the benefit from accepting the project accrues to the bondholders.

The bondholder–stockholder conflict is of course recognized by capital market participants. Rational bondholders recognize the incentives faced by the stockholders. They understand that after the bonds are issued, any action which increases the wealth of the stockholders will be taken. In ricing the bond issue, bondholders make estimates of the behavior of the stockholders, given the investment, financing, and dividend policies available to the stockholders. The price which bondholders pay for the issue will be lower to reflect the possibility of subsequent wealth transfers to stockholders.[5] The pricing of the bond issue is discussed in more detail in the appendix.

1.2. Control of the bondholder–stockholder conflict: The competing hypotheses

There seems to be general agreement within the finance profession that the bondholder–stockholder relationship entails conflict and that the prices in security markets behave as if all security-holders form rational expectations about the stockholders' behavior after the bonds are issued. However, there is disagreement about whether the total value of the firm is influenced by the way in which the bondholder–stockholder conflict is controlled. There are

---

analysis does not address the issue of the endogeneity of the stockholders' behavior because variables such as the value of the firm's assets or the variance rate are treated as fixed rather than as decision variables. Therefore, the implications drawn from the option pricing model are only suggestive. In section A.2 of the appendix, we suggest how the endogeneity of investment policy affects the optimal choice of financial structure and the value of the firm's financial claims.

[4]The mere exchange of low-risk assets for high-risk assets does not alter the value of the firm if both assets have the same net present values. However, stockholders will have incentives to purchase projects with negative net present values if the increase in the firm's variance rate from accepting those projects is sufficiently large. Even though such projects reduce the total value of the firm, the value of the equity rises.

[5]Similarly, the value of the common stock at the time the bonds are issued will be higher to reflect possible transfers which shareholders will be able to effect. However, this is not to suggest that there is always a positive price at which the bonds can be sold. If the probability of a complete wealth transfer to stockholders prior to required payments to bondholders is 1, then the bonds will sell for a zero price.

two competing hypotheses. We call them the Irrelevance Hypothesis and the Costly Contracting Hypothesis.

1.2.1. The Irrelevance Hypothesis

The Irrelevance Hypothesis is that the manner of controlling the bondholder–stockholder conflict does not change the value of the firm.

Irrelevance under a fixed investment policy. In the Modigliani/Miller (1958) or Fama/Miller (1972) models the firm's investment policy is assumed fixed.[6] As long as the firm's total net cash flows are fixed, the value of the firm will not be changed by the existence or non-existence of protective covenants; with fixed cash flows, any gain which covenants give bondholders is a loss to stockholders, and vice versa. Covenants merely alter the distribution of a set of payoffs which is fixed to the firm's claimholders as a whole, and the choice of specific financial contracts is irrelevant to the value of the firm.

Irrelevance when investment policy is not fixed. Dividend payout, asset substitution, and underinvestment all represent potential opportunities for wealth transfer to stockholders. When these opportunities are available, the firm's investment policy cannot be regarded as fixed because it is likely to be altered by the presence of risky debt. The total value of the firm could be reduced if stockholders engage in actions which maximize the value of their own claims, but not the total value of the firm. However, even if investment policy cannot be regarded as fixed, mechanisms other than covenants exist which could be sufficient to induce the firm's stockholders to choose a firm-value-maximizing production/investment policy.

The forces exerted by external markets could induce the stockholders to maximize the value of the firm. Long (1973) suggests that the firm will accept all projects with a positive net present value if recapitalization is costless. Fama (1978a) argues that if takeovers are costless, the firm's owners always have an incentive to maximize the value of the firm. Additionally, ongoing firms have other incentives to follow a value-maximizing policy. Cases can be constructed in which a firm with a long history of deviating from such a policy in order to maximize only shareholder wealth will be worth less than it would have, had a value-maximizing policy been followed and expected to continue.

Ownership of the firm's claims could be structured in a way which controls the stockholders' incentive to follow a strategy which does not maximize the total value of the firm. Galai/Masulis (1976) suggest that if all investors hold equal proportions of both the firm's debt and the firm's equity

---

[6]The mechanism by which this fixity occurs is not well specified. However, the assumption of zero transactions costs in these models suggests that contractual provisions which fix investment policy and control the bondholder–stockholder conflict can be costlessly written and enforced.

issues, wealth redistributions among claimholders leave all investors indifferent. In such a case, bondholder–stockholder conflict arising over investment policy is costlessly controlled, and, even with risky debt, the stockholders will still follow a firm-value-maximizing strategy.

Thus, even when the firm's investment policy is not fixed, under the Irrelevance Hypothesis the stockholders' behavior is not altered by the presence of the bondholder–stockholder conflict. The influence of external markets or the possibility of restructuring the firm's claims implies that the choice of financial contracts is irrelevant to the value of the firm.

1.2.2. The Costly Contracting Hypothesis

The Costly Contracting Hypothesis is that control of the bondholder–stockholder conflict through financial contracts can increase the value of the firm. Like the Irrelevance Hypothesis, the Costly Contracting Hypothesis recognizes the influence which external markets and the possibility of recapitalization exert on the firm's choice of investment policy. However, this hypothesis presupposes that those factors, while controlling to some extent the bondholder–stockholder conflict, are insufficient to induce the stockholders to maximize the value of the firm rather than maximizing the value of the equity. The Costly Contracting Hypothesis underlies the work of Jensen/Meckling (1976), Myers (1977), and Miller (1977a).

Financial contracting is assumed to be costly. However, bond covenants, even if they involve costs, can increase the value of the firm at the time bonds are issued by reducing the opportunity loss which results when stockholders of a levered firm follow a policy which does not maximize the value of the firm. Furthermore, in the case of the claim dilution problem (which involves only a wealth transfer), if covenants lower the costs which bondholders incur in monitoring stockholders, the cost-reducing benefits of the covenants accrue to the firm's owners. With such covenants, the firm is worth more at the time the bonds are issued.

Under the Costly Contracting Hypothesis, there is a unique optimal set of financial contracts which maximizes the value of the firm. Note, however, that the bondholder–stockholder conflict would be resolved and its associated costs driven to zero without bond covenants if the firm never issued any risky debt. But for the firm to follow such a policy is costly if it is optimal to have risky debt in the firm's capital structure. Thus, the Costly Contracting Hypothesis presupposes that there are benefits associated with the inclusion of risky debt. Others have suggested benefits associated with issuance of risky debt which relate to, for example, (1) information asymmetries and signalling [Stiglitz (1972) and Ross (1977)], (2) taxes [Modigliani/Miller (1958, 1966)], (3) agency costs of equity financing [Jensen/Meckling (1976)], (4) differential transactions and flotation costs, and (5) unbundling of riskbearing and capital ownership [Fama (1978b)]. We do not address the issue of the exact nature of the benefit from the issuance of risky debt.

1.3. Evidence provided by an examination of bond covenants

In this paper, we use the data base provided by the *Commentaries* to distinguish between the Irrelevance and the Costly Contracting Hypotheses. Much of our evidence is qualitative rather than quantitative. Many social scientists are reluctant to consider such observations as evidence. However, qualitative evidence such as that provided by the *Commentaries* is frequently employed in the social sciences and in particular the property rights/economic analysis of law literature [see Alchian/Demsetz (1972), Cheung (1973), Coase (1960), Demsetz (1967), Manne (1967), and Posner (1972)]. Furthermore, qualitative evidence appears to have been instrumental in the development of the natural sciences [e.g., Darwin (1859)].[7]

Observation of persisting institutions represents important empirical evidence. However, we must specify precisely the nature of the evidence afforded by the observations under a particular hypothesis. After all, evidence (whether qualitative or quantitative) is useful only if it distinguishes among competing hypotheses;[8] what separates good empirical evidence from bad is not whether it can be reduced to numbers, but whether it increases our knowledge of how the world functions.

Debt covenants are a persistent phenomenon. They have been included in debt contracts for hundreds of years,[9] and over time the corporate debt contract which contains them has evolved into 'undoubtedly the most involved financial document that has been devised'.[10] The covenants discussed in *Commentaries* are representative of the covenants found in actual practice. As discussed by Rodgers (1965) and in the preface to the *Commentaries*, specific sections of the *Commentaries* were written by those considered to be the leading practitioners in their field. To check the correspondence between *Commentaries* and observed contractual provisions, we selected a random sample of 87 public issues of debt which were

---

[7]Darwin is perhaps the most familiar example; however, it is not the best. Although Darwin presents no quantitative evidence to support his hypotheses, his discussions are typically phrased in quantitative terms, referring to testable propositions about population sizes, etc. However, other areas of biology were developed totally without quantitative evidence. For example, see von Baer's work on embryology, Barnard's work in physiology, and Cuvier's work on taxonomy. For a general description of the development of the science of biology, see Coleman (1971).

[8]This proposition is well established in the philosophy literature. See Kuhn (1970), Nagel (1961), and Popper (1959).

[9]Rodgers (1965) discusses the evolution of debt contracts; he also discusses the history of the American Bar Foundation's Corporate Trust Indenture Project, under which the *Commentaries* were written.

[10]Kennedy (1961, p. 1).

registered with the Securities and Exchange Commission between January, 1974 and December, 1975. The standardized provisions of the type discussed in *Commentaries* are used frequently: 90.8 percent of the bonds contain restrictions on the issuance of additional debt, 23.0 percent have restrictions on dividend payments, 39.1 percent restrict merger activities, and 35.6 percent constrain the firm's disposition of assets. Furthermore, we found that when a particular provision is included, a boilerplate from *Commentaries* is used almost exclusively.

It seems reasonable that the covenants discussed in *Commentaries* have not arisen merely by chance; rather, they take their current form and have survived because they represent a contractual solution which is efficient from the standpoint of the firm.[11] As Alchian (1950) indicates, 'success (survival) accompanies relative superiority';[12] and 'whenever successful enterprises are observed, the elements common to those observed successes will be associated with success and copied by others in their pursuit of profits or success'.[13] Hence the *Commentaries* represents a powerful piece of evidence on efficient forms of the financial contract.

However, Miller (1977b, p. 273) indicates an important constraint on the use of this evidence: 'The most that we can safely assert about the evolutionary process underlying market equilibrium is that harmful heuristics, like harmful mutations in nature, will die out. Neutral mutations that serve no function, but do no harm, can persist indefinitely.' In addition to observing the persistence of covenants, we must demonstrate that the covenants involve out-of-pocket or opportunity costs for the firm, since the mere existence of covenants is consistent with both the Irrelevance and the Costly Contracting Hypotheses. But if covenants are costly, as we find in this paper, we must reject the Irrelevance Hypothesis. Similarly, the existence of the costly incentive-related covenants we discuss is inconsistent with the argument that external market forces and the possibility of restructuring the firm's claims provide a sufficient incentive for stockholders to follow a firm-value-maximizing policy. On the other hand, costly incentive-related covenants are exactly what would be expected under the Costly Contracting Hypothesis.

Given that the costs of restrictive covenants are positive, an important question is whether those costs are economically significant. The costs of particular covenants cannot easily be measured, and we present no direct evidence on the dollar magnitude of the costs. In a number of instances we use the assumption that such costs are important to generate testable propositions about the firm's capital structure. Although the evidence on the

---

[11]See Alchian (1950) and Stigler (1958) for a discussion of the survivorship principle.
[12]Alchian (1950, p. 213).
[13]Alchian (1950, p. 218).

importance of the bondholder–stockholder conflict is by no means con-clusive, in several cases where the predictions of the analysis have been tested, the evidence is consistent with the theory. It appears that the Costly Contracting Hypothesis, which explains how firms reduce the costs of the bondholder–stockholder conflict, helps to account for the variation in debt contracts across firms. In contrast, the Irrelevance Hypothesis, while con-sistent with any observed set of contracts, yields no predictions about the form of the debt contract.

1.4. Overview of the paper

Observed debt covenants are discussed in section 2. To facilitate the discussion, observed covenants are grouped into four categories: produc-tion/investment covenants, dividend covenants, financing covenants, and bonding covenants. We use a common format for the discussion of each covenant; a particular type of covenant is first described, and its impact then analyzed.

Covenants which directly restrict the shareholders' choice of production/in-vestment policy, are discussed in section 2.1. These covenants impose re-strictions on the firm's holdings of financial investments, on the disposition of assets, and on the firm's merger activity. The observed constraints place few specific limitations on the firm's choice of investment policy. However, it is important to realize that, because of the cash flow identity, investment, dividend, and financing policy are not independent; they must be determined simultaneously. Thus, covenants which restrict dividend and financing policy also restrict investment policy.

Bond covenants which directly restrict the payment of dividends are considered in section 2.2. The dividend restriction does not take the form of a constant dollar limitation. Instead, the maximum allowable dividend payment is a function of both accounting earnings and the proceeds from the sale of new equity. The analysis suggests that the dividend covenant places an implicit constraint on the investment policy of the firm and provides the stockholders with incentives to follow a firm-value-maximizing produc-tion/investment policy.

Financing policy covenants are discussed in section 2.3. These covenants restrict not only the issuance of senior debt, but the issuance of debt of any priority. In addition, the firm's right to incur other fixed obligations such as leases is restricted. These restrictions appear to reduce the underinvestment incentives discussed by Myers (1977). In section 2.4, convertibility, callability, and sinking fund provisions are also examined. These provisions appear to specify payoffs to bondholders in a way which also controls bondholder-stockholder conflict.

In section 2.5, we analyze covenants which specify bonding activities –

expenditures made by the firm which control the bondholder–stockholder conflict. These bonding activities include the provision of audited financial statements, the specification of accounting techniques, the required purchase of insurance, and the periodic provision of a statement, signed by the firm's officers, indicating compliance with the covenants.

Just as the covenants described in section 2 are persistent phenomena, so are the institutions for enforcing these contractual restrictions. The enforcement of bond covenants within the existing institutional arrangements is the subject of section 3. The Trust Indenture Act of 1939 restricts the provisions of the debt contract for public issues in a way which makes the enforcement of tightly restrictive covenants very expensive. Another enforcement cost emanates from the legal liability which bondholders incur when they exercise control over the firm. Default remedies which are available to the firm, and their associated costs, are also discussed.

Our conclusions are presented in section 4.

2. A description and analysis of bond covenants

We group observed covenants into four categories: production/investment covenants, dividend covenants, financing covenants, and bonding covenants. Our discussion of the covenants covers all the restrictions reported in *Commentaries*; we have not singled out only particular types of covenants for discussion.[14]

2.1. Restrictions on the firm's production/investment policy

The stockholders' production/investment decisions could be directly constrained by explicitly specifying the projects which the firm is allowed to undertake. Alternatively, if it were costless to enforce, the debt contract could simply require the shareholders to accept all projects (and engage in only those actions) with positive net present values. Although certain covenants directly restrict the firm's investment policy, debt contracts discussed in *Commentaries* do not generally contain extensive restrictions of either form.

2.1.1. Restrictions on investments

Description.   Bond covenants frequently restrict the extent to which the firm can become a claimholder in another business enterprise. That restriction, known as the 'investment' restriction, applies to common stock investments, loans, extensions of credit, and advances.[15] Alternative forms of this cov-

---

[14]However, note that we do not discuss the standard contractual provisions governing procedural matters (e.g., face amount, redemption procedure) which are necessary to define the firm's obligations as debt.

[15]Investments in direct obligations of the United States of America, prime commercial paper, and certificates of deposit are frequently excepted. *Commentaries* (p. 461, sample covenant 1A).

enant suggested in *Commentaries* either (1) flatly prohibit financial investments of this kind, (2) permit these financial investments only if net tangible assets meet a certain minimum, or (3) permit such investments subject to either an aggregate dollar limitation or a limitation representing a prespecified percentage of the firm's capitalization (owners' equity plus long-term debt).

Analysis. We suggest that stockholders contractually restrict their ability to acquire financial assets in order to limit their ability to engage in asset substitution after the bonds are issued.[16,17] However, the inclusion of the investment covenant imposes opportunity costs. First, if there are economies of scale in raising additional capital, or costs associated with changing dividends, then allowing the purchase of financial assets can reduce these costs.[18] Second, if a firm is involved in merger activities, the purchase of equity claims of the target firm prior to the merger can also provide benefits. Thus, the Costly Contracting Hypothesis predicts that bond contracts of firms involved in merger activities, for which the opportunity cost of restricting 'investments' is therefore high, will contain less restrictive investment covenants. However, our analysis does not predict which of the above forms the investment restriction will take.

2.1.2. Restrictions on the disposition of assets

Description. 'The transfer of the assets of the obligor substantially as an entirety' can be restricted by a standard boilerplate.[19] The contract can also require that the firm not 'otherwise than in the ordinary course of business, sell, lease, transfer, or otherwise dispose of any substantial part of its properties and assets, including...any manufacturing plant or substantially all properties and assets constituting the business of a division, branch, or other unit operation'.[20] Another restriction is to permit asset disposition only

[16]Given that stockholders of most corporations are subject to double taxation of their returns, financial assets are negative net present value projects whose acquisition reduces the value of the firm. However, shareholders will have an incentive to purchase such assets if acquiring them increases the variability of the firm's cash flows by enough to offset the reduction in the value of the firm. Thus, the investments covenant raises the price to the stockholders of increasing the variability of the firm's cash flows.

[17]An alternative explanation for the investment restriction is that it reduces the conflict between managers and stockholders. The investment restriction typically applies to 'any person'. Hence managers are restricted from making loans to themselves, as well as from investing the firm's resources in firms which the managers own. We cannot reject this explanation for the investment restriction. However, it is not clear why bondholders have a comparative advantage (over stockholders) in policing managerial behavior of this form.

[18]That the purchase of short-term riskless assets is often allowed under the investments restriction is consistent with this explanation. Stockholders cannot increase the variability of cash flows with riskless assets. Furthermore, Treasury Bills dominate cash, which has a zero pecuniary return.

[19]*Commentaries* (p. 423).

[20]*Commentaries* (p. 427, sample covenant 2).

up to a fixed dollar amount, or only so long as (1) the proceeds from the sale are applied to the purchase of new fixed assets, or (2) some fraction of the proceeds is used to retire the firm's debt.[21]

Analysis.   The Costly Contracting Hypothesis suggests that restrictions on the sale of substantial units of the firm's assets are observed because, in general, the proceeds if assets are sold piecemeal will be less than if sold as a going concern.[22] By imposing the higher cost of piecemeal sale, this covenant also raises the cost to stockholders of substituting variance increasing assets for those currently owned by the firm.

One cost associated with flat prohibitions on the sale of particular assets rises from the fact that the firm is not permitted to divest itself of those assets whose value to others is greater than the value to itself. Thus the restriction which permits asset sale if the proceeds are applied to the purchase of new fixed assets lowers this opportunity cost. However, a provision which permits such asset exchange is costly because it allows for the possibility of obtaining variance increasing negative net present value assets in the exchange. The stipulation that a fraction of the proceeds from the sale of assets be used for the retirement of the firm's debt makes asset substitution more expensive for stockholders by requiring a concurrent increase in the coverage on, and thus the value of, the outstanding debt.

2.1.3. Secured debt

Description.   Securing debt gives the bondholders title to pledged assets until the bonds are paid in full. Thus, when secured debt is issued the firm cannot dispose of the pledged assets without first obtaining permission of the bondholders.

Analysis.   We suggest that the issuance of secured debt lowers the total costs of borrowing by controlling the incentives for stockholders to take projects which reduce the value of the firm; since bondholders hold title to the assets, secured debt limits asset substitution. Secured debt also lowers administrative costs and enforcement costs by ensuring that the lender has clear title to the assets and by preventing the lender's claim from being jeopardized if the borrower subsequently issues additional debt. In addition, collateralization

[21]Such provisions typically apply to the retirement of the firm's funded (i.e., long-term) debt. The covenant in a particular bond issue requires that *all* the firm's debt be retired on a prorated basis. To require that only the particular bond issue containing the covenant be retired might well violate the firm's other debt agreements.

[22]Given that selling substantial portions of the firm's assets can be illegal under, for example, the Uniform Fraudulent Conveyance Act, the standard boilerplate would seem redundant. Our theory does not explain the redundancy of the terms of the bond contract and the constraints implied by the legal system. But in the case of this boilerplate, we suggest that, should the assets of the firm be sold, subjecting the firm's managers to civil and criminal liability alone is a more costly remedy than allowing the bondholders to put the firm in default.

reduces expected foreclosure expenses because it is less expensive to tsae possession of property to which the lender already has established title.

However, secured debt involves out of pocket costs (e.g., required reports to the debt-holders, filing fees, and other administrative expenses). Securing debt also involves opportunity costs by restricting the firm from potentially profitable dispositions of collateral.

The Costly Contracting Hypothesis leads to two predictions about the use of secured debt. First, if the firm goes into bankruptcy proceedings and the collateral. is judged necessary for the continued operation of the firm, the bankruptcy judge can prohibit the bondholders from taking possession of the property. Thus for firms where liquidation is more likely than re-organization (e.g., for smaller firms), the issuance of secured debt will be greater. Second, we would expect more frequent use of secured debt the less specialized the firm's resources. To the extent that assets (such as a patent right) are highly specialized and firm-specific, their value is greater to the firm than in the market place. Consequently, it will be costly to the stockholders if they dispose of such assets in order to engage in asset substitution. The more specialized the assets, the more costly is asset substitution to stockholders, the tighter the implicit constraint on asset sale, and thus the less likely is the use of secured debt.[23]

2.1.4. Restrictions on mergers

Description. Some indenture agreements contain a flat prohibition on mergers. Others permit the acquisition of other firms provided that certain conditions are met. For example, *Commentaries* suggests restrictions in which the merger is permitted only if the net tangible assets of the firm, calculated on a post-merger basis, meet a certain dollar minimum, or are at least a certain fraction of long-term debt. The merger can also be made contingent on there being no default on any indenture provision after the transaction is completed.

The acquisition and consolidation of the firm into another can be permitted subject to certain requirements. For example, the corporation into which the company is merged must assume all of the obligations in the initial indenture. Article 800 of the American Bar Foundation *Model Debenture Indenture Provisions* also requires that there be no act of default after completion of the consolidation, and that the company certify that fact through the delivery to the trustee of an officer's certificate and an opinion of counsel.

Analysis. Since the stockholders of the two firms must approve a merger, the market value of the equity claims of both the acquired and acquiring firm must be expected to rise or the merger will not be approved by

---

[23]For a further discussion of secured debt, see Scott (1977) and Smith/Warner (1979).

stockholders of the respective firms.[24] A merger between two firms usually results in changes in the value of particular classes of outstanding claims because both the asset and liability structure of the resulting firm differ from that of the predecessor firms. The effects of a merger on the value of particular claims depend upon: (1) the degree of synergy brought about by the merger, (2) the resources consumed in accomplishing the merger, (3) the variance rates of the pre-merger firms' cash flows, (4) the correlation coefficient between the merged firms' cash flows, and (5) the capital structure (i.e., ratio of face value of debt to market value of all claims) of the respective firms. A merger leaves the value of outstanding debt claims unaffected if (1) the merger involves no synergy, (2) there are no transactions costs, (3) the pre-merger firm's cash flows have equal variance rates, (4) the correlation coefficient between the merged firms' cash flows is $+1$, and (5) the pre-merger firms have the same capital structure.

With no contractual constraints against mergers, the value of the bondholders' claims can be reduced due to the effect of a difference in variance rates or a difference in capital structures. Our analysis implies, then, that merger restrictions limit the stockholders' ability to use mergers to increase either the firm's variance rate or the debt to asset ratio to the detriment of the bondholders. Note that to the extent that synergistic mergers are prevented by this covenant, the firm suffers an opportunity loss.[25]

2.1.5. Covenants requiring the maintenance of assets

Description. The covenants we have discussed constrain production/investment policy by prohibiting certain actions. However, the firm's operating decisions can also be limited by *requiring* that it take certain actions, that it invest in certain projects, or hold particular assets. Examples of such covenants are those requiring the maintenance of the firm's properties and maintenance of the firm's working capital (i.e., current assets less current liabilities).[26] *Commentaries* offers covenants which require the firm to maintain working capital above a certain minimum level. Frequently, activities

---

[24]This is consistent with the evidence of Dodd/Ruback (1977) and Bradley (1978). They find that, on average, there is positive abnormal performance for common stocks of both acquiring and acquired firms.

[25]As we discuss in section 2.3, the indenture agreements typically require that the firm comply with one or more tests (such as minimum ratios of net tangible assets to funded debt) in order to issue additional debt. According to *Commentaries*, when additional debt obligations are incurred through a merger, for purposes of the tests, the debt incurred can be treated as having been issued as of the merger. Thus, financing policy covenants can be employed to control mergers.

[26]Another restriction on increases in the risk of the firm's activities is a covenant requiring that the firm stay in the same line of business. For example, the Associated Dry Goods Credit Corporation Notes of 1983 require that the firm 'not engage in any business other than dealing in Deferred Payment Accounts'. This covenant thus makes it more costly to engage in asset substitution.

such as mergers are made contingent upon the maintenance of working capital.

Analysis. While a covenant can require that the firm maintain its properties, such a covenant will not have much impact if it is expensive to enforce. However, if the maintenance is performed by an independent agent, enforcement costs are expected to be lower and such a restriction will be effective. For example, in the shipping industry, where maintenance services are typically provided through third parties, bond covenants frequently explicitly include service and dry-docking schedules in the indenture.

We suggest that the working capital requirement is included because any violation of the covenant provides a signal to the lender. This signal can result in renegotiation of the debt contract, an alternative preferable to default when bankruptcy is more costly than renegotiation. This hypothesis is consistent with the interpretation of the working capital covenant in *Commentaries* (p. 453): 'If a breach of the covenant occurs, the lender is in a position to use this early warning to take whatever remedial action is necessary.'

2.1.6. *Covenants which indirectly restrict production/investment policy*

Stockholder use (or misuse) of production/investment policy frequently involves not some action, but the failure to take a certain action (e.g., failure to accept a positive net present value project). Because of this, investment policy can be very expensive to monitor, since ascertaining that the firm's production/investment policy does not maximize the firm's market value depends on magnitudes which are costly to observe. Solutions to this problem are not obvious. For example, if the indenture were to require the bondholders (rather than the stockholders) to establish the firm's investment policy, the problem would not be solved; the bondholders, acting in their self interest, would choose an investment policy which maximized the value of the bonds, not the value of the firm.[27] In addition, there are other costs associated with giving bondholders a role in establishing the firm's investment policy. For instance, as we discuss in section 3, legal costs can be imposed on bondholders if they are deemed to have assumed control of the corporation.

However, direct restrictions on the stockholder's choice of production/investment policy are only one way to limit the projects in which the firm can engage. Covenants constraining the firm's dividend and financing policies can also be written in a way which serves a similar function, since the firm's production/investment, dividend, and financing policies are linked through the cash flow identity. If direct restrictions on production/investment policy

---

[27]Jensen/Meckling refer to this as the symmetry property.

were sufficiently expensive to enforce, dividend and financing policy covenants would be the only efficient way of constraining the firm's actions.

2.2. *Bond covenants restricting the payment of dividends*

Description. Cash dividend payments to stockholders, if financed by a reduction in investment, reduce the value of the firm's bonds by decreasing the expected value of the firm's assets at the maturity date of the bonds, making default more likely. Thus, it is not surprising that bond covenants frequently[28] restrict the payment of cash dividends to shareholders.[29] Since the payment of dividends *in cash* is just one form which distributions to stockholders can take, actual dividend covenants reflect alternative possibilities. For example, if the firm enters the market and repurchases its own stock the coverage on the debt decreases in exactly the same way as it would if a cash dividend were paid. The constraints discussed in *Commentaries* relate not only to cash dividends, but to 'all distributions on account of or in respect of capital stock... whether they be dividends, redemptions, purchases, retirements, partial liquidations or capital reductions and whether in cash, in kind, or in the form of debt obligations of the company'.[30]

The dividend covenant usually establishes a limit on distributions to stockholders by defining an inventory of funds available for dividend payments over the life of the bonds.[31] The inventory is not constant; rather, it is allowed to change as a function of certain variables whose values can be influenced by the stockholders. Typically, the inventory of funds available for the payment of dividends in quarter τ, D_τ^*, can be expressed as

$$D_\tau^* = k\left(\sum_{t=0}^{\tau} E_t\right) + \left(\sum_{t=0}^{\tau} S_t\right) + F - \left(\sum_{t=0}^{\tau-1} D_t\right), \tag{1}$$

[28]Kalay (1979) reports that in a sample of 150 randomly selected industrial firms, every firm had a dividend restriction in at least one of its debt instruments.

[29]According to Henn (1970, pp. 648–656) most states have also limited the source of dividends to legally prescribed funds. Various laws define the funds legally available for dividends in terms of (1) earned surplus, (2) net profits or net earnings, (3) non-impairment of capital, (4) insolvency, or some combination. Directors are often made liable by statute (and possibly subject to criminal penalties) for dividends paid out of funds not legally available. Even apart from statutes expressing such limitation, distribution of dividends which would render the corporation insolvent is probably wrongful in most jurisdictions on principles of the law of creditors' rights.

[30]*Commentaries* (p. 405). It should be noted that the problem of constraining the firm's investment in financial assets, which we discussed in section 2.1, is sometimes handled within the dividend covenant. Distributions restricted under the dividend covenant can be defined to include purchases of securities by the firm. Under this definition, the stockholders of the firm can choose to hold any amount of financial investments so long as they give up an equal amount of dividends.

[31]Kennedy (1961, p. 137). In his study of dividend covenants, Kalay (1978) finds that most of them take the form discussed here.

where, for quarter t,

E_t is net earnings,
S_t is the proceeds from the sale of common stock net of transactions costs,
F is a number which is fixed over the life of the bonds, known as the 'dip',
k is a constant, $0 \leq k \leq 1$.

Hence the inventory of funds is a positive function of the earnings which the firm has accumulated, a positive function of the extent to which the firm has sold new equity claims, and a negative function of the dividends paid since the bonds were issued at $t = 0$.

The payment of a dividend is not permitted if its payment would cause the inventory to be drawn below zero. The inventory can become negative if the firm's earnings are negative. In that case, no dividend is permitted. However, stockholders are not required to make up the deficiency.[32] Thus the dividend payment in quarter τ, D_τ, must satisfy the constraint

$$D_\tau \leq \max[0, D_\tau^*]. \tag{2}$$

Analysis. This form of dividend covenant has several interesting features. The dividend restriction is not an outright prohibition on the payment of dividends. In fact, the stockholders are permitted to have any level of dividends they choose, so long as the payment of those dividends is financed out of new earnings or through the sale of new equity claims. The dividend covenant acts as a restriction not on dividends *per se*, but on the payment of dividends financed by issuing debt or by the sale of the firm's existing assets, either of which would reduce the coverage on, and thus the value of, the debt.

The dividend covenant described in eqs. (1) and (2) coupled with the cash-flow identity that inflows equal outflows constrain investment policy.[33] The cash-flow identity for the firm can be expressed as

$$D_t + R_t + P_t + I_t \equiv \phi_t + S_t + B_t, \tag{3}$$

where, for quarter t,

D_t is the dividend paid,
R_t is interest paid,
P_t is debt principal paid,
I_t is new investment,
ϕ_t is the firm's cash flow.

---

[32]Given limited liability, a covenant requiring that a positive balance be maintained in the inventory and that individual shareholders be assessed for deficiencies is probably not enforceable without considerable cost.

[33]We would like to thank John Long for suggesting this expositional model and for helpful discussions on this point.

S_t is the proceeds from the sale of equity net of transactions cost,
B_t is the proceeds from the sale of bonds net of transactions cost.

The firm's cash flow, ϕ_t, can be expressed as[34]

$$\phi_t \equiv E_t + d_t + R_t + L_t, \tag{4}$$

where, for quarter t,

E_t is the firm's net earnings,
d_t is depreciation,
L_t is the book value of any assets liquidated.[35]

Substituting (3) into (4) and solving for D_t yields

$$D_t \equiv E_t + d_t + R_t + L_t - I_t + S_t + B_t - R_t - P_t. \tag{5}$$

To see how the dividend covenant constrains investment policy, consider the simplest case. Assume that an all equity firm sells bonds at par with a covenant that it will issue no additional debt over the life of the bonds (i.e., $B_t = 0$ for $t \neq 0$, and $P_t = 0$ for $t \neq T$). If we also assume that $F \equiv 0$, and $k \equiv 1$, then substituting (5) and (1) into (2) yields the condition for dividends in quarter τ to be positive,

$$B_0 \leqq \sum_{t=0}^{\tau} (I_t - L_t - d_t). \tag{6}$$

The right-hand side of (6) is simply the cumulative change in the book value of the firm's assets since the bonds were sold. Thus in this simple case, the dividend covenant requires that for dividends to be paid in the quarter the bonds are issued, investment must be large enough that the net change in the book value of the firm's assets be no less than the net proceeds from the sale of the debt – the firm cannot borrow to pay dividends. The constraint also requires that in subsequent quarters investment be large enough for the book value of the firm's assets to be maintained at that level.

If the assumptions that $k = 1$ and $F = 0$ are now relaxed, then eq. (6) becomes

$$B_0 + (1 - k)\left(\sum_{t=0}^{\tau} E_t\right) - F \leqq \sum_{t=0}^{\tau} (I_t - L_t - d_t). \tag{7}$$

---

[34]For purposes of illustration we assume that the accrual is depreciation and that all items other than depreciation, interest payments, and liquidations affect cash flows and earnings in the same way.

[35]L_t is defined as the book value of assets liquidated when earnings includes gains or losses on the sale of assets. If such gains or losses are not included in earnings, then L_t is the proceeds from the liquidation.

Setting k between zero and one requires that if the firm has positive earnings, the book value of the assets of the firm must actually increase in order for dividends to be paid.[36]

By placing a maximum on distributions, the dividend covenant effectively places a minimum on investment expenditures by the owners of the firm, as Myers and Kalay (1979) argue. This reduces the underinvestment problem discussed by Myers, since so long as the firm *has* to invest, profitable projects are less likely to be turned down.

While having a tight dividend constraint controls the stockholders incentives associated with the dividend payout problem, there are several associated costs. An outright prohibition on dividends or allowing dividends but setting k less than one increases the probability that the firm will be forced to invest when it has no available profitable projects. Investment in securities of other firms is not always possible, since purchases of capital market instruments (which in the absence of corporate taxes have zero net present value) are frequently prohibited by the investments covenant we discussed in section 2.1. Even if financial investments are not restricted, Kalay argues that if the firm pays income taxes on its earnings, the taxation of the returns from the financial assets makes them negative net present value projects.[37]

The tighter restriction on dividends implied by a lower k also increases the stockholders' incentives to engage in asset substitution, and increases the gain to the firm's shareholders from choosing high variance, negative net present value projects. Assume that negative net present value projects generate negative accounting earnings. Then from the first term of eq. (1), the inventory available for dividends will be reduced by taking such a project. The lower the value of k, the smaller the reduction in the inventory. To the extent that dividends transfer wealth to stockholders, the marginal impact of lowering k is thus to increase the gain (or decrease the loss) to shareholders from accepting such projects. However, as we discuss below, a lower k also confers benefits, since it reduces the stockholders' incentive to engage in 'creative accounting' to increase reported earnings.

If it is costly to restrict dividends, not all debt agreements will include a dividend restriction. Dividend covenants would be expected only if there are offsetting benefits. One prediction of our analysis is that the presence of a dividend covenant should be related to the maturity of the debt. Thus, short-

---

[36]The value of k is less than 1 in about 20 percent of the dividend covenants which Kalay (1979) examines. According to *Commentaries* (p. 414), the 'dip', F, is equal to about a year's earnings. Kalay finds that the mean value of the dip, as a fraction of earnings, is indeed approximately 1.

[37]We conjecture that the specification of a positive F in the debt contract is directed at reducing the costs of temporarily having no profitable investment projects and being unable to pay dividends. In spite of the increased payouts it allows, the dip permits a dividend to be paid to shareholders even when earnings are negative and the firm has not sold new equity.

term debt instruments (such as commercial paper) are less likely to contain dividend restrictions than long-term debt; if liquidation of the firm's assets within a short period of time is sufficiently costly to the shareholders, they are better off not selling the firm's assets for cash in order to pay themselves a dividend. This implicit constraint on dividend payout becomes less restrictive the longer the time to maturity of the debt, and the cost-offsetting benefits of an explicit dividend constraint thus become greater as a function of maturity.

Evidence. Kalay develops and tests a number of propositions about how the dividend constraint will be set. He argues that the shareholders' incentive to sell assets for cash is greater the higher the fraction of the firm consisting of debt: the higher that fraction, the greater the potential wealth transfer to stockholders. Consistent with the argument that the dividend constraint involves costs, he finds a significant negative cross-sectional relationship between the dividends which can be paid out under the constraint and the firm's debt/equity ratio.[38]

Kalay also reports that firms do not always pay out all of the dividends to which they are entitled under the indenture agreement. He argues that firms maintain such an 'inventory of payable funds' because having an inventory reduces the probability that the firm will be unable to pay dividends and thus be forced to invest when there are temporarily no profitable investment projects. However, if stockholders maintain an inventory and fail to pay out all funds available for dividends, wealth transfers from bondholders are foregone. On this basis, Kalay posits that the shareholders' incentive to maintain an inventory is lower the higher the firm's leverage. That proposition is consistent with his finding that there is a significant negative relationship between the firm's debt/equity ratio and the (size adjusted) 'inventory of payable funds'.

2.2.1. Control of investment incentives when the inventory is negative

Throughout the above analysis we have assumed that the inventory of funds available for the payment of dividends, D_τ^*, is positive. If the firm has been experiencing negative earnings, the inventory can become negative; with a negative inventory, no dividends can be paid. The negative earnings which lead to a dividend prohibition are likely to be associated with a fall in the value of the firm, and an increase in both its debt/equity ratio and the probability of default on its debt. Hence at the times when a dividend

---

[38]The effective constraint on dividends cannot be determined without considering dividend covenants across all the firm's bond issues. Kalay treats the tightness of the dividend constraint with this in mind; the negative relationship he postulates is between the amount which can be paid out (adjusted for firm size) under the firm's *most* restrictive dividend constraint and its leverage.

prohibition comes into play, the firm is also likely to be faced with greater incentives to engage in asset substitution and claim dilution.

When the firm is doing poorly, the dividend constraint is not capable of controlling the investment and financing policy problem induced by the presence of risky debt. But the direct limitations on production/investment policy we discussed in section 2.1 can limit the stockholders' actions when the inventory for payment of dividends is negative. In addition, financing policy covenants not only address the claim dilution problem, but independently reinforce the effect of the dividend covenant in restricting production/investment policy.

2.3. Bond covenants restricting subsequent financing policy

2.3.1. Limitations on debt and priority

Description. In section 1 we discussed the stockholders' incentives to reduce the value of the outstanding bonds by subsequently issuing additional debt of higher priority, thereby diluting the bondholders' claim on the assets of the firm. Covenants suggested in *Commentaries* limit stockholders actions in this area in one of two ways: either through a simple prohibition against issuing claims with a higher priority, or through a restriction on the creation of a claim with higher priority unless the existing bonds are upgraded to have equal priority. The latter restriction requires, for example, that if secured debt is sold after the issuance of the bonds, the existing bondholders must have their priority upgraded and be given an equal claim on the collateral with the secured debtholders.

In addition to restricting the issuance of debt of higher priority, there are sample covenants in *Commentaries* restricting the stockholders' right to issue *any* additional debt. Issuance of new debt can be subject to aggregate dollar limitations. Alternatively, issuing debt can be prohibited unless the firm maintains minimum prescribed ratios between (1) net tangible assets and funded (i.e., long-term) debt, (2) capitalization and funded debt, (3) tangible net worth[39] and funded debt, (4) income and interest charges (referred to as earnings tests), or (5) current assets and current debt (referred to as working capital tests). There are also provisions requiring the company to be free from debt for limited periods (referred to as 'clean-up' provisions). Combinations of two or more of these limitations are sometimes included in the indenture agreement.

It is important to note the scope of the restrictions imposed through the

---

[39]Some definitions of net worth include subordinated debt and thus treat it as equity. Thus the issuance of debt of equal priority is limited, and the constraint on the issuance of junior debt is relaxed. Our theory does not explain which alternative definition of net worth will be appropriate for a given firm.

covenants limiting the issuance of additional debt. In addition to money borrowed, the covenants also apply to other liabilities incurred by the firm. Other debt-like obligations which can be limited by the covenants are: (1) assumptions or guarantees of indebtedness of other parties,[40] (2) other contingent obligations which are analogous to, but may not technically constitute, guarantees; (3) amounts payable in installments on account of the purchase of property under purchase money mortgages, conditional sales agreements or other long-term contracts; (4) obligations secured by mortgage on property acquired by the company subject to the mortgage but without assumption of the obligations.

Since the claims of the firm in subsidiary corporations are like that of a stockholder, if a subsidiary issues debt or preferred stock the coverage afforded the bondholders of the parent firm is reduced. Thus the limitations on debt usually apply to the debt of the consolidated firm.[41]

Analysis. Our analysis suggests that it is generally not optimal to prevent all future debt issues. If, as the firm's opportunity set evolves over time, new investments must be financed by new equity issues or by reduced dividends, then with risky debt outstanding part of the gains from the investment goes to bondholders, rather than stockholders. Those investments increase the coverage on the debt, and reduce the default risk borne by the bondholders. To the extent such reductions are unanticipated, they result in an increase in the value of outstanding bonds at the expense of the stockholders. So a prohibition of all debt issues would reduce the value of the firm because wealth maximizing stockholders would not take all positive net present value projects. The possibility of asset substitution increases the costs of outright prohibition on debt issues and makes variance reducing positive net present value projects less attractive. However, our analysis suggests that contractually agreeing to have *some* degree of restriction on future debt issues is in the interests of the firm's owners. By merely restricting the total amount of *all* debt which can be issued, the perverse investment incentives associated with debt discussed by Myers (1977) are limited.

---

[40]The third edition of Dewing (1934, p. 105) discusses the Denver Rio Grande Railroad, which is the 'classic case' of a guaranteed bond which brought a severe test of the strength of the guarantor:

> 'The old Western Pacific Railway was built for strategic reasons in order to complete a Pacific coast extension for the Denver and Rio Grande Railroad – all a part of Gould's contemplated transcontinental railway system. The bonds of the Western Pacific were guaranteed, principal and interest, by the Denver and Rio Grande. When it developed that the Western Pacific failed to earn the interest charges, default occurred, and the Western Pacific passed into the hands of receivers.
>   The Denver and Rio Grande Railroad, having failed to meet the guarantees, was ordered to pay over to the trustees of the Western Pacific bonds the sum of $38,000,000. Thereupon the Denver and Rio Grande itself failed.'

[41]Borrowing by a subsidiary from the company or another subsidiary is excluded.

Financing-policy covenants also impact on investment incentives in other ways. In section 2.1, we discussed the direct limitations on financial investments included in bond covenants. Financial investments can also be restricted through the debt covenant. For example, when debt is limited to a specific percentage of net tangible assets, financial investments are sometimes excluded from the definition of net tangible assets for purposes of the covenant. This definition allows the firm to hold a portion of its assets as financial investments, but requires the firm to reduce the debt and its capital structure to do so, thus controlling the asset substitution problem associated with financial investments.

Financing policy impacts on production/investment policy through the dividend covenant. If the level of outstanding debt changes over the life of the bonds, eq. (6) (which presumes that no additional debt is either issued or repaid) must be modified,

$$\sum_{t=0}^{\tau} (B_t - P_t) \leq \sum_{t=0}^{\tau} (I_t - L_t - d_t), \tag{8}$$

where

B_t is the proceeds from the sale of bonds net of transactions costs,
P_t is debt principal paid,
I_t is new investment,
L_t is the book value of any assets liquidated,
d_t is depreciation.

The left-hand side of eq. (8) is simply the cumulative change in the book value of the firm's debt since the sale of this bond issue at $t=0$. For dividends to be paid the cumulative change in the book value of the assets must be no less than the cumulative change in the book value of the debt. Thus the stockholders cannot borrow to finance dividend payments.

2.3.2. Limitations on rentals, lease, and sale-leasebacks

Description. *Commentaries* offers alternative restrictions on the stockholders' use of lease or rental contracts. The covenant typically restricts the firm from the sale-leaseback of property owned prior to the date of the indenture.[42] Some covenants also exclude individual leases or sale-leasebacks below a specified dollar total. Lease payments can also be limited to a fraction of net income. Finally, leasing and renting can be controlled through the debt covenant by capitalizing the lease liability and including it in both

---

[42]This restriction sometimes applies only to specific property (e.g., manufacturing property or heavy equipment) or applies except for items specifically exempted (e.g., office space, warehouses, or automobiles). Alternatively, only long-term leases are covered, with a condition that for short-term leases the company discontinue the use of the property after the term of the lease.

the long-term debt definition and asset definitions. In this case, the covenant specifies the procedure for computing the capitalized value of the asset and liability.[43]

Analysis. Continued use of leased or rented assets by the firm is contingent on making the lease or rental payments. These payments represent liabilities to the firm, and are a claim senior to that of the debtholders: such obligations reduce the value of the outstanding bondholders' claim. For this reason, the Costly Contracting Hypothesis predicts restrictions on the stockholders' subsequent use of leases in the indenture agreement. However, we are unable to explain the specific form which the restriction will take for a particular set of firm characteristics.

2.4. Bond covenants modifying the pattern of payoffs to bondholders

There are several provisions which specify a particular pattern of payoffs to bondholders in a way which controls various sources of stockholder–bondholder conflict of interest.

2.4.1. Sinking funds

Description. A sinking fund is simply a means of amortizing part or all of an indebtedness prior to its maturity. A sinking fund bond is like an installment loan.[44] In the case of a public bond issue, the periodic payments can be invested either in the bonds which are to be retired by the fund or in some other securities. The sinking fund payments can be fixed, variable or contingent. For the years 1963–1965, 82 percent of all publicly-offered issues included sinking fund provisions.[45]

Analysis. A sinking fund affects the firm's production/investment policy through the dividend constraint. From eq. (8) we see that if a sinking fund is included in the indenture, principal repayment, P_t, will be positive prior to the maturity date of the bond; the book value of the assets of the firm can decline over the life of the bond issue without violating the dividend constraint. A sinking fund reduces the possibility that the dividend constraint will require investment when no profitable projects are available. One potential cost associated with the dividend constraint is thus reduced.

Myers (1977) has suggested that sinking funds are a device to reduce

---

[43]See *Commentaries* (p. 440).

[44]In a private placement, the amortization may simply require periodic partial payments to the holder. An alternative to a sinking fund it to provide for serial maturities with part of the issue maturing at fixed dates. This practice is rarely used in the corporate bond market presumably because with fewer identical contracts, maintenance of a secondary market in the bond contracts is more expensive.

[45]See Norgaard/Thompson (1967, p. 31). Note also that in enforcing the Public Utilities Holding Company Act, the SEC requires a sinking fund to be included.

creditors' exposure in parallel with the expected decline in the value of the assets supporting the debt. Myers' analysis implies that sinking funds would be more likely to be included in debt issues (1) the higher the fraction of debt in the capital structure, (2) the greater the anticipated future discretionary investment by the firm and (3) the higher the probability that the project will have a limited lifetime. One industry which illustrates an extreme of the last ot these characteristics is the gas pipeline industry. The sinking fund payments required in some gas pipeline debentures are related to the remaining available gas in the field.[46]

Not all debt issues have sinking funds; their exclusion from some contracts can be explained by anticipated costs which sinking funds can impose on the trustee if there is a default. Although the application of sinking fund monies is set forth in the covenant, should default occur the applicable law is not clear.[47] Even where only one series of bonds is involved, application of funds to the retirement of specific bonds with knowledge of a default might involve participation by the trustee in an unlawful preference for which the trustee might be held liable.

2.4.2. Convertibility provisions

Description. A convertible debenture is one which gives the holder the right to exchange the debentures for other securities of the company, usually shares of common stock and usually without payment of further compensation. The convertible must contain provisions specifying:

[46]The model indenture provision on this point from the American Bar Foundation (1971) states:

'The Company will file with the Trustee on or before..., and on or before each [insert month and day] thereafter so long as the Debentures shall remain Outstanding, a Certificate of Available Gas Supply. In the event that any such Certificate shall show that the date of exhaustion of available gas supply of the Company is a date earlier than..., the aggregate of the Sinking Fund installments due on the next succeeding Sinking Fund Date and each Sinking Fund Date thereafter up to and including the Sinking Fund Date immediately preceding a date (herein called the Margin Date) two years prior to said date of exhaustion of available gas supply shall be increased by an amount equal to the aggregate of the Sinking Fund instalments due on and after the Margin Date, each such Sinking Fund Instalment coming due between the date of such Certificate and the Margin Date being increased proportionately, as nearly as may be, so that each increased installment shall be multiple of $1,000 and the Sinking Fund installments due on and after the Margin Date shall be eliminated and the schedule of Sinking Fund installments thus revised shall constitute the schedule of Sinking Fund installments under this Indenture until further revised as hereinafter provided.'

[47]If specific bonds have been selected for purchase or redemption by the sinking fund, and all necessary steps have been taken except the actual surrender of the bonds, the funds in the hands of the trustee become specifically allocated to the selected bonds. In the event of subsequent default the holder is entitled to payment upon surrender of the bonds, regardless of the payoff to the other bondholders. If default occurs before all steps necessary for retirement of a specific bond have been concluded, all further action is typically suspended. Any preliminary steps taken are revoked, and the funds are retained by the trustee until the default is cured or the trustee receives judicial direction as to the disposition of the funds.

(1) The type of security issuable upon conversion. This is usually common stock of the company, but occasionally it has been stock of a parent or affiliated corporation.

(2) The duration of the conversion period. This may start at the time of issuance or after a specified date, and run until maturity, redemption, or some specified earlier date. The New York Bond Exchange will not permit the designation 'convertible' on the issue unless the privilege extends for the life of the debenture. The exchange will permit the formal designation to be followed by '(convertible prior to . . .)'.

(3) The conversion price at which the stock can be acquired. The conversion price may be the same for the entire period or increase at stated intervals. The conversion price is normally payable only by surrender of a like principal amount of the debentures but occasionally the payment of cash in a fixed ratio to debentures is also required.

(4) Additional Procedural Points. E.g., where must the issue be surrendered for conversion? Does the debenture holder receive accrued interest upon conversion? Will the firm issue fractional shares?

(5) Antidilution Provisions. Provisions which protect the conversion privilege against certain actions by the stockholders such as stock splits, stock dividends, rights offerings, issuance of other convertible securities, mergers, and the distribution of assets.

Analysis. Jensen/Meckling (1976) and Mikkelson (1978) discuss the use of convertible debt as a way to control aspects of the bondholder–stockholder conflict of interest. With non-convertible debt outstanding, the stockholders have the incentive to take projects which raise the variability of the firm's cash flows. The stockholders can increase the value of the equity by adding a new project· with a negative net present value if the firm's cash flow variability rises sufficiently. The inclusion of a convertibility provision in the debt reduces this incentive. The conversion privilege is like a call option written by the stockholders and attached to the debt contract. It reduces the stockholders' incentive to increase the variability of the firm's cash flows, because with a higher variance rate, the attached call option becomes more valuable. Therefore the stockholders' gain from increasing the variance rate is smaller with the convertible debt outstanding than with non-convertible debt.

However, not all debt contracts include a convertibility provision since it is costly to do so.[48] For example, the underinvestment problem is exacerbated with convertible debt outstanding.

---

[48]If part of the incentive for issuing debt comes from the tax deductibility of interest payments, then the tax treatment of interest payments by the Internal Revenue Service can be important and is affected by whether the debt is convertible. Where the capitalization of a corporation is largely debt, the IRS under Section 385 of the Tax Code can contend that some of the 'loans' are in fact capital contributions, and will deny the deduction of 'interest' on the loans. While debt-equity ratios of as much as 700 to 1 have been allowed for tax purposes, the

Evidence. Mikkelson (1978) presents cross-sectional evidence that the probability of the inclusion of the conversion privilege is positively related to (1) the firm's debt/equity ratio, (2) the firm's level of discretionary investment expenditure, and (3) the time to maturity of the debt. Each of these relationships is consistent with the Costly Contracting Hypothesis, and the hypothesis that the benefits of convertible debt are related to a reduction in the bondholder–stockholder conflict.

2.4.3. Callability provisions

Description. The firm's right to redeem the debentures before maturity at a stated price is typically included in the indenture agreement. Without the inclusion of the callability provision in the indenture agreement, a debenture holder cannot be compelled to accept payment of his debenture prior to its stated maturity date. In the usual case, the call price is not constant over the life of the bonds. The redemption price in a callable bond normally is initially set equal to the public offering price plus one year's interest on the bond. The schedule of call prices then typically scales the call premium to zero by a date one year prior to the maturity of the bonds, although it is sometimes as early as two to five years prior to maturity.

Analysis. We have suggested that if agency costs of equity are zero and recapitalization of the firm is costless, the firm will accept all projects with positive net present values and thus the stockholder–bondholder conflict of interest will be solved. One cost of buying out bondholders in a recapitalization results from the additional premium the bondholders demand for the firm to repurchase the bonds. Since the firm cannot vote bonds which it repurchases, a bilateral monopoly results from the attempt to repurchase

---

Treasury is inclined to look askance at 'loans' by stockholders in proportion to their stockholdings to a corporation with a high debt-equity ratio.

Whether stockholder advances to a corporation are loans or equity is a question of fact under the Tax Code. The taxpayer has the burden of proof as to this fact. The Treasury has issued guidelines for determining whether a corporate obligation is equity or debt. The major factors are: (1) the ratio of debt to equity of the corporation; (2) the relationship between holdings of stock and holdings of debt; (3) whether the debt is convertible into the stock of the corporation; (4) whether there is a subordination to or preference over any indebtedness of the corporation; and (5) whether there is a written, unconditional promise to pay on demand, or on a specified date a sum of money in return for adequate compensation, and to pay a fixed rate of interest.

If the IRS determines that the 'debt' is really equity there are a number of tax consequences. (1) The 'interest' deduction to the corporation is disallowed. (2) All payments of 'interest' and 'principal' are treated as dividend income to the shareholder/lender. (3) The shareholder/lender is denied a bad debt deduction if the corporation is unable to pay the principal.

The guidelines point out a potential cost in making all debt convertible. Even if the agency costs of debt are reduced to zero when stockholders and bondholders are the same, there can be an associated increase in taxes paid by the firm and its claimholders. It should be kept in mind, however, that factors other than taxes are necessary to explain why, prior to the corporate income tax, firms typically did not issue proportional claims, and not all debt was convertible.

the outstanding bonds. With a bilateral monopoly it is indeterminate how the gains will be divided between stockholders and bondholders. As Bodie/Taggart (1978) and Wier (1978) argue, a call provision places an upper limit on the gains which the bondholders can obtain. Wier notes further that if side payments can be negotiated costlessly, then the bondholder monopoly is unimportant from the standpoint of the value of the firm; the callability provision merely redistributes the property rights to the monopoly from bondholders to stockholders. Implicit in the argument that the call provision affects the total value of the firm is the notion that the bilateral monopoly implies real resource expenditures on negotiation.

It should also be noted that our argument cannot represent the only reason for callable bonds: after all, government bonds are often callable but there is no obvious investment incentive problem which such a provision addresses.[49]

2.5. Covenants specifying bonding activities by the firm

Potential bondholders estimate the costs associated with monitoring the firm to assure that the bond covenants have not been violated, and the estimate is reflected in the price when the bonds are sold. Since the value of the firm at the time the bonds are issued is influenced by anticipated monitoring costs, it is in the interests of the firm's owners to include contractual provisions which lower the costs of monitoring. For example, observed provisions often include the requirement that the firm supply audited annual financial statements to the bondholders. Jensen/Meckling call these expenditures by the firm bonding costs.

2.5.1. Required reports

Description. Indenture agreements discussed in *Commentaries* normally commit the company to supply financial and other information for as long as the debt is outstanding. Typically, the firm agrees to supply the following types of information: (1) all financial statements, reports, and proxy statements which the firm already sends to its shareholders; (2) reports and statements filed with government agencies such as the SEC or Public Utility Commissions; (3) quarterly financial statements certified by a financial officer of the firm and (4) financial statements for the fiscal year audited by an independent public accountant.

Analysis. Our analysis suggests that bondholders find financial statements to be useful in ascertaining whether the provisions of the contract have been (or are about to be) violated. If the firm can produce this information at a

---

[49]In addition, since virtually all debt is callable, there is little cross-sectional variation in its use. For a discussion of the empirical testability of arguments for callable debt, see Wier (1978).

lower cost than the bondholders (perhaps because much of the information is already being collected for internal decision making purposes), it pays the firm's stockholders to contract to provide this information to the bondholders. The market value of the firm increases by the reduction in agency costs.[50]

Jensen/Meckling (1976) and Watts (1977) point out that firms have the incentive to provide financial statements which have been audited by an external accounting firm if the increase in the market value of the bonds is greater than the present value of the auditing fees, net of any nominal benefits which accrue in internal monitoring. If bonding activities which are related to the bondholder–stockholder conflict involve incremental costs, then since the conflict increases with the debt in the firm's capital structure, the use of externally audited financial statements should be positively related to the firm's debt/equity ratio. Auditing expenditures should be associated with the extent to which covenants are specified in terms of accounting numbers from financial statements.[51,52]

2.5.2. Specification of accounting techniques

Description. As indicated, covenants restricting dividend, financing, and production/investment policy are frequently specified in terms of income or balance sheet numbers.[53] For public debt issues, other than stating that they should be consistent with generally accepted accounting principles (GAAP), covenants frequently do not specify how the accounting numbers will be computed.

Analysis. Restrictions on the shareholders' behavior can be relaxed by manipulating the accounting numbers which define the constraints.[54] For example, the impact of a change in accounting techniques on dividend and investment policy can be seen by referring to eq. (1) defining the inventory of funds for payment of dividends. The change in allowed dividend payments in quarter τ resulting from a change in earnings in quarter τ is proportional to k (i.e., $\partial D_\tau^* / \partial E_\tau = k$). If accounting earnings are overstated, then required current investment is increased by $(1-k)$ times the change in reported earnings. After the bonds have been sold, shareholders have an incentive to use whichever method of calculation inflates stated earnings. However, this

---

[50]See Jensen/Meckling (1976, p. 338) and Watts (1977).

[51]For a further discussion of the incentives to employ external auditors, see Watts (1977).

[52]Furthermore, this analysis leads Leftwich/Watts/Zimmerman (1979) to predict that voluntary public disclosure of financial statements prior to required provision by the exchanges or regulation should be associated with the level of debt in the firm's capital structure.

[53]See Holthausen (1979) and Leftwich (1979) for more comprehensive analyses of the use of accounting definitions in bond covenants.

[54]One case where accounting manipulations may have been made to prevent the firm from violating its debt covenants is that of Pan American World Airways. See Foster (1978, p. 354).

argument overstates the incentive to manipulate accounting earnings if current earnings can only be increased by reducing future earnings. To illustrate, since the total amount of depreciation on a machine is fixed, taking less depreciation now implies that future accounting earnings will be reduced. In this case the shareholders can only lower required current investment by increasing required future investment. The magnitude of the gain to the shareholders from manipulation of accounting numbers is on the order of the discount rate multiplied by k times the change in reported earnings and this is likely to be relatively small.

It is expensive to specify the accounting procedure by contract and, if the specified procedure differs from GAAP, it is expensive to prepare an additional set of accounting statements for the bondholders. Such detailed procedures can be a more costly mechanism for the bondholders to protect themselves against 'creative accounting' than by requiring external auditing and reflecting any risk of accounting manipulations in the price paid for the bonds.

Holthausen (1979) argues that the firm's decision to change depreciation methods could result in a change in reported earnings which relaxes contractual constraints and results in a transfer of wealth to stockholders. Furthermore, Leftwich (1979) argues that restricting stockholders to GAAP involves costs since over time, accounting principles change. Mandated changes in GAAP can cause the constraints on the stockholders' behavior to change and in some cases to be violated.[55] Leftwich's analysis predicts that certain changes in GAAP should be associated with wealth losses to the firm's claimholders. Moreover, the extent of the loss should be related to the extent to which the contracts are specified in terms of GAAP.

2.5.3. Officers' certificate of compliance

Description. Commentaries suggests that in addition to submitting the reports indicated above, the firm usually promises to provide an annual certificate as to whether there has been any default under the indenture. The Certificate of Compliance must be signed both by the president or vice-president, and by either the treasurer, assistant treasurer, controller or assistant controller of the company. The statement indicates that the signing officer has reviewed the activities of the company for the year, and that to the best of his knowledge the firm has fulfilled all of its obligations under the indenture. If there has been a default, the nature and status of the default must be specified. Some indentures also call for certificates or opinions as to compliance to be supplied by independent accountants. Normally it is provided that the accountants' statement certify that during the examination the accountants 'obtained no knowledge' of any default. The accountants are

---

[55]Fogelson (1978) discusses several cases where this has occurred.

often expressly relieved of all liability for failure to obtain knowledge of a default.

Analysis. The Costly Contracting Hypothesis suggests that the certificate of compliance is a way of reducing the monitoring costs of the bondholders. It is less expensive to have officers of the firm or the firm's accountants, who already will be knowledgeable of any defaults, contract to call such defaults to the attention of the bondholders than to let bondholders themselves ascertain if a default has occurred.

2.5.4. *The required purchase of insurance*

Description. Indenture agreements frequently include provisions requiring the firm to purchase insurance. The sample covenants in *Commentaries* specify that the firm will purchase insurance 'to substantially the same extent as its competitors'. The stockholders sometimes retain the right to self-insure if the plan is certified by an actuary. Typically, the indenture requires the firm to maintain liability insurance.

Analysis. In a world with perfect markets, there is no corporate demand for insurance; the corporate form effectively hedges insurable risk.[56] Our analysis suggests that the corporate purchase of insurance is a bonding activity engaged in by firms to reduce agency costs between bondholders and stockholders (as well as between the managers and the owners of a corporation). If insurance firms have a comparative advantage in monitoring aspects of the firm's activities, then a firm which purchases insurance will engage in a different set of activities from a firm which does not.

For example, a frequently purchased line of corporate insurance is boiler insurance. Insurance companies hire and train specialized inspectors to monitor the operation and maintenance of boilers, and the loss control program which is provided by the insurance company constrains the actions of the stockholders and managers of the firm. A covenant requiring the purchase of insurance gives stockholders the incentive to engage in the optimal amount of loss control projects. If the purchase of a sprinkler system were a positive net present value project it could still be rejected by stockholders of a levered firm because it reduces the variance rate of the firm's cash flows and thereby increases the value of the debt. But if the firm is contractually required to purchase insurance and if the insurance industry is competitive, the firm has the incentive to take any loss control project where the present value of the premium reductions is greater than the cost of the project. With the purchase of insurance the corporation's cash flow variability is unaffected by the purchase of loss control projects.

---

[56]See Mayers/Smith (1978).

3. The enforcement of bond covenants

The covenants we have discussed do not completely control the conflict between bondholders and stockholders; they do not go nearly so far as they could in restricting the firm's actions. The covenants could require that the firm secure permission of the bondholders for each action it takes, or that the firm 'accept all profitable projects, and only those projects'. However, as Jensen/Meckling (1976, p. 338) and Myers (1977, p. 158) argue, if such covenants are sufficiently expensive to enforce, it will not be in the interests of the firm's owners to offer them.

To specify types of enforcement costs, we must examine the institutional framework within which covenant enforcement takes place for further insight into why certain kinds of covenants are observed — and others not. Our analysis takes the institutional arragnements as given. A deeper issue relates to the endogeneity of the institutions themselves. To the extent that the existing legal institutions represent an efficient solution to the problem of financial contracting, enforcement costs are lowered. But regardless of whether or not existing institutions imply 'minimum' costs, the types of contracts we observe depend on the level of these institutionally-related costs.

3.1. The legal liability of bondholders

Description. When bondholders exercise a significant degree of 'control' over the firm, they become legally liable to both the firm (i.e., the shareholders) and to third parties for losses incurred as a result of certain of their actions.[57] Although acts such as the seizure of collateral do not, in general, subject the creditor to liability,[58] creditor liability still occurs under a variety of conditions. For example, it can arise when a creditor who controls the firm is responsible for mismanagement. One of the leading cases is *Taylor versus Standard Gas Company,*[59] in which the court held the firm's creditor responsible for abuses which resulted from the exercise of control.

Creditors whose debt contracts contain restrictions which cause the firm to breach its contract with third parties, such as suppliers, employees, and other creditors, can also be held liable. One notable case in which a covenant

---

[57]Much of the discussion of the liability issue is based on the survey article of Douglas-Hamilton (1975). The liability of bondholders depends critically on the definition of 'control'. In the case of liability for securities law violations, 'a creditor would be considered in control of a corporate debtor even it if only indirectly possessed the power to direct the management or the policies of the debtor'. See Douglas-Hamilton (pp. 346–347).

That the courts frown upon bondholder control is not a new notion. Dewing (1953, pp. 188–189) indicates that the 'exclusion of bondholders from all voice in the management of the corporation...has been sanctioned by centuries of legal authority' and is a 'time honored legal theory'.

[58]Douglas-Hamilton (p. 364).

[59]306 U.S. 307 (1939). See Douglas-Hamilton (p. 348).

violated the rights of third parties is that of *Kelly versus Central Hanover Bank and Trust Company.*[60] There, the bondholders of the debtor corporation brought suit against another class of claimants, namely the creditor banks of the debtor. The bondholders charged that the banks, in obtaining a covenant pledging stock as security for their loans, violated the terms of the indenture agreement between the bondholders and the debtor. According to Douglas-Hamilton (1975, p. 364):

> 'It appears that the case against the banks was later settled on terms which included a payment of $3,435,008 by the banks to the bondholders and the withdrawal by the banks of claims aggregating $42,887,500 in the debtor corporation's bankruptcy proceedings.'

Creditors can also incur liability for Federal Securities Law violations. For example, under Rule 10b–5 of Section 10 of the Securities Act of 1934, which deals with fraud, a creditor incurs liability for failing to disclose material information about the firm. Creditor liability even arises in cases where there has been inadequate 'policing by a creditor of press releases of its troubled debtor to insure that they do not depict an inaccurate optimistic picture to the public'.[61]

Analysis. Covenants which have the effect of assigning legal liability to the bondholders represent a real cost to the firm's owners if bondholders, or their agent, are more likely than the firm's management to be held responsible for actions which result in losses and if the legal process which establishes liability is costly. In that case, giving bondholders control is a more costly way to run the firm simply because of the legal costs involved in the determination of bondholder liability. The firm's owners are better off simply not issuing those types of debt which are likely to result in such costs being incurred. While we have no direct evidence on the costs of creditor liability, one comment from the legal literature which suggests that those costs are not trivial is the warning that 'whenever a creditor contemplates taking a hand in the management of a financially troubled debtor, it should think of its deeper pockets and keep its hands there'.[62]

3.2. The role of the trust indenture and the trustee

Description. Debt contracts discussed in *Commentaries* typically appoint an independent 'trustee' to represent the bondholders and act as their agent in covenant enforcement. This is done under a device known as a corporate trust indenture, which specifies the respective rights and obligations of the

---

[60]85 F 2d 61 (2d Cir. 1936).
[61]Douglas-Hamilton (p. 354).
[62]Douglas-Hamilton (p. 364).

firm, the individual bondholders, and the trustee. Although the trustee is an agent of the bondholders, in practice he is actually compensated by the firm.[63]

Analysis.   If the firm's debt is not held by a single borrower, then a number of problems related to enforcement of the debt contract arise. For example, any individual's holdings of the firm's debt may be so small that no single bondholder has much incentive to expend resources in covenant enforcement. But it is not the case that individual bondholders necessarily expend 'too few' resources in covenant enforcement. If the number of bondholders is small, then there can actually be overinvestment in enforcement in the sense that there is either a duplication of effort, or that creditors expend resources which simply result in change in the distribution of the proceeds. Our analysis implies that the firm's owners offer a contract which appoints a trustee to help assure that the optimal amount of covenant enforcement will take place.

Having the firm pay the trustees directly solves the 'free-rider' problem which would be inherent in making individual bondholders pay the trustee for enforcing the covenants. However after the bonds have been sold, the stockholders have an incentive to bribe the trustee so that they can violate the debt covenants. There are several factors which prevent such bribery from taking place.

Bribing the trustee is expensive if the trustee's reputation has significant value in the marketplace. *Ex ante*, it is in the interests of the firm's owners to choose an 'honest' trustee – that is, one who is expensive to bribe. This is because the value of the firm at the time it issues the debt contract reflects the probability of covenant enforcement. To the extent that enforcement by an 'honest' trustee reduces the problems of adverse borrower behavior induced by risky debt, the value of the firm is higher. Our analysis therefore implies that those chosen as trustees stand to lose much if they are caught accepting bribes. In fact, the indenture trustee is 'generally a large banking institution',[64] which has significant revenues from activities unrelated to being a trustee and which also depend on the market's perception of its trustworthiness. Furthermore, the behavior of the trustee is restricted by both trust and contract law.[65]

3.2.1. The Trust Indenture Act of 1939

Description.   Publicly issued debt obligations must comply with the requirements of the Trust Indenture Act of 1939 (TIA).[66] Although the TIA does

---

[63]For a further discussion of the trustee's compensation, see Kennedy (1961, p. 49)

[64]Obrzut (1976, p. 131).

[65]For a further discussion, see Kennedy, especially chapter 2.

[66]There are minor exceptions. For example, issues of less than $1 million are exempted. The TIA is enforced by the Securities and Exchange Commission. For the bonds to be sold, the terms of the indenture must be 'qualified' by the SEC.

not explicitly regulate the restrictive covenants which the bond contract can include, the TIA does impose certain standards of conduct on the trustee. The trustee must meet certain minimum capital requirements. The trustee is not permitted to have a serious conflict of interest; with some minor exceptions, he may not act as the agent for two different classes of bondholders of the same firm, and he may not himself be a creditor in the firm for whose debt contract he acts as trustee.[67]

Analysis.　In spite of these restrictions on the behavior of the trustee, it can still be very costly to write a contract where the bondholders are represented by such an agent. The trustee will still not act entirely in the bondholders' interest. This is particularly true because the extent to which the trustee can be held negligent is limited: while the trustee must act in good faith, his responsibilities often go no further unless there is a default. Under the TIA, when a default has occurred the trustee is only required to 'use the same degree of care and skill...as a prudent man would exercise' in enforcing the covenants. Furthermore it is not clear whether, prior to the TIA, the legal standards for either pre- or post-default conduct of trustees were significantly different.[68]

3.2.2. *Public versus private placements*

Description.　Section 4(2) of the Securities Act of 1933 provides that a sale of securities not involving any public offering is exempt from registration. Such exempt issues are referred to as private placements or direct placements. Private placements are not typically subject to the TIA. They represent an alternative to publicly placed debt.

Analysis.　Since the enforcement of tightly restrictive covenants through a trustee is difficult, the benefit from private (rather than public) placement of the firm's debt issues can be substantial. Our analysis suggests that private placements will contain more detailed restrictions on the firm's behavior than do public issues.[69] In addition, we would expect that the riskier the debt, the more likely that it will be privately placed. Because of the costs associated with the enforcement of trust indentures, the covenants in debt issues are not likely to eliminate the problems induced by the presence of risky debt.

---

[67]Kennedy (p. 35) claims that the standards of conduct contained in the TIA 'had been accepted and followed by the more responsible trust companies for a long time prior to the enactment of the legislation, so that no abrupt or sudden change was effected'. A major proponent of the legislation which resulted in the TIA was the Securities and Exchange Commission [Obrzut (1976, p. 133)].

[68]For a further discussion, see Johnson (1970).

[69]That private issues contain more restrictive covenants than public issues is consistent with the observations of the authors of *Commentaries* (p. 11 and p. 14). Note that private issues may also have trustees, even though the number of claimholders is typically small.

Evidence. Consistent with the hypothesis that privately placed debt contracts contain more extensive provisions than public, Leftwich (1979) presents evidence that variations from generally accepted accounting procedures occur more frequently in private than public debt issues. The adjustments to GAAP are systematic; they generally eliminate non-cash gains. However they do not restrict non-cash losses. For example, restatement of asset values which result in gains are typically eliminated from computed earnings while those resulting in losses are not.

Cohan (1967, p. 1) finds evidence of a shift to private placements during the 1930s: 'In the thirty-four years from 1900 to 1934, about 3 percent of all corporate debt cash offerings, or approximately $1 billion were directly (privately) placed. However, in the ensuing thirty-one years, from 1935 to 1965, 46 percent, or $85 billion, were directly placed.' While our analysis does predict such a shift to private placements after the TIA, this shift is also consistent with Benston's (1969) suggestion that the inception of the SEC in 1934 increased the cost of public versus private issues.

3.3. Default remedies

The debt contract typically gives the firm a strong incentive to live up to the restrictive covenants: any breach of the covenants is considered an act of default. Not only is the firm normally required to report any such breach, but the lender is given the right to engage in certain actions (e.g., seizure of collateral, acceleration of the maturity of the debt) to protect his interest.

3.3.1. Renegotiation

Description. Since actions such as the seizure of collateral consume real resources, the debt contract is often renegotiated in order to eliminate the default. In public debt issues the contract can be changed by the use of a 'supplemental indenture'. The supplement must be approved by the bondholders, and must meet the requirements of the TIA.

Changes in the specific covenants cannot usually be made without the consent of the holders of two-thirds in principal amount of the outstanding debt[70] (the firm itself is not allowed to vote any debt it holds). Moreover, the consent of 100 percent of the debtholders is required in order to change the maturity date or principal amount of the bonds. In private placements involving few lenders, renegotiation is typically easier.[71]

---

[70]See *Commentaries* (p. 307) and Section 902, American Bar Foundation Model Debenture Indenture Provisions   All Registered Issues.

[71]According to Zinbarg (1975): 'My own institution's experience [Prudential Insurance Co. of Am] may serve as an illustration. In any given year, we will, on average, receive one modification request per loan on the books. In no more than five per cent of these cases will we refuse the request or even require any quid pro quo, because the vast majority of corporate requests are perfectly reasonable and do not increase our risk materially.'

Analysis. The seemingly lower renegotiating costs of privately placed debt issues further re-inforce our earlier prediction that such private placements will contain tighter restrictions on the firm's behavior than will public issues.

3.3.2. *Bankruptcy*

Description. Should renegotiation fail, a default also gives the lender the right to put the firm into legal bankruptcy proceedings. Several features of the bankruptcy process bear on the enforcement of debt contracts. For example, since the bankruptcy process gives the firm temporary protection from acts of foreclosure and lien enforcement, some enforcement mechanisms are no longer available to the lender.

Analysis. Our theory suggests that it is more efficient to have some ambiguities in the initial debt contract, and to let them be resolved in bankruptcy should default ever occur. Since it is the firm's owners who bear the total costs associated with enforcing the debt contract, it is in their interests to find the most efficient balance between expenditures on drafting the debt contract and expected legal expenditures in bankruptcy. In a world where contracting is costly, that balance will imply less than complete specification of the payoff to be received by claimholders in every possible future state of the world.

As Warner (1977) discusses, bankruptcy courts recognize the priorities specified in the firm's debt agreements in only a limited sense. There are many cases where 'junior' claimants are compensated before claimants 'senior' to them are paid in full. Since 'priorities' are not always enforced, it will not always pay the firm to indicate the priority of a given debt issue with much specificity (e.g., creditor A is forty-seventh in line).

4. Conclusions

4.1. *The role of bond covenants*

We have examined the specific provisions which are included in corporate debt contracts. Since covenants are a persistent phenomena, we can therefore assume that these provisions are efficient from the standpoint of the firm's owners, and thus we can draw inferences about the role of these contractual forms in the firm's capital structure.

Observed debt covenants reduce the costs associated with the conflict of interest between bondholders and stockholders; the ingenuity with which debt contracts are written indicates the strong economic incentives for the firm's owners to lower the agency costs which can result from having risky debt in the firm's capital structure.

The existence of standardized debt contracts such as those found in

Commentaries suggests that the out-of-pocket costs of drafting observed bond contracts are small indeed. However, the direct and opportunity costs of complying with the contractual restrictions appear to be substantial. We have presented no evidence on the precise dollar magnitudes, and we emphasize that a particular covenant included in a given debt contract will not impose opportunity costs with probability one. But our analysis indicates that observed bond covenants involve expected costs which are large enough to help account for the variation in debt contracts across firms. This is consistent with the Costly Contracting Hypothesis. On the other hand, it is inconsistent with the Irrelevance Hypothesis, which predicts that total resource expenditures on control of the bondholder–stockholder conflict will be negligible.

Our analysis also sheds some light on the relative costs of the alternative types of restrictions which can be written into the debt contract. We conclude that production/investment policy is very expensive to monitor. Stockholder use (or misuse) of production/investment policy frequently involves not some explicit act, but the failure to take a certain action (e.g., failure to accept a positive net present value project). It is expensive even to ascertain when the firm's production/investment policy is not optimal, since such a determination depends on magnitudes which are difficult to observe. The high monitoring costs which would be associated with restrictive production/investment covenants, including the potential legal costs associated with bondholder control, dictate that few production/investment decisions will be contractually proscribed. For the firm's owners to go very far in directly restricting the firm's production/investment policy would be inefficient.

On the other hand, we conclude that dividend policy and financing policy involve lower monitoring costs. Stockholder use of these policies to 'hurt' bondholders involves acts (e.g., the sale of a large bond issue) which are readily observable. Because they are cheaper to monitor, it is efficient to restrict production/investment policy by writing dividend and financing policy covenants in a way which helps assure that stockholders will act to maximize the value of the firm.

4.2. Implications for capital structure

With more fixed claims in the capital structure, the benefits to the stockholders from asset substitution, claim dilution, underinvestment, and dividend payout increase; with higher benefits, the stockholders will expend more real resources 'getting around' any particular set of contractual constraints. This, in turn, will increase the benefits of increased tightness of the covenants. Accordingly, the costs associated with the bondholder–stockholder conflict rise with the firm's debt/equity ratio. Simply limiting the debt in the capital structure is an efficient mechanism for controlling this conflict. Because of this, the costs associated with writing and enforcing covenants influence the level of debt the firm chooses.

Since observed debt covenants involve real costs, there must be some benefit in having debt in the firm's capital structure; otherwise, the bondholder–stockholder conflict can be costlessly eliminated by not issuing debt. Hence our evidence indicates not only that there is an optimal form of the debt contract, but an optimal *amount* of debt as well. The benefits from issuing risky debt are not well understood, and even though the costs we have discussed in this paper provide a lower bound on their magnitude, our analysis has not permitted us to distinguish between alternative explanations of the benefits: (1) information asymmetries and signalling, (2) taxes, (3) agency costs of equity financing, (4) differential transactions and flotation costs, and (5) unbundling of riskbearing and capital ownership.

4.3. Some possible extensions

While our analysis of debt covenants is a useful start at explaining certain aspects of the firm's capital structure, there are a number of issues which have not been explored here which, we believe, merit further attention. We have attempted to indicate the interrelationship between covenants restricting dividend, financing, and production/investment policy. However, we have not developed a theory which is capable of explaining how, for a given debt issue, the total 'package' of covenants is determined. Further work on the substitutability or complementarity of the specific contractual provisions is necessary before it is possible to predict, for any set of firm-specific characteristics, the form which the debt contract will take.

Second, we emphasize that bond covenants are but one way in which the behavior of the stockholders is constrained. For example, both the legal system and the possibility of takeovers are factors which make it more expensive for stockholders to engage in actions aimed at maximizing the value of their own claim but not the total value of the firm. The relative importance of these factors, and how they affect the firm's choice of debt covenants, is not yet well understood.

Finally, it is important to remember that in focusing on the bondholder–stockholder conflict, we have ignored other conflicts, such as that between managers and stockholders, which also exist. To the extent that the contracts comprising the firm are interdependent and simultaneously determined, the bondholder–stockholder conflict should not be viewed in isolation. The impact of the bondholder–stockholder conflict on the firm's total contracting costs cannot be fully understood until the nature of these contractual interdependencies is explored.

Appendix

In this appendix, we consider in more detail the results presented in section 1. First, we discuss the valuation of the debt of a levered firm when the relevant variables in the valuation equations can be specified parametrically over the life of the bonds. We then expand the analysis to the case where stockholders can change these variables after they obtain the proceeds from the sale of the debt, and where both the stockholders and bondholders are aware of this possibility when the bonds are originally issued.

A.1. Option pricing valuation of the firm's financial claims

The valuation of the equity and debt of a levered firm is examined by Black/Scholes (1973) and Merton (1974). Where the bonds are single-payment contracts and the market is efficient and competitive, without transactions costs, information costs, other agency costs, or taxes, the analysis is straightforward. Consider a bond contract which promises to repay a lump sum, X, covering both principal and interest at a specified date in the future, t^*. When the bond issue is sold, the proceeds from the sale equal the current value of the bondholders' claim, B, on the firm's assets. Assume that the firm's financial claims consist of this bond issue and common stock. Thus, the current value of the stock, S, is the difference between the current value of the firm's assets, V, and the value of the bonds, B,

$$S \equiv V - B. \tag{A.1}$$

Given this contract, the optimal strategy for the firm's shareholders at the maturity date of the bonds can be specified: if the value of the firm's assets at the maturity date, V^*, is greater than the face value of the bonds, X, then repay the bonds; the stockholders equity at that date, S^* will be the difference between the value of the firm's assets and the face value of the bonds, $V^* - X$. On the other hand, if at the maturity date of the bonds the value of the firm's assets is less than the face value of the bonds, then default on the bonds; the bondholders do not receive the face value of the bonds, they receive only the firm's assets, V^*. Given limited liability, the shareholders' equity is zero. Thus, at t^* the value of the stock, S^*, is

$$S^* = \max[0, V^* - X], \tag{A.2}$$

and the value of the bonds is

$$B^* = \min[V^*, X]. \tag{A.3}$$

This bond issue is equivalent to the sale of the firm's assets to the bondholders for a package containing: (1) the proceeds from the sale of the bonds, B, (2) a claim which allows the stockholders to receive the dividends paid by the firm over the life of the bonds, and (3) a European call option[72] to repurchase the assets at the maturity date of the loan T time periods later ($T = t^* - t$), with an exercise price equal to the face value of the bonds, X. Those variables which affect the value of call options are also important in valuing the financial claims of firms.

To derive an explicit solution for the market value of the bonds given the other variables, make the following assumptions:

(1) There are homogeneous expectations about the dynamic behavior of the value of the firm's assets. The distribution at the end of any finite time interval is lognormal. The variance rate, σ^2, is constant.

(2) The dynamic behavior of the value of the assets is independent of the face value of the bonds, X.

(3) There are no transactions costs associated with default.

(4) The firm pays a continuous flow of dividend payments to the shareholders. The dividend payment, per unit time D, is a constant fraction, δ, of the market value of the assets: $\delta = D/V$.

(5) Capital markets are perfect. There are no transactions costs or taxes. All participants have free access to all available information. Participants are price takers.

(6) There is a known constant riskless rate of interest, r.[73]

Under these assumptions, Merton (1974) has shown that the value of the bonds, B, can be written as

$$B = Ve^{-\delta T} N \left\{ \frac{-\ln(V/X) - (r - \delta + \sigma^2/2)T}{\sigma\sqrt{T}} \right\}$$

$$+ Xe^{-rT} N \left\{ \frac{\ln(V/X) + (r - \delta - \sigma^2/2)T}{\sigma\sqrt{T}} \right\}, \tag{A.4}$$

[72] A European call option is a contract which gives the owner the right to purchase a specified asset at a specified price, called the exercise price, on a specified date, called the maturity date. Since the option is only exercised if it is in the best interest of the owner, it will be exercised only if the value of the asset is above the exercise price at the maturity date; otherwise it will expire worthless.

[73] Merton (1973) has modified the Black/Scholes contingent claims analysis to account for time series variability in interest rates. His solution retains the basic form of this analysis. Since the effects of the variability of the riskless rate and term structure are not of primary concern here, this simpler assumption will be maintained.

where $N\{\ \}$ is the cumulative standard normal distribution function. In general form,

$$B = B(V, X, T, \delta, \sigma^2, r),\qquad\qquad\qquad\text{(A.5)}$$

where

$$\frac{\partial B}{\partial V}, \frac{\partial B}{\partial X} > 0 \quad \text{and} \quad \frac{\partial B}{\partial T}, \frac{\partial B}{\partial \delta}, \frac{\partial B}{\partial \sigma^2}, \frac{\partial B}{\partial r} < 0.$$

A.2. The nature of the covenants to be included in the debt contract

As we discussed in section 1, in pricing the bonds the bondholders must ascertain the values of the variables in eq. (A.5). These variables can be changed after the bonds are issued; the bondholders make assessments of likely stockholder actions, given whatever restrictions the debt contract places on the stockholders. The particular covenants written are those which maximize the wealth of the firm's current owners. This is the set of covenants which maximizes the with-dividend value of the firm when the bonds are issued.

For explicit analysis of the incentives faced by the shareholders and bondholders in drafting the debt contract, the analysis of the valuation of claims must be expanded.[74] The firm's objective is assumed to be the maximization of current equity, S, and the current dividend, D,

$$W \equiv S + D.\qquad\qquad\qquad\text{(A.6)}$$

For an all equity firm which has decided to sell bonds, the value of the stock, S, can be expressed as the total ex-dividend value of the firm, V, minus the value of the claim sold to the new bondholders, B,

$$S \equiv V - B.\qquad\qquad\qquad\text{(A.7)}$$

The value of the claim sold to the new bondholders is a function of the projects chosen, and the terms of the contract. More specifically, let the firm choose a vector of activities, α, and a vector of provisions in its financial contracts, f (e.g., f includes the face value of the debt, X, and the time to maturity of the bonds, T, as well as covenants such as restrictions on dividend payments). In general, the value of the firm's assets, the variance rate, and the dividend payments area function of the activities and contractual provisions chosen. Thus the value to the stockholders of the claim sold to the bondholders can be expressed as

$$B = B(\alpha, f).\qquad\qquad\qquad\text{(A.8)}$$

---

[74]The following analysis was suggested by John Long.

The cash flow identity that inflows equal outflows can be used to re-express the dividend payment, D, as the sum of the internally generated cash flow before interest expense, ϕ, plus the net proceeds from the sale of the new bonds, B, minus the new investment expenditures, I,

$$D \equiv \phi + B - I. \tag{A.9}$$

The proceeds from the sale of the new bonds will depend on the financial covenants, f, chosen. Let $\alpha(f)$ represent the activity that, given the choice of financial contract, f, maximizes the with-dividend value of the shareholder's equity. The bondholders will assume that if the contractual provisions are f, then the stockholders will act in their own self-interest and choose the vector of activities, $\alpha(f)$. Thus, the proceeds from the sale of the new bonds will be

$$B = B(\alpha(f), f). \tag{A.10}$$

Substituting (A.7), (A.8), (A.9) and (A.10) into (A.6) allows us to re-express shareholder wealth as

$$W = V(\alpha, f) - B(\alpha, f) + B(\alpha(f), f) + \phi(\alpha, f) - I(\alpha, f). \tag{A.11}$$

Thus, for a given financial structure, f, the optimal activity choice, α, to maximize shareholder wealth is

$$W(\alpha(f), f) = V(\alpha(f), f) + \phi(\alpha(f), f) - I(\alpha(f), f). \tag{A.12}$$

From (A.12) it is clear that the optimal financial structure, f^*, will be that structure for which the with-dividend value of the firm is maximized subject to the available set of financial structures; i.e.,

$$V[\alpha(f^*), f^*] + \phi[\alpha(f^*), f^*] - I[\alpha(f^*), f^*]$$
$$\geq V[\alpha(f), f] + \phi[\alpha(f), f] - I[\alpha(f), f],$$

for all feasible f.

This can be illustrated graphically. Let (α^{**}, f^{**}) be the point where the with-dividend value of the firm is maximized; i.e., where

$$V(\alpha^{**}, f^{**}) + \phi(\alpha^{**}, f^{**}) - I(\alpha^{**}, f^{**})$$
$$\geq V(\alpha, f) + \phi(\alpha, f) - I(\alpha, f),$$

for all choices of financial structure and activities, assuming that the magnitudes could be independently set. We call this point the 'idealized' capital structure/activity choice for the firm. In fig. 1 the with-dividend value of the firm is represented in (α, f) space as level sets. The set of optimal activity choices as a function of financial structure, $\alpha(f)$, is also represented. The agency costs described by Jensen/Meckling (1976) are $[V(\alpha^{**}, f^{**}) + \phi(\alpha^{**}, f^{**}) - I(\alpha^{**}, f^{**})] - [V(\alpha(f^{*}), f^{*}) + \phi(\alpha(f^{*}), f^{*}) - I(\alpha(f^{*})f^{*})]$, i.e., the difference between the with-dividend value of the firm given the idealized capital structure and the idealized activity choice minus the value of the firm given the optimum (feasible) choice of activities and capital structure.

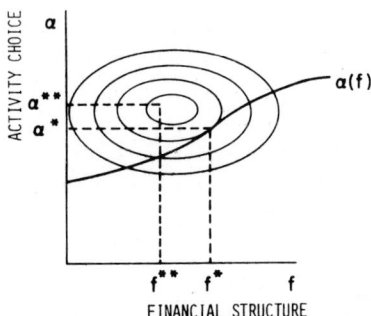

Fig. 1. Determination of the optimal financial structure, f^{*}, and activity choice, α^{*}. The collection of level sets represent different with-dividend market values of the firm, assuming the activity choice, α, and financial structure, f, can be set independently. The point (α^{**}, f^{**}) is the maximum with-dividend firm market value. The function $\alpha(f)$ represents the choice of activity which maximizes shareholder wealth for a given financial structure. Agency costs are $\{[V(\alpha^{**}, f^{**}) + \phi(\alpha^{**}, f^{**}) - I(\alpha^{**})] - [V(\alpha(f^{*}), f^{*}) + \phi(\alpha(f^{*}), f^{*}) - I(\alpha(f^{*}), f^{*})]\}$.

References

Alchian, Armen, 1950, Uncertainty, evolution, and economic theory, Journal of Political Economy 58, 211–221.

Alchian, Armen and Harold Demsetz, 1972, Production, information costs, and economic organization, American Economic Review 62, 777–795.

American Bar Foundation, 1971, Commentaries on model debenture indenture provisions 1965, Model debenture indenture provisions all registered issues 1967, and Certain negotiable provisions which may be included in a particular incorporating indenture (Chicago, IL).

Benston, George J., 1969, The effectiveness and effects of the SEC's accounting disclosure requirements, in: Henry G. Manne, ed., Economic policy and the regulation of corporate securities (American Enterprise Institute, Washington, DC), 23–79.

Black, Fischer, 1976, The dividend puzzle, Journal of Portfolio Management 2, 5–8.

Black, Fischer and John C. Cox, 1976, Valuing corporate securities: Some effects of bond indenture provisions, Journal of Finance 31, 351–367.

Black, Fischer, Merton H. Miller and Richard A. Posner, 1978, An approach to the regulation of bank holding companies, Journal of Business 51, 379–412.

Black, Fischer and Myron Scholes, 1973, The pricing of options and corporate liabilities, Journal of Political Economy 81, 637–659.

Bodie, Zvi and Robert Taggart, 1978, Future investment opportunities and the value of the call provision on a bond, Journal of Finance 23, 1187–1200.

Bradley, Michael, 1978, An analysis of interfirm cash tender offers, Unpublished manuscript (University of Chicago, Chicago, IL).

Cheung, Steven, 1973, The fable of the bees: An economic investigation, Journal of Law and Economics 16, 11–33.

Coase, Ronald, 1960, The problem of social cost, Journal of Law and Economics 3, 1–44.

Cohan, Avery G., 1967, Yields on corporate debt directly placed (National Bureau of Economic Research, New York).

Coleman, William, 1971, Biology in the nineteenth century: Problems of form, function, and transformation (Wiley, New York).

Darwin, Charles, 1859, The origin of species by means of natural selection or the preservation of favoured races in the struggle for life. Reprinted in 1962 (Collier Books, New York).

Demsetz, Harold, 1967, Toward a theory of property rights, American Economic Review 57, 347–359.

Dewing, Arthur, 1934, 1953, The financial policy of corporations (Ronald Press, New York).

Dodd, Peter and Richard Ruback, 1977, Tender offers and stockholder returns: An empirical analysis, Journal of Financial Economics 5, 351–373.

Douglas-Hamilton, Margaret H., 1975, Creditor liabilities resulting from improper interference with the management of a financially troubled debtor, Business Lawyer 31, 343–365.

Fama, Eugene F., 1978a, The effect of a firm's investment and financing decisions on the welfare of its security holders, American Economic Review 68, 272–284.

Fama, Eugene F., 1978b, Agency problems and the theory of the firm, Unpublished manuscript (University of Chicago, Chicago, IL).

Fama, Eugene F. and Merton Miller, 1972, The theory of finance (Holt, Rinehart and Winston, New York).

Fogelson, James H., 1978, The impact of changes in accounting principles on restrictive covenants in credit agreements and indentures, Business Lawyer 73, 769–787.

Foster, George, 1978, Financial statement analysis (Prentice-Hall, Englewood Cliffs, NJ).

Galai, Dan and Ronald W. Masulis, 1976, The option pricing model and the risk factor of stock, Journal of Financial Economics 3, 53–81.

Henn, Harry H., 1970, Handbook of the law of corporations and other business enterprises (West Publishing Company, St. Paul, MN).

Holthausen, Robert, 1979, Toward a positive theory of choice of accounting techniques: The case of alternative depreciation methods, Unpublished manuscript (University of Rochester, Rochester, NY).

Jensen, Michael C. and William H. Meckling, 1976, Theory of the firm: Managerial behavior, agency costs, and capital structure, Journal of Financial Economics 3, 305–360.

Johnson, William A., 1970, Default administration of corporate trust indentures: The general nature of the trustee's responsibility and events of default, St. Louis University Law Journal 15, 203–236.

Kalay, Avner, 1979, Toward a theory of corporate dividend policy, Unpublished Ph.D. thesis (University of Rochester, Rochester, NY).

Kennedy, Joseph C., 1961, Corporate trust administration (New York University Press, New York).

Kuhn, Thomas S., 1970, The structure of scientific revolutions (University of Chicago Press, Chicago, IL).

Leftwich, Richard, 1979, Accounting principles and bond indentures: The role of private contracts, Unpublished manuscript (University of Rochester, Rochester, NY).

Leftwich, Richard, Ross Watts and Jerold L. Zimmerman, 1979, A theory of voluntary corporate disclosure, Unpublished manuscript (University of Rochester, Rochester, NY).

Long, John B., 1973, Book review of the theory of finance by Eugene Fama and Merton Miller, Journal of Money, Credit and Banking 5, 229–235.

Manne, Henry, 1967, Our two corporation systems: Law and economics, Virginia Law Review 53, 259–284.

Mayers, David and Clifford W. Smith, 1978, Towards a positive theory of insurance, Unpublished manuscript (University of Rochester, Rochester, NY).

Merton, Robert C., 1973, Theory of rational option pricing, Bell Journal of Economics and Management Science 4, 141–183.

Merton, Robert C., 1974, On the pricing of corporate debt: The risk structure of interest rates, Journal of Finance 29, 449–470.

Mikkelson, Wayne, 1978, An examination of the agency cost rationale for convertible bonds, Unpublished manuscript (University of Rochester, Rochester, NY).

Miller, Merton, 1977a, The wealth transfers of bankruptcy: Some illustrative examples, Special issue on the economics of bankruptcy reform, Law and Contemporary Problems 41, Autumn, 39–46.

Miller, Merton, 1977b, Debt and taxes, Journal of Finance 22, 261–275.

Miller, Merton and Franco Modigliani, 1966, Some estimates of the cost of capital to the electric utility industry, American Economic Review 56, 334–391.

Modigliani, Franco and Merton Miller, 1958, The cost of capital, corporation finance, and the theory of investment, American Economic Review 48, 261–297.

Myers, Stewart C., 1977, Determinants of corporate borrowing, Journal of Financial Economics 5, 147–175.

Nagel, Ernest, 1961, The structure of science: Problems in the logic of scientific explanation (Harcourt, Brace & World, New York).

Norgaard, Richard L. and F. Corine Thompson, 1967, Sinking funds: Their use and value (Financial Executives Research Foundation, New York).

Obrzut, Frederica R., 1976, The trust indenture act of 1939: The corporate trustee as creditor, UCLA Law Review 24, 131–159.

Popper, Karl, 1959, The logic of scientific discovery (Hutchinson, London).

Posner, Richard A., A theory of negligence, Journal of Legal Studies 1, 29–96.

Rodgers, Churchill, 1965, The corporate trust indenture project, Business Lawyer 20, 551–571.

Ross, Stephen A., 1977, The determination of financial structure: The incentive signalling approach, Bell Journal of Economics 8, 23–40.

Scott, James H., Jr., 1977, Bankruptcy, secured debt, and optimal capital structure, Journal of Finance 32, 1–19.

Smith, Clifford W., 1976, Option pricing: A review, Journal of Financial Economics 3, 3–51.

Smith, Clifford W. and Jerold B. Warner, 1979, Bankruptcy, secured debt, and optimal capital structure: Comment, Journal of Finance 34, 247–251.

Stigler, George J., 1958, The economies of scale, Journal of Law and Economics 1, 54–71.

Stiglitz, Joseph E., 1972, Some aspects of the pure theory of corporate finance: Bankruptcies and takeovers, Bell Journal of Economics 3, 458–482.

Warner, Jerold B., 1977, Bankruptcy, absolute priority, and the pricing of risky debt claims, Journal of Financial Economics 4, 239–276.

Watts, Ross, 1977, Corporate financial statements, a product of the market and political processes, Australian Journal of Management 2, 53–75.

Wier, Peggy, 1978, Callable debt, Unpublished manuscript (University of Rochester, Rochester, NY).

Zinbarg, Edward, 1975, The private placement loan agreement, Financial Analysts Journal 31, July/Aug., 33–52.

Pricing Mortgage Originations

Clifford W. Smith, Jr.*

The general structure of observed mortgage loan contracts and the structure of firms in the industry can be explained in terms of competitive markets and rational expectations. It is not necessary to invoke disequilibrium, credit-rationing theories. Collateralization, covenants, downpayments, and other noninterest rate provisions in loan contracts are efficient mechanisms to control the conflict of interest between the borrower and lender. Finally, there are constraints lenders place on the range of contractual provisions offered because of interdependencies in payoffs across contracts and the costs they face associated with insolvency.

INTRODUCTION

A loan contract is typically a complex agreement. Provisions are frequently included which restrict the borrower's use of certain of his assets, require the disclosure of the occurrence of particular events, and in some circumstances provide for the direct supervision of certain of the borrower's activities. In the economics literature, these contractual provisions are typically explained in terms of credit rationing;[1] much of this literature emphasizes the inefficiency of moral hazard and adverse selection in the loan market.

In this paper, I examine the incentives of the borrower and lender within the context of competitive markets; rational expectations on the part of both borrowers and lenders are assumed. These contracting incentives determine the complex terms included in loan contracts. My analysis implies that contractual provisions such as collateralization of loans, limitation on renting and escrow accounts are efficient solutions to incentive problems occurring in the mortgage loan market.

* Associate Professor, Graduate School of Management, University of Rochester, Rochester, New York, 14627.

The Implications of competition among borrowers   A lender is faced with many alternative borrowers. He can loan funds to an individual through a mortgage loan or an automobile loan. He can loan funds to a corporation either by making a loan or by buying bonds. Finally, the lender can loan funds to federal, state or local governments by buying their bonds, notes, or bills. A specific alternative on which I want to focus is treasury bills.

Treasury bills are short-term obligations of the U.S. Government. They have essentially no probability of default associated with them; their purchase and sale impose minimal transactions costs; and they entail virtually zero administration costs. Thus, as long as the alternative of treasury bills is available to the lender, any other borrower whose loan contract imposes default costs, transactions costs, or administrative costs must compensate the lender for bearing these costs, or the contract will be dominated by treasury bills. For example, this means that although a mortgage loan contract may specify that the lender mails payment notices, the borrower ultimately bears the costs through a higher promised interest rate on the loan.

Control of Incentive Conflicts   Whenever cooperative action is required and utility maximizing individuals are faced with alternative activity choices, incentive conflicts exist. With frictionless markets (e.g., Coase [8]) incentive conflicts are assumed costlessly controlled: Contracts can be costlessly negotiated, administered and enforced, restricting an individual's or firm's opportunity to a single point. Thus, even with perfect markets, contracts should be expected to contain provisions controlling individuals' real activity choices.

I assume incentive conflicts are not costlessly controlled. In general, positive negotiation, information, administration and litigation costs imply optimal contracts will provide less than complete control of real activity choices. With competitive and informationally efficient financial markets, unbiased estimates of the total contracting costs (both out-of-pocket and opportunity costs) will be reflected in the prices of securities when sold.[2] Thus incentives exist to structure contracts and institutions to reduce these costs. Mortgage contracts and the structure of lending institutions are the result of a costly contracting process.

Ultimately, the loan market exists because it facilitates the intertemporal rearrangement of consumption opportunities. One cost of maintaining this market is that of contractually controlling the conflict between borrower and lender. As long as the contracting technology does not allow for control of this conflict at zero cost, the contracting costs must be incurred in order to make lending feasible.

Moral Hazard and Adverse Selection   The alteration of activities in response to changed incentives after the origination of a loan is referred to as the moral hazard problem. Moral hazard occurs as long as contractual guarantees of an individual's future actions are expensive.[3] Thus even with zero information costs (in the sense that the lender can perfectly anticipate the policyholder's actions, given his contractually restricted opportunity set), moral hazard occurs. Adverse selection refers to the tendency for those who are the worst risks to apply for loans.

Lenders recognize that borrower's incentives change when loans are negotiated; interest rates reflect rational forecasts of the contracting costs. The borrower recognizes that the lender anticipates that he will act on his own self-interest given his contractually restricted opportunity set. Hence, in the mortgage loan market the *borrower* has a strong incentive to minimize the costs of adminis- tration of the loan. Therefore, given the contracting technology and effective competition among lenders, private incentives exist for the equilibrium loan con- tract to maximize the borrower's expected utility while minimizing the total costs borne by the borrowers.

PRICING SIMPLE LOANS IN PERFECT MARKETS

To begin, I ignore costs associated with contracting to focus on implications of the possibility of default. Consider a simple loan contract: A promise to re- pay a lump sum, F, covering both principal and interest at a specified date in the future, t*, T years from now. At the maturity date of the loan, the lender will have a claim on the borrower with a face value of F dollars. If the value of the borrower's assets is greater than the promised repayment amount, then the loan can be fully repaid. On the other hand, if at the maturity date of the loan the value of the borrower's assets is less than the promised repayment amount, the borrower must default on the loan. The lender does not receive the promised repayment, he can only take the borrower's assets. Exhibit 1 illustrates the payoffs to the lender at the maturity date of the loan for each possible value of the borrower's assets.

The current value of this simple debt instrument has been examined by several authors[4] and been shown to be a positive function of: (1) the current market value of the borrower's assets, V; and (2) the face value of the loan, F; and a negative function of: (3) the time until the maturity of the loan, T; (4) the net rental rate of the borrower's assets, s; (5) the variability of the future values of the borrower's assets, σ^2; and (6) the riskless rate of interest (e.g., the treasury bill rate). Thus, the current value of the loan can be expressed as:

$$L = L(V, F, T, s, \sigma^2, r) \tag{1}$$

where $\dfrac{\partial L}{\partial V}, \dfrac{\partial L}{\partial F} > 0$ and $\dfrac{\partial L}{\partial T}, \dfrac{\partial L}{\partial s}, \dfrac{\partial L}{\partial \sigma^2}, \dfrac{\partial L}{\partial r} < 0.$

The partial effects indicated are in the expected direction and have intuitive interpretations: An increase in the value of the borrower's assets directly in- creases the value of the equity and increases the coverage of the debt, thereby

EXHIBIT 1

Value of the loan (L *) at the maturity date of the loan (t*) for each possible
value of the borrower's assets (V*) given the face value of the loan (F)

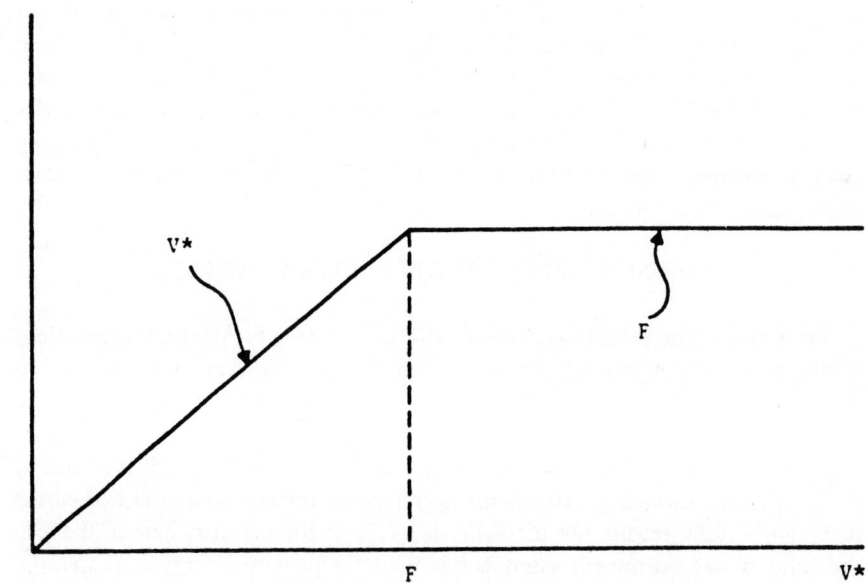

lowering the probability of default and increasing the value of the loan. An increase in the face value increases the lender's claim on the assets thus increasing the value of the debt. An increase in either the time to repayment or the riskless rate lowers the present value of the promised repayment amount, lowering the value of the debt. Given the market value of the borrower's assets, if the net rental rate increases, the expected rate of price appreciation in the assets falls. Thus, the expected value of the assets at the maturity date of the loan is less, default is more likely, and the value of the debt is less. An increase in the variance rate increases the dispersion of possible values of the borrower's asset at the repayment date. Since the lender has a maximum payment he can receive, an increase in the dispersion increases the probability that the value of the borrower's assets will be below the promised repayment, thereby lowering the value of the debt.

Equilibrium Interest Rates   The promised interest rate, f, on this simple loan can be expressed as:

$$e^{fT} = F/L(V, F, T, s, \sigma^2, r),\qquad(2)$$

or

$$\hat{r} = \ln(F/L(V, F, T, s, \sigma^2, r))/T$$

$$= \hat{r}(V, F, T, s, \sigma^2, r), \tag{3}$$

where $\dfrac{\partial \hat{r}}{\partial V} < 0. \dfrac{\partial \hat{r}}{\partial F}, \dfrac{\partial \hat{r}}{\partial s}, \dfrac{\partial \hat{r}}{\partial \sigma^2} \dfrac{\partial \hat{r}}{\partial r}$, 0, and $\dfrac{\partial \hat{r}}{\partial T} \gtrless 0.$

The interpretation of the effect on the promised interest rate of the value of the assets, the net service flow, the variance rate and the riskless rate are straight-foward: those values which increase the value of the loan reduce the promised interest payment. There is a less-than-proportional increase in the current value of a loan from an increase in the face value because of the increased probability of default; thus the promised interest rate rises. There are two effects on the promised interest rate of an increase in the time to repayment, either of which can dominate: (1) An increase in the time to repayment reduces the value of the debt, increasing the promised interest rate; (2) Given the current value of the debt and promised repayment, an increase in the life of the loan lowers the promised interest rate.

Amortization Schedule Thus far, only the simplest loan contracts have been considered, contracts which call for only one payment of principal plus interest at the maturity date of the loan. Since mortgage loans typically require monthly payments over ten, twenty, or thirty years, the impact of that simplification may be of concern. However, this modification changes none of the general form arguments in equation (1). With these required payments, the contract is like a series of loans. The first payment (loan) must be repaid as contractually agreed or the entire sequence goes into default. After that payment, the next payment (loan) must be paid. Thus, although the contract is much more complex (see Geske [10]) the same variables enter the mortgage lending decision to determine the value of the mortgage loan as in the simple case above. Furthermore, the current market value of an amortized loan is strictly greater than that of a simple, single-payment loan.

Prepayment Options Mortgage loan contracts specify prepayment rights; loans frequently can be prepaid (after some specified date) with no penalty. Thus, these contracts are like corporate bonds with a call provision. With uncertain future interest rates, the value of the prepayment option to the borrower is greater the greater the variability of future interest rates. This is because if, after the loan is made, interest rates fall, the borrower exercises his prepayment option; while if interest rates rise, he does not. Thus, more variable interest rates made a mortgage containing prepayment provisions less valuable (see Brennan/Schwartz [7]).[5]

Second Mortgages[6] Assume that two loans are outstanding, one with higher priority under default than the other, and both with the same maturity date, t*.[7] If the value of the collateral at t* is greater than the face value of the first mortgage, F_1, then the first mortgage lender is paid in full; if not, the first mortgage holder receives the collateral and the second mortgage lender and the borrower receive nothing. If the value of the collateral is greater than the sum of the face values of the first and second mortgages, $F_1 + F_2$, then both loans are repaid and the borrower keeps the residual. If the value of the collateral at t* is between F_1 and $F_1 + F_2$, the second mortgage lender receives the difference between the value of the collateral and F_1. Exhibit 2 illustrates the payoffs to the first and second mortgage holders at the maturity date of the loans for each possible value of the borrower's assets.

Inspection indicates that the pricing of the first mortgage is unaffected by the existence of the second mortgage. The current value of the second mortgage can be expressed as:

$$L_2 = L_2 (V, F_1, F_2, T, s, \sigma^2, r) \tag{4}$$

where $\quad \dfrac{\partial L_2}{\partial V}, \dfrac{\partial L_2}{\partial F_2} > 0; \dfrac{\partial L_2}{\partial F_1}, \dfrac{\partial L_2}{\partial s} < 0;$ and $\dfrac{\partial L_2}{\partial T}, \dfrac{\partial L_2}{\partial \sigma^2}, \dfrac{\partial L_2}{\partial r} \gtrless 0.$

The ambiguity of the response of the value of the second mortgage with respect to the time of maturity, the variance rate and the riskless rate arises because of the dual debt/equity behavior of the instrument. If the value of the collateral is "close to" the promised repayment of the first mortgage, the second mortgage is essentially the residual claimant, and the claim's value behaves much like an equity claim. Conversely, if the value of the collateral is significantly higher so that the probability of default on the first mortgage is "small," the second mortgage is essentially a fixed claim and behaves like debt.

Restrictions in Mortgage Loan Contracts The lender must ascertain the values of the variables in equation (3) to determine the appropriate interest rate, $\hat{r}$, to compensate him for the risk he bears. In the case of the face value of the loan and the time until maturity, this is not difficult since these are the results of direct negotiation between the borrower and lender and are explicitly stated. The riskless rate is exogenous to the entire process and is readily observable. Furthermore, if there were no transactions costs, the value of the borrower's assets could be determined as well. However, there are fundamental problems with ascertaining the net rental rate and the variance rate of the borrower's assets, for these factors are, to some extent, under the control of the borrower; and thus can be changed to benefit the borrower and hurt the lender after the loan is made.

For example, if a borrower obtains a loan for the stated purpose of purchasing a low-risk asset and the lender charges an interest rate commensurate with

EXHIBIT 2

Payoffs to first (L_1) and second (L_2) mortgage at the maturity date of the loan (t^*) for each possible value of the borrower's assets (V^*) given the face value of the first (F_1) and second (F_2) mortgages.

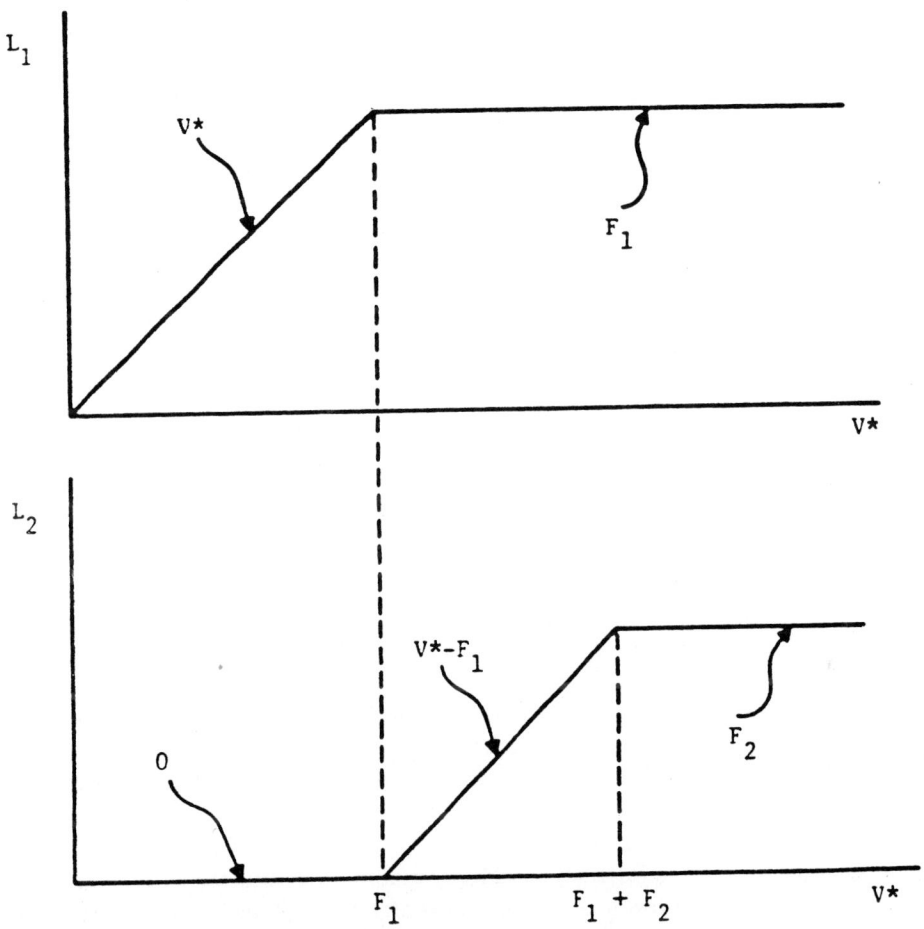

that low risk, the value of the loan would fall (the value of the borrower's equity would rise) if the borrower could sell his low-risk assets and purchase assets with a high variance rate. Especially in the case of mortgage loans, the assessment of the net rental rate on a house is very difficult. This is explicitly because this variable is so directly under the control of the borrower. Specifically, the net rental rate is the value of the rental service less the expenditures on maintenance (i.e., repairs, taxes, insurance) of the property. If the market price of the property falls below the promised repayment amount and the borrower feels that there is a greater probability of default, then he can increase the net rental rate he receives on the house by reducing maintenance expenditures to zero.

There are three major ways in which a lender can attempt to protect himself from these problems: (1) He can increase the required downpayment. This lowers the borrower's incentive to engage in activities that increase the probability of default by increasing the borrower's equity and thus his loss if default occurs. (2) He can charge an interest rate high enough to protect himself against the most unfavorable action which may be available to the borrower. For example, he might assume that the borrower will use the funds to acquire very risky assets with the proceeds of the loan or make no maintenance expenditures on the property. If the lender does this, unless the borrower acquires assets of the risk presumed by the lender and unless the borrower makes zero maintenance expenditures, the lender will be overcompensated for the actual risk borne. Therefore, if this procedure is employed, low-risk assets or assets which the owner wishes to maintain would be expensive to acquire with borrowed funds. (3) The lender can write restrictive covenants into the loan agreement. For example, escrow accounts are regularly employed with mortgage loans. This insures the lender that certain maintenance expenses, such as insurance and taxes, are met. Moreover, some mortgage loan contracts specify items such as repainting frequency. Again, this provision attempts to regulate the extent to which the borrower can hurt the lender by increasing the net service flows to himself. Finally, lenders regularly require that the loan be collateralized. If the lender holds the title to the assets, the title cannot be legally transferred without the permission of the lender. Thus, asset substitution is precluded, and the risk characteristics of this portion of the borrower's assets can be determined with much greater certainty.

So far we have seen that even if the contracting process is costless and loan markets are competitive and efficient, the use of restrictive covenants and collateral in mortgage loan contracts are important in controlling the conflict of interest that exists between borrowers and lenders. Although additional incentives are added when transactions and information are costly and are compounded when government regulations specifically prohibit the borrower and lender from including certain provisions within loan contracts, the basic incentives described here still exist. These more complex issues are considered next.

THE IMPACT OF CONTRACTING COSTS ON THE STRUCTURE OF MORTGAGE LOAN CONTRACTS

As suggested above, given that lenders have the opportunity to employ their funds in many different ways, some of which involve virtually no processing, monitoring, or administering costs (such as the purchase of treasury bills), any costs imposed on the lender through a loan contract will ultimately be paid by the borrower. Such costs as the cost of mailing payment notices may be impounded in the interest rate charged on the loan or charged to the borrower directly. But no matter how the fees are collected, as long as the lender has alternative uses of his funds, any costs imposed on the lender will ultimately be borne by the borrower. (Some of the costs are typically directly and explicitly imposed on the borrower, such as the mortgage application fee or the fee for the appraisal of the property by the lender.)

Administrative Costs, Bankruptcy Laws and Default Costs Conceptually, the total value of the borrower's assets, V, can be separated into three categories: (1) the value of the collateral, V_c, (2) the value of the "unattachable" assets,[8] V_u, and (3) the value of the "attachable" assets, V_a. (For simplicity, assume the assets can be expressed as fractions, $c + u + a \equiv 1$, of the lender's total assets.[9]) To the extent that other "attachable" assets exist, then the lender can acquire these assets in the event that the borrower defaults.

The simple model presented in the previous section also can be modified to account for various contracting costs. Assume that: (1) There are administrative costs, τ associated with processing the payment if the borrower does not default, (2) if the borrower does default, the foreclosure and other costs can be expressed as linear function of the value of the collateral. Furthermore, assume that foreclosure costs differ for assets pledged as collateral, $\Phi_c + \phi_c V_c^*$, and other attachable assets $\Phi_a + \phi_a V_a^*$.

Finally, there are other costs associated with default which are directly imposed on the borrower. If it is expensive to default on a loan, the analysis presented in the previous section must be modified to incorporate the additional incentives faced by the borrower. For example, it may be expensive to default on a real estate loan simply because it is costly to move. If that is the case, a borrower will not choose to default on his loan at the point where the value of his collateral is just equal to the promised repayment, F. If the individual would incur default costs of Δ dollars, he will not default on his loan unless the value of the house is less than the repayment amount minus the borrower-borne default costs.

Exhibit 3 illustrates the net payoffs to the lender at the maturity of the loan for each possible value of the lender's assets. The implications of these modifications are straightforward:

$$\hat{f} = \hat{f}(V^*, c, a, F, T, \sigma^2, s, \phi_c, \phi_c, \Phi_a, \phi_a, \tau, B, r) \tag{5}$$

where $\dfrac{\partial \hat{f}}{\partial c}, \dfrac{\partial \hat{f}}{\partial a}, \dfrac{\partial \hat{f}}{\partial \Delta}, < 0; \dfrac{\partial \hat{f}}{\partial \Phi_c}, \dfrac{\partial \hat{f}}{\partial \phi_c}, \dfrac{\partial \hat{f}}{\partial \Phi_a}, \dfrac{\partial \hat{f}}{\partial \phi_a}, \dfrac{\partial \hat{f}}{\partial \tau}, > 0;$ and other

effects as in equation (3).

Any form of higher transaction/administrative costs assumed by the lender makes the loan less valuable and results in a higher promised interest rate on the

EXHIBIT 3

Net payoffs to the mortgage lender (L*) at the maturity of the loan (t*) for each
possible value of the borrower's assets (V*) given the face value of the loan (F); where
the borrower has pledged the fraction, c, of his assets as collateral, and the bankruptcy
laws specify that the lender can also attach the fraction, a, of the borrower's assets if
default occurs. Foreclosure costs are assumed $\Phi_c + cV^*(1 - \phi_c)$ for collateral,
$\Phi_a + aV^*(1 - \phi_a)$ for attachable assets, administrative costs, given no attachable
assets, administrative costs, given no default are τ, and the borrower bears default
costs (Δ) if he defaults

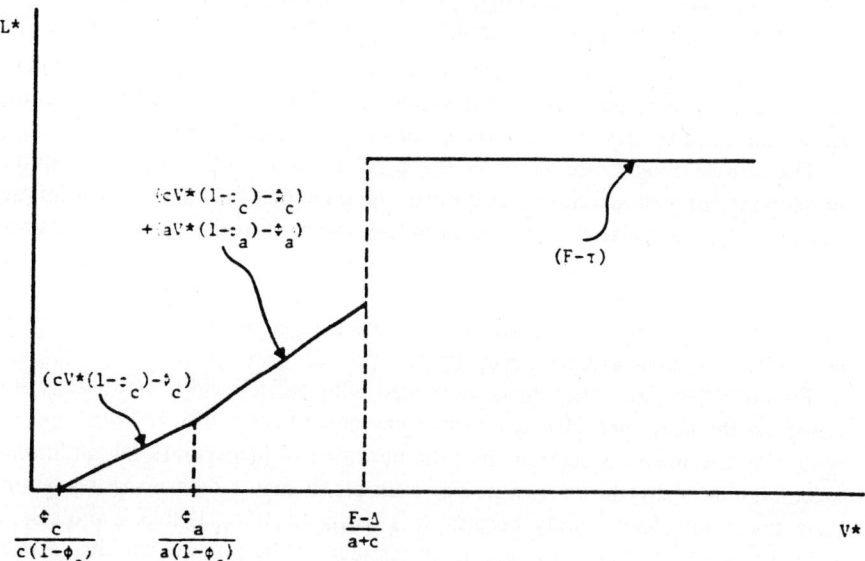

loan. However, if borrower-borne default costs are positive, the promised interest
rate will be lower because of these additional incentives facing the borrower to
avoid default. Thus, default costs borne by the borrower decrease the probability
of default, increase the value of the loan, and lower the promised interest payment. Finally, the higher the fraction of the lender's assets that are pledged as
collateral or are attachable, the more valuable the loan and the lower the required
interest rate.

Note that if a lender can lower the costs of processing, monitoring, or administering loans, he can earn abnormal returns in the short run. However, in the
long run, when other lenders also employ these less costly techniques, competition will lower the cost of borrowing. For example, since information is expensive
and it is expensive to enforce contracts, a lender will demand that a loan be
formally collateralized, establishing priority over subsequent loans. It is also
less expensive to take possession of an asset to which the lender already has

established legal claim; therefore. foreclosure expenses are reduced through collateralization. Since this form of the loan contract is less costly to administer, the effective interest rate charged the borrower will be less than for uncollateralized loans.

Another obvious way in which these costs can be reduced is by increasing the downpayment, the margin between the value of the collateral and the amount of the loan. The larger the downpayment, the lower the default risk on the loan and the lower the expected costs of processing, monitoring and administrating the loan. Thus, loans with high downpayments require lower interest rates both because the risk is lower and because the expected transactions costs to be imposed on the lender are lower.[10]

The moving costs discussed above are only an example of a much broader class of borrower-borne default costs. These costs may be either pecuniary or nonpecuniary and include the borrower's valuation of the incremental costs attributed to default which are expected to be imposed through (1) higher interest expense in anticipated future borrowing, (2) the reduction in the probability of obtaining certain types of employment in the future, (3) the loss of any consumer surplus associated with the collateral and, (4) the default procedure itself (e.g., the moving costs or opportunity cost of the borrower's time spent with collection agents).

It should be noted that the analysis without default costs or distinction between collateral, attachable and unattachable assets did not include variables which dealt with the borrower's credit record: The value of the loan was simply a function of the value of the borrower's assets, the riskiness of the assets, etc. Now we see that factors which appear in most credit reports, such as the record of previous borrowing experience and information on the length of time in previous locations, can be useful indicators of the costs associated with default on the loan. However, these variables are only important within a restricted range of possible outcomes of the value of the collateral. If the value of the collateral is greater than the promised repayment amount, the borrower could voluntarily agree with the lender to sell the property, pay off the loan (avoid the foreclosure costs) and pocket the difference; when the value of the collateral plus the default costs are less than the promised repayment, the borrowers will default.

However, if the borrower can shift assets from the attachable to the unattachable category, the value of the loan falls and the value of the borrower's equity rises. Examples of this action are purchasing a large house or putting the assets in the name of a relative.[11] For these reasons, the assets not explicitly pledged as collateral will be discounted in the lending decision. Thus, this legal provision for unattachable assets raises the contracted interest rates. This cost is borne by all borrowers who do not default on their loans.

Given these limitations on the lender's ability to take possession of any of the borrower's assets other than those which have explicitly been pledged as collateral, the value of a credit check on the borrower is limited. In the absence of regulation, it would be expected that any credit check would be confined to items for which the benefits exceed the costs. However, the form which regulation of lenders usually assumes is an examination of "bad" loans. If a regulator regularly asks to see the documentation about the loan and the "credit-worthiness" of the borrower, the lender is induced to demand a more expensive credit check. He will still obtain only those items for which the benefits exceed the costs, only now an additional benefit exists for the lender: If the loan goes "bad", he has more to show the regulator, who then imposes fewer costs on the lender.

Usury Laws   Another legislative constraint placed on many loan markets is the imposition of a usury ceiling on interest rates. If the riskless rate of interest is above the usury ceiling (ignoring tax incentives and coercion by governmental authorities) no loans will be made. This is because both a higher effective interest rate and a lower level of risk could be obtained by purchasing treasury bills.

If the riskless rate is below the usury ceiling rate loans will be made as long as the usury ceilings allows a sufficient rate of interest to compensate the lender for both the risk which he bears and for the costs of processing, administering and monitoring required by the loan. The primary way in which this is done is by increasing the downpayment required on the loan. This lowers the probability of default on the loan and brings the competitive rate of interest on the loan within the legal limit.

Typically, there are three ways in which a borrower can adjust to usury restrictions in mortgage markets: (1) He can reduce his loan demand by choosing a different house, (2) he can increase his borrowing in other forms such as automobile loans, credit card balances, (3) he can seek to lower the risk of the loan by purchasing various kinds of insurance (such as VA, FHA,[12] and MGIC) whose premiums are not subject to the usury ceilings.

When the insurance is employed to avoid the usury laws it should be clear that the insurance company accepts part of the default risk for the loan. It is compensated for accepting that risk through the insurance premiums charged.[13] However in the case of particular government administered programs which price the insurance at below its cost there is a subsidy to some group, such as VA insured loans to veterans. If the price of mortgage insurance were unregulated, riskier loans would have higher insurance premiums assessed to compensate the insurer. However with regulated price (one-half percent on FHA and zero percent on VA), the insured loans will appear more a bargain to borrowers with property in riskier neighborhoods, hence insured loans should be more prevalent there.

If there were no transactions costs, etc., the sum of the interest payments and the insurance premium on an insured loan would equal the interest rate paid if the same loan were uninsured. However, given positive costs of adminis-tration, it seems likely that the sum of the insurance premium plus the interest payments on an insured loan will be greater than the interest payments on an uninsured loan of the same risk. Thus, if the borrower employs what seems to be a relatively inexpensive method to avoid the usury ceilings, mortgage insur-ance, he still must incur higher total costs than if that restriction had been absent.

ON THE STRUCTURE OF THE INDUSTRY

The preceding analysis of provisions in mortgage loan contracts ignores any interdependence among contracts which the lending institution issues, focusing on the trade-off between promised interest rates, time to maturity, required downpayments and other contractual provisions. A general set of considerations which is important for understanding observed aspects of the organization form of lending institutions is the set of contracting costs between the firm and its claimholders.

Most mortgage loans are originated by the depository financial intermediaries. Depositors turn assets over to the firm in return for a promise to be repaid plus interest (or services) in the future. There are incentive conflicts between de-positors and stockholders over the dividend, financing, and investment policies of the firm. There are also incentive conflicts between the owners and managers over investment policy. In this section, these conflicts are analyzed and it is suggested how they can be controlled by the firm's choice of ownership and asset structure.[14]

Common Stock Firms   First, the incentives faced by the stockholders of a common stock thrift institution operated to maximize shareholder welfare are analyzed. Initially, assume that the conflict between stockholders and managers is costlessly controlled.

The stockholders of a thrift institution have incentives to engage in oppor-tunistic behavior with respect to depositors which are much the same as the incentives of borrowers discussed earlier. Assume that a bank issues a long-term certificate of deposit (CD) with an interest rate which would be appropriate for a policy of low dividends. If the bank raises its dividend and finances the dividend increase by liquidating its assets then the coverage on this fixed claim would fall, the risk of the CD would rise. In the limit, if the bank sold all its assets and paid a liquidating dividend, the depositors would be left with worth-less claims.[15] But depositors will anticipate these actions by the bank. To con-trol these incentive conflicts, stockholders would be expected to limit the firm's choice of investment, financing and dividend policies, for example, through provisions in the firm's charter.

Mutual Ownership   Another way in which the incentive conflict between depositors and stockholders can be controlled is with an alternative ownership structure, mutual ownership. In a mutual thrift institution, the depositors are also the owners of the firm. In this way conflicts arising from differential incentives between depositors and equityholders are controlled by making the members of the two groups coincident.

To this point. the owner-manager conflict has been assumed costlessly controlled. Now, that assumption is relaxed. A significant factor in controlling managers is the threat of a tender offer or proxy fight. In a mutual, since the ownership claims are not separately traded, tender offers are impossible. And proxy fights, since shares (and votes) cannot be purchased, are more expensive, and thus less effective. Therefore, it appears that the major advantage of mutuals (from controlling the incentive conflict between depositors and stockholders) is offset by reduced control of the owner-manager conflict.

In the thrift industry, both stock and mutual firms coexist. Competition between mutuals and stocks suggest for a common set of services, there should be little difference in the contracts. The main difference should be in the relative specialization in types of contracts offered. If in mutuals control of the depositor-stockholder conflict is greater while the control of the owner-manager conflict is more expensive than in stocks, then mutuals should be more prevalent in thrifts where management discretion is less important and whose liability structure would have larger depositor-stockholder conflicts. This would suggest that full service banks are more likely to be stocks because of the greater range of loan contracts offered and thus greater required management discretion. Moreover, stocks would be expected to specialize in issuing deposits with shorter effective maturity dates, deposits where the depositor-stockholder conflict is less. Conversely, mutuals would be expected to issue fewer types of loans, specializing in secured loans where management discretion is less; and the deposits in mutuals should have longer effective maturities.

Asset Maturity Structure The effective duration of the asset structure of the firm affects the depositor-stockholder incentive conflict. As Myers [15] indicates, future investment decisions of the firm can be viewed as options. He shows that with longer lived fixed liability claims in a firm's capital structure, the conflict between the fixed claimholders and stockholders over the exercise of investment options is greater; hence, the lower the demand price for the fixed claim. Myers concludes that firms can control these incentive problems by matching maturities of assets and liabilities.

Incentives to match maturities of cash flows from assets and liabilities is reinforced by bankruptcy/default costs faced by the lending institution. If the value of the lender's assets falls below the value of his maturing obligations, the lender must default on his obligations and can be forced into bankruptcy. For a regulated industry such as banking, costs associated with bankruptcy/default include a range of factors. If the bank's capital falls below a specified level, regulatory agencies can restrict the bank's activities. Limitations can be imposed on issuing additional notes, management can be removed, and in extreme cases the authority can take direct control of the bank's activities or impose a merger or other form of reorganization. Banks consume real resources in activities to avoid these sanctions.

One way to reduce this probability is to manage the bank's outstanding assets and liabilities to hedge sources of risk. Banks' liabilities, even CDs and time deposits, are of very short effective duration; for a relatively small penalty, the deposits can be withdrawn. Thus when interest rates increase many deposits are renegotiated at the new higher rates. If a bank makes thirty-year fixed interest rate loans while accepting effectively short-term deposits, it exposes itself to significant cash flow variability associated with changes in market interest rates. Matching effective maturities of assets and liabilities hedges this interest rate risk; thus, with more variable market interest rates conventional mortgages with provisions for variable rates should be expected.[16]

Although banks do not appear to have a comparative advantage in issuing long-term liabilities, life insurance companies do. Life insurance contracts have long effective duration. Thus, standard, long-term, fixed-rate mortgages are likely to be available through banks who sell the loans to insurance companies along with a contract to service the loans. To certify the quality of the loans, they are typically first insured by the FHA or VA.

Finally, the banker also may choose to geographically diversify in lending to minimize the probability that a localized event will adversely affect a large portion of his loans simultaneously. For example, a flood or a riot could, virtually by itself, force a lender into bankruptcy if a large portion of his assets were mortgage loans in the affected area (especially since many typical homeowner's insurance policies do not cover these types of losses).[17] Lenders also can diversify across different types of loans.

CONCLUSIONS

The analysis presented in this paper indicates that the general provisions of observed mortgage loan contracts can be explained in terms of competitive markets and rational expectations; it is not necessary to invoke disequilibrium, credit-rationing theories. Collateralization, covenants, downpayments and other noninterest rate provisions in loan contracts are efficient mechanisms to control the borrower/lender conflict.

To some extent, there is an implicit prediction of behavior on the part of mortgage lenders which casual empiricism would suggest is false. I have described a market in which loans on low-risk collateral are made with low interest rates and/or low downpayments, and loans on high-risk collateral are made with high interest rates or with high downpayments (or with required mortgage insurance policies). However, substantial variation in interest rates or required downpayments are not generally observed in mortgage markets.[18] Why? I think that there are three partial explanations. First, it is somewhat more expensive to make a finer differentiation among borrowers; it may be cheaper for the lender to follow a policy in which a required interest rate and downpayment are stated for all borrowers with the lender simply deciding whether or not to make a specific loan. This may be socially efficient if the costs imposed on the borrowers in terms of higher interest expense is less than the costs which would be imposed on the lenders if they were forced to differentiate among borrowers.

Second, much of the analysis in this paper has been in the context of single-payment contracts. With amortized loans conditional penalties can be imposed for default on specific payments over the life of the loan. The more effective these conditional penalties, the less required differentiation at the origination of the loan.

A third explanation of the observed behavior may be that lenders fear the political costs which might be imposed on them if they differentiated among borrowers through such well-understood means as varying the downpayment and the effective interest rate for different borrowers. For example, if the suburban residential areas were lower risk loan areas and the inner city residential areas were high-risk loan areas, similar loan contracts might be offered the two areas because the expected legal expenses which might arise from having to prove that differentiation is not "discrimination" could well outweigh any possible benefit to the lender.[19]

Notice that an implication of this argument is that without differentiation across loans on required downpayments or interest rates, the low-risk borrower is charged too high a rate. Moreover, if there are political costs associated with rejecting loans from high-risk areas, minimizing total costs (political and otherwise) calls for making more high-risk loans. Therefore, it is possible that loans in low-risk neighborhoods are overcharged and loans in high-risk neighborhoods are undercharged for the risk borne by the lender: Political costs can generate reverse discrimination. However, these costs must be borne by all mortgage borrowers—this political pressure on lending institutions can be expected to raise promised interest rates on mortgage loans.

NOTES

This research is supported by the Managerial Economics Research Center, University of Rochester.

1. See Baltensperger [1] for a review of the credit rationing literature.
2. Jensen/Meckling [12] in analyzing the contracting process define an agency relationship as "a contract under which one or more persons (the principle[s]) engage another person (the agent) to perform some service on their behalf which involves delegating some decision-making authority to the agent." They decompose the contracting (or agency) costs into three components: (1) monitoring expenditures by the principal, (2) bonding expenditures by the agent, and (3) the residual loss. Monitoring is the principal's attempt to control and assess the agent's behavior. Bonding is a form of guarantee made by the agent that he

will not harm the principal's interest, or that he will indemnify the principal. The residual loss is the opportunity cost to the principal from the agent's actions which differ from the decisions which would have been made by the principal in the absence of contracting costs.

3. In this framework, the moral hazard problem is just a special case of a positive residual loss.

4. Benston and Smith [2], Black [3], Black/Miller/Posner [5], Black/Scholes [6], and Smith [16]. For a more rigorous derivation of the results presented here, see Smith [16].

5. For an estimate of the magnitude of this effect, see Hendershott/Villani [11]. Although we abstract from the effect here, a major event triggering prepayment of mortgage loans is the sale of the property. With assumable loans, prepayment is less likely to be triggered by sale of the property. Moreover, the effects discussed here are exacerbated if, with increased interest rates, the frequency of property sales is reduced.

6. This analysis is similar to the Black/Cox [4] analysis of subordinated debt.

7. If the loans' maturity dates differ, the problem becomes more complex. See Geske [10].

8. For example, the law generally provides that a man's home or tools cannot be attached in the case of default on a loan, if those items are not pledged as collateral on that loan.

9. See Stultz [18] for an analysis of this problem where the correlation coefficient between the value of the collateral and the attachable assets is less than one.

10. The incentives for the borrower to misrepresent the value of the collateral or to attempt to change the risk characteristics or payouts of the assets are small for a high ratio of equity to debt, because of the relative insensitivity of the value of the debt to changes in these parameters in that range of the function.

11. For example, see "Promoter's Fall: After Striking It Rich, John King Sees Luck Fail, Says He's Broke," *Wall Street Journal,* August 11, 1975:

> . . .Though he says he's broke, Mr. King continues to live in the fancy home in the Denver suburb of Cherry Hills. In 1970, before his financial collapse, Mr (John M.) King transferred $3 million in assets, including property and oil and gas interests, to his children's trusts.

12. FHA and VA loans have never been subject to usury laws. However, in practice, the explicit interest rates charged are quoted at rates equal to those prevailing in the local mortgage market. "Points," a sum paid at the origination of the loan, make that quoted rate competitive.

13. See Merton [14] for an analysis of the pricing of loan guarantees.

14. See Mayers/Smith [13] and Fama/Jensen [9] for further analysis of these issues.

15. For further elaboration on this point, see Jensen/Meckling [12] or Smith/Warner [17]. Although current regulation restricts depository intermediaries from taking some of the extreme examples suggested and existing deposit insurance protects a majority of depositors, the differing organizational structures discussed here predate much of the regulation and insurance.

16. Another mechanism lenders might be expected to employ in hedging this interest rate risk is writing financial futures contracts. However existing regulation has constrained lenders from fully exploiting this option.

17. Although regulation limits the ability of the lender to diversify geographically, loan participations sold from one bank to another is a mechanism through which this can be accomplished.

18. There does seem to be differentiation through the use of mortgage insurance. However, this is a blunt tool. In some states, private mortgage insurance cannot be used if the downpayment is over 5%. FHA and VA mortgage insurance contracts are standardized external to the lender.

19. The "appraisal" of a house by a mortgage lender has somewhat of this effect. If mortgage loans are being made with "30% downpayments", and the lender receives a mortgage application on a house in a risky area, he will typically "appraise" the house for less than the selling price. He then gives the borrower a mortgage for 30% of the appraised value. This effectively raises the required downpayment.

REFERENCES

[1]   Ernst Baltensperger, "Credit Rationing: Issues and Questions," *Journal of Money, Credit and Banking* 10 (1978), 170-183.

[2]   George Benston and Clifford Smith, "A Transactions Cost Approach to the Theory of Financial Intermediation," *Journal of Finance* 31 (1976), 215-231.

[3]   Fischer Black, "Bank Funds Management in an Efficient Market," *Journal of Financial Economics* 2 (1975), 323-339.

[4]   Fischer Black and John Cox, "Valuing Corporate Securities: Some Effects of Bond Indenture Provisions," *Journal of Finance* 31 (1976), 351-367.

[5]   Fischer Black and Merton Miller and Richard Posner, "An Approach to the Regulation of Bank Holding Companies," *Journal of Business* 51 (1978), 379-412.

[6]   Fischer Black and Myron Scholes, "The Pricing of Options and Corporate Liabilities," *Journal of Political Economy* 81 (1973), 637-659.

[7]   Michael Brennan and Edwardo Schwartz, "Savings Bonds, Retractable Bonds and Callable Bonds," *Journal of Financial Economics* 5 (1977), 67-88.

[8]   Ronald Coase, "The Problem of Social Cost," *Journal of Law and Economics* 7 (1960), 1-44.

[9]   Eugene Fama and Michael Jensen, "Agency Problems and the Survival of Organizations," unpublished manuscript, University of Rochester (1982).

[10] Robert Geske, "The Value of Corporate Liabilities as Compound Options," *Journal of Financial and Quantitative Analysis* 12 (1977), 541-552.

[11] Patric Hendershott and Kevin Villani, "The Terminations Premium in Mortgage Coupon Rates: Evidence on the Integration of Mortgage and Bond Markets," *Journal of Finance,* forthcoming 1982.

[12] Michael Jensen and William Meckling, "Theory of the Firm: Managerial Behavior, Agency Costs and Ownership Structure," *Journal of Financial Economics* 3 (1976), 305-360.

[13] David Mayers and Clifford Smith, "Contractual Provisions, Organizational Structure and Conflict Control in Insurance Markets," *Journal of Business* 54, No. 3 (1981), 407-434.

[14] Robert Merton, "An Analytic Derivation of the Cost of Deposit Insurance and Loan Guarantees: An Application of Modern Option Pricing Theory," *Journal of Banking and Finance* 1 (1977), 3-11.

[15] Stewart Myers, "Determinants of Corporate Borrowing," *Journal of Financial Economics* 5 (1977), 147-175.

[16] Clifford Smith, "On the Theory of Financial Contracting," *Journal of Monetary Economics* 6 (1980), 333-357.

[17] Clifford Smith and Jerold Warner, "On Financial Contracting: An Analysis of Bond Covenants," *Journal of Financial Economics* 5 (1979), 117-161.

[18] René Stulz, "Options on the Minimum or the Maximum of Two Risky Assets: Analysis and Applications," *Journal of Financial Economics,* forthcoming.

Credit Rationing in Markets with Imperfect Information

By JOSEPH E. STIGLITZ AND ANDREW WEISS*

Why is credit rationed? Perhaps the most basic tenet of economics is that market equilibrium entails supply equalling demand; that if demand should exceed supply, prices will rise, decreasing demand and/or increasing supply until demand and supply are equated at the new equilibrium price. So if prices do their job, rationing should not exist. However, credit rationing and unemployment do in fact exist. They seem to imply an excess demand for loanable funds or an excess supply of workers.

One method of "explaining" these conditions associates them with short- or long-term disequilibrium. In the short term they are viewed as *temporary disequilibrium* phenomena; that is, the economy has incurred an exogenous shock, and for reasons not fully explained, there is some stickiness in the prices of labor or capital (wages and interest rates) so that there is a transitional period during which rationing of jobs or credit occurs. On the other hand, long-term unemployment (above some "natural rate") or credit rationing is explained by governmental constraints such as usury laws or minimum wage legislation.[1]

The object of this paper is to show that in *equilibrium* a loan market may be characterized by credit rationing. Banks making loans are concerned about the interest rate

they receive on the loan, and the riskiness of the loan. However, the interest rate a bank charges may itself affect the riskiness of the pool of loans by either: 1) sorting potential borrowers (the adverse selection effect); or 2) affecting the actions of borrowers (the incentive effect). Both effects derive directly from the residual imperfect information which is present in loan markets after banks have evaluated loan applications. When the price (interest rate) affects the nature of the transaction, it may not also clear the market.

The adverse selection aspect of interest rates is a consequence of different borrowers having different probabilities of repaying their loan. The expected return to the bank obviously depends on the probability of repayment, so the bank would like to be able to identify borrowers who are more likely to repay. It is difficult to identify "good borrowers," and to do so requires the bank to use a variety of *screening devices*. The interest rate which an individual is willing to pay may act as one such screening device: those who are willing to pay high interest rates may, on average, be worse risks; they are willing to borrow at high interest rates because they perceive their probability of repaying the loan to be low. As the interest rate rises, the average "riskiness" of those who borrow increases, possibly lowering the bank's profits.

Similarly, as the interest rate and other terms of the contract change, the behavior of the borrower is likely to change. For instance, raising the interest rate decreases the return on projects which succeed. We will show that higher interest rates induce firms to undertake projects with lower probabilities of success but higher payoffs when successful.

In a world with perfect and costless information, the bank would stipulate precisely all the actions which the borrower could

*Bell Telephone Laboratories, Inc. and Princeton University, and Bell Laboratories, Inc., respectively. We would like to thank Bruce Greenwald, Henry Landau, Rob Porter, and Andy Postlewaite for fruitful comments and suggestions. Financial support from the National Science Foundation is gratefully acknowledged. An earlier version of this paper was presented at the spring 1977 meetings of the Mathematics in the Social Sciences Board in Squam Lake, New Hampshire.

[1] Indeed, even if markets were not competitive one would not expect to find rationing; profit maximization would, for instance, lead a monopolistic bank to raise the interest rate it charges on loans to the point where excess demand for loans was eliminated.

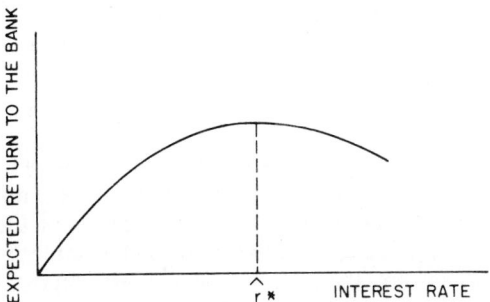

FIGURE 1. THERE EXISTS AN INTEREST RATE WHICH
MAXIMIZES THE EXPECTED RETURN TO THE BANK

undertake (which might affect the return to the loan). However, the bank is not able to directly control all the actions of the borrower; therefore, it will formulate the terms of the loan contract in a manner designed to induce the borrower to take actions which are in the interest of the bank, as well as to attract low-risk borrowers.

For both these reasons, the expected return by the bank may increase less rapidly than the interest rate; and, beyond a point, may actually decrease, as depicted in Figure 1. The interest rate at which the expected return to the bank is maximized, we refer to as the "bank-optimal" rate, $\hat{r}^*$.

Both the demand for loans and the supply of funds are functions of the interest rate (the latter being determined by the expected return at $\hat{r}^*$). Clearly, it is conceivable that at $\hat{r}^*$ the demand for funds exceeds the supply of funds. Traditional analysis would argue that, in the presence of an excess demand for loans, unsatisfied borrowers would offer to pay a higher interest rate to the bank, bidding up the interest rate until demand equals supply. But although supply does not equal demand at $\hat{r}^*$, it is the equilibrium interest rate! The bank would not lend to an individual who offered to pay more than $\hat{r}^*$. In the bank's judgment, such a loan is likely to be a worse risk than the average loan at interest rate $\hat{r}^*$, and the expected return to a loan at an interest rate above $\hat{r}^*$ is actually lower than the expected return to the loans the bank is presently making. Hence, there are

no competitive forces leading supply to equal demand, and credit is rationed.

But the interest rate is not the only term of the contract which is important. The amount of the loan, and the amount of collateral or equity the bank demands of loan applicants, will also affect both the behavior of borrowers and the distribution of borrowers. In Section III, we show that increasing the collateral requirements of lenders (beyond some point) may decrease the returns to the bank, by either decreasing the average degree of risk aversion of the pool of borrowers; or in a multiperiod model inducing individual investors to undertake riskier projects.

Consequently, it may not be profitable to raise the interest rate or collateral requirements when a bank has an excess demand for credit; instead, banks deny loans to borrowers who are observationally indistinguishable from those who receive loans.[2]

It is not our argument that credit rationing will always characterize capital markets, but rather that it may occur under not implausible assumptions concerning borrower and lender behavior.

This paper thus provides the first theoretical justification of true credit rationing. Previous studies have sought to explain why each individual faces an upward sloping interest rate schedule. The explanations offered are (a) the probability of default for any particular borrower increases as the amount borrowed increases (see Stiglitz 1970, 1972; Marshall Freimer and Myron Gordon; Dwight Jaffee; George Stigler), or (b) the mix of borrowers changes adversely (see Jaffee and Thomas Russell). In these circumstances we would not expect loans of different size to pay the same interest rate, any more than we would expect two borrowers, one of whom has a reputation for prudence and the other a reputation as a bad credit risk, to be able to borrow at the same interest rate.

We reserve the term credit rationing for circumstances in which either (a) among loan applicants who appear to be identical some

---

[2]After this paper was completed, our attention was drawn to W. Keeton's book. In chapter 3 he develops an incentive argument for credit rationing.

receive a loan and others do not, and the rejected applicants would not receive a loan even if they offered to pay a higher interest rate; or (b) there are identifiable groups of individuals in the population who, with a given supply of credit, are unable to obtain loans at any interest rate, even though with a larger supply of credit, they would.[3]

In our construction of an equilibrium model with credit rationing, we describe a market equilibrium in which there are many banks and many potential borrowers. Both borrowers and banks seek to maximize profits, the former through their choice of a project, the latter through the interest rate they charge borrowers and the collateral they require of borrowers (the interest rate received by depositors is determined by the zero-profit condition). Obviously, we are not discussing a "price-taking" equilibrium. Our equilibrium notion is competitive in that banks compete; one means by which they compete is by their choice of a price (interest rate) which maximizes their profits. The reader should notice that in the model presented below there are interest rates at which the demand for loanable funds equals the supply of loanable funds. However, these are not, in general, equilibrium interest rates. If, at those interest rates, banks could increase their profits by lowering the interest rate charged borrowers, they would do so.

Although these results are presented in the context of credit markets, we show in Section V that they are applicable to a wide class of principal-agent problems (including those describing the landlord-tenant or employer-employee relationship).

I. Interest Rate as a Screening Device

In this section we focus on the role of interest rates as screening devices for distinguishing between good and bad risks. We assume that the bank has identified a group

of projects; for each project θ there is a probability distribution of (gross) returns R. We assume for the moment that this distribution cannot be altered by the borrower.

Different firms have different probability distributions of returns. We initially assume that the bank is able to distinguish projects with different mean returns, so we will at first confine ourselves to the decision problem of a bank facing projects having the same mean return. However, the bank cannot ascertain the riskiness of a project. For simplicity, we write the distribution of returns[4] as $F(R,\theta)$ and the density function as $f(R,\theta)$, and we assume that greater θ corresponds to greater risk in the sense of mean preserving spreads[5] (see Rothschild-Stiglitz), i.e., for $\theta_1 > \theta_2$, if

$$(1) \quad \int_0^\infty Rf(R,\theta_1)\,dR = \int_0^\infty Rf(R,\theta_2)\,dR$$

then for $y \geqslant 0$,

$$(2) \quad \int_0^y F(R,\theta_1)\,dR \geqslant \int_0^y F(R,\theta_2)\,dR$$

If the individual borrows the amount B, and the interest rate is $\hat{r}$, then we say the individual defaults on his loan if the return R plus the collateral C is insufficient to pay back the promised amount,[6] i.e., if

$$(3) \quad C + R \leqslant B(1 + \hat{r})$$

---

[3] There is another form of rationing which is the subject of our 1980 paper: banks make the provision of credit in later periods contingent on performance in earlier period; banks may then refuse to lend even when these later period projects stochastically dominate earlier projects which are financed.

[4] These are subjective probability distributions; the perceptions on the part of the bank may differ from those of the firm.

[5] Michael Rothschild and Stiglitz show that conditions (1) and (2) imply that project 2 has a greater variance than project 1, although the converse is not true. That is, the mean preserving spread criterion for measuring risk is stronger than the increasing variance criterion. They also show that (1) and (2) can be interpreted equally well as: given two projects with equal means, every risk averter prefers project 1 to project 2.

[6] This is not the only possible definition. A firm might be said to be in default if $R < B(1 + \hat{r})$. Nothing critical depends on the precise definition. We assume, however, that if the firm defaults, the bank has first claim on $R + C$. The analysis may easily be generalized to include bankruptcy costs. However, to simplify the analysis, we usually shall ignore these costs. Throughout this section we assume that the project is the sole project

Thus the net return to the borrower $\pi(R,\hat{r})$ can be written as

$$(4a) \quad \pi(R,\hat{r})=max(R-(1+\hat{r})B; -C)$$

The return to the bank can be written as

$$(4b) \quad \rho(R,\hat{r})=min(R+C; B(1+\hat{r}))$$

that is, the borrower must pay back either the promised amount or the maximum he can pay back $(R+C)$.

For simplicity, we shall assume that the borrower has a given amount of equity (which he cannot increase), that borrowers and lenders are risk neutral, that the supply of loanable funds available to a bank is unaffected by the interest rate it charges borrowers, that the cost of the project is fixed, and unless the individual can borrow the difference between his equity and the cost of the project, the project will not be undertaken, that is, projects are not divisible. For notational simplicity, we assume the amount borrowed for each project is identical, so that the distribution functions describing the number of loan applications are identical to those describing the monetary value of loan applications. (In a more general model, we would make the amount borrowed by each individual a function of the terms of the contract; the quality mix could change not only as a result of a change in the mix of applicants, but also because of a change in the relative size of applications of different groups.)

We shall now prove that the interest rate acts as a screening device; more precisely we establish

THEOREM 1: *For a given interest rate $\hat{r}$, there is a critical value $\hat{\theta}$ such that a firm borrows from the bank if and only if $\theta > \hat{\theta}$.*

This follows immediately upon observing that profits are a convex function of R, as in Figure 2a. Hence expected profits increase with risk.

---

undertaken by the firm (individual) and that there is limited liability. The equilibrium extent of liability is derived in Section III.

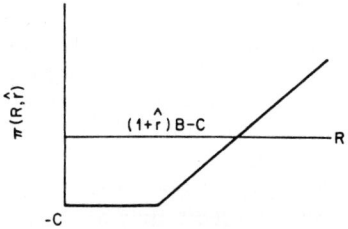

FIGURE 2a. FIRM PROFITS ARE A CONVEX FUNCTION OF THE RETURN ON THE PROJECT

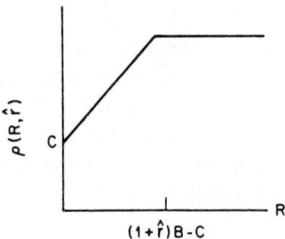

FIGURE 2b. THE RETURN TO THE BANK IS A CONCAVE FUNCTION OF THE RETURN ON THE PROJECT

The value of $\hat{\theta}$ for which expected profits are zero satisfies

$$(5) \quad \Pi(\hat{r},\hat{\theta}) \equiv$$

$$\int_0^{\infty} max[R-(\hat{r}+1)B; -C] \, dF(R,\hat{\theta})=0$$

Our argument that the adverse selection of interest rates could cause the returns to the bank to decrease with increasing interest rates hinged on the conjecture that as the interest rate increased, the mix of applicants became worse; or

THEOREM 2: *As the interest rate increases, the critical value of θ, below which individuals do not apply for loans, increases.*

This follows immediately upon differentiating (5):

$$(6) \quad \frac{d\hat{\theta}}{d\hat{r}} = \frac{B\int_{(1+\hat{r})B-C}^{\infty} dF(R,\hat{\theta})}{\partial\Pi/\partial\hat{\theta}} > 0$$

For each θ, expected profits are decreased;

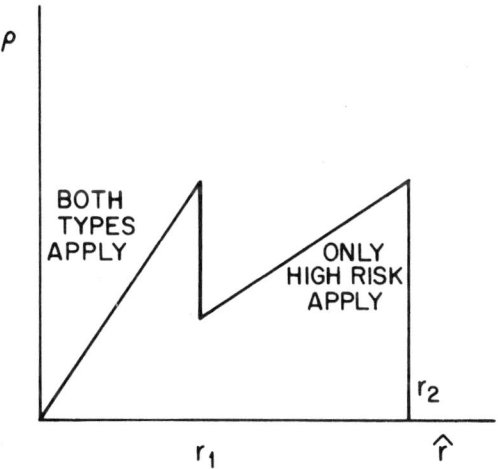

FIGURE 3. OPTIMAL INTEREST RATE r_1

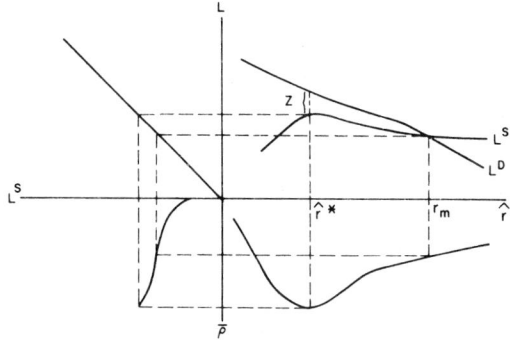

FIGURE 4. DETERMINATION OF THE MARKET EQUILIBRIUM

hence using Theorem 1, the result is immediate.

We next show:

THEOREM 3: *The expected return on a loan to a bank is a decreasing function of the riskiness of the loan.*

PROOF:

From (4b) we see that $\rho(R, \hat{r})$ is a concave function of R, hence the result is immediate. The concavity of $\rho(R, \hat{r})$ is illustrated in Figure 2b.

Theorems 2 and 3 imply that, in addition to the usual direct effect of increases in the interest rate increasing a bank's return, there is an indirect, adverse-selection effect acting in the opposite direction. We now show that this adverse-selection effect *may* outweigh the direct effect.

To see this most simply, assume there are two groups; the "safe" group will borrow only at interest rates below r_1, the "risky" group below r_2, and $r_1 < r_2$. When the interest rate is raised slightly above r_1, the mix of applicants changes dramatically: all low risk applicants withdraw. (See Figure 3.) By the same argument we can establish

THEOREM 4: *If there are a discrete number of potential borrowers (or types of borrowers) each with a different θ, $\bar{\rho}(\hat{r})$ will not be a monotonic function of $\hat{r}$, since as each succes-*

sive group drops out of the market, there is a discrete fall in $\bar{\rho}$ (where $\bar{\rho}(\hat{r})$ is the mean return to the bank from the set of applicants at the interest rate $\hat{r}$).

Other conditions for nonmonotonicity of $\bar{\rho}(\hat{r})$ will be established later. Theorems 5 and 6 show why nonmonotonicity is so important:

THEOREM 5: *Whenever $\bar{\rho}(\hat{r})$ has an interior mode, there exist supply functions of funds such that competitive equilibrium entails credit rationing.*

This will be the case whenever the "Walrasian equilibrium" interest rate—the one at which demand for funds equals supply—is such that there exists a lower interest rate for which $\bar{\rho}$, the return to the bank, is higher.

In Figure 4 we illustrate a credit rationing equilibrium. Because demand for funds depends on $\hat{r}$, the interest rate charged by banks, while the supply of funds depends on ρ, the mean return on loans, we cannot use a conventional demand/supply curve diagram. The demand for loans is a decreasing function of the interest rate charged borrowers; this relation L^D is drawn in the upper right quadrant. The nonmonotonic relation between the interest charged borrowers, and the expected return to the bank per dollar loaned $\bar{\rho}$ is drawn in the lower right quadrant. In the lower left quadrant we depict the relation between $\bar{\rho}$ and the supply of loanable funds L^S. (We have drawn L^S as if it

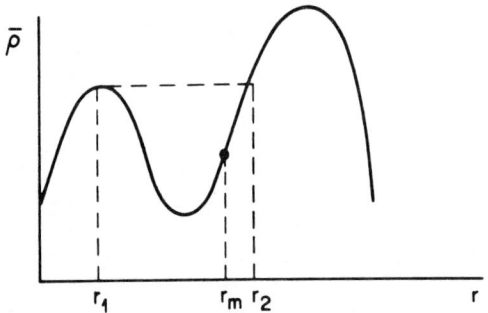

FIGURE 5. A TWO-INTEREST RATE EQUILIBRIUM

were an increasing function of $\bar{\rho}$. This is not necessary for our analysis.) If banks are free to compete for depositors, then $\bar{\rho}$ will be the interest rate received by depositors. In the upper right quadrant we plot L^S as a function of $\hat{r}$, through the impact of $\hat{r}$ on the return on each loan, and hence on the interest rate $\bar{\rho}$ banks can offer to attract loanable funds.

A credit rationing equilibrium exists given the relations drawn in Figure 4; the demand for loanable funds at $\hat{r}^*$ exceeds the supply of loanable funds at $\hat{r}^*$ and any individual bank increasing its interest rate beyond $\hat{r}^*$ would lower its return per dollar loaned. The excess demand for funds is measured by Z. Notice that there is an interest rate r_m at which the demand for loanable funds equals the supply of loanable funds; however, r_m is not an equilibrium interest rate. A bank could increase its profits by charging $\hat{r}^*$ rather than r_m: at the lower interest rate it would attract at least all the borrowers it attracted at r_m and would make larger profits from each loan (or dollar loaned).

Figure 4 can also be used to illustrate an important comparative statics property of our market equilibrium:

COROLLARY 1. *As the supply of funds increases, the excess demand for funds decreases, but the interest rate charged remains unchanged, so long as there is any credit rationing.*

Eventually, of course, Z will be reduced to zero; further increases in the supply of funds then reduce the market rate of interest.

Figure 5 illustrates a $\bar{\rho}(\hat{r})$ function with multiple modes. The nature of the equilibrium for such cases is described by Theorem 6.

THEOREM 6: *If the $\bar{\rho}(r)$ function has several modes, market equilibrium could either be characterized by a single interest rate at or below the market-clearing level, or by two interest rates, with an excess demand for credit at the lower one.*

PROOF:

Denote the lowest Walrasian equilibrium interest rate by r_m and denote by $\hat{r}$ the interest rate which maximizes $\rho(r)$. If $\hat{r} < r_m$, the analysis for Theorem 5 is unaffected by the multiplicity of modes. There will be credit rationing at interest rate $\hat{r}$. The rationed borrowers will not be able to obtain credit by offering to pay a higher interest rate.

On the other hand, if $\hat{r} > r_m$, then loans may be made at two interest rates, denoted by r_1 and r_2. r_1 is the interest rate which maximizes $\rho(r)$ conditional on $r \leqslant r_m$; r_2 is the lowest interest rate greater than r_m such that $\rho(r_2) = \rho(r_1)$. From the definition of r_m, and the downward slope of the loan demand function, there will be an excess demand for loanable funds at r_1 (unless $r_1 = r_m$, in which case there is no credit rationing). Some rejected borrowers (with reservation interest rates greater than or equal to r_2) will apply for loans at the higher interest rate. Since there would be an excess supply of loanable funds at r_2 if no loans were made at r_1, and an aggregate excess demand for funds if no loans were made at r_2, there exists a distribution of loanable funds available to borrowers at r_1 and r_2 such that all applicants who are rejected at interest rate r_1 and who apply for loans at r_2 will get credit at the higher interest rate. Similarly, all the funds available at $\rho(r_1)$ will be loaned at either r_1 or r_2. (There is, of course, an excess demand for loanable funds at r_1 since every borrower who eventually borrows at r_2 will have first applied for credit at r_1.) There is clearly no incentive for small deviations from r_1, which is a local maximum of $\rho(r)$. A bank lending at an interest rate r_3 such that $\rho(r_3) < \rho(r_1)$ would not be able to obtain credit. Thus, no bank would switch to a loan offer between r_1 and r_2. A bank offering an interest rate r_4 such that $\rho(r_4) > \rho(r_1)$ would not be able to attract any borrowers since by definition $r_4 > r_2$, and there is no excess demand at interest rate r_2.

A. *Alternative Sufficient Conditions for Credit Rationing*

Theorem 4 provided a sufficient condition for adverse selection to lead to a nonmonotonic $\bar{\rho}(\hat{r})$ function. In the remainder of this section, we investigate other circumstances under which for some levels of supply of funds there will be credit rationing.

1. *Continuum of Projects*

Let $G(\theta)$ be the distribution of projects by riskiness θ, and $\rho(\theta, r)$ be the expected return to the bank of a loan of risk θ and interest rate r. The mean return to the bank which lends at the interest rate $\hat{r}$ is simply

$$(7) \qquad \bar{\rho}(\hat{r}) = \frac{\int_{\theta(\hat{r})}^{\infty} \rho(\theta, \hat{r}) \, dG(\theta)}{1 - G(\hat{\theta})}$$

From Theorem 5 we know that $d\bar{\rho}(\hat{r})/d\hat{r} < 0$ for some value of $\hat{r}$ is a sufficient condition for credit rationing. Let $\rho(\hat{\theta}, \hat{r}) = \hat{\rho}$ so that

$$(8) \qquad \frac{d\bar{\rho}}{d\hat{r}} = -\frac{g(\hat{\theta})}{[1 - G(\hat{\theta})]} (\hat{\rho} - \bar{\rho}) \frac{d\hat{\theta}}{d\hat{r}}$$

$$+ \frac{\int_{\hat{\theta}}^{\infty} [1 - F((1 + \hat{r})B - C, \theta)] \, dG(\theta)}{1 - G(\hat{\theta})}$$

From Theorems 1 and 3, the first term is negative (representing the change in the mix of applicants), while the second term (the increase in returns, holding the applicant pool fixed, from raising the interest charges) is positive. The first term is large, in absolute value, if there is a large difference between the mean return on loans made at interest rate $\hat{r}$ and the return to the bank from the project making zero returns to the firm at interest rate $\hat{r}$ (its "safest" loan). It is also

large if $(g(\hat{\theta})/[1 - G(\hat{\theta})]) \, (d\hat{\theta}/d\hat{r})$ is large, that is, a small change in the nominal interest rate induces a large change in the applicant pool.

2. *Two Outcome Projects*

Here we consider the simplest kinds of projects (from an analytical point of view), those which either succeed and yield a return R, or fail and yield a return D. We normalize to let $B = 1$. All the projects have the same unsuccessful value (which could be the value of the plant and equipment) while R ranges between S and K (where $K > S$). We also assume that projects have been screened so that all projects within a loan category have the same expected yield, T, and there is no collateral required, that is, $C = 0$, and if $p(R)$ represents the probability that a project with a successful return of R succeeds, then

$$(9) \qquad p(R)R + [1 - p(R)]D = T$$

In addition, the bank suffers a cost of X per dollar loaned upon loans that default, which could be interpreted as the difference between the value of plant and equipment to the firm and the value of the plant and equipment to the bank. Again the density of project values is denoted by $g(R)$, the distribution function by $G(R)$.

Therefore, the expected return per dollar lent at an interest rate $\hat{r}$, if we let $J = \hat{r} + 1$, is (since individuals will borrow if and only if $R > J$):

$$(10)$$

$$\rho(J) = \frac{1}{\int_J^K g(R) \, dR} \left[J \int_J^K p(R) g(R) \, dR \right.$$

$$\left. + \int_J^K [1 - p(R)][D - X] g(R) \, dR \right]$$

Using l'Hopital's rule and (1), we can establish sufficient conditions for $\lim_{J \to K} (\partial \rho(J)/ \partial J) < 0$ (and hence for the nonmonotonicity of ρ):[7]

---

[7]The proofs of these propositions are slightly complicated. Consider 1. Since $p(R) = T - D/R - D$, the

(a) if $lim_{R \to K} g(R) \neq 0, \infty$ then a sufficient condition is $X > K - D$, or equivalently, $lim_{R \to K} p(R) + p'(R)X < 0$

(b) if $g(K) = 0$, $g'(K) \neq 0, \infty$ then a sufficient condition is $2X > K - D$, or equivalently, $lim_{R \to K} p(R) + 2p'(R)X < 0$

(c) if $g(K) = 0$, $g'(K) = 0$, $g''(K) \neq 0$, then a sufficient condition is $3X > K - K - D$, or equivalently, $lim_{R \to K} p(R) + 3p'(R)X < 0$

Condition (a) implies that if, as $1 + \hat{r} \to K$, the probability of an increase in the interest rate being repaid is outweighed by the deadweight loss of riskier loans, the bank will maximize its return per dollar loaned at an interest rate below the maximum rate at which it can loan funds $(K-1)$. The conditions for an interior bank optimal interest rate are significantly less stringent when $g(K) = 0$.

3. Differences in Attitudes Towards Risk

Some loan applicants are clearly more risk averse than others. These differences will be reflected in project choices, and thus affect

---

expected profit per dollar loaned may be rewritten as

$$\rho(J) = [J - D + X][T - D] \frac{\int_J^K \frac{g(R)}{R-D} dR}{\int_J^K g(R)\,dR} + D - X$$

Differentiating. and collecting terms

$$\frac{1}{T-D} \frac{\partial \rho}{\partial J} = \frac{\int_J^K \frac{g(R)}{R-D} dR}{\int_J^K g(R)\,dR} + [J - D + X]$$

$$\times \left[\frac{\frac{-g(J)}{J-D} \int_J^K g(R)\,dR + g(J)\int_J^K \frac{g(R)}{R-D} dR}{\left[\int_J^K g(R)\,dR\right]^2} \right]$$

Using l'Hopital's rule and the assumption that $g(K) \neq 0, \infty$

$$\lim_{J \to K} \left(\frac{1}{T-D} \frac{\partial \rho}{\partial J} \right) = \left(\frac{1}{K-D} - \frac{K-D+X}{2(K-D)^2} \right);$$

or
$$sign\left(\lim_{J \to K} \frac{1}{T-D} \frac{\partial \rho}{\partial J} \right) = sign(K - D - X)$$

Conditions 2 and 3 follow in a similar manner.

---

the bank-optimal interest rate. High interest rates may make projects with low mean returns— the projects undertaken by risk averse individuals—infeasible, but leave relatively unaffected the risky projects. The mean return to the bank, however, is lower on the riskier projects than on the safe projects. In the following example, it is systematic differences in risk aversion which results in there being an optimal interest rate.

Assume a fraction λ of the population is infinitely risk averse; each such individual undertakes the best perfectly safe project which is available to him. Within that group, the distribution of returns is $G(R)$ where $G(K) = 1$. The other group is risk neutral. For simplicity we shall assume that they all face the same risky project with probability of success p and a return, if successful, of $R^* > K$; if not their return is zero. Letting $\hat{R} = (1 + \hat{r})B$ the (expected) return to the bank is

(11)

$$\bar{\rho}(\hat{r}) = \frac{\{\lambda(1 - G(\hat{R})) + (1-\lambda)p\}}{\lambda(1 - G(\hat{R})) + (1-\lambda)}(1 + \hat{r})$$

$$= \left[1 - \frac{(1-p)(1-\lambda)}{\lambda(1 - G(\hat{R})) + (1-\lambda)} \right] \frac{\hat{R}}{B}$$

Hence for $R < K$, the upper bound on returns from the safe project

(12)
$$\frac{d \ln \bar{\rho}}{d \ln(1 + \hat{r})} = 1 -$$

$$\frac{(1-\lambda)(1-p)\lambda g(\hat{R})\hat{R}}{(1 - \lambda G(\hat{R}))(\lambda(1 - G(\hat{R})) + p(1-\lambda))}$$

A sufficient condition for the existence of an interior bank optimal interest rate is again that $lim_{R \to K} \partial \bar{\rho}/\partial \hat{r} < 0$, or from (12), $\lambda/1 - \lambda$ $lim_{R \to K} g(R)\hat{R} > p/1 - p$. The greater is the riskiness of the risky project (the lower is p), the more likely is an interior bank optimal interest rate. Similarly, the higher is the relative proportion of the risk averse individuals affected by increases in the interest rate to risk neutral borrowers, the more important is the self-selection effect, and the more likely is an interior bank optimal interest rate.

II. Interest Rate as an Incentive Mechanism

A. *Sufficient Conditions*

The second way in which the interest rate affects the bank's expected return from a loan is by changing the behavior of the borrower. The interests of the lender and the borrower do not coincide. The borrower is only concerned with returns on the investment when the firm does not go bankrupt; the lender is concerned with the actions of the firm only to the extent that they affect the probability of bankruptcy, and the returns in those states of nature in which the firm *does* go bankrupt. Because of this, and because the behavior of a borrower cannot be perfectly and costlessly monitored by the lender, banks will take into account the effect of the interest rate on the behavior of borrowers.

In this section, we show that increasing the rate of interest increases the relative attractiveness of riskier projects, for which the return to the bank may be lower. Hence, raising the rate of interest may lead borrowers to take actions which are contrary to the interests of the lender, providing another incentive for banks to ration credit rather than raise the interest rate when there is an excess demand for loanable funds.

We return to the general model presented above, but now we assume that each firm has a choice of projects. Consider any two projects, denoted by superscripts j and k. We first establish:

THEOREM 7: *If, at a given nominal interest rate r, a risk-neutral firm is indifferent between two projects, an increase in the interest rate results in the firm preferring the project with the higher probability of bankruptcy.*

PROOF:
The expected return to the ith project is given by

$$(13) \quad \pi^i = E\left[max\left(R^i - (1+\hat{r})B, -C\right)\right]$$

so

$$(14) \quad \frac{d\pi^i}{d\hat{r}} = -B\left(1 - F_i\left((1+\hat{r})B - C\right)\right)$$

Thus, if at some $\hat{r}$, $\pi^j = \pi^k$, the increase in $\hat{r}$ lowers the expected return to the borrower from the project with the higher probability of paying back the loan by more than it lowers the expected return from the project with the lower probability of the loan being repaid.

On the other hand, if the firm is indifferent between two projects with the same mean, we know from Theorem 2 that the bank prefers to lend to the safer project. Hence raising the interest rate above $\hat{r}$ could so increase the riskiness of loans as to lower the expected return to the bank.

THEOREM 8: *The expected return to the bank is lowered by an increase in the interest rate at $\hat{r}$ if, at $\hat{r}$, the firm is indifferent between two projects j and k with distributions $F_j(R)$ and $F_k(R)$, j having a higher probability of bankruptcy than k, and there exists a distribution $F_l(R)$ such that*
(a) $F_j(R)$ represents a mean preserving spread of the distribution $F_l(R)$, and
(b) $F_k(R)$ satisfies a first-order dominance relation with $F_l(R)$; i.e., $F_l(R) > F_k(R)$ for all R.

PROOF:
Since j has a higher probability of bankruptcy than does k, from Theorem 7 and the initial indifference of borrowers between j and k, an increase in the interest rate $\hat{r}$ leads firms to prefer project j to k. Because of (a) and Theorem 3, the return to the bank on a project whose return is distributed as $F_l(R)$ is higher than on project j, and because of (b) the return to the bank on project k is higher than the return on a project distributed as $F_l(R)$.

B. *An Example*

To illustrate the implications of Theorem 8, assume all firms are identical, and have a choice of two projects, yielding, if successful, returns R^a and R^b, respectively (and nothing

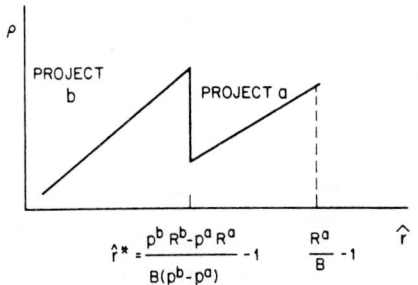

FIGURE 6. AT INTEREST RATES ABOVE $\hat{r}^*$, THE RISKY PROJECT IS UNDERTAKEN AND THE RETURN TO THE BANK IS LOWERED

otherwise) where $R^a > R^b$, and with probabilities of success of p^a and p^b, $p^a < p^b$. For simplicity assume that $C = 0$. If the firm is indifferent between the projects at interest rate $\hat{r}$, then

$$(15) \quad \left[R^a - (1+\hat{r})B \right] p^a = \left[R^b - (1+\hat{r})B \right] p^b$$

i.e.,

$$(16) \quad B(1+\hat{r}) = \frac{p^b R^b - p^a R^a}{p^b - p^a} \equiv (1+\hat{r}^*)B$$

Thus, the expected return to the bank as a function of r appears as in Figure 6.

For interest rates below $\hat{r}^*$, firms choose the safe project, while for interest rates between $\hat{r}^*$ and $(R^a/B) - 1$, firms choose the risky project. The maximum interest rate the bank could charge and still induce investments in project b is $\hat{r}^*$. The highest interest rate which attracts borrowers is $(R^a/B) - 1$, which would induce investment only in project a. Therefore the maximum expected return to a bank occurs when the bank charges an interest rate $\hat{r}^*$ if and only if

$$p^a R^a < \frac{p^b (p^b R^b - p^a R^a)}{p^b - p^a}$$

Whenever $p^b R^b > p^a R^a$, $1 + \hat{r}^* > 0$, and ρ is not monotonic in $\hat{r}$, so there may be credit rationing.

III. The Theory of Collateral and Limited Liability

An obvious objection to the analysis presented thus far is: When there is an excess demand for funds, would not the bank increase its collateral requirements (increasing the liability of the borrower in the event that the project fails); reducing the demand for funds, reducing the risk of default (or losses to the bank in the event of default) and increasing the return to the bank?

This objection will not in general hold. In this section we will discuss various reasons why banks will not decrease the debt-equity ratio of borrowers (increasing collateral requirements)[8] as a means of allocating credit.

A clear case in which reductions in the debt-equity ratio of borrowers are not optimal for the bank is when smaller projects have a higher probability of "failure," and all potential borrowers have the same amount of equity. In those circumstances, increasing the collateral requirements (or the required proportion of equity finance) of loans will imply financing smaller projects. If projects either succeed or fail, and yield a zero return when they fail, then the increase in the collateral requirement of loans will increase the riskiness of those loans.

Another obvious case where increasing collateral requirements may increase the riskiness of loans is if potential borrowers have different equity, and all projects require the same investment. Wealthy borrowers may be those who, in the past, have succeeded at risky endeavors. In that case they are likely to be less risk averse than the more conservative individuals who have in the past invested in relatively safe securities, and are consequently less able to furnish large amounts of collateral.

In both these examples collateral requirements have adverse selection effects. However, we will present a stronger result. We

---

[8] Increasing the fraction of the project financed by equity and increasing the collateral requirements both increase the expected return to the bank from any particular project. They have similar but identical risk and incentive effects. Although the analysis below focuses on collateral requirements, similar arguments apply to dept-equity ratios.

will show that even if there are no increasing returns to scale in production and all individuals have the same utility function, the sorting effect of collateral requirements can still lead to an interior bank-optimal level of collateral requirements similar to the interior bank-optimal interest rate derived in Sections I and II. In particular, since wealthier individuals are likely to be less risk averse, we would expect that those who could put up the most capital would also be willing to take the greatest risk. We show that this latter effect is sufficiently strong that increasing collateral requirements will, under plausible conditions, lower the bank's return.

To see this most clearly, we assume all borrowers are risk averse with the same utility function $U(W)$, $U'>0$, $U''<0$. Individuals differ, however, with respect to their initial wealth, W_0. Each "entrepreneur" has a set of projects which he can undertake; each project has a probability of success $p(R)$, where R is the return if successful. If the project is unsuccessful, the return is zero; $p'(R)<0$. Each individual has an alternative safe investment opportunity yielding the return ρ^*. The bank cannot observe either the individual's wealth or the project undertaken. It offers the same contract, defined by C, the amount of collateral, and $\hat{r}$, the interest rate, to all customers. The analysis proceeds as earlier; we first establish:

THEOREM 9: *The contract $\{C, \hat{r}\}$ acts as a screening mechanism: there exist two critical values of W_0, $\hat{W}_0$, and $\overset{*}{W}_0$, such that if there is decreasing absolute risk aversion all individuals with wealth $\hat{W}_0 < W_0 < \overset{*}{W}_0$ apply for loans.*

PROOF:

As before, we normalize so that all projects cost a dollar. If the individual does not borrow, he either does not undertake the project, obtaining a utility of $U(W_0\rho^*)$, or he finances it all himself, obtaining an expected utility of (assuming $W_0 \geq 1$)

$$(17) \quad \max_R \{ U((W_0-1)\rho^*+R)p(R)$$

$$+ U((W_0-1)\rho^*)(1-p(R))\}$$

$$\equiv V(W_0)$$

Define

$$(18) \quad V_0(W_0) = max\{ U(W_0\rho^*), \hat{V}(W_0)]$$

We note that

$$(19) \quad \frac{dU(W_0\rho^*)}{dW_0} = U'\rho^*$$

$$(20) \quad \frac{d\hat{V}(W_0)}{dW_0} = [U_1'p + U_2'(1-p)]\rho^*$$

(where the subscript 1 refers to the state "success" and the subscript 2 to the state "failure"). We can establish that if there is decreasing absolute risk aversion,[9]

$$\frac{dU(W_0\rho^*)}{dW_0} < \frac{d\hat{V}(W_0)}{dW_0}$$

Hence, there exists a critical value of W_0, $\hat{W}_0$, such that if $W_0 > \hat{W}_0$ individuals who do not borrow undertake the project.

For the rest of the analysis we confine ourselves to the case of decreasing absolute risk aversion and wealth less than $\hat{W}_0$.

If the individual borrows, he attains a utility level[10]

$$(21) \quad \{ \max_R U(W_0\rho^* - (1+\hat{r}) + R)p$$

$$+ U((W_0 - C)\rho^*)(1-p)\}$$

$$\equiv V_B(W_0)$$

The individual borrows if and only if

$$(22) \quad V_B(W_0) \geq V_0(W_0)$$

---

[9] To prove this, we define $\hat{W}_0$ as the wealth where undertaking the risky project is a mean-utility preserving spread (compare Peter Diamond-Stiglitz) of the safe project. But writing $U'(W(U))$, where $W(U)$ is the value of terminal wealth corresponding to utility level U,

$$\frac{dU'}{dU} = \frac{U''}{U'} = -A; \quad \frac{d^2U'}{dU^2} = -\frac{A'}{U'} \gtrless 0 \text{ as } A' \lesseqgtr 0$$

Hence with decreasing absolute risk aversion, U' is a convex function of U and therefore EU' for the risky investment exceeds $U'(\rho^*W_0)$.

[10] In this formulation, the collateral earns a return ρ^*.

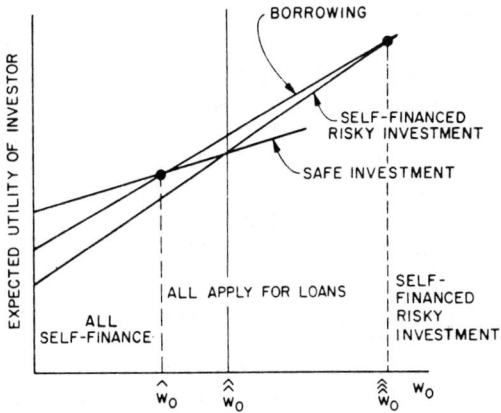

FIGURE 7. COLLATERAL SERVES AS
A SCREENING DEVICE

But

$$(23) \quad \frac{dV_B}{dW_0} = (U_1'p + U_2'(1-p))\rho^*$$

Clearly, only those with $W_0 > C$ can borrow. We assume there exists a value of $W_0 > 0$, denoted $\hat{W}_0$, such that $V_B(\hat{W}_0) = U(\rho^*\hat{W}_0)$. (This will be true for some values of ρ^*.) By the same kind of argument used earlier, it is clear that at $\hat{W}_0$, borrowing with collateral is a mean-utility preserving spread of terminal wealth in comparison to not borrowing and not undertaking the project. Thus using (20) and (23), $dV_B/dW_0 > d\hat{V}_0(W_0)/dW_0$ at $\hat{W}_0$. Hence, for $\hat{W}_0 < W_0 < \hat{\hat{W}}_0$ all individuals apply for loans, as depicted in Figure 7. Thus, restricting ourselves to $W_0 < \hat{W}_0$, we have established that if there is any borrowing, it is the wealthiest in that interval who borrow. (The restriction $W_0 < \hat{W}_0$ is weaker than the restriction that the scale of projects exceeds the wealth of any individual.)

Next, we show:

THEOREM 10: *If there is decreasing absolute risk aversion, wealthier individuals undertake riskier projects:* $dR/dW_0 > 0$.

PROOF:
From (21), we obtain the first-order condition for the choice of R:

$$(24) \quad U_1'p + (U_1 - U_2)p' = 0$$

so, using the second-order conditions for a maximum, and (24),

$$(25) \quad \frac{dR}{dW_0} \gtreqless 0 \text{ as } \frac{U_1''p + (U_1' - U_2')p'}{U_1'p}$$

$$= -A_1 - \frac{(U_1' - U_2')}{U_1 - U_2} \gtreqless 0$$

But

$$\lim_{W_1 \to W_2} -\frac{U_1' - U_2'}{U_1 - U_2} = -\frac{U_1''}{U_1'} = A_1$$

implying that, if $W_1 = W_2$, $dR/dW_0 = 0$. However,

$$\frac{\partial\left(-A_1 - \dfrac{U_1' - U_2'}{U_1 - U_2}\right)}{\partial W_1}\Bigg|_{A_1 = -\frac{U_2' - U_1'}{U_1 - U_2}}$$

$$= -A_1' - \frac{U_1''}{U_1 - U_2} + \frac{U_1' - U_2'}{U_1 - U_2}\frac{U_1'}{U_1 - U_2}$$

$$= -A_1' \gtreqless 0 \text{ as } A_1' \lesseqgtr 0$$

Hence $dR/dW_0 > 0$ if $A' < 0$.
Next we show

THEOREM 11: *Collateral increases the bank's return from any given borrower:*

$$dp/dC > 0$$

PROOF:
This follows directly from the first-order condition (24):

$$\text{sign } \frac{dR}{dC} = \text{sign } U_2'\rho^*p' < 0$$

and thus $dp/dC > 0$. But

THEOREM 12: *There is an adverse selection effect from increasing the collateral requirement, i.e., both the average and the marginal borrower who borrows is riskier,* [11] $d\hat{W}_0/dC > 0$.

---

[11] At a sufficiently high collateral, the wealthy individual will not borrow at all.

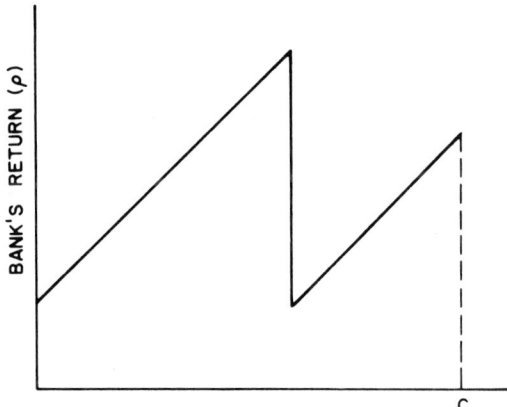

FIGURE 8. INCREASING COLLATERAL REQUIREMENT
LOWERS BANK'S RETURNS

PROOF:

This follows immediately upon differentiation of (21)

$$dV_B/dC = -U_2'\rho^*(1-p) < 0$$

It is easy to show now that this adverse selection effect *may* more than offset the positive direct effect. Assume there are two groups; for low wealth levels, increasing C has no adverse selection effect, so returns are unambiguously increased; but there is a critical level of C such that requiring further investments select against the low wealth-low risk individuals, and the bank's return is lowered.[12] (See Figure 8.)

This simple example has demonstrated[13] that although collateral may have beneficial incentive effects, it may also have countervailing adverse selection effects.

A. *Adverse Incentive Effects*

Although in the model presented above, increasing collateral has a beneficial incen-

---

[12] If we had not imposed the restriction $W_0 < \hat{W}_0$, then there may exist a value of W_0, $\hat{\hat{W}}_0 > \hat{W}_0$, such that for $W_0 > \hat{\hat{W}}_0$, individuals self-finance. It is easy to show that $\partial \hat{\hat{W}}_0/\partial C < 0$, so there is a countervailing positive selection effect. However if the density distribution of wealth is decreasing fast enough, then the adverse selection effect outweighs the positive selection effect.

[13] It also shows that the results of earlier sections can be extended to the risk averse entrepreneur.

tive effect, this is not necessarily the case. The bank has limited control over the actions of the borrowers, as we noted earlier. Thus, the response of the borrower to the increase in lending may be to take actions which, in certain contingencies, will require the bank to lend more in the future. (This argument seems implicit in many discussions of the importance of adequate initial funding for projects.) Consider, for instance, the following simplified multiperiod model. In the first period, θ occurs with probability p_1; if it does, the return to the project (realized the second period) is R_1. If it does not, either an additional amount M must be invested, or the project fails completely (has a zero return). If the bank charges an interest rate $r_2 \leq \hat{r}_2$ on these additional funds, they will invest them in "safe" ways; if $r_2 > \hat{r}_2$ those funds will be invested in risky ways. Following the analysis in Section II, we assume that the risk differences are sufficiently strong that the bank charges $\hat{r}_2$ for additional funds. Assume that there is also a set of projects (actions) which the firm can undertake in the first period, but among which the bank cannot discriminate. The individual has an equity of a dollar, which he cannot raise further, so the effect of a decrease in the loan is to affect the actions which the individual takes, that is, it affects the parameters of the projects, R_1, R_2, and M, where M is the amount of second-period financing needed if the project fails in the first period. For simplicity, we take R_2 as given, and let L be the size of the first-period loan. Thus the expected return to the firm is simply (if the additional loan M is made when needed)

$$p_1\left(R_1 - (1+\hat{r}_1)^2 L\right)$$

$$+\hat{p}\left(R_2 - \left[(1+\hat{r}_1)^2 L + (1+\hat{r}_2)M\right]\right)$$

where $\hat{p} = p_2(1-p_1)$, $(1+\hat{r}_1)^2$ is the amount paid back (per dollar borrowed) at the end of the second period on the initial loan and $\hat{r}_2$ is the interest on the additional loan M; thus the firm chooses R_1 so that

$$p_1 = \hat{p}(1+\hat{r}_2)\frac{dM}{dR_1}$$

Assume that the opportunity cost of capital to the bank per period is ρ^*. Then its net expected return to the loan is

$$p_1(1+\hat{r}_1)^2 L + \hat{p}\left[(1+\hat{r}_1)^2 L + (1+\hat{r}_2)M\right]$$

$$-\rho^*\left[\rho^* L + (1-p_1)M\right]$$

We can show that under certain circumstances, it will pay the bank to extend the line of credit M. Thus, although the bank controls L, it does not control directly the total (expected value) of its loans per customer, $L+(1-p_1)M$.

But more to the point is the fact that the expected return to the bank may not be monotonically decreasing in the size of the first-period loans. For instance, under the hypothesis that $\hat{r}_1$ and $\hat{r}_2$ are optimally chosen and at the optimum $\rho^* > p_2(1+\hat{r}_2)$, the return to the bank is a decreasing function of M/L. Thus, if the optimal response of the firm to a decrease in L is an increase in M (or a decrease in M so long as the percentage decrease in M is less than the percentage decrease in L), a decrease in L actually lowers the bank's profits.[14]

IV. Observationally Distinguishable Borrowers

Thus far we have confined ourselves to situations where all borrowers appear to be identical. Let us now extend the analysis to the case where there are n observationally distinguishable groups each with an interior bank optimal interest rate denoted by r_i^*.[15] The function $\rho_i(r_i)$ denote the gross return to a bank charging a type i borrower interest r_i. We can order the groups so that for $i>j$, $\max \rho_i(\hat{r}_i) > \max \rho_j(\hat{r}_j)$.

[14] For instance, if some of the initial investment is for "back-up" systems in case of various kinds of failure, if the reduction in initial funding leads to a reduction in investment in these back-up systems, when a failure does occur, large amounts of additional funding may be required.

[15] The analysis in this section parallels Weiss (1980) in which it was demonstrated that market equilibrium could result in the exclusion of some groups of workers from the labor market.

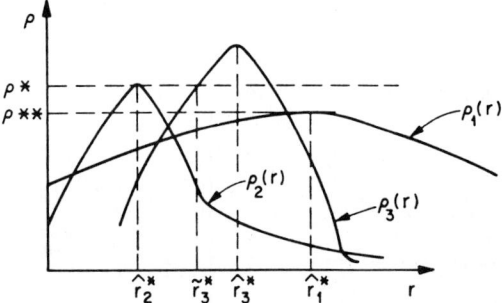

FIGURE 9. IF GROUPS DIFFER, THERE WILL EXIST RED LINING

THEOREM 13: *For $i>j$, type j borrowers will only receive loans if credit is not rationed to type i borrowers.*

PROOF:
Assume not. Since the maximum return on the loan to j is less than that to i, the bank could clearly increase its return by substituting a loan to i for a loan to j; hence the original situation could not have been profit maximizing.

We now show

THEOREM 14: *The equilibrium interest rates are such that for all i, j receiving loans, $\rho_i(\hat{r}_i) = \rho_j(\hat{r}_j)$.*

PROOF:
Again the proof is by contradiction. Let us assume that $\rho_i(\hat{r}_i) > \rho_j(\hat{r}_j)$; then a bank lending to type j borrowers would prefer to bid type i borrowers away from other banks. If ρ^* is the equilibrium return to the banks per dollar loaned, equal to the cost of loanable funds if banks compete freely for borrowers, then for all i, j receiving loans $\rho_i(r_i) = \rho_j(r_j) = \rho^*$. These results are illustrated for three types of borrowers in Figure 9.

If banks have a cost of loanable funds ρ^* then no type 1 borrower will obtain a loan; all type 3 borrowers wishing to borrow at interest rate $\tilde{r}_3$ (which is less than $\hat{r}_3^*$, the rate which maximizes the bank's return) will obtain loans—competition for those borrowers drives their interest rate down; while some, but not necessarily all, type 2 borrowers receive a loan at $\hat{r}_2^*$. If the interest rate were to fall to ρ^{**}, then all types 2 and 3 would receive loans; and some (but not all) type 1 borrowers would be extended credit.

Groups such as type 1 which are excluded from the credit market may be termed "redlined" since there is no interest rate at which they would get loans if the cost of funds is above ρ^{**}. It is possible that the investments of type 1 borrowers are especially risky so that, although $\rho_1(\hat{r}_1^*) < \rho_3(\hat{r}_3^*)$, the total expected return to type 1 investments (the return to the bank plus the return to the borrower) exceeds the expected return to type 3 investments. It may also be true that type 1 loans are unprofitable to the bank because they find it difficult to filter out risky type 1 investments. In that case it is possible that the return to the bank to an investment by a type 1 borrower would be greater than the return to a type 3 investment if the bank could exercise the same control (judgment) over each group of investors.

Another reason for $\rho_1(\hat{r}_1^*) < \rho_3(\hat{r}_3^*)$ may be that type 1 investors have a broader range of available projects. They can invest in all the projects available to type 3 borrowers, but can also invest in high-risk projects unavailable to type 3. Either because of the convexity of the profit function of borrowers, or because riskier investments have higher expected returns type 1 borrowers will choose to invest in these risky projects.

Thus, *there is no presumption that the market equilibrium allocates credit to those for whom the expected return on their investments is highest.*

IV. Debt vs. Equity Finance, Another View of the Principal-Agent Problem

Although we have phrased this paper in the context of credit markets, the analysis could apply equally well to any one of a number of principal-agent problems. For example, in agriculture the bank (principal) corresponds to the landlord and the borrower (agent) to the tenant while the loan contract corresponds to a rental agreement. The return function for the landlord and tenant appears in Figures 10a and 10b. The central concern in those principal-agent

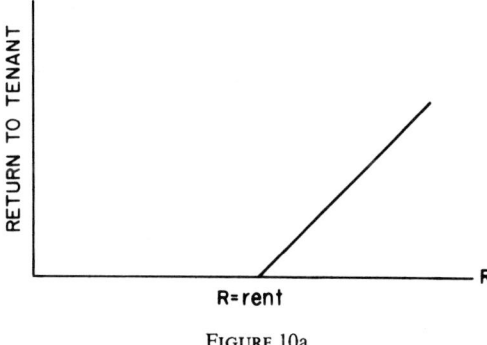

FIGURE 10a

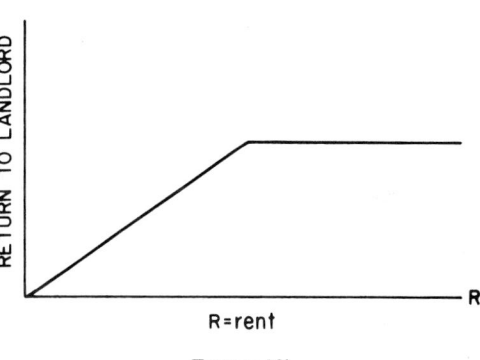

FIGURE 10b

problems is how to provide the proper incentives for the agent. In general, revenue sharing arrangements such as equity finance, or sharecropping are inefficient. Under those schemes the managers of a firm or the tenant will equate their marginal disutility of effort with their share of their marginal product rather than with their total marginal product. Therefore, too little effort will be forthcoming from agents.

Fixed-fee contracts (for example, rental agreements in agriculture, loan contracts in credit markets) have the disadvantage that they impose a heavy risk on the agent, and thus if agents are risk averse, they may not be desirable. But it has long been thought that they have a significant advantage in not distorting incentives and thus if the agent is risk neutral, fixed-fee contracts will be employed.[16] These discussions have not consid-

---

[16]See, for instance, Stiglitz (1974). For a recent formalization of the principal-agent problem, see Steven Shavell.

ered the possibility that the agent will fail to pay the fixed fee. In the particular context of the bank-borrower relationship, the assumption that the loan will always be repaid (with interest) seems most peculiar. A borrower can repay the loan in all states of nature only if the risky project's returns plus the value of the equilibrium level of collateral exceeds the safe rate of interest in all states of nature.

The consequences of this are important. Since the agent can by his actions affect the probability of bankruptcy, fixed-fee contracts do not eliminate the incentive problem.

Moreover, they do not necessarily lead to optimal resource allocations. For example, in the two-project case discussed above (Section II, Part B), if expected returns to the safe project exceed that to the risky ($p^s R^s > p' R'$) but the highest rate which the bank can charge consistent with the safe project being chosen (r^*) is too low (i.e., $p^s(1+r^*) > p' R'$) then the bank chooses an interest rate which causes all its loans to be for risky projects, although the expected total (social) returns on these projects are less than on the safe projects. In this case a usury law forbidding interest rates in excess of r^* will increase net national output. Our 1980 paper and Janusz Ordover and Weiss show that government interventions of various forms lead to Pareto improvements in the allocation of credit.

Because neither equity finance nor debt finance lead to efficient resource allocations, we would not expect to see the exclusive use of either method of financing (even with risk-neutral agents and principals). Similarly, in agriculture, we would not expect to see the exclusive use of rental or sharecropping tenancy arrangements. In general, where feasible, the payoff will be a non-linear function of output (profits). The terms of these contracts will depend on the risk preferences of the principal and agent, the extent to which their actions (both the level of effort and riskiness of outcomes) can affect the probability of bankruptcy, and actions can be specified within the contract or controlled directly by the principal.

One possible criticism of this paper is that the single period analysis presented above artificially limits the strategy space of lenders.

In a multiperiod context, for instance, banks could reward "good" borrowers by offering to lend to them at lower interest rates, and this would induce firms to undertake safer projects (just as in the labor market, the promise of promotion and pay increases is an important part of the incentive and sorting structure of firms, see Stiglitz, 1975, J. L. Guasch and Weiss, 1980, 1981). In our 1980 paper, we analyze the nature of equilibrium contracts in a dynamic context. We show that such contingency contracts may characterize the dynamic equilibrium. Indeed, we establish that the bank may want to use quantity constraints — the availability of credit — as an additional incentive device; thus, in the dynamic context there is a further argument for the existence of rationing in a competitive economy.

Even after introducing all of these additional instruments (collateral, equity, nonlinear payment schedules, contingency contracts) there may exist a contract which is optimal from the point of view of the principal; he will not respond, then, to an excess supply of agents by altering the terms of that contract; and there may then be rationing of the form discussed in this paper, that is, an excess demand for loans (capital, land) at the "competitive" contract.

VI. Conclusions

We have presented a model of credit rationing in which among observationally identical borrowers some receive loans and others do not. Potential borrowers who are denied loans would not be able to borrow even if they indicated a willingness to pay more than the market interest rate, or to put up more collateral than is demanded of recipients of loans. Increasing interest rates or increasing collateral requirements could increase the riskiness of the bank's loan portfolio, either by discouraging safer investors, or by inducing borrowers to invest in riskier projects, and therefore could decrease the bank's profits. Hence neither instrument will necessarily be used to equate the supply of loanable funds with the demand for loanable funds. Under those circumstances credit restrictions take the form of limiting the number of loans the bank will make, rather than limiting the size of each loan, or making the interest rate charged an increasing function of the magnitude of the loan, as in most previous discussions of credit rationing.

Note that in a rationing equilibrium, to the extent that monetary policy succeeds in shifting the supply of funds, it will affect the level of investment, not through the interest rate mechanism, but rather through the availability of credit. Although this is a "monetarist" result, it should be apparent that the mechanism is different from that usually put forth in the monetarist literature.

Although we have focused on analyzing the existence of excess demand equilibria in credit markets, imperfect information can lead to excess supply equilibria as well. We will sketch an outline of an argument here (a fuller discussion of the issue and of the macro-economic implications of this paper will appear in future work by the authors in conjunction with Bruce Greenwald).[17] Let us assume that banks make higher expected returns on some of their borrowers than on others: they know who their most credit worthy customers are, but competing banks do not. If a bank tries to attract the customers of its competitors by offering a lower interest rate, it will find that its offer is countered by an equally low interest rate when the customer being competed for is a "good" credit risk, and will not be matched if the borrower is not a profitable customer of the bank. Consequently, banks will seldom seek to steal the customers of their competitors, since they will only succeed in attracting the least profitable of those customers (introducing some noise in the system enables the development of an equilibrium). A bank with an excess supply of loanable funds must assess the profitability of the loans a lower interest rate would attract. In equilibrium each bank may have an excess supply of loanable funds, but no bank will lower its interest rate.

The reason we have been able to model excess demand and excess supply equilibria in credit markets is that the interest rate

directly affects the quality of the loan in a manner which matters to the bank. Other models in which prices are set competitively and non-market-clearing equilibria exist share the property that the expected quality of a commodity is a function of its price (see Weiss, 1976, 1980, or Stiglitz, 1976a, b for the labor market and C. Wilson for the used car market).

In any of these models in which, for instance, the wage affects the quality of labor, if there is an excess supply of workers at the wage which minimizes labor costs, there is not necessarily an inducement for firms to lower wages.

The Law of Supply and Demand is not in fact a law, nor should it be viewed as an assumption needed for competitive analysis. It is rather a result generated by the underlying assumptions that prices have neither sorting nor incentive effects. The usual result of economic theorizing: that prices clear markets, is model specific and is not a general property of markets—unemployment and credit rationing are not phantasms.

REFERENCES

P. Diamond and J. E. Stiglitz, "Increases in Risk and in Risk Aversion," *J. Econ. Theory*, July 1974, *8*, 337–60.

M. Freimer and M. J. Gordon, "Why Bankers Ration Credit," *Quart. J. Econ.*, Aug. 1965, *79*, 397–416.

Bruce Greenwald, *Adverse Selection in the Labor Market*, New York: Garland Press 1979.

J. L. Guasch and A. Weiss, "Wages as Sorting Mechanisms: A Theory of Testing," *Rev. Econ. Studies*, July 1980, *47*, 653–65.

_____ and _____, "Self-Selection in the Labor Market," *Amer. Econ. Rev.*, forthcoming.

Dwight Jaffee, *Credit Rationing and the Commercial Loan Market*, New York: John Wiley & Sons 1971.

_____ and T. Russell, "Imperfect Information and Credit Rationing," *Quart. J. Econ.* Nov. 1976, *90*, 651–66.

W. Keeton, *Equilibrium Credit Rationing*, New York: Garland Press 1979.

[17]A similar argument to that presented here appears in Greenwald in the context of labor markets.

J. Ordover and A. Weiss, "Information and the Law: Evaluating Legal Restrictions on Competitive Contracts," *Amer. Econ. Rev. Proc.*, May 1981, *71*, 399–404.

M. Rothschild and J. E. Stiglitz, "Increasing Risk: I, A Definition," *J. Econ. Theory*, Sept. 1970, *2*, 225–43.

S. Shavell, "Risk Sharing and Incentives in the Principal and Agent Problem," *Bell J. Econ.*, Spring 1979, *10*, 55–73.

G. Stigler, "Imperfections in the Capital Market," *J. Polit. Econ.*, June 1967, *85*, 287–92.

J. E. Stiglitz, "Incentives and Risk Sharing in Sharecropping," *Rev. Econ. Studies*, Apr. 1974, *41*, 219–55.

_____, "Incentives, Risk, and Information: Notes Towards a Theory of Hierarchy," *Bell J. Econ.*, Autumn 1975, *6*, 552–79.

_____, "Prices and Queues as Screening Devices in Competitive Markets," IMSSS tech. report no. 212, Stanford Univ.

_____, "The Efficiency Wage Hypothesis, Surplus Labor and the Distribution of Income in L.D.C.'s," *Oxford Econ. Papers*, July 1976, *28*, 185–207.

_____, "Perfect and Imperfect Capital Markets," paper presented to the New Orleans meeting of the Econometric Society, Dec. 1970.

_____, "Some Aspects of the Pure Theory of Corporate Finance: Bankruptcies and Take-Overs," *Bell J. Econ.*, Autumn 1972, *3*, 458–82.

_____ and A. Weiss, "Credit Rationing in Markets with Imperfect Information, Part II: A Theory of Contingency Contracts," mimeo. Bell Laboratories and Princeton Univ. 1980.

A. Weiss, "A Theory of Limited Labor Markets," unpublished doctoral dissertation, Stanford Univ. 1976.

_____, "Job Queues and Layoffs in Labor Markets with Flexible Wages," *J. Polit. Econ.*, June 1980, *88*, 526–38.

C. Wilson, "The Nature of Equilibrium in Markets with Adverse Selection," *Bell J. Econ.*, Spring 1980, *11*, 108–30.

Bond Covenants and Delegated Monitoring

MITCHELL BERLIN and JAN LOEYS*

ABSTRACT

This paper examines alternative contracting arrangements available to a firm seeking to finance an investment project. The authors consider the choice between loan contracts with covenants based on noisy indicators of the firm's financial health and loan contracts enforced by a monitoring specialist. In one interpretation, the specialist is a financial intermediary. The firm's choice is shown to depend upon the firm's credit rating, the accuracy of financial indicators of the firm's condition, the loss from premature liquidation of the firm's project, and the cost of monitoring.

IN RECENT YEARS, FINANCIAL theorists have made substantial progress in explaining the functions of financial intermediaries and complex financial contracts. One strand of the literature explains the existence of specialized monitoring institutions as the result of market failures in direct credit markets. For instance, financial intermediaries have been characterized as delegated monitors. (See, for example, Boyd and Prescott [3], Campbell and Kracaw [4], Chan [5], Diamond [6], and Gorton and Haubrich [7].) Another strand of the literature focuses on the role of contractual covenants as mechanisms to control agency problems between firm insiders and outside investors. (See, for instance, Ho and Singer [8], Kalay [9], and Smith and Warner [13].) Yet there has been little work on the marginal benefits and costs of using monitoring specialists when covenants are at least partially effective in controlling agency problems.

This paper presents a model of a firm's choice between two different contractual arrangements: loan contracts with covenants but no monitor and loan contracts enforced by a monitoring specialist. One possible interpretation, and the one that we shall emphasize for concreteness, is that the first type of contract is a bond and the second type is a bank loan. This links our work to the literature on financial intermediation. A second interpretation is that our monitor is a bond trustee or an auditing firm hired by a trustee to examine the firm's finances. In this interpretation, the model provides a formal analysis of the demand for bond clauses that permit the trustee to audit the firm on demand. The model portrays a credit market in which different types of firms make different contractual

* Federal Reserve Bank of Philadelphia and J. P. Morgan and Company, respectively. We have benefited from suggestions by John Boyd, Joe Haubrich, George Pennacchi, Tony Saunders, and an anonymous referee, who cannot, of course, be blamed for any mistakes. The views expressed do not necessarily represent the views of the Federal Reserve Bank of Philadelphia, the Federal Reserve System, or J. P. Morgan and Co. Research for this paper was completed while Jan Loeys was an economist at the Federal Reserve Bank of Philadelphia.

choices and in which changes in the information technology shift the margin of choice.

In our model, as in much of the literature on why banks exist, bondholders have inadequate incentives to monitor on their own. However, in place of the typical informational assumption that investors choose between becoming fully informed and remaining totally ignorant, investors are assumed to face a richer menu of choices about the quality of the information they can gather about firms. We maintain a distinction between routine accounting information that can often be gathered at low cost and detailed information about the firm's prospects, which can only be gathered by intensive and costly monitoring. In addition, we introduce observable differences between firms that can affect contractual choices. Firms have different histories, operate in different markets, and have projects likely to produce different streams of returns. When firms enter credit markets, market participants have substantial prior knowledge that permits them to distinguish different types of firms, and contractual choices will reflect this knowledge.

We permit individual investors to observe low-cost, but noisy, interim indicators of the firm's future ability to repay. These indicators might be routine financial ratios used to measure the firm's financial health or even the firm's ability to make coupon payments on time. Bond covenants are written as functions of these indicators, and the firm's inability to satisfy these covenants places the firm in default. However, since the covenants are based on imperfect information, default policies based on these covenants will be inefficient. Bond contracts will tend to be either too harsh or too lenient; harsh contracts lead to excessive default, while lenient contracts permit too many unpromising projects to mature. A detailed investigation of the firm's condition would provide more information and would thus avoid this inefficiency. However, such investigations are costly, and bondholders holding diversified portfolios have limited private incentives to monitor, even when monitoring is worthwhile for all investors taken together.

When bond covenants based on imperfect information would lead to too many mistakes, the services of a monitoring specialist—a "banker"—may be required. However, this specialist must be provided with incentives both to monitor and to choose an efficient default policy. Our model examines the tradeoff between the gains from an efficient default policy and the agency costs that arise when the task of monitoring is delegated. In particular, we examine these tradeoffs as a function of a few parameters that characterize the firm and the information technology. The most important of these are the firm's "credit rating", the predictive value of interim financial indicators of the firm's future health, the costs of a detailed investigation of the firm's financial condition, and the lost value from premature liquidation of projects.

The remainder of the paper is organized as follows. Section I presents the model. Section II describes the optimal contracts without monitoring. Section III shows that securityholders have inadequate incentives to monitor and presents the optimal contract with monitoring. Section IV describes the tradeoffs between the different types of contracts and presents comparative-statics results. The final section concludes and discusses possible extensions.

I. The Model[1]

Consider a market composed of N risk-neutral entrepreneurs who have a project but no wealth and M identical, risk-averse investors who have wealth but no projects. Throughout, we shall refer to the entrepreneurs as firms. All projects require the investment of a single unit of wealth in period 0 and yield final project returns in period 2, the final period. Assume that, together, investors have sufficient wealth to finance the projects of all firms, i.e.,

$$WM > N, \qquad (1)$$

where W is the wealth of one investor. To keep the notation simple, the model is developed in terms of a single firm. Unless otherwise noted, different firms may have different parameter values.

After contracts have been drawn up and funds transferred in period 0, each firm's project type is determined by an independent, random variable, $t \in \{t_G, t_B\}$, where t_G indicates a good project and t_B a bad project. In period 1, the decision is made either to permit the project to mature or to liquidate the project. If a project is allowed to mature until the second period, its discounted gross revenues are either X_g, with probability $f(t)$, or X_b (zero for all firms), with probability $1 - f(t)$. Thus, even if the project type becomes known, some uncertainty about the final-period returns remains. Good projects are more likely to yield positive returns than are bad projects, i.e., $f(t_G) > f(t_B)$, and all final project returns can be observed by anyone.

Alternatively, if a project of *either* type is liquidated in period 1, it yields a nonrandom, discounted liquidation value, X_d, in period 2. Alternatively, X_d might be the firm's value after a reorganization. We assume that the expected gross revenues from a good project that matures exceed the project's liquidation value and that the opposite is true of bad projects; i.e.,

$$f(t_G)X_g > X_d > f(t_B)X_g. \qquad (2)$$

In addition to investing in projects, investors may invest in a storage technology yielding a discounted return of 1 in the final period. The return to storage exceeds the liquidation value of projects; i.e., $X_d < 1$. Inequality (1) implies that, in equilibrium, some investors will store at least some of their wealth.

The information structure of the model is as follows. When funds are invested in period 0, no firm knows the type of project that it will draw. In period 1, however, each firm learns whether its project is good or bad, while investors observe costlessly an indicator of each project's type. The indicator is independent across projects and is denoted by $y \in \{y_G, y_B\}$. Everyone knows both the conditional distribution of project types for each value of the indicator and the prior distribution of the indicator. Let $p(t_i \mid y_j)$ denote the conditional probability of t_i given y_j, and let $p(y_j)$ denote the prior probability of y_j. Given the simple structure of uncertainty, a useful parameterization of the probability distributions

---

[1] For a list of symbols used in this model, see Appendix A.

is as follows:

$$\begin{bmatrix} p(t_G \,|\, y_G) \; p(t_G \,|\, y_B) \\ p(t_B \,|\, y_G) \; p(t_B \,|\, y_B) \end{bmatrix} = \begin{bmatrix} \rho + \alpha(1-\rho) & \alpha(1-\rho) \\ 1 - \rho - \alpha(1-\rho) & 1 - \alpha(1-\rho) \end{bmatrix}$$

and   (3)

$$\begin{bmatrix} p(y_G) \\ p(y_B) \end{bmatrix} = \begin{bmatrix} \alpha \\ 1 - \alpha \end{bmatrix},$$

where $0 < \alpha < 1$ and $0 < \rho < 1$. In this parameterization, α is both the prior probability of a favorable indicator and the prior probability of a good project. ρ measures the informativeness of the indicator, with $\rho = 1$ corresponding to a perfectly informative indicator and $\rho = 0$ corresponding to a totally uninformative indicator.[2] The indicator may be interpreted as a balance-sheet ratio, perhaps the working capital-asset ratio, or the firm's ability to make a coupon payment. If this indicator is a very good predictor of the firm's ultimate ability to repay, then ρ is near one.

In addition to observing the costless but noisy indicator, investors can learn any firm's project type by monitoring the firm in period 1 at a cost, e, the disutility of effort required to monitor the firm. We assume that no one is privy to the outcome of another's investigation or, for that matter, to whether any investigation was performed at all.

There are two types of lending arrangements, *bonds* and *bank loans*. Bonds are claims on the firm's final project returns sold directly by firms to investors. Alternatively, a group of investors may hire another investor—a "banker"—to contract with a single borrowing firm on their behalf. (Henceforth, the term "lender" will be used when statements might apply equally to bondholders or bankers.)

Both bonds and bank loans contain two types of clauses, *covenants* and *payments*. A covenant confers upon lenders the right to place the firm in default for specified values of the indicator, thereby forcing the firm to liquidate the project.[3] It is the contractual right to intervene under well-specified circumstances, rather than fixed contractual payments in non-default states, that distinguishes our bank loans and security contracts as debt contracts.[4] While nothing in the model requires the contracts to have fixed contractual payments in non-default states, all of our contracts are feasible if this constraint is imposed. The covenant may be conditioned both upon the indicator and upon statements

---

[2] An indicator with higher ρ is more informative in Blackwell's [2] sense. In addition, if $t_G = 2$, $t_B = 1$, and $y_G = 2$, $y_B = 1$, then ρ is the correlation coefficient beween t and y.

[3] We view the breach of a covenant restriction as an indicator of the firm's financial condition, which is exogenous in our model. Some covenants—such as restrictions on dividend payouts and priority rules—are primarily means of controlling moral-hazard problems and are best viewed as mechanisms to constrain management and equityholders' actions. This aspect of covenants is emphasized by Smith and Warner [13].

[4] Equityholders, of course, have open-ended rights of intervention as legal owners of the firm. However, outside equityholders, with limited holdings in a particular firm, will have limited incentives to bear the substantial costs of monitoring firm insiders. In fact, this is one reason why bond contracts that place clear, legally binding constraints on the firm may be preferred to equity.

made by lenders about the project's type.[5] A covenant can be written as a function:

$$d(t_i', y_j) \in \{0, 1\} \quad \text{for} \quad i, j = G, B. \tag{4}$$

The first argument of the function, t_i', is a statement made by a lender that the project is of type t_i. When $d(\cdot) = 1$, the project is permitted to mature, and, when $d(\cdot) = 0$, the firm is placed in default and the project is liquidated.

All payments are made by the firm in the final period when project returns are realized. Thus, payments may depend upon realized revenue as well as indicators and statements. For notational convenience only, payments made to the banker and to the bank's investors are written as if they were made directly by the borrowing firm. As long as final revenues are observable, there is no loss of generality. An arrangement in which the banker distributed revenues to investors (or vice versa) would yield an identical distribution of revenues among the different claimants. Thus, the total payment made by the firm to investors (other than the banker) can be written:

$$r_k(t_i', y_j) \quad \text{for} \quad i, j = G, B \quad \text{and} \quad k = g, b, d. \tag{5}$$

This is the payment made to investors when final revenues are X_k, the indicator is y_j, and a lender makes a statement t_i' about the project. Similarly, payments to the banker can be written:

$$b_k(t_i', y_j) \quad \text{for} \quad i, j = G, B \quad \text{and} \quad k = g, b, d. \tag{6}$$

Since firms have no wealth, all payments must be made out of project revenues. Thus, a feasible contract requires that

$$X_k \geq r_k(t_i', y_j) + b_k(t_i', y_j) \quad \text{for any} \quad i, j, k, \tag{7}$$

and, when the firm is placed in default (i.e., $k = d$), this holds with equality. In addition, all payments must be non-negative:

$$r_k(t_i', y_j) \geq 0 \quad \text{and} \quad b_k(t_i', y_j) \geq 0 \quad \text{for any} \quad i, j, k. \tag{8}$$

Together, (7) and (8) imply that no agent will have negative final-period consumption.

Consider now the different agents' objective functions. Assume that any statements about the type of project are truthful. Later, incentive-compatibility constraints will be imposed to make this true. A firm's expected profits at period 1, after it learns that it has project type t_i and after y_j has been observed, are

$$\pi_1^f(t_i, y_j) = d(t_i, y_j)\{f(t_i)[X_g - r_g(t_i, y_j) - b_g(t_i, y_j)]\}$$
$$+ (1 - d(t_i, y_j))\{X_d - r_d(t_i, y_j) - b_d(t_i, y_j)\}. \tag{9}$$

At period 0, the firm's expected profits are

$$\pi_0^f = \Sigma_i \Sigma_j \, \pi_1^f(t_i, y_j) p(t_i \mid y_j) p(y_j). \tag{10}$$

---

[5] In our model, truthful revelations by the borrowing firm can only be achieved by a contract that treats firms with the same indicator identically, i.e., a pooling contract. Thus, statements by firms can provide no information that is not contained in the indicator.

Now consider an investor who has placed w dollars in a firm or a bank (that has invested in a firm). w is also the investor's share of the firm's outstanding securities because each project requires a single unit of wealth. Since investors are risk averse, we assume that each invests in many firms or banks and holds a well-diversified portfolio. Thus, investors will evaluate returns as if they were risk neutral. The investor's expected payments from a firm of unknown type when y_j has been observed are

$$\pi_1^I(y_j) = w\{\textstyle\sum_i[d(t_i, y_j)f(t_i)r_g(t_i, y_j) + (1 - d(t_i, y_j))r_d(t_i, y_j)]p(t_i \mid y_j)\}, \quad (11)$$

while expected payments at period 0, before the indicator has been observed, are

$$\pi_0^I = \textstyle\sum_j \pi_1^I(y_j)p(y_j). \quad (12)$$

II. Optimal Contracts without Monitoring

When no monitoring occurs, lenders know only the public indicator. Formally, a contract without monitoring can be viewed as a pooling contract, with terms depending solely upon the value of the indicator. In fact, when no monitoring occurs, only bonds will be used since there is no function for a banker (whose sole purpose in our model is to act as a specialized monitor). The no-monitoring assumption implies that contractual terms will depend only upon the indicator, or that

$$d(t_G, y_j) = d(t_B, y_j) \quad \text{for all} \quad j \quad (13)$$

and

$$r_k(t_G, y_j) = r_k(t_B, y_j) \quad \text{for all} \quad j, k. \quad (14)$$

In a competitive market in which all investors have access to a storage technology, the bond contract must maximize the firm's expected profits subject to investors' willingness to supply funds. In Appendix B, we describe market equilibrium when there are many ex ante distinguishable firms and show that, for a firm that can pay a higher return than storage, the optimal bond contract must satisfy the following problem:

$$\max_{d(\cdot), r(\cdot)} \pi_0^f \quad (15)$$

subject to

$$\pi_0^I \geq w, \quad (16)$$

and (7), (8), (13), and (14).

Since there are two values of the indicator, there are four possible default policies, only two of which can be optimal. One contract, the *lenient bond contract* (S_L) never places the firm in default. Another contract, the *harsh bond contract* (S_H), places the firm is default only when the bad indicator, y_B, is observed. Contracts that place the firm in default when a good indicator is observed cannot be optimal for the following reasons. One that imposes default only when the good indicator is observed is never optimal because a good indicator is good news about the project; if it is optimal to impose default when $y = y_G$, then the same must be true when $y = y_B$. (See Milgrom [10] for a definition of "good news".) However, default will not always be imposed because, by assumption, storage strictly dominates any contract that always places the firm in default.

For both the lenient and harsh bond contracts, the firm's maximum expected profits can be derived by solving (16) as an equality and substituting into (15). Letting $\pi^f(S)$ denote the firm's maximum expected profits at period 0 under contract type S, we have

$$\pi^f(S_L) = p(y_G)[f(t_G)X_g p(t_G \mid y_G) + f(t_B)X_g p(t_B \mid y_G)]$$
$$+ p(y_B)[f(t_G)X_g p(t_G \mid y_B) + f(t_B)X_g p(t_B \mid y_B)] - 1 \qquad (17)$$

and

$$\pi^f(S_H) = p(y_G)[f(t_G)X_g p(t_G \mid y_G) + f(t_B)X_g p(t_B \mid y_G)] + p(y_B)X_d - 1. \qquad (18)$$

To understand these contracts, it is helpful to compare them with the first best, the optimal liquidation policy if the project type were known. The first-best policy maximizes total contractual surplus, which by (2) involves liquidating bad projects and continuing good projects. The S_L contract, however, does not liquidate bad projects, while the S_H contract liquidates good projects when the indicator is misleadingly unfavorable. Subtracting (18) from (17) and using (3) results in an expression for the relative profitability of the two contracts. For expositional purposes, we make the simplifying assumption that $f(t_B)$ is very close (but not equal) to one and that $f(t_G)$ is very close (but not equal) to zero for all firms. While nothing important hinges upon this assumption—essentially the same results have been derived for the more general case—it permits an uncluttered presentation of results.[6] Thus,

$$\pi^f(S_L) - \pi^f(S_H) = p(y_B)[p(t_G \mid y_B)X_g - X_d]$$
$$= (1 - \alpha)[\alpha(1 - \rho)X_g - X_d]. \qquad (19)$$

This difference is positive and the S_L contract is optimal when α is high and ρ is low. When α, the prior probability of a good project, is high, it is optimal to ignore even unfavorable information. When ρ is low, the indicator is an imprecise predictor of the firm's future prospects, and bad information is discounted. The difference is also positive when X_g is large and X_d is small, that is, when the liquidation value of the project is small relative to the value of the project should it succeed. This will be the case, for example, if the project involves capital goods that have no ready secondary market. When this is true, the cost of liquidating too seldom is small and the S_L contract is optimal.

III. Optimal Contracts with Monitoring

In this section, after showing that diversified bondholders will, in general, monitor too little, we derive the optimal incentive contract for a delegated monitor and

---

[6] If $f(t_B) = 0$, then the firm with a bad project could always be induced to state truthfully its project type and separation could be achieved without monitoring. The simplification creates a bias toward harsh contracts; in the general case, good projects are not quite so good and bad projects are not quite so bad. In the simple case, the "degree of goodness" is captured by varying X_g and X_d parametrically.

analyze the agency costs of contractual schemes with monitoring. At the end of the section, alternative interpretations of these contractual arrangements are discussed.

Since there are two values of the indicator, monitoring might occur for either or both of the two indicators. However, monitoring when the indicator is good can be valuable only when both the prior probability of a good project and the informativeness of the indicator are quite low, precisely those values for which storage is likely to dominate investment in the firm under any type of contract. Thus, we focus on contracts in which monitoring takes place only when the indicator is unfavorable. Such contracts permit a more efficient liquidation policy while economizing on both monitoring and agency costs.

A necessary condition for monitoring to be valuable is that the expected gross revenues from an efficient liquidation policy less monitoring costs exceed the expected gross revenues from both (i) liquidating all projects for y_B and (ii) continuing all projects; i.e.,

$$\text{i. } p(t_G | y_B) X_g + p(t_B | y_B) X_d - e \geq X_d,$$

$$\text{ii. } p(t_G | y_B) X_g + p(t_B | y_B) X_d - e \geq p(t_G | y_B) X_g, \tag{20}$$

which can be rewritten:

$$\text{i. } p(t_G | y_B)[X_g - X_d] \geq e,$$

$$\text{ii. } [1 - p(t_G | y_B)] X_d \geq e. \tag{21}$$

Securityholders, however, will have inadequate incentives to monitor when each has limited wealth invested in any one firm. Even if we abstract from the real-world problems of achieving bondholder consensus, any individual bondholder will weigh the private gains from monitoring—measured by the left-hand sides of (21.i) and (21.ii) multiplied by w—against the full costs of monitoring. When w is small, no investor will monitor even when (21) holds. We assume, henceforth, that bondholders hold a well-diversified portfolio and will not choose to monitor.[7]

We now examine the case where a delegated monitor—a banker—is provided with a compensation scheme that induces an efficient liquidation policy for y_B. The banker, like other investors, is too risk averse to invest an appreciable amount of wealth in the project he or she monitors without bearing excessive risk. Thus, the banker invests in the market portfolio and must be provided with a payment scheme to induce him or her to monitor efficiently on behalf of other investors. We make the standard assumptions that the banker's objection func-

---

[7] If there are substantial transactions costs of assembling and maintaining a diversified portfolio, then investors might be unable to diversify fully. Our model effectively assumes that these transactions costs are negligible. The reduction in brokerage fees and the rapidly expanding menu of mutual funds available to the typical investor have dramatically reduced transactions costs in recent years. We are hesitant, however, to view a mutual fund manager as a delegated monitor in our sense. The incentives for mutual fund managers to engage in detailed monitoring of the firms in the fund's portfolio are quite limited. A more typical behavior is to sell securities at the first sign of bad news.

tion,

$$U(b_k + W) - e,$$

is separable in income and monitoring effort and that $U' > 0$ and $U'' < 0$.

Incentive compatibility requires that the banker have an incentive both to monitor and to reveal truthfully the outcome of his or her investigation. It is easy to show that, if the banker has an incentive to monitor, then he or she will truthfully reveal the outcome of his or her investigation. Thus, the binding incentive-compatibility conditions are that the banker's expected utility from an efficient liquidation policy is greater than the expected utility from (i) a policy of liquidating all projects and (ii) a policy of permitting all projects to continue. These two conditions can be written:

i. $p(t_G \,|\, y_B) U[b_g(t_G, y_B) + W] + p(t_B \,|\, y_B) U[b_d(t_B, y_B) + W] - e$
$$\geq U[b_d(t_B, y_B) + W],$$

ii. $p(t_G \,|\, y_B) U[b_g(t_G, y_b) + W] + p(t_B \,|\, y_B) U[b_d(t_B, y_B) + W] - e$
$$\geq p(t_G \,|\, y_B) U[b_g(t_G, y_B) + W] + p(t_B \,|\, y_B) U[W].^{[8]} \quad (22)$$

Letting the function G denote the inverse of U, treating both as equalities, and solving for b_g and b_d, we have

i. $b_g(t_G, y_B) = G\left(\dfrac{e}{p(t_G \,|\, y_B)(1 - p(t_G \,|\, y_B))} + U[W] \right) - W,$

ii. $b_d(t_B, y_B) = G\left(\dfrac{e}{1 - p(t_G \,|\, y_B)} + U[W] \right) - W, \quad (23)$

while the banker's compensation for y_G is zero since no monitoring occurs when the indicator is favorable. Note that $b_g > b_d$. If this were not true, the banker would always choose the certain return from a policy of liquidating all projects over the uncertain return from monitoring.

Let B denote the contract in which the banker monitors and chooses an efficient liquidation policy for y_B. The optimal bank contract chooses a set of payments to maximize

$$\pi_0^f = p(y_G)[p(t_G \,|\, y_G)\{X_g - r_g(t_G, y_G) - b_g(t_G, y_G)\}]$$
$$+ p(y_B)[p(t_G \,|\, y_B)\{X_g - r_g(t_G, y_B) - b_g(t_G, y_B)\}$$
$$+ p(t_B \,|\, y_B)\{X_d - r_d(t_B, y_B) - b_d(t_B, y_B)\}] \quad (24)$$

subject to

$$\pi_0^l = p(y_G)p(t_G \,|\, y_G)r_g(t_G, y_G)$$
$$+ p(y_B)[p(t_G \,|\, y_B)r_g(t_G, y_B) + p(t_B \,|\, y_B)r_d(t_B, y_B)] \geq 1 \quad (25)$$

---

[8] Unlike Diamond [6], we do not permit the monitor to be subjected to "nonpecuniary" penalties. Although the time costs of bankruptcy for firm management and the loss of reputation are, no doubt, important, it is very doubtful that these costs can be designed as part of an optimal contract as in Diamond. Rather, they should be modeled explicitly as part of the legal or market environment.

and (23). Define $z \equiv p(t_G | y_B) = \alpha(1 - \rho)$. This variable is inversely related to the informativeness of bad information about the project. When z is low, a bad indicator is reliable evidence that the project is bad. Letting (25) be satisfied with equality and substituting this and (23) into (24), the firm's maximum expected profits are

$$\pi^f(B) = \alpha(\rho + z)X_g + (1 - \alpha)[zX_g + (1 - z)X_d - C(e, z)] - 1, \quad (26)$$

where

$$C(e, z) \equiv zG(ez^{-1}(1 - z)^{-1} + U[W]) + (1 - z)G(e(1 - z)^{-1} + U[W]) - W.$$

C denotes the total expected payments required to make the banker choose efficient liquidation decisions. If the outcome of the banker's investigation were observable, then it would suffice to pay him or her the utility cost of monitoring, e, whenever he or she monitored. However, since monitoring is unobservable, the banker must be compensated in excess of the actual costs of monitoring to induce him or her both to monitor and to make efficient liquidation decisions. This excess is the agency cost of hiring a delegated monitor.

The behavior of C is as follows. First, C is increasing in e since $G' > 0$. Second, for any strictly increasing utility function, C grows infinitely large as z approaches zero or one. The intuition is straightforward. When z is very low, the probability of finding a good project is very low. Unless the banker's payment for a successful project (b_g) is very large, he or she will choose to liquidate all projects. When z is very high, the banker will find a policy of allowing all projects to mature to be very attractive. Thus, the banker's payment when the project is liquidated (b_d) must be very large to induce him or her to monitor. Since $b_g > b_d$, so must the banker's payment be should the project succeed.

Third, C must be increasing in z for $z \geq \frac{1}{2}$. As z increases, the banker is more likely to find a good project when the indicator is bad. Thus, the banker's liquidation payment must increase to induce him or her to monitor rather than to choose a policy of allowing all projects to mature. Also, for $z \geq \frac{1}{2}$, b_g is increasing in z. Since both payments are increasing in z and since the probability of the banker receiving the larger payment is also increasing, total expected payments must be increasing. Finally, for typical utility functions such as the square root and logarithmic functions, C can be shown to be decreasing in z when z is small. For small values of z, b_g is decreasing in z, thus imparting a negative slope to C, which achieves a minimum at some value of z less than or equal to $\frac{1}{2}$.

What types of real-world contractual arrangements does our incentive-compatible scheme resemble? We consider two interpretations. One interpretation is that our monitor is a loan officer delegated to oversee part of a bank loan portfolio. This interpretation rationalizes the monitor's risk aversion and inability to invest an appreciable amount of wealth in the project.[9] The loan contract

---

[9] If the banker can invest an appreciable amount of his or her own wealth without bearing excessive risk, then the costs of inducing an efficient default policy are lowered because the banker's interests are, to some extent, harmonized with bank investors. If individual bankers can manage a very large, diversified portfolio, then even small amounts of wealth will suffice. (In the limit, a perfectly diversified portfolio could be managed efficiently with zero agency costs and no wealth posted.) If, however,

is of the following type: If the firm's financial condition as measured by the indicator is good, then the banker does not monitor and the firm pays a contractually agreed loan rate. (As noted above, this economizes on monitoring costs.) If the indicator is bad, then the banker retains the right to reorganize the firm, conditional upon the outcome of an investigation. Whenever the indicator is bad, the firm must pay a higher markup on its loan, reflecting the costs of monitoring: both direct costs and agency costs.

In a second interpretation, the monitor is not a banker but a bond trustee or an auditor hired by the trustee. In addition to distributing payments, trustees are often given the contractual right to audit the firm on demand. The audit, which is usually performed by an outside firm, is triggered by the firm's inability to satisfy promptly covenant requirements. In this interpretation, our model provides a formal analysis of the marginal benefits and costs of contractual clauses that give trustees the right to audit the firm.

While suggestive, both of these interpretations have problems. For the first interpretation to be fully consistent, the rise in the firm's markup must be paid out to the loan officer as part of a managerial compensation scheme. While de facto compensation schemes may resemble our incentive schedule, there is little evidence that formal compensation schemes take this form. (See Robert Morris Associates [12].) Also, the rise in the markup when the firm fails to satisfy covenant requirements will be the outcome of a bargaining game, perhaps constrained by implicit agreements. We are currently studying when an incentive-compatible monitoring scheme can be sustained without a binding written contract. Similarly, trustees and auditing firms are typically paid a fixed fee rather than a variable payment that depends upon the outcome of their investigations. It is clear that more work is required to bring the theoretical contracting scheme closer to those actually observed in financial markets.

IV. The Choice between Contracts with and without Monitoring

In this section, we show that the optimal contract choice depends upon the relative inefficiencies of excessively lenient or excessively harsh liquidation policies and upon the agency costs of hiring a banker to make efficient liquidation decisions. We also present comparative statics that show how contractual choice is affected by the model parameters.

Using expressions (17), (18), and (26), we can derive expressions for the differences in the firm's expected profits under the three contracts:

i. $\pi^f(B) - \pi^f(S_L) = (1 - \alpha)\{(1 - z)X_d - C(e, z)\},$

ii. $\pi^f(B) - \pi^f(S_H) = (1 - \alpha)\{z(X_g - X_d) - C(e, z)\},$

iii. $\pi^f(S_L) - \pi^f(S_H) = (1 - \alpha)\{z(X_g - X_d) - (1 - z)X_d\}.$ (27)

---

monitors have limited spans of control, as in Boyd and Prescott [3] and Ramakrishnan and Thakor [11], then diversification will require a coalition of bankers. Such coalitions face difficult tradeoffs between risk sharing and free-rider problems. We feel that real-world limits on the ability to impose risk on bank managers are sufficiently important for the limiting case we consider to be of interest.

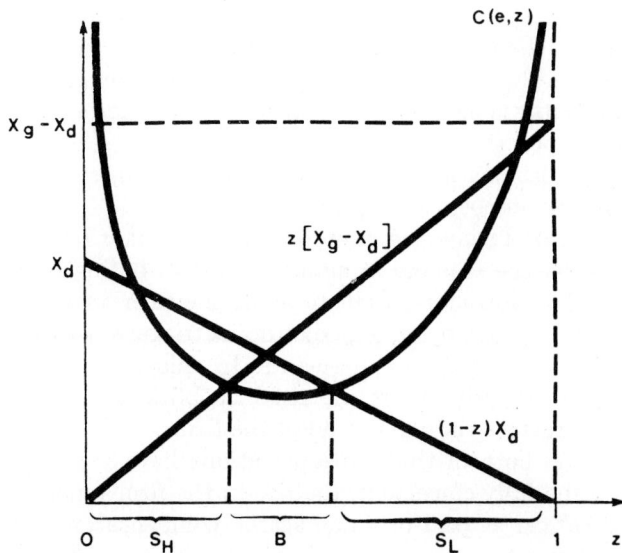

Figure 1. The Relationship between z and the Optimal Contract

A graphical analysis of these expressions is possible. There are three separate terms to consider: $(1-z)X_d$, $z(X_g - X_d)$, and C. Although it is possible for the B contract to be dominated throughout—if e is very large or $(X_g - X_d)$ is very small—we focus on those cases where banks dominate securities for some values of z; i.e., both (27.i) and (27.ii) are positive for some z.

Figure 1 shows a typical configuration for which this is true.[10] The S_H contract dominates for small z, and the S_L contract dominates for large z. For both small and large z, the agency costs of hiring a delegated monitor are very large and the marginal benefits from an efficient liquidation policy are very small; thus, one of the bond contracts will be optimal. The harsh contract will be optimal for z near zero because few good projects will be found when the indicator is bad. The lenient contract will be optimal for z near one because many of the projects with bad indicators will turn out to be good. For intermediate values of z, however, the marginal value of monitoring is large and, in turn, the expected costs of inducing efficient decision making by the banker are small. In this range, the bank contract will be chosen.

We now investigate how variations in the parameters affect the optimal contract choice. Figure 1 shows that, as long as investors have insufficient incentives to monitor, a decrease in the cost of monitoring increases the range over which bank loans dominate. This follows because $dC/de > 0$. However, as e continues to fall, it may become profitable for individual investors to monitor the firm themselves.[11] The same is true if the individual investor's share (w) of a firm's debt rises sufficiently.

---

[10] This configuration will hold if $(X_g - X_d)$ is not too small. For a more complete analysis, see Berlin and Loeys [1]. This paper also has a more detailed analysis of the comparative statics and examines the conditions under which monitoring for both values of the indicator will be optimal.

[11] Although for sufficiently small monitoring costs it may be profitable for individual investors to

Consider now the effect of changes in α or ρ. As α, the prior probability of a good project, increases, z increases. This implies that the S_L contract dominates over an increasing range. For firms that are very likely to have good projects, the incremental value of interim information is small unless the indicator is very informative. Thinking of α as a firm's credit rating, this says that a highly rated firm is more likely to secure finance using bonds with lenient covenants than a lower rated firm. Firms with lower credit ratings are likely to secure finance using bank loans or bonds with harsh covenants.

It is natural to interpret ρ as a measure of the stability of the relationship between the information upon which covenants are based and the firm's ultimate ability to repay. Thus, if the covenants specify that the firm must satisfy certain financial ratios, a large ρ indicates that these ratios bear a stable relationship to the firm's longer term project revenues. As ρ increases, either of the two contracts that are responsive to interim information, B and S_H, become relatively more attractive. For firms without very high credit ratings, it can be shown that, if $(X_g - X_d)$ is large, then the model predicts the use of bank contracts for intermediate values of ρ and the use of harsh bond contracts for high values of ρ.

Finally, Figure 1 shows that a rise in X_g or a decline in X_d enlarges the range over which lenient security contracts dominate and reduces the preference for either harsh security contracts or loan contracts. This result is no surprise. For a project with a low liquidation value, neither monitoring nor harsh covenant restrictions produce large gains because investors cannot gain much from early liquidation. Low liquidation values are likely to be found with firms that have invested mostly in firm-specific or intangible capital that does not have a secondary market.

V. Conclusion

We have examined two contractual alternatives available to a firm seeking to finance an investment. Debt contracts with covenants based on noisy indicators of the firm's financial condition tend to be either too harsh (too many good projects are liquidated) or too lenient (too many bad projects are permitted to mature). Hiring the services of a delegated monitor ensures a more efficient liquidation policy, but providing the monitor with proper incentives is costly. The firm's optimal choice reflects a tradeoff between the inefficiencies of rigid bond covenants and the agency costs of hiring a delegated monitor. This tradeoff depends upon a number of parameters characterizing the firm's production technology and the information technology.

Although our contractual choices have similarities to institutions in the real world, we are yet some distance from being able to reproduce the contractual forms actually observed in financial markets. Although we have interpreted the

---

monitor firms themselves, the actual decision to monitor has game-theoretic elements that we do not analyze. Also, in a world where individual securityholders do have incentives to monitor, a reasonable model must take account of conflicts of interest among claimants and the costs of forging consensus, which play no part in our model.

delegated monitor as a banker, to be fully convincing this interpretation requires an explicit analysis of the bank's liability side. Also, while the model treats all outcomes under the bank loan as if they arose from a binding written contract, we feel that renegotiation and implicit agreements are quite important features of delegated-monitoring arrangements. Our debt contracts without monitoring are more nearly recognizable as bonds, but the secondary market for financial assets plays no role in our model. It would be quite interesting to analyze the tradeoffs between complex covenants, which may be necessary to control agency problems, and the size of the secondary market for a firm's securities. In future work, we hope to address some of these problems.

Appendix A

List of Symbols

α: probability that a firm's project is of type t_G.

$b(\cdot)$: payment by firm to bank.

B: bank (loan) contract.

$d(\cdot)$: default covenant; $d(\cdot) = 0$: default; $d(\cdot) = 1$: no default.

e: monitoring costs.

$G(\cdot)$: inverse of $U(\cdot)$.

π_x^f: expectation at time x of firm's profits.

π_x^I: expectation at time x of investor's profits.

$\pi^f(S)$: firm's maximum expected profit if lending contract is of type S, where $S = B, S_H, S_L$.

$r(\cdot)$: payment by firm to investor (other than the bank).

ρ: informativeness of the indicator y.

S_L: lenient bond contract.

S_H: harsh bond contract.

t_i: type of project, where $i = G$ (good) or B (bad).

$U(\cdot)$: banker's utility of income.

X_k: period-2 revenues of a project, discounted to period 1, where $k = g, b, d$.

y_j: indicator about project's type, where $j = G, B$.

w: share of individual investor in total debt of a firm.

W: total wealth of an individual investor.

z: $p(t_G | y_B)$.

Appendix B

Firms are indexed by $n = 1, \cdots, N$. For simplicity, assume that each firm is different. Then n may also be used to denote the vector of observable characteristics of the nth firm:

$$n = (\alpha(n), \rho(n), X_g(n), X_d(n)).$$

We assume that firms offer contracts and that investors then allocate their wealth among firms and storage. Let w_{mn} be the wealth invested by investor m

in the nth firm, and let w_{mo} be the wealth placed by investor m in storage. Let $T(n)$ denote an incentive-compatible contract offered by the nth firm. (If this contract requires the efforts of a monitor, then it must satisfy the incentive-compatibility conditions described in the text.) The expected profits of the nth firm under a contract $T(n)$ are denoted by $\pi^f(n, T(n))$, and the contract offered by this firm, $T^*(n)$, must satisfy

$$T^*(n) = \text{argmax } \pi^f(n, T(n)) \tag{A1}$$

subject to

$$\sum_m w_{mn} \geq 1. \tag{A2}$$

If this is infeasible, the firm does not operate. Let $\pi^I_m(n, T^*(n))$ denote the expected return per unit of funds invested by investor m in the nth firm. Since each investor can store his or her wealth,

$$\pi^I_m(n, T^*(n)) \geq 1 \tag{A3}$$

for any firm that operates. In equilibrium, contracts must yield equal returns across investors and across firms; i.e.,

$$\pi^I_m(n, T^*(n)) = \pi^I_{m'}(n', T^*(n')) \quad \text{for all} \quad m, m', n, n', \tag{A4}$$

where n and n' are firms that receive funds. Let F denote the set of firms that receive funds. By (1) and (A3), F will contain all firms that have a maximum expected return at least equal to one. Then the description of equilibrium is completed by a market-clearing condition,

$$\sum_m(\sum_{n \in F} w_{mn} + w_{mo}) = Mw_m. \tag{A5}$$

Together, (A1) through (A5) describe equilibrium with heterogeneous firms.

REFERENCES

1. M. Berlin and J. Loeys. "The Choice between Bonds and Bank Loans." Working Paper No. 86-18, Federal Reserve Bank of Philadelphia, November 1986.
2. F. Blackwell. "Comparison of Experiments." In J. Neyman (ed.), *Proceedings of the Second Berkeley Symposium in Mathematical Statistics and Probability.* Berkeley: University of California Press, 1951, 93–102.
3. J. H. Boyd and E. C. Prescott. "Financial Intermediary Coalitions." *Journal of Economic Theory* 38 (April 1986), 211–32.
4. T. Campbell and W. Kracaw. "Information Production, Market Signalling, and the Theory of Financial Intermediation." *Journal of Finance* 35 (September 1980), 863–82.
4. Y. Chan. "On the Positive Role of Financial Intermediaries in the Allocation of Venture Capital in a Market with Imperfect Information." *Journal of Finance* 38 (December 1983), 1543–69.
6. D. W. Diamond. "Financial Intermediation and Delegated Monitoring." *Review of Economic Studies* 51 (July 1984), 393–414.
7. G. B. Gorton and J. G. Haubrich. "Bank Deregulation, Credit Markets, and the Control of Capital." Working Paper No. 8-86, Rodney White Center for Financial Research, February 1986.
8. T. H. Ho and R. F. Singer. "Bond Indenture Provisions and the Risk of Corporate Debt." *Journal of Financial Economics* 10 (December 1982), 375–406.
9. A. Kalay. "Stockholder-Bondholder Conflict and Dividend Constraints." *Journal of Financial Economics* 10 (July 1982), 211–33.

10. P. R. Milgrom. "Good News and Bad News: Representation Theorems and Applications." *Bell Journal of Economics* 12 (Autumn 1981), 380–91.

11. R. Ramakrishnan and A. Thakor. "Information Reliability and the Theory of Financial Intermediation." *Review of Economic Studies* 51 (July 1984), 415–32.

12. Robert Morris Associates. *Incentive Compensation Systems for Commerical Loan Officers.* Philadelphia: Robert Morris Associates, 1983.

13. C. W. Smith and J. B. Warner. "On Financial Contracting: An Analysis of Bond Covenants." *Journal of Financial Economics* 7 (June 1979), 117–61.

Insiders and Outsiders: The Choice between Informed and Arm's-Length Debt

ABSTRACT

While the benefits of bank financing are relatively well understood, the costs are not. This paper argues that while informed banks make flexible financial decisions which prevent a firm's projects from going awry, the cost of this credit is that banks have bargaining power over the firm's profits, once projects have begun. The firm's portfolio choice of borrowing source and the choice of priority for its debt claims attempt to optimally circumscribe the powers of banks.

ACCORDING TO RECEIVED THEORY, banks reduce the agency costs associated with lending to small and medium growth firms in various ways.[1] Yet in practice, many such firms diversify away from bank financing even if banks are willing to lend more.[2] Why do these firms forsake informed and seemingly more efficient sources of debt finance to borrow from less informed arm's-length sources? While the benefits of bank financing are relatively well understood, the costs are not. This paper argues that while informed banks make flexible financial decision which prevent a firm's projects from going awry, the cost of this credit is that banks have bargaining power over the firm's profits, once projects have begun. The firm's choice of borrowing sources and the choice of priority for its debt claims attempt to optimally circumscribe the powers of banks.

* Assistant Professor of Finance, University of Chicago. I am indebted to Mitchell Berlin, Douglas Diamond, Oliver Hart, Donald Lessard, Antonio Mello, Stewart Myers, John Parsons, Canice Prendergast, David Scharfstein, Steven Sharpe, Jeremy Stein, René Stulz (the editor), Miguel Villas-Boas, and an anonymous referee for valuable comments and advice. I thank David Scharfstein for directing me toward this area. All errors are, of course, my own.

[1] The bank first screens prospective clients (Diamond (1991a)). Later, by threatening to cut off credit, it provides the firm with the incentives to take the right investments (Stiglitz and Weiss (1983)). As a result of the diminished adverse selection (through information) and the reduced moral hazard (through control of the firm's investment decisions), the bank has the capacity to provide cheap 'informed' funds as opposed to costly 'uninformed' or arm's-length funds (James (1987)). Finally, a positive loan renewal signal implies that other agents with fixed-payoff claims need not undertake a similar costly evaluation (Easterbrook (1984) and Fama (1985)).

[2] For example, Anstaett, McCreary, and Monahan (1988) document the case of Trans Leasing International Inc., a growth firm with a capitalization of $60 million in 1987 and a projected investment of $245 million over the subsequent five years. Trans Leasing restructured its borrowing by issuing notes and paying down bank borrowing. This met the firm's aims of "expand(ing) available debt capacity" and "diversify(ing) the company's sources of finance."

In this paper, I consider an owner-managed firm with a project idea. The firm has to make an externally financed investment in order to obtain a stochastic payoff. After making the investment, the owner exerts costly effort which affects the distribution of project returns. The state of the world, which is privately observable by the owner, is then realized. Depending on the state of the world, continuing the project (as opposed to liquidating it) may have positive or negative net present value (NPV). As the owner has a residual claim, and all financing is through external debt, she always wants to continue the project.

I distinguish between different sources of credit by their ability to acquire information about the debtor and their accessibility. A bank that lends to the firm for a project can obtain information about the firm in the course of lending which the firm cannot easily communicate to others.[3] Further, bank debt is easily renegotiated, because the bank is a monolithic, readily accessible creditor. However, a typical arm's-length creditor like the bondholder receives only public information. It is hard to contact these dispersed holders and any renegotiation suffers from information and free-rider problems.

This paper makes a simple but fundamental point. An informed bank will be able to control the owner's decision such that the project is continued only if it has positive NPV. In the process of doing so, however, it adversely affects the owner's incentive to exert effort.

To see this, I consider two kinds of bank contracts. The short-term bank contract is one where the bank requires repayment of the loan after the state is realized. As the bank is also informed about the state, it can prevent the owner from continuing a negative NPV venture by demanding repayment. Unfortunately, it can also demand repayment when continuing is efficient. If the owner has only the bank as a source of finance, she has to share some of the surplus from the project with the bank in order to persuade it to continue lending. As the owner no longer obtains all the surplus from the project, she exerts lower effort than optimal, thus reducing the project returns.

Alternatively, the bank can require repayment only when the project is completed. This is the long-term bank contract. The bank can no longer extract surplus from the firm. However, this contract creates a new problem. The bank cannot simply demand repayment when project continuation is inefficient; it now has to bribe the owner to stop the project. States where continuation has a negative NPV are now more attractive than before. The owner's incentive to exert effort to avoid these states is reduced. From the analysis of the above contracts, I derive implications for the choice of maturity of bank debt.

The third contract I consider is a long-term contract offered by an arm's-

---

[3] This information may be generated in real-time, during the process of lending. This includes information about the firm's prior projections, ability to meet prior targets, reliability and competence of personnel, etc. It is very hard for firms to present hard data on this to outside creditors. However, once a project is completed, there are 'hard' data like sales and profits which can be presented to outside creditors.

length investor. Unlike the banks, arm's-length lenders have no control over the owner's continuation decision. However, surplus is not reallocated after the state is realized. This contract may give the owner a higher incentive to exert effort than do either of the bank contracts. I conclude that the welfare effect of borrowing from a bank rather than arm's-length sources is ambiguous; the benefit of being bank-controlled has to be weighed against the costs of distortions in the owner's incentives to exert effort.

While analyzing the short-term bank contract, I assume initially that the firm is locked in to the bank for some exogenous reason. This assumption does not merely help us present the main issues simply. It could characterize economies where the banking sector is not competitive, either because of bank collusion or because of government intervention (see Modigliani and Perotti (1990)). I relax this assumption by allowing uninformed, outside lenders to compete with the informed, inside bank to lend when the owner wants to continue to project.

Competition among potential financiers is a double-edged sword. On the one hand, the inside bank's ability to appropriate surplus is reduced, which improves the owner's incentives to exert effort. On the other hand, the bank's control over the project is also reduced because uninformed lenders may continue unprofitable projects. The firm chooses its optimal borrowing structure, with the aim of reducing the bank's ability to appropriate rents, without drastically reducing its ability to control. The two fundamental factors within the firm's choice set in doing this are the levels of initial borrowing from the two different sources and the relative priority assigned to the respective claims. I thus obtain cross-sectional implications for a firm's choice of borrowing sources as well as the relative priority of its borrowing. I also show how public revelation of information affects this choice.

There are two main contributions of this paper. The first contribution is to emphasize a cost of bank finance that stems endogenously from the monitoring and control function the bank performs. The second contribution is to show how maturity, source choice, and priority affect both the benefits and the costs of bank debt. This is in contrast to much of the literature (Diamond (1991b) is an exception), which assumes the costs of bank debt to be exogenous and invariant to attributes of debt contracts like priority.

My paper is similar to Grossman and Hart (1986) in that the ex post allocation of property rights determines ex ante incentives. I, however, endogenously obtain the division of these rights into the rights to surplus and the rights to control. Because both these rights are aspects of the bank's information-based implicit property rights, they tend to vary similarly with most factors. My model is also not the first to examine the choice between bank and arm's-length debt. In Diamond (1991a) firms build reputation by taking on costly bank-monitored debt. Firms that acquire good reputations then move on to the arm's-length market to save on monitoring costs. The important difference in this paper is that the cost of bank debt is endogenous.

This paper is similar in parts to Sharpe (1990). However, there are important differences. Sharpe restricts his analysis to examining the costs of the inside bank's rents. My paper, in addition, explores the benefits of the inside bank's control. This difference in approach is important. For example, I show that changes in the allocation of priority, in general, do not alter the inside bank's rents. A focus on only rents could lead to the misleading conclusion that priority does not matter. However, changes in priority alter the inside bank's control and thus influence the owner's incentives to exert effort. My paper is also different in content. Sharpe examines the role of implicit contracts in reducing the bank's *incentives* to extract rents. My paper emphasizes the amount of borrowing from different sources and the allocation of priority as factors that alter the bank's *ability* to extract rents as well as its ability to control the firm.

The rest of the paper is structured as follows. Section I describes the basic model. Section II analyzes the different contracts assuming that once a firm borrows from a bank, it is compelled to borrow only from it in the future. The basic trade-off is demonstrated by comparing bank debt with arm's-length debt. In Section III, the assumption of exogenous lock-in is relaxed. I show how the bank's ability to control and its ability to extract surplus emerge from its informational advantage over outside lenders. I examine the effect of multiple sourcing, priority, and interim public revelation of information on the efficacy of bank debt. Section IV examines extensions and Section V concludes.

I. The Model

A. The Project

Consider an economy with a single owner-managed firm (henceforth the 'owner' or the 'firm'). The owner has a project idea. At the initial date 0, the owner has to invest a fixed amount I. She then expends personal effort β at a unit cost of 1. Effort increases the expected value of future returns in a way to be specified. The assets purchased at date 0 can be liquidated at date 1 for value L where $L \leq I$. At date 2, these assets depreciate to value zero.

There are two possible states at date 1. The state can be good, G, with probability q and bad, B, with probability $(1 - q)$. At date 2, in the good state the project pays out X with probability 1. In the bad state it pays out X with probability p_B and zero with probability $(1 - p_B)$. I assume that $X > I \geq L > p_B X$.

Private effort $\beta \epsilon [0, \infty)$ along with an exogenous quality parameter $\theta \epsilon [0, 1]$, affect the probability q of the good state occurring. For a small firm, β is the physical or mental exertion by the management. For a large firm, β can be thought of as discretionary investment. The quality θ represents exogenous determinants of the likelihood of the project's being good.[4] I assume $q =$

---

[4] For example, a project to modify a successful car model for the new year has a high θ while the search for commercial superconductors is a low-θ project.

$q(\beta, \theta)$, where q has the following properties

$$q_1(\beta, \theta) > 0, \ q_{11}(\beta, \theta) < 0, \ q_2(\beta, \theta) > 0, \qquad \text{(A1)}$$

$$q_1(0, \theta) = 1/\epsilon, \ q_1(\infty, \theta) = 0, \qquad \text{(A2)}$$

$$q_{12}(\beta, \theta) = 0, \qquad \text{(A3)}$$

where the subscript k denotes the partial with respect to the kth argument. I also use subscripts for the date but the difference will be clear from the context.

Assumption (A1) states that the probability of the good state being realized is increasing and concave in the effort of the owner and is increasing in the quality θ. Assumption (A2) states that the marginal benefit of effort decreases to zero from a large number. Assumption (A3) is a separability assumption.

In summary, if the owner invests at date 0:

Date 0	Date 1	Date 2
Investment I made. Effort β exerted after investment made.	State realized. Owner can continue project. If not continued, project is liquidated for value L.	Project pays out X with probability 1 in the good state. In the bad state it pays X with probability p_B and zero with probability $(1 - p_B)$. Assets are worthless.

B. Financiers

This is a risk-neutral world and the riskless interest rate is 0. The owner has no money of her own. She must borrow to finance the project. There are two types of lenders in the *competitive* date 0 credit market:

i. *Banks* enter the market at each date to acquire information and make loans. If a bank makes a loan to a firm at date 0, it gains access to the internal records the firm maintains (and henceforth it will be referred to as the inside bank). During this period, the bank monitors the firm's books and the accounts the firm maintains with the bank. Much of the information obtained this way is 'soft' in nature. It cannot be credibly communicated to outsiders even if the firm wants to do so. Therefore, banks acquire information only by lending, which is consistent with the empirical evidence in Lummer and McConnell (1989). I assume, for simplicity, that the costs of monitoring are negligible.

ii. *Arm's-length investors* lend at date 0 and return to collect repayments at date 2. Even if they lend, they do not examine the books. This may be because they have a high private cost of monitoring as compared to the banks or because the size of each investor's loan is small, resulting in a free-rider problem.

C. Information

Everyone knows quality θ at date 0. Once the project starts, the owner knows the effort exerted. She also learns the state before deciding whether to continue the project at date 1. The inside bank learns the effort provided and the state at the same time as the owner. Arm's-length investors and outside banks observe only public signals, which are assumed uninformative unless otherwise specified.

D. Contracts

I assume that contracts cannot be made contingent on the liquidation decision, effort, or the state. Myers (1977) discusses in detail why it may not be possible to make contracts contingent on investment (or disinvestment). Effort and the state can be observed only by the owner and anybody privy to inside information, but not by the courts. The courts, however, can observe and verify the monetary transfers that the parties choose to record.

I allow only debt contracts, an assumption which may be justified by appealing to the costly state verification technology in Diamond (1991a) or Gale and Hellwig (1985). Without loss of generality, I consider only pure discount debt contracts, that is, contracts where the firm borrows an amount A_i at date i and is required to make a *single* repayment D_{ij} at date j. I call contracts over a single period ($j - i = 1$) *short-term contracts* and those over two periods ($j - i = 2$) *long-term contracts*. Any debt contract is a convex combination of short-term and long-term contracts.

I do not allow for contracts in which the required repayment, under any circumstance, is less than the amount borrowed, i.e., $D_{ij} < A_i$. These contracts are implausible and a minor change to the model would rule them out.[5] As the credit markets are competitive at date 0, I assume that any ex post rents accruing to a lender are paid up front to the owner at date 0. In general, such rents would be given back to the firm by reducing its cost of doing business or as perks related to the project.

II. The Basic Trade-Off

Henceforth the terms ex ante and ex post are with reference to the time the initial date 0 contract is agreed to. The following subscripts are used: L denotes long-term, S short-term, b denotes bank, and a arm's-length.

---

[5] For example, in a world with fly-by-night operators (without projects) who are ex ante indistinguishable from the genuine firm, a lender offering such contracts would be swamped by the operators. These operators would pocket the difference between the amount borrowed and the required repayment. If the operators have some costs of dissimulation, any debt contract where $D_{ij} \geq A_i$ would cause them to self-select out. Rather than carry these operators through the model, we assume the contractual restriction.

The borrower decides (i) what type of lender to approach and maturity to borrow; (ii) what effort level β to exert and, after contracting; (iii) whether to continue or liquidate after seeing the state at date 1. The lender decides (i) the contract terms offered at date 0 and, (ii) whether to renegotiate, cut off credit, continue with the old contract, or offer a new contract at date 1. The first-best solution is now characterized.

A. First-Best Solution

If financed, at date 1 the owner should continue in the good state and close the project down in the bad state. The expected surplus is $q(\beta, \theta)(X - I) - (1 - q(\beta, \theta))(I - L) - \beta$ at date 0. The first term is the surplus in the good state, the second is the depreciation losses in the bad, while the third is the cost of effort. The project should be financed only if the surplus is positive for some effort level. The effort β_{FB}^*, which maximizes this surplus, is obtained by solving the first-order condition (FOC)

$$q_1(\beta, \theta) = \frac{1}{X - L} \quad \text{for} \quad \beta = \beta_{FB}^*. \tag{1}$$

Assumptions A1 and A2 ensure existence and uniqueness of the solution.

A contract that approaches[6] first-best should have the following two features. First, the owner should have an incentive to voluntarily liquidate the project in the bad state. Alternatively, the lender should have the ability to coerce or persuade her to do so. Second, the owner should obtain all the surplus from the good state and face all the losses in the bad. As we see later, no rational contract simultaneously achieves both objectives. The resulting trade-off between project control and owner's incentives to exert effort is the main focus of the paper.

In what follows, I repeatedly use the following ideas: (a) given limited liability, the owner will never liquidate in the bad state unless refused credit or bribed and (b) the competitive date 0 market for credit *and* lender individual rationality together imply that loans are zero NPV projects. Hence, all inefficiencies are ultimately borne by the owner.

I first analyze contracts with the arm's-length lender, then contracts with the bank. To present the issues as simply as possible, I initially assume the firm can write only one type of contract at a time. In addition, once the owner has borrowed from a bank, I assume it is locked in to that bank for all future borrowing. I relax both assumptions later.

B. Arm's-Length Contract

By assumption, the arm's-length lender neither receives information nor can he act upon it. In this situation, the short-term contract is equivalent to

---

[6] If $L_0 < I_0$, no contract can achieve the first best solution. By limited liability, the owner does not face the full cost of the bad state. No contract can efficiently correct for this without ex ante transfers to the lender (to satisfy its rationality constraint). The owner's liquidity constraint rules out such transfers.

the long-term contract, and I consider only the latter. The owner borrows amount I at date 0 and promises to repay D_{02a} at date 2. As discussed before, the owner will always continue at date 1, even though it may be inefficient to do so. The lender is not present to influence this decision. Given an arm's-length contract at date 0, the owner chooses her effort level by solving

$$\max_{\beta} q(\beta, \theta)(X - D_{02a}) + (1 - q(\beta, \theta))(p_B(X - D_{02a})) - \beta. \quad (2)$$

Let β_a^* solve the corresponding FOC. Let the lender conjecture that ex post contract, the (unobservable) effort exerted by the owner will be β_a^c. The arm's-length investor lends provided he finds it individually rational,

$$D_{02a} \geq \frac{I}{[q(\beta_a^c, \theta) + (1 - q(\beta_a^c, \theta))p_B]} \quad (3)$$

and provided the contract is feasible, $X \geq D_{02a}$. In a Rational Expectations Equilibrium, the lender's conjecture must be correct, so that

$$\beta_a^c = \beta_a^*. \quad (4)$$

In a competitive credit market, (3) should be met with equality. So, if a feasible contract exists, the FOC obtained from (2), (3), and the equilibrium condition (4) taken together imply the optimal effort β_a^* is defined implicitly by

$$q_1(\beta, \theta) = \frac{1}{\left[X - I - \dfrac{(1 - q(\beta_a^*, \theta))(1 - p_B)I}{q(\beta_a^*, \theta) + (1 - q(\beta_a^*, \theta))p_B}\right](1 - p_B)}, \quad (5)$$

for $\beta = \beta_a^*$. The effort exerted is less than first best; $\beta_a^* < \beta_{FB}^*$. The rationale is simple. The owner continues in the bad state, forcing the rational lender to demand a higher face value than if the continuation decision were efficient. This reduces the surplus available to the owner in the good state. Also the residual value, $X - D_{02a}$, accruing to the owner with probability p_B increases the attractiveness of the bad state, further reducing effort. All inefficiency stems from the inability of the owner to commit to liquidate the project in the bad state.[7]

A solution β_a^* to (5) may not exist at low values of θ. Given the intrinsic poor quality of the project θ, the face value demanded could be so high as to depress the incentive to provide effort below the minimum required to satisfy

---

[7] Equation (5) is a fixed point problem. The existence of a solution is not always assured and intuitively, for low-quality projects (low θ), no solution should exist. Assumptions A1 and A2 together with a single crossing condition would ensure that if a solution exists to (5), it is unique. In the example that I construct, a unique solution always exists for the range of project qualities that I examine. All the results hold even if there are multiple solutions (as in the Laffer curve theories of the 'Less Developed Country' debt problem). I then define the solution to be the highest value of β, which implies that the face value is set at the lowest level compatible with lender individual rationality.

the lender's individual rationality condition. In other words, the returns to the lender could decrease with increasing face value. Credit is then rationed because of poor incentives for effort.

C. Bank Contracts

C.1. Short-Term Bank Contract

The owner borrows I at date 0. The bank observes the effort exerted and then the state. At date 1, in the bad state the project is liquidated and the bank recovers L. In the good state, the date 0 contract does not oblige the bank to lend. It can use this discretion to hold up the owner and demand a share of the surplus in return for the funds needed to continue the project. Solving the bargaining game, the owner gets $\mu(X - L)$ while the lender gets $(1 - \mu)(X - L) + L$, where $\mu \epsilon [0, 1]$ is the share of the unallocated surplus that the owner gets after bargaining. The currently exogenous μ will also be referred to as 'bargaining power.' Let q^*_{Sb} denote the probability of reaching the good state with the induced effort. The FOC for the owner's effort decision at date 0 is

$$q_1(\beta , \theta) = \frac{1}{\mu(X - L)} \tag{6}$$

for $\beta = \beta^*_{Sb}$, provided it is individually rational for the bank to lend:

$$\left[1 - \frac{I - L}{q^*_{Sb}(X - L)}\right] - \mu \geq 0. \tag{7}$$

This condition is merely that the bank make nonnegative profits from lending. If μ is high (≈ 1) the bank will not be able to recover the depreciation losses $(1 - q^*_{Sb})(I - L)$. If μ is low (≈ 0), the owner, faced with poor incentives, will not exert much effort. Consequently, q^*_{Sb} will be low, forcing down the term in square brackets. It will not be rational for the bank to lend in either case. As the bank rations credit when the firm's bargaining power is at extremes, arm's-length debt could be available to the firm when short-term bank debt is not. For intermediate values of μ, the bank will lend. But comparing (6) and (1), and using the monotonicity and concavity of q, there will be underprovision of effort compared to the first-best.

The short-term bank contract requires repayment at date 1. This works well in the bad state, where the bank should cut off credit. In the good state where the bank should continue to lend, the contract has to be renegotiated with resulting distortions to the firm's incentives for effort. Note that the first best may be achievable if we constrain the bargaining sufficiently by means of an external nonrenegotiable mechanism. For example, a commitment to lend at a particular interest rate with the option for the bank to pull out achieves first best under some circumstances. But these mechanisms are somewhat special and will not be explored further (see footnote 8).[8]

C.2. Long-Term Bank Contract

The bank lends I long-term to the firm, so that at date 1 the loan is renewed automatically and at date 2 the required repayment is D_{02b}. At date 1, in the good state, the optimal decision is to continue. As the surplus is fully allocated by the initial contract, there is no renegotiation. In the bad state, it is efficient to close down the project. As the bank cannot unilaterally do so the contract has to be renegotiated. The surplus (from taking the efficient decision) that they bargain over is $L - p_B X$. The owner gets $p_B(X - D_{02b}) + \mu(L - p_B X)$ while the lender gets $p_B D_{02b} + (1 - \mu)(L - p_B X)$ in the bad state. The first term in each expression is the amount allocated by the initial contract. We require that:

$$X \geq \frac{I - (1 - q_{Lb}^*)(1 - \mu)(L - p_B X)}{q_{Lb}^* + (1 - q_{Lb}^*)p_B} = D_{02b}. \qquad (8)$$

The left-hand side of the equality is the face value demanded by the bank in order to break even. The inequality requires that the project return be enough to meet this in the good state. The face value demanded increases with the bargaining power of the owner for two reasons. First, the bank gets less of the surplus in the bad state. Second, it is easily shown that increasing the owner's share in the bad state reduces her incentive to exert effort to avoid the state, thereby reducing q_{Lb}^*.

D. Choice between Contracts

The owner chooses between contracts on an ex ante basis. As the date 0 market for credit is competitive, all individually rational loans are zero NPV.

---

[8] In the absence of a commitment by the bank to relend at date 1 and the commitment mechanisms below, fixing the face value conditional on relending in the good state is vacuous, as it will always be renegotiated. When there is no commitment to relend, we can restrict ourselves without loss of generality to short-term contracts. Commitment is possible through the appropriate design of governing mechanisms (see Aghion, Dewatripont, and Rey (1989); Macleod and Malcomson (1989); or Hart and Moore (1988)). These mechanisms work by constraining the bargaining process and hence they suffer from limitations, as parties could always make unobservable offers (or threats made credible from) outside the process. The specific mechanisms described in the above papers will not work because (a) there is not obvious way in which the parties can specify a nonrenegotiable default option, (b) the owner is liquidity constrained and, (c) there is no last moment after which the gains from trade will disappear. Of course, if we make assumptions about the nature of the available mechanisms, the first-best contract can be achieved. For example, assume that the project is no longer available after a specific time at date 1. A contract which specifies bank control over the relending decision and fixes the date 2 terms for relending (at the minimum compatible with bank rationality) approaches the first best. The reason is that at the last instant, the owner can offer a contract to borrow at the above rate. The bank can do no better than accept. The owner cannot get a lower rate as the bank can assure itself of the rate in the initial contract and knows that it is in the interest of the owner to borrow (see Hart and Moore (1988) for details). Such a contract would be similar to lines of credit callable at the option of the bank under 'materially adverse circumstances.'

Any ex post rents extracted by the bank are prepaid to the owner. These payments have no effect on her incentives to exert effort. Thus the owner's ex ante expected utility with bank financing is:

$$q_b^*(X - I) - (1 - q_b^*)(I - L) - \beta_b^*. \tag{9}$$

Note that the project continuation decision at date 1 is efficient, regardless of the maturity of bank debt. However, the maturity of bank debt affects the owner's incentives for effort and $q_{Sb}^* \neq q_{Lb}^*$. The owner's ex ante contract expected utility with arm's-length financing is:

$$q_a^*(X - I) - (1 - q_a^*)(I - p_B X) - \beta_a^*. \tag{10}$$

The first term in (9) and (10) is the expected surplus in the good state. The second term in (10) is the cost of inefficient continuation, while in (9) it is just the depreciation losses (as control is efficient). A bank loan is preferred if (9) > (10), so that

$$(1 - q_a^*)(L - p_B X) - (q_a^* - q_b^*)(I - L)$$
$$- ((q_a^* - q_b^*)(X - I) - (\beta_a^* - \beta_b^*)) \geq 0. \tag{11}$$

The choice between bank debt and arm's-length debt depends on whether the ex post continuation inefficiency with the latter outweighs the possible distortion to effort incentives with the former. If $q_a^* \leq q_b^*$, bank financing dominates arm's-length financing.

The interesting case is when $q_a^* > q_b^*$, that is, when the provision of effort with arm's-length financing is greater than that with bank financing. The first term in (11) is the ex ante benefit of bank control which is positive as $p_B X < L$; the second is the additional loss due to depreciation as the bad state is reached more often with bank debt; the third is the loss in surplus because of differential ex post effort distortion. If the ex ante cost of the relative underprovision of effort from the second and third term outweighs the benefit of control (the first term), bank finance can be less efficient than arm's-length finance.

For a given function $q(\cdot, \cdot)$, the exogenous bargaining power μ and project quality θ determine the choice of maturity and source. I briefly examine the effect of changing these parameters on loan choice.

D.1. Effect of Bargaining Power

As discussed earlier, the distortion in the owner's incentives on borrowing short term from the bank *decreases* as her bargaining power increases, so that $dq_{Sb}^*/d\mu > 0$. The cost of arm's-length debt is, however, independent of μ. Consider a project for which arm's-length debt is preferred to short-term bank debt for some μ. Then

Lemma 1: *There is a $\hat{\mu}_S \epsilon [0, 1]$ such that arm's-length debt is preferred ex ante to short-term bank debt by any owner with bargaining power $\mu \leq \hat{\mu}_S$.*

The distortion to the owner's incentives on borrowing long-term from the bank *increases* as her bargaining power increases, so that $dq_{Lb}^*/d\mu < 0$. Consider a project for which arm's-length debt is preferred to long-term bank debt for some μ. It follows that

Lemma 2: There is a $\hat{\mu}_L \epsilon [0, 1]$ such that arm's-length debt is preferred ex ante to long-term bank debt by any owner with bargaining power $\mu \geq \hat{\mu}_L$.

It is easy to show that arm's-length debt is not always dominated by bank debt. For example, consider a choice between arm's-length and long-term bank debt. Assume that $q(0, \theta) = 0$ and $q(\epsilon, \theta) = 1$, so that some small effort ϵ is necessary for the project to succeed with probability 1. Let $\mu = 1$. Both types of lenders get back $p_B D_{02}$ in the bad state. However, the owner, when borrowing from the bank, gets an additional $(L - p_B X)$ in the bad state compared to what she gets when borrowing at arm's-length. For a loan of the same face value, she has less of an incentive to exert effort when borrowing from the bank. Lender rationality then demands that $D_{02a} < D_{02b}$, which further reduces the owner's incentive to reach the good state when borrowing from the bank. In fact, if $p_B(X - D_{02b}) + (L - p_B X) > X - D_{02b} > 0$, she will exert no effort. Note that in this situation, she will still exert effort when borrowing at arm's-length. The bank will not lend long term while the firm may still obtain arm's-length loans.

Proposition 1: (i) If $\hat{\mu}_S > \hat{\mu}_L$, the firm chooses short-term bank debt if $1 \geq \mu > \hat{\mu}_S$, arm's-length debt if $\hat{\mu}_S \geq \mu \geq \hat{\mu}_L$, and long-term bank debt if $\hat{\mu}_L > \mu \geq 0$. (ii) If $\hat{\mu}_L \geq \hat{\mu}_S$, then the firm never chooses arm's-length debt, borrows short term from the bank for $\mu \geq \hat{\mu}_{LS}$, and borrows long term if $\mu < \hat{\mu}_{LS}$, where $\hat{\mu}_{LS} \epsilon (\hat{\mu}_S, \hat{\mu}_L)$.

Proposition 1 suggests that the optimal maturity of bank borrowing is negatively related to μ, the share the owner obtains from bargaining. Maturity does not affect the bank's control but it alters the states in which bargaining takes place and hence the distortion to incentives. Another way to interpret this is that the postulated lock-in gives the bank property rights to the firm. With short-term bank debt, the bank has direct control rights, while with long-term bank debt, it acquires the right to control through bilateral bargaining and by giving up some right to the surplus. Because the surplus the bank acquires in different states depends on the maturity of the debt, maturity affects effort. The firm chooses maturity to give itself the best incentives for effort. Empirically, a firm should borrow long term from a bank when the latter has an exogenous source of power over the former. Examples of this power could include bank control over crucial suppliers and bank shareholdings in the firm.

D.2. Effect of Project Quality

The propositions I derive for the effect of project quality θ on the choice between either long-term bank debt and short-term bank debt or arm's-length debt and short-term bank debt are similar. I state only one:

Proposition 2: *There exists a project quality* $\bar{\theta}\epsilon[0,1]$ *such that* (*i*) *short-term bank debt is preferred to arm's-length debt when* $\theta \leq \bar{\theta}$ *and* (*ii*) *arm's-length debt is preferred to short-term bank debt when* $\theta > \bar{\theta}$.

Proof: See Appendix.

The intuition is simple. Conditional on the good state, the bank extracts the same amount, regardless of project quality. This depends crucially on the absence of interim date competition and the assumption that bargaining power is exogenous. In contrast, as the project quality improves, control becomes less important. The face value demanded by arm's-length lenders falls, improving incentives for effort. The owner's ex ante utility with either kind of financing is increasing in quality, but it increases at a faster rate with arm's-length financing, hence the proposition.

Firms with higher quality prefer arm's-length debt, a result similar to that of Diamond (1991a), who finds that firms with a higher reputation borrow from the arm's-length market. Here the finding is due to the fact that high quality firms find bank debt relatively more onerous and it holds even if monitoring costs are small.

E. How is Bargaining Power Determined?

So far I have assumed bargaining power μ to be exogenously given. This could be appropriate if lock-in between a firm and its initial bank is exogenous. For example, banks may agree not to poach each other's clients. Such collusive practices may be reinforced by a government that wants to restrain 'de-stabilizing competition' in the banking sector (see Macrae (1990), Modigliani and Perotti (1990)). In such an economy, the firm and the bank are, ex post, in a *bilateral bargaining* situation between *two fully informed* parties. If we know their discount rates (a commonly accepted exogenous primitive) and the structure of the bargaining game, we can determine the share of the surplus the firm gets.

My assumption of exogenous lock-in is less tenable if banks do not collude and government intervention is minimal. The main difference between lenders, once the project has begun, is informational. I now show that the inside bank's informational advantage over outside lenders can endogenously lock the firm to it. To derive this, I now allow competition from outside uninformed lenders at the interim date 1. Obviously, interim competition reduces the inside bank's implicit property rights in the firm and hence its share of the rents. Unfortunately, its control rights are simultaneously reduced, for outside uninformed lenders may now interfere with the inside bank's closure decisions.

I then allow the firm to borrow from multiple sources at the same time. The firm structures its borrowing so as to maximize the bank's control while minimizing the consequent rents. The firm's choice variables in doing this are the relative amounts it borrows from the bank and the arm's-length lenders at date 0 and the relative priority of sources. I obtain implications for source choice and priority structure. Finally, I examine the effect of interim public signals.

For reasons of brevity, I now drop the long-term bank contract from consideration. Henceforth, 'bank contract' refers to the short-term bank contract.

III. Interim Competition and Multiple Sources

A. Bank Debt with Interim Competition

The bank lends amount I at date 0. At date 1, the owner has to roll over the repayment on the date 0 loan, D_{01}. Instead of being locked in to the initial bank at this point, the owner bargains for the best terms with all potential lenders (including the initial bank). I make two assumptions that simplify the algebra. First, $p_B = 0$. Second, assets do not depreciate over the first period, so that $L = I$.

As the first period loan is riskless, the date 1 repayment $D_{01} = I$. The amount to be borrowed by the owner at date 1, to continue the project, is $I_S = I$. At date 1, the owner asks both the inside bank and a single outside bank (the number of outside banks is immaterial) to submit a sealed bid to the owner. The bid specifies the face value the lender demands at date 2 in return for the loan of I_S at date 1. The lowest bid is accepted. The solution to the bidding game determines the expected date 2 face value for the loan made at date 1.[9] The equilibrium solution is

Proposition 3: (i) No equilibrium exists in pure strategies. (ii) There is an equilibrium in mixed strategies where: (a) the outside bank has a mixed strategy of bidding which is independent of the state. It will not bid at all with probability π_N. It makes zero expected profits. It makes positive expected profits conditional on the good state of

$$\frac{1-q}{q} I_S (1 - \pi_N) \tag{12}$$

where

$$\pi_N = \frac{(1-q)}{q} \frac{I_S}{(X - I_S)} \tag{13}[10]$$

and q is the outside bank's conjectured probability of the good state. (b) The inside bank offers to lend only in the good state. If the outside bank bids with

---

[9] I defend my choice of bargaining game, based on what I believe is common practice. For example, "what is being contemplated in 'obtaining competitive quotations' is an approach to a limited number of banks on an open basis. Each should be told that a competitive quotation is being taken from another bank, but not the name of the bank." (Donaldson and Donaldson (1982)).

[10] More precisely, $\pi_N = \text{Min}\left[1, \dfrac{1-q}{q} \dfrac{I_S}{X - I_S}\right]$.

positive probability ($\pi_N < 1$), *the inside bank makes a conditional expected profit of*

$$\frac{(1 - q)I_S}{q}.$$ (14)

If the outside bank does not bid with positive probability, the inside bank captures all the project surplus.

Proof: See Appendix.

If the outside bank's strategy was pure and therefore predictable, the inside bank would charge a lower rate in the good state and not bid in the bad state, thus letting the outsider finance only bad projects. This is the problem of the Winner's Curse, which is why the outsider plays a mixed strategy. If the outside bank bids in the bad state, it gets to lend with certainty as the inside bank does not bid. The probability of this happening is $(1 - q)(1 - \pi_N)$ and the loss is I_S. The outsider recovers the loss by making a profit in the good state. Equation (12) is then obtained by conditioning on the good state.

The inside bank bids only in the good state where the loan is riskless. It charges a premium over the full information rate, because its competition is uninformed. If the outside bank bids in the bad state, the owner will use part of the loaned amount to pay off the inside bank. If it does not, the project is shut down and the proceeds used to pay off the inside bank.

Proposition 3 supports what I assumed previously, as it implies that information asymmetry can lead to lock-in. First, no equilibrium exists in pure strategies and even allowing for noise, the outsider does not bid if its informational disadvantage is bad enough. In general, however, the firm is not locked in to the informed bank with probability 1. The inside bank's control and rental rights are changed from the earlier analysis in interesting ways.

In the earlier analysis, the informed bank exerted control directly by cutting off credit in the bad state. But now, if the inside bank refuses the bad project credit, it will be shut down only with probability π_N, as the uninformed outside bank may decide to lend. It follows that π_N is a measure of the control rights exercised by the inside bank. As $\pi_N \leq 1$, these (weakly) decrease compared to the earlier analysis. The inside bank extracts all the surplus when it is in a bilateral bargaining position. Such a position occurs now only if $\pi_N = 1$. As the bank is assumed to make take-it-or-leave-it offers here, it is appropriate to compare the level of rents it extracts now with those that would accrue if $\mu = 0$ in the earlier analysis. Thus its ability to extract rent also (weakly) decreases.

Both the bank's rental and control rights depend on its implicit property rights or ex post monopoly power. Hence

Proposition 4: (*i*) *Both the conditional expected rents extracted by the inside bank and the control exercised by it decrease in q and* (*ii*) *increase in* I_S (*the amount rolled over at date* 1). (*iii*) *The control exercised by the inside bank increases with a reduction in the available surplus* $X - I_S$.

Proof: Follows directly by differentiating (13) and (14).

The implicit property rights of the inside bank arise because of (a) it *informational advantage*, which decreases in the outsider's estimate of the probability of success, q, and (b) the *value* of this advantage, which increases in the amount to be borrowed (or rolled over) at date 1, I_S.

A.1. Effect of Project Quality

The probability of the good state, q, depends on project quality θ, which in turn determines the inside bank's informational advantage (Proposition 4 (i)). Using Proposition 3, I can derive the share μ the firm gets as well as the control π_N exercised by the bank. The difference from the earlier analysis is that μ now depends on θ. As the analysis of a firm's choice between bank debt and arm's-length debt is similar to the one carried out earlier. I refer the reader to Rajan (1991a) for details. I present an example describing the firm's choice when its initial borrowing is entirely from the bank or from the arm's-length market.

Example 1. Let $X = 5$, $I = 1$ and $q(\beta, \theta) = \theta - e^{-2\beta}$.

As quality increases, the effort provided with bank debt approaches that with arm's-length debt (Figure 1). The control provided by the bank also decreases with quality (Figure 2). The costs and benefits of having an ex post informed lender are relatively minor for high-quality firms in a competitive, unrestricted economy. This makes firms with high-quality projects indifferent between bank debt and arm's-length debt (Figure 3). Transaction costs may entirely determine their choice of finance. This should be contrasted with my earlier analysis of an economy where lock in was exogenously mandated. In that economy, firms with high-quality projects found bank debt relatively more onerous.

The effects of having ex post informed lenders are significant for firms lower down on the quality spectrum. For medium-quality projects, the benefit of control outweighs the relative underprovision of effort, so bank debt dominates arm's-length debt. Arm's-length debt dominates for low quality firms, because both the marginal cost of the relative underprovision at low levels of effort and the magnitude of relative underprovision become significant.

B. Borrowing at Date 0 from Both the Bank and Arm's-Length Lender

Proposition 4 (ii) shows that the firm can reduce the value of the inside bank's information advantage over outsiders if the firm reduces the amount it has to roll over with the bank at date 1. It can do this by borrowing from both a bank and the arm's-length market at date 0. If bank debt is senior at date 2 to arm's-length debt, I merely substitute the amount borrowed from the bank

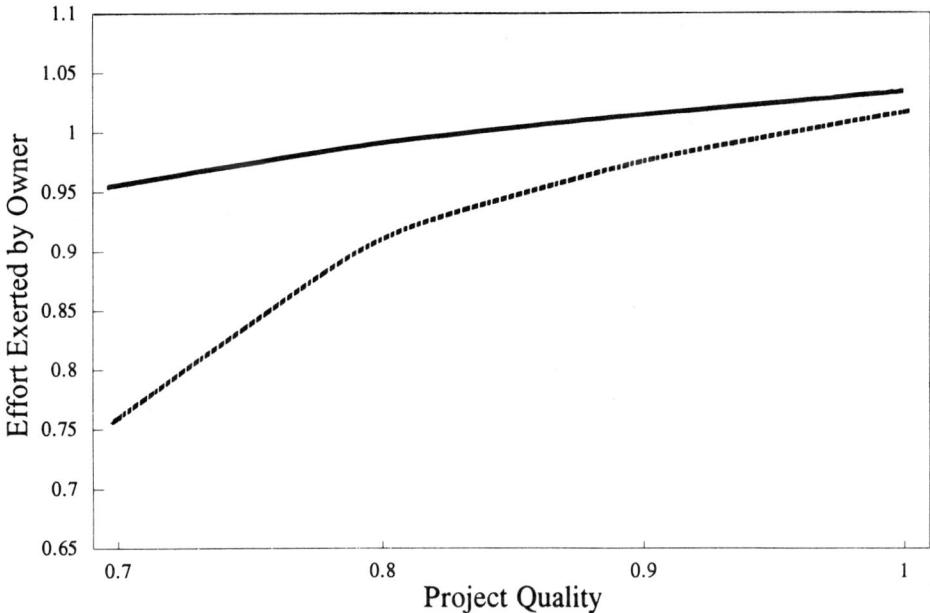

Figure 1. The effect of project quality on the effort exerted by the owner. The solid line is the effort exerted by the owner when funded entirely with arm's-length debt while the dashed line is the effort exerted when funded entirely with short-term bank debt. Calculations are based on the data in example 1.

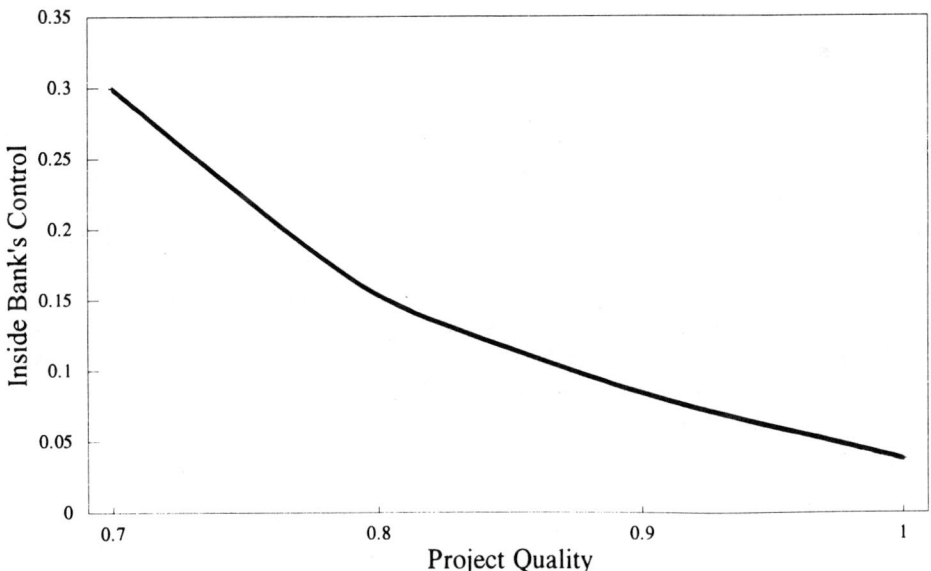

Figure 2. The effect of project quality on the control provided by the inside bank. The control provided by the inside bank is the ex ante probability that the outside bank will not bid. Calculations are based on the data in example 1.

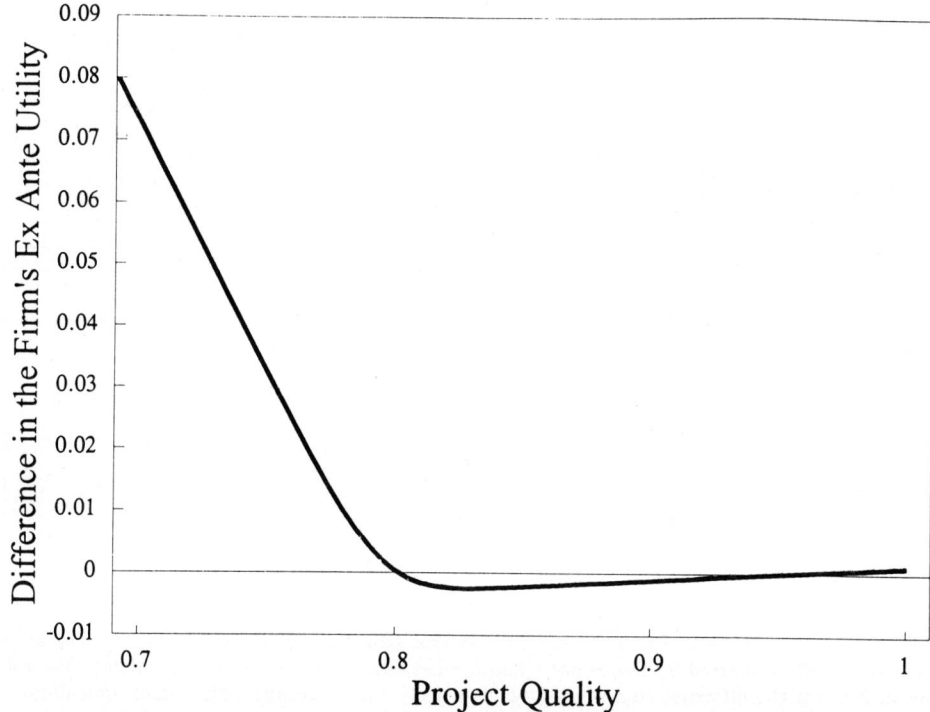

Figure 3. The effect of project quality on the difference in ex ante value to the owner of the different sources. The owner's ex ante expected utility when funded entirely with short-term bank debt is subtracted from the ex ante expected utility when funded entirely with arm's-length debt. This difference is plotted in the figure. Calculations are based on the data in example 1.

for I_S in (13) and (14) to obtain the inside bank's control and rents. The amount required to be borrowed short term, at date 1, is reduced. Outside banks are now more willing to lend the smaller amount at date 1, reducing the inside bank's rents but also its control. Note that arm's-length lenders also benefit as they get their share of the liquidation proceeds if the project is shut down at date 1. They free ride on the control provided by the inside bank. (The proof of Proposition 5, in the Appendix, formally analyzes all this.)

The relative priority[11] of each claim on date 2 revenue, is an important determinant of rents and control.[12] My model clearly defines the optimal priority schedule.

---

[11] A claim which has priority has effective legal precedence over the firm's revenues and assets. I distinguish priority from seniority, although in practice they are used interchangeably. The reason is that a claim which is collateralized with assets may be prior in the sense of this paper, although it may not be a senior claim.

[12] As the loan in the first period is riskless, date 1 priority does not matter.

B.1. Priority

Intuitively, it is clear that the lower the uncommitted date 2 surplus available to be allocated at date 1, the lower the uninformed outsider's willingness to bid. The control of the inside bank must increase (Proposition 4 (iii)). It may appear that the inside bank's ability to appropriate rents at date 1 should also be reduced if there is lower surplus to bargain over. It turns out that this is true only in the situation that the outsider does not bid at all ($\pi_N = 1$). Otherwise, the reduction in outside competition completely counters the effect of the lower available surplus on inside bank rents. The size of the date 2 uncommitted surplus has no effect on rents when the outsider bids with positive probability.[13]

A firm with multiple date 0 lenders can commit surplus away from a subset of lenders by giving priority to the other lenders. If the arm's-length claim has priority over bank debt, the uncommitted date 2 revenue is reduced by the contracted face value D_{02a}. At the time of date 1 bargaining, the bargainers face an effective project revenue of $X - D_{02a}$, instead of X. So long as debt is risky, the uncommitted date 2 surplus is also *reduced*, by the amount of the default risk premium impounded in the face value D_{02a}. On the other hand, if the bank has priority, the size of the date 1 available surplus is *increased*, by the amount borrowed from arm's-length lenders at date 0.

Allocation of priority also affects the face value demanded by the arm's-length lender. If bank debt has priority, the arm's-length lender demands a higher face value as he can be dispossessed by the banks ex post.

Ascribing priority to the arm's-length claim improves efficiency as a result of the reduced uncommitted surplus improving control, the reduced inside bank rents if $\pi_N = 1$, and the lower rate demanded by the arm's-length lender. Therefore I state

Proposition 5: *It is optimal for arm's-length debt contracted at date 0 to have a prior claim than bank debt over date 2 revenues.*

Proof: See Appendix.

This result suggests that considerations of ex post bargaining are an important determinant of capital structure. If the only difference between arm's-length debt and arm's-length equity is priority, Proposition 5 suggests that debt is preferred even if there are no information asymmetries separating management and investors at date 0. In Figure 4, I plot the fraction of the loan that the owner optimally borrows from the bank at date 0, for the data in Example 1.

---

[13] As an analogy, consider a miser with private knowledge about the size of her wealth. Let her have one favorite nephew who is informed about the size of the hoard and many uninformed relatives. If the miser publicly bequeaths a large amount to charity, the relatives lose much of their interest in her. The favorite nephew now has a *higher probability* of getting a *lower* bequest if he persists in his attentions. In our simple model, the expected size of his inheritance (rents) remains constant. But whether the miser gets any attention at all becomes more sensitive to the favorite nephew's decisions (control).

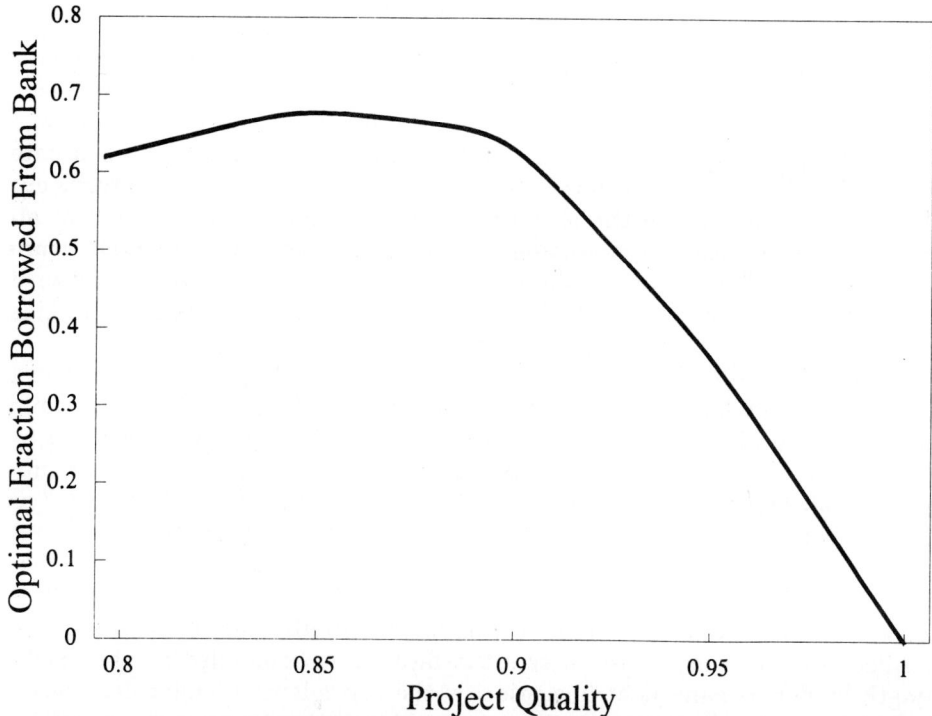

Figure 4. The effect of project quality on the optimal fraction of investment funded with short-term bank debt. The optimal fraction of short-term bank debt is calculated, assuming the arm's-length lender has priority. Calculations are based on the data in example 1.

For small and medium firms where the problem I discuss is important, arm's-length debt should be of higher priority than bank debt. In practice, there are two ways of effecting this. First, arm's-length debt could be collateralized with assets like land and buildings which are insensitive to the value of the firm.[14] Bank debt, however, could be left unsecured.[15] Second, arm's-

---

[14] Typically, this takes the form of a mortgage bond or mortgage note. Of course, firms in the United States also issue unsecured debentures. It would be interesting to determine the relative importance of each type of bond in financing small and medium firms. Note that some countries prevent firms from issuing noncollateralized bonds. For example, before 1983, Japan prohibited these issues for all companies except Toyota and Matsushita Electricals.

[15] Frank Lourenso, an executive vice president of Chemical Bank who is in charge of lending to small- and medium-sized businesses, stated that most of Chemical's loans to businesses are unsecured (*New York Times*, October 7, 1991). Even if bank debt is secured, it could be collateralized with assets like accounts receivables and inventories which are positively correlated with the value of the firm. In case of default, arm's-length debt secured on property would effectively have priority (under the implicit assumption that property values are independent of the value of the firm).

length debt could be made senior to bank debt. This may be less effective than collateralization because bank debt, by virtue of its short maturity, can dispossess the arm's-length lender before the maturity of the arm's-length loan.

In his classic empirical study of 14 reorganizations, Dewing (1920) suggests that arm's-length lenders have priority over banks. He writes

> ... there are four classes of persons who are directly interested in the financial success of a large corporation. The first is that of the bondholders who have frequently a direct lien on the corporation's physical property... The second class is the holders of short time obligations and open accounts, —the banks and the merchandise creditors. These men have been more alert to the situation than the bondholders because they have been in closer touch with the business. Their claims to earnings are usually second to those of the bondholders. The third class ... is the stockholders ... the officers of the corporation ... constitute the fourth class.

Leveraged buyouts in the United States seem a recent counterexample where banks hold a claim senior to the public junk bonds. However, it can be argued that the true monitor in a buyout is the investment bank, which usually has an equity stake.

Diamond (1991b) obtains the opposite priority rule to what I obtain, because in his model the problem is one of excessive liquidation by the bank. If the bank has higher priority, it can dispossess the arm's-length creditor, giving the bank an incentive to avoid liquidation. In a sense, giving the bank priority makes the returns to arm's-length debt more sensitive to information. In his model, symmetrically informed competition prevents the bank from getting too much power. My assumption that the bank is an insider and better informed than other potential creditors is crucial to the difference in our results.

C. Interim Public Information

So far, I have assumed that there are no interim public signals to inform outsiders about the state. Now assume the firm has borrowed from a bank at date 0. Let a public signal W about the state be seen at date 1, before the bidding takes place. If the firm is in the good state, let the public signal be w_G with probability Ω_G and w_B with probability $(1 - \Omega_G)$. In the bad state, let it be w_G with probability $1 - \Omega_B$ and w_B with probability Ω_B. I assume the signal is noisy but informative, so that $1 > \Omega_G > 1 - \Omega_B > 0$. The outside bank now updates its prior conjecture q^*. If the signal is w_G the posterior

$$q_G^+ = \frac{q^* \Omega_G}{q^* \Omega_G + (1 - q^*)(1 - \Omega_B)}, \tag{15}$$

if the signal is w_B,

$$q_B^+ = \frac{q^*(1 - \Omega_G)}{q^*(1 - \Omega_G) + (1 - q^*)\Omega_B}. \tag{16}$$

I now examine how interim information affects the firm's ex post incentives and its ex ante utility when financed with bank debt.[16] In the limit, of course, perfect interim public information achieves the first best as, at date 1, all the creditors are perfectly informed. However, an informative but noisy interim signal can have very interesting effects. Contrary to intuition, the interim signal *may not* reduce the inside bank's ex post rents but may still improve the owner's incentives.

To see this, note that the owner gets nothing in the bad state. At date 0, she cares only about the expected excess cost of bank debt conditional on the good state. She maximizes

$$\max_\beta q(\beta, \theta) \left(X - I - E_{W|G} \left[\frac{(1 - q^+)I}{q^+} + \frac{(1 - q^+)I(1 - \pi_N^+)}{q^+} \right] \right) - \beta, \tag{17}$$

where $E_{W|G}$ is the expectation in the good state over the values of the signal. The excess cost of bank debt is the term in square brackets in (17) and is direct from Proposition 3. The first term in square brackets is the rent extracted by the inside bank. The second term in square brackets is the amount recouped by outside banks in the good state, in compensation for inefficient lending in the bad state. Substituting (15) and (16) in (17), the conditional expected excess cost then is

$$\frac{(1 - q^*)I}{q^*} + \frac{(1 - q^*)I}{q^*} \left(1 - \left(\frac{1 - q^*}{q^*} \right) \left(\frac{I}{X - I} \right) \left[\frac{(1 - \Omega_B)^2}{\Omega_G} + \frac{\Omega_B^2}{1 - \Omega_G} \right] \right). \tag{18}$$

The inside bank's expected rent conditional on the good state, $E_{W|G}[(1 - q^+)I/q^+]$, turns out to be $(1 - q^*)I/q^*$. Surprisingly, this is exactly what it would be if there were no signal (keeping the market's conjectures about the effort level constant). The intuition is as follows. Conditional on seeing the good signal, outsiders bid more aggressively, and the inside bank's rents are lower than if there were no signal. However, conditional on seeing the (incorrect) bad signal, outsiders are less aggressive and the inside bank's rents are higher. The increase in rents is enough to compensate for any

---

[16] If the posterior $q^+ \leq I/X$, $\pi_N = 1$ and the outside banks stop bidding. The firm and the inside bank are in a bilateral bargaining situation. Any decrease in the posterior, below the cutoff level I/X, has no effect on rents or control because they both reach their maximum value. I have not allowed for this in my analysis but it is easily incorporated.

decrease, even allowing for the increased probability of the good signal in the good state.[17]

The second term in (18) which is the amount charged by outside banks is, however, lower as a result of the signal.[18] The outside lenders now bid so as to make zero expected profits conditional on the signal. Conditional on seeing the bad signal, they bid less often than they would bid if they saw the good signal (and less often than if they had seen no signal). As the bad signal occurs more often in the bad state, on average they bid less in the bad state and $E_{W|B}[\pi_N^+] < \pi_N$. This implies that the amount they need to recoup in the good state so as to break even is lower with the signal than without.

In sum, for fixed conjectures, the interim signal has no effect on the inside bank's rents. However, the outside bank's continuation decision becomes more state-contingent, which improves the inside bank's control. It follows that in equilibrium, the firm exerts more effort when there is an informative interim signal. Also, because the excess cost in (18) decreases with the accuracy of the signal, the effort exerted increases with the accuracy of the signal. We now examine the effect of the signal on the firm's ex ante utility.

The firm's ex ante utility is given by

$$q^*(X - I) - (1 - q^*)I(1 - E_{W|B}[\pi_N^+]) - \beta.$$

As discussed above, the equilibrium q^* is higher in the presence of an informative signal because the firm exerts more effort. Also, the inside bank's control $E_{W|B}[\pi_N^+]$ is higher, keeping the outsider's conjecture of q^* fixed. However, it is not a priori obvious that both effects taken together imply that an informative interim public signal results in higher ex ante utility for the firm.[19] But if the rate of change of ex ante utility with effort, β_{Sb}^*, is nonnegative, for the range of β_{Sb}^* induced by the interim signal, then

---

[17] Mathematically, the rents are decreasing in q^+ (Proposition 4 (i)). However, even though $E_{W|G}[q^+] > q^*$, rents do not decrease. This is because the rents are also convex in q^+. From convexity, the increase in rents conditional on the bad signal balances both the decrease in rents conditional on the good signal and the increased probability of the good signal conditional on the good state.

[18] This is easily seen. The term in square brackets in (18) is only equal to 1 when the signal is uninformative ($\Omega_G = (1 - \Omega_B)$). It is easily shown that this increases from 1 as the determinants of the accuracy of the signal, Ω_G and Ω_B, increase.

[19] Ex post, the owner makes the effort decision taking the outsider's a priori conjecture, q^*, as fixed. Even though there is underprovision of effort compared to the first best, it is not true that increased effort induced by the interim signal, always makes the firm better off ex ante. An increase in effort raises the outsider's a priori conjecture, q^*, which reduces the control of the inside bank, ceteris paribus. The reduction in control coupled with the cost of effort may outweigh any benefit from reaching the good state more often. This is clearly seen when $q^* \approx I/X$ and the interim signal is barely informative, $\Omega_G = (1 - \Omega_B) + \epsilon$. The rate of change of ex ante utility with equilibrium effort, β_{Sb}^*, is $-q_1 I - 1$ which is negative. In this case, the interim signal reduces ex ante utility, because it spurs the firm to costly effort which reduces control more than it increases surplus.

Proposition 6: *The ex ante advantage to bank debt in the presence of outside potential lenders increases with the informativeness of an interim public signal.*

The analysis above would argue that a firm should not match the maturity of its borrowing to the life of its assets but to the revelation of credible, accurate public information. For example, if the cost of information revelation increases when the firm is acting strategically in the product markets, the firm should borrow to match 'the maturity of its product market strategies.' In a similar vein, when a plant is being constructed, a substantial portion of the uncertainty is resolved when certain publicly visible output criteria are met. This could explain why such a project is financed initially with bank debt, which is then replaced by arm's-length debt.[20] The project gets the advantage of bank control at the important early stages. Public revelation of information reduces any attendant costs. Arm's-length debt replaces bank debt for subsequent stages where information is less easily revealed.

IV. Extensions

A. Relationships

I have, thus far, considered the firm to have only one project. This is the natural assumption if the size of the project is large compared to future opportunities. Typically, however, on successful completion of a project, firms have access to many new opportunities. In addition, success in a project usually leads to verifiable public information in the form of profits and demonstrable products.

In this situation, the inside bank has an incentive to 'behave' by reducing the rents it extracts during the project. It does this in the hope of getting a share of the attractive future lending opportunities. The low level of information asymmetries on completion of the project enables the firm to make the credible threat of denying these opportunities to the inside bank. Conversely, in an economy with only ex ante identical banks, a bank which 'behaves' gains reputation over other banks and is preferred as a future lender. It is easy to formalize a reputational equilibrium (see Rajan (1991a)), where such an implicit contract or 'relationship' is sustained between the bank and the firm. In a sense, the firm's share μ, while bargaining within a relationship, is greater than its share in the context of a single project. Relationships thus improve the efficiency of short-term bank contracts.

Unfortunately, such relationships are less easily sustained in an economy which contains both arm's-length lenders and banks. The reason is simple. A relationship requires two-sided commitment. In a bank-dominated economy, a bank that 'behaves' is confident that it has a superior reputation in the eyes of the firm and will in fact be preferred to other banks for future projects. In an economy which also contains arm's-length lenders, however, reputation

---

[20] See Kelor Chemicals, Harvard Business School Case.

building by the inside bank may not be enough to ensure that it gets preference over arm's-length sources. Worse still, the factors that give the bank incentives to 'behave' may be the very factors that make a firm prefer arm's-length markets. For instance, consider the earlier situation of an economy with exogenously mandated lock-in. If convinced that good behavior would be rewarded, the inside bank has the greatest incentive to behave when the firm has high-quality future opportunities (which are most profitable to the bank). Yet, a firm with high-quality opportunities prefers to borrow from arm's-length markets for them (Proposition 2). The firm will not be able to commit to staying with the bank. The latter will then have little incentive to behave.

This suggests that the effectiveness of implicit contracts in reducing the cost of bank debt varies negatively with the liquidity of arm's-length markets. Relationships may not be a sustainable way of reducing the cost of bank debt when alternative sources of finance are available.

B. Multiple Inside Banks

I have restricted the firm to borrowing from only one bank at date 0. Would borrowing at date 0 from multiple banks solve the problem I discuss? Under the assumptions that all these banks monitor closely and then compete à la Bertrand, the first best is achieved. If the decision to monitor is discretionary and not costless, the effectiveness of this solution is reduced, even under Bertrand competition.

If one of the banks has marginally easier access to the firm's books, it can preempt the others by investing the monitoring costs. As competition at date 1 is assumed Bertrand, the other banks have no incentive to invest in monitoring. Thus small monitoring costs coupled with unequal access may be enough to restore monopoly (see Rajan (1991b)).

Even if banks have equal access, it is possible to get overmonitoring (too many banks monitoring in an attempt to get the monopoly rents) or free-riding and too little control (see Rajan (1991a)). The recent experience of banks with debtors like Maxwell Corporation and Polly Peck suggests that the latter situation may be empirically more relevant.[21] This is a fruitful area for future research.

C. Explicit Contracts and Mechanism Design

Would our problem be solved by designing mechanisms to implement explicit contracts? Governments can legislate interest-rate ceilings. The ceiling limits ex post opportunism (at the cost of some credit rationing). Alternatively, a bank can offer loan commitment contracts that fix the interest rate it can charge while giving it the ability to withdraw the loan under extraordinary situations. In certain situations (see footnote 8) the loan commitment contract approaches first best.

---

[21] See, for example, "Maxwell meltdown," *The Economist*, December 7, 1991.

Again these are not perfect fixes, for there are various methods other than through the interest rate that a bank can collect its rents. The bank can direct the choice of projects, levy compensating balances, or refuse to relax covenants when the credit rating improves. This is a general problem with using mechanism design to solve problems of ex post opportunism (Hart and Moore (1989)). Bargaining and transfers take place outside the mechanism, and efforts to 'game' the mechanism make it all the more inefficient. For example, Aoki (1988) suggests that the high ratio of cash to assets observed for Japanese firms incurring high debt stems from the banks' requiring firms to maintain 'compensating balances' with the banks, in order to get around the problem of interest-rate ceilings.

V. Conclusion

The main point of this paper has been that there is a fundamental trade-off between bank debt and arm's-length debt. The bank can monitor the firm and control its investment decisions. However, in the very process of doing this, it alters the division of surplus between itself and the firm. This distorts the firm's incentives. The firm may then prefer credit from arm's-length sources, which provide neither the benefits of bank debt nor the costs.

The bank's ability to control and its ability to influence the division of surplus are both linked, because they are aspects of the bank's implicit property rights. I showed how the bank's informational advantage over outside lenders could confer on it these property rights. I then discussed how borrowing from multiple sources and appropriately setting priority are ways of circumscribing the bank's ability to extract surplus without diminishing its control.

My analysis is not restricted to commercial banks. Many investment banks have the ability to acquire information *and* negotiate with the firms—the functions that characterize the entities I call 'banks.' As firms make repeated issues and some investment banks act as delegated monitors for a stable set of investors (see Bruck (1988)), my analysis of 'bank' finance would apply there too.[22]

Finally, there has been some debate (see Meerschwam (1991)) about the relative efficiency of a *relationship*-based banking system (where a firm is locked in to a relationship with one bank) compared to a transactions-based system (where many banks bid competitively for each transaction that a firm undertakes). My paper suggests that relationships and transactions reflect

---

[22] Carosso (1970) and Dewing (1953) document the 'competitive bidding' controversy in the United States. Regulatory authorities observed that each firm was using the same investment bank(s) repeatedly for underwriting its issues. It was felt that the firms were being locked in and investment banks were exercising too much monopoly power over their clients. In response, the authorities required public utilities to put each issue up for competitive bidding by all potential underwriters. Carosso presents evidence from several studies that outside competition did not, in general, change the identity of the underwriters. This is consistent with the predictions of my model.

two extremes of the control-rent trade-off. Although there has been a movement away from relationships in the 1970s and 1980s in developed countries, my analysis suggests each system has its virtues and unidimensional comparisons are misleading. As a case in point, the deterioration in the credit rating of bank loan portfolios in the United States and Japan over this period may partly reflect the deterioration in control that accompanies the movement from a relationship-oriented system to a transactions-based competitive system. Without examining the accompanying effect on investment, statements on the efficiency implications of this phenomenon are inappropriate.

Appendix

Proof of Proposition 2: I am done if I can show that the ex ante utilities are increasing in θ and the utility with arm's-length financing increases at a faster rate. Differentiating the ex ante utilities with respect to θ, I get

$$\frac{dU_a}{d\theta} = X(1 - p_B)\left(\frac{\delta q}{\delta \beta_a^*}\frac{\delta \beta_a^*}{\delta \theta} + \frac{\delta q}{\delta \theta}\right), \tag{A1}$$

$$\frac{dU_{Sb}}{d\theta} = (X - L)\left(\frac{\delta q}{\delta \beta_{Sb}^*}\frac{\delta \beta_{Sb}^*}{\delta \theta} + \frac{\delta q}{\delta \theta}\right). \tag{A2}$$

Implicitly differentiating the first-order conditions (4) and (5) and setting $\delta^2 q/\delta\theta\delta\beta = 0$

$$\frac{\delta \beta_a^*}{\delta \theta} > 0 \qquad \frac{\delta \beta_{Sb}^*}{\delta \theta} = 0. \tag{A3}$$

By direct comparison and knowing that $p_B X < L$, $dU_a/d\theta > dU_{Sb}/d\theta$ Q.E.D.

Proof of Proposition 3: The proof extends and applies Engelbrecht-Wiggans, Milgrom, and Weber (1983) and Hendricks and Porter (1988) to a general version of the model in the text.

The owner knows the random value V of the project. V takes values in $\Re$ (set of real numbers) and has finite expectation. The two potential lenders are an informed inside lender (henceforth the insider) and an uninformed outside potential lender (outsider). The random variable Z is the private information of the insider about the value of the project. Both the insider and the outsider know the joint distribution of (V, Z).

Each lender submits a sealed bid r, which is the fraction of the project he will allow the owner to retain. The owner accepts the highest bid which exceeds her reservation bid r_0. If the bid r wins, the winner lends amount I at date 1 and in exchange gets $V(1 - r)$ at date 2.

The insider's problem, after observing $Z = z$, is to choose r to maximize Probability(Bid r wins) $(E[V|Z = z](1 - r) - I)$. The insider's private information Z enters his decision problem only through $H = E[V|Z]$. I assume without loss of generality that the insider observes the real valued random variable H rather than Z. The insider after observing the private information can be characterized by his information-induced 'type' h.

The solution method requires a one-to-one mapping between the information-induced type of the insider and his equilibrium bid. As H does not have a continuous distribution in the problem, I must 'smooth' out the types to obtain it. This is easily done by allowing the insider mixed strategies. The informed lender then randomizes, using a variable U that is independent of (V, Z). Without loss of generality U has an atomless distribution on $[0, 1]$. A mixed strategy σ for the informed bidder is a function from $\Re \times [0, 1] \to [0, 1]$ and $\sigma(h, u)$ is the bid when $H = h$ and $U = u$. I assume without loss of generality that σ is nondecreasing in u for fixed values of h.

I derive a continuous type t from the joint distribution of h and u; Let $\{(H, U) < (h, u)\}$ denote the event $\{(H < h)$ or $(H = h$ and $U < u)\}$. Let $T(h, u)$ be the probability of that event and define $T = T(H, U)$. T is the insider's distributional type and is uniformly distributed on $[0, 1]$. Also note that $H(t) = \inf\{h | \text{Prob}(H \leq h) > t\}$, $H = H(T)$ a.s. This implies that T carries all the information that H does but has the advantage of being a continuous distribution.

To summarize, I started with information Z, found the conditional H, 'smoothed' it out with U, and thus obtained T. The equilibrium strategy σ is now a function from the space of types $t \epsilon [0, 1]$ to the space of bids $[0, 1]$ and is assumed to be nondecreasing in t.

The uninformed outsider gets no signal. His bidding strategy is described by a distribution G over $[0, 1]$ representing his random choice of bids.[23] Finally I define σ^{-1} as the generalized inverse of σ, i.e., σ^{-1} is a function from the space of bids to the space of types.

Lemma A1: *The strategies (σ, G) are a Bayesian Nash equilibrium if the inside lender bids:*

$$\sigma(t) = \frac{E[H(T)|T \leq t] - I}{E[H(T)|T \leq t]} \qquad \text{for } t \geq t_0 \tag{A4}$$

$$\sigma(t) = r_0 \qquad \text{for } t_0 > t \geq \underline{t} \tag{A5}$$

$$\sigma(t) = 0 \qquad \text{for } t < \underline{t} \tag{A6}$$

where r_0 is the reservation bid set by the owner (possibly zero),

$$t_0 \text{ is sup } \{t : \{E[H(T)|T \leq t] - I\}/E[H(T)|T \leq t] = r_0\},$$

and $\underline{t}$ is $\inf\{t : H(t) \geq I\}$.

---

[23] While I introduced mixed strategies for the informed for technical reasons, the mixed strategies for the outsider are a direct consequence of the assumption that the insider knows everything the outsider knows. If the outsider tries to play according to a pure and therefore predictable strategy, the insider will respond by bidding slightly higher if worthwhile and nothing if not. On average, the uninformed will lose, which cannot happen by individual rationality.

The distribution of the uninformed bid is

$$G(r) = 1 \quad if \, r \geq \frac{\bar{H} - I}{\bar{H}} = \bar{r}, \tag{A7}$$

$$G(r) = \frac{\int_0^{\sigma^{-1}(r)} h(s) \, ds}{\int_0^1 h(s) \, ds} \quad for \, \frac{\bar{H} - I}{\bar{H}} > r > r_0, \tag{A8}$$

$$G(r) = \frac{\int_0^{t_0} h(s) \, ds}{\int_0^1 h(s) \, ds} \quad for \, r_0 \geq r > 0, \tag{A9}$$

where $\bar{H} = E[H]$.

Proof: The equilibrium strategy is such that the expected payoff to each lender conditional on his information set is maximized given the strategy of the other lender. The proof consists of the following steps: (1) Show the equilibrium bids have identical support. (2) Use this to show that the uninformed outsider makes zero profits in equilibrium. (3) Set the outsider's profit to zero to obtain the optimal bid for the informed. (4) Use the optimizing behavior of the informed to derive the bidding strategy for the uninformed.

I omit steps (1) and (2) which are identical to the argument in Engelbrecht-Wiggans, Milgrom, and Weber (1983). The expected profits of the outsider conditional on winning with a bid r (where t is the corresponding informed type such that $\sigma(t) = r$) is $E[H(T)(1 - r) - I | T \leq t]$. Setting this equal to zero,

$$r = \sigma(t) = \frac{E[H(T)|T \leq t] - I}{E[H(T)|T \leq t]}. \tag{A10}$$

This expression holds when $t \geq t_0$ (where t_0 is the type 'corresponding' to a bid of r_0 as earlier defined). When $t_0 > t \geq \underline{t}$, the optimal bid for the informed is r_0, as $\underline{t}$ is the lowest information type at which the insider still makes profits by bidding r_0. Below $\underline{t}$, the insider will not bid as any bid will result in certain losses.

The strategy of the outsider is chosen so as to induce the insider to bid according to σ. The insider after seeing t maximizes $G(r)[H(t)(1 - r) - I]$ with respect to r where $r = \sigma(t)$. Differentiating with respect to r

$$\frac{dG(r)}{dr}[H(t)(1 - r) - I] - G(r)H(t) + \lambda_1 - \lambda_2 = 0, \tag{A11}$$

where λ_1 is the Lagrangian multiplier for constraint $r \geq r_0$ and λ_2 is that for $r \leq \bar{r}$. Rearranging (when $\lambda_1 = \lambda_2 = 0$),

$$\frac{G'(r)}{G(r)} = \frac{H(t)\, dr}{H(t)(1 - r) - I}. \tag{A12}$$

Also

$$r = \sigma(t) = \frac{\int_0^t H(s)\, ds - tI}{\int_0^t H(s)\, ds}, \tag{A13}$$

$$dr = \sigma'(t)\, dt = \frac{I\left(tH(t) - \int_0^t H(s)\, ds\right)}{\left(\int_0^t H(s)\, ds\right)^2}\, dt. \tag{A14}$$

Substituting in (A12) from (A13) and (A14),

$$\frac{G'(r)}{G(r)} = \frac{H(t)\, dt}{\int_0^t H(s)\, ds}. \tag{A15}$$

Integrating between t and 1 (for $t > t_0$) and applying the boundary condition that $G(\sigma(1)) = 1$,

$$G(\sigma(t)) = \frac{\int_0^t H(s)\, ds}{\int_0^1 H(s)\, ds}. \tag{A16}$$

For any bid by the outsider corresponding to an informed type less than t_0, the outsider expects losses. Hence $G(r_0) = G(\sigma(t_0)) = G(0)$, i.e., the outsider does not bid with positive probability. The value $\pi_N = G(r_0)$ is the probability that the outsider does not bid.   Q.E.D.

Now consider the model in the text. In the good states (probability q) the project is worth X and in the bad (probability $1 - q$) it is worth $p_B X$. The insider knows the value of the project exactly, so that $\boldsymbol{H} = X$ or $p_B X$; the outsider knows the distribution. Assume without loss of generality that $\boldsymbol{U}$ is uniform on $[0, 1]$.

$$t(h, u) = \text{prob}\{(\boldsymbol{H} < h) \text{ or } (\boldsymbol{H} = h \text{ and } \boldsymbol{U} < u)\},$$

$$t(h = p_B X, u) = u(1 - q),$$

$$\text{and } t(h = X, u) = (1 - q) + uq.$$

$$H(t) = p_B X \text{ for } t \leq 1 - q$$

$$\text{and } H(t) = X \text{ for } t > 1 - q.$$

Substituting values

$$\sigma(t) = \frac{(1-q)p_B X + uqX - I(1-q+uq)}{(1-q)p_B X + uqX} \qquad \text{for } t > t_0, \quad \text{(A17)}$$

$$G(\sigma(t)) = \frac{(1-q)p_B X + uqX}{(1-q)p_B X + qX} \qquad \text{for } t > t_0, \qquad \text{(A18)}$$

$$G(\sigma(t)) = \frac{(1-q)I(X - p_B X)}{((1-r_0)X - I)((1-q)p_B X + qX)} \qquad \text{for } t \le t_0. \quad \text{(A19)}$$

Equations (A17) and (A18) follow from definitions and $G(\sigma(t_0))\ (= \pi_N)$ is obtained by substituting t_0 (the value of t at which the optimal bid of the insider is r_0) into $G(\sigma(t))$. Note that $\pi_N = 1$ when $q\{X(1-r_0) - I\} - (1-q)\{I - p_B X(1-r_0)\} \le 0$, i.e., when the outsider cannot make profits in expectation even if he were the sole bidder (and not exposed to adverse selection). The outsider does not bid and the insider grabs all the rents up to r_0.

Specializing the model further, I set $p_B X = 0$ and $r_0 = 0$ to get

Profit of the insider condition on good state:

$$= (1-q)I/q \qquad \text{when } \pi_N < 1$$
$$= X - I \qquad \text{when } \pi_N = 1$$

where $\pi_N = \text{Min}\left[1, \dfrac{(1-q)I}{q(X-I)}\right]$.

The profit to the outsider is zero on average. If $\pi_N < 1$, the outsider bids with positive probability whenever the project is bad. As the insider does not bid in these states, the outsider makes losses whenever she bids. The zero profit condition implies that these losses are equal in expectation to the profits she makes in the good state.

Loss to uninformed from bidding in bad state:

$$= (1-q)I(1-\pi_N) \quad \text{Q.E.D.}$$

Proof of Proposition 5: Assume fraction α of the total investment is financed through the bank and let arm's-length debt have lower priority than bank debt. The owner has an ex ante problem of choosing the fraction α and an ex post problem of deciding the effort level β. The ex post problem follows immediately, once I derive the expected date 2 face value demanded by the lenders. The expected face value demanded by the bank follows from Proposition 3. Substituting αI for I_s,

$$\alpha I + \frac{(1-q_{aJ}^*)}{q_{aJ}^*}\alpha I + \frac{(1-q_{aJ}^*)}{q_{aJ}^*}(1-\pi_{NJ})\alpha I, \qquad \text{(A20)}$$

where

$$q_{aJ}^* = q(\beta_{aJ}^*, \theta); \quad \pi_{NJ} = \frac{(1 - q_{aJ}^*)\alpha I}{q_{aJ}^*(X - \alpha I)}; \quad 0 \le \alpha \le 1. \quad (A21)$$

The control exerted by the bank enables the arm's-length lender to recover his money when the inefficient project is terminated at date 1. The face value demanded by the arm's-length lender can then be derived from his IR condition,

$$(1 - \alpha)I = D_{02a}q_{aJ}^* + (1 - q_{aJ}^*)\pi_{NJ}(1 - \alpha)I - h(D_{02}, \alpha, q_{aJ}^*) \quad (A22)$$

The value h is a complicated term, which I assume small.[24] As the effect of h is to increase the face value demanded by arm's-length debt, and $h = 0$ when arm's-length debt has higher priority, relaxing the assumption only strengthens the argument for giving arm's-length debt priority.

Solving for D_{02a} from (A22) and adding to (A20), I get the total expected face value of debt at date 2, whence the ex post problem follows. Ex ante, the owner chooses α to maximize

$$\max_{\alpha} U_{aJ} = q_{aJ}^*(X - I) - (1 - q_{aJ}^*)I(1 - \pi_{NJ}) - \beta_{aJ}^*. \quad (A23)$$

Under regularity conditions which ensure a unique solution, I substitute the FOC for the ex post problem:

$$q_1 \left(X - I - \frac{(1 - q_{aJ}^*)I}{q_{aJ}^*} - \frac{(1 - q_{aJ}^*)\alpha I}{q_{aJ}^*}\left(1 - \frac{\pi_{NJ}}{\alpha}\right) \right) - 1 = 0 \text{ for } \beta = \beta_{aJ}^*$$

$$(A24)$$

The program (A21), (A23), and (A24) is in the Standard Principal Agent framework and can be solved explicitly for α^* and β_{aJ}^*.

If arm's-length debt has priority, the net revenue of the project that the short-term lenders bid for at date 1 is $(X - D_{02a})$. I substitute this for X in Proposition 3. The control provided by short-term debt is now given by

$$\pi_{NS} = \frac{(1 - q_{aS}^*)\alpha I}{q_{aS}^*(X - D_{02a} - \alpha I)}. \quad (A25)$$

When the outsider bids with positive probability ($\pi_N \ne 1$), priority affects only control π_N in Proposition 3, but not the rents of the inside bank, for reasons specified in the text. Obviously π_{NS} in (A25) exceeds π_{NJ} in (A21).

---

[24] If D_{12} is the face value that the short-term lender who wins the bargaining game asks from the owner at date 1, then

$$h = q_{aJ}^* \sum_{D_{12}} 1_{[X - D_{12} < D_{02}]}(D_{02} - (X - D_{12}))\text{Prob}(D_{12}).$$

It is hard to obtain h in closed form because it involves the distribution of the winning bid.

The structure of the owner's problem remains the same. However the increased control reduces the compensatory rents demanded by the outside bank (from (A20)), and improves effort (from (A24)). For any value of α, $\beta_{aS}^* > \beta_{aJ}^*$. For any value of β, as π_{NS} is greater than π_{NJ}, a revealed preference argument establishes the superiority of giving arm's-length debt priority.

When the outsider does not bid at all, the priority of the arm's-length claim reduces the surplus available and hence the rents of the inside bank. The rest of the argument follows as above.   Q.E.D.

REFERENCES

Aghion, P., M. Dewatripont, and P. Rey, 1989, Renegotiation design under symmetric information, Mimeo, M.I.T.

Anstaett, K., D. McCreary, and S. Monahan, 1988, Practical debt considerations for growth companies: A case study approach, *Journal of Applied Corporate Finance* 1, 71–78.

Aoki, M., 1988, *Information, Incentives and Bargaining in the Japanese Economy* (Cambridge University Press, London).

Bruck, C., 1988, *The Predator's Ball: The Inside Story of Drexel Burnham and the Rise of the Junk Bond Raiders* (Simon and Schuster, New York, NY).

Carosso, V., 1970, *Investment Banking in America* (Harvard University Press, Cambridge, MA).

Dewing, A., 1920, *Corporate Promotions and Reorganization* (Harvard University Press, Cambridge, MA).

———, 1953, *The Financial Policy of Corporations* (Ronald Press Company, New York, NY).

Diamond, D., 1991a, Monitoring and reputation: The choice between bank loans and directly placed debt, *Journal of Political Economy* 99, 688–721.

———, 1991b, Seniority and maturity structure of bank loans and publicly traded debt, Mimeo, University of Chicago.

Donaldson, J. and T. Donaldson, 1982, *The Medium Term Loan Market* (St. Martin's Press, New York, NY).

Easterbook, F., 1984, Two-agency cost explanations of dividends, *American Economic Review* 74, 650–659.

Engelbrecht-Wiggans, R., P. Milgrom, and R. Weber, 1983, Competitive bidding and proprietary information, *Journal of Mathematical Economics* 11, 161–169.

Fama, E., 1985, What's different about banks?, *Journal of Monetary Economics* 15, 29–39.

Gale, D. and M. Hellwig, 1985, Incentive compatible debt contracts: The one period problem, *Review of Economic Studies* 30, 3–31.

Grossman, S. and O. Hart, 1986, The costs and benefits of ownership: A theory of vertical and lateral integration, *Journal of Political Economy* 94, 691–719.

Hart, O. and J. Moore, 1988, Incomplete contracts and renegotiation, *Econometrica* 56, 755–785.

——— and J. Moore, 1989, Debt and renegotiation, Working paper 520, M.I.T.

Hendricks, K. and R. Porter, 1988, An empirical study of an auction with asymmetric information, *American Economic Review* 78, 865–883.

James, C., 1987, Some evidence on the uniqueness of bank loans, *Journal of Financial Economics* 19, 217–235.

Lummer, S. and J. McConnell, 1989, Further evidence on the bank lending process and the reaction of the capital market to bank loan agreements, *Journal of Financial Economics* 25, 99–122.

Macleod, W. and J. Malcomson, 1989, Efficient specific investment, incomplete contracts and the role of market alternatives, Mimeo, Queen's University.

Macrae, N., 1990, Sweaty brows slippery fingers, *The Economist*, September 8, 1990, 21–24.

Meerschwam, D., 1991, *Breaking Financial Boundaries: Global Capital, National De-regulation and Financial Services Firms* (Harvard Business School Press, Cambridge, MA).

Modigliani, F. and E. Perotti, 1990, The rules of the game and the development of security markets, Mimeo, M.I.T.

Myers, S., 1977, Determinants of corporate borrowing, *Journal of Financial Economics* 5, 147–175.

Rajan, R., 1991a, Essays on banking, Unpublished Ph.D. thesis, M.I.T.

———, 1991b, Conflict of interest and the separation of commercial and investment banking, Mimeo, University of Chicago.

Sharpe, S., 1990, Asymmetric information, bank lending and implicit contracts: A stylized model of customer relationships, *Journal of Finance* 45, 1069–1087.

Stiglitz, J. and A. Weiss, 1983, Incentive effects of terminations: Applications to credit and labor markets, *American Economic Review* 73, 912–927.

III

FINANCIAL DISTRESS

"Financial distress" is a somewhat imprecise term that refers to the costs a borrower incurs when it cannot meet its currently due obligations. In the analysis of financial distress, it is important to understand the distinctions among default, bankruptcy, and liquidation. "Default" is the breach of a promise made under a contract. (Violation of a debt covenant other than one specifying promised payments conventionally is called "technical default.") In private debt agreements, default is frequently remedied through renegotiation. Default in public debt agreements is more likely to lead to bankruptcy because of the less flexible renegotiation process and the attendant higher renegotiation costs. "Bankruptcy" is a legal proceeding for the court-supervised administration of a firm in financial distress. Most large public corporations file under Chapter 11, where the firm's outstanding contracts are reorganized. Under Chapter 7, the firm is liquidated. "Liquidation" is the sale of the firm's assets with the distribution of the proceeds to the firm's claimants according to their priority.

Recent research has focused on the costs of financial distress and the role of financial institutions in resolving financial distress. In this literature, financial-distress costs are generally divided into two categories: direct and indirect. Direct costs of financial distress refer to legal, administrative, and advisory costs a firm incurs in its attempts to resolve its financial difficulties by renegotiating its claims or by filing for bankruptcy protection. Indirect costs of financial distress involve the costs associated with disruptions in the firm's input supplies, losses that arise from reduced product demand, and agency costs that arise from poorly aligned incentives. This last source of distress costs has received the most attention in the academic literature.

The first article, by **Wruck** (1990), provides a review of empirical studies concerning organizational restructuring that occurs in financial distress. Wruck makes two important points. First, information asymmetries create important impediments to restructuring firms in financial distress. In particular, in financial distress, management and/or shareholders have a strong incentive to overstate the value of the firm to induce bondholders and other claimants to accept a restructuring over liquidation. By avoiding liquidation, shareholders are able to keep their option on the firm's assets alive. As a result of these information asymmetries, there is demand for a well-informed workout specialist or financial institution to assess the firm's prospects.

A second point made by Wruck is that real benefits can arise from financial distress. Specifically, firms in financial distress make widespread and fundamental changes in their ownership and corporate-governance structures. For example, U.S. firms emerge from financial distress with ownership structures that are characterized by greater concentration of share ownership and greater involvement on the part of financial institutions in the strategic decision making of the firm. As a result, financial distress can create value both through restructuring the firm's operations and through modification of the firm's governance structure.

If, as is generally believed, the costs of financial distress are higher for reorganizations occurring in bankruptcy, then it is in the collective interests of all the firm's claimants to recontract outside of bankruptcy. This raises the important question of why private recontracting negotiations fail, resulting in a costly bankruptcy. The second article, by **Gilson, John, and Lang** (1990), addresses this issue. They argue that the incentive to recontract privately and avoid bankruptcy depends on two factors. The first factor is the potential cost savings from recontracting outside of bankruptcy. The higher these potential cost savings, the greater the collective gain from avoiding bankruptcy. The second factor affecting the choice of private recontracting is the ability of creditors to agree on a reorganization plan. A costly bankruptcy can be avoided only if claimholders can agree on how the cost savings from recontracting privately are to be allocated among the claimants of the firm.

Gilson, John, and Lang argue that Chapter 11 is more costly for firms that consist largely of intangible assets, especially when the assets generate a stream of firm-specific rents. For these firms, the greater likelihood of asset sales in bankruptcy implies that going-concern value is more likely to be reduced in bankruptcy. As a result, bankruptcy is more costly for firms with more intangible assets. A testable implication of this argument is that firms with higher ratios of market value to replacement cost will be less likely to file for Chapter 11 protection.

The success of private debt renegotiations also depends on the willingness and/or ability of creditors to recontract outside of bankruptcy. The willingness to settle privately in turn depends on the severity of holdout problems among creditors. Holdout problems refer to an individual creditor's incentives not to participate in a restructuring even though collectively creditors as a group are better off if the restructuring is successful. As Gilson, John, and Lang explain, holdout problems are more important when restructuring public debt than when restructuring private debt for two reasons. First, as discussed in Part II, public debt is more difficult to restructure because it is subject to the provisions of the Trust Indenture Act of 1939. As a result, public-debt restructurings are limited to exchange offers in which existing debt is exchanged for new claims on the firm. Second, with diffusely held public debt, free-rider problems are more likely to impede a restructuring. Specifically, if some bondholders forgive a portion of their claim in a restructuring, the value of the firm's remaining debt will increase. Thus, individual bondholders with small claims who do not view their participation as pivotal will free-ride and will not participate in the restructuring.

To empirically examine the determinants of the success of private-debt restructuring, Gilson, John, and Lang examine 169 financially distressed firms. Their evidence indicates that firms are more likely to restructure their debt outside of bankruptcy the higher the firm's market-to-book ratio, the greater the proportion of debt held by banks, and the fewer the total number of lenders. These results suggest that holdout problems are an important deterrent to private debt restructuring.

In addition to holdout problems, private recontracting attempts potentially fail because claimants are poorly informed about the future prospects of the firm. Brown, James, and Mooradian (1993) examine how the composition of securities offered to public claimholders and the presence of a well-informed bank lender can overcome the information problems associated with private recontracting.

Additional evidence that free-rider problems and information asymmetries make it difficult to renegotiate in times of financial distress is provided in the third article, by **Hoshi, Kashyap, and Scharfstein** (1990). The authors examine the effects of financial distress on investment activity and product sales among Japanese firms. The authors focus on Japanese firms because many firms in Japan have close ties to commercial banks through groups called *Keiretsus*. For a firm in one of these groups, banks provide most of the debt financing, own a portion of the firm's equity, and in many cases have representatives on the firm's board of directors. The authors argue that free-rider and information problems will be less severe for firms in *Keiretsus*. As a result, conditional on financial distress, these firms are expected to perform better than firms without strong banking relationships. Consistent with this argument the authors find that among financially distressed firms (defined as those with cash flows insufficient to meet interest payments), firms in strong bank relationships reduce their investment expenditures less and experience a smaller decline in product sales than do firms that are not part of a *Keiretsu*.

In the final article, **Gertner and Scharfstein** (1991) examine the effects of financial distress on firms' investment and liquidation incentives. If financial contracts could be costlessly renegotiated and there were no information asymmetries between outside debtholders and the management of the firm, then the Coase (1960) theorem implies that financial distress would have no impact on real investment decisions of the firm. If the financially distressed firm's assets are more valuable when employed by some other firm, then the firm should be liquidated and the creditors paid off according to the priority of their claim. If the firm's assets are more valuable in their present use, then they should continue as a going concern.

Gertner and Scharfstein examine the effects on operating performance of institutional constraints on financial recontracting. The authors examine the firm's investment policy both in the context of private debt restructuring and within the Chapter 11 bankruptcy proceedings. In their model, the firm is assumed to have both private debt and public debt outstanding. Private debt is assumed to be substantially easier to renegotiate than public debt for the reasons discussed above.

Gertner and Scharfstein examine the implications of these impediments to private debt restructuring for the efficiency of the firm's investment and liquidation decisions. They show that even if bank debt can be restructured, investment policy will be inefficient when the firm has public debt outstanding. The inefficiency arises because with public debt outstanding, shareholder wealth maximization differs from firm value maximization. Firms will forgo positive net present value (NPV) projects that involve large wealth transfers to bondholders; that is, firms will underinvest. Likewise, firms will pursue negative NPV projects that involve transfers from bondholders to shareholders (or the bank); that is, firms will overinvest.

Introducing the possibility of an exchange offer involving public debt does not eliminate their costs. For exchange offers to be successful, bondholders must be offered a claim whose value exceeds the expected value of the existing debt, conditional on the success of the offer. This generally requires giving bondholders a senior claim. However, priority-increasing exchange offers can lead to overinvestment since they have the potential to transfer wealth from bondholders to shareholders.

Financial distress, reorganization, and organizational efficiency

Karen Hopper Wruck*

Harvard Business School, Boston, MA 02163, USA

Received June 1990, final version received January 1991

This paper examines financial distress and its effect on organizational efficiency. Imperfect information and conflicts of interest among the firm's claimholders influence the outcome of financial distress. Methods for resolving distress and controlling conflicts of interest are discussed. New evidence on financial restructuring and distress costs is presented along with evidence on the organizational restructuring that accompanies financial distress. The evidence demonstrates that financial distress has benefits as well as costs, and that financial and ownership structure affect the net costs.

1. Introduction

Financial distress has changed dramatically over the last decade, in part because of major changes in the law and in financial markets. Since the adoption of the Bankruptcy Reform Act in October 1979, the number of Chapter 11 petitions has increased greatly. In 1980, the first full year after the new bankruptcy act, the number of bankruptcy petition filings increased 85% to 5,637, up from 3,042 in 1979. In addition, since October 1979 there have been more than 20 Chapter 11 filings involving over $1 billion in liabilities.[1] Texaco's Chapter 11 filing in April 1987 was the largest in U.S. history, with $21.6 billion in liabilities; Campeau filed the second largest bankruptcy petition, in January 1990, with $9.9 billion in liabilities. The size of the liabilities and the circumstances surrounding many of the filings – legal

---

*I would like to thank George Baker, Michael Gibbs, Krishna Palepu, Richard Ruback, Eric Wruck, the participants in the conference on the Structure and Governance of Enterprise, and especially Michael Jensen (the editor) and Jerold Warner (the referee) for their comments and suggestions. I would also like to thank Chris Allen, Karen Fuller, and Amy Smith for providing research assistance.

[1] Altman (1983) and Altman (1990).

Journal of Financial Economics 27 (1990) 419–444. North-Holland

judgments, product-liability claims, labor problems, leveraged acquisitions and leveraged buyouts – have stimulated debate and controversy among the press, investors, and researchers.

In financial markets over the last decade, firms began to substitute public original-issue high-yield debt, so-called junk bonds, for commercial loans from the banking and insurance sector. The number of new high-yield debt offerings increased from 22 in 1977 to a peak of 217 in 1986, falling to 111 in 1989.[2] Through both takeovers and voluntary changes in capital structure, high-yield debt has facilitated the restructuring of many U.S. corporations. In addition, the development of a liquid market for high-yield debt focused attention on private workouts and exchange offers often used by firms to resolve financial distress. The number of investors buying and selling the securities of distressed firms and the capital available for such investments has grown spectacularly. Some of these 'vulture capitalists' accumulate positions and participate directly in negotiations to reorganize the firm.

Financial distress is an emerging field steeped in confusion and complexity. Some of the confusion can be resolved by understanding the diverse nature of financial distress; it is not synonymous with corporate death. Firms in distress face a variety of situations having very different effects on their values and claimholders. This diversity, in conjunction with conflicts of interest among claimholders, leads to an information problem that makes valuing a distressed firm difficult. The valuation problems exacerbate the conflicts of interest. Section 2 of this paper discusses the nature of financial distress, conflicts of interest, and the information problem facing a distressed firm's claimholders. Firms can resolve financial distress privately through a workout or liquidation, or under the supervision of the Bankruptcy Court. Section 3 discussed the methods available for resolving distress and evidence on the factors affecting their use.

Until recently, research on financial distress focused on distress costs and financial restructuring. The possibility that financial distress could result in beneficial outcomes was generally ignored. New empirical evidence demonstrates that financial distress has both benefits and costs, and that financial and ownership structure affect the net costs. Financial distress is often accompanied by comprehensive organizational changes in management, governance, and structure. This organizational restructuring can create value by improving the use of resources. For example, individual firms in declining industries tend to continue to operate and invest in economic activities even though efficiency dictates a capacity reduction. Financial distress frees resources to move to higher-valued uses by forcing managers and directors to reduce capacity and to rethink operating policies and strategy decisions. This kind of organizational change is unlikely to occur in an all-equity firm,

----

[2]Cheung, Bencivenga, and Fabozzi (1990).

because without leverage, poor performance does not lead to financial distress. It is financial distress that gives creditors a legal right to demand restructuring. Section 4 discusses the benefits and costs of financial distress, and presents evidence on the performance of distressed firms in Japan. Section 5 concludes.

2. Financial distress, the information problem, and conflicts of interests

2.1. A definition of financial distress

This paper defines financial distress as a situation where cash flow is insufficient to cover current obligations. These obligations can include unpaid debts to suppliers and employees, actual or potential damages from litigation, and missed principal or interest payments under borrowing agreements (default). Technical default, the violation of a debt covenant other than one specifying principal and interest payments (e.g., minimum-net-worth requirements or working-capital constraints), can be a warning that distress is imminent. Financial distress generally leads to negotiations with at least one of the firm's creditors. Cross-default provisions are debt covenants in which default on one debt security is a condition for technical default on another. Such provisions result in much more complicated negotiations to resolve distress.

Some confusion arises because the word insolvent is often used as a synonym for financial distress. Insolvency can be interpreted as pertaining to stocks or flows, and the two are often confused. For example, *Webster's New World Dictionary* (*Second College Edition*) defines 'insolvent' first as 'not enough to pay all debts' and then as 'unable to pay debts as they become due'. A stock-based definition describes as insolvent a firm with a negative economic net worth: the present value of its cash flows is less that its total obligations.[3] A firm in financial distress is insolvent on a flow basis, it is unable to meet current cash obligations.[4] Flow-based insolvency gives unpaid creditors the right to demand restructuring because their contract with the firm has been breached. If a firm is insolvent on a stock basis, but solvent on a flow basis, it creditors have little power, because their claims are paid to date. Creditors can expect little help from shareholders in such a situation

---

[3]This should not be confused with negative net worth in an accounting sense. The accounting balance sheet for a healthy firm can show total assets less than total liabilities. For example, Sealed Air Corporation, a New York Stock Exchange firm, completed a leveraged recapitalization in July 1989 that left it with a negative accounting net worth of over $160 million. The company has had no problems meeting debt service and is a year ahead of schedule in paying off its debt [Wruck (1990)].

[4]Altman (1983) discusses in detail the different ways insolvency is defined. He labels the flow definition of insolvency 'technical insolvency' and the stock definition as 'insolvency in a bankruptcy sense'.

because their equity claims are still valuable. In the unlikely event that firm value increases dramatically, shareholders capture the benefits.

Bankruptcy and liquidation are also used as synonyms for financial distress. In this paper, bankruptcy refers to the court-supervised process for breaking and rewriting contracts. Liquidation refers to a sale of the firm's assets and distribution of proceeds to claimants.

2.2. The information problem and conflicts of interest

The information problem faced by a distressed firm's claimholders is how to obtain reliable data to determine whether the firm is insolvent on a stock, as well as a flow basis. The extreme examples presented in fig. 1 help illustrate the problem. It shows actual cash flows for two firms. At time 1 the firms have identical historical cash flows, and future cash flows through time 2 are identical. It is only after time 2 that cash flows will differ. At time 1 both firms become distressed. The firm in panel A is insolvent on both a stock and a flow basis – cash flow after time 1 is permanently lower than the level of obligations. The panel B firm is insolvent on a flow basis only. Its cash flow will return to pre-distress levels after time 2.

The information problem boils down to deciding whether a distressed firm's situation is better described by panel A or panel B. It is important because the value-maximizing way to resolve distress differs between panels. The panel B firm can meet its obligations by persuading claimants to agree to a new payment schedule. Except for the costs of renegotiating, it suffers no penalty for financial distress. Resolving distress for the panel A firm requires major effort, including reducing fixed claims or reorganizing (if feasible) in a way that creates enough value to cover the claims.

At the time of financial distress (time 1) investors know the history of actual cash flows, but must make predictions about future cash flows with incomplete information. This can lead to honest disagreement about the firm's future prospects. Even if all parties could accurately predict future cash flows, there would still be conflict over the best way to resolve distress, because different reorganization policies distribute wealth across managers, creditors, and shareholders differently. Therefore, reorganization policies are advocated both out of concern for value maximization and out of self-interest. Where the two differ, there is potential for value-destroying behavior. As discussed in detail in section 4.4.1, the rules of the game for reorganization in the U.S. exacerbate these conflicts.

In pursuing their own interests, claimants have incentives to present biased and inaccurate data as though it were unbiased and accurate. Shareholders have incentives to claim the firm is insolvent only on a flow basis (like the panel B firm) because it increases the likelihood that they will retain their equity stake and therefore preserve the option value of their claim. Creditors

Panel A

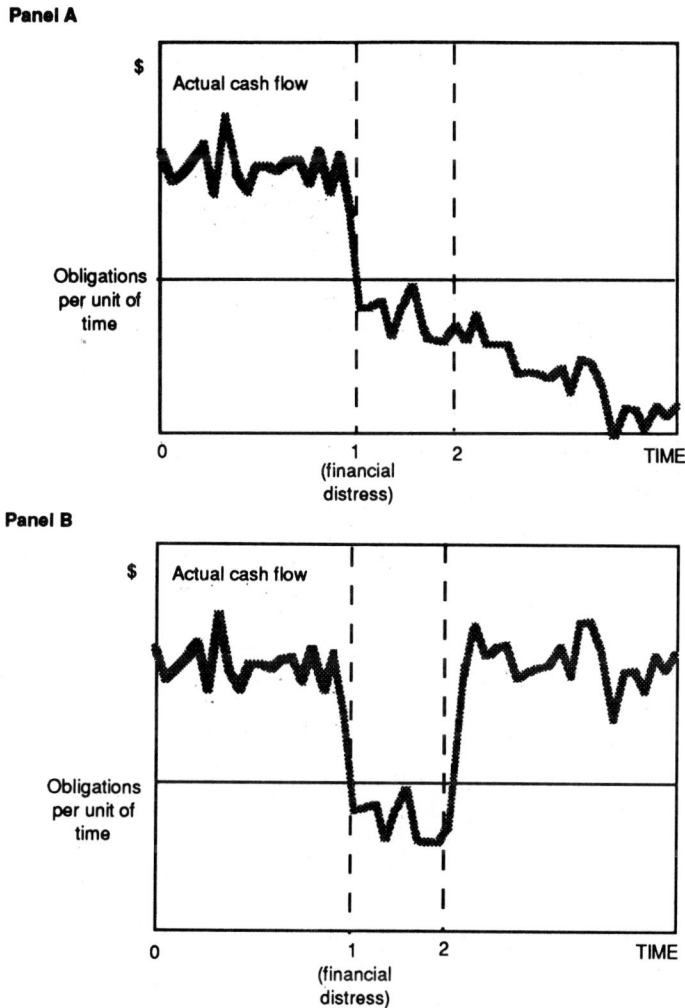

Panel B

Fig. 1. The information problem and conflicts of interest in financial distress.

Panels A and B illustrate actual cash flows for two firms that become flow-based insolvent at time 1. Investors in a distressed firm face an information problem – they cannot tell whether their firm has cash flows more like those in panel A or B. The firm in panel A is insolvent due to a permanent reduction in cash flow, while the firm in panel B is insolvent due to a temporary reduction in cash flow – at time 2 its cash flow returns to a pre-distress level. Cash flows at the time of financial distress are identical for the two firms. At time 1, no one has both the relevant information about cash flows and the incentive to reveal it to the firm's claimholders. Out of self-interest shareholders will argue that panel B represents the firm's situation, while creditors will argue that panel A is more realistic. Managers will tend to side with the party less likely to fire them.

have incentives to claim the firm is insolvent on a stock basis (like the panel A firm) because it increases the likelihood that they will be awarded the equity. Managers have an incentive to side with the party less likely to fire them. Resolving these conflicts consumes resources and in the extreme can destroy huge amounts of value. For example, a panel B firm can be turned into a panel A firm as claimants fight over the distribution of wealth, or if a value-reducing reorganization policy is chosen because it furthers the interests of a persuasive class of claimants.

The most reliable estimate of future cash flows can be obtained when accurate information is shared by managers and claimholders. Managers generally have better information about the firm's internal operations than outside investors, but they may lack the ability or incentives to make the best use of that information. A management team committed to a poor strategy or to preserving its control over the firm is using its superior information to make poor decisions. Despite their lack of detailed information about the firm's operations, both creditors and shareholders are often better able to assess the firm's situation. Large creditors have employees who are expert analysts, and in addition creditors sometimes receive special reports from the firm containing information not available to the public. Active shareholders are often better able to assess industry trends, the firm's strategy, and the effectiveness of top management. Unfortunately, no party has both the information and incentives to reveal that information to others.

Workout specialists, whose reputation suffers if they mislead claimholders, could help solve the information problem. As such a specialist, Drexel Burnham Lambert's ability to execute hundreds of exchange offers in the high-yield market suggests that its reputation played a role in attenuating information problems. The role of specialists in resolving financial distress quickly and inexpensively has been drastically curtailed with the demise of Drexel and by recent court decisions. In particular, Judge Lifland's January 1990 decision in the LTV bankruptcy case makes it more costly to resolve distress outside the courtroom. He ruled that LTV's bondholders who participated in out-of-court exchange offers before the firm's Chapter 11 filing were not entitled to a claim equal to the face value of their old bonds. Instead their claims were limited to the market value of their new bonds. Since this decision only one major private workout has been successfully completed, and it was structured to circumvent the effect of his ruling should the firm later file Chapter 11.[5]

---

[5]See 'U.S. Bankruptcy Judge Rules in Favor of LTV', January 31, 1990, Reuters Newswire. The successful workout referred to above was an exchange offer completed on February 5, 1990 by SCI TV. The company, formerly owned by Storer, went private and was later taken public by KKR and George Gillett in 1987. All of SCI's banks and 95% of its publicly traded debt participated in the restructuring. Each creditor class agreed to approximately the same proportional reduction in its claims, so that in the event of Chapter 11 it would suffer the same percentage reduction in its allowable claims. (See 'SCI TV Completes Exchange Offer or Notes, Debentures', February 5, 1990, Reuters Newswire.)

3. Resolving financial distress

Financial distress is resolved in an environment of imperfect information and conflicts of interest. Yet evidence on the frequency distribution of outcomes for firms in distress proves that it is not synonymous with corporate death. Financial distress is often resolved through private workouts or legal reorganization under Chapter 11 of the U.S. Bankruptcy Code. Only much more rarely are distressed firms liquidated under Chapter 7 of the code. Fig. 2 traces firms in financial distress to their final outcomes based on data from five empirical studies. From left to right the figure presents the sample criteria for each study and follows each set of sample firms to their final outcomes. Gilson (1989, 1990) and Gilson, John, and Lang (1990) provide evidence on the fate of firms that experienced extremely poor stock-price performance. Weiss (1990) and Morse and Shaw (1988) provide evidence on outcomes for firms filing Chapter 11.

3.1. Outcomes conditional on poor stock-price performance

Gilson (1989, 1990) and Gilson, John, and Lang (1990) study New York (NYSE) and American Stock Exchange (AMEX) firms whose three-year cumulative stock-price performance is in the bottom 5% of all firms listed on the two exchanges between 1978 and 1987. Of these firms 51% become distressed, either defaulting or restructuring their debt. The remaining 49% do not default or restructure their debt.[6] Of the distressed firms with available data, 47% (80) are able to resolve distress through a private workout.

In a workout, the firm and its creditors renegotiate their contracts privately, resolving distress without resorting to the bankruptcy courts.[7] The outcome of a workout can range from a one-time waiver of payment to a restructuring of all liabilities and equity claims. With publicly traded debt securities, the restructuring is often achieved through an exchange offer in which the distressed debt securities are exchanged for new debt securities and sometimes preferred or common stock. The remaining 53% (89) of the sample firms file for protection under Chapter 11 of the U.S. Bankruptcy Code.

3.2. Outcomes conditional on legal bankruptcy

Fig. 2 also follows firms that file Chapter 11 from the Weiss (1990) and Morse and Shaw (1988) samples, respectively. Their samples include firms

---

[6] These data were obtained in private conversation with Gilson.

[7] Firms sometimes liquidate privately. Hite, Owers, and Rogers' (1987) sample contains 49 NYSE and AMEX firms that liquidated voluntarily and privately between 1963 and 1983. Their study does not provide evidence on the proportion of sample firms in financial distress.

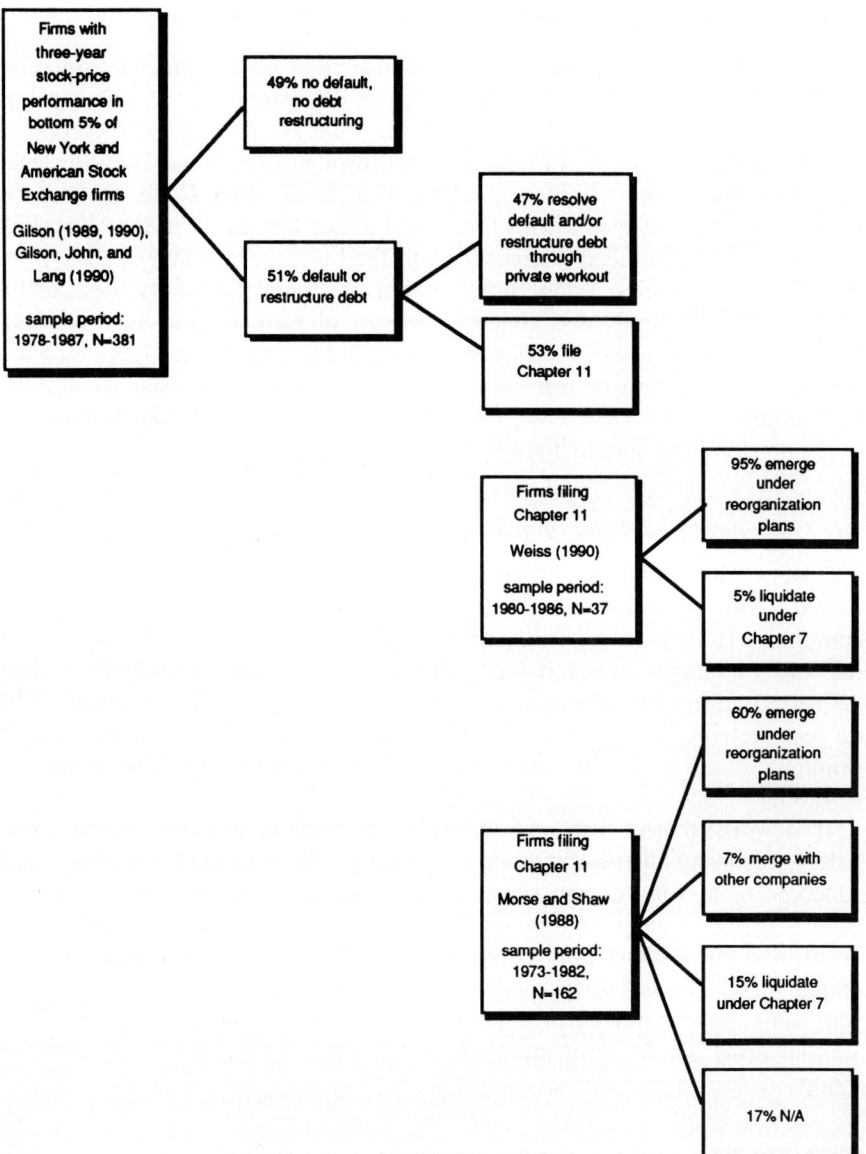

Fig. 2. Evidence on the outcomes of financial distress based on data from five empirical studies.

The trees trace the frequency distribution of outcomes for firms in financial distress. The first box in each tree presents authors of the studies and summarizes their sample period, size, and selection criteria. Gilson (1989, 1990) and Gilson, John, and Lang (1990) study a sample of 381 NYSE and AMEX firms with very poor three-year cumulative stock returns during the period 1978–1987. Weiss (1990) and Morse and Shaw (1988) study samples of 37 and 162 firms filing bankruptcy petitions in the periods 1980–1986 and 1973–1982, respectively.

that file Chapter 11 whether or not they had extremely poor stock-price performance. A firm or its creditors can file for bankruptcy protection, which provides a court-supervised setting in which to rewrite contracts with creditors. After a firm files for bankruptcy, it continues to be run by the incumbent management team, although if management has committed fraud or is proven incompetent, the court appoints a trustee to manage the company.

Most firms entering Chapter 11 emerge after debtholders have agreed to exchange their original claims for new debt and/or equity in the company. The new debt usually has smaller payments spread over more years. Weiss (1990) studies the reorganization plans of 37 NYSE and AMEX firms that enter Chapter 11. Of the 37 firms, 95% (35) emerged from Chapter 11 under accepted reorganization plans and 5% (2) are eventually liquidated under Chapter 7. Morse and Shaw (1988) study post-Chapter 11 stock-price performance of 162 firms filing between 1973 and 1982. Of their sample firms, 60% (98) emerge from Chapter 11 under reorganization plans, 7% (11) merge with other companies, and 15% (25) liquidate under Chapter 7. Morse and Shaw could not determine with certainty the outcome for the remaining 17% (28) of their sample firms.

A firm liquidates by converting some or all of its assets to cash and distributing that cash to its claimants. When assets are less valuable to the firm than to a third party, they can be sold piecemeal or as a productive group, whichever yields the highest proceeds. Under Chapter 7 of the Bankruptcy Code, liquidation is supervised by the court. This means the bankruptcy court judge oversees the conversion of the firm's assets into cash and the distribution of the proceeds to claimholders in order of their priority.

3.3. The role of organizational form and creditors

3.3.1. Evidence from the United States

Many previous studies of financial distress focus on estimating the unconditional probability that a firm will file bankruptcy.[8] These studies generally analyze matched samples of bankrupt and nonbankrupt firms, using accounting information and other firm characteristics as explanatory variables. Gilson, John, and Lang (1990) estimate the probability of Chapter 11 conditional on poor stock-price performance. They study how asset and liability structures help predict whether financial distress is resolved through a private workout or through formal bankruptcy under Chapter 11.

Financial Structure
By design, Gilson, John, and Lang's sample contains firms for which a large percentage of the equity value has been destroyed before a default. At the

[8]See, for example, Altman (1968) and Beaver (1966).

median, firms in their sample that renegotiate their liabilities privately lose 50% of their equity value over the three years before the default, and firms filing for Chapter 11 lose over 60% of their equity value. Gilson et al. find that private renegotiation is more likely the higher the ratio of bank debt to total liabilities. The more complex the firm's capital structure (as represented by the number of classes of debt), the less likely private renegotiation is to be successful. These findings confirm some intuitive insights about bargaining and negotiation: more concentrated borrowings are easier to renegotiate, and it is easier to negotiate with fewer groups. For managers concerned about their firm's ability to reorganize privately, these results highlight the factors to consider when choosing a financing strategy.

Asset Structure

Gilson et al. also find that when Tobin's Q (the ratio of market value to replacement cost of assets) is higher, private renegotiation is more likely. They interpret their results as evidence that private reorganization is more likely in distressed firms whose economic activities generate substantial intangible assets. This is true, they argue, because the value of intangible assets is more likely to be destroyed in bankruptcy than in a private workout.[9] An alternative explanation for their results is that cross-sectional differences in Q reflect variation in the pre-distress capital structure as well as in the nature of firms' assets.

A simple numerical example illustrates how this happens. Consider two firms each worth $100, with an asset replacement cost of $10 (equal to liquidation value). Firm 1 finances itself with $90 of debt and $10 of equity, whereas firm 2 finances itself with $10 of debt and $90 of equity. Suppose that for each firm half the equity value is lost and the firm defaults, entering the Gilson et al. sample. Firm 1 is worth $95 and has a Q of 9.5. Firm 2 is worth $55 and has a Q of 5.5. If firm 1 liquidates, $85 of value is destroyed and debtholders receive only 11% of their claim. If firm 2 liquidates, only $45 of value is destroyed and debtholders receive 100% of their claim. Firm 1's debt and equityholders have stronger incentives to reorganize quickly, and probably privately, once default occurs. This has nothing to do with the nature of the firm's assets, but rather with the control function of debt.[10]

---

[9]Of course, if the value of intangible assets could be realized through a sale, this would not be true.

[10]This simple example assumes a gradual deterioration of value leading to distress rather than an exogenous shock affecting both firms simultaneously and identically. If, for example, a shock instantaneously reduced the value of both firms by $90, they would both be worth $10 at the time of distress and would probably resolve distress similarly.

3.3.2. International evidence

Most of the available evidence on financial distress is based on the experience of U.S. firms. Hoshi, Kashyap, and Scharfstein (1990) provide evidence on the experience of firms in Japan. They examine the industry-adjusted investment and sales performance of 121 Japanese firms approaching financial distress between April 1978 and March 1985.[11] In selecting their sample, Hoshi, Kashyap, and Scharfstein assume a firm is approaching distress when the ratio of operating income to interest expense (interest coverage) falls below one. Sample firms have one year of healthy coverage followed by two years of poor coverage.

The evidence of Hoshi et al. indicates that cross-sectional differences in financial structure explain differences in sample firms' performance. Strong ties to financial institutions and other firms are associated with higher investment and sales performance during distress. The 49 sample firms that are members of a keiretsu – a group of firms with product-market ties and cross-share ownership that are centered around a set of banks and financial institutions – invest and sell more during periods of financial distress. Highly concentrated bank borrowings are also associated with superior performance. For Japanese firms, close bank lending relationships and equity ownership go together. On average, the largest lender holds 23% of the firm's bank debt and 4% of its equity. The shareholdings of the top lender, however, are not statistically significant as an explanatory variable for firm performance.

The implications of the results in Hoshi et al. for U.S. firms are difficult to determine because the financial structures associated with superior performance by Japanese firms in financial distress are illegal in the U.S. The Glass–Steagall Act prevents banks from holding large equity positions in firms, including the firms that borrow from them. Prowse (1990) reports that in Japan, commercial banks own 20.5% of equity securities. Japanese insurance companies own 17.7% and pension funds 5.3%. In the U.S., insurance companies and pension funds own 5.2% and 14.5%, respectively. For antitrust reasons, U.S. regulations also discourage cross-share ownership within industries [Roe (1990)].

Following financial distress, U.S. firms adopt ownership structures that look more like those of Japanese firms. Gilson (1990) finds that the concentration of equity ownership by outsiders (including creditors) increases following financial distress. The holdings of all 5% and greater outside blockholders increase from an average of 12.3% one year before distress to

---

[11]A disadvantage of using sales and investment as measures of firm performance is that they are not always positively associated with changes in value. Increased sales are not necessarily more profitable, and increased investment does not necessarily have a positive net present value. Unless systematically bad decisions are being made by sample firms, however, these performance measures should not pose a large problem.

27.9% two years following distress. Creditors obtain an equity interest in the firm as part of the reorganization, while outsiders assemble blocks of shares through open market trading. Under Glass–Steagall, a bank working out a loan is granted a temporary exemption from the prohibition against equity ownership, although it must sell any equity position it receives in exchange for debt forgiveness within two years. In addition, the priority status of a lender can be reduced if the lender attempts to control decision-making at the borrowing firm. Gilson (1990) shows that banks take advantage of the exemption. Two years after the beginning of financial distress, banks and insurance companies own 18.7% of sample firms' equity. For 20% of Gilson's sample firms, banks receive equity as part of a private debt restructuring. In these firms, banks hold an average of 24% of the firm's equity.

The financial and ownership structures chosen by Japanese firms raise important issues for U.S. firms. If the keiretsu, as an organizational form, is superior to organizational forms allowed in the U.S. and if bank equity ownership (common not only in Japan, but in Europe as well) improves firm performance, then the U.S. regulatory system imposes large costs on domestic firms and on the economy.

4. Benefits and costs of financial distress

Previous studies of financial distress focus on the costs and ignore the possibility that distress can result in beneficial outcomes. This stems in part from a widely accepted model of the firm's capital-structure decision. For example, in their textbook, Brealey and Myers (1988, p. 421) present the following simple formula for the value of a leveraged firm:

$$\textit{Value of firm} = \textit{Value if all equity financed} + \textit{PV tax shield}$$

$$- \textit{PV cost of financial distress},$$

where the *PV cost of financial distress* is the probability of financial distress multiplied by the expected costs (out-of-pocket plus indirect costs). According to this formula, the firm chooses how much to borrow by balancing the tax benefits of leverage against the costs of an increased probability of financial distress. But this analysis is incomplete because it ignores both the nontax benefits of leverage and the benefits of financial distress. Therefore, it understates the amount a firm should borrow.

4.1. Nontax benefits of leverage

Leverage provides discipline and monitoring not available to an all equity firm. According to free-cash-flow theory it creates value by imposing a discipline on organizations that reduces agency costs [Jensen (1986)]. The value created by leverage does not necessarily come at the price of an increased probability of financial distress. A more efficiently run firm can carry a higher debt burden with an equal or reduced probability of financial distress.

Evidence on the improved operating performance of leveraged-buyout firms is consistent with this theory. Kaplan (1989b) and Smith (1990) find operating income increases by over 40% during the two to three years following a leveraged buyout. Baker and Wruck (1989) find that The O.M. Scott & Sons Company managed assets differently after its leveraged buyout than it had as an ITT subsidiary. Managers tried to increase value rather than 'make budget'. Production efficiency and working-capital management improved. Kaplan and Stein (1990) find that asset betas fall by 40% following leveraged recapitalizations. Evidence from Wisconsin Central Ltd. Railroad's (WCL) leveraged buyout indicates that asset-beta reductions result from organizational changes.[12] WCL's post-buyout strategy reduced operating leverage in a number of ways, including reducing the number of yards and cars and running a 'just-in-time' railroad.

When liquidation or reorganization is the firm's highest-valued alternative, default creates value by providing an event that triggers change. Financial distress gives creditors the right to demand restructuring because their contract with the firm has been breached. They can push the firm to liquidate or reorganize. Leverage can, therefore, lead to value maximization by triggering liquidation [Titman (1984)]. The value of a firm likely to liquidate too soon or linger too long is reduced.

Where firm value is deteriorating, high leverage leads to an earlier default, and simultaneously accomplishes two objectives. It preserves value when the alternative is a continued erosion of value, and in doing so increases the likelihood that the firm will reorganize quickly and efficiently. Fig. 3 helps to illustrate this point. It shows two firms in the same business with the same liquidation value. One has chosen a high-leverage capital structure, while the other has chosen low leverage. Assume the debt covenants are such that the firm defaults when the net present value of the firm's cash flows falls below the face value of its obligations. The value that triggers default is higher for the highly leveraged firm than for the less leveraged firm.

At the time of default the claimholders of the high- and low-leverage firms face very different situations. If the high-leverage firm liquidates, the value represented by area A is destroyed. A much smaller value represented by area B is destroyed if the low-leverage firm liquidates. The larger value at risk in liquidation gives the high-leverage firm's claimholders stronger incentives to reorganize quickly, and probably privately, once default occurs.

---

[12]See Burkhardt, Jensen, and Barry (1990).

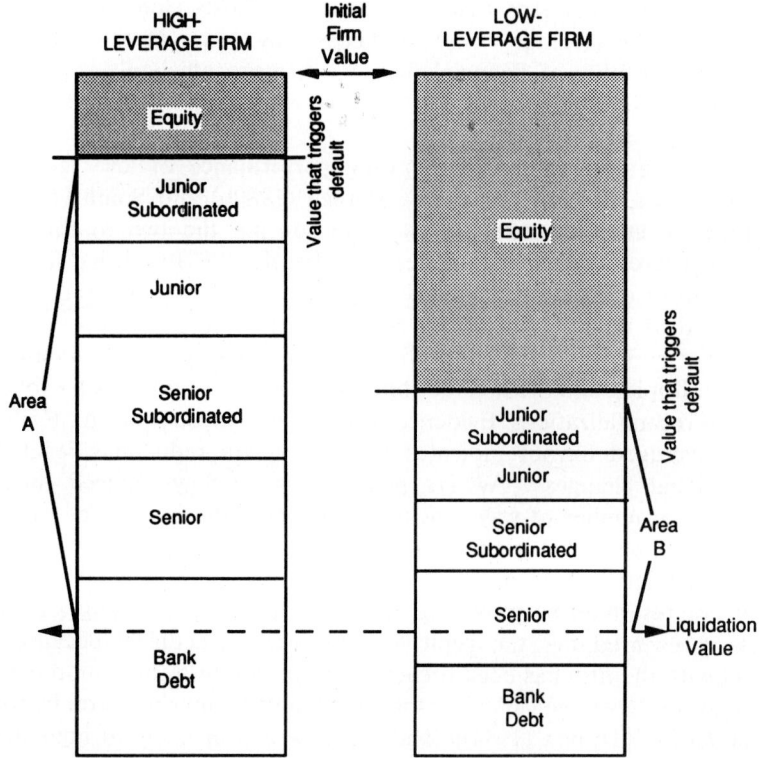

Fig. 3. Illustration of the incentive for more highly leveraged firms to reorganize privately.

The figure presents capital structures for high- and low-leverage firms with identical initial values and liquidation values. Each firm defaults when the net present value of its cash flow falls below the face value of its obligations (firm value at default is denoted by the line labeled 'value that triggers default'). The high-leverage firm defaults at a value that is much higher than that for the low-leverage firm. Areas A and B represent the values that would be destroyed if the high- or low-leverage firms, respectively, were liquidated after default. Because liquidation and bankruptcy costs can destroy more value in the high-leverage firm (in other words because area A > area B), the high-leverage firm's claimholders have stronger incentives to reorganize quickly and outside bankruptcy court. In some situations, however, private reorganization is not a viable option. When the firm has a large number of independent and widely scattered claimants, private reorganization is extremely difficult and costly. For example, a retailer with thousands of suppliers or a firm with product-liability problems might find private reorganization impossible. Even in this situation the incentives to resolve financial distress quickly are stronger for the high-leverage firm.

Though the high-leverage firm has a higher trigger value, both firms could have the same value at default if an exogenous shock caused a substantial value reduction. If such exogenous shocks were the primary cause of distress, the theory that debt preserves value by triggering early default would be suspect. Not all financial distress, however, is caused by exogenous shocks. If value declines gradually as the firm's industry deteriorates or as management wastes resources by pursuing a poor strategy, the high-leverage firm defaults at a higher value and the waste and poor strategy are more likely to be eliminated. These causes of decline in value – exogenous shocks, gradual deterioration, and poor management decisionmaking – provide a beginning descriptive taxonomy of the causes of financial distress. The available empirical evidence on both the benefits and costs of distress, and the importance of each of these causes, are discussed below.

4.2. Benefits of financial distress

4.2.1. Changes in management and governance

Poor management decisionmaking and weak governance can lead to financial distress. Incumbent managers and directors can also inhibit a firm's ability to recover if new or special skills are required to turn the firm's performance around. Gilson (1989, 1990) documents changes in top management and boards of directors following financial distress. His sample includes firms whose cumulative three-year stock return is in the bottom 5% of all firms on the NYSE and AMEX. In spite of their poor performance, over half of his sample firms do not default. These firms have an average three-year stock return of −50.2%, whereas the three-year stock return for firms experiencing distress is −68.9%. The nondistressed firms have a 19% annual turnover in top management – somewhat higher than the normal turnover rate of 12% for a random sample of NYSE and AMEX firms [Warner, Watts, and Wruck (1988)]. On the other hand, the distressed firms experience a 52% annual turnover of top management. These results are consistent with the idea that leverage acts as a catalyst for organizational change. Poor stock-price performance is not enough to remove incumbent managers, but financial distress provides a mechanism to initiate top-management changes.

Turnover among directors is also high following distress. Gilson finds that within four years after the onset of financial distress only 47% of old directors still hold their seats. Eight percent of the firms replace their entire board. He also finds that boards of directors are restructured following financial distress; for 60% of his sample firms, the size of the board shrinks following distress. Consistent with a loss of reputation, departing directors subsequently serve on fewer boards.

4.2.2. Changes in organizational strategy and structure

Some firms in financial distress undergo dramatic organizational changes as part of their recovery, refocusing their strategy and undertaking restructurings. Often some assets are sold, while others are reorganized and restaffed. The U.S. steel industry is an example. Increased international competition in steel during the 1980s forced many U.S. steel firms into financial distress. Some firms, such as Wheeling-Pittsburgh, filed under Chapter 11. Others, such as Inland Steel, restructured privately. These firms reduced their fixed obligations and employment, and refocused operations to produce primarily specialty steel products.

Such reorganizations illustrate how financial structure interacts with investment decisions; financial distress forces a change in the firm's economic activities and the way these activities are organized. These restructurings often create value for the firm's claimholders. The same reorganizations probably would have created value before financial distress, but the impetus for change provided by distress was absent. Financial distress can, therefore, force managers to undertake value-increasing organizational changes they would not have otherwise undertaken. For example, in its August 1990 *Preliminary Report on the Financial Condition of the Donald J. Trump Organization Post Restructuring*, the State of New Jersey Department of Law and Public Safety reported that financial distress had forced management to rethink its strategy:

> [financial distress has] created a crisis atmosphere wherein debt service payments cannot now be satisfied out of the operating cash flow and has forced the Company to rethink its entire strategy and capital structure. In this case, excessive debt has acted as a powerful agent for change and, ironically, has served as a brake on management mistakes. It may very well be that the greatest hope for preserving value lies in a quick and efficient reorganization and workout process – a privatized bankruptcy of sorts – outside the courtroom.

Without outside intervention, management often fails to change strategy, or is unaware that the company's strategy is the wrong one. Examples of situations in which financial distress forced managers to refocus, or where the absence of distress allowed managers to preside over a deteriorating firm, illustrate this point. Revco is an example of the former. Shortly after Revco's LBO, a new CEO was appointed who changed the company's strategy from one of 'everyday low prices' to mini-department stores (a cash-intensive strategy change). Revco's stores began carrying television sets and small appliances. The merchandise didn't sell and the strategy was a failure. Within six months the firm defaulted and another new CEO was appointed to change it strategic direction.

Massey Ferguson exemplifies the management of a deteriorating firm in the absence of financial distress. Baldwin and Mason (1983) report that the market value of the company's equity fell from $505 million to $100 million between 1976 and 1980. During this period management closed facilities, laid off employees and sold assets, but made no major change in how the firm was run. Finally, in March 1979, the CEO resigned and a new manager was appointed. In late 1980 the firm began restructuring its claims through a private workout.

When firm value deteriorates as a result of poor management or when firm value is highest in liquidation and management refuses to liquidate, financial distress creates value. But the process of recovering from distress can create value even if the events leading to distress are out of management's control. For example, consider a firm pushed into financial distress by an exogenous shock. The process of recovery provides an opportunity to create value by reassessing the firm's strategy and restructuring its operations. This does not mean that the effects of the shock can be completely reversed, but rather that management can make decisions that improve the firm's depressed state.

4.2.3. Benefits of Chapter 11

In their analysis, Gilson et al. assume that Chapter 11 is always a worse outcome than a private renegotiation. In some special situations, however, the ability to enter Chapter 11 is a valuable alternative for securityholders. For example, trade creditors and claimants in product-liability suits, are numerous and have heterogenous claims. Reaching a private agreement with all of them is very difficult. Under Chapter 11, diffuse creditors can be dealt with as a single class, making negotiation manageable and settling protracted disputes once and for all. For example, before filing under Chapter 11, Manville Corporation faced 20,000 asbestos-related lawsuits and estimated that eventually another 32,000 would be filed. Under Chapter 11, all damage suits were stayed, and present and future asbestos claimants were put in a single class.[13] A.H. Robbins filed under Chapter 11 following liability problems with its Dalkon Shield birth-control device. Other companies, such as Braniff and Eastern Airlines, have filed under Chapter 11 when faced with labor contracts that management viewed as too costly to allow the firm to survive.

---

[13]See Lewin (1990). As part of Manville's reorganization plan, a trust was established to satisfy the claims of asbestos victims. The recent cash crisis in this trust calls into question the ability of Chapter 11 to resolve continuing litigation permanently, since the reorganized company might be required to contribute additional funds to the trust.

Chapter 11 also allows for the issuance of new senior credit, called 'debtor-in-possession financing', which can be crucial to the firm, especially in retail businesses where trade credit is often necessary for survival. Pre-Chapter 11 trade creditors and other unsecured creditors have low priority, coming just before equityholders. Claims of creditors lending to the firm after it files under Chapter 11 are second in priority only to legal and administrative expenses. Distressed firms that require new credit have incentives to file under Chapter 11, and potential creditors have incentives to withhold credit until after the filing. Campeau, for example, was able to secure new credit quickly after it filed under Chapter 11. In less than a month, Campeau obtained a $700 million debtor-in-possession credit facility, $400 million for Federated from Citibank and $300 million for Allied from Chemical Bank.

4.3. Costs of financial distress

4.3.1. Out-of-pocket costs

The out-of-pocket or direct costs of financial distress are the easiest to measure. They include legal, administrative, and advisory fees paid by the company. Data on out-of-pocket costs are available for firms that restructure debt through an exchange offer or that file for bankruptcy. Gilson, John, and Lang (1990) present the only available evidence on the direct costs of private workouts. With a sample of 18 private debt restructurings, they find that the median out-of-pocket cost of restructuring debt through an exchange offer is 0.32% of total assets measured at the fiscal year-end closest to the exchange-offer date.

A number of studies provide evidence on the direct costs of bankruptcy. The findings of four of them are summarized in table 1. Warner (1977a), Altman (1984), and Weiss (1990) all measure direct costs as a percentage of the market value of the firm one year before bankruptcy. They find that direct costs are quite small, averaging between 3% and 4.5% of market value. For firms that liquidate at the end of the bankruptcy process, Ang, Chua, and McConnell (1982) find that out-of-pocket costs are 7.5% of the liquidated value of the firm. The maximum out-of-pocket costs are 6.6% of market value in Weiss' sample and 9.8% in Warner's sample. Comparing the direct costs of private workouts with direct costs of bankruptcy suggests that out-of-pocket costs are almost ten times less when the firm is able to restructure debt privately.[14]

[14]Evidence relating the direct costs of bankruptcy to firm size is contradictory. In his sample of railroads, Warner finds that direct costs as a percentage of market value are inversely related to size. He concludes that there are significant fixed costs of bankruptcy. Ang, Chua, and McConnell (1982) test for and find evidence supporting Warner's results in a sample of smaller firms. Weiss, however, does not find evidence of significant fixed costs. He argues that changes in

Table 1

Summary of evidence on the direct costs of bankruptcy from four studies covering 1933–1986.

Study	Sample selection criteria	Mean cost	As a percent of	Sample period	Sample size
Warner (1977a)	Railroad bankruptcies	4 %	Market value one year before bankruptcy	1933–1955	11
Ang, Chua, and McConnell (1982)	Bankruptcies filed in the western district of Oklahoma [all eventually liquidated]	7.5%	Liquidated value of firms at end of bankruptcy process	1963–1978	55
Altman (1984)	11 retail and 7 industrial firms	4.3%	Market value one year before bankruptcy	1970–1978	18
Weiss (1990)	Bankruptcies filed in: Central CA, Southern FL NY, Northern IL MI OH, District of MA	3.1%	Market value at end of fiscal year before bankruptcy	1980–1986	31

4.3.2. Indirect costs

Indirect costs are opportunity costs imposed on the firm because financial distress affects its ability to conduct business as usual. A distressed firm is hampered on three fronts. First, it loses the right to make certain decisions without legal approval. For example, a firm in Chapter 11 cannot spend money or sell assets without court approval.

Second, financial distress can reduce demand for the firm's product and increase its production costs. Demand falls if the value of the product to consumers depends on the firm's future performance and financial distress threatens the firm's ability to survive. Production costs increase if financial distress affects the firm's ability to negotiate favorable input prices or credit terms. Worried about the distressed firm's ability to pay its debts, suppliers often charge a risk premium through increased prices, tightened credit terms, or poorer service. In addition, it may be difficult to negotiate favorable terms, prices, and service if suppliers begin to view their relationship with the firm as a short-term one. The time that elapses between the first indication of distress and its resolution – a little over a year for private negotiations and a little under two and a half years for bankruptcies [Gilson, John, and Lang (1990) and Weiss (1990)] – indicates these issues can be persistent.

---

the bankruptcy code, new financing techniques, and differences in samples probably explain the differing results.

Third, management spends considerable time resolving financial distress. The value of this time is generally considered an indirect cost, but not all the time is lost. When management is engaged in productive restructuring and in implementing strategic change, it is using its time to increase firm value. Unless the time could have been spent more productively elsewhere, its value should not be considered an indirect cost.

Estimating the indirect costs of financial distress is difficult because the costs represent lost opportunities. Available evidence is very mixed. Altman (1984) estimates the unexpected loss in profits for three years before a Chapter 11 filing for eleven retailing and five industrial firms and uses this loss as a measure of the indirect costs of financial distress. This interpretation is problematic because it is impossible to tell whether the loss in profits is in fact caused by financial distress or whether financial distress is caused by the loss in profits. He finds the sum of direct and indirect costs (loss in profits) averages 8.7% of market value one year before bankruptcy for the retailing firms and 15.0% for the industrial firms. It is not surprising that the loss in profits should be smaller for retailing firms. Industrial firms are more likely to be selling products for which the future availability of service, guarantees, warranties, parts, and support is very important. In contrast to Altman, Kaplan (1989) finds that the Campeau's sales were unharmed by its Chapter 11 filing. He concludes that the indirect costs of distress for this retailer were small.

Cutler and Summers (1988) estimate the indirect costs of Texaco's April 1987 bankruptcy filing using bond and stock-price data. Texaco acquired all of Getty Oil's common stock during a period when Getty had agreed to allow Pennzoil to acquire about 43% of its common stock at a lower price. Because Texaco had agreed to indemnify Getty against all lawsuits, it was liable for damages when Pennzoil sued Getty for breach of contract. The litigation resulted in a court order that Texaco pay Pennzoil $12 billion in damages. After the damages were upheld in appeals court, Texaco filed a Chapter 11 petition. The companies attempted to agree on a settlement amount, but failed until Carl Icahn purchased stock in both companies and helped bring about a final settlement of $3 billion.

The loss in the combined market values of Texaco and Pennzoil across all litigation and settlement events is the sum of the direct and indirect costs of financial distress. Cutler and Summers estimate the abnormal change in market value of debt and equity to be $2.1 billion. (Before Icahn's involvement in the settlement, combined losses in market value were over $3 billion.) Subtracting total legal costs provides an estimate of the indirect costs of financial distress for Texaco. Cutler and Summers estimate the after-tax legal costs for both firms to be $525 million. Subtracting the direct costs from the total loss in value provides an estimate of $1.575 billion in indirect costs. Texaco's market value was approximately $17 billion before the litigation (book value of debt plus market value of equity). Therefore, the indirect costs implied by stock-price changes amount to about 9% of firm value.

4.4. Enforcement of absolute priority under bankruptcy law

According to the absolute priority rule, Chapter 11 reorganization plans must satisfy senior claimants completely before more junior claimants receive anything. The extent to which absolute priority is enforced by bankruptcy courts has implications for the costs of financial distress as well as the pricing of securities; the value of contractually specified priority is negligible if the court does not systematically enforce it. Studies of reorganization plans consistently reveal, however, that absolute priority is not enforced. Warner (1977a, b) studies a sample of railroad bankruptcies between 1926 and 1955. He finds that absolute priority is not enforced and that this fact is reflected in the market prices of the firm's debt securities. In studying how the court determines whether a creditor's claim is satisfied, he finds that accounting face values, not market values, are the basis for comparing old and new securities.

More recent reorganization plans for industrial companies are studied by Franks and Torous (1989) and Weiss (1990). Franks and Torous (1989) study the reorganization plans of 27 firms emerging from bankruptcy between 1971 and 1986. The Bankruptcy Reform Act went into effect in October 1979, so some of their sample firms reorganized under the old Chapter 10 and others under the new Chapter 11. They find that of the 27 plans 78% (21) show deviations from priority, and that in 67% (18) shareholders receive some consideration when more senior claimants are not paid in full.

Evidence on the enforcement of absolute priority under Chapter 11 is presented in Weiss (1990). He studies the reorganization plans of 37 firms filing under Chapter 11 between 1980 and 1986. Each plan states the claims of each creditor class, what each class receives under the plan, and whether a class is 'impaired'. A class of creditors is impaired if its claims are not satisfied in full. If a plan describes a class as unimpaired and the class disagrees, it can protest to the judge who makes the final decision. No rules specify acceptable valuation methods, but in general accounting and not market values are the standard.

To study the violation of priority, Weiss divides claimants into three classes – secured creditors, unsecured creditors, and equityholders – and studies whether absolute priority is enforced by noting which classes are impaired. If a class of claimants is impaired and a more junior class receives any value on its claims, priority is violated. Weiss finds that absolute priority is enforced only 22% of the time. Seventy-eight percent of the reorganization plans violate absolute priority, 70% by giving a valuable claim to equityholders when unsecured creditors are impaired and 8% by giving a valuable claim to equityholders when both secured and unsecured creditors are impaired. The detail on individual firms in Weiss' study shows some surprising outcomes. For example, he finds that the reorganization plans of Imperial Industries and Richton International allowed equityholders to retain 100% of the firm's common stock even though Imperial Industries' unsecured creditors received only 37% of their claims and Richton International's only 60%.

Weiss demonstrates that absolute priority is violated more frequently for relatively large firms and for firms filing in the Southern District of New York. Among the 18 sample firms filing in New York's Southern District, in only one case was absolute priority upheld. New York filings partially explain the results for large firms as well. Of the 20 firms in Weiss's sample with assets over $100 million where priority was violated, 14 filed under Chapter 11 in the Southern District of New York.

4.5. Why deviations from priority arise

The rules governing bankruptcy in the U.S. encourage outcomes that deviate from absolute priority. Two factors are especially important in these outcomes: (i) the rights given to the firm's managers after it has filed for bankruptcy and (ii) the reliance on a consensual voting process, rather than a market process, to reorganize the firm.

The U.S. is one of the few countries that leaves incumbent management in charge of a bankrupt firm.[15] Once the firm is in bankruptcy, not only do managers continue to make operating decisions, but for 120 days after the Chapter 11 filing the managers have an exclusive right to propose a reorganization plan. The court often grants several extensions of this deadline. Management has an additional 180 days from the filing date to obtain creditor and shareholder approval. If the firm fails to propose a plan or has had a plan rejected, creditors can propose their own plan. For creditors to propose a plan, however, they must provide proof of values for claims to be issued and assets to be retained or sold. This requires costly appraisals and hearings. Management need only obtain the judge's agreement that the values assigned under its plan are 'fair and reasonable'. The higher cost to creditors of proposing their own plan, in both time and money, can lead them to accept a plan that results in a lower firm value, i.e., that is inefficient and violates priority.

U.S. bankruptcy rules allow managers to make trade-offs between firm value and their personal well-being at the expense of the firm's claimholders. For example, if liquidation is the highest-valued strategy, it is hard to imagine managers proposing it, because they would lose their jobs. In addition, it

---

[15]See 'Bankruptcy Law: A Sticky End', The Economist, February 24, 1990, pp. 77–78.

becomes difficult for claimants to fire managers because the judge must approve the decision. In light of the information and incentive problems mentioned earlier, it is clear that granting hiring and firing rights to shareholders or creditors is not a solution. A claimant class prefers managers that further its interests over managers that maximize value. It is hard to believe, however, that a bankruptcy judge is most qualified to make hiring and firing decisions.

Chapter 11's consensual reorganization process allows both impaired creditors and shareholders to vote on a plan. Because only impaired creditor classes and shareholders vote, the plan determines who votes and which claimants vote together. Acceptance of a plan generally requires approval by all impaired creditor classes and shareholders. For each impaired class, acceptance of a plan requires the approval of two-thirds in amount and a majority in number of the claims voted. For equityholders, two-thirds of the shares voted must favor the plan. The court can 'cram-down' a reorganization plan, however, even if some impaired creditor classes or shareholders refuse to approve it, if it views the plan as fair and equitable to all impaired classes. This is generally interpreted as meaning that claimholders receive at least what they would have received in liquidation [Altman (1983, pp. 13 – 31)].

Granting shareholders the right to vote gives them power to transfer value from creditors. For example, if the firm is insolvent on a stock basis, there is no value left for shareholders after creditors are paid. The right to vote and to hold up the process allows shareholders to extract valuable claims. On the other hand, excluding shareholders from the voting implies that, if the firm were insolvent on a flow basis only, creditors would be overcompensated because they would be awarded the entire value of the firm.

Information and incentive problems could be solved if a reliable third-party estimate of firm value could be obtained. Were firm value known, the court could distribute it to claimants in order of priority. As discussed earlier, creditor, shareholder, and management estimates are unreliable. Easterbrook (1990) suggests that if the market for distressed corporate assets is not too thin, auctioning the firm's assets to a third party and distributing the proceeds to claimholders would improve the efficiency of the U.S. bankruptcy process. Holding an auction that allowed the firm's claimholders to bid would quickly eliminate the opportunistic value estimates promoted by the current bankruptcy process; to back up an estimate each group would have to put its own money on the table. The winning bidder would decide whether to keep the incumbent management team. In some countries, such as Germany, bankrupt companies are auctioned routinely. The U.S. legal system, however, refuses to rely on markets to determine values. Out-of-court workouts can circumvent some of the problems with Chapter 11 but, as mentioned earlier, recent court decisions are discouraging this activity.

5. Conclusions

Financial distress affects more than the firm's financial structure. It triggers a process of organizational change that has the potential to create value for the firm's claimholders. The costs of financial distress must be weighed against the benefits to determine its net effect on the organization's claimholders. Direct costs of financial distress average 3.5% of market value. Estimates of indirect costs are less reliable, but evidence to date indicates they lie in the range of 9% to 15% of market value. Financial distress triggers changes in management and governance. Although the benefits of distress have not yet been quantified, turnover in top management and changes in governance indicate that corporate insiders are disciplined for poor performance. Evidence from clinical studies and case studies documents changes in strategy and organizational structure following financial distress that are consistent with a process of corporate revitalization.

The legal rules of the game in bankruptcy create conflicts of interest among claimholders. The conflicts lead to complex information and inference problems for claimholders trying to value a distressed firm. These problems can be solved by encouraging the development of a liquid market for distressed companies' assets and allowing bankrupt firms to be auctioned. Other countries, such as Germany, have successfully developed such systems. In the absence of the legal system's willingness to rely on markets, the information and incentive problems associated with Chapter 11 can be attenuated by encouraging private workouts. Creating an environment friendly to workouts helps firms avoid Chapter 11 and allows actors in financial markets to play a role in resolving distress. Unfortunately, recent court decisions suggest the U.S. is moving away from, rather than toward, this solution. New tax laws further damage distressed companies. The 1990 tax act imposes new taxes on troubled companies by, among other things, making it more difficult to structure nontaxable exchange offers and making debt forgiveness taxable to the firm. The result will be more bankruptcy filings.

Management can affect the difficulty of recontracting through its financing decisions. A financial structure that aligns the interests of various claimholders, for example strip financing where creditors hold equity, reduces incentives for claimants to jockey for advantage in the event of distress. Financial structures in which creditors hold equity are common in Japan and Germany, and in both of these countries financial distress is generally resolved through private workouts.

Finally, it is important to consider whether there is a value-maximizing way to avoid distress entirely. Arbitrarily reducing leverage will succeed in avoiding distress, but is unlikely to results in value maximization. Both tax benefits and the organizational and incentive benefits of leverage would be lost. Rather the solution lies in aligning the interests of management with the interests of the firm's shareholders. The firm's financing policy, governance structure, and compensation policies can all be used to bring about this solution.

References

Altman, Edward I., 1968, Financial ratios, discriminant analysis and the prediction of corporate bankruptcy, Journal of Finance 23, 589–609.

Altman, Edward I., 1983, Corporate financial distress (Wiley, New York, NY).

Altman, Edward I., 1984, A further empirical investigation of the bankruptcy cost question, Journal of Finance 39, 1067–1089.

Altman, Edward I., 1990, Investing in distressed securities, The Altman/Foothilll report on the anatomy of defaulted debt and equities.

Ang, James S., Jess H. Chua, and John J. McConnell, 1982, The administrative costs of corporate bankruptcy: A note, Journal of Finance 37, 219–226.

Baker, George P. and Karen H. Wruck, 1989, Organizational changes and value creation in leveraged buyouts: The case of the O.M. Scott & Sons Company, Journal of Financial Economics 24, 163–190.

Baldwin, Carliss Y. and Scott P. Mason, 1983, The resolution of claims in financial distress: The case of Massey Ferguson, Journal of Finance 38, 505–523.

Bankruptcy law: A sticky end, The Economist, February 24, 1990, 77–78.

Beaver, William H., 1966, Financial ratios as predictors of failures, Empirical Research in Accounting, Supplement to Journal of Accounting Research, 71–111.

Beck, Susan, 1990, Revco in ruins, The American Lawyer, June, 56–64.

Berman, Adam M., Michael C. Jensen, Mark Wolsey-Paige, and Karen H. Wruck, Revco D.S. Incorporated, Harvard Business School case study 9-190-202 (Harvard University, Cambridge, MA).

Brealey, Richard A. and Stewart C. Myers, 1988, Principles of corporate finance, 3rd ed. (McGraw-Hill, New York, NY).

Burkhardt, Willey, Michael C. Jensen, and Brian Barry, Wisconsin Central Ltd. Railroad and Berkshire Partners (A) and (B), Harvard Business School case study 9-190-062, 9-190-070 (Harvard University, Cambridge, MA).

Cheung, Rayner, Joseph C. Bencivenga, and Frank J. Fabozzi, 1990, Original issue high yield bonds: Total returns and historical default experience 1977–1989, Working paper (Massachusetts Institute of Technology, Cambridge, MA).

Cutler, David M., and Lawrence H. Summers, 1988, The costs of conflict resolution and financial distress: Evidence from the Texaco–Pennzoil litigation, Rand Journal of Economics 19, no. 2, 157–172.

Easterbrook, Frank H., 1990, Is corporate bankruptcy efficient?, Journal of Financial Economics, this volume.

Franks, Julian R. and Walter N. Torous, 1989, an empirical investigation of U.S. firms in reorganization, Journal of Finance 44, 747–779.

Gilson, Stuart C., 1989, Management turnover and financial distress, Journal of Financial Economics 25, 241–262.

Gilson, Stuart C., 1990, Bankruptcy, boards, banks, and blockholders, Journal of Financial Economics, this volume.

Gilson, Stuart C., Kose John, and Larry H.P. Lang, 1990, Troubled debt restructurings, Journal of Financial Economics, this volume.

Harlan, Christi, 1990, Eastern Airlines' creditors seek sales proceeds, Wall Street Journal, May 18, B 11.

Hite, Gailen L., James E. Owers, and Ronald C. Rogers, 1987, The market for interfirm asset sales: Partial sell-offs and total liquidations, Journal of Financial Economics 18, 229–252.

Hoshi, Takeo, Anil Kashyap, and David Scharfstein, 1990, Troubled debt restructurings, Journal of Financial Economics, this volume.

Jensen, Michael C., 1986, Agency costs of free cash flow, corporate finance and takeovers, American Economic Review 76, 323–329.

Jensen, Michael C., 1989, The eclipse of the public corporation, Harvard Business Review, Sept.–Oct., 61–74.

Kaplan, Steven N., 1989a, Campeau's acquisition of Federated: Value added or destroyed, Journal of Financial Economics 25, 191–212.

Kaplan, Steven N., 1989b, The effects of management buyouts on operating performance and value, Journal of Financial Economics 24, 217–254.

Kaplan, Steven N. and Jeremy C. Stein, 1990, How risky is the debt in highly leveraged transactions? Evidence from public recapitalizations, Journal of Financial Economics, this volume.

Lewin, Tamar, 1982, The legal issues in Manville's move, New York Times, August 27, D 1, 6.

Morse, Dale and Wayne Shaw, 1988, Investing in bankrupt firms, Journal of Finance 43, 1193–1206.

Preliminary report on the financial condition of the Donald J. Trump organization post-restructuring, Public report by the State of New Jersey Department of Law and Public Safety, August 1990.

Prowse, Stephen D., 1990, Institutional investment patterns and corporate financial behavior in the U.S. and Japan, Journal of Financial Economics, this volume.

Roe, Mark J., 1990, Legal restraints on ownership and control of public companies, Journal of Financial Economics, this volume.

Smith, Abbie, 1990, Corporate ownership structure and performance: The case of management buyouts, Journal of Financial Economics, this volume.

Titman, Sheridan, 1984, The effect of capital structure on a firm's liquidation decision, Journal of Financial Economics 13, 137–151.

Verma, Kiran, Inland Steel Industries, Inc, Harvard Business School case study 9-188-040 (Harvard University, Cambridge, MA).

Warner, Jerold B., 1977a, Bankruptcy costs: Some evidence, Journal of Finance 32, 337–347.

Warner, Jerold B., 1977b, Bankruptcy and the pricing of risky debt, Journal of Financial Economics 4, 39–276.

Warner, Jerold B., Ross L. Watts, and Karen H. Wruck, 1988, Stock-price performance and top-management changes, Journal of Financial Economics 20, 461–492.

Weiss, Lawrence A., 1990, Priority of claims and ex post re-contracting in bankruptcy, Journal of Financial Economics, this volume.

White, Michelle J., 1980, Public policy toward bankruptcy: Me-first and other priority rules, Bell Journal of Economics 11, 550–564.

White, Michelle J., 1983, Bankruptcy costs and the new bankruptcy code, Journal of Finance 38, 477–504.

Wruck, Karen H., Sealed Air Corporation's leveraged recapitalization, Harvard Business School case study 9-391-067 (Harvard University, Cambridge, MA).

Troubled debt restructurings

An empirical study of private reorganization of firms in default*

Stuart C. Gilson

The University of Texas at Austin, Austin, TX 78712, USA

Kose John and Larry H.P. Lang

New York University, New York, NY 10003, USA

Received November 1989, final version received May 1990

This study investigates the incentives of financially distressed firms to restructure their debt privately rather than through formal bankruptcy. In a sample of 169 financially distressed companies, about half successfully restructure their debt outside of Chapter 11. Firms more likely to restructure their debt privately have more intangible assets, owe more of their debt to banks, and owe fewer lenders. Analysis of stock returns suggests that the market is also able to discriminate *ex ante* between the two sets of firms, and that stockholders are systematically better off when debt is restructured privately.

1. Introduction

With the proliferation of leveraged buyouts (LBOs) and other highly leveraged transactions, there has been growing popular concern that the corporate sector is being burdened with too much debt. Much of this concern

*We would like to thank Edward Altman, Yakov Amihud, Sugato Bhattacharya, Keith Brown, Robert Bruner, T. Ronald Casper, Charles D'Ambrosio, Larry Dann, Oliver Hart, Gailen Hite, Max Holmes, Scott Lee, Gershon Mandelker, Scott Mason, Robert Merton, Wayne Mikkelson, Megan Partch, Ramesh Rao, Roy Smith, Chester Spatt, Gopala Vasudevan, and Richard West for their helpful comments. We are especially grateful to Michael Jensen (the editor) and Karen Wruck (the referee) for their many detailed and thoughtful suggestions. This paper has also benefited from the comments of participants at the 1989 American Economic Association Meetings, the conference on 'The Structure of Governance of Enterprise' at the Harvard Business School, and seminars at Dartmouth College, the Harvard Business School, the University of Oregon, and the University of Pittsburgh. The second author acknowledges support from the Yamaichi Faculty Fellowship and the Garn Institute of Finance.

Journal of Financial Economics 27 (1990) 315–353. North-Holland

is founded in the belief that highly levered firms could default in large numbers in a major recession (*Wall Street Journal*, 25 October 1988). At issue is whether corporate default is costly, and whether, as recently suggested by Jensen (1989a, b), private contractual arrangements for resolving default represent a viable (and less costly) alternative to the legal remedies provided by Chapter 11.

This study investigates the incentives of financially distressed firms to choose between private renegotiation and Chapter 11. We analyze the experience of 169 publicly traded companies that experienced severe financial distress during 1978–1987. Our investigation yields a number of insights into the corporate debt restructuring decision. In about half of all cases, financially distressed firms successfully restructure their debt outside of Chapter 11. Financial distress is more likely to be resolved through private renegotiation when more of the firm's assets are intangible, and relatively more debt is owed to banks; private negotiation is less likely to succeed when there are more distinct classes of debt outstanding.

An analysis of common stock returns provides complementary evidence on firms' incentives to settle out of court. Abnormal stock-price performance suggests stockholders generally fare better under private renegotiation than bankruptcy. In advance of the outcome, the market appears to be able to identify which firms are more likely to succeed at restructuring their debt outside of Chapter 11.

Finally, we present detailed descriptive evidence of how debt is restructured outside of bankruptcy. Previous empirical research in corporate financial distress has dealt largely with formal reorganization in Chapter 11. Detailed case analyses of selected firms in our sample provide additional insights into firms' incentives to choose between private renegotiation and Chapter 11.

The study is organized as follows. Section 2 discusses firms' incentives to choose between private renegotiation and bankruptcy as alternative mechanisms for dealing with default. Section 3 describes the data and methodology. Section 4 presents the empirical analysis of troubled debt restructurings. Section 5 concludes with a summary of the results. The appendix presents ten detailed case studies of firms that attempted to restructure their debt privately.

2. Corporate default and debt restructuring

A firm that must restructure the terms of its debt contracts to remedy or avoid default is faced with two choices; it can either file for bankruptcy or attempt or renegotiate with its creditors privately in a 'workout'. The alternatives are similar in that relief from default is obtained when creditors consent to exchange their impaired claims for new securities in the firm. Sometimes this exchange is implicit, as when the terms of a debt contract are modified.

If bankruptcy is the alternative to private renegotiation, then firms' incentives to settle with creditors out of court, and the settlement terms, will reflect the legal and institutional constraints of the bankruptcy process. The remainder of this section briefly describes relevant bankruptcy law, and identifies some important economic factors that affect the choice between bankruptcy and private debt renegotiation.

2.1. Rules and procedures of bankruptcy

For most companies, bankruptcy practices are governed by Chapter 11 of the U.S. Bankruptcy Code (henceforth, the 'Code'). Filings under Chapter 11 are treated as corporate reorganizations, and the bankrupt firm is expected to continue as a going concern after leaving bankruptcy. To protect the firm from creditor harassment while it tries to reorganize, Chapter 11 imposes an automatic stay that prevents creditors from collecting on their debt or foreclosing on their collateral until the firm leaves bankruptcy.[1]

In Chapter 11, an exchange of securities is formally proposed in a reorganization plan. The plan assigns claimholders to various classes, and a separate exchange is proposed for each class. All claims placed within a given class must be substantially similar. Thus, for example, trade debt might be placed in one class, secured bank debt in another, and so forth, although finer partitioning of claims is possible.

The value of new securities distributed to any class is in principle determined by the absolute priority rule, under which each creditor class is compensated for the face value of its prebankruptcy claims only after all other classes designated as senior are paid in full. Franks and Torous (1989), Eberhart et al. (1990), and Weiss (1990) show that significant deviations from absolute priority occur in practice. All three studies document cases where stockholders participate in a reorganization plan that provides for less than full payment of senior claims.

The filing firm, or debtor, has the exclusive right to propose the first plan. If this plan is not filed within 120 days of the initial Chapter 11 filing, or accepted by creditors within 60 additional days, any claimholder class can propose its own plan. Acceptance of the plan requires an affirmative vote by a majority (two-thirds in value and one-half in number) of the claimholders in each impaired class. To break deadlocks, the court can unilaterally impose or 'cram down' the plan on dissenting classes if the plan is 'fair and

---

[1]Alternatively, firms can elect to liquidate by filing under Chapter 7 of the Code. Before the Code was enacted on October 1, 1979, bankruptcy practices were governed by the Bankruptcy Act, under which corporations could choose to either liquidate under Chapter VII, or reorganize under Chapters X or XI. Filing for Chapter 11 is not always the exclusive right of stockholders. Creditors may file an 'involuntary' Chapter 11 petition, if they can demonstrate that the firm has been delinquent in making payments on its debt. Following a default, creditors can generally accelerate full payment on their debt after 30 days have elapsed, thus giving the firm little option but to file for bankruptcy.

equitable' – that is, if the market value of new securities distributed to each class under the plan at least equals what the class would receive a liquidation. In practice, cram-downs are extremely rare [Klee (1979)]. It is in the joint interest of all classes to avoid a cram-down, because application of the fair and equitable standard requires the court to determine the firm's liquidation value and going-concern value in a special hearing. These hearings are considered extremely time-consuming and costly. Avoidance of cram-down also explains observed deviations from absolute priority, since classes that receive nothing under the plan (including stockholders) are deemed not to have accepted the plan, giving creditors an incentive to voluntarily relinquish part of their claims.

Chapter 11 also provides for the appointment of committees to represent the interests of certain claimholder classes before the court. Committees normally consist of the seven largest members of a particular class who are willing to serve, and are empowered to hire legal counsel and other professional help. Committees' operating expenses are paid out of the bankrupt firm's assets. Appointment of a committee of unsecured creditors is mandatory in Chapter 11 cases; additional committees can be appointed to represent other classes, including stockholders, at the discretion of the judge [DeNatale (1981)].

2.2. Determinants of the choice between bankruptcy and private renegotiation

Whether financial distress is resolved through bankruptcy or private renegotiation depends on two factors. First, stockholders and creditors will collectively benefit from settling out of court when private renegotiation generates lower costs than bankruptcy. Under the lower-cost alternative, the resulting value of the firm will be higher, and the firm's claims can be restructured on terms that leave each of the original claimholders better off. Claimholders' incentives to settle privately will increase with the size of the potential cost savings from recontracting outside of Chapter 11. Second, the lower-cost alternative will be adopted only if claimholders can agree on how to share the cost savings. Attempts to settle privately are more likely to fail when individual creditors have stronger incentives to hold out for more favorable treatment under the debt restructuring plan.

The remainder of the section develops this simple economic model of the corporate debt-restructuring decision, and derives empirical proxies for firms' incentives to restructure their debt privately.[2]

---

[2]Previous empirical studies of out-of-court restructuring include Gilson (1989, 1990), who analyzes changes in corporate ownership and governance structure during financial distress, and Hoshi et al. (1990), who investigate the resolution of financial distress in Japan. Previous theoretical research into the choice between bankruptcy and private renegotiation includes

2.2.1. Relative cost of formal bankruptcy versus private renegotiation

Although attempts have been made to measure the costs of Chapter 11 empirically [Warner (1977b), Ang et al. (1982), Altman (1984), Weiss (1990)], we currently know little about how these costs compare with the costs of private renegotiation. In analyzing the costs of financial distress, it has become common to distinguish between direct and indirect costs. Direct costs are out-of-pocket transactions cost (such as charges for legal and investment banking services). Indirect costs include all other costs related to the firm's bankruptcy or debt restructuring. For example, managers may forego profitable investment opportunities because they are distracted by dealings with creditors or the bankruptcy court. Indirect costs also include the value of managers' time spent in such dealings.

It is widely believed among practitioners that direct costs are significantly higher for bankruptcy than private renegotiation, because the procedural demands and legal complexity of Chapter 11 result in inflated lawyers' fees [Stein (1989)]. Formal legal motions must be drafted and argued before the bankruptcy judge at each step of the reorganization. An inordinate amount of time may be required to make any decision that lies outside the ordinary course of the firm's business.[3] When debt is restructured privately, legal costs are reduced because such decisions can be made more quickly. In addition, bankruptcy lawyers have an incentive to prolong the firm's stay in Chapter 11, because their compensation is treated as a priority claim, which entitles them to be paid before any of the firm's general unsecured creditors or shareholders. These arguments suggest that indirect costs (as measured by the expenditure of managers' time) are also higher for bankruptcy than for private renegotiation.

The relative cost disadvantage of bankruptcy is offset by two factors. First, the Code's automatic stay provision ameliorates the common pool problem inherent in distressed situations, by imposing a well-defined queuing order on creditors (who would otherwise rush to be first in line to collect payment on

---

Haugen and Senbet (1978), Bulow and Shoven (1978), White (1983), Aivazian and Callen (1983), Green and Laffont (1987), Roe (1987), Kahn and Huberman (1988), Brown (1989), Giammarino (1989), Hart and Moore (1989), and Mooradian (1989). Much of this research views the firm's bankruptcy decision as the outcome of a strategic game played between stockholders and creditors. An analogous problem is addressed in the 'theory of litigation', which analyzes the choice faced by plaintiffs and defendants between settling out of court or going to trial [Gould (1973)].

[3] For example, if a debtor wishes to retain the services of an investment bank, it must first file an application with the bankruptcy court. Applications can be made only after appropriate 'notice and hearing' has been given, which requires the firm to inform all creditors of the application in writing, and allow sufficient time for any objections to be filed. The court rules on the application at a special hearing. The time required for approval can be shortened if the debtor requires creditors to show cause, allowing the application to be approved within a few days if no objections are raised.

their debt and seize collateral). Such activity will be wasteful if it results in costly duplication of effort or creates additional distraction for management [Jackson (1986)].

Second, firms in Chapter 11 can grant new lenders superpriority status, or a security interest equal or senior to that of existing debt (also known as debtor-in-possession financing). In the absence of this provision, firm value could be reduced because stockholders have an incentive to underinvest in positive-NPV projects that enrich senior claimholders [Myers (1977), Smith and Warner (1979)]. In principle, an equivalent provision could be negotiated among creditors and stockholders privately; however, senior creditors would have to voluntarily consent to subordinate their claims. The option to grant new lenders superpriority status will be especially valuable for firms that are in need of short-term trade financing and have few free assets to pledge as security.

Data limitations preclude direct measurement of relative recontracting costs (see section 3). In the following analysis, we assume that firms and creditors expect private renegotiation to be less costly than bankruptcy. Empirical justification for this assumption is provided in section 4, although we recognize that bankruptcy will dominate private renegotiation for some firms. The importance of relative recontracting costs is assessed by relating the firm's choice of recontracting method (i.e., private or legal) to a variable that measures cross-sectional variation in this assumed cost difference.

Such a test requires us to discriminate among firms on the basis of their expected cost savings from settling privately. This forced us to exclude certain costs (for example, legal fees and management's time costs) for which we were unable to find suitable empirical proxies. The cost that we use to test our model is the destruction of going-concern value that occurs when assets are sold to pay down debt and remedy default [Jensen (1989a, b)]. This loss of value will be greater for intangible assets and assets that generate firm-specific rents (e.g., growth opportunities, managerial firm-specific human capital, monopoly power, and operating synergies whose value depends on the firm's assets being kept together). If, as argued below, assets are more likely to be sold when debt is restructured in Chapter 11 rather than privately, then Chapter 11 will be relatively most costly for firms whose assets are more intangible or firm-specific. We measure the potential loss of going-concern value due to asset sales by the ratio of the firm's market value to the replacement cost of its assets; replacement cost approximates what the firm's assets could be sold for piecemeal. Firms with a higher market value/replacement cost ratio will be more likely to restructure their debt privately, because Chapter 11 is relatively more costly for such firms.

For several reasons, assets are more likely to be sold when debt is restructured in Chapter 11 rather than privately. First, automatic stay gives the debtor more power over the disposition of the firm's assets, by enjoining creditors from exercising their nonbankruptcy right to sue the firm and seize collateral. Asset sales that would normally be in violation of the firm's debt covenants will be allowed if the firm can convince the bankruptcy judge that such sales are necessary for the continued operation of the business.

Second, since the debtor can undermine the value of lenders' collateral and grant new lenders superpriority standing, fully secured lenders will in general prefer liquidation over reorganization. This may create additional pressure for asset sales in bankruptcy. In Chapter 11, creditors can initiate asset sales by 'making a motion to sell assets' before the court. In addition, Chapter 11 cases can be converted into Chapter 7 liquidations. Although conversion to Chapter 7 occurs for only about 5% of the bankruptcies that we examine, other studies have found much higher rates of liquidation. For a sample of Chapter 11 filings in the Southern District of New York (including nonpublic firms), White (1989) finds that about one-third either end up in Chapter 7 or as liquidating reorganizations.

Finally, purchasing assets from a financially distressed firm is less risky in Chapter 11, because asset sales are executed by a court order and are thus free from legal challenge. In addition, assets that are purchased from an insolvent firm that subsequently files for Chapter 11 may have to be returned as a 'voidable preference' or 'fraudulent transfer'. Given the costs incurred if an asset sale is later challenged or cancelled, potential purchasers of an asset will prefer to deal with firms in Chapter 11.

2.2.2. Factors affecting creditors' willingness to settle outside of Chapter 11

Even if stockholders and creditors believe that their combined wealth will be higher if debt is restructured outside of Chapter 11, negotiations can break down if particular creditors hold out for more generous terms. The severity of the holdout problem will depend on the voting rules for determining acceptance of the plan, the number of creditors who participate in the plan, and the type of debt that is restructured (bank loans, publicly traded debt, etc.). In addition, creditors may withhold their consent from a restructuring plan if they dispute the value of the new securities being offered under the plan.

Adopting a debt restructuring plan outside of bankruptcy generally requires the unanimous consent of all creditors whose claims are in default. Impaired creditors who are excluded from the plan can accelerate payment of their claims, or force the firm into bankruptcy by filing an involuntary Chapter 11 petition. Cross-default provisions in the firm's debt contracts will increase the proportion of creditors who participate in the plan. Thus in a typical workout the potential holdout problem is quite severe because of the veto power held by individual creditors. This problem is less severe in Chapter 11, where approval for a reorganization plan is required only from a specified majority of the creditors in each class of claims, and dissenting classes can be forced to comply with the plan under the Code's cram-down provision.

We hypothesize that the holdout problem is more severe (and the probability of successful private renegotiation, lower) when relatively more creditors are allowed to participate in the restructuring plan. An increase in the number of total votes to be cast increases the probability that at least one of the votes will be negative. Reasoning along similar lines, Smith and Warner (1979) conjecture that private negotiation of debt will be easier when the debt is privately placed (and owed to fewer lenders). On the other hand, having fewer creditors could result in more frequent bargaining deadlocks, if smallness of numbers causes individual creditors to feel more powerful and perceive greater dollar benefits to holding out. When there are few creditors – as in any bilateral bargaining situation involving few buyers and sellers – mutually beneficial trades will not always take place. If a negotiated solution is not forthcoming, the only way to break the deadlock may be to file for bankruptcy.

A related consideration is the heterogeneity of the firm's financial claims, or the complexity of its capital structure. Firms with more complex capital structures are hypothesized to succeed less often at restructuring their debt privately. The more that creditors' claims differ in seniority rights, security, and other features, the more likely different claims are to be treated differently under any proposal restructuring plan (in the package of new securities offered to holders of each type of claim). As a result, there may be greater disagreement over whether the plan is equitable in its treatment of different claims. In practice, inter-creditor disputes are extremely common, even among creditors who hold the same general type of security (for example, members of a bank lending consortium).

Achieving a consensus among creditors outside of bankruptcy will also depend upon what type of debt is being restructured. The holdout problem is especially severe for publicly traded bonds. Under the Trust Indenture Act of 1939, firms are prohibited from changing any of the 'core' terms of the bond indenture (the principal amount, interest rate, or stated maturity) unless every bondholder gives his/her consent. Although only a simple or two-thirds majority is generally required to change other covenants in the bond, amendment of the core terms is often critical to resolving financial distress.

As a result, restructuring of publicly traded debt almost always takes the form of an exchange offer. In return for tendering their old bonds, bondholders receive a package of new securities (often including some form of equity) that offers a lower cash payout. Since participation in the offer is voluntary, bondholders will have incentives to hold out if their individual tendering decision has little impact on whether the offer is successful; such incentives will be stronger when the bonds are more widely held. To encourage bondholders to tender, exchange offers are structured to penalize holdouts. The new bonds are generally more senior, and mature sooner, than the old bonds. In addition, holders can be asked to jointly tender their bonds and vote for the elimination of protective covenants in the old bonds; for this reason the success of an exchange offer is often conditional on a stipulated voting majority of bonds being tendered.

In our sample, publicly traded debt is always restructured through exchange offers. These offers are typically completed in under two months. This time can be further reduced if the firm qualifies under Section 3(a)(9) of the 1933 Securities Act for an exemption from ordinary registration requirements for any new securities issued under the offer. These so-called 3(a)(9) offers were pioneered by Drexel Burnham Lambert in the early 1980s. A company will generally qualify to make such an exchange if it is not paying anyone to solicit the exchange, and if both new and old securities involved in the offer have the same issuer. These offers can be made by any firm that qualifies, even if it is not financially distressed. Over the period 1981–1986, approximately 30% of the 184 offers for which Drexel served as advisor were made by financially distressed companies. Currently, virtually all exchange offers made by distressed companies are structured as 3(a)(9) offers.

Bankruptcy practitioners assert that attempts to settle outside of Chapter 11 are more likely to succeed when relatively less debt is owed to trade creditors, and more is owed to bank lenders. The holdout problem is particularly severe for trade debt because the number of trade creditors is often quite large, and their claims are relatively heterogeneous, precluding the use of exchange offers to restructure this debt in the same manner as publicly traded bonds. Securing a consensus among trade creditors is also thought to be more difficult because they tend to be 'acrimonious' and 'unsophisticated'. By similar reasoning, private renegotiation is less likely to succeed when the firm has significant contingent liabilities, such as those arising from product liability suits, where individual tort claims can number in the tens of thousands. Bank lenders, in contrast, tend to be more sophisticated and fewer in number than other kinds of lenders, and are more amenable to settling outside of Chapter 11 [Stein (1989)]. Similar arguments would seem to apply to insurance companies that hold privately placed debt.

Finally, creditors' consent to a restructuring plan will be harder to obtain when there is greater asymmetry in the information used by stockholders and creditors to value the firm. Through their control over the supply of such information, stockholders have incentives to influence creditors' perception of firm value to gain more favorable terms in the restructuring plan. DeAngelo et al. (1990) present evidence that is consistent with financially distressed firms using accounting accruals to influence their negotiations with bank lenders. Since rational creditors are aware of stockholders' incentives to misstate the value of the firm, private renegotiation may fail because of the resulting 'lemons' problem. In Chapter 11, stockholders have a much smaller information advantage over creditors. Firms are required to make extensive, regular disclosures of their financial and operating data to the court. Additional information is contained in the court testimony of expert witnesses and management, and creditors can exercise their 'rights of discovery' to require additional disclosures from the debtor. Any continuing disputes over value can be arbitrated by the court.

We use three variables as proxies for the severity of the holdout problem. First, troubled debt is more likely to be restructured outside Chapter 11 when there are fewer creditors. Second, debt is more likely to be restructured privately when relatively more of the debt is privately held by banks and insurance companies. In addition to the reasons discussed above, bank and insurance company debt is hypothesized to have this effect because such debt reduces the amount of information asymmetry between stockholders and creditors. Since these lenders are generally few in number, they have stronger incentives to monitor the firm than other kinds of creditors. Also, privately placed debt typically includes more financial covenants than other types of debt; even when firms are fully in compliance with these covenants, more information is implicitly revealed about firms' financial and operating characteristics.

Finally, holdouts by junior creditors will be less common when the firm's market value is high in relation to the replacement cost of its assets. As discussed in section 2.2.1, more going-concern value is dissipated in bankruptcy than in private workouts when more of the firm's assets are sold in bankruptcy. Junior creditors' position in the absolute priority ranking ensures that they bear most of this cost, and they will offer less resistance to any proposed restructuring plan. Thus, firms with a higher market value/replacement cost ratio will be more likely to restructure their debt outside of Chapter 11.

2.3. 'Prepackaged' Chapter 11

The preceding analysis is based on a simple dichotomy between bankruptcy and private renegotiation. However, the Code also permits firms to make a 'prepackaged' Chapter 11 filing, in which the bankruptcy petition and reorganization plan are filed together. Terms of the plan are negotiated in advance between the firm and its creditors, and a vote is taken almost immediately.[4]

---

[4]Under section 1126(b) of the Code, any claimholder who accepts or rejects a reorganization plan that is proposed prior to filing for Chapter 11 is deemed also to have accepted or rejected the plan for purposes of plan confirmation, provided that the debtor has disclosed all relevant information for making an informed decision as provided under nonbankruptcy law.

Prepackaged Chapter 11 is thus a hybrid of conventional bankruptcy and private renegotiation that incorporates certain features of each recontracting alternative. In practice, successful prepackaged filings are extremely rare. Although prepackaged filings can significantly reduce the time that firms spend in court and obviate the need for costly creditors' committees, disputes involving the plan are still possible after filing. We were informed by a professional bankruptcy consultant that only 5% to 10% of the largest bankruptcies begin as prepackaged filings, and that fewer than half of these are successful (the original plan is accepted). Only one firm in the sample made a prepackaged Chapter 11 filing [see the case of Crystal Oil in the appendix]. The company spent a total of only three months in bankruptcy, compared with a median of eighteen months for all bankrupt firms in the sample.

3. Data and sample selection

Although identifying bankrupt firms is fairly straightforward, there are few legal or institutional guideposts for deciding what constitutes a debt restructuring. In contrast to Chapter 11 cases, most debt restructurings do not have a well-defined beginning or ending date. Restructuring rarely begins or ends with a formal public announcement, and no special documents have to be filed with any government agency. Information about the restructuring disclosed in normal Securities and Exchange Commission (SEC) filings often lacks detail. Sometimes the same debt is restructured on a number of successive occasions, or different classes of debt are restructured concurrently as separate transactions.

This study uses the same sampling procedure and definition of a debt restructuring as Gilson (1989, 1990). This definition emphasizes the economic similarities between Chapter 11 and private renegotiation as alternative mechanisms for dealing with financial distress. A firm is financially distressed if it has insufficient cash flows to meet the payments on its debt. To avoid or remedy a default, the firm must reduce or defer the payments, or replace the debt with securities having residual rather than fixed payoffs. Consistent with this simple intuition, a debt restructuring is defined as a transaction in which an existing debt contract is replaced by a new contract, with one of the following consequences: (i) required interest or principal payments on the debt are reduced; (ii) the maturity of the debt is extended; or (iii) creditors are given equity securities (common stock or securities convertible into common stock). In addition, the restructuring must be undertaken in response to an anticipated or actual default. This last requirement ensures that the sample includes only restructurings that are undertaken by financially distressed firms. As reported later in table 3, approximately two-thirds of sampled firms that privately restructure their debt are in default at some point during their restructuring.[5]

A debt restructuring is assumed to take place over the interval defined by the first and last reference to the restructuring in the *Wall Street Journal* (*WSJ*), unless more accurate dates are available from other sources. Event-study tests undertaken below measure stock returns in relation to these two dates. If a firm restructures its debt in several discrete periods, these are treated as a single restructuring transaction if less than a year separates adjoining periods. A debt restructuring plan is considered successful if the firm does not file for bankruptcy within a year of the last reference to the restructuring.[6] Consistent with the joint reorganization of claims under Chapter 11, concurrent restructuring of the firm's publicly traded and privately placed debt is treated as a single debt restructuring.

This study analyzes a sample of 169 exchange-listed companies that were in severe financial distress during 1978–1987; 80 firms privately restructured their debt, and 89 firms filed for Chapter 11. Selection of the sample was a two-step process. First, for a given year, firms listed on the New York and American Stock Exchanges were ranked by unadjusted common stock returns at year-end (cumulated over three years), and a stratum was formed consisting of those firms in the bottom five percent. Second, financially distressed firms within this stratum were identified by searching through the *WSJ Index* for any reference to a default, bankruptcy, or debt restructuring in each of the surrounding five years. This two-step procedure was repeated for each of the years 1979–1985, resulting in an initial stratified sample of 793 firm-years (447 firms). Under the assumption that extreme stock-price declines reflect extreme declines in firms' cash flows, this sampling procedure replicates the sequence of actual events that lead to financial distress.

This sampling method has two principal advantages. First, since we are interested in contrasting private renegotiation and bankruptcy as alternative mechanisms for dealing with extreme financial distress, we want to exclude debt restructuring by nondistressed firms. For example, a highly levered but

---

[5]Defaults on technical convenants (for example, those requiring firms to maintain a minimum level of net worth) are not explicitly considered in this definition because such covenants are frequently renegotiated by financially healthy firms when debt is privately placed. As Zinbarg (1975, p. 35) notes: 'My own institution's experience (Prudential Insurance Company of America) may serve as an illustration. In any given year, we will, on average, receive one modification request per loan on the books. In no more than five percent of these cases will we refuse the request or even require any quid pro quo, because the vast majority of corporate requests are perfectly reasonable and do not increase our risk materially.' For a detailed discussion of the economic function of covenants, see Smith and Warner (1979).

[6]Thus, for example, if the last reference to an ongoing restructuring of a firm's bank debt was on June 15, 1982, and the next such reference occurs on September 12, 1983, these would be treated as references to two separate restructurings. Similarly, if a firm's bank debt is successfully restructured on March 22, 1980, and it begins to restructure its publicly traded debt on November 2, 1980, these would be treated as two references to the same ongoing restructuring. Five firms in the sample appear twice as two separate restructurings, and four firms appear as both a debt restructuring and a bankruptcy.

profitable firm may wish to amend certain terms in its debt to enable it to invest in a positive-NPV project. Extreme negative stock returns are a relatively unambiguous indicator of poor financial performance. Inspection of the source documents reveals that 56% of firms in the sample explicitly restructured their debt to avoid bankruptcy. The remaining firms either received a going concern qualification from their auditors during the restructuring, where in default, or experienced a change in control at the hands of creditors (as evidenced by a creditor-initiated senior-management change or placement of stock with creditors).

A second advantage is that the sample contains a more representative cross-section of debt restructurings than if the search had been based on reported cases of default. The latter criterion would exclude firms that restructure their debt to avoid default; evidence reported in the next section suggests that such preemptive restructuring is fairly common. Similarly, a sample that consists of defaults reported by *Moody's* or *Standard and Poor's* would exclude firms that have no publicly traded debt; such firms make up 54% of the current sample. Potential biases inherent in the sampling procedure are discussed in the next section.

Information on debt restructuring plans and other relevant data are obtained from the *WSJ*, the *Moody's* manuals, the *Capital Changes Reporter*, and the *Q-File* directory of 10k reports and proxy statements. Additional data are obtained from the exchange-offer circulars issued by firms that restructured their publicly traded bonds. The market value/replacement cost ratio is constructed using data from the COMPUSTAT data base, and is described in Lang et al. (1989). Because stock returns (and market values) of highly levered firms are extremely volatile, we use a three-year average of this variable in the empirical analysis. The bank-debt ratio is defined as the book value of debt owed to banks and insurance companies divided by the book value of total liabilities. Eighty-five percent of all firms in the sample owe debt to banks, while only eleven percent owe debt to insurance companies; results are qualitatively the same when the numerator includes only bank debt. The number of creditors is approximated by the number of distinct classes of debt referenced in the long-term debt section of *Moody's*. Data used to construct these variables predate as closely as possible the start of the firm's debt restructuring or bankruptcy.

4. Results

4.1. Sample characteristics

Most of the debt-restructuring activity in the sample is clustered in the years 1981–1985 (see table 1). This is consistent with the timing of the general economic recession of the early 1980s, when one would expect there

Table 1

Time series of corporate debt-restructuring activity, by starting date and eventual outcome of restructuring. Sample consists of 80 firms that successfully avoid bankruptcy by restructuring their debt out of court, and 89 firms that are unsuccessful in restructuring their debt and file under Chapter 11 of the U.S. Bankruptcy Code. The sample period is 1978–1987.[a]

Year	Number of attempted debt restructurings	Percentage of restructuring attempts that end in bankruptcy
1978	9	11.1
1979	8	50.0
1980	11	63.6
1981	18	66.7
1982	38	47.4
1983	28	46.4
1984	25	60.0
1985	20	60.0
1986	10	50.0
1987	2	100.0
Total	169	52.7

[a]A debt restructuring is defined as a transaction in which an existing debt contract is replaced by a new contract, with one of the following consequences: (i) required interest or principal payments on the debt are reduced, (ii) the maturity of the debt is extended, or (iii) creditors are given equity securities (common stock or securities convertible into common stock). All restructurings are undertaken in response to an anticipated or actual default. Sources used to determine firms' financial status include the *WSJ*, Commerce Clearing House's *Capital Changes Reporter*, the *Moody's* manuals, and the *Q-file* directory of annual 10k reports and proxy statements.

to be relatively more reported cases of financial distress. Seventy-six percent of the debt restructurings in the sample begin in this period. Also indicated is the percentage of restructuring attempts that eventually fail, and end with a Chapter 11 filing. The sample is about evenly divided between successful and failed attempts. Except in the first and last years of the sample period (when the number of events is extremely small), there does not appear to be any time trend in the observed failure rate.

The frequency of events corresponding to the beginning and conclusion of debt restructurings is listed in table 2. Separate figures are reported for successful and failed restructuring attempts. Primary sources used to identify these events include the *WSJ* and firms' 10k reports. Panel A of the table reveals that in a number of cases, negotiations took place prior to the starting date identified from public sources. Forty-seven initial references in fact pertain to the final resolution of a debt restructuring. We believe that we have come reasonably close to identifying the true starting dates for 90 firms (53 percent of the sample), where the initial event either takes the form of a default (52 firms) or an announcement that the firm has just commenced (or

Table 2

Frequency distribution of events used to identify the beginning and conclusion of 80 successful and 89 unsuccessful attempts by firms to restructure their debt privately to avoid bankruptcy. All transactions take place between 1978 and 1987. Figures in the table are based on information contained in the *Wall Street Journal*, the *Moody's* manuals, Commerce Clearing House's *Capital Changes Reporter*, and the *Q-file* directory of annual 10k reports and proxy statements.[a]

	Outcome of debt-restructuring attempt	
	Success-ful	Unsuccess-ful
Panel A: Events that identify the beginning of debt restructuring		
Default	29	23
Final resolution of debt restructuring announced	20	27
Initial announcement of debt restructuring	18	20
Reference to a debt restructuring that is already in progress	11	16
Creditor-initiated senior-management change	1	1
Firm receives a going-concern qualification from its auditors	1	0
Firm engages investment banker to lead debt restructuring	0	1
Senior management denies that bankruptcy is imminent	0	1
Panel B: Events that identify the conclusion of debt restructuring		
Restructuring agreement formally consummated	46	0
Last public reference to an ongoing restructuring in progress	13	0
Sale of equity or debt securities as part of restructuring plan	10	0
Merged into another company	4	0
Creditors receive equity securities under restructuring plan	4	0
Shareholder approval obtained for restructuring plan	3	0
Chapter 11 filing	0	89
Totals	80	89

[a]See table 1 for a definition of debt restructuring and bankruptcy.

will shortly commence) restructuring its debt (38 firms). Of the 52 default announcements, 34 refer to payment defaults and 18 to technical defaults on financial covenants. Over the course of a restructuring, firms can be associated with more than one event listed in panel A. Although a default normally allows the debtor a 30-day grace period before creditors can exercise their right to accelerate full payment of the debt, negotiations to restructure the debt are assumed to begin immediately after the firm defaults.

Panel B of table 2 reports the frequency of events used to identify the conclusion of a debt restructuring. By definition, all 89 restructuring attempts that fail end with a Chapter 11 bankruptcy filing. Of the remaining 80 successful debt restructurings, for 44 firms it was possible to identify the date on which the restructuring agreement was formally consummated. For 13 firms there was no clear concluding date, only some final reference in the *WSJ* to a restructuring that was still in progress. For ten firms the restructur-

Table 3

Selected attributes of 80 successful corporate debt restructurings undertaken to avoid bankruptcy between 1978 and 1987.[a]

Attribute	Percentage of sample
Panel A: Incidence of default during debt restructuring [b]	
Payment default	36.3
Technical default	21.3
Unspecified default	17.5
All defaults	66.3
Panel B: Stockholder approval for restructuring plan	
Approval for issuance of new common stock specified under plan	17.5
Approval of asset sales specified under plan	1.3
No stockholder approval required	81.2
Panel C: Type of debt restructured	
Bank debt (by firms that have bank debt outstanding)	90.0
Publicly traded debt (by firms that have publicly traded debt outstanding)	69.8

[a]See table 1 for a definition of debt restructuring and bankruptcy.

[b]A *payment default* is defined as a default on an interest or principal payment; included are cases where a firm unilaterally suspends payment on its debt, even though no default is formally declared by creditors. A *technical default* is defined as a default on a financial covenant in the firm's debt. Sources used to determine whether debt is in default include the *Moody's* manuals, Commerce Clearing House's *Capital Changes Reporter*, the *Q-file* directory of annual 10k reports and proxy statements, and Standard and Poor's *Bond Owner's Guide*.

ing concluded with the sale of new debt or equity securities, with the issue proceeds used to help finance the restructuring. In four additional cases the restructuring ended with creditors receiving an equity interest in the firm, either directly or as a result of interest being paid in equity securities instead of cash.

Starting and ending dates for bankruptcy are generally better defined. Of the 89 firms in the sample that filed for Chapter 11, 42 leave bankruptcy when their reorganization plans are formally confirmed by the court. An additional ten firms are merged into nonbankrupt firms, and four are liquidated following the conversion of their cases to Chapter 7 proceedings. For the remaining 33 firms, either bankruptcy was still in progress at the time of this writing (eight firms), or it was not possible to determine precisely when or how the firm emerged from Chapter 11.

Some general attributes of the 80 successful debt restructurings in the sample are presented in table 3. Reported default rates in panel A indicate whether any of the firm's outstanding debt is in default; data limitations preclude a finer breakdown by particular classes of debt (secured debt, trade debt, etc.). Although defaults on senior securities and related 'material' events must be reported in the firm's 10k report, the amount and detail of disclosure vary significantly. For example, a firm is not required to report when it first started to restructure its debt, or that it has been in discussion with creditors concerning a possible default. A firm might disclose that it has restructured its 'subordinated debt', without specifying how particular claims in this category have been restructured. A default may go unreported if the firm does not file its 10k report; filing omissions by financially distressed firms are fairly common [Gilson (1990)]. As well, firms and creditors exhibit a penchant for secrecy in these transactions. For example, the debt restructuring of Tiger International Inc. (included in the appendix) began when the *WSJ* reported that the firm unilaterally suspended payments on about half of its $1.8 billion in debt:

> Tiger said that a total of $350 million in interest and principal on its bank and institutional debt is scheduled for payment in 1983. But the company wouldn't disclose how much of the $350 million would be affected by its decision to 'temporarily defer' debt service on $900 million of its total debt. Tiger also wouldn't disclose when specific payments were due on any of the $350 million. Asked for elaboration ... a company spokeswoman said she didn't know whether the company had missed a deadline for any payments on the $900 million in debt .... Tiger's lenders, whom the company declined to identify, were informed of the decision at yesterday's meeting.
>
> (*WSJ*, 15 February 1983, 5)

Fifty-three firms (66.3 percent of the sample) were in default before successfully restructuring their debt. Since 29 of these restructurings begin with a default (see table 2), 24 firms did not default until after entering negotiations with creditors to restructure their debt. In 51 firms (64 percent of the sample), no default occurred, or occurred after the debt restructuring began. Thus, firms often begin restructuring their debt before any actual default (or without any default occurring).

Explicit stockholder approval was required for only 18.8 percent of all restructuring plans that were adopted (panel B). In most of these cases, approval was required to issue common stock under the plan, either as a requirement imposed by the firm's stock exchange, or because it was necessary to increase the number of authorized shares. For the remaining 81.2 percent of all cases where such approval was not obtained, the possibility exists that adoption of these plans was not always in the best interests of stockholders. Where managers have the authority to accept or reject a restructuring plan, there is no assurance that they will make the decision that maximizes stockholders' wealth. Gilson (1989, 1990) finds that turnover of senior managers and directors is lower when firms restructure their debt outside of Chapter 11. Thus, managers could have incentives to settle with

Table 4

Summary of restructuring terms for 80 successful corporate debt restructurings undertaken between 1978 and 1987, by general class of debt restructured (bank, publicly traded, and other debt).[a]

Restructuring terms	Percentage of debt within a given class restructured on specified terms			Percentage of firms that restructure any debt on specified terms
	Bank	Public	Other	
Extension of maturity	48.6	6.7	25.0	48.8
Reduction of interest or principal	54.2	56.7	75.0	72.5
Distribution of equity securities	51.4	86.7	75.0	73.8
Percentage of firms that restructure debt in a given class	90.0	37.5	20.0	

[a]*Extension of maturity* includes deferral of promised interest or principal payments. *Reduction of interest or principal* includes foregiveness of overdue or future promised payments, in addition to reductions in the stated rate of interest. *Distribution of equity securities* includes distributions of common or preferred stock, as well as securities that can be converted into either class of stock (e.g., warrants and convertible bonds); also included are provisions in the debt contract that give firms the option to make payments either in cash or in equity securities. *Bank debt* includes debt owed to commercial banks and insurance companies. *Other debt* includes debt owed to suppliers, trade creditors, and other nonbank companies.

creditors on overly generous terms to secure their consent to a plan, even though stockholders would be better off in bankruptcy. Stock-return evidence presented below, however, suggests that the market on average reacts positively to events that increase the probability of successful private renegotiation and negatively to events that increase the probability of bankruptcy. This suggests that potential agency conflicts between managers and stockholders are not a deciding factor in whether firms privately restructure or file for Chapter 11.

Finally, firms that restructure their debt privately sometimes restructure only a subset of their outstanding debt contracts (panel C). Only 90.0 percent of firms in the sample with bank debt outstanding, and 69.8 percent of firms with publicly traded debt, actually restructure such debt. In contrast, Chapter 11 cases necessarily require participation by all impaired claimholder classes, which in practical terms generally means all of the firm's outstanding claims. This suggests that private renegotiation may be less costly than Chapter 11 if the firm is able to recontract only with those creditors whose claims are in default, thus conserving on transactions costs.

Table 4 summarizes the principal terms on which firms in the sample restructure their debt, based on the three criteria used to define a debt restructuring (that is, there must either be a reduction in interest or principal payments, an extension of the debt's maturity, or a distribution of equity securities to creditors). Since firms do not always disclose the exact terms on which debt is restructured, figures in the table represent lower bounds on the frequency with which these terms are actually incorporated in restructuring plans.

New equity securities are distributed to creditors in almost 74 percent of all successful restructurings. A similar percentage of restructurings results in a reduction in promised payments on the debt. The least common provision in these agreements is an extension of maturity. Different classes of debt also appear to be restructured on substantially different terms. Approximately 49 percent of bank debt restructurings provide for an extension of maturity, compared with only 6.7 percent of restructurings of publicly traded debt; this latter result is consistent with firms offering shorter-maturity debt in exchange offers to discourage holdouts (see section 2.2.2). Although 51.4 percent of bank debt restructurings result in bank lenders receiving equity in the firm, holders of publicly traded debt are given equity securities 86.7 percent of the time. The latter difference is a likely consequence of various legal and regulatory factors that make it prohibitively costly for banks to hold large amounts of equity in publicly traded companies.

In particular, banks are constrained from holding significant blocks of stock in other firms by section 16 of the Glass-Steagall Act, the Bank Holding Company Act and the Federal Reserve Board's Regulation Y, although temporary exceptions are granted when stock is obtained in a debt restructuring. In general, banks must divest their stockholdings after approximately two years, although extensions are possible. Second, creditors can be held legally liable to other claimholders if the firm's financial condition deteriorates subsequent to their assuming a controlling interest in the firm and exercising 'undue influence' over its business [Douglas-Hamilton (1975), Smith and Warner (1979)]. A given percentage equity ownership in a firm might, for purposes of proving legal liability, be assumed to confer greater control on a small group of bank lenders than a dispersed group of public bondholders. Finally, a controlling shareholding in a firm could be construed as an 'insider relationship', thus obliging banks to return any monetary consideration received from the firm as a 'preference item' if it later files for bankruptcy. Banks may prefer to receive relatively less equity in a debt restructuring if they assess a high probability that the firm will subsequently become bankrupt.

The preceding simple classification of restructuring terms provides a general overview of how these deals are structured. Given the complexity and idiosyncratic nature of these transactions, some useful insights can also be gained by direct examination of individual cases. The appendix presents detailed case descriptions of ten debt restructurings in the sample. The cases are intended to be a representative cross-section of various restructuring plan types and outcomes. These case descriptions provide evidence that complements evidence presented in the next section, where we attempt to identify factors conducive to restructuring debt outside of Chapter 11.

Table 5 contrasts selected characteristics of firms by whether or not they successfully restructure their debt outside of Chapter 11. Firms that privately restructure their debt have a higher market value/replacement cost ratio and have relatively more bank debt than firms in Chapter 11. The means and medians of both variables are significantly different between subsamples at the 1 percent level of significance. Both differences are consistent with the theory developed in section 2. Firms with a higher market value/replacement cost ratio are hypothesized to find bankruptcy more costly than private renegotiation, and to be less prone to holdouts by junior creditors. Firms with more bank debt outstanding can more easily renegotiate their debt because banks are more sophisticated and less numerous than other kinds of creditors, resulting in fewer holdouts.

The mean number of debt contracts (approximated by the number of entries in the long-term debt section of *Moody's*) is marginally higher for firms that restructure their debt privately, but the difference is not statistically significant, and the medians are identical. Alternatively, we define the standardized number of debt contracts as the number of contracts divided by the book value of total liabilities. This variable is significantly lower for firms that restructure successfully; mean and median differences (not shown) are significant at the 2 percent and 7 percent levels, respectively. The standardized number of debt contracts, or the number of creditors per dollar of debt, is arguably a better proxy for creditors' incentives to hold out. Anecdotal evidence suggests that holdouts are relatively more common among smaller creditors, possibly because they have less wealth at risk if the restructuring attempt fails.

Firms that restructure their debt privately are also generally larger, as measured by the book value of assets and the number of shareholders and employees. Both mean and median book values of assets are higher for firms that restructure successfully, although only the difference in medians is statistically significant using a Wilcoxon rank-sum test (p-value of 0.02). Firm size may be a proxy for the number of creditors or the complexity of the firm's capital structure; the simple correlation between the book value of assets and the (nonstandardized) number of debt contracts is positive and significant (0.72, with a p-value of 0.00).

The two groups of firms are fairly similar in overall leverage (measured by the ratio of total liabilities or long-term debt to total assets), and mean stock-price performance (measured over the current and preceding two years). On the other hand, median unadjusted and net-of-market returns are significantly higher for the firms that restructure privately, according to a Wilcoxon rank-sum test for differences in medians (p-values of 0.04 and 0.05,

Table 5

Selected firm and debt characteristics for 80 firms that successfully restructure their debt out of court, and 89 firms that are unsuccessful in restructuring their debt and file under Chapter 11 of the U.S. Bankruptcy Code. Beginning dates for attempted debt restructurings all take place between 1978 and 1987.[a]

Characteristic	80 successful restructurings				89 unsuccessful restructurings				p-value of t-test (Wilcoxon rank sum test) for difference in:	
	Mean	Median	Min.	Max.	Mean	Median	Min.	Max.	Mean	Median
Market value/replacement cost ratio	0.83	0.65	0.23	2.92	0.61	0.56	0.20	1.75	0.01	0.01
Debt ÷ total liabilities (book values)										
(i) Bank debt	0.40	0.36	0.00	0.88	0.25	0.20	0.00	0.83	0.00	0.00
(ii) Public debt	0.13	0.02	0.00	0.66	0.08	0.00	0.00	0.61	0.08	0.08
(iii) Secured debt	0.14	0.00	0.00	0.82	0.12	0.00	0.00	0.70	0.51	0.91
(iv) Convertible debt	0.07	0.00	0.00	0.68	0.06	0.00	0.00	0.77	0.67	0.65
Number of debt contracts outstanding	7.0	5.0	1.0	28.0	6.0	5.0	1.0	31.0	0.22	0.18
Book value of total assets ($millions)	633	101	9	10,209	317	49	6	9,383	0.15	0.02
Number of shareholders (1,000s)	14	4	1	207	3	3	1	34	0.04	0.08
Number of employees (1,000s)	5	1	0	76	3	2	0	32	0.26	0.88
Total liabilities ÷ book value of assets	0.94	0.83	0.43	4.92	1.01	0.86	0.39	10.00	0.65	0.99
Long-term debt ÷ book value of assets	0.64	0.55	0.00	4.23	0.58	0.45	0.00	8.70	0.63	0.02
Prior 3-year common stock return (%)										
(i) Unadjusted	−36.4	−50.3	−93.3	360.0	−48.6	−60.7	−98.0	179.3	0.17	0.04
(ii) Less market return	−134.0	−142.0	−230.4	273.8	−147.7	−160.4	−249.9	62.0	0.15	0.05
Length of debt restructuring attempt (months)	15.4	11.0	1.0	72.0	8.1	3.0	1.0	42.0	0.00	0.00
Length of bankruptcy proceedings after unsuccessful restructuring attempt (months)	—	—	—	—	20.4	18.0	3.0	43.0	—	—

[a]See table 1 for a definition of debt restructuring and bankruptcy. When applicable, figures are those that most closely predate the beginning of firms' debt restructuring or bankruptcy. Figures defined in terms of firms' assets and liabilities are all based on reported book values in the *Moody's* manuals. *Bank debt* includes outstanding liabilities to both commercial banks and insurance companies. The *market value/replacement cost ratio* equals the three-year average ratio of the market value of assets to their replacement value. The *number of debt contracts* equals the number of separate descriptive headings in the long-term debt section of the *Moody's* manuals. The *market return* is the equally weighted market portfolio return in the CRSP daily returns file.

respectively). A comparison of medians is probably more appropriate given the extreme nonnormality of the sample (drawn from the left-hand tail of unconditional returns distribution). One explanation for this difference is that superior performance is associated with a smaller reduction in going-concern value, resulting in a higher market value/replacement cost ratio and increased incentives to renegotiate debt privately. Consistent with this posited relationship, the correlation between prior unadjusted stock returns and the market value/replacement cost ratio is positive and significant (0.19, with a *p*-value of 0.04).

Finally, firms that restructure their debt privately require an average of 15.4 months, and a median of 11 months, to complete the restructuring. Restructuring of publicly traded debt is completed in a much shorter time than restructuring of nontraded debt. The 30 exchange offers in the present sample take an average of 6.6 months to complete (not shown), compared with 15.9 months for all other debt; corresponding median times are 2 and 10.5 months. Differences in both means and medians are statistically significant using a *t*-test and Wilcoxon rank sum test (*p*-values of less than 0.01).

Firms that file for Chapter 11 spend an average of 8.1 (median of 3) months attempting to restructure their debt before seeking bankruptcy protection, and an average of 20.4 (median of 18) additional months in Chapter 11. In the present sample, Chapter 11 cases take significantly longer to complete than successful debt restructurings; differences in the mean and median number of months elapsed under each alternative are significantly different from zero (*p*-values of less than 0.01).

4.2. Direct measurement of debt-restructuring costs

We argued in section 2 that relative restructuring costs are an important determinant of whether firms restructure their debt privately or in Chapter 11. Because firms are generally not required to disclose the total costs incurred in a private workout, explicit measurement of these costs is generally not possible. Only four firms in the present sample reported debt-restructuring expenses in their 10k reports (and only for restructuring of publicly traded debt). Data on bankruptcy costs are available only at considerable expense, by direct examination of court records [Weiss (1990)].

It is possible, however, to estimate the direct costs of exchange offers for publicly traded debt. Firms must provide an estimate of offer-related costs in the exchange offer circular distributed to bondholders. We obtained the circulars for 26 of the 32 exchange offers in the sample (including two made by firms that ultimately went bankrupt). For 18 of these offers, the circular provided an estimate of out-of-pocket costs (including payments made to the exchange and information agent, and related legal, accounting, brokerage, and investment banking fees). Firms were omitted when only a subset of the

Table 6

Direct costs of troubled exchange offers for publicly traded debt. Sample consists of 18 exchange offers undertaken between 1981 and 1988. Costs consist of compensation paid to the exchange and information agent, and all legal, accounting, brokerage, and investment banking fees incurred by the firm in connection with the offer.[a]

	Mean	Median	Min.	Max.
Exchange offer costs ($1,000s)	799	424	200	2,500
Offer costs as a percentage of the book value of assets	0.65	0.32	0.01	3.40
Offer costs as a percentage of the face value of bonds restructured under offer	2.16	2.29	0.27	6.84

[a]These 18 exchange offers represent all offers in the sample for which an estimate of total offer-related costs was disclosed in either the exchange offer circular of the firm's 10k report. Such documentation was obtained for 26 of the 32 exchange offers in the entire sample (two of which were undertaken by firms that ultimately filed for bankruptcy). The book value of assets and the face amount of debt are the figures that most closely predate the commencement of the offer.

offer's total costs were presented, to avoid biasing the cost estimates downward (several circulars reported only that certain costs would be of some 'customary' amount; another circular contained only blank spaces where offer costs were to have been reported). Firms were also omitted if the investment bank that served as financial advisor to the offer was paid in warrants or common stock, unless a dollar estimate of the value of this payment was provided in the circular.

In economic terms, exchange-offer costs appear to be trivial (table 6). Mean and median exchange-offer costs as a percentage of the book value of assets prior to the offer are only 0.65 and 0.32 percent, respectively. In relation to the face amount of the debt involved in the exchange offer, the corresponding figures are 2.16 and 2.29 percent. These estimates do not include any indirect costs of exchange offers or the costs of restructuring nonpublic debt.

There is evidence that direct bankruptcy costs are also relatively small. Warner (1977b) reports that direct costs for a sample of 11 railroad bankruptcies from the period 1933–1955 represent, on average, 5.3 percent of firms' market value at the time of the bankruptcy filing. Ang et al. (1982) investigate a sample of 86 firms that filed for bankruptcy (and eventually liquidated) in the Western District of Oklahoma between 1963 and 1979. They report mean and median direct costs (as a percentage of total liquidation proceeds) of 7.5 and 1.7 percent, respectively. Weiss (1990) analyzes a sample of 37 New York- and American Stock Exchange-listed firms that filed for bankruptcy between 1980 and 1986, and finds that average direct costs are, on average, 2.9 percent of the book value of assets prior to filing.

Direct costs of exchange offers in our sample also exhibit economies of scale. Average offer costs decline with both the book value of assets and the face value of debt involved in the offer. The correlation between average costs and the book value of assets (not shown) is -0.42 (p-value of 0.08); the correlation between average costs and the face value of debt is -0.57 (p-value of 0.01). A statistically significant negative relation is also found when average costs are regressed against each deflator in ordinary least-squares regressions. Economies of scale have previously been documented for direct bankruptcy costs [Warner (1977b), Ang et al. (1982)].

4.3. Prediction of successful private renegotiation

This section presents a logit regression analysis that relates the probability of successful private renegotiation to our empirical proxies for relative bankruptcy costs and the magnitude of the potential holdout problem. The dependent variable equals 1 if a firm successfully restructures its debt without entering Chapter 11, and equals 0 if the restructuring attempt fails and the firm files for bankruptcy. Thus, a positive coefficient on an independent variable in the regressions implies that firms for which this variable takes on a higher value are more likely to settle with creditors privately. Our explanatory variables are the firm's market/replacement cost ratio, the bank-debt ratio, and the standardized number of debt contracts outstanding (scaled by the book value of total liabilities).

Four estimated specifications of the model are shown in table 7; in the first, all three explanatory variables are included, and in the remaining three, the variables are included separately. In general, all three variables have significant explanatory power, and are consistent with the univariate comparisons made in table 5. The estimated coefficient on the market value/ replacement cost ratio is positive and highly significant in both the combined and univariate regressions (both coefficients have p-values of 0.01). The positive coefficient has two non-mutually-exclusive interpretations, since this ratio is a proxy for both relative recontracting costs and the magnitude of junior creditors' losses if the firm files for Chapter 11 (greater expected losses will increase creditors' willingness to settle privately). The logit regression tests do not allow us to distinguish between these two hypotheses.

The estimated coefficient on the bank debt ratio is positive and significant in both of the regressions in which it appears, although it is somewhat more significant when included separately (with a p-value of 0.00, versus 0.05 for the combined regression). The standardized number of debt contracts is negatively related to the probability of successful private renegotiation, although the estimated coefficient is only marginally significant when included in the combined regression (p-value of 0.12). When this variable appears alone, the estimated coefficient is negative and significant (p-value

Table 7

Logit regressions relating firm characteristics to outcome of debt restructuring. Sample consists of 80 firms that successfully avoided bankruptcy by restructuring their debt out of court, and 89 firms that were forced to seek protection under Chapter 11 of the U.S. Bankruptcy Code. All transactions take place between 1978 and 1987. The dependent variable equals 1 if a firm successfully restructures its debt out of court, and equals 0 if the restructuring attempt fails and the firm files for bankruptcy. Asymptotic *p*-values are shown in parentheses.[a]

Independent variables	(1)	(2)	(3)	(4)
Intercept	-1.40^b (0.01)	-1.16^b (0.01)	-0.82^b (0.00)	0.21 (0.33)
Market value/replacement cost ratio	1.51^b (0.01)	1.49^b (0.01)	—	—
Bank-debt ratio	1.59^c (0.05)	—	2.20^b (0.00)	—
Number of debt contracts outstanding	-2.60 (0.12)	—	—	-2.91^c (0.03)
Sample size	112	119	159	157
Model *p*-value	0.0012	0.0030	0.0005	0.0163
Pseudo *R*-square	0.051	0.026	0.026	0.013

[a]See table 1 for a definition of debt restructuring and bankruptcy. Explanatory variables predate as closely as possible the start of each firm's debt restructuring or bankruptcy. The *market value/replacement cost ratio* equals the three-year average ratio of the market value of assets to their replacement value. The *bank-debt ratio* equals the book value of debt owed to banks and insurance companies, divided by the book value of total liabilities. The *number of debt contracts outstanding* equals the number of distinct descriptive headings under the long-term debt section of the *Moody's* manuals, divided by the book value of total liabilities; to facilitate reporting in the table, the estimated coefficient on this variable is divided by 1,000.
[b]*p*-value ≤ 0.01.
[c]*p*-value ≤ 0.05.

of 0.03). These results suggest that creditor holdouts are less common when relatively more debt is owed to banks, and there are fewer creditors.

The results in table 7 hold with the addition of alternative explanatory variables. Earlier, we hypothesized that private renegotiation is less likely to succeed when relatively more debt is owed to trade creditors, because it is more difficult to obtain their unanimous consent to a restructuring plan. In addition, firms that are more reliant on trade credit may view Chapter 11 more favorably, because the Code's superpriority provision makes it easier to raise new working capital. As a proxy for the importance of trade credit, we use the ratio of accounts payable to total liabilities observed before restructuring activity begins. The trade-debt ratio is negatively correlated with the bank-debt ratio (not shown), and positively correlated with the standardized number of debt contracts (correlations are -0.29 and 0.31, respectively, with *p*-values of 0.00). It is insignificant in the regressions, however, whether included alone or in combination with other variables.

Although the estimated coefficients are consistent with the hypotheses developed in section 2, the overall explanatory power of the regressions is small. 'Pseudo' R-squares [Madalla (1983)] calculated for each regression indicate that the logit regressions explain no more than about 5 percent of the total variation in the dependent variable, although model p-values are generally less than 1 percent. The lack of overall power may be due to the relatively small sample size and the use of cross-sectional data. In addition, a number of other economic factors that may be critical to the success of private renegotiation are either unsystematic or impossible to quantify (e.g., the relative bargaining abilities and personalities of the parties involved). This last consideration underlies the analysis of stock returns in the next section.

A final concern is that the logit results may be subject to two possible biases. First, our empirical tests assume that private renegotiation is less costly than bankruptcy. Although we do not presume this to be true for all firms, general support for this assumption is found in anecdotal accounts of the bankruptcy process [Stein (1989)] and in stock-return evidence presented in the next section. In addition, a bankruptcy filing represents the first public announcement of financial distress for only 27 firms in the sample (see table 2); for 14 of these firms the *WSJ* report of the filing refers to a previous failed restructuring attempt. Thus 92 percent of firms in the sample first attempted to settle privately with creditors. It can be shown that creditors and stockholders will never attempt to settle privately if bankruptcy is less costly (assuming full participation by all creditors).

A second possible source of bias is the use of a nonrandom sample to estimate the logit regressions. The coefficient estimates in table 7 will be biased if the relative frequency of private restructuring and Chapter 11 in the sample differs from the population frequency [Manski and McFadden (1983)]. Since firms are sampled on extreme negative stock returns, these relative frequencies could differ if the probability of successful private renegotiation depends on prior stock-price performance. Prior stock returns are insignificant when added to the regressions, however, and the remaining coefficient estimates are qualitatively unchanged.

4.4. Evidence from stock returns

Ideally, claimholders' incentives to choose between private renegotiation and bankruptcy could be assessed directly by comparing the value of the securities distributed under each alternative to various claimholder classes (secured lenders, public bondholders, etc.). Although such direct comparisons are precluded by a lack of relevant price data, analysis of common stock returns provides some insights into what determines claimholders' incentives to settle privately.

Given evidence in the last section that certain firm characteristics can be used to predict whether attempted private renegotiation will be successful, we are interested in knowing whether the stock market also forms such a prediction. By examining abnormal stock returns around the initial announcement of a restructuring attempt, one can assess whether the market uses similar information to predict the likelihood of successful private renegotiation.

To investigate this possibility, we perform two related analyses of stock returns. First, we partition the sample by whether or not firms are ultimately successful in privately restructuring their debt. If the market is correct on average in predicting this outcome, we should observe a different stock-price reaction for the two subsamples. This approach imposes no prior constraints on the information set that the market uses in making its forecast. The same approach is used by Bradley et al. (1983) in analyzing target companies' stock-price performance following a failed tender offer. Second, we use cross-sectional regression analysis to relate announcement-day returns to variables that were used in the logit analysis to predict the success of private renegotiation. This approach implicitly constrains the market's information set to contain only some subset of these variables.

By analyzing cumulative stock returns over the entire restructuring interval, it is also possible to make certain inferences about relative recontracting costs. Positive cumulative abnormal returns for successful restructurings are consistent with the hypothesis that fewer total costs are incurred (firm value is higher) under private renegotiation than bankruptcy. This allows us to contrast the costs of private renegotiation and bankruptcy without having to measure these costs directly. Baldwin and Mason (1983) undertake a similar analysis of the debt restructuring of Massey Ferguson (included in the current sample).

Stock returns observed around the outcome announcement will contain more information about relative recontracting costs when more of the firm's debt is restructured under the plan. If the unanimous consent of all creditors is required, abnormal returns at the announcement of a successful restructuring must reflect total savings in recontracting costs from avoiding bankruptcy. Given that all creditors (and stockholders) consent to the plan, the wealth of each claimholder, and thus the value of the firm, will be higher under private renegotiation than bankruptcy.

If only a subset of the firm's debt is restructured, adoption of a restructuring plan could in principle reduce the wealth of nonparticipating creditors (by granting participating creditors increased seniority interests, for example). The size of these wealth transfers will be limited, however, by the right of nonparticipating creditors to sue the firm (and other creditors), covenants that restrict the issuance of more senior debt, and cross-default provisions that restrict the firm's ability to exclude certain creditors from participation in the plan.

Abnormal common stock returns around the initial announcement of a restructuring attempt are reported in table 8. We exclude the 27 bankrupt firms in the sample (see table 2) for which the Chapter 11 filing was the first public announcement of financial distress, since it is not known for these firms when (or whether) private renegotiation was attempted before the bankruptcy filing. Reported returns are two-day mean market-model residuals, estimated using Center for Research in Security Prices (CRSP) daily returns for the period 250 days to 50 days prior to the announcement date, and the equally weighted market return. Since infrequent trading is an especially common problem for measuring stock returns of financially distressed firms, abnormal returns are based on Scholes–Williams estimates of the market-model parameters [Scholes and Williams (1977)].

Separate results are presented for the total sample, and for a subsample of 90 restructuring attempts (including 38 successful and 52 failed restructurings) where the initial public announcement contains a reference to either a default or what appears to be the actual commencement of negotiations with lenders. Announcements in the latter sample may contain relatively more surprise, and therefore provide a more powerful test of the market's ability to discriminate between firms that ultimately either succeed or fail to restructure their debt privately.

For the total sample, two-day average returns associated with the initial announcement of a debt restructuring equal -1.6 percent for firms that successfully restructure their debt, and -6.3 percent for firms whose restructuring attempt ultimately fails. These returns are significantly different at the 5 percent level (t-statistic of 2.50). Corresponding returns estimated for the sample of 'surprise' announcements are -3.0 and -8.7 percent, and are significantly different at the 10 percent level (t-statistic of 1.90). Although less significant results are obtained for the 'surprise' sample (which may be attributable to the smaller sample size), both sets of results are consistent with the market being able to distinguish in advance which firms are more likely to be successful at restructuring their debt privately. As pointed out above, these results do not allow us to identify what specific information the market uses in forming its prediction.

Table 8 also reports two-day abnormal returns for the announcement of the outcome of a debt restructuring. For unsuccessful attempts to restructure, this is the announcement of a firm's Chapter 11 filing. For successful restructurings, abnormal returns around the outcome announcement are insignificantly different from zero, for both samples. For unsuccessful restructurings, abnormal returns are significantly negative around the announce-

Table 8

Two-day average returns associated with the initial announcement of a private debt restructuring, and of the first announcement of the restructuring's resolution. Figures are based on a sample of 80 firms that successfully restructured their debt to avoid bankruptcy, and 89 firms that were ultimately unsuccessful in restructuring their debt and filed under Chapter 11 of the U.S. Bankrutpcy Code. Announcement dates are determined from the *Wall Street Journal*. All announcements take place between 1978 and 1988. In panel B, results are based on a subsample of 90 debt restructurings (47 successful and 43 unsuccessful) that begin with the announcement of a default or for which the actual commencement date of the restructuring is known. *t*-statistics are given in parentheses.[a]

Announcement type	(1) Successful debt restructuring	(2) Unsuccessful debt restructuring	*t*-statistic of (2) minus (1)
Panel A: Total sample			
(A) Initiation of debt restructuring	−0.016 (1.53)	−0.063 (4.03)[b]	(2.50)[c]
Sample size	68	57	
(B) Resolution of debt restructuring	0.007 (0.63)	−0.167 (6.68)[b]	(6.37)[b]
Sample size	66	38	
t-statistic of (A) minus (B)	(1.51)	(3.53)[b]	
Panel B: Restructurings that begin with a default or for which actual commencement date is known			
(A) Initiation of debt restructuring	−0.030 (1.94)[d]	−0.087 (3.39)[b]	(1.90)[d]
Sample size	37	31	
(B) Resolution of debt restructuring	−0.009 (0.70)	−0.166 (5.98)[b]	(5.16)[b]
Sample size	34	19	
t-statistic of (A) minus (B)	(1.07)	(2.09)[c]	

[a]See table 1 for a definition of debt restructuring and bankruptcy. The two-day average return is an average of daily returns realized on the *Wall Street Journal* announcement day and the preceding day. Stock returns are obtained from the 1988 CRSP daily returns file.
[b]*p*-value ≤ 0.01.
[c]*p*-value ≤ 0.05.
[d]*p*-value ≤ 0.10.

ment of the Chapter 11 filing, again for both samples (respective abnormal returns are −16.7 and −16.6 percent, with corresponding *t*-statistics of 6.68 and 5.98).

When these results are combined with the initial-announcement returns, it appears that stockholders do better over the entire restructuring interval when their firms ultimately settle with creditors out of court. This impression

Table 9

Average cumulative returns for successful and unsuccessful debt restructurings. Returns are measured from one day before the commencement of restructuring to day on which success of restructuring attempt is determined. Figures are based on a sample of 80 firms that successfully restructured their debt to avoid bankruptcy, and 89 firms that were ultimately unsuccessful in restructuring their debt and filed under Chapter 11 of the U.S. Bankruptcy Code. Announcement dates are determined from the *Wall Street Journal*. All announcements take place between 1978 and 1988. In panel B, results are based on a subsample of 90 debt restructurings (47 successful and 43 unsuccessful) that begin with the announcement of a default or for which the actual commencement date of the restructuring is known. *t*-statistics are given in parentheses.[a]

Outcome of debt restructuring	Average cumulative return
Panel A: Total sample	
(A) Successful	0.414
	(2.71)[c]
Sample size	69
(B) Unsuccessful	−0.399
	(3.28)[b]
Sample size	55
t-statistic of (A) minus (B)	(4.17)[b]
Panel B: Restructurings that begin with a default or for which actual commencement date is known	
(A) Successful	0.713
	(3.21)[b]
Sample size	38
(B) Unsuccessful	−0.361
	(2.19)[c]
Sample size	30
t-statistic of (A) minus (B)	(3.88)[b]

[a]See table 1 for a definition of debt restructuring and bankruptcy. Stock return data are obtained from the 1988 CRSP daily returns file.
[b]p-value ≤ 0.01.
[c]p-value ≤ 0.05.

is confirmed in table 9, which reports average cumulative abnormal returns for the entire restructuring interval. For the total sample, stockholders of firms that successfully restructured realized average abnormal returns of 41.4 percent over the restructuring interval, whereas stockholders of ultimately bankrupt firms realized abnormal returns of −39.9 percent. Corresponding returns for the 'surprise' subsample are 71.3 and −36.1 percent. For both panels, differences in returns are significant at the 5 percent level. These results are not driven by outliers. Seventy-two percent of cumulative returns are negative for firms that ultimately file for Chapter 11, and 58 percent are positive for firms that successfully restructure. The percentage of negative returns is significantly different between the two subsamples at the 5 percent level.

These results suggest that, for whatever reason, stockholders on average fare less well in bankruptcy than in private renegotiation, and thus have incentives to settle with creditors privately. Consistent with this possibility, stockholders seldom exercise their option to file for Chapter 11 without first attempting to restructure the firm's debt privately (see table 2). An alternative interpretation, however, is that firms that file for bankruptcy experience unexpectedly worse operating performance than firms that ultimately restructure their debt privately. Thus larger stock-price declines for bankrupt firms may not be due to the recontracting process itself, but instead reflect a selection bias resulting from the fact that bankrupt firms are inherently less profitable (subsequent to the bankruptcy filing).

Finally, attempts to relate abnormal stock returns to the explanatory variables used in the logit regressions yielded insignificant results. Cross-sectional regressions of abnormal returns against various combinations of these variables generally produced adjusted R-squares of less than 5 percent, and individual coefficient estimates were almost always insignificant. The insignificant results cannot be attributed to multicollinearity or heteroskedasticity of the error terms. The low explanatory power of these regressions is consistent with the market's using more information to forecast the outcome of private renegotiation than is captured by the explanatory variables.

5. Conclusion

In this study we investigate how financially distressed firms restructure their debt. For a sample of 169 distressed companies, we investigate firms' economic incentives to choose between private renegotiation and formal bankruptcy as alternative mechanisms for dealing with default. In about half of all cases, financially distressed firms successfully restructure their debt outside of Chapter 11. Financial distress is more likely to be resolved through private renegotiation when more of the firm's assets are intangible, and relatively more debt is owed to banks; private renegotiation is less likely to succeed when there are more distinct classes of debt outstanding. Analysis of stock returns suggests that the market is also able to identify in advance which firms are more likely to succeed in restructuring their debt privately. Cumulative stock returns are significantly higher when debt is restructured privately; thus on average stockholders have incentives to avoid bankruptcy and settle out of court.

One implication of our results is that troubled companies are likely to find informal alternatives to bankruptcy increasingly attractive in dealing with financial distress. As recently argued by Jensen (1989a, b), companies that have relatively more debt outstanding will default sooner if they are being mismanaged. This has the virtue of forcing management to undertake corrective changes in corporate policy sooner, thus preserving more of the firm's going-concern value. Consistent with this, the present study finds that insolvent firms with relatively high going-concern value are more likely to restructure their debt privately, because more of this value tends to be lost for a variety of reasons (including through asset sales) when debt and the firm's operations are reorganized in Chapter 11. Thus, future defaults by the current generation of highly levered companies may be increasingly resolved through private renegotiation.

Our results also have important implications for interpreting recent evidence that shows an increase in the default rate of high-yield publicly traded bonds [Altman (1989), Asquith et al. (1989)]. We present evidence that restructuring of publicly traded debt almost always takes the form of an exchange offer, and is generally completed within two months. The out-of-pocket costs incurred in connection with these offers are economically insignificant (amounting on average to less than 1 percent of the firm's book value of assets). It remains an unanswered empirical question whether other default-related costs are sufficiently high to warrant continued concern over the recent rise in defaults.

Appendix

Case studies of attempts by ten firms to restructure their debt privately to avoid bankruptcy

This appendix presents brief case studies describing the experience of ten firms that attempted to restructure their debt privately to avoid bankruptcy. Each case study describes major events relating to the restructuring, general terms (either proposed or adopted) for restructuring the firm's debt, and other relevant information. The cases are based on information contained in published reports in the *Wall Street Journal* and disclosed in firms' 10k reports, shareholder proxy statements, and exchange-offer prospectuses. The ten firms examined here represent a cross-section of various possible restructuring plan types and outcomes. At the beginning of each case we classify the debt restructuring according to the principal types of debt involved, and whether the restructuring attempt was successful (i.e., whether the firm avoided having to file for Chapter 11). In addition, for each case we report (i) the period over which the restructuring took place (as defined in section 3 of the text), (ii) the Scholes–Williams cumulative abnormal common stock return over the restructuring interval (labeled *car*), and (iii) the firm's common stock price at the beginning and end of the restructuring, or the most recent prices reported inside the restructuring interval (labelled *p0* and *p1*, respectively). Stock prices are obtained from Standard and Poor's *Daily*

Stock Price Record. Reported time intervals are all rounded to the nearest month. 'n.a.' means that cumulative abnormal returns could not be calculated because there were insufficient stock returns available as a result of nontrading.

Brock Hotel Corporation Classification: *Successful restructuring of bank and publicly traded debt, accompanied by stock placement with financial advisor to restructuring and common stock rights offering (6/28/85–6/26/86; car = n.a.; p0 = $2\frac{7}{8}$, p1 = $\frac{2}{8}$).*

The company made an exchange offer to holders of its eight publicly traded debenture issues, offering a package of common stock and new debentures (having a lower coupon rate, payable in cash or common stock). Although 86 percent of the debentures were tendered under the offer, it was decided that the offer would not be sufficient to resolve the company's financial problems. As a result, the company implemented a comprehensive plan to restructure all of its long-term debt. Under the plan, all of the new debentures issued under the previous exchange offer were converted into various amounts of common and preferred stock, common stock options, and cash. In addition, the company acquired the bank debt and capitalized lease obligations of its operating subsidiaries (using a combination of cash, warrants, and common stock options), and exchanged new debentures for all of the preferred stock of a partly owned subsidiary. Various other debt was also restructured, including liabilities arising from canceled operating leases and company guarantees, and the lease agreement on the company's headquarters building. A critical feature of the plan was a rights offering of 266 million common shares to current stockholders (only about 13 million shares were outstanding before the offering). Following a vote of the common stockholders, the plan was adopted one year from the announcement of the initial exchange offer. A major role in the restructuring was played by The Hallwood Group Inc., which the company engaged as a financial advisor to the restructuring. In addition to managing the rights offering, Hallwood obtained secured lenders' consent to the plan by agreeing to guarantee the minimum proceeds that would be realized from selling various assets under the plan. In return for providing these and other services. Hallwood received the right to elect a majority of the company's board of directors (including its chairman), and was issued 14 percent of the company's common stock.

Crawford Energy Inc. Classification: *Unsuccessful restructuring of bank and trade debt (10/20/83–9/30/85; car = −63.3%; p0 = $3\frac{1}{8}$, p1 = $\frac{2}{8}$).*

Following eight months of negotiations, the company eliminated most of its $10 million in trade debt by offering new common stock to its 44 trade creditors in a negotiated exchange offer. In return for canceling almost half of the debt, trade creditors received 21 percent of the company's common stock. Also participating in the plan was A. Gail Crawford, the company's founder, chairman, and CEO. Mr Crawford, who before the offer held 79 percent of the company's stock, was issued new stock representing 33 percent of the total shares outstanding after the offer, in return for his personally assuming the remainder of the debt. Four months later, the company announced an agreement in principle with its two banks to restructure its bank loans. Although payment on these loans was four months overdue, neither bank had yet formally declared the company in default. This agreement, which provided for an extension of the loans' due date, was in default eight months later. The banks then agreed to fund the company on a monthly basis while it sought to sell off assets or obtain an infusion of outside equity. Four months after that, the company filed for Chapter 11.

Crystal Oil Company Classification: *Unsuccessful restructuring of bank, trade, and publicly traded debt (6/11/85–10/1/86; car = n.a.; p0 = 2, p1 = $\frac{3}{8}$).*

The company entered into an agreement with a major supplier to extend payment on its trade debt, in return for issuing the supplier a secured note. As disclosed in the company's 10k report, it was also in technical default on a secured mortgage note held by a bank, although details concerning how (or whether) the default was resolved were not reported. At the same time, the company undertook an exchange offer for its six publicly traded debenture issues, offering a package of common stock and new secured notes (having a higher coupon rate, payable in either cash or common stock). The old debentures represented approximately 80 percent of the company's long-term debt. Four months later, after extending and sweetening the offer seven times, the company accepted all 70 percent of the debentures that were tendered, resulting in the issuance to noteholders of approximately 26 percent of the company's common stock (following payment of interest on the new notes with common stock, noteholders' ownership increased to 59 percent within three months). Despite the success of the exchange offer, the company subsequently found it necessary to again restructure its debt. Within approximately a year of the conclusion of its exchange offer, the company made a 'prepackaged' Chapter 11 filing, after having first obtained creditors' consent to a reorganization plan. The company emerged from Chapter 11 after only three months.

Dunes Hotels and Casinos Inc. Classification: *Successful restructuring of bank and other privately-placed debt, accompanied by outside stock placement* $(8/31/83-2/6/84$; car $= 102.9\%$; $p0 = 4\frac{4}{8}$, $p1 = 6\frac{4}{8})$.

For six months, the company attempted to restructure a $30 million debt held by two private investors, Ronald and Stuart Perlman. Initially, the Perlmans agreed to acquire the company for $80 million in notes and the assumption of $105 million in debt. This agreement was replaced by another under which the Perlmans were to convert their debt into approximately 45 percent of the company's common stock. The restructuring of this and other debt was deemed essential to avert a bankruptcy filing. Finally, the company reached an agreement to place 41 percent of its common stock with John Jack Anderson, a private investor with prior management experience in the industry. At about the same time, the company restructured approximately $80 million of debt owed to its three institutional lenders (a bank, a leasing company, and American Financial Corporation), resulting in various payment deferrals. Terms of the agreement gave Mr. Anderson effective voting control over additional shares held by management, increasing the percentage of common shares he either owned or controlled to 51 percent. Mr. Anderson was named chairman of the company, succeeding Morris Shenker, who prior to the restructuring held 41 percent of the company's stock. Mr. Shenker, who remained CEO, had filed for personal bankruptcy four months previously.

Lamson & Sessions Co. Classification: *Successful restructuring of bank debt, accompanied by new private debt placement* $(12/31/82-4/29/85$; car $= 51.3\%$; $p0 = 3\frac{1}{8}$, $p1 = 3\frac{6}{8})$.

The company disclosed in its annual report that it was not in compliance with 'certain' covenants in its loan agreements, and had been attempting to restructure its debt to 24 bank and insurance company lenders. The company had no publicly traded debt. Ten months into the negotiations, the company announced that the restructuring effort had stalled because of disagreements among lenders over terms. The company refused to explain what the differences were, or disclose the identity of the lenders. A debt restructuring plan was announced five months later. Under the plan, the company's institutional debt was to be converted into cash, new secured notes, and convertible preferred stock (with dividends payable in either cash or common stock). Assuming full conversion of the preferred stock, the lenders would hold 34 percent of the firm's common stock. The cash payment, representing 24 percent of the balance owed, was raised through a new short-term secured credit facility with Congress Financial Corp. As part of the plan, borrowings under this facility were to be reduced by applying part of the proceeds raised from the subsequent divestiture of an operating subsidiary. The plan was adopted three months later at the company's annual meeting, where stockholders approved a requisite increase in the number of authorized common shares. At the same meeting, the company's chairman relinquished the post of CEO to the company president, and announced that he would soon also step down as chairman. Ten months later, the company repurchased (with cash) all of the new notes for 60 percent of their face value, and exchanged new common stock warrants for approximately a third of the preferred stock held by lenders.

Oak Industries Inc. Classification: *Successful restructuring of publicly traded debt, accompanied by outside stock placement* ($2/11/85$–$5/6/86$; $car = -33.3\%$; $p0 = 2\frac{1}{8}$, $p1 = 1\frac{4}{8}$).

The company, which had no bank debt, offered to exchange a package of notes, warrants, and common stock for its three outstanding publicly traded debenture issues. The new notes had a lower promised coupon rate and identical face value, and were to mature approximately ten years before the old debentures. The notes also allowed payment of interest in either cash or common stock (the company indicated that interest would be paid in common stock for the 'foreseeable future'). After extending the offer three times, the company accepted all 79 percent of the old debentures tendered, two months following the initial announcement of the offer. Approximately one week before the offer's expiration, the company's president resigned to 'pursue other business interests', amid an SEC investigation into alleged disclosure violations by the company. Seven months after the first exchange offer concluded, the company announced a new exchange offer for all of its publicly traded debt, in which holders were offered a package of cash and common stock. The cash part of the offer was financed by the sale of a major operating division and block of new equity securities to Allied-Signal Inc. (not previously a stockholder). The equity placement, which was made conditional on the success of the debt restructuring, consisted of common stock and warrants, representing about 20 percent of the company's common stock outstanding at the conclusion of the offer (assuming full exercise of the warrants). As part of the agreement, Allied-Signal also received three seats on the company's seven-member board of directors. The second exchange offer and the transaction with Allied-Signal were completed five months later, resulting in a doubling of the total number of common shares outstanding.

Petro Lewis Corp. Classification: *Successful restructuring of publicly traded debt, effected through acquisition of the company* ($3/28/85$–$12/31/86$; $car = -50.2\%$; $p0 = 4\frac{1}{8}$, $p1 = 2\frac{1}{8}$).

The company attempted to restructure its publicly traded debt through a series of three exchange offers. Approximately 75 percent of the company's long-term debt was publicly traded. In the first offer, which took two months to complete, the company sought to exchange new (secured and unsecured) notes and common stock for one of its note issues and three issues of preferred stock. Approximately 80 percent of the notes, and on average 58 percent of the preferred-stock issues, were tendered and accepted. Five months later, the company undertook a new exchange offer for four of its outstanding issues of subordinated notes and debentures. Holders were offered a package of new secured notes (carrying a higher coupon rate but lower face value), common stock, and cash. After several extensions of the expiration date, the offer concluded two months later, with about 50 percent of holders tendering. The third and final offer was announced five months later, and consisted of an offer to exchange a package of new secured and convertible notes and common stock for all nine of the company's publicly traded debt issues outstanding (including those that were issued under the earlier exchange offers). The company terminated this offer four months later, after deciding that it did not 'represent a viable alternative for the company'. Two months previously, an agreement had been announced in which Freeport-McMoRan Inc. would acquire the company to enable it to avert a bankruptcy filing, for a total price of about $770 million. Ultimately Freeport purchased the company by making a public tender offer for all of its outstanding publicly traded securities (debt as well as equity). The time that elapsed between the initial exchange offer and the consummation of the merger was approximately 20 months.

Seiscom Delta Inc. Classification: *Successful restructuring of bank debt, followed by bankruptcy more than one year later (5/12/83–4/26/85; car = −65.3%; p0 = 5$\frac{3}{8}$, p1 = 1$\frac{1}{8}$).*

The company announced that it restructured its bank debt by obtaining a one-year extension of the date on which its revolving bank loans would convert to term loans. In the *WSJ* story that reported the restructuring, the company refused to identify which banks were involved, and no mention of the transaction was made in the firm's 10k report for that year. The company had no publicly traded debt outstanding. Fourteen months later, the company was granted a 'second' waiver on a bank loan covenant (the first was not reported) that was in default because the company had exceeded the borrowing limit specified in its revolving credit agreement. Two weeks later, D. Gale Reese, chairman and CEO of the company, resigned under pressure from its banks. The *WSJ* quoted a company spokesman as saying: 'It's just a matter of the bank being willing to do certain things provided Gale Reese was not on the team.' In the same story that reported Mr. Reese's resignation, it was revealed that one of the company's banks granted a third waiver of the same loan covenant. Nine months later, a definitive agreement was reached to restructure the company's bank debt. The agreement provided for the banks to forgive 52 percent of the outstanding bank-loan balance, and grant a seven-month waiver of interest and nineteen-month waiver of principal owed on the remaining balance. In return, the banks were given a package of common stock, convertible preferred stock, and warrants, which together represented 77 percent of the company's outstanding common stock (assuming full conversion of preferred stock and warrants). In addition, the banks were granted an increased security interest in all of the company's assets. The agreement also provided for forgiveness of certain lease payments owed on the company's headquarters building. Seventeen months later, the company and four of its wholly owned subsidiaries filed for Chapter 11.

Tiger International Inc. Classification: *Successful restructuring of bank and publicly traded debt by parent company, accompanied by bankruptcy of subsidiary (2/14/83–3/25/85; car = 18.3%; p0 = 7$\frac{1}{8}$, p1 = 8$\frac{6}{8}$).*

The company and its bank lenders agreed on a tentative restructuring plan four months following the company's decision to unilaterally suspend interest and principal payments on about half of its total $1.8 billion in debt. Regarding the company's decision to suspend payments on its debt, a company spokesman was paraphrased by the *WSJ* as saying that 'the company chose to announce suspension of interest and principal on debt, rather than issue a joint release with lenders, because of the large number of banks involved (60, including certain other unspecified 'lending institutions') and the complexity of the loan agreements'. Under the proposed plan, the company was to be granted an extension on scheduled payments owed by three operating subsidiaries, receive a new revolving credit line from an existing lender, and implement an exchange offer for its two publicly traded issues of debentures. Regarding lenders' reaction to the plan, the firm's chairman noted: 'It's in the lenders' interest to do this. All of them agree that the going concern is the important thing.' On the day before the announcement of the plan, it was announced that the company's president and financial vice president had both resigned; the company denied allegations that this action had been prompted by its lenders. Interest on the new credit line was tied to the company's future earnings performance. The exchange offer took three months to complete, with approximately 81 percent of all bonds being tendered. Tendering debenture-holders received a package of new debentures (having a lower face value, shorter average maturity, and identical coupon rate), common stock, and warrants; interest on the new debentures was payable in either cash or common stock. Final agreement on the restructuring of subsidiary debt was reached by two of the subsidiaries seven months after the initial plan was proposed, and by the third, a year after the plan proposal date. Shortly thereafter the company undertook an additional exchange offer for two issues of publicly traded debt owed by one of its subsidiaries, offering a package of common stock and warrants. Fourteen months following the initial suspension of debt payments, the company revealed in its annual report that it was still attempting to restructure the debt of a subsidiary. Eight months later, the subsidiary independently filed for Chapter 11, after it failed to reach a standstill agreement with its banks on a $132 million secured note that was in default.

Verna Corp. Classification: *Successful restructuring of bank and privately placed debt (12/31/ 82–4/29/85; car = –136.7%; $p0 = 4\frac{7}{8}$, $p1 = \frac{13}{16}$).*

After reporting a quarterly loss, the company granted its two banks a security interest in 39 drilling rigs (although no default was reported). Six months later the company announced that it had restructured its bank debt. The banks, which were owed approximately $28 million, were given warrants convertible into 13 percent of the company's common stock, a security interest in accounts receivable, and a 'fee' of $850,000. In return, the company was granted a thirteen-month deferral of interest and principal payments, and an increase in its borrowing limit under an existing revolving loan. Concurrently with the bank debt restructuring, the company privately placed $1 million of new secured subordinated notes with a group of three venture capital companies. In return for purchasing the notes, said companies were given common stock warrants for 8 percent of the common stock and three permanent seats on the board of directors. Ten months later, both the bank debt and new notes hadto be restructured, resulting in various payment deferrals and increased grants of security. Among other things, the banks were given the right to force certain asset sales to effect repayment of the debt. Eighteen months later, the company restructured its debt for a third and final time, following stockholder approval of the transaction. Debt owed to the two banks was converted into an issue of new secured notes, convertible preferred stock, and preferred stock warrants, representing 56 percent of the company's common stock (assuming full conversion of the banks' claims). The notes held by the three venture capital lenders were exchanged for new common stock, representing 24 percent of the common stock then outstanding. Three months later, four of the firm's five outside directors resigned after the company's insurer withdrew its liability coverage.

References

Altman, Edward, 1984, A further investigation of the bankruptcy cost question, Journal of Finance 39, 1067–1089.

Altman, Edward, 1989, Measuring corporate bond mortality and performance, Journal of Finance 44, 909–922.

Ang, James, Jess Chua, and John McConnell, 1982, The administrative costs of corporate bankruptcy: A note, Journal of Finance 37, 219–226.

Asquith, Paul, David Mullins, Jr., and Eric Wolff, 1989, Original issue high yield bonds: Aging analyses of defaults, exchanges and calls, Journal of Finance 44, 923–952.

Aivazian, Varouj and Jeffrey Callen, 1983, Reorganization in bankruptcy and the issue of strategic risk, Journal of Banking and Finance 7, 119–133.

Baldwin, Carliss and Scott Mason, 1983, The resolution of claims in financial distress: The case of Massey Ferguson, Journal of Finance 38, 505–516.

Bradley, Michael, Anand Desai, and E. Han Kim, 1983, The rationale behind interfirm tender offers, Journal of Financial Economics 11, 183–206.

Brown, David, 1989, Claimholder incentive conflicts in reorganization: The role of bankruptcy law, Review of Financial Studies 2, 109–123.

Bulow, Jeremy and John Shoven, 1978, The bankruptcy decision, Bell Journal of Economics 9, 436–445.

DeAngelo, Linda, 1988, Managerial competition, information costs, and corporate governance: The use of accounting performance measures in proxy contests, Journal of Accounting and Economics 10, 3–36.

DeAngelo, Harry, Linda DeAngelo, and Douglas Skinner, 1990, An empirical investigation of the relation between accounting choice and dividend policy in troubled companies, Unpublished paper (University of Michigan, Ann Arbor, MI).

DeNatale, Andrew, 1981, The creditors' committee under the Bankruptcy Code: A primer, American Bankruptcy Law Journal 55, 43–62.

Douglas-Hamilton, Margaret, 1975, Creditor liabilities resulting from improper interference with the management of a financially troubled debtor, Business Lawyer 31, 343–365.

Eberhart, Allan, William Moore, and Rodney Roenfeldt, 1990, Security pricing and deviations from the absolute priority rule in bankruptcy proceedings, Journal of Finance, forthcoming.

Franks, Julian and Walter Torous, 1989, An empirical investigation of U.S. firms in reorganization, Journal of Finance 44, 747–769.

Giammarino, Ronald, 1989, The resolution of financial distress, Review of Financial Studies 2, 25–47.

Gilson, Stuart, 1989, Management turnover and financial distress, Journal of Financial Economics 25, 241–262.

Gilson, Stuart, 1990, Bankruptcy, boards, banks, and blockholders, Journal of Financial Economics, this volume.

Gould, John, 1973, The economics of legal conflicts, Journal of Legal Studies 2, 279–300.

Green, Jerry and Jean-Jacques Laffont, 1987, Renegotiation and the form of efficient contracts, Unpublished paper (Harvard University, Cambridge, MA).

Hart, Oliver and John Moore, 1989, Default and renegotiation: A dynamic model of debt, Unpublished paper (Massachusetts Institute of Technology, Cambridge, MA).

Haugen, Robert and Lemma Senbet, 1978, The insignificance of bankruptcy costs to the theory of optimal capital structure, Journal of Finance 33, 383–393.

Hoshi, Takeo, Anil Kashyap, and David Scharfstein, 1990, The role of banks in reducing the costs of financial distress in Japan, Journal of Financial Economics, this volume.

Jackson, Thomas, 1986, The logic and limits of bankruptcy law (Harvard University Press, Cambridge, MA).

James, Christopher, 1987, Some evidence on the uniqueness of bank loans, Journal of Financial Economics 19, 217–235.

Jensen, Michael, 1989a, Active investors, LBOs, and the privatization of bankruptcy, Journal of Applied Corporate Finance 2, 35–44.

Jensen, Michael, 1989b, Eclipse of the public corporation, Harvard Business Review, Sept./Oct., 61–74.

Huberman, Gur and Charles Kahn, 1988, Default, foreclosure, and strategic renegotation, Unpublished paper (Columbia University, New York, NY).

King, Lawrence, 1979, Chapter 11 of the 1978 Bankrutpcy Code, American Bankruptcy Law Journal 53, 107–131.

Klee, Kenneth, 1979, All you ever wanted to know about cram down under the new bankruptcy code, American Bankruptcy Law Journal 53, 133–171.

Lang, Larry, Rene Stulz, and Ralph Walkling, 1988, Managerial performance, Tobin's q and the gains from successful tender offers, Journal of Financial Economics 24, 137–154.

Maddala, G., 1983, Limited-dependent and qualitative variables in econometrics (Cambridge University Press, Cambridge).

Manski, Charles and Daniel McFadden, 1983, Alternative estimators and sample designs for discrete choice analysis, in: Charles Manski and Daniel McFadden, eds., Structural analysis of discrete data with econometric applications (MIT Press, Boston, MA).

Mooradian, Robert, 1989, Recapitalizations and the free-rider problem, Unpublished paper (University of Florida, Gainesville, FL).

Myers, Stewart, 1977, Determinants of corporate borrowing, Journal of Financial Economics 5, 147–176.

Roe, Mark, 1987, The voting prohibition in bond workouts, The Yale Law Journal 97, 232–279.

Scholes, Myron and Joseph Williams, 1977, Estimating betas from non-synchronous data, Journal of Financial Economics 5, 309–327.

Smith, C. and Jerold Warner, 1979, On financial contracting: An analysis of bond covenants, Journal of Financial Economics 7, 117–161.

Stein, Sol, 1989, A feast for lawyers (M. Evans and Company, Inc., New York, NY).

Titman, Sheridan, 1984, The effect of capital structure on a firm's liquidation decision, Journal of Financial Economics 13, 137–151.

Trost, Ronald, 1979, Business reorganizations under Chapter 11 of the new Bankruptcy Code, Business Lawyer, April, 1309–1346.

Wall Street Journal, 1988, Corporate finance, 'leveraged to the hilt', October 25, p. A11.

Warner, Jerold, 1977a, Bankruptcy, absolute priority and the pricing of risky debt claims, Journal of Financial Economics 4, 239–276.

Warner, Jerold, 1977b, Bankruptcy costs: Some evidence, Journal of Finance 32, 337–347.

Weiss, Lawrence, 1990, Bankruptcy resolution: Direct costs and violation of priority of claims, Journal of Financial Economics, this volume.

White, Michelle, 1989, The corporate bankruptcy decision, The Journal of Economic Perspectives 3, 129–151.

Zinbarg, Edward, 1975, The private placement loan agreement, Financial Analysts Journal 31, 33–52.

The role of banks in reducing the costs of financial distress in Japan*

Takeo Hoshi

University of California, San Diego, CA 92093, USA

Anil Kashyap

Board of Governors, Federal Reserve System, Washington, DC 20551, USA

David Scharfstein

Massachusetts Institute of Technology, Cambridge, MA 02139, USA
National Bureau of Economic Research, Cambridge, MA 02138, USA

Received November 1989, final version received August 1990

We explore the idea that financial distress is costly because free-rider problems and information asymmetries make it difficult for firms to renegotiate with their creditors. We present evidence that Japanese firms with financial structures in which these problems are likely to be small perform better than other firms after the onset of distress. In particular, we show that firms in industrial groups – those with close financial relationships to their banks, suppliers, and customers – invest more and sell more after the onset of distress than nongroup firms. We find similar results for nongroup firms that nevertheless have strong ties to a main bank.

1. Introduction

The increase in leverage of many U.S. corporations in the 1980s has touched off a public debate about its effect on economic activity.[1] In one

*We thank Ben Bernanke, Wayne Ferson, Kenneth Froot, Robert Gertner, David Hirshleifer, Michael Jensen, John McMillan, Koichi Sakamoto, Steven Sharpe, Walter Torous, Robert Vishny, Karen Wruck, and seminar participants at the Harvard Business School, the National Bureau of Economic Research, Princeton University, University of California at Los Angeles, University of California at San Diego, University of Chicago, The Wharton School, and Yale University for helpful comments, Fumie Kojima, Koichi Sakurada, and Andrew Wiedlin for very able research assistance, MIT's International Financial Services Research Center for financial support, and the Nikkei Data Bank Bureau for allowing us to use their data. Scharfstein is grateful for research support from a John M. Olin Fellowship at the National Bureau of Economic Research and a fellowship from Batterymarch Financial Management. Any opinions expressed are those of the authors, not those of the Federal Reserve Board of Governors or its staff.

[1]There has been little change in average debt/equity ratios, but a dramatic increase in the leverage of the most highly leveraged companies. See Bernanke, Campbell, and Whited (1990).

Journal of Financial Economics 27 (1990) 67–88. North-Holland

view, large debt burdens constrain investment and threaten financial stability; in another, they prevent corporate waste and improve economic performance. Either way, high leverage increases the likelihood that firms will be unable to make their debt payments, and it raises concern about what happens to these distressed firms. Some argue that, as long as a firm has good prospects, financial distress will have no real impact; the firm's debt will be renegotiated to ensure its survival.[2] Others take a less sanguine view: creditors' conflicting claims make renegotiation difficult and may lead creditors to liquidate the firm even though it is collectively inefficient for them to do so.[3]

Both theories of financial distress have some appeal, but there are virtually no facts to lead us to one or the other. In this paper, we attempt to bring some evidence to bear on this question. We analyze how financial distress affects firms' investment behavior and their performance in product markets. Our empirical evidence suggests that financial distress is costly for firms that are likely to have significant conflicts among their creditors.

The evidence is from Japan. We focus on Japanese firms because of the kind of financial environment in which they operate. Many firms in Japan have very close ties to a 'main bank'. The bank provides debt financing to the firm, owns some of its equity, and may even place bank executives in top management positions. For many of these firms, the main-bank relationship is part of a larger industrial structure known as the *keiretsu*, a group of firms centered around affiliated banks and financial institutions. Firms in industrial groups also have strong product-market ties to each other that are strengthened by cross-share ownership.

This financial and industrial structure can reduce the costs of financial distress. These costs stem from the inherent difficulty of renegotiating financial claims, particularly when there are many creditors. As Bulow and Shoven (1978) and Gertner and Scharfstein (1990) point out, free-rider problems reduce the incentive for creditors to grant financial relief or extend credit: an individual creditor bears the full costs, but shares the benefits. Moreover, when debt is diffusely held, bondholders are not likely to be well informed about the firm and may not know whether it is profitable to provide new capital or to give interest and principal concessions. These problems can also spill over and disrupt supplies and sales: suppliers may not be willing to provide trade credit and make long-term commitments; and customers may be wary about whether the firm will be able to meet its implicit and explicit warranties.

---

[2]This version of the Coase Theorem has been espoused by Haugen and Senbet (1978) and, more recently, by Jensen (1989).

[3]This view is implicit in theories of leverage that argue that firms balance the tax advantage of debt and the greater costs of financial distress.

Such problems are probably less severe for firms with strong relationships to banks. Because substantial debt and equity stakes are held by just a few financial institutions, free-rider problems are less prevalent. In addition, since the main bank is probably well informed about the firm and its prospects, problems stemming from asymmetric information between creditors and firms are likely to be small. Finally, the customers and suppliers of group firms in which they own equity are more likely to maintain their product-market ties.

Thus, our approach is to see whether firms that have close financial relationships to banks and their trading partners can more effectively avoid the problems associated with financial distress. Our main empirical finding is that financially distressed group firms invest more and sell more than non-group firms in the years following the onset of financial distress. Moreover, firms that receive a larger fraction of their debt financing from their largest lender invest and sell more, even if they are not group members. These findings suggest that, when financial claims are spread among many creditors, financial distress is more costly than when they are concentrated.

This evidence on the costs of financial distress differs from findings in previous studies. Warner (1977) focuses on the administrative costs of the bankruptcy process. He estimates that bankrupt railroads between 1933 and 1955 incurred administrative expenses during bankruptcy of 4% of their prebankruptcy market value. Weiss (1990) finds administrative costs of about 3% of market value for a subsample of firms that filed for Chapter 11 bankruptcy protection between 1980 and 1986. As the authors indicate, given that bankruptcy filings are relatively uncommon even for financially distressed firms, these expenses do not amount to a significant cost of financial distress.

Thus, if the costs of financial distress are large, they must stem from real efficiency costs in the product market. Cutler and Summers (1988) try to detect these costs in the events following Pennzoil's successful $10 billion judgement against Texaco and Texaco's subsequent attempts to have this judgement overturned. One might expect that the outcome of litigation favoring one company over the other would not change their combined value because they were fighting over a lump-sum transfer. Cutler and Summers, however, found that when the court ruled against Texaco, thereby increasing Texaco's expected liability to Pennzoil, the combined value of the two firms fell. The cumulative losses were over $3 million, much larger than any reasonable expectation of the administrative costs incurred in the dispute. The authors interpret this finding as evidence that the financial distress brought on by Texaco's $10 billion liability made it less able to raise capital and operate efficiently. This finding supports our evidence, but it is only suggestive: it would be useful to have more direct evidence on the sources of inefficiency and more systematic evidence from other cases.

Altman (1984) tries to measure the losses from financial distress by calculating the extent to which firms' profits are abnormally low in the three years before they file for bankruptcy. He attributes the lower profits to efficiency losses from financial distress. Unfortunately, this empirical finding does not distinguish between the cause of financial distress and its consequences: a firm's performance may be poor because it is financially distressed, but the firm also may be financially distressed because its performance is poor.

We try to distinguish between these effects. Our point is *not* that financially distressed firms perform worse than financially sound firms, although this is certainly true. Rather, if a firm is financially distressed, it performs better than other financially distressed firms if its financial structure makes it relatively easy to renegotiate its liabilities. This differential response suggests there may be efficiency losses during financial distress for some firms.

This evidence complements our earlier work [Hoshi, Kashyap, and Scharfstein (1990, 1991)] examining the role of bank relationships in facilitating corporate investment. We showed that investment by group firms is less sensitive to their liquidity than it is for nongroup firms. We interpreted this finding as evidence that bank relationships relax liquidity constraints by lessening information and incentive problems in the capital market. The results of this paper can help to explain our earlier findings for at least two reasons. First, because group firms can take on more debt (since their costs of distress are lower), they are better able to exploit its tax advantages. This lowers their cost of capital. Second, group firms that need to raise capital can do so by issuing debt. They then avoid equity issues which tend to depress share prices [Myers and Majluf (1984) and Asquith and Mullins (1986)]. Thus, reducing the costs of financial distress facilitates investment and relaxes liquidity constraints even when firms are not distressed.

The paper is organized as follows. The next section describes Japanese corporate financing patterns in more detail. We also summarize the evidence – largely case studies – on the role of Japanese banking relationships in moderating the costs of financial distress. Section 3 describes our data, and we present our empirical findings in section 4. Section 5 concludes with a discussion of the implications of these findings.

2. Japanese corporate finance and financial distress

One of the most important features of Japanese corporate financing arrangements is associated with an organizational structure known as the *keiretsu*, or industrial group. We focus on the six largest industrial groups (Mitsubishi, Mitsui, Sumitomo, Fuyo, Dai-ichi Kangyo, and Sanwa), which have their origins in the 1950s. The former three emerged from the remains of the *zaibatsu* that were outlawed after World War II. The latter three were established somewhat later by the banks now at their core. Most large Japanese companies in the 1950s developed some affiliation with an industrial group. Membership in these groups have been remarkably stable for over three decades.

The six groups we examine are both diversified and vertically integrated. Almost half of the 200 largest firms in Japan are members of one of these groups. The six groups account for roughly 40% to 55% of sales in the natural resources, primary metal, industrial machinery, chemical, and cement industries [Gerlach (1987)]. As evidence of vertical integration, Gerlach notes that group firms are three times as likely to trade with group members as with nonmembers. These trading relationships are reinforced by cross-shareholdings in the group; firms with close product-market ties often hold significant stakes in each other.

From our perspective, the most important aspect of the group is the relationship between its manufacturing firms and financial institutions, both banks and insurance companies. For example, a Mitsubishi manufacturing firm may have ties to the Mitsubishi Bank, Mitsubishi Trust Bank, Meiji Life Insurance, and Tokio Fire and Marine Insurance, all core financial institutions of the Mitsubishi group. This relationship has several aspects. First, group firms do a substantial fraction of their borrowing from group financial institutions. Usually, one of these institutions is considered the firm's 'main bank': it takes a more active role in arranging financing for the firm, even though the firm borrows from other institutions in and out of the group. Using a loose definition of group affiliation, Sheard (1985) estimates that in 1980 group firms did 21% of their borrowing from their group's financial institutions.

In addition, group financial institutions typically own equity in the firms to which they lend. In our sample period, financial institutions were allowed to hold up to 10% of a firm's outstanding shares. By 1987, they were forced to reduce their holdings to no more than 5%. Sheard (1985) calculates that for 72% of Japanese firms the largest lender was one of the firm's top five shareholders.

Finally, the placement of key bank personnel in top managerial positions of group firms reinforces the banks' power as shareholders and creditors. In addition, former and current bank executives sit on the boards of many firms. Using information in the 1982 edition of the publication *Kigyo Keiretsu Soran*, we find that of the 1103 Japanese firms listed on the Tokyo Stock Exchange 8% have at least one director from the firm's main bank and 34% have a former main bank executive as a director (and often a top manager). As we discuss below, board representation and transfer of management personnel are particularly common in times of financial distress.

The question we focus on is whether these close financial links reduce the costs of financial distress. These costs can come from at least three sources.

First, when there are many creditors it is difficult to negotiate with all of them simultaneously.[4] Holdout creditors can then free-ride on others. As discussed by Myers (1977), Bulow and Shoven (1978), and Gertner and Scharfstein (1990), difficulties in negotiating with creditors may lead to underinvestment and inefficient liquidation. Even if the firm has valuable investment opportunities, an individual creditor may be reluctant to finance them because part of the greater future cash flows accrue to the holdout creditors. Similarly, even if it is efficient for creditors collectively to write down the debt, a sole creditor may be unwilling to do so because he bears all the cost and receives only part of the benefit.

Second, these problems are exacerbated when creditors are not well informed about the firm's prospects. In this case it is difficult to raise capital from one creditot,[5] let alone get numerous creditors to agree to a financial restructuring that promotes investment and avoids inefficient liquidation.[6]

Finally, there are more subtle forms of credit that are difficult to obtain when a firm is in financial distress. Consumers deciding whether to buy a durable good must also decide whether the firm will be able to meet its implicit and explicit warranties.[7] This confidence is a form of credit that consumers may be unwilling to extend to firms in financial distress. Moreover, suppliers may be unwilling to extend trade credit.[8] And, when it is not clear whether a firm will remain in business, product-market competitors may compete aggressively to convince creditors that it is indeed unprofitable for the firm to remain in business.[9]

In theory, group financing arrangements can moderate these problems in several ways. First, because there are fewer creditors and the main bank

---

[4]In fact, in the United States, the Trust Indenture Act prohibits bondholders from renegotiating with the firm. See Roe (1987) and Gertner and Scharfstein (1990) for an analysis.

[5]See Bolton and Scharfstein (1989) for a model in which financial distress leads to inefficient liquidation even though there is only one creditor.

[6]Gertner (1989) explores the added inefficiencies when there are more than two parties bargaining and there is asymmetric information.

[7]See Titman (1984).

[8]Cutler and Summers (1988) quote from an affidavit Texaco filed with the bankruptcy court:

> The increasing deterioration of Texaco's credit and financial condition has made it more and more difficult, with each passing day, for Texaco to finance and operate its business... As normal supply sources become inaccessible and other financing is unavailable, Texaco's operations will begin to grind to a halt. In fact, Texaco is already having to consider the prospect of shutting down one of its largest domestic refineries because of its growing inability to acquire crude and feedstock.

[9]See Bolton and Scharfstein (1989). An example of this is the case of Massey Ferguson. Its main competitor, John Deere, used Massey's financial distress as an opportunity to compete more agressively making it even more difficult for Massey to resolve its short-term financial problems.

holds a large financial stake in the firm, free-rider problems are less severe. In addition, because of its financial stake, the main bank is probably well informed about the firm's financial position and its prospects. Problems in obtaining credit because of information asymmetries are therefore reduced.

A more subtle reason that free-rider problems may be less severe stems from the repeated participation of banks in lending consortiums. For example, the Mitsubishi Bank may be the main bank for a firm in the Mitsubishi group, but the firm will typically borrow from banks outside the group as well. The Mitsubishi Bank will in turn participate in lending consortiums headed by other banks that serve as the main lenders to firms outside the Mitsubishi group. It is clear to all members of the consortium that the main bank is responsible for helping the firm in times of distress. Repeated participation in these consortiums ensures that the main bank fulfills its implicit contract to provide relief even though doing so may not seem best in the short run.[10]

Finally, there are numerous direct and indirect financial links between suppliers, customers, and financially distressed firms. Suppliers and customers often have an equity stake in the firm, and the firm may even have a stake in its suppliers and customers. Moreover, the firm's main bank may also be the main bank for the suppliers and customers. This financial web could make suppliers more willing to extend trade credit and invest in long-term supply relationships, and customers more willing to buy from the firm.

Group affiliation may be sufficient to overcome some of the problems associated with financial distress, but it is by no means necessary. There are firms that do not belong to a group that nevertheless have very strong ties to a single bank. For example, one of the nongroup firms in our sample, Meiji Leather Tanning, received 36% of its bank financing and 10% of its equity financing (the legal maximum) from its largest lender.[11] Such firms may not receive financial support from the other manufacturing firms in a group, but in theory they should receive help from closely affiliated financial institutions. We try to detect this possibility by collecting data on how much firms borrow from their largest lender and how much equity these lenders hold.

Before determining whether our hypotheses are supported by the data, we discuss a number of cases of financial distress. These cases highlight the main bank's role in helping firms work out of financial distress. They are discussed at greater length in Sheard (1985).

Perhaps the best-known case in which banking ties and group affiliation played a crucial role in helping a firm through financial distress is

---

[10]Aoki (1988, p. 149) makes a similar point, arguing that the main bank bears a disproportionate share of the costs because its reputation as a responsible monitor is at stake.

[11]In fact, Meiji Leather Tanning did quite well after the onset of financial distress: both its investment and sales growth exceeded its industry's average.

Sumitomo Bank's restructuring of Mazda, the automobile manufacturer.[12] Mazda experienced considerable financial difficulty after the 1973 oil shock sharply reduced the demand for its gas-guzzling rotary-engine cars. In response to these troubles, Sumitomo Bank and Sumitomo Trust sent a number of their top executives to serve as Mazda directors and others to manage key divisions of the company. They lent Mazda money at favorable rates and encouraged the company to sell its shares in the banks. Sumitomo Corporation, the large trading company of the Sumitomo group, took charge of distribution and the newly appointed management team implemented efficiency improvements in production. The banks, along with Sumitomo Corporation, also promoted Mazda sales among their customer firms and employees and leaned on suppliers to sell to the firm at favorable prices. Mazda is now a profitable company. The combination of bank-induced managerial changes, financial support, and pressure on suppliers is typical of the role banks play when their clients are in financial distress.

We know that several firms in our sample received help from group financial institutions when they were in financial distress. For example, Nippon Light Metal benefited from interest-rate reductions from Dai-ichi Kangyo Bank, saving the company about Y900 million per year (approximately $4.5 million at exchange rates prevailing then). Mitsui Toatsu received interest concessions from the Mitsui Bank. Sumitomo Bank implemented a large-scale restructuring of Daishowa Paper, placing bank executives in top managerial positions, writing down half its outstanding debt, and moving the firm into more profitable lines of business.

Although there are numerous anecdotes suggesting that main banks play an important role when Japanese firms are in financial distress, there is little statistical evidence along these lines. Indeed, Miwa (1985) fails to find changes in the lending behavior of the main banks of 134 financially distressed firms. The only statistical evidence we know that is consistent with the anecdotal evidence is presented by Suzuki and Wright (1985). They identify a set of Japanese firms that filed for bankruptcy liquidation or reorganization and a set that was given interest or principal concessions by creditors. They find that group firms with close ties to banks are more likely to fall into the latter set. This suggests that the concentration of financial claims enables firms to avoid the bankruptcy courts and yet still work out of financial distress. This finding is consistent with Gilson, John, and Lang's (1990) analysis of U.S. firms showing that firms that rely more on bank financing than on bond financing are more likely to restructure outside the bankruptcy courts.[13]

---

[12] See Pascale and Rohlen (1983) for details.

[13] The Corporate Reorganization Law of 1952 resembles the reorganization code that existed in the U.S. before the recent bankruptcy reform. This is not a coincidence because the Japanese code was adopted during the U.S. post-war occupation.

3. Data

The data on which our empirical analysis is based come mostly from the Nikkei Financial Data Tapes. This source contains financial data on all Japanese companies listed on the Tokyo Stock Exchange. We restrict our attention to manufacturing firms. The tapes also contain data on some, but not all, companies that were once on the Tokyo Stock Exchange and were subsequently delisted. We augmented these data with other data available from Nikkei on delisted firms. Thus, in principle we can analyze the entire sample of financially distressed firms. In many cases, however, distressed firms are restructured through liquidations, asset sales, spinoffs, or mergers, making it virtually impossible to track their subsequent performance. This introduces the possibility of selection bias in our results; we discuss this possibility in more detail below.

The choice of sample also depends on how financial distress is defined. Among the many possible definitions, we chose one that selects firms experiencing an immediate cash-flow crisis. In particular, we identified all firms whose operating income was greater than their interest payments in one year (coverage ratio greater than one), but less in the next two. We also required that the firm be listed on the Tokyo Stock Exchange at the onset of distress. The requirement that the firm was healthy at least once in the sample helps weed out firms that were distressed even at the beginning of the sample. We tried to exclude these distressed firms because we wanted to begin tracking firms at the start of their troubles. We also considered an alternative procedure that required that all firms have no history of financial distress for at least four years. This stricter selection rule left us with only 78 firms, but did not have much effect on the empirical results.

In describing the data, we compare various performance measures before, during, and after the onset of financial difficulty. As a convention, we date the second year in which the coverage ratio is below one as period t. Thus, for example, period $t - 2$ refers to the year of healthy performance preceding the two years of distress and period $t + 3$ is three years after the second year in which the coverage ratio is below one.

The sample period in which firms could enter our sample as distressed begins in April 1978 and ends in March 1985. For most firms, the fiscal year runs from April 1 to the following March 31. As the first entry in table 1 shows, over the entire sample of 6,209 observations, 12.3% of the observations have coverage ratios below one. As the next line shows, however, in 2.9% of the observations, a company has one healthy year followed by two distressed years. A firm can fall into this latter category more than once during the sample. We take the first time this occurs as the onset of distress. Of the roughly 950 listed manufacturing companies in the Nikkei database and the other delisted firms, 168 experience at least one bout of financial distress under this selection rule.

Table 1

Selected summary statistics of firms listed on the Tokyo Stock Exchange between 1978 and 1985. Number of firms varies from year to year, but averages almost 950. Coverage is the ratio of operating income to interest expense. Depressed industries are those targeted for structural adjustment by Japan's Ministry of International Trade and Industry.

Firm characteristic	Percent of sample
Coverage < 1	12.3%
Coverage < 1 for two straight years	2.9
Depressed industry	8.3
Of observations in depressed industry those with coverage < 1	20.6
Of observations in depressed industry those with coverage < 1 for two straight years	4.1
Of observations in healthy industry those with coverage < 1	11.6
Of observations in healthy industry those with coverage < 1 for two straight years	2.8

A natural question is whether this rule reliably identifies distressed firms. To assess this question, we sort the sample on the basis of whether the firm is classified by the Ministry of International Trade and Industry (MITI) as being in a structurally depressed industry and therefore targeted for structural adjustment.[14] Overall, firms in these industries account for 8.3% of the observations. The incidence of distress is higher in these industries than in others. As the table shows, for more than 20% of the observations, firms in depressed industries have a coverage ratio below one and for 4.1% of the observations a previously healthy firm runs into financial difficulty two years in a row. These percentages are larger than the percentages for firms in healthy industries, 11.6% and 2.8%, respectively.

In the remainder of the paper we focus on the performance of the distressed firms. For some of the 168 companies that we identify as distressed, we cannot get complete or consistent data. The data shortages leave us with a sample of 125 firms. Before describing the results of the analysis, we explain why the other 43 firms are omitted and discuss how the omissions could bias the results.

The main data difficulty arises when firms in financial distress participate in some kind of restructuring: a merger or takeover, a spinoff of a division, or a sale of a major asset. These changes make it virtually impossible to track performance after the onset of distress because the size of the firm changes discontinuously. The Nikkei database codes 25 firms as having undergone restructurings of this sort. These firms are dropped from the sample.

[14]These industries are reported in Ueksa (1987, p. 493). The Depressed Industries Law covering 1978 to 1983 identified 14 industries as depressed and in need of structural adjustment. This industry classification is more narrowly defined than ours. Under our scheme we identify 9 industries as depressed. The Structural Reform Law covering 1983–1988 identifies 23 industries as depressed; in our classification scheme this amounts to 11 industries.

An additional 3 firms are dropped because they were liquidated and then delisted according to *Nihon Keizai Shimbun*, the leading Japanese financial daily. Another firm was dropped from the Nikkei database, but we could not determine whether this was because of a merger or a bankruptcy. Finally, we had incomplete or unreliable data on certain key variables of interest for 14 other firms. In four cases, the data indicated more than a 200% increase in the capital stock in a single year. We assume that these data were misreported (or that there had been an unrecorded merger), so we exclude these four firms. We were also unable to obtain complete data on depreciable asset for four firms, making the construction of the investment variable impossible. The data omission occurred well before these firms became financially distressed. For six companies we were unable to collect detailed shareholding information.

Omission of these 14 firms is not likely to introduce selection bias. The omission of the 30 other companies that were restructured or liquidated is potentially more troubling. If, for example, all of the restructured firms were relatively unhealthy group firms, their omission could explain why group firms tend to outperform nongroup firms. To address this concern we collected information on these restructurings from *Nihon Keizai Shimbun*. From the articles we find no reason to believe that there is any systematic pattern that might bias the results. Of the 25 mergers, spinoffs, or asset sales, 16 are nongroup firms and nine are group firms (according to a loose classification scheme that we discuss below). These proportions reflect the roughly 2 to 1 proportion of nongroup to group firms in the entire sample of distressed firms. There is no obvious selection bias that we can detect, but nevertheless we cannot rule it out.

One piece of evidence suggests that, if anything, there may be a selection bias against finding a difference between group and nongroup firms. Of the three bankruptcy liquidations, all were nongroup firms. This is consistent with Suzuki and Wright's (1985) finding that financially distressed unaffiliated firms are more likely to go bankrupt than financially distressed group firms. If these unaffiliated bankrupt firms are worse on average than the rest of the sample, the sample of unaffiliated firms that we actually analyze is probably biased slightly toward relatively healthy ones.

The next step in forming the data is to classify firms as either group or nongroup firms. The dichotomous nature of this classification probably overstates the extent to which the two sets of firms differ. Membership is not clearly defined, but there are varying degrees of affiliation, which we try to pick up with this classification scheme. One indication of group affiliation is whether the firm sits on the group's President's Council, the set of firms that meets regularly to discuss issues facing the group. We consider these firms part of the group.

There are firms, however, that have some group affiliation, but do not sit on the President's Council. Identifying them requires some judgement. One approach is to use the affiliations as identified by publications that provide analyses of the *keiretsu*. *Keiretsu no Kenkyu* stands out as one that focuses on the financial ties between firms and banks. *Keiretsu no Kenkyu*'s classification scheme is fairly loose, however, and tends to classify as group firms those with only marginal affiliations.

As a result, we use Nakatani's (1984) refinement of *Keiretsu no Kenkyu*'s classification scheme. Nakatani's refinement selects firms with stable group ties. Unfortunately, Nakatani does not classify firms that were involved in merger activity. Since his sample ends in 1983, we verified that the affiliations he identified were unchanged in the 1986 edition of *Keiretsu no Kenkyu*.[15] Thus, our set of group firms includes this updated list of Nakatani-identified group firms and the President's Council firms.

The remaining firms in the sample that do not fit these criteria are classified as nongroup firms. Although some of them are actually classified by *Keiretsu no Kenkyu* as being related to a group, their ties are weaker. Thus, we lump them together with the smaller number of firms that have no relationship with a group. In the end, we are left with 45 group firms and 80 nongroup firms.

For further information on the strength of a firm's bank relationship, we use detailed bank-borrowing and equity data. The Nikkei database contains data back to 1977 on the amount each firm borrows from each bank in Japan. Thus, for both group and nongroup firms, we calculate the fraction of all bank borrowing that comes from the firm's largest lender in period t. We call this variable *TOPLEND*.[16] In addition, from *Keiretsu no Kenkyu*, we calculate the fraction of the firm's outstanding shares held by the largest lender in year t. We call this variable *SHARE*.

Table 2 lists summary statistics on the 125 firms in our sample. The first two rows compare the mean (gross) investment rate of financially distressed firms with the industry average. The investment rate in period t is the change in the capital stock of depreciable assets during the period plus depreciation normalized by the capital stock at the beginning of the period. The capital stock numbers from which the investment series are derived are estimates of the replacement cost of capital. These estimates require converting book values of capital to market values through an iterative procedure. The calculations are described in more detail in Hoshi and Kashyap (1990).

The cumulative investment rate listed in the table is the sum of the investment rates in periods $t + 1$ through $t + 3$. As the table indicates, financially distressed firms invest substantially less than the industry average

---

[15]We found two firms whose affiliation weakened by 1986.

[16]Some of the firms in our sample had no bank borrowing. We set *TOPLEND* equal to zero for these firms. An alternative procedure is to calculate *TOPLEND* as the ratio of group borrowing to total debt. This has no substantive effects on the empirical results.

Table 2

Definitions and summary statistics of variables in the sample of 125 financially distressed Japanese firms from 1978 to 1985. Year t denotes the second consecutive year in which a firm's coverage ratio (operating income divided by interest expense) is below one. Financially distressed firms are those for which coverage is less than one in year t and $t-1$, but not in $t-2$.

Variable	Definition	Mean	Std. dev.
Cumulative investment	Sum of gross investment from $t+1$ to $t+3$	0.329	0.341
Industry mean cum. investment	Sum of industry mean gross investment from $t+1$ to $t+3$	0.528	0.151
Cum. sales[a] growth	Sum of sales growth from $t+1$ to $t+3$	0.139	0.260
Industry mean[a] cum. sales growth	Sum of industry mean sales growth from $t+1$ to $t+3$	0.181	0.145
GROUP	Dummy variable = 1 if firm is member of group	0.359	—
TOPLEND	Fraction of bank loans from largest lender	0.219	0.126
SHARE	Fraction of shares owned by largest lender	0.041	0.026w
Debt/capital ratio	Based on book value measured at t	3.30	2.12
Coverage ratio	Operating income in t /interest payments in t	0.180	0.795
Depressed industry dummy	Dummy = 1 if firm is in depressed industry as determined by MITI	0.160	—

[a]These numbers include only 124 firms because we eliminated an outlier.

in the three years following the onset of distress. Assuming depreciation rates of about 10% [Hoshi and Kashyap (1990)], the average financially distressed firm barely keeps pace with depreciation, while the capital stock of the average firm grows by over 20%. The sales growth rates reported in the next two rows reveal a similar pattern of relatively poor performance by financially distressed firms.

Table 2 also reports some financial statistics on the firms in our sample. On average the largest lender holds about 21.9% of the firm's bank debt and 4.1% of its equity. The average coverage ratio in period t is 0.180, considerably less than one. Of the 125 firms in our sample, 16.0% are in depressed industries and 35.9% are group members.

Table 3

Average annual investment rates of 125 financially distressed Japanese group and nongroup firms in years $t-3$ through $t+3$, subtracting the mean investment rate of firms in the same industry. Standard errors in parentheses. Year t denotes the second year in a row in which the firm's coverage ratio is below one. Financially distressed firms are those for which coverage is less than one in year t and $t-1$, but not in $t-2$. Year t is any year from 1978 to 1985.

Firm type	Year						
	$t-3$	$t-2$	$t-1$	t	$t+1$	$t+2$	$t+3$
Group firms ($n=45$)	−0.035 (0.019)	−0.030 (0.021)	−0.041[a] (0.024)	−0.067[a] (0.014)	−0.051[a] (0.025)	−0.062[a] (0.017)	−0.012 (0.022)
Nongroup firms ($n=80$)	−0.045[a] (0.018)	−0.038 (0.025)	−0.046 (0.026)	−0.053 (0.022)	−0.125[a] (0.016)	−0.085[a] (0.018)	−0.030 (0.024)
Difference (group vs. nongroup)	0.010 (0.026)	0.008 (0.033)	0.005 (0.035)	−0.014 (0.026)	0.074[a] (0.030)	0.023 (0.025)	0.018 (0.033)

[a]Statistically significant difference from zero at the 5% confidence level.

4. Empirical findings

To learn whether the process of financial distress lowers firm efficiency, we examine whether distressed firms perform better if their financial structure facilitates renegotiation in time of distress. We provide details of our empirical results for investment and briefly report the results for sales performance. We first compare the behavior of group and nongroup firms and then present a regression analysis that focuses on how the details of firms' financial structures affect their investment or sales performance.

Table 3 reports the mean deviation of the firm's investment level from its industry's average investment level three years before and after period t. We report the results for group and nongroup firms separately. The table corroborates the results reported in table 2, that in general financially distressed firms invest less than the industry average.

More interesting, however, are the differences in the investment rates for the group and nongroup firms. In six of the seven years, the industry-adjusted investment rates are higher for group than for nongroup firms. These differences are smallest before the onset of distress and largest after. The only statistically significant difference in investment rates is in year $t+1$; the mean industry-adjusted investment rate of group firms exceeds that of nongroup firms by 0.074. This difference is quite large. Financially distressed group firms invest on average at about 10% per year. Thus, a difference of 0.075 means that nongroup firms invest roughly 75% less than group firms.

Group affiliation is not the only difference in the financial structures of financially distressed firms that might affect their ability to work out of

Table 4

Estimated coefficients from regressing the sum of investment in years $t + 1$ through $t + 3$ of 125 financially distressed Japanese firms on the mean investment rate in the firm's industry during the same period and various measures of corporate and financial structure. Year t denotes the second consecutive year in which a firm's coverage ratio is below one. Financially distressed firms are those for which coverage is below one in years t and $t - 1$, but not in year $t - 2$. Variables are defined in table 2. t-statistics are in parentheses.[a]

Variable	Model 1	Model 2	Model 3
Constant	−0.138	−0.309	−0.439
	(−1.10)	(−1.89)	(−2.81)
Industry mean cum. investment	0.687	0.674	0.576
	(3.27)	(3.19)	(2.84)
Depressed industry dummy	−0.076	−0.111	−0.102
	(−1.12)	(−1.56)	(−1.39)
GROUP	0.131	0.404	0.464
	(2.28)	(2.62)	(3.03)
TOPLEND	0.378	1.284	1.333
	(1.35)	(2.42)	(2.49)
SHARE	−0.312	3.591	1.961
	(−0.25)	(1.29)	(0.61)
GROUP * TOPLEND		−1.390	−1.365
		(−2.07)	(−2.10)
GROUP * SHARE		−0.332	−1.233
		(−0.14)	(−0.56)
TOPLEND * SHARE		−17.267	−13.811
		(−2.02)	(−1.37)
Cum. investment $t - 2$ to t			0.217
			(2.34)
Coverage ratio			−0.027
			(−0.74)
Debt/equity ratio			0.037
			(2.57)
Adjusted R^2	0.114	0.145	0.224

[a]t-statistics are calculated using White's (1980) heteroskedastic-consistent standard errors.

distress. To address this issue we regress a measure of the firm's investment on a number of financial factors that should be related to the costs of organizing a workout.

Table 4 reports a series of regressions in which the dependent variable is the sum of the investment rates in years $t + 1$ through $t + 3$, which we call cumulative investment. The first column reports the results from regressing cumulative investment on a dummy variable that equals one if the firm is in a group (labeled GROUP), on TOPLEND and on SHARE. We also include the industry's average investment rate to control for industrywide shifts in the expected value of investment and a dummy variable equal to one if the firm is in a depressed industry as determined by MITI.

As expected, the coefficient of the industry's average investment rate is statistically significant and large. All else being equal, a 10% increase in industry average investment leads to an increase of nearly 7% in investment by financially distressed firms. The coefficient of the depressed industry dummy is negative, but statistically insignificant. We would expect a negative sign because depressed industries are those in which the government tries to reduce capacity. [See Ueksa (1987).]

The main findings of this table are that the coefficients of *GROUP* and *TOPLEND* are both positive, although only the coefficient of *GROUP* is statistically significant. The positive coefficients are what one would expect if financial distress is costly. By contrast, the coefficient of *SHARE* is negative, the opposite of the predicted sign, although it is statistically insignificant.

More importantly, the point estimates of both *GROUP* and *TOPLEND* suggest that they have economically important effects on investment. To see this consider two firms that are identical except that one is in a group and the other is not. Suppose that the industry these firms are in has an investment rate equal to the sample mean of 0.528 and that the *SHARE* and *TOPLEND* variables are equal to their sample means of 0.041 and 0.219. From the regression results, we predict that the nongroup firm will invest a cumulative 0.282 over the three years $t + 1$ to $t + 3$. Given estimated depreciation rates of about 10% [Hoshi and Kashyap (1990)], this means that its capital stock would depreciate by roughly 2%. By contrast, the group firm's cumulative investment would be 0.413, still below the industry investment rate, but 46% larger than the nongroup firm. Note that instead of eroding, the group firm's capital stock would actually grow by roughly 11% during the three years.

A similar calculation for *TOPLEND* indicates that its effect is also large. Of course, the coefficient estimate is measured with considerable noise in this regression, so it is difficult to be confident of this effect. Consider a hypothetical firm with all the variables in the regression equal to their sample means. Now suppose that *TOPLEND* increases from the sample mean of 0.219 to 0.345, one standard deviation away. Our regression analysis predicts that this increase of 58% would increase cumulative investment from the sample mean of 0.329 to 0.377, an increase of 14%. Put differently, the elasticity of investment with respect to *TOPLEND* is 0.24: a 1% increase in the fraction of lending by the largest bank translates into an increase in investment of 0.24%.

The second column of table 4 reports a regression that adds three interaction terms of the variables *GROUP*, *TOPLEND*, and *SHARE*. The first two, *GROUP* ∗ *TOPLEND* and *GROUP* ∗ *SHARE*, tell us whether concentrated bank borrowing and share ownership are more or less important for group firms than for nongroup firms. There are two reasons to believe that both of these coefficients will be negative. First, our measure of group affiliation is based on the strength of the firm's affiliation with its main bank. Thus, the group dummy already captures some of the effects of concentrated bank borrowing and share ownership. Second, group firms may have other ways of moderating the costs of financial distress that are not available to nongroup firms with close ties to banks. As we discussed in the previous section, group firms have close financial links to their customers and suppliers. These firms may be more willing to extend trade credit and to continue buying in times of distress, providing a degree of financial relief unavailable to nongroup firms lacking these product-market ties. Unfortunately, we cannot distinguish between these two explanations.

The second column of table 4 establishes that the coefficients of both interaction terms have the predicted negative sign, but only the coefficient of *GROUP * TOPLEND* is statistically significant. The sum of the coefficient of this interaction term and the *TOPLEND* coefficient itself measures the total effect of *TOPLEND* for group firms (assuming for the moment that *SHARE* is zero). The sum of these coefficients is -0.106, but it is not significantly different from zero. In contrast, for nongroup firms, the direct effect of concentrated bank borrowing as measured by the coefficient of *TOPLEND* is large and statistically significant.

The second column of table 4 also includes the interaction term *TOPLEND * SHARE*. This variable is a rough indication of whether concentrated bank borrowing and share ownership are substitutes or complements. One hypothesis (substitutability) is that if firms borrow a lot from one bank, an increase in share ownership by that bank has little effect on the costs of financial distress because the bank already has a large enough debt stake in the firm to provide incentives for efficient renegotiation. Conversely, banks with large equity stakes do not need to hold much debt. This suggests a negative sign for the coefficient of *TOPLEND * SHARE*. Alternatively, it is possible that concentrated bank borrowing is effective only if the bank also owns shares in the firm (complementarity). This might be the case because banks that have only debt claims receive little of the benefit if the firm succeeds. Equity ownership would allow them to reap more of the benefits of good future performance.

The data are more consistent with the substitutability hypothesis. The coefficient is negative and statistically significant. Once this interaction term is included in the regression equation, the coefficient of *SHARE* shifts from being negative (in the first regression equation) to being positive, although this is statistically insignificant.

The regression estimates suggest that the cumulative effect of *TOPLEND* on investment is large for nongroup firms. To see that its effect is important, we note that the predicted cumulative investment of a nongroup firm is 0.301 when evaluated at the sample means of the regressors for a nongroup firm. A one standard deviation increase of *TOPLEND* from its mean for nongroup firms of 0.235 to 0.381 increases cumulative investment by 0.085 to 0.386. This increase is the sum of a positive direct effect and a negative indirect effect that lowers the positive impact of *SHARE* on investment.[17] Thus, the 62% increase in *TOPLEND* increases cumulative investment by 28%, indicating an elasticity of investment with respect to *TOPLEND* of 0.45 at the sample means.

The last column of table 4 reports the results of including a set of variables that are intended to address some alternative explanations of our results. The inclusion of these variables does not affect the results in the second column substantially.

First, we include the firm's cumulative investment from $t - 2$ to t. Table 2 suggests that group firms invest more than nongroup firms even before they get into trouble, although the mean differences are smaller and statistically insignificant in this earlier period. It is possible that group firms tend to invest more than nongroup firms in any event (for example, because their bank relationships lower their cost of capital). If this is true, our findings have little to do with financial distress and more to do with the overall distinction between group and nongroup firms. Of course, this explanation does not address the findings on other variables such as *TOPLEND*. We find that the estimated coefficient is indeed positive and statistically significant; however, its inclusion does not substantially affect our previous findings.

We also include the firm's coverage ratio in period t to measure the extent of the firm's distress. All else being equal, we would expect firms with relatively high coverage ratios to invest more; they are less distressed and their investment prospects are likely to be better. In contrast to this prediction, the point estimate of the coefficient is slightly negative but statistically indistinguishable from zero.

Finally, we include the debt/capital ratio at time t, where debt is measured in book values and capital is measured as the replacement value of the physical capital stock.[18] The idea is that the higher a firm's leverage, the more likely it will be to get into financial trouble. Thus, the average profitability of a financially distressed firm increases with its leverage. We would therefore expect highly leveraged firms to invest more because their investment prospects are better on average. If leverage is correlated with

---

[17]There are two competing effects. The direct effect increases investment by (1.423)(0.147) and the indirect effect lowers investment by (19.496)(0.147)(0.041), where 0.041 is the mean value of *SHARE* for nongroup firms.

[18]We use replacement costs of capital rather than the asset market's valuation (debt plus the market value of equity) for the following reason. Equity values contain information about the ability of firms to work out of financial distress and they should be higher for firms that are expected to invest more. This will tend to induce a negative relationship between market-value debt/capital ratios and investment which would dampen the effect we are interested in.

GROUP, *TOPLEND*, or *SHARE*, its omission would induce spurious correlation between these variables and investment. In line with the prediction, the coefficient of the debt/capital ratio is positive and statistically significant. Together, none of the results of interest are materially affected by these additions.

We perform similar analyses using sales growth as our performance measure. Because the findings are similar to those for investment, we review them briefly.

As with investment, financially distressed firms experience slower sales growth than the industry average in each of the years $t - 2$ through $t + 3$. More importantly, in each year the point estimates of the means for group firms are larger than those for nongroup firms, although the only statistically significant differences are in years t and $t + 1$. The regression evidence is also consistent with our findings on cumulative investment. We use the sum of sales growth in years $t + 1$ through $t + 3$ as the dependent variable in our regressions. We also use the same basic regressors as those reported in table 4 for cumulative investment, substituting industry average sales growth for industry average investment as a control.

The same basic results hold for sales growth. The coefficients of *GROUP* and *TOPLEND* are positive and statistically significant, while the coefficient of *SHARE* is negative and statistically insignificant. A comparative static exercise similar to the one performed for investment establishes that the effects of the *GROUP* and *TOPLEND* variables are economically important. The results predict that a group firm will sell roughly 58% more than an otherwise identical nongroup firm (evaluated at the sample means). In addition, the regression indicates that a 1% increase in borrowing from the largest lender raises the sales of a typical nongroup firm by about 0.5%. The effects of *GROUP* and *TOPLEND* on sales growth are similar to their effects on investment.

We add the interaction terms (*GROUP* ∗ *TOPLEND*, *GROUP* ∗ *SHARE*, and *TOPLEND* ∗ *SHARE*), as well as the coverage ratio, the debt/equity ratio, and lagged sales growth. The interaction terms have the same negative sign as in the investment regression equations; only *TOPLEND* ∗ *SHARE* is statistically significant. *GROUP* and *TOPLEND* continue to be statistically significant in both of these equations. Finally, none of these results are overturned by the inclusion of lagged sales growth, the debt/capital ratio, and the coverage ratio.

5. Concluding remarks

This paper explores the idea that financial distress is costly because free-rider problems and information asymmetries make it difficult for firms to renegotiate with their creditors in times of distress. We present evidence consistent with this view by showing that firms with financial structures in which free-rider and information problems are likely to be small perform better than other firms after the onset of distress. In particular, we show that firms in industrial groups – those with close financial relationships to their banks, suppliers, and customers – invest and sell more after the onset of distress than nongroup firms. Moreover, firms that are not group members, but nevertheless have strong ties to a main bank, also invest and sell more than firms without strong bank ties.

An alternative view is that group firms are helped in times of financial distress not because it is efficient to help them, but simply because the group is unwilling to let one of its members fail. This could be because bankruptcy reflects badly on other group firms; because the managers of other group firms feel a personal loyalty to the managers of the troubled company; or because bank executives are reluctant to admit that they made a mistake in extending credit. This view is similar to the view that conglomerates are often reluctant to liquidate unprofitable divisions. Thus, the group may be bailing out indiscriminately both good and bad firms, with ambiguous efficiency effects. We can think of no clearcut way of distinguishing between this interpretation and the one put forth in the paper. But, it is worth noting that when members of the group help troubled companies they do not just infuse money; as the examples discussed in section 2 indicate, they also actively try to restructure the company. This behavior is inconsistent with the view that they just throw good money after bad.

Our analysis may help to explain some differences between Japanese and U.S. firms. In the United States, debt is more diffusely held, with large companies relying more heavily on bond financing. This form of financing exacerbates problems stemming from financial distress and suggests that it may have been wise for U.S. firms to shy away from high debt levels. Japanese firms have taken on a larger amount of risky debt, but have established an institutional structure to cope with high leverage.

Interestingly, while leverage has been increasing in the U.S., it has been declining in Japan. Deregulation of Japanese capital markets has enabled Japanese firms to issue bonds domestically and abroad. They have exploited this new opportunity by substituting bond financing for bank borrowing [Hoshi, Kashyap, and Scharfstein (1990)]. This shift toward the public capital markets means that Japanese corporate debt is becoming more diffusely held and that relationships with banks are weakening. Thus, it is possible that leverage ratios have declined in part in response to a perceived increase in the costs of financial distress. It is too early to tell whether this is the case.

At the same time, of course, the recent leveraged buyout wave has increased corporate debt burdens in the U.S. The central question is whether this increase in leverage also comes with a change in the institutions that are needed to cope with financial distress. On the one hand, the senior bank debt and high-yield (junk) debt used to finance these acquisition, appear to be diffusely held, at least much more so than Japanese corporate debt. On the other hand, as the incidence of financial distress increases, U.S. companies and their investment bankers are trying to find new ways to reorganize outside of bankruptcy court.

References

Aoki, Masahiko, 1988, Information, incentives, and bargaining in the Japanese economy (Cambridge University Press, Cambridge, MA).

Altman, Edward, 1984, A further empirical investigation of the bankruptcy cost question, Journal of Finance 39, 1067–1089.

Asquith, Paul and David Mullins, 1986, Equity issues and offering dilution, Journal of Financial Economics 15, 61–89.

Bernanke, Ben, John Campbell, and Toni Whited, 1990, U.S. corporate leverage: Developments in 1987 and 1988, Brookings Papers on Economic Activity 1, 255–278.

Bolton, Patrick and David Scharfstein, 1990, A theory of predation based on agency problems in financial contracting, American Economic Review 80, 93–106.

Bulow, Jeremy and John Shoven, 1978, The bankruptcy decision, Bell Journal of Economics 9, 437–456.

Cutler, David and Lawrence Summers, 1988, The costs of conflict resolution and financial distress: Evidence from the Texaco–Pennzoil litigation, Rand Journal of Economics 19, 157–172.

Gerlach, Michael, 1987, Alliances and the social organization of business, Working paper (University of California, Berkeley, CA).

Gertner, Robert, 1989, Inefficiency in three-person bargaining, Working paper (University of Chicago, Chicago, IL).

Gertner, Robert and David Scharfstein, 1989, A theory of workouts and the effects of reorganization law, Working paper (University of Chicago, Chicago, IL).

Gilson, Stuart, John Kose, and Larry Lang, 1990, Troubled debt restructurings: An empirical study of private reorganization of firms in default, Journal of Financial Economics, this volume.

Haugen, Robert and Lemma Senbet, 1978, The insignificance of bankruptcy costs to the theory of optimal capital structure, Journal of Finance 70, 383–393.

Hoshi, Takeo and Anil Kashyap, 1990, Evidence on q and investment for Japanese firms, Journal of the Japanese and International Economies, forthcoming.

Hoshi, Takeo, Anil Kashyap, and David Scharfstein, 1990, Bank monitoring and investment: Evidence from the changing structure of Japanese corporate banking relationships, in: R. Glenn Hubbard, ed., Asymmetric information, corporate finance, and investment (University of Chicago Press, Chicago, IL) 105–126.

Hoshi, Takeo, Anil Kashyap, and David Scharfstein, 1991, Corporate structure liquidity and investment: Evidence from Japanese industrial groups, Quarterly Journal of Economics 106, forthcoming.

Kigyo Keiretsu Soran, 1983, Annual publication (Toyo Keizai).

Miwa, Yoshiro, 1985, Mein banku to sono kinoh (Main bank and its role), in: Takafusa Nakamura, Shunsaku Nishikawa, and Yutaka Kosai, eds., Gendai hihon keizai shisutemu (Contemporary Japanese economic system) (University of Tokyo Press, Tokyo) 170–199.

Myers, Stewart, 1977, The determinants of corporate borrowing, Journal of Financial Economics 5, 147–175.

Myers, Stewart and Nicholas Majluf, 1984, Corporate financing and investment decisions when firms have information investors do not have, Journal of Financial Economics 13, 187–222.

Nakatani, Iwao, 1984, The economic role of financial corporate grouping, in: M. Aoki, ed., The economic analysis of the Japanese firm (North-Holland, Amsterdam).

Pascale, Richard and Thomas P. Rohlen, 1983, The Mazda turnaround, Journal of Japanese Studies 9, 219–263.

Roe, Mark, 1987, The voting prohibition in bond workouts, Yale Law Journal 97, 232–278.

Sheard, Paul, 1985, Main banks and structural adjustment in Japan, Research paper no. 129 (Australia–Japan Research Centre).

Suzuki, Sadahiko and Richard Wright, 1985, Financial structure and bankruptcy risk in Japanese companies, Journal of International Business Studies, 97–110.

Titman, Sheridan, 1984, The effect of capital structure on a firm's liquidation decision, Journal of Financial Economics 13, 137–151.

Ueksa, Masu, 1987, Industry organization: The 1970s to the present, in: Kozo Yamamura and Yasukichi Yasuba, eds., The political economy of Japan, Volume 1: The domestic transformation (Stanford University Press, Stanford, CA).

Warner, Jerold, 1977, Bankruptcy costs: Some evidence, Journal of Finance 32, 337–347.

Weiss, Lawrence A., 1990, Bankruptcy resolution: Direct costs and violation of priority claims, Journal of Financial Economics, this volume.

White, Halbert, 1980, Heteroskedasticity-consistent covariance matrix estimator and a direct test for heteroskedasticity, Econometrica 48, 817–838.

A Theory of Workouts and the Effects of Reorganization Law[*]

ROBERT GERTNER and DAVID SCHARFSTEIN

ABSTRACT

We present a model of a financially distressed firm with outstanding bank debt and
public debt. Coordination problems among public debtholders introduce investment
inefficiencies in the workout process. In most cases, these inefficiencies are not
mitigated by the ability of firms to buy back their public debt with cash and other
securities—the only feasible way that firms can restructure their public debt. We
show that Chapter 11 reorganization law increases investment, and we characterize
the types of corporate financial structures for which this increased investment
enhances efficiency.

DURING THE LATE 1980s there was a dramatic increase in the leverage of U.S.
corporations, raising concerns about the corporate sector's financial stability.[1]
Indeed, by June 1990, 156 (24%) of the 662 companies that issued high-yield
bonds between 1977 and 1988 had either defaulted, gone bankrupt, or
restructured their public debt. The face value of these distressed bonds
amounts to nearly 21 billion dollars.[2]

The central question raised by these distressed firms is easy to put but
hard to answer: What is the effect of financial distress on a firm's operating
performance? There are two competing views. The first, an application of the

[*] This is a greatly revised version of "The Effects of Reorganization Law on Investment
Efficiency." Gertner is with the Graduate School of Business and the Law School, University of
Chicago; Scharfstein is with the Sloan School of Management, Massachusetts Institute of
Technology, and with the National Bureau of Economic Research. We thank Ian Ayres, Doug
Baird, Walter Blum, Keith Cohon, Doug Diamond, Ken Froot, Bob Gibbons, Steve Kaplan, Ron
Masulis, Kevin Murphy, Randy Picker, Mark Roe, Jeremy Stein, René Stulz, Robert Sydow, Rob
Vishny, an anonymous referee, and seminar participants at the NBER, University of Chicago,
the Federal Reserve Bank of Richmond, Ohio State, University of Michigan, Boston University,
and Princeton for helpful comments. We especially thank Paul Asquith for comments and
providing the data for some of the summary statistics. Gertner is grateful to the John M. Olin
Foundation Fellowship in Law and Economics at The University of Chicago Law School, the
NSF, Grant SES-8911334, and the IBM Faculty Research Fund at the Graduate School of
Business, University of Chicago for financial support. Scharfstein is grateful for fellowships from
the Olin Foundation and Batterymarch Financial Management and for financial support from
the International Financial Services Research Center at MIT.

[1] Bernanke and Campbell (1988) and Bernanke, Campbell, and Whited (1990) document the
increases in corporate leverage in the 1980s. The most significant increase occurs in the leverage
of the most highly indebted companies.

[2] These numbers were calculated from data made available to us by Paul Asquith. For a more
complete analysis of default rates on high-yield bonds, see Asquith, Mullins, and Wolff (1989).

Coase Theorem, holds that there are no real effects of financial distress.[3] Critical to this view is the distinction between financial and economic distress. Admittedly, most firms in financial trouble also suffer from poor operating performance. But, no financial maneuvering can save these economically distressed firms. If, however, a firm's capital structure prevents it from pursuing its value-maximizing operating strategy, creditors will restructure their claims to maximize firm value. We should expect financially distressed firms to do poorly on average, but no worse than if they had no leverage.

The second view—implicit in the leading theory of capital structure—is that financial distress hampers operating performance. In this view, the Coase Theorem fails; financial renegotiation is inefficient and operating distortions are introduced.

Distinguishing between these two views is important for understanding a variety of issues: capital structure decisions; the costs of tax policies which affect the level of corporate debt; the impact of wide-scale financial distress during a recession; and the role and effects of specific provisions of bankruptcy law.

Unfortunately, it is difficult to distinguish empirically between financial and economic distress. Is a financially distressed firm liquidated because renegotiation is inefficient or because the firm is not economically viable? Is a firm's poor operating performance the result of underlying business problems or an inappropriate capital structure? Unfortunately, the empirical attempts to distinguish between financial and economic distress are limited to specific environments in which it is relatively easy to make such a distinction.[4]

The theoretical distinction between financial and economic distress emerges in the important work of Bulow and Shoven (1978) and the follow-up work of White (1980, 1983).[5] These models demonstrate how conflicts among creditors can lead to inefficiencies when a firm is in financial distress. The impediment to efficient renegotiation in these models is the assumption that

---

[3] This view has been argued by Haugen and Senbet (1978), Roe (1983), Baird (1986), and Jensen (1986).

[4] Cutler and Summers (1988) study the stock price reactions to the events following Pennzoil's successful 10 billion dollar lawsuit against Texaco. Events which should have zero-sum effects resulted in a larger market value loss to Texaco than gain to Pennzoil. They interpret this finding as evidence that Texaco's financial distress was costly; Texaco was in financial but not economic distress. Hoshi, Kashyap, and Scharfstein (1990) show, in a sample of distressed Japanese firms, that those with financial structures that are easier to renegotiate a priori—those which borrow a lot from a single bank—invest more and have higher sales than firms with more complex financial structures.

[5] More recent contributions include Aivazian and Callen (1983), Titman (1984), Brown (1989), Giammarino (1989), Bergman and Callen (1990), and Baird and Picker (1991). With the exception of Titman, which assumes it is impossible to negotiate with customers who rely on the firm for product maintenance and Giammarino which analyzes a signaling model of debt restructuring, these papers assume efficient renegotiation and therefore focus on how value is divided.

the firm cannot renegotiate with public debtholders, although they can renegotiate efficiently with a bank. There are two types of inefficiencies that can result. On the one hand, because public debtholders claim part of the cash flows from new investment, distressed firms can have difficulty issuing equity or debt for new investment. Thus, they may pass up positive net present value investments.[6] On the other hand, a distressed company may actually overinvest because shareholders receive much of the upside benefits of risky investment but bear little of the downside costs. As a result, they may take negative net present value projects which increase the riskiness of the firm's cash flow.[7]

There are two primary contributions of this paper. The first is to show that these investment inefficiencies are still a problem even when firms can renegotiate with public debtholders. We analyze the implicit renegotiation that takes place when firms offer a package of new securities and cash in exchange for the original public debt. Public debt restructurings almost always take this form because the Trust Indenture Act of 1939 requires unanimous debtholder consent before a firm can alter the principal, interest, or maturity of its public debt. Exchange offers effectively alter these features but, since nontendering public debtholders maintain their original claim for payments from the firm, the Trust Indenture Act is not violated.

Despite the frequency with which exchange offers have been made—73 of 156 distressed junk bond issuers have successfully completed exchanges between 1977 and 1990—there is at least one substantial obstacle to successfully completing an exchange.[8] Those debtholders who do not tender can see the value of their bonds rise if the exchange offer is successful since tendering creditors forgive some of the debt and reduce the default risk of the original debt. Although public debtholders as a group would be better off if the exchange offer goes through, those with small stakes have an incentive to hold out. Thus, it can be very difficult to complete an exchange.

This free-rider problem can be, and often is, mitigated by offering a more senior security in exchange for the public debt, one with shorter maturity, or, when it is available, cash. Moreover, in these types of exchanges public debtholders may be willing to tender at below-market prices because they fear that holding out will make them effectively junior to the new securities. But, the important point is that even though these types of offers enable firms to restructure their public debt profitably, they do not, in general, result in efficient investment. The problem is that in deciding whether to tender, public debtholders take the firm's investment policy as given. Thus, individual debtholders—each with small stakes—fail to take into account their effect on the firm's investment decision, despite the fact that their decisions, taken as a whole, affect investment behavior.

---

[6] This is the effect first analyzed by Myers (1977).

[7] This risk-taking effect is analyzed in detail by Jensen and Meckling (1976).

[8] Of the 73 firms that successfully completed exchange offers 23 have subsequently filed for bankruptcy. Also, many firms have attempted exchange offers which failed.

The second principal contribution is to analyze the effects of reorganization law on investment. We show that key features of the law—the automatic stay, the voting rules for plan approval, and the power of equity holders to retain value for themselves—all act to increase investment both in and out of Chapter 11. Whether this increases efficiency depends on whether the firm would otherwise have underinvested or overinvested as a result of financial distress. We characterize the aspects of the firm's debt structure—the priority of bank debt relative to public debt, the maturity structure, and the existence of covenants restricting senior debt issues—that lead to underinvestment or overinvestment. We are then able to identify the situations in which Chapter 11 increases or decreases investment efficiency.

Our paper is organized as follows. Section I presents our benchmark model of workouts when public debt restructurings are not possible and bankrupt firms are liquidated, not reorganized. We build on the Bulow and Shoven model to analyze the effects of priority and maturity on investment after the onset of financial distress. Section II introduces the possibility of public debt restructurings through exchange offers and compares the results of this model to those of Section I's benchmark model. We show that if there is no restriction on senior debt issues, exchange offers do not affect the costs of financial distress but do place more of the burden of distress on public debtholders. If there are covenants restricting senior debt issues, however, exchange offers can be used to eliminate them and thereby increase investment. In this case, exchange offers may reduce the debt burden so much that they lead to overinvestment and actually exacerbate inefficiencies. We show that it is sometimes efficient to eliminate seniority covenants, but investment efficiency is greater if a firm can only remove them with a vote that is separate from an exchange offer. Section III introduces the possibility of reorganization rather than liquidation upon default. We review some of the key features of Chapter 11 reorganization law and analyze their effects on investment. We conclude in Section IV.

I. A Simple Model of Workouts and Investment

In this section, we consider a simple model of a financially distressed firm with both privately-placed debt and publicly-traded debt. We think of the private debt as bank debt (although it could be held by any large creditor) and the public debt as debentures.[9] We model the idea that it is easier to renegotiate with a bank (or a small syndicate of banks) than with numerous public debtholders by assuming at first that the firm cannot renegotiate with public debtholders. We relax this assumption in Section II where we present a model of exchange offers.

An important issue is how the debt's maturity structure affects the ability of firms to work out of distress. We assume that all of the bank debt, with face value B, is short-term, maturing at date 1. By contrast, fraction q of the

---

[9] We model public debt as unsecured, so we use the term debentures to distinguish them from bonds, which in the legal literature exclusively refers to secured debt.

face value of the public debt D, is due at date 1, and fraction $1 - q$ is due at a later date 2. This timing reflects the fact that bank debt generally has a shorter maturity than public debt.

The firm has two assets: cash and/or liquid assets of Y; and an investment project which requires an investment of I at date 1 and returns a stochastic cash flow of X at date 2 distributed over the support $[0, \infty)$. We denote the cumulative distribution of X as $F(X)$, the density as $f(X)$, and the mean as $\overline{X}$. For simplicity, we assume the firm has no fixed assets such as plant and equipment. All parties are risk neutral, and the riskless interest rate is zero.

Finally, we assume that the firm is in financial distress at date 1; its assets in place are worth less than the face value of its debt obligations: $Y < B + D$. Thus, if the firm is liquidated, and if absolute priority rules are followed, shareholders receive nothing, and public debtholders and the bank share Y between them. Assuming equal priority of bank and public debt in liquidation, the bank gets $[B/(B + D)]Y$, which we denote L_B and the public debtholders get $[D/(B + D)]Y$, which we denote L_D.[10] If the firm is liquidated, the public debt maturing at date 2 is accelerated to date 1, consistent with the Bankruptcy Code. In this section, we assume that bankruptcy is equivalent to liquidation; reorganization in Chapter 11 is ruled out. In Section III, we analyze how reorganization law affects investment incentives in this model.

The central question is whether the financially distressed firm invests in the project at date 1. If $Y > I + B + qD$, the firm has enough cash to invest in the project and pay off both the bank debt and the public debt maturing at date 1. In this case, the firm invests regardless of whether the project has positive or negative net present value: if the firm does not invest, equity gets nothing; if the firm does invest, there is some chance that equity's payoff would be positive. We assume instead that $Y < I + B + qD$ so that the firm needs an additional $I + B + qD - Y$ to meet its date-1 obligations and invest in the project.

The firm has several options in meeting its cash shortfall. It can try to raise new funds by issuing debt or equity, or it can try to restructure its existing bank debt or public debt. We focus here on debt restructurings—first on bank debt restructurings and, in Section II, on public debt restructurings. We show later that the firm prefers to restructure than to issue new debt or equity.

A. Bank Debt Restructurings

We consider bank debt restructurings first because they are substantially easier to organize than public debt restructurings.[11] Indeed, the Trust Indenture Act of 1939 *prohibits* public debtholders from changing the principal,

---

[10] In bankruptcy, creditors do not have a claim for unmatured interest. So, for simplicity, we assume that the contractual interest rate on the public debt is zero.

[11] Gilson, John, and Lang (1990) show empirically that the existence of public debt is the most significant determinant of whether a financially distressed firm restructures successfully out of court or files for Chapter 11 reorganization.

interest, or maturity of public debt without public debtholders' unanimous consent. Even without the Trust Indenture Act, free rider problems can impede successful renegotiation. For example, if some public debtholders forgive part of their debt, the value of the remaining debt rises. If each public debtholder is small, and thus has no effect on the outcome of the negotiations, then each will refuse to restructure his portion of the debt. We discuss these issues in detail in Section II.

In a bank debt restructuring the firm effectively rolls over its initial loan of B and borrows an additional $I + qD - Y$ for the investment and to pay off the public debt due at date 1. Our analysis is simplified if we assume that the interest on this loan has lower priority than all outstanding debt while the principal has equal priority. This assumption is not realistic since bankruptcy law does not distinguish between principal and matured interest. But, any other assumption complicates the analysis because the fraction of the firm that the public debtholders get depends on the interest rate on the new loan. On the other hand, if we assume the new interest has lower priority, the combined return to the bank and the firm is independent of the interest rate. This permits us to complete the analysis without determining the interest rate on the bank debt. The issue this raises for the ability to renegotiate with the bank is interesting, but it is an unnecessary complication for the basic analysis.

If the firm invests, and $X < I + B + D - Y$, the bank receives

$$\frac{I + B + qD - Y}{I + B + D - Y} X.$$

If $X > I + B + D - Y$, the shareholders and the bank together get to split $X - (1 - q)D$. The bank agrees to finance the firm provided:

$$\int_0^Z \frac{I + B + qD - Y}{I + B + D - Y} Xf(X) \, dX$$

$$+ \int_Z^\infty [X - (1 - q)D] f(X) \, dX - (I + qD - Y) \ge L_B, \quad (1)$$

where $Z \equiv I + B + D - Y$.

The right-hand side of inequality (1) is what the bank receives in liquidation. There are two important assumptions implicit in this formulation. First, the firm liquidates and cannot invest in bankruptcy. In Section III, we introduce the possibility of investment in Chapter 11 bankruptcy proceedings. Second, we assume that if the bank does not lend money, the firm goes bankrupt; the firm cannot raise the necessary cash from an outside source. We will see below that, although it may be possible to raise outside funds, the bank has a greater incentive to provide funds than any outsider. Since we wish to derive conditions under which investment occurs, not how the gains from the investment are split, our analysis is unaffected by this assumption.

Inequality (1) is equivalent to:

$$\overline{X} - I \geq qD + \int_0^Z \frac{(1-q)D}{Z} Xf(X)\, dX$$

$$+ \int_Z^\infty (1-q)Df(X)\, dX + L_B - Y. \quad (2)$$

The first three terms on the right-hand side sum to the market value of the public debt conditional on bank lending and investment. Thus, we write (2) as:

$$\overline{X} - I \geq V_D - L_D, \quad (3)$$

where V_D is the market value of the public debt in this case.

Inequality (3) captures a simple but important idea. V_D is the value of the public debt conditional on investment while L_D is its value if no investment occurs. So the difference of the two measures the transfer from the bank and equity holders to public debtholders if the firm invests. If the net present value of the project, $\overline{X} - I$, is greater than this transfer, then the firm restructures its bank debt and invests.

Interestingly, this transfer can be positive or negative. If it is positive, the firm will tend to forego positive NPV projects, those with NPV between zero and $V_D - L_D$; the debt obligations act as a tax on the project, discouraging investment. If it is negative, the firm may adopt negative NPV projects, those with NPV between $V_D - L_D$ and zero; creditors effectively subsidize the project, encouraging investment. So, inefficiencies can involve either under-investment or overinvestment.

This wedge is introduced because the value of the public debt conditional on investment can be greater or less than its liquidation value. If, for example, Y is close to zero, public debt is worth almost nothing in a liquidation, so public debtholders benefit from investment. In this case, the existence of public debt discourages investment. By contrast, if Y is close to $B + D$, public debtholders would get paid off nearly in full if the firm is liquidated. But, if it is not liquidated, public debtholders own a risky claim, the value of which could well be below D. Here, public debt promotes investment, though it may be inefficient

The discussion suggests that there are two effects at work. On the one hand, the debt obligations tend to make investment look unattractive because existing creditors can siphon off cash flow from the project. This is Myers' (1977) well-known argument; the existence of a "debt overhang" discourages investment. On the other hand, debt obligations can lead the firm to take excessive risks: equity receives nothing if the firm is liquidated but has some value if the firm invests, even if it is in a negative NPV investment, a point made clear by Jensen and Meckling (1976).

The maturity structure of the debt has important effects on the efficiency of investment. As the maturity of the public debt shortens (q increases), its value increases because the date-1 portion is safe and the date-2 portion is risky: $dV_D/dq > 0$. This increases the transfer to public debtholders and reduces the firm's incentive to invest. In the limit as all the public debt becomes due at date 1, the transfer approaches $D - L_D > 0$. In this case, the firm may pass up positive NPV investments but will never choose negative NPV investments. The efficiency effect of shortening the public debt's maturity is ambiguous. The increase in q may force the firm to pass up positive NPV projects, but it also may deter investment in negative NPV projects.

An increase in bank debt, holding fixed the total amount of indebtedness, $B + D$, has an unambiguously positive effect on efficiency. The increase in B decreases the right-hand side of expression (3) if it is positive and increases it if it is negative. So, the shift toward bank debt away from public debt can either induce the firm to take positive NPV projects it would not have taken or turn down negative NPV projects it would have taken. Clearly, if all debt were held by the bank, investment would always be efficient; bank renegotiation is assumed to be costless so the conditions of the Coase Theorem are satisfied.

B. New Capital Infusions

Instead of restructuring its bank debt, the firm could try to raise new money from another bank or by issuing equity. Neither of these alternatives is as attractive as a restructuring. Like a restructuring, the new bank lends $I + B + qD - Y$ and receives the same date-2 payoffs. But, unlike a restructuring, some of the new money goes to pay off the existing bank debt of B at face value. One can show that the firm will be able to raise new debt financing provided

$$\overline{X} - I \geq V_D - L_D + B - L_B, \tag{4}$$

or, in words, if the net present value of the investment exceeds the sum of the transfer to the public debtholders, $V_D - L_D$, and the transfer to the bank, $B - L_B$. The condition differs from a bank debt restructuring because in a restructuring the bank takes into account the fact that its debt is worth only $L_B < B$ in a liquidation. With a new loan the bank receives a transfer of $B - L_B > 0$. This subsidy means that the set of investment projects that can be financed without outside debt is a strict subset of those which can be financed with a bank debt restructuring.

Investment is even less attractive if the firm issues equity rather than debt. The bank continues to receive a subsidy of $B - L_B$, but the transfer to the public debtholders rises. The public debt conditional on investment is worth more because the date-2 portion of the debt is paid off before equity is paid anything. By contrast, when the firm issues debt, the public debtholders and the new debtholders are on equal footing at date 2. So, the condition for investment takes the same form as inequality (4) except that V_D is greater when the firm issues equity.

The analysis implies that the firm never issues equity since an equity issue transfers value to public debtholders not transferred by a debt issue. The prediction is less clear about the choice between debt issues and a bank loan restructuring. Clearly, when inequality (3) is satisfied but inequality (4) is not, the firm will restructure its bank debt. But, if both inequalities are satisfied the model has no prediction. The bank knows that if there is no restructuring, the firm will issue new debt and the bank will receive B. So, in a debt restructuring, the bank will settle for nothing less than B. As a result, equity holders are indifferent between a debt issue and a bank debt restructuring because they must transfer B to the bank in both situations.

C. Effects of Priority

So far, we have assumed that all debt has equal priority in bankruptcy. However, firms can explicitly contract for certain debts to be paid before others in bankruptcy. There are two ways in which priority can affect the ability of distressed firms to raise capital in our model. First, the seniority of the existing bank debt affects what the bank would get in bankruptcy liquidation if it did not lend new money, thereby determining the value of the bank's next best alternative. The more junior the existing bank debt, the worse off the bank is in liquidation, so the more willing it is to lend. Second, the seniority of the new bank debt affects what the bank can get if it lends new money. In general, the more senior the new bank debt, the better off the bank is at any chosen interest rate. Thus, if they could, the firm and the bank would like to issue debt that is senior to the existing public debt. Of course, there are often constraints on their ability to do so; the public debt may contain covenants restricting the issuance of any debt senior to the public debt. These covenants may prohibit such issuance altogether, may limit the amount, or may allow it if certain cash flow and net worth conditions are satisfied.

To see this more formally, suppose there is no covenant prohibiting a senior debt issue. Then the interest rate on the new bank debt can be set so high that the firm always defaults at date 2 and the senior debt gets all of the date-2 cash flow X. This means that the value of the public debt conditional on new senior lending is just qD and public debtholders only receive their date-1 payment. The value of the public debt if the firm is liquidated is L_D, assuming, as before, that the existing bank debt and public debt have equal priority. Based on the previous section we know that the project's net present value must exceed the net subsidy to public debtholders from investment. So the bank will be willing to lend provided

$$\overline{X} - I \geq qD - L_D. \tag{5}$$

The right-hand side of (5) is strictly less than the right-hand side of expression (3) since $qD < V_D$; the firm is more prone to invest when there is no covenant restricting senior debt issuance.[12] It can have positive or negative efficiency effects by reducing the underinvestment problem or exacerbating the overinvestment problem.

This analysis can tell us something about the interaction between maturity structure and seniority covenants. If the public debt has a relatively short maturity (q near 1), the firm is likely to underinvest. In this case, a seniority covenant tends to worsen the problem, making it more difficult for the firm to raise capital. If the firm leaves out the covenant, we would expect to see the bank lend new money that is senior to the old debentures. The ability to issue such debt can counteract the inefficiency created by the short maturity of the public debt. In contrast, if the debt has a relatively long maturity, the firm is more prone to overinvest. In this case, a seniority covenant makes it more difficult to raise capital and could eliminate the tendency toward overinvestment. Thus, if capital structure is chosen partly to minimize the costs of financial distress, we would expect long-term public debt to contain seniority covenants in the indentures and short-term public debt to omit such covenants.

This framework can also tell us something about the interaction between public debt maturity and the priority of the existing debt. Suppose that there is no seniority covenant. Then if the original public debt is pari passu (equal priority) with the bank debt, the investment condition is given by expression (5). But, if the initial bank debt is senior to the public debt, the condition becomes

$$\overline{X} - I \geq qD - \max(Y - B, 0) \qquad (6)$$

because the value of the junior public debt in liquidation is now $\max(Y - B, 0)$. Since this is less than $L_D \equiv [D/(B + D)]Y$, the value of the public debt if it is pari passu with the old bank debt, the firm is now less prone to invest; the bank does better in liquidation, so financing new investment is less attractive.

The shorter the maturity of the public debt, the more likely the firm is to underinvest. Thus, the model suggests that when the public debt is relatively short term, existing senior bank debt is likely to worsen the underinvestment problem. But, when the public debt is long term, the seniority of bank debt can be a useful way of curbing the overinvestment problem. If the costs of financial distress drive capital structure choices, our model predicts that the bank debt will be senior if the public debt is long term and junior if it is short term.

---

[12] Stulz and Johnson (1985) develop this point in a model where the ability to use secured debt for new borrowing mitigates the Myers (1977) underinvestment problem. Berkovitch and Kim (1990) analyze how priority structure affects investment efficiency under both symmetric and asymmetric information.

Although the model predicts that the bank debt will be junior if the public debt is short term, in a more realistic formulation, it is difficult to make short-term bank debt effectively junior. To see this, suppose that if the firm does not invest and is not liquidated at date 1, it nevertheless has positive, stochastic cash flows at date 2. Thus, unlike the model above, if the firm pays off its debts at date 1, the value of equity is positive even if the firm does not invest. The firm has three alternatives: invest, continue without investing, or be liquidated.

Now suppose that $Y \geq qD + B$ so that it is feasible for the firm to meet its date-1 debt obligations and continue in operation without investing. The value of the bank debt is B, which is what it is worth in liquidation if the bank debt is senior. The bank refuses to provide new funds for investment, but demands payment of B in period 1. This is more than $\max(Y - D, 0)$, the bank's payoff if the firm is liquidated and the bank is junior to the public debt. Thus, even though the bank debt is contractually junior to the public debt, the bank acts as if it is senior. This makes the bank reluctant to lend new money, a more efficient outcome. So, in this model, if q is small enough so that $Y > qD + B$, the bank acts as a senior lender. But, if q is very close to one, it is possible to induce the bank to act as if it was junior to the public debt.

II. Distressed Exchange Offers for Public Debt

So far, we have assumed that it is impossible to renegotiate with public debtholders. This assumption is not too far off the mark; the Trust Indenture Act's prohibitions on changes in the timing or amount of public debt payments forces public debt restructurings to take the form of exchange offers.[13] Firms offer cash and/or a package of debt and equity securities, with the offer typically contingent on the acceptance of a specified fraction of the debt.[14]

In this section, we analyze the extent to which this limited form of renegotiation affects the inefficiencies discussed in the previous section. The key assumption of the model is that each debtholder's stake is small enough that he ignores the effect of his tender decision on both the firm's investment decision and the value of the firm's securities. This assumption is unrealistically strong for firms with a large portion of their debt held by just a few institutional investors, an admittedly common situation. We make this assumption to highlight the problems that arise when creditors cannot fully

---

[13] There are some similarities between corporate debt exchange offers and buybacks of developing country debt. See Froot (1989) and Bulow and Rogoff (1989) for analyses of developing country debt exchanges.

[14] For example, in early 1990, AP Industries offered $50 in cash, one share of common stock, and $340.91 principal amount of new zero-coupon senior subordinated notes due in 1997 in exchange for each $1000 principal amount of its 12 $^3/_8$% subordinated debentures due in 2001. The offer was conditioned on 95% of the outstanding principal amount being tendered.

coordinate their actions. We believe that similar effects would be present in a model in which debtholders have substantial stakes.[15]

We proceed in two stages. First, we analyze the profitability of exchanges assuming that the firm has ample cash to finance the investment even without a debt restructuring. We will show that an exchange is profitable only if the debt is exchanged for cash or for debt that has higher priority than the original debt. Although this analysis has no efficiency implications—the firm invests even without an exchange—it is helpful in answering the second more interesting question: when can an exchange reduce cash obligations and enable the firm to invest? We will show that the bank is generally better off if the firm can exchange its debentures, that investment incentives are unaffected by the ability to exchange debt in most circumstances, and that the ability to exchange is not equivalent to efficient renegotiation of the public debt.

A. *Exchanges Assuming No Cash Shortage*

In this subsection we assume that, while the firm is in financial distress, it does not need an exchange or a bank concession in order to invest and meet its date-1 debt obligations: $Y > I + B + qD$. We first consider an exchange for debt due at date 2 with a face value of p for each dollar in face value of the existing debt. Let X_b be the breakeven value of X, so the firm defaults at date 2 for all $X < X_b$. Shareholders receive nothing if $X < X_b$ and receive $X - X_b$ otherwise. Thus, an exchange is profitable if and only if it lowers X_b.

Let β denote the fraction of public debt the firm exchanges. Without an exchange, $X_b = I + D + B - Y$. By contrast, if the firm exchanges, it owes the nontendering debtholders $(1 - \beta)D$ and the tendering debtholders βpD, so $X_b = I + (1 - \beta)D + \beta pD + B - Y$. Here, X_b is decreasing in β if and only if $p < 1$, i.e., the firm can exchange a dollar of old debt for less than a dollar of new debt. So if $p < 1$ an exchange is profitable and if $p > 1$ an exchange is unprofitable.

Proposition 1: *It is unprofitable to offer an exchange for new debt with equal priority to the old public debt.*

Proof: See Appendix.

The exchange is unprofitable because of a classic holdout problem.[16] If other debtholders tender, the value of the existing debt rises, creating an incentive to hold out. To see this, consider the decision facing the holder of \$1 of debt who is offered \$1 of the new debenture ($p = 1$) due at date 2.[17] Will the holdout have an incentive to tender, assuming that all the other

---

[15] Gertner (1990) analyzes a bargaining model in which one party needs to reach agreement with two others under asymmetric information. Holdout problems similar to those analyzed here are also present. In addition, he shows that it may not be in the private interest of bargaining parties to form coalitions, even though the coalitions improve overall bargaining efficiency.

[16] Roe (1987) contains the first discussion of this holdout problem.

[17] We assume that \$1 is a negligible portion of the overall public debt.

debtholders tender? If so, then it is an equilibrium for all debtholders to exchange.

The answer depends on the payoffs of the two debentures when the firm is in default at date 2. If the firm does not default, the debtholder is just as happy with the new debentures as with the old debentures. But if the firm does default at date 2, the payoffs are quite different. Those who tender receive their pro rata share of the firm at date 2, $(X + Y - I - B)/D$, but the holdout receives q at date 1 and receives a pro rata share of the firm at date 2, $(1 - q)(X + Y - I - B)/D$. Since $(X + Y - I - B)/D < 1$, the debtholder is better off holding out.

The holdout is better off because the earlier payment on the old debenture is effectively senior to the new debenture. Tendering debtholders share ratably in a risky date-2 claim. But, by holding out, the debtholder receives a safe date-1 payment while still sharing pro rata in the date-2 portion of payoffs.

This logic rests crucially on the assumption that the debtholders do not act collectively. Suppose they could. Then the question becomes: are we all better off if we all tender than if we all hold out? This is quite different from the individual question: am I better off if I tender than if I hold out assuming everyone else tenders? In the collective case, if everyone tenders then the payoff is again $(X + Y - I - B)/D$ when the firm defaults. But, if no one tenders then the payoff is q at date 1 and $(X + Y - I - B - qD)/D$ at date 2. This is equal to the payoff from tendering, so debtholders as a group are indifferent between the two options when $p = 1$.

The holdout problem is even more pronounced if the firm offers to exchange junior debt or equity for the old debentures. There are now two reasons why debtholders want to hold out. As before, holdouts are senior in that some of their claim is paid at date 1 before the uncertainty is realized and tendering debtholders are paid. In addition, holdouts also have seniority at date 2 since the new security is junior debt or equity. If all debtholders tender, a holdout's claim would be riskless since the holdout gets q at date 1, and the $1 - q$ that is owed at date 2 is senior to the claims of all tendering debtholders, making it riskless as well. Thus, a corollary of Proposition 1 is that exchange offers for junior debt or equity are also unprofitable.

Quite the opposite result holds if the firm can offer a more senior debenture in exchange for the old debt. These types of exchanges are quite common. In a sample of 169 exchange offers by 67 companies, we discovered at least 48 instances in which a firm offered a debenture that is senior to the old debentures.[18]

---

[18] These 67 companies are a subsample of the 73 original issue high-yield debt companies that completed exchange offers between 1977 and June 1990. We found information on the exchange offers from two sources: *First Boston High Yield Handbook*, 1988 and 1989, and the S&P Called Bond Record, 1977–1990. We could not find detailed information on the exchange offers of the remaining 6 companies. This may be an underestimate of the frequency of exchanges for senior securities because classification is based on a security's title. In some case cases, the new security may have the same title but be senior.

Proposition 2: *It is profitable to offer an exchange for new debt which is senior to the old public debt.*

Proof: See Appendix.

There are two competing effects at work. Again, the difference in the payoffs from tendering and holding out depends on the payoffs of the old and new debentures when the firm is in default at date 2. As before, consider the decision facing the holder of \$1 of debt, assuming that all others tender when $p = 1$. On the one hand, the holdout's date-2 claim is worthless when the firm defaults. Since the new debt is senior, each new debenture holder is paid $(X + Y - I - B)/D$ and there are insufficient funds to pay the old junior debenture holder. On the other hand, the portion q of the holdout's claim is paid at date 1, making it effectively senior to the new debentures. On the whole, given our assumptions that $X > 0$ and $Y > I + B + qD$, the increased seniority at date 2 is worth more than the earlier maturity of the q portion of the claim. Instead of a holdout problem there is a *hold-in* problem; debt holders would tender for $p < 1$ despite the fact that they are made worse off as a group.

The hold-in problem is more severe when the public debt is relatively long term. Very short maturity debt is paid off almost in full at date 1. So only a small portion of the debt can be leapfrogged in the capital structure. The short maturity of the debt effectively gives it a degree of seniority that cannot be erased by a senior debt issue. Indeed, one can show that as the debt becomes shorter-term, p increases and exchanges become less attractive to the firm.[19]

We have shown that the firm prefers exchanges for senior debt to exchanges for pari passu or junior debt. But in many cases there are seniority covenants in the public debt prohibiting senior debt issues. Yet firms with such covenants do issue more senior debt in exchanges.[20] How is this possible? The indenture for the debt issue typically specifies that covenants can be changed or eliminated by either a simple or super majority vote of the

---

[19] The property of longer maturity debt that makes the hold-in problem relevant is that a greater fraction of promised payments come after the resolution of uncertain cash flows. Extending maturity from date 1 to date 1.5 would have no effect if there were no chance of insolvency before date 2.

[20] For example, in March 1987, Michigan General offered \$500 principal amount of 6% Increasing Rate Senior Subordinated Notes due in 1992, \$200 principal amount of Zero Coupon Delayed Convertible Senior Subordinated Notes due in 1997, and 12 shares of \$2 Delayed Convertible Preferred Stock in exchange for each \$1000 principal amount of 10 $\frac{3}{4}$% Senior Subordinated Debentures due in 1998. Both new Senior Subordinated Notes were made senior to the old debentures even though there was a covenant in its indenture stating, "the Company will not incur, create, issue, assume or guarantee any full recourse indebtedness which is both senior in right of payment to the Debentures and subordinate or junior in right of payment to any other Senior Indebtedness." This covenant protects the public debtholders from being leapfrogged by new public debt but does not, by itself, restrict issuing new senior bank debt. The bank loan agreement or other covenants in the public debt indenture may restrict the amount of new senior bank debt.

face value of the debt.[21] The exchange is then made contingent on a so-called *exit consent* in which the required fraction of the debt votes to strip the old debenture of the seniority and perhaps other covenants. The act of tendering consists of two actions: first, a vote to strip the debt of its covenant protection, and second, an acceptance of the exchange for the now legally-issued senior debt.[22] In Section II.B below, we discuss the efficiency consequences of tying the covenant waiver to the exchange offer via an exit consent.

There are at least two other ways firms commonly structure an exchange. One is to offer cash instead of a security such as debt or equity. Another is to offer debt with a shorter maturity than the existing debt. It turns out that in our two-period model these alternatives are equivalent. Debt due at date 1 is paid off with certainty, so exchanges for short-term debt are equivalent to cash exchanges.[23]

Proposition 3: *It is profitable to offer an exchange for cash.*

Proof: See Appendix.

Exchange offers for cash are profitable for similar reasons that senior debt exchanges are profitable. As more debtholders tender, more cash is paid out at date 1, reducing the value of the old debt at date 2. Tendering debtholders are paid cash for the $1 - q$ portion of their claim at date 1. Since this is paid before a holdout receives payment on the $1 - q$ portion of his claim, the tendering debtholders are effectively senior to the nontendering debtholders. As a result, the date-2 portion of the old debt claim is less valuable. Faced with this hold-in problem, old debtholders are willing to tender at a low price.

Recall that throughout the analysis we have assumed that the firm does not have a cash shortage. If the firm does not have sufficient cash, it will use all of its cash in excess of $B + I$ to buy back debt. It is important to note that the firm would not find it profitable to issue outside equity or debt (with equal or junior priority to the old debt) in order to buy back the public debt. The outside capital would not be senior to the untendered debt, so the required interest rate on the outside capital would more than make up for the savings on the exchange offer.

In this model, the ability to exchange for cash does not lead to any added inefficiencies since the firm will always invest in the single project. However, in a model in which there are either several projects or the level of investment is a choice variable, significant inefficiencies can result. The firm may choose to use cash which could be invested in positive net present value

---

[21] Since the vote does not change the timing or amount of payments it is not prohibited by the Trust Indenture Act. See Roe (1987).

[22] The legal status of exit consents is quite uncertain. Although an exit consent was upheld in Katz versus Oak Industries Inc. 508 A.2d 873 (Del. Ch. 1986), several potential legal arguments against them have not been tried. See Coffee and Klein (1990).

[23] Both alternatives are quite common. In our sample of 169 exchange offers, 39 involved some cash. Of the 101 cases in which a debt security was offered, 74 offered debt with a shorter maturity than the old debt.

projects to buy back public debt if the reduction in payments to creditors exceeds the NPV of a project. But, this inefficiency is limited in scope; financially distressed firms tend not to have a great deal of excess cash available for this type of activity.

As we discussed above, there is no difference between an exchange for cash and an exchange for shorter maturity debt of any priority in this model. In a model with more than two periods, there may be a difference because the firm may not have enough cash to exchange all the debt for cash immediately but may be able to achieve a similar effect with an exchange for shorter maturity debt. Our analysis suggests that an exchange for shorter maturity debt is profitable when the firm can make the debtholders who tender effectively senior to those who do not tender. This is possible if the realization of the risky project occurs after the new debt matures, but there are some relatively certain cash flows before the new debt matures. This allows the new debt to have low default risk and be paid off before the old debt matures.

B. Exchanges When There Is a Cash Shortage

The above analysis assumes that the firm does not need to restructure its debt in order to invest at date 1. Exchanges have no effect on efficiency; they just redistribute value from public debtholders to shareholders. We now suppose the firm needs a concession from either the bank or public debtholders to invest at date 1. We start by assuming that $I + B < Y < I + B + qD$; the firm needs some concession to invest but has enough cash to pay off the bank and invest.

We explicitly model bank renegotiation and public debt exchanges. The firm first approaches the bank seeking a concession. It makes a take-it-or-leave-it offer to postpone some or all of B until date 2, perhaps along with some debt forgiveness. The firm then has the option of offering an exchange for the public debt. This timing captures the idea that a firm is unable to commit to the bank not to pursue a profitable exchange offer.

Suppose the bank refuses to give the firm a concession. At this point, the firm can propose to exchange the public debt for a more senior debenture. (As we saw in the previous section this is preferred to offering a debenture that is pari passu with the old debt.) We assume for the moment that there is no seniority covenant. Because the new debt is senior to the old, the firm can set p, the face value of the new debenture, so that it is paid all of the date-2 cash flows. Thus, the maximum value of a unit of the new debenture is $(\overline{X} - Y - I - B)/D$, provided the firm buys back all of the debt.[24] If a debtholder does not tender, he receives only the date-1 payment q. So, if $(\overline{X} + Y - I - B)/D > q$ or, equivalently, if

$$\overline{X} - I \geq B + qD - Y \tag{7}$$

---

[24] The proof that the firm will wish to buy back all of the debt applies in this case as well.

an exchange offer for senior debt is feasible. In this case, the firm will want
to buy back its public debt because the alternative is liquidation in which
case shareholders get nothing.

Now consider the first stage of the model in which the firm approaches the
bank to receive a concession. The bank knows that if it turns down the firm's
offer, the firm will be able to exchange its debentures provided expression (7)
is met. In this case, the bank receives B. So, the bank will turn down any
offer which has an expected value less than B.

It is possible that the firm might prefer to renegotiate with the bank to
receive some date-1 debt relief rather than restructure its public debt. As
long as it can defer enough of its bank debt to pay off the date-1 portion of the
public debt, this strategy is feasible. So, suppose the bank extends the
maturity of its loan but requires the firm to pay B' at date 2. Assume for the
moment that there is no public debt covenant prohibiting the issuance of
senior debt; B' can be senior to the date-2 payments on the public debt. In
addition, if $Y < I + qD$ the bank has to provide a cash infusion of $I + qD -
Y$. If $Y > I + qD$, the remaining cash of $Y - I - qD$ is available to pay off
the bank at date 1. Since the new bank debt is senior, the minimum B' that
the bank would accept satisfies

$$\int_0^{B'} Xf(X)\,dX + \int_{B'}^{\infty} B'f(X)\,dX + Y - I - qD = B. \qquad (8)$$

The question is whether the firm prefers renegotiating with the bank or
renegotiating with the public debtholders via an exchange offer. Proposition
4 establishes that, when feasible, the firm prefers a public debt restructuring
to a bank debt restructuring.

Proposition 4: *If $I + B < Y < I + B + qD$ and there are no contractual restrictions on issuing senior debt, the firm prefers a public debt exchange to a bank
debt restructuring.*

Proof: See Appendix.

In both an exchange offer and a bank debt restructuring, the bank ends up
with a claim worth B. However, the exchange is less costly because the firm
can take advantage of the hold-in problem; by exchanging for senior debt and
leaving holdouts with a junior security, the firm induces public debtholders
to tender for a claim that the bank would not accept.

Now suppose instead that $\overline{X} - I < B + qD - Y$, so expression (7) is violated. In this case, an exchange offer is not feasible without a bank concession. Thus, if the bank turns down the firm's take-it-or-leave-it offer, the firm
is liquidated and the bank gets L_B. This means that the firm can offer the
bank a claim worth L_B, and the bank will accept the offer. Note also that
when $Y < I + B$ the bank would also accept an offer of L_B because without
such a writedown the firm would be unable to invest at date 1.

Given an offer worth L_B and the bank's acceptance, the firm may be able
to exchange its public debt. In an exchange, the maximum value of each new

senior debenture is $(\overline{X} + Y - I - L_B)/D$, while each untendered debenture is worth q because there will no funds available at date 2 to pay off the untendered junior debt. Thus, the firm can complete an exchange provided

$$\overline{X} - I \geq qD - L_D. \tag{9}$$

Note that if the exchange is successful, the firm will be able to make its date-1 bank payment of L_B and invest I since we have assumed that $Y > I + B > I + L_B$. If (9) is violated, however, the firm does not offer to exchange and thus is liquidated at date 1.

There will tend to be underinvestment if the current portion of the public debt qD exceeds its liquidation value L_D and overinvestment if the current portion is less than its liquidation value. The minimum transfer to the public debtholders from investment is the least that they can be given with investment qD minus what they get in liquidation L_D. If the transfer is positive, there is underinvestment, and if the net subsidy is negative, there is overinvestment.

The condition for investment is exactly the same as in the model of Section I in which exchange offers were ruled out, but it is possible for the firm to issue senior bank debt. In both cases, investment occurs if the net present value of the project exceeds $qD - L_D$. Although investment behavior is no different, the parties who pay for the investment are different. If (9) is a strict inequality, the public debtholders are worse off with an exchange than with a bank debt restructuring. In the bank debt restructuring, they keep their old securities, while in an exchange the hold-in problem leads public debtholders to accept a lower value security. Since, in both cases, the bank gets a claim worth L_B, equity is the beneficiary of the exchange offer.

Thus, exchange offers can be profitable for the firm if it is able to exchange the debt for more senior securities or has excess cash it can use to exchange the debt for cash. But note the ability to exchange does nothing to improve the efficiency of investment decisions of financially distressed firms if there is no seniority covenant in the public debt; it just affects who bears the costs of financial distress.[25] The reason is that public debtholders take the success of the exchange as given in making their tender decision. Therefore, they do not consider how a change in operating policy made possible by the exchange, affects their claim.

We summarize these results in the following proposition.

Proposition 5: *If the firm has insufficient cash to invest, there are three possible outcomes. If the NPV of the investment $\overline{X} - I$ is sufficiently large, the bank is paid in full, the public debtholders accept an exchange, and the firm invests. For intermediate NPVs, the bank debt is forgiven to L_B, the public debtholders accept an exchange, and the firm invests. If the NPV is suffi-*

---

[25] Although the basic idea that exchange offers give limited possibilities to increase investment incentives is quite robust, the strong result of no effect is somewhat model-specific. For example, if management were only willing to invest if equity value exceeded some threshold level, the concessions from public debtholders would increase the ability to invest.

ciently small, the firm is liquidated and does not invest. The possibility of a public debt exchange does not alter investment when there are no covenants prohibiting senior debt issues.

The analysis assumes that there is no covenant in the public debt prohibiting a senior debt issue. As discussed in Section II.A, however, firms can get around this covenant through an exit consent in which debtholders simultaneously tender their debentures for more senior ones and, as a condition of the exchange, vote to remove the seniority covenant on the original debt issue. The condition for investment continues to be given by inequality (9).

Thus, exchange offers combined with exit consents can be used to strip seniority covenants that would otherwise prevent a public debt restructuring and constrain investment; in this case, exchange offers have real investment effects. But, the firm can go too far; exit consents and exchange offers can reduce the value of the public debt so much that the firm actually overinvests. Coffee and Klein (1990) have argued that the "coercive" character of exit consents leads to inefficiencies and have called for a ban on exit consents. As a result of a ban, debtholders would still be able to vote to remove covenants, but the vote would not be a condition for tendering in an exchange.

Such a ban on exit consents is efficient in our model. To see this, suppose there is a seniority covenant in the public debt. The interesting case is where the firm cannot raise new bank financing that is pari passu with the existing debt: $\overline{X} - I < V_D - L_D$ and $V_D - L_D > 0$, so that the firm potentially under-invests. If the firm could renegotiate directly with public debtholders they would be willing to reduce the value of their debt conditional on investment to L_D through a reduction of principal or interest. Of course, the Trust Indenture Act does not permit public debtholders to reduce V_D in this way. But, they can effectively reduce V_D by voting to waive the seniority covenant. At the same time, the bank lends new money senior to the public debt, and the interest rate is chosen so that the value of the public debt V_D' is anywhere from a minimum of qD to a maximum of V_D. (Note that V_D' cannot be below qD because if the firm invests the payment of qD is required.)

Public debtholders will accept a covenant waiver only if they know they will receive at least L_D as a result of the restructuring. If $qD < L_D$, the firm can offer L_D, and the public debtholders will accept; if $qD > L_D$, the value of the debt cannot be reduced all the way to L_D, and the offer will be qD. So $V_D' = \max\{qD, L_D\}$. Thus, the condition for investment with a covenant waiver is

$$\overline{X} - I \geq \max\{qD, L_D\} - L_D = \max\{qD - L_D, 0\}. \qquad (10)$$

Contrast this condition to inequality (9) which determines investment when exit consents are possible. The two conditions are the same when $qD > L_D$. In both cases underinvestment may result because there are limits on how much debt reduction is feasible via exit consents or covenant waivers. But, when $qD < L_D$, exit consents allow some negative NPV projects to be taken while covenant waivers do not. The firm can reduce the value of the public debt to below its liquidation value when exit consents are possible but cannot do this when debtholders vote separately on the covenant waiver. Thus, in some situations, exit consents go too far in lowering the debt burden. We have only focused on the case where $\overline{X} - I < V_D - L_D$ and $V_D - L_D > 0$, but in the other cases covenant waivers also lead to weakly more efficient investment outcomes than exit consents.[26]

The conclusion is that exchange offers only alter investment behavior when there is a covenant in the public debt prohibiting senior debt issues. In these cases, firms can use exit consents to remove covenants, issue senior debt, and increase investment. But, exit consents can result in excessive investment. By contrast, if the firm is prohibited from using exit consents and instead must ask for a separate vote to waive a seniority covenant, investment decisions are improved.

The results of this section indicate that the firm would never propose an exchange for more junior securities. This is difficult to reconcile with empirical observations. There are two promising explanations. First, if the firm has private information, it may signal its information by the type of security offered in an exchange. As Myers and Majluf (1984) show, equity issues can signal that the firm's value is low. The firm may then offer an exchange for equity so that debtholders lower the value of the claim they require in exchange.[27] This may offset the losses the firm incurs from the holdout problem created by an exchange for a more junior security.

A second reason why firms may offer junior securities is that public creditors are not really atomistic. In this case, the firm may be able to convince a sufficient number of large debtholders that their acceptance of equity is necessary for a successful restructuring. Equity may be preferred because it reduces the cash drainage from the firm.

Finally, we note two recent developments that have made exchanges less attractive. In the LTV bankruptcy, Judge Lifland disallowed a portion of the claims of public debtholders who participated in a previously completed exchange. He ruled that the admissible claim was the market value of the debentures at the time of the exchange, not its face value. Thus, there may be some reluctance to exchange for fear that the firm would file for Chapter 11 in the future. In addition, the tax treatment of exchanges was changed as part of the Revenue Reconciliation Act of 1990, requiring the firm to recognize cancellation of debt income based on the market value of new securities, not their face value. Firms may be able to avoid this tax liability in Chapter 11.

---

[26] For completeness, consider the case where $\overline{X} - I < V_D - L_D < 0$. In this case the public debtholders would never agree to lower the value of their debt further below its liquidation value. In contrast, an exit consent could allow negative NPV projects to be taken. Also consider the case where $\overline{X} - I > V_D - L_D$. Neither covenant waivers nor exit consents change investment behavior. Public debtholders reject any covenant waiver, but an exit consent can be used to extract value from public bondholders.

[27] See Gertner (1990) and Brown, James, and Mooradian (1991). The latter paper provides empirical evidence consistent with the signaling view.

III. Reorganization Law and Investment

In the U.S., financially distressed companies often seek court protection under the provisions of Chapter 11 of the Bankruptcy Code. These provisions in the Code are intended to promote reorganization of economically viable firms as going-concerns and thereby avoid inefficient liquidation of distressed firms. When a firm files for bankruptcy, all of its debts become due, but an *automatic stay* is invoked stopping all principal and interest payments, and secured creditors lose the right to take possession of their collateral.

In Chapter 11, control of a firm, known as the *debtor in possession*, typically remains with the current management and board of directors. This contrasts with Chapter 7 bankruptcy proceedings in which a trustee takes control and manages the company while organizing a piecemeal liquidation or sale of the firm as a going concern. Creditors are paid in accordance with the absolute priority rule, so equity gets nothing unless all creditors are paid in full. In Chapter 11, management is permitted to continue operating the firm, but all significant decisions are subject to court review and legal motions by creditors to disallow the proposed policy.[28] In reviewing the debtor's policies, the court's objective is to approve policies which maximize the value of the estate. The court has the charge of promoting "equitable" resolutions. This gives the court significant latitude in overseeing the debtor's operations. In addition, the fiduciary responsibility of management is to maximize the value of the estate, not the value of equity.

Operations proceed with court oversight until a reorganization plan is approved through a voting procedure of creditors or the firm is liquidated (piecemeal or as a going concern) either in Chapter 11 or after a conversion to Chapter 7. A reorganization plan specifies a new capital structure for the firm, delineating how creditors are paid in terms of cash or securities of the reorganized firm.

In this section, we focus on three aspects of Chapter 11 that we believe are fundamental for understanding its effect on operating and investment decisions: the automatic stay, the voting rules that determine whether a reorganization plan is approved, and the maintenance of equity value despite the fact that creditors are not paid in full. In general, Chapter 11 has ambiguous effects on efficiency, but the analysis characterizes the situations in which efficiency is enhanced or diminished.

A. The Automatic Stay

The automatic stay increases the firm's incentive to invest. To see this suppose the firm files for Chapter 11 and that the automatic stay is the only feature of Chapter 11. The public debtholders' claims are delayed until date 2, at which time they are either paid in full or share the firm's assets with the bank if the firm is unable to make its debt payment.

---

[28] Control of the corporation can be given to a trustee if creditors can show that current management has acted fraudulently.

Effectively, the automatic stay extends the maturity of the public debt from $q > 0$ to $q = 0$. As we have seen, the firm has a greater incentive to invest when the debt has longer maturity. There are two separate effects. First, the firm may now have the cash needed for investment, so it may not have to borrow funds at date 1: Y may be less than $I + B + qD$ but greater than $I + B$. And even if the firm must borrow ($Y < I + B$), investment is more attractive because the automatic stay forces public debtholders to bear more risk.

The firm may be more willing to invest, but it is not necessarily efficient for it to do so. Public debtholders may be forced to bear too much risk, leading the firm to overinvest. The oversight of the court and the ability of public debtholders to object to the firm's investment plans may prevent large abuses of this type.

This analysis assumes that the new money comes from the bank and is pari passu with the outstanding public debt. But, the debtor will generally try to get the court to approve financing senior to all existing debt. Such financing—known as *debtor in possession* (*DIP*) *financing*—is considered an administrative cost which is paid ahead of all other creditors. The court can even make post-petition debt senior to other administrative costs. In addition, the court can approve a *cash collateral* agreement, allowing the debtor to use liquid assets to finance its operations even if these assets are pledged as collateral to a creditor. Thus, the court can effectively strip seniority covenants and security from existing debt. This leads to even greater investment incentives, although the junior creditors who are potentially hurt by the new senior investment can try to petition the court to reject the new financing.

The automatic stay also affects the incentives of the bank to lend outside of bankruptcy. Since the subsidy to the public debtholders from investment is reduced by the automatic stay, the bank and the firm have an incentive to restructure inside bankruptcy rather than outside bankruptcy. If the deadweight losses associated with bankruptcy are less than the reduction in the net subsidy to debtholders, firms will file for bankruptcy even though they could have successfully restructured outside of bankruptcy. In this case, the Chapter 11 option can reduce efficiency. Investment is unchanged by the filing, but the firm is willing to incur a deadweight cost to extract value from public debtholders.[29]

B. Chapter 11 Voting

Investment inefficiencies arise in our model because of the inability to negotiate directly with public debtholders. Exchange offers do little to improve investment efficiency. The underlying problem is that unlike the bank,

---

[29] This implicitly assumes that a firm which defaults must file for bankruptcy. However, in this situation, if bankruptcy proceedings are costly, public bondholders may choose not to force the firm into bankruptcy despite default. They know that bankruptcy results in imposition of the automatic stay which may delay payment as much as default. In this case, the automatic stay can effectively be achieved without an actual filing.

public debtholders do not take into account their effect on the firm's investment policy.

Chapter 11 voting rules can get around this problem. Reorganization plans must be approved by all classes of creditors and the court. Classes are determined by grouping creditors with essentially equivalent claims. So, for example, secured and unsecured creditors are always assigned to different classes. A class approves a plan if two-thirds of the allowed monetary interests and a majority in number within the class accepts the plan. A dissenting member of a class can object to a plan if he gets a claim worth less than his claim in liquidation.

To see how the voting procedure affects restructuring and investment, suppose that the firm files for Chapter 11 reorganization and immediately proposes a reorganization plan that gives public debtholders a claim on the reorganized company which, conditional on investment, is worth $L_D + \varepsilon$, a little more than the return to public debtholders under liquidation. Furthermore, suppose that this is a take-it-or-leave-it offer and that if the plan is rejected the firm is liquidated. In deciding how to vote, a public debtholder compares his return if the plan is successful with his return if it is not. If the plan is successful, all public debtholders share $L_D + \varepsilon$. If the plan is unsuccessful, all public debtholders share L_D in liquidation. Thus, they all vote for the plan. The debtor can offer the holders of the public debt a claim just above its liquidation value, so there is no subsidy to or from public debtholders. The result is efficient investment.

Why does this voting mechanism work while an exchange offer does not? The answer is that the voting procedure does not allow public debtholders to be treated differently depending on their vote, whereas tendering and non-tendering public debtholders are treated differently. In an exchange offer, a public debtholder compares the value of the new claim with the value of the old claim *conditional on success* of the exchange offer because it is possible for the debtholder to keep his old claim even if the tender offer is successful. But if the conditions for acceptance under the voting procedure are met, those who do not vote for the plan are compelled to accept the offer.[30] Thus, the voting procedure can be used to internalize the effects of the investment decision and get around the holdout and hold-in problems, thereby improving investment efficiency.[31]

The voting procedure is unlikely to work as smoothly as we have modeled it. In practice, the debtor does not have all the bargaining power. The threat to liquidate the firm if the plan is rejected may not be credible; the debtor may choose to continue operating the firm in Chapter 11. Asymmetric

---

[30] A dissenting member of an approving class who gets less than the liquidation value of its claim can object to the plan. If successful, this will cause the plan to be defeated. This does not accomplish the same thing as holding out in a successful exchange offer. In that situation, other creditors make concessions while the holdout's claim is unchanged.

[31] A similar problem arises in the context of takeovers. Shareholders that do not tender may be able to free-ride on the acquirer's value gains. One way around this problem has been proposed by Bebchuk (1985): let the shareholders vote whether to accept the offer and make a successful vote binding on all shareholders. This reduces inefficiency for the same reason it does here.

information may lead to inefficiencies through strategic behavior and delay. Nevertheless, an important feature of voting is its capacity to overcome the holdout and hold-in problems.

This analysis raises a natural question: if Chapter 11 voting procedures enhance efficiency, why can the firm not include in its debt covenants a provision that mimics the Chapter 11 voting procedures for exchange offers by the firm. The answer is that, as discussed above, the Trust Indenture Act of 1939 prohibits it.[32]

This voting rule can help the firm to obtain concessions from public debtholders. Even if the bank is willing to lend outside Chapter 11, the firm may be better off filing for bankruptcy and taking advantage of the voting procedure to obtain a transfer from public debtholders. This is more likely to be the best strategy when these concessions are large. Thus, if the public debt is relatively short term, senior, or protected by seniority covenants, the public debt is generally more valuable outside Chapter 11 than inside. In these cases, we would expect firms to file.

C. Maintenance of Equity Value

One of the most salient features of Chapter 11 reorganizations is that shareholders typically retain a stake in the firm, even though debtholders are not paid in full. Franks and Torous (1989) find that, in a sample of 28 Chapter 11 filings, equity holders retain some equity in the reorganized firm in 21 cases.

The debtor's bargaining power in Chapter 11 is derived from a number of procedural rules on the formation and acceptance of a reorganization plan. The *debtor in possession* has the exclusive right to propose a plan for the first 120 days after filing the bankruptcy petition. This exclusivity period can be, and often is, extended by the judge for long periods. Only once exclusivity is lifted can creditors propose a plan.

The debtor's threat to delay a plan is often credible; the debtor wishes to protract bankruptcy proceedings on the chance that the debtor will turn solvent and that shareholders will receive a larger payoff in the liquidation or reorganization. These debtor bargaining powers help explain why shareholders typically retain a stake in the reorganized firm even though creditors are not paid in full.

---

[32] 'The Act was initially promoted to protect public debtholders from being exploited by the firm. The fear was that a large shareholder would have an incentive to secretly buy up the bonds and vote to eliminate principal and interest payments. Roe (1987) argues that this provision of the Trust Indenture Act no longer serves any useful purpose and is inconsistent with the voting procedures used in Chapter 11 reorganizations. Fraud statutes can be used to avoid manipulation by large shareholders. The Act may force firms to file for bankruptcy with all its other baggage in order to restructure its public debt. Currently, "pre-packaged" or "1126b" plans, in which reorganization plans are already approved when the firm files for bankruptcy, are becoming popular. They are used mainly to compel holdouts to go along with other members of their creditor class. Republic Health used a pre-package plan successfully.

This threat is damaging to creditors because they usually want the proceedings to end as soon as possible in order to receive principal and interest payments on their debt. In addition, all creditors face the risk that the estate's value will decline dramatically during bankruptcy. Secured creditors also face the risk that the secured assets will depreciate during Chapter 11.

Clearly, the decision to accept or reject a plan depends on what happens if the plan is not approved, i.e., on the threat points in this game.[33] One threat point of a plan's sponsor is that the plan will be approved by the court even in the presence of a dissenting class of creditors. The procedure is referred to as *cramdown*. Section 1129 of the Bankruptcy Code provides for cramdown if a class receives a claim with value equivalent to full payment or if every class junior to the dissenting class receives nothing.[34]

Creditors also have threats. They can propose a plan of their own which can be crammed down on the equity holders. Perhaps, even more important, secured creditors can try to lift the automatic stay.[35] They can also file for dismissal of the case or conversion to Chapter 7 liquidation.[36] Creditors can fight management's operating and investment decisions. They can refuse to lend new money, and they can try to block asset sales.

The fact that equity retains value in many reorganizations even if creditors are not paid in full can have important implications for behavior outside of Chapter 11, in particular for incentive to lend new money outside of bankruptcy. In our model, the firm has only two alternatives: to obtain new funds and invest, or to go bankrupt and liquidate the firm. In practice, however, there is generally a third option: to file for Chapter 11 protection, invoke the automatic stay, and maintain control, continuing in operation without new funds for investment. This threat is often both harmful to creditors and perfectly credible: in liquidation equity value is almost certain to be wiped out, while in Chapter 11 equity value is positive if there is any possibility of solvency. Faced with this threat, the creditors' best alternative may be to extend further funds for investment. Thus, reorganization law provides a distressed firm with a credible threat that increases the creditors' incentives to provide new funds. In essence, the law affects the bargaining

---

[33] See Brown (1989) and Baird and Picker (1991) for analyses of how various bankruptcy rules affect the way in which firm value is divided between shareholders and creditors.

[34] Some jurisdictions have allowed equity to maintain value in cramdown even if all creditors are not paid in full. This rule, known as the *new value exception*, permits old equity holders to maintain control as long as it pays creditors the liquidation value of the assets and the old equity holders contribute new capital equal to the value of the equity of the reorganized company. The existence of the new value exception under the Bankruptcy Code is a controversial and unsettled legal issue. See Norwest Bank Worthington versus Ahlers 485 U.S. 197 (1988) and the discussion in Baird and Jackson (1990).

[35] Causes to lift the automatic stay include lack of adequate protection, or a showing that the creditor is undersecured and the collateral is not necessary for an effective reorganization.

[36] The court can convert a Chapter 11 case to Chapter 7 if it is in the best interest of the creditors and the estate as long as certain conditions are met. These conditions, listed in Section 1112 of the Code, include continuing losses with "no reasonable likelihood of rehabilitation," unreasonable delay by the debtor, and failure to consummate a plan.

process outside of bankruptcy, changing not just how surplus is split but the efficiency of outcomes as well.

To develop this idea in more detail, we consider the following simple extension of our model in Section I. Suppose that if the firm continues in operation without investing, it receives a stochastic date-2 payoff of X_c (with mean $\bar{x}_c$) in addition to the date-1 liquidation value of Y. In order to focus on continuation as a threat rather than a value-maximizing strategy, we assume that continuation is inefficient; total value is higher if the firm liquidates than if it continues without investment, $\overline{X}_c < 0$. The value of the public debt if the firm follows the continuation strategy is V_D^c. The bank and the firm together get $\overline{X}_c + Y - V_D^c$ if the firm continues without investing. If the firm invests, their combined payoff, as before, is $\overline{X} - I + Y - V_D$. Finally, if the firm is liquidated, their combined payoff is L_B, with equity getting nothing.

Suppose that among these three alternatives liquidation is the most attractive to the bank and equity combined, so that

$$L_B > \max\left(\overline{X} - I + Y - V_D, \overline{X}_c + Y - V_D^c \right) \tag{11}$$

Then, absent Chapter 11 reorganization, the firm will be liquidated.

But, now suppose the firm can file in Chapter 11, invoke the automatic stay, defer debt payments until date 2, and stay in control of the firm. This is collectively inefficient for the bank and shareholders since $L_B > \overline{X}_c + Y - V_D^c$. The bank would like to pay the firm to liquidate instead of continue, but it cannot. Any payment from the bank to the firm cannot go to shareholders before it goes to the firm's other creditors; this would be a fraudulent conveyance and declared illegal. Given this restriction, the firm's threat is credible; shareholders are better off continuing in operation in the hope that X_c is sufficient to pay creditors at date 2, thereby giving equity a positive return, which exceeds equity's zero return in liquidation.

So the bank has two options. It can let the firm file Chapter 11 or it can provide new money for investment. If the joint returns from investing are larger than those from continuation in Chapter 11, i.e.,

$$\overline{X} - I - V_D \geq \overline{X}_c - V_D^c, \tag{12}$$

the bank will lend money for investment. If not, the firm will file for Chapter 11 protection.

The option to file for Chapter 11 protection can increase efficiency. If (12) is satisfied, the firm will be more prone to invest. This is efficient if $V_D - L_B > 0$, the case in which the firm underinvests without Chapter 11. If, however, $V_D - L_D < 0$, the firm would otherwise overinvest, and Chapter 11 merely exacerbates the inefficiency. By contrast, if (12) is violated, Chapter 11 always reduces efficiency since the firm continues rather than liquidates, and $\overline{X}_c < 0 < Y$.

The overall efficiency effects of this aspect of Chapter 11 are ambiguous, but we can identify the situations in which it is likely to be helpful or harmful. First, when the public debt is short term, the bank debt is senior, and the public debt is protected by seniority covenants, underinvestment is likely to be a problem, and Chapter 11 can be helpful. Second, when investment is risky relative to continuation, investment tends to be more attractive to the bank and equity because the public debt is worth less. In this case, the likely effect of Chapter 11 is to promote investment rather than to give the firm an easy way of avoiding efficient liquidation.

Another out-of-bankruptcy effect of the maintenance of equity value in Chapter 11 is to reduce the incentives to take risk. In a Chapter 7 liquidation, shareholders generally receive nothing, making Chapter 7 very unattractive to shareholders and management. So, as the firm's financial position gradually deteriorates, management has a strong incentive to take risk-increasing investments and to pay out as much firm value as possible to themselves. This incentive is obviously diminished the higher the return to equity and management in Chapter 11. Of course, if public debtholders are aware of the law, they must be promised a higher interest rate to compensate them for their lower return when the firm is in distress. If the investment decisions of a financially distressed firm are more efficient, there will be more than enough increased value to pay the higher interest rates and yet increase equity value.

IV. Concluding Remarks

This paper outlines some of the characteristics of corporate financial structure that can make financial distress more or less costly. We focus on coordination problems among numerous public debtholders as the main source of inefficiency. This problem can lead to underinvestment when bank debt is senior, when public debt is short term, or when it is protected by seniority covenants. Overinvestment tends to be a problem with junior bank debt, long-term public debt, and when a firm can strip seniority covenants with exit consents.

Exchange offers can be used to restructure public debt, but they do not, in general, lead to efficient investment. So, financial distress may result in inefficient operating policy even though banks are perfectly informed and exchanges are possible with public creditors. If there are no seniority covenants in the public debt, exchange offers do not change the firm's investment behavior but simply force public debtholders to bear more of the burden of financial distress. If there is a seniority covenant, however, investment can be increased through an exchange offer that strips public debt of its covenant and enables a firm to issue senior debt to finance investment. However, such exchange offers can go too far, resulting in overinvestment in some cases. Efficiency is increased if exit consents are not allowed, and, instead, debtholders vote separately to eliminate seniority covenants.

The Trust Indenture Act gives rise to investment inefficiencies because it forces firms to make exchange offers rather than bargain directly with public debtholders. In our model, all investment inefficiencies would be eliminated if the Trust Indenture Act was repealed. Of course, this result follows from our assumption of complete information in which case bargaining is efficient in the absence of transaction costs. In a more realistic model with asymmetric information and other transaction costs, investment inefficiencies are likely to result.

There are a number of empirical implications of our model. First, the model predicts that, conditional on an out-of-court workout, distressed firms with senior bank debt, short-term public debt, and effective seniority covenants will invest less. Second, the model predicts that exchanges are more likely when the public debt is relatively long term. And, when possible, exchanges should shorten the maturity of public debt, strip existing covenants, and offer more senior securities.

Our model is also a useful starting point to think about the tradeoffs firms face in deciding whether to file for Chapter 11 rather than seek an out-of-court restructuring. We have outlined how debt structure affects the payoffs from an out-of-court restructuring. To complete the theory, we need a model of the reorganization process, one that tells us how debt structure affects investment behavior and the division of firm value in Chapter 11.

We conclude by noting that while we have analyzed the effects of Chapter 11 on distressed firms, we have sidestepped an important point made by legal scholars. Roe (1983), Baird (1986), and Jackson (1986) have all argued that the manipulation that is possible in Chapter 11 can be avoided by eliminating Chapter 11 reorganization altogether and relying on Chapter 7.

The basic thrust of the argument is as follows. Consider a firm in financial distress much like the firm we have modeled. Suppose the firm goes into Chapter 7 and the trustee sells the firm in its entirety, either through an auction or through negotiations with investors and other firms. The proceeds from the sale are then used to pay off creditors using the same priority rules that apply if the assets are sold piecemeal. Any funds that are left after paying off all the creditors in full go to the original shareholders. The newly created firm has none of its previous debts and should be able to invest efficiently. If the original managers of the firm are essential for the investment project, the new owners can hire them to run the company, or the old managers could buy the firm themselves, borrowing against the firm's now unencumbered assets. In effect, the Chapter 7 effects a swap of all the outstanding debt for a package of new securities.

Our analysis suggests that the issues are more complex than these authors suggest. The important point is that the maintenance of equity value in Chapter 11 affects both investment and bargaining outside of bankruptcy. It makes creditors more willing to lend, and it can reduce managerial moral hazard outside of bankruptcy. Moreover, if the market for the sale of distressed firms is thin and inefficient, the buyer will get some rents. This will inefficiently increase the firm's ex ante cost of capital since neither original shareholders nor creditors receive these rents. And, the forced sale envisioned by these authors can lead to different operating and investment policies. So, the normative question of whether a forced sales regime is more or less efficient than some form of reorganization law is an empirical one, given the potential allocative distortions of both systems.

Appendix

Proof of Proposition 1: For a given p and β, the value of the firm in default is: $X + Y - I - B - (1 - \beta)qD$. Total outstanding claims at date 2 are $(1 - \beta)(1 - q)D + \beta pD$ of which tendering debtholders collectively receive a fraction $\beta pD/[(1 - \beta)(1 - q)D + \beta pD]$. Thus, the value of each of the βD tendered debentures is:

$$\int_0^{X_b} \frac{p}{(1 - \beta)(1 - q)D + \beta pD} \left[X + Y - I - B - (1 - \beta)qD\right] f(X)\,\mathrm{d}X$$

$$+ \int_{X_b}^{\infty} pf(X)\,\mathrm{d}X. \quad \text{(A1)}$$

Each nontendering debtholder receives a certain payment of q at date 1 and a risky claim at date 2 comprised of his share of the insolvent firm if $X < X_b$ and full payment of $(1 - q)$ if $X > X_b$:

$$q + \int_0^{X_b} (1 - q)\frac{X + Y - I - B - (1 - \beta)qD}{(1 - \beta)(1 - q)D + \beta pD} f(X)\,\mathrm{d}X$$

$$+ \int_{X_b}^{\infty} (1 - q)f(X)\,\mathrm{d}X. \quad \text{(A2)}$$

Equating (A1) and (A2) determines, for any given β, the p at which debtholders are just indifferent between tendering and not tendering. This equation can be rewritten as:

$$\int_0^{X_b} \frac{(X + Y - I - B)(1 - q - p) + pqD}{(1 - \beta)(1 - q)D + \beta pD} f(X)\,\mathrm{d}X$$

$$+ \int_{X_b}^{\infty} (1 - p)f(X)\,\mathrm{d}X = 0. \quad \text{(A3)}$$

At $p = 1$, the left-hand side is

$$\int_0^{X_b} \frac{q[D - (X + Y - I - B)]}{(1 - \beta)(1 - q)D + \beta pD} f(X)\,\mathrm{d}X. \quad \text{(A4)}$$

The integrand is 0 at $X = X_b$ and positive for $X < X_b$, so (A4) is positive at $p = 1$. Since the left-hand side of (A3) is decreasing in p, the p that solves (A3) is greater than one. Q.E.D.

Proof of Proposition 2: The value of the old debentures given β and p when the firm exchanges for senior debt is given by:

$$q + \int_{X_1}^{X_b} \frac{X + Y - I - B - (1 - \beta)qD - \beta pD}{(1 - \beta)D} f(X) \, dX$$

$$+ \int_{X_b}^{\infty} (1 - q) f(X) \, dX, \quad \text{(A5)}$$

where $X_1 \equiv I + B + (1 - \beta)qD + \beta pD - Y$ is the cutoff value of X above which the new debentures are paid in full and $X_b \equiv I + B + (1 - \beta)D + \beta pD - Y$ is the cutoff value of X above which the old debt is paid in full and the firm is solvent; $X_1 \leq X_b$, with equality if and only if $\beta = 1$. Since the new debt is senior to the old debt, for X between X_1 and X_b holdouts share $X + Y - I - B - (1 - \beta)qD - \beta pD$, the cash left after date-1 payments and date-2 payments of βpD to the new senior debt.

Tendering debtholders do not receive q at date 1 but do receive a senior claim at date 2. The value of their debt is

$$\int_0^{X_1} \frac{X + Y - I - B - (1 - \beta)qD}{\beta D} f(X) \, dX + \int_{X_1}^{\infty} pf(X) \, dX. \quad \text{(A6)}$$

We now show that the value to the firm of an exchange is increasing in β. Equating (A5) and (A6) and combining terms gives,

$$\int_0^{X_1} \frac{X + Y - I - B - qD}{\beta D} f(X) \, dX - \int_{X_1}^{X_b} \frac{X + Y - I - B - pD}{(1 - \beta)D} f(X) \, dX$$

$$- \int_{X_b}^{\infty} (1 - p) f(X) \, dX = 0. \quad \text{(A7)}$$

Since $X_b = I + B - Y + (1 - \beta)D + p\beta D$,

$$\frac{dX_b}{d\beta} = D \left[\beta \frac{\partial p}{\partial \beta} - (1 - p) \right]. \quad \text{(A8)}$$

Differentiating (A7),

$$\frac{\partial p}{\partial \beta} = \frac{\displaystyle \int_0^{X_1} \frac{X + Y - I - B - qD}{\beta^2 D} f(X) \, dX + \int_{X_1}^{X_b} \frac{X + Y - I - B - pD}{(1 - \beta)^2 D} f(X) \, dX}{\displaystyle \int_{X_1}^{X_b} \frac{1}{1 - \beta} f(X) \, dX + \int_{X_b}^{\infty} f(X) \, dX}. \quad \text{(A9)}$$

Multiplying by β and substituting from (A7),

$$\beta \frac{\partial p}{\partial \beta} = \frac{\dfrac{1}{1-\beta} \displaystyle\int_{X_1}^{X_b} \frac{X + Y - I - B - pD}{(1-\beta)D} f(X)\,dX + \displaystyle\int_{X_b}^{\infty} (1-p)f(X)\,dX}{\displaystyle\int_{X_1}^{X_b} \frac{1}{1-\beta} f(X)\,dX + \displaystyle\int_{X_b}^{\infty} f(X)\,dX},$$

$$(A10)$$

and

$$\beta \frac{\partial p}{\partial \beta} - (1-p) = \frac{\dfrac{1}{1-\beta} \displaystyle\int_{X_1}^{X_b} \frac{X + Y - I - B - pD}{(1-\beta)D} f(X)\,dX - \displaystyle\int_{X_1}^{X_b} \frac{1-p}{1-\beta} f(X)\,dX}{\displaystyle\int_{X_1}^{X_b} \frac{1}{1-\beta} f(X)\,dX + \displaystyle\int_{X_b}^{\infty} f(X)\,dX}. \quad (A11)$$

The denominator is clearly positive. The numerator is equal to

$$\frac{1}{(1-\beta)^2 D} \int_{X_1}^{X_b} \left[X + Y - I - B - D(1 - \beta + \beta p) \right] f(X)\,dX.$$

At X_1 the integrand is $(1 - \beta)(q - 1)D$, which is negative. Since the integrand is increasing in X, the numerator is negative, and X_b is decreasing in β. Thus, one can determine whether an exchange offer is profitable by checking to see whether p is greater or less than one at $\beta = 1$.

If we set $\beta = 1$, $X_1 = X_b$ and we can rewrite (A7) as

$$\int_0^{X_b} \frac{X + Y - I - B - qD}{D} f(X)\,dX - \int_{X_b}^{\infty} (1 - p)f(X)\,dX = 0. \quad (A13)$$

Since $Y > I + B + qD$ by assumption, the first term in (A13) is positive. Thus, to satisfy (A13), p must be less than one.   Q.E.D.

Proof of Proposition 3: Suppose the firm offers to exchange each dollar of old debt for V dollars of cash or new short-term debt. Debtholders will be indifferent between tendering and not for any V and β provided,

$$q + \int_0^{X_b} \frac{X + Y - I - B - (1 - \beta)qD - V\beta D}{(1-\beta)D} f(X)\,dX$$

$$+ \int_{X_b}^{\infty} (1 - q)f(X)\,dX = V, \quad (A14)$$

where $X_b \equiv I + B + (1 - \beta)qD + V\beta D - Y$. We can rewrite (A14) as

$$\int_0^{X_b} \frac{X + Y - I - B - VD}{(1 - \beta)D} f(X)\, dX + \int_{X_b}^{\infty} (1 - V)f(X)\, dX = 0. \quad \text{(A15)}$$

Totally differentiating (A15) yields,

$$\frac{dV}{d\beta} = \frac{\displaystyle\int_0^{X_b} \frac{X + Y - I - B - VD}{(1 - \beta)^2 D} f(X)\, dX}{F(X_b) + (1 - \beta)[1 - F(X_b)]} \quad \text{(A16)}$$

$$= \frac{-(1 - V)[1 - F(X_b)]}{\beta\{F(X_b) + (1 - \beta)[1 - F(X_b)]\}}, \quad \text{(A17)}$$

where the second equality follows from substituting (A15) into (A16). From (A14), $V < 1$, so (A17) implies that $V'(\beta) < 0$. The cost to the firm of the exchange is $\beta D V(\beta)$. Since debtholders are indifferent between tendering and not, the expected payments to the nontendering debtholders must be $(1 - \beta)D V(\beta)$. Adding, the expected payments to all public debtholders is $V(\beta)D$. So, the firm maximizes profits by choosing β to minimize $V(\beta)$. Since $V'(\beta) < 0$, an exchange for cash is profitable.   Q.E.D.

Proof of Proposition 4: From (A13), the exchange offer terms for senior debt are determined by

$$\int_0^{X_b} (X + Y - I - B - qD)f(X)\, dX - \int_{X_b}^{\infty} (1 - p)Df(X)\, dX = 0, \quad \text{(A18)}$$

where $X_b = X + Y - I - B - pD$.

In an exchange, the shareholders receive $X - X_b$ if it is positive and zero otherwise. In a bank renegotiation, shareholders receive $X - B' - (1 - q)D$ if it is positive and zero otherwise. So an exchange is more profitable provided $X_b < B' + (1 - q)D$.

To show that this is indeed the case, we assume, to the contrary, that $X_b \geq B' + (1 - q)D$. Thus, let $B' \equiv X_b - (1 - q)D - \varepsilon$, $\varepsilon \geq 0$. Then equation (8) can be rewritten as

$$\int_0^{X_b - (1-q)D - \varepsilon} Xf(X)\, dX + \int_{X_b - (1-q)D - \varepsilon}^{\infty} [X_b - (1 - q)D - \varepsilon]f(X)\, dX$$

$$+ Y - I - qD - B = 0. \quad \text{(A19)}$$

Using the definition of X_b and rearranging, (A19) becomes

$$\int_0^{X_b - (1-q)D - \varepsilon} (X + Y - I - qD - B)f(X)\, dX$$

$$- \int_{X_b - (1-q)D - \varepsilon}^{\infty} (1 - p)D = 0. \quad \text{(A20)}$$

Now compare (A20) and (A18). The only difference is the limits of integration. Note that the left-hand side of (A18) is increasing in X_b and since $X_b - (1 - q)D - \varepsilon < X_b$, the left-hand side of (A20) is less than that of (A18). Thus, if (A18) is satisfied with equality, (A20) must be violated. Thus, B' must be greater than $X_b + (1 - q)D$.   Q.E.D.

REFERENCES

Aivazian, V. and J. Callen, 1983, Reorganization in bankruptcy and the issue of strategic risk, *Journal of Banking and Finance* 7, 1989, 119–133.

Asquith, P., D. Mullins, and E. Wolff, 1989, Original issue high yield bonds: Aging analyses of defaults, exchanges, and calls, *Journal of Finance* 44, 923–952.

Baird, D., 1986, The uneasy case for corporate reorganization, *Journal of Legal Studies* 15, 127–147.

—— and T. Jackson, 1990, *Cases, Problems, and Materials on Bankruptcy*, 2nd Edition (Little Brown and Company, Boston).

—— and R. Picker, 1991, A simple noncooperative bargaining model of corporate reorganizations, *Journal of Legal Studies*, Forthcoming.

Bebchuk, L., 1985, Towards an undistorted choice and equal treatment in corporate takeovers, *Harvard Law Review* 98, 1693–1808.

Bergman, Y. and J. Callen, 1990, Opportunistic behavior in debt renegotiations and an interior optimal capital structure of the firm without deadweight costs, Unpublished manuscript, Brown University Department of Economics.

Berkovitch, E. and E. H. Kim, 1990, Financial contracting and leverage induced over- and under-investment incentives, *Journal of Finance* 45, 765–794.

Bernanke, B. and J. Campbell, 1988, Is there a corporate debt crisis? *Brookings Papers on Economic Activity*, pp. 83–139.

——, J. Campbell, and T. Whited, 1990, U.S. corporate leverage: Developments in 1987 and 1988, *Brookings Papers on Economic Activity*, pp. 255–278.

Brown, D., 1989, Claimholder incentive conflicts in reorganization: The role of bankruptcy law, *The Review of Financial Studies* 2, 109–123.

——, C. James, and R. Mooradian, 1991, The information content of exchange offers made by distressed firms, Unpublished manuscript, Graduate School of Business, University of Florida.

Bulow, J. and J. Shoven, 1978, The bankruptcy decision, *Bell Journal of Economics* 9, 437–456.

—— and K. Rogoff, 1989, Sovereign debt repurchases: No cure for overhang, Working paper 2850, National Bureau of Economic Research.

Coffee, J. and W. Klein, 1990, Protection of bondholders from unfair constrained-choice tender offers, Unpublished manuscript, UCLA Law School.

Cutler, D. and L. Summers, 1988, The costs of conflict resolution and financial distress: Evidence from the Texaco-Pennzoil litigation, *Rand Journal of Economics* 19, 157–172.

Franks, J. and W. Torous, 1989, An empirical investigation of firms in reorganization, *Journal of Finance* 44, 747–779.

Froot, K., 1989, Buybacks, exit bonds, and the optimality of debt and liquidity relief, *International Economic Review* 30, 49–70.

——, D. Scharfstein, and J. Stein, 1989, LDC debt: Forgiveness, indexation, and investment incentives, *Journal of Finance* 44, 1335–1350.

Gertner, R., 1990, Inefficiency in three-person bargaining, Unpublished manuscript, University of Chicago, Graduate School of Business.

Giammarino, R., 1989, The resolution of financial distress, *The Review of Financial Studies* 2, 25–47.

Gilson, S., K. John, and L. Lang, 1990, Troubled debt restructurings: An empirical study of private reorganization of firms in default, *Journal of Financial Economics* 27, 315–354.

Haugen, R. and L. Senbet, 1978, The insignificance of bankruptcy costs to the theory of optimal capital structure, *Journal of Finance* 33, 383–393.

Hoshi, T., A. Kashyap, and D. Scharfstein, 1990, The role of banks in reducing the costs of financial distress in Japan, *Journal of Financial Economics* 27, 67–88.

Jackson, T., 1986, *The Logic and Limits of Bankruptcy Law.* (Harvard University Press, Cambridge.)

Jensen, M., 1986, Agency costs of free cash flow, corporate finance, and takeovers, *American Economic Review* 76, 323–329.

—— and W. Meckling, 1976, Theory of the firm: Managerial behavior, agency costs, and ownership structure, *Journal of Financial Economics* 3, 305–360.

Myers, S., 1977, "Determinants of corporate borrowing, *Journal of Financial Economics* 5, 147–175.

—— and N. Majluf, 1984, Corporate financing and investment decisions when firms have information that investors do not have, *Journal of Financial Economics* 13, 187–221.

Roe, M., 1983, Bankruptcy and debt: A new model for corporate reorganization, *Columbia Law Review* 83, 528–602.

——, 1987, The voting prohibition in bond workouts, *The Yale Law Journal* 97, 232–279.

Stulz, R. and H. Johnson, 1985, An analysis of secured debt, *Journal of Financial Economics* 14, 501–521.

Titman, S., 1984, The effect of capital structure on a firm's liquidation dec ision, *Journal of Financial Economics* 13, 137–151.

White, M., 1980, Public policy toward bankruptcy: Me-first and other priority rules, *Bell Journal of Economics* 11, 550–564.

——, 1983, Bankruptcy costs and the new bankruptcy code, *Journal of Finance* 38, 477–487.

IV

INTEREST RATE EXPOSURE MANAGEMENT

During the past ten years the use of "off-balance-sheet" commitments by commercial banks has increased dramatically. Off-balance-sheet commitments include interest rate and currency swap agreements, futures and forward contracts, standby letters of credit, and loan sales and loan commitments. These items are commitments because they represent a promise by the bank to purchase or sell a financial claim at some future date. They are called off-balance-sheet because prior to 1992 (when the new capital requirements were fully implemented), these commitments were not included on bank balance sheets for the purpose of computing minimum capital requirements.

One explanation for the growth of off-balance-sheet commitments is that they provide a means by which banks can control their interest rate risk exposure. Interest rate risk refers to changes in the market value of the bank arising from unanticipated changes in the level of interest rates. In the first article, **Flannery and James** (1984) examine the determinants of the sensitivity of bank stocks to interest rate changes. They argue that the interest rate sensitivity of a financial institution's stock depends on both the maturity structure of the firm's nominal contracts and leverage. The greater the maturity mismatch between the firm's nominal assets and liabilities and the greater the leverage, the greater the interest sensitivity of the firm's stock.

Flannery and James examine empirically the determinants of the interest rate sensitivity of a set of commercial banks and savings and loans during the 1980s. To estimate the interest sensitivity of bank common stock returns, they propose a two-factor market model in which bank stock returns are related to the returns on an equally weighted market portfolio of common stocks and unanticipated changes in interest rates. The estimated coefficient

399

on unanticipated interest rate changes then is used in a cross-sectional regression relating interest sensitivity to the maturity composition of the bank's assets and liabilities. The authors find that on average the longer the maturity of assets relative to liabilities, the greater the interest sensitivity of bank common-stock returns.

A subsequent paper by Kane and Unal (1990) finds that the interest sensitivities of bank stock returns are not stable over the period 1975 through 1985. Kane and Unal argue that the lack of stability results from the fact that bank interest sensitivity is determined by the effect of interest rate changes both on the value of on-balance-sheet assets and liabilities and on the value of unbooked assets or liabilities such as the value of the bank's charter and the value of access to deposit insurance. If interest rate changes affect the value of booked and unbooked assets differently, then bank interest rate sensitivity will vary as the value of the unbooked assets and liabilities vary relative to on-balance-sheet items. However, if banks' use of interest rate hedging instruments vary over this period, measured interest sensitivities will also be unstable.

In the second paper, **Brickley and James** (1986) examine how access to deposit insurance affected the common stock returns of savings and loans during the mid-1980s. They argue that during this period, S&L regulators relaxed insolvency rules, which significantly increased the value of access to deposit insurance (an important off-balance-sheet asset for savings and loans). Moreover, Brickley and James show that changes in the value of access to deposit insurance were negatively correlated with the value of other S&L assets. Specifically, a decline in the value of S&L on-balance-sheet assets increased the S&L's leverage, thereby increasing the value of access to deposit insurance. As a result, relaxing insolvency rules and increasing the value of access to deposit insurance decreased the observed co-movement of the S&L's stock returns with the tangible assets of the S&L. The decrease in the co-movement of the stock returns with respect to the S&L's underlying assets was manifested in a decrease in the interest sensitivity of S&L stock returns. Consistent with this argument, Brickley and James find a significant decrease in the interest sensitivity of S&L stocks following the relaxation of insolvency rules in the mid-1980s.

Although banks and S&Ls are exposed to interest rate risk, it is not apparent that expending resources to reduce interest rate risk through hedging will increase bank value. Specifically, if risk-averse shareholders of a bank can hedge interest rate risk themselves or if interest rate risk is priced in the marketplace, then hedging is not necessarily a value-enhancing strategy. **Smith and Stulz** (1985) examine the conditions under which hedging by the financial institution increases firm value. They demonstrate that hedging can increase firm value for three reasons: (1) taxes, (2) costs of financial distress, and (3) managerial risk aversion.

A progressive tax code can make it advantageous for a firm to hedge through the use of forwards, futures, swaps, or options. With a progressive tax system, the after-tax value of the firm is a concave function of the firm's pretax income. By reducing the volatility of taxable income through hedging, the firm can lower its expected tax liability. A similar argument applies when financial distress involves significant dead-weight costs. By reducing the variability of cash flows (and thereby reducing the likelihood of financial distress), the firm will increase its value by the expected value of the cost savings. As discussed in Part V, the costs of regulatory intervention are a component of financial-distress costs for banks and savings and loans. As a result, these institutions hedge to reduce the likelihood of violating regulatory capital requirements or other regulatory standards that are tied to accounting measures of income or net worth.

A final reason for hedging, discussed in Smith and Stulz, is managerial risk aversion. Managerial risk aversion can lead to hedging if the compensation schedule is not too convex in firm value (that is, the convexity in the compensation schedule does not fully offset managerial risk aversion). As a result, the more option-like features in the compensation plan, the less likely one would be to observe hedging.

One of the most popular tools used by commercial banks to hedge interest rate risk is interest rate swaps. The article by **Smith, Smithson, and Wakeman** (1988) describes the market for interest rate swaps, the factors affecting the value of swap contracts, and reasons for the growth in the swap market. As the authors explain, an interest rate swap involves the exchange of cash flows between the two parties, one agreeing to make periodic payments to the other based on a fixed interest rate and to receive cash flows based on a floating interest rate index. The authors show that the cash flows associated with a swap agreement are equivalent to a set of loan contracts: borrowing at a fixed interest rate and lending at a floating interest rate index. Using this relation, they show that the interest rate sensitivity of a swap is equal to the interest rate sensitivity of a bond of the same maturity. However, they indicate that the default risk of a swap differs substantially from that of a bond. The crucial difference between the default risk of an interest rate swap and of a bond is that the principal in the swap is only notional. As a result, the default risk of swaps resembles that of a strip of forward contracts, each with a different maturity date.

The last three articles in this part examine the use of loan sales and standby letters of credit by commercial banks. The article by **Pennacchi** (1988) examines the market for commercial loan sales, which increased dramatically in the 1980s. Commercial loan sales, generally by large money center and regional banks, involve the sale of new commercial loans to smaller banks, foreign banks, and nonbank institutions. The paper by **Hess and Smith** (1988) examines mortgage securitization where individual principal and interest payments in a portfolio of mortgage loans are rebundled to create new securities. The growth of securitization and loan sales is significant in part because they unbundle the origination and monitoring functions associated with the lending process from the actual funding of loans.

Pennacchi argues that the growth of commercial loan sales is attributable largely to the effects of bank regulation. Specifically, he argues that minimum capital requirements act like a tax on bank loan financing. This tax arises from the fact that capital requirements, when binding, force banks to operate with an inefficient mix of debt and equity. In Pennacchi's model, capital requirements limit banks from realizing the full relative tax advantage of debt financing.

If regulation places some banks at a comparative disadvantage in funding loans and if those banks nevertheless retain a comparative advantage in monitoring and originating loans, then separating funding activities from loan servicing will be value-enhancing. Loan sales are limited, however, by the effects of sales on the incentive that the selling bank has to monitor. Selling loans with recourse (wherein the selling bank retains liability for any losses from default) solves the moral-hazard problem associated with the separation of monitoring from funding. However, loans sold with recourse do not avoid capital requirements for the seller since the guarantee is treated as a liability for the purposes of computing capital requirements. As a result, only loans sold without recourse effectively avoid capital requirements for the selling bank. But sales without recourse reduce the seller's incentives to monitor.

Both Pennacchi and Hess and Smith discuss the optimal contract for selling loans without recourse. The optimal contract is a contract in which the bank retains an equity interest in the proceeds from the loan. This arrangement resembles one in which the bank sells short-term strips of loans and retains a junior claim on the longer-term cash flows.

Hess and Smith argue that if the effective maturity of a bank's asset portfolio is greater than that of its liabilities, then with higher interest rates, the market value of the bank falls. By facilitating the sale of long-term loans, securitization reduces the sensitivity of bank value to interest rate changes. Moreover, they note that mortgage loan contracts historically have included an option to prepay the loan prior to maturity. The value of this prepayment option depends on interest rates; it also depends on the volatility of rates. Securitization allows the bank to resell this prepayment option to reduce its exposure to this volatility risk.

In the final article, **James** (1988) examines the market for commercial loan sales and standby letters of credit. A standby letter of credit is a bank-issued commitment to pay one party (called the beneficiary) in the event that the bank's customer defaults on a contractual obligation. James argues that both standby letters of credit and loan sales have payoff characteristics that are similar to the payoff characteristics of secured debt. For example, consider a loan sale with recourse. In the event of default on the loan, the purchaser has a claim on any proceeds from the loan plus a general claim on the assets of the bank. Only in the event that the loan defaults and the bank fails will the purchaser experience a loss. But this is also the condition in which a secured creditor (with the loan as collateral) would experience a loss. A similar argument can be made for a loan guaranteed by a standby letter of credit. The lender in this case has a claim on the proceeds from the loan plus, in the event of default, a general claim on the assets of the bank issuing the standby letter of credit.

Given the similarities among loan sales, standby letters of credit, and secured debt, James argues that the incentives banks have to engage in loan sales and to issue standby letters of credit are similar to the incentives nonbank firms have to issue secured debt. Specifically, as Stulz and Johnson (1985) argue, the issuance of secured debt can serve to control underinvestment problems that arise when a firm has risky debt in its capital structure. When a firm has a risky debt outstanding, issuing secured debt limits the wealth transfer from shareholders to debtholders associated with undertaking profitable but relatively low-risk investment opportunities. James's analysis is useful because he provides a motive for the growth of loan sales and standby letters of credit based on issues other than the avoidance of capital requirements or other regulatory taxes.

The Effect of Interest Rate Changes on the Common Stock Returns of Financial Institutions

MARK J. FLANNERY and CHRISTOPHER M. JAMES*

ABSTRACT

This paper examines the relation between the interest rate sensitivity of common stock returns and the maturity composition of the firm's nominal contracts. Using a sample of actively traded commerical banks and stock savings and loan associations, common stock returns are found to be correlated with interest rate changes. The co-movement of stock returns and interest rate changes is positively related to the size of the maturity difference between the firm's nominal assets and liabilities.

THE RELATION BETWEEN interest rate movements and common stock returns has been the focus of a considerable amount of research in recent years. Empirical research has found that inclusion of an interest rate factor adds substantial explanatory power to the simple single-factor market model, where the return on an index of common stocks is used as a proxy for the market portfolio (see, for example, Folger et al. [10] and Fama and Schwert [7]). However, a common deficiency of empirical research in this area is that no specific hypotheses are presented to explain why the effect of interest rate movements on common stock returns should vary among stocks.[1]

In this paper, we examine whether the interest rate sensitivity of common stock returns is related to the maturity composition of the firm's holdings of nominal contracts. We draw on recent research concerning the relation between inflation and stock returns to provide a theoretical rationale for why the interest rate sensitivity of a firm's common stocks should be related to the maturity composition of the firm's nominal assets and liabilities. The empirical relation between the interest rate sensitivity of common stock returns and the maturity composition of nominal contracts is examined for a set of actively traded commercial banks and stock savings and loan associations (S&Ls). These firms

---

* University of North Carolina and University of Oregon, respectively. Special thanks go to Ron Masulis and Wayne Ferson for lengthy discussions on the subject of this paper. We would also like to thank Larry Dann, Mike Hopewell, Megan Partch, George Racette, Richard Startz, Alden Toevs, and Peggy Wier for helpful discussion and criticisms. Sally Collier, Kathi Martell, and Diane Mayer provided excellent research assistance. A portion of this study was undertaken while the first author was a research advisor to the Federal Reserve Bank of Philadelphia and the second author was a consultant to the Comptroller of the Currency. The views expressed here in no way represent those of the Federal Reserve Bank of Philadelphia or the Comptroller of the Currency.

[1] Inclusion of interest rates as a separate factor can be justified by specifying an intertemporal capital asset pricing model, where the investment opportunity set is permitted to vary and the level of interest rates describes changes in the opportunity set (see Merton [16]). Fama and Schwert [7] analyze the relation between asset returns and interest rates where interest rates are assumed to reflect expected inflation.

were chosen because of the detail and consistency with which the maturity of their assets and liabilities is reported. We find that the common stock returns of these firms are highly correlated with interest rate changes. Moreover, the co-movement of bank stock returns with interest rate changes is found to be positively related to the size of the maturity difference between the bank's nominal assets and liabilities. Our results are consistent with the hypothesis that cross-sectional differences in the interest rate sensitivity of common stocks result, in part, from differences in the maturity composition of the firm's nominal assets and liabilities.

The paper is organized as follows. Section I derives a relation between the maturity composition of a firm's balance sheet and the co-movement of its stock returns with interest rate changes and provides a statement of the hypothesis to be tested. Section II describes the methodology used to estimate interest rate sensitivity, our data, and sample selection procedures. Interest rate sensitivity estimates for commercial banks are presented in Section III. Section IV presents evidence that the interest rate sensitivity of a firm's common stock is related to the maturity composition of the firm's nominal assets and liabilities. The final section contains a brief summary of our results.

I. The Relation Between Interest Rates and Common Stock Returns

To examine the effect of interest rate changes on common stock returns, it is useful to consider the nominal return of a firm's common stock as consisting of two components: (1) the return on nominal assets and (2) the return associated with real or physical assets (liabilities, excluding equity, can be viewed as negative assets). Nominal assets are simply assets with cash flows that are fixed in nominal terms (for example, accounts receivable, most contracts, debt, and certain input contracts), while the cash flows generated by real assets fluctuate with the price level. In general, we may write

$$\tilde{R}_{jt} \equiv \gamma_j \tilde{R}_{jt}^N + (1 - \gamma_j)\tilde{R}_{jt}^P \tag{1}$$

where

$\tilde{R}_{jt}$ = nominal return on the common stock of firm j at time t
$\tilde{R}_{jt}^N$ = nominal return on the nominal assets held by firm j at time t
$\tilde{R}_{jt}^P$ = nominal return on the real assets of firm j at time t
γ_j = net nominal assets held by firm j as a proportion of total assets.

In words, the nominal return on the stock of the jth firm at time t is defined as a weighted average of the returns on the firm's nominal and real assets.

The nominal contracting hypothesis postulates that a firm's holdings of nominal assets plays an important role in explaining the behavior of common stock returns through the redistributive effects of unanticipated inflation and unanticipated changes in expected inflation.[2] Since unanticipated inflation *ceteris*

---

[2] French et al. [11] were the first to describe the nominal contracting hypothesis as we do here. Christie [1] examines the relation between interest rate changes, variance in stock returns, and firm value within the context of the nominal contracting hypothesis. Christie finds a positive relation between interest rates and volatility of stock returns (and therefore a negative relation between interest rates and firm value).

paribus affects the real value of nominal but not real assets, stockholders of firms with fewer nominal assets than nominal liabilities should benefit from unexpected inflation, while if nominal liabilities are less than nominal assets the value of equity should decline with unexpected inflation. Unexpected changes in *expected* inflation will affect the nominal (as well as real) value of nominal contracts through the effect of changes in expected inflation on the nominal interest rate used to discount the cash flows. The effect of changes in expected inflation on the value of nominal assets and liabilities will vary directly with the term to maturity of the nominal contract.[3] The effect of an unanticipated change in expected inflation on the value of equity will be greater, therefore, the longer the maturity of the firm's nominal assets relative to its nominal liabilities (see Grove [12]).

If, as Fama [3, 4], Fama and Gibbons [6], and Nelson and Schwert [17] argue, movements in the term structure of interest rates (i.e., unanticipated changes in the level of interest rates) result primarily from changes in inflationary expectations, then the nominal contracting hypothesis implies a relation between common stock returns and interest rate changes. In particular, the interest rate sensitivity of a firm's common stock returns will depend upon the firm's holdings of net nominal assets (γ_j) and the maturity composition of net nominal assets held. The higher the proportion of the net nominal assets and the longer the maturity of net nominal assets held, the more sensitive should be the firm's common stock returns to interest rate changes.[4] For example, as interest rates change, the common stock returns of a firm financed entirely by equity and holding only nominal assets should behave exactly like a bond with a maturity equal to the average maturity of the firm's assets. To summarize, the nominal contracting hypothesis predicts that cross-sectional variation in the effect of unanticipated interest rate changes on stock prices should be related to differences in balance sheet composition.

Testing the nominal contracting hypothesis requires detailed balance sheet information concerning the proportion of net nominal assets held (γ_j) and the maturity composition of nominal contract holdings. Sufficiently detailed balance sheet information to test this hypothesis is generally not available for nonfinancial firms.[5] However, commercial banks are required to provide federal regulators with detailed information concerning the maturity compositions of their assets and liabilities. Since commercial banks hold assets and liabilities consisting almost entirely of nominal contracts, we need not be concerned with cross-sectional variations in γ_j and can focus instead on the relation between the

[3] As demonstrated by Hopewell and Kaufman [14], the effect of changes in the level of interest rates on the value of a bond will depend upon the duration and not the maturity of the bond. For simplicity, we assume in the following discussion that nominal contracts have a single risk-free payment at maturity so that duration and maturity are identical.

[4] It is important to note that the maturity composition of nominal assets will affect the interest rate sensitivity of equity regardless of whether the change in the level of interest rates results from changes in the expected real interest rate or changes in price expectations. Note also that the maturity composition of real assets will affect interest rate sensitivity only if the expected *real* interest rate changes.

[5] Inadequate data may partially explain the inability of recent studies such as French et al. [11] to find a significant relation for nonfinancial firms among nominal contract holdings, common stock returns, and changes in inflationary expectations.

interest rate sensitivity of stock prices and differences in the maturity of net nominal assets held.[6]

Using a sample of commercial bank stocks, we test an implication of the nominal contracting hypothesis that we call the *maturity mismatch hypothesis*. The maturity mismatch hypothesis postulates that differences in the maturity composition of net nominal assets cause differences in the interest rate sensitivity of common stock returns. (This assumes parallel shifts in the entire term structure.) A testable implication of the maturity mismatch hypothesis is that the effect of a change in the level of interest rates on the equity value of the firm will vary directly with the difference between the average maturity of the firm's nominal assets and liabilities. In particular, for a given unexpected increase in the level of interest rates, an increase in the maturity of net nominal assets should *ceteris paribus* result in a larger decrease in the value of equity.

II. Measuring the Effect of Interest Rate Changes on Common Stock Returns

The procedure we employ to test the maturity mismatch hypothesis is to first estimate the sensitivity of common stock returns to interest rate changes and then examine whether our measure of interest rate sensitivity is related to the maturity composition of the firm's nominal assets. We estimate the following model to measure interest rate sensitivity:

$$\tilde{R}_{jt} = \beta_{0j} + \beta_{mj}\tilde{R}_{mt} + \beta_{Ij}\tilde{R}_{It} + \tilde{\varepsilon}_{jt} \qquad (2)$$

where

$\tilde{R}_{jt}$ = the holding period return to the jth stock over the period ending at time t

$\tilde{R}_{mt}$ = the holding period return on an equally weighted portfolio of common stocks over the period ending at time t

$\tilde{R}_{It}$ = the holding period return on an index of constant maturity default-free bonds over the period ending at time t.

The estimated β_{Ij} from Equation (2) provides an unbiased measure of the effect of nominal interest rate changes on the common stock returns of firm j given its relation to the market index. Since the holding period returns on bonds are negatively correlated with changes in the level of interest rates, a positive value for β_{Ij} implies that the firm's market value declines when interest rates rise. The market index $\tilde{R}_{mt}$ in Equation (2) may fluctuate, in part, because of movements in $\tilde{R}_{It}$ and vice versa. To be certain that our findings are not significantly affected by the model as specified in Equation (2), we estimated variations of the model in which the stock market index was first orthogonalized to R_{It}. In all cases, the results using these alternative specifications were qualitatively similar to the results reported here.

---

[6] For the banks in our sample, real assets (in terms of bank buildings and equipment) averaged less than 2 percent of total bank assets. Equity was less than 6 percent of total assets.

Equation (2) was estimated using weekly return data for the period January 1, 1976 to November 1, 1981. Weekly common stock returns were obtained for a sample of 67 commercial banks from the Data Resources Incorporated (DRI) Security Price File. Banks were included in the sample if they met the following criteria: (1) traded continuously (every week) during the period January 1976 to November 1981, (2) had an identifiable lead bank in the case of multibank holding companies, and (3) the lead bank filed the large bank supplement to the FDIC Call Report during the 1976 to 1981 period. Only banks that traded continuously during the sample period were included to minimize bias in the coefficient estimates arising from infrequent trading (see Dimson [2]). Only bank holding companies with an identifiable lead bank were included in the sample so that balance sheet items obtained from the lead bank's Call Report would adequately reflect the holding company's balance sheet. (For the bank holding companies included in our sample, the lead bank constituted on average 84 percent of the total banking assets of the holding company.) The requirement that the lead bank file the large bank supplement was imposed to obtain sufficient reporting detail about asset and liability maturities.

The equity market index and interest rate indices were also obtained from DRI. The equity portfolio employed in this study was the weekly return on the NYSE composite index. There is no obviously superior interest rate index to use in estimating Equation (2). To avoid changes in the series due to changes in default premia, only indices consisting of U.S. Treasury or U.S. Government guaranteed debt obligations were used. Several alternative interest rate indices were used to check the robustness of our results.

(1) The return on Government National Mortgage Association (GNMA) 8 percent certificates calculated as the weekly holding period return, using the price of the most recently issued GNMA 8 percent certificate at the close of trading on Friday of each week. (Denoted as R_{GNMA}.)

(2) The weekly percentage change in the yield relative on an index of 7-year Treasury bonds. (Denoted as R_{G7}.)[7]

(3) The return on 1-year Treasury bills calculated as the weekly holding period return, using the price of the most recently issued bill at the close of trading on Friday of each week. (Denoted as R_{TB}.)

Descriptive statistics for these series are contained in Part A of Table I.

If these three interest rate indices measure unanticipated changes in interest rates, then the series should be white noise processes. To examine this issue, the autocorrelation functions for each series were estimated using lags of up to 15 weeks. The autocorrelations for lags 1 through 6 are presented in Part B of Table I (lags 4 to 15 were not significantly different from zero). A Box-Pierce Q-statistic

---

[7] The yield relative is defined as

$$-\left[\frac{Y_t - Y_{t-1}}{Y_{t-1}}\right]$$

where Y_t is the yield to maturity. For long-term bonds the change in the yield relative is approximately equal to the holding period return.

Table I

Interest Rate Indices[a]

A. Descriptive Statistics

| Index | Mean Weekly Return | Std. Dev. | Correlation Coefficients | | |
			R_{GNMA}	R_{G7}	R_{TB}
R_{GNMA}	−0.16%	0.015	1.00	0.746	0.698
R_{G7}	−0.26%	0.021	0.746	1.00	0.794
R_{TB}	−0.018%	0.004	0.698	0.794	1.00

B. Autocorrelation Coefficients

Index	r_1	r_2	r_3	r_4	r_5	r_6	$S(r)$[b]
R_{GNMA}	−0.002	0.068	0.041	−0.024	0.101	0.085	0.06
R_{G7}	0.055	0.133	0.076	0.057	0.047	0.010	0.06
R_{TB}	0.170	0.214	0.200	0.085	−0.001	0.056	0.06

[a] Based on weekly data for the period January 1, 1976 to November 1981.
[b] Standard error of the autocorrelation coefficients.

was used to test whether the autocorrelation coefficients (lags 1 to 15) are jointly different from zero. For the R_{GNMA} series, the autocorrelation coefficients are not either individually or jointly different from zero. On the other hand, for the Treasury bill series, the first three autocorrelations are significantly different from zero (at the 0.01 level). The R_{G7} series is indeterminate; r_2 is significantly different from zero, although the Box-Pierce Q-statistic is not.

To obtain a measure of unanticipated interest rate changes, a third-order autoregressive model (AR(3)) was estimated for each series.[8] Part A of Table II contains the parameter estimates for the AR(3) models. The autocorrelation coefficients for the residuals of the models (reported in Part B) indicate that the residual autocorrelations are small and insignificantly different from zero, consistent with the series being generated by a white noise process.[9] (A series consisting of unanticipated interest rate changes must have this property.) The residuals of these AR(3) models were therefore used as the interest rate indices in estimating Equation (2).[10]

III. Bank Interest Rate Sensitivity Estimates

Table III contains the results of estimating Equation (2) for an equally weighted portfolio of commercial bank stocks. The estimated value of β_I for the portfolio represents the cross-sectional average value of the $\hat{\beta}_{Ij}$. Our results indicate commercial bank stock returns are very sensitive to interest rate changes regard-

---

[8] An AR (3) model was chosen through inspection of the partial autocorrelation and autocorrelation coefficients associated with the T-Bill series. An AR(3) model was estimated for the R_{GNMA} and R_G series for consistency.

[9] Autocorrelation coefficients were calculated for up to 15-week lags. The magnitude of these coefficients and the pattern are similar to the results reported in Part B of Table I.

[10] Equation (2) was also estimated without whitening the interest rate series. The results obtained are virtually identical to the results reported in Sections III and IV.

Table II

Estimates of Unanticipated Interest Rate Changes

A. AR(3) Model[a]

$$R_t = \alpha_0 + \alpha_1 R_{t-1} + \alpha_2 R_{t-2} + \alpha R_{t-3} + U_t$$

Index	α_0	α_1	α_2	α_3	$S(U)$[b]
R_{GNMA}	−0.0015	−0.0053	0.0685	0.0425	0.015
	(0.0009)	(0.0587)	(0.0588)	(0.0591)	
R_{G7}	−0.0020	0.0443	0.1261	0.0617	0.021
	(0.0012)	(0.0584)	(0.0583)	(0.0586)	
R_{TB}	−0.0002	0.1138	0.1657	0.1463	0.003
	(0.0020)	(0.0577)	(0.0575)	(0.0578)	

B. Autocorrelation Coefficients

Index	r_1	r_2	r_3	r_4	r_5	r_6	$S(r)$[c]
R_{GNMA}	0.001	−0.002	−0.010	−0.031	0.106	0.083	0.06
R_{G7}	−0.002	−0.006	−0.006	0.042	0.047	0.011	0.06
R_{TB}	0.000	0.013	0.011	0.041	−0.031	0.061	0.06

[a] Standard errors are in parentheses.
[b] Standard errors of the residuals.
[c] Standard error of the autocorrelation coefficients.

Table III

Estimates of Interest Rate Sensitivity for a Portfolio of Commercial Bank Stocks[a]

$$\tilde{R}_t = \beta_0 + \beta_m \tilde{R}_{mt} + \beta_I \tilde{R}_{It} + \tilde{\epsilon}_t$$

Index[b,c]	$\hat{\beta}_0$	$\hat{\beta}_m$	$\hat{\beta}_I$	$\bar{R}^2$	Durbin-Watson Statistic
R_{GNMA}	0.002	0.556	0.133	0.57	1.74
	(0.001)	(0.030)	(0.038)		
R_{G7}	0.002	0.560	0.069	0.56	1.73
	(0.001)	(0.031)	(0.027)		
R_{TB}	0.001	0.555	0.515	0.57	1.73
	(0.001)	(0.031)	(0.160)		

[a] Estimated using weekly data for the period January 1, 1976 to November 1981, $N = 302$.
[b] Interest rate series are the residuals of the AR(3) models.
[c] Standard errors are in parentheses.

less of the interest rate index employed. Equation (2) was also estimated separately for each of the 67 banks in our sample. Note that the positive coefficients associated with $\tilde{R}_{It}$ indicate an inverse relation between unanticipated interest rate changes and the return on bank stocks. Note also that the value of $\hat{\beta}_I$ associated with the T-Bill index is substantially larger than the value of $\hat{\beta}_I$ obtained using longer term bond series. The difference in the estimates of $\hat{\beta}_I$ result in part from the fact that long-term bond prices respond more to a given change in the level of interest rates than do short-term bond prices.[11]

[11] This finding is consistent with our interpretation of $\hat{\beta}_I$ as a measure of interest sensitivity resulting from maturity mismatch.

IV. Interest Rate Sensitivity and the Maturity Composition of Nominal Contracts

The results obtained from estimating Equation (2) indicate that the returns on bank stocks are highly correlated with interest rate changes. These results are used to examine two testable implications of the maturity mismatch hypothesis. First, if the interest rate sensitivity of bank stocks is related to the maturity composition of net nominal assets, then $\hat{\beta}_{1j}$ is expected to vary directly with the difference between the average maturities of the bank's nominal assets and liabilities. Second, if Equation (2) is estimated for a set of firms with the same proportion of nominal assets as commercial banks (effectively 100 percent) but with net nominal assets of significantly longer maturity, then the average value of $\hat{\beta}_1$ for these firms is expected to be significantly larger than $\hat{\beta}_1$ estimated for the portfolio of bank stocks.

A. Bank Cross-Section Results

If cross-sectional differences in interest rate sensitivity arise from differences in the maturity composition of nominal assets, $\hat{\beta}_{1j}$ should be larger *ceteris paribus* the longer the maturity of the bank's net nominal assets. A measure of maturity mismatch was constructed by subtracting the dollar value of liabilities subject to repricing within one year from the dollar value of assets subject to repricing within the same period. This net short asset position is called "Short." By construction, assets and liabilities excluded from this measure are assumed to mature in more than one year. (Reporting requirements of bank regulatory agencies dictate the use of one year as the dividing line between short and long assets and liabilities.) A positive value of Short corresponds to a situation where the bank's short-term assets exceed the value of its short-term liabilities (which implies the value of long-term liabilities exceed the value of long-term assets). A negative value of Short implies that the value of short-term assets is less than the value of short-term liabilities.

While the maturity of most balance sheet items is well-defined, some assets and liabilities could not be sorted unambiguously into the "over one year" or "under one year" category. The most important items in this group were demand deposits, savings (passbook) accounts, time deposits under $100,000, and cash assets (including Federal Reserve balances, vault cash, demand deposits due from other banks, and cash items in the process of collection). On the one hand, some of these items (savings and demand deposits) can be withdrawn at any time and might therefore be considered short-term and subject to repricing within one year. Alternatively, there exists considerable evidence that these deposit stocks adjust slowly to interest rate changes, giving these items longer effective maturities.[12] In this paper, these items were treated as long-term items and therefore were excluded from our measure of net short assets.[13] The definition of Short

[12] See, for example, Flannery [8] or Hester and Pierce [13]. Deposit rate ceilings also impose the equivalent of a regulatory lag on commercial banks similar in impact to the effect of regulatory lags on utility stock prices (see Keran [15]).

[13] Our definition is consistent with the definition of short assets used in Salomon Brothers' *Quarterly Bank Stock Reports*. Related research [9] also confirms that these items behave as long-term assets and liabilities.

used is: (net federal funds sold + investments maturing in less than one year + floating rate loans + trading account securities + customers' liabilities to the bank for outstanding acceptances) − (domestic and foreign certificates of deposits in excess of $100,000 maturing in less than one year + other liabilities for borrowed money + the bank's liabilities on customers' acceptances outstanding).

To test the maturity mismatch hypothesis, we estimate the following cross-sectional regression:

$$\hat{\beta}_{Ij} + \alpha_0 + \alpha_1 \left(\frac{\text{Short}}{\text{MV}} \right)_j + \tilde{\omega}_j \tag{3}$$

where

Short = the jth bank's average net short position over the 1976–81 period
MV = average market value of the jth bank's equity
$\tilde{\omega}_j$ = error term.

An appropriate scale variable is required to put the dollar measure of maturity mismatch in the same units of measurement as our measure of interest rate sensitivity. We therefore deflated Short by the market value of the bank's (or holding company's) common stock outstanding, calculated as the average of 1975 and 1980 year-end market values. (We also deflated by book value of bank equity and obtained similar cross-sectional results.)

Implicit in the estimation of Equation (3) is the assumption that the effect of unexpected interest rate changes on firm value is proportional to the value of Short. The intercept term is intended to capture the effect of factors other than Short on the firm's interest rate sensitivity (which are assumed to be constant across banks). For each bank, we obtained balance sheet data from the March 31 *FDIC Report of Condition* in each sample year. A potential source of error arises because stock price data in many instances are for the bank holding company, whereas Short is computed only for the lead bank. Our sample selection techniques should minimize the effects of this error since our sample of stocks includes only holding companies with a large, well-defined lead bank. Under the maturity mismatch hypothesis the expected sign of α_1 is negative. An increase, for example, in net short-term assets $\left(\frac{\text{Short}}{\text{MV}} \right)$ implies a corresponding decrease in long-term assets and/or increase on long-term liabilities. This change should make equity less negatively correlated with interest rate changes. Since our interest rate indices ($\hat{R}_{It}$) are negatively correlated with changes in the level of interest rates, an increase in Short should correspond to a smaller value of $\hat{\beta}_{Ij}$.

The cross-sectional regression results are reported in Table IV. Regardless of the rate index employed, a negative and statistically significant relation is found between our measure of bank rate sensitivity and the bank's net short asset position. The positive and significant intercept suggests that even when the bank's net short-term assets are zero (so that short-term liabilities are equal to short-term assets) the bank's market value will fluctuate with interest rate changes. This may result from a mismatch in the maturity of assets and liabilities within the long-term category (over one year). The evidence presented in Table IV therefore supports with the prediction of the maturity mismatch hypothesis

Table IV

Cross-Section Results[a,b]

$$\hat{\beta}_{Ij} = \alpha_0 + \alpha_1\left(\frac{\text{Short}}{MV}\right)_j + \hat{\omega}_j$$

Dependent Variable	α_0	α_1	$\bar{R}^2$	F-statistic
$\hat{\beta}_{\text{GNMA}}$	0.143	−0.031	0.30	25.17
	(0.018)	(0.006)		
$\hat{\beta}_{\text{G7}}$	0.054	−0.019	0.25	19.10
	(0.013)	(0.004)		
$\hat{\beta}_{\text{TB}}$	0.538	−0.124	0.25	19.43
	(0.083)	(0.028)		

[a] Standard errors are in parentheses.
[b] Estimated using cross-sectional data for 67 banks.

that an increase in the maturity of net nominal assets corresponds to greater interest rate sensitivity of stock prices.[14]

In interpreting our cross-sectional results, several caveats should be made. First, our two-step procedure of estimating interest rate sensitivity for each bank using Equation (2) and then analyzing the cross-sectional relation between $\hat{\beta}_{Ij}$ and the firm's net short position introduces measurement error in our dependent variable in Equation (3). More importantly, since Equation (2) was estimated over the same time period and for firms in the same industry, the errors in estimating (2) may be contemporaneously correlated. This would in turn induce (presumably positive) correlation among the estimates of $\hat{\beta}_{Ij}$ and therefore among the $\tilde{\omega}_j$ in Equation (3). This will result in a downward bias in the estimated variance of $\hat{\alpha}_1$ and consequently an overstatement of significance levels. Since the source of this potential problem is the contemporaneous correlation in residuals associated with estimating Equation (2) across banks in our sample, we estimated for a random sample of 10 of our banks a correlation matrix for the residuals obtained in estimating (2). The average correlation coefficient was 0.11 (not significantly different from zero) with the maximum value being only 0.24 (all but one were positive). Since the pairwise correlation of the errors in estimating Equation (2) appears small, the estimates of β_{Ij} are not likely to be highly correlated, and the loss of efficiency is likely to be small.[15]

---

[14] To test the structural stability of the model, Equations (2) and (3) were estimated using data for two subperiods: 1976 to January 1979 and January 1979 to November 1981. These subperiods were chosen because certain regulatory changes (such as the introduction of money market CDs) may have significantly changed the effective maturity of certain balance sheet items (e.g., retail time deposits). Using an F-test, we cannot reject the hypothesis of structural stability in Equation (2) over these two subperiods. In addition, estimates of Equation (3) for these subperiods yields results similar to those in Table IV.

[15] Note, however, that a linear combination of the error terms in Equation (2) could be highly correlated with one another even though the pairwise correlations are small. An alternative way to test the maturity mismatch hypotheses would be to utilize a technique similar to the one employed by French et al. [11]. This would involve a one-step estimation procedure of including the Short measure in Equation (2) and estimating the system of 67 time series equations using Zellner's [19] seemingly unrelated regressions technique.

Table V

Estimates of Interest Rate Sensitivity for Stock S&Ls[a,b]

$$\tilde{R}_t = \beta_0 = \beta_m \tilde{R}_{mt} + \beta_I \tilde{R}_{It} + \tilde{\epsilon}_t$$

Index[c]	$\hat{\beta}_0$	$\hat{\beta}_m$	$\hat{\beta}_I$	$\bar{R}^2$	Durbin-Watson Statistic
R_{GNMA}	0.004	1.113	0.474	0.50	1.92
	(0.001)	(0.073)	(0.093)		
R_{G7}	0.004	1.082	0.320	0.49	1.87
	(0.001)	(0.076)	(0.069)		
R_{TB}	0.004	1.094	2.022	0.50	1.84
	(0.001)	(0.074)	(0.414)		

[a] Standard errors are in parentheses.
[b] Estimated using weekly data for the period January 1976 to November 1981, $N = 302$.
[c] Interest rate series are the residuals of the AR(3) models.

A second potential problem arises from the fact that the measurement (sampling) error associated with $\hat{\beta}_{Ij}$ may vary cross-sectionally. This may introduce heteroskedasticity into Equation (3) which would cause inefficient (though unbiased) coefficient estimates. To examine the effect of heteroskedasticity, we re-estimated Equation (3) with a heteroskedasticity correction based on the estimated standard errors of $\hat{\beta}_{Ij}$. The results were very similar to those reported in Table IV.

B. Evidence from an Analysis of Savings and Loan Stocks

We obtained additional evidence in support of the maturity mismatch hypothesis from examining the interest rate sensitivity of stock savings and loan associations. Since substantial evidence exists (see, for example, (3)) that S&Ls are less well hedged than are commercial banks (i.e., S&Ls have longer term net nominal assets), the maturity mismatch hypothesis would predict that the average value of $\hat{\beta}_{Ij}$ will be greater for S&Ls than for commercial banks. To examine this question, Equation (2) was estimated for an equally weighted portfolio of 26 actively traded S&L stocks over the period January 1976 to November 1981 using weekly returns. Table V contains the results. As in the case of commercial banks, movements in interest rates are highly correlated with S&L common stock returns (French et al. [11] report similar results). Note also that $\hat{\beta}_I$ is positive, indicating that the market value of S&Ls moves inversely with interest rates. In addition, Equation (2) was estimated for each of the S&Ls individually. The estimated value of $\hat{\beta}_{Ij}$ was positive and statistically significant for all the S&Ls in our sample. A comparison of the coefficient estimates for the interest rate indices for commercial banks, reported in Table III, to the estimates of $\hat{\beta}_I$ for S&Ls indicates that the S&L coefficients are over twice as large as those for commercial banks.

To test formally whether the difference in $\hat{\beta}_I$'s is statistically significant, we employed the following procedure. Equation (2) was estimated simultaneously for the portfolios of S&L and commercial bank stocks using Zellner's [19] seemingly unrelated regression technique. Since the independent variables are the same in both equations, this procedure provides no efficiency gain. However, it does produce an estimate of the covariance of the $\hat{\beta}_j$'s for the bank and S&L portfolios.[16] The estimated covariance was then used in computing the t-statistic to test the difference in coefficients. For the test involving R_{GNMA}, the calculated t-statistic is 5.68, significantly different from zero at the 0.01 level.

V. Summary and Conclusion

Our evidence supports the hypothesis that the effect of nominal interest rate changes on common stock prices is related to the maturity composition of a firm's net nominal asset holding. For commercial bank and S&L stocks, changes in interest rates were found to be significantly related to stock price movements. In addition, cross-sectional variation in the interest rate sensitivity measure is significantly related to the maturity mismatch of the bank assets and liabilities. Consistent with the nominal contracting hypothesis, the maturity composition of nominal contracts is found to be a significant factor affecting common stock returns.

---

[16] The estimated residuals from (2) for the S&L and bank portfolios are much more highly correlated than the residuals obtained when (2) was estimated for individual stocks. The contemporaneous correlation of residuals for the two portfolios is 0.52.

REFERENCES

1. Andrew A. Christie. "The Stochastic Behavior of Common Stock Variances: Value, Leverage and Interest Rate Effects." *Journal of Financial Economics* (December 1981), 407–32.
2. Elroy Dimson. "Risk Measurement When Shares Are Subject to Infrequent Trading." *Journal of Financial Economics* (June 1980), 197–226.
3. Robert O. Edmister. *Financial Institutions: Markets and Management.* New York: McGraw-Hill, 1980.
4. Eugene F. Fama. "Short-term Interest Rates as Predictors of Inflation." *American Economic Review* (June 1975), 269–82.
5. ———. "Inflation Uncertainty and the Expected Return on Treasury Bills." *Journal of Political Economy* (June 1976), 427–48.
6. ——— and Michael Gibbons. "Inflation, Real Returns and Capital Investment." *Journal of Monetary Economics* (May 1982), 397–424.
7. ——— and William G. Schwert. "Asset Returns and Inflation." *Journal of Financial Economics* (November 1977), 115–46.
8. Mark J. Flannery. "Retail Bank Deposits as Quasi-Fixed Factors of Production." *American Economic Review* (June 1982), 527–36.
9. ——— and Christopher James. "Market Evidence on the Effective Maturity of Bank Assets and Liabilities." Forthcoming, *Journal of Money, Credit and Banking*, 1984.
10. H. Russel Folger, Kose John, and James Tipton. "Three Factors, Interest Rate Differentials and Stock Groups." *Journal of Finance* 36 (May 1981), 323–35.
11. Kenneth R. French, Richard C. Ruback, and G. William Schwert. "Effects of Nominal Contracting on Stock Returns." *Journal of Political Economy* (January 1983), 70–96.
12. Michael Grove. "On Duration and the Optimal Maturity Structure of the Balance Sheet." *Bell Journal of Economics* (Autumn 1974), 696–707.
13. Donald D. Hester and James L. Pierce. *Bank Management and Portfolio Behavior.* New Haven: Yale University Press, 1975.

14. Michael Hopewell and George G. Kaufman. "Bond Price Volatility and Term to Maturity: A Generalized Respecification." *American Economic Review* (September 1973), 749–53.

15. Michael Keran. "Inflation, Regulation and Utility Stock Prices." *Bell Journal of Economics* (Spring 1976), 268–80.

16. Robert C. Merton. "An Intertemporal Capital Asset Pricing Model." *Econometrica* (September 1973), 867–87.

17. Charles R. Nelson and G. William Schwert. "On Testing the Hypothesis That the Real Rate of Interest is Constant." *American Economic Review* (June 1977), 478–86.

18. Salomon Brothers. *Quarterly Bank Stock Reports.*

19. Arnold Zellner. "An Efficient Method of Estimating Seemingly Unrelated Regressions and Tests for Aggregation Bias." *Journal of the American Statistical Association* (June 1962), 348–68.

ACCESS TO DEPOSIT INSURANCE, INSOLVENCY RULES AND THE STOCK RETURNS OF FINANCIAL INSTITUTIONS*

James A. BRICKLEY

University of Utah, Salt Lake City, UT 84112, USA

Christopher M. JAMES

University of Oregon, Eugene, OR 97403-1208, USA

Received June 1984, final version received September 1985

This paper analyzes how access to deposit insurance affects the common stock returns of financial institutions during periods of financial distress. During periods of distress the definition of insolvency used by insuring agencies may be modified to avoid a substantial number of bank failures. These modifications can increase the value of future deposit guarantees and affect the behavior of stock returns of banks and S&Ls. This hypothesis is examined using S&L data for the 1976 through 1983 period. Modification of insolvency rules applied to S&Ls appears to have reduced significantly the co-movement of S&L stock returns with S&L portfolio holdings.

1. Introduction

Under the current system of deposit insurance, insurance agencies and bank regulators are given broad discretion in defining insolvency.[1] This discretion, afforded both the Federal Deposit Insurance Corporation (FDIC) for banks and the Federal Savings and Loan Insurance Corporation (FSLIC) for savings and loans (S&Ls), is particularly important during 'crisis periods', when enforcing restrictive covenants or applying existing insolvency rules would result in a substantial number of failures. During such periods, to avoid

---

*Financial support for this study was provided by a grant from the Federal Home Loan Bank Board and McGraw Hill Corporation which provided us access to the Data Resources Incorporated's *Securities Price File*. The authors thank S. Bhagat, A. Hess, M. Hopewell, S. Manaster, R. Masulis, J. McConnell, W. Mikkelson, J. Schallheim, C. Smith and an anonymous referee for comments.

[1] Insolvency for an insured financial institution occurs when the insurer will no longer provide deposit guarantees and the bank's charter is revoked. Prior to failure, however, the activities of the financially distressed institution may be restricted by regulators [see Smith (1982, pp. 326–327)]. For non-financial firms, insolvency is traditionally defined as a situation in which the firm is unable to meet its currently due debt obligations [see for example Haugen and Senbet (1978)]. For a depository institution with debt immediately putable at par value, a sufficient condition for insolvency *without* deposit insurance is when the market value of the bank's assets falls below the present value of its contractual obligations, i.e., net worth is zero. With deposit insurance, insolvency may not occur when net worth (as defined above) is zero, but rather is determined by the insuring agency.

---

failures, the FDIC or FSLIC may modify its definition of insolvency. Changes in FSLIC capital requirements and the capital certificate program begun in 1980 are examples of modifications in the solvency criteria for S&Ls.

Modification of the rules governing insolvency can affect the value of access to federal deposit insurance. Recent studies by Merton (1977) and Buser, Chen and Kane (1981) show that providing deposit guarantees at less than their market value provides banks with a subsidy. The value of this subsidy equals the difference between the cost of risky and riskless (guaranteed) deposit claims less the premium charged for insurance. Access to future deposit guarantees, under these circumstances, is an asset of the bank. The value of this asset is equal to the present value of the stream of subsidies the bank or S&L expects to receive. The rules used to determine insolvency affect the value of access to insurance by defining the states in which insurance will be provided. Relaxing insolvency rules under these circumstances will increase the value of access to deposit insurance.[2]

In this paper we examine how modification of insolvency rules, together with access to fixed premium deposit insurance, affect the common stock returns of financial institutions. Because a decrease in the value of the bank's portfolio holdings increases the risk of deposits, the value of access to fixed premium deposit insurance will be negatively correlated with the value of the bank's portfolio holdings. Relaxing insolvency rules, by increasing the value of access to deposit insurance, may result in a decrease in the co-movement of bank stock returns with the return on the bank's portfolio holdings. Therefore, during crisis periods, the co-movement of bank stock returns with the underlying assets of the bank (i.e., assets exclusive of deposit guarantees) may decrease.[3] We refer to this prediction as the *subsidy hypothesis*.

In the absence of the modification of insolvency rules, contingent claims analysis predicts that the elasticity or co-movement of stock prices with respect to the value of the underlying assets will *increase* as insolvency is approached.[4] This prediction is based, however, on the assumption that insolvency rules are adhered to, i.e., 'me first' rules providing debt strict priority over equity are enforced. Therefore, examining the co-movement of bank stock returns with the returns on the bank's portfolio holdings provides a means of testing the subsidy hypothesis.[5]

---

[2] Similarly relaxing insolvency rules may increase the value of access to other government subsidies, e.g., government loans at below market rates and tax subsidies. These additional gains due to forebearance are discussed in detail in section 6.5.

[3] The decrease in the co-movement of bank stock returns with the return on the bank's portfolio holdings may also result in a decrease in the estimated beta and the variance of bank stock returns.

[4] See Black and Cox (1976) and Galai and Masulis (1976).

[5] Only under the subsidy hypothesis will the elasticity *decrease* during financial distress. The lack of a significant increase in the elasticity is also consistent with our subsidy hypothesis. Formulating the subsidy hypothesis in terms of a decrease in the elasticity provides therefore a strong test of the subsidy hypothesis.

To test the subsidy hypothesis, we examine the stock returns of S&Ls during the period 1976 through 1982. We focus our analysis on S&Ls for four reasons. First, as a result of the unexpected increase in the level of interest rates in the late 1970's S&Ls entered into a period of financial distress. Second, in response to this crisis, there is evidence of vast recontracting between the FSLIC and S&Ls involving modifications of insolvency rules. Third, the portfolios of S&Ls consist primarily of mortgages. This permits us to develop a measure of changes in the market value of S&L portfolio holdings. Using this measure we can examine the relation between common stock returns and the returns on the underlying assets of the S&L. Finally, the uniformity in financial reporting required by the Federal Home Loan Bank Board (FHLBB) facilitates our analysis.

Our empirical analysis reveals a significant decrease in the co-movement of S&L stock returns with the returns on their underlying assets (as proxied by the return on an index of mortgages) after 1979. Moreover, estimates of betas for S&L stocks drop significantly after 1979. These changes coincide with a substantial decrease in the value of S&L assets and as a result an increase in S&L leverage.

While the evidence from the S&L industry is consistent with the subsidy hypothesis, we cannot rule out the possibility that some other factors, not related to forebearance and government subsidies, explain the behavior of S&L stock returns. For example, during the period in which insolvency rules were changed, S&Ls were provided broader asset powers and broader authority to use interest rate futures for hedging. A careful examination of the changes in S&L assets and futures market suggests that these factors are not the major source of the change in the behavior of S&L stock returns. In addition, an examination of the stock returns of other financial institutions during this period suggests that the change in the behavior of S&L stock returns is not the result of some other factors affecting all financial institutions.

The paper is organized as follows: Section 2 discusses the nature of federal recontracting during the 1976 through 1982 period and formally states the hypotheses to be tested. Section 3 describes our methodology. Section 4 describes our sample design. Section 5 presents results concerning the behavior of S&L risk measures. In section 6 we examine the effect of other factors that may explain the results. Section 7 provides our conclusions.

2. The crisis in the thrift industry and FSLIC forebearance

2.1. FSLIC policies concerning insolvency

The financial distress of the thrift industry, which began in the late 1970's is well documented.[6] As a result of the increase in the level of interest rates

---

[6]See Kane (1981, 1983) and Balderston (1981).

during this period, the market value of S&L portfolio holdings (primarily mortgages) decreased substantially. The resulting deterioration of the financial condition of S&Ls is reflected in the decrease in S&L earnings during the 1980–1982 period and in the negative spread between mortgage interest income and S&L cost of funds. The return on book value of equity and the relation between mortgage interest income and S&L cost of funds during the period 1976 through 1983 are presented in table 1. Another indicator of the financial problems of thrift institutions is the relation between the market value of S&L portfolio holdings and the value of S&L deposit liabilities. Estimates by Kane (1983) indicate that the face value of S&L deposit liabilities exceeded the market value of S&L booked assets by $150 billion (or 25 percent of S&L assets) by year end 1981.

As a result of the crisis in the thrift industry, the FSLIC implemented a series of policies, beginning in 1980, that changed the rules used in determining insolvency. In particular, prior to 1980 S&Ls were required to maintain a ratio of *book value* of net worth to deposits of at least 5 percent as a condition for obtaining deposit insurance.[7] However, these requirements were reduced by the FSLIC in June of 1980 to 3 percent.[8]

In addition to the changes in net worth requirements, the FSLIC implemented several other regulatory changes designed to forestall S&L failures. First, in September 1981, the deferred accounting for losses on the sale of mortgages and securities was authorized, which permitted S&Ls to sell assets and realize capital losses for tax purposes without reducing their capital account for regulatory purposes. Second, beginning in 1981, certain S&Ls were permitted to issue to the FHLBB capital certificates which were counted as net worth.[9] Third, in many instances the FHLBB did not enforce the net worth requirements [see Kane (1983)]. Evidence from the S&Ls in our sample (described below) is consistent with this contention. Of the 48 individual S&Ls in our sample, four had a negative book value of equity during the 1980

---

[7] Bank regulators have traditionally defined insolvency for insured S&Ls and commercial banks in terms of book value of net worth [see Campbell and Glenn (1984)]. Since federal regulatory agencies do not require S&Ls to carry their mortgage portfolios at market value on their balance sheets, S&Ls may continue to operate even though they would be insolvent in the absence of insurance (i.e., the market value of their underlying or booked assets is less than the value of their contracted liabilities).

[8] See *Savings and Loan Fact Book*, 1982. Horton (1979) provides evidence that net worth requirements were strictly enforced for all S&Ls prior to 1980. For S&Ls less than 20 years old, statutory net worth is calculated in a more complex manner. For these S&Ls net worth requirements are determined by dividing the age of the S&L by twenty and multiplying this number by the statutory net worth requirement. Four of the S&Ls in our sample were less than 20 years old. Of these four, the most recently chartered was in 1973.

[9] Capital certificates represent the clearest form of modifying S&L insolvency rules. For S&Ls that failed to meet net worth requirements and were in danger of being declared insolvent by state regulators, the FHLBB purchased capital certificates in exchange for promissory notes. A capital certificate is similar to cumulative preferred stock, with a dividend requirement equal to the interest paid on the FHLBB's promissory note. Dividends are payable *only* if the net income of the S&L is positive. Thus, insurance was provided to S&Ls with negative *book* net worth.

Table 1

Average return on book equity and the average spread between S&L cost of funds and the return on mortgages 1976 through 1983 for all federally insured S&Ls.[a]

Year	Average return on equity (percent)[b]	Spread between mortgage returns and cost of funds (percent)		
		Interest income on mortgages	Average cost of funds	Spread[c]
1976	11.11	8.00	6.38	1.62
1977	13.99	8.26	6.44	1.82
1978	14.21	8.50	6.79	1.81
1979	12.11	8.86	7.47	1.39
1980	2.45	9.34	8.94	0.40
1981	−15.39	9.91	10.92	−1.01
1982	−16.20	10.68	11.38	−1.70
1983	7.05	11.04	9.81	1.23

[a] Source: *U.S. Savings and Loan Fact Book*, U.S. League of Savings and Loans, 1984.

[b] Represents net income as a percent of the book value of equity.

[c] Spread equals the difference between interest income on mortgages and the average cost of funds.

through 1982 period. Moreover, in our sample the average ratio of book equity to deposits was 2 percent (the median value was 2.3 percent) less than the regulatory requirement of 3 percent.

2.2. Statement of hypotheses

The primary hypothesis examined in this paper is that changes in insolvency rules during the 1980–1982 period significantly affected the behavior of S&L stock returns by increasing the value of access to deposit insurance and other government subsidies. The subsidy hypothesis predicts that these changes reduced the elasticity of S&L stock prices with respect to the underlying assets of the S&L.

The subsidy hypothesis can be tested empirically by examining the relation between the stock returns of S&Ls and the return on their underlying assets. Using option pricing theory Galai and Masulis (1976) show that the following relation exists between the return on equity and the return on the assets of the firm:

$$r_s = \eta_s r_v,$$

where

r_s = return on equity,

η_s = the elasticity of equity (S) with respect to the value of the assets of the firm (V), and

r_v = return of the firm's assets.

Under absolute 'me first' priority rules, as the value of the underlying assets of the S&L (V) approaches the value of deposits (D), the elasticity η_s will increase without limit. Therefore, as insolvency approaches, the sensitivity of r_s to changes in r_v will increase. Moreover, the elasticity of equity relates the systematic risk of the stock to the systematic risk of the firm's assets and the standard deviation of the return on equity to the standard deviation of the return on the firm's assets. In particular,

$$\beta_s = \eta_s \beta_v \quad \text{and} \quad \sigma_s = \eta_s \sigma_v,$$

where β_s and β_v denote the beta of equity and the beta of the firm's assets, respectively, and σ_s and σ_v denote the standard deviation of the return on equity and the return on the firm's assets.[10] Given the asset composition of S&Ls and the enforcement of 'me first' priority rules, the elasticity of S&L stock prices (η_s) and therefore the beta and standard deviation of S&L stocks should increase during the 1980 through 1982 period.

The subsidy hypothesis predicts, however, that failure to enforce 'me first' rules and the continued provision of fixed premium deposit insurance results in a decrease in the S&L stock price elasticities. With access to fixed premium deposit insurance an S&L consists of two types of assets, its portfolio holdings and access to deposit insurance. Relaxation of insolvency rules increase the value of access to deposit insurance (V') relative to the S&Ls portfolio holdings (V). Because the common stock returns of S&Ls reflect the return on both types of assets and because the return on access to insurance is negatively correlated with the return on S&L portfolio holdings, relaxing insolvency rules reduces the co-movement of the S&L's stock returns with the return on its portfolio holdings.

The effect of changing insolvency rules when deposit insurance is provided at fixed premiums can be illustrated within the option pricing framework. Merton (1977) has shown that the value of a deposit guarantee is equal to the value of a European put option on the assets of the bank with a striking price equal to the face value of debt and an expiration date equal to the date when the bank's debt matures (time t). Assuming access to insurance is guaranteed, the value of future deposit guarantees is equal to the value of a put option written at some future date (t) with an expiration date of $t + r$. The value of this option is simply equal to the value of a European put expiring in $t + r$ periods. The elasticity of the put (access to insurance) with respect to the underlying assets of the bank (denoted as η_I) is strictly less than zero [see Jarrow and Rudd (1983)]. Therefore, with access to insurance the elasticity of

---

[10] See Black and Scholes (1973) and Smith (1976). Similar results can be obtained without the use of options pricing theory. See Hamada (1969).

equity (denoted as η_s) with respect to the assets of the S&L is

$$\eta_s = \frac{V}{V + V'}\eta_w + \frac{V'}{V + V'}\eta_I, \tag{1}$$

where η_w is the elasticity of equity in the absence of insurance (and $\eta_w \geq 1$). Increasing the value of V' relative to V results therefore in a decrease in the elasticity of the S&L's stock.[11] In general as long as the value of this access to insurance and other subsidies is less than perfectly correlated with the market value of the S&L's portfolio holdings, relaxing insolvency conditions will reduce the S&L's stock elasticity with respect to its underlying (booked) assets.

In addition to affecting the value of access to deposit insurance modifying insolvency rules may affect the value of other subsidies provided thrifts. In particular, relaxing insolvency rules provided thrifts with continued access to Federal Home Loan Bank (FHLB) advances. Since the interest rate on FHLB advances is determined by the FHLB's own borrowing costs, advances represent a source of government subsidized borrowing.[12]

Changes in insolvency rules also affected the ability of S&Ls to utilize tax loss carry backs. By permitting certain S&Ls to continue to operate and through permitting S&Ls to realize losses on the sale of mortgages for tax purposes (but not for purposes of determining net worth requirements), access to tax refunds was preserved.[13] The effects of these other subsidies together with access to deposit insurance are examined as part of the subsidy hypothesis.

3. Methodology

Testing the subsidy hypothesis requires a measure of the return on the S&L's underlying assets. Since S&Ls invest primarily in mortgages we assume that the primary factor affecting the value of S&L portfolio holdings is

[11] Note that the subsidy hypothesis involves testing the joint hypothesis of changes in insolvency rules and S&L asset returns and equity returns follow a log normal diffusion process, so that the relation in eq. (1) holds. The options pricing framework is used only to illustrate the effect of deposit insurance on S&L equity returns. A formal model of the effect of access to insurance would need to incorporate how insurance effects η_s through changes in the boundary conditions.

[12] In this way the effect of access to advances on S&L stock returns is similar to access to deposit insurance. A decrease in the value of S&L assets increases the difference between the S&L's own uninsured borrowing rate and the advance rate. However, given the importance of insured deposits as a funding source, access to deposit insurance is likely to be a more important government subsidy. For a description of the advance program, see *FHLBB Journal*, December 1983.

[13] Prior to 1981 S&Ls could not realize losses from the sale of mortgages without reducing their regulatory net worth. As a result S&Ls paid federal taxes in 1978 through 1980 though they would have had no federal tax liability if losses on their mortgage portfolio had been realized. See Kane (1981).

changes in the market value of mortgages. (The average proportion of mortgage loans to total assets for S&Ls during the 1976 through 1982 period was 0.89.)[14] Weekly holding period returns associated with Government National Mortgage Association (GNMA) eight percent certificates are used to measure changes in the market value of mortgages. The GNMA index was obtained from Data Resources Incorporated (DRI). The index consists of price quotes for the most recently issued eight percent certificates at the close of trading on Friday of each week. Weekly holding period returns were calculated from changes in the price quotes.[15]

Our methodology involves first estimating the relation between stock returns and the return on GNMA certificates. This provides an estimate of the S&L's stock price elasticity with respect to the value of its underlying assets. Next, we examine the effect of FSLIC policy changes on the S&L's stock price elasticity.

To obtain an estimate of an S&L's stock elasticity we estimated the following model:

$$R_{jt} = \alpha_j + \beta_{Ij} R_{It} + \varepsilon_{jt}, \tag{2}$$

where

R_{jt} = the holding period return on the jth S&L stock over the period ending at the time t,

R_{It} = the holding period return on an index of mortgage bonds ending at time t, and

ε_{jt} = error term.

The coefficient on the mortgage index β_{Ij} measures the co-movement between an S&L's stock returns (R_{jt}) and the underlying assets of the S&L.[16]

---

[14]*Savings and Loan Fact Book*, 1982.

[15]DRI obtains price quotes from Telstat which supplies price information to *The Wall Street Journal* and other sources. GNMA eight percent certificates were used because price data was available from January 1976. A potential problem with using GNMA certificates is interest and principle payments are insured, whereas S&L mortgages have positive default probabilities. For this reason the GNMA index only measures changes in the value of S&L portfolio resulting from interest rate changes. Moreover, since the last GNMA eight percent certificate was issued in April 1982 after this date price quotes are for a security with a decreasing term to maturity. After April 1982, the GNMA quotes represent prices in the secondary market for seasoned GNMA eight percent pools. A third problem with the GNMA index is that because of prepayments its maturity or duration may change with the level of interest rates. As discussed in section 6.4, to avoid these last two problems a Treasury Bill index was also used.

[16]Note that by definition
$$\beta_{Ij} = dR_j/dR_I.$$
Since R_I serves as a proxy for r_v, the above relation may be rewritten as
$$\beta_{Ij} = (dR_j/dr_v)(dr_v/dR_I) = \eta_s (dr_v/dR_I).$$
Clearly β_{Ij} will differ from the elasticity of the stock to the extent that there is not a one-to-one correspondence between r_v and R_I.

In conducting our empirical analysis, we chose January 1980 as the date that insolvency rules were relaxed.[17] Our hypothesis is that the average value of the β_{1j} will be lower in the 1980–1982 period than in the 1976–1979 period.

4. Sample design

Eq. (2) was estimated using weekly common stock returns data over the period January 1, 1976 to January 7, 1983. Weekly common stock returns were obtained for a sample of 30 S&L holding companies owning a total of 48 individual S&Ls. Common stock returns were calculated using price and dividend data obtained from DRI's Security Price File. S&L holding companies were included in the sample if they met the following criteria: (1) had SIC codes between 6120 and 6129 (operation of a S&L is the firm's primary line of business) and had common stock price and trading information contained in the DRI Securities File; (2) traded continuously (every week) for at least four consecutive years (208 weeks) during the 1976 to 1983 period; and (3) the S&Ls within the holding company comprised at least 80 percent of the S&L holding company assets.[18]

The sample of S&Ls used in this study consists principally of large S&Ls. The median asset size for S&Ls in our sample was $1.7 billion in 1981. S&Ls ranged in size from $248 million to $13 billion. In contrast the median size of all federally insured S&Ls was $50 million in 1981.

Since our sample consists of large S&Ls, our results may not be applicable to all S&Ls. In particular, the S&Ls in our sample may be more likely to receive government subsidies through modification of insolvency rules than smaller S&Ls. In particular, federal regulators may be less willing to close relatively large financial institutions in financial distress than smaller institutions.[19] Appendix 1 contains a list of the S&Ls in our sample and information concerning their size and trading activity.

[17] Choice of this date is arbitrary. Greater specificity in terms of dates for these regulatory changes is difficult to obtain since regulatory proceedings concerning the crisis in the thrift industry occurred over an extended period of time.

[18] The median ratio of S&L assets to holding company assets is 0.97. No significant change in this ratio occurred during our sample period. For example, the median ratio was 0.96 during the 1976 through 1979 period and was 0.97 during the 1980 through 1982 period. For multiple S&L holding companies the assets of the individual S&L subsidiaries were summed in constructing this ratio. In the case of mergers assets of the acquired S&L were included in the holding company's assets following the merger. Assets for the holding companies were obtained from Moody's *Banking and Finance Manual.*

[19] See Kane (1983). For example, in a recent report to Congress the Comptroller of the Currency indicated that he would not permit the ten largest commercial banks to fail. This statement, made after the financial distress of Continental Illinois, implies a willingness to modify insolvency rules if necessary to avoid large bank failures (*The Wall Street Journal*, Sept. 20, 1984, p. 2). The extension of federal guarantees to all depositors at American Savings and Loan, following the financial distress of the parent, Financial Corporation of America, provides another example (see *The Wall Street Journal*, Aug. 30, 1984, p. 3).

5. Behavior of S&L risk measures

5.1. Elasticity estimates

Eq. (2) was estimated for each of the 30 S&Ls in our sample. As a way of summarizing those results, estimates for an equally weighted portfolio of these S&Ls are reported below (standard errors are in parentheses):[20]

$$R_{Pt} = 0.004 + 0.835 \, R_I, \qquad R^2 = 0.151, \quad D.W. = 1.76,$$
$$\quad\;\; (0.002) \quad (0.110)$$

where $D.W.$ stands for Durbin–Watson statistic.

The positive and highly significant coefficient on the mortgage index indicates, as expected, S&L stock prices move contemporaneously with mortgage bond prices (the value of β_I describes this co-movement).

Our hypothesis is that recontracting resulted in a decrease in the co-movement of S&L stock prices with the return on their asset portfolios (R_I) during the 1980 through 1982 period. We test this hypothesis by estimating the following model:

$$R_{Pt} = \alpha_{P0} + \beta_{PI} R_{It} + \beta_{Ps} R_{It} * D + w_{Pt}, \tag{3}$$

where

R_{Pt} = weekly holding period return on an equally weighted portfolio of S&L stocks in week t,

R_{It} = weekly holding period return on the GNMA index in week t, and

D = a binary variable taking on the value of zero during the period January through December 1979, one otherwise.

The coefficient on the interactive dummy variable (β_{ps}) is intended to measure any change in the co-movement of S&L stocks prices with the return on their assets over the two periods. The subsidy hypothesis predicts a reduction in the stock price elasticity so that the expected sign of β_{ps} is negative. To avoid shifts in the parameter estimates of (3) due to changes in portfolio composition, eq. (3) was estimated using a portfolio of 20 S&L stocks which traded over the entire seven-year period. The estimate of eq. (3) is provided below:

$$R_{pt} = 0.004 + 1.41 \, R_{It} - 0.874 \, R_{It} * D,$$
$$\quad (0.02) \quad (0.287) \quad\;\; (0.281)$$

$$R^2 = 0.142, \quad D.W. = 1.67.$$

[20] The number of S&L stocks in the portfolio varied, depending on the availability of price data, from 30 to 20 stocks. Appendix 1 contains elasticity estimates for each of the S&Ls in our sample.

Consistent with the subsidy hypothesis, the coefficient associated with the interaction variable is negative and statistically significant at the 0.01 level.[21]

This decrease in the elasticity estimate occurred during a period in which the market value of S&L 'booked' assets decreased significantly. This decline in asset values resulted in a substantial increase in S&L leverage. For the S&Ls in our sample (as discussed below), the mean ratio of debt to the market value of common stock increased from 24.19 in the 1976 to 1980 period to 40.53 in the 1980 through 1982 period (the difference in means is statistically significant; the *t*-statistic is 4.34).[22] The increase in leverage in the absence of FSLIC policy changes would be expected to increase the elasticity of S&L stocks. We observe, however, a significant decrease in the co-movement of S&L stocks with interest rate changes.

5.2. Changes in other risk measures

To examine changes in the beta of S&Ls we estimated the following market model:

$$R_{pt} = \alpha_1 + \beta_m R_m + \beta_{ms} R_{mt} * D + \varepsilon_t, \qquad (4)$$

where

R_{pt} = weekly holding period return on an equally weighted portfolio of S&L stocks trading from 1976 through 1982,

R_{mt} = weekly holding period return on the NYSE composite index, and

D = binary variable which is one for the period January 1980 to January 1983, zero otherwise.

An estimate of eq. (4) is provided below (standard errors are in parentheses):

$$R_{pt} = (0.002) + 1.51\, R_{mt} - 0.25\, R_{mt} * D,$$
$$\phantom{R_{pt} = }(0.001) \quad (0.125) \qquad (0.110)$$

$$R^2 = 0.48, \quad D.W. = 1.67.$$

Consistent with the subsidy hypothesis the coefficient associated with the market portfolio (β_m) declined significantly in the post-1979 period.[23]

---

[21]All 20 S&Ls that traded continuously over the 1976 through 1982 period had lower estimated values for β_I in the 1980 through 1982 period. See appendix 1. Similar results were obtained when eq. (3) was estimated over the two subperiods and the equality of coefficients associated with R_I examined using an *F*-test. The *F*-statistic is 6.32.

[22]Kane (1983) estimates that the unrealized losses on mortgages during the 1979 through 1982 period for all S&Ls was $21 billion dollars or about 15 percent of total S&L assets. For all federally insured S&Ls the ratio of debt to book value of equity increased from 17.02 in the 1976 to 1980 period to 28.25 in the 1980 through 1982 period.

[23]Similar results are obtained if the market model is estimated separately in both periods and an *F*-test is used. The *F*-statistic is 3.87.

Table 2

An analysis of changes in the ratio of standard deviations of returns for an equally weighted portfolio of 20 S&L stocks and the Government National Mortgage Association (GNMA) index over the 1976 through 1982 period.[a]

	1976	1977	1978	1979	1980	1981	1982
σ_s/σ_I	4.63	5.18	5.34	3.48	1.66	1.28	1.86
		1976 to 1980			1980 to 1983		
σ_s/σ_I		4.14			1.58		

[a] σ_s and σ_I are estimates of the standard deviation of weekly stock returns for a portfolio of 20 S&L stocks and the standard deviation of the weekly return on the GNMA index, respectively. S&L holding companies included in the sample are those with common stock price and trading information contained in the DRI *Securities File* and which traded over the entire study period. The return on the GNMA index represents the holding period return on an index of GNMA eight percent certificates.

The decrease in the beta for S&L stocks may result from a change in the systematic risk of the mortgage index [see eq. (1)]. We therefore estimated eq. (4) using the return on the GNMA index as the dependent variable. The results of this estimation are provided below (standard errors are in parentheses):

$$R_{It} = 0.000 + 0.19\,R_{mt} + 0.11\,R_{mt} * D,$$
$$(0.001)\quad (0.065)\qquad (0.086)$$

$$R^2 = 0.11, \quad D.W. = 2.08.$$

These results indicate the absence of any significant decrease in the beta for the GNMA index.

We also calculated the ratio of the standard deviation of S&L stock returns to the standard deviation of the return on the GNMA index. A decrease in the elasticity of the stock returns should result in a decrease in this ratio after 1979. These ratios are reported in table 2. Consistent with our hypothesis the ratio declines after 1979. In addition, the ratio of the standard deviation of each S&L's returns to the standard deviation of R_I was calculated for the two subperiods, 1976–1979 and 1980–1982.[24] Using a paired *t*-test the mean ratio of standard deviations was found to be significantly lower during the 1980 through 1982 period (for the 20 S&Ls that traded over both periods). The calculated *t*-statistic is -4.86.

[24] We analyze the ratio of the standard deviations because our concern is with the variability of S&L stock returns *relative* to the return on S&L underlying assets. The decrease in the ratio of standard deviations results primarily from the increased volatility of interest rates (R_I). The standard deviation of the returns on the S&L portfolios during the 1976 to 1982 period are:

	1976	1977	1978	1979	1980	1981	1982
σ_s	0.036	0.024	0.040	0.042	0.041	0.040	0.051

6. Contemporaneous factors affecting the S&L industry

In this section we explore alternative explanations for the change in the behavior of S&L stock prices. In particular, we examine the effect of (1) changes in the composition of the S&L assets and liabilities, (2) S&L activity in financial future markets, and (3) changes in the level of interest rates.[25] Our analysis suggests these factors are not the source of the decrease in S&L stock price elasticities. We also examine the effect of FHLB advances and tax subsidies on S&L stock returns. These factors may have contributed to the change in S&L stock price behavior as discussed below.

6.1. Changes in the asset and liability composition of S&Ls

During the early 1980's S&Ls were given broader powers to issue variable rate mortgages and to expand their nonmortgage lending activities. If S&Ls significantly altered the maturity composition of their assets (moving, for example, from fixed rate mortgages to variable rate mortgages), this may change the relation between S&L stock returns and R_I. In particular, since changes in the value of mortgages occur primarily because of changes in the level of interest rates, the shorter the maturity of S&L assets, the less S&L stock prices will respond to interest rate changes like a long-term mortgage certificate and the lower the β_{I_j}. We examined this issue by analyzing the relation between the maturity mismatch (the difference between the average maturity of assets and liabilities of S&Ls) and cross-sectional, as well as intertemporal, differences in the β_{I_j}'s.

A measure of maturity mismatch was constructed by subtracting the dollar value of S&L liabilities maturing or subject to repricing within one year from the dollar value of assets subject to repricing within the same period. This measure is denoted as '*Short*'. By construction, assets and liabilities excluded from this measure are assumed to mature or be repriced in more than one year, and will be referred to as '*Long*'. A negative value of *Short* implies that the value of short-term assets is less than the value of short-term liabilities. This, in turn, implies the value of long-term assets exceeds the value of long-term liabilities. Appendix 2 describes how we constructed *Short*.

The *Short* measure was computed for each S&L in our sample using the FHLBB *Report of Condition* for December of each year. (Consistent balance sheet information could be obtained from the FHLBB for December 1977 through December 1982.) In the case of multiple S&L holding companies *Short* was computed by summing the *Short* measure for each of the S&Ls within the holding company. Finally, we deflated *Short* by the year-end market value of the S&L holding company's outstanding common stock so that the

---

[25]See Eisenbeis (1983) for a discussion of these changes.

dollar measure of maturity mismatch is in the same units of measure as β_{Ij}. Our *Short* measure is denoted as *Short/MV*, where *MV* is the market value of the S&L's common stock.

If the β_{Ij} decline because of an increase in the net short assets of S&Ls (so that S&L stocks move less with long-term bonds), then one would expect a significant increase in *Short/MV* during the period 1980 to 1983. Table 3 summarizes the behavior of the average value of *Short/MV* for the S&Ls in our sample during the period 1977 through 1982. The data in table 3 indicate an *increase* in the maturity of S&L assets relative to the maturity of liabilities.[26] Therefore, the behavior of *Short/MV* does not appear to explain the decrease in β_I after 1979.

An alternative explanation for the decrease in the elasticity of S&L stock returns is a decrease in S&L leverage. To examine this issue we computed the market value of the common stock outstanding for each S&L at the end of each year. We also calculated the book value of S&L debt obligations (all deposits plus other debt obligations for December of each year). We then calculated the debt to equity ratio of each S&L (denoted as *Debt/MV*). To the extent that S&Ls have risky debt obligations *Debt/MV* will represent an upward biased estimate of S&L leverage.

Table 4 provides the mean leverage ratio for the S&Ls in our sample over the period 1977 through 1982. As shown in table 4 the leverage ratio *increased* during the 1980–1982 period. In the absence of changes in FSLIC policies the increase in leverage would be expected to *increase* the elasticity measures, however the elasticity measures decrease during the 1980–1982 period.[27]

To analyze further the relation among β_{Ij} the maturity composition of S&Ls and leverage we estimated the following pooled cross-section time series model:

$$\beta_{Ijt} = \alpha_0 + \alpha_1 (Short/MV)_{jt} + \alpha_2 (Short/MV)_{jt} * D$$

$$+ \alpha_3 (Debt/MV)_{jt} + \varepsilon_{jt}, \tag{5}$$

---

[26] The mean value of *Short/MV* during the period 1980 to 1982 is significantly smaller than the mean value of *Short/MV* for the 1976 to 1979 period. The *t*-statistic for the difference in means test is -5.95. The decrease in *Short* is not attributable primarily to a decrease in *MV* during the 1980 to 1982 period. Scaling *Short* by the book value of total assets yields a similar pattern.

[27] The median elasticity coefficients for S&L in our sample over the 1977 through 1983 period are:

	1977	1978	1979	1980	1981	1982
$\hat{\beta}_I$	2.18	3.54	1.28	0.78	0.45	0.94

Table 3

The average ratio of net short-term assets to the market value of S&L equity from 1977 through 1982.[a]

	1977	1978	1979	1980	1981	1982
Short/MV[b]	−4.85	−6.65	−10.04	−12.16	−22.39	−17.61

[a]Sample size ranged from 20 S&Ls to 30 S&Ls. Holding companies in the sample are those with common stock and trading information contained in the DRI *Securities File* and which traded for at least four consecutive years during the study period. To be included in the sample the S&Ls within the holding company must have comprised at least 80 percent of the holding company's assets.

[b]*Short/MV* equals the ratio of short-term assets minus short-term liabilities to the market value of the common stock of the S&L. Short-term assets and liabilities are defined as claims maturing or being repriced within one year.

Table 4

Average debt to market value ratios for S&Ls 1977 through 1982.[a]

	1977	1978	1979	1980	1981	1982
Debt/MV[b]	24.27	24.02	24.37	28.64	30.90	42.80

[a]Sample size ranged from 20 S&Ls to 30 S&Ls. Holding companies included in the sample are those with common stock and trading information contained in the DRI *Securities File* and which traded for at least four consecutive years during the study period. To be included in the sample the S&Ls within the holding company must have comprised at least 80 percent of the holding company's assets.

[b]*Debt/MV* equals the ratio of the book value of S&L debt to the market value of equity. The book value of the S&Ls debt was obtained from Moody's *Banking and Finance Manual*. The market value of equity (MV) was computed based on shares outstanding and price data for December, 31 of each year. All information pertains to S&L holding companies where applicable.

where

β_{Ijt} = the estimated coefficient associated with R_I for the jth S&L over the period t,

$Debt/MV_{jt}$ = debt to equity ratio for the jth S&L over the period t, where the dollar value of debt includes all deposit and other debt obligations and equity represents the market value of equity,

D = binary variable taking on the value of zero for the 1976 through 1979, one otherwise, and

ε_{jt} = error term.

In eq. (5) *Short/MV* is intended to measure the effect of differences in the maturity composition of S&L assets and liabilities on the relation between R_I and S&L stock returns. The expected sign of α_1 is negative. If our measure of *Short* captures maturity mismatch, an increase in net short-term assets (implying a corresponding decrease in long-term assets and/or an increase in long-term liabilities) should result in a decrease in β_I.

An interactive binary variable, $Short/MV * D$, is included in the model to measure any change in the relation between β_I and maturity composition of $Short/MV$. After insolvency rules were changed $Short/MV$ is expected to be less important in the determination of β_{Ij}. Therefore, the expected sign of α_2 is positive.

If investors expect the FSLIC to enforce 'me first' priority rules, the expected sign on the leverage variable is positive. Under the subsidy hypothesis, however, leverage increases do not necessarily imply an increase in the elasticity of the stock. In particular, since increases in leverage increase the risk borne by the FSLIC, an increase in leverage may increase the value of access to insurance and therefore lower β_{Ij}. Thus, including $Debt/MV$ provides an additional test of the subsidy hypothesis.

In estimating eq. (5) we used estimates of β_{Ij} obtained over two subperiods: 1976 through 1979 and 1980 to 1983. Average values for $Short/MV$ and $Debt/MV$ were obtained for each S&L for each of the two subperiods (1977 through 1979 and 1980 through 1982). These values were calculated using data for December, 31 of each year.

Eq. (5) was estimated using OLS techniques for our sample of 30 S&L holding companies over the two time periods. The results are presented below (standard errors are in parentheses):

$$\hat{\beta}_{Ijt} = 1.36 - \underset{(0.531)}{1.48}(Short/MV)_{jt} + \underset{(0.053)}{0.17}(Short/MV)_{jt} * D$$

$$- \underset{(0.257)}{0.62}(Debt/MV)_{jt}, \qquad R^2 = 0.35.$$

The negative and statistically significant coefficient on $Short/MV$ is consistent with the hypothesis that cross-sectional differences in the effect of changes in mortgage interest rates on the stock returns of S&Ls result, in part, from differences in the maturity composition of S&L assets and liabilities. An increase in $Short$ (or decrease in net long-term assets) results in a decrease in the co-movement of S&L stock returns with the return on long-term mortgages. In addition, the coefficient on the interaction variable (α_2) is positive and statistically significant. This indicates that $Short/MV$ is significantly less important during the 1980 and 1983 period than before the changes in insolvency rules. Changes in the maturity composition of S&Ls do not appear to explain the significant decrease in sensitivity of S&L stock prices to mortgage rate changes after 1979. Indeed, changes in the maturity composition of S&Ls would indicate that the co-movement should have increased after 1979.

Finally, consistent with the subsidy hypothesis, the coefficient on the $Debt/MV$ variable is negative and statistically significant at the 0.01 level (one-tailed test). Increases in leverage, given fixed insurance premium, increase the value of access to insurance and thereby result in a reduction of β_I.[28]

While the changes in S&L asset and liability composition do not appear to explain the behavior of the elasticity of S&L stocks during the 1976 to 1983 period, changes in the elasticity of S&L stocks may reflect changes in S&L activities that are not reflected on S&L balance sheets. One such activity is the origination and sale of mortgages. The origination and sale of mortgages may generate fee income while reducing S&L exposure to unexpected interest rate changes. To investigate this issue, information on mortgage loans and participations purchased and sold by insured S&Ls was obtained for the period 1976 through 1982.

Net mortgages sold increased during the 1976 through 1979 period and in 1982. If increased mortgage sales are the source of the decline in the elasticity of S&Ls one would expect to observe a decrease in $\hat{\beta}_{Ij}$ in 1976 through 1977 and in 1982. However, $\hat{\beta}_I$ increased in both of these periods (see footnote 27).[29]

A final piece of evidence as to whether changes in S&L stock price behavior is the result of changes in asset composition is obtained from estimating elasticity coefficients for the 25 S&Ls in our sample with stock price data available for 1983 (balance sheet data was not available from the FHLBB for 1983). If the decrease in S&L elasticities is the result of changes in asset composition (resulting from regulatory changes), then our elasticity measure would not be expected to increase in 1983. However, if changes in insolvency rules and the resulting increase in the value of insurance is the source of the decrease in β_{Ij}, then as the earnings of thrifts improved in 1983 (see table 1) the estimates of β_{Ij} should increase.

We estimated eq. (2) was estimated using data for 1983. The median value of $\hat{\beta}_{Ij}$ increased in 1983 to 1.90 (from 0.94 in 1982). Moreover, the average value of $\hat{\beta}_{Ij}$ increased to 1.63 (from 0.92 in 1982). This change in the average value

---

[28] Because the dependent variable in eq. (5) is measured with error and given the shift in $\hat{\beta}_{Ij}$ over the two periods, the errors in eq. (5) may be cross-sectionally heteroskedastic. To correct for possible heteroskedasticity, we re-estimated eq. (5) using a generalized least squares model which utilizes estimates of the cross-sectional variances from the OLS regression [see Kmenta (1971, pp. 510–512)]. The results using this procedure are similar to those obtained using OLS estimates.

[29] Net mortgages sold (mortgages sold less mortgages purchased) during the 1976 to 1982 for all S&Ls are given below (in millions) (source: *FHLBB Journal*, table 54.5):

1976	1977	1978	1979	1980	1981	1982
$ − 4,352	$ − 651	$4,501	$6,299	$2,901	$2,094	$30,118

The decrease in $\hat{\beta}_I$ may result from commitments to sell mortgages (particularly during 1980 and 1981). We were unable to obtain information on commitments to sell mortgages. However, since most commitments are for delivery within one year, commitments to sell mortgages does not appear to be the primary reason for the decrease in S&L stock elasticities.

of $\hat{\beta}_I$ is significantly different from zero using a paired t-test at the 0.01 level (the t-statistic is 5.56). The increase in the elasticity in 1983 appears therefore consistent with the subsidy hypothesis.

6.2. Futures market activity

A potential alternative explanation for the decrease in our elasticity measure is the expanded use of financial futures by S&Ls as a means of hedging interest rate risk. During July 1981, the FHLBB implemented regulations permitting S&Ls to transact in futures markets.[30] While increased use of interest futures may reduce S&L interest rate risk, S&L use of interest rate futures during the period appears limited even among large S&Ls. A recent survey of futures activity reveals only 47 percent of S&Ls with assets over $1 billion transacted in financial futures. [See Booth, Smith and Stolz (1984).] The net short position for all S&Ls as of March 1984 was only $1.702 billion (based on par value of securities).[31]

To examine whether hedging in the futures market might explain the decrease in the elasticity estimate for the S&Ls in our sample, we estimated the relation between β_I and *Short/MV* during the period 1976 through 1979 (a period during which futures activity was almost non-existent). We next used these coefficient estimates, together with the estimated value of β_I for the 1980 through 1982 period, to determine the average *Short/MV* implied by the lower elasticity estimates in the 1980 through 1982 period. Given the market value of S&L equity, the lower estimates for β_I imply an increase in average short-term assets of $1.2 billion (i.e., the estimates of β_{Ij} imply short-term assets of $1.2 billion *greater* than the actual level observed; the average asset size of S&Ls in our sample during this period was $2.6 billion and average short-term assets were $881 million). Based on a sample of 30 S&Ls this implies an aggregate increase in short assets of $36 billion in the 1980 through 1982 period. This required increase in short-term assets exceeds the net short position of *all* S&Ls in GNMA futures contracts held as of March 1984 by $34 billion. These, admittedly crude estimates, suggest that S&L activity in the futures market is not the source of the decline in elasticity estimates.

6.3. Changes in the level of interest rates

While the change in the relation between S&L stock returns and R_I appears consistent with the subsidy hypothesis, the decrease in the elasticity estimates might result from some contemporaneous economy-wide event-unrelated to FSLIC policies. For example, the level of interest rates rose dramatically after

---

[30]*Savings and Loan Fact Book*, 1982.

[31] Federal Home Loan Board, *Report of Condition*, March 1984.

Table 5

An analysis of shifts in market model parameters and elasticity estimates for portfolios of commercial bank and life insurance stocks over the period 1976 through 1982.[a]

Panel A: Bank analysis

Relation between bank stock returns and the return on GNMA index

$$R_{Bt} = \underset{(0.001)}{0.002} + \underset{(0.106)}{0.245R_I} - \underset{(0.133)}{0.145R_I * D}, \qquad R^2 = 0.03, \quad D.W. = 1.67$$

Market model estimates for banks

$$R_{Bt} = \underset{(0.000)}{0.112} + \underset{(0.038)}{0.370R_m} - \underset{(0.049)}{0.030R_m * D}, \qquad R^2 = 0.37, \quad D.W. = 1.85$$

Panel B: Life insurance analysis

Relation between life insurance stock returns and the return on GNMA index

$$R_{In} = \underset{(0.001)}{0.003} + \underset{(0.076)}{0.204R_I} - \underset{(0.165)}{0.000R_I * D}, \qquad R^2 = 0.04, \quad D.W. = 1.23$$

Market model estimates for life insurance stocks

$$R_{In} = \underset{(0.001)}{0.004} + \underset{(0.062)}{0.431R_m} + \underset{(0.043)}{0.001R_m * D}, \qquad R^2 = 0.28, \quad D.W. = 2.03$$

---

[a] R_B = weekly return on an equally weighted portfolio of bank stocks obtained from Data Resources Incorporated (DRI),

R_I = weekly holding period return on an index of Government National Mortgage Association (GNMA) eight percent certificates,

D = binary variable taking on the value of zero for the period 1976 to 1980, one otherwise,

R_{mt} = weekly return for the NYSE composite index, and

R_{In} = weekly return on an equally weighted portfolio of life insurance stocks obtained from DRI.

1979. The effect of a change in the level of interest rates on the elasticity of a stock in the absence of deposit insurance is an empirical issue.[32] Christie (1982) finds for common stocks in general a *positive* relation between η_s and interest rates. Christie's results suggest therefore that in the absence of access to insurance, the elasticity of S&L stocks should increase as interest rates increase.

To examine whether the change in the relation between S&L stock returns and the return on mortgages is due to some event-unrelated to changes in insolvency rules (such as the level of interest rates), we analyze the relation between the stock returns of other types of financial institutions and R_I. We chose as control groups commercial banks and life insurance companies. Since

---

[32] Galai and Masulis (1976) demonstrate that there exists *ceteris paribus* an inverse relation between the level of interest rates and η_s. However, changes in the level of interest rates also affect the value of the firm's assets. Fama and Schwert (1977) find on average a negative relation between stock returns and interest rate changes. An increase in interest rates may therefore reduce the value of the firm's assets leading to an increase in elasticity.

Flannery and James (1984b), using a model similar to eq. (2), find a significant relation between bank stock returns and R_I and given the similarity between the portfolio composition of banks and S&Ls (i.e., both consist primarily of financial contracts), commercial banks provide an appropriate control group. Life insurance companies were selected because of their specialization in mortgage lending and their portfolio of other relatively long-term assets.[33] Finding a significant reduction in β_I for commercial banks and insurance companies in the period 1980 through 1982 would suggest that the decline in β_I for S&Ls is *not* the result of changes in insurance administration.[34]

Table 5 presents estimates of eq. (3) for a portfolio of commercial bank stocks and life insurance companies.[35] Unlike the results for S&Ls, the interactive dummy for both banks and insurance companies is not significantly different from zero at the 0.10 level. Moreover, an analysis of the behavior of the market model parameters for these firms indicates no significant change in β_m during the period 1980 to 1983.

6.4. Other factors

Another factor that may affect our elasticity estimates is a change in the behavior of our mortgage index. Since our index is constructed from newly issued GNMA eight percent certificates, changes in the level of interest rates may affect the price volatility of the GNMA series. In particular, because prepayments on mortgages in GNMA pools may decrease as interest rates rise the duration of the GNMA index may increase as interest rates rise. If similar changes in prepayments for mortgages held by the S&Ls in our sample did not occur, this may reduce the estimate of β_I. To insure that our findings are not the result of a change in the behavior of the returns on GNMA certificates, we reestimated eq. (3) using a series constructed from six-month Treasury bill returns. Treasury bill returns were used because Treasury bills have a known and constant duration. To insure that the Treasury bill return series reflected unanticipated interest rate changes, the series was whitened using an AR(3) process. Eq. (3) was estimated using as an interest rate series the residuals of the AR(3) model. The interactive dummy variable is again negative and significantly different from zero at the 0.01 level (the t-statistic is -2.79).

---

[33] In 1983 life insurance companies held an average of 50 percent of their assets in corporate bonds and 30 percent of their assets in mortgages. *Source*: Board of Governors of the Federal Reserve System, *Flow of Funds Account*, 1983.

[34] No changes in capital requirements for insured commercial banks occurred during the 1976–1982 period. Commercial banks and S&Ls benefited from the introduction of All Saver Certificates in 1981 and personal interest tax exemptions in 1980. If these events are significant factors in the decrease in S&L stock elasticity, a similar change should be observed for commercial banks.

[35] Equally weighted portfolios of bank and life insurance stocks were obtained from DRI.

6.5. Other subsidies

While our focus has been on the effect of changes in insolvency rules on the value of access to deposit insurance, these changes may also affect the value of other subsidies provided thrifts during crisis periods. Two potentially important sources of subsidies during the 1980 through 1982 period were FHLB advances and tax refunds associated with tax loss carry-back provisions of the corporate tax code. By modifying insolvency rules, the FSLIC provided S&Ls continued access to these subsidies.[36]

The FHLB advance program permits S&Ls with qualifying collateral to borrow up to 25 percent of their assets at rates determined by each FHLB's cost of funds. Since FHLB borrowing carries an implied guarantee of the federal government, advances represent a source of federally subsidized borrowing for S&Ls.[37]

The S&Ls in our sample increased their borrowing under advances from 8 percent of their liabilities during the 1976–1979 period to 14.2 percent of their liabilities during the 1980–1982 period. The increased use of advances is therefore a potential explanation for the decline in β_I. Because the effect of access to advances should be similar to the effect of access to deposit guarantees on the elasticity of S&L stocks, the subsidy hypothesis predicts a negative cross-sectional relation between changes in β_I and advances during the 1976 through 1982 period.

To test this implication of the subsidy hypothesis, we obtained data of advances for the 20 S&Ls in our sample that traded over the entire seven-year period. We then examined the relation between β_{Ij} and the ratio of advances to market value of common stock outstanding. The results of this analysis are presented below (standard errors are in parentheses):

$$\hat{\beta}_{Ijt} = 1.30 - \underset{(0.08)}{0.18} (ADV/MV)_{jt}, \qquad R^2 = 0.12,$$

---

[36] Changes in insolvency rules not only permitted S&Ls to continue to utilize these subsidies, but also permitted expanded access. In particular, by permitting S&Ls to realize losses from the sale of mortgages for tax purposes while deferring the loss for purposes of determining regulatory net worth, S&Ls were provided greater access to tax loss carry-backs. Kane (1981) argues that net worth requirements limited the use of carry backs during 1979 and 1980.

[37] Advance policy is outlined in the Federal Home Loan Bank Board's Office of District Bank's *Advance Guidelines*. Advances are collateralized primarily by residential mortgages at market value. District Banks require S&Ls to specify the use for which the advance will be used and to demonstrate 'sound management'. In the event of failure, the District Bank has first claim on the collateralized assets. During the 1976 through 1981 period S&Ls increased their use of advances primarily to obtain liquidity due to disintermediation caused by deposit rate ceilings on longer-term deposits [see Kent (1981)].

where

$\hat{\beta}_{Ijt}$ = the estimated coefficient associated with R_I for the jth S&L in period t, and

$(ADV/MV)_{jt}$ = ratio of FHLB advances to total market value of equity for the jth S&L in period t.

Consistent with the subsidy hypothesis we find a negative and significant relation between $\hat{\beta}_I$ and advance activity.[38]

In estimating S&L stock price elasticities, we use the changes in the market value of GNMA certificates as a proxy for changes in the market value of S&L portfolios. Increased use of tax loss carry-backs in the 1980–1982 period may alter the relation between before-tax earnings (proxied by R_I) and S&L stock returns. In this way use of tax loss carry-backs may contribute to the decrease in β_I during the 1980–1982 period.

Evaluating the importance of tax refunds in explaining the decrease in β_I is complicated by the fact that S&L tax payments are related to earnings. Earnings, in turn, are negatively correlated with the value of access to deposit guarantees. Disentangling the influence of tax subsidies from access to deposit insurance is therefore extremely difficult. Finding a positive relation between β_I and tax payments is consistent with changes in the value of access to deposit insurance as well as increased access to tax refunds.[39]

For the S&Ls in our sample tax payments as a percent of total assets decreased from 0.5 percent during the 1976 through 1979 period to -0.16 percent during the 1980 through 1982 period. This change in tax payments is a potential explanation for the decline in $\hat{\beta}_I$.[40]

7. Summary

Consistent with the subsidy hypothesis we find a significant decrease in the co-movement of S&L stock returns with the returns of S&L portfolio holdings following the reduction of net worth requirements in 1980. Moreover, we find

[38] Several caveats concerning the interpretation of these results are required. First, to the extent that advances are used simply to substitute for deposits, an increase in advances should *ceteris paribus* not affect β_{Ij}. New financing with advances does imply an increase in subsidies. Second, because the FHLB's claim to S&L assets is senior to that of the FSLIC, increases in advances increase the risk of the FSLIC's position and thereby increases insurance subsidies. Discussions with the Seattle FHLB indicate that advances were used by financially distressed thrifts to replace outflows of large certificates of deposit (see also *The Wall Street Journal*, Aug. 30, 1982, p. 3). However, in these circumstances, the District Bank required the FSLIC to guarantee the advances.

[39] Failure to find a significant relation between tax payments and β_{Ij} would suggest that reported net income for tax purposes serves as a poor proxy for changes in the market value of S&L portfolio holdings. We find a positive and statistically significant relation between β_I and tax payments (refunds).

[40] The ability to utilize tax loss carry-back was in part the result of changes in insolvency rules [see Kane (1981)]. Tax refunds were not, however, sufficient to offset operating losses for S&Ls (see table 1). If the entire drop in $\hat{\beta}_I$ were the result of expanded access to tax refunds, one would *not* expect to observe the negative relation between $\hat{\beta}_{Ij}$ and leverage.

cross-sectionally, a negative relation between leverage and the sensitivity of S&L stock returns to changes in the value of the firm's assets. This finding is inconsistent with the enforcement of 'me first' priority rules.

An important implication of our analysis is that inferences regarding the risk of insured financial institutions, based on the behavior of their stock returns, should be made with caution.[41] In particular, since their stock returns reflect investor expectations concerning the reaction of the insuring agent to changes in risk (in terms of insurance availability), changes in the value of their portfolio holdings need not be reflected fully in changes in the equity value of the institution.

Finally, our analysis provides further evidence concerning the behavior of the stocks of firms in financial distress. Consistent with the findings of Aharony, Jones and Swary (1980) and Baldwin and Mason (1983), we find a decrease in the beta estimates of financially distressed firms. However, because of the relative simplicity of S&L balance sheets we are able to trace this decrease in beta to a decrease in the elasticity of S&L stock prices with respect to the value of underlying assets. In this way our analysis contributes to the understanding of the stock price behavior of firms in financial distress.

Appendix 1

Table A.1 contains a listing of the 30 S&Ls in our sample. For each observation: (1) the years included in the sample, (2) the asset size (from *Moody's*, 1982), (3) the stock exchange, and (4) the state where the lead S&L is located are listed. The table also includes the elasticities of the stock prices with respect to the underlying assets estimated over the periods: 1976–1979 and 1980–1982. The technique for estimating elasticities is described in section 3.

The table indicates that the sample includes large S&Ls, based predominately in California. The median asset size for the sample is approximately $1.7 billion, ranging from a low of $248 million to a high of $13 billion. The median asset size of all insured S&Ls in 1982 was $50 million. Seventeen of the S&Ls operated in California. Twenty were listed on national exchanges (fifteen NYSE and five ASE). The remaining ten S&Ls traded over-the-counter.

The elasticity estimates contained in the last two columns document the shift in elasticities between the 1976–1979 and 1980–1982 periods. In all cases where sufficient data existed to provide estimates in both subperiods, the elasticities were lower in the later period.

---

[41] For example, Marcus and Shaked (1984) utilize estimates of the variance of equity returns in the Black–Scholes put option pricing formula to obtain an estimate of the market value of FDIC insurance. However, our analysis suggests the variance of equity returns may provide a downward biased estimate of the variance of asset returns, resulting in an underestimate of the value of insurance.

Table A.1

Sample of 30 savings and loans used in the study: Years included in sample, asset size, stock exchange, state of lead S&L, and elasticity estimates for 1976–1979 and 1980–1982 periods.

Name	Years in sample	Asset size[a] (000's)	Stock exchange[a]	State[b]	Elasticity[c]	
					1976 to 1979	1980 to 1982
Ahmanson, H.F. (AHM)	1976–83	13,109,603	NYSE	CA	2.00	1.02
Alamo Savings Association (ALMO)	1979–83	313,781	NASDAQ	TX	—	0.58
American Savings and Loan (AAA)	1976–83	2,225,894	NYSE	FL	1.79	0.71
Beverly Hills Savings and Loan (BHSL)	1980–83	490,560	NASDAQ	CA	—	0.62
Biscayne Federal Savings and Loan (BIS)	1976–83	1,784,267	NYSE	FL	1.20	0.68
Downey Savings and Loan (DSL)	1976–83	1,388,128	ASE	CA	1.81	1.08
Equitable Savings and Loan (EQIB)	1976–82	1,519,018	NASDAQ	OR	2.23	0.38
Far West Financial Corporation (FWF)	1976–83	908,381	NYSE	CA	1.12	0.50
Fidelity Financial Corporation (FDY)	1976–82	2,852,623	NYSE	CA	2.75	0.31
Financial Corporation of America (FIN)	1976–83	3,757,352	NYSE	CA	1.18	0.74
Financial Corporation of Santa Barbara (FSB)	1980–83	1,898,018	NYSE	CA	—	0.84
Financial Federation (FFI)	1976–83	2,455,617	NYSE	CA	1.51	0.64
First Charter Financial Corporation (FCF)	1976–83	9,750,034	NYSE	CA	1.94	0.95
First Federal Savings and Loan Raleigh (FFSR)	1980–83	248,137	NASDAQ	NC	—	0.20
First Savings and Loan Shares (FSX)	1976–82	1,310,636	ASE	CO	1.35	0.28
First Western Financial Corporation (FWES)	1978–83	703,401	NASDAQ	NV	1.27	0.53
Frontier Savings and Loan Association (FRNT)	1979–83	N.L.	NASDAQ	NV	—	0.67
Gibralter Financial Corporation (GFC)	1976–83	4,771,371	NYSE	CA	2.23	1.02
Golden West Financial Corporation (GDW)	1976–83	5,541,347	NYSE	CA	2.10	0.90
Guarantee Financial Corporation (GFCC)	1978–83	1,693,073	NASDAQ	CA	1.13	0.94
Homestead Financial Corporation (HOMF)	1978–83	513,161	NASDAQ	CA	0.76	0.34
Imperial Corporation of America (ICA)	1976–83	5,169,203	NYSE	CA	2.17	0.98
Land of Lincoln Savings and Loan	1980–83	586,889	NASDAQ	IL	—	0.24
Mercury Savings and Loan (MSL)	1976–83	1,122,741	ASE	CA	1.28	0.86
Nevada Savings and Loan Association (NEV)	1976–83	654,014	NYSE	NV	1.93	0.69
North Carolina Federal Savings and Loan (NCES)	1980–83	367,580	NASDAQ	NC	—	0.26
Northern California Savings and Loan (NCX)	1976–82	1,912,394	NYSE	CA	1.81	0.93
Transohio Financial Corporation (TFC)	1976–83	5,169,203	NYSE	OH	0.83	0.68
Wesco Financial Corporation (WSC)	1976–83	361,525	ASE	CA	1.01	0.16
Western Financial Corporation (WFN)	1976–82	1,904,272	ASE	AZ	1.04	0.84

[a] As shown in Moody's, 1982.
[b] State where the lead S&L is located.
[c] Estimated by regressing weekly S&L stock returns on an index of GNMA securities.

Table A.2

Definition of variables.

I. Assets

(A) *Cash and short-term investments*: Cash includes vault cash, demand deposits at commercial banks, deposits at a Federal Home Loan bank or at Federal Reserve banks which are unpledged. Short-term investments represent the book value of unpledged investments which are defined as liquid assets for regulatory purposes (Regulation 523.10g). Included are certificates of deposit, repurchase agreements, US government obligations, and other debt obligations with a maturity of less than one year.

(B) *Variable rate mortgages*: Any mortgage on a one-to-four-family dwelling with non-graduated payments with a contracted interest which may be adjusted over the life of the mortgage. All variable rate mortgages regardless of restriction on interest or payment adjustments are included in this category.

(C) *Open-end consumer loans*: Credit extended in connection with credit cards, overdrafts on NOW and demand deposit accounts, other open end credit extended.

(D) *Unsecured construction loans*: All unsecured loans made for the purpose of constructing new residential property.

(E) *Accrued interest receivable*: Accrued interest receivable on all loans where interest is maintained in separate accounts plus interest receivable on investments.

(F) *Loans on savings accounts*: Loans fully secured by the pledge or assignment of the borrowers' savings accounts.

(G) *Advances on customer borrowing*: Payments due for taxes and insurance payments made on loan security properties.

II. Liabilities

(A) *FHLBB advances due in less than one year*: All advances maturing within one year.

(B) *Commercial paper*: Commercial paper issued by the S&L.

(C) *Other borrowing due in less than one year*: Borrowing from all sources other than the FHL bank due in less than one year.

(D) *Overdrafts on demand deposit accounts*: Negative demand deposit balances and cashiers checks outstanding.

(E) *Other accounts payable*: Amounts owed and accrued for services supplies and other expenses including advance payments for borrowers taxes and insurance.

(F) *CDs greater than $100,000*: Certificates of deposit's earning excess of the passbook rate issued in denominations of 100,000 or more.

(G) *Repurchase agreements and accounts paying more than passbook rate maturing in less than one year*: Repurchase agreements plus accounts with maturities less than one year with minimum deposits of less than $100,000 and earning in excess of the passbook rate.

Appendix 2

Methodology used to construct a measure of net current claims ('Short')

The definition of *Short* used is: (cash and short-term investments + variable rate mortgages + open end consumer loans + accrued interest receivable + advances for customer borrowing + unsecured construction loans + loans on savings accounts) − (FHLBB advances due in less than one year + commercial paper + overdrafts on demand deposit accounts + CD's greater than $100,000 + bank loans due in less than one year + other borrowing due in less than one year + other accounts payable + repurchase agreements and accounts paying more than the passbook rate maturing in less than one year). A detailed description of each of these items is provided in table A.2.

Excluded from *Short* are deposits under $100,000 paying the passbook rate or less. While these deposits can be withdrawn on short notices and might therefore be considered short-term, there exists considerable evidence that these deposit stocks adjust slowly to interest rate changes, giving them longer effective maturities [see Flannery and James (1984b) and Hester and Pierce (1975)]. Including these items in the *Short* measure does not significantly affect the results reported in this paper.

Included in *Short* are all variable rate mortgages. Most variable rate mortgages issued by S&Ls contain no limits on interest rate adjustment or monthly payment adjustment [see *FHLBB Journal*, December 1982). Excluding mortgages with caps from our *Short* measure does not affect our basic results.

References

Aharony, J., C.P. Jones and I. Swary, 1980, An analysis of risk and return of corporate bankruptcy using capital market data, Journal of Finance 35, 1001–1016.

Balderston, F., 1981, The savings and loan mortgage discount and the effective maturity of mortgage loans, Working paper no. 81-41 (University of California, Berkeley, CA).

Baldwin, C. and S.P. Mason, 1983, The resolution of claims in financial distress: The case of Massey Ferguson, Journal of Finance 38, 505–516.

Black, F. and M. Scholes, 1973, The pricing of options and corporate liabilities, Journal of Political Economy 81, 637–659.

Black, F. and J.C. Cox, 1976, Valuing corporate securities: Some effects of bond indenture provisions, Journal of Finance 31, 351–368.

Booth, J.R., R. Smith and R.W. Stolz, 1984, Use of interest rate futures by financial institutions, Journal of Bank Research 15, 15–25.

Buser, S.A., A.H. Chen and E.J. Kane, 1981, Federal deposit insurance, regulatory policy and optimal bank capital, Journal of Finance 36, 51–60.

Campbell, T.S. and D. Glenn, 1984, Deposit insurance in a deregulated environment, Journal of Finance 39, 775–787.

Christie, A., 1982, The stochastic behavior of common stock variances: Value, leverage and interest rate effects, Journal of Financial Economics 10, 407–432.

Dimson, E., 1980, Risk measurement when shares are subject to infrequent trading, Journal of Financial Economics 8, 297–326.

Eisenbeis, R.A., 1982, New investment powers: Diversification or specialization, Proceedings of the Eighth Annual Conference, Federal Home Loan Bank of San Francisco, 107–122.

Fama, E. and G.W. Schwert, 1977, Assets returns and inflation, Journal of Financial Economics 5, 115–146.

Flannery, M.J. and C. James, 1984, The effect of interest rate changes on the common stock returns of financial institutions, Journal of Finance 39, 1141–1153.

Flannery, M.J. and C. James, 1984, Market evidence of the effective maturity of bank assets and liabilities, Journal of Money Credit and Banking 16, 435–445.

Galai, D. and R. Masulis, 1976, The option pricing model and the risk factor of stock, Journal of Financial Economics 3, 53–81.

Hamada, R., 1969, Portfolio analysis, market equilibrium and corporate finance, Journal of Finance 24, 13–32.

Haugen, R.A. and L.W. Senbet, 1978, The insignificance of bankruptcy costs to the theory of optimal capital structure, Journal of Finance 33, 383–393.

Hester, D.D. and J.L. Pierce, 1975, Bank management and portfolio behavior (Yale University Press, New Haven, CT).

Horton, J., 1979, A critical analysis of asset-based risk related capital requirements for savings and loan associations, Working paper no. 83 (Federal Home Loan Bank Board, Washington, DC).

Jarrow, R.A. and A. Rudd, 1983, Option pricing (Irwin, Homewood, IL).

Kane, E.J., 1983, The role of government in the thrift industry's net-worth crisis, in: George Benston, ed., Financial services (Prentice-Hall, Englewood Cliffs, NJ).

Kane, E.J., 1981, S&Ls and interest rate re-regulation: The FSLIC as an in-place bailout program, Unpublished manuscript (Ohio State University, Columbus, OH).

Kaufman, G.G., 1983, The US financial system (Prentice-Hall, Englewood Cliffs, NJ).

Kent, R.A., An analysis of counter-cyclical policies of the FHLBB, Journal of Finance 36, 61–81.

Kmenta, J., 1971, Elements of econometrics (MacMillan, New York).

Marcus, A.J. and I. Shaked, 1984, The valuation of FDIC insurance using option-pricing estimates, Journal of Money Credit and Banking 16, 446–460.

Merton, R.C., 1977, An analytical derivation of the cost of deposit insurance and loan guarantees: An application of modern option pricing theory, Journal of Banking and Finance 1, 3–11.

Merton, R.C., 1983, Theory of rational option pricing, Bell Journal of Economics 4, 141–183.

Sharpe, W.F., 1978, Bank capital adequacy, deposit insurance and security values, Journal of Financial and Quantitative Analysis 13, 701–718.

Smith, C.W., 1976, Option pricing: A review, Journal of Financial Economics 3, 3–52.

Smith, C.W., 1982, Pricing mortgage obligations, AREUEA Journal 10, 313–330.

U.S. League of Savings and Loan Association, 1982, Savings and loan source book.

Warner, J.B., 1977, Bankruptcy, absolute priority and the pricing of risking debt claims, Journal of Financial Economics 4, 239–276.

The Determinants of Firms' Hedging Policies

Clifford W. Smith and René M. Stulz*

Abstract

We develop a positive theory of the hedging behavior of value-maximizing corporations. We treat hedging by corporations simply as one part of the firm's financing decisions. We examine (1) taxes, (2) contracting costs, and (3) the impact of hedging policy on the firm's investment decisions as explanations of the observed wide diversity of hedging practices among large, widely-held corporations. Our theory provides answers to the questions: (1) why some firms hedge and others do not; (2) why firms hedge some risks but not others; and (3) why some firms hedge their accounting risk exposure while others hedge their economic value.

I. Introduction

There is a considerable literature on the hedging practices of firms;[1] however, the focus is generally on risk-averse producers who use forward or futures markets to reduce the variability of their income.[2] Although this literature provides a useful basis for the analysis of hedging in closely-held corporations, partnerships, or individual proprietorships, it is not as applicable to large, widely-held corporations whose owners, the stockholders and bondholders, have the ability to hold diversified portfolios of securities.[3] In this paper, we develop a positive theory of hedging by value-maximizing corporations in which hedging is part of overall corporate financing policy.

* Graduate School of Management, University of Rochester, Rochester, NY 14627, and College of Administrative Science, Ohio State University, Columbus, OH 43210, respectively. The authors thank P. Meyers, L. Wakeman, and two anonymous *JFQA* referees for their comments and suggestions. Clifford Smith receives support from the Managerial Economics Research Center, Graduate School of Management, University of Rochester.

[1] A recent review of papers on hedging foreign exchange risks by Jacques [15] contains 80 references.

[2] References that consider the hedging problems for risk-averse agents include [1], [2], [10], [12], [13], [19], and [24].

[3] Notice that the literature on the demand for insurance addresses a problem that is similar to the problem discussed by the literature on hedging. However, for corporations, the determinants of the demand for insurance differ crucially from the determinants of hedging policies. For a corporation, the purchase of insurance provides real services due to the expertise of insurance companies in evaluating some types of risks and administering claims settlement procedures (for an analysis of these services, see [20]), while forward or futures contracts provide no apparent real services.

Modigliani/Miller [21] show that, with fixed investment policy and with no contracting costs or taxes, corporate financing policy is irrelevant. Their argument implies that if a firm chooses to change its hedging policy, investors who hold claims issued by the firm can change their holdings of risky assets to offset any change in the firm's hedging policy, leaving the distribution of their future wealth unaffected.[4] Thus, if the hedging policy affects the value of the firm, it must do so through (1) taxes, (2) contracting costs, or (3) the impact of hedging policy on the firm's investment decisions. We examine each of these potential explanations of the observed diversity of hedging practices among large widely-held corporations.[5] Our analysis provides answers to the following questions: (1) Why do some firms hedge while others do not? (2) Why do firms hedge some risks, but not others? (3) Why do some firms hedge accounting exposure, while others hedge economic values?

A definition of hedging. A firm can hedge by trading in a particular futures, forward, or option market even though it has no identifiable cash position in the underlying commodity. Furthermore, a firm can hedge by altering real operating decisions; for instance, a merger can produce effects similar to those of hedging through financial contracts. Thus, we adopt a fairly general definition of hedging in terms of the market value of the firm. Let $V(\underline{S})$ be the value of a firm if it does not hedge, where $\underline{S}$ is a vector of state variables. Consider two firms, a and b, that differ from the firm with value $V(\underline{S})$ only in their hedging policies. We say that firm a hedges more with respect to state variable i than firm b if the absolute value of the covariance of the value of firm a with state variable i is less than or equal to that of firm b. Therefore, hedging reduces the dependence of firm value on changes in the state variable. Alternatively, we say that firm a hedges more than firm b if the absolute value of the covariance of the value of firm a with the value of an unhedged firm with the same production policy and capital structure is less than or equal to that of firm b.

II. Taxes and Hedging

The structure of the tax code can make it advantageous for firms to take positions in futures, forward, or options markets. If effective marginal tax rates on corporations are an increasing function of the corporation's pre-tax value, then the after-tax value of the firm is a concave function of its pre-tax value. If hedging reduces the variability of pre-tax firm values, then the expected corporate tax liability is reduced and the expected post-tax value of the firm is increased, as long as the cost of the hedge is not too large. See Figure 1.

---

[4] If markets are perfect and complete, the value of the firm is independent of its hedging policy for other reasons, as well. For example, if a firm hedges the value of an input by purchasing forward contracts and that input price rises, the firm's pricing and production policies should not be affected by the existence of the hedge. The opportunity cost of the input is its current price, not the (sunk) cost of the forward contract.

[5] This diversity has been well documented in the case of foreign exchange risks. See, for instance, [23].

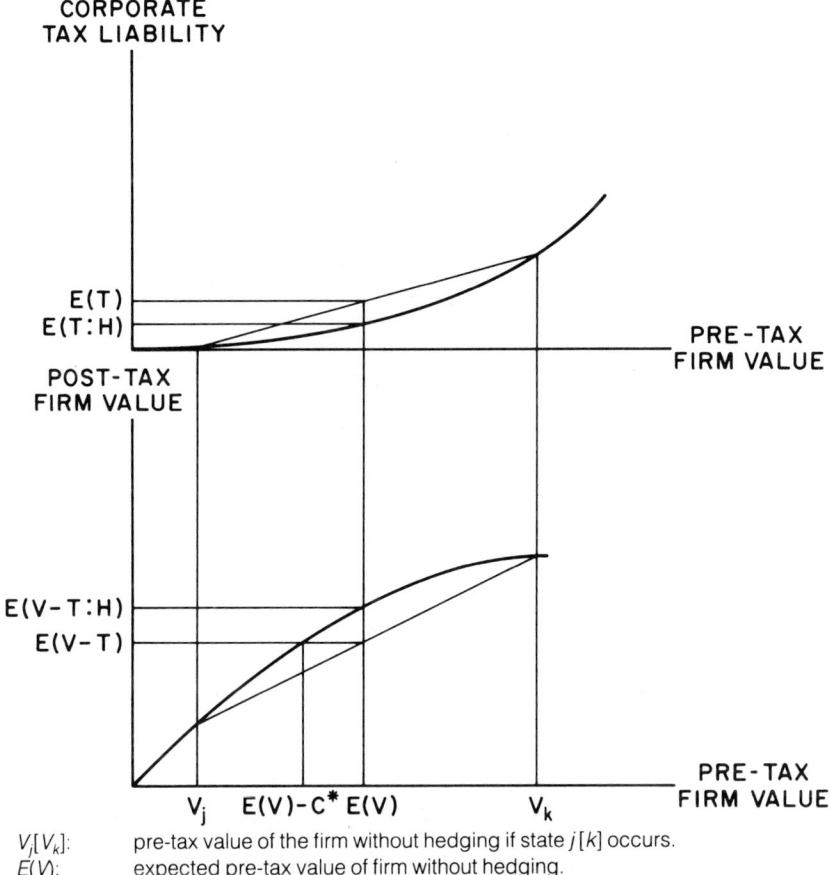

CORPORATE
TAX LIABILITY

E(T)
E(T:H)

PRE-TAX
FIRM VALUE

POST-TAX
FIRM VALUE

E(V−T:H)
E(V−T)

PRE-TAX
FIRM VALUE

V_j $E(V)-C^* E(V)$ V_k

$V_j[V_k]$:	pre-tax value of the firm without hedging if state $j[k]$ occurs.
$E(V)$:	expected pre-tax value of firm without hedging.
$E(T)$:	expected corporate tax liability without hedging.
$E(T:H)$:	corporate tax liability with a costless, perfect hedge.
$E(V-T)$:	expected post-tax firm value without hedging.
$E(V-T:H)$:	post-tax firm value with a costless, perfect hedge.
C^*:	maximum cost of hedging where hedging is profitable.

FIGURE 1

Corporate Tax Liability and Post-Tax Firm Value as a Function of Pre-Tax Firm
Value
(If costless hedging reduces the variability of pre-tax firm value, then the firm's
expected tax liability falls and its expected post-tax value rises.)

A. Hedging and Corporate Tax Liabilities

To analyze the effect of hedging on the present value of the firm's after-tax
cash flow, we employ a state-preference model of firm value. We assume that
there are s states of the world, with V_i defined as the pre-tax value of the firm in
state of the world i. States of the world are numbered so that $V_i \le V_j$, if $i < j$. Let

P_i be the price today of one dollar to be delivered in state of the world i, and $T(V_i)$ be the tax rate if the before-tax value of the firm is V_i. In the absence of leverage, the value of the firm after taxes, $V(0)$, is given by

$$(1) \qquad V(0) = \sum_{i=1}^{S} P_i\left(V_i - T\left(V_i\right)V_i\right).$$

Hedging can increase the value of the firm if there are two states of the world, j and k, such that $T(V_j) < T(V_k)$. To demonstrate this, suppose that the firm holds a hedge portfolio such that $V_j + H_j = V_k + H_k$, and that the hedge portfolio is self-financing in the sense that $P_j H_j + P_k H_k = 0$. (Such a portfolio is feasible if it is possible to create a portfolio that pays one dollar in state j and a portfolio that pays one dollar in state k.) Let $V^H(0)$ be the value of the hedged firm. It follows that

$$(2) \qquad \begin{aligned} V^H(0) - V(0) = &\; P_j\left(T\left(V_j\right)V_j - T\left(V_j + H_j\right)\left(V_j + H_j\right)\right) \\ &+ P_k\left(T\left(V_k\right)V_k - T\left(V_k + H_k\right)\left(V_k + H_k\right)\right) > 0. \end{aligned}$$

(The inequality is implied by the definition of a concave function.) Therefore, costless hedging increases the value of the firm. This analysis also implies that incomplete hedging (i.e., hedging that does not eliminate all uncertainty in future cash flows) also raises firm value.

The previous analysis must be modified if hedging is costly. If transactions costs of hedging do not exceed the benefits identified in (2), i.e., $V^H(0) - V(0)$, hedging increases firm value. The amount of hedging undertaken by the firm depends on the transactions cost structure of hedging. If transactions costs exhibit scale economies, then the firm either hedges completely, if the cost is low enough, or hedges nothing.

Hedging can be costly because the firm purchases before-tax cash flows from investors who receive after-tax cash flows. If the marginal investor's tax function is linear in the payoffs of the hedging instruments, our analysis still holds; the self-financing hedge portfolio analysis is still valid. However, if investors' tax functions are nonlinear and investors face different tax rates across states, the analysis is more complex. It could be the case that the decrease in the firm's expected tax liability from hedging is offset by an increase in the expected tax liability of the investors who enable the firm to hedge. Thus, there may be no impact on expected taxes. Hedging instruments would be priced accordingly and there would be no benefit from hedging. However, in this case, it would pay firms that expect to face a constant tax rate to offer hedging instruments to firms that expect their tax rate to be an increasing function of their cash flow. This mechanism tends to produce hedging instrument prices as if the marginal investor faces a linear tax function.[6]

---

[6] Cornell [6] offers some supporting evidence for this conjecture.

The basic provisions of the corporate tax code (a zero tax rate on negative taxable income, moderate progressivity for taxable income under $100,000 and a constant rate thereafter) yield a convex statutory tax function. The convex region is extended by tax preference items like the investment tax credit that offset a stated maximum fraction, x, of a corporation's tax liability.[7] The effective marginal tax rate is constant only if taxable income exceeds $1/x$ times the corporation's accumulated investment tax credits, a number that can substantially exceed $100,000. DeAngelo and Masulis [7] report that over the period 1964-1973, in any year an average of 27 percent of the firms filing tax returns paid no taxes; for the largest corporations, the average was between 10 percent and 20 percent.

The tax-reducing benefits of hedging increase if the function that yields after-tax income becomes more concave. Thus, if excess-profits taxes or investment-tax credits increase the convexity of the tax function, then such a tax will induce firms to hedge more. Conversely, allowing trading in tax credits reduces the convexity of the tax function and reduces the tax benefits of hedging.[8]

The three-year carry-back, fifteen-year carry-forward provision and the progressivity provisions of the tax code produce local concavities in the tax function.[9] A firm that faces concavities in the tax function finds it profitable to "reverse hedge," increasing the variability of its taxable income over that range of outcomes.

III. Debt and Hedging Policies

A. Transactions Costs of Bankruptcy

Transactions costs of bankruptcy can induce widely-held corporations to hedge.[10] Consider a levered firm that pays taxes on its cash flows net of interest payments to the bondholders. Let F be the face value of debt. If the value of the firm is below F at maturity, the bondholders receive F minus the transactions costs of bankruptcy. Otherwise, the shareholders receive firm value minus both taxes paid and the bondholders' payment, F. The lower are expected bankruptcy

---

[7] For tax years 1983 and 1984, the maximum tax offset by the investment tax credit is 85 percent. It was 50 percent in 1978, and increased by 10 percent per year until it reached 90 percent in 1982.

[8] Regulations are equivalent to in-kind taxes. For example, if unexpectedly large changes in firm value lead politicians to impose additional constraints on the firm, then these additional regulatory costs are like taxes even though they do not result from the filing of a tax form. Note also that if regulations typically impose constraints on firms expressed in terms of accounting numbers, then this establishes incentives for firms to hedge accounting rather than economic values.

[9] The fifteen-year carry forward provision applies only for operating losses. Notice that the existence of a minimum tax introduces further complications. However, the minimum tax tends to make after-tax income more of a concave function of before-tax income, as it implies that some taxes will be paid on positive cash flows. Cordes and Sheffrin [5] present evidence on the use of these provisions.

[10] Diamond [8] also argues that bankruptcy costs lead to hedging. In his model of financial intermediaries, financial intermediaries hedge all systematic risks, i.e., all risks that have no incentive effects. His inclusions are stronger than ours because in his model there are no cases in which it does not pay to hedge, either because of transaction costs or for other reasons discussed in this paper.

costs, the higher the expected payoffs to the firm's claimholders. By reducing the variability of the future value of the firm, hedging lowers the probability of incurring bankruptcy costs. This decrease in expected bankruptcy costs benefits shareholders. Figure 2 illustrates this point. If transactions costs of bankruptcy are a decreasing function of firm value, and the tax rate is either constant or an increasing function of firm value, expected after-tax firm value net of bankruptcy costs is higher if the firm can costlessly hedge.

To extend our analysis, we consider a simple model in which a firm issues debt to create a tax shield. Again, let P_i be the price today of one dollar delivered in state i and $T(V_i)$ be the tax rate, if the before-tax value of the firm is V_i. In the absence of leverage, the after-tax value of the firm is $V(0)$. We assume a leveraged firm issues pure discount bonds with face value F, and pays taxes on its before-tax value net of its payment to the bondholders. The after-tax value of a levered firm with the same investment policy as the unlevered firm is $V(F)$. For simplicity, it is assumed that $V_j < F < V_k$. If $V_i < F$, bankruptcy costs are given by $C(V_i) \leq V_i$. The difference in the value of the levered firm and the unlevered firm is given by

$$(3) \qquad V(F) - V(0) = \sum_{i=1}^{j} P_i \big(T(V_i)V_i - C(V_i) \big) + \sum_{i=k}^{s} P_i T(V_i) F,$$

where F corresponds to the payment to the bondholders in the absence of bankruptcy. By inspection, the value of the levered firm equals the value of the unlevered firm minus the present value of bankruptcy costs plus the present value of the tax shield from interest payments.[11] From equation (3), the value of the levered firm increases with decreases in the present value of expected bankruptcy costs.[12]

To analyze the effects of hedging on expected bankruptcy costs, we examine an unlevered firm whose shareholders plan to issue debt. Since potential bondholders have no market power, shareholders capture any increase in firm value from bond issuance. We assume that investment policy is fixed, ($V_i(0)$ is given for all is), and that any proceeds of a debt issue are distributed to the shareholders as a dividend.

The firm can reduce bankruptcy costs by holding a hedge portfolio that pays positive amounts when the firm would be bankrupt without hedging. To analyze the benefits of hedging, consider a hedge that pays $H_g < 0$ in state g and $H_m > 0$ in state m. We assume the hedge portfolio involves no current cash flows (i.e., $P_g H_g + P_m H_m = 0$) and that $V_g + H_g > F$ and $V_m + H_m > F$. By construction, $V_g < F$. Let $V^H(F)$ be the value of the leveraged firm if the firm hedges. Then, assuming a constant tax rate T, we have

$$(4) \qquad V^H(F) - V(F) = P_g C(V_g) + P_g T(F - V_g).$$

---

[11] The model we employ is similar to those developed by Kraus and Litzenberger [17] and Brennan and Schwartz [4]. While our treatment of taxes is not very sophisticated, it is important to understand that the role played by taxes in this analysis is simply to justify the existence of debt. A more realistic treatment of taxes would not add important insights to our analysis.

[12] Note that with a more sophisticated treatment of taxes the analysis becomes more complex. As the probability of bankruptcy decreases, the promised yield of the debt decreases and so does its tax shield.

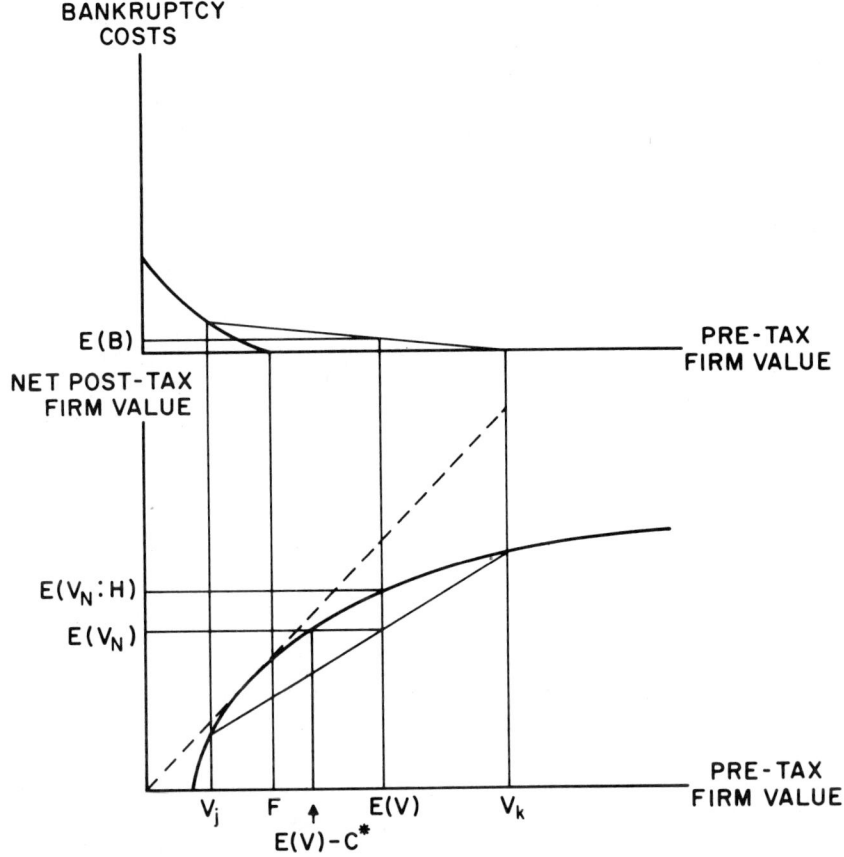

$V_j[V_k]$: pre-tax value of the firm without hedging if state $j[k]$ occurs.
F: face value of the debt.
$E(V)$: expected pre-tax value of the firm without hedging.
$E(V_N)$: net expected post-tax value of the firm without hedging.
$E(V_N{:}H)$: net expected post-tax value of the firm with a perfect, costless hedge.
$E(B)$: expected bankruptcy cost without hedging.
$E(B{:}H)$: expected bankruptcy cost with perfect hedging will be zero in this case.
C^*: maximum cost of hedging where hedging is profitable.

FIGURE 2

Post-Tax Firm Value as a Function of Pre-Tax Firm Value in the Presence of
Bankruptcy Costs
(If costless hedging reduces the variability of pre-tax firm value, then the firm's
expected bankruptcy costs fall and its net (of bankruptcy costs) expected post-tax
value of the firm increases.)

Since $C(V_g) > 0$ and $V_g < F$, $V^H(F) - V(F)$ is always positive. Thus, the hedge decreases the present value of bankruptcy costs and increases the present value of the tax shield of debt. (With a constant tax rate, expected tax payments from the hedge are zero unless the firm is bankrupt when the hedge pays off.) Shareholders benefit from hedging only because bankruptcy involves real costs to stock-holders and bondholders—the direct bankruptcy costs and the loss of debt tax shields.

Again, with costly hedging it is still generally profitable to hedge. However, shareholders must account for hedging costs when they decide among alternative hedging strategies.

B. Bond Covenants and Costs of Financial Distress

For hedging to increase shareholder wealth, the firm must convince poten-tial bondholders that it will hedge after the bond sale and, hence, that expected bankruptcy costs are not as high as the firm's investment policy would otherwise suggest. But potential bondholders recognize that hedging after the sale of the debt is not in the stockholders' best interests. Although hedging increases the value of the firm, it also redistributes wealth from shareholders to bondholders in a way that makes shareholders worse off.[13] Without an incentive to hedge, de-spite promising to do so, it will be difficult for the firm to make a credible an-nouncement that it will hedge.[14]

There are at least two ways that market forces create incentives for share-holders to pursue a hedging policy. First, if the firm borrows frequently, it bene-fits from a reputation for hedging since that reputation increases the price for its new debt. Yet, such a reputation is not likely to be sufficient to insure that the firm will hedge when the probability of bankruptcy is large. Then, the gain from no longer hedging is likely to outweigh the cost of lost reputation, since the repu-tation is valuable only if the firm successfully avoids bankruptcy. Second, hedg-ing provides a means whereby the firm can reduce the costs of financial distress imposed by bond covenants that constrain the shareholders to take actions they would otherwise avoid. For instance, binding bond covenants can force the firm to alter its investment policy; hedging can reduce the likelihood that covenants become binding.

C. Empirical Implications

Warner [28] suggests that transactions costs of bankruptcy are a small frac-tion of large firms' assets. Yet, small bankruptcy costs can be sufficient to induce large firms to hedge, if the reduction in expected bankruptcy costs exceeds the costs of hedging. Warner also indicates that the bankruptcy costs are less than proportional to firm size. If hedging costs are proportional, the reduction in ex-pected bankruptcy costs is greater for the small corporation, and, hence, small firms are more likely to hedge.

A firm can hedge to reduce the expected costs of financial distress. Because bond covenants use accounting numbers to define states where the firm's activi-

---

[13] In this context, the decision not to hedge after debt has been sold has the same effect on the shareholders' wealth as a decision by the firm to substitute a more risky asset for a less risky asset. See [25].

[14] Note that this is an example of a time-inconsistent optimal policy. See [18].

ties are restricted,[15] a firm that wants to decrease the probability of financial distress must manage its accounting numbers so that bond covenants do not become binding. It is thus possible for a value-maximizing firm to choose to reduce the variance of its accounting earnings, even if this increases the variance of economic earnings.[16]

IV. Managerial Compensation, Risk Aversion, and Hedging

The corporation's managers, employees, suppliers, and customers are frequently unable to diversify risks specific to their claims on the corporation. Because they are risk averse, these individuals require extra compensation to bear the nondiversifiable risk of the claims.[17] With limited liability, the amount of risk that can be allocated to the stockholders is restricted by the company's capital stock. But the firm can reduce the risk imposed on other claimholders by hedging. Thus, as long as the reduction in compensation of managers and employees and other suppliers plus the increased revenues from customers exceed the costs of hedging, hedging increases the value of the firm.

A. Managerial Risk Aversion and Hedging

Shareholders hire managers because they have specialized resources that increase the value of the firm. Managers cannot use their expertise unless they have some discretion in the choice of their actions. Yet, unless faced with proper incentives, managers will not maximize shareholder wealth. The managerial compensation contract must be designed so that when managers increase the value of the firm, they also increase their expected utility. Frequently observed provisions of managerial compensation contracts make the manager's total current compensation an increasing function of firm value.[18]

The managers' expected utility depends on the distribution of the firm's payoffs. Hedging changes the distribution of the firm's payoffs and, therefore, changes the managers' expected utility. To analyze the managers' hedging choices, we define hedging as the acquisition of financial assets that reduce the variance of the firm's payoffs. The firm is assumed to acquire a hedge portfolio

---

[15] See [25] for a description and analysis of bond covenants.

[16] One also would expect firms to hedge more if accounting rules are changed to increase the variance of accounting earnings. Thus, firms will hedge less under FASB 52 than under FASB 8, as translation gains and losses are not recognized in earnings when they occur under FASB 52 while they were under FASB 8.

[17] Employees demand higher wages if the probability of layoff is greater. Managers demand higher salaries (or perhaps even an equity stake in the company) if the risks of failure, insolvency, and financial embarrassment are great. Suppliers set more unfavorable terms in long-term contracts with companies whose prospects are more uncertain. And customers, concerned about a company's ability to service their products in the future or fulfill warranty obligations, will be reluctant to buy its products. Reagan and Stulz [22] provide an analysis of risk-sharing when one party of the contract has a comparative advantage in using capital markets to diversify risks away.

[18] See [26] for a description and analysis of the provisions of management compensation contracts and see [11] for a discussion of the specification of bonus plans. Note also that we assume the manager's marginal tax rate is constant. Progressive tax rates only make managerial wealth a more concave function of firm value and thus reinforce our results based on risk aversion alone.

that creates neither a cash inflow nor outflow at acquisition. Let H_i be the payoff of the hedge portfolio in state of the world i so that

$$(5) \qquad H_i = \sum_j N_j \cdot Q_{ij},$$

where N_j is the number of shares of asset j purchased, and Q_{ij} is the payoff of one share of asset j in state of the world i.

To derive the optional hedge portfolio, we assume a two-period world in which the manager's end-of-period wealth equals the sum of his pecuniary compensation plus the payoff of his nontradeable investment in the firm. This implies that the manager's indirect utility function in state i is a function only of his end-of-period wealth in state i, written W_i; and his wealth is an increasing function of the total value of the firm in state i, i.e., $V_i + H_i$,

$$(6) \qquad U_i = U\Big(W\big(V_i + H_i\big)\Big); \quad i = 1, \ldots, S.$$

The indirect utility function of wealth is assumed to be strictly concave; thus, the manager is risk averse. With these assumptions, the manager maximizes expected utility

$$(7) \qquad U = \sum_i P_i \cdot U\Big(W\big(V_i + H_i\big)\Big),$$

where p_i is the probability of state i occurring, subject to the budget condition that

$$(8) \qquad \Sigma_j N_j \cdot Q_{0j} = 0,$$

where Q_{0j} is the price at the beginning of the period of a share of asset j. To obtain the optimal number of shares of each security, N_j, the first-order conditions are

$$(9) \qquad \sum_i P_i \frac{\partial U}{\partial W} W' \frac{Q_{ij}}{Q_{0j}} = \sum_j P_i \frac{\partial U}{\partial W} W' \frac{Q_{ik}}{Q_{0k}}, \quad \text{for all } j \text{ and } k,$$

where W' is the first derivative of function $W(\cdot)$. The first-order conditions state that the marginal increase in expected utility per dollar of security j purchased must equal the marginal increase in expected utility per dollar of security k purchased. To simplify, we assume that all financial assets have equal expected rates of return and that the firm incurs no transactions costs when it purchases or sells financial assets.

The solution to the hedging problem has several interesting properties. First, if the manager's end-of-period wealth is a concave function of the end-of-period firm value, the optimal hedging strategy is to hedge the firm completely, if this is feasible. The expected income of the manager is maximized if the firm is completely hedged, because the expected value of a concave function of a random variable is smaller than the value of the function evaluated at the expected value of the random variable (Jensen's Inequality). As the manager is risk averse, he will choose to bear risk only if he is rewarded for doing so by higher expected income. Since his expected income is maximized when the firm is completely hedged, the manager will choose to bear no risk.[19]

Second, if the manager's end-of-period wealth is a convex functon of the end-of-period firm value, but the manager's expected utility is still a concave function of the end-of-period value of the firm, the optimal strategy generally will be to eliminate some, but not all, uncertainty through hedging. In this case, the expected income of the manager is higher if the firm does not hedge, since his income is a convex function of the value of the firm. However, because the manager is risk averse, he will want to give up some expected income to reduce risk. Faced with a trade off between expected income and risk of income, the manager will not, in general, choose a policy that makes his income riskless.

Third, if the manager's end-of-period utility is a convex function of the end-of-period firm value, Jensen's Inequality implies that the manager's end-of-period utility has a higher expected value if the firm is not hedged at all. Bonus or stock option provisions of compensation plans can make the manager's expected utility a convex function of the value of the firm. If the manager's expected utility is a convex function of the value of the firm, the manager will behave like a risk-seeker even though his expected utility function is a concave function of his end-of-period wealth.

An example of a situation in which a firm does not hedge even though the manager is risk averse can make this point clearer. We assume that the compensation contract promises a payment equal to $T + \text{Max}(V_i - K_i, 0)$. The option-like feature of this contract can be found in many compensation contracts. For simplicity, we assume that $S = 2$ and $V_2 > K > V_1 > T$. The manager is assumed to maximize an expected utility function of the form

$$(10) \qquad U = P_1 \frac{1}{d} W_1^d + P_2 \frac{1}{d} W_2^d; \quad d < 1 .$$

The firm hedges if it purchases financial assets that pay a positive amount in state 1 and a negative amount in state 2. Given our assumptions, the expected payoff of the hedge portfolio must equal zero, which implies that $H_2 = (-p_1/p_2)H_1$. By eliminating H_2 in equation (7) and taking the partial derivative of the manager's expected utility with respect to H_1, one can easily verify that U is a decreasing function of H_1 for positive values of H_1 equal to or smaller than the value of H_1 required to hedge the value of the firm completely. Thus, the structure of the manager's compensation package can induce him not to hedge the firm at all.

Frequently, compensation packages make the manager's end-of-period wealth a concave function of the firm value in some regions and a convex function in others. This suggests that hedging will take place for some values of the firm and not others. Furthermore, for values of the firm that make the manager's end-of-period wealth a convex function of firm value, the manager may choose

---

[19] This result is equivalent to Arrow's [3] proposition that a risk-averse individual offered fairly priced insurance fully insures. See also [14].

454

to "reverse-hedge" (make the value of the firm even more dependent on the realization of some state variable).

We have assumed that the expected rates of return on all financial assets are equal and that transactions costs are negligible.[20] If expected returns to financial assets vary, the manager faces a trade off between expected income and risk of income. In such cases, he will hedge less if hedging involves going short in a portfolio with a high expected return. If transactions costs increase, the firm will hedge less, as hedging decreases the manager's expected end-of-period wealth. We also must assume that the firm has a comparative advantage in hedging over the manager. In other words, it should not pay for the manager to hedge his end-of-period wealth on his personal account. The combination of transactions costs, economies of scale, and the large number of managers within any firm make this comparative advantage likely.[21]

B. Managerial Compensation and Hedging

Our analysis has, thus far, taken as given the form of the management compensation contract. This analysis is interesting in itself since it produces positive statements about the firm's hedging policies. In reality, however, shareholders choose the management compensation package and, thereby, affect the hedging managers undertake. Making managerial wealth a concave function of firm value bonds the firm to a hedging policy. This should be important for a firm with debt or other fixed claims, as it offers greater assurance that the firm will hedge as long as that compensation policy is followed.

Managers whose compensation is a concave (or not too convex) function of firm value have incentives to reduce firm cash flow variability. Hence, such managers might reject variance-increasing positive net present value (NPV) projects. If hedging costs are negligible, it pays to let managers hedge as this increases incentives to take variance-increasing positive NPV projects. If shareholders instead try to prohibit hedging, managers will focus more on nonpriced risks. Still, as long as their compensation depends on firm value, managers have incentives to consider market valuation in evaluating projects.

With costly hedging, shareholders have incentives to devise a compensation plan that discourages managers from devoting excessive resources to hedging. This can be accomplished when computing the manager's compensation by filtering out those changes in firm value that are not under the manager's control and by making the manager's compensation a more convex function of firm value. However, it will generally not be efficient to eliminate all incentives to hedge. Earlier sections have demonstrated that hedging can be profitable. Moreover, a compensation plan that eliminates all hedging incentives would be costly to negotiate and implement.[22]

---

[20] Stulz [27] derives optimal hedging strategies in a continuous-time framework when holding costs for forward contracts are positive and when expected rates of return differ across assets for the case of foreign exchange exposure.

[21] If there is a single manager, scale economies can still induce the manager to hedge through the firm. Note that the size of most futures contracts is too large to make them useful to hedge a manager's income.

[22] The Diamond/Verrecchia [9] analysis suggests that bonus schemes would filter out the effect

A manager's compensation often includes a payment whose value depends on accounting earnings. It follows that the manager's expected utility depends on both the firm's market value and its accounting earnings. If the manager's expected utility depends heavily on accounting earnings and is a concave function of accounting earnings, one would expect the firm to principally hedge accounting earnings even if doing so increases the variance of the firm's economic value.

Managers' risk aversion can lead them to hedge, but it does not necessarily do so. If the compensation package of the manager is such that his income is a convex function of the value of the firm, it can be the case that the manager is better off if the firm does not hedge. Hence, the more option-like features in a firm's compensation plan, the less the firm is expected to hedge. For instance, bonus plans that make a payment to managers only if accounting earnings exceed some target number will induce managers to hedge less since this payment is a convex function of accounting earnings.

If the manager owns a significant fraction of the firm, one would expect the firm to hedge more, as the manager's end-of-period wealth is more a linear function of the value of the firm. This reinforces the incentive for closely-held firms to hedge since the owners are unlikely to hold well-diversified portfolios and, thus, have incentives to induce managers to reduce the variance of the firm's returns.

V. Summary and Conclusions

This paper presents an analysis of the hedging behavior of firms that differs fundamentally from the existing literature. Rather than assuming that the firm is risk averse, we follow modern finance theory and assume that incentives exist within the contracting process to maximize the market value of the firm. We then show that a value-maximizing firm can hedge for three reasons: (1) taxes, (2) costs of financial distress, and (3) managerial risk aversion. Our analysis offers a framework within which the wide diversity of hedging practices among firms can be understood.

Further research should focus on empirical tests of the implications of our analysis. To implement the tests, however, more detailed data are required than are available from sources such as *Compustat,* in which firms' hedging activities are aggregated with other contingent outcomes such as insurance contracts and outstanding lawsuits. Transactions, such as mergers, also accomplish some of the same results as hedging, although it is likely to be difficult to appropriately control for other changes in investment and financing policy to focus on these hedging characteristics.

---

of variables over which management has no control. However, the difficulty in administering such a scheme must explain why they are rarely observed.

456 References

[1] Anderson, R. W., and J. P. Danthine. "Hedging and Joint Production: Theory and Illustrations." *Journal of Finance*. Vol. 35 (May 1980), pp. 487-497.

[2] _____. "Cross Hedging." *Journal of Political Economy,* Vol. 89 (December 1981), pp. 1182-1196.

[3] Arrow, Kenneth J. "Uncertainty and the Welfare Economics of Medical Care." *American Economic Review,* Vol. 53 (December 1963), pp. 943-973.

[4] Brennan, Michael, and Eduardo Schwartz. "Corporate Income Taxes, Valuation, and the Problem of Optimal Capital Structure." *Journal of Business,* Vol. 51 (January 1978), pp. 103-114.

[5] Cordes, J. J., and S. M. Sheffrin. "Estimating the Tax Advantage of Corporate Debt." *Journal of Finance,* Vol. 38 (March 1983), pp. 95-105.

[6] Cornell, B. "Taxes and the Pricing of Treasury Bill Futures Contracts: A Note." *Journal of Finance,* Vol. 36 (December 1981), pp. 1169-1176.

[7] DeAngelo, Harry, and Ronald Masulis. "Optimal Capital Structure under Corporate and Personal Taxation." *Journal of Financial Economics,* Vol. 8 (March 1980), pp. 3-29.

[8] Diamond, D. W. "Financial Intermediation and Delegated Monitoring." *Review of Economic Studies,* Vol. 51 (July 1984), pp. 393-414.

[9] Diamond, Douglas, and Robert Verrecchia. "Optimal Managerial Contracts and Equilibrium Security Prices." *Journal of Finance,* Vol. 37 (May 1982), pp. 275-287.

[10] Feder, G.; R. E. Just; and A. Schmitz. "Futures Market and the Theory of the Firm under Uncertainty." *Quarterly Journal of Economics,* Vol. 94 (March 1980), pp. 317-328.

[11] Healy, Paul. "The Impact of Accounting Bonus Schemes on the Selection of Accounting Principles." University of Rochester, Unpublished Ph.D. Dissertation (1983).

[12] Ho, Thomas S. Y., and Anthony Saunders. "Fixed Rate Loan Commitments, Take-Down Risk, and the Dynamics of Hedging with Futures." *Journal of Financial and Quantitative Analysis,* Vol. 18 (December 1983), pp. 499-516.

[13] Holthausen, J. M. "Hedging and the Competitive Firm under Uncertainty." *American Economic Review,* Vol. 69 (December 1979), pp. 989-995.

[14] Huberman, Gur; David Mayers; and Clifford W. Smith, Jr. "Optimal Insurance Policy Indemnity Schedules." *Bell Journal of Economics,* Vol. 14 (Autumn 1983), pp. 415-426.

[15] Jacques, L. "Management of Foreign Exchange Risk: A Review Article." *Journal of International Business Studies,* Vol. 11 (Spring-Summer 1981), pp. 81-101.

[16] Jagannathan, Ravi. "Call Options and the Risk of Underlying Securities." *Journal of Financial Economics,* Vol. 13 (September 1984), pp. 425-434.

[17] Kraus, Alan, and Robert Litzenberger. "A State Preference Model of Optimal Financial Leverage." *Journal of Finance,* Vol. 28 (September 1973), pp. 911-922.

[18] Kydland, R. E., and E. C. Prescott. "Rules Rather than Discretion: The Inconsistency of Optimal Plans." *Journal of Political Economy,* Vol. 85 (June 1977), pp. 513-548.

[19] Makin, J. H. "Portfolio Theory and the Problem of Foreign Exchange Risk." *Journal of Finance,* Vol. 33 (May 1978), pp. 517-534.

[20] Mayers, David, and Clifford Smith. "On the Corporate Demand for Insurance." *Journal of Business,* Vol. 55 (April 1982), pp. 281-296.

[21] Modigliani, Franco, and Merton Miller. "The Cost of Capital, Corporation Finance and the Theory of Investment." *American Economic Review,* Vol. 48 (June 1958), pp. 261-297.

[22] Reagan, Patricia B., and René M. Stulz. "Risk Sharing, Labor Contracts and Capital Markets." University of Rochester, Unpublished Manuscript (1983).

[23] Rodriguez, R. *Foreign Exchange Management in U.S. Multinationals*. Lexington, Massachusetts: D. C. Heath (1980).

[24] Rolfo, Jacques. "Optimal Hedging under Price and Quantity Uncertainty: The Case of a Cocoa Producer." *Journal of Political Economy*, Vol. 88 (February 1980), pp. 100-116.

[25] Smith, Clifford, and Jerold Warner. "On Financial Contracting: An Analysis of Bond Covenants." *Journal of Financial Economics*, Vol. 7 (June 1979), pp. 117-161.

[26] Smith, Clifford, and Ross Watts. "Incentive and Tax Effects of U.S. Executive Compensation Plans." *Australian Journal of Management*, Vol. 7 (December 1982), pp. 139-157.

[27] Stulz, René. "Optimal Hedging Policies." *Journal of Financial and Quantitative Analysis*, Vol. 19 (June 1984), pp. 127-140.

[28] Warner, Jerold. "Bankruptcy Costs: Some Evidence." *Journal of Finance*, Vol. 32 (May 1977), pp. 337-348.

The Market for Interest Rate Swaps

Clifford W. Smith, Jr., Charles W. Smithson, and Lee Macdonald Wakeman

Clifford W. Smith, Jr. is a Professor of Finance at the William E. Simon Graduate School of Business Administration, University of Rochester, Rochester, NY. Charles W. Smithson is a Vice President at Continental Bank, Chicago, IL. Lee Macdonald Wakeman is a Vice President at Chemical Bank, New York, NY.

■ A swap involves an exchange of cash flows between the parties to the contract; in an interest rate swap, one party periodically pays a cash flow determined by a fixed interest rate and receives a cash flow determined by a floating interest rate. Although the instrument only first appeared in 1982,[1] U.S. dollar interest rate swaps have grown into a market with 1987 volume estimated at $542 billion.[2] With such growth has come concern about the risks in this market. Indeed, in their capital adequacy proposal, the Federal Reserve and the Bank of England suggest, "The credit risks inherent in such contracts now constitute a significant element of the risk profiles of some banking organizations, notab-

ly the large multinational banking organizations that act as intermediaries between end-users of these contracts."[3] The Bank for International Settlements asserts that the credit risk of swaps is underpriced, "gross income from the transaction is insufficient, on average, to compensate fully for their inherent risks."[4] These statements reflect a misconception about default risks inherent in interest rate swaps as well as about the motivation for the growth of the market—misconcep-

---

This research was partially supported by the John M. Olin Foundation and the Managerial Economics Research Center, William E. Simon Graduate School of Business Administration, University of Rochester. We thank George Benston, Wayne Marr, David Mayers, Ren Stulz, our colleagues at the Simon School, and the two referees of this journal for their comments.

---

[1]The first swap contract to appear was the currency swap, publicly introduced via the transaction between IBM and the World Bank in 1981 (although several private currency swaps had been arranged earlier). The currency coupon swap extended the fixed-fixed nature of a currency swap to the exchange of a cash flow based on a fixed interest rate in one currency for one based on a floating interest rate in another. The interest rate swap evolved as a special case of a currency coupon swap in which all payments are made in a single currency. For more on these and other swap contracts see Smith, Smithson, and Wakeman [23].

Exhibit 1. Decomposition of a Simple Interest Rate Swap

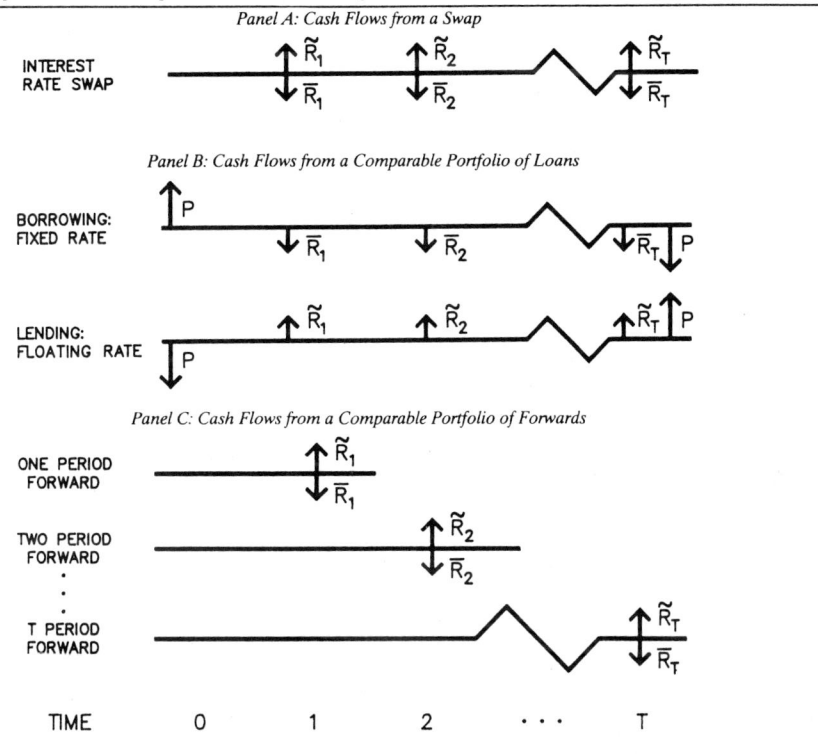

In Panel A the party receives cash flows $(\tilde{R}_t)$ determined by the relevant floating interest rate and pays cash flows $(\bar{R}_t)$ determined by the fixed interest rate at origination. Note that inflows are denoted by up arrows and outflows by down arrows; the magnitude of the cash flow is indicated by the length of the arrow. In Panel B the swap is decomposed into a portfolio of two loan contracts: borrowing at a fixed-rate and lending at a floating-rate, where $\bar{R}_t$ are the fixed coupon payments, $\tilde{R}_t$ are the floating coupon payments, and P is the principal. In Panel C, the swap is decomposed into a portfolio of T forward contracts in which the party illustrated has agreed at origination to pay at period t in the future a known amount $(\bar{R}_t)$ to receive an amount determined by the prevailing single-period interest rate $(\tilde{R}_t)$.

tions that have their root in misunderstandings of the instrument.

I. Analysis of an Interest Rate Swap

A simple interest rate swap contract is illustrated in Panel A of Exhibit 1. The cash flows are based on a "notional" principle, P, which is used to calculate the cash

flows but normally is not exchanged. At stipulated settlement dates (typically every six months) the firm in Exhibit 1 pays a "coupon" determined by the fixed interest rate prevailing at contract origination $(\bar{R}_t)$. In return, the firm receives a "coupon" based on the re-

---

[2]The notional principal of outstanding US dollar interest rate swaps as reported in the International Swap Dealers Association, Survey of Members, July 1988.

[3]See the Federal Reserve Bank and Bank of England ([7], p. 3). Also see, E.N. Berg, "Fed Urges Swap Plan for Banks," New York Times, (March 3, 1987).

[4]See the Bank for International Settlements ([1], p. 3).

levant floating interest rate, $\tilde{R}_t$ (the six-month rate in effect at $t - 1$).[5] Hence, throughout the swap the cash flow at the next settlement is non-stochastic. Operationally, gross cash flows are not exchanged; only the net is paid as a difference check from the party that would have received the smaller payment. Thus, the firm illustrated in Exhibit 1 receives a difference check, $D_t = \tilde{R}_t - \bar{R}_t$, at time t.[6]

A. An Interest Rate Swap as a Portfolio of Loans

As illustrated in Exhibit 1, the swap cash flows in Panel A are equivalent to the pair of loan contracts in Panel B—borrowing at a fixed-rate and simultaneously lending at a floating-rate. To prevent arbitrage, the value at origination of the T-period swap, $S(O,T)$, must equal the difference between the values of a T-period floating-rate note, $\tilde{L}(O,T)$, and a T-period fixed-rate note, $\bar{L}(O,T)$,[7]

$$S(O,T) = \tilde{L}(O,T) - \bar{L}(O,T). \qquad (1)$$

Employing market rates, the value of each loan is zero at origination; hence, the value of the swap contract also must be zero at origination, $S(O,T) = O$. After origination the swap value is determined by realized rates.

The value of the fixed-rate loan, $\bar{L}(O,T)$, can be decomposed into the net present value of a fixed-rate annuity with a vector of payments $\bar{R}_T$ and a T-period zero coupon bond with face value P_T,

$$\bar{L}(O,T) = NPV[\bar{R}_T] + NPV[P_T]. \qquad (2)$$

The value of the floating-rate loan, $\tilde{L}(O,T)$, can be decomposed into the values of a vector of floating-rate annuity payments $\tilde{R}_T$ and the same T-period zero,

$$\tilde{L}(O,T) = NPV[\tilde{R}_T] + NPV[P_T]. \qquad (3)$$

Thus, the value of the swap in Exhibit 1 also is the difference between the values of floating and fixed-rate annuities,

$$S(O,T) = NPV[\tilde{R}_T] - NPV[\bar{R}_T]. \qquad (4)$$

The Impact of Interest Rate Changes on Swap Value

Increases in market rates reduce the value of the fixed-rate loan by reducing the value of both the fixed-rate annuity and the embedded zero-coupon bond,

$$\frac{\partial \bar{L}(O,T)}{\partial \tilde{r}(t,t+1)} = \frac{\partial NPV[\bar{R}_T]}{\partial \tilde{r}(t,t+1)} + \frac{\partial NPV[P_T]}{\partial \tilde{r}(t,t+1)} < 0. \qquad (5)$$

However, on interest rate reset dates, rate increases leave the value of a default-free floating-rate note unaffected. That is, at a settlement date,

$$\frac{\partial \tilde{L}(O,T)}{\partial \tilde{r}(t,t+1)} = \frac{\partial NPV[\tilde{R}_T]}{\partial \tilde{r}(t,t+1)} - \frac{\partial NPV[P_T]}{\partial \tilde{r}(t,t+1)} = 0. \qquad (6)$$

Since increases in rates unambiguously reduce the value of the imbedded zero, they must increase the value of the floating-rate annuity by an equal amount. Thus, higher rates increase the swap value,

$$\frac{\partial S(O,T)}{\partial \tilde{r}(t,t+1)} = \frac{\partial NPV[\tilde{R}_T]}{\partial \tilde{r}(t,t+1)} - \frac{\partial NPV[\bar{R}_T]}{\partial \tilde{r}(t,t+1)} > 0. \qquad (7)$$

As Equation (7) indicates, the derivative of the swap value with respect to rate changes is greater than that of either the fixed or floating-rate annuity. The relative contribution of the fixed and floating-rate terms to interest-rate responsiveness depends on the maturity of the swap. For shorter term swaps, the change in the value of the floating-rate annuity dominates, but for longer term swaps, the change in the fixed-rate annuity dominates.

Equation (7) demonstrates that on reset dates the value of the Exhibit 1 swap is inversely related to the value of a comparable maturity fixed-rate bond. This is obvious from using Equation (5) to combine Equations (6) and (7) to obtain,

---

[5]Swaps generally specify that the rate for the next period is set using the appropriate floating interest rate two days prior to the current period's settlement date.

[6]An expected coupon payment for the floating rate loan is $\tilde{R}_t = \tilde{r}(t-1,t)P$, where $\tilde{r}(t-1,t)$ is the forward rate. The coupon payments for the fixed rate loan are $\bar{R}_t = r(O,T)P$, where $r(O,T)$ is the par rate—i.e., the rate for T-period bond that pays a level coupon and sells at par at origination. Therefore, the difference checks for the swap in Exhibit 1 are $D_t = [\tilde{r}(t-1,t) \, r(O,T)]P$.

---

[7]Note that this arbitrage result does not depend on the assumption that the contracts are default-risk free. With default risk, as long as the borrowing is collateralized with the lending agreement, the cash flows in Panels A and B are always equivalent.

Exhibit 2. Payoff Profile for a Swap at a Representative Settlement Date

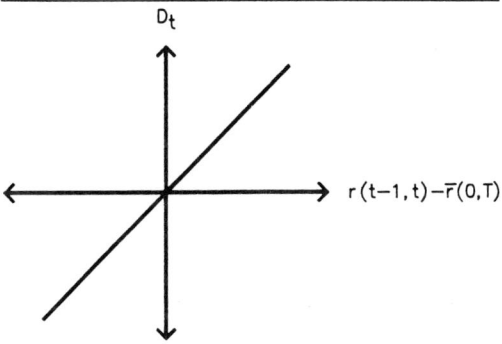

The value of a typical swap difference check, D_t, received by the party paying fixed and receiving floating. The value of the check increases as the realized forward rate, $r(t - 1,t)$, is greater than the par rate at origination, $\bar{r}(O,T)$. This exhibit also can be used to illustrate the relation between swap, forward, and futures contracts. The value to the seller of a forward contract behaves similarly; but, the par rate is replaced by the forward rate, $\bar{r}(t - 1,t)$. The value of the day t settlement to the seller for a futures contract also behaves similarly; but, the rate difference is between the futures rate calculated on day t and that from day $t - 1$.

$$\frac{\partial S(O,T)}{\partial \bar{r}(t,t+1)} = -\frac{\partial \bar{L}(O,T)}{\partial \bar{r}(t,t+1)}. \qquad (8)$$

This restatement of the relation explains why, at rate-reset dates, the interest rate sensitivity of a swap is equal in magnitude to the interest rate sensitivity of a fixed-rate bond of the same maturity and coupon, even though the swap principal is only notional.

Thus far we have focused on rate-induced changes in the value of the swap at a settlement date. Between settlement dates, the amount of the next floating-rate payment is known. Therefore, Equation (6) does not hold for all $r(t,t+1)$ and the responsiveness of the swap value to interest-rate changes is reduced, since the derivative of the floating-rate loan value with respect to the spot rate is negative. Thus, the sign of the Equation (7) derivative can be reversed. For example, in period T if the party in Exhibit 1 is to receive the final difference check, subsequent increases in interest rates lower the remaining swap value.

B. An Interest Rate Swap as a Portfolio of Forward Contracts

Panel C of Exhibit 1 illustrates that a default-free interest rate swap can also be decomposed into a portfolio of forwards, one maturing at each settlement date. Exhibit 2 illustrates the payoff profile for one settlement date. If rates rise, the firm receives an inflow; if rates fall, the firm makes an outflow. Hence, a swap is like a portfolio of forward contracts, with maturities corresponding to the settlement dates specified in the swap. At each settlement the losses or gains in the currently maturing forward are realized. However, since a swap specifies the T-period par rate, $\bar{r}(O,T)$, in each embedded forward rather than the individual time-zero forward rates, $\bar{r}(t,t+1)$, the cash flows from a swap and that from a portfolio of forwards will differ unless the term structure is flat.

II. Swaps And Default Risk

The appropriate swap default premium is an issue of major concern to market participants. The chairman of the International Swap Dealers Association or ISDA effectively summarized the views of many market participants when he asserted: "The credit aspect of swaps is not being adequately remunerated in the market. There's a credit spread of 150 basis points in the loan market but of only 5 to 10 basis points in swaps. The weakest credits are getting a terrific deal."[8] This assertion that the credit/default risk of swaps is mispriced relative to that of loans requires that we examine the differences between default on a loan versus a swap. Yet it is by viewing swaps as a portfolio of forward contracts that we gain the most insights into the default risk of an interest rate swap.

A. Default Risk of Swaps vs. Loans

A crucial difference between default on interest rate swaps and default on loans is that the principal in an interest rate swap is only notional, whereas a major component of the expected loss in lending involves principal repayment. Suppose the firm in Exhibit 1 defaults at time t. For default on a fixed-rate loan like the one in Panel B, the loss to the counterparty is the sum of the present values of the principal, P, and the coupon payments, $\bar{R},...,\bar{R}_T$. In contrast, Panel A de-

[8]A quote from Patrick de Saint-Aignan as reported in David Shirreff, "The Fearsome Growth of Swaps," *Euromoney* (October 1985), pp. 247–261.

Exhibit 3. An Off-Market-Rate Swap

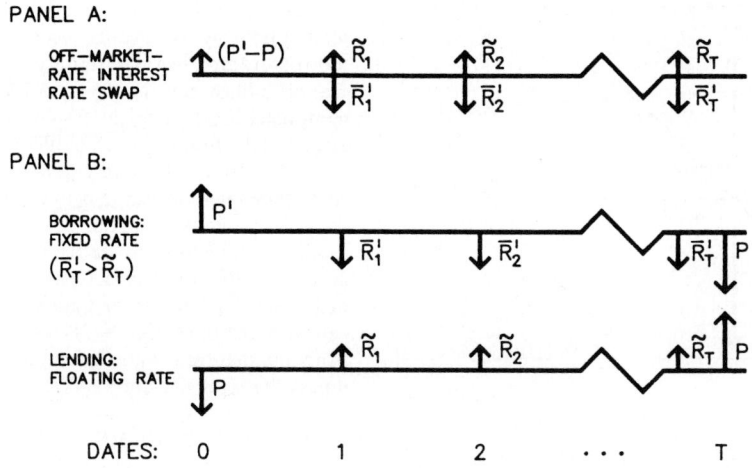

The party pays cash flows $(\bar{R}'_t)$ determined by a fixed interest rate above the current market rate and receives cash flows $(\tilde{R}_t)$ determined by the relevant floating interest rate. In Panel A, a principal exchange $(P' - P)$ occurs at origination, with P' equal to the market value of a bond with coupons $\bar{R}'_t$ and a principal repayment of P. In Panel B this swap is decomposed into two loan contracts: borrowing at a fixed rate higher than the prevailing market rate and lending at the market floating rate.

monstrates that the counterparty in a swap will suffer no principal loss.

Moreover, in a swap the lost cash flow in periods $t,...,T$ is reduced from $\bar{R}_t$ to $\bar{R}_t - \tilde{R}_t$—the difference between fixed and floating-rates rather than the level of the rate. If rates have fallen since the contract was originated, the remaining cash flows look like those of an off-market-rate swap. Consider again the swap in Exhibit 1, but suppose the specified fixed-rate exceeds the current rate, producing off-market coupons, $\bar{R}'_i > \bar{R}_i$. Defining P' as the value of a bond with coupons of $\bar{R}'_i$ and a principal repayment of P, this off-market swap with a net principal inflow at origination is illustrated in Panel A of Exhibit 3. Panel B decomposes the swap into two loans where the coupon payment $\bar{R}'_i$ is higher than $\bar{R}_i$ and the final principal payment, P, is less than P'. Hence, in an off-market-rate swap, the party receives a principle inflow at origination and expects to pay difference checks over the term of the swap. Thus the required initial principal exchange, $P' - P$, reflects the current market loss to the floating-rate payer were the fixed-rate payer to default.

Finally, when comparing swaps and loans, it must be remembered that rational default requires the remaining value of the contract to be negative. For example, if rates have risen since origination, then for the swap in Exhibit 1 the remaining net present value of the contract is positive. Therefore, default by the fixed-rate payer would be irrational since it would result in the cancellation of a profitable contract.[9] Consequently, the pricing implications of default are significantly smaller for a swap than for a loan.

B. Default Risk in Forwards, Futures, and Swaps

In many ways, the probability of default on a swap is more like the default problem in forward and futures contracts than loans. As with forwards and futures,

---

[9]In the special case where the term structure is flat and interest rates have remained unchanged since origination of the swap, $\bar{R}_t - \tilde{R}_t = O$ for all $t = 1,...t$; so, the remaining value of the swap is the same as the value at origination $[S(t,T) = S(O,T) = O]$. Hence in this special case, default costs are limited to the transaction costs of locating a replacement counterparty.

swap default risk is two-sided. However, loans, annuities, deposits, and non-assessable insurance policies are structured so that after origination, payments only go in one direction—one of the parties to the contract bears all the default risk. Consequently, insights into swap default risk can be gained by comparing default control mechanisms for swaps with those of forwards and futures.[10] We examine three of these mechanisms: the way contract value is distributed, the way the contract is traded, and performance bonds.

Distributing Contract Value The way value changes are distributed to the contracting parties differs across forward, futures, and swap contracts. At one extreme is the futures contract, where the total change in the value of the contract is distributed daily. At the other extreme is the forward contract, where value is distributed to the owners only at contract maturity. Swaps fall between these extremes; difference checks distribute value changes periodically over the contract life, not just at maturity. However, since the difference check in an interest rate swap only reflects the maturing embedded forward contract, a difference check generally does not distribute the entire value change.

These differences in the distribution of contract value have implications for the probability of default. Since a futures contract is cash-settled daily, losses from default are limited to a one-day value change. Conversely, since a forward contract requires no settlement prior to maturity, the value change can be significantly larger. Hence, potential default risk is greater for forward contracts than futures contracts, all else being equal. Swaps are again an intermediate case; difference checks provide a periodic partial settlement. Moreover, default on any of the required difference-check payment accelerates the remaining payments. With default, the swap reverts from a portfolio of forward contracts to a single, currently due contract.

Trading the Contracts Forward, futures, and swap contracts differ with respect to the manner in which they are traded. Futures contracts are always exchange traded. While the exchange itself takes no positions, it guarantees the performance of all participants through its clearinghouse. Hence, the problem of two-sided default risk is addressed by the exchange interposing itself between parties in each transaction. Most forward contracts (for example, on foreign exchange and interest rates) are marketed by financial institutions. Since a bank is one of the counterparties to every transaction, economies of scale in credit evaluation can be achieved, but default risk is still counterparty specific. Some forward contracts are exchange traded, notably forward contracts on tin and several other metals on the London Metal Exchange. That exchange's recent experience demonstrates that the existence of an exchange does not eliminate default risk (the "tin cartel" defaulted on contracts for tin delivery, making the exchange liable for the loss.[11] With an exchange, the cost of default is spread over all the traded contracts rather than imposed on a specific counterparty (as with most forward contracts).

Early in their evolution, swaps were negotiated on an individual basis (particularly currency swaps). A financial intermediary would arrange a swap between two parties known to each other. Development of a secondary market allowing firms to trade swaps was necessarily limited. With matched counterparties, there was an understandable reluctance to permit transferring swap contracts, since such transference would rationally induce the uninvolved party to expend resources to evaluate the prospective new counterparty's default risk.

As the interest rate swap market has evolved, banks have taken more of the intermediary role. Today, the majority of interest rate swaps involve a bank as a counterparty, thereby achieving significant economies in credit evaluation. Furthermore, problems related to the transferring of swaps have been reduced, since the firm can cancel an interest rate swap contract with a bank via a cash settlement or by "unwinding" the contract (entering into another swap with provisions the reverse of the first).

Performance Bonds The exchange-traded futures contracts require an explicit performance bond to be posted. This bond, the initial margin, typically is equal to the maximum daily fluctuation permitted in the value of the contract. Each day, the contract is settled by drawing down or adding to the margin account. The futures contract also requires that the margin account balance exceed a specified minimum (the maintenance margin). If, as the result of daily settlements the ac-

---

[10]There exists a wealth of literature on the valuation of default-free forward and futures contracts. See Black [3], Oldfield/Messina [17], Kane [11], Jarrow/Oldfield [9], Cox, Ingersoll, and Ross [6], and Richard Sundaresan [19]. French [8] provides empirical tests of the relation between forward prices and futures prices.

[11]See "Tin Crisis in London Roils Metal Exchange" in *The Wall Street Journal* of November 13, 1985.

Exhibit 4. The Impact of a Rising Structure of Interest Rates on Swap Payments and Default

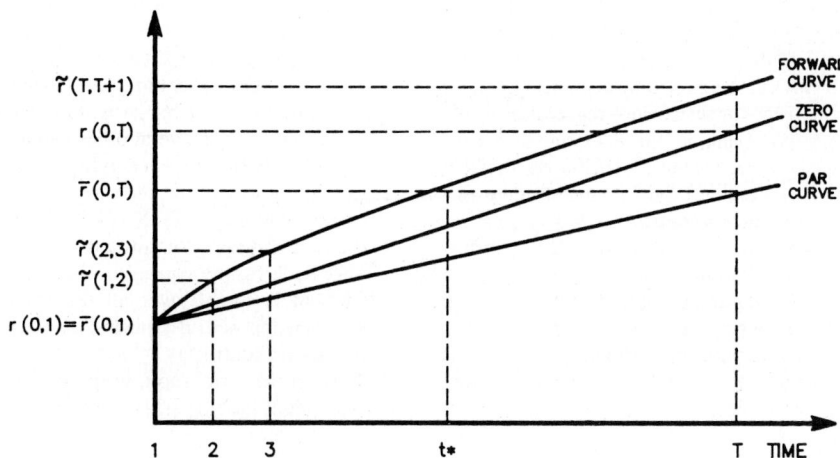

The zero curve displays the yields to maturity of zero coupon bonds. The forward curve displays the implied one period forward interest rates. The par curve displays the per period rate for a bond which pays a level coupon and sells at par for different maturities. At time t^*, the implied forward rate, $\tilde{r}(t^* - 1, t)$, equals the T-period par rate.

count balance falls below that minimum, the contract owner is required to bring the margin account back to the initial level or the contract is closed out. These mechanisms, in place and functioning, substantially reduce the threat of default for futures contracts.

Exchanges also impose other rules to reduce default risk. Some markets allow collateralization as a substitute for posting margin, thereby lowering the cost of market participation to hedgers. Futures exchanges impose limits on daily price moves, a practice which Brennan [4] argues is a partial substitute for posting margin (but one that is less effective in financial markets where alternative sources of information about equilibrium prices are available). Finally, exchange transactions must be executed through a member firm which endorses the transaction—and thus effectively imposes a potential liability on itself should its customer fail to perform. Hence, this broker endorsement increases the broker's incentive to monitor its customers' margin accounts (Sharpe [21], p. 528).

In the swap market, margin or other forms of explicit performance bonds are not required for good credits, but they are employed for poor credits. The most fre-

quently employed performance bond is to require a poor credit to post collateral in the form of a portfolio of financial securities.

In addition, performance bonding through insurance has also been employed. The World Bank established a swap insurance program which divides the cash flows from the swap between the World Bank and the Aetna Casualty and Surety Company—the World Bank retains the interest-rate risk and Aetna assumes the default risk. This swap insurance program acts like private mortgage insurance; the insurer (here Aetna) bonds the counterparty against default.

C. Other Determinants of Default Risk for Interest Rate Swaps

The Use of the Swap As suggested above, default requires that both the contract value be negative and the contract owner be in bankruptcy. An interest rate swap could be used either to speculate on or hedge against changes in interest rates. Clearly, the risk of default on the contract is influenced by the use to which instrument is put. If a firm's cash flows are sensitive to interest rate changes, and if it enters into a swap con-

Exhibit 5. Illustration of the Purported Gains from Credit Risk Arbitrage via an Interest Rate Swap

Credit Rating of Firm	AAA	BBB
Cost of Directly Borrowing Fixed	10.8%	12.0%
Cost of Directly Borrowing Floating	LIBOR + 0.25%	LIBOR + 0.75%
Fund		
AAA Borrows Fixed	10.8%	
BBB Borrows Floating		LIBOR + 0.75%
Swap		
AAA Receives Fixed	10.9%	
AAA Pays Floating	LIBOR	
BBB Receives Floating		LIBOR
BBB Pays Fixed		10.9%
All-in cost of funding	LIBOR - 0.1%	11.65%
Savings	0.35%	0.35%

tract as a hedge, the probability of financial distress and bankruptcy is reduced—and outflow is required only when the hedging firm's other net cash flows are expected to be higher. In contrast, if a swap contract is used to speculate, an outflow may well be required when the firm is in financial distress. Thus, with a swap contract, default risk is endogenous, so the default risk and therefore the appropriate risk premium is partially determined by the use to which the instrument is put.

Term Structure Given that the credit risk assessment process is in place, default implies a deterioration in the firm's financial position since contract origination. Hence, the probability of default is a positive function of the time since contract initiation. As we note above, a fixed-rate payer like the one illustrated in Exhibit 1 will make payments determined by the par rate at origination and will receive payments determined by future floating-rates. If the term structure is upward sloping, as in Exhibit 4, the fixed-rate payer expects to pay difference checks for periods $1,2,...,t^*$ and receive difference checks thereafter. Hence, if the term structure is upward sloping, the expectation is that the party paying fixed and receiving floating (the party in Exhibit 1) will pay difference checks early in the term of the swap and receive net payments in the later periods. In terms of Exhibit 4, this means that $\bar{r}(t - 1,t) - r(O,T)$ is expected to be negative in the early periods and positive in the later periods. Thus, the probability that the

fixed-rate payer will default is less than would be the case if the term structure were flat or had a negative slope.

III. The Rationale for Interest-Rate Swaps

So far we have seen that interest rate swaps fit on a continuum between forward and futures contracts. But this relation between swaps, forwards, and futures raises another question: since forwards and futures are substitutes for swaps, what explains the dramatic growth of the interest rate swap market?

A. Financial Arbitrage

The most frequently advanced argument to explain the growth of the swap market is that swaps exploit market inefficiencies. For example, Mr. Robin Leigh-Pemberton, governor of the Bank of England, argued that swaps enable borrowers to "arbitrage" the credit markets, allowing "...a good credit rating in one part of the currency/maturity matrix to be translated into relatively cheap borrowing in another."[12] Bicksler/Chen [2] reiterated this position by asserting that pricing is inconsistent across financial markets and that the "difference in the quality spreads presents a market arbitrage opportunity" which can be exploited via a swap. An illustration of borrowers taking advantage of the differential quality spreads to which Bicksler/Chen alluded is provided in Exhibit 5.[13] In this exhibit, the quality spread in the fixed-rate market is 1.2%, but only 0.5% in the floating-rate market. The assertion is this quality-spread differential can be "arbitraged"—the AAA borrows fixed, the BBB borrows floating, and via a swap each ends up with lower borrowing costs.[14]

The illustration in Exhibit 5 is consistent with both available data on quality differentials and the observation that fixed-rate payers are predominantly the less creditworthy counterparty. However, it is less clear that this behavior is consistent with classic financial arbitrage. First, arbitrage should lead to decreasing, not

---

[12]A quote in "The Risk Game: A Survey of International Banking," by Merril Stevenson in *The Economist*, March 21, 1987.

[13]This illustration was taken from "The International Swap Market," an advertising supplement by Bankers Trust Company to *Euromoney Corporate Finance*, September 1985.

[14]The implicit assertion that the quality differential can be used to the benefit of all parties—the two borrowers and the financial intermediary—was examined by Turnbull [27]. He shows that with perfect markets, swaps must be a zero sum game.

increasing, swap volumes; as the quality spread is arbitraged, the rate differences would be eliminated and this rationale for interest rate swaps should disappear. Second, the underlying reason for the quality differentials is ignored.

Comparative Advantage The trade press explains quality differentials by asserting that firms have a "comparative advantage" in one of the credit markets. The AAA has a comparative advantage in the fixed-rate market, and the BBB in the floating-rate market. The interest rate swap permits them to exploit their comparative advantages and produce interest rate savings. However, the comparative-advantage argument does neglect arbitrage. With no barriers to capital flows, this argument from elementary trade theory cannot hold. Arbitrage eliminates any comparative advantage.

Underpriced Credit Risk It has been suggested that fixed-rate and that floating-rate lenders assess risk differently. For example, Ramaswamy/Sundaresan [18] find that default premiums for floating-rate loans are lower than predicted. While underpriced credit risk for floating-rate loans would explain the growth of interest rate swaps, swaps effectively increase the demand for floating-rate debt by lower-rated companies and the demand for fixed-rate debt by higher-rated companies. This should eliminate the supposed differential pricing.

Differential Prepayment Options The apparent savings from obtaining funding via a swap can be explained by considering options available to the borrower. Most fixed-rate loans also include a prepayment option.[15] In contrast, interest rate swaps normally contain no such prepayment option. Early termination of a swap agreement requires that the remaining contract be marked to market and paid in full.[16]

Hence, the positions of the firm which has borrowed fixed directly and the one which has borrowed floating and swapped to fixed are quite different. The former owns a put option on interest rates; the latter does not. And, in this context, the transaction between the AAA firm and the BBB firm looks less like financial arbitrage and more like an option transaction. The BBB firm can borrow at a fixed-rate more cheaply by swapping from floating because the borrowing-floating/swap-to-fixed

alternative does not include the interest rate option contained in the borrow-fixed alternative. The BBB firm, in effect, has sold an interest rate option. The funding cost "savings" obtained by the BBB firm (and the AAA firm) come from the premium on this option.[17]

B. Liquidity

An important factor in the growth in this market is the substantial reduction in bid/ask spreads. In 1982, spreads exceeded 200 basis points; now they are frequently less than ten. Thus, the dramatic increase in volume has been accompanied by an equally dramatic increase in the liquidity of the market.

C. Exposure Management

Since swaps can be used to manage a corporation's exposure to interest rate risk, part of the growth in interest rate swaps simply reflects the general increase in corporate hedging activities. In addition to risk-aversion of the owner of a closely-held firm, Smith/Stulz [24] demonstrate that value-maximizing firms can have incentives to hedge because: *(i)* convexities in the corporate tax schedule makes the expected after-tax value of the firm a decreasing function of the volatility of taxable income; *(ii)* expected costs of financial distress are increasing in the volatility of firm value; and *(iii)* managerial risk aversion reduces the value of ill-diversified fixed compensation claims. Mayers/Smith [15] show that hedging can control an aspect of Myers' [16] underinvestment problem, thus reducing expected costs of financial distress. And Shapiro/Titman [20] point out that firms with product warranties, service networks, etc., have greater incentives to hedge. To this list we offer two additions. First, given current and anticipated future asset structure, corporations have incentives to carefully structure the liability side of their balance sheet to control potential incentive problems.[18] Consider then the firm's long-term debt. When realizations deviate from forecasts, recapitalization of the firm is sometimes beneficial, but most long-term bond contracts include penalties for prepaying or call-

---

[15]This is the call provision in standard corporate bonds. See Smith/Warner [25].

[16]See Article 12 of the International Swap Dealers Association's *Code of Standard Wording, Assumptions and Provisions for Swaps,* 1986 edition.

---

[17]It is important to ensure that the quoted rates in Exhibit 5 are complete and consistent. In addition to differential prepayment options, differential fees, commissions, or expenses can eliminate the apparent advantage. It is also important to ensure the rates are quoted employing the same compounding and days-of-the-year conventions. See Smith [26].

[18]See Myers [16] and Jensen/Smith [10].

ing the bonds. Interest rate swaps allow the financial manager additional flexibility to restructure the firm's long term fixed-rate obligations while avoiding the costs of calling the bonds. Second, thrifts have a comparative advantage in attracting short-term deposits, but in placing long-term mortgage loans. However, a policy of simply exploiting this institutional advantage exposes them to significant interest rate risk (Smith [22]). As an alternative to offering adjustable-rate mortgages or selling mortgages and reinvesting the proceeds in short-term assets, this risk can be managed by using interest rate swaps to manage the gap between asset and liability maturities.[19]

D. Synthetic Instruments

A final reason for the growth of the swap market is their usefulness in the creation of new financial instruments. For example, the market for long-dated interest rate forward contracts was historically very illiquid. But since interest rate swaps can be viewed as portfolios of forward interest rate contracts, long-term swaps have been stripped to increase liquidity in the market for long-dated forward rate agreements. Conversely, interest rate swaps have been combined with other instruments to create new products. For example, the combination of a fixed-rate loan and an interest rate swap where the party pays fixed produces a "reverse floating-rate loan;" if interest rates rise, then the coupon payments on the loan fall.

IV. Conclusions

One must be struck by the growth of the U.S. dollar interest rate swap market—from zero in 1981 to an outstanding volume of $542 billion at the end of 1987. The argument that arbitrage of quality spreads is the reason for this growth is unsatisfying. Since swap cash flows are equivalent to those from portfolios of existing financial products, arbitrage among inconsistently priced instruments is feasible. But successful arbitrage should eliminate pricing inconsistencies and should therefore lead to decreasing volume rather than the observed increase. Moreover, we see no convincing evidence that swaps are mispriced—that the quality spread for swaps is lower than for loans is not sufficient

to imply mispriced credit risk. Indeed, credit spreads should be lower for swaps than for loans because (i) the principal in a swap is only notional; (ii) the difference check is a function of the difference rather than the level of rates; and (iii) rational default requires that both the firm be in bankruptcy and the remaining swap value be negative. Indeed, the apparent funding cost savings may well reflect differential prepayment options rather than arbitrage profit. Instead, we propose that the growth of this market has been the result of reductions in the bid/ask spread, a general increase in the corporate demand for risk management instruments (including swaps), and the ability to use swaps to create synthetic financial instruments.

With the dramatic growth in volume has come concern about the credit risk of swaps, including proposals from the Fed and the Bank of England for the imposition of capital-adequacy requirements on banks that intermediate swaps. Intermediation in the swap market imposes claims on a firm's capital, so additional capital would perform a potentially valuable bonding function. However, since banks can fully capture the benefits of an increase in demand for their market-making services from better bonding, there will exist a market-determined optimal capital reserve. Therefore, the rationale for the proposed requirements must be based on the non-actuarial pricing of FDIC insurance (see Busser, Chen, and Kane [5]) or on the subsidization of risk-taking behavior that results when government regulators are reluctant to liquidate large financial institutions (see Kane [12, 14]).

While our analysis is not sufficient to permit the quantification of the optimal capital requirement, two general conclusions seem warranted. First, the appropriate capital requirement should be related to the default characteristics of those swaps that the bank intermediates. Our analysis indicates that the default risk of an individual swap is dramatically less than that of a comparable loan, and is more closely related to the default risk of forward and futures contracts. By contrasting the swap with forward and a futures contracts, it becomes clear that the default risk for an interest rate swap is determined by the credit rating of the contracting firm, correlation between the contracting firm's value and interest rates, the volatility of interest rates, the slope of the term structure, the maturity of the swap, the frequency of the difference checks, and whether some form of performance bond is posted.

Second, the cash flow implications of default for a portfolio of swaps are significantly different than those of a single contract. If a bank maintains a relatively

---

[19]We believe that these exposure-management arguments help explain the active participation of thrift institutions and insurance companies in the interest rate swap market. And, in addition to those thrifts wanting to hedge their exposures, Edward Kane reminded us that there are hundreds of "zombie" thrifts whose managers want to make endgame plays. See Kane [13].

balanced portfolio of swaps, it will generally receive payments from half its book and make payments to the other half. Thus, at any time only half its outstanding swaps would be candidates for default. Moreover, since default on the swap requires both that the firm be in financial distress and that the remaining value of the contract be negative, default on swaps by hedgers should be more idiosyncratic than default on loans. Therefore, default risk faced by a bank in the interest rate swap market seems especially well-suited to be managed through diversification by holding a portfolio of swaps.

References

1. Bank for International Settlements, *Recent Innovations in International Banking*, Basle, 1986.

2. J. Bicksler and A.H. Chen, "An Economic Analysis of Interest Rate Swaps," *The Journal of Finance* (July 1986), pp. 645–655.

3. F. Black, "The Pricing of Commodity Contracts," *Journal of Financial Economics* (January 1976) pp. 167–179.

4. M.J. Brennen, "A Theory of Price Limits in Futures Markets," *Journal of Financial Economics* (June 1986), pp. 213–233.

5. S.A. Busser, A.H. Chen, and E.J. Kane, "Federal Deposit Insurance, Regulatory Policy, and Optimal Bank Capital," *Journal of Finance* (March 1981), pp. 51–60.

6. J.C. Cox, J.E. Ingersoll, Jr., and S.A. Ross, "The Relation Between Forward Prices and Futures Prices," *Journal of Financial Economics* (December 1981), pp. 321–346.

7. Federal Reserve Board and Bank of England, "Agreed Proposal of the United States Federal Banking Supervisory Authorities and the Bank of England on Primary Capital and Capital Adequacy Assessment" and Staff Memo: "Treatment of Interest Rate and Exchange Rate Contracts in the Risk Asset Ratio," March 3, 1987.

8. K.R. French, "A Comparison of Futures and Forward Prices," *Journal of Financial Economics* (November 1983), pp. 311–342.

9. R.A. Jarrow and G.S. Oldfield, "Forward Contracts and Futures Contracts," *Journal of Financial Economics* (December 1981), pp. 373–382.

10. M.C. Jensen and C.W. Smith, Jr., "Stockholder, Manager, and Creditor Interests: Applications of Agency Theory," *Recent Advances in Corporate Finance*, E. Altman and M. Subrahmanyam (eds.), Homewood, IL, Irwin, 1987, pp. 93–131.

11. E.J. Kane, "Market Incompleteness and Divergences Between Forward and Futures Interest Rates," *Journal of Finance* (May 1980), pp. 221–234.

12. ———, "Appearance and Reality in Deposit Insurance: The Case for Reform," *Journal of Banking and Finance* (June 1986), pp. 175–188.

13. ———, "Dangers of Capital Forbearance: The Case of the FSLIC and 'Zombie' S&Ls," *Contemporary Policy Issues* (January 1987), pp. 77–83.

14. ———, "How Incentive-Incompatible Deposit Insurance Funds Fail," working paper, Ohio State University, 1988.

15. D. Mayers and C.W. Smith, Jr., "Corporate Insurance and the Underinvestment Problem," *Journal of Risk and Insurance* (March 1987), pp. 45–54.

16. S. Myers, "Determinants of Corporate Borrowing," *Journal of Financial Economics* (November 1977), pp. 147–175.

17. G. Oldfield and R. Messina, "Forward Exchange Price Determination in Continuous Time," *Journal of Financial and Quantitative Analysis* (September 1977), pp. 473–479.

18. K. Ramaswamy and S.M. Sundaresan, "The Valuation of Floating Rate Instruments: Theory and Evidence," *Journal of Financial Economics* (December 1986), pp. 251–272.

19. S.F. Richard and M. Sundareson, "A Continuous Time Equilibrium Model of Forward Prices and Futures Prices in a Multigood Economy," *Journal of Financial Economics* (December 1981), pp. 347–371.

20. A.C. Shapiro and S. Titman, "An Integrated Approach to Corporate Risk Management," *Midland Corporate Finance Journal* (Summer 1985), pp. 41–56.

21. W. Sharpe, *Investments*, Englewood Cliffs, NJ, Prentice-Hall, 1985.

22. C.W. Smith, Jr., "Pricing Mortgage Originations," *American Real Estate and Urban Economics Association Journal* (Fall 1982), pp. 313–330.

23. C.W. Smith, Jr., C.W. Smithson, and L.M. Wakeman, "The Evolving Market for Swaps," *Midland Corporate Finance Journal* (Winter 1986), pp. 20–32.

24. C.W. Smith, Jr., and R. Stulz, "The Determinants of Firm's Hedging Policies," *Journal of Financial and Quantitative Analysis* (December 1985), pp. 391–405.

25. C.W. Smith, Jr., and J. Warner, "On Financial Contracting: An Analysis of Bond Covenants," *Journal of Financial Economics* (June 1979), pp. 117–161.

26. D.J. Smith, "Measuring the Gains from 'Arbitraging' the Swap Market," unpublished manuscript, Boston University, 1987.

27. S.M. Turnbull, "Swaps: A Zero Sum Game?" *Financial Management* (Spring 1987), pp. 15–21.

Loan Sales and the Cost of Bank Capital

GEORGE G. PENNACCHI*

ABSTRACT

This paper considers a model where banks may improve the returns on loans by monitoring borrowers. Bank regulation, together with competitive deposit and equity financing, can give banks an incentive to sell loans, but the extent of their loan selling is limited by a moral-hazard problem. A solution is given for the optimal design of the bank-loan buyer contract that alleviates this moral-hazard problem. An explanation is also given as to why some banks might buy loans and why loan sales volume has recently increased.

BANKS' PRACTICE OF MAKING loans and then selling them to other institutions and individuals has grown in popularity. An important example in the development of loan selling has been the increase in banks' mortgage loans that are insured and pooled under the authority of the Government National Mortgage Association (GNMA) and then sold to secondary market investors. Recently, however, there has been a dramatic rise in the volume of other types of loans being sold, especially by money-center banks. Portions of commercial loans originated by these larger banks are being sold to smaller banks, foreign banks, and other financial and nonfinancial institutions. In addition, banks' car loans and credit card receivables have also been pooled and sold to institutions and individuals.[1] Selling loans that were once considered nonmarketable assets, a process that has been termed "asset securitization", may be signalling the start of a fundamental change in the commercial banking business. The leading banks in loan-selling operations now view themselves more as originators and distributors of loans rather than as institutions holding loans as assets.

The potentially large impact of loan sales on the future of commercial banking naturally evokes the question of what incentives exist for banks to sell loans. In this paper, we show that loan sales allow some banks to finance loans less expensively than by traditional deposit or equity issue because bank funds received via loan sales can avoid costs associated with required reserves and

* Department of Finance, University of Pennsylvania. I am grateful for useful comments from the participants of seminars at the University of Pennsylvania, the Conference on Asset Securitization at Northwestern, and the European Finance Meetings in Madrid, Spain. Comments by Franklin Allen, Mitchell Berlin, Michael Fishman, Joseph Haubrich, Robert Litzenberger, David Pyle, Krishna Ramaswamy, Michael Smirlock, and an anonymous referee are also appreciated. Funding was provided by the Herbert V. Prochnow Educational Foundation of the Graduate School of Banking, Madison, Wisconsin.

[1] See Salem [30, 31] and Pavel [26] for a description of current developments regarding bank loan selling and the more general phenomenon known as "asset securitization." Also relevant is *The New York Times*, January 20, 1986, "Loan Sales Market Swelling," and February 11, 1985, "Repackaging of Car Loans is Increasing."

required capital. However, it is worth noting that current research suggests that there may be additional reasons why funding through loan sales can be less expensive than bank deposits and equity. Greenbaum and Thakor [14] show that signalling information regarding loan quality may be enhanced when loans are sold rather than funded by deposits. Another recent paper by James [17] demonstrates that loan sales can provide lower cost financing for bank equity-holders and enable the bank to avoid a possible underinvestment problem when it has risky debt outstanding. In addition, Flannery [11] shows how current bank-examination procedures may induce banks to hold only certain risk classes of loans while profitably selling the rest.

Our paper goes on to demonstrate that the extent of banks' loan selling is limited by a moral-hazard problem that arises from the diminished incentive by banks to efficiently monitor and service loans after they have been sold. Banks can help alleviate this problem by optimally designing their contracts with loan buyers. By offering loan buyers an incentive-efficient loan sales contract, a bank's loan sales volume, and hence its profitability, can be maximized.

The plan of the paper is as follows. In Section I, we present a simple state-preference model of the banking firm. The bank chooses its optimal quantity of loans to originate along with its levels of monitoring borrowers. The bank also decides whether to finance its asset holdings by issuing deposits or equity. We examine optimal portfolio and capital-structure decisions, first when loan sales are prohibited and second when they are allowed. In order to determine a bank's equilibrium quantity of loan sales, the optimal bank-loan buyer contract is studied next. In Section II, we analyze the optimal design of this contract when the level of loan monitoring by banks is unobservable and agents are risk neutral. Contracts are considered where the loan buyer has no recourse to the bank for losses and also where recourse is permitted. Section III generalizes the model to allow banks market power in deposit financing. We show that equilibria exist where some banks will choose to sell loans while other banks may choose to purchase loans. This analysis leads to an explanation for why the aggregate volume of loan selling has recently increased. A conclusion follows in Section IV.

I. A Model of the Banking Firm

This model concentrates on the loan-making activities of banks. Originating loans, as well as possibly holding marketable securities, is what we will define as the "portfolio" services provided by banks—the process of channeling funds between savers and borrowers. It is assumed that banks can expend real resources in gathering information on loan applicants and monitoring loans so as to improve the return (quality) on these loans. The information-gathering and monitoring functions of banks have been stressed in the papers by Campbell and Kracaw [4] and Diamond [6]. Other services provided by banks, particularly transactions services such as check clearing and deposit-to-currency convertibility, are ignored in this paper. As in Black [2], Fama [8], and Fischer [10], it is assumed that no necessary connection exists between the portfolio and transactions services of banks, and hence they can be separated into different "departments" of the banking organization.[2]

A. Equilibrium with No Loan Sales

Consider a one-period state-preference model where banks choose investments in loans or marketable securities. Let N denote a bank's total amount of funds initially invested in these assets. We assume that a technology exists where a bank can improve the (uncertain) return on its loans by expending resources on gathering information and monitoring its borrowers.

(A1) Banks can make unit investments such that one dollar lent to borrower i at the beginning of the period entitles the bank to an end-of-period cash flow equalling $x_i(s, a_i)$, where s indexes the state of nature at the end of the period and a_i is the level of "monitoring" chosen by the bank at the beginning of the period.[3] Assuming a possibly infinite number of states, s can be designated as $s \in [0, 1]$, i.e., real numbers on the unit closed interval. $x_i(s, a_i)$ is a concave function of a_i.

(A2) Banks produce monitoring services, a_i, via a constant-returns-to-scale technology so that their cost function is $c(a_i) = ca_i$, where c is a positive constant.

Assumptions (A1) and (A2) describe the bank's investment opportunities. For investments such as loans to small firms and consumers, it is reasonable to believe that $\partial x_i(s, a_i)/\partial a_i \geq 0$; i.e., monitoring services, produced from inputs such as the labor of loan officers and assessors and computer hardware and software, can improve the bank's return on these loans. However, in the case of loans to well-known investment-grade corporations and investments in money-market assets such as Treasury bills, it is more reasonable to assume that bank monitoring would have no effect on these marketable assets' cash flows, so that $\partial x_i(s, a_i)/\partial a_i = 0$ for these assets.

A bank can finance its investments by issuing deposits or equity. Let D denote the bank's total level of deposit financing, and let E equal the amount of equity funds raised by the bank.

(A3) Banks are price takers in both deposit (debt) and equity financing markets. Assuming complete markets, let $p^d(s)$ denote the equilibrium price (density) paid by depositors (debtholders) for a security having no agency costs that pays one dollar in state s at the end of the period, where the return on this security is treated as debt for personal tax purposes.

---

[2] Extending the model to allow for a transactions technology and for transactions deposit accounts produces no substantive changes in the model's results concerning loan sales.

[3] While this effort expended by the bank for a given loan, a_i, is referred to as the bank's level of monitoring activities, this effort could also be interpreted to include the bank's information-gathering and credit-checking activities necessary to select a better quality loan from a pool of applicants. Therefore, our reference to a moral-hazard problem of inefficient monitoring caused by the unobservability of the bank's effort by loan buyers, which is explained in Section I, Subsection B, and treated in Section II, could be interpreted to refer also to an adverse-selection problem of inefficient information gathering by the bank.

Similarly, $p^e(s)$ denotes the equilibrium price density paid by equity-holders for a security paying one dollar in state s and with a return taxed as equity.

(A4) Banks are subject to a corporate income tax, with proportional tax rate equal to t. They are also required to hold non-interest-bearing reserves on deposits where ρ is the required reserve/deposit ratio.

Assumption (A3) assumes perfect competition in financing bank investments. However, we will generalize the analysis to consider imperfect competition in deposit markets later in Section III. Since this paper disregards transactions services of banks, one should think of banks' deposits as being in non-transactions accounts, such as money-market deposit accounts, certificates of deposit, or other "purchased funds," that thus can be regarded simply as (short-term) debt instruments. In practice, non-transactions deposits have either zero or small reserve requirements. For example, money-market deposit accounts have no required reserves, while most certificates of deposit have a three percent requirement. Whether ρ is zero or small will not be critical in terms of our qualitative results.

Using the price of a security that pays one dollar in all states, $s \in [0, 1]$, we can define r_d and r_e as the certainty-equivalent required returns to debtholders and equityholders, respectively:

$$\frac{1}{1 + r_i} \equiv \int_0^1 p^i(s) \, ds, \quad i = d, e. \tag{1}$$

Bank deposits are assumed to be insured by a government regulator who also imposes an initial capital requirement on the bank.

(A5) Deposits are insured by a government agency that charges the bank a (risk-sensitive) premium covering the value of the agency's end-of-period deposit guarantee. However, the insurer limits banks' selection of a deposit (debt)-equity ratio to a maximum of ς. Because of the insurer's special legal and regulatory authority over banks, we assume that it can costlessly monitor a bank's activities such that the bank's investment and financial decisions are fixed after its insurance premium is set.

The assumption that deposit insurance is fairly priced is made for a number of reasons. First, while distortions created by mispriced deposit insurance have been studied in a number of papers, whether deposit insurance is actually over- or underpriced for most banks is an unresolved issue.[4] Second, less-than-substantial mispricing does not lead to qualitatively different results but adds more clutter to the analysis. While risk-insensitive deposit insurance may influence a bank's desire to sell loans, we show that this is not a necessary condition for a bank loan-selling incentive.[5] Third, the fair-pricing assumption may be

---

[4] In a similar state-preference framework, Dothan and Williams [7] analyze distortions arising from the mispricing of deposit insurance. Pennacchi [29] examines whether deposit insurance provided by the FDIC is generally over- or underpriced.

[5] Because of the presence of a capital-adequacy constraint in our model, unlike Dothan and Williams [7], the incentive for banks to pursue greater risk, normally associated with fixed-rate or

justified by appealing to the analysis of Buser, Chen, and Kane [3], who suggest that a riskier bank faces a greater regulatory cost imposed on it by the FDIC. From the bank's point of view, this cost serves the same function as a risk-sensitive (implicit) deposit insurance premium.

The assumption of costless monitoring by the insuring agency is meant to capture one effect of the existence of deposit insurance and bank regulation. Deposit insurance can be viewed as an institutional structure that results in the agency costs associated with uninsured deposits being reduced. Merton [22, p. 3] states, "Hence, for the small depositor particularly, there are large information and surveillance costs to be saved if the institutional structure of the bank were such that the safety of the deposits was assured . . . ." A deposit insurer such as the FDIC has the regulatory authority to audit banks at will, require capital, issue cease-and-desist orders, and close banks, which will likely give it a monitoring cost substantially lower than that of uninsured debtholders or depositors who may be subject to free-rider problems. The imposition of a capital requirement also makes the zero-monitoring-cost assumption more reasonable since a capital constraint can be used to limit banks to leverage ratios where monitoring costs are sufficiently small.

The Appendix to this paper shows that, if the bank's objective is to maximize the after-tax gain to shareholders' equity, assumptions (A1) to (A5) lead to its objective function having the following form:[6]

$$\max_{\{N,(a_i),D,E\}} \left\{ \sum_{i=1}^{N} \left[(1+r_e) \int_0^1 p^e(s)x_i(s,a_i)\,ds - 1 - ca_i \right] - r_d D \right\}(1-t) - r_e E, \quad (2)$$

subject to the constraints:

$$N + \rho D \leq D + E \quad \text{(financing constraint)}, \quad (3)$$

$$D \leq \zeta E \quad \text{(capital constraint)}. \quad (4)$$

In expression (2), we choose the bank's assets i, $i = 1, \cdots, N$, to be ordered from the highest valued asset to the lowest.[7] Thus, loan or security $i = N$ is the "marginal" investment made by the bank, i.e., the investment that the bank is (approximately) indifferent to making.

Differentiating with respect to each of the bank's choice variables, this leads

---

subsidized deposit insurance, is reduced because greater risk cannot be obtained via higher leverage. Banks may increase their risk by less stringent monitoring of loans, but, in our model, this would result in a decrease in the loan's value. If, by lowering monitoring, the loss to the bank from a fall in loan value exceeds the bank's gain from a greater value of deposit insurance, banks may still follow firm value-maximizing behavior as in the case of the fair pricing of insurance. However, as is shown in Section II, banks may increase their financial risk by selling loans, and, thus, mispricing of deposit insurance may create other incentives for loan sales in addition to those analyzed in this paper.

[6] The assumption of fair deposit insurance induces the bank to maximize the after-tax value of the firm. The fair insurance premium simply equals the value of the insurer's end-of-period liability since the insurer's monitoring costs are assumed to be zero. If monitoring costs were positive, they would need to be included in the calculation of a fair premium. However, sufficiently small costs would not overturn our results.

[7] This is assuming that each a_i is chosen optimally according to condition (6).

to the first-order Kuhn-Tucker conditions:[8]

$$\left\{ \left[(1 + r_e) \int_0^1 p^e(s) x_N(s, a_N) \, ds - 1 - c a_N \right] (1 - t) - \lambda_1 \right\} N = 0, \qquad (5)$$

$$\left\{ (1 + r_e) \int_0^1 p^e(s) \frac{\partial x_i}{\partial a_i} (s, a_i) \, ds - c \right\} a_i = 0, \qquad (6)$$

$$\{ -r_d (1 - t) + \lambda_1 (1 - \rho) - \lambda_2 \} D = 0, \qquad (7)$$

$$\{ -r_e + \lambda_1 + \zeta \lambda_2 \} E = 0, \qquad (8)$$

where λ_1 and λ_2 are the multipliers associated with constraints (3) and (4), respectively, and the expressions in brackets are all nonpositive.

The bank's optimal choice of debt versus equity financing is given by conditions (7) and (8). The capital constraint of the bank will be binding; i.e., it will choose to be at its maximum debt/equity ratio, ζ, if

$$r_d \frac{(1 - t)}{(1 - \rho)} < r_e, \qquad (9)$$

while reversal of this inequality implies that an all-equity capital structure is optimal.

A net tax advantage to debt financing (condition (9) for sufficiently small ρ) is supported by empirical evidence.[9] Moreover, in a theoretical model where the typical firm experiences agency costs of debt issue, Barnea, Haugen, and Senbet [1] derive condition (9) (for $\rho = 0$) as a general-equilibrium result. In that model, a firm chooses its debt/equity ratio where its rising marginal agency cost of debt issue equals the marginal net tax benefit to debt financing. It then follows (see Orgler and Taggart [25, p. 218]) that, if insured banks have zero or negligible agency costs of deposit issue, they will choose to be at their maximum allowed debt/equity ratio. By assuming fairly priced deposit insurance with costless monitoring by the insurer, which is equivalent to assuming zero agency costs of debt issue, the relative tax advantages of debt are not fully realized at the binding debt/equity ratio.

Thus, with a binding capital constraint, the bank's choice of investments can now be determined. From the first-order conditions (5), (6), (7), and (8), we have

---

[8] Condition (5) is obtained by differentiating with respect to N but ignoring the integer constraint on loans.

[9] Empirical evidence by Gordon and Malkiel [12] and Skelton [32] generally supports the hypothesis of a net tax advantage to debt. For example, Gordon and Malkiel find that (personal) tax-exempt yields are approximately seventy-five percent of taxable yields. If $(1 - t)$ is approximately fifty-two to fifty-four percent during their sample period, this implies a net tax advantage to debt. Also, with current tax-law changes resulting in a thirty-four percent corporate tax rate, which exceeds the top twenty-eight percent marginal tax rate for high-income individuals, it can be argued that the model by Miller [23], in which firms are indifferent between debt and equity financing, cannot possibly hold. Casual evidence also suggests that bankers view equity as more expensive than debt or deposits since many bankers see increases in capital requirements as costly. For example, see *The Wall Street Journal*, December 2, 1985, "Capital-Ratio Rise Sours Bank Growth."

that the bank's optimal asset volume, N, will satisfy

$$(1 + r_e) \int_0^1 p^e(s) x_N(s, a_N^*) \, ds - 1$$

$$= ca_N^* + \left[\frac{r_e}{1 - t} + \zeta r_d \right] \bigg/ (1 + \zeta(1 - \rho)). \quad (10)$$

The left-hand side of (10) is the value of contingent interest income received from the marginal one-dollar bank investment when the level of monitoring, a_N^*, is optimally chosen according to condition (6). The right-hand side of (10) is simply the cost of making this marginal one-dollar investment. The first term on the right is the additional resource cost of monitoring the borrower, while the second term is the bank's weighted marginal cost of debt and equity issue.

Consider the implications of condition (10) for a bank's choice of marketable securities such as Treasury bills or similar money market instruments. Since $\partial x_i(s, a_i)/\partial a_i = 0$ for these securities, we know that $a_i^* = 0$. Further, if insured bank deposits, such as certificates of deposit, are competitively priced and have virtually the same risk, liquidity, and personal tax treatment as other money-market instruments, we can treat them as perfect substitutes, as does Fama [9]. In a competitive equilibrium, they must have the same yield, so that marginal revenue from money-market instruments, i.e., the left-hand side of (10), must equal r_d. However, from (9), r_d is less than the marginal cost of bank financing, the right-hand side of (10), implying that, if bank deposits require a similar yield to money-market assets, it is unprofitable for banks to hold these assets solely for portfolio (non-transactions) purposes.[10] Banks' added costs from required reserves and/or relatively expensive equity capital imply that, if their deposits are competitively priced, then their asset portfolios must yield more than just the return on marketable assets. Banks facing competitive financing must make other types of investments such as loans that require monitoring and credit checking—specialized activities not in direct competition with (unregulated) money market funds or individual investors. The next section shows how loan selling can be a profitable arrangement for banks that originate loans.

B. Equilibrium with Loan Sales

Consider a bank selling a claim on the return of a loan it originates. The interest on the loan buyer's funds used to buy this claim is assumed to be taxed in the same manner as interest on a standard (taxable) bond. While the optimal bank-loan buyer contract will be examined in more detail in the next section, here we simply assume that a share, b_i, of the return from each loan i is sold to a loan buyer. Thus, if loan i requires one dollar of initial financing and returns $x_i(s, a_i)$ dollars if state s occurs and the bank monitors at level a_i, loan buyers

---

[10] Fama [9] gives empirical evidence and a theoretical explanation similar to this paper's to show why certificates of deposit will have a yield nearly identical to similar money-market instruments, in spite of certificates of deposit required reserves. Because the "reserve tax" falls not on depositors but on the bank, Fama reaches the same conclusion as this paper, that banks issuing certificates of deposit will choose to "hold no open-market securities."

receive $b_i x_i(s, a_i)$ while the bank receives $(1 - b_i)x_i(s, a_i)$. The amount paid by loan buyers for a share, b_i, of loan i is then

$$\bar{b}_i \equiv b_i \int_0^1 p^d(s)x_i(s, a_i) \; ds. \tag{11}$$

Suppose that banks finance a proportion, $\bar{b}$, of each one-dollar loan through loan sales; i.e., $\bar{b}_i = \bar{b}$, $i = 1, \cdots, N$. Assuming fairly priced deposit insurance, the objective function for the bank is

$$\max_{\{N,(a_i),D,E\}} \left\{ \sum_{i=1}^N \left[(1+r_e) \int_0^1 p^e(s)(1 - b_i)x_i(s, a_i) \; ds - (1 - \bar{b}) - ca_i \right] - r_d D \right\}$$
$$\times (1 - t) - r_e E, \tag{12}$$

subject to the same constraints (3) and (4) as before, except that now $(1 - \bar{b})N$ replaces N in (3).

The bank's optimization problem now involves the following equilibrium condition regarding its choice of loans originated, N;

$$(1 + r_e) \int_0^1 p^e(s)x_N(s, a_N) \; ds - 1 = ca_N + r_I$$
$$- b_N \left[(1 + r_I) \int_0^1 p^d(s)x_N(s, a_N) \; ds - (1 + r_e) \int_0^1 p^e(s)x_N(s, a_N) \; ds \right], \tag{13}$$

where $r_I \equiv [r_e/(1 - t) + \varsigma r_m]/[1 + \varsigma(1 - \rho)]$ is the bank's weighted marginal cost of internal financing, equal to the bank's marginal cost of capital for the no-loan-sales case. Comparing the form of equation (13) with the analogous condition (10) for the no-loan-sales case, we see that the marginal cost of originating a loan, which is the right-hand side of (13), differs from that of (10) because of an additional final term. This term represents a possible savings to the bank in its marginal cost of capital due to raising funds via loan sales.

Under reasonable circumstances, this last term on the right-hand side of (13) will be less than zero. To see this, note from equation (1) that

$$\int_0^1 p^d(s) \; ds \; \Big/ \; \int_0^1 p^e(s) \; ds = (1 + r_e)/(1 + r_d). \tag{14}$$

This implies that the ratio of the "averages" of the primitive security prices for debt and equity equals the ratio of the certainty-equivalent rates of return on equity versus debt. An additional assumption that is sufficient, though not necessary, for loan sales to lower the marginal cost of capital would be that the debt/equity security price ratio be uniform across states:[11]

$$p^d(s)/p^e(s) = (1 + r_e)/(1 + r_d) \quad \text{for all} \quad s. \tag{15}$$

---

[11] Litzenberger and Van Horne [19] show that, in a Miller [23] type of world with investors in different tax clienteles, the ratio of the rates of return for a primitive debt and equity security would equal the ratio of the complements of personal tax rates for equity and debt for the "marginal" investor. DeAngelo and Masulis [5] show that investor risk neutrality would imply this uniformity.

Employing this stronger assumption, the last term in equation (13) can be rewritten as

$$-b_N \left[(1 + r_e) \int_0^1 p^e(s) x_N(s, a_N) \, ds \, \frac{(r_I - r_d)}{(1 + r_d)} \right] < 0 \qquad (16)$$

since $r_I > r_d$ from condition (9).

The loan-sales equilibrium condition (13) indicates that, if the price paid by loan buyers for their loan share sufficiently reflects the higher average relative price paid for debt securities over equity securities, then the bank can lower its cost of financing by selling loans. Note that this always holds in the certainty case, i.e., a single end-of-period state of the world. By selling loans, banks can raise funds at the same cost, r_d, as deposits, but the funds acquired through loan sales do not appear as a larger level of deposits on the balance sheet of the bank. Therefore, the bank will not be required to issue more relatively expensive equity in order to stay within its capital adequacy constraint or be required to hold non-interest-paying reserves against these funds. Ceteris paribus, with a lower cost of capital, banks will choose to expand their loan-originating and monitoring activities, leading to a lower competitive interest rate on loans. From a macro-economic perspective, an economy-wide increase in the proportion of loans sold would decrease the demand for high-powered money, tending to raise nominal measures of output.

Thus far, we have not addressed an important issue that affects the bank's choice of monitoring when it decides to sell loans. If the bank's monitoring levels, a_i, $i = 1, \cdots, N$, are observable by loan buyers, enabling the bank to commit to given levels of monitoring, then loan sales can indeed lead to increased bank profits and loan originations.[12] However, when loan monitoring is unobservable by loan buyers, a potential moral-hazard problem arises that can limit the proportion of loans sold. By selling a share of a loan, the bank's incentive to monitor is diminished since its monitoring level will satisfy

$$(1 + r_e)(1 - b_i) \int_0^1 p^e(s) \frac{\partial x_i}{\partial a_i} (s, a_i) \, ds = c. \qquad (17)$$

With the marginal benefit from monitoring discounted by the factor $(1 - b_i)$, monitoring will be less than in the no-loan-sales case. Rational loan buyers will infer this diminished level of monitoring and hence expect a smaller state-contingent loan cash flow, $x_i(s, a_i)$. Thus, they will pay the bank less per dollar of the loan the greater the total share of the loan sold.[13] However, by optimally

---

[12] To see this, suppose that banks can commit to the same levels of monitoring as in the no-loan-sales case, given by condition (6), i.e., $a_i = a_i^*$. Then a comparison of the marginal loan equilibrium conditions (10) and (13) will imply a lower total marginal cost of an additional one-dollar loan, given the negativity of the last term on the right-hand side of (13). Furthermore, when monitoring is observable, if it is profitable to sell any share of a loan, it must be even more profitable to sell the entire loan.

[13] The amount paid by loan buyers is still given by equation (11), but now loan buyers infer that the bank's level of monitoring, a_i, is that which satisfies equation (17), not equation (6). Since loan buyers can deduce this monitoring level with certainty, they know each $x_i(s, a_i)$ with certainty, which justifies discounting these state-contingent cash flows by $p^d(s)$.

structuring the bank-loan buyer contract, this moral-hazard problem can be reduced. Determining this optimal contract will help to explain the proportion of loans that can be sold.

II. Bank-Loan Buyer Contract Choice

A bank's decision to originate and monitor a given loan can be made independently of the same decisions for other loans, as can be verified from the banks' objective function (12) and conditions (13) and (17). Therefore, a separate objective function for each loan can be obtained. Taking condition (12) for the case of $N = 1$, multiplying by $(1 - t)$, and substituting in the equilibrium condition of $D = \zeta E$, one obtains the individual loan objective function:

$$(1 + r_e) \int_0^1 p^e(s)(1 - b)x(s, a) \, ds - ca - (1 + r_I)I, \tag{18}$$

where $I \equiv (1 - \rho)D + E = 1 - \bar{b}$ is the amount of internal financing used in originating the one-dollar loan.

In order to add more structure to our problem and keep the analysis tractable, the case in which security valuation by shareholders and loan buyers reflects risk neutrality is considered. In this case, investors will be concerned only with the expected return on their contingent claim to the loan. In addition, we make the following assumptions regarding the return distribution of the bank loan, the cost of monitoring, and observability.

(A1′) The stochastic return on the loan, x, has a distribution such that $x \in [0, L]$, where L is the promised end-of-period payment on the loan. The bank can alter the loan's return distribution by monitoring, so that the probability density function of the loan's return has the form $f(x, a)$. It is assumed, as in Hart and Holmström [15], that the loan's distribution function, $F(x, a)$, satisfies the convexity-of-distribution-function condition:

$$F(x, \lambda a + (1 - \lambda)a')$$

$$\leq \lambda F(x, a) + (1 - \lambda)F(x, a'), \quad \forall a, a'; \quad \lambda \in (0, 1). \tag{19}$$

(A2′) Let the bank's cost of monitoring a loan be given by $c(a)$, where $c'(a) > 0$ and $c''(a) \geq 0$.
(A3′) Bank-loan monitoring is unobservable by loan buyers. However, they can observe the loan's actual return, and, hence, their share of the loan's return may be contingent on the loan's actual return, i.e., $b = b(x)$.

The bank's problem of choosing the optimal loan sales contract and level of monitoring can then be written as

$$\max_{\{b(x), I, a\}} \int_0^L (1 - b(x))x \, dF(x, a) - c(a) - (1 + r_I)I, \tag{20}$$

subject to

$$\int_0^L b(x)x \, dF(x, a)/(1 + r_d) + I = 1 \quad \text{(financing constraint),} \quad (21)$$

$$\int_0^L (1 - b(x))x \, dF(x, a) - c(a) \geq \int_0^L (1 - b(x))x \, dF(x, a') - c(a'),$$

$$\forall a' \neq a \text{ (incentive-compatibility constraint).} \quad (22)$$

However, if condition (19) holds, Hart and Holmström [15] show that the incentive-compatibility constraint, (22), can be converted into the more convenient form:

$$\int_0^L (1 - b(x))x \, dF_a(x, a) = c'(a). \quad (23)$$

We are now prepared to consider a variety of contractual arrangements between the bank and the loan buyer.

A. Loan Sales without Recourse

We will define a bank-loan buyer contract with no recourse as one in which the bank cannot pledge outside assets as a potential payment to the loan buyer. Only the proceeds of the loan return are permitted to be split between the bank and loan buyer. As will be discussed in greater detail in the next section, the Federal Reserve places restrictions on loans sold with recourse, and in practice the great majority of loan sales are made without recourse. Therefore, it is of interest to consider this case. The no-recourse restriction on the loan sales contract takes the form:

$$b(x) \leq 1 \quad \text{for all} \quad x. \quad (24)$$

Conditions (20), (21), (23), and (24) then characterize the bank's problem of selecting the optimal no-recourse contract. Let ω and λ be the Lagrange multipliers for the constraints (21) and (23), respectively, and let $\mu(x)$ be the multipliers for the inequalities in (24).

The first-order conditions with respect to the bank's choice of $b(x)$, I, and a are

$$\left\{\left(\frac{\omega}{1 + r_d} - 1\right)xf(x, a) - \lambda xf_a(x, a) - \mu(x)\right\}b(x) = 0, \quad (25)$$

$$\{-(1 + r_I) + \omega\}I = 0, \quad (26)$$

$$\left\{\frac{\omega}{1 + r_d}\int_0^L b(x)x \, dF_a(x, a) + \lambda\left[\int_0^L (1 - b(x))x \, dF_{aa}(x, a) - c''(a)\right]\right\}a = 0, \quad (27)$$

where the expressions in brackets must be nonpositive.

For the case where, in equilibrium, the entire loan is not financed through loan sales, i.e., $I > 0$, then from condition (26) we have that $\omega = 1 + r_I$. Condition

(25) can then be written as

$$\{\theta x f(x, a) - \lambda x f_a(x, a) - \mu(x)\} b(x) = 0, \tag{28}$$

where $\theta = (r_I - r_d)/(1 + r_d) > 0$ is the present value of savings by financing through loan sales rather than internal funds.

Before attempting to analyze equations (27) and (28), let us consider the characteristics of the probability density function, $f(x, a)$, for a typical bank loan, as this will prove insightful in interpreting these optimality conditions. Assume that the bank loan is made to an otherwise all-equity-financed firm that invests its funds in assets (projects) with an uncertain return. If V is the value of this firm's assets when its loan with promised payment L becomes due, then at maturity the value of this bank loan will be

$$x = \min[L, V]. \tag{29}$$

A reasonable assumption concerning the range of the distribution of V is that it is bounded below at zero. In addition, we assume that the bank's monitoring level, a, affects the form of the firm's asset density function such that a lower level of a implies a "fatter" lower tail of the density function of V. Figure 1 gives a plausible form for this probability density function of V; $g(V, a_1)$ is the density if the firm is monitored by the bank at level a_1, while $g(V, a_0)$ is the density if the firm is monitored at level a_0, where $a_1 > a_0$.

Given the density function for V, the density function for the loan return, x, is determined. The loan-return density when the bank monitors at level a_1, $f(x, a_1)$, is simply equal to $g(V, a_1)$ for $V < L$, with all the probability mass of $g(V, a_1)$ for $V \geq L$ "piled" together at point L. Thus, the value of $f(L, a_1)$ is a Dirac delta function spike with area equal to prob$(V \geq L)$. $f(x, a_0)$ over the range $[0, L]$ will bear a similar relationship to $g(V, a_0)$.

Note in Figure 1 that, if the promised loan payment, L, is not too large relative to the density of V, then $g(V, a_0) > g(V, a_1)$ and, hence, $f(x, a_0) > f(x, a_1)$ for

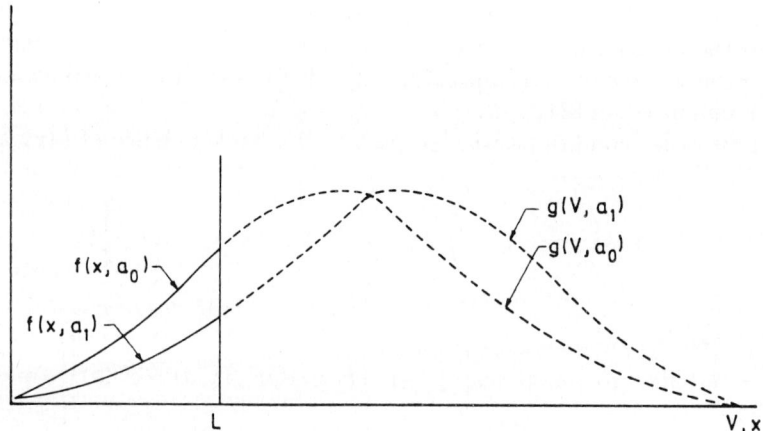

Figure 1. Firm asset (V) and loan return (x) probability density functions. - - - $(g(V, a))$, density of firm's assets; —— $(f(x, a))$, density of loan return; L, promised loan payment; a_1, a_0, monitoring levels, where $a_1 > a_0$.

all V and x less than L. In other words, if the promised loan payment is sufficiently in the lower tail of the firm's asset return, then, over the range zero to L, the density is a decreasing function of the bank's monitoring level; i.e., less monitoring makes the tail "fatter".[14] The casual observation that banks rarely make commercial loans carrying exorbitant interest rates, e.g., twenty points above prime, lends support to the proposition that L is typically in the lower tail of the firm's asset distribution, where $g_a(V, a) < 0$.

Now assuming, as in Figure 1, that $f_a(x, a) < 0$ for all $x < L$, we see from condition (28) that the expression within brackets must be non-negative for all $x < L$ such that

$$\mu(x) = \theta x f(x, a) - \lambda x f_a(x, a) \geq 0, \quad \forall x < L. \tag{30}$$

Therefore, $b(x) = 1$ for all $x < L$; i.e., the optimal loan sale contract gives the loan buyer the entire loan return whenever a loan default occurs. Hence, the bank will receive a return from the loan only when the loan does not default since only when $x = L$ will $f_a(L, a)$ be positive. Only in this case will $\mu(L) = 0$ so that $b(L) < 1$ and

$$\lambda = \theta \frac{f(L, a)}{f_a(L, a)}. \tag{31}$$

Thus, our assumptions on the loan distribution and preferences lead to a unique piecewise-linear optimal sharing rule that looks very similar to the loan buyer having a debt position and the bank an equity position in the loan.[15] The contract is characterized by penalizing the bank if low loan outcomes occur and rewarding the bank if high loan outcomes (no default) occur. Giving the bank a disproportionate share of the risk allows the bank to reap a disproportionate share of the gains from monitoring, enabling a greater amount of the loan to be sold while maintaining monitoring-incentive efficiency.

There is evidence that actual non-recourse loan sales contracts follow this principle of giving the selling bank a disporportionate share of the loan's risk. Melvin [20, p. 41] cites the example of Bank One's sale of promised payments from a pool of credit card receivables in which the selling bank retained an equity position in the pool equal to twice the historical default level of the receivables. A similar contract was designed to sell a senior interest in a pool of adjustable-rate commercial mortgages.[16] Coast Savings and Loan, a California thrift that originated the mortgages, retained a junior twenty percent interest in the pool. Another example is the practice of many money-center banks of selling short-

---

[14] One can think of the function of the bank's monitoring to be that of limiting the risk of the borrowing firm's projects (assets). The bank, by reducing the "fatness" of the tail of the firm's asset distribution, is improving the expected return on its loan.

[15] The contract is not exactly debt-equity division of the loan return. Note that, for small loan default, i.e., $x = L - \varepsilon$, where ε is a small positive quantity, the loan buyers could receive a total return greater than their return when the loan did not default at all since $b(x) = 1$ for $x < L$ and $b(x) < 1$ for $x = L$. The framework of Holmström [16] can be used to derive contract optimality conditions under an alternative assumption that bank-loan buyer asset choice displays risk aversion.

[16] See *The Wall Street Journal*, February 26, 1987, "S&L's Issue Puts an Unusual Twist on Credit Support."

term "strips" of longer term loans.[17] Typically, the originating bank negotiates a lending commitment of between one and seven years with a borrowing firm. This loan is then financed by selling short-term obligations of between one and three months, called "strips", to a loan buyer. When the strip matures, the loan buyer is under no obligation to renew this short-term financing. While the buyer of the strip is exposed to default risk in the short run before the maturity date of the strip, the originating bank retains greater exposure to default in the longer run because of its commitment to refinance the loan.[18] This arrangement would therefore preserve much of the bank's incentive to monitor.

It is straightforward to show that the equilibrium level of bank monitoring that results under the optimal loan sales contract will be less than the most economically efficient (first-best) level of monitoring. Note that the terms in square brackets in equation (27) are just the second-order condition regarding the bank's optimal monitoring choice, which is assumed to hold and therefore is negative. This implies that the loan buyer's expected benefit from greater monitoring is positive:

$$\int_0^L b(x)x \, dF_a(x, a) > 0. \tag{32}$$

Rearranging the bank's incentive-compatibility condition (23), it follows that

$$\int_0^L x \, dF_a(x, a) = c'(a) + \int_0^L b(x)x \, dF_a(x, a) > c'(a). \tag{33}$$

Therefore, in equilibrium, the expected marginal return on the loan from additional monitoring exceeds the marginal cost to greater monitoring.

Certain loans may not require any internal financing under the equilibrium bank-loan buyer contract, i.e., $I = 0$. In this case, the structure of the contract remains qualitatively the same, however, with a return going to the bank only if the loan return is high.[19] Clearly, loans for which the benefits from monitoring are negligible or zero would be fully sold. For example, the polar case in which $f_a(x, a) = 0$ for all (x, a) would imply an equilibrium level of monitoring of $a = 0$. No problem of moral hazard would exist, and the bank would optimally choose

---

[17] See *The Wall Street Journal*, January 23, 1986, "Major New York Banks Initiate Tactic of Selling Short-Term 'Strips' of Loans."

[18] Merton [21] shows that the risk premium on a promised corporate payment rises as the time until payment is received increases. Note, however, that it may not be the case that the bank has made a firm commitment to the borrower to renew the loan. As with other types of loan commitments, these contracts typically contain a rather vague condition whereby the bank would not be obligated to relend, such as "if there was a materially adverse change in the borrower's condition." In practice, banks seldom utilize this condition even if it appears to be in their best interests at the time. Gorton and Haubrich [13] argue that there may still exist an implicit firm commitment to renew the loan that is bound by the bank's reputation as a dependable provider of loan commitment services.

[19] When $I = 0$, condition (26) implies that $\omega \leq 1 + r_l$. For $1 + r_d \leq \omega \leq 1 + r_l$, condition (25) indicates that the bank will again receive a share of the loan's return only when no default occurs. For $0 \leq \omega \leq 1 + r_d$, $b(x)$ will tend to be less than one for large values of x and equal to one for smaller values of x.

to finance the loan entirely through funding from loan sales.[20] This (degenerate) case could be viewed as the bank performing solely an underwriting function. Of course, this makes sense since, if there were no benefits to monitoring a borrowing firm's loan, the loan would be essentially a marketable asset.

B. Loan Sales with Recourse

One simple contractual arrangement that could provide a first-best solution to the above problem (20) to (22) would be for the bank simply to guarantee the loan buyer a rate of return of r_d regardless of the actual loan payoff. This contract, similar to the bank-depositor contract in Diamond [6], would be feasible if the bank were able to maintain sufficient asset (loan) diversification such that the probability of the bank's failure were negligible. Giving the loan buyer recourse to claims on other bank assets conceivably would allow the bank to sell the entire loan and still retain the incentive to monitor at the economically efficient level.

However, the Federal Reserve has sought to place restrictions on direct guarantees on loan sales.[21] With only a few exceptions, guarantees by banks to reimburse loan buyers for loan losses, even if a ceiling on the amount of the bank's reimbursement were made, would lead the Fed to treat the bank's proceeds from a loan sale as a "deposit" subject to inclusion in calculations of required capital and possibly subject to required reserves. Federal Reserve proposals do allow for loans to be sold with recourse in the following manner. If a bank agrees to guarantee a given *percentage* of loan sales losses, say l, where l is less than seventy-five percent, then this bank will be permitted to classify only a proportion $(1 - l)$ of the proceeds from the loan buyer as a loan sale. The other proportion, l, of the proceeds must be classified as a deposit, again subject to required capital. However, the Federal Reserve has stated that, as long as the percent losses guaranteed, l, is less than seventy-five percent, no required reserves need be held against the proceeds of the loan sale.

Under this arrangement, where the loan buyer's payment is $b(x)x = bx + bl(L - x)$, one might ask what the bank's optimal choice of b and l is. For this type of recourse loan, the bank's problem is

$$\max_{\{b,l,a\}} \bar{x}(a) - b[\bar{x}(a) + l(L - \bar{x}(a))] - c(a) - (1 + r_I)I, \qquad (34)$$

---

[20] While Greenbaum and Thakor's [14] signalling model produces a distinct (and perhaps complementary) rationale for loan sales, they arrive at a result similar to that of this paper—namely, that better quality assets are funded by loan sales while poorer quality assets (cf. those needing more monitoring) are funded with deposits.

[21] See Federal Reserve regulations 12 CFR Part 204 Regulation D; Docket No. R-0571 and the instructions for filing Reports of Condition and Income, as well as the explanations of these regulations in Pavel [26]. While the Federal Reserve places restrictions on direct guarantees by banks of loan sales, they have not acted to restrict loan sales that are guaranteed by third-party insurance companies, even if the bank and insurance company negotiate an agreement that obligates the bank to reimburse ex post the insurance company for any payments it must make to the loan buyer. Under these circumstances, third-party insurance of loan sales appears to be the optimal arrangement from the bank's and loan buyer's points of view. However, it is reasonable to believe that the existence of this loophole will be short-lived.

subject to

$$b[\bar{x}(a) + l(L - \bar{x}(a))]\left(\frac{1 - l}{1 + r_d} + \frac{l}{1 + r_c}\right) + I = 1, \tag{35}$$

$$[1 - b(1 - l)]\bar{x}_a = c'(a), \tag{36}$$

$$0 \leq l \leq \bar{l} = 0.75, \tag{37}$$

$$0 \leq b \leq 1, \tag{38}$$

where $\bar{x}(a) = \int_0^L x\, dF(x, a)$, $\bar{x}_a = \int_0^L x\, dF_a(x, a)$, and r_c denotes the cost of bank funds from loan sales that are subject to capital constraints but not required reserves. r_c will be the cost of capital on the proportion l of loan-sale proceeds when the proportion of loan losses guaranteed is less than seventy-five percent. Therefore, r_c equals the expression for r_l but where required reserves, ρ, have been set equal to zero, and hence $r_c \leq r_l$.

Assuming that the incentive-compatibility constraint (36) is binding in equilibrium, it is clear from (37) and (38) that the equilibrium level of bank monitoring, a, will be less than the economically efficient (first-best) level. Interpreting the Kuhn-Tucker conditions from (34) to (38), it is straightforward to show that possible optima exist only for two sets of (b, l) combinations: where constraints (36) and (37) bind and where constraints (36) and (38) bind. Therefore, banks will always choose a positive level of loss guarantees under these regulations. Depending on the magnitude of the parameters of the model, the bank will either sell the entire loan with $l < \bar{l}$ or choose to sell somewhat less than the entire loan with $l = \bar{l}$.

III. Loan Sales and Imperfect Competition in Deposit Markets

Money-center and large regional banks account for virtually all the recent growth in commercial and industrial loans sold in the U.S.[22] The majority of these sales are portions of short-term loans or loan strips of investment-grade borrowers, implying that these assets are similar in quality to money-market instruments such as commercial paper. It could be argued that some of this loan selling substitutes for commercial-paper underwriting, an activity where commercial banks face restrictions.

Purchasers of these loans include a growing number of non-bank financial institutions and nonfinancial corporations. However, the bulk of these assets are bought by smaller domestic banks and foreign banks. One explanation for why other banks might wish to purchase these short-term loans is that they serve to enhance a bank's liquidity, reducing the cost of providing transactions services such as check clearing and currency-to-deposit convertibility.[23] A second expla-

---

[22] The Board of Governores of the Federal Reserve System's February 1986 Senior Loan Officer Opinion Survey gives information on the sixty largest U.S. banks' commercial loan sales activities, including their loan sales volume and the principal purchasing institutions. The nine largest banks accounted for more than half of the $26 billion loan sales outstanding as of year-end 1985.

[23] A transactions demand for liquid or marketable assets could be derived similarly to the inventory-theoretic transactions demand for money modeled by Miller and Orr [24].

nation for banks purchasing loans emerges by generalizing the model in Section I to consider imperfect competition in banks' deposit markets. The analysis is similar to that of Fama [9]. Banks with market power in deposit financing, but with relatively weak loan-origination opportunities, become candidates for loan purchases.

To illustrate this point in a simple manner, assume that, if an originating bank monitors a loan at level $a = \tilde{a}$, there is zero probability of default and the loan returns $x(s, \tilde{a}) = 1 + r_n$. Monitoring at any level $a < \tilde{a}$ results in a loan default, with the loan returning $1 + r_n - z$, where $z > \tilde{a}c$ is constant for all states. Let $\bar{b}$ equal the proportion of financing obtained through selling a share of the loan's return, where $\bar{b}$ is assumed sufficiently small to maintain the bank's incentive to monitor. In addition, let r_m denote the yield on money-market instruments and competitively priced deposits, and, as before, let r_I equal the cost of internal financing when bank deposits are competitively priced.

Figure 2 depicts an equilibrium that corresponds to the loan sales equilibrium previously analyzed in Section I, Subsection *B*. *NN'* denotes the marginal-revenue curve for loans, while *NAA'* denotes the bank's marginal-revenue curve for all assets, assuming that the bank can always purchase marketable assets bearing a return of r_m instead of originating loans past the point $r_n - c\tilde{a} < r_m$. The marginal cost of funds is given by *DD'* when the bank does not sell loans and *DSS'* when the bank does. Note that, for this case, the point *S* is to the left of point *A*, indicating that the marginal cost of funds rises above the level r_m prior to the marginal-revenue curve, *NAA'*, and implying that the bank will optimally begin selling loans at point *S*. Therefore, the case depicted in Figure 2 describes a bank that has relatively greater loan-origination opportunities than core-deposit funding opportunities.

In contrast, Figure 3 depicts an equilibrium in which a bank has relatively less loan-origination than deposit-funding opportunities. Here, the marginal-cost-of-funding curve *DSS'* reaches the level r_m at point *S*, which is to the right of where

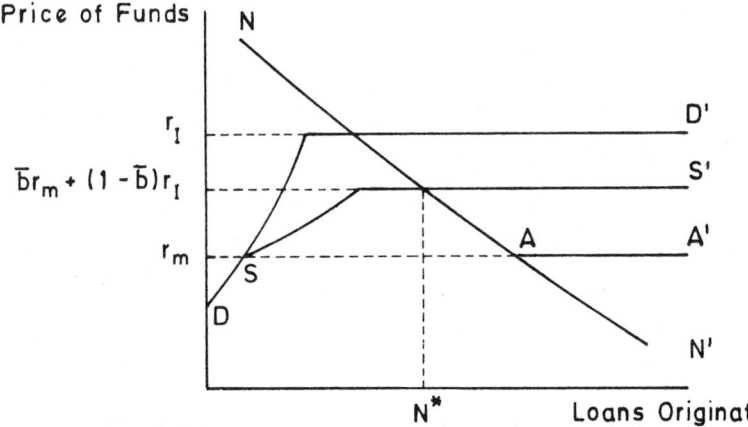

Figure 2. Loan-selling bank. *NN'*, marginal revenue from loan origination = $r_n(N) - c\tilde{a}$; *NAA'*, marginal revenue for all assets; *DD'*, marginal cost of funds without loan sales; *DSS'*, marginal cost of funds with loan sales.

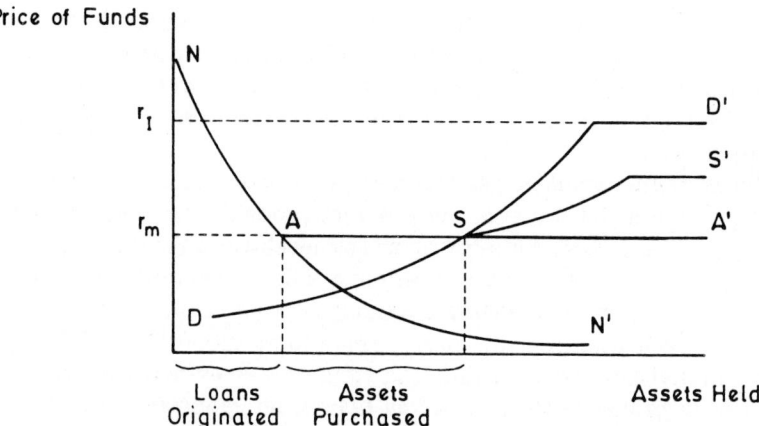

Figure 3. Loan-purchasing bank. NN', marginal revenue from loan origination $= r_n(N) - c\bar{a}$; NAA', marginal revenue for all assets; DD', marginal cost of funds without loan sales; DSS', marginal cost of funds with loan sales.

the marginal-revenue curve NAA' reaches r_m at the point A. This bank will optimally purchase marketable assets, which pay return r_m, equal in value to the length AS. Some of these marketable assets could take the form of loan shares sold by a bank with a situation of that of Figure 2. Therefore, the analysis in Figures 2 and 3 provides testable implications regarding which banks would choose to sell versus buy loans or hold marketable securities. Furthermore, the model predicts that a decline in inexpensive deposit-funding opportunities would tend to result in an expansion of loan sales.

These implications are roughly consistent with the stylized facts of loan sales. Large money-center banks, which originate the lion's share of loans sold, generally acquire funding in wholesale markets, through issuing large certificates of deposit and other purchased funds, paying competitive rates. Smaller banks have a much greater proportion of their liabilities in small time and savings deposits—approximately sixty-nine percent for banks with assets of less than \$100 million versus thirty-six percent for banks with assets exceeding \$100 million.[24] Peltzman [28, p. 562] states, "If small banks have had a cost advantage anywhere, it has been in securing deposits. ... [time] deposit cost differences between small and large banks running on the order of 200 to 400 basis points."

While larger banks are at a relative disadvantage in terms of deposit funding, one would expect that their loan-origination opportunities might exceed those of many smaller banks. Because of their location in large financial centers throughout the world, money-center banks would appear to have access to many potential borrowers. Small banks constrained to local lending markets might also have the amount of their lending opportunities limited because of an inability to achieve diversification, which purchasing loans can help to remedy. A recent empirical

[24] See Waldrop [33] for a comparison of large and small banks' liability compositions. Note that Banker's Trust is one of the first and largest banks to expand its loan-sales activities. In 1979, it sold eighty branches in its retail network having combined deposits of \$934 million, receiving a \$65 million sales premium on these deposits.

study by Pavel and Phillis [27] finds that a bank's comparative advantage in originating and servicing loans has the largest impact in determining the amount of loans that it will sell. The size of a bank's assets, its ability to diversify, and whether its capital constraint is binding are also significant factors in determining the amount of its loan sales. James [17] also finds that banks with a large volume of off-balance-sheet activities tend to have high leverage.

Finally, the growth in the aggregate volume of loan sales has roughly coincided with a general decline in banks' market power in deposit financing. The 1970's and early 1980's saw a disintegration of the monopolistic price-fixing effects of Regulation Q as unregulated intermediaries such as money-market mutual funds provided competitive returns to small investors. Securitization of mortgage loans showed steady growth over this period, while commercial, credit card, and auto loan sales totaling a relatively negligible amount in 1983 are estimated by Salem [31] to stand at roughly $35 billion in 1986, up approximately one hundred percent from the previous year.

IV. Conclusion

This paper demonstrated that banks faced with significant competition for deposit financing, as well as regulatory constraints in the form of required capital and/or reserves, cannot profit by simply holding money-market assets but must provide other services, such as information gathering and monitoring activities related to making loans. Loan sales can reduce the cost of funding these loans. However, we showed that other banks with substantial market power in deposit financing, but with limited loan-origination opportunities, may choose to hold marketable assets. These assets can take the form of loan shares purchased from those banks facing competitive financing.

A bank's ability to sell loans depends on loan buyers' perception of the bank's incentive to monitor those loans. By designing the loan sales contract in a way that gives the bank a disproportionate share of the gains to monitoring, it was shown that a greater share of the loan can be sold and, hence, a greater level of bank profits can be attained.

There is another issue that this paper has touched upon but not adequately treated. Determining what effect greater loan sales has on overall bank risk would be a productive area of research. Because the optimal loan-sales contract attempts to give the bank a disproportionate share of the gains to monitoring, the bank will generally be assuming a disproportionate share of a given loan's risk. Thus, it might appear that loan sales would increase the volatility of the bank's asset portfolio. However, for a given bank capital structure, the benefits of asset diversification, deriving from a greater number of loans originated when loan selling occurs, might outweigh the higher risk incurred on each individual loan. It may be unwise for regulators to unconditionally discourage loan sales.

Appendix

Below is a derivation of the bank's objective function when banks maximize the after-tax rate of return to shareholders and deposit insurance is fairly priced.

Using the notation in the text, the bank's end-of-period after-tax asset value, when state s occurs, is

$$\{\textstyle\sum_{i=1}^{N} (x_i(s, a_i) - 1 - ca_i) - r_d D\}(1 - t) + N + \rho D + r_d D. \quad \text{(A1)}$$

Letting ϕ be the premium charged for deposit insurance, the payoff to equity-holders when the bank is solvent is

$$\{\textstyle\sum_{i=1}^{N} (x_i(s, a_i) - 1 - ca_i) - r_d D\}(1 - t) + E - \phi D \equiv W(s) - \phi D. \quad \text{(A2)}$$

Of course, equityholders receive nothing when bankruptcy occurs. The end-of-period payoff to the deposit insurer is ϕD when the bank is solvent and $W(s)$ when the bank is insolvent. The insurer receiving $W(s)$ implicitly assumes that the value of the bank's tax shield is preserved when the bank fails. This is not unrealistic since Kane [18, p. 38] points out that, when a failed bank is merged with an acquiring bank, the failed bank's losses can be used to reduce the acquiring bank's tax liability.

It is assumed that the deposit insurer's regulatory authority enables it to costlessly audit the bank's risk just after the start of the period. Let S_0 denote the set of solvency states and S_1 the set of insolvency states. Also let $\{p(s)\}$ denote the set of primitive security prices that the deposit insurer uses to value its end-of-period cash flow. Then a fair premium, ϕ, is such that

$$\phi D \int_{S_0} p(s)\ ds + \int_{S_1} p(s) W(s)\ ds = 0. \quad \text{(A3)}$$

Substituting this value for ϕ in (A2) and taking the shareholders' present value of (A2) over all solvency states, S_0, one obtains

$$\int_{S_0} W(s) p^e(s)\ ds + \frac{\int_{S_1} p(s) W(s)\ ds}{\int_{S_0} p(s)\ ds} \int_{S_0} p^e(s)\ ds. \quad \text{(A4)}$$

Finally, the assumption is made that $p(s)$ is a constant proportion of $p^e(s)$ for all s. For example, if the insuring agency's valuation of contingent claims reflected that of depositors (debtholders) with state-contingent prices $\{p^d(s)\}$, then, as shown by Litzenberger and Van Horne [19, p. 739], the quantity $p^d(s)/p^e(s)$ would be constant across states if the personal tax bracket of the "marginal" investor indifferent between holding debt and equity were constant across states. This assumption is also made in DeAngelo and Masulis [5].

Expression (A4) can then be written as

$$\left\{\textstyle\sum_{i=1}^{N} \left[(1 + r_e) \int_0^1 p^e(s) x_i(s, a_i)\ ds - 1 - ca_i\right] - r_d D\right\} \frac{(1 - t)}{(1 + r_e)} + \frac{E}{1 + r_e}. \quad \text{(A5)}$$

If the bank is assumed to maximize the difference between the present value of equityholders' payment (A4) and the amount of equity that must initially be raised, E, then, by subtracting E from (A4) and multiplying by $(1 + r_e)$, one obtains equation (2) in the text.

REFERENCES

1. A. Barnea, R. Haugen, and L. Senbet. "An Equilibrium Analysis of Debt Financing under Costly Tax Arbitrage and Agency Problems." *Journal of Finance* 36 (June 1981), 569–81.
2. F. Black. "Banking and Interest Rates in a World without Money." *Journal of Bank Research* 1 (Autumn 1970), 8–20.
3. S. Buser, A. Chen, and E. Kane. "Federal Deposit Insurance, Regulatory Policy, and Optimal Bank Capital." *Journal of Finance* 36 (March 1981), 51–60.
4. T. Campbell and W. Kracaw. "Information Production, Market Signalling and the Theory of Financial Intermediation." *Journal of Finance* 35 (September 1980), 863–81.
5. H. DeAngelo and R. Masulis. "Optimal Capital Structure under Corporate and Personal Taxation." *Journal of Financial Economics* 8 (March 1980), 3–29.
6. D. Diamond. "Financial Intermediation and Delegated Monitoring." *Review of Economic Studies* 51 (July 1984), 393–414.
7. U. Dothan and J. Williams. "Banks, Bankruptcy, and Public Regulation." *Journal of Banking and Finance* 4 (March 1980), 65–87.
8. E. Fama. "Banking in the Theory of Finance." *Journal of Monetary Economics* 6 (January 1980), 39–57.
9. ———. "What's Different about Banks?" *Journal of Monetary Economics* 15 (January 1985), 29–39.
10. S. Fischer. "A Framework for Monetary and Banking Analysis." *Economic Journal* 93 (March 1983), supplement, 1–16.
11. M. Flannery. "Deposit Insurance, Capital Regulation, and the Choice of Bank Loan Default Rates." Mimeo, University of North Carolina at Chapel Hill, 1987.
12. R. Gorton and B. Malkiel. "Corporation Finance." In H. J. Aaron and J. A. Pechman (eds.), *How Taxes Affect Economic Behavior.* Washington, D.C.: Brookings, 1981, 131–98.
13. G. Gorton and J. Haubrich. "Loan Sales, Recourse, and Reputation: An Analysis of Secondary Loan Participations." Working Paper No. 14-87, Rodney L. White Center for Financial Research, University of Pennsylvania, 1987.
14. S. Greenbaum and A. Thakor. "Bank Funding Modes: Securitization versus Deposits." *Journal of Banking and Finance* 11 (September 1987), 379–402.
15. O. Hart and B. Holmström. "The Theory of Contracts." Working Paper No. 418, Massachusetts Institute of Technology, 1986.
16. B. Holmström. "Moral Hazard and Observability." *Bell Journal of Economics* 10 (Spring 1979), 74–91.
17. C. James. "An Analysis of the Use of Loan Sales, Standby Letters of Credit and Secured Debt by Commmercial Banks." Mimeo, University of Oregon, 1987.
18. E. Kane. *The Gathering Crisis in Federal Deposit Insurance.* Cambridge: MIT Press, 1985.
19. R. Litzenberger and J. Van Horne. "Elimination of the Double Taxation of Dividends and Corporate Financial Policy." *Journal of Finance* 33 (June 1978), 737–57.
20. D. Melvin. *A Primer for RMA Staff on Legal and Regulatory Concepts and Standards in the Securitization of Loans.* Philadelphia: Robert Morris Associates, 1986.
21. R. Merton. "On the Pricing of Corporate Debt: The Risk Structure of Interest Rates." *Journal of Finance* 29 (May 1974), 449–70.
22. ———. "An Analytical Derivation of the Cost of Deposit Insurance and Loan Guarantees: An Application of Modern Option Pricing Theory." *Journal of Banking and Finance* 1 (June 1977), 3–11.
23. M. Miller. "Debt and Taxes." *Journal of Finance* 32 (June 1977), 261–75.
24. ——— and D. Orr. "A Model of the Demand for Money by Firms." *Quarterly Journal of Economics* 80 (August 1966), 413–35.
25. Y. Orgler and R. Taggart. "Implications of Corporate Capital Structure Theory for Banking Institutions." *Journal of Money, Credit, and Banking* 15 (May 1983), 212–21.
26. C. Pavel. "Securitization." In *Economic Perspectives.* Chicago: Federal Reserve Bank of Chicago, July/August 1986, 16–31.
27. ——— and D. Phillis. "To Sell or Not to Sell: Loan Sales by Commercial Banks." Mimeo, Federal Reserve Bank of Chicago, 1987.

28. S. Peltzman. "Comment on Bank Market Structure and Competition: A Survey." *Journal of Money, Credit, and Banking* 16 (November 1984), 650–56.

29. G. Pennacchi. "A Reexamination of the Over (or Under) Pricing of Deposit Insurance." *Journal of Money, Credit, and Banking* 19 (August 1987).

30. G. Salem. "Selling Commercial Loans: A Significant New Activity for Money Center Banks." *Journal of Commercial Bank Lending* 68 (April 1985), 2–19.

31. ———. "Loan Selling: A Banking Revolution." Mimeo, Donaldson, Lufkin & Jenrette Securities Corporation, October 1986.

32. J. Skelton. "The Relative Pricing of Tax-Exempt and Taxable Debt." Working paper, University of California-Berkeley, 1982.

33. R. Waldrop. "Interest Rate Deregulation and Its Impact on the Cost of Funds at Commercial Banks." *Banking and Economic Review* 4 Federal Deposit Insurance Corporation (March 1986), 19–22.

Elements of Mortgage Securitization

ALAN C. HESS
Washington Mutual Professor of Financial Markets, Graduate School of Business Administration, University of Washington

CLIFFORD W. SMITH, JR.
Professor, William E. Simon Graduate School of Business Administration, University of Rochester

Abstract

In this paper we review the forms of mortgage securitization, analyze the demand for securitization, and demonstrate how securitization meets these demands by reducing intermediation costs. We argue that the increased use of securitization is a response to increased interest rate volatility and represents a contractual innovation that facilitates an efficient allocation of risk-bearing among households and intermediaries.

1. Introduction

Securitization is a wholesale financial intermediation process which rebundles individual principal and interest payments of existing financial instruments to create new securities. In this paper we argue that securitization is a cost-effective way for financial intermediaries to manage their interest-rate risk exposure. Our analysis of securitization builds on and integrates three extant arguments in the intermediation literature: (1) financial intermediaries exist because they reduce transaction and information costs to borrowers and lenders (Benston and Smith, 1976); (2) the supply of intermediation services by short-funded, mortgage lenders exposes them to significant interest rate risk (Hess, 1987); and (3) hedging is a value increasing response to increased interest rate uncertainty (Mayers and Smith, 1982, 1987, and Smith and Stulz, 1985). We accept points one and three, and develop point two: securitization lowers the cost of separating the supply of intermediation services from interest rate risk management. We argue that the gains from securitization are increased by the implicit put option on interest rates embedded in mortgage loans and the implicit call option on interest rates embedded in long term deposits.

2. Intermediation services

Financial intermediaries provide four types of services to financial market participants: they originate financial assets and liabilities, they enforce the rights and

Journal of Real Estate Finance and Economics, 1: 331–346 (1988)
© 1988 Kluwer Academic Publishers

obligations of the parties specified in the financial contracts, they make markets in financial instruments, and they manage the risks associated with the contractually generated cash flows. The intermediary's cash flows come from both the supply of intermediation services and capital gains or losses from risk management; the risks include interest-rate risk, prepayment risk, and default risk.

2.1. Production of mortgage loans

Mortgage lending, a particular type of financial intermediation, can be divided into three separable activities: loan origination, loan servicing, and ownership of the loan's cash flow rights. Intermediation costs are potentially lowest when each of these three activities is produced by its lowest cost supplier. A local financial institution, a bank or savings and loan association, has geographically specific knowledge that tends to make it the lowest cost estimator of the credit worthiness of borrowers and the market value of the underlying real property being mortgaged. As a result, it typically has a comparative advantage in mortgage origination. It is also frequently the lowest cost servicer of mortgages through its local branch network. This comparative advantage in the origination and service components of the lending process generally is enhanced by continuing investments in human and informational capital that help it maintain a cost advantage over other potential originators and servicers.

An intermediary that makes a mortgage loan does not have to hold the mortgage and manage its attendant interest-rate risk until it is redeemed (Deshmukh, Greenbaum and Kanatas, 1983). The potentially harmful results of failing to separate interest-rate risk management from intermediation service supply were demonstrated in the early 1980s. Approximately 1,200 short-funded, mortgage-lending savings and loan associations ceased to exist as independent economic entities, even though estimates suggest that as a group savings and loans were viable suppliers of intermediation services. For example, Hess (1987) decomposes savings and loan industry income into that due to the supply of intermediation services (defined as income absent capital gains and losses due to unexpected changes in interest rates) and that due to interest-rate risk exposure. The industry's intermediation profit margin was positive even though its measured income was negative due to the effect of unexpected increases in market interest rates given their interest-rate risk exposure. This evidence suggests that savings and loans could have benefited from separating the supply of intermediation services from interest-rate risk management.

Failure to separate the transaction components of mortgage lending from its funding can increase intermediation costs even in periods of stable interest rates because of the local nature of mortgage and deposit markets. Areas with fast-growing populations and consequently a large number of new homes being built have experienced shortages of mortgage lending from deposit intermediaries at permitted interest rates. This has created pressure to find alternative sources of mortgage loan financing. In other areas at different stages of development, local housing construction has been less than local deposit additions at prevailing interest rates. There, pressures have existed to find alternative uses of savings. In addition to lending and saving imbalances, savings and loans traditionally have lacked geographical risk diversification in both their mortgage loans and deposits. Therefore, changes in local economic conditions lead to increases in the risk of supplying intermediation services that could be reduced through geographic diversification.

2.2. Exposure to interest-rate changes

Mortgage lending deposit intermediaries have supplied financial contracts with the maturities demanded by their customers. These have tended to be relatively short-term deposits but long-term loans. Long-term, fixed-rate mortgages reduce households' exposures to interest-rate risk as compared to short-term or variable-rate mortgages. With a long-term, fixed-rate mortgage, the duration of a house times its value more closely approximates the duration of its mortgage times its value.[1] This reduces the response of the housing component of household wealth to changes in market interest rates and partially immunizes the household against unexpected changes in interest rates (Hess, 1984).

Deposits also allow households to transfer some of their interest rate risk to deposit intermediaries. Households have a variety of holding periods for their savings. Some savings are held for near-term spending while other savings are held for distant spending such as during retirement. In principle, if deposit intermediaries offered an unlimited array of savings instruments they could attract more long-term savings. This would allow the intermediary to lengthen the duration of its liability portfolio and reduce its interest-rate risk exposure. However, partially for regulatory reasons, deposits have tended to be primarily short-term instruments. Moreover, markets for interest-rate risk management tools such as forwards, futures, options, and swaps have been fairly illiquid, especially in long maturity contracts. As a result, mortgage-lending deposit intermediaries have been exposed to interest-rate risk and have faced substantial costs due to the difference between the effective maturities of their assets and liabilities.

3. Effects of changes in interest rates

Management of interest-rate risk exposure becomes increasingly important as interest-rate volatility increases. Figure 1 and Table 1 indicate that interest rates (as represented by the secondary market yield on U.S. Treasury bills with three months to maturity) have increased and become more variable since 1947. The variance of the change in interest rates increased by more than a factor of four

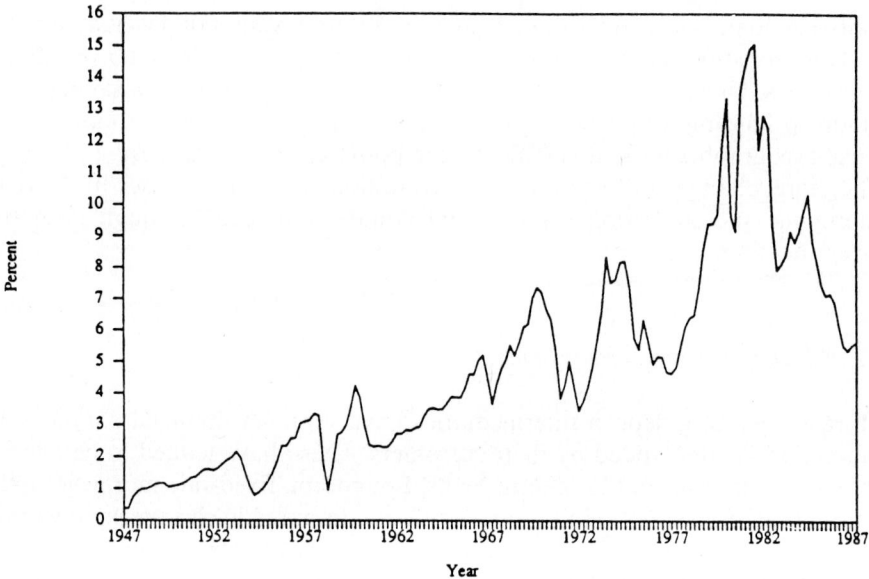

Fig. 1. Yields on 3-month Treasury Bills from 1947 to 1987.

Table 1. Summary statistics for the secondary market yield on 3-month Treasury Bills (% per year)

Variable	Mean	Standard Deviation	Minimum	Maximum
		1950s		
R	2.00	0.85	0.79	4.23
dR	0.08	0.41	−1.54	1.01
		1960s		
R	3.98	1.33	2.30	7.35
dR	0.08	0.37	−0.88	0.83
		1970s		
R	6.29	1.87	3.44	11.84
dR	0.11	0.81	−1.61	2.17
		1980s		
R	9.40	2.92	5.35	15.05
dR	−0.21	1.51	−3.74	4.46

R is the level of the yield on 3-month Treasury bills, and dR is its first difference.

from the 1960s to the 1970s, and by more than a factor of three in the 1980s over the 1970s.

3.1. Response of lender value to interest-rate changes

If interest rates rise unexpectedly, market values of short-funded intermediaries fall because the market values of long-term, fixed-rate mortgages fall relative to the market values of short-term deposits. Without prepayment options in the financial contracts the response of value to unexpected interest rate changes is generally symmetric. If interest rates fall unexpectedly, the values of deposit intermediaries rise. Figure 2 illustrates the effect of interest rate changes on the value of a deposit intermediary that finances long-term, fixed-rate mortgages with short-term deposits. The horizontal axis records changes in market interest rates (dR) and the vertical axis records the corresponding change in the market value of the intermediary (dV). With no prepayment options in the loan or deposit contracts, Grove (1974) shows that the approximate formula linking dV to dR is

$$dV/dR = (L*DL - A*DA)/(1 + R). \tag{1}$$

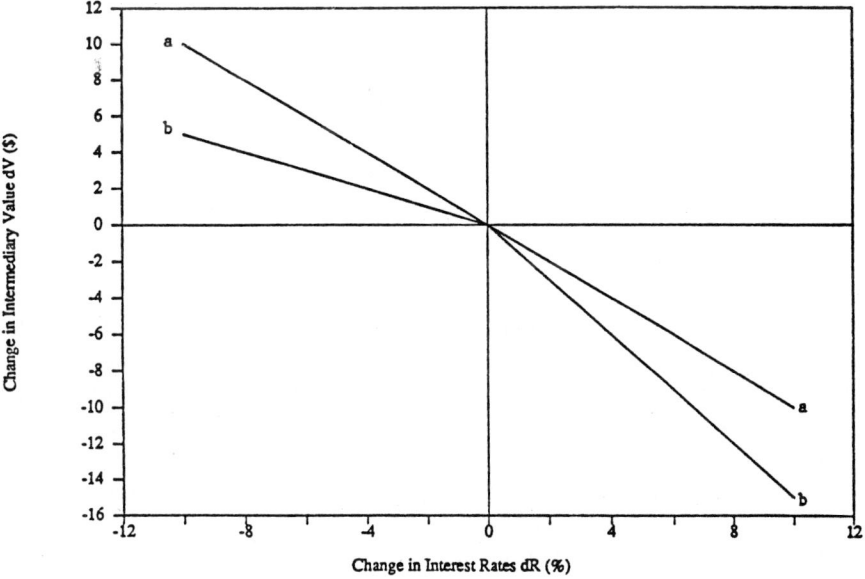

Fig. 2. The effect on lender value of interest-rate changes for a short-funded intermediary. Line *aa* illustrates the negative relation between firm value and interest rates. Line *bb* illustrates the effect of the embedded prepayment options sold loan customers and withdrawal options sold depositors.

Here, L is the market value of liabilites,
$\quad\quad A$ is the market value of assets,
$\quad\quad DL$ is the duration of liabilities,
$\quad\quad DA$ is the duration of assets, and
$\quad\quad R$ is the initial market interest rate.

Line aa in Figure 2 depicts equation (1) for a short-funded mortgage lender. In this case, the market value of liabilities times the duration of liabilities, $L*DL$, is less than the market value of assets times the duration of assets, $A*DA$; hence the change in the value of the intermediary due to a change in interest rates, dV/dR, is negative. If the duration imbalance, $(L*DL - A*DA)$ is reduced, the line becomes flatter and the response of value to a change in interest rates, dV/dR, falls. Conversely, if the duration imbalance increases, line aa becomes steeper and the sensitivity of value to interest rates increases.[2]

3.2. Effects of embedded options in loans and deposits

Historically, intermediaries have offered loan and deposit contracts which typically have given the customer the option to prepay the loan or withdraw the deposit prior to maturity. Unexpected mortgage prepayments and deposit withdrawals present an important complication to analysis of the effects of interest-rate changes on intermediary value. A mortgage consists of an underlying asset, the market value of its remaining principal and interest payments, plus a sequence of call options on these payments. Mortgage lenders have written these call options: generally, each option has an exercise price equal to the book value of the remaining principal payments.

Because of the call options, line aa in Figure 2 is not appropriate during periods of falling interest rates. If interest rates fall, homeowners can exercise their right to prepay (call) an existing mortgage at its book value. In many cases they refinance at the then prevailing interest rate. Mortgage prepayments and refinancing have two separate effects on the value of short-funded mortgage lenders. First, when a mortgage is prepaid at book, the lender gives up a capital gain equal to the difference between the market and book values of the mortgage. Second, the lender must reinvest the cash in some new financial instrument; for simplicity, assume this is a new mortgage on the same property. The new instrument yields the then prevailing lower market rate and, other market conditions being constant, has a longer duration than the prepaid mortgage.

If mortgage contracts allow prepayment, the mortgage lender receives capital gains only on the mortgages which are not prepaid. Line bb to the left of the origin in Figure 2 represents these capital gains. Prepayments reduce the response of the value of the intermediary to interest-rate changes. To the left of the origin, the vertical distance between lines aa and bb reflects the difference between the market and book values of prepaid mortgages. It is the intermediary's foregone value increase due to prepayments.[3] Assuming that the prepaid mortgages are refinanced at the then prevailing lower interest rate, the duration of the intermediary's assets increases. In equation (1) the asset duration, DA, increases, making the intermediary's value more responsive to interest-rate changes.[4]

Since long-term certificates of deposit (CDs) also include early withdrawal provisions, line aa in Figure 2 is also incorrect for increases in interest rates. With higher rates, holders of long-term CDs will redeem their low rate CDs and take out new higher rate CDs. The value of this option is shown in line bb to the right of the origin.

Because of the maturity options offered in both loan and deposit instruments, value changes produced by interest rate changes are not symmetric. Unexpected increases in rates lead to reductions in loan prepayments and a lengthening of the effective maturity of the loan portfolio. This increases the fall in the value of the intermediary from the rate rise. At the same time, depositors roll over their long-term deposits at the higher rates, again increasing the fall in the value of the intermediary. These options cause the gains to the mortgage lender from declines in market interest rates to be less than the losses associated with increases in interest rates. As a result, expected intermediary value is reduced by increases in interest rate volatility.

3.3. Incentives to hedge interest-rate risk

Securitization is a special case of corporate hedging since it transfers interest-rate risk from short-funded mortgage lenders to other parties which have a comparative advantage in managing the risk.[5] Since the typical mortgage lender is a corporation, not an individual, risk aversion does not provide a satisfactory rationale for corporate hedging. We treat hedging by a value-maximizing intermediary as a special case of corporate financial policy. Modigliani and Miller (1958) demonstrate that with fixed investment decisions, no taxes, and no contracting costs, a firm's choice of financing policy does not affect its current market value. Thus, hedging policy (as well as the rest of corporate financing policy) can affect a firm's value only if the policy changes the firm's tax liability, its contracting costs, or its incentives regarding current or future real investment. We believe that each of these arguments provides a partial explanation of a short-funded mortgage lender's incentives to hedge.

If there are fixed costs of hedging, intermediaries have a comparative advantage over individuals in hedging. Consequently, the increased variance of changes in interest rates that has occurred in each decade since World War II has increased the benefits of hedging by intermediaries.

Progressivity in the tax code provides opportunities for some lenders to raise their after-tax expected net cash flows through securitization.[6] For example, in a simple tax system with a positive marginal tax rate on profits and a zero rate on losses, the function relating taxes to taxable income resembles a call option on taxable income. The government is long the call, and the firm and its shareholders are short the call. Option pricing theory implies that the value of this call increases with the variance in taxable income. Securitization allows the intermediary to reduce its exposure to interest rate risk, reduce the variation in its taxable income, lower its expected tax liability, raise its expected after-tax cash flows, and thus increase its market value. (Note that carry-backs and carry-forward provisions reduce the convexity of the tax code and thus reduce the firm's incentives to hedge.) The investment tax credit and the alternative minimum tax are other tax code provisions that introduce convexities into the tax schedule and offer profitable hedging opportunities to value maximizing corporations.[7]

Myers (1977) argues that a firm's investment incentives can be affected by its capital structure. A firm with substantial debt can have incentives to reject positive net present value investment projects if the cost of acquisition falls primarily on the stockholders but the benefits accrue primarily to the bondholders. In the case of insured deposit intermediaries, the major beneficiary is the insuring agency. Mayers and Smith (1987) show that hedging can control a form of the underinvestment problem for a firm which has risky debt outstanding. If the value of the firm's assets falls unexpectedly, the firm's leverage rises unexpectedly, and the underinvestment incentives become potentially severe. By reducing the volatility of firm value, securitization reduces the probability of rejecting profitable projects.

In addition to stockholders and bondholders, a firm has a vast network of contracts among parties with common as well as conflicting interests. Managers, employees, customers, and suppliers are sometimes less able to diversify firm-specific investments than are stockholders and bondholders. Like the owners of a closely-held corporation, these claim holders' risk aversion can motivate mortgage loan securitization. However, the specific incentives of corporate managers to engage in securitization depends on the particular form of their compensation package and its relation to firm value. While risk aversion motivates a manager compensated primarily through salary to lobby for securitization, a manager with substantial compensation through stock options or bonus plans has fewer incentives to hedge. This results from the option-like character of the manager's payoffs under both stock option and standard bonus plans (Smith and Watts, 1982).

4. Types of securitized mortgage instruments

The principal and interest payments on a mortgage pool constitute a cash flow stream of uncertain size, duration, and value. Changes in market interest rates change the market value of a mortgage pool absent any changes in its expected repayments of principal and interest. This exposes mortgage lenders to price risk. In addition, unexpected variation over time in prepayment rates causes actual cash flows to differ from their expected values. Homeowners prepay mortgages both in response to specific factors that affect homeowners differently, as well as in response to economy wide factors (such as declines in interest rates) that affect many homeowners similarly. This prepayment uncertainty exposes investors in mortgage-backed securities to reinvestment risk. Securitized mortgage instruments are designed to help investors manage both price risk and reinvestment risk.

Strips, senior/subordinated claims, and collateralized mortgage obligations (CMOs) are bonds that are collateralized by an underlying pool of mortgages which is usually guaranteed by one of the federal housing agencies. They are issued by investment banks, home builders, federal mortgage agencies, savings and loan associations, mortgage bankers, insurance companies, and commercial banks. The issuer either originates or purchases a mortgage pool and then issues a set of new securities that rebundle the principal and interest payments from the pool.

4.1. Strips

A simple way to construct new securities from a mortgage pool is to separate interest payments from principal payments and sell separate rights to each. The rights to the principal only payments are called POs and the rights to the interest only payments are called IOs.

Because of prepayments and the sensitivity of prepayments to interest rates, changes in interest rates have substantially different effects on the cash flows accruing to POs and IOs and thus on their market values. Prepayments do not affect the total cash flow to POs, but they do shorten the duration of this cash flow. On the other hand, prepayments reduce the total cash flow going to the IO. Figure 3 shows the responses of the prices of POs and IOs to changes in market interest rates. As market interest rates fall, prepayments increase. These prepayments go to the PO. The value of a PO rises both because its cash flows are received sooner and because the appropriate discount rate is lower. In contrast, the total cash flows going to the IO are reduced. This reduction more than offsets the effect of a lower discount rate. Hence, the value of an IO falls when market interest rates fall.

4.2. Senior and subordinated claims

A second way to unbundle mortgages is along their credit dimension. A mortgage originator with a package of loans ready for resale in the secondary market can have valuable inside information on the probability of prepayment and the credit quality of these loans. If a loan pool is more likely to be held to maturity or if its credit quality is above average but the market is unaware of these favorable

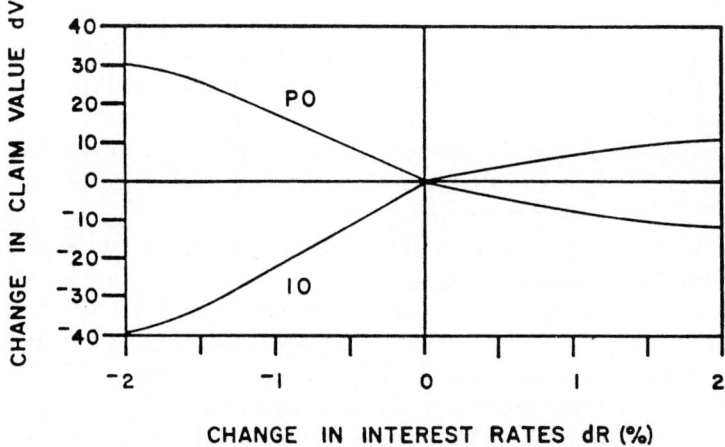

Fig. 3. Responses of the values of principal only (PO) and interest only (IO) claims to changes in market interest rates.

characteristics, the market will price the loans to reflect the average value of all loans. Thus, it is to the originator's advantage to signal their higher quality to the market so as to reduce their price discount in the secondary market. Senior/subordinated transactions provide a way to do this. The originator sells a senior claim on, say, 90% of the cash flows and keeps a subordinated claim on the remaining 10%. By issuing a subordinated claim, the senior claim has greater cash flow rights in case of default or delinquency on the underlying pool. The subordinated claim is typically retained by the originator who has a comparative advantage in assessing loan quality.

4.3. Collateralized mortgage obligations

CMOs are analogous to a dual-purpose mutual fund. A closed-end fund issues a fixed number of shares, and uses the proceeds of the sale to finance the purchase of a pool of assets (typically equities.) Dual purpose funds have two types of claims: income shares and capital shares. Owners of income shares have the first rights to all the dividends plus a fixed portion of the principal at the specified date when the fund is dissolved. Capital claim holders are the residual claimants: they receive everything left over (Ingersoll, 1976). Dual-purpose mutual funds repackage existing cash flows to provide customized cash flows to meet the demands of specific financial market participants. CMOs similarly allow the sale of separate ownership rights to sequential pieces of the principal and interest payments, and the proceeds from the sale of the claims are invested in a pool of mortgages.

Figure 4 illustrates a mortgage pool that has four classes of securities plus a

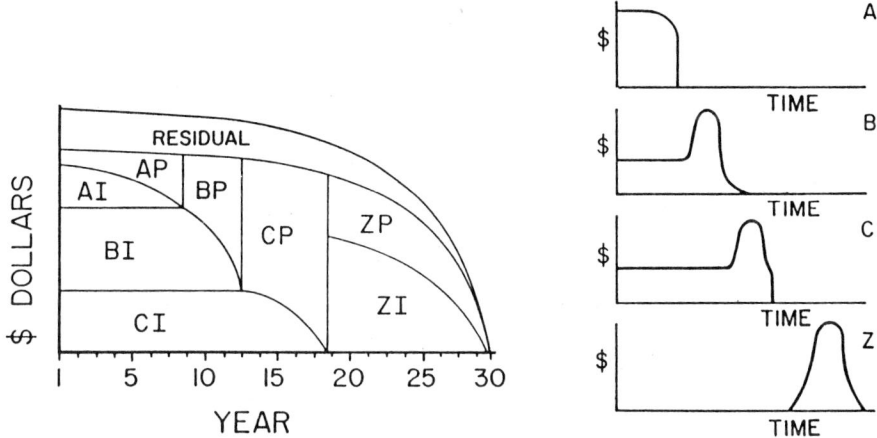

Fig. 4. The promised cash flows to a mortgage pool with four classes of securities plus a residual. Class *A* receives all the initial principal payments (*AP*) and a portion of the interest payments (*AI*). While the principal payments are going to the class *A* security holders, class *B* and *C* security holders initially receive only interest payments (*BI* and *CI*). Principal repayments go to *B* holders after class *A* are paid (*BP*) and then to class *C* (*CP*). *Z* holders receive interest and principal payments (*ZI* and *ZP*) only after the *A*, *B*, and *C* claimholders are paid.

residual. Class *A* receives all of the initial principal payments, the section labeled *AP,* and a portion of the interest payments, labeled *AI.* All prepayments up to an amount specified in the contract are paid to class *A* security holders. If prepayments rise because of a fall in market interest rates, the cash flows to class *A* securities rise because principal repayments accelerate. While the principal payments are going to the class *A* security holders, class *B* and *C* security holders initially receive only interest payments. After the class *A* securities are redeemed in full, principal payments flow to the class *B* securities. After the class *B* securities are redeemed in full, principal payments are directed to the class *C* securities. The *Z* class of securities, typically called a "modified" zero, recieves no payments, neither principal nor interest payments, until the previous three classes have been redeemed.

The four panels along the right hand of Figure 4 display the time profiles of the cash flows to each security. The class *A* cash flow resembles a short-term mortgage. The cash flows to classes *B* and *C* resemble those on corporate and government bonds, where there are initially level interest payments followed by larger flows from repayment of principal. The class *Z* cash flow is similar to that of a zero coupon security, in that over the early years of its life its cash flow is zero.

The residual is the remaining cash flow arising from a CMO. The cash flows to the residual are similar to the payoffs to the equity holders in a standard corporation. The residual arises in part because credit rating agencies require CMOs to be overcollateralized in order to receive a AAA credit rating. With overcollateralization, non-residual CMO investors have a higher probability of receiving their promised payments.

5. Hedging through securitization

5.1. Changing durations

To reduce the response of firm value to interest rate changes, hedging must reduce the duration of assets or increase the duration of liabilities.[8] Securitization does this by reducing the duration of assets held by deposit intermediaries. For example, a short-funded mortgage lender can use CMOs in three ways to manage its interest rate risk exposure: (1) it can convert its mortgage assets into CMOs and sell them; (2) it can buy or retain class *A* securities and hold them in their portfolios; and (3) it can buy or retain the residual portion. The first two shorten the asset duration and reduce the change in intermediary value caused by a change in market interest rates. The value of the residual, unlike most mortgage market instruments, is constructed to be positively correlated with market interest rates.[9] If market interest rates rise, prepayments decline and cash flows to the residual increase. Thus, its market value increases. This increase in market value can be used to offset the concomitant losses that are incurred on the short-funded mortgage portfolio.

Short-funded mortgage lenders can also use strips to hedge their interest rate risk. They have accentuated convexities. Short-funded mortgage lenders are more likely to be interested in IOs. If interest rates rise, the value of fixed-rate, long-term mortgages declines. Holding IOs offsets the effect of this fall in the value of its whole mortgage loans on the market value of the institution. Its exposure to interest-rate risk is reduced. Institutions that service but do not hold long-term, fixed-rate mortgages might be interested in POs. When interest rates decline and mortgages are prepaid, income from servicing mortgage payments declines. The increased value of POs tends to offset this service income decline. This results in less market-value sensitivity to interest rate changes.

IOs and POs, senior/subordinated claims, and CMOs help to complete financial markets by unbundling existing instruments and permitting their cash flows to be rebundled in ways that expand hedging and speculating opportunities. For example, strips permit market participants to trade on market interest rate or mortgage prepayment expectations.

5.2. Hedging volatility changes

Line *bb* in Figure 2 illustrates an important incentive for the mortgage lender to hedge against changes in interest rate volatility. By selling embedded interest-rate options to both its loan and deposit customers, the lender is vulnerable to increases in interest-rate volatility. The asymmetry in the lender's value profile implies that the firm loses more from a given interest-rate increase than it gains from a comparable interest-rate reduction. To reduce its exposure to unexpected increases in interest-rate volatility, the lender must purchase offsetting interest-rate options. Through securitization, the lender resells its position in the prepayment options it originally sold its mortgage loan customers. This makes line *bb* more nearly linear and reduces lender exposure to interest-rate volatility.[10]

5.3. Ownership structure and bonding

Gains from securitization are limited if the owner of the cash flow rights also bears the default risk. Separating the credit rater from the credit risk bearer tends to induce the credit rater to make too many low quality loans to receive the origination fee, loans that it would not make if it had to bear the default risk. The simple solution of having the mortgage loan originator retain the default risk is limited by Federal Reserve regulations. If the mortgage originator retains the default risk, it must meet certain reserve requirements and capital adequacy standards. These act as a tax on mortgage origination, causing mortgage costs to be higher and their quantity demanded to be lower. This reduction in loan volume results in a dead weight loss.

A partial solution to this problem of altering credit standards is to have a third party (for example, a private mortgage insurer) bear the default risk. If the mortgage originator and the insurer can negotiate an effective long-term contract, the mortgage originator can be charged on an experience rated basis. This provides an incentive to the originator to identify good credit risks and package mortgages into pools that have lower than average default risks. The saving in insurance fees will offset the increase in the costs required to make accurate ratings. The reserve requirement and capital adequacy taxes will be eliminated and the deadweight loss will be reduced.[11]

5.4. Pricing securitized claims

Prepayments complicate the pricing of mortgages and mortgage-backed securities. Most analyses treat the prepayment provision in mortgage loans as a call option written by the lender and owned by the mortgage borrower. Sophisticated models of the optimal exercise of these prepayment options based on changes in the level and structure of interest rates have been derived from modern analysis of the term structure of interest rates (Hendershott and van Order, 1987).

These macroeconomic models of prepayments can be complemented by including microeconomic analyses of demographic factors that affect households differently. Major reasons for mortgage loan prepayments other than interest rate reductions are marriage, divorce, births, promotions, transfers, retirements, and deaths. Since these events are more likely among some identifiable population subgroups than others, actuarial techniques like cohort analysis should be productive in examining how age, income marital status, and family size affect prepayment probabilities and through them prices of mortgage-backed securities.

Mortgage prepayments should also be related to the provisions of the underlying mortgage. For example, in a given area a 10% mortgage with three points may be offered simultaneously with a 10½% mortgage with no points. Individuals choosing the first mortgage are more likely to have a longer expected housing tenure to allow them to amortize the fixed points charge over a longer period of time. Conversely, individuals with shorter expected tenures would choose the second mortgage because it minimizes their expected housing costs. Empirical investigation is necessary to determine the magnitude of the prepayment variation associated with these characteristics of the mortgage. With that information, these factors can be taken into account in pricing mortgage backed securities more accurately.

6. Summary

Mortgage securitization has grown rapidly in the 1980s. This growth is a combination of (1) an ever present demand by value maximizing financial intermediaries to hedge changes in their values; (2) a demand by households to have puttable short-term deposits and callable long-term mortgages; and (3) large increases in interest-rate volatility. Mortgages have been securitized into CMOs, strips, and senior/subordinated claims. Each of these increases the array of traded financial instruments and reduces the costs of managing the interest rate, credit, and prepayment risks of mortgages and deposits. Hedging can reduce a firm's operating costs by (1) reducing expected taxes if the function linking taxes to taxable income is nonlinear; (2) reducing the compensating differential necessary to induce contracting parties with ill diversified, firm-specific claims to do business with the firm; (3) reducing the underinvestment problem; and (4) reducing bankruptcy costs.

Deposit intermediaries originate and service mortgages and deposits and manage the cash flow risks associated with these instruments. Prime among these risks is the interest rate risk that results from intermediaries funding long-term mortgages with short-term deposits. Increased interest-rate volatility increases the costs of managing these risks and lowers the value of short-funded mortgage lenders. To maintain their cost advantage, intermediaries devise and use new lower cost hedging instruments. Securitization is one instrument in an array of hedging vehicles.

Notes

1. Kendrick (1976) uses a 70-year average life for residential housing in estimating the housing stock. While the duration of a 70-year house is longer than the duration of a 30-year, fixed-rate mortgage, the 30-year mortgage is closer than a variable rate mortgage to the duration of a house.

2. Convexity, the effect of changes in interest rates on the duration of assets and liabilities, is ignored in this analysis.

3. In a well functioning market this opportunity cost is reflected in the pricing of the mortgage at origination.

4. This could be shown in Figure 2 by increasing the steepness of lines *aa* and *bb*. Subsequent changes in interest rates have larger effects on the intermediary's value than preceding changes. This process repeats itself if interest rates continue to decline.

5. Since life insurance companies and pension funds have long-term commitments, they have a comparative advantage in owning the cash flow rights to long-lived mortgages. However, neither type of institution typically has local knowledge of borrowers or property values nor do they generally have loan servicing facilities. Thus, a useful exchange is made by having mortgage originators and servicers sell the cash flow rights to insurance companies and pension funds.

6. See Mayers and Smith (1982), Gurel and Pyle (1984), and Smith and Stulz (1985).

7. DeAngelo and Masulis (1980) examine the investment tax credit, and Smith, Smithson, and Wakeman (1987) analyze the alternative minimum tax.

8. In the context of equation (1), this will reduce the slope of the line linking firm value changes to interest-rate changes.

9. This is true of the typical CMO residual. However, CMO claims can be constructed with other correlations between the residual and market interest rates.

10. Purchasing deposit insurance from the FDIC or FSLIC also helps to make line *bb* less nonlinear. See Brickley and James (1986).

11. Mayers and Smith (1982) provide a similar argument on the comparative advantage of insurers in monitoring.

References

Benston, George and Smith, Clifford. "A Transactions Cost Approach to the Theory of Financial Intermediation." *Journal of Finance* 31 (1976), 215–231.

Brickley, James and James, Christopher. "Access to Deposit Insurance, Insolvency Rules and the Stock Returns of Financial Institutions." *Journal of Financial Economics* 16 (1986), 345–371.

DeAngelo, Harry and Masulis, Ronald. "Optimal Capital Structure Under Corporate and Personal Taxation." *Journal of Financial Economics* 8 (1980), 3–29.

Deshmukh, Sudhakar D.; Greenbaum, Stuart I.; and Kanatas, George. "Interest Rate Uncertainty and the Financial Intermediary's Choice of Exposure." *Journal of Finance* 38 (1983), 141–147.

Grove, M. A. "On 'Duration' and the Optimal Maturity Structure of the Balance Sheet." *The Bell Journal of Economics and Management Science* 5 (1974), 696–709.

Gurel, Eitan and Pyle, David. "Bank Income Taxes and Interest Rate Risk Management: A Note." *Journal of Finance* 34 (1984), 1199–1206.

Hendershott, Patric H. and Van Order, Robert. "Pricing Mortgages: An Interpretation of the Models and Results." *Journal of Financial Services Research* 1 (1987), 77–111.

Hess, Alan C. "Variable Rate Mortgages: Confusion of Means and Ends." *Financial Analysts Journal* (January/February 1984), 67–70.

Hess, Alan C. "Could Thrifts be Profitable? Theoretical and Empirical Evidence." *Carnegie-Rochester Conference Series on Public Policy* 26 (1987), 223–282.

Ingersoll, Jonathan. "A Theoretical and Empirical Investigation of the Dual Purpose Funds: An Application of contingent-claims Analysis." *Journal of Financial Economics* 3 (1976), 83–123.

Kendrick, John. *The Formation and Stocks of Total Capital.* National Bureau of Economic Research, distributed by Columbia University Press, 1976.

Mayers, David and Smith, Clifford. "On the Corporate Demand for Insurance." *Journal of Business* 55 (2) (1982), 281–296.

Mayers, David and Smith, Clifford. "Corporate Insurance and the Underinvestment Problem." *Journal of Risk and Insurance* 54 (1987), 45–54.

Modigliani, Franco and Miller, Merton. "The Cost of Capital, Corporation Finance and the Theory of Investment." *American Economic Review* 48 (1958), 261–297.

Myers, Stewart. "Determinants of Corporate Borrowing," *Journal of Financial Economics* 5 (1977), 147–175.

Smith, Clifford; Smithson, Charles W.; and Wakeman, Lee Macdonald. "The Market of Interest Rate Swaps." Unpublished manuscript, University of Rochester, (1987).

Smith, Clifford and Stulz, Rene. "The Determinants of Firms' Hedging Policies." *Journal of Financial and Quantitative Analysis* 20 (1985), 391–405.

Smith, Clifford and Watts, Ross. "Incentive and Tax Effects of U.S. Executive Compensation Plans." *Australian Journal of Management* 7 (1982), 139–157.

THE USE OF LOAN SALES AND STANDBY LETTERS OF CREDIT BY COMMERCIAL BANKS*

Christopher JAMES

University of Oregon, Eugene, OR 97403, USA

Received February 1988, final version received June 1988

This paper examines the incentives banks have to engage in 'off balance sheet' activities such as commercial loan sales and the issuance of standby letters of credit (SLCs). I show that loan sales and loans backed by SLCs have payoff characteristics similar to secured debt. Like secured debt, off balance sheet activities permit banks to sell a portion of the cash flows associated with new investment opportunities. This ability permits banks to invest in loans with positive net present values that they would pass up if restricted to deposit financing. An examination of the risk premium on large certificates of deposit provides evidence consistent with the model.

1. Introduction

Over the past decade there has been a dramatic increase in what is called 'off balance sheet' banking. Examples include the issuance of standby letters of credit (SLCs) and commercial loan sales.[1] An SLC is a bank-issued commitment to pay one party (called the beneficiary) in the event that the bank's customer (called the account party) fails to repay a loan or defaults on some other contractual obligation. In the event of default, the bank advances funds to the beneficiary in the amount of beneficiary's loss. Commercial loan sales involve the sale of newly originated bank loans to a third party. Loan sales are structured so that the selling bank continues to service the loan even though title to the loan is transferred to the purchaser.

*Thanks to A. Berger, M. Flannery, F. Furlong, T. Hannan, M. Keeley, G. Pennacchi, P. Wier, the participants of the finance workshop at the University of Pennsylvania, the referee, and the editors for helpful comments. The research assistance of Bill Robertson is greatly appreciated. This paper was written while I was a visiting scholar at the Federal Reserve Bank of San Francisco.

[1] For example, SLCs outstanding grew at an annual rate of 24 percent during the period 1974 to 1985, whereas commercial loans at commercial banks increased at an annual rate of 3 percent during this period. See Benveniste and Berger (1986) or Bennett (1986). Information on loan sales comes from two sources: Schedule L of the Call Report and senior loan officer surveys (LPS) conducted by the Federal Reserve Board. Call Report information indicates that loans sold increased from $23 billion in 1983 to $111 billion in 1986. A similar pattern of growth is observable in the LPS survey data.

Journal of Monetary Economics 22 (1988) 395–422. North-Holland

Loan sales and SLCs have two features in common. First, they involve the separation of many of the services associated with bank lending, such as credit risk evaluation and underwriting, from the funding of a loan. For example, in a loan sale with recourse or in a loan backed by an SLC, the bank underwrites the credit risk and may service the loan, but the purchaser or beneficiary funds the loan. By separating the funding of a loan from these other activities, a bank can earn fee income without putting an asset or corresponding liability on its balance sheet. Second, as I demonstrate in this paper, loan sales and SLC-backed loans have payoff characteristics similar to collateralized or secured debt.

This paper examines two questions as they pertain to commercial loan sales and the issuance of SLCs. The first question concerns the incentives a bank has to separate the funding of a loan from the other services associated with lending. Recent research on loan sales and SLCs has focused on bank regulation as the primary motivation for these activities and the reason for their recent growth. [See for example Pennacchi (1987) and Pavel and Phillis (1987).] In this paper I argue that the incentives to undertake commercial loan sales or to issue SLCs do not derive solely from bank regulation or deposit insurance. Specifically, the observation that SLC-backed loan sales have payoff characteristics similar to secured debt suggests that the incentives banks have to sell loans or issue SLCs are similar to the incentives firms in general have to issue secured debt. Drawing on work by Stulz and Johnson (1985), I show that the use of loan sales and SLCs can avoid the underinvestment problem that arises when a firm has risky debt outstanding. By an underinvestment problem I mean the tendency for firms with debt outstanding to pass up new positive net present value investments. This problem, described in detail in Myers (1977), arises when new investment opportunities reduce the risk of outstanding debt claims and effect a wealth transfer from stockholders to debtholders.

I show that loan sales and SLC issues, like secured debt, can reduce this transfer by permitting the bank to sell a portion of the cash flows associated with new investment opportunities. By providing investors a senior claim to these cash flows, the wealth transfer from stockholders to existing depositors is reduced. Moreover, because banks are generally prohibited from issuing collateralized deposits, loan sales and SLCs serve as substitutes.[2] The hypothesis that loan sales and SLCs are a substitute for collateralized debt claims is referred to as the *Collateralization Hypothesis*.

The model of loan sales and SLC issues is used to analyze the effect of capital requirements and deposit insurance on the incentive to engage in 'off balance sheet' activities. In particular, I show that capital requirements and

---

[2] Under Federal law and regulation (12 USC 90 and 12 CRF 7.7410) national banks may pledge assets against public but not private deposits. See Hayes (1987).

fixed rate deposit insurance exacerbate the underinvestment problem and increase the incentives to engage in these activities. Capital requirements, which limit bank leverage, exacerbate the underinvestment problem by restricting a bank's ability to offset reductions in asset risk with an increase in financial leverage. Fixed rate deposit insurance can increase the underinvestment problem because with insurance the rate paid on a portion of the bank's liabilities will not adjust to reflect the marginal risk associated with new investment opportunities.

A second question examined in this paper concerns the effect of loan sales and SLC issues on the default risk of deposits. The effect of these activities on the risk of deposits depends on the reasons banks undertake them. One explanation for the growth of 'off balance sheet' banking is that it is a manifestation of a moral hazard problem that is endemic to a system of fixed rate deposit insurance pricing [see, for example, Pyle (1985)]. Because SLCs and certain loan sales are not subject to capital requirements, these contingent liabilities provide a way for a bank to increase leverage. By increasing leverage, a bank can generate or enhance subsidies arising from deposit insurance. This argument, referred to as the *Moral Hazard Hypothesis*, implies that off balance sheet activities increase the risk of deposits.

The Collateralization Hypothesis implies that because the ability to issue collateralized claims affects a bank's investment policy, depositors (and/or the FDIC) are not necessarily worse off when loans are sold or SLCs are issued. The effect, therefore, of loan sales and SLC issues on bank risk is an empirical issue. To address this question, the relation between the interest rate paid on large bank CDs (greater than $100,000) and bank asset risk, financial leverage, and the volume of SLCs and loan sales is examined. This examination reveals that the risk premium on large CDs increases with asset risk and financial leverage. However, no significant relation is found between the rate paid on CDs and either the volume of SLCs or loans sold.

The model developed in this paper has important implications concerning the regulation of 'off balance sheet' activities. If the ability to issue secured debt substitutes (such as SLCs) can increase the value of the bank, regulation designed to limit these activities may prove counterproductive by increasing the risk borne by the FDIC. More generally, the analysis suggests that regulations that restrict the type of financing used by banks (e.g., capital requirements) and are intended to limit FDIC risk exposure may have the unintended effect of altering bank investment decisions and increasing the FDIC's risk exposure.

The paper is organized as follows. Section 2 provides a brief description of the loan sales and SLC markets and the current regulatory treatment of these activities. Section 3 presents the model of the payoff characteristics of loan sales, SLCs, and secured debt. This model is used to show how the option to use secured debt or its equivalent can increase the value of the bank. Section 4 discusses the empirical implications and provides the empirical tests of the model. The final section concludes.

2. Background

2.1. The market for commercial loan sales and SLCs

Commercial loan sales involve the sale by banks of newly originated commercial loans. Most commercial loan sales are structured contractually as participations so that the selling bank maintains a creditor–debtor relationship with the borrower.[3] This means that the selling bank continues to be responsible for servicing the loan, enforcing covenants, monitoring the financial condition of the borrower, and handling workouts and other problems that might arise in the event of default. In exchange for performing these services, the selling bank is compensated through a 'spread'. The spread represents the difference between the rate paid by the borrower to the bank and the return promised to the purchaser of the loan.

The payments the purchaser receives will depend on the recourse provisions associated with the sale. In a loan sale without recourse, the purchaser receives the right to a set of contracted loan payments. In the event of a default on the loan sold, the purchaser receives whatever cash flows the loan generates. A loan sale with recourse provides the purchaser in the event of the default a general claim on the bank's assets equal to the amount of loss guaranteed by the selling bank. Existing bank regulations require that loans sold with recourse be treated as assets when calculating capital requirements. Moreover, the proceeds of loans sold with recourse are also subject to reserve requirements. As a result of these regulations, commercial loans are rarely sold with full recourse.[4]

---

[3] Loan sales, structured as participations, differ from what has traditionally been referred to as a participation in the banking literature. The older form of participation is better described as a syndication or assignment. This involves a lead bank negotiating for each bank in the syndicate. However, each of the banks in the syndicate make a separate loan to the borrowing firm. Recent loan sales, structured as participations, involve the creation of a new contract between the bank and the purchaser of the loan. The purchaser's contract is with the originating bank and not with the bank's loan customer. See Gorton and Haubrich (1987) for a discussion of the contractual aspects of loan participations. See Melvin (1986) for a description of the regulatory treatment of loan sales.

[4] The 1985 LPS Survey indicates that 13 percent of loans sold were sold with a put option, allowing the purchaser to sell back the loan. Loans sold without recourse raise concerns with the purchaser regarding both the quality of loans sold (an adverse selection problem) and the diligence with which the selling bank will monitor the borrower after a sale (a moral hazard problem). See Pennacchi (1987). One technique used to provide the purchaser a credible assurance of quality is for the selling bank to maintain or fund a portion of the loan sold. A second technique involves selling short-term 'strips' of longer-term loans. While the buyer of the strip is exposed to default risk in the short run, before the maturity date of the strip, the originating bank retains exposure to default in the longer run if it is committed to refinancing the loan. Finally, because most commercial loans sold are short-term and selling banks are repeatedly in the market, 'reputational' capital may assure quality. [See Gorton and Haubrich (1987).]

An SLC is a guarantee by a bank to pay the beneficiary if the bank's customer fails to repay a loan or perform some other contractual obligation [for a description of the SLC market see Bennett (1986) or Koppenhaver (1987)]. The majority of SLCs are used to back financial contracts such as commercial paper, municipal bonds, and direct loans. The issuer of an SLC agrees to advance funds to make the beneficiary whole in the event the account party defaults on the loan.[5] As in a loan sale with recourse, the beneficiary will receive less than the contracted rate on the loan only in the event that the loan defaults and the bank issuing the SLC fails.

If the bank could issue uninsured deposits secured by a specific loan, precisely the same factors would determine the cash flows to secured depositors. Specifically, the secured depositor would receive less than the contracted payment only when the bank failed and the cash flows from the collateral were less than the contracted payments due on the debt.

2.2. Incentives for loan sales and SLCs

Recent research has focused on bank regulation as the primary motivation for these activities. Two arguments have been made concerning the effects of regulation. The first argument will be referred to as the *Moral Hazard Hypothesis*. Pyle (1985), Benveniste and Berger (1986), and others argue that fixed rate deposit insurance together with capital requirements provide incentives to increase financial leverage through the issuance of contingent liabilities that are not subject to capital requirements. By increasing financial leverage in this way, a bank can enhance whatever subsidy it receives from deposit insurance. The moral hazard hypothesis therefore predicts that 'off balance sheet' activities increase the risk of deposits.

An alternative argument concerning the effect of regulation is referred to as the *Regulatory Tax Hypothesis*. Loan sales and SLCs, it is argued, permit banks to avoid reserve requirements and capital requirements. Specifically, it is argued that the cost of meeting capital requirements and holding noninterest earning reserves raise the cost of funds for a bank above what a nonbank institution must pay. [See for example Pennacchi (1987) and Pavel and Phillis (1987).] While reserve requirements unambiguously increase the cost of funds, the theoretical arguments for how capital requirements affect the cost of funding a loan are not well developed. Specifically without a well developed theory of bank capital structure (in the absence of deposit insurance), it is

---

[5]Because the bank's obligation is contingent on the default or nonperformance of the account party, most SLCs expire unused. For example, a special survey conducted by the Federal Reserve Board [Federal Reserve Bulletin (1979)] found that defaults by account parties constituted only 2.03 percent of SLCs outstanding in 1978. While SLCs represent a contingent liability of the bank the volume of SLCs reported represents the volume of loans and other contractual obligations backed or guaranteed by SLCs and not the market value of the bank's contingent liability.

unclear how capital requirements affect the cost of capital (independent of their effect on the value of deposit guarantees).

While regulation may enhance the incentives to sell loans and issue SLCs, as discussed in section 3, it is unlikely that regulation is solely responsible. Several institutional facts support this conjecture. First, nonbank financial institutions which are not subject to the same regulations as banks and do not issue insured deposits are active in the loan sales and financial guarantees market.[6] Moreover, recent surveys conducted by the Federal Reserve Board indicate that a substantial portion of loans sold are purchased by other banks. For example, the 1985 Lending Practices Survey (LPS) indicates that 53 percent of loans sold were purchased by other domestic commercial banks (and 36.5 percent were purchased by banks with assets of over $1 billion). Because most banks are subject to the same marginal reserve requirement on deposits and to the same minimum capital requirement, it is unclear why the regulatory tax burden should vary among banks for financing the *same* loan.

Nonregulatory motives also exist for loan sales and SLC issues. The model developed in this paper shows that the incentives banks have to sell loans or issue SLCs are similar to the incentives nonfinancial firms have to issue secured debt. Other nonregulatory motives for loan sales have also been advanced. For example, Pavel and Phillis (1987) argue that loan sales permit banks to invest in and diversify across a broader set of loans than they originate and service. Moreover, as Hess and Smith (1987) point out, banks may have a comparative advantage in originating and servicing loans but not in loan ownership (funding) or in interest rate risk management. It is important to emphasize that the model developed in this paper complements rather than contradicts these explanations for loan sales and SLC issues.

3. The model

In this section I present a framework for analyzing the payoff characteristics of SLCs and loan sales. I show that collateralized claims (i.e., loan sales or SLCs) permit a bank to sell claims to a portion of the payoffs associated with a new loan and thereby reduce the wealth transfer from shareholders to uninsured depositors (or the FDIC) associated with undertaking a new investment. The effect of capital requirements on a bank's investment decision is also analyzed.

3.1. Assumptions and notations

I employ a two-period framework in which a bank has at $t = 0$ one 'booked' loan, with a face value of $1 and an option or opportunity to invest in a

---

[6]For example, insurance companies issue financial guarantees that compete with bank-issued SLCs. According to Hirtle (1987), the volume of these guarantees has grown at approximately the same rate as bank-issued SLCs (i.e., 20 percent per year).

second loan requiring an investment of $1 at time $t = 0$. If the opportunity to make the loan is *not* undertaken at time $t = 0$, the option expires and is worthless. Both the existing loan and the loan prospect, if undertaken, pay off in the second period (time $t = 1$). The bank's booked loan is financed with both equity and deposits, with e and $1 - e$ representing the amount of equity and deposits used.

The payoff characteristics of a bank's currently booked loan and loan opportunity are as follows: The booked loan is used to finance a risky project that has a continuous payoff function $g_1(s)$, where s represents a given state of nature. I assume s is distributed uniformly over the interval $[0, \bar{s}]$. The bank, in making the loan, is assumed to incur monitoring and origination costs of c. I assume that banks have a comparative advantage in originating and monitoring loans so that for the same level of exogenously determined monitoring activity, nonbank lenders would incur costs of c^*, where $c^* > c$. [See Fama (1985) for empirical support for this assumption.] All market participants are assumed to be risk-neutral. Finally, deposit and equity markets are assumed to be perfectly competitive and all taxes (including reserve requirements) are ignored.

These assumptions imply that the contracted payment (interest plus principal) on the bank's existing or booked loan, r_L, satisfies[7]

$$\int_0^{\bar{s}} \min\left[g_1(s) - c, r_L - c\right] f(s) \, ds = r_f + d, \tag{1}$$

where

$f(s)$ = probability density function of s,
r_f = one plus the risk-free rate of interest,
d = $c^* - c$.

The payoff schedule for booked loans in any state is therefore

$$a_1(s) = \min\left[g_1(s) - c, r_L - c\right] \geq 0. \tag{2}$$

Deposits, used to finance booked loans, are assumed to be fairly priced when issued. This assumption is consistent with either actuarially fair deposit insurance prices or the absence of deposit guarantees. The effect of fixed price deposit insurance is discussed later. The promised payment associated with

---

[7]I assume, for simplicity, that the bank captures the entire surplus generated by the difference in origination costs. In addition I assume $g(s) > c$. The framework I employ is similar to the framework used by Benveniste and Berger (1986). They show that the ability to issue securitized claims can improve the allocation of risk-sharing among a bank's debtholders and depositors. In particular, securitization provides some bank claimants a senior claim to certain assets. If investors were to vary in their degree of risk aversion, securitization may result in a lower cost of funds by providing richer risk-sharing opportunities. Benveniste and Berger's model is based on an assumption that investors' risk-sharing opportunities outside the bank are limited. Their model does, however, yield implications similar to the model developed in this paper.

deposits used to finance 'booked' loans, denoted as r_d, satisfies

$$\int_0^{\bar{s}} \min[r_d(1-e), a_1(s)] f(s)\,ds = r_f(1-e). \tag{3}$$

The contracted payoff on deposits (r_d) is assumed fixed until time $t = 1$. Finally, the expected payoff to bank stockholders, associated with 'booked' loans, is

$$\int_0^{\bar{s}} a_1(s) f(s)\,ds - \int_0^{\bar{s}} \min[r_d(1-e), a_1(s)] f(s)\,ds, \tag{4}$$

which is assumed to be greater than zero.

As indicated earlier, the bank has an option to make a second loan at time $t = 0$. The loan is assumed to be a positive net present value investment for the bank. The existence of the lending opportunity might arise, for example, from existing customer relations acquired through the bank's *past* investment in firm-specific credit information [see Kane and Malkiel (1965)] and does not necessarily imply imperfect competition in the loan market. The option to make this loan is equivalent to the growth opportunity discussed in Myers (1977).

The payoff characteristic of the lending opportunity can be derived as follows. Let $g_2(s)$ represent the state-contingent payoff function of the risky project the new bank loan will be used to finance. The contracted payment associated with this loan, r_L^N, is set so that

$$\int_0^{\bar{s}} \min\left[g_2(s) - c, r_L^N - c\right] f(s)\,ds \geq r_f. \tag{5}$$

The payoff in a given state for this loan will be denoted as $a_2(s)$.

3.2. Payoff characteristics of secured debt, loan sales, and SLC-backed loans

In this section I show that the payoff characteristics of loan sales and SLC-backed loans are similar to the payoffs associated with a secured debt claim. I assume in the analysis that the new loan serves as collateral or is sold or backed by an SLC.

Consider first the case of a deposit or debt claim secured by the new loan. The contracted payment on secured debt, denoted as r_s, must in equilibrium satisfy

$$\int_0^{\bar{s}} \min\left[r_s, a_2(s) + \frac{r_s}{L_s} a_1(s)\right] f(s)\,ds = r_f, \tag{6}$$

where

$$L_s = r_s + r_d(1-e).$$

In words, a secured debtholder receives the contracted payment r_s as long as the bank does not fail. In the event the bank fails, the purchaser receives the minimum of the contracted payment, r_s, or the cash flows from the new loan plus a proportion of the cash flows from the bank's other assets. In equilibrium the expected payoff must equal r_f.

The payoff characteristics of a loan sold with full recourse are identical to those of secured debt. Specifically, assume that the bank makes the new loan and subsequently sells. If the bank continues to service the loan, the purchase price of the loan will be set so that the expected payoff is r_f. The promised payment on the loan sale, r_{SR}, is determined so that

$$\int_0^{\bar{s}} \min\left[r_{SR}, a_2(s) + \frac{r_{SR}}{L_{SR}} a_1(s) \right] f(s)\, ds = r_f,$$

where

$$L_{SR} = r_d(1-e) + r_{SR}.$$

In words, the loan sold serves as the primary source of cash flows. In the event of selling bank's failure, the purchaser will receive the minimum of r_{SR} or the cash flows from the loan sold plus a proportion of the cash flows from the bank's other assets. In equilibrium, ignoring differences in contracting costs (discussed below), $r_{SR} = r_s$.

In the case of a loan sale with partial recourse, the underlying loan sold serves as the primary source of cash flows. Let λ represent the proportion of the loan's losses guaranteed by the bank and r_{SL} as the contracted payment to the purchaser. The payoff to the purchaser of the loan in any state is

$$\min\left[r_{SL}, a_2(s) + \min\left[\lambda(r_{SL} - a_2(s)), \lambda \frac{r_{SL} - a_2(s)}{L_{SL}} a_1(s) \right] \right]. \qquad (7)$$

As Pennacchi (1987) points out, the contracted payoff on loan sales with partial recourse may reflect moral hazard problems associated with reduced incentives a bank has to monitor loans that it sells. The agency costs of loan sales are discussed in section 3.5.

Finally, consider an SLC-backed loan. I assume that the cost of creating and monitoring an SLC-backed loan is identical to a bank loan. If r_{SC} represents the contracted payment the borrower must make on the SLC-backed loan, then the maximum fee the account party will pay is determined so that

$$r_{SC} + \text{Fee} = r_L^N.$$

Given this fee, the account party's (borrower's) payment to the bank and lender is

$$a_2(s) = \min\left[g_2(s), r_L^N\right].$$

The contracted payment on the SLC-backed loan therefore satisfies

$$\int_0^{\bar{s}} \min\left[r_{SC}, \frac{r_{SC}}{L_{SC}}a_1(s) + a_2(s)\right]f(s)\,\mathrm{d}s = r_f. \tag{8}$$

Note that the payoff characteristics of the SLC-backed loan to the lender are identical to secured debt.[8] Therefore, in equilibrium $r_{SC} = r_s$.

3.3. *The underinvestment problem as a rationale for collateralization*

This section draws on recent research by Stulz and Johnson (1985) concerning the rationale for secured debt issues. They argue that the ability to issue collateralized claims can affect a firm's investment policy and therefore the size as well as the distribution of a firm's cash flows among various claimants. In particular, the ability to issue collateralized debt may enable a firm to undertake investment opportunities it would pass up if constrained to issue unsecured claims. This will occur when the issuance of a collateralized claim reduces the transfer from stockholders to existing debtholders associated with undertaking a new investment project. This argument will be referred to as the *Collateralization Hypothesis*.

A similar argument can be made for the use of off balance sheet activities by banks. Indeed, deposit insurance and bank regulation are likely to make the underinvestment problem particularly important in banking. To determine when banks will find it advantageous to engage in off balance sheet activities, I first show that a bank will not undertake some profitable new loan opportunities if constrained to deposit financing. Next I show that, if the contracted rate on secured debt (or the rate on loan sales or SLC-backed loans) is less than the promised rate on deposits, secured debt reduces the underinvestment problem.

---

[8]The equivalence of SLC financing and secured debt can be demonstrated by noting that the lender on an SLC-backed loan will receive less than r_{SC} if

$$r_{SC} > g_2(s) - \text{Fee or} \quad r_L^N > g_2(s)$$

(default occurs on the SLC-backed loan) and

$$r_d(1-e) + r_{SC} > A(s)$$

(claims on the bank exceed cash flow from existing assets and collateral). In the case of secured debt, payments will be less than r_S if

$$r_d(1-e) + r_s \geq A(s)$$

(default occurs) and

$$r_s > a_2(s)$$

or, since $r_s \leq r_L^N$, $r_L^N > g_2(s)$.

To abstract from the effect of bank regulation and deposit insurance, off balance sheet activities are analyzed first in the context of a deregulated environment, without deposit insurance. The effects of deposit insurance and regulation are then examined.

Assume at time $t = 0$ the bank exercises its option and undertakes the new loan opportunity (described earlier) funding it entirely with deposits. Because all depositors are assumed to have the same priority claim to the bank's assets, if the promised payments to existing depositors are fixed, then the promised payment on new deposits, r_d^N, must satisfy

$$\int_0^{\bar{s}} \min\left[r_d^N, \frac{r_d^N}{L_d} A(s)\right] f(s)\, ds = r_f, \tag{9}$$

where

$$L_d = r_d^N + r_d(1 - e),$$

and

$$A(s) = a_1(s) + a_2(s).$$

An important assumption in the analysis which follows is that r_d is fixed at the time the new loan opportunity must be undertaken. This assumption is required for the underinvestment problem to occur [see Myers (1977)].[9] As shown later, if the rate of new deposits (r_d^N) is constrained to equal r_d (as in the case of fixed premium deposit guarantees), the results discussed in the following sections hold.

The bank will forego the investment opportunity if constrained to deposit financing if the gains from undertaking the opportunity accrue primarily to existing depositors. Specifically, the bank will not fund the loan if

$$\int_0^{\bar{s}} a_2(s) f(s)\, ds - \int_0^{\bar{s}} \min\left[r_d^N, \frac{r_d^N}{L_d} A(s)\right] f(s)\, ds$$

$$- \left\{ \int_0^{\bar{s}} \min\left[r_d(1-e), \frac{r_d(1-e)}{L_d} A(s)\right] f(s)\, ds \right.$$

$$\left. - \int_0^{\bar{s}} \min[r_d(1-e), a_1(s)] f(s)\, ds \right\} \le 0. \tag{10}$$

[9] r_d may be fixed because deposits are insured at a fixed premium or because the maturity of deposits exceeds one period. Alternatively, r_d may be fixed even though deposits are short-term, if for example an information asymmetry exists between the investment opportunities, as perceived by bank managers, and outside depositors. Finally, an underinvestment problem may arise even though r_d varies (as in the case of a variable risk-based deposit insurance premium) if the bank is contractually obligated to invest in a new loan at $t = 0$ (because of outstanding loan commitments) at a fixed rate and it has a second loan opportunity with characteristics like those discussed in the text.

Expression (10) represents the change in shareholders' wealth resulting from the new loan.

The term in brackets represents the change in the value of outstanding deposits as a result of funding the loan. Notice that by assumption the first term in (10) is greater than r_f. In addition, because new deposits are fairly priced, the second term in (10) equals r_f. Therefore (10) will be less than zero if and only if outstanding deposits are risky (so that the term in brackets can be greater than zero). Finally (10) suggests that the underinvestment problem will be greater (i.e., the likelihood of passing up a positive net present value loan) the greater the default probability of the bank's existing deposits.[10]

Intuitively, existing depositors gain from either a reduction in the probability of default and/or increased cash flows in the event of default. The gain existing depositors realize reduces the return bank shareholders receive from the new loan and therefore reduces their incentives to undertake the loan. This transfer from bank shareholders to existing depositors results in the underinvestment problem identified by Myers (1977).

Suppose that instead of deposit financing the new loan is financed by issuing a claim collateralized by the new loan. The contracted or promised payment on the collateralized debt, r_s (or the loan sold with recourse or the SLC-backed loan), will be less than the contracted payment on new deposits, r_d^N, if and only if there exists a state such that

(i) $\quad a_1(s) + a_2(s) < r_d^N + r_d(1 - e),$

and

(ii) $\quad \min\left[r_s, a_2(s) + \dfrac{r_s}{L_s} a_1(s) \right] > \dfrac{r_d^N}{L_d} [a_1(s) + a_2(s)].$

In the case of a loan sold with partial recourse condition (ii) becomes

(ii′) $\quad \min\left[r_{SL}, a_2(s) + \min\left[\lambda(r_{SL} - a_2(s)), \lambda \dfrac{r_{SL} - a_2(s)}{L_{SL}} a_1(s) \right] \right]$

$$> \dfrac{r_d^N}{L_d} [a_1(s) + a_2(s)].$$

The proof of this proposition is contained in the appendix. In words, the promised or contracted payment on secured claims to be less than the promised payment on deposits requires that new deposits have a positive probability of default [condition (i)]. In addition, if investors are risk-neutral,

---

[10] Myers (1977) derives this result for debt claims generally.

the *expected return* on deposits or collateralized debt must be equal. For the contracted payoff on collateralized debt (i.e., the promised payment investors receive if default does not occur) to be less than the contracted payment on deposit requires that collateralized debtholders receive higher payments in the event of default. This is condition (ii) or (ii′). Note that the difference between the contracted rate on collateralized claims (r_s) and deposits (r_d) will be greater the higher the probability of failure (i.e., the riskier a bank's deposits) and the lower the risk of the collateral (i.e., the default risk of the new loan).

The next issue concerns how issuing collateralized claims affects a bank's investment policy. The following proposition describes how issuing collateralized claims affects shareholder wealth.

Proposition 1. If there exists a wealth transfer from shareholders to existing depositors associated with financing a new loan with deposits and if the contracted rate on collateralized claims is less than the contracted rate on new deposit claims, then issuing collateralized claims will reduce the transfer from shareholders to existing depositors associated with investing in the new loan.

Proposition 1 implies that there are loans with positive net present values that a bank would make if it can issue collateralized claims but would pass up if only deposit financing were available.

Proof. The proof focuses on collateralized claims with recourse, although similar results are obtained for nonrecourse claims (see footnote 11). Existing depositors' gains when new deposits are issued are [from (10)]

$$\int_0^{\bar{s}} \left[r_d(1-e), \frac{r_d(1-e)}{L_d} A(s) \right] f(s)\, ds$$

$$- \int_0^{\bar{s}} \min[r_d(1-e), a_1(s)] f(s)\, ds > 0. \tag{11}$$

Secured debt will reduce the transfer to existing depositors if

$$\int_0^{\bar{s}} \min\left[r_d(1-e), \frac{r_d(1-e)}{L_d} A(s) \right] f(s)\, ds$$

$$> \int_0^{\bar{s}} \min\left[r_d(1-e), \max\left[\frac{r_d(1-e)}{L_s} a_1(s), \right. \right.$$

$$\left. \left. a_1(s) + a_2(s) - r_s \right] \right] f(s)\, ds, \tag{12}$$

where the right-hand side of (12) represents the expected payoff to existing depositors given secured debt (or a claim with recourse) is issued and the left-hand side of (12) represents the payoff to existing depositors if new deposits are issued.[11] For all states in which default does not occur the payoffs to existing depositors are the same whether deposits or secured debt is used.[12] Consider next the default states where $a_1(s) + a_2(s) < r_d^N + (1-e)r_d$ (this set is not empty by the assumption that the $r_s < r_d^N$). Assume these states are distributed over the interval $[0, \hat{s}]$. For the default states the expected payoffs to secured debtholders exceed the payoffs new depositors expect to receive (since secured debt is profitable), i.e.,

$$\int_0^{\hat{s}} \min\left[r_s, a_2(s) + \frac{r_s}{L_s}a_1(s)\right]f(s)\,ds > \int_0^{\hat{s}} \frac{r_d^N}{L_d}A(s)f(s)\,ds. \qquad (13)$$

This implies that existing depositors receive less in these states than they receive when deposit financing is used. Therefore, (12) holds.[13]

The intuition behind Proposition 1 is as follows. If existing deposits pay a contractually fixed interest rate, then the market value of the deposits will increase either because the new loan lowers the probability of default or increases the level of the bank's cash flows in the event of default. Recall that the promised payment on secured debt, r_s, will be lower than the promised payment on new deposits only when the payoffs to secured debtholders are

---

[11] If a nonrecourse claim is issued the transfer is reduced if

$$\int_0^{\hat{s}} \min\left[r_d(1-e), \frac{r_d}{L_d}A(s)\right]f(s)\,ds$$

$$> \int_0^{\hat{s}} \min[r_d(1-e), \max(a_1(s), a_1(s) + a_2(s) - r_{SL})]f(s)\,ds. \qquad (12')$$

The proof is unaffected by substituting (12') for (12) in the text.

[12] Because $r_s < r_d^N$, the default states with secured debt financing are a subset of the default states with deposit financing.

[13] In default,

$$\int_0^{\hat{s}} \min\left[r_s, a_2(s) + \frac{r_s}{L_s}a_1(s)\right]f(s)\,ds$$

$$+ \int_0^{\hat{s}} \max\left[\frac{r_d}{L_s}(1-e)a_1(s), a_1(s) + a_2(s) - r_s\right]f(s)\,ds$$

$$= \int_0^{\hat{s}} A(S)f(s)\,ds$$

$$= \int_0^{\hat{s}}\left[\frac{r_d^N}{L_d}A(S) + \frac{r_d(1-e)}{L_d}A(s)\right]f(s)\,ds.$$

Therefore (13) implies (12) holds. For a nonrecourse loan expression (13) becomes

$$\int_0^{\hat{s}} \min[r_{SL}, a_2(s)]f(s)\,ds > \int_0^{\hat{s}} \frac{r_d^N}{L_d}A(s)f(s)\,ds.$$

larger in the event of failure [i.e., condition (ii) or (ii′) hold]. However, this implies that existing depositors receive less than if new deposit claims are issued. Therefore, the wealth transfer to existing depositors is less when collateralized claims are issued.

The profitability of selling loans or issuing SLCs or secured debt claims does not necessarily imply existing depositors are worse off. Since use of secured claims will result in the bank making loans it might otherwise pass up, the payoffs to existing depositors can be greater when a secured claim is issued. As Stulz and Johnson (1985) point out, this may explain why unsecured debtholders (or depositors) permit secured debt issues.[14]

3.4. Capital requirements and deposit insurance

Bank regulation, particularly capital requirements and fixed rate deposit insurance, can exacerbate the underinvestment problem. For example, if capital regulation requires a new loan be financed with at most $1 - e$ of deposits, then the increase in the value of existing deposits [the bracketed term in (10)] is larger.[15] In other words, capital requirements prohibit the bank from offsetting a reduction in *asset* risk with an increase in *financial* risk. The Collateralization Hypothesis therefore predicts that binding capital requirement will increase the incentives to issue collateralized claims.

Fixed price deposit insurance can also exacerbate the underinvestment problem. With complete (100 percent) insurance, an underinvestment problem will arise so long as the cost of deposits including insurance premiums and reserve requirements exceeds the risk-free rate.[16] In this case, if the contracted rate on secured claims is less than r_d, then issuing secured claims will reduce

---

[14] Issuance of junior secured debts or loans sold without recourse will never make existing depositors worse off relative to their position when the loan opportunity is not undertaken. The payoff to junior secured claimants is

$$\min[\, r_J, a_2(s) + \max(\, a_1(s) - r_d(1-e), 0)\,],$$

and the payoff to existing depositors is

$$\min[\, r_s(1-e), \max(\, a_1(s), a_1(s) + a_2(s) - r_J)\,] \geq \min[\, r_d(1-e), a_1(s)\,].$$

For loan sale without recourse the payoff to existing depositors is

$$\min[\, r_d(1-e), \max(\, a_1(s), a_1(s) + a_2(s) - r_{SR})\,],$$

which is greater than or equal to the payoff depositors receive without loan sales.

[15] Note that if new equity is fairly priced the first two terms in (10) are no smaller. Because an increase in capital requirements can reduce the market value of the bank they may have the unintended effect of increasing the risk of existing deposits.

[16] In a competitive deposit market with deposit insurance the rate paid on deposits will equal the risk-free rate. The cost of deposits to the bank will equal the risk-free rate plus the insurance premium and the cost associated with meeting reserve requirements. If deposit insurance is fairly priced on average then, as Fama (1985) points out, the reserve requirement tax is sustainable only if there is something special about bank loans. The model presented in this paper assumes that banks have a comparative advantage in originating and monitoring loans [see eq. (2)] (i.e., bank loans are special).

the transfer from shareholders to the deposit insurance agency. With less than complete deposit insurance and risky uninsured deposits outstanding, an underinvestment problem can arise because the rate on existing deposits will not adjust fully to reflect the marginal contribution of the new loan to the overall risk of a bank's deposit claims. Specifically, while uninsured rates will adjust to reflect the risk of new loans, the cost of insured deposits will not. Therefore, the cost of deposit financing will not fully reflect the marginal risk of the new loan. In this case one obtains the result that a bank with risky deposits outstanding will tend to underinvest in relatively low-risk loans and overinvest in high-risk loans. [See for example Kareken and Wallace (1978).]

3.5. Contracting cost, legal and regulatory issues

In the previous section, loan sales and SLCs were shown to be similar to secured debt in the absence of contracting and other agency costs. These costs may, however, differ among financing techniques and will vary with the recourse provided. For example, as Pennacchi (1987) argues, the bank's incentives to monitor are lower where loans are sold with partial recourse rather than maintained on the bank's balance sheet. This is an agency cost associated with loan sales. Contracting and monitoring costs associated with registering collateral and monitoring bank loan-servicing performance may also increase the cost of secured debt, loan sales, and SLCs relative to deposit financing [see Smith and Warner (1977)].

An advantage of loan sales (as well as SLCs) is that because title to the collateral is transferred, there is no uncertainty concerning the purchaser's claim to the collateral in the event of bankruptcy.[17] More importantly, commercial banks are generally prohibited from pledging assets against deposits or issuing collateralized deposits (see footnote 2). In addition, loan sales and SLCs may provide banks a means of avoiding regulatory taxes associated with deposit financing such as reserve requirements and capital requirements.

4. Empirical implications

The model developed in section 3 establishes that there are some loans, if they are undertaken and financed with secured debt or secured debt substitutes, which benefit both existing depositors and shareholders. Moreover the model establishes that these loans would not be made if these financing vehicles were not available.

The analysis presented in section 3 also provides insights into when one would expect SLCs and loan sales to be used. Assume, for the moment, that

---

[17]Warner (1979) finds that in bankruptcy proceedings of nonfinancial firms priority rules are in many instances not followed. Because insured commercial banks are not subject to the Federal bankruptcy code there is additional uncertainty concerning the treatment of collateral in the event of bankruptcy. See Hayes (1987).

SLCs and loan sales provide no benefits other than to reduce the underinvestment problem. First, the underinvestment problem is not likely to be serious when a bank's existing deposits are not very risky. Therefore loan sales and SLCs are likely to increase the higher the default probability associated with deposits. Specifically, SLCs and loan sales are expected to be used more frequently by banks with greater leverage and greater asset risk. Second, the underinvestment problem is not likely to be serious for high-NPV or high-risk loans. Thus, loan sales and SLCs are likely to be used more frequently for low-risk loans to customers with a small amount of bank specific capital (e.g., loans to investment grade borrowers). Finally, because the underinvestment problem is exacerbated by binding capital requirements, banks with equity capital at or below the legal limit are expected to use SLCs and loan sales more frequently.

As discussed in section 3.5, loan sales and SLC may impose additional contracting costs. SLCs and loan sales are expected to be used for loans where these costs are lowest. Purchasers of loans will expend resources on verifying collateral (the underlying loans in a package) and on monitoring the bank's servicing performance. These costs are likely to be smallest for loans to the bank's least risky customers. For these types of loans, the value of the bank's centralized monitoring is least valuable.

The institutional arrangements are consistent with the predictions of my model. Commercial loan sales and SLCs consist primarily of loans to the bank's most credit-worthy customers (i.e., investment grade credits). For example, the Federal Reserve's Lending Practices Survey for February 1986 found that approximately two thirds of the loans sold by respondents were obligations of investment grade credits. Moreover, several studies have found default rates on SLC-backed loans to be lower than commercial loans [see Goldberg and Lloyd-Davies (1985) and Bennet (1986)]. Empirical studies of the SLCs and loan sales have found the probability of SLC issuance or loan sales to be positively related to bank leverage and whether capital requirements are binding. [See Benveniste and Berger (1986) and Goldberg and Lloyd-Davies (1985).] These results are consistent also with the predictions of the model developed here.

There is, however, another hypothesis consistent with these findings. The Moral Hazard Hypothesis also predicts that the frequency of loan sales and SLCs will be positively related to capital requirements and the risk of existing bank deposits. Although not capable of explaining SLC issues or loan sales by nonbank intermediaries, the testable implications of the Moral Hazard Hypothesis concerning the use of SLCs and loan sales within the banking industry are similar to those of my model.

The model developed in this paper does yield one important and testable implication that differs from the predictions of the Moral Hazard Hypothesis. If the *sole* motive for SLCs or loan sales is to avoid regulations designed to limit FDIC risk exposure, one would expect a positive relation between the

FDIC's risk exposure and a bank's use of SLCs or loan sales. While the FDIC's risk exposure is not directly observable, one can obtain a measure of the FDIC's exposure from the risk premium on a bank's uninsured (or partially insured) deposits. Assuming uninsured depositors behave as if they are not implicitly fully insured, the Moral Hazard Hypothesis predicts a positive relation between the risk premium on uninsured CDs and the volume of SLCs and loan sales. However, if one motive for loan sales or SLCs is to avoid an underinvestment problem, existing depositors as well as bank stockholders may be better off given SLCs and loan sales. Therefore, finding no significant relation (or a negative relation) between the risk premium on bank CDs and the volume of SLCs and/or loan sales is consistent with the Underinvestment Hypothesis.[18]

4.1. Empirical tests

Two empirical tests are performed. The first involves examining the relation between the interest cost on large CDs (deposits in excess of $100,000), the volume of loan sales and SLCs outstanding and a set of variables designed to proxy for factors affecting the risk premium on CDs. The second test involves examining the relation between the volume of SLCs and loan sales and the leverage of the bank and the risk of the bank's existing assets.

The interest cost of large CDs is estimated from information contained in the Consolidated Report of Condition and Income. The average rate paid on CDs is estimated by dividing the total interest paid on large domestic CDs during a quarter by the average dollar value of domestic CDs outstanding during the quarter (only the interest cost of domestic CDs is reported). There are two problems with using the average rate paid on CDs as a proxy for CD rates. [See Baer and Brewer (1986).] First, this measure fails to account for differences in maturity of CDs outstanding. However, the large bank supplement to the Report of Condition contains information on the maturity structure of CDs outstanding. From this information a weighted average maturity of a bank's CDs can be computed.[19]

A second problem with this measure is that it may reflect the rate offered on CDs in previous quarters as well as the rate on newly issued CDs. To

---

[18]As pointed out by the referee, the moral hazard and collateralization hypotheses are not mutually exclusive. Therefore, an analysis of CD rates can only identify the net effect of off balance sheet activities on bank risk.

[19]The dollar volume of time deposits of $100,000 or more is reported for six maturity categories: one day, three months or less, over three months to six months, over six months to twelve months, over one year to five years, and over five years. The weighted average maturity is calculated in months, with deposits of one day and three months or less assigned a value of one month. For the remaining categories, the maturity of CDs is assumed to be the longest maturity in that category. For deposits over five years, a maturity of sixty months was assigned.

determine whether the average interest cost of CDs is a reasonable proxy for the rate offered on CDs in a given quarter, I obtained the Innerline Survey of rates paid on newly issued CDs by three hundred banks for the first quarter of 1985. [See Hannan and Hanweck (1987) for a description of the survey.] Thirty-nine of the banks in my sample reported offer rates to Innerline. The average rate reported by these banks in the Innerline Survey is 9.28 percent. The average interest on CDs cost from the Call Report is 9.12 percent for that quarter. The difference is not statistically significant at the 0.10 level.

The interest cost on large CDs in a quarter is assumed to be a function of several factors: (1) the average maturity of the CDs outstanding, (2) the general level of interest rates as measured by average yield on ninety-day Treasury bills over the quarter, (3) the leverage of the bank, (4) the default or credit risk of the bank's loan portfolio, and (5) the interest rate risk of the bank.

Month-end quotes for the yield on ninety-day Treasury bills in the secondary markets are used to calculate the average yield on Treasury bills during each quarter. Financial leverage is estimated as the ratio of total assets of the bank (or bank-holding company) to the market value of total bank capital. The total market value of capital is estimated as the sum of the book value of subordinated debt and preferred stock of the bank or bank-holding company and the market value of common stock of the bank or bank-holding company. The market value of common stock outstanding is calculated by multiplying the number of shares outstanding at the beginning of the quarter by the price of the bank's stock at the beginning of the quarter.

Two variables are used to measure the risk of a bank's asset portfolio. The first measure is the provision for loan and lease losses in each quarter divided by the end of the quarter total of loans and leases outstanding.[20] A second measure is the variance of the bank's or bank-holding company's monthly common stock returns for the twelve months prior to the end of each quarter. The variance in stock returns is multiplied by the square of the ratio of the market value of equity to asset. This adjusted variance measure provides an estimate of the variance of the bank's asset returns.[21]

The interest rate risk of the bank is measured by the maturity mismatch between the bank's assets and liabilities. A measure of maturity mismatch, identical to the one used in Flannery and James (1984), is constructed from the Call Report. This measure, denoted as Short, represents the absolute value of the difference between dollar value of assets subject to repricing within one

---

[20] The Report of Income defines the provision for loan and leases losses as 'the amount needed to make the allowance for loan and lease losses adequate to absorb expected loan and lease losses'. Source: 1986 instructions to Consolidated Report of Income.

[21] This calculation is based on a simplifying assumption that the variance of the return on uninsured deposits is zero.

year and the dollar value of liabilities subject to repricing within the same period, divided by the book value of equity.[22]

4.2. Data

The empirical analysis is based on a sample of fifty-eight banks. Banks were included in the sample if they met the following criteria: (1) information for the bank or bank-holding company was contained in the Compustat Quarterly Bank File during the period 1984 through 1986, and (2) a lead bank was identifiable in the case of a multibank-holding company.

Only banks contained in the Compustat Quarterly Bank File were included because Compustat was used to obtain monthly stock prices and balance sheet information for the bank-holding companies. Only bank-holding companies with an identifiable lead bank are included in the sample so balance sheet items obtained from the lead bank's Call Report will adequately reflect the holding company's balance sheet. (Only bank-holding companies with the lead bank constituting 75 percent or more of the holding companies' assets in 1986 are included in the sample. For holding companies in the sample, the assets of the lead bank average 90 percent of the holding company assets.)

Quarterly data over the period 1985 through 1986 are used to test the model. This period was chosen because the first full year loan sales are reported in the Call Report is 1984.[23]

4.3. Empirical results

Table 1 provides descriptive statistics for banks in the sample. It is interesting to note that SLCs and loan sales constitute a sizable proportion of the total capital of the bank-holding company. Total SLCs (the sum of SLCs issued from foreign and domestic offices) average 95 percent of total capital, with a maximum value of twelve times total capital. The average ratio of loan sales to total capital is 24 percent.

The empirical test of the model, described in the previous subsection, is based on an assumption that the rate paid on CDs reflects a risk premium. The first step therefore is to investigate the relation between average CD rates and the measures of bank leverage and asset risk described in the previous

---

[22]A larger value of Short implies a greater maturity mismatch between bank assets and liabilities. The absolute value of the difference between short-term assets and liabilities is used to account for the fact that earnings variability induced from interest rate changes can arise through either short-term assets exceeding short-term liabilities or the converse. Reporting requirements necessitate using a one-year dividing line between short- and long-term assets. See Flannery and James (1984) for a description of how Short is constructed.

[23]Unfortunately, as discussed in Salem (1986) and described in the instructions to the Call Report, only loans sold without recourse are included in the Call Report as loan sales. Information on the proportion of these loans backed by SLCs or which have other performance guarantees is not provided.

Table 1

Summary statistics for fifty-eight commercial banks for the period 1984 through 1986 (quarterly data).

	Mean	Max.	Min.
Assets of holding company (millions)	$18,292	$196,124	$1,196
Assets of lead bank (millions)	$16,288	$153,293	$551
Market value of total capital/Assets[a]	0.072	0.220	0.012
Book value of total capital/Assets[b]	0.061	0.114	0.036
Loan loss/Total loans	0.0022	0.0487	−0.0004
Absolute value of the ratio of net short-term assets to book value of equity	4.69	11.99	0.006
Average maturity of CDs (months)	8.03	39.33	1.04
Interest cost of CDs	0.087	0.195	0.024
SLCs/Market value of total capital	0.948	12.54	0.000
Loan sales/Market value of total capital	0.239	4.07	0.000

[a] Market value of total capital equals the market value of common stock plus the book value of preferred stock and subordinated debt for the holding company. Assets refer to assets of the holding company.
[b] Book value of total capital equals the book value of common stock plus the book value of preferred stock and subordinated debt for the lead bank. Assets refer to the assets of the lead bank.

section. Two models are estimated. One model relates the average rate paid on CDs to balance sheet measures of credit risk, interest rate risk, and financial leverage. The second model relates CD rates to the variance in the bank's stock returns over the preceding twelve months (which should reflect both interest rate risk and credit risk) as well as financial leverage. The results of this analysis are reported in table 2. The first two columns of table 2 contain the results of an OLS and generalized least squares regression relating the rate paid on CDs to Treasury bill yields, the average maturity of the bank's CDs, and balance sheet measures of risk. The generalized least squares regression is based on an error components model, described in Kmenta (1986), which permits independent time series and cross-sectional components of the disturbance term. The second two columns present the results of regressions in which the adjusted variance in the monthly return on the bank's common stock is used a proxy for asset risk.

The results in table 2 are generally consistent with the hypothesis that CD rates reflect a default risk premium. For both models, a positive and statistically significant relation is found between the interest cost on CDs and the ratio of assets to total capital of the holding company. Moreover, the coefficients on the loan loss variable and on Short (which measures interest rate risk) are positive and statistically significant. (This result is consistent with the hypothesis that CD rates reflect both the credit risk and interest rate risk of the bank.) In the second two columns the coefficient on the adjusted variance in monthly stock returns is positive and statistically significant.

Table 2

Pooled cross-section time series regression relating interest cost of large CDs to the risk of the issuing bank (t-statistics in parentheses); dependent variable = interest cost on large CDs.[a]

Independent variable	OLS (1)	GLS[b] (2)	OLS (3)	GLS[b] (4)
Intercept	0.0147 (5.238)	0.0094 (5.058)	0.0189 (7.803)	0.0116 (8.014)
T-bill rate	0.8402 (28.67)	0.8366 (29.88)	0.8224 (28.17)	0.8182 (29.89)
Average maturity CDs	0.0004 (6.049)	0.0004 (4.357)	0.0005 (7.803)	0.0004 (4.357)
Assets/Market value of total capital[c]	6.220×10^{-5} (5.494)	6.031×10^{-5} (5.517)	6.427×10^{-5} (5.625)	6.200×10^{-5} (5.642)
Adjusted variance in monthly stock returns	—	—	1.633×10^{-3} (2.812)	1.846×10^{-3} (2.936)
Loan loss provision/ Total loans	0.7252 (4.646)	0.6696 (4.389)	—	—
Short	0.0004 (1.706)	0.0003 (1.612)	—	—
R^2	0.58	0.60	0.57	0.60
Number of observations	679	679	679	679

[a]Analysis based on quarterly data for fifty-eight bank-holding companies over the period 1984 through 1986.
[b]GLS estimates are obtained from an errors component model.
[c]Market value of total capital equals the sum of the market value of the holding companies' common stock, the book value of the preferred stock, and subordinated debt.

To investigate whether 'off balance sheet' activities affect the risk premium on large CDs, the regressions reported in table 2 were re-estimated with two additional independent variables: (1) the ratio of SLCs outstanding to total market value of capital and (2) the ratio of loan sales to total market − value of capital. If the volume of SLCs outstanding or loan sales relative to total capital increases the risk borne by uninsured depositors (and the FDIC), a positive relation is expected between CD rates and SLCs outstanding as well as loan sales. No significant relation is expected under the underinvestment hypothesis. The results of this analysis are reported in table 3.

No statistically significant relation is found between the rate paid on CDs and either SLCs outstanding or loan sales during the quarter. Moreover, using an F-test one cannot reject, at the 0.10 level, the hypothesis that the coefficients on SLCs and loan sales are jointly equal to zero in either model. The results presented in table 3 are consistent with the prediction of the model developed in section 3. The evidence presented is not consistent with the hypothesis that increased SLC or loan sales activity increases the risk borne by

Table 3

Pooled cross-section time series regression relating interest cost of CDs to the risk of the issuing bank and the volume of SLCs and loan sales (t-statistics in parentheses); dependent variable = interest cost on large CDs.[a]

Independent variable	OLS (1)	GLS[b] (2)	OLS (3)	GLS[b] (4)
Intercept	0.0142 (4.954)	0.0096 (5.033)	0.0180 (7.783)	0.0116 (8.007)
T-bill rate	0.8396 (28.35)	0.8386 (29.43)	0.8207 (27.73)	0.8178 (29.14)
Average maturity CDs	0.0004 (5.890)	0.0004 (4.389)	0.0005 (6.208)	0.0004 (4.350)
Assets/Market value of total capital[c]	6.145×10^{-5} (5.387)	6.067×10^{-5} (5.524)	6.386×10^{-5} (5.555)	6.192×10^{-5} (5.613)
Adjusted variance in monthly stock returns	—	—	1.588×10^{-3} (2.670)	1.841×10^{-3} (2.922)
Loan loss provision/ Total loans	0.7055 (4.401)	0.6867 (4.336)	—	—
Short	0.0004 (1.861)	0.0003 (0.9532)	—	—
SLC/Total market value of capital	−0.0002 (−0.4921)	−0.0002 (−0.3836)	−0.0001 (−0.3733)	−0.0001 (−0.1244)
Loan sales/Total market capital	−0.0004 (−0.3892)	−0.0004 (−0.0039)	−0.0001 (−0.1048)	−0.0005 (−0.4013)
R^2	0.57	0.60	0.57	0.60
Observations	679	679	679	679

[a]Analysis based on quarterly data for fifty-eight bank-holding companies over the period 1984 through 1986.
[b]GLS estimates are from an errors component model.
[c]Market value of total capital equals the sum of the market value of the holding companies' common stock, the book value of preferred stock, and subordinated debt.

uninsured depositors. The conclusion requires, however, an important caveat. Because loan sales reported in the Call Report are sales without explicit recourse (see footnote 23), it is uncertain whether loan sales generally adversely affect the risk of deposits.

A second test of the model involves examining the relation between SLCs outstanding, the risk of the bank's existing assets, and the leverage of the bank. The model developed in section 3 predicts a larger volume of SLCs relative to total capital the riskier the bank's assets and the lower the ratio of total capital to assets. While riskier banks are expected to be more active participants in the SLC market, two additional factors may affect a bank's activity in the SLC market. The first factor is the dollar volume of foreign deposits. Because approximately 10 percent of SLCs are issued by foreign

Table 4

Pooled cross-section time series regression relating SLCs outstanding to the bank risk and capital requirements (t-statistics in parentheses); dependent variable = SLC/Total market value of capital.[a]

Independent variable	(1)	(2)
Intercept	0.01313	0.1606
	(0.4524)	(2.463)
Assets/Total market value of capital[b]	0.0017	0.0019
	(1.891)	(2.129)
Provision for loan loss/Total loans	79.81	
	(6.213)	
Short	0.0385	
	(3.250)	
Adjusted variance in monthly stock returns		0.0031
		(6.781)
Bind	0.5496	0.5587
	(6.896)	(7.002)
Foreign office deposits	7.58×10^{-5}	7.321×10^{-5}
	(20.48)	(19.881)
R^2	0.49	0.47
Number of observations	683	683

[a]Analysis based on quarterly data for fifty-eight bank-holding companies over the period 1984 through 1986.
[b]Market value of total capital equals the sum of the market value of the holding companies' common stock, the book value of preferred stock, and subordinated debt.

branch offices of banks in the sample, activity in foreign banking markets may influence the total volume of SLCs outstanding.

The second factor affecting SLC issues is the capital adequacy requirement. One rationale for SLC issues, discussed earlier, is the avoidance of capital requirements (because SLCs are not included when determining regulatory capital requirements). To account for this motive, I constructed a dummy variable, which takes on a value of one if the bank's book value of equity is less than 6 percent, zero otherwise. This variable is denoted as Bind. If avoiding capital requirements is a motive for issuing SLCs (or because capital requirements exacerbate the underinvestment problem), a larger volume of SLC outstanding is expected for banks with binding capital requirements.

Table 4 presents the results of an OLS regression relating the volume of SLCs outstanding relative to the market value of total capital to bank financial leverage, asset risk, foreign office deposits outstanding, and capital requirements. (An error components model was also estimated, yielding similar results.) The results reported in column 1 are based on balance sheet measures of risk, while the results in column 2 are based on the adjusted variance in the bank's monthly stock returns as a measure of risk.

The results in both columns of table 4 indicate a positive and statistically significant relation between SLCs outstanding and the ratio of assets to total capital. This relation is not simply the result of capital adequacy requirements since these are included elsewhere in the regression. The positive and significant coefficients on the loan loss and the Short variables are also consistent with the hypothesis that riskier banks issue larger relative amounts of SLCs. The positive and statistically significant relation between SLC outstanding and the adjusted variance of the bank's stock return, reported in column 2, is also consistent with the model. Finally, the positive and significant coefficient on the capital requirement variable, 'Bind', is consistent with the hypothesis that SLC are used to avoid capital requirements.

The relation between the ratio of loan sales to total capital and bank risk is also examined. While a negative relation is found between loan sales, the ratio of assets to total capital and the dummy variable for capital requirements, no significant relation is found between loan sale and the other measures of bank risk.[24]

5. Summary and conclusion

The model demonstrates that one motive for loan sales and SLC issues is to avoid an underinvestment problem that arises when a firm (bank) has risky debt outstanding. I show that SLCs and loan sales can, like secured debt, reduce the underinvestment problem by permitting the bank to sell claims to portion payoffs of new loans that would otherwise accrue to existing depositors.

This explanation for the use of SLCs and loan sales yields two testable implications. First, unlike the explanations for loan sales and SLCs based solely on regulatory avoidance, my model indicates that depositor and/or the FDIC are not *necessarily* made worse off by these activities. Second, since the underinvestment problem is likely to be more severe the riskier the bank's existing deposits and the greater the amount of equity capital the bank is required to use for new loans, the volume of SLCs and loan sales are expected to be greater the riskier the bank and for banks with binding capital requirements.

An analysis of CD rates paid by fifty-eight banks over the period 1984 through 1986 reveals no statistically significant relation between the risk premium on uninsured deposits and the amount of SLCs outstanding or loans sold. Moreover, the volume of SLCs relative to bank capital is found to be positively related to balance sheet measures of bank risk as well as financial leverage. These results are consistent with the predictions of the model presented in this paper.

---

[24] In the loan sale analysis, the asset size of the bank was included in the regression. A positive and significant relation between loan sales and bank size is found.

Appendix

Proposition. *In equilibrium secured debt is profitable (i.e., the contracted rate,* r_s, *is less than* r_d^N) *if and only if there exists a state such that*

(i) $a_1(s) + a_2(s) < r_d^N + r_d(1 - e)$

(default occurs with deposit financing) and

(ii) $\min\left[r_s, a_2(s) + \dfrac{r_s}{L_s}a_1(s)\right] > \dfrac{r_d^N}{L_d}\left[a_1(s) + a_2(s)\right].$

Proof.   Consider the case where

$$r_s = r_d^N$$

(i.e., secured debt is not profitable) and condition (i) holds. This implies that for all states

$$\min\left[r_s, a_2(s) + \dfrac{r_s}{L_s}a_1(s)\right] \geq \min\left[r_d^N \dfrac{r_d^N}{L_s}A(s)\right].$$

However, since

$$a_2(s) + \dfrac{r_s}{L_s}a_1(s) > \dfrac{r_d^N}{L_d}A(s),$$

for all default states, the assumption that $r_s = r_d^N$ implies either

$$\int_0^{\bar{s}}\min\left[r_d^N\dfrac{r_d^N}{L_d}A(s)\right]f(s)\,\mathrm{d}s \neq r_f,$$

or

$$\int_0^{\bar{s}}\min\left[r_s, a_2(s) + \dfrac{r_s}{L_s}a_1(s)\right]f(s)\,\mathrm{d}s \neq r_f,$$

which contradicts the assumption of equilibrium in the market for bank debt. Now suppose

$$r_s < r_d^N$$

(i.e., secured debt is profitable). In equilibrium this holds only if for some state

$$\min\left[r_s, a_2(s) + \frac{r_s}{L_s}a_1(s)\right] > \min\left[r_d^N \frac{r_d^N}{L_d}A(s)\right]$$

[i.e., condition (ii) holds]. Given the payoff structure for secured debt and the fact that $r_s < r_d^N$, this can hold only if for some state

$$r_d^N + r_d(1 - e) > A(s)$$

[i.e., condition (i) holds].

References

Baer, Herbert and Elijan Brewer, 1986, Uninsured deposits as a source of market discipline: Some new evidence, Federal Reserve Bank of Chicago Economic Perspectives 10, 23–31.

Bennett, Barbara, 1986, Off balance sheet risk in banking: The case of standby letters of credit, San Francisco Federal Reserve Bank Economic Review 1, 19–29.

Benveniste, Lawrence and Allen N. Berger, 1986, Standby letters of credit: Benefits of financing loans off a bank's balance sheet, Research papers in banking and financial economics (Board of Governors of the Federal Reserve System, Washington, DC).

Fama, Eugene, 1985, What's different about banks, Journal of Monetary Economics 10, 10–19.

Flannery, Mark and Christopher James, 1984, The effect of interest rate changes on the common stock returns of financial institutions, Journal of Finance 39, 1141–1153.

Goldberg, Michael and Peter Lloyd-Davies, 1985, Standby letters of credit: Are banks overextending themselves?, Journal of Bank Research 16, 28–39.

Gorton, Gary and Joseph G. Haubrich, 1987, Loan sales, recourse and reputation: An analysis of secondary loan participations, Working paper (University of Pennsylvania, Philadelphia, PA).

Greenbaum, Stewart and Anjan Thakor, 1987, Bank funding modes: Securitization versus deposits, Banking Research Center working paper no. 146 (Northwestern University, Evanston, IL).

Hayes, David C., 1987, Some issues in asset securitization by national banks, Issues in Bank Regulation 10, 5–24.

Hannan, Timothy and Gerald Hanweck, 1987, Bank insolvency risk and the market for large certificates of deposit, Journal of Money, Credit and Banking, forthcoming.

Hess, Alan and Clifford Smith, 1987, Elements of mortgage securitization, Center for the Study of Banking and Financial Markets working paper no. 60 (University of Washington, Seattle, WA).

Hirtle, Beverly, 1987, The growth of the financial guarantee market, Federal Reserve Bank of New York Quarterly Review 12, 10–18.

Kane, Edward and Burton Malkiel, 1965, Bank portfolio allocation, deposit variability and the availability doctrine, Quarterly Journal of Economics 79, 113–134.

Kareken, John and Neil Wallace, 1978, Deposit insurance and bank regulation: A partial equilibrium exposition, Journal of Business 51, 413–438.

Kmenta, Jan, 1986, Elements of econometrics, 2nd ed. (Macmillan, New York).

Koppenhaver, Gary, 1987, Standby letters of credit, Federal Reserve Bank of Chicago Economic Perspectives 11, 28–35.

Melvin, Donald, 1986, A primer for RMA staff on legal and regulatory concepts and standards in the securitization of loans (Robert Morris Associates, Philadelphia, PA).

Myers, Stewart, 1977, Determinants of corporate borrowing, Journal of Financial Economics 5, 147–175.

Pavel, Christine, 1986, Securitization, Federal Reserve Bank of Chicago Economic Perspectives 10, 16–31.

Pavel, Christine and David Phillis, 1987, Why commercial banks sell loans: An empirical analysis, Federal Reserve Bank of Chicago Economic Perspectives 11, 3–14.

Pennacchi, George, 1987, Loan sales and the cost of bank capital, Working paper (University of Pennsylvania, Philadelphia, PA).

Pyle, David, 1985, Discussion of off balance sheet banking, in: The search for financial stability: The past fifty years (Federal Reserve Bank of San Francisco, CA).

Salem, George, 1986, Selling commerical loans: A significant new activity for money center banks, Journal of Commerical Bank Lending, 12–22.

Salem, George, 1987, Loan selling: A growing revolution that can affect your bank, Journal of Commercial Bank Lending, 12–22.

Smith, Clifford and Jerold Warner, 1977, On financial contracting: An analysis of bond covenants, Journal of Financial Economics 7, 117–161.

Stulz, Rene and Herb Johnson, 1985, An analysis of secured debt, Journal of Financial Economics 14, 501–521.

Warner, Jerold, 1977, Bankruptcy, absolute priority and the pricing of risky debt claims, Journal of Financial Economics 4, 329–350.

V

BANK REGULATION

Bank regulation is pervasive in that virtually all aspects of a bank's operation are subject to government oversight and regulation. Government regulation and oversight of commercial banks reflect a variety of stated objectives—from promoting "fairness" to promoting bank "safety and soundness." The readings in this part focus on the rationale for and the effects of bank safety and soundness regulation.

Bank safety and soundness regulation is intended to control bank risk taking. Government concern with bank risk taking arises primarily from the provision of deposit insurance to commercial banks by the Federal Deposit Insurance Corporation. In particular, by law, deposits up to $100,000 are insured against loss, with *de facto* coverage extending to even larger deposits. As the agency of the federal government that insures bank deposits, the FDIC assumes the liability for insured deposits in the event that the bank fails. As a result, just like the creditor of any corporation, the FDIC is concerned with the activities of banks that affect the risk of default. Indeed, much of bank safety and soundness regulation resembles the covenants found in debt contracts to control stockholder/bondholder conflicts in nonbank firms [see **Smith and Warner** (1979)].

While deposit insurance may create a demand for safety and soundness regulation, the more basic question is why the government provides deposit insurance. The primary rationale for deposit insurance is that without it, banks are subject to socially destructive runs by depositors. Research has focused on two important characteristics of bank operations that contribute to deposit runs. First, as a result of the lending activities described in Part II, banks' primary assets (loans) are informationally intensive, illiquid investments. Second, a significant proportion of bank liabilities are deposits redeemable on demand at par value. The ability of depositors to redeem their claims on demand at par means that the deposit contract calls for sequential servicing. The amount the bank pays depositors seeking withdrawal depends on the par value of the depositor's claim and the depositor's place in the queue of bank customers seeking to withdraw their funds. In the absence of deposit insurance, this sequential-servicing feature of deposits can lead to situations in which all or most of the depositors seek to withdraw their funds.

In the first article, **Diamond and Dybvig** (1983) provide a model to illustrate: (1) how offering deposits enhances welfare, and (2) why rational depositors would participate in a bank run that makes depositors collectively worse off. Diamond and Dybvig argue that deposits provide individual depositors insurance against liquidity shocks (unexpected demands for current consumption). Specifically, banks provide risk sharing among depositors; they invest in long-term, illiquid investment projects and offer deposit contracts that pay a fixed amount and permit early withdrawal in the event that an individual depositor wants liquidity. The bank thus promises a higher payment to depositors in the event of early withdrawal than could be received were the depositor to invest directly in illiquid assets, and since depositors are risk-averse, they prefer a smoother pattern of returns through time.

While banks provide valuable liquidity, there is the unfortunate possibility of a deposit run in which all depositors seek early withdrawal. Within Diamond and Dybvig's model, anything might trigger a deposit run; all that is required for a run to start is for individual depositors to believe that other depositors will withdraw. In this case, even though it is in the collective interest of all depositors not to withdraw (since a run induces the costly liquidations of productive investments), individually it is in each depositor's interest to withdraw.

One way to avoid deposit runs is through deposit insurance. With insurance, the value of a depositor's claim on the bank no longer depends on the depositor's place in the queue of depositors seeking to withdraw their funds. Thus, deposit insurance eliminates the incentive of depositors to participate in a run.

An issue not specifically addressed in Diamond and Dybvig is the reason for banking panics. Banking panics are simultaneous deposit runs on a number of banks. One view (consistent with Diamond and Dybvig's model) is that banking panics are random events caused by shifts in the beliefs of depositors. An alternative view is that bank panics are linked to events in the macroeconomy. Specifically, Gorton (1988) has argued that information asymmetries make it difficult and costly for individual depositors to assess the value of a bank's loan portfolio. In this case, depositors will rely in part on information about the macroeconomy in making this assessment. As a result, in the absence of deposit insurance, banking panics occur as systematic responses to depositor's changing perceptions of bank risk. Consistent with this view, Gorton finds in the pre-1914 era that banking panics were closely linked to changes in the business cycle.

While bank failures may be precipitated by declines in economic activity (as Gorton finds), to what extent do bank failures contribute to further declines in business activity? This question is addressed in **Bernanke** (1983). One way in which bank failures potentially worsen an economic contraction is through declines in the money supply. Specifically, bank runs result in an exchange of deposits for currency which, absent offsetting actions by the central bank, leads to a decrease in the money supply.

Bernanke examines an alternate way in which bank failures might affect real economic activity: through reducing real investment activity. In particular, Bernanke argues that commercial banks provide important information-gathering and monitoring services for borrowers and lenders. Focusing on the 1930s, Bernanke argues that widespread bank failures disrupted the normal channels through which credit flowed in the economy. Actual bank failures together with the fear of runs in the 1930s forced a contraction in the banking system's role in the intermediation of credit. This contraction led to higher costs of credit intermediation and as a result a higher effective cost of credit for some borrowers. Higher borrowing costs in turn resulted in reduced investment activity and slower economic growth. Consistent with this argument, Bernanke finds evidence that bank failures caused further declines in economic activity in the period 1919 through 1941.

While deposit insurance has been effective in eliminating deposit runs and panics, it creates a role for bank safety and soundness regulation. As discussed, the need for regulation arises from the fact that with deposit insurance, the FDIC assumes the liability for losses on insured deposits. Safety and soundness regulation is especially important because in the United States deposit insurance is not priced (explicitly) on the basis of bank risk. In particular, in the United States, banks are charged a fixed premium per dollar of deposits for insurance. Absent regulation, this pricing scheme creates powerful incentives for banks to take on additional risk. As Merton (1977) shows, deposit insurance can be viewed as a put option on the value of the bank's assets with a strike price equal to the face value of the bank's deposits. With fixed-rate deposit insurance, banks seeking to maximize the value of shareholder wealth have incentives to increase the value of this insurance put option by increasing asset risk or increasing leverage.

Fixed-rate deposit insurance will generate a subsidy for the insured bank whenever the premium charged for insurance is less than the actuarially fair rate based on the risk of the bank's assets and the leverage of the bank. As **Buser, Chen, and Kane** (1981) point out, the explicit premium on deposit insurance is only part of the cost of the coverage. They argue that precisely because the explicit premium on deposit insurance is invariant to bank risk, the FDIC is forced to establish an implicit premium for insurance. Regulations imposed on banks as a condition for receiving insurance reduce the value of the bank and thus act as an implicit premium.

Buser, Chen, and Kane argue that since explicit premiums are not risk-rated to control risk taking, implicit premiums must be risk-related. Moreover, they argue that banks will only submit to regulation as a requirement for receiving insurance if they are at least as well off with insurance (inclusive of these indirect costs) as they would be without insurance and government regulation. Thus, subsidized insurance serves to induce banks to submit to government regulation.

One important way in which bank regulators attempt to constrain bank risk taking is through minimum capital standards. Current capital standards set limits on the use of deposit and debt financing as a percentage of bank assets (and under the new risk-based capital standards as a percentage of "risk-adjusted" bank assets). In **Flannery** (1989), the influence of capital standards and the bank-examination process on bank asset-portfolio choice is examined. As Flannery explains, a substantial part of the examination process is devoted to assessing the credit quality of a bank's loan and investment portfolios. As part of the examination process, bank examiners seek to identify assets whose timely and full repayment are unlikely. These assets are classified by examiners. More important, a proportion of the estimated losses from these assets is deducted from the regulator's assessment of the bank's capital. This deduction is intended to represent the decline in the value of the classified assets.

An important observation made by Flannery is that the examination process is one-sided in selectively marking to market only assets whose market value has fallen. Assets with market values that have risen continue to be valued at historical cost for the purpose of computing bank capital. One obvious effect of this process is to create an incentive for banks to sell assets that have appreciated in value. Moreover, Flannery shows that the interaction of deposit insurance, capital standards, and examination procedures leads banks to prefer a unique level of asset risk. Increasing asset risk increases the value of deposit insurance to the bank; however, it also makes asset markdowns more likely, thus reducing the permissible level of bank leverage. The optimal level of asset risk for the bank is a result of balancing these two conflicting effects.

The importance of bank capital in constraining bank risk taking is examined empirically in **Keeley** (1990). Keeley's analysis is motivated in part by the increase in the number of savings and loan and bank failures in the late 1980s and early 1990s. One explanation for the increase in the number of bank failures is the moral-hazard problem associated with the provision of fixed-rate deposit insurance. However, deposit insurance has been provided since the 1930s; the question arises as to why it took 50 years for major problems to arise.

Keeley argues that historically, bank charter values served to constrain bank risk taking. Specifically, Keeley argues that an important component of the market value of bank equity is the value of a bank's charter. The value of a bank's license to operate represents the present discounted value of rents arising from operating a bank. These rents depend, in turn, on the degree of competition within the banking industry. Greater competition in local banking markets (through, say, elimination of branching restrictions or through entry by nonbank competitors) serves to reduce bank charter values.

While the value of a bank's charter is an important component of the market value of bank equity capital, it does not directly contribute to regulatory "book" capital. Regulatory book capital is simply the difference between the book value of bank assets and liabilities. More important, bank capital-adequacy requirements and ultimately the regulator's decision to close a bank depend on the book and not the market value of a bank's capital. Since a bank's owners lose the rights to the charter if the bank fails, Keeley argues that the possession of a valuable bank charter serves as a bankruptcy cost borne by the owners of the bank. As a result, Keeley argues that the gains from increased risk taking (through enhancing the value of the deposit insurance put option) are offset by decreases in the expected value of the bank's charter. The higher the charter value of the bank, the lower the optimal level of risk for the bank.

Keeley examines empirically the relation between bank risk and measures of bank charter value. He finds that bank risk taking is negatively related to the ratio of the market to book value of bank assets (a proxy for bank charter value). One implication of Keeley's analysis is that the increase in the number of bank failures in the 1980s resulted from a decline in bank charter values.

The apparent failure of bank regulation and examinations to constrain risk taking in the 1980s has led to proposals for explicit risk-based deposit-insurance pricing. One argument in favor of explicit risk-based pricing is that this type of insurance pricing will result in less reliance on bank regulation and examination to control risk taking. This question is addressed in **Chan, Greenbaum, and Thakor** (1992). In particular, they examine whether risk-based deposit insurance together with bank capital requirements can be used to elicit accurate private information about bank default risk that is costly for the regulator to observe. They show that unless banks receive some deposit-linked subsidies, an incentive-compatible, risk-sensitive deposit-insurance scheme is not possible. Intuitively, for a risk-sensitive deposit-insurance pricing scheme to be incentive-compatible, it must be costly for high-risk banks to mimic the leverage choice of low-risk banks. One mechanism that makes mimicry costly is a valuable bank charter that is lost if the bank fails.

Bank Runs, Deposit Insurance, and Liquidity

Douglas W. Diamond
University of Chicago

Philip H. Dybvig
Yale University

This paper shows that bank deposit contracts can provide allocations superior to those of exchange markets, offering an explanation of how banks subject to runs can attract deposits. Investors face privately observed risks which lead to a demand for liquidity. Traditional demand deposit contracts which provide liquidity have multiple equilibria, one of which is a bank run. Bank runs in the model cause real economic damage, rather than simply reflecting other problems. Contracts which can prevent runs are studied, and the analysis shows that there are circumstances when government provision of deposit insurance can produce superior contracts.

I. Introduction

Bank runs are a common feature of the extreme crises that have played a prominent role in monetary history. During a bank run, depositors rush to withdraw their deposits because they expect the bank to fail. In fact, the sudden withdrawals can force the bank to liquidate many of its assets at a loss and to fail. In a panic with many bank failures, there is a disruption of the monetary system and a reduction in production.

Institutions in place since the Great Depression have successfully prevented bank runs in the United States since the 1930s. Nonethe-

We are grateful for helpful comments from Milt Harris, Burt Malkiel, Mike Mussa, Art Raviv, and seminar participants at Chicago, Northwestern, Stanford, and Yale.

[*Journal of Political Economy*, 1983, vol. 91, no. 3]

less, current deregulation and the dire financial condition of savings and loans make bank runs and institutions to prevent them a current policy issue, as shown by recent aborted runs.[1] (Internationally, Eurodollar deposits tend to be uninsured and are therefore subject to runs, and this is true in the United States as well for deposits above the insured amount.) It is good that deregulation will leave banking more competitive, but we must ensure that banks will not be left vulnerable to runs.

Through careful description and analysis, Friedman and Schwartz (1963) have provided substantial insight into the properties of past bank runs in the United States. Existing theoretical analysis has neglected to explain why bank contracts are less stable than other types of financial contracts or to investigate the strategic decisions that depositors face. The model we present has an explicit economic role for banks to perform: the transformation of illiquid assets into liquid liabilities. The analyses of Patinkin (1965, chap. 5), Tobin (1965), and Niehans (1978) provide insights into characterizing the liquidity of assets. This paper gives the first explicit analysis of the demand for liquidity and the "transformation" service provided by banks. Uninsured demand deposit contracts are able to provide liquidity but leave banks vulnerable to runs. This vulnerability occurs because there are multiple equilibria with differing levels of confidence.

Our model demonstrates three important points. First, banks issuing demand deposits can improve on a competitive market by providing better risk sharing among people who need to consume at different random times. Second, the demand deposit contract providing this improvement has an undesirable equilibrium (a bank run) in which all depositors panic and withdraw immediately, including even those who would prefer to leave their deposits in if they were not concerned about the bank failing. Third, bank runs cause real economic problems because even "healthy" banks can fail, causing the recall of loans and the termination of productive investment. In addition, our model provides a suitable framework for analysis of the devices traditionally used to stop or prevent bank runs, namely, suspension of convertibility and demand deposit insurance (which works similarly to a central bank serving as "lender of last resort").

The illiquidity of assets enters our model through the economy's riskless production activity. The technology provides low levels of output per unit of input if operated for a single period but high levels

---

[1] The aborted runs on Hartford Federal Savings and Loan (Hartford, Conn., February 1982) and on Abilene National Bank (Abilene, Texas, July 1982) are two recent examples. The large amounts of uninsured deposits in the recently failed Penn Square Bank (Oklahoma City, July 1982) and its repercussions are another symptom of banks' current problems.

of output if operated for two periods. The analysis would be the same if the asset were illiquid because of selling costs: one receives a low return if unexpectedly forced to "liquidate" early. In fact, this illiquidity is a property of the financial assets in the economy in our model, even though they are traded in competitive markets with no transaction costs. Agents will be concerned about the cost of being forced into early liquidation of these assets and will write contracts which reflect this cost. Investors face private risks which are not directly insurable because they are not publicly verifiable. Under optimal risk sharing, this private risk implies that agents have different time patterns of return in different private information states and that agents want to allocate wealth unequally across private information states. Because only the agent ever observes the private information state, it is impossible to write insurance contracts in which the payoff depends directly on private information, without an explicit mechanism for information flow. Therefore, simple competitive markets cannot provide this liquidity insurance.

Banks are able to transform illiquid assets by offering liabilities with a different, smoother pattern of returns over time than the illiquid assets offer. These contracts have multiple equilibria. If confidence is maintained, there can be efficient risk sharing, because in that equilibrium a withdrawal will indicate that a depositor should withdraw under optimal risk sharing. If agents panic, there is a bank run and incentives are distorted. In that equilibrium, everyone rushes in to withdraw their deposits before the bank gives out all of its assets. The bank must liquidate all its assets, even if not all depositors withdraw, because liquidated assets are sold at a loss.

Illiquidity of assets provides the rationale both for the existence of banks and for their vulnerability to runs. An important property of our model of banks and bank runs is that runs are costly and reduce social welfare by interrupting production (when loans are called) and by destroying optimal risk sharing among depositors. Runs in many banks would cause economy-wide economic problems. This is consistent with the Friedman and Schwartz (1963) observation of large costs imposed on the U.S. economy by the bank runs in the 1930s, although they attribute the real damage from bank runs as occurring through the money supply.

Another contrast with our view of how bank runs do economic damage is discussed by Fisher (1911, p. 64).[2] In this view, a run occurs because the bank's assets, which are liquid but risky, no longer cover the nominally fixed liability (demand deposits), so depositors withdraw quickly to cut their losses. The real losses are indirect, through

[2] Bryant (1980) also takes this view.

the loss of collateral caused by falling prices. In contrast, a bank run in our model is caused by a shift in expectations, which could depend on almost anything, consistent with the apparently irrational observed behavior of people running on banks.

We analyze bank contracts that can prevent runs and examine their optimality. We show that there is a feasible contract that allows banks both to prevent runs and to provide optimal risk sharing by converting illiquid assets. The contract corresponds to suspension of convertibility of deposits (to currency), a weapon banks have historically used against runs. Under other conditions, the best contract that banks can offer (roughly, the suspension-of-convertibility contract) does not achieve optimal risk sharing. However, in this more general case there is a contract which achieves the unconstrained optimum when government deposit insurance is available. Deposit insurance is shown to be able to rule out runs without reducing the ability of banks to transform assets. What is crucial is that deposit insurance frees the asset liquidation policy from strict dependence on the volume of withdrawals. Other institutions such as the discount window ("lender of last resort") may serve a similar function; however, we do not model this here. The taxation authority of the government makes it a natural provider of the insurance, although there may be a competitive fringe of private insurance.

Government deposit insurance can improve on the best allocations that private markets provide. Most of the existing literature on deposit insurance assumes away any real service from deposit insurance, concentrating instead on the question of pricing the insurance, taking as given the likelihood of failure (see, e.g., Merton 1977, 1978; Kareken and Wallace 1978; Dothan and Williams 1980).

Our results have far-reaching policy implications, because they imply that the real damage from bank runs is primarily from the direct damage occurring when recalling loans interrupts production. This implies that much of the economic damage in the Great Depression was *caused* directly by bank runs. A study by Bernanke (in press) supports our thesis, as it shows that bank runs give a better predictor of economic distress than money supply.

The paper proceeds as follows. In the next section, we analyze a simple economy which shows that banks can improve the risk sharing of simple competitive markets by transforming illiquid assets. We show that such banks are always vulnerable to runs. In Section III, we analyze the optimal bank contracts that prevent runs. In Section IV, we analyze bank contracts, dropping the previous assumption that the volume of withdrawals is deterministic. Deposit insurance is analyzed in Section V. Section VI concludes the paper.

II. The Bank's Role in Providing Liquidity

Banks have issued demand deposits throughout their history, and economists have long had the intuition that demand deposits are a vehicle through which banks fulfill their role of turning illiquid assets into liquid assets. In this role, banks can be viewed as providing insurance that allows agents to consume when they need to most. Our simple model shows that asymmetric information lies at the root of liquidity demand, a point not explicitly noted in the previous literature.

The model has three periods ($T = 0, 1, 2$) and a single homogeneous good. The productive technology yields $R > 1$ units of output in period 2 for each unit of input in period 0. If production is interrupted in period 1, the salvage value is just the initial investment. Therefore, the productive technology is represented by

$$
\begin{array}{ccc}
T = 0 & T = 1 & T = 2 \\
-1 & \begin{cases} 0 \\ 1 \end{cases} & \begin{array}{c} R \\ 0, \end{array}
\end{array}
$$

where the choice between $(0, R)$ and $(1, 0)$ is made in period 1. (Of course, constant returns to scale implies that a fraction can be done in each option.)

One interpretation of the technology is that long-term capital investments are somewhat irreversible, which appears to be a reasonable characterization. The results would be reinforced (or can be alternatively motivated) by any type of transaction cost associated with selling a bank's assets before maturity. See Diamond (1980) for a model of the costly monitoring of loan contracts by banks, which implies such a cost.

All consumers are identical as of period 0. Each faces a privately observed, uninsurable risk of being of type 1 or of type 2. In period 1, each agent (consumer) learns his type. Type 1 agents care only about consumption in period 1 and type 2 agents care only about consumption in period 2. In addition, all agents can privately store (or "hoard") consumption goods at no cost. This storage is not publicly observable. No one would store between $T = 0$ and $T = 1$, because the productive technology does at least as well (and better if held until $T = 2$). If an agent of type 2 obtains consumption goods at $T = 1$, he will store them until $T = 2$ to consume them. Let c_T represent goods "received" (to store or consume) by an agent at period T. The privately observed consumption at $T = 2$ of a type 2 agent is then what he stores from $T = 1$ plus what he obtains at $T = 2$, or $c_1 + c_2$. In terms of this publicly observed variable c_T the discussion above implies that each agent has a state-dependent utility function (with the state private information), which we assume has the form

$$U(c_1, c_2; \Theta) = \begin{cases} u(c_1) & \text{if } j \text{ is of type 1 in state } \Theta \\ \rho u(c_1 + c_2) & \text{if } j \text{ is of type 2 in state } \Theta, \end{cases}$$

where $1 \geq \rho > R^{-1}$ and $u : R_{++} \to R$ is twice continuously differentiable, increasing, strictly concave, and satisfies Inada conditions $u'(0) = \infty$ and $u'(\infty) = 0$. Also, we assume that the relative risk-aversion coefficient $-cu''(c)/u'(c) > 1$ everywhere. Agents maximize expected utility, $E[u(c_1, c_2; \Theta)]$, conditional on their information (if any).

A fraction $t \in (0, 1)$ of the continuum of agents are of type 1 and, conditional on t, each agent has an equal and independent chance of being of type 1. Later sections will allow t to be random (in which case, at period 1, consumers know their own type but not t), but for now we take t to be constant.

To complete the model, we give each consumer an endowment of 1 unit in period 0 (and none at other times). We consider first the competitive solution where agents hold the assets directly, and in each period there is a competitive market in claims on future goods. It is easy to show that because of the constant returns technology, prices are determined: the period 0 price of period 1 consumption is 1, and the period 0 and 1 prices of period 2 consumption are R^{-1}. This is because agents can write only uncontingent contracts as there is no public information on which to condition. Contracting in period $T = 0$, all agents (who are then identical) will establish the same trades and each will invest his endowment in the production technology. Given this identical position of each agent at $T = 0$, there will be trade in claims on goods for consumption at $T = 1$ and at $T = 2$. Each has access to the same technology and each can choose any positive linear combination of $c_1 = 1$ and $c_2 = R$. Each individual's production set is proportional to the aggregate set, and for there to be positive production of both c_1 and c_2, the period $T = 1$ price of c_2 must be R^{-1}. Given these prices, there is never any trade, and agents can do no better or worse than if they produced only for their own consumption. Letting c_k^i be consumption in period k of an agent who is of type i, the agents choose $c_1^1 = 1$, $c_2^1 = c_1^2 = 0$, and $c_2^2 = R$, since type 1's always interrupt production but type 2's never do.

By comparison, if types were *publicly* observable as of period 1, it would be possible to write optimal insurance contracts that give the ex ante (as of period 0) optimal sharing of output between type 1 and type 2 agents. The optimal consumption $\{c_k^{i*}\}$ satisfies

$$c_1^{2*} = c_2^{1*} = 0 \tag{1a}$$

(those who can, delay consumption),

$$u'(c_1^{1*}) = \rho R u'(c_2^{2*}) \tag{1b}$$

(marginal utility in line with marginal productivity), and

$$tc_1^{1*} + [(1 - t)c_2^{2*}/R] = 1 \tag{1c}$$

(the resource constraint).

By assumption, $\rho R > 1$, and since relative risk aversion always exceeds unity, equation (1) implies that the optimal consumption levels satisfy $c_1^{1*} > 1$ and $c_2^{2*} < R$.[3] Therefore, there is room for improvement on the competitive outcome ($c_1^1 = 1$ and $c_2^2 = R$). Also, note that $c_2^{2*} > c_1^{1*}$ by equation (1b), since $\rho R > 1$.

   The optimal insurance contract just described would allow agents to insure against the unlucky outcome of being a type 1 agent. This contract is not available in the simple contingent-claims market. Also, the lack of observability of agents' types rules out a complete market of Arrow-Debreu state-contingent claims, because this market would require claims that depend on the nonverifiable private information. Fortunately it is potentially possible to achieve the optimal insurance contract, since the optimal contract satisfies the self-selection constraints.[4] We argue that banks can provide this insurance: by provid-

---

[3] The proof of this is as follows:

$$\rho R u'(R) < R u'(R)$$

$$= 1 \cdot u'(1) + \int_{\gamma=1}^{R} \frac{\partial}{\partial \gamma} [\gamma u'(\gamma)] d\gamma$$

$$= u'(1) + \int_{\gamma=1}^{R} [u'(\gamma) + u''(\gamma)] d\gamma$$

$$< u'(1),$$

as $u' > 0$ and $(\forall \gamma) -u''(\gamma)\gamma/u'(\gamma) > 1$. Because $u'(\cdot)$ is decreasing and the resource constraint (1c) trades off c_1^{1*} against c_2^{2*}, the solution to (1) must have $c_1^{1*} > 1$ and $c_2^{2*} < R$.

[4] The self-selection constraints state that no agent envies the treatment by the market of other indistinguishable agents. In our model, agents' utilities depend on only their consumption vectors across time and all have identical endowments. Therefore, the self-selection constraints are satisfied if no agent envies the consumption bundle of any other agent. This can be shown for optimal risk sharing using the properties described after (1). Because $c_1^{1*} > 1$ and $c_1^{2*} = 0$, type 1 agents do not envy type 2 agents. Furthermore, because $c_1^{2*} + c_2^{2*} = c_2^{2*} > c_1^{1*} = c_1^{1*} + c_2^{1*}$, type 2 agents do not envy type 1 agents. Because the optimal contract satisfies the self-selection constraints, there is necessarily a contract structure which implements it as a Nash equilibrium—the ordinary demand deposit is a contract which will work. However, the optimal allocation is not the unique Nash equilibrium under the ordinary demand deposit contract. Another inferior equilibrium is what we identify as a bank run. Our model gives a real-world example of a situation in which the distinction between implementation as a Nash equilibrium and implementation as a *unique* Nash equilibrium is crucial (see also Dybvig and Spatt, in press, and Dybvig and Jaynes 1980).

ing liquidity, banks guarantee a reasonable return when the investor cashes in before maturity, as is required for optimal risk sharing. To illustrate how banks provide this insurance, we first examine the traditional demand deposit contract, which is of particular interest because of its ubiquitous use by banks. Studying the demand deposit contract in our framework also indicates why banks are susceptible to runs.

In our model, the demand deposit contract gives each agent withdrawing in period 1 a fixed claim of r_1 per unit deposited at time 0. Withdrawal tenders are served sequentially in random order until the bank runs out of assets. This approach allows us to capture the flavor of continuous time (in which depositors deposit and withdraw at different random times) in a discrete model. Note that the demand deposit contract satisfies a *sequential service constraint*, which specifies that a bank's payoff to any agent can depend only on the agent's place in line and not on future information about agents behind him in line.

We are assuming throughout this paper that the bank is mutually owned (a "mutual") and liquidated in period 2, so that agents not withdrawing in period 1 get a pro rata share of the bank's assets in period 2. Let V_1 be the period 1 payoff per unit deposit withdrawn which depends on one's place in line at $T = 1$, and let V_2 be the period 2 payoff per unit deposit not withdrawn at $T = 2$, which depends on total withdrawals at $T = 1$. These are given by

$$V_1(f_j, r_1) = \begin{cases} r_1 & \text{if } f_j < r_1^{-1} \\ 0 & \text{if } f_j \geq r_1^{-1} \end{cases} \tag{2}$$

and

$$V_2(f, r_1) = \max \{R(1 - r_1 f)/(1 - f), 0\}, \tag{3}$$

where f_j is the number of withdrawers' deposits serviced before agent j as a fraction of total demand deposits; f is the total number of demand deposits withdrawn. Let w_j be the fraction of agent j's deposits that he attempts to withdraw at $T = 1$. The consumption from deposit proceeds, per unit of deposit of a type 1 agent, is thus given by $w_j V_1(f_j, r_1)$, while the total consumption, from deposit proceeds, per unit of deposit of a type 2 agent is given by $w_j V_1(f_j, r_1) + (1 - w_j)V_2(f, r_1)$.

Equilibrium Decisions

The demand deposit contract can achieve the full-information optimal risk sharing as an equilibrium. (By equilibrium, we will always refer to pure strategy Nash equilibrium[5]—and for now we will assume all agents are required to deposit initially.) This occurs when $r_1 = c_1^{1*}$, that is, when the fixed payment per dollar of deposits withdrawn at $T = 1$ is equal to the optimal consumption of a type 1 agent given full information. If this contract is in place, it is an equilibrium for type 1 agents to withdraw at $T = 1$ and for type 2 agents to wait, provided this is what is anticipated. This "good" equilibrium achieves optimal risk sharing.[6]

Another equilibrium (a bank run) has all agents panicking and trying to withdraw their deposits at $T = 1$: if this is anticipated, all agents will prefer to withdraw at $T = 1$. This is because the face value of deposits is larger than the liquidation value of the bank's assets.

It is precisely the "transformation" of illiquid assets into liquid assets that is responsible both for the liquidity service provided by banks and for their susceptibility to runs. For all $r_1 > 1$, runs are an equilibrium.[7] If $r_1 = 1$, a bank would not be susceptible to runs because $V_1(f_j, 1) < V_2(f, 1)$ for all values of $0 \leq f_j \leq f$; but if $r_1 = 1$, the bank simply mimics direct holding of the assets and is therefore no improvement on simple competitive claims markets. A demand deposit contract which is not subject to runs provides no liquidity services.

The bank run equilibrium provides allocations that are worse for all agents than they would have obtained without the bank (trading in the competitive claims market). In the bank run equilibrium, everyone receives a risky return that has a mean one. Holding assets directly provides a riskless return that is at least one (and equal to $R > 1$ if an agent becomes a type 2). Bank runs ruin the risk sharing between agents and take a toll on the efficiency of production because all production is interrupted at $T = 1$ when it is optimal for some to continue until $T = 2$.

If we take the position that outcomes must match anticipations, the inferiority of bank runs seems to rule out observed runs, since no one would deposit anticipating a run. However, agents will choose to deposit at least some of their wealth in the bank even if they anticipate a positive probability of a run, provided that the probability is small enough, because the good equilibrium dominates holding assets di-

---

[5] This assumption rules out a mixed strategy equilibrium which is not economically meaningful.

[6] To verify this, substitute $f = t$ and $r_1 = c_1^{1*}$ into (2) and (3), noting that this leads to $V_1(\cdot) = c_1^{1*}$ and $V_2(\cdot) = c_2^{2*}$. Because $c_2^{2*} > c_1^{1*}$, all type 2's prefer to wait until time 2 while type 1's withdraw at 1, implying that $f = t$ is an equilibrium.

[7] The value $r_1 = 1$ is the value which rules out runs and mimics the competitive market because that is the per unit $T = 1$ liquidating value of the technology. If that liquidating value were $\Theta < 1$, then $r_1 = \Theta$ would have this property. It has nothing directly to do with the zero rate of interest on deposits.

rectly. This could happen if the selection between the bank run equilibrium and the good equilibrium depended on some commonly observed random variable in the economy. This could be a bad earnings report, a commonly observed run at some other bank, a negative government forecast, or even sunspots.[8] It need not be anything fundamental about the bank's condition. The problem is that once they have deposited, anything that causes them to anticipate a run will lead to a run. This implies that banks with pure demand deposit contracts will be very concerned about maintaining confidence because they realize that the good equilibrium is very fragile.

The pure demand deposit contract is feasible, and we have seen that it can attract deposits even if the perceived probability of a run is positive. This explains why the contract has actually been used by banks in spite of the danger of runs. Next, we examine a closely related contract that can help to eliminate the problem of runs.

III. Improving on Demand Deposits: Suspension of Convertibility

The pure demand deposit contract has a good equilibrium that achieves the full-information optimum when t is not stochastic. However, in its bank run equilibrium, it is worse than direct ownership of assets. It is illuminating to begin the analysis of optimal bank contracts by demonstrating that there is a simple variation on the demand deposit contract which gives banks a defense against runs: suspension of allowing withdrawal of deposits, referred to as suspension of convertibility (of deposits to cash). Our results are consistent with the claim by Friedman and Schwartz (1963) that the newly organized Federal Reserve Board may have made runs in the 1930s worse by preventing banks from suspending convertibility: the total week-long banking "holiday" that followed was more severe than any of the previous suspensions.

If banks can suspend convertibility when withdrawals are too numerous at $T = 1$, anticipation of this policy prevents runs by removing the incentive of type 2 agents to withdraw early. The following contract is identical to the pure demand deposit contract described in (2) and (3), except that it states that any agent will receive nothing at $T = 1$ if he attempts to withdraw at $T = 1$ after a fraction $\hat{f} < r_1^{-1}$ of all deposits have already been withdrawn—note that we

---

[8] Analysis of this point in a general setting is given in Azariadis (1980) and Cass and Shell (1983).

redefine $V_1(\cdot)$ and $V_2(\cdot)$,

$$V_1(f_j, r_1) = \begin{cases} r_1 & \text{if } f_j \leq \hat{f} \\ 0 & \text{if } f_j > \hat{f} \end{cases}$$

$$V_2(f, r_1) = \max\left\{\frac{(1 - fr_1)R}{1 - f}, \frac{(1 - \hat{f}r_1)R}{1 - \hat{f}}\right\},$$

where the expression for V_2 assumes that $1 - \hat{f}r_1 > 0$.

Convertibility is suspended when $f_j = \hat{f}$, and then no one else "in line" is allowed to withdraw at $T = 1$. To demonstrate that this contract can achieve the optimal allocation, let $r_1 = c_1^{1*}$ and choose any $\hat{f} \in \{t, [(R - r_1)/r_1(R - 1)]\}$. Given this contract, no type 2 agent will withdraw at $T = 1$ because no matter what he anticipates about others' withdrawals, he receives higher proceeds by waiting until $T = 2$ to withdraw; that is, for all f and $f_j \leq f$, $V_2(\cdot) > V_1(\cdot)$. All of the type 1's will withdraw everything at period 1 because period 2 consumption is worthless to them. Therefore, there is a unique Nash equilibrium which has $f = t$. In fact, this is a dominant strategy equilibrium, because each agent will choose his equilibrium action even if he anticipates that other agents will choose nonequilibrium or even irrational actions. This makes this contract very "stable." This equilibrium is essentially the good demand deposit equilibrium that achieves optimal risk sharing.

A policy of suspension of convertibility at $\hat{f}$ guarantees that it will never be profitable to participate in a bank run because the liquidation of the bank's assets is terminated while type 2's still have an incentive not to withdraw. This contract works perfectly only in the case where the normal volume of withdrawals, t, is known and not stochastic. The more general case, where t can vary, is analyzed next.

IV. Optimal Contracts with Stochastic Withdrawals

The suspension of convertibility contract achieves optimal risk sharing when t is known ex ante because suspension never occurs in equilibrium and the bank can follow the optimal asset liquidation policy. This is possible because the bank knows exactly how many withdrawals will occur when confidence is maintained. We now allow the fraction of type 1's to be an unobserved random variable, $\tilde{t}$. We consider a general class of bank contracts where payments to those who withdraw at $T = 1$ are any function of f_j and payments to those who withdraw at $T = 2$ are any function of f. Analyzing this general class will show the shortcomings of suspension of convertibility.

The full-information optimal risk sharing is the same as before, except that in equation (1) the actual realization of $\bar{\imath} = t$ is used in place of the fixed t. As no single agent has information crucial to learning the value of t, the arguments of footnote 3 still show that optimal risk sharing is consistent with self-selection, so there must be some mechanism which has optimal risk sharing as a Nash equilibrium. We now explore whether banks (which are subject to the constraint of sequential service) can do this too.

From equation (1) we obtain full-information optimal consumption levels, given the realization of $\bar{\imath} = t$, of $c_1^{1*}(t)$ and $c_2^{2*}(t)$. Recall that $c_2^{1*}(t) = c_1^{2*}(t) = 0$. At the optimum, consumption is equal for all agents of a given type and depends on the realization of t. This implies a unique optimal asset liquidation policy given $\bar{\imath} = t$. This turns out to imply that uninsured bank deposit contracts cannot achieve optimal risk sharing.

PROPOSITION 1: Bank contracts (which must obey the sequential service constraint) cannot achieve optimal risk sharing when t is stochastic and has a nondegenerate distribution.

Proposition 1 holds for all equilibria of uninsured bank contracts of the general form $V_1(f_j)$ and $V_2(f)$, where these can be any function. It obviously remains true that uninsured pure demand deposit contracts are subject to runs. Any run equilibrium does not achieve optimal risk sharing, because both types of agents receive the same consumption. Consider the good equilibrium for any feasible contract. We prove that no bank contract can attain the full-information optimal risk sharing. The proof is straightforward, a two-part proof by contradiction. Recall that the "place in line" f_j is uniformly distributed over $[0, t]$ if only type 1 agents withdraw at $T = 1$. First, suppose that the payments to those who withdraw at $T = 1$ is a nonconstant function of f_j over feasible values of t: for two possible values of $\bar{\imath}$, t_1 and t_2, the value of a period 1 withdrawal varies, that is, $V_1(t_1) \neq V_1(t_2)$. This immediately implies that there is a positive probability of different consumption levels by two type 1 agents who will withdraw at $T = 1$, and this contradicts an unconstrained optimum. Second, assume the contrary: that for all possible realizations of $\bar{\imath} = t$, $V_1(f_j)$ is constant for all $f_j \in [0, t]$. This implies that $c_1^1(t)$ is a constant independent of the realization of $\bar{\imath}$, while the budget constraint, equation (1c), shows that $c_2^2(t)$ will vary with t (unless $r_1 = 1$, which is itself inconsistent with optimal risk sharing). Constant $c_1^1(t)$ and varying $c_2^2(t)$ contradict optimal risk sharing, equation (1b). Thus, optimal risk sharing is inconsistent with sequential service.

Proposition 1 implies that no bank contract, including suspension convertibility, can achieve the full-information optimum. Nonetheless, suspension can generally improve on the uninsured demand deposit contract by preventing runs. The main problem occurs when convertibility is suspended in equilibrium, that is, when the point $\hat{f}$ where suspension occurs is less than the largest possible realization of t. In that case, some type 1 agents cannot withdraw, which is inefficient ex post. This can be desirable ex ante, however, because the threat of suspension prevents runs and allows a relatively high value of r_1. This result is consistent with contemporary views about suspension in the United States in the period before deposit insurance. Although suspensions served to short-circuit runs, they were "regarded as anything but a satisfactory solution by those who experienced them, which is why they produced so much strong pressure for monetary and banking reform" (Friedman and Schwartz 1963, p. 329). The most important reform that followed was federal deposit insurance. Its impact is analyzed in Section V.

V.   Government Deposit Insurance

Deposit insurance provided by the government allows bank contracts that can dominate the best that can be offered without insurance and never do worse. We need to introduce deposit insurance into the analysis in a way that keeps the model closed and assures that no aggregate resource constraints are violated. Deposit insurance guarantees that the promised return will be paid to all who withdraw. If this is a guarantee of a real value, the amount that can be guaranteed is constrained: the government must impose real taxes to honor a deposit guarantee. If the deposit guarantee is nominal, the tax is the (inflation) tax on nominal assets caused by money creation. (Such taxation occurs even if no inflation results; in any case the price level is higher than it would have been otherwise, so some nominally denominated wealth is appropriated.) Because a private insurance company is constrained by its reserves in the scale of unconditional guarantees which it can offer, we argue that deposit insurance probably ought to be governmental for this reason. Of course, the deposit guarantee could be made by a private organization with some authority to tax or create money to pay deposit insurance claims, although we would usually think of such an organization as being a branch of government. However, there can be a small competitive fringe of commercially insured deposits, limited by the amount of private collateral.

The government is assumed to be able to levy any tax that charges every agent in the economy the same amount. In particular, it can tax those agents who withdrew "early" in period $T = 1$, namely, those with low values of f_j. How much tax must be raised depends on how many deposits are withdrawn at $T = 1$ and what amount r_1 was promised to them. For example, if every deposit of one dollar were withdrawn at $T = 1$ (implying $f = 1$) and $r_1 = 2$ were promised, a tax of at least one per capita would need to be raised because totally liquidating the bank's assets will raise at most one per capita at $T = 1$. As the government can impose a tax on an agent *after* he or she has withdrawn, the government can base its tax on f, the realized total value of $T = 1$ withdrawals. This is in marked contrast to a bank, which must provide sequential service and cannot reduce the amount of a withdrawal after it has been made. This asymmetry allows a potential benefit from government intervention. The realistic sequential-service constraint represents some services that a bank provides but which we do not explicitly model. With deposit insurance we will see that imposing this constraint does not reduce social welfare.

Agents are concerned with the after-tax value of the proceeds from their withdrawals because that is the amount that they can consume. A very strong result (which may be too strong) about the optimality of deposit insurance will illuminate the more general reasons why it is desirable. We argue in the conclusion that deposit insurance and the Federal Reserve discount window provide nearly identical services in the context of our model but confine current discussion to deposit insurance.

PROPOSITION 2: Demand deposit contracts with government deposit insurance achieve the unconstrained optimum as a unique Nash equilibrium (in fact, a dominant strategies equilibrium) if the government imposes an optimal tax to finance the deposit insurance.

Proposition 2 follows from the ability of tax-financed deposit insurance to duplicate the optimal consumptions $c_1^1(t) = c_1^{1*}(t)$, $c_2^2(t) = c_2^{2*}(t)$, $c_2^1(t) = 0$, $c_1^2(t) = 0$ from the optimal risk sharing characterized in equation (1). Let the government impose a tax on all wealth held at the beginning of period $T = 1$, which is payable either in goods or in deposits. Let deposits be accepted for taxes at the pretax amount of goods which could be obtained if withdrawn at $T = 1$. The amount of tax that must be raised at $T = 1$ depends on the number of withdrawals then and the asset liquidation policy. Consider the proportionate tax as a function of f, $\tau: [0, 1] \rightarrow [0, 1]$ given by

$$\tau(f) = \begin{cases} 1 - \dfrac{c_1^{1*}(f)}{r_1} & \text{if } f \leq \bar{t} \\[2mm] 1 - r_1^{-1} & \text{if } f > \bar{t}, \end{cases}$$

where $\bar{t}$ is the greatest possible realization of $\tilde{t}$.

The after-tax proceeds, per dollar of initial deposit, of a withdrawal at $T = 1$ depend on f through the tax payment and are identical for all $f_j \leq f$. Denote these after-tax proceeds by $\hat{V}_1(f)$, given by

$$\hat{V}_1(f) = \begin{cases} c_1^{1*}(f) & \text{if } f \leq \bar{t} \\ 1 & \text{if } f > \bar{t}. \end{cases}$$

The net payments to those who withdraw at $T = 1$ determine the asset liquidation policy and the after-tax value a withdrawal at $T = 2$. Any tax collected in excess of that needed to meet withdrawals at $T = 1$ is plowed back into the bank (to minimize the fraction of assets liquidated). This implies that the after-tax proceeds, per dollar of initial deposit, of a withdrawal at $T = 2$, denoted by $\hat{V}_2(f)$, are given by

$$\hat{V}_2(f) = \begin{cases} \dfrac{R\{1 - [c_1^{1*}(f)f]\}}{1 - f} = c_2^{2*}(f) & \text{if } f \leq \bar{t} \\ \dfrac{R(1 - f)}{1 - f} = R & \text{if } f > \bar{t}. \end{cases}$$

Notice that $\hat{V}_1(f) < \hat{V}_2(f)$ for all $f \in [0, 1]$, implying that no type 2 agents will withdraw at $T = 1$ no matter what they expect others to do. For all $f \in [0, 1]$, $\hat{V}_1(f) > 0$, implying that all type 1 agents will withdraw at $T = 1$. Therefore, the unique dominant strategy equilibrium is $f = t$, the realization of $\bar{t}$. Evaluated at a realization t,

$$\hat{V}_1(f = t) = c_1^{1*}(t)$$

and

$$\hat{V}_2(f = t) = \frac{[1 - tc_1^{1*}(t)]R}{1 - t} = c_2^{2*}(t),$$

and the optimum is achieved.

Proposition 2 highlights the key social benefit of government deposit insurance. It allows the bank to follow a desirable asset liquidation policy, which can be separated from the cash-flow constraint imposed directly by withdrawals. Furthermore, it prevents runs because, for all possible anticipated withdrawal policies of other agents, it never pays to participate in a bank run. As a result, no strategic issues of confidence arise. This is a general result of many deposit insurance schemes. The proposition may be too strong, as it allows the government to follow an unconstrained tax policy. If a nonoptimal tax must be imposed, then when t is stochastic there will be some tax distortions and resource costs associated with government deposit insurance. If a sufficiently perverse tax provided the revenues for insurance, social welfare could be higher without the insurance.

Deposit insurance can be provided costlessly in the simpler case where t is nonstochastic, for the same reason that there need not be a suspension of convertibility in equilibrium. The deposit insurance guarantees that type 2 agents will never participate in a run; without runs, withdrawals are deterministic and this feature is never used. In particular, so long as the government can impose *some* tax to finance the insurance, no matter how distortionary, there will be no runs and the distorting tax need never be imposed. This feature is shared by a model of adoption externalities (see Dybvig and Spatt, in press) in which a Pareto-inferior equilibrium can be averted by an insurance policy which is costless in equilibrium. In both models, the credible promise to provide the insurance means that the promise will not need to be fulfilled. This is in contrast to privately provided deposit insurance. Because insurance companies do not have the power of taxation, they must hold reserves to make their promise credible. This illustrates a reason why the government may have a natural advantage in providing deposit insurance. The role of government policy in our model focuses on providing an institution to prevent a bad equilibrium rather than a policy to move an existing equilibrium. Generally, such a policy need not cause distortion.

VI. Conclusions and Implications

The model serves as a useful framework for analyzing the economics of banking and associated policy issues. It is interesting that the problems of runs and the differing effects of suspension of convertibility and deposit insurance manifest themselves in a model which does not introduce currency or risky technology. This demonstrates that many of the important problems in banking are not necessarily related to those factors, although a general model will require their introduction.

We analyze an economy with a single bank. The interpretation is that it represents the financial intermediary industry, and withdrawals represent net withdrawals from the system. If many banks were introduced into the model, then there would be a role for liquidity risk sharing between banks, and phenomena such as the Federal Funds market or the impact of "bank-specific risk" on deposit insurance could be analyzed.

The result that deposit insurance dominates contracts which the bank alone can enforce shows that there is a potential benefit from government intervention into banking markets. In contrast to common tax and subsidy schemes, the intervention we are recommending provides an institutional framework under which banks can operate smoothly, much as enforcement of contracts does more generally.

The riskless technology used in the model isolates the rationale for deposit insurance, but in addition it abstracts from the choice of bank loan portfolio risk. If the risk of bank portfolios could be selected by a bank manager, unobserved by outsiders (to some extent), then a moral hazard problem would exist. In this case there is a trade-off between optimal risk sharing and proper incentives for portfolio choice, and introducing deposit insurance can influence the portfolio choice. The moral hazard problem has been analyzed in complete market settings where deposit insurance is redundant and can provide no social improvement (see Kareken and Wallace 1978; Dothan and Williams 1980), but of course in this case there is no trade-off. Introducing risky assets and moral hazard would be an interesting extension of our model. It appears likely that some form of government deposit insurance could again be desirable but that it would be accompanied by some sort of bank regulation. Such bank regulation would serve a function similar to restrictive covenants in bond indentures. Interesting but hard to model are questions of regulator "discretion" which then arise.

The Federal Reserve discount window can, as a lender of last resort, provide a service similar to deposit insurance. It would buy bank assets with (money creation) tax revenues at $T = 1$ for prices greater than their liquidating value. If the taxes and transfers were set to be identical to that of the optimal deposit insurance, it would have the same effect. The identity of deposit insurance and discount window services occurs because the technology is riskless.

If the technology is risky, the lender of last resort can no longer be as credible as deposit insurance. If the lender of last resort were *always* required to bail out banks with liquidity problems, there would be perverse incentives for banks to take on risk, even if bailouts occurred only when many banks fail together. For instance, if a bailout is anticipated, all banks have an incentive to take on interest rate risk by mismatching maturities of assets and liabilities, because they will all be bailed out together.

If the lender of last resort is not required to bail out banks unconditionally, a bank run can occur in response to changes in depositor expectations about the bank's credit worthiness. A run can even occur in response to expectations about the general willingness of the lender of last resort to rescue failing banks, as illustrated by the unfortunate experience of the 1930s when the Federal Reserve misused its discretion and did not allow much discounting. In contrast, deposit insurance is a binding commitment which can be structured to retain punishment of the bank's owners, board of directors, and officers in the case of a failure.

The potential for multiple equilibria when a firm's liabilities are more liquid than its assets applies more generally, not simply to banks. Consider a firm with illiquid technology which issues very short-term bonds as a large part of its capital structure. Suppose one lender expects all other lenders to refuse to roll over their loans to the firm. Then, it may be his best response to refuse to roll over his loans even if the firm would be solvent if all loans were rolled over. Such liquidity crises are similar to bank runs. The protection from creditors provided by the bankruptcy laws serves a function similar to the suspension of convertibility. The firm which is viable but illiquid is guaranteed survival. This suggests that the "transformation" could be carried out directly by firms rather than by financial intermediaries. Our focus on intermediaries is supported by the fact that banks directly hold a substantial fraction of the short-term debt of corporations. Also, there is frequently a requirement (or custom) that a firm issuing short-term commercial paper obtain a bank line of credit sufficient to pay off the issue if it cannot "roll it over." A bank with deposit insurance can provide "liquidity insurance" to a firm, which can prevent a liquidity crisis for a firm with short-term debt and limit the firm's need to use bankruptcy to stop such crises. This suggests that most of the aggregate liquidity risk in the U.S. economy is channeled through its insured financial intermediaries, to the extent that lines of credit represent binding commitments.

We hope that this model will prove to be useful in understanding issues in banking and corporate finance.

References

Azariadis, Costas. "Self-fulfilling Prophecies." *J. Econ. Theory* 25 (December 1980): 380–96.

Bernanke, Ben. "Nonmonetary Effects of the Financial Crisis in the Propagation of the Great Depression." *A.E.R.* (in press).

Bryant, John. "A Model of Reserves, Bank Runs, and Deposit Insurance." *J. Banking and Finance* 4 (1980): 335–44.

Cass, David, and Shell, Karl. "Do Sunspots Matter?" *J.P.E.* 91 (April 1983): 193–227.

Diamond. Douglas W. "Financial Intermediation and Delegated Monitoring." Working Paper, Graduate School Bus., Univ. Chicago, 1980.

Dothan, U., and Williams, J. "Banks, Bankruptcy and Public Regulations." *J. Banking and Finance* 4 (March 1980): 65–87.

Dybvig, Philip H., and Jaynes, G. "Microfoundations of Wage Rigidity." Working Paper, Yale Univ., 1980.

Dybvig, Philip H., and Spatt, Chester S. "Adoption Externalities as Public Goods." *J. Public Econ.* (in press).

Fisher, Irving. *The Purchasing Power of Money: Its Determination and Relation to Credit, Interest and Crises.* New York: Macmillan, 1911.

Friedman, Milton, and Schwartz, Anna J. *A Monetary History of the United States, 1867–1960.* Princeton, N.J.: Princeton Univ. Press (for Nat. Bur. Econ. Res.), 1963.

Kareken, John H., and Wallace, Neil. "Deposit Insurance and Bank Regulation: A Partial-Equilibrium Exposition." *J. Bus.* 51 (July 1978): 413–38.

Merton, Robert C. "An Analytic Derivation of the Cost of Deposit Insurance and Loan Guarantees: An Application of Modern Option Pricing Theory." *J. Banking and Finance* 1 (June 1977): 3–11.

————. "On the Cost of Deposit Insurance When There Are Surveillance Costs." *J. Bus.* 51 (July 1978): 439–52.

Niehans, Jürg. *The Theory of Money.* Baltimore: Johns Hopkins Univ. Press, 1978.

Patinkin, Don. *Money, Interest, and Prices: An Integration of Monetary and Value Theory.* 2d ed. New York: Harper & Row, 1965.

Tobin, James. "The Theory of Portfolio Selection." In *The Theory of Interest Rates,* edited by Frank H. Hahn and F. P. R. Brechling. London: Macmillan, 1965.

Nonmonetary Effects of the Financial Crisis in the Propagation of the Great Depression

By BEN S. BERNANKE*

During 1930–33, the U.S. financial system experienced conditions that were among the most difficult and chaotic in its history. Waves of bank failures culminated in the shutdown of the banking system (and of a number of other intermediaries and markets) in March 1933. On the other side of the ledger, exceptionally high rates of default and bankruptcy affected every class of borrower except the federal government.

An interesting aspect of the general financial crises—most clearly, of the bank failures—was their coincidence in timing with adverse developments in the macroeconomy.[1] Notably, an apparent attempt at recovery from the 1929–30 recession[2] was stalled at the time of the first banking crisis (November–December 1930); the incipient recovery degenerated into a new slump during the mid-1931 panics; and the economy and the financial system both reached their respective low points at the time of the bank "holiday" of March 1933. Only with the New Deal's rehabilitation of the financial system in 1933–35 did the economy begin its slow emergence from the Great Depression.

A possible explanation of these synchronous movements is that the financial system simply responded, without feedback, to the declines in aggregate output. This is contradicted by the facts that problems of the financial system tended to lead output declines, and that sources of financial panics unconnected with the fall in U.S. output have been documented by many writers. (See Section IV below.)

Among explanations that emphasize the opposite direction of causality, the most prominent is the one due to Friedman and Schwartz. Concentrating on the difficulties of the banks, they pointed out two ways in which these worsened the general economic contraction: first, by reducing the wealth of bank shareholders; second, and much more important, by leading to a rapid fall in the supply of money. There is much support for the monetary view. However, it is not a complete explanation of the link between the financial sector and aggregate output in the 1930's. One problem is that there is no theory of monetary effects on the real economy that can explain *protracted* nonneutrality. Another is that the reductions of the money supply in this period seems quantitatively insufficient to explain the subsequent falls in output. (Again, see Section IV.)

The present paper builds on the Friedman-Schwartz work by considering a third way in which the financial crises (in which we include debtor bankruptcies as well as the failures of banks and other lenders) may have affected output. The basic premise is that, because markets for financial claims are incomplete, intermediation between some classes of borrowers and lenders requires nontrivial market-making and information-gathering services. The disruptions of 1930–33 (as I shall try to show) reduced the effectiveness of the financial sector as a whole in performing these services. As the real costs of intermediation increased, some borrowers (especially households, farmers, and small firms) found credit to be expensive and difficult to obtain. The effects of this credit squeeze on aggregate demand helped convert the severe but not unprecedented downturn of 1929–30 into a protracted depression.

*Stanford Graduate School of Business and Hoover Institution. I received useful comments from too many people to list here by name, but I am grateful to each of them. The National Science Foundation provided partial research support.

[1] This is documented more carefully in Sections I.C and IV below.

[2] This paper does not address the causes of the initial 1929–30 downturn. Milton Friedman and Anna Schwartz (1963) have stressed the importance of the Federal Reserve's "anti-speculative" monetary tightening. Others, such as Peter Temin (1976), have pointed out autonomous expenditure effects.

It should be stated at the outset that my theory does not offer a complete explanation of the Great Depression (for example, nothing is said about 1929–30). Nor is it necessarily inconsistent with some existing explanations.[3] However, it does have the virtues that, first, it seems capable (in a way in which existing theories are not) of explaining the unusual length and depth of the depression; and, second, it can do this without assuming markedly irrational behavior by private economic agents. Since the reconciliation of the obvious inefficiency of the depression with the postulate of rational private behavior remains a leading unsolved puzzle of macroeconomics, these two virtues alone provide motivation for serious consideration of this theory.

There do not seem to be any exact antecedents of the present paper in the formal economics literature.[4] The work of Lester Chandler (1970, 1971) provides the best historical discussions of the general financial crisis extant; however, he does not develop very far the link to macroeconomic performance. Beginning with Irving Fisher (1933) and A. G. Hart (1938), there is a literature on the macroeconomic role of inside debt; an interesting recent example is the paper by Frederic Mishkin (1978), which stresses household balance sheets and liquidity. Benjamin Friedman (1981) has written on the relationship of credit and aggregate activity. Hyman Minsky (1977) and Charles Kindleberger (1978) have in several places argued for the inherent instability of the financial system, but in doing so have had to depart from the assumption of rational economic behavior.[5] None of the above authors has emphasized the effects of financial crisis on

the real costs of credit intermediation, the focus of the present work.

The paper is organized as follows: Section I presents some background on the 1930–33 financial crisis, its sources, and its correspondence with aggregate output movements. Section II begins the principal argument of the paper. I explain how the runs on banks and the extensive defaults could have reduced the efficiency of the financial sector in performing its intermediary functions. Some evidence of these effects is introduced.

Possible channels by which reduced financial efficiency might have affected output are discussed in Section III. Reduced-form estimation results, reported in Section IV, suggest that augmenting a purely monetary approach by my theory significantly improves the explanation of the financial sector-output connection in the short run. Section V looks at the persistence of these effects.

Some international aspects of the financial sector-aggregate output link are briefly discussed in Section VI and Section VII concludes.

I. The Financial Collapse: Some Background

The problems faced by the U.S. financial system between October 1930 and March 1933 have been described in detail by earlier authors,[6] but it will be useful to recapitulate some principal facts here. Given this background, attention will be turned to the more central issues of the paper.

The two major components of the financial collapse were the loss of confidence in financial institutions, primarily commercial banks, and the widespread insolvency of debtors. I give short discussions of each of these components and of their joint relation to aggregate fluctuations.

A. *The Failure of Financial Institutions*

Most financial institutions (even semipublic ones, like the Joint Stock Land Banks) came under pressure in the 1930's. Some,

---

[3]See Karl Brunner (1981) for a useful overview of contemporary theories of the depression. Also, see Robert Lucas and Leonard Rapping's article in Lucas (1981).

[4]This is especially true of the more recent work, which tends to ignore the nonmonetary effects of the financial crisis. Older writers often seemed to take the disruptive impact of the financial breakdown for granted.

[5]I do not deny the possible importance of irrationality in economic life; however, it seems that the best research strategy is to push the rationality postulate as far as it will go.

[6]See especially Chandler (1970, 1971) and Friedman and Schwartz.

such as the insurance companies and the mutual savings banks, managed to maintain something close to normal operations. Others, like the building-and-loans (which, despite their ability to restrict withdrawals by depositors, failed in significant numbers) were greatly hampered in their attempts to carry on their business.[7] Of most importance, however, were the problems of the commercial banks. The significance of the banking difficulties derived both from their magnitude and from the central role commercial banks played in the financial system.[8]

The great severity of the banking crises in the Great Depression is well known to students of the period. The percentages of operating banks which failed in each year from 1930 to 1933 inclusive were 5.6, 10.5, 7.8, and 12.9; because of failures and mergers, the number of banks operating at the end of 1933 was only just above half the number that existed in 1929.[9] Banks that survived experienced heavy losses.

The sources of the banking collapse are best understood in the historical context. The first point to be made is that bank failures were hardly a novelty at the time of the depression. The U.S. system, made up as it was primarily of small, independent banks, had always been particularly vulnerable. (Countries with only a few large banks, such as Britain, France, and Canada, never had banking difficulties on the American scale.) The dominance of small banks in the United States was due in large part to a regulatory environment which reflected popular fears of large banks and "trusts"; for example, there were numerous laws restricting branch banking at both the state and national level. Com-

petition between the state and national banking systems for member banks also tended to keep the legal barriers to entry in banking very low.[10] In this sort of environment, a significant number of failures was to be expected and probably was even desirable. Failures due to "natural causes" (such as the agricultural depression of the 1920's upon which many small, rural banks foundered) were common.[11]

Besides the simple lack of economic viability of some marginal banks, however, the U.S. system historically suffered also from a more malign source of bank failures; namely, financial panics. The fact that liabilities of banks were principally in the form of fixed-price, callable debt (i.e., demand deposits), while many assets were highly illiquid, created the possibility of the perverse expectational equilibrium known as a "run" on the banks. In a run, fear that a bank may fail induces depositors to withdraw their money, which in turn forces liquidation of the bank's assets. The need to liquidate hastily, or to dump assets on the market when other banks are also liquidating, may generate losses that actually do cause the bank to fail. Thus the expectation of failure, by the mechanism of the run, tends to become self-confirming.[12]

An interesting question is why banks at this time relied on fixed-price demand deposits, when alternative instruments might have reduced or prevented the problem of runs.[13] An answer is provided by Friedman and Schwartz: They pointed out that, before the establishment of the Federal Reserve in 1913, panics were usually contained by the practice of suspending convertibility of bank deposits into currency. This practice, typically initiated by loose organizations of urban

---

[7]Hart describes the problems of the building-and-loans. An interesting sidelight here is the additional strain on housing lenders caused by the existence of the Postal Savings System; see Maureen O'Hara and David Easley (1979).

[8]According to Raymond Goldsmith (1958), commercial banks held 39.6 percent of the assets of all financial intermediaries, broadly defined, in 1929. See his Table 11.

[9]Cyril Upham and Edwin Lamke (1934, p. 247). Since smaller banks were more likely to fail, the fraction of deposits represented by suspended banks was somewhat less. Eventual recovery by depositors was about 75 percent; see Friedman and Schwartz, p. 438.

[10]Benjamin Klebaner (1974) gives a good brief history of U.S. commercial banking.

[11]Upham and Lamke, p. 247, report that approximately 2–3 percent of all banks in operation failed in each year of the 1920's.

[12]Douglas Diamond and Philip Dybvig (1981) formalize this argument. For an alternative analysis of the phenomenon of runs, see Robert Flood and Peter Garber (1981).

[13]For example, equity-like instruments, such as those used by modern money-market mutual funds, could have been used as the transactions medium. See Kenneth Cone (1982).

banks called clearinghouses, moderated the dangers of runs by making hasty liquidation unnecessary. In conjunction with the suspension of convertibility practice, the use of demand deposits created relatively little instability.[14]

However, with the advent of the Federal Reserve (according to Friedman-Schwartz), this roughly stable institutional arrangement was upset. Although the Federal Reserve introduced no specific injunctions against the suspension of convertibility, the clearinghouses apparently felt that the existence of the new institution relieved them of the responsibility of fighting runs. Unfortunately, the Federal Reserve turned out to be unable or unwilling to assume this responsibility.

No serious runs occurred between World War I and 1930; but the many pieces of bad financial news that came in from around the world in 1930–32 were like sparks around tinder. Runs were clearly an important part of the banking problems of this period. Some evidence emerges from contemporary accounts, including descriptions of specific events precipitating runs. Also notable is the fact that bank failures tended to occur in short spasms, rather than in a steady stream (see Table 1, col. 2, for monthly data on the deposits of failing banks). The problem was not arrested until government intervention became important in late 1932 and early 1933.

We see, then, that the banking crises of the early 1930's differed from earlier recorded experience both in magnitude and in the degree of danger posed by the phenomenon of runs. The result of this was that the behavior of almost the entire system was adversely affected, not just that of marginal banks. The bankers' fear of runs, as I shall argue below, had important macroeconomic effects.

B. Defaults and Bankruptcies

The second major aspect of the financial crisis (one that is currently neglected by historians) was the pervasiveness of debtor insolvency. Given that debt contracts were written in nominal terms,[15] the protracted fall in prices and money incomes greatly increased debt burdens. According to Evans Clark (1933), the ratio of debt service to national income went from 9 percent in 1929 to 19.8 percent in 1932–33. The resulting high rates of default caused problems for both borrowers and lenders.

The "debt crisis" touched all sectors. For example, about half of all residential properties were mortgaged at the beginning of the Great Depression; according to the *Financial Survey of Urban Housing* (reported in Hart), as of January 1, 1934,

> The proportion of mortgaged owner-occupied houses with some interest or principal in default was in none of the twenty-two cities [surveyed] less than 21 percent (the figure for Richmond, Virginia); in half it was above 38 percent; in two (Indianapolis and Birmingham, Alabama) between 50 percent and 60 percent; and in one (Cleveland), 62 percent. For rented properties, percentages in default ran slightly higher. [p. 164]

Because of the long spell of low food prices, farmers were in more difficulty than homeowners. At the beginning of 1933, owners of 45 percent of all U.S. farms, holding 52 percent of the value of farm mortgage debt, were delinquent in payments (Hart, p. 138). State and local governments—many of whom tried to provide relief for the unemployed—also had problems paying their debts: As of March 1934, the governments of 37 of the 310 cities with populations over 30,000 and of three states had defaulted on obligations (Hart, p. 225).

In the business sector, the incidence of financial distress was very uneven. Aggregate corporate profits before tax were negative in 1931 and 1932, and after-tax retained earnings were negative in each year from 1930 to 1933 (Chandler, 1971, p. 102). But the subset

---

[14] Diamond and Dybvig derive this point formally, with some caveats.

[15] Finding an explanation for the lack of indexed debt during the deflationary 1930's—as in the inflationary 1970's—is a point on which I stumble.

of corporations holding more than $50 million in assets maintained positive profits throughout this period, leaving the brunt to be borne by smaller companies. Solomon Fabricant (1935) reported that, in 1932 alone, the losses of corporations with assets of $50,000 or less equalled 33 percent of total capitalization; for corporations with assets in the $50,000–$100,000 range, the comparable figure was 14 percent. This led to high rates of failure among small firms.

Although the deflation of the 1930's was unusually protracted, there had been a similar episode as recently as 1921–22 which had not led to mass insolvency. The seriousness of the problem in the Great Depression was due not only to the extent of the deflation, but also to the large and broad-based expansion of inside debt in the 1920's. Charles Persons surveyed the credit expansion of the predepression decade in a 1930 article: He reported that outstanding corporate bonds and notes increased from $26.1 billion in 1920 to $47.1 billion in 1928, and that nonfederal public securities grew from $11.8 billion to $33.6 billion over the same period. (This may be compared with a 1929 national income of $86.8 billion.) Perhaps more significantly, during the 1920's, small borrowers, such as households and unincorporated businesses, greatly increased their debts. For example, the value of urban real estate mortgages outstanding increased from $11 billion in 1920 to $27 billion in 1929, while the growth of consumer installment debt reflected the introduction of major consumer durables to the mass market.

Like the banking crises, then, the debt crisis of the 1930's was not qualitatively a new phenomenon; but it represented a break with the past in terms of its severity and pervasiveness.

C. *Correlation of the Financial Crisis with Macroeconomic Activity*

The close connection of the stages of the financial crisis (especially the bank failures) with changes in real output has been noted by Friedman and Schwartz and by others. An informal review of this connection is facilitated by the monthly data in Table 1. Column 1 is an index of real industrial production. Columns 2 and 3 are the (nominal) liabilities of failing banks and nonbank commercial businesses, respectively.

The industrial production series reveals that a recession began in the United States during 1929. By late 1930, the downturn, although serious, was still comparable in magnitude to the recession of 1920–22; as the decline slowed, it would have been reasonable to expect a brisk recovery, just as in 1922.

With the first banking crisis, however, there came what Friedman and Schwartz called a "change in the character of the contraction" (p. 311). The economy first flattened out, then went into a new tailspin just as the banks began to fail again in June 1931.

A lengthy slide of both the general economy and the financial system followed. The banking situation calmed in early 1932, and nonbank failures peaked shortly thereafter. A new recovery attempt began in August, but failed within a few months.[16] In March 1933, the bottom was reached for both the financial system and the economy as a whole. Measures taken after the banking holiday ended the bank runs and greatly reduced the burden of debt. Simultaneously aggregate output began a recovery that was sustained until 1937.

The leading explanation of the correlation between the conditions of the financial sector and of the general economy is that of Friedman and Schwartz, who stressed the effects of the banking crises on the supply of money. I agree that money was an important factor in 1930–33, but, because of reservations cited in the introduction, I doubt that it completely explains the financial sector-aggregate output connection. This motivates

---

[16] Judging by Table 1 the failure of this recovery seems to be unrelated to financial sector difficulties. However, accounts from the time suggest that the banking crisis of late 1932 and early 1933 (which ended in the banking holiday) was in fact quite severe; see Susan Kennedy (1973). The relatively low reported rate of bank failures at this time may be an artifact of state moratoria, restrictions on withdrawals, and other interventions.

TABLE 1—SELECTED MACROECONOMIC DATA, JULY 1929–MARCH 1933

Month	IP	Banks	Fails	$\Delta L/IP$	L/DEP	DIF
1929J	114	60.8	32.4	.163	.851	2.31
A	114	6.7	33.7	.007	.855	2.33
S	112	9.7	34.1	.079	.860	2.33
O	110	12.5	31.3	.177	.865	2.50
N	105	22.3	52.0	.121	.854	2.68
D	100	15.5	62.5	−.214	.851	2.59
1930J	100	26.5	61.2	−.228	.837	2.49
F	100	32.4	51.3	−.102	.834	2.48
M	98	23.2	56.8	.076	.835	2.44
A	98	31.9	49.1	.058	.826	2.33
M	96	19.4	55.5	−.028	.820	2.41
J	93	57.9	63.1	.085	.818	2.53
J	89	29.8	29.8	−.055	.802	2.52
A	86	22.8	49.2	−.027	.800	2.47
S	85	21.6	46.7	.008	.799	2.41
O	83	19.7	56.3	−.010	.791	2.73
N	81	179.9	55.3	−.067	.777	3.06
D	79	372.1	83.7	−.144	.775	3.49
1931J	78	75.7	94.6	−.187	.763	3.21
F	79	34.2	59.6	−.144	.747	3.08
M	80	34.3	60.4	−.043	.738	3.17
A	80	41.7	50.9	−.104	.722	3.45
M	80	43.2	53.4	−.133	.706	3.99
J	77	190.5	51.7	−.120	.707	4.23
J	76	40.7	61.0	−.013	.704	3.93
A	73	180.0	53.0	−.103	.706	4.29
S	70	233.5	47.3	−.050	.713	4.82
O	68	471.4	70.7	−.310	.716	5.41
N	67	67.9	60.7	−.101	.726	5.30
D	66	277.1	73.2	−.120	.732	6.49
1932J	64	218.9	96.9	−.117	.745	4.87
F	63	51.7	84.9	−.138	.757	4.76
M	62	10.9	93.8	−.183	.744	4.91
A	58	31.6	101.1	−.225	.718	6.78
M	56	34.4	83.8	−.154	.696	7.87
J	54	132.7	76.9	−.170	.689	7.93
J	53	48.7	87.2	−.219	.677	7.21
A	54	29.5	77.0	−.130	.662	4.77
S	58	13.5	56.1	−.091	.641	4.19
O	60	20.1	52.9	−.095	.623	4.44
N	59	43.3	53.6	−.133	.602	4.79
D	58	70.9	64.2	−.039	.596	5.07
1933J	58	133.1	79.1	−.139	.576	4.79
F	57	62.2	65.6	−.059	.583	4.09
M	54	3276.3[a]	48.5	−.767[a]	.607[a]	4.03

Notes: IP = seasonally adjusted index of industrial production, 1935–39 = 100; *Federal Reserve Bulletin.*

  Banks = deposits of failing banks, $millions; *Federal Reserve Bulletin.*

  Fails = liabilities of failing commercial businesses, $millions; *Survey of Current Business.*

 $\Delta L/PI$ = ratio of net extensions of commercial bank loans to (monthly) personal income; from *Banking and Monetary Statistics* and *National Income.*

  L/D = ratio of loans outstanding to the sum of demand and time deposits, weekly reporting banks; *Banking and Monetary Statistics.*

  DIF = difference (in percentage points) between yields on Baa corporate bonds and long-term U.S. government bonds; *Banking and Monetary Statistics.*

[a] A national bank holiday was declared in March 1933.

my study of a nonmonetary channel through which an additional impact of the financial crisis may have been felt.

II. The Effect of the Crisis on the Cost of Credit Intermediation

This paper posits that, in addition to its effects via the money supply, the financial crisis of 1930–33 affected the macroeconomy by reducing the quality of certain financial services, primarily credit intermediation. The basic argument is to be made in two steps. First, it must be shown that the disruption of the financial sector by the banking and debt crises raised the real cost of intermediation between lenders and certain classes of borrowers. Second, the link between higher intermediation costs and the decline in aggregate output must be established. I present here the first step of the argument, leaving the second to be developed in Sections III–V.

In order to discuss the quality of performance of the financial sector, I must first describe the real services that the sector is supposed to provide. The specification of these services depends on the model of the economy one has in mind. We shall clearly not be interested in economies of the sort described by Eugene Fama (1980), in which financial markets are complete and information/transactions costs can be neglected. In such a world, banks and other intermediaries are merely passive holders of portfolios. Banks' choice of portfolios or the scale of the banking system can never make any difference in this case, since depositors can offset any action taken by banks through private portfolio decisions.[17]

As an alternative to the Fama complete-markets world, consider the following stylized description of the economy. Let us suppose that savers have many ways of transferring resources from present to future, such as holding real assets or buying the liabilities of

governments or corporations on well-organized exchanges. One of the options savers have is to lend resources to a banking system. The banks also have a menu of different assets to choose from. Assume, however, that banks specialize in making loans to small, idiosyncratic borrowers whose liabilities are too few in number to be publicly traded. (Here is where the complete-markets assumption is dropped.)

The small borrowers to whom the banks lend will be taken, for simplicity, to be of two extreme types, "good" and "bad." Good borrowers desire loans in order to undertake individual-specific investment projects. These projects generate a random return from a distribution whose mean will be assumed always to exceed the social opportunity cost of investment. If this risk is nonsystematic, lending to good borrowers is socially desirable. Bad borrowers try to look like good borrowers, but in fact they have no "project." Bad borrowers are assumed to squander any loan received in profligate consumption, then to default. Loans to bad borrowers are socially undesirable.

In this model, the real service performed by the banking system is the differentiation between good and bad borrowers.[18] For a competitive banking system, I define the *cost of credit intermediation* (*CCI*) as being the cost of channeling funds from the ultimate savers/lenders into the hands of good borrowers. The *CCI* includes screening, monitoring, and accounting costs, as well as the expected losses inflicted by bad borrowers. Banks presumably choose operating procedures that minimize the *CCI*. This is done by developing expertise at evaluating potential borrowers; establishing long-term relationships with customers; and offering loan conditions that encourage potential borrowers to self-select in a favorable way.[19]

Given this simple paradigm, I can describe the effects of the two main components of

---

[17] It should be noted that the phenomena emphasized by Friedman and Schwartz—the effects of the contraction of the banking system on the quantity of the transactions medium and on real output—are also impossible in a complete-markets world.

[18] To concentrate on credit intermediation, I neglect the transactions and other services performed by banks.

[19] See Dwight Jaffee and Thomas Russell (1976) and Joseph Stiglitz and Andrew Weiss (1981) on the way banks induce favorable borrower self-selection.

the financial crisis on the efficiency of the credit allocation process (i.e., on the *CCI*).

A. *Effect of the Banking Crises on the CCI*

The banking problems of 1930–33 disrupted the credit allocation process by creating large, unplanned changes in the channels of credit flow. Fear of runs led to large withdrawals of deposits, precautionary increases in reserve-deposit ratios, and an increased desire by banks for very liquid or rediscountable assets. These factors, plus the actual failures, forced a contraction of the banking system's role in the intermediation of credit.[20] Some of the slack was taken up by the growing importance of alternative channels of credit (see below). However, the rapid switch away from the banks (given the banks' accumulated expertise, information, and customer relationships) no doubt impaired financial efficiency and raised the *CCI*.[21]

It would be useful to have a direct measure of the *CCI*; unfortunately, no really satisfactory empirical representation of this concept is available. Reported commercial loan rates reflect loans that are actually made, not the shadow cost of bank funds to a representative potential borrower; since banks in a period of retrenchment make only the safest and highest-quality loans, measured loan rates may well move inversely to the *CCI*. I obtained a number of interesting results using the yield differential between Baa corporate bonds and U.S. government bonds as a proxy for the *CCI*; however, the use of the Baa rate is not consistent with my story that bank borrowers are those whose liabilities are too few to be publicly traded.

While we cannot observe directly the effects of the banking troubles on the *CCI*, we can see their impact on the extension of bank credit: Table 1 gives some illustrative data. Column 4 gives, as a measure of the flow of

bank credit, the monthly change in bank loans outstanding, normalized by monthly personal income.[22] One might have expected the loan-change-to-income ratio to be driven primarily by loan demand and thus by the rate of production. Comparison with the first two columns of Table 2 shows, however, that the banking crises were as important a determinant of this variable as output. For example, except for a brief period of liquidation of speculation loans after the stock market crash, credit outstanding declined very little before October 1930—this despite a 25 percent fall in industrial production that had occurred by that time. With the first banking crisis of November 1930, however, a long period of credit contraction was initiated. The shrinkage of credit shared the rhythm of the banking crises; for example, in October 1931, the worst month for bank failure before the bank holiday, net credit reduction was a record 31 percent of personal income.[23]

The fall in bank loans after November 1930 was not simply a balance sheet reflection of the decline in deposits. Column 5 in Table 1 gives the monthly ratio of outstanding bank loans to the sum of demand and time deposits. This ratio declined sharply as banks switched out of loans and into more liquid investments.

The perception that the banking crises and the associated scrambles for liquidity exerted a deflationary force on bank credit was shared by writers of the time. A 1932 National Industrial Conference Board survey of

---

[20] For an interesting contemporary account of this process, see the article by Eugene H. Burris in the *American Banker*, October 15, 1931.

[21] Since intermediation resources could have been shifted out of the beleaguered banking sector (given enough time), mine is basically a costs-of-adjustment argument.

[22] In the construction of the bank loans series, data from weekly reporting member banks (which held about 40 percent of all bank loans) were used to interpolate between less frequent aggregate observations. Note that, for our purposes, looking at the change in loans is preferable to considering the stock of real loans outstanding: In a regime of nominally contracted debt and sharp unanticipated deflation, stability of the stock of real debt does *not* signal a comfortable situation for borrowers.

[23] The effect of bank failures on credit outstanding is somewhat exaggerated by the fact that the credit contraction measure includes the loans of suspending banks that were not transferred to other banks; however, I estimate that this accounting convention is responsible for less than one-eighth of the total (measured) credit contraction between October 1930 and February 1933.

credit conditions reported that "During 1930, the shrinkage of commercial loans no more than reflected business recession. During 1931 and the first half of 1932 (the period studied), it unquestionably represented pressure by banks on customers for repayment of loans and refusal by banks to grant new loans" (p. 28). Other contemporary sources tended to agree (see, for example, Chandler, 1971, pp. 233–39, for references).

Two other observations about the contraction of bank credit can be made. First, the class of borrowers most affected by credit reductions were households, farmers, unincorporated businesses, and small corporations; this group had the highest direct or indirect reliance on bank credit. Second, the contraction of bank credit was twice as large as that of other major countries, even those which experienced comparable output declines (Klebaner, p. 145).

The fall in bank loans outstanding was partly offset by the relative expansion of alternative forms of credit. In the area of consumer finance, retail merchants, service creditors, and nonbank lending agencies improved their position relative to banks and primarily bank-supported installment finance companies (Rolf Nugent, 1939, pp. 114–16). Small firms during this period significantly reduced their traditional reliance on banks in favor of trade credit (Charles Merwin, 1942, pp. 5 and 75). But, as argued above, in a world with transactions costs and the need to discriminate among borrowers, these shifts in the loci of credit intermediation must have at least temporarily reduced the efficiency of the credit allocation process, thereby raising the effective cost of credit to potential borrowers.

B. *The Effect of Bankruptcies on the CCI*

I turn now to a brief discussion of the impact of the increase in defaults and bankruptcies during this period on the cost of credit intermediation.

The very existence of bankruptcy proceedings, rather than being an obvious or natural phenomenon, raises deep questions of economic theory. Why, for example, do the

creditor and defaulted debtor make the payments to third parties (lawyers, administrators) that these proceedings entail, instead of somehow agreeing to divide those payments between themselves? In a complete-markets world, bankruptcy would never be observed; this is because complete state-contingent loan agreements would uniquely define each party's obligations in all possible circumstances, rendering third-party arbitration unnecessary. That we do observe bankruptcies, in our incomplete-markets world, suggests that creditors and debtors have found the combination of simple loan arrangements and *ex post* adjudication by bankruptcy (when necessary) to be cheaper than attempting to write and enforce complete state-contingent contracts.

To be more concrete, let us use the "good borrower-bad borrower" example. In writing a loan contract with a potential borrower, the bank has two polar options. First, it might try to approximate the complete state-contingent contract by making the borrower's actions part of the agreement and by allowing repayment to depend on the outcome of the borrower's project. This contract, if properly written and enforced, would completely eliminate the possibility of either side not being able to meet its obligations; its obvious drawback is the cost of monitoring which it involves. The bank's other option is to write a very simple agreement ("payment of such-amount to be made on such-date"), then to make the loan only if it believes that the borrower is likely to repay. The second approach usually dominates the first, of course, especially for small borrowers.

A device which makes the cost advantage of the simpler approach even greater is the use of collateral. If the borrower has wealth that can be attached by the bank in the event of nonpayment, the bank's risk is low. Moreover, the threat of loss of collateral provides the right incentives for borrowers to use loans only for profitable projects. Thus, the combination of collateral and simple loan contracts helps to create a low effective *CCI*.

A useful way to think of the 1930–33 debt crisis is as the progressive erosion of borrowers' collateral relative to debt burdens.

As the representative borrower became more and more insolvent, banks (and other lenders as well) faced a dilemma. Simple, noncontingent loans faced increasingly higher risks of default; yet a return to the more complex type of contract involved many other costs. Either way, debtor insolvency necessarily raised the *CCI* for banks.

One way for banks to adjust to a higher *CCI* is to increase the rate that they charge borrowers. This may be counterproductive, however, if higher interest charges increase the risk of default. The more usual response is for banks just not to make loans to some people that they might have lent to in better times. This was certainly the pattern in the 1930's. For example, it was reported that the extraordinary rate of default on residential mortgages forced banks and life insurance companies to "practically stop making mortgage loans, except for renewals" (Hart, p. 163). This situation precluded many borrowers, even with good projects, from getting funds, while lenders rushed to compete for existing high-grade assets. As one writer of the time, D. M. Frederiksen, put it:

> We see money accumulating at the centers, with difficulty of finding safe investment for it; interest rates dropping down lower than ever before; money available in great plenty for things that are obviously safe, but not available at all for things that are in fact safe, and which under normal conditions would be entirely safe (and there are a great many such), but which are now viewed with suspicion by lenders.
> [1931, p. 139]

As this quote suggests, the idea that the low yields on Treasury or blue-chip corporation liabilities during this time signalled a general state of "easy money" is mistaken; money was easy for a few safe borrowers, but difficult for everyone else.

An indicator of the strength of lender preferences for safe, liquid assets (and hence of the difficulty of risky borrowers in obtaining funds) is the yield differential between Baa corporate bonds and Treasury bonds (Table 1, column 6). Because this variable contains no adjustment for the reclassification of firms into higher risk categories, it tends to understate the true difference in yields between representative risky and safe assets. Nevertheless, this indicator showed some impressive shifts, going from 2.5 percent during 1929–30 to nearly 8 percent in mid-1932. (The differential never exceeded 3.5 percent in the sharp 1920–22 recession.) The yield differential reflected changing perceptions of default risk, of course; but note also the close relationship of the differential and the banking crises (a fact first pointed out by Friedman and Schwartz). Bank crises depressed the prices of lower-quality investments as the fear of runs drove banks into assets that could be used as reserves or for rediscounting. This effect of bank portfolio choices on an asset price could not happen in a Fama-type, complete-markets world.

Finally, it is instructive to consider the experience of a country that had a debt crisis without a banking crisis. Canada entered the Great Depression with a large external debt, much of it payable in foreign currencies. The combination of deflation and the devaluation of the Canadian dollar led to many defaults. Internally, debt problems in agriculture and in mortgage markets were as severe as in the United States, while major industries (notably pulp and paper) experienced many bankruptcies (A. E. Safarian, 1959, ch. 7). Although Canadian bankers did not face serious danger of runs, they shifted away from loans to safer assets. This shift toward safety and liquidity, though less pronounced than in the U.S. case, drew criticism from all facets of Canadian society. The *American Banker* of December 6, 1932, reported the following complaint from a non-populist Canadiàn politician:

> The chief criticism of our present system appears to be that in good times credit is expanded to great extremes... but, when the pinch of hard times is first being felt, credit is suddenly and drastically restricted by the banks... At the present time, loans are only being made when the banks have a very wide

margin of security and every effort is being made to collect outstanding loans. All our banks are reaching out in an endeavor to liquefy their assets....

[p. 1]

Canadian lenders other than banks also tried to retrench: According to the *Financial Post*, May 14, 1932, "Insurance, trust, and loan companies were increasingly unwilling to lend funds with real estate and rental values falling, a growing number of defaults of interest and principal, the increasing burden of property taxes, and legislation which adversely affected creditors" (quoted in Safarian, p. 130).

More careful study of the Canadian experience in the Great Depression would be useful. However, on first appraisal, that experience does not seem to be inconsistent with the point that even good borrowers may find it more difficult or costly to obtain credit when there is extensive insolvency. The debt crisis should be added to the banking crises as a potential source of disruption of the credit system.

III. Credit Markets and Macroeconomic Performance

If it is taken as given that the financial crises during the depression did interfere with the normal flows of credit, it still must be shown how this might have had an effect on the course of the aggregate economy.

There are many ways in which problems in credit markets might potentially affect the macroeconomy. Several of these could be grouped under the heading of "effects on aggregate supply." For example, if credit flows are dammed up, potential borrowers in the economy may not be able to secure funds to undertake worthwhile activities or investments; at the same time, savers may have to devote their funds to inferior uses. Other possible problems resulting from poorly functioning credit markets include a reduced feasibility of effective risk sharing and greater difficulties in funding large, indivisible projects. Each of these might limit the economy's productive capacity.

These arguments are reminiscent of some ideas advanced by John Gurley and E. S. Shaw (1955), Ronald McKinnon (1973), and others in an economic development context. The claim of this literature is that immature or repressed financial sectors cause the "fragmentation" of less developed economies, reducing the effective set of production possibilities available to the society.

Did the financial crisis of the 1930's turn the United States into a "temporarily underdeveloped economy" (to use Bob Hall's felicitous phrase)? Although this possibility is intriguing, the answer to the question is probably no. While many businesses did suffer drains of working capital and investment funds, most larger corporations entered the decade with sufficient cash and liquid reserves to finance operations and any desired expansion (see, for example, Friedrich Lutz, 1945). Unless it is believed that the outputs of large and of small businesses are not potentially substitutes, the aggregate supply effect must be regarded as not of great quantitative importance.

The reluctance of even cash-rich corporations to expand production during the depression suggests that consideration of the aggregate demand channel for credit market effects on output may be more fruitful. The aggregate demand argument is in fact easy to make: A higher cost of credit intermediation for some borrowers (for example, households and smaller firms) implies that, for a given *safe* interest rate, these borrowers must face a higher effective cost of credit. (Indeed, they may not be able to borrow at all.) If this higher rate applies to household and small firm borrowing but not to their saving (they may only earn the safe rate on their savings), then the effect of higher borrowing costs is unambiguously to reduce their demands for current-period goods and services. This pure substitution effect (of future for present consumption) is easily derived from the classical two-period model of savings.[24]

---

[24] The classical model may be augmented, if the reader desires, by considerations of liquidity constraints, bankruptcy costs, or risk aversion; see my 1981 paper.

Assume that the behavior of borrowers unaffected by credit market problems is unchanged. Then the paragraph above implies that, for a given safe rate, an increase in the cost of credit intermediation reduces the total quantity of goods and services currently demanded. That is, the aggregate demand curve, drawn as a function of the safe rate, is shifted downward by a financial crisis. In any macroeconomic model one cares to use, this implies lower output and lower safe interest rates. Both of these outcomes characterized 1930–33, of course.

Some evidence on the magnitude of the effect of the financial market problems on aggregate output is now presented.

IV. Short-Run Macroeconomic Impacts of the Financial Crisis

This section studies the short-run or "impact" effects of the financial crisis. For this purpose, I use only monthly data on the relevant variables. In addition, rather than consider the 1929–33 episode outside of its context, I have widened the sample to include the entire interwar period (January 1919–December 1941).

Section I.C above has already given some evidence of the relationship between the troubles of the financial sector and those of the economy as a whole. However, support for the thesis of this paper requires that nonmonetary effects of the financial crisis on output be distinguished from the monetary effects studied by Friedman and Schwartz. My approach will be to fit output equations using monetary variables, then to show that adding proxies for the financial crisis substantially improves the performance of these equations. Comparison of financial to totally nonfinancial sources of the Great Depression, such as those suggested by Temin, is left to future research.

To isolate the purely monetary influences on the economy, one needs a structural explanation of the money-income relationship. Lucas (1972) has presented a formal model in which monetary shocks affect production decisions by causing confusion about the price level. Influenced by this work, most recent empirical studies of the role of money

have related national income to measures of "unanticipated" changes in money or prices.[25]

The most familiar way of constructing a proxy for unanticipated components of a variable is the two-step method of Robert Barro (1978), in which the residuals from a first-stage prediction equation for (say) money are employed as the independent variables in a second-stage regression. I experimented with both the Barro approach and some alternatives.[26] Since my conclusions were unaffected by choice of technique, I report here only the Barro-type results.

In the spirit of the Lucas-Barro analysis, I considered the effects of both "money shocks" and "price shocks" on output. Money shocks $(M - M^e)$ were defined as the residuals from a regression of the rate of growth of $M1$ on four lags of the growth rates of industrial production, wholesale prices, and $M1$ itself; price shocks $(P - P^e)$ were defined symmetrically.[27] I used ordinary least squares to estimate the effects of money and price shocks on the rate of growth of industrial production, relative to trend.

The basic regression results for the interwar sample period are given as equations (1) and (2) in Table 2. These two equations are of interest, independently of the other results of this paper. The estimated "Lucas supply curve," equation (2), shows an effect of price shocks on output that is statistically and economically significant. As such, it complements the results of Thomas Sargent (1976), who found a similar relationship for the postwar. The relationship of output to money surprises, equation (1), is a bit weaker. The fact that we discover a smaller role for money in the monthly data than does Paul Evans (1981) is primarily the result of our inclusion of lagged values of production on the right-hand side. This inclusion seems justified both on statistical grounds and for

---

[25] A notable exception is Mishkin (1982).

[26] Principal alternatives tried were 1) the use of anticipated as well as unanticipated quantities as explanatory variables; and 2) reestimation of some equations by the more efficient but computationally more complex method of Andrew Abel and Mishkin (1981).

[27] The first-stage regressions were unsurprising and, for the sake of space, are not reported.

TABLE 2—ESTIMATED OUTPUT EQUATIONS

$$(1) \quad Y_t = \underset{(10.21)}{.623} \ Y_{t-1} - \underset{(-2.37)}{.144} \ Y_{t-2} + \underset{(3.42)}{.407} \ (M-M^e)_t + \underset{(1.16)}{.141} \ (M-M^e)_{t-1}$$

$$+ \underset{(0.42)}{.051} \ (M-M^e)_{t-2} + \underset{(1.19)}{.144} \ (M-M^e)_{t-3}$$

$$s.e. = .0272 \quad D.W. = 2.02 \quad \text{Sample: } 1/19-12/41$$

$$(2) \quad Y_t = \underset{(9.50)}{.582} \ Y_{t-1} - \underset{(-1.76)}{.118} \ Y_{t-2} + \underset{(5.33)}{.533} \ (P-P^e)_t + \underset{(3.33)}{.350} \ (P-P^e)_{t-1}$$

$$+ \underset{(0.34)}{.036} \ (P-P^e)_{t-2} + \underset{(0.66)}{.069} \ (P-P^e)_{t-3}$$

$$s.e. = .0260 \quad D.W. = 2.01 \quad \text{Sample: } 1/19-12/41$$

$$(3) \quad Y_t = \underset{(9.86)}{.613} \ Y_{t-1} - \underset{(-2.63)}{.159} \ Y_{t-2} + \underset{(2.92)}{.332} \ (M-M^e)_t + \underset{(0.99)}{.113} \ (M-M^e)_{t-1} + \underset{(0.96)}{.110} \ (M-M^e)_{t-2}$$

$$+ \underset{(1.38)}{.156} \ (M-M^e)_{t-3} - \underset{(-4.24)}{.869E-04} \ DBANKS_t - \underset{(-1.93)}{.406E-04} \ DBANKS_{t-1}$$

$$- \underset{(-1.95)}{.258E-03} \ DFAILS_t - \underset{(-2.47)}{.325E-03} \ DFAILS_{t-1}$$

$$s.e. = .0249 \quad D.W. = 1.99 \quad \text{Sample: } 1/21-12/41$$

$$(4) \quad Y_t = \underset{(9.76)}{.615} \ Y_{t-1} - \underset{(-2.13)}{.131} \ Y_{t-2} + \underset{(3.99)}{.455} \ (P-P^e)_t + \underset{(1.97)}{.231} \ (P-P^e)_{t-1} - \underset{(-0.03)}{.004} \ (P-P^e)_{t-2}$$

$$+ \underset{(0.22)}{.024} \ (P-P^e)_{t-3} - \underset{(-4.03)}{.799E-04} \ DBANKS_t - \underset{(-1.66)}{.337E-04} \ DBANKS_{t-1}$$

$$- \underset{(-1.52)}{.202E-03} \ DFAILS_t - \underset{(-1.83)}{.242E-03} \ DFAILS_{t-1}$$

$$s.e. = .0246 \quad D.W. = 1.98 \quad \text{Sample: } 1/21-2/41$$

Notes: Y_t = rate of growth of industrial production (*Federal Reserve Bulletin*), relative to exponential trend.
$(M-M^e)_t$ = rate of growth of M1, nominal and seasonally adjusted (Friedman and Schwartz, Table 4-1), less predicted rate of growth.
$(P-P^e)_t$ = rate of growth of wholesale price index (*Federal Reserve Bulletin*), less predicted rate of growth.
$DBANKS_t$ = first difference of deposits of failing banks (deflated by wholesale price index).
$DFAILS_t$ = first difference of liabilities of failing businesses (deflated by wholesale price index).
Data are monthly; *t*-statistics are shown in parentheses.

the economic reason that costs of adjusting production can be presumed to create a serial dependence in output. Like Evans, I was not able to find effects of money (or prices) lagged more than three months.

While these regression results exhibit statistical significance and the expected signs for coefficients, they are disappointing in the following sense: When equations (1) and (2) are used to perform dynamic simulations of the path of output between mid-1930 and the bank holiday of March 1933, they capture no more than half of the total decline of output during the period. This is the basis of the comment in the introduction that the declines in money seem "quantitatively insufficient" to explain what happened to output in 1930–33.

Given the basic regressions (1) and (2), the next step was to examine the effects of including proxies for the nonmonetary financial impact as explanators of output. Based on the earlier analysis of this paper, the most obvious such proxies are the deposits of failing banks and the liabilities of failing businesses.

A preliminary problem with the bank deposits series that needs to be discussed is the value for March 1933, the month of the bank holiday. As can be seen in Table 1, the deposits of banks suspended in March 1933 is seven times that of the next worse month. The question arises if any adjustment should be made to that figure before running the regressions.

We believe that it would be a mistake to eliminate totally the bank holiday episode from the sample. According to contemporary accounts, rather than being an orderly and planned-in-advance policy, the imposition of the holiday was a forced response to the most panicky and chaotic financial conditions of the period. The deposits of suspended banks figure for March, as large as it is, reflects not all closed banks but only those not licensed to reopen by June 30, 1933. Of these banks, most were liquidated or placed in receivership; less than 25 percent had been licensed to reopen as of December 31, 1936.[28] Qualitatively, then, the March 1933 episode resembled the earlier crises; it would be throwing away information not to include in some way the effects of this crisis and of its resolution on the economy.

On the other hand, the mass closing of banks by government action probably created less confusion and fear of future crises than would have a similar number of suspensions occurring without government intervention. As a conservative compromise, I assumed that the "supervised" bank closings of March 1933 had the same effect as an "unsupervised" bank crisis involving 15 percent as much in frozen deposits. This scales down the March 1933 episode to about the size of the events of October 1931. The sensitivity of the results to this assumption is as follows:

increasing the amount of importance attributed to the March 1933 crisis raises the magnitude and statistical significance of the measured effects of the financial crises on output. (It is in this sense that the 15 percent figure is conservative.) However, the bank failure coefficients in the regressions retained high significance even when less weight was given to March 1933.

I turn now to the results of adding (real) deposits of failing banks and liabilities of failing businesses to the output equations (see equations (3) and (4) in Table 2). The sample period begins in 1921 because of the unavailability of data on monthly bank failures before then. In both regressions, current and lagged first differences of the added variables enter the explanation of the growth rate of industrial production (relative to trend) with the expected sign and, taken jointly, with a high level of statistical significance. The magnitudes and significance of the coefficients of money and price shocks are not much changed. This provides at least a tentative confirmation that nonmonetary effects of the financial crisis augmented monetary effects in the short-run determination of output.

Some alternative proxies for the nonmonetary component of the financial crisis were also tried. For the sake of space, only a summary of these results is given. 1) To examine the direct effects of the contraction of bank credit on the economy, I began by regressing the rate of growth of bank loans on current and lagged values of suspended bank deposits and of failing business liabilities. (This regression indicated a powerful negative effect of financial crisis on bank loans.) The fitted series from this regression was used as a proxy for the portion of the credit contraction induced by the financial crisis. In the presence of money or price shocks, the effect of a decline in this variable on output was found to be negative for two months, positive for the next two months, then strongly negative for the fifth and sixth months after the decline. For the period from 1921 until the bank holiday, and with monetary variables included, the total effect of credit contraction on output (as measured by the sum of lag coefficients in a polynomial

[28]*Federal Reserve Bulletin*, 1937, pp. 866–67.

distributed lag) was large (comparable to the monetary effect), negative, and significant at the 95 percent level. For the entire interwar sample, however, the statistical significance of this variable was much reduced. This last result is due to the fact that the recovery of 1933–41 was financed by nonbank sources, with bank loans remaining at a low level.

2) Another proxy for the financial crisis that was tried was the differential between Baa corporate bond yields and the yields on U.S. bonds. As described in Section I.C, this variable responded strongly to both bank crises and the problems of debtors, and as such was a sensitive indicator of financial market conditions. The yield differential variable turned out to enter very strongly as an explanator of current and future output growth, overall and in every subsample. As much of this predictive power was no doubt due to pure financial market anticipations of future output declines, I also put the differential variable through a first-stage regression on the liabilities of bank and business failures. Assuming that these latter variables themselves were not determined by anticipations of future output declines (see below), the use of the fitted series from this regression "purged" the differential variable of its pure anticipatory component. The fitted series entered the output equations less strongly than the raw series, but it retained the right sign and statistical significance at the 95 percent confidence level.

In almost every case, then, the addition of proxies for the general financial crisis improved the purely monetary explanation of short-run (monthly) output movements. This finding was robust to the obvious experiments. For example, with the above-noted exception of the credit variable in 1933–41, coefficients remained roughly stable over subsamples. Another experiment was to include free dummy variables for each quarter from 1931:I to 1932:IV in the above regressions. The purpose of this was to test the suggestion that our results are only a reflection of the fact that both the output and financial crisis variables "moved a lot" during 1930–33. The rather surprising discovery was that the inclusion of the dummies *increased* the magnitude and statistical sig-

nificance of the coefficients on bank and business failures. Finally, the economic significance of the results was tested by using the various estimated equations to run dynamic simulations of monthly levels of industrial production (relative to trend) for mid-1930 to March 1933. Relative to the pure money-shock and price-shock simulations described above, the equations including financial crisis proxies did well. Equations (3) and (4) reduced the mean squared simulation error over (1) and (2) by about 50 percent. The other (nonreported) equations did better; for example, those using the yield differential variable reduced the *MSE* of simulation from 90 to 95 percent.

These results are promising. However, a caveat must be added: To conclude that the observed correlations support the theory outlined in this paper requires an additional assumption, that failures of banks and commercial firms are not caused by anticipations of (future) changes in output. To the extent that, say, bank runs are caused by the receipt of bad news about next month's industrial production, the fact that bank failures tend to lead production declines does not prove that the bank problems are helping to cause the declines.[29]

While it may not be possible to convince the determined skeptic that bank and business failures are not purely anticipatory phenomena, a good case can be made against that position. For example, while in some cases a bad sales forecast may induce a firm to declare bankruptcy, more often that option is forced by insolvency (a result of past business conditions). For banks, it might well be argued that not only are failures relatively independent of anticipations about output, but that they are not simply the product of current and past output performance either: First, banking crises had never previous to this time been a necessary result of declines in output.[30] Second, Friedman and Schwartz, as well as other writers, have identified

---

[29] Actually, a similar criticism might be made of Barro's work and my own money and price regressions.

[30] Philip Cagan (1965) makes this point; see pp. 216, 227–28. The 1920–22 recession, for example, did not generate any banking problems.

specific events that were important sources of bank runs during 1930–33. These include the revelation of scandal at the Bank of the United States (a private bank, which in December 1930 became the largest bank to fail up to that time); the collapse of the Kreditanstalt in Austria and the ensuing financial panics in central Europe; Britain's going off gold; the exposure of huge pyramiding schemes in the United States and Europe; and others, all connected very indirectly (if at all) with the path of industrial production in the United States.

If it is accepted that bank suspensions and business bankruptcies were the product of factors beyond pure anticipations of output decline, then the evidence of this section supports the view that nonmonetary aspects of the financial crisis were at least part of the propagatory mechanism of the Great Depression. If it is further accepted that the financial crisis contained large exogenous components (there is evidence for this in the case of the banking panics), then there are elements of causality in the story as well.

V. Persistence of the Financial Crisis

The claim was made in the introduction that my theory seems capable, unlike the major alternatives, of explaining the unusual length and depth of the Great Depression. In the previous section, I attempted to deal with the issue of depth; simulations of the estimated regressions suggested that the combined monetary and nonmonetary effects of the financial crisis can explain much of the severity of the decline in output. In this section, the question of the length of the Great Depression is addressed.

As a matter of theory, the duration of the credit effects described in Section II above depends on the amount of time it takes to 1) establish new or revive old channels of credit flow after a major disruption, and 2) rehabilitate insolvent debtors. Since these processes may be difficult and slow, the persistence of nonmonetary effects of financial crisis has a plausible basis. (In contrast, persistence of purely monetary effects relies on the slow diffusion of information or unexplained stickiness of wages and prices.) Of

course, plausibility is not enough; some evidence on the speed of financial recovery should be adduced.

After struggling through 1931 and 1932, the financial system hit its low point in March 1933, when the newly elected President Roosevelt's "bank holiday" closed down most financial intermediaries and markets. March 1933 was a watershed month in several ways: It marked not only the beginning of economic and financial recovery but also the introduction of truly extensive government involvement in all aspects of the financial system.[31] It might be argued that the federally directed financial rehabilitation—which took strong measures against the problems of both creditors and debtors—was the only major New Deal program that successfully promoted economic recovery.[32] In any case, the large government intervention is prima facie evidence that by this time the public had lost confidence in the self-correcting powers of the financial structure.

Although the government's actions set the financial system on its way back to health, recovery was neither rapid nor complete. Many banks did not reopen after the holiday, and many that did open did so on a restricted basis or with marginally solvent balance sheets. Deposits did not flow back into the banks in great quantities until 1934, and the government (through the Reconstruction Finance Corporation and other agencies) had to continue to pump large sums into banks and other intermediaries. Most important, however, was a noticeable change in attitude among lenders; they emerged from the 1930–33 episode chastened and conservative. Friedman and Schwartz (pp. 449–62) have documented the shift of banks during this time away from making loans toward holding safe and liquid investments. The growing level of bank liquidity created an illusion (as Friedman and Schwartz pointed out) of easy money;

---

[31]See Chandler (1970), ch. 15, and Friedman and Schwartz, ch. 8.

[32]E. Carey Brown (1956) has argued that New Deal fiscal policy was not very constructive. A paper by Michael Weinstein in Brunner (1981) points out counterproductive aspects of the N.R.A.

however, the combination of lender reluctance and continued debtor insolvency interfered with credit flows for several years after 1933.

Evidence of postholiday credit problems is not hard to find. For example, small businesses, which (as I have noted) suffered disproportionately during the Contraction, had continuing difficulties with credit during recovery. Lewis Kimmel (1939) carried out a survey of credit availability during 1933–38 as a companion to the National Industrial Conference Board's 1932 survey. His conclusions are generally sanguine (this may reflect the fact that the work was commissioned by the American Bankers Association). However, his survey results (p. 65) show that, of responding manufacturing firms normally dependent on banks, refusal or restriction of bank credit was reported by 30.2 percent of very small firms (capitalization less than $50,000); 14.3 percent of small firms ($50,001–$500,000); 10.3 percent of medium firms ($500,001–$1,000,000); and 3.2 percent of the largest companies (capital over $1 million). (The corresponding results from the 1932 NICB survey were 41.3, 22.2, 12.5, and 9.7 percent.)

Two well-known economists, Hardy and Viner, conducted a credit survey in the Seventh Federal Reserve District in 1934–35. Based on "intensive coverage of 2600 individual cases," they found "a genuine unsatisfied demand for credit by solvent borrowers, many of whom could make economically sound use of working capital.... The total amount of this unsatisfied demand for credit is a significant factor, among many others, in retarding business recovery." They added, "So far as small business is concerned, the difficulty in getting bank credit has increased more, as compared with a few years ago, than has the difficulty of getting trade credit." (These passages are quoted in W. L. Stoddard, 1940.)

Finally, another credit survey for the 1933–38 period was done by the Small Business Review Committee for the U.S. Department of Commerce. This study surveyed 6,000 firms with between 21 and 150 employees. From these they chose a special sample of 600 companies "selected because of their high ratings by a standard commercial rating agency." Even within the elite sample, 45 percent of the firms reported difficulty in securing funds for working capital purposes during this period; and 75 percent could not obtain capital or long-term loan requirements through regular markets. (See Stoddard.)

The reader may wish to view the American Bankers Association and Small Business Review Committee surveys as lower and upper bounds, with the Hardy-Viner study in the middle. In any case, the consensus from surveys, as well as the opinion of careful students such as Chandler, is that credit difficulties for small business persisted for at least two years after the bank holiday.[33]

Home mortgage lending was another important area of credit activity. In this sphere, private lenders were even more cautious after 1933 than in business lending. They had a reason for conservatism; while business failures fell quite a bit during the recovery, real estate defaults and foreclosures continued high through 1935.[34] As has been noted, some traditional mortgage lenders nearly left the market: life insurance companies, which made $525 million in mortgage loans in 1929, made $10 million in new loans in 1933 and $16 million in 1934.[35] During this period, mortgage loans that were made by private institutions went only to the very best potential borrowers. Evidence for this is the sharp drop in default rates of loans made in the early 1930's as compared to loans made in earlier years (see Carl Behrens, 1952, p. 11); this decline was too large to be explained by the improvement in business conditions alone.

To the extent that the home mortgage market did function in the years immediately following 1933, it was largely due to the direct involvement of the federal government. Besides establishing some important new institutions (such as the FSLIC and the system of federally chartered savings and loans), the government "readjusted" existing debts, made investments in the shares of

[33] See Chandler (1970), pp. 150–51.
[34] U.S. Department of Commerce (1975), series N301.
[35] U.S. Department of Commerce (1975), N282.

thrift institutions, and substituted for recalcitrant private institutions in the provision of direct credit. In 1934, the government-sponsored Home Owners' Loan Corporation made 71 percent of all mortgage loans extended.[36]

Similar conditions obtained for farm credit and in other markets, but space does not permit this to be pursued here. Summarizing the reading of all of the evidence by economists and by other students of the period, it seems safe to say that the return of the private financial system to normal conditions after March 1933 was not rapid; and that the financial recovery would have been more difficult without extensive government intervention and assistance. A moderate estimate is that the U.S. financial system operated under handicap for about five years (from the beginning of 1931 to the end of 1935), a period which covers most of the time between the recessions of 1929–30 and 1937–38. This is consistent with the claim that the effects of financial crisis can help explain the persistence of the depression.

VI. International Aspects

The Great Depression was a worldwide phenomenon; banking crises, though occurring in a number of important countries besides the United States, were not so ubiquitous. A number of large countries had no serious domestic banking problems, yet experienced severe drops in real income in the early 1930's. Can this be made consistent with the important role we have ascribed to the financial crisis in the United States? A complete answer would require another paper; but I offer some observations:

1) The experience of different countries and the mix of depressive forces each faced varied significantly. For example, Britain, suffering from an overvalued pound, had high unemployment throughout the 1920's; after leaving gold in 1931, it was one of the first countries to recover. The biggest problems of food and raw materials exporters were falling prices and the drying up of overseas markets. Thus we need not look to the domestic financial system as an important cause in every case.

2) The countries in which banking crises occurred (the United States, Germany, Austria, Hungary, and others) were among the worst hit by the depression. Moreover, these countries held a large share of world trade and output. The United States alone accounted for almost half of world industrial output in 1925–29, and its imports of basic raw materials and foodstuffs in 1927–28 made up almost 40 percent of the trade in these commodities.[37] The reduction of imports as these economies weakened exerted downward pressure on trading partners.

3) There were interesting parallels between the troubles of the domestic financial system and those of the international system. One of the Federal Reserve's proudest accomplishments had been the establishment, during the 1920's, of an international gold-exchange standard. Unfortunately, like domestic banking, the gold-exchange standard had the instability of a fractional-reserve system. International reserves included not only gold but also foreign currencies, notably the dollar and the pound; for countries other than the United States and the United Kingdom, foreign exchange was 35 percent of total reserves.

In 1931, the expectations that the international financial system would collapse became self-fulfilling. A general attempt to convert currencies into gold drove one currency after another off the gold-exchange standard. Restrictions on the movement of capital or gold were widely imposed. By 1932, only the United States and a small number of other countries remained on gold.

As the fall of the gold standard parallelled domestic bank failures, the domestic insolvency problem had an international analogue as well. Largely due to fixed exchange rates, the deflation of prices was worldwide. Countries with large nominal debts, notably agricultural exporters (the case of Canada has been mentioned), became unable to pay. Foreign bond values in the United States were extremely depressed.

[36]U.S. Department of Commerce (1975), N278 and N283.

[37]U.S. Department of Commerce (1947), pp. 29–31.

As in the domestic economy, these problems disrupted the worldwide mechanism of credit. International capital flows were reduced to a trickle. This represented a serious problem for many countries.

To summarize these observations: the fact that the Great Depression hit countries which did not have banking crises does not preclude the possibility that banking and debt problems were important in the United States (or, for that matter, that countries with strong banks had problems with debtor insolvency). Moreover, my analysis of the domestic financial system may be able to shed light on some of the international financial difficulties of the period.

VII. Conclusion

Did the financial collapse of the early 1930's have real effects on the macroeconomy, other than through monetary channels? The evidence is at least not inconsistent with this proposition. However, a stronger reason for giving this view consideration is the one stated in the introduction: this theory has hope of achieving a reconciliation of the obvious suboptimality of this period with the postulate of reasonably rational, market-constrained agents. The solution to this paradox lies in recognizing that economic institutions, rather than being a "veil," can affect costs of transactions and thus market opportunities and allocations. Institutions which evolve and perform well in normal times may become counterproductive during periods when exogenous shocks or policy mistakes drive the economy off course. The malfunctioning of financial institutions during the early 1930's exemplifies this point.

REFERENCES

Abel, Andrew and Mishkin, Frederic, "An Integrated View of Tests of Rationality, Market Efficiency, and the Short-Run Neutrality of Monetary Policy," Working Paper 726, National Bureau of Economic Research, 1981.

Barro, Robert, "Unanticipated Money, Output, and the Price Level in the United States," *Journal of Political Economy*, August 1978, *86*, 549–80.

Behrens, Carl, *Commercial Bank Activities in Urban Mortgage Financing*, New York: National Bureau of Economic Research, 1952.

Bernanke, Ben, "Bankruptcy, Liquidity, and Recession," *American Economic Review Proceedings*, May 1981, *71*, 155–59.

Brown, E. Carey, "Fiscal Policy in the 'Thirties: A Reappraisal," *American Economic Review*, December 1956, *46*, 857–79.

Brunner, Karl, *The Great Depression Revisited*, Boston: Martinus Nijhoff, 1981.

Cagan, Philip, *Determinants and Effects of Changes in the Stock of Money, 1875–1960*, New York: National Bureau of Economic Research, 1965.

Chandler, Lester, *America's Greatest Depression*, New York: Harper & Row, 1970.

_____, *American Monetary Policy, 1928–1941*, New York: Harper & Row, 1971.

Clark, Evans, *The Internal Debts of the United States*, New York: Macmillan Co., 1933.

Cone, Kenneth, "Regulation of Depository Financial Intermediaries," unpublished doctoral dissertation, Stanford University, 1982.

Diamond, Douglas and Dybvig, Philip, "Bank Runs, Deposit Insurance, and Liquidity," mimeo., University of Chicago, 1981.

Evans, Paul, "An Econometric Analysis of the Causes of the Great Depression in the U.S.," mimeo., Stanford University, 1981.

Fabricant, Solomon, *Profits, Losses, and Business Assets, 1929–1934*, Bulletin 55, National Bureau of Economic Research, 1935.

Fama, Eugene, "Banking in the Theory of Finance," *Journal of Monetary Economics*, January 1980, *6*, 39–57.

Fisher, Irving, "The Debt-Deflation Theory of Great Depressions," *Econometrica*, October 1933, *1*, 337–57.

Flood, Robert and Garber, Peter, "A Systematic Banking Collapse in a Perfect Foresight World," Working Paper No. 691, National Bureau of Economic Research, 1981.

Frederiksen, D. M., "Two Financial Roads Leading Out of Depression," *Harvard Business Review*, October 1931, *10*, 131–48.

Friedman, Benjamin, "Debt and Economic Activity in the United States," Working Paper

No. 704, National Bureau of Economic Research, 1981.

Friedman, Milton, and Schwartz, Anna J., *A Monetary History of the United States, 1867–1960*, Princeton: Princeton University Press, 1963.

Goldsmith, Raymond, *Financial Institutions in the American Economy Since 1900*, Princeton: Princeton University Press, 1958.

Gurley, John G. and Shaw, E. S., "Financial Aspects of Economic Development," *American Economic Review*, September 1955, *45*, 515–38.

Hart, A. G., *Debts and Recovery, 1929–1937*, New York: Twentieth Century Fund, 1938.

Jaffee, Dwight, and Russell, Thomas, "Imperfect Information and Credit Rationing," *Quarterly Journal of Economics*, November 1976, *90*, 651–66.

Kennedy, Susan E., *The Banking Crisis of 1933*, Lexington: University Press of Kentucky, 1973.

Kimmel, Lewis H., *The Availability of Bank Credit, 1933–1938*, New York: National Industrial Conference Board, 1939.

Kindleberger, Charles P., *Manias, Panics, and Crashes*, New York: Basic Books, 1978.

Klebaner, Benjamin, *Commercial Banking in the United States: A History*, Hinsdale: Dryden Press, 1974.

Lucas, Robert E., Jr., "Expectations and the Neutrality of Money," *Journal of Economic Theory*, April 1972, *4*, 103–24.

_____, *Studies in Business Cycle Theory*, Cambridge: Massachusetts Institute of Technology Press, 1981.

Lutz, Friedrich, *Corporate Cash Balances, 1914–43*, New York: National Bureau of Economic Research, 1945.

McKinnon, Ronald J., *Money and Capital in Economic Development*, Washington: The Brookings Institution, 1973.

Merwin, Charles L., *Financing Small Corporations*, New York: National Bureau of Economic Research, 1942.

Minsky, Hyman P., "A Theory of Systematic Fragility," in E. I. Altman and A. W. Sametz, eds., *Financial Crises*, New York: Wiley-Interscience, 1977.

Mishkin, Frederic, "The Household Balance Sheet and the Great Depression," *Journal*

of *Economic History*, December 1978, *38*, 918–37.

_____, "Does Anticipated Money Matter? An Econometric Investigation," *Journal of Political Economy*, February 1982, *90*, 22–51.

Nugent, Rolf, *Consumer Credit and Economic Stability*, New York: Russell Sage Foundation, 1939.

O'Hara, Maureen and Easley, David, "The Postal Savings System in Depression," *Journal of Economic History*, September 1979, *39*, 741–53.

Persons, Charles E., "Credit Expansion, 1920 to 1929 and Its Lessons," *Quarterly Journal of Economics*, November 1930, *45*, 94–130.

Safarian, A. E., *The Canadian Economy in the Great Depression*, Toronto: University of Toronto Press, 1959.

Sargent, Thomas J., "A Classical Macroeconometric Model for the United States," *Journal of Political Economy*, April 1976, *84*, 207–38.

Stiglitz, Joseph E. and Weiss, Andrew, "Credit Rationing in Markets with Imperfect Information," *American Economic Review*, June 1981, *71*, 393–410.

Stoddard, W. L., "Small Business Wants Capital," *Harvard Business Review*, Spring 1940, *18*, 265–74.

Temin, Peter, *Did Monetary Forces Cause the Great Depression?*, New York: W. W. Norton, 1976.

Upham, Cyril B. and Lamke, Edwin, *Closed and Distressed Banks: A Study in Public Administration*, Washington: The Brookings Institution, 1934.

Board of Governors of the Federal Reserve System, *Banking and Monetary Statistics*, 1943.

Federal Reserve Bulletin, various issues.

National Industrial Conference Board, *The Availability of Bank Credit*, New York, 1932.

Survey of Current Business, various issues.

U.S. Department of Commerce, *Historical Statistics of the United States*, Washington: USGPO, 1975.

_____, *National Income*, Washington: USGPO, 1954.

_____, *The United States in the World Economy*, Washington: USGPO, 1947.

Federal Deposit Insurance, Regulatory Policy, and Optimal Bank Capital*

STEPHEN A. BUSER, ANDREW H. CHEN, and EDWARD J. KANE**

ABSTRACT

This paper seeks to explain the combination of explicit and implicit pricing for deposit insurance employed by the FDIC. Essentially, the FDIC sells two products—insurance *and* regulation. To span the product space, it must and does set two prices. We argue that the need to establish regulatory disincentives to bank risk-taking is the heart of the controversy over the adequacy of bank capital and that the ability to close risky banks before exhausting their *charter value* (i.e., the value of their right to continue in business) stands at the center of these disincentives and in front of the FDIC's insurance reserves.

JUST AS A BOOK shouldn't be judged by its cover, a government agency shouldn't be judged by the words behind its initials. With the FDIC (Federal Deposit Insurance Corporation), the agency's name describes only *part* of its formal operations: the FDIC is quasi-governmental, has a regional structure and sells deposit insurance. However, the initials fail to convey the FDIC's critical place in the governmental regulatory structure as the sole federal overseer of the approximately 8900 state-chartered commercial banks that have chosen not to belong the Federal Reserve System.[1] Reflecting the Federal Reserve's membership problem, the number of these banks is growing year by year.

Besides selling deposit insurance at bargain explicit rates, the FDIC performs four regulatory functions: (1) *Entry regulation.* It passes on new banks' applications for deposit insurance and on branch and merger proposals as well, thereby protecting the value of existing bank charters; (2) *Examination.* Two-thirds of FDIC employees are concerned with inspecting bank records and supervising managerial activity; (3) *Regulation of deposit rates and conditions for withdrawal.* By tradition, FDIC policies on these matters conform entirely with regulations applicable to Federal Reserve member banks; and (4) *Disposition of failed banks.* When an insured bank fails, the FDIC usually chooses not to liquidate it.[2]

* An earlier version of this paper was delivered at the June, 1979 meetings of the Western Economics Association. The authors wish to thank Edward H. Bowman, Michael Bordo, K.C. Chen, Jeffrey Fisher, Patrick Hess, E. Han Kim, Joseph Sinkey, Benjamin M. Friedman and Anthony M. Santomero of this *Journal* for helpful criticism.

** Associate Professor of finance, Professor of Finance, and Reese Professor of Banking and Monetary Economics (respectively) at The Ohio State University.

[1] In December 1979, there were 14,364 insured commercial banks, of which 5425 were member banks. Until 1980, when federal charters became possible for mutual savings banks under the Federal Home Loan Bank Board, the FDIC was also the only federal agency regulating mutual savings banks.

[2] The FDIC may handle a bank failure in any of three basic ways: (1) it may liquidate a failed bank, paying off its depositors in full; (2) it may arrange a merger or sell some or all of the bank's assets to

With the exception of Merton's [14] effort to incorporate surveillance costs, previous models of the FDIC contract for deposit insurance [13, 22, 12] neglect the agency's regulatory functions. In the literature of bank regulation, studies of FDIC efforts to bolster bank capital [20, 17, 18, 6, 3, 2, 19, 10] have not integrated into their analyses the costs and benefits of deposit insurance *per se*. Our goal is to erect a descriptively realistic unified framework for analyzing the regulatory and insurance dimensions of FDIC activity. With Kareken and Wallace [8] (whose model can be viewed as a special case of ours), we believe that only such a framework can identify the true justification of FDIC attempts to regulate bank capital.

We believe that the FDIC deliberately sets its *explicit* insurance premium below market value to entice state-chartered nonmember banks to submit themselves voluntarily to FDIC regulatory dominion. Precisely because the explicit price of its product is subsidized, to control excess demand for insurance services (i.e., expanded risk-taking) the FDIC is forced to develop an *implicit* price structure. To restrain bank risk-taking, the FDIC must raise (or restructure) its explicit fees or maintain an active regulatory posture. Regulations imposed on client banks as a condition for receiving FDIC insurance reduce the value of deposit insurance to owners of the banking firm. In Section I, we interpret this deadweight loss in value as an additional *implicit* premium that banks "pay" for insurance. This charge develops over and above the FDIC's *explicit* fees.

Adopting Posner's [18] conception of regulation as a tax, we perceive the FDIC to organize its examination and supervisory functions in ways that establish disincentives to "excessive" risk-taking by client banks. FDIC procedures ensure that the regulatory tax on an insured bank increases with the bank's portfolio risk. Bankers that resist these incentives may be made to forfeit their bank's charter well before its value approaches zero. We argue that a bank's charter value serves the comparatively small FDIC insurance fund (which amounts to only about 0.80 per cent of total deposits in insured banks) as its first line of defense against losses arising out of a bank's operations. From this perspective, FDIC entry regulation and periodic examination of individual banks' balance-sheet ratios function *in tandem* to maintain charter value and to control the moral hazard inherent in the FDIC's insurance business.

Seeing FDIC regulatory activities as foci for implicit price discrimination gives further insight into the function performed by its explicit premium. The implicit dimensions of the FDIC pricing strategy convert the explicit premium into a convenient device for adjusting the net insurance subsidy that the FDIC finances in any year from tax-exempt earnings on its insurance fund. Currently the FDIC expresses its explicit gross annual premium as a *rebatable* fraction (1/12 of one per cent) of a bank's total domestic deposits. In 1977 (a year representative of recent experience), the rebate reduced the net assessment to 1/27 of one per cent [5].

From a corporate-finance perspective, rational bank managers must consider both explicit *and* implicit fees when analyzing the costs and benefits of deposit

---

another bank, which then assumes liability for the bank's deposits; or (3) it may operate the bank itself or reorganize it. FDIC officials strive to choose the approach that appears least expensive for the FDIC insurance fund [1].

insurance and when optimizing the amount of their bank's capital funds. Our approach exemplifies Kane's [7] "Regulatory Dialectic" in that the equilibrium value of deposit insurance—both for the bank and for the FDIC—depends on the joint responses of regulator and regulatee. Banks respond to the structure of implicit and explicit insurance premia set by the FDIC, and the FDIC adjusts its implicit and explicit fee structure to recover its costs and to achieve supplementary objectives of public policy. However, because of the deadweight losses involved, it is unlikely that the FDIC's interactive strategy is *socially* optimal. We discuss the interactive process but stop short of modeling optimal FDIC response.

I. Deposit Insurance and the Value of the Banking Firm

In the absence of bankruptcy costs, corporate income taxation, or other market imperfections, Modigliani and Miller (M&M) [15] have shown that in competitive capital markets the value of a firm is independent of its financial structure. Restoring one or more of these excluded conditions can produce an optimal debt-equity ratio. For example, M&M have also shown that allowing interest on debt to be tax-deductible provides an incentive (in the form of tax savings) for firms to substitute debt for equity in their financial structure. Kareken and Wallace [8] generate a debt-incentive effect by assuming that entry restrictions permit banks to earn monopoly profits by attaching transaction services to the debt claims held by depositors. By themselves, positive incentives for debt would produce a zero-equity corner solution. However, when bankruptcy is costly, increasing leverage (which, for a firm with a risky asset portfolio, increases the probability of bankruptcy) provides a growing offset to the incentives to expand debt. Under these twin conditions, a value-maximizing firm may reach an internal optimum, with positive equity in its financial structure[3] [11, 9, 4, 24]. This is illustrated in Figure 1.

In the diagram, V_u denotes the value of the firm in an unlevered state (pure equity) and the V curve shows how the value of the firm would vary with increasing leverage. At the point of zero equity (D^{max}), debt-capital by itself is sufficient to finance the firm's entire asset portfolio. In the case illustrated, the value of the firm is maximized at V^0 and D^0, which also represent optimal values for an uninsured bank.

Deposit Insurance Provided Free of Charge by an External Guarantor

In corporate finance, banks have traditionally been conceived of as more than just another business firm. They are alleged to offer a unique combination of product services. They hold some specialized assets, notably commercial loans, and issue some specialized liabilities, notably demand deposits. They operate under unusual regulatory restrictions, including entry limitations, interest-rate ceilings, reserve requirements, and governmental guarantees on their deposit-liabilities. In this paper, we analyze the effects of having a governmental agency

---

[3] Strictly speaking, an internal optimum occurs only if, at zero equity, the deadweight loss due to costly bankruptcy dominates the tax subsidy. However, the existence of an internal optimum is not critical to our analysis.

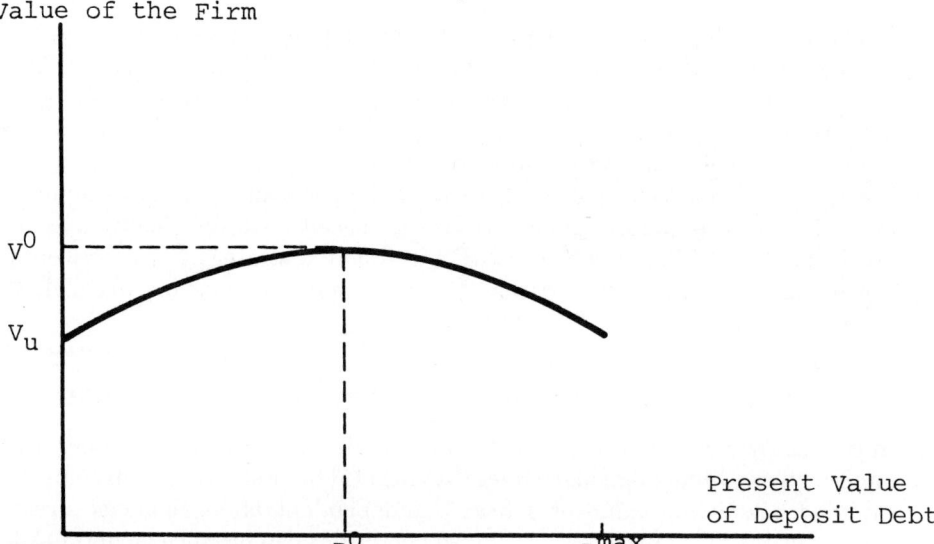

Figure 1. Value of the Banking Firm as a Function of Its Financial Structure with Costly Bankruptcy and Tax-Deductible Interest on Deposits

(the FDIC) guarantee a bank's debt. Under existing arrangements, only deposit liabilities are covered by insurance, and these only up to a specific limit per account. However, we abstract from these complications, by neglecting nondeposit debts and assuming that insurance coverage extends to *all* deposit balances. We also assume away any doubts about the ability or willingness of the guarantor (the FDIC) to meet its insurance obligations.

As the foundation of our subsequent analysis, we focus first on the case where FDIC insurance coverage is offered without charge; i.e., without either explicit fees or regulatory interference of any kind. With free deposit insurance, the FDIC commits itself to satisfy depositor claims in the event of bank insolvency without levying prior charges on the bank. In effect, free insurance reinstates the zero-equity corner solution that arises when bankruptcy is costless to the firm.

In Figure 2 we compare the value of the firm with free insurance (V_I) and without any insurance at all (V). At any level of deposits, the vertical distance between the two curves (V_I and V) portrays the value of free insurance as assessed by the banking firm. Merton [13] and Sharpe [22] join others in suggesting that the FDIC should charge an explicit insurance premium sufficient to exhaust this increase in value. When insurance fees are set according to this "fair-value" rule, the cum-insurance value of the bank, net of the explicit insurance premium, would coincide with its uninsured value at each and every level of deposits. With or without insurance, bank management that strives to maximize the value of the firm would under these circumstances operate at the debt level, D^0, and the firm would be worth V^0.

Although such a neutral insurance contract might arise in a competitive market for deposit insurance, it should be clear that a "fair-value" rule does little to persuade banks to accept FDIC regulation. This objective is euphemistically expressed in the FDIC's mandate from Congress, which focuses on protecting depositors and promoting sound banking practices.

To establish regulatory dominion, the FDIC must structure its insurance contract so that, on balance, deposit insurance offers a bank at least one opportunity to increase firm value above the bank's maximal value as an uninsured firm. In Figure 3, the boundary for bank indifference to deposit insurance is plotted as a horizontal line at V^0.

At the same time, maximum feasible increases in value are given by V_I, the locus of firm value under free insurance. As a way to close the opportunity set for illustrative purposes only, in drawing Figure 3 we assume that the FDIC insists that its insurance contracts carry incentives that prevent a bank from increasing

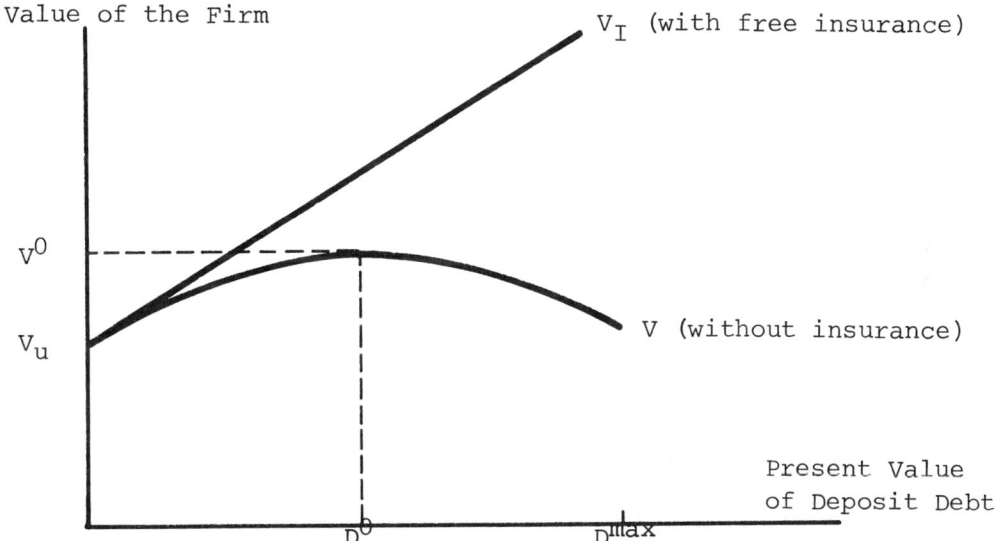

Figure 2. Impact of "free" Insurance on the Value of the Firm

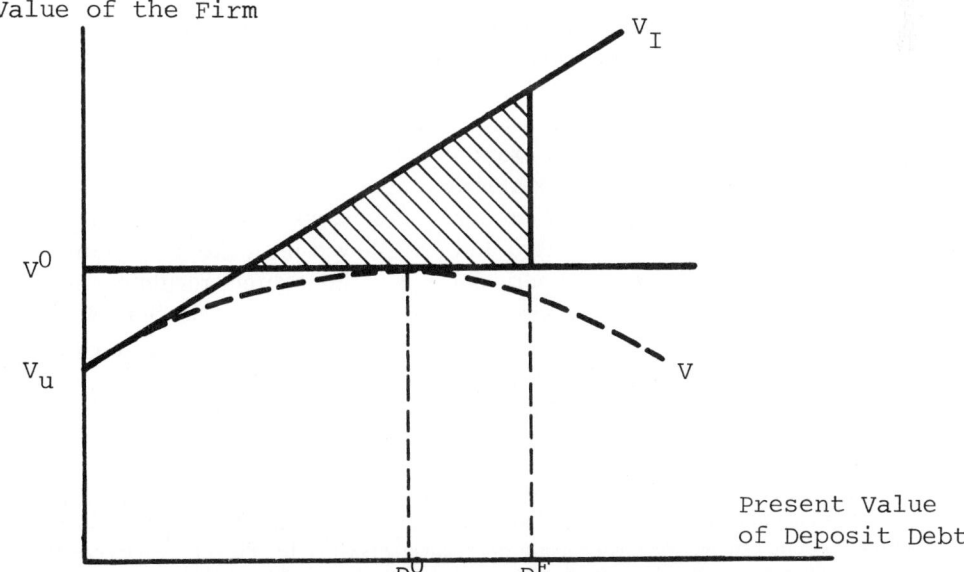

Figure 3. Limits on "Acceptable" Insurance Contracting

its deposit leverage beyond some maximum acceptable level, D^F. Taken together, these three boundaries mark off a shaded triangle of mutually acceptable contracting opportunities.

It is interesting to note that the "fair-value" pricing rules assumed by Merton [13], Sharpe [22], McCulloch [12], and Kareken and Wallace [8] do not permit contracts to be negotiated that would correspond to points strictly in the interior of this set.

The Value of the Banking Firm with FDIC Insurance and Regulation

In the real world, even uninsured banks are subject to regulation by state banking commissioners. To qualify for FDIC insurance, banks open themselves to federal examination and supervision.[4] Our model of FDIC behavior presumes that the FDIC imposes tougher restriction on a bank's activities and organization than state commissioners do. To keep the model simple, we neglect enforcement and compliance costs and assume that the FDIC's differentially severe regulation focuses along the single dimension of bank capital. In principle, other regulatory penalties may be subsumed in this regulatory-tax concept.

In the model, FDIC bank examiners appraise the economic value of the bank's assets and liabilities on an appointed date. The residual capital position (which includes an appropriate allowance for the value of the bank's charter or right to continue in business) is then compared to the FDIC's standard for capital adequacy, which may be unique for each bank. For example, a formula developed at the New York Federal Reserve Bank assigns a specific weight, ranging from zero to one, to each asset category and calculates the sum of these weighted values as the minimum level for capital adequacy. A more complex formula developed at the Board of Governors employs a liquidity test as well, making the standard for capital adequacy sensitive to the bank's mix of liabilities as well as its mix of assets.[5] In our model, we specify only that the standard is set by the FDIC and is known to bank management in advance of the examination date.

FDIC bank examinations place a bank into one of three basic states. These states range along the horizontal axis of Figure 4, which plots the probability density (conditional on the bank's current portfolio) against every possible value of the bank's capital on the next examination date.

Boundaries between different states are imposed by the FDIC. In state I, bank capital is judged to be *adequate*. In our model, banks with adequate capital are presumed to pose no moral hazard and are allowed until the next examination date to operate under broad supervision but without direct regulatory interference. When a bank's capital proves to be inadequate, its classification varies with the extent of the deficiency. As a condition for continued insurance (or to avoid undefined sanctions), we assume that in state II bank managers are asked to strengthen the bank's asset and liability portfolios to reduce its need for capital under the FDIC adequacy norms. Alternatively, the bank might be expected to

---

[4] In the modern U.S., many federal bank examiners operate under the auspices of the Comptroller of the Currency and the Federal Reserve. Moreover, in a few states the FDIC has experimented with letting the state banking commission perform examinations on its behalf. For convenience, the text portrays the FDIC as directly conducting examinations of all insured banks.

[5] Sinkey [23] offers a detailed discussion of standards for adequate bank capital.

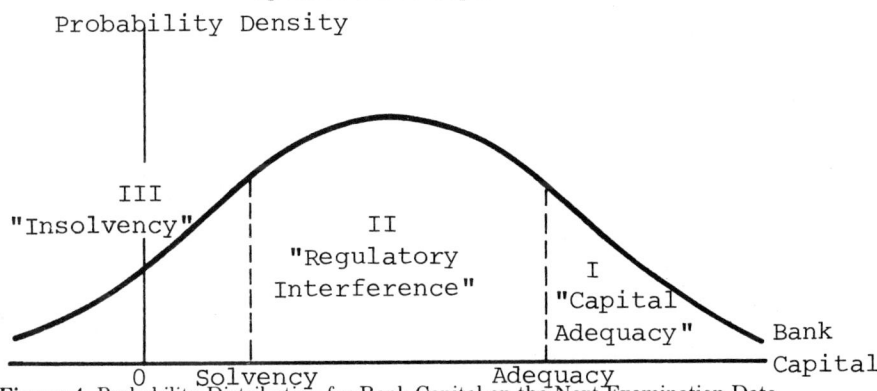

Figure 4. Probability Distribution for Bank Capital on the Next Examination Date

make up some of the equity deficiency by raising new capital or restricting current and subsequent dividend payments.

Whenever the *book value* of stockholder equity is assessed to be zero, the FDIC must declare the bank "technically insolvent." Since federal authorities can assist a bank to avoid this condition, a critical point cannot be strictly displayed in Figure 4. However, we assume that the FDIC forces a bank to technical insolvency only when the *market value* of its portfolio and physical assets (i.e., excluding the value of the charter) falls seriously below that of its deposit liabilities. This lets us bound state II at some positive fraction of the value of the bank's charter to continue in operation for future periods.

Although the FDIC must ask chartering authorities to close a technically insolvent bank, it need not liquidate it. The FDIC may permit the failed bank to merge with another institution; the FDIC may sell off the bank charter to another bank, which then accepts some subset of bank assets and assumes the failed bank's deposits; the FDIC may operate the bank itself for an interim period; it may assist the bank to reorganize under new management. Our model suggests that the FDIC would try to preserve the value of the bank charter, since the value of the charter reduces the FDIC's net liability to the depositors.

If the goal of the FDIC were only to minimize its own liability, the FDIC would pay off the depositors of a failed bank only as a last resort, and then only in markets where the costs of arranging a deposit assumption were high and/or the value of the bank's charter was very low. The FDIC would seek to effect a deposit assumption and asset transfer to one or more banks whenever this would be less than the costs of liquidating the bank.

Capital Regulation as an Implicit Premium for Deposit Insurance

For analytic convenience, we portray FDIC regulatory interference as restricting the set of profit opportunities that an affected bank's management may exploit in states II and III. We assume that throughout state II direct regulatory interference results in a reduction in firm value that increases with the size of the FDIC-assessed capital deficiency. In state III, we presume that the bank would be closed, with the residual value of its lost charter serving as the firm's cost of bankruptcy.

Prior to examination, the bank can, through its capital decision, influence the probabilities of ending up in states I, II, and III as well as the magnitude of the anticipated regulatory tax applicable in state II. The regulatory structure we describe reduces the bank's incentive to substitute deposit debt for capital, since increased leverage increases the expected costs of being discovered either to be insolvent or to have inadequate capital. Referring back to the V_I curve (shown originally in Figure 2), for every positive value of debt, the value of the insured firm cum-regulation would be reduced by the corresponding deadweight losses as indicated by the curve, V_{IR}, in Figure 5.

In the diagram, the vertical distance between the V_I and V_{IR} curves portrays the varying value of *implicit* FDIC premiums for insurance levied in the form of contingent regulatory interference accepted as a condition for insurance. The vertical distance between V_{IR} and V measures the net benefit to the firm from trading prospective losses from costly bankruptcy without insurance for FDIC regulation. In Figure 5, this net benefit is favorable to the firm at low debt levels, but unfavorable at high debt levels.

Optimal Capital Structure with Implicit and Explicit Insurance Premia

When the explicit premium is fixed per dollar of deposits, the cum-regulation value of the insured firm may be shown in Figure 5 simply as the curve V_{IR} reduced by the appropriate constant fraction (w) of deposit levels.

In the diagram, D^* denotes the optimal level of insured deposits with implicit and explicit insurance premia. The corresponding point (V^*) on the curve denoting the cum-insurance value of the banking firm net of the explicit premium (V_{IR}-wD) denotes the new optimum firm value. As noted previously, unless V^* is strictly greater than V^0 a value-maximizing firm would not voluntarily sign up for federal deposit insurance at all.

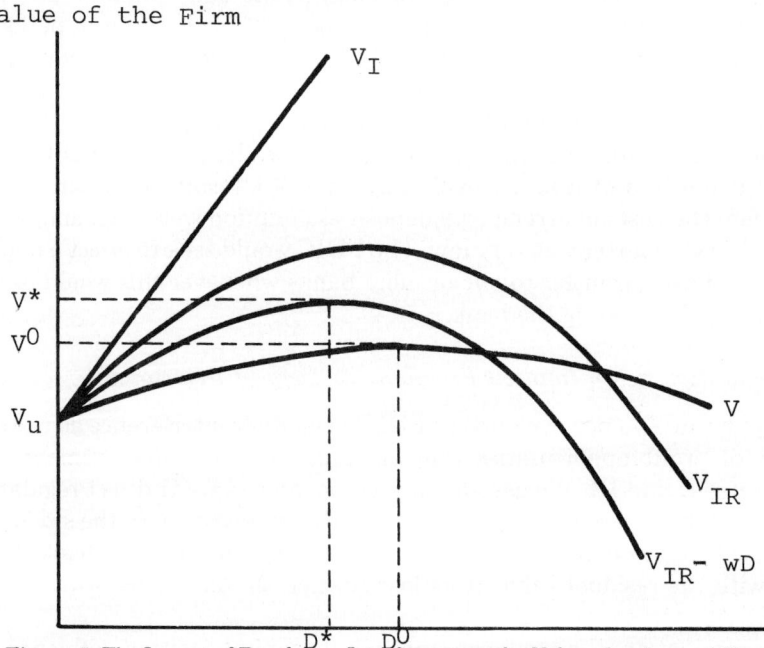

Figure 5. The Impact of Regulatory Interference on the Value of an Insured Banking Firm

Although our assumptions fix the size of the individual banking firm, in the real world the tax-cum-insurance net subsidy both helps to explain and serves to complicate regulatory policies with respect to entry, branching, mergers, and acquisitions. Supernormal profits rooted in this net subsidy tend to attract new competitors and to encourage existing firms to expand their scale of operations. If it is truly to manage its insurance liabilities, the FDIC cannot afford to be indifferent to entry and expansion in individual banking markets.

II. Summary and Implications

Exclusive reliance on an explicit flat-rate premium would interfere with the FDIC's simultaneous promotion of sound banking practices and federal regulatory oversight for nonmember banks. A value-maximizing nonmember bank would not join the FDIC if the explicit insurance premium per dollar exceeded the per-dollar tax subsidy on deposit borrowings. At flat rates below its break-even level, an insured bank would reap subsidies from taxes *and* insurance. In this situation, the combined subsidy would be a strictly increasing function of bank leverage.

To offset this structural incentive towards inordinate leverage, other authors (e.g., Scott and Mayer [21]) propose that the FDIC levy a risk-rated structure of explicit premia that would vary FDIC charges with a bank's portfolio risk. Recognizing the existence of implicit as well as explicit prices for FDIC insurance, we see that the FDIC currently achieves a comparable effect by employing a risk-rated structure of *implicit* premia in the form of regulatory interference. Regulatory standards for capital adequacy emerge as the critical element in the FDIC's pricing strategy, in that these standards determine the anticipated net value of deposit insurance to stockholders as a function of bank leverage.

Implications for the Capital-Shortage Controversy in Banking

Viewing capital standards as risk-rated implicit premia explains why managers of individual banks seem more concerned about capital standards than about the FDIC's explicit charges. These explicit charges serve mainly to align the overall FDIC subsidy to insured banks with the tax-exempt earnings of the agency's insurance fund.

Our model predicts that many insured banks would operate at leverage levels that closely border the FDIC's regulatory norm. At the margin, the net explicit subsidy for deposit debt is constant. Internal equilibrium is achieved only when this subsidy is offset by the risk-rated implicit premium. Since the implicit premium is triggered by proximity to regulatory standards for capital adequacy, this balance figures to be struck at a similar distance for every insured bank. This argument helps to explain why banks frequently shift on and off the FDIC's "problem list" in large numbers [23]. Their capital positions are carried across the adequacy threshold by unanticipated cyclical swings in economic activity.

REFERENCES

1. Ross E. Barnett, Paul M. Horvitz, and Stanley C. Silverberg, "Deposit Insurance: The Present System and Some Alternatives," *The Banking Law Journal*, 94 (April 1977), pp. 304–32.
2. H. Prescott Beighley, John H. Boyd, and Donald P. Jacobs, "Bank Equities and Investor Risk

Perceptions: Some Entailments for Capital Adequacy Regulation," *Journal of Bank Research*, 6 (Autumn 1975), pp. 190–207.

3. Roger Blair, and Arnold Heggestad, "Bank Portfolio Regulation and the Probability of Bank Failure," *Journal of Money, Credit and Banking*, 10 (February 1978), pp. 88–93.

4. Andrew H. Chen, "Recent Developments in the Cost of Debt Capital," *Journal of Finance*, 33 (June 1978), pp. 863–77.

5. Federal Deposit Insurance Corporation, *1977 Annual Report*, Washington: 1978.

6. Benjamin M. Friedman, and Peter Formuzis, "Bank Capital: The Deposit-Protection Incentive," *Journal of Bank Research*, 6 (Autumn 1975), pp. 208–18.

7. Edward J. Kane, "Good Intentions and Unintended Evil: The Case Against Selective Credit Allocation," *Journal of Money, Credit and Banking*, 9 (February 1977), pp. 55–69.

8. John H. Kareken, and Neil Wallace, "Deposit Insurance and Bank Regulation: A Partial-Equilibrium Exposition," *Journal of Business*, 51 (July 1978), pp. 413–38.

9. E. Han Kim, "A Mean-Variance Theory of Optimal Capital Structure and Corporate Debt Capacity," *Journal of Finance*, 33 (March 1978), pp. 45–63.

10. Michael Koehn, and Anthony M. Santomero, "Regulation of Bank Capital and Portfolio Risk," Working Paper No. 9–79 (mimeographed), Rodney White Center for Financial Research, The Wharton School, 1979.

11. Alan Kraus, and Robert Litzenberger, "A State-Preference Theory of Optimal Financial Leverage," *Journal of Finance*, 28 (September 1973), pp. 911–22.

12. J. Huston McCulloch, "Interest Rate Risk and Capital Adequacy for Traditional Banks and Financial Intermediaries," NBER Working Paper No. 237 (revised), Stanford, CA, July 1978.

13. Robert C. Merton, "An Analytic Derivation of the Cost of Deposit Insurance Loan Guarantees: An Application of Modern Option Pricing Theory," *Journal of Banking and Finance*, 1 (June 1977), pp. 3–11.

14. Robert C. Merton, "On the Cost of Deposit Insurance When There Are Surveillance Costs," *Journal of Business*, 51 (July 1978), pp. 439–52.

15. Franco Modigliani, and Merton Miller, "The Cost of Capital, Corporation Finance and the Theory of Investment," *American Economic Review*, 48 (June 1958), pp. 261–97.

16. Franco Modigliani, and Merton Miller, "Corporate Income Taxes and the Cost of Capital: A Correction," *American Economic Review*, 53 (June 1963), pp. 433–43.

17. Sam Peltzman, "Capital Investment in Commercial Banking and Its Relationship to Portfolio Regulation," *Journal of Political Economy*, 78 (Jan./Feb. 1970), pp. 1–26.

18. Richard A. Posner, "Taxation by Regulation," *Bell Journal of Economics and Management Science*, 1 (Spring 1971), pp. 22–50.

19. John J. Pringle, "The Capital Decision in Commercial Banks," *Journal of Finance*, 29 (June 1974), pp. 779–95.

20. Anthony M. Santomero, and Ronald D. Watson, "Determining the Optimal Capital Standards for the Banking Industry," *Journal of Finance*, 32 (September 1977), pp. 1267–82.

21. Kenneth E. Scott, and Thomas Mayer, "Risk and Regulation in Banking: Some Proposals for Deposit Insurance Reform," *Stanford Law Review*, 23 (May 1971), pp. 857–902.

22. William F. Sharpe, "Bank Capital Adequacy, Deposit Insurance and Security Values," *Journal of Financial and Quantitative Analysis*, 13 (November 1978), pp. 701–18.

23. Joseph F. Sinkey, Jr. *Problem and Failed Institutions in the Commerical Banking Industry*, Greenwich: JAI Press, 1979.

24. Stuart M. Turnbull, "Debt Capacity," *Journal of Finance*, 34 (September 1979), pp. 931–940.

CAPITAL REGULATION AND INSURED BANKS' CHOICE OF INDIVIDUAL LOAN DEFAULT RISKS

Mark J. FLANNERY*

University of Florida, Gainesville, FL 32611, USA

Received July 1988, final version received May 1989

How bankers choose the riskiness of their individual assets is an important question. It is well known that fixed-premium deposit insurance leads a bank to prefer a high-variance asset portfolio, but its effect on individual asset choice has not been carefully evaluated. This paper demonstrates how bank examination procedures and capital adequacy standards can make the value of a bank's deposit insurance contract concave in individual asset risks. Insured bankers may therefore have a rational preference (ceteris paribus) for relatively safe individual loans, even while they prefer risky portfolio returns. The model's implications for loan securitization and the Federal regulators' new risk-based capital standards are discussed.

1. Introduction

Understanding how financial intermediary firms ('banks') choose their portfolios is important for addressing a broad range of managerial, investor, and regulatory issues. The substantial existing literature on bank portfolio choice can be broadly divided into two categories. Initially, writers addressed the issue of *individual asset* selection, often as if banks were atomistic agents like any other capital market investor. Subsequently, Merton (1977) interpreted deposit insurance as a put option, and the bank investment literature shifted its focus to selecting the optimal level of *portfolio* risk. This aggregated view of the bank investment problem has tended to obscure the question of how individual assets are selected. The present paper combines the intuitive insights of Merton's approach to bank valuation with a more traditional concern about the individual assets in a bank's portfolio. I argue that the combination of loan examination procedures and capital adequacy regu-

*I acknowledge with thanks the helpful comments of Yuk-Shee Chan, Jennifer Conrad, Robert Eisenbeis, Christopher James, George Pennacchi, Anthony Saunders, Richard Startz, and finance seminar participants at INSEAD, the London Business School, and the University of North Carolina. Financial support was provided by the North Carolina Business Foundation. This paper was completed while I was at the University of North Carolina and a visiting professor at the London Business School.

Journal of Monetary Economics 24 (1989) 235–258. North-Holland

lation leads insured banks to prefer relatively low-risk individual loans (*ceteris paribus*), even while they pursue high portfolio risk in order to maximize their deposit insurance put option value.

Prior to Merton's (1977) path-breaking contribution, the bank investment literature focused primarily on the selection of individual assets.[1] The 'microeconomic' strand of this literature tended to emphasize market power [e.g., Klein (1977), Monti (1971, 1972)], firm liquidity needs [e.g., Edgeworth (1888), Porter (1961)], or scale and scope economies in originating loans [e.g., Baltensperger and Milde (1977), Sealey and Lindley (1977)] as important determinants of bank portfolio composition. The 'finance' strand of the literature frequently focused on firm risk aversion [e.g., Parkin (1970), Hart and Jaffee (1974)] or the impact of deposit insurance and regulatory restrictions [e.g., Kahane (1977), Blair and Heggestad (1978), Koehn and Santomero (1980), Kim and Santomero (1988)].

Klein (1971) and Monti (1971, 1972) demonstrated that a risk-neutral bank with market power will maximize its monopoly rents with a unique portfolio composition. An alternative way to produce a unique optimal portfolio allocation is to assume that risk-averse banks operate as atomistic investors in the capital market. An excellent example of this approach is Hart and Jaffee (1974), whose bank chooses asset and liability portfolio shares from a set of exogenously specified alternatives. The unique portfolio composition implies an endogenous bankruptcy probability. Because the optimal portfolio is affected by regulatory constraints, these models can indicate the impact of regulation on bank safety and soundness.

These portfolio-selection models suffer from two serious shortcomings. First, bank risk aversion represents an awkward assumption for at least some banking firms. [Santomero (1984, pp. 581–582) discusses the issues involved in selecting a bank objective function.] Diversified bank shareholders should be indifferent to the variance of their individual security returns, and managerial risk aversion can be substantially mitigated via appropriate compensation packages, the takeover mechanism, and so forth. At least for large, publicly traded banking firms – which represent the bulk of the industry's assets and innovational ability – it therefore seems important to develop an alternative firm objective function. Second, portfolio selection models specify that bank asset returns are exogenously determined. But this assumption fails to recognize that bankers design and negotiate the securities they eventually hold in their own portfolios. Even though permissible bank assets are largely limited to 'loans', the risk level of these loans can be endogenized by varying collateral, maturity, or restrictive covenants. In other words, a model of bank

---

[1]Baltensperger (1980, esp. pp. 19–29) and Santomero (1984, esp. pp. 586–590) provide reviews of the earlier literature.

asset selection should recognize that banks frequently *originate* securities with endogenous characteristics, as opposed to simply *investing* in assets with exogenous properties.

Merton's (1977) formulation of deposit insurance as a put option almost totally suppresses the question of bank portfolio composition. Operating in perfect capital markets, insured banks seek to maximize the value of their deposit insurance options by selecting the riskiest available asset portfolio. Any asset combination that produces a particular level of portfolio risk is equally valuable to bank shareholders. Subsequent papers [including Merton (1978), Buser, Chen, and Kane (1981), Marcus (1984), and Pyle (1986)] specified conditions under which insured banks would seek less than maximal portfolio risk – but still without concern for the properties of individual assets within the portfolio.

Neither historical perspective on the bank investment problem reflects the strong conventional wisdom that bankers prefer low-risk individual assets. That is, a 'bankable' asset is one with low *ex ante* default probability. This conventional wisdom is consistent with Fama's (1985) contention that uninformed capital market participants can infer something positive about a firm's credit quality from the simple observation that a bank has lent to the firm:

> Bank loans are short-term and the renewal process triggers periodic evaluations of the organization's ability to meet low-priority fixed payoff contracts. Positive renewal signals from bank loans mean that other agents with higher-priority fixed payoff claims *need not undertake similar costly evaluations of their claims.* Bank signals are credible since the bank backs its opinions with resources, or by declining resources. [Fama (1985, p. 36), emphasis added]

If bankers prefer relatively low-risk loans (for whatever reason), their willingness to take a 'low-priority fixed payoff' claim implies that senior claimants are subject to very low default risk.[2] By contrast, if bankers will accept any default risk at an appropriate price (as would diversified, unregulated capital market lenders), simply observing a loan renewal conveys little to outsiders.

This paper presents a model of bank portfolio selection that is embedded in Merton's (1977) basic framework. Individual asset riskiness influences the insurance put option's value because the bank's required capitalization varies with the level of low-quality loans detected in its portfolio. (I argue that this property results from the loan examination process and capital adequacy

---

[2]Empirical support for this view is provided by James (1987), who reports that the announcement of a bank borrowing arrangement is associated with positive excess returns to the borrower's common stock. Lummer and McConnell (1988) report that the initial loan announcement causes no excess return, but the market interprets subsequent loan renewals as positive signals.

regulations.) Unlike the standard analysis of FDIC insurance as a put, therefore, increased asset risk has an ambiguous impact on the value of a bank's deposit insurance coverage: it *raises* the option's value directly, but it also *reduces* option value by lowering the strike price. The option value's concavity substitutes for earlier models' utility function concavity as a device for generating a unique optimal portfolio. The paper thus unifies the two prior strands of the bank investment literature – the option pricing strand and the risk-averse investor strand – and identifies a new channel by which capital adequacy regulations can influence bank risk. This view of bank portfolio selection also broadens the earlier literature by emphasizing the endogeneity of bank loan risk characteristics. Finally, the model has implications for the recent phenomenon of loan securitization.

The paper is organized as follows. Section 2 presents a simple model of insured bank profit maximization with risk neutrality and perfect competition. The model illustrates several well-known conclusions and provides a vehicle for relating this paper's innovations to the existing literature. The loan examination process is described in section 3, which explains how loan classifications combine with (existing and proposed) capital standards to make permissible bank leverage depend on the riskiness of a bank's individual loans. The next section indicates how banks will originate loans with (endogenous) risk characteristics that maximize the value of their deposit insurance put option. An illustrative model of the maximization process is presented. Section 5 then solves a 'standard' portfolio selection model in which asset return characteristics are exogenously fixed. The bank chooses portfolio shares that maximize its put option value, again taking account of its risk-sensitive leverage restrictions. The implications of the model for the recent phenomenon of loan securitization are described in section 6. The final section summarizes and concludes.

2. A model of bank maximization

The economy is populated exclusively by risk-neutral investors. Deficit spending units borrow to finance current consumption and/or investment plans, and all such loans have the same (finite) maturity. Loan returns are normally distributed, with individual loans differing in the variance of their final payout. Bankers may make individual loans with any desired level of risk (i.e., return variance), but competition with other bankers and with nonbank lenders assures that each loan carries a contract rate that provides an expected return equal to the riskless rate of interest (R_f). Banks fund their loan portfolios partly with owners' equity and partly with deposit funds. The one advantage bankers have over other capital market participants is free Federal deposit insurance on all their liabilities, so the contract rate on deposits is R_f. Banks hold no reserves against deposits.

2.1. The bank's decisions

Each representative bank is assumed to have an exogenously fixed amount of equity (K). Federal deposit insurance makes depositors willing to supply an unlimited amount of deposits at the riskless rate, regardless of the bank's asset risk or leverage. With a (nondegenerate) normally distributed return on the loan portfolio (R_L), the bank has a nonzero probability of bankruptcy associated with any positive level of deposits (D). Risk-neutral bank shareholders then seek to maximize their expected end-of-period wealth (W) by choosing D and the loan portfolio's riskiness (σ_p). Expected terminal wealth is given by

$$E(W) = \int_{R_L^*}^{\infty} \left[\tilde{R}_L (D+K) - R_f D \right] f(\tilde{R}_L) \, dR_L, \tag{1}$$

where

R_f = one plus the riskless interest rate,
$\tilde{R}_L$ = one plus the realized loan rate,
R_L^* = $R_f D / (D+K)$ is the lowest loan return for which depositors can be fully repaid, and
$f(\tilde{R}_L)$ = the density function for $\tilde{R}_L$ (which depends on σ_p).

Dividing (1) through by K gives the expected return on invested capital,

$$E(W/K) = E(R_E) = \int_{R_L^*}^{\infty} \left[\tilde{R}_L (D+K)/K - R_f (D/K) \right] f(\tilde{R}_L) \, dR_L, \tag{2}$$

which bank shareholders are assumed to maximize. Adding the bank's expected return in the bankruptcy states to (2), and then subtracting out the same quantity, yields a useful alternative expression for the shareholders' maximand:

$$E(R_E) = \int_{-\infty}^{\infty} \left[\tilde{R}_L (D+K)/K - R_f (D/K) \right] f(\tilde{R}_L) \, dR_L$$

$$- \int_{-\infty}^{R_L^*} \left[\tilde{R}_L (D+K)/K - R_f (D/K) \right] f(\tilde{R}_L) \, dR_L. \tag{3}$$

Because capital market equilibrium requires $E(R_L) = R_f$,[3] (3) can be rewritten

---

[3] This equilibrium condition for loan pricing assumes that bankers are collectively 'small' relative to the uninsured capital market. Any benefits of subsidized FDIC insurance therefore accrue to bank shareholders, rather than being conveyed to their customers. This is the standard assumption employed in the existing literature [e.g., Merton (1977), Buser, Chen, and Kane (1981), Marcus (1984), or Pyle (1986)]. Flannery and James (1989) evaluate the implications of alternative assumptions about banking industry structure and entry for the impact of deposit insurance on bank risk.

as

$$E(R_E) = R_f + \int_{-\infty}^{R_L^*} \left[R_f(D/K) - \tilde{R}_L(D+K)/K \right] f(\tilde{R}_L) \, dR_L. \quad (4)$$

The expected return to equityholders in (4) has two parts. First, invested capital must earn the riskless rate. [If $E(R_E) < R_f$, equityholders would issue no deposits and invest their unlevered capital directly in loans.] The second component of (4) is the excess of contractual debt obligations over earnings in the bankruptcy states. This term corresponds to Merton's (1977) option value of Federal deposit insurance.

The Federal deposit insurance option is written on the bank's asset portfolio, with an exercise price equal to the (end-of-period) face value of outstanding deposits. This option value, which is expressed per dollar of invested equity in (4), can be rewritten in terms of a put option value (V):

$$E(R_E) = R_f + V(\sigma_p, R_f(D/K)), \quad (5)$$

where $R_f(D/K)$ is the exercise price. The put option's value is increasing in both asset variance and the exercise price,

$$V_1 > 0, \qquad V_2 > 0.$$

Accordingly, in the absence of restrictive regulations, expected bank profits will be maximized by selecting the greatest feasible levels of asset risk (σ_p) and financial leverage (D/K).

2.2. Implications for capital adequacy and deposit insurance pricing

Several well-known consequences of deposit insurance are readily illustrated in this framework. First, (5) makes it clear that the 'actuarially fair' FDIC premium equals the option value V. With this cost of deposit insurance, equityholders earn an expected return just equal to R_f. Given the dependence of V on σ_p and D, risk-related insurance premia would have to vary similarly with changes in those decision variables.

Second, regulators charged with assuring financial safety and soundness are unwilling to allow private bankers unrestricted choice of their σ_p and D/K. Kahane (1977), Blair and Heggestad (1978), and Koehn and Santomero (1980) have shown how regulatory restrictions on permissible assets and/or capital ratios can be used to influence the probability of bank failure. In other words, regulators attempt to bound σ_p and (D/K) in ways that reduce the attainable option value in (5). Buser, Chen, and Kane (1981) interpret the private cost of these regulatory restrictions as an *implicit* insurance premium. Without such regulations (of which capital adequacy is an important component) the deposit insurance fund would not be viable.

Finally, Sharpe (1978) demonstrates that 'adequate' capital is the amount that makes the insurance premium actuarially fair. A risk-related capital standard can be interpreted as an additional constraint on bank maximization of the form

$$\ell = \ell(\sigma_p), \qquad \ell' < 0, \tag{6}$$

where $\ell(\sigma_p)$ is the permissible leverage as a function of portfolio risk. Under this type of capital constraint the bank's insurance option value would become

$$V = V\big(\sigma_p, R_f \ell(\sigma_p)\big). \tag{7}$$

Unlike the standard option in (5), this put option's value can be *concave* in σ_p. Regulators can constrain the bank's maximum attainable option value (V^*) by choosing a $\ell(\sigma_p)$ schedule that equates V^* with the insurance premium for all possible levels of σ_p.

3. Loan examinations and capital adequacy regulation

U.S. bank regulators have never imposed a capital standard that varies with portfolio risk, as in (6). However, they have recently agreed with central banks in the Group of Ten to impose a risk-related capital standard under which banks must hold more capital against assets that are considered more volatile. [See Board of Governors (January 19, 1989).] In other words, new Federal regulations make permissible bank leverage vary inversely with the risk of individual assets in the portfolio. This new risk-related capital standard resembles historical U.S. procedures, under which bank examination standards and capital adequacy regulations are combined to vary permissible leverage with the perceived quality of *individual* bank assets. The bank examination process evaluates individual asset risks, and the examiner's overall assessment of asset quality influences the leverage a bank is permitted to undertake. This type of (historic and prospective) capital regulation makes bankers select particular loan risk levels that maximize the option value of their FDIC insurance.

3.1. The loan examination process

For purposes of capital adequacy regulation, bank 'capital' has historically included equity accounts, subordinated debentures, *and* the allowance for loan and lease losses (ALL).[4] The ALL account is intended to reflect the management's best estimate of future loan losses from the existing portfolio.[5] As a check on these loan quality assessments, 'an evaluation of capital adequacy is one of the major purposes of a bank or bank holding company examination' [Federal Reserve *Commercial Bank Examination Manual* (section 303.1, p. 5)]. That is, the examination seeks to assure that the bank's ALL fairly represents the loan portfolio's true condition.

This is a substantial task because many bank assets have no secondary market from which current value can be determined readily. Consequently, a substantial proportion of the bank examination process is devoted to assessing the credit quality of an institution's loan portfolio. Examiners seek to identify loans whose timely and full repayment is unlikely. Such loans are 'classified' or 'criticized' in the examination report.[6] The ALL must be sufficient to cover (at least) the anticipated losses on classified loans, and some proportion of these

---

[4] In fact, a bank's reported ALL includes both estimated future loan losses and additional charges that are made to minimize Federal income tax liabilities. The ALL thus has three separate components:

    a valuation portion,
    a deferred tax portion,
    a contingency portion.

This paper deals with the valuation portion alone, which banks report in their quarterly Income and Condition Reports as a contra-account to total loans. The latter two components reflect differences between the loan loss provision reported for tax purposes and that reported in other financial statements. For further details, see Schweitzer (1975) or the *Comptrollers Handbook for the National Bank Examiners* (Feb. 1984, section 217.1, pp. 1–2).

[5] The new risk-based capital standard [Board of Governors (1989)] relegates general loss reserves to the Second Tier of capital, and limits the proportion of capital that may be composed of such reserves. This treatment of the ALL may be revised before the final (1992) implementation of risk-based capital standards.

[6] The Federal Reserve (1985, section 217.1, p. 2) *Commercial Bank Examination Manual* defines three categories of classified loans:

    '*Substandard Assets* – A substandard asset is inadequately protected by the current sound worth and paying capacity of the obligor or of the collateral pledge, if any... They are characterized by the distinct possibility that the bank will sustain some loss if the deficiencies are not corrected.

    '*Doubtful Assets* – An asset classified doubtful has all the weaknesses inherent in one classified substandard with the added characteristic that the weaknesses make collection or liquidation in full, on the basis of currently existing facts, conditions, and values, highly questionable and improbable.

    '*Loss Assets* – Assets classified loss are considered uncollectible and of such little value that their continuance as bankable assets is not warranted. This classification does not mean that the asset has absolutely no recovery or salvage value, but rather it is not practical or desirable to defer writing off this basically worthless asset even though partial recovery may be effected in the future.'

anticipated losses are (formally or informally) deducted from the regulator's assessment of bank capital. By contrast, however, no recognition is given to credits whose values have increased above their acquisition cost.[7]

The examination process is thus one-sided in an important way: it *selectively marks to market* bank loan assets. The regulatory assessment of adequate capital recognizes the effect of credits whose market values have fallen (due to increased default probability), while loans whose values have risen continue to be valued at historic cost.[8]

3.2. Defining 'adequate' capital

Regulators have offered broad guidelines about what constitutes 'adequate' capital, but each bank's permissible leverage is in fact defined on a case-by-case basis. The extent of classified assets has an important influence on the level of capital a bank is required to hold. For example, the Board of Governors explains:

> In the assessment of capital adequacy, *asset quality considerations are especially critical*. These include the risk composition and profile of the loan portfolio, credit and sovereign risk concentrations and the level and severity of examiner classified and criticized assets. Before an overall assessment of capital adequacy can be made, therefore, examiners must take into account all of these factors, *including, in particular, the level and severity of classified assets*. [January 24, 1986, Press Release, p. 22, emphasis added]

This perspective on low-quality assets reflects a general regulatory view that bank capital should be conceptually divided into two components: capital required to absorb known loan problems and capital required to cover unanticipated developments elsewhere on the balance sheet (unforeseen credit

---

[7]Borrowers whose loan obligations have risen in value have an incentive to refinance. The bank will retain these loans at the initial contract rate if some market imperfection makes it infeasible for borrowers to renegotiate. Alternatively, if the loan contract includes appropriate prepayment penalties, the bank will reap the benefits of creditors' quality improvements.

[8]Several readers have incorrectly conjectured that this institutional arrangement should make bank equity systematically sell at a *premium over* book value, which has not occurred (at least for large banks) during the past decade. What must be realized is that the ALL, like other reserve accounts, is *included in* 'book equity'. Classifying a loan may alter the composition of bank equity (between retained earnings and the ALL), but does not change the total book value of equity. By contrast, of course, the market value of equity promptly reflects new information about bank asset values. It is the regulatory treatment of classified loans, not their accounting treatment, that influences *ex ante* bank risk preferences. See the following section.

losses, interest rate, and other operating risks, etc.).[9] This view is also represented in the new U.S. risk-related capital standards:

> General provisions or general loan-loss reserves are created against the
> possibility of future losses. Where they are not ascribed to particular
> assets and do not reflect a reduction in the valuation of particular assets,
> these reserves qualify for inclusion in capital... Where, however, provi-
> sions have been created *against identified losses or in respect of a demon-
> strable deterioration in the value of particular assets*, they are not freely
> available to meet unidentified losses which may subsequently arise else-
> where in the portfolio and *do not possess an essential characteristic of
> capital*. Such specific or earmarked provisions should therefore not be
> included in the capital base. [Committee on Banking Regulations (July
> 1988, p. 6), emphasis added]

When the U.S. regulations are fully implemented in 1992, it appears that
banks will be required to deduct from measured capital any loan loss al-
lowances associated with specific problem loans. An increase in classified loans
will therefore reduce a bank's regulatory capital, with corresponding implications for the scale of its borrowed obligations.

Existing and pending institutional arrangements thus constitute a type of
risk-related capital standard in which *individual asset* risks negatively influence
permissible leverage. A portfolio of loans with higher return variances will
tend to generate a higher volume of classified assets, and regulators remove
some portion of classified assets from their estimate of available bank capital.
Because the loan examination process *selectively* marks to market loans whose
values have declined, a portfolio of riskier (that is, more variable) loans
therefore requires higher capitalization.

3.3. Modeling the capital adequacy constraint

The model presented in section 2 requires only slight modification to include
this connection between asset risk and permissible leverage. All the assumptions underlying that model continue to hold, except that now the bank's
decision horizon is assumed to be two periods (rather than one), and all loans

---

[9]Historically, the examining agencies formally adjusted a bank's book capital ratio to reflect
perceived loan quality. [See Altman (1985, p. 502), Hempel, Coleman, and Simonson (1983, pp.
300–302), or Sinkey (1986, p. 529).] For example, FDIC examiners computed a Net Capital Ratio
(NCR) defined as

$$NCR = [K - L - D - S]/[A - L - D - S],$$

where K = book capital, L = assets classified 'loss', D = assets classified 'doubtful', S = assets
classified 'substandard', and A = total assets. Sinkey (1978) shows that this capital measure was
the best predictor of membership on the FDIC's problem bank list.

and deposits have a fixed maturity of two periods. R_f should also be interpreted as the two-period riskless rate. The model has three dates. At $t = 0$, the bank assembles its loan portfolio. At $t = 1$, an examination occurs, losing loans are marked to market, and the capital adequacy standard is applied. At $t = 2$, loans and deposits repay and the bank is terminated.

Consider a loan with return standard deviation σ_i. Initially, this loan is priced to yield an expected return R_f. As time proceeds and new information arrives about the borrower, however, the loan's expected return will rise or fall. When examiners arrive at $t = 1$, there is some probability they will find it has fallen in value enough to be classified. Let the probability of this occurring be given by the function $c(\sigma_i)$, with $c'(\sigma_i) > 0$. Then in a portfolio of N equal-sized loans the expected dollar value of classified assets (C) will be

$$C = \sum_{i=1}^{N} \frac{c(\sigma_i)}{N} (D + K). \tag{8}$$

There are two important points to emphasize about (8). First, the dollar volume of loan classifications increases with the riskiness of individual assets. Second, classifications depend *linearly* on portfolio composition. Because return covariances are ignored, classified loans do not fully reflect portfolio risk.

Regulators are assumed to require a minimum amount of unencumbered capital as protection against unforeseen risks. Following a bank examination, capital adequacy is assessed by subtracting from gross capital some proportion (β) of classified loans. Banks may issue liabilities up to a multiple of this unencumbered capital. Permissible leverage is thus implicitly given by

$$(D + K) = M(K - \beta C), \tag{9}$$

where M is the leverage permitted on unencumbered capital and β is the proportion of classified loans subtracted from book capital.[10] Substituting (8) into (9) and re-arranging gives the permissible leverage a bank expects to have at $t = 1$ as a function of the asset risk it selects at $t = 0$:

$$\frac{D}{K} \equiv d(S) = \frac{M}{1 + \beta M \Gamma} - 1, \tag{10}$$

---

[10] The model's intuition requires that an increase in σ_i causes more loans to be classified, which seems uncontroversial. However, different types of loans (e.g., consumer vs. commercial, domestic vs. foreign) or banks with different levels of collection expertise might have different values of β. One extreme example of this differentiation is the statutory requirement that classified foreign loans to countries that are subject to substantial transfer risk have $\beta = 1$. See Federal Reserve (1985, section 708) *Commercial Bank Examination Manual*.

where S is a vector of loan standard deviations in the bank's portfolio and

$$\Gamma = \sum_{i=1}^{N} \frac{c(\sigma_i)}{N}.$$

Note that $d'(S) < 0$, indicating that more leverage (that is, a higher exercise price for the deposit insurance option) can be attained only with less asset risk.

Substituting this leverage constraint (10) into (5) gives a well-defined maximization problem: at $t = 0$, the banker selects a portfolio of loans to maximize her expected return on equity.[11,12] The banker's return is importantly affected by the value of her deposit insurance option, which depends on permissible leverage (10).

4. Optimal endogenous loan risks

Unlike many other capital market investors (e.g., mutual funds), bankers generally undertake meaningful negotiations with a borrower before making a loan. Loan terms can be adjusted (with compensating variations in the contract rate) to influence risk if either the borrower or the bank wishes to do so. Therefore, an important component of a banker's portfolio selection problem is her ability to customize loan contracts to provide the desired level of risk. The most general form of the maximization problem in (5) would permit the banker to select individual loan risks (σ_i), pairwise loan covariances (ρ_{ij}), and individual asset portfolio shares (X_i). This is a complex problem

[11] When the banker is assembling her asset portfolio at $t = 0$, I assume that she plans (expects) to satisfy capital adequacy regulations at $t = 1$, though there is no feature of the model to assure this. [Note that a sufficiently severe penalty for banks with inadequate capital would make it rational for bankers to plan on satisfying (10).] The analysis in the text makes two additional assumptions about actions at $t = 1$. First, the possibility that examiners would close the bank after completing their examination is ignored. Second, bank owners may not add any new equity at $t = 1$, nor may they sell 'winner' loans to compensate for the examiner selectively marking the 'losers' to market. (This inability to sell seasoned loans seems quite realistic, given the potential for adverse selection by an informed initial lender.)

[12] Another, more complex, way to model the interaction between examinations and capital adequacy would incorporate the time dimension more explicitly. With correlated loan returns, actual classifications will be distributed around their expected value (8) even for large values of N. Thus, the option's value is not determined until *after* the assets have been put into place. If adequate capital is assessed using the actual classifications, permissible leverage (10) becomes a random variable at the time asset risks are selected by the bank. Therefore, the maximization problem at $t = 0$ becomes

$$\max_{\{\sigma_i\}} \Psi = E\left(V\left[\sigma_p, R_f \tilde{\delta}\right]\right),$$

where the random variable $\tilde{\delta}$ is the realization of $d(S)$ in (10). In other words, the bank chooses asset risks to maximize its expected option value, though the actual option value will not be determined until $t = 1$.

with no particularly enlightening general solution. But the model's basic intuition can be illustrated under more restrictive assumptions.

4.1. A simplified model solution

Assume that the correlation coefficient between all pairs of possible loans is exogenously fixed at ρ. Under plausible circumstances, it will then be optimal to assemble a loan portfolio composed entirely of loans with a single default risk σ_i.[13] As $N \to \infty$ the loan portfolio's variance goes to

$$\sigma_p^2 = \rho\sigma_i^2, \tag{11}$$

and permissible leverage is

$$d(S) = d(\sigma_i) = \frac{M}{1 + \beta Mc(\sigma_i)} - 1. \tag{12}$$

Substituting (11) and (12) into (5) shows how individual loan riskiness influences the expected return on bank equity:

$$E(R_E) = R_f + V\left(\sigma_i\sqrt{\rho}, R_f d(\sigma_i)\right). \tag{13}$$

Bank shareholders choose a loan risk class (σ_i) at $t = 0$ which maximizes the expected value of their deposit insurance put option. Maximizing (13) with respect to σ_i yields

$$V_1\sqrt{\rho} + V_2 d' = 0. \tag{14}$$

With $V_1 > 0$, $V_2 > 0$, and $d' < 0$, (14) can yield an interior solution, σ_i^*, for suitable parameter values.

The novel implication here is that *an insured, regulated bank may prefer a unique default risk for the individual loans on its books*. The permissible leverage function $d(\sigma_i)$ conveys a comparative advantage to banks in funding loans of one particular riskiness, because that default-risk level maximizes their deposit insurance option value. The intuition underlying this conclusion is straightforward. A bank's option value increases with asset risk, *ceteris paribus*.

---

[13] Because σ_i is freely adjustable, any level of portfolio risk can be attained with a single loan risk class. The bank will then choose the portfolio that permits it the greatest degree of leverage. If the classification function $c(\sigma_i)$ is concave, two (or more) loan risk classes will permit more leverage than a single risk class located between the two. But the choice of two different loan types may also provide diversification, which reduces portfolio variance. Whether the single-risk portfolio will be preferred then depends on the local convexity of the put option valuation formula, relative to the concavity of $c(\sigma_i)$.

However, when permissible leverage (which also increases option value) is negatively related to asset risk, an increase in σ_i has an ambiguous impact on V. The optimal default risk balances the positive (direct) impact of asset risk on V against its negative (indirect) impact via permissible leverage.[14]

4.2. Simulation results

It would be encouraging if reasonable model parameters implied 'realistic' levels of optimal loan default risk. To investigate this, take the classification function to be

$$c(\sigma_i) = N(-A/\sigma_i), \tag{15}$$

where A is a positive constant and N is the c.d.f. of a standard unit normal. According to (15), a loan with standard deviation σ_i will be classified if its value falls A percent below par. This is more likely to occur the higher is σ_i. A lower value of A corresponds to more stringent examination standards.

Substituting (15), (11), and (12) into (5) gives a specific maximand that can be solved for alternative parameters values. Figs. 1 and 2 plot the put option's value per dollar of equity against discrete values of σ_i and for alternative combinations of the other model parameters. Since the model embodies no charter value for the bank beyond what is earned at $t = 2$, Merton's (1977) model would indicate that the put option's value increases monotonically in portfolio variance. In this model, however, the risk sensitivity of permissible leverage induces a local maximum at a relatively low σ_i. For sufficiently high levels of portfolio variance, the direct effect of variance on option value becomes dominant. This pattern emerges for a variety of parameter values (not all of which are illustrated here).

If banks are unrestricted by portfolio regulations, figs. 1 and 2 indicate that they will take maximum advantage of mispriced deposit insurance by seeking maximal portfolio risk. But very high values of σ_i are unlikely to be either feasible or privately optimal. Prudential bank regulation effectively limits

---

[14]If the bank in this model could choose loan correlations as well as σ_i, it would select $\rho = 1$ to maximize portfolio variance. But suppose regulators also consider asset correlations in determining permissible leverage. Then (10) would be rewritten as

$$d = d(S, \rho), \tag{10'}$$

with $d_1 < 0$ and $d_2 < 0$. Condition (14) is then rewritten as

$$E(R_L) = R_f + V(\sigma_i\sqrt{\rho}, d(S, \rho)). \tag{13'}$$

Maximizing (14') with respect to σ_i and ρ yields the first-order conditions

$$V_1\sqrt{\rho} + V_2 d_1 = 0, \tag{14a}$$

$$\tfrac{1}{2}V_1\sigma_i/\sqrt{\rho} + V_2 d_2 = 0, \tag{14b}$$

which can be solved for interior optimum values of both σ_i and ρ.

banks to holding fixed-income claims on their customers. From a private managerial perspective, monitoring costs and moral hazard problems increase substantially with loan risk, which creates an incentive to avoid extremely risky debt-like claims. [See, for example, Stiglitz and Weiss (1981).] Moreover, there are strong, though largely unwritten, conventions among regulators about what constitutes a loan of 'bankable' quality. If we take the 'relevant range' of asset risks as $\sigma_i < 0.15$ (or so), the FDIC put option is roughly concave in σ_i for all the cases illustrated in figs. 1 and 2. In short, simulation results indicate that historical examination and capital adequacy controls could largely explain the observed tendency of insured banks to specialize in relatively low-risk assets.

Figs. 1 and 2 indicate that the option value increases in maximum permissible leverage (M). The option is also rather sensitive to the regulator's treatment of classified loans: reducing β from 1.0 (in fig. 1) to 0.5 (in fig. 2) substantially raises the attainable option value and reduces the range of σ_i values for which the leverage sensitivity dominates the option's value.[15]

Finally, these (and other) simulation results indicate the following comparative static properties for the simplified model:

1. $\partial \sigma_i^* / \partial \beta < 0$. An increase in β reduces the optimal portfolio risk. As regulators penalize permissible leverage more aggressively for classified loans, bankers reduce their loan risks in an effort to protect their ability to lever equity capital with deposits.
2. $\partial \sigma_i^* / \partial A > 0$. A higher A indicates that examiners will classify a smaller proportion of loans, *ceteris paribus*. As the classification standard weakens, the leverage penalty for high-risk assets declines, which leads bankers to take on greater portfolio risks.
3. $\partial \sigma_i^* / \partial M < 0$. An increase in the maximum permissible leverage reduces portfolio risk. This occurs because each dollar of equity is more valuable the higher is M. Bankers are therefore more reluctant to impair capital via classified loans when M is large.

To summarize, simulations illustrate two important dimensions of the model. First, its implied loan risk levels are reasonably close to reality. Second, changes in the regulatory environment plausibly influence the preferred level of loan risk.

---

[15]Comparing figs. 1 and 2 indicates the potential importance of capital forbearance in controlling FDIC exposure. When only 50% of classified loans are deducted from capital (fig. 2), deposit insurance values are much higher than in fig. 1. Moreover, in fig. 2 a bank would maximize its option value with a high loan risk level. Restrictive regulations are therefore very important for bounding bank asset risks. By contrast, when the entire balance of classified loans is deducted from capital (fig. 1), a bank's best strategy is to hold relatively low-risk individual loans, even in the absence of other restrictive regulations.

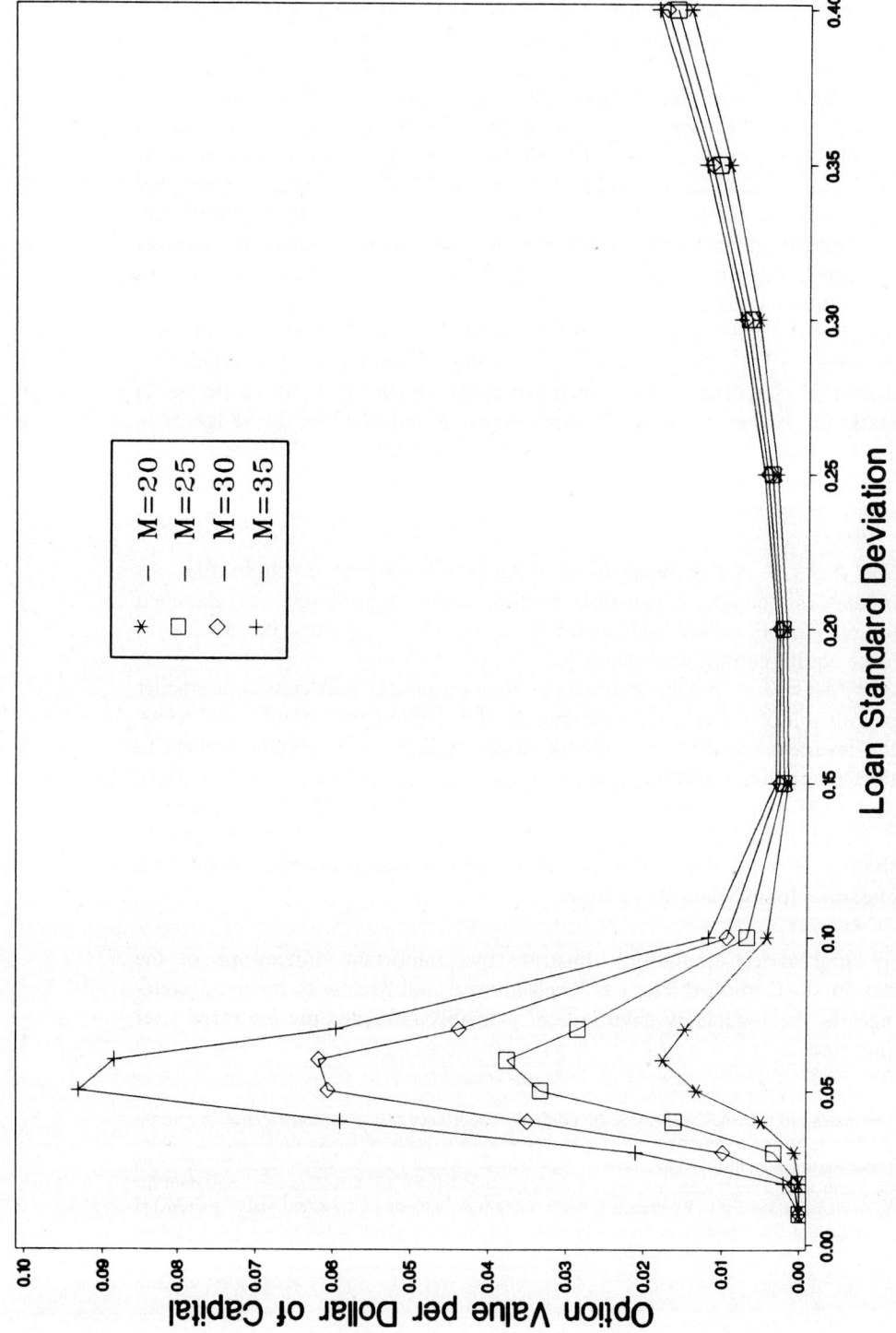

Fig. 1. FDIC option values; $\beta = 1.0$, $\rho = 0.5$, $A = 0.1$, $R_f = 1.1$.

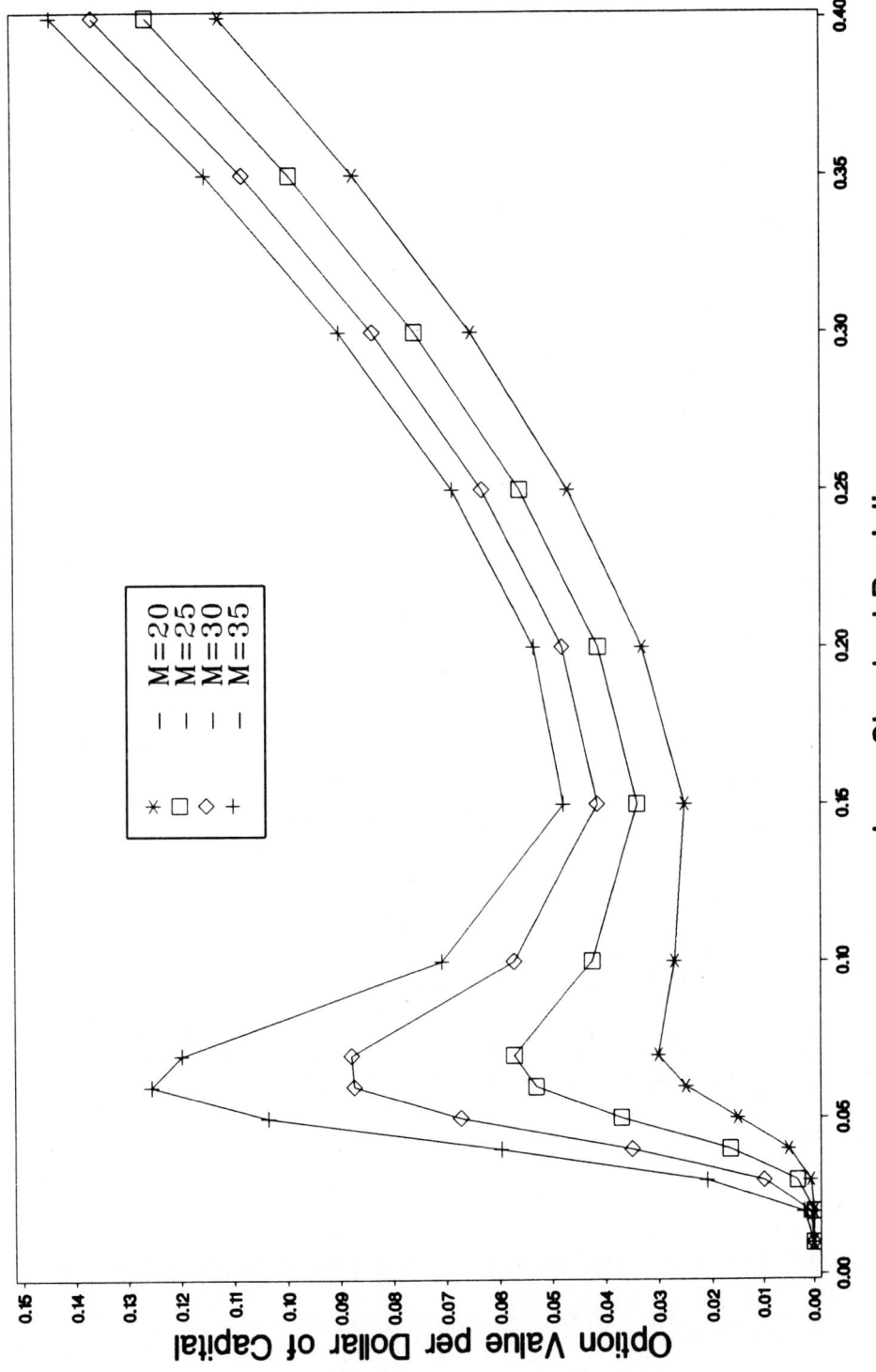

Fig. 2. FDIC option values; $\beta = 0.5$, $\rho = 0.5$, $A = 0.1$, $R_f = 1.1$.

4.3. Portfolio diversification

This simplified version of the model implies that banks will specialize in a single loan risk class. However, permitting ρ_{ij} to vary across possible loan pairs could imply an optimal portfolio containing a variety of loan risk levels. Furthermore, this model's connection between permissible leverage and bank loan risks is unlikely to be the sole determinant of portfolio composition. Other factors that might influence bank asset choice include monopoly power, liquidity, scale or scope economies, risk aversion, or special information availability. In short, examination and capital adequacy effects most likely interact with other factors to determine an individual bank's optimal portfolio. The regulatory effects identified here tend to lower a bank's preferred loan risk, *ceteris paribus*.

5. Optimal portfolio composition with exogenous asset characteristics

The impact of loan classifications on bank risk preferences can also be illustrated in the context of a more traditional portfolio selection model. Instead of taking loan risks as endogenous, assume each of the bank's permissible investments has exogenously fixed stochastic properties. The bank's maximization of (5) now becomes a standard portfolio choice problem, subject to a leverage constraint. Consider the two-asset case. Portfolio variance is

$$\sigma_p^2 = X_1^2\sigma_1^2 + X_2^2\sigma_2^2 + 2X_1X_2\rho_{12}\sigma_1\sigma_2, \tag{16}$$

where

X_i = portfolio share of asset i: $0 \leq X_i \leq 1$, $X_1 + X_2 = 1$,
σ_i = (exogenous) standard deviation of asset i, and
ρ_{12} = (exogenous) correlation between the two assets' returns.

Federal regulators' new risk-based capital standards require that [from (9)]

$$D + K = M\big(K - \beta(D + K)\big[X_1 c(\sigma_1) + X_2 c(\sigma_2)\big]\big). \tag{17}$$

Recognizing that $X_2 = (1 - X_1)$, (17) can be transformed to give the bank's permissible leverage in terms of portfolio composition:

$$\frac{D}{K} = \frac{M}{1 + \beta M\big[c(\sigma_2) + X_1(c(\sigma_1) - c(\sigma_2))\big]} - 1. \tag{18}$$

Without loss of generality, assume that $\sigma_1 > \sigma_2$, which implies that $c(\sigma_1) >$

$c(\sigma_2)$. It follows that $\partial(D/K)/\partial X_1 < 0$. As in (10), shifting toward the riskier asset reduces permissible leverage.

Substituting (16) and (18) into (5) gives the bank's maximization problem as

$$\max_{\{X_1\}} V = V\left(\sigma_p, R_f(D/K)\right). \tag{19}$$

The usual interpretation of an insured bank's incentives would have it plunge into X_1 in order to attain the greatest portfolio risk. However, with a risk-sensitive capital requirement the negative impact of portfolio risk on permissible leverage may temper this incentive. Maximizing (19) gives the first-order condition

$$\frac{\partial V}{\partial X_1} = V_1 \frac{\partial \sigma_p}{\partial X_1} + V_2 R_f \frac{\partial[D/K]}{\partial X_1} = 0. \tag{20}$$

This expression may yield an interior equilibrium value of X_1, though it need not. Fig. 3 plots portfolio risk as a function of X_1, for $\rho_{12} = -0.5$. A bank maximizing its option value will never select a portfolio in the range $(A, B]$. The reason is that the point A offers greater leverage and at least as much portfolio variance as all the points up to and including B. Consequently, an optimal portfolio corresponds to point A or to some point in the region $(B, C]$. The private incentive to diversify is reduced by capital adequacy regulation of the form (18).[16]

Note that the optimal value of X_1 in (20) depends on the model parameters. A change in the regulatory environment $[M, \beta, \text{ or } c(\sigma_i)]$ or market conditions $[\sigma_i, \rho_{12}, \text{ or } R_f]$ will generally alter the bank's preferred portfolio composition.

6. Loan securitization

The preceding discussion has assumed that all loans originated by the bank are also financed in its own portfolio. With limited exceptions (loan participations or syndications), institutional arrangements prior to about 1981 did not permit banks to originate commercial loans for sale to others. Recently, however, large U.S. money center banks have begun selling loans out of their portfolios [see Salem (1986, 1987) or Gorton and Haubrich (1988)]. These 'securitized' loans are primarily high-quality, short-term credits, sold to smaller domestic banks and to U.S. subsidiaries of foreign banks. This development *separates* the bank's financing decision from the process of negotiating and structuring a loan agreement. A practitioner's explanation for the incentive to

---

[16]Schaefer (1987) argues that a capital constraint that is linear in individual asset risks cannot generally be efficient because it ignores return covariances that can importantly influence portfolio risk.

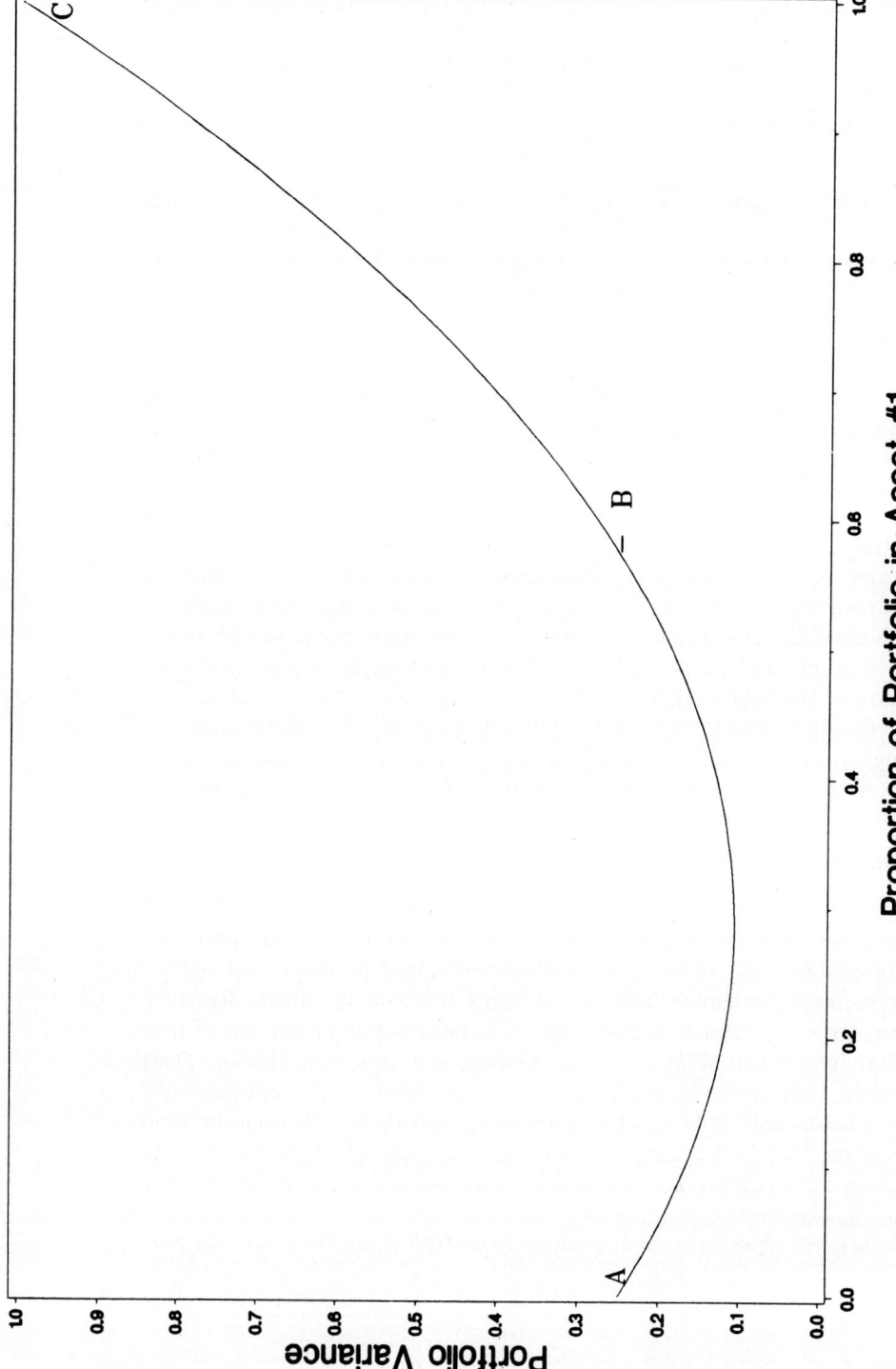

Fig. 3. Partial portfolio dominance.

securitize high-quality loans is that

> banks have become high-cost providers of credit to large creditworthy borrowers... The crux of the matter is that holding these high-quality loans on banks' balance sheets is simply no longer profitable and is an inefficient use of scarce equity capital. [Salem (1987, p. 13)]

The Bank for International Settlements (1986) reached a similar conclusion in evaluating the international banking environment (see pp. 12–13, 129). Some observers have been troubled by this trend toward securitization. For example, a recent report of the Congressional Committee on Government Operations asserts that, as bankers have withdrawn from lending to large blue-chip corporations

> in order to keep their deposit resources fully invested, [they] have turned to making riskier loans, and that this shift toward riskier loans by major banks has hurt the stability and soundness of the entire banking system. [U.S. Congress (1987, p. 5)]

If the indicated portfolio shift toward higher-risk credit has in fact occurred, the policy implications could be substantial. But an important question is whether any such reduction in bank asset quality is *due to* securitization.

The private incentives to securitize loans can be readily discussed in the context of the model presented here. If bankers can efficiently originate loans of one default risk, it seems likely that they will be (among the) minimum-cost originators of loans across a spectrum of default risks. This ability to originate loans competitively means that banks will sell the loans for which they possess no comparative advantage in financing. Prevailing regulatory standards *partly* determine which loans a bank can best finance, and loans with other default risks will be sold to unregulated (or differentially regulated) capital market lenders.

The model's focus on capital adequacy and examination standards might naively suggest that loans will be sold by regulated banks primarily to nonbanking firms. However, many loan sales occur *within* the banking sector [Salem (1986, 1987), BIS (1986)]. There are several possible reasons why such intra-industry transfers would be rational. First, if regulators apply different capital standards to different banks, each group will have its own optimal loan risks. Some loans originated by large banks could be more advantageously financed by smaller banks, and vice versa. Second, classified loans may be evaluated differently at different banks. In assessing capital adequacy, examiners are specifically instructed to consider a bank's historical ability to collect on classified assets. In terms of the model, this means that β may differ cross-sectionally (perhaps for reasons purely of historical accident), producing

cross-sectional variation in optimal loan risks. Finally, cross-sectional variation in local loan market conditions may create imbalances between the loans
bankers can profitably make and the loans they find it optimal to finance. For
all these reasons, bank loan sales need not necessarily be made to unregulated
firms alone.

Other models in the literature can explain loan sales by banking firms.
James (1988) argues that bank loan sales perform the function that securitized
debt issues perform for nonfinancial firms – but banks are prohibited from
securing their debt. Pennacchi (1987) and Greenbaum and Thakor (1987) view
bank loans as importantly different from marketable securities, because monitoring the borrower creates value. The decision to sell such loans therefore
raises incentive and agency-cost issues: loan sales compromise the seller's
incentive to monitor, which limits the loans that can be securitized. As a
consequence, these papers indicate that banks will securitize the loans for
which the value of specialized, centralized monitoring is least. Generally, such
loans are thought to be a bank's most (obviously) creditworthy. This paper's
model complements rather than competes with other models of loan securitization.

7. Summary and conclusions

This paper has combined the option view of bank value maximization with a
more traditional concern for the determinants of bank portfolio composition.
It is argued that the historical combination of loan examination standards and
capital adequacy regulation amounted to a type of risk-related capital standard, under which individual loan risks influence a bank's permissible leverage. In fact, this traditional arrangement resembles the formal risk-based
capital standards that are now being implemented by U.S. regulators. Both the
existing and the proposed capital standards provide an incentive for bankers
to prefer relatively low-variance individual securities, *ceteris paribus*. As Fama
(1985) has suggested, alert capital market participants might be able to infer
valuable information from a bank's decision to grant or renew credit to a
borrowing firm.

This characterization of bank risk preferences also has important implications in the broader context of capital market equilibrium. Since insured
bankers compete with unregulated lenders in making loans, regulations will
partly determine which loans bankers have a comparative advantage in financing. If bank technology for originating loans can be applied across a
reasonably wide range of loan risks, bankers will securitize the loans that they
cannot efficiently finance in their own portfolios. As regulatory restrictions
change over time, the bank's preferred loan risks also change, influencing the
type of loans they sell to the market.

References

Altman, Edward I., 1985, Managing the commercial lending process, in: Richard C. Aspinwall and Robert A. Eisenbeis, eds., Handbook for banking strategy (Wiley, New York, NY) 473–510.

Baltensperger, Ernst 1980, Alternative approaches to the theory of the banking firm, Journal of Monetary Economics 6, 1–37.

Baltensperger, Ernst and H. Milde, 1976, Predictability of reserve demand, information costs, and portfolio behavior of commercial banks, Journal of Finance 31, 835–843.

Bank for International Settlements, 1986, Recent innovations in international banking (BIS, Basel).

Blair, R. and A. Heggestad, 1978, Bank portfolio regulation and the probability of bank failure, Journal of Money, Credit and Banking 10, 88–93.

Board of Governors of the Federal Reserve System, 1985, Commercial bank examination manual (Federal Reserve System, Washington, DC).

Board of Governors of the Federal Reserve System, 1989, Final risk-based capital guidelines, Press release, Jan. 19 (Federal Reserve System, Washington, DC).

Buser, Stephen A., Andrew H. Chen, and Edward J. Kane, 1981, Federal deposit insurance, regulatory policy, and optimal bank capital, Journal of Finance 36, 51–60.

Committee on Banking Regulations and Supervisory Practices, 1988, International convergence of capital measurement and capital standards, Mimeo. (CBRSP, Basel).

Edgeworth, F.Y., 1888, The mathematical theory of banking, Journal of Royal Statistical Society 51, 113–127.

Fama, Eugene F., 1985, What's different about banks?, Journal of Monetary Economics 15, 29–39.

Flannery, Mark J. and Christopher M. James, 1989, On the incidence of deposit insurance subsidies, Mimeo. (University of Florida, Gainesville, FL).

Gorton, Gary and Joseph Haubrich, 1988, The loan sales market, in: George G. Kaufman, ed., Research in financial services (JAI Press, Greenwich, CT).

Greenbaum, Stuart I. and Anjan V. Thakor, 1987, Bank funding modes: Securitization versus deposits, Journal of Banking and Finance 11, 379–401.

Hart, O.D. and D.M. Jaffee, 1974, On the application of portfolio theory to depository financial intermediaries, Review of Economic Studies 41, 129–147.

Hempel, George H., Alan B. Coleman, and Donald G. Simonson, 1983, Bank management (Wiley, New York, NY).

James, Christopher M., 1987, Some evidence on the uniqueness of bank loans, Journal of Financial Economics 19, 217–236.

James, Christopher M., 1988, The use of loan sales and standby letters of credit by commercial banks, Journal of Monetary Economics 22, 395–422.

Kahane, Yehuda, 1977, Capital adequacy and the regulation of financial intermediaries, Journal of Banking and Finance 1, 207–218.

Kim, Daesik and Anthony M. Santomero, 1988, Risk in banking and capital regulation, Journal of Finance 43, 1219–1233.

Klein, M.A., 1971, A theory of the banking firm, Journal of Money, Credit and Banking 3, 205–218.

Koehn, Michael and Anthony M. Santomero, 1980, Regulation of bank capital and portfolio risk, Journal of Finance 35, 1235–1244.

Lummer, Scott and John McConnell, 1988, Further evidence on the bank lending process and the capital market response to bank loan agreements (Purdue University, West Lafayette, IN).

Marcus, Alan J., 1984, Deregulation and bank financial policy, Journal of Banking and Finance 8, 557–565.

Merton, Robert C., 1978, On the cost of deposit insurance when there are surveillance costs, Journal of Business 51, 439–452.

Merton, Robert C., 1977, An analytic derivation of the cost of deposit insurance and loan guarantes, Journal of Banking and Finance 1, 3–11.

Monti, M., 1971, A theoretical model of bank behavior and its implications for monetary policy, L'Industria 2, 3–29.

Monti, M., 1972, Deposit, credit and interest rate determination under alternative bank objective functions, in: G.P. Szego and K. Shell, eds., Mathematical methods in investment and finance (North-Holland, Amsterdam).

Parkin, Michael J., 1970, Discount house portfolio and debt selection, Review of Economic Studies 37, 469–497.

Pennacchi, George, 1988, Loan sales and the cost of bank capital, Journal of Finance 43, 375–395.

Porter, R.C., 1961, A model of bank portfolio selection, Yale Economic Essays 1, 323–369.

Pyle, David H., 1986, Capital regulation and deposit insurance, Journal of Banking and Finance 10, 189–201.

Salem, George M., 1987, Loan selling: A growing revolution that can affect your bank, Journal of Commercial Bank Lending 69, no. 5, 12–24.

Salem, George M., 1986, Selling commercial loans: A significant new activity for money center banks, Journal of Commercial Bank Lending 68, no. 8, 2–13.

Santomero, Anthony M., 1984, Modeling the banking firm, Journal of Money, Credit and Banking 16, 576–602.

Schaefer, Stephen M., 1987, The design of bank regulation and supervision: Some lessons from the theory of finance, in: R. Porter and A.K. Swaboda, eds., Threats to international financial stability (Cambridge University Press, Cambridge).

Schweitzer, Stuart A., 1975, Bank loan losses: A fresh perspective, Federal Reserve Bank of Philadelphia Business Review, 18–28.

Sealey, C.W. and J.T. Lindley, 1977, Inputs, outputs, and a theory of production and cost at depository financial institutions, Journal of Finance 32, 1251–1266.

Sharpe, William F., 1978, Bank capital adequacy, deposit insurance and security values, Journal of Financial and Quantitative Analysis 13, 701–718.

Sinkey, Joseph E., Jr., 1986, Commercial bank financial management (MacMillan, New York, NY).

Sinkey, Joseph E., Jr., 1978, Identifying problem banks, Journal of Money, Credit and Banking 10, 184–193.

Stiglitz, Joseph and Andrew Weiss, 1981, Credit rationing in markets with imperfect information, American Economic Review 71, 393–410.

U.S. Congress, House Committee on Government Operations, 1987, Modernization of the financial services industry: A plan for capital mobility within a framework of safe and sound banking (U.S. Congress, Washington, DC).

Deposit Insurance, Risk, and Market Power in Banking

By Michael C. Keeley*

A fixed-rate deposit insurance system provides a moral hazard for excessive risk taking and is not viable absent regulation. Although the deposit insurance system appears to have worked remarkably well over most of its 50-year history, major problems began to appear in the early 1980's. This paper tests the hypothesis that increases in competition caused bank charter values to decline, which in turn caused banks to increase default risk through increases in asset risk and reductions in capital. (JEL 600)

It has long been recognized that a fixed-rate deposit insurance system, such as the Federal Deposit Insurance Corporation's (FDIC's), or the Federal Savings and Loan Insurance Corporation's (FSLIC's) can pose a moral hazard for excessive risk taking. The reason is that banks or thrifts can borrow at or below the risk-free rate by issuing insured deposits and then investing the proceeds in risky assets with higher expected yields.

As Robert C. Merton (1977) has shown, deposit insurance can be viewed as a put option on the value of a bank's assets at a strike price equal to the promised maturity value of its debt. Under a fixed-rate system, banks potentially can transfer wealth from the insuring agency, and, absent regulation, banks seeking to maximize the value of their equity will maximize the value of the put by increasing asset risk and/or minimizing invested capital relative to assets.

Empirical research, however, does not seem to show that banks in general maximize the put option value. For one thing, many banks hold substantially more capital than the required amounts (Michael C. Keeley, 1988) and for another, researchers have found that for many banks, the value of the deposit insurance option is less than its price (Allan J. Marcus and Israel Shaked, 1984; Ehud Ronn and Avinash K. Verma, 1986; George Pennacchi, 1987), assuming that at the expiration of the option insolvent banks are closed. Moreover, for most of its 50-year history, the insurance system has been characterized by low failure rates and low payouts–just the opposite of what might be expected if banks were maximizing the value of the put option successfully.

Recently, bank and thrift failures and deposit insurance payouts have reached record highs (see Chart 1); the FSLIC has liabilities far in excess of its assets, and even the FDIC faces threats to its solvency. Although many have argued that these recent problems are in part due to the moral hazard of deposit insurance, the question is why it has taken 50 years for major problems to arise.

One explanation (Arnold Kling, 1986) is that the recent episode simply reflects an increasingly risky economy, which in turn has increased the risk of bank portfolios. In the last few years, whole sectors and regions of the national and even the world economy have encountered serious downturns that

*Vice President, Cornerstone Research, 1000 El Camino Real, Menlo Park, CA 94025. Much of the research in this paper was conducted while the author was a research officer at the Federal Reserve Bank of San Francisco. However, opinions expressed herein are those of the author and do not necessarily reflect the view of the Federal Reserve Bank of San Francisco, the Board of Governors of the Federal Reserve System, or Cornerstone Research. An earlier version of this paper was presented at Garn Institute of Finance's academic symposium on deposit insurance. Comments from William Beaver, Jack Beebe, Barbara Bennett, Mark Flannery, Christopher James, Ed Kane, Stuart Myers, Randall Pozdena, Anthony Saunders, and two anonymous referees are greatly appreciated. Alice Jacobson provided expert research assistance. The usual caveats apply, however.

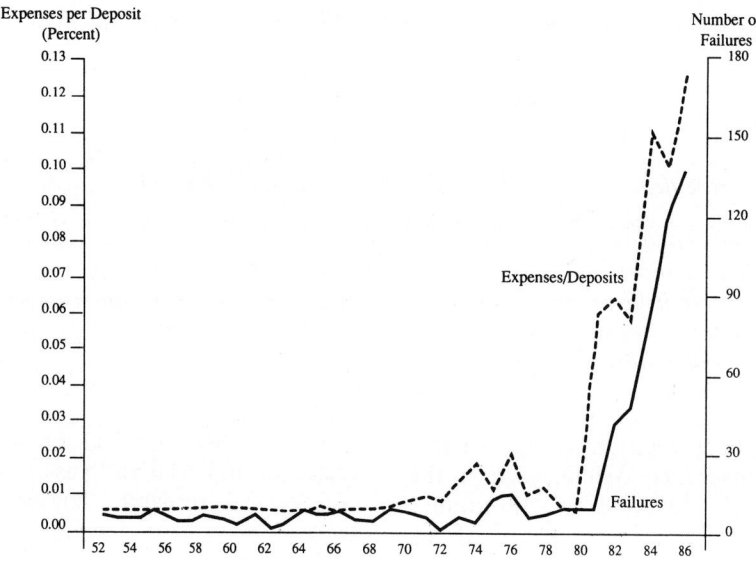

CHART 1. DEPOSIT INSURANCE EXPENSES PER DOLLAR OF DEPOSITS AND
BANK FAILURES

have affected the values of bank and thrift assets. Similarly, interest rates have become more volatile, increasing the riskiness of banks', and especially thrifts', portfolios.

The rise in bank and thrift failures in recent years also may reflect the secular decline in capital-to-asset ratios over the past two decades. As Chart 2 shows, both market and book capital ratios of the 25 largest bank holding companies have fallen well below their levels in the mid-1950's, when only a handful of banks and thrifts failed each year, as opposed to several hundred per year recently. Moreover, beginning in about 1974, market values of the 25 largest bank holding companies in the aggregate fell below book capital ratios.

There are two reasons why declining capital ratios could lead to an increased rate of bank failures. First, lower capital, holding asset risk constant, leads to less protection against failure. Second, as shown in Frederick T. Furlong and Keeley (1987, 1989), lower capital ratios increase the incentive for banks to increase asset risk. Thus, even if overall risk in the economy did not increase, banks would have a greater incentive to increase asset portfolio risk due to the decline in capital ratios.

There is little doubt that increased risk in the economy and declining capital ratios have had a lot to do with the increase in bank and especially thrift failures in recent years. But these developments do not explain why banks and thrifts allowed bankruptcy risk to increase. After all, depository institutions have considerable control over the riskiness of their asset portfolios and perhaps even more control over their capital ratios. Thus, these explanations beg the question of why capital ratios behaved as they did.

Specifically, why did banks on average hold so much capital during the 1950's and early 1960's, and why did capital ratios fall during the 1960's and 1970's? It seems difficult to pinpoint any explicit regulatory changes that would have made it easier for banks to increase default risk, and banks had access to fixed-rate deposit insurance throughout the period.[1] A similar puzzle

---

[1]Although the percentage of deposits explicitly covered by deposit insurance has increased, in theory, even partial deposit insurance coverage provides an incentive for banks to minimize capital and maximize asset risk (as long as they can share losses with the deposit insurance fund).

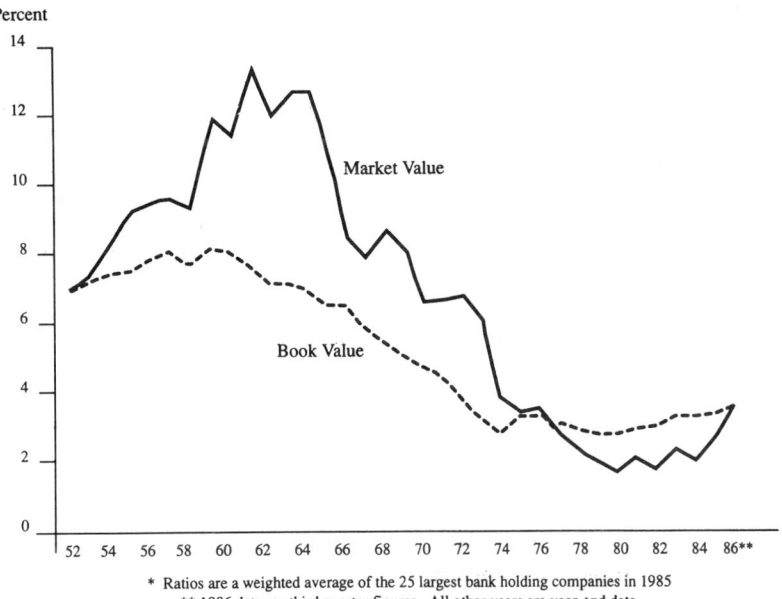

* Ratios are a weighted average of the 25 largest bank holding companies in 1985
** 1986 data are third quarter figures. All other years are year-end data.

CHART 2. CAPITAL-TO-ASSET RATIOS, MARKET AND BOOK VALUES

arises in trying to explain the cross-sectional variation in bank capital ratios. Some banks, for example, hold much more capital than others and much more than regulators require.

This paper argues that one explanation for these apparent puzzles involves differences and changes in the degree of competition faced by banks. In the 1950's and even early 1960's banks partially were protected from competition by a variety of regulatory barriers. For example, chartering was very restrictive (Sam Peltzman, 1965) until the mid-1960's when James Saxton, then comptroller of the currency, greatly liberalized it (Keeley, 1985a, b). Moreover, some banks were protected by various state laws that limited or prohibited branching, multibank holding company, and interstate bank expansion. However, these laws have been greatly liberalized over the last few years, possibly eroding banks' charter values. Likewise, deposit rate deregulation may have diminished charter values by increasing competition, especially for institutions in protected local markets that had been relying on nonprice service competition to attract funds. In addition, beginning in the

early 1980's, thrifts were given expanded powers that enabled them to compete more fully with banks. Finally, many argue that changes in technology have increased the competition that banks face from nonbank financial firms, such as investment banks, brokerage firms, and insurance companies. Such developments as money market mutual funds, cash management accounts, and increased use of commercial paper have all made competitive inroads in banks' traditional product markets.

Increased competition may have reduced banks' incentives to act prudently with regard to risk taking. In fact, the evidence in Chart 2 of declining market values (which would reflect capitalized charter values) relative to book values (which would not) suggests that bank charter values were declining. In the 1950's and early 1960's, regulatory restrictions on entry and competition made bank charters valuable. With valuable charters as assets, banks had an incentive not to risk failure since the owners of the banks cannot sell the charter once the bank is declared insolvent. Instead, a bank that was insolvent on a book-value basis still had a valuable charter that the FDIC could sell in a purchase and assumption (P&A). (In calculating primary book capital, intangible assets, generally representing the excess of the purchase price of assets that had been acquired over their book value, are subtracted from capital.) This may explain why P&A's typically are less costly than liquidations. Also, banks would apparently be willing to overpay for deposit insurance if it were needed to obtain and maintain a valuable charter.

The possession of a valuable charter thus made it difficult for banks to shift losses to the FDIC, and its potential loss in essence created a regulatory bankruptcy cost from the point of view of bank owners. This is especially so since regulators focus on book value when assessing a bank's solvency, not market value. Thus, the gains from feasible increases in risk taking would be offset by the diminished expected value of the charter. As a result, a bank will not have an incentive on the margin to increase default risk (either through reducing capital relative to assets or increasing asset risk) as long as the expected loss of the charter exceeds the gain to the bank of the enhanced value of the deposit insurance put option. Moreover, regulation limited the feasible increases in risk taking so as to prevent banks from potentially imposing losses that would have exceeded their charter values. This idea is established formally below using a state preference model.

In the empirical analysis below a simultaneous equations model of bank risk taking and charter value is developed and estimated. Changes in the laws governing branching, multibank holding company expansion, and interstate entry are used to identify the model statistically. Over the last 20 years or so, these anticompetitive laws have been liberalized greatly, and there are virtually no cases of states increasing their stringency (Dean F. Amel and Daniel G. Keane, 1987). Although the liberalization of these laws is not necessarily the most important factor in increasing the degree of bank competition, it is an easily observed exogenous factor with respect to bank risk taking. Thus, changes in these laws over time provide an opportunity to examine their

influence on market power in banks and whether exogenous variations in market power are related to bank risk taking.

This paper first examines the relationship between changes in regulatory entry barriers and the market power of banks in order to create an instrument for charter value. Then the relationship between market power and risk taking is estimated. This paper employs James Tobin's q, as suggested by Eric Lindenberg and Stephen Ross (1981), as a measure of a bank's market power (monopoly rents). Two measures of bank risk are then related to exogenous variations in q: the market-value capital-to-asset ratio and the interest cost on large, uninsured CD's. I find that q appears to be a useful proxy for market power and that banks with greater market power hold more capital and pay lower rates on CD's.

The remainder of the paper is organized as follows. In Section I, a state preference model is employed to show how market power can affect bank risk taking and how it can be measured. Section II presents the empirical results. Finally, Section III contains a summary and conclusions.

I. Theoretical Framework

Below, a state preference model is used to develop the major results.[2] The model described below closely follows that presented in Furlong and Keeley (1989). Marcus (1984) has developed similar results using an options model, but the state preference model clarifies the conditions under which a bank can benefit from increasing default risk and also illustrates the relationship between charter value and Tobin's q.

A two-period (current and future period), two-state model is used where P_1 and P_2 are the current values of a dollar payment in future states 1 and 2, respectively. (Thus, the risk-free interest rate is $1/(P_1 + P_2) - 1$).

---

[2]State preference models have been widely used in the analysis of banking and deposit insurance—see John H. Kareken and Neil Wallace (1978), William F. Sharpe (1978), Uri Dothan and Joseph Williams (1980), and Furlong and Keeley (1987, 1989).

The state prices are assumed to be exogenously given. To fund its assets, a bank uses an initial capital of C_0 dollars and issues deposits with a current value of D_0 dollars. Initially, the bank is assumed to issue risk-free deposits that pay off \$1 in each state, although this assumption is relaxed later to allow for the issuance of risky deposits. Also, it is assumed that initially the bank is not insured, although this assumption is relaxed later too. The bank invests in an asset security A that pays A_1 dollars in state 1 and A_2 dollars in state 2.

The current value of the bank's equity, V_0, is found by valuing the various cash flows at the state prices. It is assumed that the bank can acquire security A at a price P_A and issue deposits at a price P_d. Thus, the bank can purchase $(C_0 + D_0)/P_A$ units of A. The current value of the bank's equity, V_0, is the value of the cash flows from the assets acquired minus those of the liabilities issued:

$$(1) \quad V_0 = [(C_0 + D_0)/P_A][P_1 A_1 + P_2 A_2]$$
$$- (D_0/P_d)(P_1 + P_2).$$

If the bank is competitive in both the asset market and the deposit market, then $P_A = P_1 A_1 + P_2 A_2$ and $P_d = P_1 + P_2$, and equation (1) above reduces to

$$(2) \quad V_0 = C_0.$$

If the bank is not insured, the value of its equity is independent of its (*ex ante*) risk taking. The reason is that if the bank were to default in state 1 and not meet its promised obligations to depositors, the depositors would demand sufficiently higher payments in state 2 so as to leave the costs unchanged at P_d.

However, with deposit insurance, depositors would not demand a higher payment in state 2, because the insuring agency would pay them the difference between the promised obligations and the asset value in the event of bankruptcy. But with fixed-rate underpriced deposit insurance with a premium, assumed for expositional purposes to be zero, banks pay less than the promised

amount if bankruptcy occurs in state 1, and only the promised amount in state 2. If the bank were to go bankrupt in state 1, then the future value of the bank's equity in state 1 is zero, and its current equity value is

$$(3) \quad V_0 = (C_0 + D_0)(P_2 A_2)/P_A$$
$$- P_2 D_0/P_d > C_0.$$

The current value of the bank's equity when bankruptcy would occur in state 1 (that is, when bankruptcy is possible) equals the value of the excess of its deposit obligations over asset returns (the option value of deposit insurance) I_0, plus its invested capital, C_0. That is,

$$(4) \quad V_0 = I_0 + C_0$$

where

$$(5) \quad I_0 = D_0 P_1/P_d - (C_0 + D_0)P_1 A_1/P_A$$

and $I_0 > 0$.

As is well known, increasing capital, holding constant deposits, reduces the value of the deposit insurance option, and hence equity, and increasing asset risk (increasing the payment in state 2 while reducing that in state 1 so as to hold the price of the asset constant) increases the option value.[3] Thus, the problem facing bank regulators is to constrain banks' incentives to reduce capital relative to assets and to increase asset risk. The puzzle is why regulators apparently succeeded throughout much of the last 50 years but in recent years apparently have failed.

---

[3]Since $I_0 > 0$, the value of the bank exceeds its initial capital investment. Thus,

$$dI_0/dC_0|D_0 = -P_1 A_1/P_A < 0$$

and

$$dI_0/dA_2|P_A = -(C_0 + D_0)(P_1/P_A)(dA_1/dA_2) > 0$$

since

$$dA_1/dA_2 < 0.$$

A. Charter Values

If banks can operate only with charters that are limited in supply, banks may be able to acquire assets at below-market prices (that is, bank loans would earn higher risk-adjusted rates than would market securities) and/or they may be able to make below-market-value payments on deposits (that is, deposits would pay below the risk-adjusted rate). Bank charters have been made valuable by limiting their supply and by protecting banks through various regulations that limited interbank competition as well as competition by nonbank firms.

In the model below, banks are assumed to be insured (at zero cost)[4] but face periodic examinations. At the end of the period, if the bank is insolvent (that is, its assets, not including the charter value, are less than deposit obligations), equity holders receive nothing, depositors receive their promised obligations, and the insurance agency receives the bank's assets, including the charter. If the bank is solvent, however, the bank retains its charter value and continues to operate for another period.

If a bank chooses capital and asset risk so that it will not default in either state, the current value of the bank's equity is

$$(6) \quad V_0 = (C_0 + D_0)(P_1 A_1 + P_2 A_2)/P_A$$
$$- D_0(P_1 + P_2)/P_d + X_0$$

where

$$(7) \qquad X_0 = P_1 X_1 + P_2 X_2$$

in which $P_1 X_1$ is the current value of the charter to operate one more period if state 1 occurs, and $P_2 X_2$ is the current value of the charter to operate one more period if state 2 occurs. Thus, the bank must balance the gains from increased risk taking (I_0) with the loss of the charter value if bankruptcy occurs ($P_1 X_1$). The bank will risk

bankruptcy only if

$$(8) \qquad I_0 > P_1 X_1.$$

Consider a bank just on the verge of insolvency in state 1 (that is, when a marginal increase in asset risk or reduction in capital would cause bankruptcy). The value of such a bank is

$$(9) \qquad V_0 = (C_0 + D_0)(P_2 A_2)/P_A$$
$$- D_0 P_2/P_d + X_0.$$

However,

$$(10) \quad dV_0/dD_0 | C_0 = - P_1 X_1 < 0.$$

That is, a marginal increase in deposits holding capital constant, which causes bankruptcy in state 1, in turn causes the bank to lose the value of its charter if state 1 occurs, $P_1 X_1$. Similarly,

$$(11) \quad dV_0/dA_2 | P_A, C_0 = - P_1 X_1 < 0.$$

Thus, a bank initially at a position where solvency is guaranteed in both states will not have an incentive on the margin to increase risk either through increases in leverage (that is, increases in deposits holding capital constant) or increases in asset risk.[5] This remains true throughout the region where $P_1 X_1 > I_0$.

Although valuable bank charters do not obviate the need for bank regulation because I_0 is unbounded in the absence of

----

[4]Similar results are obtained if deposit insurance has a positive cost not related to default risk. The assumption of zero cost is employed to simplify the analysis.

[5]Marcus (1984) shows that dV_0/dD_0 can be positive for banks with low charter values and negative for banks with high charter values using an options pricing formula. Although he argues that $dV_0/d\sigma$ (the equivalent of dV_0/dA_2) can be negative, his figure 2 implies that, for banks with high charter values, $dV_0/d\sigma$ is positive. Moreover, in his model, it is unclear what determines the critical value of whether a marginal increase in default risk will be beneficial.

In contrast, the state preference model shows that the choice is one of balancing the gains in the option value of deposit insurance with loss of the expected value of the charter. Marginal increases in default risk will not benefit the bank until default risk is sufficiently high so that $I_0 = P_1 X_1$.

regulation, they make the regulator's job much easier. If a bank's capital and asset risk were initially set so that solvency were assured in both states, a large discrete increase in asset risk or reduction in capital sufficient to make $I_0 > P_1 X_1$ would be required if the value of the bank's equity were to increase. Since such large discrete changes presumably would be easy to detect, banks would be discouraged from trying to increase default risk in the first place, and regulators would not need to be concerned with small changes in asset risk or capital.

B. Market Power

An uninsured bank that has market (monopoly) power in its asset market can make positive net present value loans. That is, the loans' future payoffs, when valued at the exogenously given state prices, exceed their current cost. For a such a bank,

(12) $(P_1 A_1 + P_2 A_2)/P_A = \varepsilon > 1.$

However, the bank does not face an inexhaustible supply of such loan opportunities, and as assets A_0 (which equal $C_0 + D_0$) increase, ε, the ratio of cash flows from an asset to its price diminishes. (That is, $\varepsilon = \varepsilon(A_0)$ and $\varepsilon' < 0$.) Assuming such a bank maximizes its net-of-capital investment value, it will expand until the current value of its marginal revenue equals the marginal cost of its deposits (which is 1). That is, $\varepsilon(1 + n) = 1$, where n is the elasticity of ε with respect to A_0. (For an uninsured bank, this condition holds regardless of whether bankruptcy occurs, assuming no bankruptcy costs, since the costs of deposits are unaffected by the risk of bankruptcy.) Similar conditions hold for market power on the deposit side.[6]

For banks that have market power in either the asset or deposit market, as suggested originally by George Stigler (1964) and later and more formally by Lindenberg

and Ross (1981), Tobin's q is an ideal measure of market power. In this paper, Tobin's q is defined as the current market value of a firm's assets (the market value of its equity plus debt) divided by their current cost to a firm. The reason that q is an ideal measure of monopoly rents is that the capitalized value of such rents, whether they arise from market power in the asset market, deposit market, or both, will be reflected in the market value of the firm's equity, and thus assets, but not in the costs of acquired assets. The reasons for q's superiority as a measure of market power are spelled out in more detail in Michael Salinger (1984) and Michael Smirlock et al. (1984). To see why Tobin's q is a measure of market power in the above model, note that q is given by

(13) $q = \dfrac{[(C_0 + D_0)\varepsilon - D_0 + X_0] + D_0}{C_0 + D_0}$

  $= \varepsilon + X_0/(C_0 + D_0).$

(The terms in brackets [ ] represent the market value of the bank's equity to which the current value of debt D_0 is added.) Equation (13) shows that q is equal to the current plus future degree of market power as reflected in current and future ε. For a competitive firm, $\varepsilon = 1$ and $X_0 = 0$, but for a firm with market power, as discussed above, $\varepsilon > 1$ and $X_0 > 0$. Thus, an uninsured bank with no market power in either the asset or deposit market would have a q of 1.[7]

II. Empirical Evidence

The data used to estimate the model are from several sources. The bank holding company data are from the Compustat bank

---

[6] For a bank with market power on the deposit side, $(P_1 + P_2)/P_d = f < 1.$

[7] For a bank with market power on the deposit side as well,

$q = \varepsilon + \dfrac{D_0}{C_0 + D_0}(1 - f) + \dfrac{X_0}{C_0 + D_0}$ where $f < 1$

is inversely related to the degree of market power on the deposit side (see footnote 6). Thus, a bank with market power on the deposit side also will have a q greater than one.

tapes, which contain balance sheets, income statements, and monthly stock prices for the 150 largest bank holding companies (BHC's). Although this sample is not representative of the entire population of all banks or bank holding companies, which comprises many smaller and often privately held organizations, the BHC's in this sample hold about 40 percent of all bank assets and thus are of interest in their own right. Data on the interest cost of large, uninsured CD's are from the Bank Consolidated Report of Conditions and Income (the Bank Call Report). Data on state branching, multibank holding company expansion, and interstate entry laws are from Amel and Keane (1987) and various Federal Reserve Annual Statistical Digests.

A. Measuring Market Power

As discussed above, q is used to measure the degree of market power in banking. The measure q is defined as the market value of assets (calculated as the sum of the market value of common equity—price per share times number of shares—and the book value of liabilities) divided by the book value of assets.[8] The assumption is that the capitalized value of the bank charter will be reflected in the market value of equity (and thus the market value of assets as defined above), but not the book value of equity or assets.[9] Thus, banks with larger charter val-

ues due to market power in asset and/or deposit markets should have greater market-to-book asset ratios. Note that the ability to issue deposits at below-market rates is an asset, the value of which will be reflected in the market value of the bank's equity and thus the market value of assets as I define them.

Several difficulties arise in using q as a measure of a bank's market power. First, the book value of assets represents the historical costs of assets acquired and sold over time, not the current costs of the assets. Thus, *ex post* market-to-book ratios that differ from 1 may reflect different asset return realizations rather than the degree of market power, which would be reflected in the *ex ante* q. Thus, the theoretically appropriate *ex ante* q is measured with error when using the *ex post* q. Another reason that q may not accurately reflect the degree of market power is that the value of potentially underpriced deposit insurance could be capitalized into a bank's market value.[10] Several methods are used in the empirical analysis to control for these possibilities.

First, and most importantly, simultaneous equations techniques are used. In the first stage, an instrument is created for q, and then the predicted ratio is used as an explanatory variable in second-stage equations of bank risk taking. Thus, the empirical model allows for both the possible endogeneity of q and the fact that q is measured with error.

Second, a sample of banking organizations is selected to have similar histories. To do this, the sample is restricted to banking organizations for which data are continuously available from 1970 through 1986. Moreover, two variables are included to control for different asset histories: a dummy variable for banks that were on the Compustat tapes in 1964 and survived to be included in the sample (about 38 percent of

---

[8] Banks use an accounting convention in which loan loss reserves are counted as book capital. However, since loan loss reserves are often taken only when asset losses either have already occurred or when they are anticipated, they in fact often do not represent book capital since the addition to capital usually would be offset at least fully by asset losses if they were realized on the books. Thus, in this paper, loan loss reserves are not counted as book capital. (This procedure follows generally accepted accounting procedures as followed by bank holding companies in their 10-K and 10-Q reports filed with the Securities and Exchange Commission.)

[9] Although a firm that acquired a bank originally endowed with a valuable charter would record that charter's value (i.e., the excess of the purchase price over the book value) as an intangible asset, intangible assets are not counted as primary book equity, the measure of book equity used in this paper.

[10] As Smirlock and Gilligan (1984) argue, a q greater than 1 also could reflect the capitalized value of a firm-specific efficiency enhancing factor of production. However, a firm possessing such a factor would have the same incentives to protect its value as would a firm possessing market power.

the sample) and each bank's asset growth rate since 1970.

B. *Model Structure*

The empirical model consists of two sets of equations. In the first set of regressions, q is regressed on dummy variables that equal 1 during a given period if there was a liberalization in the laws governing state branching, multibank holding company, and interstate expansion, respectively, during any previous period. These regressions also contain a set of control variables and other proxies for market power such as the ratio of demand deposits to total deposits, the ratio of foreign deposits to total deposits, and the ratio of loans to assets. (The branching variables are constructed based on data in Amel and Keane [1987] and various Federal Reserve Statistical Abstracts.) The balance sheet data are from Compustat and refer to the consolidated holding company.

The hypotheses are that unanticipated liberalization of legal entry barriers should erode banks' market power and thus negatively affect q and that greater deposit funding and loan making also might be related to market power and thus positively affect q.

In a second set of regressions, both actual q and an instrument for q are explanatory variables in equations that attempt to explain bank risk taking. The hypotheses are that the banks with greater market power should have larger capital-to-asset ratios and lower risks of default.

The system to be estimated can be represented as

$$(14) \qquad q_{it} = X_{1it}\beta_1 + \epsilon_{1it}$$

$$(15) \qquad \text{risk}_{it} = X_{2t}\beta_2 + q_{it}\beta_3 + \epsilon_{2it}$$

where
X_{1it} is a vector of branching, financial, control, and other variables for bank i at time t;
X_{2t} is a vector of financial and other control variables at time t;

q_{it} is the bank's market-to-book asset ratio at time t [in the two-stage least-squares estimates, equation (14) is used to construct an instrument for q_{it}];
risk_{it} is a measure of bank default risk (two measures are used: the market-value capital-to-asset ratio [the market value of common equity divided by the market value of equity plus the book value of liabilities] and the interest cost on large CD's);
β_1 and β_2 are vectors of coefficients;
β_3 is the effect of q on risk; and
ϵ_{1it} and ϵ_{2it} are random error terms.

C. *Empirical Results*

Table 1 contains descriptive summary statistics for the bank holding companies in the sample using fourth-quarter (year-end) data for the 1970–86 period.[11] It is interesting to note that market-to-book asset ratios range from 0.95 to 1.18 and that market-value capital-to-asset ratios range from 0.0075 to 0.21. Although it is not shown in the table, about 32 percent of the bank holding companies were in states that liberalized branching laws, 44 percent were in states that liberalized multibank holding company expansion laws, and 78 percent were in states that liberalized interstate entry laws by 1986.

D. *Market-to-Book Asset Ratios*

Table 2 contains the results of the estimates of equation (14) over the 1971–86 period using fourth-quarter data. Estimates of the effects of four different types of variables are reported: branching variables, control variables, balance sheet variables, and financial variables. The branching variables are dummies reflecting the liberalization during a previous period of branching,

---

[11]Some of the data items were missing on the Compustat tapes for particular bank holding companies in particular quarters. Rather than exclude the entire observation, missing values were forecast on the basis of quadratic time-trend OLS regressions estimated separately for each bank. For variables known a priori to be nonnegative, forecast values were constrained to be nonnegative.

TABLE 1—SUMMARY STATISTICS FOR 85 LARGE BANK HOLDING COMPANIES
(POOLED 1970–86, FOURTH-QUARTER DATA)

Characteristic	Mean	Minimum	Maximum
Liberalization of Branching Law (Dummy Variable)	0.19	0	1
Liberalization of Multibank Holding Co. Law (Dummy Variable)	0.26	0	1
Liberalization of Interstate Entry Law (Dummy Variable)	0.12	0	1
Book Value of Assets (Net of Loan Loss Reserves in $ Millions)	$10,587	$278	$195,147
Market-to-Book Asset Ratio, q	1.00	0.95	1.18
Multinational Regulatory Status (Dummy Variable)	0.19	0	1
Foreign Deposits/Total Deposits	14 percent	0 percent	89 percent
(Cash + Treasury Securities)/Total Assets	24 percent	7.8 percent	50.1 percent
Annual Assets Growth Rate Since 1970	12 percent	−1 percent	63 percent
Demand Deposits/Total Deposits	35.9 percent	0 percent	72.3 percent
Market-Value Capital-to-Asset Ratio	0.056	0.0075	0.21
Book-Value Capital-to-Asset Ratio	0.055	0.010	0.14
New York Composite Index	70.8	35.4	142.1
3-Month Treasury-Bill Rate	7.64 percent	4.02 percent	15.66 percent
20-Year Treasury-Bond Rate	9.03 percent	5.96 percent	13.73 percent
Average Maturity of CD's (Months)	6.45	1.19	19.81
Interest Cost of CD's	0.085	0.050	0.13

multibank holding company, and interstate expansion laws in the state in which the bank is located. The financial variables are the New York Composite Index, the three-month Treasury-bill rate, and the 20-year Treasury-bond rate. They are included to control for the effects of general interest rate and stock market trends on the market-to-book ratio that would not be related to changes in market power.

Other variables are included as proxies for market power. While some of them might be endogenous, the coefficient estimates of branching variables are not sensitive to their inclusion. The estimated coefficients generally conform with a priori expectations. Liberalization of branching or multibank holding company expansion laws in a previous period is associated with a statistically significantly (at the 1-percent level) lower market-to-book asset ratio. This suggests that both branching and multibank holding company expansion restrictions do provide banks a degree of protection from competition. This finding is consistent with a study by Mark J. Flannery (1984) that finds that unit banks in unit banking states

earn monopoly profits approximately 20 percent above those reported by similar banks in branching states, as well as other studies that have found that branching and multibank holding company expansion restrictions lead to higher loan rates and lower deposit rates.[12] (See Allen N. Berger and Timothy H. Hannan [1987] for recent evidence that restricted branching leads to lower deposit rates.) However, no significant effect of liberalization of interstate entry restrictions is found. This may reflect the fact that these laws generally allow entry only by acquisition (which would increase market prices) and do not allow de novo entry, which would directly increase competition and thus diminish market prices.

---

[12] There is an extensive literature on the effects of branching restrictions on competition. Generally, these studies show that branching restrictions are associated with reduced competition. For example, Donald T. Savage and Stephen A. Rhoades (1979) found banks in statewide branching states paid higher rates on deposits. Also, a survey by George J. Benston (1973) finds general gains in service for the banking public. See Savage and Elinor H. Solomon (1980) for a discussion of the literature.

TABLE 2—POOLED TIME-SERIES CROSS-SECTION REGRESSION FOR 85 LARGE BANK
HOLDING COMPANIES RELATING THE MARKET-TO-BOOK ASSET RATIO TO VARIOUS
DETERMINANTS OF MARKET POWER 1971–86, FOURTH-QUARTER DATA
(STANDARD ERRORS IN PARENTHESES)

$\overline{R}^2$	0.42
Number of Observations	1360
Dependent Variable Mean	1.00
(Market-to-Book Asset Ratio, q)	
Intercept	−0.94***
	(0.011)
Branching Variables	
Liberalization of Branching Law	−0.0046***
	(0.0017)
Liberalization of Multibank Holding Co. Law	−0.0074***
	(0.0015)
Liberalization of Interstate Entry Law	0.00050
	(0.0024)
Control Variables	
Dummy for Being on Compustat in 1964	0.0054***
	(0.0013)
Dummy for Multinational Status	−0.0053**
	(0.0023)
Balance Sheet Variables	
Book-Value Asset Growth Since 1970	0.21***
	(0.010)
Demand Deposits/Total Deposits (×100)	0.00056***
	(0.000067)
Loans/Total Assets	0.0098
	(0.012)
Foreign Deposits/Total Deposits (×100)	0.00019***
	(0.000045)
Book Value of Assets	−4.09E^{-9}
	(4.49E^{-8})
(Cash and Treasury Securities)/Total Assets	−0.000027
	(0.00013)
Financial Variables	
N.Y. Composite Index	0.0038***
	(0.000030)
3-Month Treasury-Bill Rate	−0.00078**
	(0.00032)
20-Year Treasury-Bond Rate	−0.0019***
	(0.00047)

*Significant at the 10-percent level.
**Significant at the 5-percent level.
***Significant at the 1-percent level.

The balance sheet variables generally have signs consistent with the notion that market power arises in deposit and loan markets, although statistically significant effects are found only for deposit markets. The fraction of demand and the fraction of foreign deposits in total deposits are positively and significantly related to the market-to-book asset ratio. The point estimate of the effect of the fraction of loans in total assets on the market-to-book ratio is positive, and the estimate of the effect of the ratio of cash and treasury securities to total assets is negative, although neither variable is significant. Banks with more rapid asset growth in the past have significantly higher market-to-book ratios, perhaps because more rapid growth is associated with lack of competition or success due to other factors. Asset size per se, however, is not significant.

The control variable, whether a bank was on Compustat in 1964, is positively and significantly related to the market-to-book ratio, perhaps indicating that older, prominent bank holding companies that survived to be included in the sample have higher market values than bank holding companies that entered the sample later. The variable for multinational status is negatively related to the market-to-book ratio, which might be due to the very competitive international environment in which these 16 money center banks (as defined by the Federal Reserve) operate.

Finally, the effects of the financial variables are much as one might expect. Stock market values are positively related to the market-to-book ratio, and interest rates are negatively related.

Overall, the high correspondence between the expected effects of the variables and their estimated effects suggests that the market-to-book ratio is in fact a proxy for market power. Next, I test whether this proxy for market power is negatively related to bank risk taking.

E. *Bank Risk*

Below, the effects of the market-to-book asset ratio on two measures of bank default risk are examined. As discussed above, a key hypothesis is that the decline in banks' market power, as proxied by their market-to-book ratios, was a primary cause of the decline in banks' capital-to-asset ratios. Moreover, the theory implies that the cross-sectional variation in bank capital ratios would be influenced by variations in market power—banks with greater market power should have higher capital ratios.

F. *Market-Value Capital-to-Asset Ratios*

Table 3 presents coefficient estimates of equation (15), in which the market-value capital-to-asset ratio (i.e., the market value of capital divided by the market value of assets, defined as the market value of equity divided by the market value of equity plus the book value of liabilities) is regressed on the market-to-book asset ratio, q, holding

stock market and interest rate trends constant. It is necessary to hold stock market and interest rate trends constant since these trends potentially could influence both the dependent and independent variables, thus leading to spurious correlation. In addition, dummies for being on Compustat in 1964 and for multinational status are included.

In the first column of Table 3, ordinary least squares (OLS) estimates from a pooled time-series cross-section regression are reported. The OLS results suggest a strong, positive, and statistically significant relationship between the proxy for market power, the market-to-book asset ratio, and the market-value capital-to-asset ratio. Thus, as predicted, banks with more market power appear to hold more capital relative to assets. Moreover, the estimated magnitude of the effect is large, with a 10 percentage point increment in the market-to-book asset ratio leading to a 0.09 increase in the market-value capital-to-asset ratio, and is not sensitive to whether the variation in the market-to-book ratio is due to changes over time or differences across banks.[13]

There are, however, several reasons why the OLS estimates should be viewed with caution. First, endogeneity between q and bank risk is possible. For example, a bank

---

[13]To assess how sensitive the results were to pooling the cross sections over time, separate cross section regressions were run for each year from 1971 to 1986. Each of the OLS point estimates of the effect of the market-to-book asset ratio on the market-value capital-to-asset ratio were significantly different from zero at the 1-percent level and ranged from 0.62 to 1.19, approximately the same magnitude as the pooled time-series cross section results reported in Table 3.

Since different banks can have different responses to the market index (as proxied by the New York Composite), I also estimated an unconstrained version of equation (15) with separate intercepts and separate slope coefficients for the New York Composite Index for all 85 bank holding companies. However, the estimate of the effect of the market-to-book ratio was statistically significant and about the same magnitude as in the constrained model estimates reported in Table 3. Thus, the results appear robust regarding the source of variation in the market-to-book capital ratio —both the time-series and cross-sectional variation in banks' market-value capital-to-asset ratios are positively associated with time-series and cross-sectional variation in banks' market-to-book capital ratios.

TABLE 3—POOLED TIME-SERIES CROSS SECTION REGRESSION RELATING THE MARKET-VALUE
CAPITAL-TO-ASSET RATIO TO THE MARKET-TO-BOOK ASSET RATIO AS A
PROXY FOR MARKET POWER, FOURTH-QUARTER DATA, 1971–86
(STANDARD ERRORS IN PARENTHESES)

	OLS	TSLS[a]	TSLS[b]
$\bar{R}^2$	0.83	0.66	0.15
Number of Observations	1360	1360	1360
Dependent Variable Mean (Market-Value Capital-to-Asset Ratio)	0.054	0.054	0.054
Intercept	−0.85***	−0.70**	−1.00***
	(0.014)	(0.026)	(0.29)
N.Y. Composite Index	−0.0000044	0.000032**	−0.000052
	(0.000013)	(0.000015)	(0.000029)
3-Month Treasury-Bill Rate	−0.00042**	−0.00043**	−0.00042
	(0.00018)	(0.00018)	(0.00051)
20-Year Treasury-Note Rate	−0.00023	−0.00091***	0.00065
	(0.00025)	(0.00028)	(0.0015)
Dummy for Being on Compustat in 1965	0.0018**	0.0021	−0.054
	(0.00073)	(0.00076)	(0.046)
Dummy for Multinational Status	−0.018***	−0.018***	−0.032**
	(0.00094)	(0.00098)	(0.015)
Market-to-Book Asset Ratio (q)	0.91***	0.77***	1.09***
	(0.013)	(0.025)	(0.27)

*Significant at the 10-percent level.
**Significant at the 5-percent level.
***Significant at the 1-percent level.
[a] Includes as instruments all variables on right-hand side of regression reported in Table 2.
[b] Includes as instruments only the branching, multibank holding company, and interstate expansion dummies, the financial variables, the on-Compustat dummy, and the dummy for multinational status.

with greater default risk could have a greater market-to-book asset ratio if deposit insurance were underpriced and its value were capitalized in a bank's market (but not book) value. Second, the market-to-book asset ratio measures market power with error due to *ex post* asset return realizations that are different from *ex ante* expectations. Third, q and the market-value capital-to-asset ratio might be spuriously correlated due to the presence of the market value of the bank's equity on both sides of the equation. Although the equation is not an identity, to the extent the ratio of the book value of liabilities to the book value of assets were approximately constant or much less variable than the ratio of the market value of equity to the book value assets, the estimated OLS coefficient on q would be biased toward 1. For these reasons, a simultaneous equations model is employed, and two-stage least squares (TSLS) estimates also are displayed in Table 3. By employing

TSLS techniques, exogenous variation in q is related to actual variation in market-value capital-to-asset ratios thus avoiding the potential endogeneity and measurement error problems associated with q. TSLS techniques also solve the problem of potential spurious correlation since the actual market value of common equity is not a right-hand-side variable. (The method of estimation employed produces standard errors corrected for the two-step nature of the procedure.)

In the first-column TSLS estimates, the instruments used to predict the market-to-book capital ratio include all of the explanatory variables in equation (14). In the second-column TSLS estimates, only the branching, multibank holding company and interstate expansion dummies, the financial variables, the on-Compustat dummy, and the multinational dummy were included as instruments, variables believed to be exogenous. Thus, in these second-column esti-

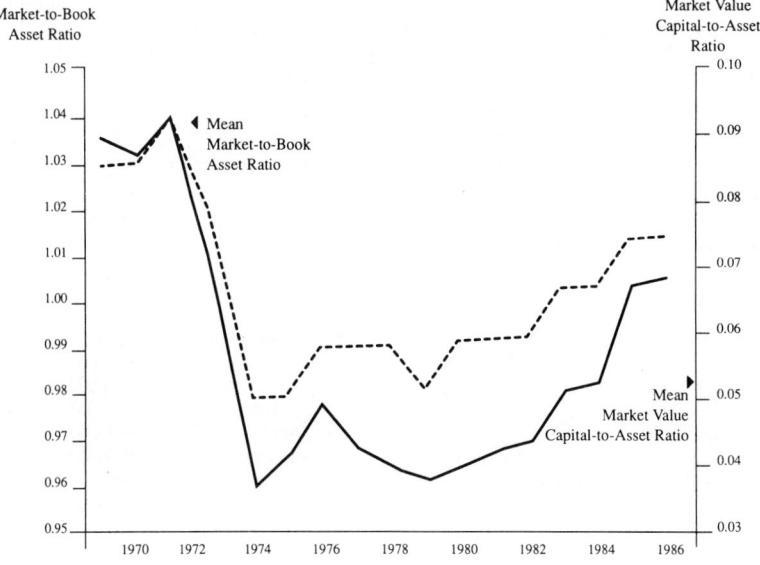

CHART 3. MEAN MARKET-TO-BOOK ASSET RATIO AND MARKET-VALUE
CAPITAL-TO-ASSET RATIO

mates, the exogenous variation in q is due mainly to exogenous variation in the branching variables. However, the TSLS estimates of the effect of the market-to-book capital ratio on the market-value capital-to-asset ratio are very similar to the OLS estimate, especially the second TSLS estimate. This may be because the biases due to measurement error and endogeneity due to the capitalization of underpriced deposit insurance are offsetting. Thus, the finding that banks with more market power hold more capital relative to assets is robust with respect to the estimation method and specification of the model.

Moreover, the decline over time in banks' market-value capital-to-asset ratios is strongly associated with the decline in their market-to-book asset ratios. Chart 3 shows that the mean of banks' market-value capital-to-asset ratios follows the mean of their market-to-book ratios over time. According to the theory developed in Furlong and Keeley (1987, 1989), banks with more capital have less incentive to increase asset risk. Thus, as long as the stringency of asset risk regulation is not less at banks with stronger capital positions, such banks should have

lower default rates and thus represent lower risk exposures to the FDIC.[14] In the next section, I present a test of this hypothesis, proxying risk exposure with the interest cost on large, uninsured CD's.

G. Interest Cost of Large CD's

Ideally, one would like to relate market power in banking directly to the risk exposure of the FDIC and a bank's uninsured depositors. While the FDIC's risk exposure is not directly observable,[15] one can obtain a

[14]As Furlong and Keeley (1987a, 1989) show, the incentive to increase asset risk declines as leverage declines because the second derivative of the value of the insurance put option with respect to asset risk with respect to leverage is positive. This result holds in a multistate state preference or a continuous option pricing framework, but it does not hold for the simple two-state model presented in this paper.

[15]As Marcus and Shaked (1984) and Ronn and Verma (1986) have shown, it is possible to estimate the FDIC's risk exposure by using an options pricing model that relates the observed risk of bank equity (with deposit insurance) to the unobserved risk of bank assets (absent deposit insurance). However, such estimates require assumptions about bank closure policy, which bank and bank holding company liabilities are

measure of the risk premium on a bank's uninsured deposits, assuming that uninsured depositors behave as if they are not implicitly fully insured. The hypothesis is that the rate on large (over $100,000) certificates of deposit (CD's) contain a risk premium related to the bank's default risk, which should be negatively related to a bank's market power as reflected in its market-to-book asset ratio, q.

Although there is a debate regarding whether, in fact, large CD's are implicitly fully insured (and thus whether they contain a risk premium), recent empirical evidence in Timothy H. Hannan and Gerald Hanweck (1988) and Christopher James (1987) strongly suggests that they do contain a risk premium. Moreover, if large CD's are sold in a national (or international) market, it is hard to imagine other factors that could explain the rate differences among banks on CD's of identical maturity.

The interest cost of large CD's is estimated from information contained in the Bank Consolidated Report of Condition and Income (the Bank Call Report). The average rate on large CD's is estimated by dividing the total interest paid (by all of the banks in the bank holding company) by the average dollar value outstanding during the year. Because of difficulties in constructing consolidated interest costs and amounts outstanding for all of the 85 bank holding companies in the previous sample, the sample had to be restricted to 77 bank holding companies for which complete information could be obtained.

Following James (1987), a weighted average maturity of CD's also is constructed to control for differences in the maturities of CD's outstanding. Since the data needed to construct this variable have only been collected since 1984, only the 1984–86 data are

used. Following James, I also control for time-series variation in the level of interest rates by including the average yield on three-month Treasury bills in the CD rate regressions.

The regression results are reported in Table 4. In the first column, estimates of the effect of the market-value capital-to-asset ratio on the CD rates are presented. As mentioned above, banks with more market power, as reflected in higher market-to-book asset ratios, hold more capital relative to assets, in theory, in order to protect their valuable charters. If this theory is correct, banks with more capital relative to assets should have lower default probabilities and thus should have lower CD rates. The results in the first column of Table 4 confirm this hypothesis: banks with greater market-value capital-to-asset ratios pay lower CD rates. In fact, a 1 percentage point increase in a bank's capital-to-asset ratio would lower its CD rate by 14 basis points.[16] This result is somewhat larger but comparable to the 8-basis-point effect Hannan and Hanweck (1988) found using the book-value capital-to-asset rates in a somewhat different specification.

In the second and third columns of Table 4, estimates of the effects of the market-to-book asset ratio on the CD rate are presented. As in the previous equations reported in Table 3, both OLS and TSLS results are presented. The TSLS results are obtained by using all of the right-hand-side variables in equation (14) (less one interest rate trend variable, due to degrees of freedom limitations) as instruments. The results confirm the hypothesis that banks with more market power have lower default risk.

As expected, the coefficient on the market-to-book asset ratio is negative and significantly different from zero at the 1-percent level. Moreover, the effect, while not large, is economically meaningful (each 1 percentage point increment in the market-to-book asset ratio reduces the average CD

---

insured, and a number of other factors (such as the market value of preferred stock, whether bank holding company assets will be used to support a failing bank, etc.). Because of uncertainty regarding just what assumptions might be appropriate and possible changes in a number of these factors over time, I focus on CD rates, a more directly observable proxy for bank default risk.

[16]This result is also consistent with the hypothesis that banks with larger capital-to-asset ratios have less incentive to increase asset risk.

TABLE 4—POOLED TIME-SERIES CROSS SECTION REGRESSION RELATING INTEREST COST OF LARGE CD'S
TO THE MARKET-TO-BOOK ASSET RATIO AS A PROXY FOR MARKET POWER AND THE MARKET-VALUE
CAPITAL-TO-ASSET RATIO, FOURTH-QUARTER DATA, 1984–86 (77 BANK HOLDING COMPANIES)
(STANDARD ERRORS IN PARENTHESES)

	OLS	OLS	TSLS
$\bar{R}^2$	0.43	0.43	0.39
Number of Observations	231	231	231
Dependent Variable Mean	0.085	0.085	0.085
(Interest Cost of CD's Divided by CD's Outstanding)			
Intercept	0.029***	0.020***	0.19***
	(0.0064)	(0.0043)	(0.070)
3-Month Treasury-Bill Rate	0.83***	0.82***	0.81***
	(0.074)	(0.074)	(0.084)
Average Maturity of CD's	0.0011***	0.0011***	0.00073
	(0.00025)	(0.00025)	(0.00055)
Market-to-Book Asset Ratio (q)		−0.18***	−0.16**
		(0.042)	(0.066)
Market-Value Capital-to-Asset Ratio	−0.14***		
	(0.034)		

*Significant at the 10-percent level.
**Significant at the 5-percent level.
***Significant at the 1-percent level.

cost by 16–18 basis points). It is important to recognize that this estimated effect arises from both the time-series as well as the cross-sectional variation in CD costs. This result is consistent with the significant positive effect of the market-to-book ratio on the market-value capital-to-asset ratio reported in Table 3 and the significant negative relationship between the market-value capital-to-asset ratio and the CD risk premium reported in column one of Table 4.

III. Summary and Conclusion

This paper addresses two major empirical puzzles. Why has the deposit insurance system worked as well as it has over much of its history even though it provides a moral hazard for excessive risk taking, and why is the cross-sectional distribution of bank risk taking nonuniform? The hypothesis is that various anticompetitive restrictions endowed banks with market power and made banking charters valuable. The potential loss of a charter in the event of bankruptcy created, in effect, a regulatory bankruptcy cost, which counterbalanced the incentive

for excessive risk taking due to fixed-rate deposit insurance.

The empirical results are consistent with this hypothesis. Banks with more market power, as reflected in larger market-to-book asset ratios, hold more capital relative to assets (on a market-value basis) and they have a lower default risk as reflected in lower risk premiums on large, uninsured CD's. Thus, at least some of the increase in bank and thrift failures and payouts from the deposit insurance funds may be due to a general decline in the value of bank charters associated with increased competition within the banking and financial service industry.

In the past, the perverse incentives created by the deposit insurance system were countervailed by the potential loss of a valuable charter that induced banks to limit their own risk taking. This does not mean that it is desirable or even possible to return to a system of anticompetitive restrictions in order to reduce banking risk. But it does mean that the deposit insurance system must be reformed to reduce the rewards it provides for excessive risk taking.

REFERENCES

Amel, Dean F., and Keane, Daniel G., "State Laws Affecting Commercial Bank Branching, Multibank Holding Companies, and Interstate Banking," Working Paper, Board of Governors of the Federal Reserve System, 1987.

Benston, George J., "The Optimal Banking Structure," *Journal of Bank Research*, Winter 1973, *3*, 220–37.

Berger, Allen N. and Hannan, Timothy H. "The Price Concentration Relationship in Banking," Working Paper No. 100, Board of Governors of the Federal Reserve System, June 1987.

Dothan, Uri and Williams, Joseph, "Banks, Bankruptcy, and Public Regulation," *Journal of Banking and Finance*, March 1980, *4*, 65–87.

Flannery, Mark J., "The Social Costs of Unit Banking Restrictions," *Journal of Monetary Economics*, March 1984, *13*, 237–49.

Furlong, Frederick T. and Keeley, Michael C., "Bank Capital Regulation and Asset Risk," *Economic Review*, Federal Reserve Bank of San Francisco, Spring 1987, 20–40.

_____, "Bank Capital Regulation and Risk Taking: A Note," *Journal of Banking and Finance*, November 1989, *13*, 883–91.

Hannan, Timothy H. and Hanweck, Gerald, "Bank Insolvency Risk and the Market for Large CDs," *Journal of Money, Credit, and Banking*, May 1988, *20*, 438–46.

James, Christopher, "Off-Balance-Sheet Banking," *Economic Review*, Federal Reserve Bank of San Francisco, Fall 1987, 21–36.

Kareken, John H. and Wallace, Neil, "Deposit Insurance and Bank Regulation: A Partial Equilibrium Exposition," *Journal of Business*, July 1978, *51*, 413–38.

Keeley, Michael C., (1985a) "The Regulation of Bank Entry," *Economic Review*, Federal Reserve Bank of San Francisco, Summer 1985, 5–13.

_____, (1985b) "Bank Entry and Deregulation," *Weekly Letter*, Federal Reserve Bank of San Francisco, August 25, 1985.

_____, "Bank Capital Regulation in the 1980s: Effective or Ineffective," *Economic Review*, Federal Reserve Bank of San Francisco, Winter 1988, 1–20.

Kling, Arnold, "The Banking Crisis from a Macroeconomic Perspective," Working Paper, Board of Governors of the Federal Reserve System, 1986.

Lindenberg, Eric and Ross, Stephen, "Tobin's *q* Ratio and Industrial Organization," *Journal of Business*, January 1981, *54*, 1–32.

Marcus, Alan J., "Deregulation and Bank Financial Policy," *Journal of Banking and Finance*, December 1984, *8*, 557–65.

_____ **and Shaked, Israel**, "The Valuation of FDIC Deposit Insurance Using Option-Pricing Estimates," *The Journal of Money, Credit, and Banking*, November 1984, Part 1, *16*, 446–60.

Merton, Robert C., "An Analytic Derivation of the Cost of Deposit Insurance Loan Guarantees," *Journal of Banking and Finance*, June 1977, *1*, 3–11.

Peltzman, Sam, "Entry into Commerical Banking," *Journal of Law and Economics*, October 1965, *8*, 11–50.

Pennacchi, George, "A Reexamination of the Over- (or Under-) Pricing of Deposit Insurance," *Journal of Money, Credit, and Banking*, August 1987, *19*, 340–60.

Ronn, Ehud and Verma, Avinash K., "Pricing Risk-Adjusted Deposit Insurance: An Option-Based Model," *Journal of Finance*, September 1986, *41*, 871–94.

Salinger, Michael, "Tobin's *q*, Unionization, and the Concentration-Profits Relationship," *Rand Journal of Economics*, Summer 1984, *15*, 159–70.

Savage, Donald T. and Rhoades, Stephen A., "The Effect of Branch Banking on Pricing, Profits, and Efficiency of Unit Banks," in *Proceedings of a Conference on Bank Structure and Competition*, Federal Reserve Bank of Chicago, 1979.

_____ **and Solomon, Elinor H.**, "Branch Banking: The Competitive Issues," *Journal of Bank Research*, Summer 1980, *11*, 110–21.

Sharpe, William F., "Bank Capital Adequacy, Deposit Insurance, and Security Values," *Journal of Financial and Quantitative*

Analysis Proceedings, November 1978, *13*, 701–18.

Smirlock, Michael, Gilligan, Thomas and Marshall, William, "Tobin's *q* and the Structure Performance Relationship,"

American Economic Review, December 1984, *74*, 1051–60.

Stigler, George, "A Theory of Oligopoly," *Journal of Political Economy*, February 1964, *72*, 44–61.

Is Fairly Priced Deposit Insurance Possible?

YUK-SHEE CHAN, STUART I. GREENBAUM, and
ANJAN V. THAKOR*

ABSTRACT

We analyze risk-sensitive, incentive-compatible deposit insurance in the presence of private information and moral hazard. Without deposit-linked subsidies it is impossible to implement risk-sensitive, incentive-compatible deposit insurance pricing in a competitive, deregulated environment, except when the deposit insurer is the least risk averse agent in the economy. We establish this formally in the context of an insurance scheme in which privately informed depository institutions are offered deposit insurance premia contingent on reported capital; the result holds for alternative sorting instruments as well. This suggests a contradiction between deregulation and fairly priced, risk-sensitive deposit insurance.

THIS PAPER EXPOSES A conflict between a deregulated, competitive financial services industry on the one hand and fairly priced, risk-sensitive deposit insurance on the other. We show that if depository institutions (DIs) are perfectly competitive, i.e., each makes zero profits on average, then it is impossible to implement incentive-compatible, risk-sensitive deposit insurance pricing.[1]

Recent distress among DIs has fueled debate about reform of the existing deposit insurance system. Many believe that the prevailing risk-insensitive premium structure encourages DIs to choose excessively risky assets, and that it should be replaced by deposit insurance premia linked to the DIs' choices of risk.[2] Risk-sensitive deposit insurance pricing, however, imposes greater informational demands on the deposit insurer, and runs afoul of both

*University of Southern California, J. L. Kellogg Graduate School of Management, Northwestern University, and School of Business, Indiana University, respectively. For their many helpful comments, we wish to express our gratitude to Stephen Buser (the editor), an anonymous referee of this Journal, Arnoud Boot, Lawrence Benveniste, David Besanko, Sudipto Bhattacharya, John Boyd, Mark Flannery, Christopher James, George Kanatas, Edward Kane, Anthony Saunders, Larry Wall, and participants at the 1988 Garn Institute Symposium and workshops at the Federal Reserve Bank of Atlanta, University of Florida, and Tulane University. The usual disclaimer applies.

[1] The only exception is the case in which the provider of deposit insurance enjoys a monopoly in the supply of risk sharing, as would be true if it was strictly less risk averse than any other agent in the economy.

[2] See Black, Miller, and Posner (1978), Chan and Mak (1985), Cummins (1988), Edwards and Scott (1979), Kane (1982), Maisel (1981), Marcus and Shaked (1984), McCulloch (1985), Merton (1977, 1978), Pennachi (1984), Ronn and Verma (1986), and Taggart and Greenbaum (1978).

measurement and implementation problems owing to observability considerations (Pyle (1984)). In particular, a DI's assets normally embody private
information, and as a practical matter this precludes conditioning the deposit
insurance premium directly on the DI's risk profile (Fama (1985), James
(1987), and Lucas and McDonald (1987, 1992)). Of course, the insurer can
attempt to learn the riskiness of a DI's asset portfolio through audits and
examinations. However, monitoring is costly, especially if it seeks to eliminate all informational asymmetry. Alternatively, the insurer could design an
incentive-compatible, risk-sensitive deposit insurance pricing system that
elicits voluntary disclosure of each DI's private information. But in administering any such system, the insurer needs to be mindful of the DI's possible
incentive to increase asset risk after the deposit insurance terms are fixed.

We focus on the two basic problems facing the deposit insurer: *private
information* (the possibility that the DI will misrepresent its asset risk in
order to obtain more favorable insurance pricing) and *moral hazard* (the
possibility that the DI will skew its asset choice in favor of more risk). To
resolve the private information problem, we examine the feasibility of using
the DI's readily observable reported capital as the attribute on which to base
the deposit insurance premium.[3] An incentive-compatible, risk-sensitive deposit insurance pricing structure may be implemented by requiring each DI
to simultaneously choose its capital requirement and its periodic deposit
insurance premium per dollar of deposits from a proffered schedule. Imagine
two types of privately informed DIs, one with high and the other with low
probability of insolvency.[4] Since the capital of an insolvent DI is forfeited, it
will be more costly for the high-risk institution to provide capital. Therefore,
if the deposit insurer requires a reporting of risk from each DI, accurate
information can be elicited if those indicating low risk are offered a lower
deposit insurance premium per dollar of insured deposits together with a
higher capital requirement. We show that the optimal arrangement will
indeed take this form.

Further, we demonstrate that in a competitive environment such a program can succeed only if there are deposit-linked subsidies. Without such
subsidies, DIs will be indifferent to capital structure, and if the deposit
insurance premium is fairly priced and thus increasing in risk, high-risk DIs
will find it profitable to mimic their low-risk peers.[5] This incentive to
misrepresent persists unless the insurer requires that a low-risk DI finance
itself exclusively with equity, in which case no surplus can be earned from

[3] The recent Treasury proposal for banking reform (1991) recommends that deposit insurance premia be linked to accounting capital. Like the Treasury, we sidestep the many issues of GAAP and RAP accounting. See White (1988).
[4] Throughout the paper, when there is private information, it is the insured DI that is privately informed about its asset risk. Thus, the deposit insurer—private or public—is as informationally disadvantaged as other investors.
[5] Fair pricing in the present context is taken to mean that the insurer will break even on each insured institution, individually. The only other examination of incentive compatible deposit insurance we are aware of is Kanatas' (1986).

mispriced deposit insurance.[6] But then the issue of deposit insurance disappears. Thus, so long as every DI finances itself with deposits, an incentive-compatible, capital-based premium schedule with fairly priced deposit insurance is a contradiction in the context of deregulated, perfectly competitive markets.

Three points deserve emphasis. First, rather than merely illustrating that a particular regulatory instrument (capital) cannot provide sorting, our analysis shows that in a competitive environment, incentive-compatible, risk-sensitive deposit insurance is impossible with any sorting instrument. Second, our results do not depend on the dimensionality of the sorting and attribute spaces. For example, a DI may have private information on more payoff-relevant attributes than there are observable DI choices on which to condition the premium. This might itself preclude incentive-compatible insurance premia that accurately reflect risk. Our point, however, is that even when sorting instruments exceed privately known attributes, separation by risk is impossible in a competitive environment. Third, taxes do not invalidate our conclusion. A DI need not be indifferent between deposits and equity, as in Modigliani and Miller (1958), for our conclusion to be sustained. With perfectly competitive credit markets, subsidies are necessary for sorting, even when interest payments are tax-deductible and dividends are not.

Resolving the problem of moral hazard requires multi-period contracting as well as rents. The moral hazard can be controlled only if the insurer can credibly threaten a DI operating with excessive risk, and this requires that the DI's license has value. Only when the deposit insurer is less risk averse than any other agent in the economy will subsidies prove to be unnecessary. The insurer then can break even while preserving a positive surplus associated with deposits due to the standard risk-sharing argument. This will make deposits special relative to DI equity, and will permit the design of incentive-compatible deposit insurance.

Our analysis assumes that the deposit insurer is an agency of the government. This has two implications. First, default by the insurer is not an issue. Second, the governmental insurer has the authority to tax, so that it is able to subsidize the insured. With a private insurer, subsidies are unavailable, default is an issue, and the supply of deposits is imperfectly elastic.[7] Implementing an incentive-compatible, risk-sensitive deposit insurance pricing scheme therefore is impossible.

Our analysis relates to Buser, Chen, and Kane (BCK) (1981) wherein deposit insurance includes both an explicit and an implicit price. The explicit price is a subsidized risk-insensitive insurance premium. The implicit price derives from regulatory restrictions and monitoring aimed at mitigating

---

[6] As we point out later, our results are sustained even if regulatory subsidies are transmitted through channels other than underpriced insurance, provided that the subsidies remain deposit-linked.

[7] We assume that private insurers are not subsidized by the government, so that they must price deposit insurance fairly, although not necessarily on each DI.

moral hazard. BCK's subsidies permit the insurer to influence the DI, and thereby address the moral hazard arising from risk-insensitive deposit insurance pricing. We show that subsidies are needed to resolve private information and moral hazard problems, even when deposit insurance pricing is risk-sensitive. In addition, whereas BCK explain the sufficiency of subsidies in controlling incentives, we explain their necessity. Our analysis also relates to Bhattacharya's (1982), which shows that deposit interest rate ceilings and entry restrictions are necessary to control moral hazard relating to asset risk.[8]

Section I describes the model. Section II analyzes incentive-compatible deposit insurance pricing with private information. Moral hazard is considered in Section III. Section IV discusses the robustness of the analysis, and Section V summarizes.

I. The Model

Consider a representative DI with access to insured deposits provided in infinitely elastic supply at the riskless interest rate. For simplicity, the DI is viewed as lending to a single borrower.[9], We take the loan size, I, to be fixed, and the DI therefore chooses a mix of deposits, D, and equity, E, to satisfy the balance sheet constraint, $D + E = I$. All of the formal analysis assumes pervasive risk neutrality, but alternative preferences are discussed in Section IV.

The borrower uses the loan to finance a single-period project with a two-state probability distribution.[10] The project returns $R > 0$ with probability (w.p.) θ, and zero w.p. $1 - \theta$. The return is observable by the DI and the borrower, but not by the deposit insurer. Since all agents are risk neutral, a necessary and sufficient condition for the borrower's project to be socially optimal is

$$\theta R - Ir_f > 0,$$

where r_f is the riskless interest factor (one plus the riskless interest rate). This condition is assumed to be satisfied throughout.

Since depositors earn the riskless interest rate—a yield consistent with other competitively priced financial instruments—the surplus available from the borrower's project will be shared by the DI and the borrower, and the competitive structure of the market will determine the sharing. If the credit market is perfectly competitive, the standard Bertrand undercutting logic will dictate that all of the surplus accrues to the borrower. With an imper-

---

[8] In a paper that came to our attention while revising this one, Giammarino, Lewis, and Sappington (1990) show that if the DI is a monopoly, an incentive-compatible deposit insurance pricing scheme is possible, but that the distortions necessary to achieve incentive compatibility may not make it worthwhile.

[9] Multiple borrowers are considered in Section IV.

[10] The results generalize to multiple-state or continuous distributions, as discussed in Section IV.

fectly competitive credit market, a more complex distribution of the surplus obtains.[11] To avoid tying our results to a particular market structure, we assume that a fraction, $\alpha \in [0, 1]$, of the project surplus accrues to the DI.[12]

Let $p \in (0, 1)$ represent the periodic deposit insurance premium per dollar of deposits. We can either treat p as a constant, as under prevailing arrangements, or make it a function of some observable instrument of DI choice (e.g., capital) and/or some ex post outcome (e.g., default).[13] For simplicity, we abstract from all regulatory restrictions other than capital requirements.

II. Optimal Risk-Sensitive Pricing with Private Information

Assume that each DI lends to one borrower, and that each DI can be one of two types.[14] Type "H" lends to a borrower with success probability θ_H and return R_H in the successful state. Type "L" lends to a borrower with success probability θ_L and return R_L in the successful state. The returns are zero in unsuccessful states with probabilities $1 - \theta_H$ and $1 - \theta_L$, respectively. Let $\theta_H < \theta_L$, and $R_H > R_L$. Since we wish to focus on the private information aspect, we assume that the DI does not choose its borrower and that its knowledge of the borrower's payoff distribution is not available to either the deposit insurer or any other DI. The assumption that the DI knows its own borrower's payoff distribution is not intended to suggest that informational problems between the DI and its borrower are trivial. Rather, it is made to focus on the informational asymmetry between the DI and the deposit insurer. Pre-contract private information therefore is the sole problem. Moral hazard issues will be addressed in Section III.

Deposit insurance premia are assumed to be paid in advance.[15] At the end of the period, if the borrower's project succeeds, the loan is repaid and the DI compensates its depositors. If the project fails, the borrower defaults and the deposit insurer repays depositors.[16]

Consider a risk-sensitive deposit insurance pricing scheme designed by the insurer to elicit the DI's private information. If the deposit insurer wishes to

---

[11] Besanko and Thakor (1990) show how the surplus from investment projects is shared in imperfectly competitive credit markets.

[12] We assume that there are alternative risky investments available that yield an expected return of r_f. Therefore, a DI will not invest in a loan with $\alpha < 0$. The implicit loan rate is $(1 - \alpha)(r_f/\theta) + \alpha(R/I)$, and when $\alpha = 0$ the borrower is charged the risk-adjusted, risk-free loan rate. This point will be revisited later.

[13] Note that the premium charged in the past has varied from year to year because of rebates. Nevertheless, every DI was charged the same premium per dollar of deposits, before and after the rebate. That is, the premium did not depend on the individual DI's choice of risk.

[14] Each type may have numerous members.

[15] The deposit insurance premium presumably is paid from the DI's retained earnings prior to the receipt of deposits and equity. Remaining retained earnings are paid out as dividends. An alternative would be to assume that $D + E$ equals I plus the deposit insurance premium. This makes the algebra messier without altering the results.

[16] Loans are assumed to be unsecured; secured lending is examined in Besanko and Thakor (1987).

avoid cross-subsidization of a riskier by a safer DI, linking capital requirements to the deposit insurance premia offers one possibility. The deposit
insurer can offer each DI a choice between combinations of insurance premia
and capital requirements, $\{p_H, E_H\}$ and $\{p_L, E_L\}$, whereby each type of DI
selects a distinct pair that maximizes its own welfare and thereby reveals its
type. Since the revelation principle (Myerson (1981)) indicates that the
optimal scheme is equivalent to one that induces truthful revelation, an
alternative is for the DI to report its risk parameter to the insurer, which
then charges a premium and specifies a capital requirement based on the
report.

The expected payoff to a DI of type i choosing $\{p_j, E_j\}$ is

$$\alpha_i(\theta_i R_i - Ir_f) + D_j r_f(1 - \theta_i - p_j), \tag{1}$$

where D_j is determined residually from the budget constraint, given E_j. The
first term in (1) is that portion of the project surplus that accrues to the DI.
The second is the subsidy from deposit insurance. Incentive compatibility
requires that the following non-mimicry constraints be satisfied:

$$\alpha_H(\theta_H R_H - Ir_f) + D_H r_f(1 - \theta_H - p_H)$$
$$\geq \alpha_H(\theta_H R_H - Ir_f) + D_L r_f(1 - \theta_H - p_L),$$

or

$$D_H(1 - \theta_H - p_H) \geq D_L(1 - \theta_H - p_L); \tag{2}$$

and similarly

$$D_L(1 - \theta_L - p_L) \geq D_H(1 - \theta_L - p_H). \tag{3}$$

Conditions (2) and (3) ensure that each type of DI will select the contract
intended for it.[17] In (2), the left-hand side (LHS) is the expected payoff to the
high-risk DI if it reports its type truthfully and the right-hand side (RHS) is
its expected payoff if it misrepresents; thus, when (2) holds, the high-risk DI
(weakly) prefers truth telling. Similarly, in (3), the LHS is the expected
payoff if the low-risk DI reports truthfully and the RHS is its expected payoff
if it misrepresents.

Although we have not yet specified a regulatory objective function, a
standard result is that the non-mimicry constraint for the potential mimic,
(2) in our case, holds tightly in equilibrium. Now suppose that deposit
insurance is fairly priced for each type, so that $P_H = 1 - \theta_H$ and $P_L = 1 - \theta_L$.
With (2) as an equality, we see that the constraint becomes

$$D_L(\theta_L - \theta_H) = 0.$$

---

[17] Note that (2) and (3) constrain strategies to those that induce truth-telling by the DIs.
Assuming that a Nash equilibrium exists in any general reporting game (possibly without these
constraints), the revelation principle asserts that without loss of generality the same Nash
equilibrium outcomes can be implemented in a game with truth-telling constraints.

The only way that this constraint can hold is with $D_L = 0$. Thus, incentive compatibility requires that the low-risk institution fund itself entirely with equity, in which case it is no longer a DI. Note that this result obtains because the DI is indifferent between deposits and capital. Thus, it will prefer a lower deposit insurance premium for any positive level of deposits. Consequently, the high-risk DI will always prefer the premium and capital requirement choice of the low-risk DI, as long as the low-risk DI has any deposits.[18] Since this conclusion holds for all $\alpha_i \geq 0$, the conflict between fairly priced deposit insurance linked to capital requirements and incentive compatibility remains, regardless of the competitive structure of the credit market.

How can the incentive compatibility of a risk-sensitive pricing structure be restored? In the absence of deposit-related rents, stemming from either subsidies or monopsonistic pricing in the deposit market, incentive-compatible pricing that links deposit insurance premia to capital levels is impossible. However, if the credit market is imperfectly competitive, so that $\alpha_i > 0$, there will be other possibilities for restoring incentive compatibility. The most emphatic may be to use the threat of charter revocation as a sorting instrument. That is, suppose the charter value of a DI of type i at the end of the period is V_i; for simplicity, let V_i be independent of the first-period state realization. This charter value can be thought of as the present value of all prospective rents expected to accrue to the DI due to $\alpha_i > 0$. Now the insurer can ask each DI to report its type. A DI indicating high risk is charged $p_H = 1 - \theta_H$ per dollar of deposits and is assured that its charter is inviolate. A DI indicating low risk is charged $p_L = 1 - \theta_L$ per dollar of deposits, but the DI's charter will be revoked with probability β if the deposit insurer is forced to repay depositors at the end of the period. This scheme will be incentive-compatible with $\beta = Dr_f(\theta_L - \theta_H)/V_H(1 - \theta_H)$, for a given D.[19] If V_H is sufficiently high, β can be a probability, i.e., take a value in [0, 1]. Note that this arrangement does not require that capital requirements vary across DIs. However, if each DI is perfectly competitive and $\alpha_i = 0$, sorting based on threat of charter revocation will not succeed. More generally, incentive-compatible risk-sensitive deposit insurance pricing is impossible even with

---

[18] With an arbitrarily large number of DI types, our analysis implies that without subsidies the only type allowed to fund with deposits will be that with the highest risk. Kareken (1983) and Niehans (1982), among others, have suggested that the deposit contract be replaced with mutual funds which could provide most of the services of deposits. Runs would be unlikely (Chari and Jagannathan (1988) and Diamond and Dybvig (1983)), but the claims would not be riskless. This raises the question of whether the pervasive availability of a risk-free claim is socially important, if at a cost (Kareken and Wallace (1978)). We do not attempt to settle that issue here. Our objective is limited to explaining that if insured deposits are socially desirable, then risk-sensitive deposit insurance may be impossible in a setting without subsidies.

[19] To see this, note that β is determined by the incentive compatibility constraint that the high-risk DI does not envy the allocation of the low-risk DI; this constraint holds tightly in a Pareto efficient equilibrium. Thus, we solve $\alpha_H[\theta_H R_H - Ir_f] + Dr_f[1 - \theta_H - p_H] + V_H = \alpha_H[\theta_H R_H - Ir_f] + Dr_f[1 - \theta_H - p_L] + \{\theta_H + [1 - \theta_H][1 - \beta]\}V_H$, with $p_H = 1 - \theta_H$ and $p_L = 1 - \theta_L$.

other sorting instruments, given perfectly competitive factor and output markets.

We now examine the role of subsidized deposit insurance in resolving the incentive compatibility problem for a competitive DI. Assume that $p_H = 1 - \theta_H - \varepsilon$ and $p_L = 1 - \theta_L - \varepsilon$, where the subsidy ε is a positive scalar. Since ε is risk-insensitive, the subsidies are invariant across DI types. Note again that the subsidy need not be embedded in the deposit insurance, but some kind of deposit-linked subsidy is essential. For example, the subsidy could arise from a deposit interest rate ceiling.[20]

The insurer's task is to minimize the cost of the deposit subsidy,

$$S \equiv \Sigma_i \lambda_i \{\varepsilon D_i\} = \varepsilon \{\lambda_H D_H + \lambda_L D_L\}, \tag{4}$$

where the λ's are scalar weighting factors, subject to the fixed-subsidy insurance premium pricing conditions

$$p_i = 1 - \theta_i - \varepsilon, \qquad i = H, L,$$

and the constraints (2) and (3). Treating (2) as an equality in equilibrium, substituting $p_H = 1 - \theta_H - \varepsilon$ and $p_L = 1 - \theta_L - \varepsilon$, and rearranging yields

$$\varepsilon[I - E_H] = [I - E_L][\theta_L - \theta_H + \varepsilon], \tag{5}$$

or equivalently,

$$\varepsilon(D_H - D_L) = D_L(\theta_L - \theta_H). \tag{5'}$$

Since $\theta_H < \theta_L$ and $\varepsilon > 0$, (5) implies that $D_H > D_L$. This means that $E_L > E_H$, since $D_H + E_H = D_L + E_L = I$. Thus, the incentive-compatible scheme has the deposit insurer offering the low-risk DI a lower periodic insurance premium ($p_L < p_H$) per dollar of deposits coupled with a higher capital requirement ($E_L > E_H$). To verify that this necessary condition for incentive compatibility is also sufficient, we need to check whether (3) is satisfied. Proving that (3) holds reduces to showing that

$$D_H(\theta_L - \theta_H) \geq \varepsilon(D_H - D_L). \tag{6}$$

Since $D_H > D_L$ and $\theta_L - \theta_H > 0$, (5') implies that (6) holds as a strict inequality. The intuition is as follows. With a subsidy that is invariant across DIs, fairness requires that the insurance premium be positively related to DI risk. However, such a schedule would not be incentive-compatible since all DIs would be encouraged to describe themselves as low risk. Incentive compatibility is retrieved, however, by linking capital requirements to the insurance premia. In order to persuade the high-risk DI to truthfully reveal its type, it

---

[20] In the case of private information, the value of α does not affect the ability to design an incentive-compatible deposit insurance pricing scheme that uses the capital requirement as a sorting variable; the deposit-linked subsidy is the essential element. However, a positive α may be a necessary precondition for using an alternative sorting instrument such as the bank's loan volume. Note also that either $\alpha > 0$ or positive subsidies will be needed in the moral hazard case.

can be subjected to a lower capital requirement. Recall that a higher capital requirement is less onerous for a low-risk DI. Thus, the optimal risk-sensitive insurance pricing structure relates capital requirements inversely to deposit insurance premia.[21]

To verify the need for subsidies, note that if $\varepsilon = 0$, (5) can hold only if $E_L = I$. Moreover, the cost (defined as the amount of subsidies) of eliciting truthful revelation will increase in the volume of deposits that the regulator wants the low-risk DI to maintain.[22]

Thus far we have assumed that deposit-linked subsidies accrue entirely to the DI. But in a competitive credit market these subsidies might be shared with the borrower, and this could affect our conclusion. For example, incentive compatibility would be jeopardized if DIs were to compete away *all* deposit-linked subsidies. However, a DI can be expected to retain deposit-linked subsidies, perfect competition notwithstanding. To see this, recall that the DI can invest in marketable securities as well as loans. Provided that the markets offer investment opportunities with payoff distributions that span the payoff distributions of loans, no DI will have an incentive to offer a loan with a repayment obligation of less than r_f/θ per dollar.[23] Consequently, the DI can be expected to retain deposit-linked subsidies.

In addition to private information, the deposit insurer must address moral hazard.

III. Moral Hazard

A. Motivation

We have thus far assumed that the DI's payoff distribution is not an instrument of choice. If the DI can make unobservable asset choices, however, the deposit insurer must be concerned about moral hazard. In the case of a perfectly competitive DI, subsidies will be shown to serve an essential role in coping with moral hazard. However, in contrast with the private information case, even with subsidies it is impossible to control moral hazard in a single-period setting. With both private information and moral hazard, subsidy-based, risk-sensitive deposit insurance pricing linked to capital requirements could be incentive-compatible in a static setting, in the sense that each DI would truthfully reveal its risk. However, each DI would choose excessive risk relative to the first best. To discourage excessive risk, the deposit insurer must contract over more than one period. We show that in a two-period setting, second-period subsidies can motivate the appropriate

---

[21] Note that the incentive-compatible schedule, unlike the prevailing arrangement, generates total premium income to the insurer, pD, which is nonlinear in D. Also, given the assumed payoff distribution, the liability of the deposit insurer is independent of the DI's capital, *conditional* on the failure of the DI.

[22] Solving for ε from (5) and substituting into (4), we can see that S is increasing in D_L.

[23] With risk-neutral investors, θ is the actual probability of success. If investors are risk averse, θ can be viewed as the risk-neutral version of the probability, derived through the equivalent martingale representation argument of Harrison and Kreps (1979).

first-period asset choice by a perfectly competitive DI. Although our formal analysis assumes away pre-contract private information, we indicate how the results would be affected by modeling private information and moral hazard jointly.

B. Single-Period Model

To focus on moral hazard, we assume only one type of DI, but it chooses assets from a continuum of investment opportunities. Each is a single-period loan used to purchase a single-period project returning $R(\theta)$ if successful, and nothing otherwise; θ is the probability of success. Cross-sectionally, $\theta \in [\underline{\theta}, \bar{\theta}] \subset (0, 1)$. We assume $R'(\theta) < 0$ and consider two cases: (1) θR is constant, and (2) θR is concave in θ with a unique maximizer at $\theta^0 \in (\underline{\theta}, \bar{\theta})$.

The deposit insurer's problem is to design a pair (p, D), where p is the periodic deposit insurance premium per dollar of deposits and D is the amount of permissible deposits. As indicated earlier, the deposit limit is equivalent to a capital requirement. Since there is no private information, p is a scalar and any DI with deposits in the amount D must pay a premium of pD at the start of the period. Moreover, as we will show in the following discussion, p can be defined so that the deposit insurer breaks even. We assume that the DI's asset choice cannot be observed by the insurer, and likewise cannot be verified ex post. The insurer can only observe whether it must settle depositors' claims; it cannot observe the project outcome (payoff). This establishes preconditions for moral hazard.

For a given (p, D), the DI chooses θ so as to maximize

$$\pi = \alpha(\theta R - Ir_f) + Dr_f[1 - \theta - p]. \tag{7}$$

The maximizing value of θ is given by the first-order condition

$$\partial \pi / \partial \theta = \alpha \, \partial(\theta R) / \partial \theta - Dr_f = 0. \tag{8}$$

Let the θ satisfying (8) be θ^*. Then we see from (8) that for Case 1, $\theta^* = \underline{\theta}$ unless $D = 0$. That is, for any (p, D), the DI chooses the riskiest project. The insurer can set its breakeven (zero subsidy) policy as follows: (i) fix some D and assume $\theta^* = \underline{\theta}$, and then (ii) set $p = 1 - \theta^* = 1 - \underline{\theta}$. This will be a breakeven pricing policy since the DI will choose the riskiest project when faced with this (p, D) combination.

For Case 2, we see from (8) that $\theta^* < \theta^0$ unless $D = 0$. Once again, the deposit insurer can set its breakeven policy as in Case 1. Thus, we find that distortions induced by moral hazard are unavoidable in a single-period setting with insured deposits. The DI chooses higher asset risk than the (socially optimal) first best because the choice of θ is independent of the insurance premium p.[24]

---

[24] The moral hazard and private information problems are not isomorphic. In the private information case, we want the deposit insurance premium to accurately reflect each DI's risk. In the moral hazard case, we want to coax each DI to choose a risk in a desired proximity of the social optimum.

If two a priori indistinguishable types of DI can choose assets from a continuum of investment opportunities, then the deposit insurer confronts both private information and moral hazard. We could think of the high-risk DI choosing θ from $[\underline{\theta}_H, \bar{\theta}_H]$ and the low-risk DI choosing from $[\underline{\theta}_L, \bar{\theta}_L]$, with $\bar{\theta}_H < \underline{\theta}_L$. To induce each DI to truthfully reveal its type, the deposit insurer can offer a choice between $\{p_H, D_H\}$ and $\{p_L, D_L\}$, as in the private information case. If the deposit insurance premium is appropriately subsidized, this will resolve the private information problem. However, each DI will choose the highest risk. In anticipation of this, the insurer must set $p_H = 1 - \underline{\theta}_H - \varepsilon$ and $p_L = 1 - \underline{\theta}_L - \varepsilon$. We will now examine the resolution of moral hazard with multiperiod contracting.

C. Two-Period Model

Again assume that there is only one type of DI and consider Case 1 where $\theta R = $ constant. At $t = 0$, the DI lends against a project that at $t = 1$ yields $R(\theta_1)$ w.p. θ_1, and zero w.p. $1 - \theta_1$. If the project fails, the borrower defaults at $t = 1$, yielding the DI nothing. The deposit insurer then repays the depositors, and the DI expires. If the project succeeds, the loan is repaid and the DI compensates depositors and continues in business for another period. At $t = 1$, new deposits are obtained and a new loan is made. At $t = 2$, the second loan yields $R(\theta_2)$ w.p. θ_2, and zero w.p. $1 - \theta_2$. For simplicity, we assume that α is invariant from period to period. We also assume that it is not feasible for the DI to operate with a negative expected profit in any period.[25]

The deposit insurer's problem is to design $((p_1, D_1), (p_2, D_2))$, where (p_i, D_i) is the combination of a premium per dollar of deposits and deposits for period i. Of course, (p_2, D_2) is offered conditional on first-period success. The DI's expected return for period i is

$$\pi_i(p_i, D_i) = \alpha\big[\theta_i R(\theta_i) - Ir_f\big] + D_i r_f\big[1 - \theta_i - p_i\big]. \tag{9}$$

The DI's objective at $t = 0$ is to maximize.

$$\tilde{\pi} = \pi_1(p_1, D_1) + \theta_1 r_f^{-1}\pi_2(p_2, D_2), \tag{10}$$

where all returns are normalized in time $t = 1$ dollars. The first-order condition governing the optimal choice of θ_1 is

$$\partial\tilde{\pi}/\partial\theta_1 = \alpha\partial\big(\theta_1 R(\theta_1)\big)/\partial\theta_1 - D_1 r_f + r_f^{-1}\big[\pi_2(p_2, D_2)\big] = 0. \tag{11}$$

Note that π_2 may include a subsidy for the second-period deposit insurance.

[25] If it were possible for the DI to operate with negative expected profit, then we could design a pricing scheme that taxes the DI heavily in the first period (which, in the absence of subsidies, would mean negative expected profit for the DI), and promises success-contingent second-period subsidies sufficient to resolve the moral hazard problem.

The deposit insurer can select (D_1, p_2, D_2) so that

$$D_1 r_f \le r_f^{-1} \big[\pi_2 (p_2, D_2) \big]. \tag{12}$$

Since $\partial \{ \theta_1 R(\theta_1) \} / \partial \theta_1 = 0$ by assumption of Case 1, (11) implies that the insurer can induce a choice of $\theta^* = \bar{\theta}$ (the project with the lowest risk) if (12) is satisfied. That is, in the first period, first-best project choice incentives can be enforced with the appropriate choices of D_1, D_2, and p_2. To further analyze (12), write

$$\pi_2 = \alpha \big[\theta_2 R_2 - I r_f \big] + D_2 r_f \big[1 - \theta_2 - p_2 \big],$$

and defining

$$\Delta(\theta_2) \equiv \alpha \big[\theta_2 R_2 - I r_f \big],$$

we have

$$\pi_2 = \Delta(\theta_2) + D_2 r_f \big[1 - \theta_2 - p_2 \big]. \tag{13}$$

Substituting (13) into (12), we obtain

$$\Delta r_f^{-1} + D_2 \big[1 - \theta_2 - p_2 \big] \ge D_1 r_f. \tag{14}$$

Note that in the second period, the DI will choose $\theta_2 = \underline{\theta}$ for any $D_2 > 0$. That is, the end-game problem precludes a resolution of the moral hazard in the second period. Thus, we can write (14) as

$$D_2 \big[1 - \underline{\theta} - p_2 \big] \ge D_1 r_f - \Delta r_f^{-1}. \tag{15}$$

Suppose $\Delta(\theta_2) = 0$; i.e., the credit market is perfectly competitive and $\alpha = 0$. Then, (15) implies that a subsidy in the second period is necessary to ensure that the DI will choose the low-risk project in the first period, provided that $D_1 > 0$. With $\Delta(\theta_2) > 0$, a second-period subsidy will be necessary to control the first-period moral hazard when the contractual payout on the first-period deposits exceeds the discounted value of the surplus accruing to the DI from the second-period project evaluated at time 1.

For Case 2, from the results of the single-period model, the DI will choose $\theta_2^* < \theta^0$ in the second period unless $D_2 = 0$. The DI's first-period asset choice, θ_1^*, is determined by the first-order condition, (11). Substituting (13) into (11), we see that $\theta_1^* = \theta^0$ if and only if

$$D_1 r_f - \Delta(\theta_2^*) r_f^{-1} = D_2 (1 - \theta_2^* - p_2).$$

The interpretation is similar to that for Case 1. If $\Delta(\theta_2^*) = 0$, a subsidy in the second period is necessary to assure first best in the first period as long as $D_1 > 0$. In general, with $\Delta(\theta_2^*) > 0$, a second-period subsidy is necessary when the contractual return on the first-period deposits exceeds the surplus accruing to the DI from the second-period project evaluated at time 1.

Thus, we find that a deposit insurance premium linked to a capital requirement will not solve the moral hazard problem in a one-period setting.[26] In a two-period setting, the moral hazard problem can be resolved only with restrictions on D_1 and D_2, and possibly with a second-period deposit-linked subsidy. A longer time horizon than two periods provides yet greater flexibility in addressing the moral hazard since subsidies can be strung out to create appropriate asset choice incentives.

By linking insurance premia and capital requirements in the way suggested, the insurer can achieve ex ante efficiency with respect to first-period asset choice. Ex post inferences by the deposit insurer are not required. Thus, the insurer need not verify the DI's asset selection.[27] Because of ex ante efficiency, the insurer knows that a rational DI will choose the socially optimal risk when offered appropriate premia/capital alternatives.

Were the insurer to design a policy to address both private information and moral hazard, each DI could be asked to choose a schedule from the pair $\{ p_1(H), D_1(H); p_2(H), D_2(H)\}$ and $\{ p_1(L), D_1(L); p_2(L), D_2(L)\}$. Schedules would be designed so that both the first- and the second-period deposit insurance premia are subsidized, and continued operation of the DI in the second period would be conditional on first-period success. Each DI would truthfully reveal its type and first-period moral hazard would be restrained. For a perfectly competitive DI, our conclusion regarding the essentiality of subsidies remains unchanged.

IV. Robustness of Results

A. Taxes

Capital structure is irrelevant in our model without taxes and deposit-linked subsidies. This suggests that with taxes the finding that subsidies are necessary for sorting may be vitiated. Leverage signaling requires that it must be costly for the high-risk DI to mimic. This, in turn, requires that the costs of debt and equity differ so that capital structure can affect the cost of capital.[28]

---

[26] Kim and Santomero (1988) consider deposit insurance designed to control asset choices and show that by tying future insurance premia to ex post asset returns, the insurer can induce the DI to undertake less risky projects. Our model differs in that we assume that the asset return cannot be verifiably deduced ex post; all that the regulator knows is whether or not it is required to settle depositors' claims.

[27] This is just as well since knowing only whether or not it is required to settle depositors' claims will not generally permit the regulator to infer the probability distribution from which the outcome was drawn.

[28] The intuition is akin to that in Shah and Thakor (1987) where incentive-compatible capital structure contracts can be designed to induce a perfectly separating equilibrium in which firms with levels of risk that vary along a continuum choose distinct debt-equity ratios. In that model, it is essential that interest payments be tax-deductible; the tax advantage of debt permits separation.

This intuition, however, is misleading in the present context. We will show that, with perfectly competitive credit markets, subsidies are necessary for sorting, even with taxes.[29] Consider the model in Section II with corporate taxes and let T denote the tax rate. Since both the interest expenses (when paid) and the insurance premium are tax-deductible, the expected return to a DI of type i choosing the pair $\{p_j, E_j\}$ will be

$$(1 - T)\{\alpha_i[\theta_i R_i - Ir_f] + D_j r_f(1 - \theta_i - p_j)\} - TE_j r_f. \tag{16}$$

If the credit market is perfectly competitive, $\alpha_i = 0$, and the DI's expected return is

$$D_j r_f(1 - \theta_i - p_j)(1 - T) - TE_j r_f.$$

Note that the first term reflects the value of the deposit insurance subsidy and the second indicates that bank equity, since it allows for no tax benefit, is a dominated instrument. Hence, unless E_j is set to zero for every DI, fairly priced deposit insurance will not be viable since it violates the DI's participation constraint (zero profits). In the Modigliani and Miller setting with taxes, extreme leverage is the optimal capital structure. In our perfectly competitive credit market, extreme leverage is the *only* feasible capital structure with taxes and without deposit-linked subsidies. Therefore, with fairly priced deposit insurance, every DI will choose extreme leverage, but then sorting becomes impossible. Thus, subsidies are necessary to restore sorting incentives.

To see how the premium/capital combinations sort DIs, consider the incentive compatibility conditions. Substituting for $p_i = 1 - \theta_i - \varepsilon$ and $E_i = I - D_i$, the conditions analogous to (2) and (3) are:

$$\varepsilon(1 - T)D_H + TD_H \geq (1 - T)D_L[\theta_L - \theta_H + \varepsilon] + TD_L, \tag{17}$$

and

$$\varepsilon(1 - T)D_L + TD_L \geq (1 - T)D_H[\theta_H - \theta_L + \varepsilon] + TD_H. \tag{18}$$

As is standard in such analyses, (17) can be shown to hold tightly in equilibrium, and therefore

$$D_H/D_L = \{1 + (1 - T)(\theta_L - \theta_H)/[T + (1 - T)\varepsilon]\}, \tag{19}$$

and $D_H > D_L$. Thus, the incentive-compatible premium/capital contracts must satisfy $E_L > E_H$ and $p_H > p_L$. As in the asymmetric information case without taxes, an incentive-compatible design inversely relates capital requirements to deposit insurance premia. Moreover, arguments similar to

---

[29] Note that the tax deductibility of deposit interest payments does not necessarily permit separation in the present setting. Taxes only make deposits different from shareholders' equity, but not from debt claims subordinated to deposits. Within limits, these latter claims satisfy the regulatory definition of capital. Thus, we again have indifference between deposits and capital in the absence of subsidies. Since our basic model assumes that taxes are zero, without loss of generality, capital can be defined as equity exclusively.

those made previously establish that deposit-linked subsidies are retained, even by perfectly competitive DIs.

B. Multiple DI Types and Arbitrary Return Distributions

We assumed only two DI types in the private information case. Suppose instead a continuum of types capable of being ranked according to risk. Then only the riskiest will have deposits in the absence of deposit-linked subsidies. All others will be required to fund exclusively with capital, since the riskiest will covet the lower deposit insurance premium offered to the less risky that have any deposits. Thus, subsidies are necessary in this more general case.

Subsidies also are necessary when each borrower's payoff is described by an arbitrary probability distribution. To see this, suppose returns are described by a continuous density function and borrowers can be ranked on the basis of first- or second-order stochastic dominance. Then the deposit insurer's liability per dollar of insured deposits will be greater for riskier DIs, implying a higher periodic premium per dollar of deposits. Subsidies will once again be required for incentive-compatible, risk-sensitive deposit insurance pricing that permits DIs, other than just the riskiest, to use deposits.

C. Risk Aversion

Since we assume risk neutrality, one might reasonably question the need for deposit insurance. We can imagine, however, that depositors are risk averse and investments embody systematic as well as unsystematic risks. Since DI equity will be priced as if shareholders are well-diversified, only the systematic component of risk will require a premium. Completely insured depositors will require a return equal to the riskless interest rate. Fairly priced deposit insurance will require that the insurance premium compensate the insurer for the difference between the yield on uninsured deposits and the riskless interest rate (Merton (1977)). Given fair pricing, however, the effective risk-adjusted yield on deposits will equal that on DI equity, and capital structure is again irrelevant.[30] Anything less than such a premium should be viewed as a deposit insurance subsidy. Our main result is then sustained in this more general framework.

Incentive-compatible, risk-sensitive deposit insurance pricing seems possible in a competitive milieu without insurer losses only if the insurer is less risk averse than all other agents. Deposit insurance priced to enable the insurer to just break even then can generate a surplus for the DI due to risk-sharing benefits. Deposits would be special relative to (uninsured) equity, and a risk-sensitive pricing structure that overcomes private information problems would be attainable. However, the deposit insurer must be the most efficient risk absorber in the economy. If others in the private sector were equally efficient, they could provide competitively priced insurance

---

[30] In this framework, governmental deposit insurance may arise because diversified shareholders are unable to provide a credible commitment to make the stipulated depositor payoffs.

with as much risk-sharing surplus for *shareholders* as governmental deposit insurance provides for depositors. Once again, DI capital structure becomes irrelevant.

D. Monitoring

In practice, deposit insurers rely on monitoring to address private information and moral hazard problems. Could risk-sensitive deposit insurance pricing be designed to exploit monitoring in lieu of direct reporting by DIs? Without subsidies, monitoring is likely to be inadequate for two reasons. First, it should be more costly than direct reporting and the deposit insurer therefore will need to gross up the premium. Unless deposits provide a surplus relative to equity, DIs will prefer to fund entirely with equity or uninsured debt rather than pay the monitoring cost of insured deposits. Second, monitoring can be effective only if the insurer can credibly threaten to punish excessive risk taking. However, in a competitive environment without subsidies, charter termination, arguably the most severe sanction available, imposes no loss on the DI and thus would not deter risk taking.

E. Private Deposit Insurance

We have assumed thus far that deposit insurance is governmental. Because of the demonstrated role of subsidies in resolving private information and moral hazard problems, private deposit insurance would not be able to implement incentive-compatible, risk-sensitive insurance pricing. Even if the DI earns monopoly rents so that subsidies are unnecessary, depositors would be concerned about the possible default of the insurer.[31] The deposit interest rate that an individual DI would need to offer depositors would then be increasing in the total of insured deposits as well as in the deposits of the individual DI. Depositors would need to monitor the insurer, and the monitoring cost would be reflected in a mark-up of the deposit interest rate. A DI therefore would find private deposit insurance inferior to governmentally provided deposit insurance.

V. Summary Remarks

This paper considers the problem of designing an incentive-compatible, risk-sensitive deposit insurance pricing scheme when the insurer confronts private information and moral hazard problems. It is shown that the insurer can elicit truthful disclosure regarding asset portfolio risk from each DI, without intrusive regulatory monitoring. This is achieved by offering DIs a schedule of capital requirements that are inversely related to deposit insurance premia and each DI is permitted to choose its most preferred combination. We show that deposit-linked subsidies are necessary if such a system is to succeed in a competitive banking industry. Since even perfectly

---

[31] We thank the referee for pointing this out to us.

competitive DIs do not completely dissipate deposit subsidies in pricing loans, positive charter values are maintained, making incentive compatibility feasible. Subsidies are also shown to be necessary to cope with the moral hazard associated with deposit insurance. Thus, fairly priced deposit insurance and, by implication, competitive private-sector insurance of deposits is impossible in a competitive banking system in which private information and moral hazard distort equilibria.

Risk-sensitive deposit insurance pricing might have been possible earlier when DIs enjoyed greater deposit-linked rents.[32] Moral hazard was less of a problem when deposit rents discouraged high-risk strategies. The value of the DI charter served as bankruptcy cost, conditioning asset selection as well as capital structure (Chan, Greenbaum, and Thakor (1986)). With the erosion of deposit rents, however, DIs had less incentive to avoid risky assets. The variety of DIs' assets expanded, increasing the informational burden of the deposit insurer, and thereby making risk-sensitive premia more compelling. But without subsidies to replace previously available deposit rents, fairly priced deposit insurance is impossible. Thus, deregulation and risk-sensitive deposit insurance pricing may be incompatible, and we confront the nice irony that risk-sensitive premia are most compelling when they are least attainable.

Recent increases, and the prospect for further increases in insurance premia, indicate continued erosion of deposit subsidies. Growing global competition together with the momentum of deregulation suggest that any future implementation of risk-sensitive deposit insurance pricing faces serious impediments. To the extent that incentive compatibility is jeopardized, more intrusive and costly supervision may become necessary with negative implications for DI competitiveness. To be sure, there are alternatives such as the narrow bank, but the restoration of a system with minimal failures, benign regulation, and risk-insensitive premia seems increasingly unlikely.

REFERENCES

Besanko, David and Anjan V. Thakor, 1987, Collateral and rationing: Sorting equilibria in monopolistic and competitive credit markets, *International Economic Review* 28, 671-689.

————, 1990, Banking deregulation: Allocational consequences of relaxing entry barriers, *Journal of Banking and Finance*, Forthcoming, 1992.

Bhattacharya, Sudipto, 1982, Aspects of monetary and banking theory and moral hazard, *Journal of Finance* 37, 371-384.

Black, Fisher, Merton H. Miller, and Robert A. Posner, 1978, An approach to the regulation of bank holding companies, *Journal of Business* 51, 379-412.

Buser, Stephen D., Andrew H. Chen, and Edward Kane, 1981, Federal deposit insurance, regulatory policy and optimal bank capital, *Journal of Finance* 36, 51-60.

[32] This is one explanation offered for the recent growth of securitization. When deposits provided greater rents, it was advantageous for DIs to unify the origination and funding functions of credit transactions. Dissipation of these rents, however, has eroded the DI's funding advantage, leading to the separation of the two credit functions with DIs concentrating on origination (Greenbaum and Thakor (1987)).

Chan, Yuk-Shee, Stuart I. Greenbaum, and Anjan V. Thakor, 1986, Information reusability, competition and bank asset quality, *Journal of Banking and Finance* 10, 242-253.

—— and Kim T. Mak, 1985, Depositors' welfare, deposit insurance, and deregulation, *Journal of Finance* 39, 959-974.

Chari, V. V. and Ravi Jagannathan, 1988, Banking panics, information and rational expectations equilibrium, *Journal of Finance* 43, 749-763.

Cummins, J. David, 1988, Risk-based premiums for insurance guaranty funds, *Journal of Finance* 43, 823-839.

Diamond, Douglas W. and Philip H. Dybvig, 1983, Bank runs, deposit insurance and liquidity, *Journal of Political Economy* 91, 401-419.

Edwards, Franklin R. and James Scott, 1979, Regulating the solvency of depository institutions: A perspective for deregulation, in Franklin R. Edwards, ed.: *Issues in Financial Regulation* (McGraw-Hill, New York, NY).

Fama, Eugene, 1985, What's different about banks? *Journal of Monetary Economics* 15, 29-39.

Giammarino, Ron, Tracy Lewis, and David E. M. Sappington, 1990, An incentive approach to banking regulation, Working paper, University of British Columbia, October.

Greenbaum, Stuart I. and Anjan V. Thakor, 1986, Bank funding modes: Securitization versus deposits, *Journal of Banking and Finance* 11, 379-402.

Harrison, Michael and David Kreps, 1979, Martingales and multiperiod securities markets, *Journal of Economic Theory* 20, 381-408.

James, Christopher, 1987, Some evidence on the uniqueness of bank loans, *Journal of Financial Economics* 19, 217-235.

Kanatas, George, 1986, Deposit insurance and the discount window: Pricing under asymmetric information, *Journal of Finance* 61, 437-450.

Kane, Edward J., 1982, S&Ls and interest rate regulation: The FSLIC as in-place bailout program, *Housing Finance Review* 1, 219-243.

Kareken, John H., 1983, Deposit insurance reform or deregulation is the cart, not the horse, *Federal Reserve Bank of Minneapolis Quarterly Review*, 1-9.

—— and Neil Wallace, 1978, Deposit insurance and bank regulation: A partial equilibrium exposition, *Journal of Business* 51, 413-438.

Kim, Deasung and Anthony Santomero, 1988, Deposit insurance under asymmetric and imperfect information, Working paper, Wharton School, University of Pennsylvania.

Lucas, Deborah and Robert McDonald, 1992, Bank financing and investment decisions with asymmetric information, *Rand Journal of Economics*, Forthcoming, October.

——, 1987, Bank portfolio choice with private information about loan quality, *Journal of Banking and Finance* 11, 473-498.

Maisel, Sherman J., 1981, The theory and measurement of risk and capital adequacy, in Scott J. Maisel, ed.: *Risk and Capital Adequacy in Commercial Banks* (NBER) (University of Chicago Press).

Marcus, Alan J. and Israel Shaked, 1984, The valuation of FDIC deposit insurance: Empirical estimates using the options pricing framework, *Journal of Money, Credit and Banking* 16, 446-460.

McCulloch, J. Huston, 1985, Interest-risk sensitive deposit insurance premia: Stable ACH estimates, *Journal of Banking and Finance* 9, 137-156.

Merton, Robert C., 1977, An analytic derivation of the cost of deposit insurance and loan guarantees, *Journal of Banking and Finance* 1, 512-520.

——, 1978, On the cost of deposit insurance when there are surveillance costs, *Journal of Business* 51, 439-452.

Modigliani, Franco and Merton H. Miller, 1958, The cost of capital, corporation finance and the theory of investment, *American Economic Review* 48, 261-297.

Myerson, Roger B., 1981, Optimal auction design, *Mathematics of Operations Research* 6, 58-73.

Niehans, Jurg, 1982, Information in monetary policy: Challenge and response, *Journal of Banking and Finance* 6, 9-28.

Pennachi, George G., 1984, Valuing alternative forms of deposit insurance for intermediaries subject to interest rate risk, Working paper, Wharton School, University of Pennsylvania.

Pyle, David, 1984, Deregulation and deposit insurance reform, *Economic Review*, Federal Reserve Bank of San Francisco, Spring, 5–15.

Ronn, Ehud and Avinash K. Verma, 1986, Pricing risk-adjusted deposit insurance: An option-based model, *Journal of Finance* 41, 871–895.

Shah, Salman and Anjan V. Thakor, 1987, Optimal capital structure and project financing, *Journal of Economic Theory* 42-2, 209–243.

Taggart, Robert A. and Stuart I. Greenbaum, 1978, Bank capital and public regulation, *Journal of Money, Credit and Banking* 10, 158–169.

U.S. Treasury, 1991, *Modernizing the Financial System: Recommendations for Safer, More Competitive Banks* (U.S.G.P.O., Washington, D.C.).

White, Lawrence, 1988, Market value accounting: An important part of the reform of the deposit insurance system, in Stuart I. Greenbaum, ed.: *Capital Issues in Banking* (Trustees of the Banking Research Fund of the Association of Reserve City Bankers and the Banking Research Center, J. L. Kellogg Graduate School of Management, Northwestern University, Evanston, IL, December).

REFERENCES

Benston, George, and Clifford Smith, 1976, "A Transactions Cost Approach to the Theory of Financial Intermediation," *Journal of Finance* **31**, 215–231.

Berlin, Mitchell, and Jan Loeys, 1988, "Bond Covenants and Delegated Monitoring," *Journal of Finance* **43**(2), 397–412.

Bernanke, Ben, 1983, "Nonmonetary Effects of the Financial Crisis in the Propagation of the Great Depression," *American Economic Review* **73**, 257–276.

Black, Fischer, 1975, "Bank Funds Management in an Efficient Market," *Journal of Financial Economics* **2**, 323–339.

Boyd, J., and E. C. Prescott, 1986, "Financial Intermediary Coalitions," *Journal of Economic Theory* **38**, 211–232.

Brown, David, Christopher James, and Robert Mooradian, 1993, "The Information Content of Distressed Restructurings Involving Public and Private Debt Claims," *Journal of Financial Economics* **33**, 93–118.

Buser, Steven, Andrew Chen, and Edward Kane, 1981, "Federal Deposit Insurance Regulatory Policy and Optimal Bank Capital," *Journal of Finance* **36**, 51–60.

Campbell, Tim S., and William A. Kracaw, 1980, "Information Production, Market Signalling, and the Theory of Financial Intermediation," *Journal of Finance* **35**(4), 863–882.

Chan, Yuk-Shee, Stuart Greenbaum, and Anjan Thakor, 1992, "Is Fairly Priced Deposit Insurance Possible?" *Journal of Finance* **47**(1), 227–246.

Coase, Ronald, 1937, "The Nature of the Firm," *Economica* n.s. **4**, 386–405.

Coase, Ronald, 1960, "The Problem of Social Cost," *Journal of Law & Economics* **3**, 1–44.

Diamond, Douglas, 1984, "Financial Intermediation and Delegated Monitoring," *Review of Economic Studies* **51**, 393–414.

Diamond, Douglas, and Paul Dybvig, 1983, "Bank Runs, Deposit Insurance, and Liquidity," *Journal of Political Economy* **91**, 401–419.

Fama, Eugene, 1985, "What's Different about Banks?" *Journal of Monetary Economics* **15**, 29–36.

Flannery, Mark, 1989, "Capital Regulation and Insured Banks' Choice of Individual Loan Default Risks," *Journal of Monetary Economics* **24**(2), 235–258.

Flannery, Mark, and Christopher James, 1984, "The Effect of Interest Rate Changes on the Common Stock Returns of Financial Institutions," *Journal of Finance* **39**, 1141–1153.

Gertner, Robert, and David Scharfstein, 1991, "A Theory of Workouts and the Effects of Reorganization Law," *Journal of Finance* **46**, 1189–1222.

Gilson, Stuart, Kose John, and Larry Lang, 1990, "Troubled Debt Restructurings: An Empirical Study of Private Reorganization of Firms in Default," *Journal of Financial Economics* **27**, 315–353.

Gorton, Gary, 1988, "Banking Panics and Business Cycles," *Oxford Economic Papers* **40**, 751–781.

Hess, Alan, and Clifford Smith, 1988, "Elements of Mortgage Securitization," *Journal of Real Estate Finance and Economics* **1**(4), 331–346.

Hoshi, Takeo, Anil Kashyap, and David Scharfstein, 1990, "The Role of Banks in Reducing the Costs of Financial Distress in Japan," *Journal of Financial Economics* **27**(1), 67–88.

James, Christopher, 1987, "Some Evidence on the Uniqueness of Bank Loans," *Journal of Financial Economics* **19**, 217–235.

James, Christopher, 1988, "The Use of Loan Sales and Standby Letters of Credit by Commercial Banks," *Journal of Monetary Economics* **22**, 395–422.

Jensen, Michael C., and William H. Meckling, 1976, "Theory of the Firm: Managerial Behavior, Agency Costs, and Ownership Structure," *Journal of Financial Economics* **3**, 305–360.

Kane, Edward, and Haluk Unal, 1990, "Modeling Structural and Temporal Variation in the Market's Valuation of Banking Firms," *Journal of Finance* **45**(1), 113–136.

Keeley, Michael, 1990, "Deposit Insurance, Risk, and Market Power in Banking," *American Economic Review* **80**, 1183–1200.

Leland, Hayne, and David Pyle, 1977, "Information Asymmetries, Financial Structure, and Financial Intermediaries," *Journal of Finance* **32**(2), 371–387.

Merton, Robert, 1977, "An Analytic Derivation of the Cost of Deposit Insurance Loan Guarantees," *Journal of Banking and Finance* **1,** 3–11.

Modigliani, Franco, and Merton Miller, 1958, "The Cost of Capital, Corporate Finance, and the Theory of Investment," *American Economic Review* **48,** 261–297.

Myers, Stewart, and Nicholas Majluf, 1984, "Corporate Financing and Investment Decisions When Firms Have Information That Investors Do Not Have," *Journal of Financial Economics* **13,** 187–222.

Pennacchi, George, 1988, "Loan Sales and the Cost of Bank Capital," *Journal of Finance* **43**(2), 375–396.

Rajan, Raghuram, 1992, "Insiders and Outsiders: The Choice between Informed and Arm's-Length Debt," *Journal of Finance* **47**(4), 1367–1400.

Santomero, Anthony, 1984, "Modeling the Banking Firm: A Survey," *Journal of Money, Credit and Banking* **16**(4) pt 2, 576–602.

Smith, Clifford, 1982, "Pricing Mortgage Originations," *Journal of the American Real Estate & Urban Economics Association* **10**(3), 313–330.

Smith, Clifford, 1986, "Investment Banking and the Capital Acquisition Process," *Journal of Financial Economics* **15**(1/2), 3–29.

Smith, Clifford, Charles Smithson, and Lee Wakeman, 1988, "The Market for Interest Rate Swaps," *Financial Management* **17**(4), 34–44.

Smith, Clifford, and Rene Stulz, 1985, "The Determinants of Firms' Hedging Policies," *Journal of Financial and Quantitative Analysis* **20**(4), 391–405.

Smith, Clifford, and Jerold Warner, 1979, "On Financial Contracting: An Analysis of Bond Covenants," *Journal of Financial Economics* **7,** 111–161.

Stiglitz, Joseph, and Andrew Weiss, 1981, "Credit Rationing in Markets with Imperfect Information," *American Economic Review* **71**(3), 393–410.

Stulz, Rene, and Herb Johnson, 1985, "An Analysis of Secured Debt," *Journal of Financial Economics* **14,** 501–521.

Wruck, Karen Hopper, 1990, "Financial Distress, Reorganization, and Organizational Efficiency," *Journal of Financial Economics* **27**(2), 419–444.